CCH® CPELink
We Bring the Experts to You

Self-Study Courses

Self-study courses are easy to use, engaging and mobile friendly! Work at your own pace and enjoy instant access to your online self-study courses immediately after purchase.

Live Webinars

Live webinars are the most convenient way to earn CPE credit — without taking a test. You get coverage of today's hot topics along with high quality, interactive courses led by expert instructors. Plus you have the flexibility to log in and listen from anywhere. It doesn't get any easier than that!

Learn more at **CCHCPELink.com**

2019

GOVERNMENTAL GAAP GUIDE
FOR STATE AND LOCAL GOVERNMENTS

ERIC S. BERMAN, MSA, CPA, CGMA

Wolters Kluwer

Editorial Staff

Editor . . . . Mary P. Taylor

Production . . . . Jennifer Schencker, Vijayalakshmi Suresh, and
Anbarasu Anbumani

This publication is designed to provide accurate and authoritative information in regard to the subject matter covered. It is sold with the understanding that the publisher is not engaged in rendering legal, accounting, or other professional services. If legal advice or other professional assistance is required, the services of a competent professional person should be sought.

—From a *Declaration of Principles* jointly adopted by a Committee of the American Bar Association and a Committee of Publishers and Associations

ISBN: 978-0-8080-4801-5

No claim is made to original government works; however, within this Product or Publication, the following are subject to CCH Incorporated's copyright: (1) the gathering, compilation, and arrangement of such government materials; (2) the magnetic translation and digital conversion of data, if applicable; (3) the historical, statutory and other notes and references; and (4) the commentary and other materials.

Portions of this work were published in a previous edition.

Printed in the United States of America

Governmental GAAP Guide

By Eric S. Berman, MSA, CPA, CGMA

Highlights

Financial professionals who work with state and local governments must stay current with emerging governmental standards or face unfortunate consequences. This one-of-a-kind tool discusses all the promulgated principles that are applicable to accounting and financial reporting by state and local governments. CCH's *Governmental GAAP Guide* delivers a thorough analysis of GASB Statements, GASB Interpretations, GASB Technical Bulletins as well as releases of the National Council on Governmental Accounting (NCGA) that remain in effect as of the date of publication, including Statements and NCGA Interpretations. Certain AICPA Audit and Accounting Guide *State and Local Governments* concepts are also discussed. Everything is analyzed and restated in plain English and is supported by timesaving examples and illustrations.

2019 Edition

To assist preparers and auditors in meeting the requirements of generally accepted accounting principles, the 2019 edition of CCH's *Governmental GAAP Guide* includes an updated comprehensive financial statement presentation, glossary and disclosure checklist, complete with cross-references to the applicable professional standards, and a series of practice alerts for pending GASB projects and recently issued GASB pronouncements. This edition of the *Governmental GAAP Guide* has been updated throughout with the very latest information on the following GASB standards either recently implemented or in the process of being implemented as of the date of this publication:

- GASB-90 (*Accounting and Financial Reporting for Majority Equity Interests—an amendment of GASB Statement No. 14*)
- GASB-89 (*Accounting for Interest Cost Incurred before the end of a Construction Period*)
- GASB-88 (*Certain Disclosures Related to Debt, including Direct Borrowings and Direct Placements*)
- GASB-87 (*Leases*)
- GASB-86 (*Certain Debt Extinguishment Issues*)
- GASB-85 (*Omnibus*)
- GASB-84 (*Fiduciary Activities*)
- GASB-83 (*Certain Asset Retirement Obligations*)
- GASB-81 (*Irrevocable Split-Interest Agreements*)
- GASB-75 (*Accounting and Financial Reporting for Postemployment Benefits Other Than Pensions*)

Implementation issues continuing to be encountered for:

- GASB-82 (*Pension Issues—an amendment of GASB Statements No. 67, No. 68, and No. 73*)

- GASB-80 (*Blending Requirements for Certain Component Units—an Amendment of GASB Statement No. 14*)

- GASB-77 (*Tax Abatement Disclosures*)

- GASB-74 (*Financial Reporting for Postemployment Benefit Plans Other than Pensions*)

- GASB-73 (*Accounting and Financial Reporting for Assets That Are Not within the Scope of GASB Statement No. 68, and Amendments to Certain Provisions of GASB Statements 67 and 68*)

- GASB-72 (*Fair Value Measurement and Application*)

- GASB-71 (*Pension Transition for Contributions Made Subsequent to the Measurement Date—an amendment of GASB Statement No. 68*)

- GASB-68 (*Accounting and Financial Reporting for Pensions—an amendment of GASB Statement No. 27*)

At the end of each chapter the *Guide* includes questions and answers, which may be used by readers to refresh themselves on the concepts contained within the chapter. The questions and answers may also be used by educators in the teaching of governmental GAAP to students. For a complete course in governmental accounting and auditing, educators may also use the companion *Governmental GAAP Practice Manual*, the newly issued *Governmental GAAP Disclosures Manual* as well as *Knowledge-Based Audits*™ of State and Local Governments with Single Audits as part of the curriculum.

New for 2019

With the publication of CCH's *Governmental GAAP Disclosures Manual*, some of the lengthier disclosures and disclosure information contained within the *Guide* has been transitioned to the *Disclosures Manual* as it is redundant. For example, Exhibit 13-7 in the 2018 *Guide* was an example of note disclosures and required supplementary information for a cost-sharing employer that has a special funding situation (no other nonemployer contributing entities) in accordance with GASB-68, as amended [GASB Cod. Secs. P20 and P21]. This same information is now presented as part of Chapter 19 in the newly issued *Disclosures Manual*.

As a result of this new *Manual*, Chapter 24 has been changed. In prior years, Chapter 24 was a checklist of disclosures, which was primarily presented from an audit perspective. This checklist is available through Wolters Kluwer's *Accounting Research Manager*® and is more up-to-date than in a printed form in a book. The new Chapter 24 focuses on special purpose entities, primarily from GASB Statement No. 62 (*Codification of Accounting and Financial Reporting Guidance Contained in Pre-November 30, 1989 FASB and AICPA Pronouncements*). State and Local Governments and other practitioners that use the *Guide* may be public broadcasters, cable systems, hospitals, insurance entities other than public risk pools, entities that are subject to regulatory accounting or utilities, all having provisions in GAAP. These are detailed in the new Chapter 24.

Similarly to past years, any GAAP that has been superseded by the time of this release, inclusive of the majority of governments that are implementing the newly adopted standards has been removed. An example of this is the removal of an Appendix in Chapter 13 containing the former GASB-45 and GASB-57 [GASB Cod. Secs. P50, .51, .52 and .54] guidance. The updated guidance is now contained in GASB-75.

Finally, wherever possible, references to individual GASB Statements also now include references to the GASB *Codification of Governmental Accounting and Financial Reporting Standards* (Codification), which is authoritative. As portrayed in the previous paragraphs, the nomenclature includes a reference to the GASB Statement (GASB-##) and then a reference to the GASB Codification Section [GASB Cod. Sec. ####]. The Codification also includes any related *Implementation Guide* questions as part of each section. Information from those questions and answers may be incorporated where necessary as part of the *Guide*.

Accounting Research Manager®

Accounting Research Manager® is the accounting industry's largest and most comprehensive online database, providing easy access to objective and insightful government, accounting, auditing, and SEC information. While other research tools simply summarize the authoritative literature, leaving you to decipher often-complex information, Accounting Research Manager® goes the extra mile to give you the clearest possible picture. We bring clarity to your government and financial reporting research.

The *Accounting Research Manager*® *Government Library* provides one-stop access to governmental authoritative and proposal stage literature, including:

- **GASB (Governmental Accounting Standards Board)** Statements & Interpretations, Technical Bulletins, Implementation Guides & related proposal stage literature

- **GAO (Government Accountability Office)** Government Auditing Standards, Financial Audit Manual

- **OMB (Office of Management and Budget)** Circulars, Compliance Supplements

The Government Library also offers in-depth, interpretive guidance. Users can access our government titles that include the *Governmental GAAP Guide*, *Governmental GAAP Practice Manual*, the *Governmental GAAP Disclosure Manual, Knowledge-Based Audits™ of State and Local Governments with Single Audits*, and the *Governmental GAAP Update Service*.

Learn more about Accounting Research Manager® by visiting www.accountingresearchmanager.com.

CCH Learning Center

CCH's goal is to provide you with the clearest, most concise, and up-to-date accounting and auditing information to help further your professional development, as well as a convenient method to help you satisfy your continuing professional education requirements. The CCH Learning Center* offers a complete line of self-study courses covering complex and constantly evolving accounting and auditing issues. We are continually adding new courses to the library to help you stay current on all the latest developments. The CCH Learning Center courses are available 24 hours a day, seven days a week. You'll get immediate exam results and certification. To view our complete accounting and auditing course catalog, go to: **http://CCHGroup.com/LearningCenter.**

9/18

For questions concerning this shipment, billing, or other customer service matters, call our Customer Service department at 1 800 344 3734.

Contents

Preface

Integrated Approach to Governmental Financial Reporting

Governmental Accounting Standards Board (GASB) Statement No. 34 (GASB-34) (*Basic Financial Statements—and Management's Discussion and Analysis—for State and Local Governments*) and GASB-35 (*Basic Financial Statements—and Management's Discussion and Analysis—for Public Colleges and Universities*) [GASB Cod. Sec. Co5], along with many amendments to those standards, continue to serve as the primary guidance for those who prepare, audit, and use government financial reports. In addition, the GASB continues to work on the further development and clarification of other accounting standards for state and local government entities. CCH's *Governmental GAAP Guide* provides interpretive guidance on the application of the core principles of U.S. generally accepted accounting principles (U.S. GAAP), and the other accounting and financial reporting pronouncements applicable to state and local governments.

PRACTICE ALERT: The GASB is in the midst of a wide-ranging multiple-year project reexamining the financial reporting model, a related project reexamining revenue and expense recognition principles and note disclosure. In late 2016, the GASB issued an Invitation to Comment, *Financial Reporting Model Improvements—Governmental Funds.* The release represented the first due process document and asked respondents for comment on a large portion of the current financial reporting model. An Invitation to Comment is a GASB staff document, asking for comments at a relatively early stage of a project prior to the GASB Board reaching a consensus view. The topics included in this initial phase included:

- Recognition approaches (measurement focus and basis of accounting) for governmental funds,
- The format of the governmental funds statement of resource flows (also known as the statement of revenues, expenditures, and changes in fund balances),
- Specific terminology,
- Reconciliation of the governmental fund statements to the government-wide statements, and
- For certain recognition approaches, a statement of cash flows.

In September 2018, the GASB released a second due process document consisting of the Board's Preliminary Views on the *Financial Reporting Model—Reexamination* project. Most notably, the GASB is focusing on a proposed one-year (operating cycle) period of availability for governmental funds with a goal of resolving inconsistencies in the recognition of prepaid items, inventory, tax and revenue anticipation notes, and grant receivables. Topics discussed in this phase include:

- Refinement of the management's discussion and analysis
- The format of the government-wide statement of activities, including whether additional information should be presented in a "natural classification" (salaries, employee benefits, etc.) schedule in the notes
- Debt service fund presentations, potentially elevating them to major fund status, similarly to the general fund
- The status and reporting of permanent funds
- Proprietary fund and business-type activity financial statements, especially the presentation of operating and non-operating revenues and expenses
- The presentation of fiduciary fund financial statements and whether the statements should be presented in the basic financial statements
- Consistency of presentation of budgetary comparisons within required supplementary information.

PRACTICE ALERTs: are inserted where necessary in the *Governmental GAAP Guide* to discuss various aspects of the GASB's preliminary views.

Additional related projects to the reexamination of the financial reporting model include a reexamination of the current revenue and expense/expenditure recognition model (primarily contained in GASB-33 and GASB-36, as amended). During January 2018, the GASB issued an Invitation to Comment entitled *Revenue and Expense Recognition*. Two models were included in the staff document. GASB staff have sought comment on a model based on whether an exchange/nonexchange model (similar to current pronouncements) or a performance obligation/nonperformance obligation model (similar to the Financial Accounting Standard Board updated provisions) was preferred by practitioners. Staff are also considering alternative models. Comments were accepted until April 2018 and public hearings were held in May. The GASB will deliberate on the responses until a Preliminary Views document is released, sometime in early 2020.

A third project reexamining note disclosure issued prior to the issuance of GASB Statement No. 72 (*Fair Value Measurement and Application*) [GASB Cod. Secs. I50, 3100] is also underway. Focus areas include, but are not limited to:

- Summary of Significant Accounting Policies including general descriptions and definitions and those related to component units,
- Information about Discretely Presented Component Units, including Related Parties, Related Organizations, Joint Ventures, and Jointly Governed Organizations,
- Investment disclosures prior to GASB-72 (GASB-31, GASB-40, GASB-59),
- Potential new or redesigned note disclosures on receivables and payables, and
- Other potential changes to other required notes.

The GASB is also in the midst of due process on a GASB Concepts Statement related to the Conceptual Framework for recognizing transactions (which was started in 2010, but stalled in 2011).

The entirety of these related projects may not be finalized until at least 2023.

New Pronouncements and Outstanding Due Process Documents

Updated annually, the GASB's *Implementation Guide 2015-1* (also referred to as the *Comprehensive Implementation Guide*) was developed to assist financial statement preparers and attesters in the implementation and application of a number of GASB pronouncements. This edition includes various changes from the GASB's 2015 guide. Additional changes were made in 2016 through 2018 with the releases of the annual *Implementation Guidance Updates* (IGU) (IGU 2016-1 and IGU 2018-1) and have been reflected where possible in the *Governmental GAAP Guide*.

The AICPA issues two annually updated guides that provide guidance for state and local governments and their auditors. The AICPA Audit and Accounting Guide *State and Local Governments* presents recommendations of the AICPA State and Local Government Audit Guide Revision Task Force on the application of generally accepted auditing standards to audits of financial statements of state and local governments.

The second guide, AICPA Audit Guide *Government Auditing Standards and Single Audits* presents recommendations of the AICPA State and Local Government Audit Guide Revision Task Force on the application of generally accepted government auditing standards (GAGAS) to audits of financial statements of state and local governments, and audits of compliance with major federal award programs under the Single Audit Act of 1996, as amended, most recently by the *Uniform Administrative Requirements, Cost Principles, and Audit Requirements for Federal Awards* (Title 2 Code of Federal Regulations Part 200). As of the publication date of this edition of CCH's *Governmental GAAP Guide*, the AICPA had issued the March 1, 2018 edition of the Audit and Accounting Guide—*State and Local Governments*, and the 2018 edition of *Government Auditing Standards and Single Audits*.

The following GASB pronouncements, issued in 2017 and 2018 through the date of publication, are discussed in the present edition and are to be implemented over the coming years along with the following implementation dates:

Statement	Title	Implementation Date
GASB-75	*Accounting and Financial Reporting for Postemployment Benefits Other Than Pensions*	Financial statements for periods beginning after June 15, 2017 (for June 30th governments, July 1, 2017).
GASB-81	*Irrevocable Split-Interest Agreements*	Reporting periods beginning after December 15, 2016 (for June 30th governments, July 1, 2017).
GASB-83	*Certain Asset Retirement Obligations*	Reporting periods beginning after June 15, 2018 (for June 30th governments, July 1, 2019).
GASB-84	*Fiduciary Activities*	Reporting periods beginning after December 15, 2018 (for June 30th governments, July 1, 2020).
GASB-85	*Omnibus*	Reporting periods beginning after June 15, 2017 (for June 30th governments, July 1, 2017).
GASB-86	*Certain Debt Extinguishment Issues*	Reporting periods beginning after December 15, 2019 (for June 30th governments, July 1, 2021).
GASB-87	*Leases*	Reporting periods beginning after December 15, 2019 (for June 30th governments, July 1, 2021).
GASB-88	*Certain Disclosures Related to Debt, including Direct Borrowings and Direct Placements*	Reporting periods beginning after June 15, 2018 (for June 30th governments, July 1, 2019).
GASB-89	*Accounting for Interest Cost Incurred before the end of a Construction Period*	Reporting periods beginning after December 15, 2019 (for June 30th governments, July 1, 2020).

Statement	Title	Implementation Date
GASB-90	*Accounting and Financial Reporting for Majority Equity Interests—an amendment of GASB Statement No. 14*	Reporting periods beginning after December 15, 2018 (for June 30th governments, July 1, 2019).

At the time of this publication, no other GASB due process documents were outstanding (excluding the aforementioned financial reporting model reexamination project).

OBSERVATION: Many new GASB standards require changes to conform to their provisions. Such changes are to be applied retroactively by restating financial statements, if *practicable* (as opposed to practical), for all prior periods presented. If restatement of prior periods is not *practicable*, the cumulative effect, if any, of implementing a statement should be reported as a restatement of beginning net position (or fund balance or fund net position, as applicable) for the earliest period restated. In the first period that the new statement is applied, the notes to the financial statements should disclose the nature of the restatement and its effect. Also, the reason for not restating prior periods presented should be disclosed.

During 2015, the GASB changed the wording of implementation from *practical* to *practicable*. The GASB believes that reasonable efforts should be deployed before a government determines that restatement of all prior periods presented is not practicable. In other words, *inconvenient* should not be considered equivalent to *not practicable*.

Other GASB Projects Discussed

The GASB also has other ongoing projects that are discussed where applicable in CCH's *Governmental GAAP Guide*. Initial deliberations and research are occurring as of the date of publication on projects involving:

- Going Concern Disclosures—Reexamination of Statement 56
- Information Technology Arrangements, including Cloud Computing
- Note Disclosures
- Public-Private Partnerships—Reexamination of Statement 60.

Codification of Governmental Accounting and Financial Reporting Standards References

Many practitioners use the GASB's annual *Codification of Governmental Accounting and Financial Reporting Standards*. The codification presents another view of GASB standards, providing authoritative accounting and financial reporting guidance. However, practitioners are cautioned that the codification may not have the most up to date information as it is only updated annually and for issued standards. The codification is organized into five parts:

I. General Principles

II. Financial Reporting

III. Measurement

IV. Specific Balance Sheet and Operating Statement Items

Section	*Topic*
A10	Asset Retirement Obligations
B50	Bond, Tax, and Revenue Anticipation Notes
C20	Cash Deposits with Financial Institutions
C50	Claims and Judgments
C55	Common Stock—Cost Method
C60	Compensated Absences
C65	Conduit Debt Obligations
C75	Construction-Type Contracts—Long-Term
D20	Debt Extinguishments and Troubled Debt Restructuring
D25	Deferred Compensation Plans (IRC Section 457)
D30	Demand Bonds
D40	Derivative Instruments
E70	Escheat Property
F60	Food Stamps
F70	Foreign Currency Transactions
I30	Interest Costs-Imputation
I40	Inventory
I50	Investments
I55	Investments—Reverse Repurchase Agreements
I60	Investments—Securities Lending
J50	Accounting for Participation in Joint Ventures and Jointly Governed Organizations
L10	Landfill Closure and Postclosure Care Costs
L20	Leases
L30	Lending Activities
N30	Nonexchange Financial Guarantees
N70	Nonmonetary Transactions
P20	Pension Activities—Reporting for Benefits Provided through Trusts That Meet Specified Criteria

V. Stand-Alone Reporting—Specialized Units and Activities.

Section	Topic
Pe5	Pension Plans Administered through Trusts That Meet Specified Criteria—Defined Benefit
Pe6	Pension Plans Administered through Trusts That Meet Specified Criteria—Defined Contribution
Po20	Public Entity Risk Pools
Po50	Postemployment Benefit Plans Administered through Trusts That Meet Specified Criteria—Defined Benefit
Po51	Postemployment Benefit Plans Administered through Trusts That Meet Specified Criteria—Defined Contribution
Re10	Regulated Operations
Sp20	Special-Purpose Governments
Ut5	Utilities

Parts I–III are of generalized interest in accounting and financial reporting, while the remaining parts are organized similarly to an encyclopedia in alphabetical order (e.g., pensions are under "P"). Paragraphs within each section are numbered consecutively, with the following structure:

Paragraphs	Topics
Paragraphs .101-.499:	Standards
Paragraphs .501-.599:	Definitions
Paragraphs .601-.699:	GASB Technical Bulletins
Paragraphs .701-.799:	GASB Implementation Guides
Paragraphs .801-.899:	AICPA Literature cleared by the GASB
Paragraphs .901-.999:	Nonauthoritative discussion (supplemental guidance and illustrations)

Sources references included in the codification are recognizeable by most practitioners such as "GASBS" meaning "GASB Statement No." Wherever possible, or when it adds clarity, the *Governmental GAAP Guide* not only references a GASB statement when discussing a topic, but also the codification section.

How to Use CCH's *Governmental GAAP Guide*

CCH's *Governmental GAAP Guide* is a single reference that discusses all of the promulgated accounting principles applicable to financial reporting by state and local governments that are in use today (not superseded): GASB Statements,

GASB Interpretations, GASB Technical Bulletins, NCGA Statements, and NCGA Interpretations. These original pronouncements have been analyzed and are restated in straightforward language to allow preparers and auditors of governmental financial statements to better understand the original promulgations. To facilitate research, major topics in the text are cross-referenced to the pertinent paragraphs of the original pronouncements. Illustrations, figures, and paragraphs called "Observations" demonstrate and clarify specific accounting principles.

The *Governmental GAAP Guide* alerts readers to and discusses financial accounting and reporting standards necessary to prepare the basic external financial statements of a governmental entity. A companion text, CCH's *Governmental GAAP Practice Manual*, illustrates how governmental financial statements are prepared based on the standards established by GASB-34 and beyond.

The comprehensive glossary of governmental accounting terms and acronyms continues to be updated. Although it is not meant to be all-inclusive, the glossary references nearly every term contained in GASB standards through GASB-90.

Finally, questions and answers are presented within the text to assist educators, students, and experienced users of the *Governmental GAAP Guide* to further explore and understand concepts and elements discussed.

Acknowledgments

The preparation of this book was made possible by the efforts of a number of dedicated people. My thanks to Mary P. Taylor for her editing and attention to detail and Jack Georger, CPA, for his technical review of the 2019 edition.

Although other individuals played an important role in the preparation of Wolters Kluwer's *Governmental GAAP Guide*, any errors or omissions are the responsibility of the author. The *Governmental GAAP Guide* continues to evolve as new pronouncements are issued and as we strive to better explain governmental accounting and reporting standards. If you have suggestions you believe will improve the quality of the material, please send them to the editor:

Mary P. Taylor
Wolters Kluwer
2700 Lake Cook Road
Riverwoods, Illinois 60015
mary.taylor@wolterskluwer.com

Eric S. Berman

Brookline, Massachusetts

and Boise, Idaho

About the Author

Eric S. Berman, MSA, CPA, CGMA, has over 27 years of governmental accounting and auditing experience and is a Partner with Eide Bailly LLP. Previous to Eide Bailly LLP, he was a quality control principal with a public accounting firm in California.

Eric is the author of the *Governmental Library* for CCH. The Government Library also offers in-depth, interpretive guidance. In addition to this *Governmental GAAP Guide,* users can access CCH's *Governmental GAAP Practice Manual,* the newly released *Governmental GAAP Disclosures Manual, Knowledge-Based Audits™ of State and Local Governments with Single Audits,* and the *Governmental GAAP Update Service.*

Eric's public sector experience includes being a Deputy Comptroller for the Commonwealth of Massachusetts from 1999 to 2010, and the Chief Financial Officer of the Massachusetts Water Pollution Abatement Trust from 1994 to 1999. Eric is a licensed CPA in Massachusetts. He obtained an M.S. in Accountancy from Bentley University. Eric recently represented the Association of Government Accountants (AGA) as the Vice Chairman of the Government Accounting Standards Advisory Council to GASB. He chairs the AGA's Audit Committee. Previously, he chaired the AGA's Financial Management Standards Board. He also is a previous chair of the American Institute of Certified Public Accountants (AICPA) Governmental Performance and Accountability Committee and is a former member of the AICPA's State and Local Government Expert Panel. Eric is currently a member of the GASB's task force reexamining the state and local governmental financial reporting model and has served on previous GASB task forces and working groups assisting in the development and implementation of standards.

Eric is also a past member of the California Society of CPA's Governmental Accounting and Auditing Committee and is past chair of the same committee for the Massachusetts Society of CPAs. He was also the founder and treasurer of a not-for-profit performing arts organization in Pennsylvania. Eric is frequently called upon to consult and train state and local governments throughout the country on governmental accounting and auditing.

I. BASIC GOVERNMENTAL ACCOUNTING CONCEPTS AND STANDARDS

CHAPTER 1
FOUNDATION AND OVERVIEW OF GOVERNMENTAL GENERALLY ACCEPTED ACCOUNTING PRINCIPLES

CONTENTS

INTRODUCTION

The National Council on Governmental Accounting (NCGA) in 1979 defined "generally accepted accounting principles" (GAAP) as it applied to governments in its first statement (NCGA-1, pars. 3–4, as amended by GASB-34, pars. 6, 15, 80, and 82) [GASB Cod. Secs. 1200.101–.102] as:

> [The] uniform minimum standards of and guidelines to financial accounting and reporting. Adherence to U.S. GAAP assures that financial reports of all state and local governments—regardless of jurisdictional legal provisions and customs—contain the same types of financial statements and disclosures, for the same categories and types of funds based on the measurement and classification criteria. Adherence to U.S. GAAP is essential to assuring a reasonable degree of comparability among the financial reports of state and local governments.

Standards have evolved dramatically in the last four decades. The NCGA was replaced by the Governmental Accounting Standards Board (GASB) five years after the statement was released. Technology and practices have changed state and local governmental operations at breakneck speed. Yet, also unchanged is the importance of reporting entities following generally accepted accounting principles in the preparation of their financial statements, which is embodied in the AICPA's *Code of Professional Conduct—Revised*, ET Section 2.320.001 (AICPA ET-2.320.001) which states:

> A member shall not (1) express an opinion or state affirmatively that the financial statements or other financial data of any entity are presented in conformity with generally accepted accounting principles or (2) state that he or she is not aware of any material modifications that should be made to such statements or data in order for them to be in conformity with generally accepted accounting principles, if such statements or data contain any departure from an accounting principle promulgated by bodies designated by Council to establish such principles that has a material effect on the statements or data taken as a whole. If, however, the statements or data contain such a departure and the member can demonstrate that due to unusual circumstances the financial statements or data would otherwise have been misleading, the member can comply with the rule by describing the departure, its approximate effects, if practicable, and the reasons why compliance with the principle would result in a misleading statement.

Part 2 of the *Code of Professional Conduct—Revised* (ET Section 2.320.001) applies to members in *business*. ET Section 0.400.32 defines *members in business* as members of the AICPA who are employed or engaged on a contractual or volunteer basis in a(n) executive, staff, governance, advisory, or administrative capacity in such areas as industry, *the public sector* (emphasis added), education, the not-for-profit sector, and regulatory or professional bodies. This does not include a member engaged in public practice. This definition, coupled with ET Section 1.320.001 which applies to members in public practice—namely independent auditors, means that members of the AICPA who prepare financial statements and work for state and local governments, or who volunteer as an executive, staff, governance, advisory, or administrative capacity (e.g., serving on a school board or a city advisory committee) must follow generally accepted accounting principles or risk an ethics violation. If a regulatory or statutory basis of accounting is used, the departure from U.S. GAAP must be described in the notes to the basic financial statements.

The AICPA Council has designated the Financial Accounting Standards Board (FASB) as the body to establish accounting principles for both for-profit and not-for-profit organizations, the Governmental Accounting Standards Board (GASB) as the body to establish accounting principles for state and local governments, and the Federal Accounting Standards Advisory Board (FASAB) as the body to establish accounting principles for the federal government as well as the Public Company Accounting Oversight Board (PCAOB) for publicly traded entities and the International Accounting Standards Board (IASB) for non-United States entities (AICPA *Code of Professional Conduct—Revised*, app. A).

The Financial Accounting Foundation (FAF) has agreed that the GASB has the authority to issue generally accepted accounting principles for state and local governmental units. Thus, the GASB establishes accounting principles for state and local governments, and the FASB establishes accounting principles for all other reporting entities, including not-for-profit organizations other than state and local governments.

Although not recognized as a standard setter for accounting principles generally accepted in the United States of America, the International Public Sector Accounting Standards Board (IPSASB) focuses on accounting and financial reporting needs of governmental entities at an international level. The IPSASB issues and promotes benchmark guidance and facilitates the exchange of information among governmental accountants and their organizations through the issuance of International Public Sector Accounting Standards (IPSAS) and related guidance. A key part of the IPSASB's strategy is to ultimately converge the IPSASs with the International Financial Reporting Standards (IFRS) issued by the International Accounting Standards Board (IASB). However, at the present time there are no discussions under way to converge the accounting principles generally accepted in the United States of America, as established by the GASB, with the IFRS or IPSASs, even though a few standards (e.g., GASB-42 (*Accounting and Financial Reporting for Impairment of Capital Assets and for Insurance Recoveries*)) have some elements of IPSASs.

GASB-62 (*Codification of Accounting and Financial Reporting Guidance Contained in Pre-November 30, 1989 FASB and AICPA Pronouncements*) incorporates into the GASB's literature all former relevant FASB Statements and Interpretations, APB Opinions, and ARBs issued prior to November 30, 1989, except those that conflict with a GASB pronouncement. The omnibus statement also incorporated all relevant AICPA pronouncements also issued prior to November 30, 1989. Therefore, all non-GASB literature issued prior to November 30, 1989, that has not been codified in GASB-62, is not authoritative.

As discussed in a September 2017 GASB revised white paper entitled *Why Governmental Accounting and Financial Reporting is—and Should Be—Different*, governments are structured differently than for-profit and not-for-profit entities. One central theme of the white paper is that the GASB's continued existence is vital to individuals and organizations who are interested in the financial performance of state and local governments, who have substantially different information needs than those who are interested in the financial performance of for-profit entities. For-profit entities, whose accounting standards are established by the FASB, are environmentally different from government entities. According to the white paper, governments enhance or maintain the well-being of citizens by providing services in accordance with public-policy goals. In contrast, for-profit business enterprises focus primarily on wealth creation, interacting principally with those segments of society that fulfill their mission of generating a financial return on investment for shareholders.

Governments are unique because:

- The entities serve a broader group of stakeholders, including taxpayers, citizens, elected representatives, oversight groups, bondholders, and others in the financial community.

- Most government revenues are raised through involuntary taxes rather than a willing exchange of comparable value between two parties in a typical business transaction.

- Monitoring actual compliance with budgeted public-policy priorities is central to government public-accountability reporting.

- Governments exist longer than for-profit businesses and are less subject to bankruptcy and dissolution, even during the latest recession.

With regard to this last point, GASB-58 (*Accounting and Financial Reporting for Chapter 9 Bankruptcies*) provides accounting and financial reporting guidance for municipal (non-state) governments that have been granted protection from creditors under Chapter 9 of the United States Bankruptcy Code. "Protection" may include modifications to the terms and conditions of certain of the government's debt issuances and relief from burdensome provisions of certain executory contracts and unexpired lease commitments. Although the number of Chapter 9 filings has been very limited in the 70 years since the federal legislation was passed and they only occur in the limited number of states that have approved Chapter 9, recent high-profile and threatened filings have brought the process to the public's attention (e.g., the cities of Detroit, Michigan, the Commonwealth of Puerto Rico, Stockton and San Bernardino, California).

PRACTICE ALERT: The Auditing Standards Board (ASB) of the AICPA has issued Statement on Auditing Standards (SAS) No. 132 [AU-C Section 570] (*The Auditor's Consideration of an Entity's Ability to Continue as a Going Concern*). SAS 132 addresses the auditor's responsibilities in the audit of financial statements relating to the entity's ability to continue as a going concern and the implications for the auditor's report. SAS 132 applies to all audits of a complete set of financial statements (including governments) regardless of whether the financial statements are prepared in accordance with a general purpose or a special purpose framework. SAS 132 requires the auditor to conclude whether substantial doubt exists about an entity's ability to continue as a going concern for a reasonable period of time based on the audit evidence obtained and evaluate the possible financial statement effects, including the adequacy of disclosure related to that disclosure. These provisions are similar to the provisions of GASB Statement No. 56 (*Codification of Accounting and Financial Reporting Guidance Contained in the AICPA Statements on Auditing Standards*), par. 16 [GASB Cod. Sec. 2250.117]. A significant difference between SAS 132 and GASB-56 is that GASB-56 not only looks forward 12 months beyond the date of the financial statements, but further requires that if a governmental entity currently knows information that may raise substantial doubt *shortly* thereafter (usually interpreted to be an additional three months), such information should also be considered. SAS 132 also contemplates so-called "close call" situations, where a third party provides support to the organization to alleviate a going concern. Such situations may be common in governments that do not have Chapter 9. SAS 132 became effective of financial statements for periods ending on or after December 15, 2017. The GASB is also in the midst of pre-agenda research potentially aligning the standards.

THE STATE AND LOCAL GOVERNMENT ACCOUNTING HIERARCHY

A governmental entity may be involved in a variety of activities that have characteristics similar to commercial enterprises and to not-for-profit entities, as well as to governmental activities. Determining which accounting standards should be observed to account for these varied activities has been confusing at times and somewhat complex. GASB-76 (*The Hierarchy of Generally Accepted Accounting Principles for State and Local Governments*) [GASB Cod. Sec. 1000] provides the fundamental guidance for determining which accounting standards governmental entities should observe to prepare their financial statements.

The U.S. GAAP hierarchy for states and local governments contains two categories of principles. The first category of authoritative U.S. GAAP consists of GASB Statements of Governmental Accounting Standards (Category A). The second category of authoritative U.S. GAAP (Category B) consists of GASB *Technical Bulletins* and *Implementation Guides*, as well as guidance from the AICPA that is specifically cleared by the GASB. Such literature contains a statement saying that it has been cleared (the majority of the GASB members did not object to its issuance) by the GASB. The GASB updates *Implementation Guide* 2015-1 annually with new or amended questions, answers, and illustrations after a public due process. Other *Implementation Guides* are issued for specific statements and after implementation of the related GASB Statement(s), are then incorporated into a future update of *Implementation Guide 2015-1.*

PRACTICE POINT: Every effort has been made to reference questions and answers in the *Implementation Guide* where it is essential to magnify, clarify, and elaborate on elements contained within the various chapters of the *Governmental GAAP Guide*. Readers should always use the U.S. GAAP Hierarchy as it is intended, referencing "Category A" U.S. GAAP prior to "Category B" and non-authoritative U.S. GAAP. Preparers of financial statements (and auditors) should also review illustrations within the *Implementation Guide* as more "background" or illustrative material than a GASB Statement—meaning, practitioners should always follow the Hierarchy to decide on the implementation to answer a particular issue, starting with GASB Statements, before referencing the *Implementation*

Guide or a GASB Technical Bulletin and certainly prior to referencing nonauthoritative matter.

Exhibit 1-1 shows the state and local government accounting hierarchy in GASB-76. The hierarchy consists of two categories, with Category B subordinate to Category A. For example, if an accounting issue is addressed in both Category A and Category B, the guidance established in Category A must be followed because it is the highest source of accounting principles for the particular accounting issue (GASB-76, par. 3) [GASB Cod. Sec. 1000.101].

EXHIBIT 1-1
STATE AND LOCAL GOVERNMENT ACCOUNTING HIERARCHY

Category A	• Officially established accounting principles—GASB Statements
Category B	• GASB *Technical Bulletins*, GASB *Implementation Guides*, and literature of the AICPA if specifically cleared by the GASB.

GASB *Interpretations* have been infrequently issued and are largely incorporated into Statements. The statement includes a footnote to Category A on the status of interpretations:

> All GASB Interpretations heretofore issued and currently in effect also are considered as being included within Category A and are continued in force until altered, amended, supplemented, revoked, or superseded by subsequent GASB pronouncements. Category A standards, including GASB Interpretations heretofore issued and currently in effect, are the subject of the Accounting Principles Rule of the American Institute of Certified Public Accountants' (AICPA) *Code of Professional Conduct,* and this Statement does not affect the application of that rule.

Therefore, GASB-76 incorporates GASB's Interpretations by reference into Category A.

PRACTICE POINT: GASB-76, paragraph 3(b) (Category B) [GASB Cod. Sec. 1000.101(b)], incorporates literature of the AICPA "cleared by the GASB," inclusive of literature specifically made applicable to state and local government entities. This literature includes elements primarily found in the AICPA Audit and Accounting Guide *State and Local Governments* (*AICPA Audit Guide*) as well as the AICPA Audit and Accounting Guide *Health Care Entities* and referenced in the GASB *Codification of Governmental Accounting and Financial Reporting Standards* (the *Codification*) as follows:

Nature of Guidance in the AICPA Audit and Accounting Guide – State and Local Governments—Appendix B	GASB Codification Reference [GASB Cod. Sec]
• Definition of "government"	1000.801, 1000 fn. 4
• Annual calculation of an arbitrage liability	1500.801
• Overdrafts of internal investment pools and of cash accounts	1800.801–.802
• Interfund balances relating to agency funds with negative cash balances	1800.803
• Reporting nonoperating revenue for certain nonexchange revenues for operating purposes or for operating purposes or capital outlay at the recipient's discretion	N50.802, 1800.804, 2200.801, P80.804
• When to report the issuance of debt	1500.802
• Reporting revenue for fees received for administering pass-through grants	N50.801
• Accounting for customer deposits for utility services	Ut5.801, P80.806
• Accounting for payments to the refunding agent for current refundings as an other financing use	D20.801
• Definition of "commitment"	2300.801
• Disclosure in the notes to the financial statements if a budget is not adopted for the general or a major special revenue fund because it is not legally required when a government presents required budgetary comparison information in the basic financial statements	1700.801, 2300.802, 2400.801
• Revenues and expenses that financing authorities should report in their financial statements, including when involved with conduit debt	P80.805, C65.801
• Reporting nonoperating revenue for appropriations for operating purposes or for operating purposes or capital outlay at the recipient's discretion	1800.804, 2200.801, N50.802, P80.804
• Accounting for lottery prize costs	P80.807, Sp20.801
• Accounting for prize liabilities for which annuities have been purchased	P80.808–.809, Sp20.802–.803
• Using present value to measure lottery prize liabilities	P80.810, Sp20.804
• Disclosure in the notes to the financial statements if a budget is not adopted for the general or a major special revenue fund because it is not legally required when a government presents required budgetary comparison information in the basic financial statements	1700.801, 2200.802, 2400.801

In addition, the *AICPA Audit Guides* contain Category B GAAP on capital asset impairment considerations for gaming entities, reporting by gaming entities, and charity care reported by public hospitals.

Authoritative U.S. GAAP is incorporated annually into the *Codification*. Many practitioners reference the *Codification* as it may be easier to find information. However, due to the annual updating, there may be a time lag in between the issuance of a GASB Statement and the incorporation of the information from the new Statement into the *Codification*. So practitioners may want to initiate research by starting with the applicable GASB Statement and if it is easier to follow, review the applicable *Codification* sections to provide an answer to a problem in accounting or financial reporting. The *Codification* also incorporates the *Implementation Guide* questions and answers.

GASB-76, par. 7 [GASB Cod. Sec. 1000.104], lists nonauthoritative literature that may be referenced, including:

- GASB Concepts Statements;
- Pronouncements and other literature of the FASB, FASAB, IPSASB, IASB, and AICPA (other than AICPA literature cleared by the GASB); practices that are widely recognized and prevalent in state and local government;
- Literature of other professional associations or regulatory agencies; and
- Accounting textbooks (including CCH's *Governmental GAAP Guide*), handbooks, and articles.

GASB-76, par. 8 [GASB Cod. Sec. 1000.105], directs practitioners to evaluate the appropriateness of nonauthoritative accounting literature by considering the consistency of the literature to GASB Concepts Statements, the relevance of the literature to particular circumstances, the specificity of the literature, and the general recognition of the issuer or author as an authority.

Application Guidance

The structure contained in GASB-76 is a hierarchy. Standards established in the highest category take precedence over those contained in a lower category. For example, accounting issues related to environmental liabilities are addressed in both GASB-49 (*Accounting and Financial Reporting for Pollution Remediation Obligations*) [GASB Cod. Sec. P40] and Statement of Federal Financial Accounting Standards 5 (*Accounting for Liabilities of the Federal Government*), as amended. When preparing financial statements for a governmental entity, the accountant must observe the standards established in GASB-49 because GASB Statements are part of Category A of the hierarchy and Federal Accounting Standards Advisory Board (FASAB) Statements are nonauthoritative (GASB-76, par. 7) [GASB Cod. Sec. 1000.104].

When an accounting issue is not addressed in a GASB Statement, the Category B of the hierarchy must be considered. For example, if a matter is addressed in an AICPA Industry Audit and Accounting Guide that has been made applicable by the AICPA and cleared by the GASB, the guidance established in the publication should be used to prepare the financial statements of a state or local governmental entity (GASB-76, pars. 4–6) [GASB Cod. Secs. 1000.101–.103].

OBSERVATION: The state and local government accounting hierarchy does not apply to the federal government. Accounting standards for the federal government are established by the Federal Accounting Standards Advisory Board (FASAB).

Accounting Principles Other Than U.S. GAAP (formerly known as OCBOA) ("Special Purpose Framework")

CCH's *Governmental GAAP Guide* focuses on accounting and financial reporting in accordance with U.S. GAAP; however, certain state and local governments that are not legally required to prepare financial statements in accordance with U.S. GAAP may elect to prepare their financial statements in accordance with a framework formerly known as an "other comprehensive basis of accounting" (OCBOA). It is known more properly known as a "special purpose framework" (SPF). Included in the definition of an SPF are various non-GAAP bases of accounting, including the cash basis, modified cash basis, regulatory basis, and income tax basis of accounting. Some state and local laws do not recognize GASB or FASB pronouncements as the required basis for preparing their governmental financial statements. For example, a governmental unit through a charter or constitution may require that a governmental reporting entity prepare its budget and financial statements on a cash basis, modified cash basis, or regulatory basis of accounting. In addition, state regulatory requirements may specify a basis of accounting other than U.S. GAAP for the preparation and filing of a government's financial statements with a specific regulatory agency. In these circumstances, the government unit should follow the guidance applicable to SPFs in the preparation of their annual financial statements.

OBSERVATION: The AICPA practice aid *State and Local Governments (TIS Section 6950.21-.22) (referring to AU-C section 800, Special Considerations—Audits of Financial Statements Prepared in Accordance with Special Purpose Frameworks)* may be helpful in preparing cash basis, modified cash basis, and regulatory basis financial statements for state and local government entities. TIS Section 9110, *Special Reports*, also has explanatory information on auditors' reports based on the provisions of Special Purpose Frameworks.

Many budgets prepared by state and local governments are developed on a basis of accounting other than U.S. GAAP. As a result, the government's internal accounting records are likely maintained on that same non-GAAP basis in order to track legal compliance. Although the governmental unit maintains its accounting records on a non-GAAP basis for legal compliance purposes, the GASB has stated that the government may still adopt a supplementary accounting system that will enable it to report on a U.S. GAAP basis in its annual financial statements (NCGA-1, par. 5).

HIERARCHY FOR PROPRIETARY FUND ACCOUNTING ACTIVITIES

From the inception of the GASB in 1984 to the release of GASB-62, there was periodic confusion among financial statement preparers, auditors, and users over its role and that of the Financial Accounting Standards Board (FASB) in the promulgation of generally accepted accounting principles for governmental entities that conduct business-type activities (such as municipal utilities) or that can take the form of either a public or a private entity (such as public health care entities, colleges, and universities).

In general, proprietary funds use the same measurement focus (flow of economic resources) and accounting basis (accrual) as commercial enterprises. Thus, governmental entities formerly had to observe all FASB Statements and Interpretations in the preparation of financial statements for proprietary funds unless the GASB has specifically addressed an accounting issue involved in one of its own pronouncements.

In practice, some proprietary funds and government entities applying proprietary fund principles previous to the issuance of GASB-62 chose to follow all FASB pronouncements while others chose to ignore those FASB pronouncements that have not been made specifically applicable to the governmental entities or cleared by the GASB. GASB-62, GASB-34 (*Basic Financial Statements—and Management's Discussion and Analysis—for State and Local Governments*), and GASB-37 (*Basic Financial Statements—and Management's Discussion and Analysis—for State and Local Governments: Omnibus*) address the issue of the applicability of FASB pronouncements.

GASB-62 not only applies to proprietary funds (enterprise and internal service funds) and governmental entities that follow proprietary fund accounting, including public benefit corporations and authorities, governmental utilities, and governmental hospital or other health-care activities, but also certain governmental activities. Based on the guidance in GASB-62, the items listed in Exhibit 1-2 are now codified for both governmental and proprietary activities.

EXHIBIT 1-2
WHICH PARTS OF GASB-62 APPLY TO WHICH BASIS OF ACCOUNTING

Both Governmental and Business Type Apply	Business-Type Activities/Fund Types Only
Special and extraordinary items, subject to the reporting distinctions of governmental funds	Capitalization of interest (see **PRACTICE ALERT** in this chapter).
Contingencies, subject to the reporting distinctions of governmental funds	Revenue recognition with a right of return.
Related parties, subject to the reporting distinctions of governmental funds	Inventory
Leases, subject to the reporting distinctions of governmental funds	Regulated operations—can apply to certain business-type activities that meet all of the following criteria (established in GASB-62, par. 476):
	• The activity's rates for regulated services provided to its customers are established by or subject to approval by an independent, third-party regulator or by its own governing board empowered by statute or contract to establish rates that bind customers.

Both Governmental and Business Type Apply	Business-Type Activities/Fund Types Only
	• The rates are designed to recover the specific regulated business-type activity's costs of providing the regulated services.
	• It is reasonable to assume that rates are set at levels that will recover the regulated business-type activity's costs and they can be charged and collected from customers. Changes in level of demand or competition during the recovery period for capitalized costs are considered.

Besides what is named in Exhibit 1-2, the scope of GASB-62 also includes the transactions set forth in Exhibit 1-3:

EXHIBIT 1-3
GASB-62 PARTS THAT APPLY TO ALL BASES OF ACCOUNTING

- Revenue recognition for exchange transactions
- Statement of net position classification
- Comparative financial statements
- Prior period adjustments
- Accounting changes and error corrections
- Disclosure of accounting policies
- Construction contracts—long term
- Extinguishments of debt
- Cable television systems
- Insurance entities—other than public entity risk pools

- Troubled debt restructuring
- Foreign currency transactions
- Interest costs—imputation
- Investments in common stock
- Nonmonetary transactions
- Sales of real estate
- Research and development operations
- Broadcasters
- Lending activities
- Mortgage banking activities

PRACTICE ALERT: The GASB recently issued GASB Statement No. 89, *Accounting for Interest Cost Incurred before the end of a Construction Period*. Upon implementation, interest will no longer need to be capitalized during the period of construction. Any interest capitalized for construction in process will no longer be part of the historical cost of the asset, but instead expensed. The provisions of the Statement are effective for periods beginning after December 15, 2019 and implemented prospectively. It is anticipated that many governments will implement these provisions early.

Applicability of GASB-62, pars. 476–500, to Proprietary Fund Accounting—*Regulated Operations*

As introduced in Exhibit 1-2, GASB-62, pars. 476–500, on *Regulated Operations* [GASB Cod. Sec. Re10], applies to governmental entities that meet *all* the following criteria:

- The regulated business-type activity's rates for regulated services provided to its customers are established by or are subject to approval by an independent, third-party regulator or by its own governing board empowered by statute or contract to establish rates that bind customers.

- The regulated rates are designed to recover the specific regulated business-type activity's costs of providing the regulated services.

- In view of the demand for the regulated services or products and the level of competition, direct and indirect, it is reasonable to assume that rates set at levels that will recover the regulated business-type activity's costs can be charged to and collected from customers. This criterion requires consideration of anticipated changes in levels of demand or competition during the recovery period for any capitalized costs (GASB-62, par. 476) [GASB Cod. Sec. Re10.101].

The various provisions of the paragraphs related to regulatory operations discuss when an asset exists and when all or part of incurred costs may be capitalized and the manner in which those costs may be recovered. Regulatory provisions may also govern asset impairment or imposition of a liability. Profits and surpluses may also be regulated.

All of the provisions within the various paragraphs of GASB-62 related to regulatory accounting are not new. They are simply edited versions of the former FAS-71 (FASB Accounting Standards Codification® (ASC™) Topic 980, *Regulated Operations*), as amended.

PRACTICE POINT: Chapter 24, "Other Special-Purpose Governments," contains a further discussion on regulated operations and accounting.

Applicability of ASC™ 958, *Not-for-Profit Entities*, and the AICPA Not-for-Profit Model (GASB-29)

GASB-29 (*The Use of Not-for-Profit Accounting and Financial Reporting Principles by Governmental Entities*) allowed *some* governmental entities to use the AICPA not-for-profit model as described in the former AICPA's Statement of Position 78-10 (SOP 78-10) (*Accounting Principles and Reporting Practices for Certain Nonprofit Organizations*). GASB-34, par. 147 and ultimately GASB-62, par. 4 superseded the use of that model. The remaining guidance for component units that are not-for-profits is largely contained in the GASB *Implementation Guide* questions 4.33.1–4.33.4, which reference GASB-14, footnote 4 and paragraph 43.

Footnote 4 to GASB-14 (*The Financial Reporting Entity*) (as amended) [GASB Cod. Sec. 2100, fn. 3] discusses how component units and other related entities to a government may be organized as not-for-profit or for-profit entities. Not-for-profit entities (e.g., foundations) are typically related to public healthcare and higher education institutions. For-profit component units may be limited liability corporations related to the public healthcare, higher education, or post-employment benefit fund entities. Paragraph 43 of GASB-14 [GASB Cod. Sec. 2100.143] requires governments to apply "the definition and display provisions of this Statement." To accomplish this, translation may have to occur between the basis of accounting of the component units and the primary government. Questions 4.33.1–4.33.4 of the *GASB Implementation Guide 2015-1* discuss translation between the bases of accounting and presentation. However, there is no requirement to change the recognition, measurement, or disclosure standards applied in a nongovernmental component unit's separately issued financial statements. Further discussion on these issues may be found in Chapter 4, "Governmental Financial Reporting Entity."

PRACTICE POINT: GASB Statement No. 80 (*Blending Requirements for Certain Component Units—an amendment of GASB Statement No. 14*) became effective for fiscal years that began after June 15, 2016. The statement required component units that are organized as not-for-profit corporations in which the primary government is the *sole corporate member* to be blended. The effect of the change may have caused many entities related to institutions of higher education and healthcare facilities to no longer be recognized either as discretely presented component units or related organizations.

CAUTION: The phrase *sole corporate member* may have slight variations in practice dependent upon state law. Practitioners should review related state laws as part of the implementation process of GASB-80.

PRACTICE ALERT: The FASB has recently issued an accounting standards update for Topic 958 (as well as Topic 954 for Health Care Entities), revising the reporting model for not-for-profit entities. The FASB proposes to present on the face of the Statement of Financial Position and the Statement of Activities amounts for two classes of net assets at the end of the period, rather than the currently required three (eliminating the temporarily restricted category). The Statement of Activities would also be amended presenting two additional subtotals of the operating activities that are associated with changes in net assets without donor restrictions. Other amendments are also proposed. As (if not more) importantly, the FASB recently approved Accounting Standards Update (ASU) 2014-09 (subsequently delayed by Accounting Standards Update 2015-14, *Revenue from Contracts with Customers*) (amending Topic 606) containing a major revision to the revenue recognition principles. This amendment is effective for annual reporting periods beginning after December 15, 2016 through December 15, 2019, depending upon aspects of the entity. ASU 2014-09 completely revises the revenue recognition model for all non-governmental entities for all goods and services. As such, governments that believe they should apply the not-for-profit model should be very aware of the changes forthcoming and be very sure of the accounting model to apply for their particular entity.

IDENTIFYING A GOVERNMENTAL ENTITY

To determine whether the state and local government accounting hierarchy or the nongovernmental accounting hierarchy applies to a particular entity, the entity must be classified as governmental or nongovernmental. In most instances it is obvious how an entity should be classified, but there are occasions in which classification is not so obvious. These issues are addressed in Chapter 1 of the AICPA's Audit and Accounting Guide *State and Local Governments* (AICPA Audit Guide) and have now been incorporated by reference into the GASB *Codification* due to GASB-76.

The AICPA Audit Guide defines "governmental entities" as "public corporations and bodies corporate and politic." In addition, other entities are governmental if they have one or more of the following three characteristics:

1. Popular election of officers or appointment (or approval) of a controlling majority of the members of the organization's governing body by officials of one or more state or local governments;

2. The potential for unilateral dissolution by a government with net position reverting to a government; or

3. The power to enact and enforce a tax levy.

Footnote 4 to GASB-76 [GASB Cod. Sec. 1000.801 fn. 4] references *Black's Law Dictionary* in defining a "public corporation" as: "An artificial person (e.g., [a] municipality or a governmental corporation) created for the administration of public affairs. Unlike a private corporation it has no protection against legislative acts altering or even repealing its charter. Instrumentalities created by [the] state, formed and owned by it in [the] public interest, supported in whole or part by public funds, and governed by managers deriving their authority from [the] state." Further, "a public corporation is an instrumentality of the state, founded and owned in the public interest, supported by public funds and governed by those deriving their authority from the state" in the definition.

Entities are presumed to be governmental if they have the ability to issue federal tax-exempt debt that is exempt from federal tax. However, entities possessing only this characteristic and none of the other three noted above, may consider themselves nongovernmental if their determination is supported by compelling, relevant evidence.

OBSERVATION: The fact that an entity is incorporated as a not-for-profit organization and exempt from federal income taxation under Section 501 of the Internal Revenue Code is not a criterion for classifying it as governmental.

According to information available from the U.S. Bureau of Census' *2012 Census of Governments*, there are over 90,100 units of state and local governments in the United States that were in existence as of June 30, 2012. Generally, these governmental entities can be classified into one of two categories:

1. General-purpose governments, including the 50 states, territories, and the District of Columbia, over 3,000 counties, 19,500 municipalities, and 16,300 townships.

2. Special-purpose governments including nearly 13,000 independent school districts and 38,000 other special districts.

The Census is in the process of finalizing the 2017 *Census of Governments* with a first data release scheduled for late 2018.

General-Purpose Governments

General-purpose governments provide a wide range of services (often including both governmental and business-type activities) and include states, counties, cities, towns, villages, and similar governmental entities. Although recognized Indian tribes may not specifically meet the criteria to be defined as a governmental entity, most tribal governments prepare their financial statements in accordance with the principles applicable to general-purpose state and local governments. Also included in the description of general-purpose governments are U.S. territories and the District of Columbia.

> **OBSERVATION:** For the purposes of federal relationships and classification, Title 2, Code of Federal Regulations, Part 200, *Uniform Administrative Requirements, Cost Principles, and Audit Requirements* (2CFR200), Indian Tribes, including Alaskan Natives, are separately defined from other governments and recipients of federal funds as long as they are recognized as eligible for the special programs and services provided by the United States to Indians because of their status as Indians (see also 25 USC 450(b)(e)). Throughout 2CFR200, guidance for Tribes and Alaskan Natives is largely similar to states as they are sovereign entities from other governments. Tribal governments may offer similar services to general-purpose governments or special-purpose governments (discussed in the next section). They may provide subsidized housing, operate a public health facility, and provide for public safety, education, sanitation, and other functions similar to states and other governments. Throughout this *Guide*, minimal further information specifically directed at Tribes and Alaska Natives is included. Tribal governments may follow GASB, or they may follow FASB, especially if they have a casino, or both.

Special-Purpose Governments

Special-purpose governments are defined as legally separate governmental entities that perform only one or a few activities and include colleges and universities, school districts, water and other utility districts or authorities, fire protection districts, cemetery districts, public employee retirement systems, public entity risk pools, governmental hospital or health-care organizations, public housing authorities, airport authorities, and similar entities.

The accounting and financial reporting treatment for a special-purpose government depends on the type of activities conducted by the entity. For example, some special-purpose governments are engaged only in business-type activities (e.g., a water district), some are engaged only in governmental activities (e.g., a library district), and others may be involved in a combination of activities (e.g., a school district).

Accounting and financial reporting for special-purpose governments are discussed in more detail elsewhere:

- Comprehensive Annual Financial Report (Chapter 20)
- Public Colleges and Universities (Chapter 21)
- Pension and Other Postemployment Benefit Plans (Chapter 22)
- Public Entity Risk Pools (Chapter 23)
- Other Special-Purpose Governments (Chapter 24).

GASB PRINCIPLE SETTING PROCESS

The GASB has established a due process for the promulgation of governmental generally accepted accounting principles that encourages participation by parties interested in a particular accounting issue. Once a governmental accounting issue has been identified, the due process generally consists of the following potential stages:

- Pre-agenda research;
- Invitation to Comment (staff document);
- Preliminary views;
- Exposure draft; and
- Standard setting.

Pre-Agenda Research Stage

The GASB may direct its staff to perform initial research on various accounting and reporting issues with a goal of presenting a memorandum to the GASB to decide upon whether the issue falls under its Scope of Authority and should be added to its current project agenda for further research. The research may include questionnaires, interviews with knowledgeable individuals, research of archival information from state and local government financial reports, and inquiry on industry practices. The GASB needs to vote affirmatively to add any pre-agenda research to the current agenda.

Once a project is added to the technical agenda, more research is performed by staff. Additional surveys, questionnaires, task force meetings, focus group interviews, and other information may be brought to the GASB's attention for deliberation.

Invitation to Comment

For complex projects, an Invitation to Comment document may be released. An invitation to comment is a document produced by GASB's staff designed to seek comments from interested parties at a relatively early stage of a project before the Board has reached a consensus view. Comments are usually in writing but public hearings may take place. An Invitation to Comment is a step before a Preliminary Views document, with a goal of providing GASB staff and the Board additional information on a project. It does not represent a consensus view of the Board.

Examples of recent Invitations to Comment have occurred in the *Financial Reporting Model Improvements—Governmental Funds* and the *Revenue and Expense Recognition* projects. In both cases, the next step is a preliminary views document.

Preliminary Views Stage

A Preliminary Views document is issued by the GASB when they desire to solicit opinions from constituents on accounting and reporting alternatives and the preliminary views of the GASB members in the early stages of accounting standards setting. This document is usually used if there is an issue that is complex or controversial. Otherwise, an Exposure Draft is developed. A Preliminary Views document may even have an alternative view that may be shared by two or more GASB members. Comments are made by responding parties. In addition, public hearings on the issue may be held where participants can present their views orally and respond to questions raised by members of the GASB. Upon receipt of comments on the GASB's Preliminary Views, further deliberation and research occurs.

Exposure Draft Stage

After research and GASB deliberation, *or* the receipt of responses from interested parties based on the description of the issue in the Preliminary Views document (if issued), an Exposure Draft may be developed. When the GASB reaches its tentative conclusion to the issue, it issues an Exposure Draft for public comment.

> **OBSERVATION:** Copies of current due process documents can be obtained from the GASB's website (www.gasb.org). Responses to Preliminary Views and Exposure Drafts are also posted on the website. GASB may also release a "plain language" document to encourage more stakeholders to participate in commenting on the due process document.

Standard-Setting Stage

After receiving comments on the Exposure Draft, the GASB may hold another public hearing. Once the GASB reaches a consensus on the accounting issue, it promulgates a standard that becomes part of generally accepted accounting principles for state and local governments. The GASB observes due process for major governmental accounting issues.

Occasionally, the GASB revisits a previous standard and decides that an omnibus statement is needed to clarify an issue in a Statement, provide technical corrections, or more closely align an issue to current practice. The last technical corrections standard that was released was GASB Statement No. 85 (*Omnibus 2017*). If issues arise during implementation of a new Statement, the GASB may approve corrections or amendments to previously issued Statements may be placed into new Statements as they are released. For example, GASB Statement

No. 78 (*Pensions Provided through Certain Multiple-Employer Defined Benefit Pension Plans*) amends certain provisions of GASB Statement No. 68 for certain entities, based upon questions and concerns received by GASB staff during the implementation of GASB-68.

In December 2010, the GASB issued a unique document suggesting guidelines on Service Efforts and Accomplishments (SEA) reporting that are voluntarily reported by governments. Suggested guidelines were used because although SEA performance reporting is not universally defined or required, the GASB believes it is an essential element of communicating basic information about a government. GASB's extensive research and monitoring indicate that it is appropriate at this time for the GASB to set forth conceptually based suggested guidelines for voluntary reporting of SEA performance information. However, it is beyond the scope of the GASB to establish the goals and objectives of state and local government services, specific nonfinancial measures or indicators of service performance, or standards of, or benchmarks for, service performance. Conversely, according to GASB:CS-1, par. 77c, "financial reporting should provide information to assist users in assessing the service efforts, costs, and accomplishments of the governmental entity." Therefore, the GASB believes that it is proper to issue guidance, even if SEA performance reporting is voluntary.

GASB Pronouncements

The GASB may express its position on a particular governmental accounting topic by issuing one or more of the following pronouncements:

- GASB Statement;
- GASB Technical Bulletins; and
- GASB Implementation Guides.

GASB Statement (Category A GAAP)

The GASB addresses major governmental accounting issues by issuing a GASB Statement, but only after all aspects of the due process have occurred.

Previously, the GASB addressed issues of lesser scope by issuing Interpretations. An Interpretation was subject to due process, although the procedures were not as formal as those for the promulgation of a Statement. Interpretations were directly voted on by the GASB and, if accepted by a majority of its members, become part of governmental generally accepted accounting principles. These have largely been included as part of Statements and are no longer being issued.

GASB-76, par. 4, also includes information on the GASB *Codification*. The *Codification* is typically updated annually for new statements and other matter issued by the GASB. GASB-76, par. 4, discusses the *Codification*, noting that upon incorporation of new statements and other matter, the information, when presented in the *Codification*, retains its authoritative status (GASB-76, par. 4) [GASB Cod. Sec. 1000.101].

GASB Technical Bulletins (Category B GAAP)

The GASB recognizes that under certain circumstances it may not need to follow the due process used for issuing a Statement or an Interpretation. The GASB has authorized its staff to provide timely guidance on governmental accounting issues by preparing a Technical Bulletin Series. The nature and purpose of GASB Technical Bulletins were addressed in GASB Technical Bulletin 84-1 (Purpose and Scope of GASB Technical Bulletins and Procedures for Issuance) (GASB:TB 84-1, par. 2).

GASB:TB 84-1 states that a Technical Bulletin, rather than a Statement or Interpretation, may be issued under the following general criteria:

- The guidance is not expected to cause a major change in accounting practice for a significant number of entities.
- The administrative cost involved in implementing the guidance is not expected to be significant for most affected entities.
- The guidance does not conflict with a broad fundamental principle or create a novel accounting practice (GASB:TB 84-1, par. 5).

The GASB follows due process before it issues a Technical Bulletin. Before the GASB releases an initial draft of a Technical Bulletin to the public for comment, members of the GASB are furnished with a copy. If a majority of the members do not object to the initial draft, the proposed Technical Bulletin is released to interested parties. Responses from the interested parties are given to the GASB for its consideration at a public meeting. If a majority of the GASB members do not object to the proposed Technical Bulletin, the GASB will issue it as a formal Technical Bulletin. Each Technical Bulletin is published with a legend that reads, "The GASB has reviewed this Technical Bulletin and a majority of its members do not object to its issuance" (GASB:TB 84-1, pars. 6–12).

PRACTICE POINT: GASB:TB 84-1 was not codified due to its foundational subject matter. Other technical bulletins have been codified. GASB:TB 2004-1, *Tobacco Settlement Recognition and Financial Reporting Entity Issues*, is still in effect as of the date of publication. GASB:TB 2004-1 is codified at GASB Cod. Secs. 2100.601, 2600.601, and T50.

Implementation Guides (Category B)

The GASB's *Implementation Guide* is a compendium of questions and answers providing explanatory material to practitioners, assisting in understanding GASB standards. The GASB may also issue freestanding *Implementation Guides* related to specific statements. As previously discussed, the Board now issues *Implementation Guide Updates*, for any new questions and answers developed as well as amendments needed to previous questions and answers due to new GASB Statement issuances. All of these are collected and incorporated annually as part of the *Implementation Guide*. The initial *Implementation Guide 2015-1* contained more than 1,200 questions and answers related to GASB standards, including those for which no individual Guides have been issued. (See previous **PRACTICE POINT** on the usage of *Implementation Guides*, especially illustrations.) Subsequent guides have added hundreds more questions and answers and edited those previously released.

> **PRACTICE POINT:** A more "user-friendly" way to find *Implementation Guide* questions and answers, including updates, may be in the *Codification.* In each section of the *Codification*, subsections .701–.799 contain *Implementation Guide* questions and answers for each subject. The illustrations and other nonauthoritative matter from *Implementation Guides* (and Statements) are contained in subsections .901–.999 of each section.

Governmental Accounting Standards Advisory Council (GASAC)

The GASB is assisted in its standards-setting process by the Governmental Accounting Standards Advisory Council (GASAC). The GASAC is responsible for consulting with the GASB on technical issues on the GASB's agenda, project priorities, matters likely to require the attention of the GASB, selection and organization of task forces, and such other matters as requested by the GASB or its chairman. The GASAC is also responsible for helping to develop the GASB's annual budget and aiding the Financial Accounting Foundation in raising funds for the GASB. The GASAC has 30 members, who are broadly representative of preparers, attesters, and users of financial information. In addition, the Comptroller General of the United States serves as an official observer.

GASB Resource Aids

The GASB staff spends considerable time helping constituents to understand and implement existing standards. Highlighted below are many of the resources the GASB makes available to help constituents apply changes in U.S. generally accepted accounting principles (U.S. GAAP) for state and local governments.

Online Technical Inquiry System

A constituent with a question about GASB standards or state and local government financial statements can fill out and submit a technical inquiry form (which may be accessed through a link in the Technical Issues section of the GASB website) and gain access to input on technical matters from the GASB staff. As resources allow, the staff responds to inquires in the interest of promoting the uniform application of U.S. GAAP and of fostering relations with the GASB constituency. Inquiries are generally responded to within a few days and are typically resolved in less than two weeks.

Governmental Accounting Research System Online

The GASB's *Governmental Accounting Research System* (GARS) is available on a subscription basis from the GASB on the internet. The complete set of original pronouncements, the GASB codification and implementation guides, as well as an index are included and are completely searchable by keyword or query.

GASB has a free, basic, online version of GARS (https://gars.gasb.org), with browsing by a table of contents. Academics have access to a subscription-based professional view, which is free for accounting program faculty and students that enroll in the program and are approved by the FAF. The professional view contains the entirety of GASB's guidance, advanced navigation, search and connection features, the ability to go back and forth between documents, and many other features, including printing and the ability to share content through social media.

Plain Language Articles and Explanatory Videos on Demand

Since 2005, many proposed GASB standards or new GASB standards have been accompanied by a relatively short explanatory article that uses a minimum of technical language. The GASB is committed to communicating in plain language with constituents about its standards and standards-setting activities. All of the articles, fact sheets, and publications in the Plain Language section of the GASB website are available for download free of charge. GASB has also started to post on its website videos on demand that explain proposed standards.

Speeches

The GASB staff, as well as its chairman, board members, and director of research and technical activities, as well as GASAC members, make appearances across the country each year to provide training regarding the proper application of GASB standards and other pronouncements, and to provide updates on GASB activities.

PRACTICE POINT: Many practitioners point to speeches and other communications from the GASB staff, its chairman, board members, and others as authoritative. These communications are *not authoritative* and usually bear a "disclaimer" as part of the communication, reminding receivers of the communication that it has not been subject to due process.

Website

The GASB makes a variety of resources available through its easy-to-navigate website, which provides click-through links to the GASB News Center, free copies of all current proposals, GASB Project Pages detailing current agenda projects and pronouncements. To be added to the GASB's constituent database, be included in GASB research and outreach activities, receive periodic e-mail updates, and be considered for GASB task forces and advisory committees, a constituent can fill out the Visitors' Register on the website.

User Guides

The GASB's nontechnical User Guides series, which are plain-language, nontechnical introductions to the financial reports of state and local governments, have been as useful to accountants and finance officers as they have been to users, both for understanding financial reports and explaining them to clients and elected officials. The nontechnical User Guides are designed for broad accessibility to anyone from the government finance novice to the longtime public manager. All of the editions in the series—the What You Should Know Guides, An Analyst's Guide, the guide to notes and supporting information, and the quick guides for elected officials—are available through the GASB store on its website.

OVERVIEW OF GOVERNMENTAL GENERALLY ACCEPTED ACCOUNTING PRINCIPLES CONCEPT STATEMENTS

As previously mentioned, NCGA-1 (*Governmental Accounting and Financial Reporting Principles*), adopted by the GASB upon its establishment in 1984, states that financial statements of a state or local government should be prepared in accordance with generally accepted accounting principles. Certain governments may be required or permitted to prepare their financial statements on a regulatory basis of accounting or another comprehensive basis of accounting; however, generally accepted accounting principles continue to be the primary criteria for preparation of financial statements of states and local governments. The generally accepted accounting principles that are applicable to state and local governments can be found primarily in the statements, interpretations, and other due-process documents remaining in effect of the NCGA, the GASB, and the applicable principles of the FASB and AICPA contained in GASB-62. The framework for such principles is established in the Concepts Statements of the GASB.

Although not considered generally accepted accounting principles themselves, Concepts Statements are intended to provide a conceptual framework that can be used as a basis for establishing consistent accounting and financial reporting standards and serve multiple purposes, including the following:

- Identifying the objectives and fundamental principles of financial reporting that can be applied to solve numerous financial accounting and reporting issues;

- Providing the GASB with the basic conceptual foundation for considering the merits of alternative approaches to financial reporting and helping the GASB develop well-reasoned financial reporting standards; and

- Assisting preparers, auditors, and users in better understanding the fundamental concepts underlying financial reporting standards.

The GASB has issued six Concepts Statements, as follows:

Concept Statement Number	Title
Concepts Statement No. 1	Objectives of Financial Reporting (GASB:CS-1)
Concepts Statement No. 2	Service Efforts and Accomplishments (GASB:CS-2)
Concepts Statement No. 3	Communication Methods in General Purpose External Financial Reports that Contain Basic Financial Statements (GASB:CS-3)
Concepts Statement No. 4	Elements of Financial Statements (GASB:CS-4)
Concepts Statement No. 5	Services Efforts and Accomplishments Reporting (an amendment to GASB Concepts Statement No. 2) (GASB:CS-5)
Concepts Statement No. 6	Measurement of Elements of Financial Statements (GASB:CS-6)

PRACTICE ALERT: The GASB has restarted a dormant project originally began prior to 2011, updating the conceptual framework for recognition and measurement of elements of financial statements. The goal of the project is to develop recognition criteria for whether information should be reported in state and local governmental financial statements and when that information should be reported. This project ultimately will lead to a Concepts Statement on recognition of elements of financial statements. A preliminary views document was being released as this publication went to press. An exposure draft is expected by 2020 and potential approval of a final Concepts Statement during 2022.

The following discussion describes these Concepts Statements and their accounting and reporting framework objectives.

Objectives of Financial Reporting

The purpose of financial reporting by state and local governmental entities is to provide information to facilitate decision making by various user groups. GASB:CS-1 identifies the following primary user groups of governmental financial reports (GASB:CS-1, par. 30):

- Citizens of the governmental entity;
- Direct representatives of the citizens (legislatures and oversight bodies); and
- Investors, creditors, and others who are involved in the lending process.

Although not specifically identified in the above listing, GASB:CS-1 states that intergovernmental grantors and other users have informational needs similar to the three primary user groups (GASB:CS-1, par. 31).

The financial reporting objectives identified by the GASB in GASB:CS-1 are to be used as a framework for establishing accounting and reporting standards for general-purpose financial statements (GPFS) (more commonly known as the basic financial statements); however, the framework may also be used by the GASB to establish standards for financial information presented outside of the GPFS. In addition, the financial reporting standards are applicable to general-purpose financial information presented in special-purpose financial reports prepared by state and local governmental entities (GASB:CS-1, pars. 8–9).

Although the governmental-type activities and business-type activities of a governmental entity can differ significantly, the GASB concluded that financial reporting objectives identified in GASB:CS-1 are applicable to both types of activities. Although financial reporting objectives are applicable to both governmental-type and business-type activities, the GASB does recognize that a specific objective may vary in its application to a particular reporting situation depending on the business-type activity and the user group that is evaluating the activity. For example, both creditors and a legislative body may be interested in a business-type activity, but creditors may be more concerned with the ability of the activity to generate cash flow from operations to service future debt requirements, whereas the legislature may be more concerned with the likelihood of future operations requiring subsidies from general revenues (GASB:CS-1, par. 43).

GASB:CS-1 identifies *accountability* as the paramount objective of financial reporting by state and local governments. Accountability is based on the transfer of responsibility for resources or actions from the citizenry to another party, such as the management of a governmental entity. Financial reporting should communicate adequate information to user groups to enable them to assess the performance of those parties empowered to act in the place of the citizenry (GASB:CS-1, pars. 56–58).

The GASB states (1) that accountability is a more important concept in governmental financial reporting than in business enterprise financial reporting and (2) that all governmental financial reporting objectives are derived from the accountability concept. The objectives of governmental financial reporting identified in GASB:CS-1 are summarized in Exhibit 1-4. In addition to the overall objective of accountability, GASB:CS-1 identified the following as objectives of governmental financial reporting (GASB:CS-1, pars. 56–58):

- Financial reporting should assist in fulfilling a government's duty to be publicly accountable and should enable users to assess that accountability.

- Financial reporting should assist users in evaluating the operating results of the governmental entity for the year.

- Financial reporting should assist users in assessing the level of services that can be provided by the governmental entity and its ability to meet its obligations as they become due.

The GASB noted that although accountability is referred to only in the first objective, *accountability is implicit in all of the listed objectives.*

Assessment of Accountability

The assessment of accountability is fulfilled in part when financial reporting enables user groups to determine to what extent current-period expenses are financed by current-period revenues. This reporting objective is based on the concept of communicating the extent to which the government achieved "interperiod equity," which is based on the position that the citizenry that benefits from an expense should pay for the expenses. Financial reporting should provide a basis for determining whether, during a budgetary period, (1) a surplus was created (a benefit to the future citizenry), (2) a deficit was incurred (a burden to the future citizenry), (3) a surplus from a previous budgetary period was used to finance current expenditures (a benefit to the current citizenry), (4) a deficit from a previous budgetary period was satisfied with current revenues (a burden to the current citizenry), or (5) current and only current expenses were financed by using current and only current revenues (interperiod equity) (GASB:CS-1, pars. 59–61).

Financial reporting by a state or local government should provide a basis for user groups to determine whether (1) the governmental entity obtained and used resources consistent with the legally adopted budget and (2) finance-related legal or contractual requirements have been met. A budget reflects myriad public policies adopted by a legislative body and generally has the force of law as its basis for authority. The legally adopted budget is an important document in establishing and assessing the accountability of those responsible for the management of a governmental entity. While finance-related legal or contractual requirements are not as fundamental as the legally adopted budget, they nonetheless provide a basis for accountability, and financial reporting should demonstrate that accountability either has or has not been achieved with respect to the requirements (GASB:CS-1, pars. 39–41).

PRACTICE ALERT: The status of budgetary reporting is an integral part of the GASB's *Financial Reporting Model—Reexamination* project. The GASB is expected to determine the appropriate method of communication. Current GAAP requires presentation of comparisons of budget to actual amounts for the General Fund and each major special revenue fund with a legally adopted budget at a minimum. U.S. GAAP allows the budget to be reported as either basic financial statements *or* required supplementary information. Current U.S. GAAP also presents the adopted budget, the final (amended) budget and actual amounts (using the budget's basis of accounting) with a variance column between the final and actual amounts. The project will also reexamine what budgetary information is essential for users. There are auditing considerations to this decision due to the different levels of assurance provided between a basic financials statement versus required supplementary information (which is less assurance). However, there are those who say budgetary information is the definition of compliance in a government and has minimal relationship to GAAP-based financial statements. The GASB has tentatively concluded and presented in the preliminary views document that budgetary reporting should be required supplementary information (RSI).

Assessing accountability of the management of a governmental entity encompasses qualitative analysis (economy, efficiency, and effectiveness) as well as quantitative analysis. GASB:CS-1 states that accountability relates to service efforts, costs, and accomplishments. Financial reporting, when combined with other information, may enable user groups, for example, to determine whether certain efforts should be funded or whether elected officials should be continued in office. The information used to measure the economy, efficiency, and effectiveness of a governmental entity should be based on objective criteria. Such information may be used to compare a governmental entity's current operating results with its prior period operating results or with other governmental entities' current operating results (GASB:CS-1, par. 79).

OBSERVATION: Accountability and the release of basic financial statements are not directly correlated, because a government may be involved in financial statement fraud. A number of well-known scandals in state and local governments have involved governments changing the results of operations to make results look better than fiscal reality. Some of these governments even won awards for financial reporting disclosure only to have it be discovered that they were involved in financial statement fraud. Care must be taken to understand all of a government's operations to properly gauge accountability. For many users, that understanding is nearly impossible. Many citizens may demand more transparency and immediacy in reporting in the future as a result.

EXHIBIT 1-4

HIERARCHY OF OBJECTIVES

GASB Concepts Statement No. 1 (GASB:CS-1)

Accountability

OVERALL GOAL:

Assist in fulfilling government's duty to be publicly accountable and enable users to assess that accountability

BASIC OBJECTIVES:

Assist users in evaluating the operating results of the governmental entity for the year

Assist users in assessing the level of services that can be provided by governmental entity and its ability to meet its obligations as they become due

COMPONENT OBJECTIVES:

- Sufficiency of current-year revenue
- Compliance with budget and finance-related and contractual requirements
- Assessment of governmental service efforts, costs, and accomplishments

- Sources and uses of financial resources
- Financing of activities and sources of cash
- Effect of current-year operations on financial position

- Financial position and condition
- Information related to physical and other non-financial resources
- Legal or contractual restrictions on resources and risk of loss of resources

Evaluation of Operating Results

Financial reporting should enable user groups to evaluate the operations of a state or local governmental entity. One aspect of operations evaluation is concerned with presenting information about sources and uses of financial resources. With respect to financial resource outflows, financial information presentations should identify all outflows and classify them by function (public health, public safety, etc.) and purpose (adult education, crime prevention, etc.). All financial resource inflows should be presented and identified by source (grants, bond proceeds, etc.) and type (taxes, fees, etc.). Resource inflows and outflows should be presented in a manner that enables user groups to determine the extent to which inflows are sufficient to finance outflows. In addition, nonrecurring inflows and outflows of resources should be disclosed in the financial report (GASB:CS-1, par. 78).

GASB:CS-1 also states that to evaluate operating results, financial reporting should enable user groups to determine how a governmental entity financed its activities and met its cash requirements (GASB:CS-1, par. 78).

OBSERVATION: To some extent, this component objective overlaps with the previous component objective (identification of sources and types of resource inflows). However, the objective of determining how cash requirements were met may require the preparation of a specific cash flow analysis, including the currently required preparation of a statement of cash flows for business-type activities.

Another element used in evaluating operations is the ability of the financial reporting to provide a basis for determining whether results of current operations improved or worsened the governmental entity's financial position as of the end of the current period (GASB:CS-1, par. 78).

Assessment of Fiscal Potential

Financial reporting should provide information concerning the financial position and condition of a state or local governmental entity. Resources should be described as current or noncurrent, and contingent liabilities should be disclosed. To assess the ability of an entity to raise resources from taxation, disclosure should include tax limitations, burdens, and sources. Likewise, the viability of issuing debt to raise revenues would require that an entity disclose debt limitations (GASB:CS-1, par. 79).

Disclosures in a financial report should enable user groups to assess current and long-term capital needs of the governmental entity. To this end, descriptions of physical and other nonfinancial resources with lives that extend beyond the current period should be included in the financial report. Such descriptions should include information that can be used to determine the service potential of such assets (GASB:CS-1, par. 79).

Finally, to allow financial statement users to assess the ability of a governmental entity to meet its obligations, the legal and contractual restrictions on resources and the potential loss of an entity's resources should be disclosed in the financial report (GASB:CS-1, par. 79).

Service Efforts and Accomplishments (GASB Concepts Statement No. 2—as amended by GASB Concepts Statements No. 3 and 5)

National Council on Governmental Accounting (NCGA) Concepts Statement 1 (*Objectives of Accounting and Financial Reporting for Governmental Units*) listed as one of its framework objectives "to provide information useful for evaluating managerial and organizational performance." The GASB was required by its 1984 structural agreement, which led in part to the Board's establishment, to recognize all NCGA statements until they were modified by the GASB. The GASB's Service Efforts and Accomplishments (SEA) reporting project has been a direct response to this mandated objective.

The GASB followed up the 1984 mandate to include in its accounting and financial reporting framework the objective "to provide information useful for evaluating managerial and organizational performance" with the issuance of Concepts Statement 2 (Service Efforts and Accomplishments) (GASB:CS-2) in 1994. GASB:CS-2 established the elements of SEA reporting, the objective and characteristics of SEA reporting, and the limitations of SEA information. The intent of GASB:CS-2 was to establish a framework for the development of "reporting standards" for performance measurement, not the establishment of the "performance standards." In December 2008, the GASB issued GASB:CS-5, which amended certain portions of GASB:CS-2.

The desired end result of GASB SEA guidance is to provide guidelines on what might be reported with regard to the foregoing categories of information and how to present or report it if a government voluntarily elects to do so.

Although the GASB conducted research and issuing documents regarding reporting for Service Efforts and Accomplishments (SEA) for over 20 years, several of the GASB's constituent groups expressed their opposition to the GASB's placing of SEA reporting project items on its technical agenda citing concern that doing so would lead to the development of performance measurement standards by the GASB. One of the central issues in the SEA controversy is the contention that the GASB does not have the fundamental jurisdictional authority to provide guidance on SEA reporting, and that providing such guidance is contrary to the GASB's mission.

In response to this concern, in November 2006, the Financial Accounting Foundation (FAF) Board of Trustees, which serves as the oversight body for both the GASB and FASB, reaffirmed that the GASB *does* have the jurisdictional authority to include SEA in its financial accounting and reporting standards-setting activities. The GASB issued a guide, *Suggested Guidelines for Voluntary Reporting: SEA Performance Information*, which contains topics on the applicability of the guidance, the essential components of SEA reports, qualitative characteristics of SEA performance information and effective communication of results. Its three appendices include illustration, background information, and board considerations.

GASB:CS-5 separates the "elements" of SEA performance measurement from the "related factors," clarifies the elements of SEA performance measures, and states that the elements of SEA reporting consist of three different types of measures:

1. Measures of service efforts (i.e., inputs);
2. Measures of service accomplishment (i.e., outputs and outcomes); and
3. Measures that relate service efforts to service accomplishments (i.e., efficiency).

In addition, GASB:CS-5 provides examples of SEA information, which include the following performance measurement data for a governmental entity's operation:

- Inputs (e.g., tons of asphalt used to repair roads or number of teachers);
- Outputs (e.g., number of potholes filled or number of students promoted);
- Outcomes (e.g., physical condition rating of roads or percentage of students entering college); and
- Efficiency (e.g., cost per pothole filled or cost per pupil educated).

There are other factors that affect external issues that influence the results and are related to SEA reporting but are not considered part of the basic measurement elements. The discussion of these related factors is expanded in GASB:CS-5 to address the following:

- Value of comparisons;
- Secondary effects of providing services;
- Relevance of demand for services;
- External or internal factors that influence SEA performance; and
- Explanatory information provided with SEA performance measures.

Communication Methods in Financial Reporting

The GASB's Concepts Statement No. 3 (GASB:CS-3) (Communication Methods in General Purpose External Financial Reports That Contain Basic Financial Statements) provides a conceptual basis for selecting communication methods to present items of information within general-purpose external financial reports that contain basic financial statements. These communication methods include reporting in basic financial statements, disclosure in notes to basic financial statements, presentation as required supplementary information (RSI), and presentation as supplementary information (SI).

GASB:CS-3 defines the communication methods commonly used in general-purpose external financial reports, develops criteria for each communication method, and provides a hierarchy for their use. These definitions, criteria, and hierarchy should help the GASB and all government financial statement preparers determine the appropriate methods to use to communicate information.

Once an item of information is considered appropriate for inclusion within general-purpose external financial reports, the appropriate communication method (placement) to be used to convey particular financial information should be determined. GASB:CS-3 states that this placement decision should be based on a hierarchy in the following order:

1. Recognition in basic financial statements;
2. Disclosure in notes to basic financial statements;
3. Presentation as required supplementary information (RSI); and
4. Presentation as supplementary information (SI).

Recognition in the Basic Financial Statements

The financial statements provide a tabular presentation of amounts derived from the accounting records reflecting either the financial position of the reporting unit at a moment in time or inflows and outflows of resources during a period of time.

The criteria for financial information that is reported within the basic financial statements is as follows:

• Items are intended to provide reliable representation of the effects of transactions and other events; and

• Items are measurable with sufficient reliability.

   Example: Reporting a government's revenues and receivables from taxable events or transactions

Disclosure in Notes to Basic Financial Statements

The notes to the financial statements are an integral part of the financial statements and are essential to users' understanding of a reporting unit's financial position and inflows and outflows of resources.

The criteria for financial information that is reported within the notes to the financial statements is as follows:

• Information has a clear and demonstrable relationship to information in the financial statements; and

• Information is *essential* to users' understanding of the statements.

   Example: Reporting the deposit and investment risks of the government that relate to the reported cash and investment balances and transactions.

OBSERVATION: The concept of "essentiality" should be tantamount to all note disclosure of a government. Many sections of notes to the basic financial statements are verbose, boilerplate or have not been updated for recent events. The GASB strives to limit note disclosure to be in concurrence with the provisions of GASB:CS-3 at every discussion of new or amended note disclosure. Preparers should review continuously notes with an eye toward streamlining text for readability and clarity, updating for current events and foremost, compliance with standards. Preparers should especially review discretely presented component unit disclosures in the primary government again, asking if the notes from the discretely presented component unit are absolutely essential for the user's understanding.

PRACTICE ALERT: The GASB has begun reexamining the effectiveness of note disclosures with a primary focus on:

- Note disclosures required by pronouncements that have not been effective for at least three years.

- Note disclosures added more recently (mainly relating to disclosures implemented in the last three years, including *Certain Disclosures Related to Debt, Including Direct Borrowings and Direct Placements, Leases* and *Certain Debt Extinguishments*) [GASB Statement Nos. 88, 87, and 86, respectively].

- Note disclosures that are the subject of other pre-agenda research projects on going concern disclosures and conduit debt.

It is estimated that an initial due process document on this project may be released in 2019.

GASB:CS-3 states that the notes should not include either subjective assessments of the effects of reported information on the reporting unit's future financial position or predictions about the effects of future events on future financial position.

Presentation as Required Supplementary Information

Required supplementary information (RSI) is supporting information that the GASB has concluded is essential for placing basic financial statements and notes in an appropriate operational, economic, or historical context.

The criteria for financial information that is reported as required supplementary information is as follows:

- Information that has a clear and demonstrable relationship to information in the financial statements or the notes to the basic statements; and

- Information that provides a context that enhances the decision-usefulness of the basic statements or notes.

Example: 10-year schedules of net pension liability and notes to required supplementary information for defined benefit pension plans.

As is the case for the notes to the financial statements, GASB:CS-3 states that RSI should not include either subjective assessments of the effects of reported information on the reporting unit's future financial position or predictions about the effects of future events on future financial position. GASB:CS-3 also states that RSI should not include information unrelated to the financial statements.

As of the date of this publication, the GASB currently requires supplementary information as follows:

Required Supplementary Information	GASB Statement Reference	GASB Codification Reference
Management's Discussion and Analysis	GASB-34, pars. 8–11, as amended	GASB Cod. Secs. 2200.106–.109.
Budgetary Comparisons	GASB-34, pars. 130–131, as amended by GASB-41	GASB Cod. Secs. 2200.206–.207, 2400.102, .103, and .119.
Public entity risk pools—certain revenue and claims development information	GASB-10, as amended by GASB 30, par. 7.	GASB Cod. Sec. Po20.147–.148.
Schedules of assessed condition and estimated and actual maintenance and preservation costs for governments that use the modified approach for infrastructure reporting	GASB Statement No. 34, pars. 132–133.	GASB Cod. Secs. 1400.118–.119.
Various pension information schedules presented by defined benefit pension plans, along with related notes.	GASB Statement No. 67, pars. 32–34, as amended	GASB Cod. Secs. Pe5.128–.130
Various pension information schedules presented by employers that are members of defined benefit pension plans, along with related notes.	GASB Statement No. 68, pars. 46 and 81, as amended.	GASB Cod. Secs. P20.145, .181, .191, .197, .210, .216, .219, .229–.230.
Various pension information schedules for employers that are *not* within the scope of GASB Statement No. 68 or GASB Statement No. 78, along with related notes.	GASB Statement No. 73, pars. 45 and 66.	GASB Cod. Secs. P22.136, .157, .168, .180, .184–.187.
Various other post-employment benefit plan schedules presented by such plans, along with related notes.	GASB Statement No. 74, pars. 34 and 36.	GASB Cod. Secs. Po50.130–.132, also P53.
Various other post-employment benefit information schedules presented by employers who are members of post-employment benefit plans, along with related notes.	GASB Statement No. 75, pars. 57–58, 97–98, 108, 115, 127, 134, 137, 170–171, 191–192, 218–221.	GASB Cod. Secs. P50 and P53—various throughout.

Presentation as Supplementary Information

Supplementary information (SI) is information that is considered to be useful for placing the financial statements and notes in an appropriate context; however, the GASB does not require the information to be presented in a reporting unit's general-purpose external financial report. However, if the government elects to prepare a comprehensive annual financial report (CAFR), certain supplemental information should be presented. See Chapter 20, "Comprehensive Annual Financial Report," for a further discussion of the CAFR.

The criteria for information that is reported as supplementary information is as follows:

- Information that is useful for placing basic financial statements and notes in an appropriate operational, economic, or historical context; and

- Information that is voluntarily included in a general-purpose external financial report.

   Example: Reporting combining and individual fund financial statements for nonmajor funds.

PRACTICE POINT: Part of the determination of whether information should be presented as required supplementary information or supplementary information almost always includes the assurance placed on the different types of information. Two different sections of generally accepted auditing standards contain audit guidance related to each type of information—AU-C Section 725, *Supplementary Information in Relation to the Financial Statements as a Whole*, and AU-C Section 730, *Required Supplementary Information*. Section 730 includes increased procedures and reporting assurance due to the emphasis placed on the information required by (in this case) a GASB standard.

   PRACTICE POINT: Many governments have statutory requirements or bond covenants for continuing disclosure (see Chapter 12, "Long-Term Debt"). Even if the schedules are in accordance with laws and regulations, they are supplementary information as they are not required by the GASB.

Elements of Financial Statements

The GASB white paper *Why Governmental Accounting and Financial Reporting Is—and Should Be—Different* makes a persuasive argument that public sector (governmental) accounting is fundamentally different from accounting outside the public sector (non-governmental). For this reason, the elements reported within the financial statements of state and local governments and their measurement and recognition criteria deserve different consideration. To provide the framework for establishing accounting principles related to the elements of financial statements and their measurement and recognition within the financial statements, the GASB has issued GASB:CS-4 (Elements of Financial Statements), and is deliberating another concepts statement on measurement and recognition attributes.

GASB:CS-4 identifies and defines seven elements, and it states that the definitions of the elements are to be applied to a governmental unit (i.e., a separate legal entity that is an organization created as, for example, a body corporate or a body corporate and politic). A reporting entity may include more than one governmental unit, and a governmental unit may consist of one or more reporting units. The rationale behind this entity concept is that control over resources and obligations to sacrifice resources, which are inherent characteristics of elements of financial statements, are manifested only at the governmental unit level, not at the reporting unit level. When financial statements are prepared for a reporting unit (e.g., a fund, a segment, or other subset of a legally separate entity, such as a state department of transportation), the elements of the reporting unit (e.g., the state department of transportation) are the elements of the governmental unit (e.g., the state) that have been assigned to that reporting unit for control, management, or financial reporting purposes.

The seven elements are the fundamental components of financial statements and can be organized by the specific financial statement to which they relate.

Elements of the Statement of Financial Position

GASB:CS-4 provides that the elements of a "statement of financial position" be defined as follows:

- "Assets"—Resources with a present service capacity that the entity presently controls.

- "Liabilities"—Present obligations to sacrifice resources that the entity has little or no discretion to avoid.

- "Deferred outflow of resources"—consumption of net position by the entity that is applicable to a future reporting period.

- "Deferred inflow of resources"—acquisition of net position by the entity that is applicable to a future reporting period.

- "Net position"—the residual of all other elements presented in a statement of financial position.

Because of the importance placed on the concept of interperiod equity (i.e., the idea that current costs are financed with current resources), the GASB concluded that two new elements were necessary: (1) deferred outflow of resources and (2) deferred inflow of resources. These deferrals can be thought of as future revenues and expenses waiting to be reported when required conditions have been met or a point in time has been reached. Although GASB:CS-4 does not provide specific examples of deferred inflows or outflow of resources, such elements are introduced in GASB-53 (*Accounting and Financial Reporting for Derivative Instruments*) with regard to the change in fair value of hedging derivatives as discussed in Chapter 9, "Deposits, Investments, and Derivative Instruments." Additional changes were introduced by GASB-60 (*Accounting and Financial Reporting for Service Concession Arrangements*) and GASB-65 (discussed below), along with the various pensions and other postemployment benefit standards, asset retirement obligations, irrevocable split-interest agreements and other standards. Each issued GASB standard indicates whether a deferred outflow of resources or a deferred inflow of resources may result from recognition of an accounting event.

OBSERVATION: The use of the term "deferred" in financial statements has changed due to the implementation of GASB-65 (*Items Previously Reported as Assets and Liabilities*). For example, the formerly recognized deferred revenue resulting from grant funds received in advance of an entity's meeting the eligibility requirements is actually a transaction that meets the definition of a liability, not a deferred inflow of resources as defined in GASB:CS-4. This transaction does not meet the definition of a deferred inflow of resources because an acquisition of net position has not occurred. An asset (cash) increased at the same time that the liability to perform under the terms of the grant increased. Thus, net position is unchanged. The GASB believes that items such as these should be described in financial statements without using the term "deferred" in the caption. For instance, in the foregoing example, the captions "Advances from grantors" or "unearned revenue" should be used, rather than "deferred revenue." The GASB believes that financial statements would be more understandable to users if the term "deferred" was reserved for items meeting the definition of deferred inflows or outflows of resources. GASB-65 requires that the term "deferred" only be used in conjunction with deferred inflows of resources or deferred outflows of resources.

Though seemingly mature in definition, the term "liability" is often misunderstood as contained within it are the concepts of obligations and, to some extent, time. An obligation is a social, legal, or moral requirement, such as a duty, contract, or promise that compels one to follow or avoid a particular course of action. Obligations can be legally enforceable as exemplified when a court compels the government to fulfill its obligation. Obligations could arise from legislation or contractual obligations. They may differ, though, based on whether exchange transactions (value for value) or nonexchange transactions take place. Constructive liabilities may occur in exchange transactions when resources are transferred to a government. In this case, the government must fulfill its obligations. The concept of "little or no discretion to avoid" arises when no power exists to decline sacrificing of resources or penalty/consequences of not doing the action is more than minor. One of the consistent themes in all of these nuances is that the parties to an obligation that may be a liability are usually external to the government.

The language originally contained in GASB Interpretation 6 (GASBI-6), *Recognition and Measurement of Certain Liabilities and Expenditures in Governmental Fund Financial Statements*, was one of the reasons why the clarification of the concepts of the term liability and obligation needed to be released. The former GASBI-6, par. 10, describes "matured liabilities" in governmental funds only (not associated with proprietary funds) as those that are normally due and payable in full when incurred or the matured portion of general long-term indebtedness (the portion that has come due for payment). In paragraph 11 of the interpretation, the GASB also interpreted matured liabilities to include debt service on formal debt issued when due (matured) and compensated absences, claims and judgments, special termination benefits, and landfill closure and post-closure care costs. All of these should be recognized as governmental fund liabilities and expenditures to the extent the liabilities are "normally expected to be liquidated with expendable available financial resources." In its basis for conclusions, the GASB considered but rejected an alternative interpretation that "other commitments" are the long-term portion of any other liabilities, provided that the government has entered into a multilateral agreement to defer payment to a future period. The GASB concluded that there is no accrual modification that would permit deferring to a future period the recognition of fund liabilities (such as salaries and utilities) that normally are paid in a timely manner and in full from current financial resources when incurred. Rather, the GASB proposed that such transactions should be reported as governmental fund liabilities and expenditures when incurred.

PRACTICE POINT: As part of the issuance of GASB-76, the GASB considered the role of Interpretations in the standards-setting process—specifically, the infrequency of their use and the commonality of their purpose with that of GASB *Technical Bulletins* and *Implementation Guides*—and concluded that GASB Interpretations are no longer needed. The GASB believes that the purpose that GASB Interpretations serve can be met in the future through other authoritative literature. Existing interpretations remain authoritative, but no future interpretations will be issued.

OBSERVATION: The controversy of recognition of a liability stems somewhat from the changing landscape of government operations. For example, postemployment benefits in many jurisdictions may be changed in law without collective bargaining, leading to the notion that these benefits may not be liabilities. The GASB's conclusions, mentioned above, are also leading to the interpretation (perhaps, rightfully so) that no liability would exist in a governmental fund that normally pays salary escalations that cannot be paid out of current financial resources due to economic conditions. The escalations are then renegotiated to be paid in a future period, even though in a statement of net position, a liability may be declared for the same circumstance.

Elements of the Resource Flow Statement

GASB:CS-4 provides that the elements of the "resource flows (change) statements" be defined as follows:

- "Outflow of resources"—a consumption of net position by the entity that is applicable to the reporting period (expenses as used in non-governmental funds and government-wide financial statements or expenditures as used in governmental funds).

- "Inflow of resources"—an acquisition of net position by the entity that is applicable to the reporting period (revenues).

The consumption of net position (outflow) is defined as the using up of net position that result in: (1) a decrease in assets in excess of any related decrease in liabilities or (2) an increase in liabilities in excess of any related increase in assets. Examples of consumption of resources include (1) using cash resources to make direct aid payments to eligible recipients (because existing cash resources of the entity have been consumed) and (2) using the labor of employees to provide government services for which payment will be made in the next reporting period (because the entity has consumed employee labor resources that were directly acquired from the employees).

The acquisition of net position (inflow) is defined as net position coming under the control of the entity or net position becoming newly available to the entity even if the resources are consumed directly when acquired. An acquisition of net position results in (1) an increase in assets in excess of any related increase in liabilities or (2) a decrease in liabilities in excess of any related decrease in assets. Examples of acquisition of net position include (1) imposing a tax (because the resources have newly come under the control of the entity) and (2) performing under the conditions of a grant received in advance (because liabilities of the entity have been satisfied, thereby increasing the entity's net position).

> **OBSERVATION:** The GASB has taken an approach to defining the elements of the financial statements that is different from the approaches used by other standards-setting bodies to date. Other standard setters, such as the Financial Accounting Standards Board (FASB) and the International Accounting Standards Board (IASB) define financial statement elements in relation to each other. For example, revenues are defined as an inflow of or increase in assets; thereby making the definition of revenues dependent on the definition of assets. Because of the inherent differences between private companies and governments, and the importance of assessing interperiod equity in government, the GASB developed its financial statement elements independent of each other to the extent possible.

Measurement of Elements of Financial Statements

GASB Concepts Statement No. 6 (GASB:CS-6), *Measurement of Elements of Financial Statements*, was released in March 2014. GASB:CS-6 addresses both measurement approaches and measurement attributes. A "measurement approach" determines whether an asset or liability presented in a financial statement should be either (*a*) reported at an amount that reflects a value at the date that the asset was acquired or the liability was incurred or (*b*) remeasured and reported at an amount that reflects a value at the date of the financial statements. A "measurement attribute" is the feature or characteristic of the asset or liability that is measured.

GASB:CS-6 establishes the two measurement approaches that would be used in financial statements, as follows:

1. *Initial-Transaction-Date-Based Measurement (Initial Amount)* This is commonly known as "historical cost." GASB:CS-6 defines the "initial amount" as the transaction price or amount assigned when an asset was acquired or a liability was incurred, including subsequent modifications to that price or amount, such as through depreciation or impairment.

2. *Current-Financial-Statement-Date-Based Measurement (Remeasured Amount)* This is commonly known as "current value" but may be at fair value, replacement value, or settlement price. The commonality among the values is that they are defined as the amount assigned when an asset or liability is remeasured as of the financial statement date.

GASB:CS-6 establishes the four measurement attributes that would be used in financial statements, as follows:

1. *Historical cost* is the price paid to acquire an asset or the amount received pursuant to the incurrence of a liability in an actual exchange transaction.

2. *Fair value* is the price that would be received to sell an asset or paid to transfer a liability in an orderly transaction between market participants at the measurement date.

3. *Replacement cost* is the price that would be paid to acquire an asset with equivalent service potential in an orderly market transaction at the measurement date.

4. *Settlement amount* is the amount at which an asset could be realized or a liability could be liquidated with the counterparty other than in an active market.

The GASB frequently must decide whether an item of information should be recognized in the financial statements, when such an item should be recognized, and at what amount it should be recognized. In the past, the GASB has relied on the conceptual framework of other standards setters and analogous examples from practice or previous standards to make such decisions.

This method of making decisions can lead to certain inconsistencies in financial reporting standards and could result in too much reliance being placed on accounting concepts that were not developed for a governmental environment. The concepts statement project on recognition and measurement attributes will ultimately provide the GASB with conceptual guidance as to when elements of financial statements should be reported in particular financial statements and at what amount (including the development of recognition criteria and a discussion of when elements of financial statements are recognized using different measurement focuses). With the issuance of GASB:CS-4 on the elements of financial statements, a conceptual framework project on recognition and measurement attributes is necessary to complete the conceptual basis for reporting items in traditional financial statements.

The accounting and reporting issues to be considered in this measurement and recognition project include the following:

• What messages are financial statements conceptually attempting to convey? (In other words, what is the story that the financial statements attempt to communicate or what questions should be answered by reading different financial statements? For example, the statement of cash flows answers the question, "What happened to cash during the year?")

• What is the relationship among objectives of financial reporting (user needs), financial statements, measurement focuses, and measurement attributes at the conceptual level?

• How does when an element is recognized affect the meaning that is to be conveyed by a particular financial statement?

• What are the fundamental recognition criteria necessary to report an element in a financial statement?

• What measurement attributes best convey the message intended for financial statements? What is the role of historical cost and fair value information in conveying these messages?

- Should the application of fair value be different for the statement of net position and the statement of activities? How does fair value relate to the cost-of-service model of the statement of activities?

SUMMARY OF BASIC GOVERNMENTAL ACCOUNTING PRINCIPLES

The objectives for governmental financial reporting discussed earlier in this chapter are the basis for determining specific accounting principles to be used by a governmental entity. Certain general principles of accounting and reporting are applicable to governmental entities. These principles, which are established by NCGA-1, as amended by GASB-34 as well as many other GASB pronouncements, provide a broad overview of financial reporting and are as follows:

1. Accounting and reporting capabilities;
2. Fund accounting systems;
3. Fund types;
4. Number of funds;
5. Reporting, valuing, and depreciating capital assets;
6. Reporting long-term liabilities;
7. Measurement focus and basis of accounting in basic financial statements;
8. To some extent, budgeting, budgetary control, and budgetary reporting;
9. Transfer, revenue, expenditure, and expense account classification;
10. Common terminology and classification; and
11. Annual financial reports.

Accounting and Reporting Capabilities

A governmental entity's accounting system should be designed to achieve the following:

- Present fairly and with full disclosure the funds and activities of the government in conformity with applicable generally accepted accounting principles; and
- Determine and demonstrate compliance with finance-related legal and contractual provisions.

Fund Accounting Systems

NCGA-1 (as amended) defines a "fund" as follows:

> A fiscal and accounting entity with a self-balancing set of accounts recording cash and other financial resources, together with all related liabilities and residual equities or balances, and changes therein, which are segregated for the purpose of carrying on specific activities or attaining certain objectives in accordance with special regulations, restrictions, or limitations. [GASB Cod. Sec. 1300, introduction].

The detailed transactions and resulting balances of a governmental entity (the primary government as well as its blended component units) are generally recorded in individual funds; however, GASB-34 requires that only major funds be reported individually in a governmental entity's basic financial statements.

Fund Types

Fund-based financial statements must be included in a governmental entity's financial report in order to demonstrate that restrictions imposed by statutes, regulations, or contracts have been followed. GASB-34 identifies the following as fund types that are to be used to record a governmental entity's activities during an accounting period (GASB-34, par. 63) [GASB Cod. Sec. 1300.103]:

- Governmental Funds (emphasizing major funds)
  — General Fund
  — Special Revenue Funds
  — Capital Projects Funds
  — Debt Service Funds
  — Permanent Funds
- Proprietary Funds
  — Enterprise Funds (emphasizing major funds)
  — Internal Service Funds
- Fiduciary Funds and Similar Component Units
  — Pension (and other employee benefit) Trust Funds
  — Investment Trust Funds
  — Private-Purpose Trust Funds
  — Agency Funds (see **PRACTICE ALERT** later in the chapter)

OBSERVATION: The fund classification provisions described in this section are for *external reporting*. The GASB does not direct how a governmental entity should construct its internal accounting structure to fulfill legal requirements or satisfy management strategies. For example, a government may maintain an account for a separate fund in its internal accounting system for resources administratively set aside for replacement of equipment. For external financial reporting purposes, this fund could be consolidated within the General Fund.

Governmental Funds

Financial statements for governmental funds have a short-term emphasis and generally measure and account for cash and "other assets that can easily be converted to cash." GASB-34 requires fund reporting be restricted to a governmental entity's General Fund and its "major" funds (GASB-34, par. 64) [GASB Cod. Sec. 1300.102].

Governmental funds primarily deal with general purpose activities and are funded largely from taxation, grants, transfers from other funds, and special assessments. In the case of a capital project, bonds are also a funding source and for permanent funds, donations are a funding source.

GASB-54 (*Fund Balance Reporting and Governmental Fund Type Definitions*) established new definitions for governmental funds types based on certain criteria. If use of a fund type is generally discretionary, specific situations under which a fund of that type should be used are identified either in the definitions in GASB-54 (i.e., debt service funds) or by requirements established in other authoritative pronouncements (i.e., special revenue and capital projects funds). The fund balance classification section of GASB-54 defines the terminology "restricted," "committed," and "assigned."

Below are the definitions of governmental fund type (GASB-54, pars. 21–35) [GASB Cod. Secs. 1300.104–.108]:

Fund Type	Definition
General Fund	To account for and report all financial resources not accounted for and reported in another fund.
Special Revenue Funds	To account for and report the proceeds of specific revenue sources that are restricted or committed to expenditure for specified purposes other than debt service or capital projects.
Capital Project Funds	To account for and report financial resources that are restricted, committed, or assigned to expenditure for capital outlays, including the acquisition or construction of capital facilities or other capital assets.
Debt Service Funds	To account for and report financial resources that are restricted, committed, or assigned to expenditure for principal and interest.
Permanent Funds	To account for and report resources that are restricted to the extent that only earnings, and not principal, may be used for purposes that support the reporting government's programs— that is, for the benefit of the government or its citizenry.

PRACTICE ALERT: The GASB's *Financial Reporting Model—Reexamination* project may redefine (or eliminate) permanent funds.

GASB-66 (*Technical Corrections—2012—an amendment of GASB Statements No. 10 and No. 62*) amended certain provisions of internal service funds related to risk management. Implementation of GASB-54 resulted in a conflict with regard to risk management activities as to fund type. GASB-10 (*Accounting and Financial Reporting for Risk Financing and Related Insurance Issues*) requires that a government's risk financing activities be accounted for either in the general fund or an internal service fund. GASB-66 resolves the conflict by removing the limitation on the type of fund to use for risk financing activities, removing the so-called "single fund principle" contained in GASB-54.

Proprietary Funds

Financial statements for proprietary funds should be based on the flow of economic resources measurement focus and the accrual basis of accounting. The proprietary fund category includes Enterprise Funds and Internal Service Funds.

Enterprise Funds. This fund type may be used to "report any activity for which a fee is charged to external users for goods or services." GASB-34 states that an Enterprise Fund *must* be used to account for an activity if any one of the following three criteria is satisfied (GASB-34, par. 67) [GASB Cod. Sec. 1300.109]:

1. The activity is financed with debt that is secured *solely* by a pledge of the net revenues from fees and charges of the activity.

2. Laws or regulations require that the activity's costs of providing services, including capital costs (such as depreciation or capital debt service), be recovered with fees and charges, rather than with taxes or similar revenues.

3. The pricing policies of the activity establish fees and charges designed to recover its costs, including capital costs (such as depreciation or debt service).

The first criterion refers to debt secured solely by fees and charges. If that debt is secured by a pledge of fees and charges from the activity and the full faith and credit of the primary government or component unit, this arrangement does not satisfy the "sole source of debt security" criterion and the activity does not have to be accounted for (assuming the other two criteria are not satisfied) in an Enterprise Fund. This conclusion is not changed even if it is anticipated that the primary government or component unit is not expected to make debt payments under the arrangement.

Footnote 34 to GASB-34, par. 67(b), states that State Unemployment Compensation Funds meet the definition of an Enterprise Fund due to the second criterion.

The third criterion is similar to the previous standard for determining when an Enterprise Fund should be used to account for an activity except that in this case, U.S. GAAP is based on "established policies" rather than management's intent.

The three criteria should be applied to a governmental entity's principal revenue sources; however, the criteria do not have to be applied to "insignificant activities" of a governmental entity. If none of the criteria apply, the activity can be accounted for in a governmental fund.

It should be noted that GASB-34 states that a fee-based activity can be accounted for in an Enterprise Fund even if the three criteria described above do not exist. The three criteria apply to fee-based activities that must be accounted for in an Enterprise Fund.

Internal Service Funds. An Internal Service Fund may be used to account for activities that involve the governmental entity providing goods or services to (1) other funds or activities of the primary government or its component units, or other governments on a cost reimbursement basis and (2) the reporting entity is the *predominant* participant in the activity. If the reporting entity is not the predominant participant, the activity should be reported in an Enterprise Fund (GASB-34, par. 68) [GASB Cod. Sec. 1300.110] (See previous discussion with regard to GASB-66).

Fiduciary Funds

Assets held by a governmental entity for other parties (either as a trustee or as an agent) and that cannot be used to finance the governmental entity's own operating programs should be reported in the fiduciary fund category, which includes (1) Pension (and other employee benefit) Trust Funds, (2) Investment Trust Funds, (3) Private Trust Funds, and (4) Agency Funds. The three trust funds are used to report resources and activities when the governmental entity is acting as a trustee (i.e., a fiduciary capacity) for individuals, private organizations, and other governments. GASB-34 states that the three trust funds are distinguished from an Agency Fund in that the trust funds are generally characterized "by the existence of a trust agreement that affects the degree of management involvement and the length of time that the resources are held."

Pension (or other Employee Benefit) Trust Funds. This fund type is used to account for resources held in trust for employees and their beneficiaries based on defined benefit pension agreements, defined contribution agreements, other postemployment benefit agreements, and other employee benefit arrangements (GASB-34, par. 70) [GASB Cod. Sec. 1300.111].

OBSERVATION: GASB-34 requires fiduciary funds to only include resources that are required to be held in trust for the members and beneficiaries of defined benefit pension plans, defined contribution plans, other postemployment benefit plans, or other employee benefit plans. GASB-34, par. 106 discusses "Fiduciary fund statements should include information about all fiduciary funds of the primary government, as well as component units that are fiduciary in nature." The paragraph further discusses "If separate, GAAP financial reports have been issued, the notes should include information about how to obtain those separate reports." Only the information that is truly of the employer and not the Plan as a whole should be included in fiduciary fund information (unless the Plan is a single employer Plan). This point was magnified by a recently released AICPA "white paper" *Governmental Employer Participation in Agent Multiple-Employer Plans: Issues Related to Information for Employer Reporting*, which states, in part:

> Another challenge... is that the financial statements of agent plans only report fiduciary net position for the plan as a whole. As fiduciary net position is a component necessary to calculate net pension liability employers need their specific interest in the agent plan's fiduciary net position (that is, their separate account information) which the plan is not required to report in its financial statements. Participating employers will need information beyond what is provided in the audited financial statements of the plan to determine their specific pension amounts.

PRACTICE ALERT: GASB Statement No. 84 (*Fiduciary Activities*) was released in 2017. GASB-84 identifies the requirements for reporting an activity as a fiduciary activity focusing on whether a government is controlling the assets of the fiduciary activity and the beneficiaries with whom a fiduciary relationship exists. An activity meeting the criteria in GASB-84 is to be reported in the fiduciary funds. An exception is provided for a business-type activity that normally expects to hold custodial assets (as defined) for three months or less.

Fiduciary component units are combined with information from fiduciary funds (as described in Chapter 4, "Governmental Financial Reporting Entity"). GASB-84 is effective for reporting periods beginning after December 15, 2018. For June 30th governments, the Statement is effective beginning on July 1, 2019, applied retroactively by restating financial statements, if practicable for all prior periods presented. Further information on GASB-84 is contained in Chapter 8, "Fiduciary Funds."

Investment Trust Funds. An Investment Trust Fund is used by a governmental entity to report the *external portion* of an investment pool as defined in GASB-31 (*Accounting and Financial Reporting for Certain Investments and for External Investment Pools*), paragraph 18 (GASB-34, par. 71) [GASB Cod. Sec.1300.112].

OBSERVATION: The GASB recently released GASB Statement No. 79 (*Certain External Investment Pools and Pool Participants*) (GASB-79). State and local government treasurers that manage investment pools or participate in external investment pools should review GASB-79 carefully and expediently. The provisions of GASB-79 address the regulatory amendments to Rule 2a7 of the Investment Company Act of 1940 issued by the Securities and Exchange Commission (SEC) to money market funds that took effect in April 2016. Further discussion of this issue is presented in Chapter 9, "Deposits, Investments, and Derivative Instruments."

Private-Purpose Trust Funds. This fund type is used to account for the principal and income for all other trust arrangements that benefit individuals, private organizations, or other governments. For example, a Private-Purpose Trust Fund would be used to account for escheat property as currently described in GASB-21 (*Accounting for Escheat Property*) (GASB-34, par. 72) [GASB Cod. Sec. 1300.113].

Agency Funds. An Agency Fund is used by a governmental entity to report assets that are held in a custodial relationship. In a typical custodial relationship, a governmental entity receives assets, may temporarily invest those assets, and then remits those assets to individuals, private organizations, or other governments (GASB-34, par. 73) [GASB Cod. Sec. 1300.114]. (See previous **PRACTICE ALERT**.)

OBSERVATION: If a government constructs what will be a capital asset on behalf of another government that will ultimately have ownership of the capital asset, this type of activity should be accounted for either in an agency fund, or if the project is funded from specific revenue sources that are restricted or committed to expenditure for specified purposes then a special revenue fund. The use of an agency fund may call into question the ability to bond for such activities because the bond proceeds may be in one fund and then transferred to an agency fund for spending on the project.

Public-purpose funds may be a term used in legislation. For financial reporting purposes, they are classified as Special Revenue Funds. Nonexpendable Trust Funds are classified as Permanent Funds.

PRACTICE ALERT: Part of the GASB's *Financial Reporting Model—Reexamination* project includes an exploration where the fiduciary fund financial statements should be presented in the basic financial statements. Some practitioners want a more prominent presentation while others prefer the Financial Accounting Standards Board (FASB) model of presenting fiduciary activities as part of note disclosure.

Governmental and Proprietary Fund Financial Statements

A governmental entity should report financial statements for its governmental and proprietary funds, but the basis for reporting these funds is not by fund type but rather by major funds (GASB-34, par. 74) [GASB Cod. Sec. 2200.157].

A significant focus of reporting governmental funds and proprietary funds is that major funds for these type funds are reported separately; while other funds defined as nonmajor are combined for reporting purposes. Internal service funds are not separated by major or nonmajor and are reported in one column, but they may be separated in a combining statement.

Fund financial statements must present in a separate column a (major) fund that satisfies both of the following criteria (GASB-34, pars. 75–76) [GASB Cod. Secs. 2200.158–.159]:

- Total assets, liabilities, revenues, or expenditures/expenses of the governmental (enterprise) fund are equal to or greater than 10% of the corresponding total (assets, liability, and so forth) for all funds that are considered governmental funds (enterprise funds).

- Total assets, liabilities, revenues, or expenditures/expenses of the governmental fund (enterprise fund) are equal to or greater than 5% of the corresponding total for all governmental and enterprise funds combined.

Due to the change in the use of deferred inflows and outflows of resources with regard to governmental funds with the implementation of GASB-65, a change in the major fund measurement criteria was required. These criteria were previously described in paragraph 76 of GASB-34 (*Basic Financial Statements—and Management's Discussion and Analysis—for State and Local Governments*). Assets are now combined with deferred outflows of resources, and liabilities are now combined with deferred inflows of resources to facilitate the major fund calculation.

PRACTICE ALERT: One of the aspects of the GASB's *Financial Reporting Model—Reexamination* project is to determine whether a change is warranted in the major fund measurement criteria, particularly in the reporting of debt service funds, which are seldom reported as major funds.

Major fund determination calculations are performed on a yearly basis. In determining total revenues and expenditures/expenses, each year extraordinary items are excluded.

The General Fund is always considered a major fund and therefore must be presented in a separate column. Major fund reporting requirements do not apply to Internal Service Funds or Fiduciary Funds.

If a fund does not satisfy the conditions described above, it can still be presented as a major fund if the governmental entity believes it is important to do so. All other funds that are not considered major funds must be combined in a separate column and labeled as nonmajor funds. Thus, there could be a nonmajor funds column for governmental funds and enterprise funds.

PRACTICE POINT: The importance of the major fund calculation/adjudication by the preparer cannot be underestimated. The number of major funds has a direct relationship to the amount of major funds presented in the balance sheet (or statement of fund net position) and the statement of revenues, expenditures and changes in fund balance (or statement of revenues, expenses and changes in fund net position) and also the level of auditing on those funds. Care must be taken in the determination of these funds and the presentation to the auditor as part of the commencement of fieldwork on the engagement.

Number of Funds

A basic principle of governmental generally accepted accounting principles is that the actual number of funds used by a governmental entity should be kept to a minimum to avoid the creation of an inefficient financial system. In general, the number of funds established must be sufficient to meet operational needs and legal restrictions imposed on the organization. For example, only one General Fund should be maintained. In some circumstances it may be possible to account for restricted resources in the General Fund and still meet imposed legal requirements. Also, there may be no need to establish a Special Revenue Fund unless specifically required by law (NCGAI-9, par. 10, and NCGA-1, par. 29) [GASB Cod. Secs. 1300.116–.117].

Reporting, Valuing, and Depreciating Capital Assets

At the fund-financial statement level, capital assets are not reported in governmental funds but are reported in proprietary funds and fiduciary funds (if any). All of a governmental entity's capital assets (with the exception of those of fiduciary funds) are reported in the government-wide financial statements and identified as related to either governmental activities or business-type activities (NCGA-1, par. 32, and GASB-34, pars. 6 and 80) [GASB Cod. Sec. 1400].

The governmental entity should report all of its capital assets, based on their original historical cost plus ancillary charges such as transportation, installation, and site preparation costs.

> **OBSERVATION:** GASB Statement No. 72 (*Fair Value Measurement and Application*) changes the recognition of donated capital assets, donated works of art, historical treasurers, and similar assets as well as capital assets received in a service concession arrangement. These assets were previously required to be measured at fair value at the date of receipt in accordance with GASB-34, par. 19. They are now to be recognized at acquisition value. Acquisition value is an entry price, whereas fair value is an "exit price." GASB-72, par. 79 defines acquisition value as the price that would be paid to acquire an asset with equivalent service potential in an orderly market transaction at the acquisition date, or the amount at which a liability could be liquidated with the counterparty at the acquisition date.

Under certain conditions works of art, historical treasures, and similar assets do not have to be capitalized. This exception is discussed in Chapter 18, "Expenses/Expenditures: Nonexchange and Exchange Transactions."

The cost (net of estimated salvage value) of capital assets (except for certain infrastructure assets) should be depreciated over the estimated useful lives of the assets. Inexhaustible capital assets (such as land, land improvements, and certain infrastructure assets where a government has elected to take a modified approach availed in GASB-34 are further discussed in Chapter 10, "Capital Assets") should not be depreciated. Depreciation expenses should be reported in the government-wide financial statements (statement of activities), financial statements for proprietary funds (statement of revenues, expenses, and changes in fund net position), and financial statements for fiduciary funds (statement of changes in fiduciary net position). Depreciation expense is not reported in governmental funds (the General Fund, Special Revenue Funds, and so forth) (GASB-34, par. 21).

Capital assets should also be evaluated for impairment when events or changes in circumstances suggest that the service utility of a capital asset may have been significantly and unexpectedly declined (GASB-42, par. 5) [GASB Cod. Sec. 1400.181].

> **PRACTICE ALERT:** GASB Statement No. 83 (*Certain Asset Retirement Obligations*) was issued in late 2016 clarifying financial reporting requirements on recognition and measurement of activities involving tangible capital assets and legally enforceable liability recognition for their retirement. Until implementation of GASB-83, there will be inconsistent reporting of asset retirement obligations (AROs), largely in conjunction with public utility entities. GASB-83 establishes the criteria for determining the timing and recognition of a liability and a corresponding deferred outflow of resources for AROs. GASB-83 became effective for periods beginning after June 15, 2018, applied retroactively by restating financial statements if practicable, for all periods presented. Earlier application is encouraged. Further information on GASB-83 is contained in Chapter 10, "Capital Assets."

Reporting Long-Term Liabilities

There are three broad but distinct categories of long-term liabilities. Long-term liabilities related to proprietary funds should be reported both in government-wide financial statements and the fund financial statements. Long-term liabilities related to fiduciary funds would be rare given the nature of fiduciary activities. (Instances of borrowings for real estate investments may be an exception, but presenting elements of post-employment benefit liabilities as part of fiduciary funds are inconsistently presented.) All other long-term liabilities that are not properly presented in either proprietary funds or fiduciary funds are general long-term liabilities and should be reported only in the governmental activities column of the statement of net position (a government-wide financial statement) (NCGA-1, pars. 32 and 42; GASB-34, pars. 6 and 82) [GASB Cod. Sec. 1500].

Measurement Focus and Basis of Accounting in Basic Financial Statements

Government-wide financial statements have been established by GASB-34 in order to provide a basis for determining (1) the extent to which current services provided by the entity were financed with current revenues and (2) the degree to which a governmental entity's financial position has changed during the fiscal year. In order to achieve these objectives, government-wide financial statements should include a statement of net position and a statement of activities.

Flow of Economic Resources: Accrual Basis of Accounting

Government-wide financial statements are based on a flow of all economic resources applied on the accrual basis of accounting. The flow of economic resources refers to all of the assets available to the governmental unit for the purpose of providing goods and services to the public. When the flow of economic resources and the accrual basis of accounting are combined, they provide the foundation for U.S. generally accepted accounting principles (U.S. GAAP) used by business enterprises in that essentially all economic assets and liabilities, both current and long-term, are presented in the statement of net position.

The governmental entity's statement of activities includes all costs of providing goods and services during the period. These costs include depreciation, the cost of inventories consumed during the period, and other operating expenses. On the activity statement, revenues earned during the period are matched with the expenses incurred for exchange or exchange-like transactions. Nonexchange transactions are accounted for based on the standards established by GASB-33 (*Accounting and Financial Reporting for Nonexchange Transactions*).

Modified Accrual Basis of Accounting

Governmental fund-based financial statements must be included in a governmental entity's financial report in order to demonstrate that restrictions imposed by statutes, regulations, contracts, or similar forces of law have been followed. These financial statements are based on the modified accrual accounting basis and the flow of current financial resources and therefore have a short-term emphasis and generally measure and account for cash and "other assets that can easily be converted to cash" (NCGA-1, par. 57; GASB-34, pars. 15, 16, 92, and 107) [GASB Cod. Sec. 1600]. (See previous **PRACTICE ALERTs** on the GASB's Invitation to Comment *Financial Reporting Model Improvements—Governmental Funds* and Chapter 3, "Basis of Accounting and Measurement Focus.")

Expenditures differ from *expenses*. *Expenditures* are decreases in (uses of) governmental fund financial resources other than interfund transfers and expiration of bond takeout agreements. Revenue and expenditure accounts thus reflect the changes in the financial condition of a governmental fund that occur during a given time period except those arising from transfers and general long-term debt issuance and issuances of special assessment bonds, refunding bonds, and certain demand bonds (NCGA-1, pars. 70 and 109, as amended by GASB-6, pars. 19–20, and GASB-7, par. 8, GASBI-1, par. 13) [GASB Cod. Sec. 1800.130].

In contrast, *expenses* are utilized in the government-wide financial statements and in proprietary and fiduciary fund financial statements. Financial statements of proprietary and fiduciary funds are based on the economic resources measurement focus and the accrual basis of accounting (GASB-34, par. 92, as amended by GASB-63, par. 8) [GASB Cod. Sec. 1600.130]. Chapter 3, "Basis of Accounting and Measurement Focus," contains a more in-depth discussion of these differences.

The GASB-34 financial statements require a reconciliation between the government-wide and fund statements, which present financial information using different bases of accounting and measurement focuses. The process by which fund financial statements are converted to government-wide financial statements is illustrated in CCH's *Governmental GAAP Practice Manual.*

Budgeting, Budgetary Control, and Budgetary Reporting

The following guidance should be followed as part of the budgetary process for a governmental entity (NCGA-1, pars. 76 and 123) [GASB Cod. Sec. 1700]:

- An annual budget should be adopted by every governmental entity;
- The accounting system should provide the basis for appropriate budgetary control;
- Budgetary comparisons should be provided for the general fund and each major special revenue fund that has a legally adopted annual budget, and governments are encouraged to present a comparison of amounts budgeted to amounts received or expended as part of RSI; and
- A government with significant budgetary perspective differences, such as program or organizational-based budgets rather than fund budgets, are to present budgetary comparison information consistent with the perspective that provides for comparison with its legally adopted budget.

Beyond this guidance and the reporting guidance of budgetary perspective differences contained in GASB-41 (*Budgetary Comparison Schedules—Perspective Differences*), GASB standards do not dictate the basis of accounting for budgets. Budgets are based upon legal definitions (not accounting principles) that are likely not standard between governments. However, GASB-41 does require presentation of budgetary comparison information for the general fund and major special revenue funds as required supplementary information based on the fund, organization, or program structure that the government uses for its legally adopted budget, reconciled to U.S. GAAP.

Transfer, Revenue, Expenditure, and Expense Account Classification

The following guidance should be followed in the preparation of governmental financial reports (NCGA-1, par. 99; GASB-34, pars. 6, 39, 53, 88, 100, and 112) [GASB Cod. Sec. 1800]:

- Transfers should be reported separately from revenues and expenditures/ expenses;
- Proceeds from the issuance of general long-term debt should be recorded separately from revenues in the governmental fund financial statements;
- Governmental fund revenues should be reported by fund and source at the fund-financial statement level;
- Governmental expenditures should be reported by fund and at least by function;
- Proprietary fund revenues should be reported by major sources, and expense should be classified in a manner like that used by similar business activities;
- The statement of activities should report governmental activities at least at the level of detail required in the governmental fund statement of revenues, expenditures, and changes in fund balances;
- Governments should present business-type activities at least by segment; and
- Contributions to term and permanent endowments, contributions to permanent fund principal, other contributions, special and extraordinary items, and transfers between governmental and business-type activities should each be separately reported.

Common Terminology and Classification

Governmental financial information is reported in budgets and external financial reports. NCGA-1 notes that it is advantageous to use common terminology and classification schemes throughout the "budget, the accounts, and the financial reports of each fund" (NCGA-1, par. 123) [GASB Cod. Sec. 1800].

Annual Financial Reports

The GASB *recommends but does not require* that a governmental financial reporting entity prepare and publish a comprehensive annual financial report (CAFR) "as a matter of public record." The CAFR is discussed in Chapter 20, "Comprehensive Annual Financial Report."

The minimum external financial reporting requirements include the following:

- Management's discussion and analysis
- Basic financial statements

— Government-wide financial statements

— Fund financial statements

— Notes to the financial statements

- Required supplementary information

The financial reporting entity consists of (1) the primary government, (2) other entities for which the primary government is financially accountable, and (3) other entities that have a relationship with the primary government whose "exclusion would cause the reporting entity's basic financial statements to be misleading or incomplete." The reporting entity concept is discussed in Chapter 4, "Governmental Financial Reporting Entity."

OBSERVATION: Governance boards, laws, or ordinances may require preparation of a CAFR.

OTHER GENERAL ACCOUNTING PRINCIPLES

With the issuance of GASB-56, certain previous accounting guidance found only in AICPA Statements on Auditing Standards was incorporated in the GASB literature. The three accounting topics incorporated by GASB-56 are (1) related-party transactions, (2) subsequent events, and (3) going-concern considerations. Remaining applicable AICPA guidance issued prior to November 30, 1989 is contained in GASB-62, as amended.

Related-Party Transactions

State and local governments are required to disclose certain related-party transactions. Generally, the accounting principle dealing with related-party transactions is that if the substance of a particular transaction is significantly different from its form because of the involvement of related parties, the financial statements should recognize the substance of the transaction, rather than its legal form. GASB-56 incorporates the previous AICPA disclosure guidance that references National Council on Governmental Accounting Interpretation No. 6 (NC-GAI-6) (Notes to the Financial Statements) as its basis for disclosing related-party transactions.

The AICPA Audit and Accounting Guide *State and Local Governments* states that in a governmental entity, related parties may include members of the governing board, administrative boards or commissions, administrative officials and their immediate families, component units and joint ventures, and affiliated or related organizations that are not included as part of the financial reporting entity. Many governments require their officials and employees to periodically file statements to disclose related-party relationships and transactions.

Examples of related-party transactions that may require consideration as to whether they involve form-over-substance conditions include:

- Borrowing or lending on an interest-free basis or rate of interest well above or below prevailing market prices;
- Real estate sold at a price that differs significantly from the appraised value;
- Exchanging similar property in a nonmonetary transaction; and
- Making loans where there is no scheduled terms or plan for repayment (GASB-56, par. 5) [GASB Cod. Sec. 2250.104].

GASB-56 also concurs with the AICPA assessment that such related-party considerations should focus on substance over form, but it recognizes that such assessments may pose challenges in a governmental context. For example, governments often enter into transactions to engage in activities that are motivated by the needs of the public good or society concerns; and, therefore may not have similar characteristics to the same transactions or activities occurring in an arm's-length transaction in the non-governmental sector or with unrelated parties. As a result, a comparison to arm's-length transactions may not be appropriate in these circumstances.

GASB-48 (*Sales and Pledges of Receivables and Future Revenues and Intra-Entity Transfers of Assets and Future Revenues*) requires that assets transferred within the same financial reporting entity be recognized at the carrying value of the transferor. This requirement results in a measurement that may be different from what may have occurred in an arm's-length transaction with an outside party.

Subsequent Events

Events or transactions that affect financial statement amounts or disclosures sometimes occur subsequent to period end but before the financial statements are issued. These transactions or events are referred to as "subsequent events." Previous accounting guidance related to subsequent events was found only in AICPA Statements on Auditing Standards. GASB-56 incorporated the basic principles of the AICPA guidance that identifies and describes the accounting and disclosure treatment for two types of subsequent events: (1) "type one events," which require adjustments to the financial statements (renamed "recognized" events in GASB-56), and (2) "type two events," which do not require financial statement adjustments but may require disclosure in the notes to the financial statements (renamed "nonrecognized" events in GASB-56):

- *Recognized events*—This type of subsequent event provides additional evidence with respect to conditions that existed at the date of the financial statements and affects the estimates that were used in the preparation of the financial statements (e.g., the settlement of a lawsuit related to an event that occurred prior to the date of the financial statements). For recognized subsequent events, the financial statements should be adjusted for any changes in estimates resulting from this new evidence.
- *Nonrecognized events*—This type of subsequent event provides evidence with respect to conditions that did not exist at the financial statement date but arose subsequent to that date. These subsequent events do not result in adjustment to financial statement amounts but should be disclosed in the notes to the financial statements if considered essential to a user's understanding of the statements. For example, changes in the quoted

market prices of a government's investments subsequent to year-end would generally not require adjustment to the financial statement amounts because the change in market value typically reflects a concurrent evaluation of new conditions.

GASB-56 also states that subsequent events may need to be included in management's discussion and analysis required by GASB-34 depending on the specific facts and circumstances (GASB-56, pars. 8–15) [GASB Cod. Secs. 2250.109–.116].

Going-Concern Considerations

The continuation of a state or local government entity as a going concern is assumed in financial reporting unless significant information exists to the contrary. For governmental entities, information that would be contrary to this assumption includes evidence that indicates the government's inability to meet obligations that are due without substantial disposition of assets outside the normal course of operations, debt restructuring, required financial oversight, or similar actions. Indicators of substantial doubt about a government's ability to continue as a going concern could include the following:

- Negative trends such as recurring declines in net position or fund balances, consistent working capital deficiencies, or operating cash flow declines;

- Significant noncompliance with debt covenants, legal reserve requirements, or other requirements that can negatively affect continued operations;

- Inabilities to raise resources or borrow monies resulting from proximity to legal debt or revenue limits;

- Internal matters such as major work stoppages, labor disputes, or excessively burdensome contracts, significant reliance on a particular program's success, the need to significantly revise operations; and

- External matters such as legal proceedings, legislative mandates, potential loss of significant intergovernmental resources or revenues, loss of principal taxpayers or customers, or the effects of natural disasters.

GASB-56 incorporated previous AICPA guidance that defines the financial statement preparer's responsibility to evaluate whether there is substantial doubt about the government's ability to continue as a going concern for a reasonable period of time beyond the date of the financial statements. The GASB essentially retained the SAS definition of "reasonable period of time" of 12 months beyond the financial statement date and added some language stating that if there is information that is currently known to the government that may raise substantial doubt shortly after the 12-month period (e.g., within an additional three months), it should also be considered.

If it is concluded that there is substantial doubt about the government's ability to continue as a going concern, GASB-56 requires specific note disclosures and discussion of such issues in management's discussion and analysis. GASB-56 also clarifies that the going-concern considerations are to be applied to the "legal entity level" or, in other words, to a "legally separate governmental entity," and not for the reporting units within the legally separate government entity. Therefore, a going concern may be assessed at a primary government that is having financial difficulties even though a component unit of a primary government may be solvent or vice versa (GASB-56, pars. 16–19) [GASB Cod. Secs. 2250.117–.120].

PRACTICE ALERT: The GASB is considering reexamination of going concern disclosures. The current note disclosures stem from AICPA guidance issued in 1988. Since then, not only has the AICPA updated its going concern provisions (see previous **PRACTICE ALERT** discussing AU-C Section 570 and SAS-132) but many different indicators of fiscal stress may be present even though few governments cease to operate. GASB staff do not plan to present initial research to the Board until July 2019. (See also next section on bankruptcy.)

Bankruptcy

Recently, municipal governments have come increasingly under fiscal distress. Tax bases have eroded while the costs of replacing aging infrastructure and funding ongoing operations have skyrocketed, causing governments to reassess programs, benefit provisions (especially postemployment benefits) and services, which some governments cannot change without legal or state fiscal oversight.

Chapter 9, Title 11, of the United States Bankruptcy Code allows a government to restructure its debts under the oversight of a fiscal monitor. GASB-58 (*Accounting and Financial Reporting for Chapter 9 Bankruptcies*) details the adjustments needed when Chapter 9 is exercised.

OBSERVATION: Chapter 9 is only available for municipal governments within states that have adopted Chapter 9 of the Bankruptcy Code and not the states themselves. Only Arkansas, Arizona, California, Florida, Missouri, Nebraska, New York, and Oklahoma have statutes that have no restrictions on filing under Chapter 9. Alaska and Alabama have no related statutes. Georgia and Iowa prohibit Chapter 9 filings. Connecticut, Kentucky, New Jersey, and Pennsylvania place preconditions on filing. In addition, New York and Pennsylvania have municipal distress statutes. Due to these limitations, according to federal court system records, fewer than 600 municipal bankruptcy cases have been filed since the legislation was enacted in 1934 and revised in 1937.

A government that falls into bankruptcy is in theory not a going concern. A "Plan of Adjustment" is usually a court-affirmed instrument that details the obligations of the government and how it will be restructured. Accounts payable, notes, and other debt obligations that are within a Plan of Adjustment would result in lower interest costs and potentially result in gains to the extent that principal and interest payable amounts are less than preplan carrying amounts of debts and other payables. Unamortized premiums and discounts should be included as part of the calculation of gains and losses. If capital leases are adjusted as part of the plan in a way that changes the amounts of the remaining minimum lease payments, then the balances of the capital asset and the obligation need to be adjusted by the difference of the present value of the future minimum lease payments and the carrying amount of the lease prepetition.

Restructuring may occur in pensions and other postemployment benefit plans. The Plan of Adjustment could reject the pension and other postemployment benefit plans themselves or amend them so they remain intact. If a rejection occurs, then effectively any liability becomes general unsecured debt and a termination of the plan occurs. Because of the termination, a gain or loss could occur because the assets and liabilities within the plan would be eliminated. If the plan is amended, no gain or loss would occur, but prospective costs would have to be remeasured through an actuarial valuation.

If a government is not expected to emerge from bankruptcy, then all assets and liabilities need to be adjusted to fair market, which is generally the amount expected to be received as of the date of the Plan of Adjustment. Gains and losses should be reported as an extraordinary item. Professional fees are expensed.

Disclosure in the notes to the basic financial statements entails the conditions that gave rise to the bankruptcy, any expected or known terms, contingencies and conditions of the bankruptcy Plan of Adjustment, changes in services provided by the government, any possibility of termination of the government, and how to obtain a copy of the Plan of Adjustment (GASB-58) [GASB Cod. Sec. Bn5].

As government employers implemented GASB-68 (*Accounting and Financial Reporting for Pensions—an amendment of GASB Statement No. 27*) and GASB-75 (*Accounting and Financial Reporting for Postemployment Benefits Other than Pensions*), as applicable, a legitimate question has been asked by virtue of recording a net pension or OPEB liability and a resulting degradation of net position of the government: does a going concern exist? A fund balance or net position deficit may not necessarily meet the criteria of going concern under GASB-56 (discussed previously). A negative balance in net position resulting from a government beginning to report its pension liability in the financial statements essentially means that the government does not currently have all of the resources needed to pay off its liabilities. Like other long-term liabilities, the net pension liability is an obligation that the government will have to repay over future years. A negative balance in net position is an issue that a municipal bond analyst, taxpayer group, or other financial statement user would focus on when evaluating a government's financial status. However, it is not necessarily a sign that a government is in dire financial difficulties. Operationally, a government's ability to provide services could be curtailed and may be reported in an "emphasis of matter" paragraph in an auditor's report to assist readers in understanding the issue. Part of the answer to *Implementation Guide* question 7.23.10 encourages governments to disclose additional details of unrestricted net position in the notes to the financial statements to isolate the effect of such issues. In addition, the government may wish to disclose an explanation in the management's discussion and analysis [GASB Cod. Sec. 2200.708-12].

Nonexchange Financial Guarantees

An unexpected consequence of going concern considerations and bankruptcy (or other fiscal stress) is the exercising of nonexchange financial guarantees. These occur when governments extend financial guarantees for the obligations of another government (or private entities, not-for-profit corporations, or individuals). As a part of this nonexchange financial guarantee, a government commits to indemnify the holder of the obligation if the entity or individual that issued the obligation does not fulfill its payment requirements. Also, some governments issue obligations that are guaranteed by other entities in a nonexchange transaction.

GASB-70 (*Accounting and Financial Reporting for Nonexchange Financial Guarantees*) requires governments that extend a nonexchange financial guarantee to recognize a liability when qualitative factors and historical data, if any, indicate that it is more likely than not (defined as greater than 50%) that the government will be required to make a payment on the guarantee. The qualitative factors largely mirror governments that have going concern indictors or are facing bankruptcy or other oversight. The amount of the liability to be recognized should be the discounted present value of the best estimate of the future outflows expected to be incurred as a result of the guarantee. When there is no best estimate but a range of the estimated future outflows can be established, the amount of the liability to be recognized should be the discounted present value of the minimum amount within the range.

A government that has issued an obligation guaranteed in a nonexchange transaction must report the obligation until legally released as an obligor (usually through the judicial process). GASB-70 also requires a government that is required to repay a guarantor for making a payment on a guaranteed obligation or legally assuming the guaranteed obligation to continue to recognize a liability until legally released as an obligor. When a government is released as an obligor, the government recognizes revenue as a result of being relieved of the obligation. An additional discussion on nonexchange financial guarantees is found in Chapter 16, "Other Liabilities."

QUESTIONS

1. According to GASB Concepts Statement No. 4 and GASB-63, which of the following elements the statement of net position does *not* contain?

    a. Assets

    b. Deferred revenue

    c. Deferred inflows of resources

    d. Net position

2. Which body promulgates standards for accounting and financial reporting for states, local governments, and other nonfederal governmental bodies and is recognized as a standard-setter by the American Institute of Certified Public Accountants in its *Code of Professional Conduct?*

    a. The American Institute of Certified Public Accountants

    b. The Financial Accounting Standards Board

    c. The Government Finance Officers Association

    d. The Governmental Accounting Standards Board (succeeding the National Council on Governmental Accounting)

3. Basic governmental accounting principles providing a broad overview on financial reporting, focus primarily on:

    a. Service efforts and accomplishments

    b. Financial accounting and reporting primarily with regard to funds and fund operations, capital assets, liabilities, including long-term debts, other accruals, and systems of records

    c. Cash flow of transactions

    d. Taxation policy

4. What type of governmental fund is used to account for and report the proceeds of specific revenue sources that are restricted or committed to expenditure?

    a. Capital projects fund

    b. Special revenue fund

    c. Restricted fund

    d. General fund

5. Which of the following is *not* an aspect of why governments are different from not-for-profit or for profit enterprises?

    a. Governments have the power to issue options, warrants, and other, similar financial instruments as long as those charged with governance approve the issuance.

    b. Governments serve a broader group of stakeholders, including taxpayers, citizens, elected representatives, oversight groups, bondholders, and others in the financial community.

c. Monitoring actual compliance with budgeted public-policy priorities is central to government public-accountability reporting.

d. Governments exist longer than for-profit businesses and are less subject to bankruptcy and dissolution, even during the latest recession.

6. Which of the following is *not* a type of GASB Pronouncement?

a. Statement

b. Technical Bulletin

c. Exposure Draft

d. Interpretation

7. Which of the following is *not* included as part of guidance provided in NCGA-1 on budgeting, budgetary control, and budgetary reporting?

a. An annual budget should be adopted by a higher level of government in addition to the governmental entity.

b. The accounting system should provide the basis for appropriate budgetary control.

c. Budgetary comparisons should be provided for the general fund and each major special revenue fund that has a legally adopted annual budget, and governments are encouraged to present a comparison of amounts budgeted to amounts received or expended as part of RSI.

d. A government with significant budgetary perspective differences, such as program- or organizational-based budgets rather than fund budgets, are to present budgetary comparison information consistent with the perspective that provides for comparison with its legally adopted budget.

8. Which of the following is not a criterion for recognition as an Enterprise Fund contained within GASB-34?

a. The activity is financed with debt that is secured *solely* by a pledge of the net revenues from fees and charges of the activity.

b. The legislative body of the government deemed it to be an enterprise fund, irrespective of the nature of operations of the fund.

c. Laws or regulations require that the activity's costs of providing services, including capital costs (such as depreciation or capital debt service), be recovered with fees and charges rather than with taxes or similar revenues.

d. The pricing policies of the activity establish fees and charges designed to recover its costs, including capital costs (such as depreciation or debt service).

9. GASB Concepts Statement No. 1 identifies the following objectives of financial reporting:

• Financial reporting should assist in fulfilling a government's duty to be publicly accountable and should enable users to assess that accountability.

- Financial reporting should assist users in evaluating the operating results of the governmental entity for the year.
- Financial reporting should assist users in assessing the level of services that can be provided by the governmental entity and its ability to meet its obligations as they become due.

Which aspect of operations is named by Concepts Statement No. 1 as being paramount in meeting the aforementioned objectives?

a. Affordability.

b. Cost vs. benefit.

c. Due professional care.

d. Accountability.

10. Which of the following is *not* an indicator of substantial doubt about a government's ability to continue as a going concern?

a. Negative trends such as recurring declines in net position or fund balances, consistent working capital deficiencies, or operating cash flow declines.

b. Recognition of a net pension liability in accordance with GASB-68.

c. Inabilities to raise resources or borrow monies resulting from proximity to legal debt or revenue limits.

d. Internal matters such as major work stoppages, labor disputes, or excessively burdensome contracts, significant reliance on a particular program's success, the need to significantly revise operations.

ANSWERS

1. According to GASB Concepts Statement No. 4 and GASB-63, which of the following elements is not contained in the statement of net position?

   Answer – B: Deferred revenue is no longer recognized upon implementation of GASB-63 within the statement of net position. All other items are found in a statement of net position.

2. Which body promulgates standards for accounting and financial reporting for states, local governments and other nonfederal governmental bodies and is recognized as a standard-setter by the American Institute of Certified Public Accountants in its *Code of Professional Conduct*?

   Answer – D: The Governmental Accounting Standards Board (succeeding the National Council on Governmental Accounting) is named within the AICPA's *Code of Professional Conduct—Revised* as being a recognized standard-setter for states, local governments, and other nonfederal governmental bodies. The FASB is a recognized standard setter within the *Code of Professional Conduct—Revised*, but not for governments. The AICPA is not a recognized standard setter with regard to accounting and financial reporting—it is recognized only for auditing. The Government Finance Officers Association is not a recognized standard setter within the *Code of Professional Conduct—Revised*.

3. Basic governmental accounting principles providing a broad overview on financial reporting, focus primarily on:

   Answer – B: Financial accounting and reporting focus primarily on funds and fund operations, capital assets, systems of records, and liabilities, including long-term and debts other accruals. Service efforts and accomplishments are not widely used principles. Cash flows of transactions are important with regard to the special purpose framework of the cash basis, but are not part of basic governmental accounting principles. Taxation policy varies from government to government.

4. What type of governmental fund is defined as the one that is used to account for and report the proceeds of specific revenue sources that are restricted or committed to expenditure?

   Answer – B: Special Revenue Fund. GASB-54 defines capital projects funds and the general fund differently than above. A restricted fund is not contained within U.S. GAAP.

5. Which of the following is *not* an aspect of why governments are different from not-for-profit or for profit enterprises?

   Answer – A: Governments do not issue options, warrants and other financial instruments. Answers B, C, and D are core differences between governments and other entities.

6. Which of the following is *not* a type of GASB Pronouncement?

   Answer – C: Exposure drafts are only part of the due process. Statements, technical bulletins, and interpretations are final pronouncements.

7. Which of the following is *not* included as part of guidance provided in NCGA-1 on budgeting, budgetary control and budgetary reporting?

   Answer – A: Approval by a higher level of government in addition to the governmental entity is only used if the government is under some form of receivership or fiscal control by another government. The other elements are common in budgeting, budgetary control, and budgetary reporting.

8. Which of the following is not a criterion for recognition as an Enterprise Fund contained within GASB-34?

   Answer – B: Even though a legislative body has the power to pass legislation, accounting principles are different from the legislative process. Activities financed with debt that is secured solely by a pledge of net revenues, laws, or regulations requiring cost recovery and pricing policies designed to recover costs are all criteria for recognition as an Enterprise Fund in accordance GASB-34.

9. GASB Concepts Statement No. 1 identifies the following objectives of financial reporting:

   - Financial reporting should assist in fulfilling a government's duty to be publicly accountable and should enable users to assess that accountability.

   - Financial reporting should assist users in evaluating the operating results of the governmental entity for the year.

   - Financial reporting should assist users in assessing the level of services that can be provided by the governmental entity and its ability to meet its obligations as they become due.

   Which aspect of operations is named by Concepts Statement No. 1 as being paramount in meeting the aforementioned objectives?

   Answer – D: Accountability is named as a paramount aspect of operations of a state or local government due to citizen and stakeholder involvement. Affordability and cost vs. benefit are important, but not as much as accountability. Due professional care is a standard of ethics and auditing.

10. Which of the following is *not* an indicator of substantial doubt about a government's ability to continue as a going concern?

    Answer – B: The recognition of a net pension liability in accordance with GASB-68, *in and of itself* may not be an indicator of a government's ability to continue as a going concern. The government may have sufficient net position to not have a deficit. Furthermore, the government may have the ability to raise revenues in the future to pay for the liability similarly to other long-term liabilities.

CHAPTER 2
BUDGETARY ACCOUNTING

CONTENTS

INTRODUCTION

A budget is a plan of financial operations that provides a basis for the planning, controlling, and evaluating of governmental activities. The budget process is a political process that usually begins with the chief executive of a governmental unit submitting a budget to the unit's legislative branch for consideration. Ultimately, the legal authority for governmental expenditures is reflected in an annual or biennial appropriations bill, act, or other form of legal adoption (NCGA-1, par. 77) [GASB Cod. Sec. 1700.101].

NCGA-1 (*Governmental Accounting and Financial Reporting Principles*), as supplemented by GASB-34 and GASB-41 (*Budgetary Comparison Schedules—Perspective Differences—an amendment of GASB Statement No. 34*), provides the basic guidance for budgetary accounting and reporting. Other than these pronouncements, there is little in U.S. GAAP on budgetary accounting and reporting due to the focus on control. Control is vitally important to a government's operations. However, many recent U.S. GAAP pronouncements, notably GASB-68 (*Accounting and Financial Reporting for Pensions—an amendment of GASB-27*), have migrated away from accounting transactions that primarily stem from budgetary decisions to those that are based upon accrual accounting principles. With the implementation of GASB-68, pension expense will likely not equal pension contributions calculated in accordance with GASB-27, creating a major budget-to-GAAP difference if the government's budget is not prepared in accordance with the economic resources measurement focus and the accrual basis of accounting (colloquially described as "full accrual accounting"). This chapter focuses on budgetary accounting and its role in government financial reporting. Chapter 20, "Comprehensive Annual Financial Report," discusses reporting budgetary comparison information in the annual financial statements.

The budgetary process for governmental units is far more significant than it is for commercial enterprises because of the public nature of the process and the fiduciary responsibility of public officials. The importance of the budgetary process is emphasized by the fact that NCGA-1 states that every governmental unit should prepare an annual comprehensive budget. The statement further recommended that the annual budget serve as a basis for control and evaluation of a fund even if the fund was not legally required to adopt a budget (NCGA-1, pars. 77–78 and 80) [GASB Cod. Secs. 1700.101–.102, .107].

Budgetary Accounting System

Budgetary control is enhanced when the legally adopted budget is integrated into the governmental unit's formal accounting system. The integration of the budget and accounting system is referred to as the budgetary accounting system. Budgetary accounts are used in a budgetary accounting system.

A budgetary accounting system should be used by certain governmental fund types. NCGA-1 states that budgetary accounts should be used in the General Fund and Special Revenue Funds. Other governmental funds that should employ a budgetary accounting system are those subject to the controls of an annually adopted budget, and those processing numerous revenue, expenditure, and transfer transactions through the fund. For example, it may be appropriate to use budgetary accounts in a Permanent Fund when activities are being financed annually through the investment earnings of the fund (NCGA-1, par. 89) [GASB Cod. Sec. 1700.118].

Conversely, budgetary accounts may be unnecessary in the following situations:

- *Debt Service Fund*—Receipts and expenditures for a period are established by the sinking fund provisions of a debt agreement or legal requirement, and few transactions are processed each period.

- *Capital Projects Fund*—Various construction projects are under contract with independent contractors who are exclusively responsible for the progress of their project (turnkey projects). However, many governments may choose to budget for capital projects individually or an entire capital program over a number of years.

Ultimately, professional judgment must be used to determine if a budgetary accounting system is necessary to provide adequate control over revenues and expenditures of a particular governmental fund (NCGA-1, par. 90) [GASB Cod. Sec. 1700.119]. Governments may also be subject to legal requirements requiring some form of budgetary system.

Budgetary accounts are used exclusively for control and therefore do not affect the actual results of operations for the accounting period. Two important aspects of a budgetary accounting system are (1) accounting for the budget and (2) accounting for encumbrances (NCGA-1, par. 91) [GASB Cod. Sec. 1700.127].

OBSERVATION: Many governments use some form of software to control spending against budget due to the internal controls necessary for compliance.

Governments with large amounts of capital spending may control spending in a fashion similar to operating accounts within capital accounts. Capital spending controls have become especially important when capital spending is financed with bonds issued related to a federal program, or similar bonds, which have purpose restrictions to financing capital assets. To assure that spending is in line with established laws, ordinances, and other legal requirements, an audit of a government might involve a large component of fieldwork centered on the control mechanisms that are established within a budgetary system.

Accounting for the Budget

In some instances, an *executive budget* is prepared, reflective of a chief executive of a government's desired policies, procedures, goals, and objectives. It is usually prepared by the executive official or budgetary office of the executive official and submitted to a legislative branch for consideration. The legislative branch may also prepare its own budget(s) for enactment and then approval (or not) by the executive branch.

GASB-34, pars. 130–131, define "original budget" and "final budget" as follows:

- The *original budget* is the first complete appropriated budget. The original budget may be adjusted by reserves, transfers, allocations, supplemental appropriations, and other legally authorized legislative and executive changes *before* the beginning of the fiscal year. The original budget should also include actual appropriation amounts automatically carried over from prior years by law. For example, a legal provision may require the automatic rolling forward of appropriations to cover prior-year encumbrances.

- The *final budget* is the original budget adjusted by all reserves, transfers, allocations, supplemental appropriations, and other legally authorized legislative and executive changes applicable to the fiscal year, whenever signed into law or otherwise legally authorized [GASB Cod. Sec. 1700.114].

As introduced, the original budget and the final budget contain individual elements or line items known as *appropriations*, which are meant to control spending at an individual action level. Most jurisdictions have laws, regulations, or ordinances that do not allow spending in excess of appropriation, except in emergencies.

In some instances, accounts or funds may be *nonappropriated* and may have a budget. Such accounts or funds may be established by enabling legislation, constitution, or federal provisions. Accounts or funds supported by grants or fees may be nonappropriated. *Flexible* budgets are similar to nonappropriated accounts or funds as they may raise (or lower) depending upon some other activity (receipt of revenue, economic conditions, etc.).

Budgets are also at different levels of operations. They may be by agency, by program within an agency, by accounting period, or even by activities within a particular budget. Some activities may be known as *objects* and may have a code or a class for reporting purposes. Common objects are salaries, benefits, expenses of employees, employee benefits, equipment, leases, and many others. Revenues may also be by code or class, with separate elements for taxation, fees, fines, grants, and investment revenues, among others.

Paragraph 131 of GASB-34 discusses how budgetary comparison schedules are presented (1) using the same format, terminology, and classifications as the budget document *or* (2) using the format, terminology, and classifications in a statement of revenues, expenditures, and changes in fund balances and accompanied by a reconciliation of the budgetary information to U.S. GAAP information [GASB Cod. Sec. 2200.207].

PRACTICE ALERT: The status of budgetary reporting is an integral part of the GASB's *Financial Reporting Model—Reexamination* project. The GASB is expected to determine the appropriate method of communication. Current U.S. GAAP requires presentation of comparisons of budget to actual amounts for the General Fund and each major special revenue fund with a legally adopted budget at a minimum. U.S. GAAP allows the budget to be reported as either basic financial statements or required supplementary information. Current U.S. GAAP also presents the adopted budget, the final (amended) budget and actual amounts (using the budget's basis of accounting) with a variance column between the final and actual amounts. The project will also reexamine what budgetary information is essential for users. There are auditing considerations to this decision due to the different levels of assurance provided between a basic financials statement versus required supplementary information (which is less assurance). However, there are those who say budgetary information is the definition of compliance in a government and has minimal relationship to GAAP-based financial statements. The preliminary views phase of the project proposed to be released in 2018 may include the Board's initial views on the status of budgetary reporting in the future, which are tentatively in favor of presenting such comparisons as required supplementary information (RSI).

The appropriated budget for the current fiscal year may be recorded in a fund using control accounts (accounts that are closed at period end and not reported in the financial statements) in the following manner:

	Debit	Credit
Estimated Revenues (Budgetary Control)	800,000,000	
Appropriations (Budgetary Control)		780,000,000
Fund Balance (Budgetary Control)		20,000,000
To record operating budget in control accounts.		

The foregoing example general ledger entry for these budgetary control accounts reflects the fact that the adopted budget anticipates estimated revenues of $800,000,000, has approved appropriations of $780,000,000, and expects a $20,000,000 increase in fund balance if those estimates are achieved.

The estimated revenues control account is a budgetary account that represents the total anticipated revenues expected to be available during the fiscal year on a budgetary basis. The estimated revenues account functions as an overall control account, and the specific revenue sources, such as property taxes, fines, and intergovernmental revenues, would be recorded in revenue subsidiary ledgers. Actual revenues are recorded in non-budgetary accounts as they are recognized throughout the accounting period. Also, as actual revenues are recorded, similar postings are made to the subsidiary ledgers. The overall control account and the subsidiary ledgers provide a basis for the subsequent comparison of the estimated revenues with the actual revenues for the period. Thus, the estimated revenues account (a budgetary account) is used to compare estimated revenues with actual revenues for the period, but it does not function as a control account for actual revenues.

The appropriations control account is a budgetary account that represents the total authorized expenditures for a current fiscal period within the budgeted fund. The appropriations account is a control account, with the details of the approved encumbrances and expenditures being recorded in appropriations subsidiary ledgers. During the year, encumbrances and expenditures are recorded both in (1) non-budgetary accounts such as public safety and health and welfare expenditures and in (2) appropriations subsidiary ledger accounts. Throughout the fiscal year, the appropriations account and its subsidiary ledger accounts can be used to control the level of encumbrances and expenditures to avoid exceeding appropriated amounts. Thus, the appropriations control account (a budgetary account) is used for both control and comparative purposes.

OBSERVATION: In order to maintain fiscal balance (otherwise known as a balanced budget) in times of fiscal stress, most government executives have the power to reduce appropriations if estimated revenues decrease. If appropriations are reduced, a debit to appropriations (budgetary control) would be necessary along with a credit to estimated revenues (budgetary control). These debits and credits would likely occur at a line item level if the government has a system with this capability.

The difference between estimated revenues and appropriations as authorized in the budget is debited or credited to the fund's fund balance budgetary control account. The entry in the fund balance account reflects either an anticipated operating surplus (credit) or a deficit (debit) for the current budgetary period.

The use of budgetary control accounts in the general ledger does not affect the actual revenues and expenditures recognized during the accounting period. This is accomplished by simply reversing, at the end of the reporting period, the budgetary control accounts created when the budget was initially recorded.

For example, assuming there were no budget amendments affecting the budgetary control totals, the earlier entry used to illustrate the recording of the budget would be reversed as follows:

	Debit	Credit
Fund Balance (Budgetary Control)	20,000,000	
Appropriations (Budgetary Control)	780,000,000	
Estimated Revenues (Budgetary Control)		800,000,000
To close budgetary control accounts.		

The budgetary control accounts can be grouped with related actual control accounts as part of the period closing to emphasize the comparative purpose of using the budgetary accounting system. The following example illustrates this type of closing, along with the use of other budgetary control accounts:

	Debit	Credit
Revenues (Actual)	795,000,000	
Estimated Revenues (Budgetary)		800,000,000
Appropriations (Budgetary)	780,000,000	
Expenditures (Actual)		770,000,000
Fund Balance (Budgetary)	20,000,000	
Fund Balance (Actual)		25,000,000
To close all revenue and expenditure related budgetary and actual control accounts.		

Accounting for Encumbrances

Encumbrances represent commitments related to contracts not yet performed, and orders not yet filled (executory contracts, open purchase orders), and they are used to control expenditure commitments for the year and to enhance cash management. A governmental unit often issues purchase orders or signs contracts for the purchase of goods and services to be received in the future.

Encumbrances may or may not carry from one period to the next. If encumbrances *do not* carry forward, they are known as "lapsing." Otherwise, they are known as "nonlapsing." Any amount that carries forward to the next period is an estimated amount of expenditures to finalize a contract. However, since the goods or services have not been provided, under most budgetary accounting principles, they do not represent expenditures or liabilities. Therefore, for accounting and *internal* financial reporting purposes (see **OBSERVATION**), the encumbered amount that carries forward needs to be reestablished in the new period.

At the time these commitments are made the following budgetary entry should be made for control purposes based upon the estimated size of each contract that is encumbered. For example, if the annual audit of a government is estimated to cost $100,000, the following entry is made upon signing of the engagement letter with the auditor (NCGA-1, par. 91) [GASB Cod. Sec. 1700.127]:

	Debit	Credit
Encumbrances (Budgetary Control)	100,000	
Reserve for Encumbrances (Budgetary Control)		100,000
To record the issuance of a contract for the annual audit.		

OBSERVATION: GASB-54 (*Fund Balance Reporting and Governmental Fund Type Definitions*) eliminated reserves for encumbrances for general purpose external financial reporting purposes. However, they may still be used for control purposes and internal reporting to management or those charged with governance. This section remains in the *Guide* due to governments still using the encumbrance method for operations management. Governments will need to be careful to translate reserves into the proper categories of fund balance for financial reporting purposes if reserves will remain in place.

The provisions of GASB-54 require *significant encumbrances* to be disclosed in the notes to the financial statements by major funds and non-major funds in the aggregate in conjunction with required disclosures about other significant commitments. Encumbered amounts for specific purposes for which resources already have been restricted, committed, or assigned do not result in separate display of the encumbered amounts within those classifications. Encumbered amounts for specific purposes for which amounts have not been previously restricted, committed, or assigned should not be classified as unassigned but, rather, should be included within committed or assigned fund balance, as appropriate. This is because the encumbrances account does not represent an expenditure for the period, only a commitment to expend resources. Likewise, the account reserve for encumbrances is not synonymous with a liability account since the liability is recognized only when the goods are received or the services performed (NCGA-1, par. 91, as amended by GASB-54, par. 24) [GASB Cod. Sec. 1700.127].

OBSERVATION: Many governments may be using systems that have predated the implementation of GASB-54 or have chosen not to update them to stop recording encumbrances and are instead recording transactions within the various categories of fund balances. Complex enterprise resource planning (ERP) systems have very detailed accounting that may be difficult to customize. In these situations, governments would then journal voucher fund balance segregation after the year-end, calculated by analyzing transactions and acts of those charged with governance, while leaving detailed transactions intact.

When an executed contract for audit services is completed or virtually completed, the budgetary encumbrance control accounts are liquidated or reduced and the actual expenditure and related liability are recorded, illustrated as follows:

	Debit	Credit
Reserve for Encumbrances (Budgetary Control)	100,000	
Encumbrances (Budgetary Control)		100,000
To record the receipts of audit services and liquidation of the outstanding encumbrance, where the encumbrance was estimated at $100,000 but the final actual expenditure was only $97,000.		
Expenditures—Professional Services	97,000	
Vouchers Payable		97,000
To record the actual expenditure for audit services.		

In the example above, because the expenditure described above is the final cost to be incurred related to this purchase, the original encumbrance amount is liquidated based on the estimated cost of goods and services, which differed from the eventual cost of the item.

During the budgetary period, the governmental unit can determine the remaining amount of the new commitments that can be signed by comparing the amount of appropriations to the sum of expenditures recognized and encumbrances outstanding.

At the end of the fiscal year, some encumbrances may be outstanding. NCGA-1 states that encumbrances outstanding at the end of the year are not expenditures for the year, and the reserve for encumbrances account is not to be treated as a liability. The treatment of the two encumbrance budgetary accounts (encumbrances and reserve for encumbrances) at the end of the year depends on whether appropriations, even if encumbered at the year-end, are allowed to lapse (NCGA-1, par. 91, as amended by GASB-54, par. 24) [GASB Cod. Sec. 1700.127].

Lapsing appropriations. When there are outstanding encumbrances at the end of the fiscal year, it is likely that the governmental unit will honor the open purchase orders or contracts that support the encumbrances. For U.S. GAAP-basis financial statement reporting purposes, outstanding encumbrances are not considered expenditures for the fiscal year. If the governmental unit allows encumbrances to lapse, even though it plans to honor them, the appropriations authority expires and the items represented by the encumbrances are usually re-appropriated in the following year's budget and re-encumbered in the new budget year.

NCGA-1 stated that when outstanding encumbrances and their related appropriations are allowed to lapse at year-end but the state or local government intends to honor the commitment, the encumbrances were to be disclosed either as a reservation of the fund balance or in a note to the financial statements, and authorization for the eventual expenditure was included in the following year's budget appropriations. However, GASB-38 (*Certain Financial Statement Note Disclosures*) rescinded the requirement to disclose the accounting policy for encumbrances in the notes to the basic financial statements. Though it is no longer required, in practice many governments still disclose the accounting policy for encumbrances due to the focus on control.

To illustrate the accounting necessary to portray the lapsing appropriations process, assume that encumbrances of $100,000 are outstanding at December 31, 20X8, but the governmental unit passes a law to commit the funds to pay for the contracts in the 20X9 fiscal year. At the end of 20X8, the following entries should be made into the books of the government but not displayed on the face of the basic financial statements:

	Debit	Credit
Reserve for Encumbrances (Budgetary Control)	100,000	
Encumbrances (Budgetary Control)		100,000

To close control accounts for encumbrances outstanding at the end of the fiscal year.

Fund Balance—Unassigned	100,000	
Fund Balance—Committed		100,000

To commit the fund balance by the estimated amount that will be re-appropriated in 20X8 for outstanding encumbrance period.

The first entry closes the encumbrance budgetary controls accounts because they are strictly budgetary accounts. The second entry meets the period-end reporting requirement of GASB-54 in that the fund balance is committed by the government for the amount of the outstanding encumbrances to be honored in the subsequent period.

At the beginning of the next fiscal year (January 1, 20X9), the following entries are made:

	Debit	Credit
Encumbrances (Budgetary Control)	100,000	
Reserve for Encumbrances (Budgetary Control)		100,000

To recognize outstanding encumbrances to be honored from the prior year.

Fund Balance—Committed	100,000	
Fund Balance—Unassigned		100,000

To reclassify fund balance in accordance with GASB-54.

In accordance with GASB-54, the above entry to remove the amount for fund balance reserved for outstanding encumbrances has been replaced with an entry to debit Fund Balance—Committed or Fund Balance—Assigned, as appropriate, and credit Fund Balance—Unassigned, assuming the encumbered amounts are not already reported within the committed or assigned classifications.

NOTE: The *GASB Implementation Guide 2015-1*, questions Z.54.13-14 [GASB Cod. Sec. 1800.744-2-3], discusses the adoption of a budget and appropriation documents in a subsequent fiscal year and their effect on fund balance classification. The GASB notes that the adopted appropriation or similar legislation generally authorizes a government to spend budgeted revenues and other financing sources and, therefore, does not impose constraints on the use of *existing resources*. However, if a portion of existing fund balance is included as a budgetary resource in the subsequent year's budget to eliminate a projected excess of expected expenditures over expected revenues, then that portion of fund balance (in an amount no greater than is necessary to eliminate the excess) should be classified as assigned. The amount should not be classified as committed, because the governing body does not have to take formal action to remove or modify that specific use—the purpose assignment expires with the appropriation. GASB further discusses in the next question that the assignment of fund balance terminates at the effective date of the following year's budget (the year after carry-over.)

The first entry reestablishes budgetary control over the outstanding encumbrances, and the next entry removes the fund balance reservation, which is no longer needed with the reestablishment of budgetary control. The appropriations control account created in the January 1, 20X9, budget will need to include the $100,000 because an expenditure for this amount is anticipated during 20X9.

From this point the normal entries for encumbrances and expenditures are followed. For example, if the goods or services are received on January 28, 20X9, and the final cost is $99,000 of the $100,000 encumbered, the following entries would be made:

	Debit	Credit
Expenditures	99,000	
Vouchers Payable		99,000
To record the receipts of goods or services.		
Reserve for Encumbrances (Budgetary Control)	100,000	
Encumbrances (Budgetary Control)		100,000
To remove encumbrances on vouchered commitments.		

The expenditures are reflected in the 20X9 GAAP-basis financial statements as required by NCGA-1.

When lapsed encumbrances are re-appropriated and treated in the manner described in the previous example, there are no differences between the budgetary accounting basis and the GAAP basis. The budgetary expenditures represented by the encumbrances are reflected in the budget in the same year that the expenditures are shown in the U.S. (GAAP) statement of revenues, expenditures, and changes in fund balances.

Nonlapsing appropriations. Appropriations for encumbrances that are outstanding at year-end and are considered nonlapsing (i.e., the legal authority to commit against them does not expire) do not require re-appropriation the following year because the appropriation authority does not expire. Typically, nonlapsing appropriations are used for long-term contracts involving construction. NCGA-1 requires that outstanding encumbrances that are charged against nonlapsing appropriations be reported as a fund balance reserve at period end. However, this NCGA-1 treatment was changed upon the implementation of GASB-54.

To illustrate the treatment under the NCGA-1 guidance, assume that encumbrances of $100,000 are outstanding as of December 31, 20X9. At the end of 20X9, the following entries would be made:

	Debit	Credit
Fund Balance—Unassigned	100,000	
Encumbrances (Budgetary Control)		100,000

To close encumbrances outstanding at the end of the fiscal year.

	Debit	Credit
Reserve for Encumbrances—20X9 (Budgetary Control)	100,000	
Fund Balance—(Restricted, Committed, or Assigned)		100,000

To reserve the fund balance by the amount that represents outstanding encumbrances at the end of the fiscal year (pursuant to NCGA-1 guidance prior to implementation of GASB-54).

OBSERVATION: Due to GASB-54, the above entries to reserve fund balance for outstanding encumbrances are modified to debit Fund Balance—Unassigned (rather than Fund Balance—Unreserved) and credit Fund Balance—Committed or Fund Balance—Assigned, as appropriate (rather than Fund Balance—Reserved for Encumbrances), assuming the encumbered amounts are not already reported within the committed or assigned classifications.

The two entries close the encumbrance budgetary control accounts to avoid reporting budgetary accounts in the GAAP-basis financial statements. The first entry closes the encumbrances control account directly to the fund balance so that as required by U.S. GAAP they are not shown as expenditures in the current fiscal year. The second entry establishes a fund balance reserve as required by NCGA-1.

At the beginning of the next fiscal year (January 1, 20X9), the following entry would be made:

	Debit	Credit
Fund Balance—(Restricted, Committed, or Assigned)	100,000	
Reserve for Encumbrances—20X9 (Budgetary Control)		100,000

*To recognize outstanding encumbrances from the prior year (see **OBSERVATION**, below).*

OBSERVATION: GASB-54 requires the above entry to recognize prior-year encumbrances to be modified to debit Fund Balance—Committed or Fund Balance—Assigned, as appropriate, rather than debiting Fund Balance—Reserved for Encumbrances, assuming the encumbered amounts are not already reported within the committed or assigned classifications.

This entry reestablishes the reserve for encumbrances account (a budgetary control account), but indicates that the reserve is applicable to amounts appropriated in the previous year's budget.

For example, if the goods or services are received on January 28, 20X9, and the final cost is $99,000 of the $100,000 encumbered, the following entry would be made during 20X9:

	Debit	Credit
Expenditures	99,000	
Vouchers Payable		99,000
To record the receipt of goods or services.		

At the end of 20X9, the following closing entry would be made:

	Debit	Credit
Reserve for Encumbrances—20X8 (Budgetary Control)	100,000	
Expenditures		99,000
Fund Balance—Unreserved		1,000
*To close expenditures encumbered during the prior year; see **OBSERVATION**, below.*		

OBSERVATION: Similarly to previous OBSERVATIONS, the above entry to close expenditures encumbered in the prior year has been modified to credit Fund Balance—Unassigned, rather than crediting Fund Balance—Unreserved.

This closing entry enables 20X9 encumbered expenditures to be reported as expenditures in 20X9 as required by U.S. GAAP when the goods or services are received.

When encumbrances are charged against nonlapsing appropriations in the manner illustrated, there are differences between the budgetary accounting amounts and the GAAP-basis amounts. The budget-based information reflects expenditures based on liabilities incurred adjusted for the effect of encumbrances outstanding, whereas the actual (GAAP-basis) financial statements reflect expenditures that do not include amounts encumbered at the end of the fiscal year. When budget-basis revenues and expenditures differ from GAAP-basis revenues and expenditures, there must be a reconciliation between budgetary information presented with the financial statements and the actual financial statements, which must be presented on a GAAP basis (NCGAI-10, pars. 15–17), as amended by GASB-14 and GASB-34. An example budgetary reconciliation, is illustrated in Exhibit 20-13, "Budget to GAAP Reconciliation," in Chapter 20, "Comprehensive Annual Financial Report."

Once a method of accounting for encumbrances is established based on the entity's appropriation lapsing policy, it should be used on a consistent basis.

BUDGETARY ACCOUNTING BY FUND TYPE

Although the NCGA recommended that all funds adopt a budget for control purposes, the nature of budgeting is different for each of the three types of funds: governmental, proprietary, and fiduciary (NCGA-1, par. 78) [GASB Cod. Sec. 1300.102].

Budgeting for Governmental Funds

Governmental funds (General Fund, Special Revenue Funds, Capital Projects Funds, Debt Service Funds, and Permanent Funds) generally use a legally adopted fixed budget, which reflects a specific estimate for revenues and appropriations for expenditures. Once expenditures and revenues are incorporated into the budget, the total appropriation amounts usually become a legal limit for current expenditures, and the estimated revenue amounts become the basis for comparison with actual revenues (NCGA-1, pars. 78 and 83–89) [GASB Cod. Sec. 1300.102, GASB Cod. Secs. 1700.110–.118].

To simplify the presentation and understanding of budget-and-actual comparison, the basis for preparing the budget would need to be the same as the governmental fund's GAAP-basis of accounting. The modified accrual basis is the GAAP basis of accounting for governmental fund types; and to simplify the accounting, the budget would reflect a similar basis for establishing expenditures and estimating revenues. However, many governments adopt a budget on a basis of accounting other than U.S. GAAP, such as a cash basis, modified cash basis, or regulatory basis of accounting. When the budgetary basis and GAAP basis of accounting are different, a governmental unit usually maintains its records on the budgetary basis (legal basis) and uses supplementary information to convert the budget-based information to the modified accrual basis (GAAP basis) for financial reporting purposes. Also, to facilitate the comparison of budgeted amounts and actual expenditures and revenues, similar terms and classifications should be used in the preparation of the budget and the presentation of the financial report (NCGA-1, par. 90) [GASB Cod. Sec. 1700.119].

> **OBSERVATION:** From an accounting perspective, it is preferable (but not required) that the budgetary system be on the same basis as the financial accounting system; namely, the modified accrual basis. However, some argue that a budget should be based on the cash basis, modified cash basis, or regulatory basis because those bases are more consistent with the statutory requirements and the financing of a governmental unit and are better understood by legislators. Financial reporting standards do not require that a budget be prepared on a GAAP basis. The largest state or local government to do so is New York City.

Budgeting for Proprietary Funds

Generally, proprietary funds adopt a flexible budget, which changes as the activity level changes. In a proprietary fund, overall activity is measured in terms of revenues and expenses and fluctuates, in part, depending on the demand for goods and services by the public (Enterprise Fund) or by other governmental departments or agencies (Internal Service Fund). The flexible budget items are generally not considered appropriations (legal spending limits) but, rather, an approved financial plan that can facilitate budgetary control and operational evaluations. A proprietary fund allows the governmental unit to prepare several budgets at different activity levels to establish an acceptable comparative basis for planned activity and actual results (NCGA-1, pars. 95–97) [GASB Cod. Secs. 1700.121–.123].

OBSERVATION: NCGA-1 discusses the preparation of several budgets based on anticipated activity levels. Even if several budgets are prepared, the budget ultimately used as a comparison with actual results should be based on the actual, not the anticipated, activity level. The preparation of the budget based on actual activity is feasible because the flexible budgeting approach can be expressed in terms of a formula (Total Expenses = Fixed Expenses + Variable Expenses) and should be applicable at any activity level.

The basis of accounting used to prepare a budget for a proprietary fund should generally be the same as the basis used to record the results of actual transactions. It is not appropriate to integrate the budgetary system into the proprietary fund's accounting system when a flexible budget system is used. However, if a fixed budget is used, perhaps due to a preference or legal requirement, it may be useful to integrate the budgetary system into the proprietary fund's accounting system, similar to governmental funds (NCGA-1, pars. 78 and 94) [GASB Cod. Sec. 1700.120].

Budgeting for Fiduciary Funds

Fiduciary funds include Pension and Other Employee Benefit Trust Funds, Investment Trust Funds, Private-Purpose Trust Funds, and (currently) Agency Funds (see **PRACTICE ALERTS** in Chapter 1, "Foundation and Overview of Governmental Generally Accepted *Accounting* Principles," and Chapter 8, "Fiduciary Funds," on GASB Statement No. 84 (*Fiduciary Activities*)). The first three fund types are similar to proprietary funds and may use budgetary controls, although these resources are not available for governmental operations. Such controls are rare due to the nature of fiduciary activities which commonly have outflows based on demand and inflows based on investing activity or contributions based on payroll that is out of the control of the fiduciary activity. Budgets are not appropriate for Agency Funds, because the government entity functions only as a custodial agent and Agency Funds record no revenues or expenditures.

Budgeting by Program or Purpose

Subsequent to the issuance of GASB-34, issues were raised about presenting budgetary comparisons when perspective differences exist. Perspective differences exist when the structure of financial information for budgetary purposes differs from the fund structure that is defined in GASB-34. For example, a government may develop a purpose-based budget that provides appropriation by project or purpose irrespective of the funds that will be used to account for those projects or purposes (in other words a cross-fund budget). In response to these issues, GASB issued GASB-41 (*Budgetary Comparison Schedules—Perspective Difference—an amendment to GASB-34*).

Essentially, GASB-41 provides an alternative budgetary comparison presentation for governments that legally adopt a budget by program or purpose that may cross funds. (See an example presentation within the discussion of perspective differences for budgetary comparisons in Chapter 20, "Comprehensive Annual Financial Report.")

OBSERVATION: One of the more thoughtful and distinguished budget presentations focusing on purposes, functions and justification for services rather than appropriations in a general government has to be the City of Portland, Oregon's budget. The City utilizes a very open, community-focused budgeting system that justifies each expenditure in an open manner. Terms are easily understood for the average citizen. For example, the Portland Water Bureau's budget shows "resources" and "requirements" all in five-year trends. Debt service and transfers are included as changes in fund balances. The requirements are then apportioned to programs, including administrative. A capital budget is then included and finally a list of full time, part time and limited term positions ledger is included. Further information on the City's budgeting documents and process may be found at https://www.portlandoregon.gov/cbo/.

QUESTIONS

1. According to NCGA-1, par. 89 [GASB Cod. Sec. 1700.118], which of the following types of funds usually *do not* include a legally adopted budget?

    a. General fund.

    b. Special revenue fund.

    c. Debt service fund.

    d. Capital projects fund.

2. According to GASB-34, pars. 130–131 [GASB Cod. Sec. 1700.114, GASB Cod. Sec. 2200.207], which of the following *are not usually* found in an adopted original budget?

    a. The mayor's State of the City speech.

    b. Appropriations.

    c. Appropriated amounts carried over from prior years as allowed under law.

    d. Reserves, transfers, allocations, supplemental appropriations, and other legally authorized legislative and executive changes before the beginning of the fiscal year.

3. With regard to budgetary financial reporting, in accordance with GASB-54, which of the following items are *not* presented as part of general purpose external financial reports?

    a. Revenues.

    b. Reserves for encumbrances.

    c. Expenditures.

    d. Transfers.

4. According to NCGA-1, what type of budget is usually adopted by a legislative body for a governmental fund?

    a. Legally adopted flexible budget.

    b. Capital improvement wish lists.

    c. Legally adopted fixed budget.

    d. Hybrid budget.

5. According to NCGA-1, what type of budget is usually adopted by a legislative body for a proprietary fund?

    a. Legally adopted fixed budget.

    b. Capital improvement wish lists.

    c. Legally adopted flexible budget.

    d. Hybrid budget.

ANSWERS

1. According to NCGA-1, par. 89 [GASB Cod. Sec. 1700.118], which of the following types of funds usually *do not* include a legally adopted budget?

   Answer – B: Debt service funds contain receipts and expenditures for a period established by the sinking fund provisions of a debt agreement or legal requirement, and few transactions are processed each period. The general fund and special revenue funds usually have a legally adopted budget. Capital projects funds usually have either a legally adopted budget or a separately adopted capital improvement program budget.

2. According to GASB-34, pars. 130–131 [GASB Cod. Sec. 1700.114, GASB Cod. Sec. 2200.207], which of the following *are not usually* found in an adopted original budget?

   Answer – A: The mayor's State of the City speech is not usually adopted by a legislative body as part of a budget, even though it may be posted on a website. Appropriations, amounts carried over from prior years as allowed under law, reserves, transfers, allocations, supplemental appropriations, and other legally authorized legislative and executive changes before the beginning of the fiscal year are all part of an adopted original budget.

3. With regard to budgetary financial reporting, in accordance with GASB-54, which of the following items are *not* presented as part of general purpose external financial reports?

   Answer – B: Reserves of any type are no longer presented as part of general purpose external financial reports. Revenues, expenditures and transfers are commonplace.

4. According to NCGA-1, what type of budget is usually adopted by a legislative body for a governmental fund?

   Answer – C: Legally adopted fixed budgets are usually required to be adopted for governmental funds. Flexible budgets may be legally adopted or not (depending on law) for proprietary funds. Capital improvement wish lists are not budgets. Hybrid budgets are undefined in U.S. GAAP.

5. According to NCGA-1, what type of budget is usually adopted by a legislative body for a proprietary fund?

   Answer – C: Legally adopted flexible budgets are commonplace for proprietary funds. For the reasons stated in the answer to question 4, the others are not used.

CHAPTER 3
BASIS OF ACCOUNTING AND MEASUREMENT FOCUS

CONTENTS

INTRODUCTION

For state and local governments, a prime area of focus of accounting and financial reporting is *accountability*. Financial reporting of state and local governments provides information to assist users in assessing accountability and making decisions. Accountability is a core element of governmental operations as the operations are funded directly or indirectly by the public. The GASB considers accountability to be the primary objective from which all other objectives are derived.

In addition to the overall objective of accountability, Governmental Accounting Standards Board Concepts Statement No. 1 (GASB:CS-1) (*Objectives of Financial Reporting*) identified the following as objectives of governmental financial reporting (GASB:CS-1, pars. 76–79):

Objective of Governmental Financial Reporting	How Objective is Met in GASB Standards
	• Reporting provides information to determine whether current-year revenues were sufficient to pay for current-year services (known as inter-period equity).
Financial reporting should fulfill a government's duty to be publicly accountable and should enable users of the financial statements to assess that accountability.	• Reporting demonstrates whether resources were obtained and used with the entity's legally adopted budget and compliance with finance-related legal or contractual requirements.
	• Reporting provides information to assist users in assessing service efforts, costs, and accomplishments of the government.
	• Reporting provides information on sources and uses of resources.
Financial reporting should assist users in evaluating the operating results of the governmental entity for the year.	• Reporting also provides information on how the government finances its activities and meets its cash requirements.
	• The net result of reporting determines whether the government's financial position improved or deteriorated as a result of the year's operations.
	• Reporting provides information about the financial position or condition of a governmental entity (as of a point in time).
Financial reporting should assist users in assessing the level of services that can be provided by the governmental entity and its ability to meet its obligations.	• Reporting also provides information about a government's physical and other nonfinancial resources that extend beyond the current year, including whether those resources still have a potential to provide services, or are impaired.
	• Finally, reporting discloses legal or other restrictions on resources and risks of potential loss of those resources.

The GASB noted that although accountability is referred to only in the first objective, accountability is implicit in all of the listed objectives.

Although most interested observers may agree with the overall goal of financial reporting, implementing the goal is the subject of much debate. The overall goal of accounting and financial reporting can be summarized as follows: to provide (1) financial information useful for making economic, political, and social decisions and demonstrating accountability and stewardship and (2) information useful for evaluating managerial and organizational performance. An important element in implementing this overall goal in a governmental environment is selecting a basis of accounting and a measurement focus for governmental funds. The selection of a basis of accounting and measurement focus affects the establishment of specific accounting principles for state and local governments (NCGA:CS-1, par. 13).

An appreciation of the unique character of governmental financial reporting can be developed only when the concepts of basis of accounting and measurement focus are fully understood. For this reason, this chapter is a foundation chapter and does not discuss governmental U.S. generally accepted accounting principles U.S. (GAAP) except to illustrate basis of accounting and measurement focus.

GASB Concepts Statement No. 6 (GASB:CS-6) (*Measurement of Elements of Financial Statements*) addresses both measurement approaches and measurement attributes. A measurement approach determines whether an asset or liability presented in a financial statement should be either (1) reported at an amount that reflects a value at the date that the asset was acquired or the liability was incurred or (2) remeasured and reported at an amount that reflects a value at the date of the financial statements. A measurement attribute is the feature or characteristic of the asset or liability that is measured. An additional project related to elements of financial statements on recognition has been merged into the reexamination of the financial reporting model.

Two primary approaches are discussed in GASB:CS-6: (1) initial transaction date-based measurement amounts (commonly known as historical cost) and (2) current financial statement date-based measurement (commonly known as remeasured amounts). The measurement attributes are defined as follows:

- *Historical cost (proceeds)*: The amount paid to acquire an asset or the amount received pursuant to the incurrence of a liability in an actual exchange transaction.

- *Fair value*: The price that would be received to sell an asset or paid to transfer a liability in an orderly transaction between market participants at the measurement date.

- *Replacement cost*: The price that would be paid to acquire an asset with equivalent service potential in an orderly market transaction at a measurement date.

- *Settlement amount*: The amount at which an asset could be realized or a liability could be liquidated with the counterparty rather than through an active market.

OBSERVATION: GASB Statement No. 72 (*Fair Value Measurement and Application*) introduces the concept of *unit of account*. *Unit of account* is defined as the level at which an asset or a liability is aggregated or disaggregated. In deliberating what became GASB-72, the GASB concluded that a government should consider the unit of account at which the fair value measurement is made because accounting standards vary in the way assets and liabilities are measured. The unit of account may be a single asset or liability (e.g., a financial instrument), a group of assets, a group of liabilities, or a group of related assets and liabilities (e.g., a partnership). The unit of account is not unique to fair value measurements; once the unit of account is established—whether at an individual account level or an aggregated level—relevant measurement attributes can be applied (GASB-72, par. 8) [GASB Cod. Sec. 3100.105].

In addition to the unit of account concept, the GASB also changed the measurement for certain donated assets with the release of GASB-72 to a concept that is not contained within GASB:CS-6. Consistent with GASB:CS-6, many assets are measured based on measurement attributes other than fair value. In its deliberations, the GASB agreed that fair value should be replaced by *acquisition value* for *certain transactions.*

Acquisition value is the price that would be paid to acquire an asset with equivalent service potential in an orderly market transaction at the acquisition date, or the amount at which a liability could be liquidated with the counterparty at the acquisition date (GASB-72, pars. 79 and 86) [GASB Cod. Sec. 1400, fn. 1]. Acquisition value is a market-based entry price. Fair value, on the other hand, is an exit price—the price that would be received to sell an asset or paid to transfer a liability. Acquisition value is a measurement at the initial transaction date using the replacement cost or the settlement amount measurement attribute.

The GASB believes that an entry price measurement is more appropriate than an exit price because (*a*) the transaction represents the government acquiring the asset and (*b*) it would result in a similar measurement as if the government had purchased the asset. Based on this conclusion, acquisition value should be used for the following assets *only*:

- Donated capital assets;
- Donated works of art, historical treasures, and similar assets; and
- Capital assets that a government receives in a service concession arrangement.

The notion of an acquisition price is further supported by the view that those assets generally will be used in providing services, rather than converted to cash (GASB-72, pars. 68 and 79, GASB-37, par. 6) [GASB Cod. Secs. 1400.102 and .109, fn. 12].

BASIS OF ACCOUNTING

An entity's accounting basis determines when transactions and economic events are reflected in its financial statements. NCGA-1 (*Governmental Accounting and Financial Reporting Principles*) states that basis of accounting refers to "when revenues, expenditures, expenses, and transfers—and the related assets and liabilities—are recognized in the accounts and reported in the financial statements." All operating transactions are the result of expected or unexpected resource flows (usually, but not exclusively, cash flows). Because of specific contractual agreements and accepted business practices, commitments that create eventual resource flows may not coincide with the actual flow of resources. For example, goods may be purchased on one date, consumed on another date, and paid for on still a third date. The accounting basis determines when the economic consequences of transactions and events are reflected in financial statements. Generally, accounting transactions and events of state and local governments are recorded on an accrual basis or modified accrual basis in accordance with U.S. GAAP depending on the fund type involved or, for non-GAAP presentations, another comprehensive basis of accounting, such as cash, modified cash, or regulatory basis.

Flow of Economic Resources (Applied on an Accrual Basis) (also known as "Full Accrual")

GASB-34 (*Basic Financial Statements—and Management's Discussion and Analysis—for State and Local Governments*) describes the measurement focus and basis of accounting of the government-wide and the proprietary (or business-type) financial statements as including revenues, expenses, gains, losses, assets, and liabilities recognized when an exchange takes place. An exchange is when value or resources is received or delivered for value or resources. Value or resources may not equate to a cash transaction. Goods and services being received or delivered may signify value (GASB-34, par. 16, as amended by GASB 63, pars. 7–8, and GASB-81, pars. 24–29) [GASB Cod. Sec. 1600.103].

Some of the essential elements of the accrual accounting method include the recognition of assets, liabilities, inflows, outflows and deferred inflows of resources or deferred outflows of resources when directed by U.S. GAAP in accordance with transaction type. Expenses are recognized when incurred unless U.S. GAAP allows deferral and amortization over a period of time. For example, GASB-68 (*Accounting and Financial Reporting for Pensions—an amendment of GASB Statement No. 27*) allows for differences between expected amounts and actual experience to be deferred and amortized over the remaining service life of an employee. However, if the difference is related to a retiree, because the retiree has no service life as an employee, then an expense is recognized immediately. Revenues are recognized similarly unless deferred due to their applicability to a future reporting period. For example, resources that are received by a government from another government before time requirements are met (e.g., prior to a fiscal year beginning) but after all other eligibility requirements are met, are declared as a deferred inflow of resources by the receiving government.

In the accrual basis of accounting, revenues from *exchange transactions* are recognized when an exchange of value for value occurs in the ordinary course of operations. The recognition may be adjusted if the circumstances are such that the collection of the exchange price is *not* reasonably assured. The exchange would result in a credit transaction to revenue and a related debit to receivable, along with any appropriate provision for uncollectible accounts. Guidance for specific transactions may adjust recognition, including for the right of return of a product sold (GASB-62, par. 23) [GASB Cod. Sec. 1600.104].

For expenses, recognition occurs when the underlying transaction occurs, regardless of when cash is disbursed. (NCGA-1, par. 59, as amended by GASB-34, par. 6) [GASB Cod. Sec. 1600.102].

PRACTICE ALERT: The GASB staff's Invitation to Comment *Revenue and Expense Recognition* presents two potential models that may become the components of a comprehensive revenue and expense model. The initial model focuses on exchange/nonexchange transactions which is primarily based on existing standards contained in GASB Statement No. 33 (*Accounting and Finan-*

cial Reporting for Nonexchange Revenues) and GASB Statement No. 36 (*Recipient Reporting for Certain Shared Nonexchange Transactions*), both as amended. The second model is similar to the newly updated Financial Accounting Standards Board (FASB) revenue recognition model which is based on whether or not a performance obligation is present. GASB staff also asked for alternatives to the two models presented. Comments were due in April 2018 with public hearings held in May 2018. A further due process document is not expected until 2020.

A summary comparison of both models is as follows:

	Exchange/Nonexchange Model	*Performance Obligation/No Performance Obligation Model*
Classification	Is the transaction an exchange or a nonexchange transaction?	Does the transaction contain a performance obligation? (Example—does the government's ambulance service have to transport a patient prior to revenue recognition)?
Recognition	*Exchange Transaction*—recognize based on earnings approach, where the government controls the asset (or incurs a liability) *and* an inflow of resources (or outflow of resources) is applicable to the period. *Nonexchange Transaction*—recognize based on GASB-33 provisions for derived tax revenues, imposed nonexchange revenues, government-mandated nonexchange transactions or voluntary nonexchange transactions. (See Chapter 17 "Revenues: Nonexchange and Exchange Transactions" and 18 "Expenses/Expenditures: Nonexchange and Exchange Transactions.")	*Transaction Contains a Performance Obligation* (*or obligations*)—recognize based on performing the service or delivery. Determine consideration, allocate the consideration to the performance obligation and recognize revenue or expense as obligation is satisfied. *Transaction does not contain a performance obligation*—recognize based on GASB-33 provisions.
Measurement	To be determined for both models as a result of further due process.	

Current Financial Resources and Modified Accrual Basis of Accounting (also known as "Modified Accrual")

The modified accrual basis of accounting is a variation of the accrual basis that modifies the basis for certain cash flow considerations.

Revenues

Revenues, including funds received from other governmental units, should be recorded when they are "susceptible to accrual." GASB-65 (*Items Previously Reported as Assets and Liabilities*), paragraph 30 [GASB Cod. Sec. S40.108], describes part of the accrual as:

When an asset is recorded in governmental fund financial statements but the revenue is not available, the government should report a deferred inflow of resources until such time as the revenue becomes available.

If revenue is not available in a governmental fund, the fund should report a deferred inflow of resources until time passes and revenue is available. For revenue to be considered susceptible to accrual, it must be both measurable and available to finance current expenditures of the fund. Some governments consider this susceptibility of accrual of revenue if it is collectible during the current period and the actual collection occurred either (1) during the current period or (2) soon enough after the end of the period to be used to pay current year-end liabilities (NCGA-1, pars. 62–63 and 69). For example, revenues may be accrued at the end of the year only if a cash flow occurs within sixty, ninety, or some other number of days after the period end date (NCGA-1, par. 62) [GASB Cod. Secs. 1600.106–.108 and P70.103].

OBSERVATION: There is no explicit definition of "measurable" in the pronouncements, but the term undoubtedly refers to the ability to quantify the amount of revenue expected to be collected. Thus, "measurable" can be interpreted as the ability to provide a reasonable estimate of actual cash flow.

PRACTICE ALERT: The GASB is in the process of updating the conceptual framework with regard to the recognition of transactions, which may clarify the word "measurable." The objective of the project is to develop criteria for *whether* information should be reported and *when* the information should be reported. A new concepts statement may result from this project. The GASB's Preliminary Views were released just prior to publication. Redeliberation is expected to occur during 2019 and an Exposure Draft is expected in 2020. A final Concepts Statement is not expected until 2022.

Examples of revenue recognition under the modified accrual basis of accounting include the following:

- *Taxes and similar nonexchange revenue* should generally be recognized as revenue when levied to the extent they are collected within the availability period as described above. Deferred inflows of resources should be reported when resources are receivable before either:
  — The period for which the property taxes are levied or
  — The period when resources are required to be used or
  — When first permitted, in which a statute includes time requirements.

  For example, if a government levies amounts in its current property tax levy for *future* debt service payments, there may not be a prohibition on recognizing the levy in current revenues. The *GASB Implementation Guide 2015-1*, question Z.33.12 [GASB Cod. Sec. N50.708-3], discloses that unless a legal requirement specifies otherwise, the period for which these amounts are levied is the same as the period for which the rest of the taxes are levied.

- *Interest and investment income,* including changes in fair value of investments, should be recognized as revenue when earned and available.

OBSERVATION: The basis for conclusions (paragraph B57) of GASB-72 (*Fair Value Measurement and Application*) makes no distinction between the bases of accounting in recognizing the fair value of investments. Investments reported in governmental fund financial statements, prepared using the current financial resources measurement focus and modified accrual basis of accounting, should be measured at fair value. The GASB also believes that gains and losses from the changes in fair value cannot be separately realized from the underlying investment and, therefore, the changes in fair value are a faithful reflection of the increase or decrease in the financial resources available to the government to fund its activities.

- *Recreation fees, parking fees, business licenses, and similar revenue* should generally be recognized when received in cash as that is likely when the exchange occurs.

Expenditures

Expenditures are recorded on a modified accrual basis when they are normally expected to be liquidated with current financial resources (referred to as a governmental fund liability). Expenditures differ from expenses in that they represent a "decrease in net financial resources." Expenditures include salaries, wages, and other operating expenditures; payments for supplies; transfers to other funds; capital outlays; and payments for the service of debt. Although most expenditures are recorded when the liability is incurred, the current financial resources measurement focus of a governmental fund significantly affects what items are to be considered expenditures in the governmental fund. Thus, expenditures for a governmental fund cannot be equated to expenses of a business enterprise (NCGA-1, par. 70) [GASB Cod. Secs. 1500.122, 1600.116]. GASB-34 did not change this model.

Examples of expenditure recognition under the modified accrual basis of accounting include the following:

- *Capital outlay* (purchases or construction of land, buildings, improvements, infrastructure, and equipment) are *not* capitalized and depreciated but are recognized as expenditures in the period that the liability is incurred.

- *Debt principal and interest payments* are recognized as expenditures when due and payable from current financial resources. Interest is not accrued on the modified accrual basis.

- *Costs incurred related to accrued expenses* such as compensated-absence obligations, pension and OPEB obligations, claims and judgments, termination benefits, landfill closure and postclosure care costs, and pollution remediation obligations are not recognized as expenditures when incurred; they are only recognized when they are normally expected to be liquidated with current financial resources.

Special Purpose Frameworks (SPFs)

Either by choice or to meet a regulatory requirement, many small government entities account for transactions and prepare their financial statements in accordance with a special purpose framework (SPF). Special purpose frameworks (formerly known as other comprehensive bases of accounting or "OCBOA"), which are commonly used by smaller state and local governments, include the following:

- Basis of cash receipts and disbursements (cash basis);

- Cash basis with modifications having substantial support (modified cash basis); and

- Basis to comply with requirements of a regulatory agency whose jurisdiction the entity is subject to (regulatory basis).

The AICPA's Audit and Accounting Guide *State and Local Governments* provides guidance on the use of these bases of accounting for government entities.

PRACTICE POINT: The focus of CCH's *Governmental GAAP Guide* is on accounting and financial reporting in accordance with U.S. GAAP; therefore, it does not address the accounting and financial reporting treatment and issues for governments that account and report in accordance with an SPF. Most accounting systems record daily transactions on a cash basis or a statutory or legislative basis, with conversions performed either manually or automatically to a U.S. GAAP basis at the end of an accounting period (either monthly or yearly). CCH's *Governmental GAAP Practice Manual* contains entries that may be needed to convert from a modified accrual to a full accrual basis of accounting.

MEASUREMENT FOCUS

The second critical element in the establishment of U.S. generally accepted accounting principles (U.S. GAAP) for governments is the selection of a measurement focus. Unlike the selection of an accounting basis, which is concerned with the timing of transactions and events, a measurement focus identifies what (and how) transactions and events should be recorded. The measurement focus is concerned with the inflow and outflow of resources that affect an entity. The balance sheet or statement of net position should reflect those resources available to meet current obligations and to be used in the delivery of goods and services in subsequent periods. The activity statement for the period should summarize those resources received and those consumed during the current period. Although there are a number of measurement focuses, the two measurement focuses recognized as generally accepted for government transactions are as follows:

1. Flow of economic resources; and

2. Flow of current financial resources.

Flow of Economic Resources (Applied on an Accrual Basis)

The flow of economic resources refers to the reporting of all of the net positions available to the governmental unit for the purpose of providing goods and services to the public. When the flow of economic resources and the accrual basis of accounting are combined, they provide the foundation for U.S. GAAP used by proprietary funds and business-type activities and in the government-wide financial statements. This approach recognizes the deferral and capitalization of certain expenditures and the deferral of certain revenues.

When the flow of economic resources is applied on an accrual basis for a fund, or for the government-wide statements, all assets, deferred outflows of resources, liabilities and deferred inflows of resources, are presented in the fund's balance sheet or statement of net position. The key differences between this approach and the current financial resources measurement focus as it applies to individual governmental funds are summarized as follows:

- Capital assets are recorded in the proprietary, enterprise, or internal service fund statement of net position or the government-wide statement of net position net of accumulated depreciation.

- Long-term debts are recorded in the proprietary, enterprise, or internal service fund statement of net position or the government-wide statement of net position.

- The fund's equity represents the net position (assets plus deferred outflows of resources less liabilities and deferred inflows of resources) available to the fund rather than the fund balance. Similarly, the government-wide equity represents the net position (assets plus deferred outflows of resources less liabilities and deferred inflows of resources) available to the government rather than any cumulative fund balances.

The activity statement includes all costs of providing goods and services during the period. These costs include depreciation, the cost of inventories consumed during the period, and other operating expenses. On the activity statement, revenues during the period are recognized along with the total cost of the particular segment (function) of government. There is a smoothing effect on the activity statement. For example, expenses do not include the full cost of purchasing depreciable property during the period and other financing sources do not include the proceeds from the issuance of long-term debt, as is the case in governmental funds under the current financial resources measurement focus.

Flow of Current Financial Resources (Applied on a Modified Accrual Basis)

The flow of current financial resources applied on a modified accrual basis is a narrow interpretation of what constitutes assets and liabilities for an accounting entity. Assets include only those considered current *financial resources*, such as cash and claims to cash, investments, receivables, inventory, and other, similar current financial assets.

PRACTICE ALERT: As part of the GASB's *Financial Reporting Model— Reexamination* project, the GASB has tentatively proposed the definition of *financial resources* to include "cash, resources that are expected to be converted to cash, and resources that are consumable in lieu of cash." The proposal is contained in the Preliminary Views due process document. It is unclear whether the change may result in more or less elements recognized in governmental funds.

Liabilities include those defined as governmental fund liabilities, which are liabilities normally expected to be liquidated with current financial resources. Deferred inflows of resources may be present in the flow of current financial resources, but only where revenue cannot be recognized but funds have been received. Revenues, and the resulting assets, are accrued at the end of the year only if the revenues are earned and are expected to be collected in time to pay for liabilities in existence at the end of the period. Expenditures, and the related liabilities, are accrued when they are normally expected to be paid out of revenues recognized during the current period. To determine which revenues and expenditures should be accrued, an arbitrary date after the end of the year must be established.

The measurement focus used for governmental funds is defined in NCGA-1, par. 18 [GASB Cod. Sec. 1300.102], as involving the "determination of financial position and changes in financial position (sources, uses, and balances of financial resources). Governmental funds are, in essence, accounting segregations of financial resources. Expendable assets are assigned to the various governmental funds according to the purposes for which they may or must be used." Due to these limitations, capital assets do not represent financial resources available for expenditure, but are items for which financial resources have been used and are thus reported as capital outlay *of governmental funds*. However, adjustments are presented to reconcile governmental fund balances and results of operations to the statement of net position and statement of activities, respectively. These adjustments may be very material.

Paragraph 87 of GASB-34 [GASB Cod. Secs. 1800.126, 2200.166], states that debt issuance costs paid out of debt proceeds, inclusive of underwriting fees are to be reported as expenditures of *governmental funds* and not capitalized and amortized. Issuance costs such as attorney and rating agency fees or bond insurance paid from existing resources should be reported as expenditures of a governmental fund when the related liability is incurred.

However, beyond these references there is no clear definition of "financial resources" or "current financial resources" as the measurement focus is referred to in the GASB literature. For example, there is little guidance on whether a long-term note receivable of a governmental fund represents a financial resource to be reported as a governmental fund asset other than the inference that fixed assets are the only assets specifically excluded from the definition (see previous **PRACTICE ALERT**).

Under the flow of current financial resources measurement focus, capital expenditures are recorded as capital outlay expenditures. In addition, prepayments and purchases of inventories may be recorded as of when the expenditures are made. Thus, the activity statement reflects only those expenditures that were made during the current period, and ignores cost allocations that might arise from expenditures incurred prior to the current period. The balance sheet or statement of net position under the flow of current financial resources approach reflects the entity's financial resource position and includes only those assets available to pay future expenditures and the fund liabilities *normally payable* from those financial assets (NCGA-1, par. 70) [GASB Cod. Secs. 1500.122, 1600.116].

GASBI-6, par. 10 [GASB Cod. Sec. 1500.118], describes "matured liabilities" in governmental funds (not associated with proprietary funds) as being only those that are normally due and payable in full when incurred or the matured portion of general long-term indebtedness (the portion that has come due for payment). GASBI-6, par. 11 [GASB Cod. Sec. 1500.119], also interprets matured liabilities to include debt service on formal debt issued when due (matured) and compensated absences, claims and judgments, special termination benefits, and landfill closure and postclosure care costs.

These liabilities should be recognized as governmental fund liabilities and expenditures to the extent the liabilities are "normally expected to be liquidated with expendable available financial resources." In its basis for conclusions, the GASB considered but rejected an alternative interpretation that "other commitments" are the long-term portion of any other liabilities, provided that the government has entered into a multilateral agreement to defer payment to a future period. The GASB concluded that there is no accrual modification that would permit deferring to a future period the recognition of fund liabilities (such as salaries and utilities) that are normally paid in a timely manner and in full from current financial resources when incurred. Rather, the GASB proposed that such transactions be reported as governmental fund liabilities and expenditures when incurred.

PRACTICE POINT: An example of potential delayed liability recognition in a fund is that post-retirement health care benefits (OPEB) in many jurisdictions may be changed in law without collective bargaining, leading to the notion that these benefits may not be liabilities. The GASB's conclusions mentioned above are also leading to the interpretation (perhaps, rightfully so) that no liability would exist in a governmental fund that normally pays salary escalations that cannot be paid out of current financial resources due to economic conditions. The escalations are then renegotiated to be paid in a future period, even though in a statement of net position, a liability may be declared for the same circumstance.

GASB-75 (*Accounting and Financial Reporting for Postemployment Benefits Other than Pensions*), paragraph B150 (in the basis for conclusions), continues this approach with regard to OPEB by requiring an OPEB liability to be recognized to the extent the liability is normally expected to be liquidated with expendable financial resources. In addition, GASB-75 requires OPEB expenditures to be recognized equal to the total of:

- Amounts paid by the employer to the OPEB plan, including amounts paid for OPEB as the benefits come due; and
- The change between the beginning and ending balances of amounts normally expected to be liquidated with expendable financial resources.

These requirements are consistent with the requirements of GASB-45 (*Accounting and Financial Reporting by Employers for Postemployment Benefits Other than Pensions*) and the requirements for recognition of other long-term liabilities and related expenditures in financial statements prepared using the current financial resources measurement focus and modified accrual basis of accounting in GASBI-6 (*Recognition and Measurement of Certain Liabilities and Expenditures in Governmental Fund Financial Statements*). To clarify the application of those requirements, the GASB decided to specify the point at which OPEB liabilities are normally expected to be liquidated with expendable available resources.

PRACTICE ALERT: The GASB's *Financial Reporting Model—Reexamination* project has recently entered a new phase. Three recognition approaches were presented in the Invitation to Comment due process document issued in 2016 for governmental funds (near-term financial resources, short-term financial resources, and long-term financial resources). No consensus was reached by the GASB to tentatively approve any of the approaches presented. Instead, the GASB issued a Preliminary Views document in 2018 including an approach for governmental funds focusing on *financial resources* (see previous **PRACTICE ALERT**) with an accrual period for one year. At the time of publication, redeliberations had not finalized on this aspect.

Basis of Accounting/Measurement Focus Illustration

The differences and similarities of the flow of economic resources (applied on the accrual basis) and the flow of current financial resources (applied on the modified accrual basis) are illustrated in the following example, which uses the following assumptions:

Activity	Amount
Fiscal Year ended June 30, 20X8 (for simplicity it is assumed that this is the first year of operations for the fund)	
Revenues:	
Billed during year	$30,000
Collected during year (one-half of the remaining balance (i.e., $2,000) is expected to be collected within 60 days of the year end and the remainder within 180 days)	26,000
Salaries:	
Paid during year	9,000
Payable (accrued) at the end of year and expected to be paid within 30 days	1,000

Activity	Amount
Property, Plant, and Equipment:	
Purchased equipment on July 1, 20X7, at a cost of $20,000, estimated four-year life, no salvage value, straight-line method for depreciation	20,000
Noncurrent Note Payable:	
Equipment purchased was financed by issuing a 10% note whereby all interest and principal are paid four years from date of issuance, but $2,000 of interest has accrued at June 30, 20X8	20,000
Supplies:	
Purchased during year	8,000
Consumed during year	6,000
Paid during year (balance to be paid 90 days after year-end date)	7,000
Pension:	
Annual required contribution	5,000
Amount funded during year	3,000

The financial statements for the governmental fund with the above financial information are presented in Exhibit 3-1.

EXHIBIT 3-1
FINANCIAL STATEMENTS

Fund Name **Statement of Revenues, Expenditures (Expenses), and Changes in Fund Balance (Net position) for Year Ended June 30, 20X8**

	Flow of economic resources	Flow of current financial resources (60-day availability assumption)*
Revenues	$ 30,000	$ 28,000
Expenditures/Expenses:		
Capital outlays	—	—
Salaries	10,000	10,000
Interest	2,000	—
Supplies	6,000	7,000
Pensions	5,000	3,000
Depreciation expense	5,000	—
Total Expenditures/Expenses	28,000	20,000
Excess of revenues over expenditures/expenses	2,000	8,000
Net position/Fund balance 7/1/X7	—	—
Net position/Fund balance 6/30/X8	$ 2,000	$ 8,000

Fund Name Statement of Net Position/Balance Sheet June 30, 20X8

	Flow of economic resources	Flow of current financial resources (60-day assumption)*
Assets		
Current assets		
Cash	$ 7,000	$ 7,000
Receivables	4,000	2,000
Supplies	2,000	—
Total Current assets	13,000	9,000
Capital assets		
Equipment	20,000	—
Accumulated Depreciation	(5,000)	—
Equipment, Net of Accumulated Depreciation	15,000	—
Total assets	$ 28,000	$ 9,000
Liabilities and Net position/Fund Balance		
Current liabilities		
Accounts payable	$ 1,000	—
Salaries payable	1,000	$ 1,000
Total Current Liabilities	2,000	1,000
Noncurrent liabilities		
Notes payable	22,000	—
Net pension obligation	2,000	—
Total Noncurrent liabilities	24,000	—
Total liabilities	26,000	1,000
Net Position/Fund balance	2,000	8,000
Total liabilities and net position/fund balance	$ 28,000	$ 9,000

* It is assumed that assets must be realizable in cash within 60 days of the end of the fiscal year to be considered available to finance current expenditures.

Basic Financial Statements: Different Measurement Focuses

Government-Wide Financial Statements

Government-wide financial statements were established by GASB-34 in order to provide a basis for determining (1) the extent to which current services provided by the entity were financed with current revenues and (2) the degree to which a governmental entity's overall financial position has changed during the fiscal year. In order to achieve these objectives, government-wide financial statements should include a statement of net position and a statement of activities.

Government-wide financial statements are reported on a flow of economic resources applied on the accrual basis of accounting. The flow of economic resources refers to all of the assets available to the governmental unit for the purpose of providing goods and services to the public. When the flow of economic resources and the accrual basis of accounting are combined, they provide a foundation for U.S. generally accepted accounting principles (U.S. GAAP) that is similar to that used by business enterprises. Businesses present essentially all assets and liabilities, both current and long-term, in their balance sheet. A governmental entity's statement of activities includes all costs of providing goods and services during a period. These costs include depreciation, the cost of inventories consumed during the period, and other operating expenses. On the activity statement, revenues earned during the period are matched with the expenses incurred for exchange or exchange-like transactions. Nonexchange transactions are accounted for based on the standards established by GASB-33 (*Accounting and Financial Reporting for Nonexchange Transactions*).

Fund Types and Financial Statements

A governmental entity can use (and report) three broad categories of funds: governmental funds, proprietary funds, and fiduciary funds.

Governmental funds. The governmental funds grouping includes five fund types (General Fund, Special Revenue Funds, Capital Projects Funds, Debt Service Funds, and Permanent Funds), which are used to record the more or less normal (non-business-like) operations of a governmental entity. The financial statements for these funds have a short-term emphasis and generally measure and account for cash and "other assets that can easily be converted to cash." These fund types are accounted for using the modified accrual accounting basis and the flow of current financial resources measurement focus.

Proprietary funds. Financial statements for proprietary funds are based on the flow of economic resources measurement focus and the accrual basis of accounting. The proprietary fund category includes Enterprise Funds and Internal Service Funds. An Enterprise Fund is used to report any activity for which a fee is charged to external users for goods or services. An Internal Service Fund may be used to account for activities that involve the governmental entity providing goods or services to other funds or activities of the primary government or its component units, or other governments on a cost-reimbursement basis where the reporting entity is the *predominant* participant in the activity. If the reporting entity is not the predominant participant, the activity should be reported in an Enterprise Fund.

Fiduciary funds. Assets held by a governmental entity for other parties (either as a trustee or as an agent) and that cannot be used to finance the governmental entity's own operating programs should be reported in the entity's fiduciary fund financial statements category. This fund grouping includes four fund types (Pension [and other employee benefit] Trust Funds, Investment Trust Funds, Private-Purpose Trust Funds, and Agency Funds). The financial statements for fiduciary funds should be reported on the flow of economic resources measurement focus and the accrual basis of accounting (with the exception of certain liabilities of defined benefit pension plans and certain postemployment health care plans). Fiduciary fund financial statements are not reported by major fund (which is required for governmental funds and enterprise funds) but must be reported by fund type (NCGA-1, par. 18, GASB-34, pars. 63–64, 66, 69, 78–79, 91–92, and 106, as amended by GASB-63, pars. 7–8 and 12, GASB-34, par. 107, as amended by GASB-67, par. 20, GASB-73, pars. 115–116, and GASB-74, par. 26) [GASB Cod. Sec. 1300.102].

PRACTICE ALERT: GASB Statement No. 84 (*Fiduciary Activities*) will redefine those activities and funds upon implementation for reporting periods beginning after December 15, 2018. For June 30 governments, the transition will take place on July 1, 2019. The basis of accounting and measurement focus for fiduciary funds will not change. However, the fund types and recognition as a fiduciary activity may change. GASB-84 recognizes a fiduciary activity that is not a component unit being present if the government controls the assets of the arrangement (described herein) and is *any* of the following:

- A pension plan that is administered through a trust in accordance with the provisions of GASB Statement No. 67 (*Financial Reporting for Pension Plans*) (see Chapter 22, "Pension and Other Postemployment Benefit Plans");

- An other postemployment benefits (OPEB) plan administered through a trust in accordance with the provisions of GASB Statement No. 74 (*Financial Reporting for Postemployment Benefit Plans Other than Pension Plans*) (also see Chapter 22); or

- A circumstance in which assets from entities that are not part of the reporting entity are accumulated for pensions as described in GASB Statement No. 73 (*Accounting and Financial Reporting for Pensions and Related Assets That Are Not within the Scope of GASB Statement 68*) and Amendments to GASB Statements 67 and 68 or OPEB as described in GASB-74 (see Chapter 13, "Pension, Postemployment, and Other Employee Benefit Liabilities").

If the activity is not a pension or OPEB plan or where assets are accumulated for pensions or OPEB as described, the activity is a fiduciary activity if all of the following criteria are met:

1. The assets associated with the activity are controlled by the government.

2. The assets associated with the activity are not derived either:

   a. Solely from the government's own—source revenues, or

   b. From government-mandated nonexchange transactions or voluntary nonexchange transactions with the exception of pass-through grants for which the government does not have administrative or direct financial involvement (see Chapter 17, "Revenues, Nonexchange and Exchange Transactions").

3. The assets associated with the activity have one or more of the following characteristics:

    a. The assets are (like many trusts or benefit plans):

        (1) Administered through a trust agreement or equivalent arrangement in which the government itself is not a beneficiary,

        (2) Dedicated to providing benefits to recipients in accordance with the benefit terms, and

        (3) Legally protected from the creditors of the government.

    b. The assets are for the benefit of individuals and the government does not have administrative involvement with the assets or direct financial involvement over the assets. In addition, the assets are not derived from the government's provision of goods or services to those individuals (situations where governments may serve as a custodian of funds).

    c. The assets are for the benefit of organizations or other governments that are not part of the financial reporting entity. In addition, the assets are not derived from the government's provisions of goods or services to those organizations or other governments (e.g., Internal Revenue Code Section 529 plans).

A government *controls* the assets of an activity if the government (*a*) holds the assets or (*b*) has the ability to direct the use, exchange or employment of the assets in a manner that provides benefits to the specified or intended recipients. Restrictions from legal or other external constraints that stipulate the assets can be used only for a specific purpose do not negate control.

Own-source revenues are revenues generated by the government itself. These may be water and sewer charges, investment earnings, sales and income taxes, property taxes and other inflows.

The types of fiduciary funds that will be reported in the basic financial statements include:

- *Pension (and Other Employee Benefit) Trust Funds* –similar to current reporting, including pension and OPEB plans administered through trusts;

- *Investment Trust Funds* –similar to current reporting including the external portion of investment pools and individual investment accounts that are held in trust;

- *Private-Purpose Trust Funds* –similar to current reporting of all fiduciary activities that are not pension arrangements, OPEB arrangements or activities required to be reported in investment trust funds and are held in trust; and

- *Custodial Funds* –a new category to report fiduciary activities that are not required to be reported in the previous types of funds. Within the custodial funds, a subcategory may be present where investment pools exist without a trust or similar arrangement.

Upon implementation, agency fund reporting will be discontinued and likely presented in custodial funds. Statements of Fiduciary Net Position and Statements of Changes in Fiduciary Net Position will continue to be used to report fiduciary activities.

Fund financial statements *may* include governmental, proprietary, and fiduciary funds to the extent that they have activities that meet the criteria of using those funds. If no activity or legal authorization is present to use a particular fund, it is not presented. In summation, the fund types used in state and local governments are as follows:

Fund Type	Funds Within Type	Balance Sheet/Net Position Title	Flows Statement Title
Governmental Funds (emphasizing major funds)	• General Fund • Special Revenue Funds • Capital Project Funds • Debt Service Funds • Permanent Funds	Balance Sheet	Statement of Revenues, Expenditures and Changes in Fund Balance
Proprietary Funds	• Enterprise funds (emphasizing major funds) • Internal Service Funds	Statement of Fund Net Position	Statement of Revenues, Expenses and Changes in Fund Net Position
Fiduciary Funds (and similar component units)	• Pension (and other employee benefit) trust funds • Investment trust funds • Private-purpose trust funds • Agency Funds	Statement of Fiduciary Net Position	Statement of Changes in Fiduciary Net Position

(GASB-34, par. 63, GASB-54, par. 28) [GASB Cod. Sec. 1300.103].

The various fund types, activities, and financial reporting for each are discussed in Chapters 6 through 8 of the *Governmental GAAP Guide*.

Exhibit 3-2 presents the basis of accounting and measurement focus that is required by U.S. GAAP accounting principles for each fund category and type of government-wide activity.

EXHIBIT 3-2
BASIS OF ACCOUNTING AND MEASUREMENT FOCUS

Fund Category/ Activity Type	Basis of Accounting	Measurement Focus
Governmental activities	Accrual basis	Economic resources
Business-type activities	Accrual basis	Economic resources
Governmental funds	Modified accrual basis	Current financial resources
Proprietary funds	Accrual basis	Economic resources
Fiduciary funds	Accrual basis	Economic resources

QUESTIONS

1. GASB Concepts Statement No. 6 does *not* include which of the following attributes as part of current financial statement date-based measurement (commonly known as remeasured amounts)?

   a. Historical cost.

   b. Fair value.

   c. Replacement cost.

   d. Settlement amount.

2. According to NCGA-1, why is a basis of accounting important to financial reporting?

   a. The basis of accounting dictates when to buy or sell bonds.

   b. The basis of accounting decides taxation policy.

   c. The basis of accounting refers to when revenues, expenditures, expenses, and transfers—and the related assets and liabilities—are recognized in the accounts and reported in the financial statements.

   d. The basis of accounting refers to when term limits are enforced.

3. According to GASB-34, when are transactions recognized in accordance with the accrual basis of accounting?

   a. When cash is received.

   b. When laws and regulations decide accounting activities.

   c. When debt is sold.

   d. When an exchange takes place.

4. According to GASB-65, what is recorded when an asset is recorded in governmental fund financial statements in accordance with the modified accrual basis of accounting but the revenue is not available?

   a. Deferred inflows of resources.

   b. Deferred revenue.

   c. Deferred charges.

   d. Deferred outflows of resources.

5. Which of the following is *not* a special purpose framework?

   a. Basis of cash receipts and disbursements (cash basis).

   b. Cash basis with modifications having substantial support (modified cash basis).

   c. Basis to comply with requirements of a regulatory agency whose jurisdiction the entity is subject to (regulatory basis).

   d. Modified accrual basis of accounting.

ANSWERS

1. GASB Concepts Statement No. 6 does *not* include which of the following attributes as part of current financial statement date–based measurement (commonly known as remeasured amounts)?

   Answer – A: Historical cost. Remeasured amounts include fair value, replacement cost, and settlement amount.

2. According to NCGA-1, why is a basis of accounting important to financial reporting?

   Answer – C: The basis of accounting refers directly to when accounting transactions are recognized in accounts and when reported on the financial statements. The buying and selling of bonds, decisions about tax policy, and the enforcement of term limits have minimal (if anything) to do with the basis of accounting.

3. According to GASB-34, when are transactions recognized in accordance with the accrual basis of accounting?

   Answer – D: Transactions are recognized under the accrual basis of accounting when an exchange takes place. Cash receipts, debt sales, and compliance with laws and regulations are not primary concerns related to the accrual basis of accounting.

4. According to GASB-65, what is recorded when an asset is recorded in governmental fund financial statements in accordance with the modified accrual basis of accounting but the revenue is not available?

   Answer – A: Deferred inflows of resources are recognized within governmental fund financial statements when an asset is recorded but revenue is not available. Deferred revenue and deferred charges are no longer used. Deferred outflows of resources are unlikely to occur in governmental funds.

5. Which of the following is *not* a special purpose framework?

   Answer – D: Cash basis, modified cash basis, and regulatory basis are all special purpose frameworks.

CHAPTER 4
GOVERNMENTAL FINANCIAL REPORTING ENTITY

CONTENTS

INTRODUCTION

The fund is the basic unit for establishing accountability for activities specifically established by laws, regulations, and other governmental mandates. Each fund consists of self-balancing accounts, including accounts for the fund's assets, liabilities, potentially deferred inflows of resources or deferred outflows of resources and residual fund balance or net position. A governmental unit's activities may be reflected in a number of governmental funds, proprietary funds, or fiduciary funds. In addition, agencies, authorities, and other governmental entities exist with their various funds that may be created by a state or local government. Ultimately, overall financial statements of the state or local government must be prepared, which raises the question of which separate legal entities and funds should be included in these broad-based financial statements.

The initial step in resolving this question is concerned with the conceptual definition of a financial reporting entity.

GASB-14 (*The Financial Reporting Entity*), GASB-39 (*Determining Whether Certain Organizations Are Component Units*), and GASB-61 (*The Financial Reporting Entity: Omnibus, an amendment of GASB Statements No. 14 and No. 34*) establish criteria for determining which organizations should be included in a governmental financial reporting entity.

PRACTICE POINT: GASB Statement No. 80 (*Blending Requirements for Certain Component Units*) amended GASB-14 further by establishing an additional blending criterion for the financial statement presentation of component units of all state and local governments. Component units incorporated as not-for-profit corporations for situations in which the primary government is the sole corporate member of the corporation are required to be blended. The sole corporate member is usually identified and defined in the articles of incorporation, bylaws, or statute. The term "sole corporate member" may not be the same as any other situation that may be considered similarly, such as when the primary government is the residual equity interest owner. (See **PRACTICE ALERT** in this chapter on the GASB's project on majority equity interests.) The entity is also required to be first adjudicated as a component unit and reported in the financial reporting entity in accordance with GASB-14, pars. 21–37, as amended [GASB Cod. Sec. 2600.113(d), fn. 6, GASB Cod. Secs. 2100.120–.136].

The AICPA Audit and Accounting Guide *State and Local Governments* contains a framework for defining a government that has been adopted by GASB as "Category B" GAAP in GASB Statement No. 76 (*The Hierarchy of Generally Accepted Accounting Principles for State and Local Governments*) [GASB Cod. Sec. 1000.101(b)]. As stated in paragraph 1.01 of the AICPA's Guide, governmental organizations have one or more of the following characteristics:

- Popular election of officers or appointment (or approval) of a controlling majority of the members of the organization's governing body by officials of one or more state or local governments;

- The potential for unilateral dissolution by a government with the net position reverting to a government; or

- The power to enact and enforce a tax levy [GASB Cod. Sec. 1000.801].

Organizations are presumed to be governmental if they have the ability to issue directly (rather than through a state or municipal authority) debt that pays interest exempt from federal taxation. However, due to the definitions in GASB-14, as amended, not-for-profit organizations may indeed be included in a primary government's financial reporting entity.

The focal point for preparing financial statements of a financial reporting entity is the *primary government*. Primary governments include states, general-purpose local governments, and certain special-purpose governmental entities.

The identification of a financial reporting entity is built around the concept of financial accountability. If a primary government is financially accountable for another entity, that entity's financial statements should be included in the financial statements of:

- The primary government; and
- If applicable, the primary government's component units.

GASB-14 and GASB-39 provide some flexibility in determining the components of the financial reporting entity. Although financial accountability is central to the identification of component units, an entity will be considered a component unit even if financial accountability does not exist if the nature and significance of its entity's economic relationship with the primary government is such that its exclusion would create misleading or incomplete financial statements or it is considered closely related or financially integrated.

The amendments to GASB-14 (and GASB-34) made by GASB-61 present guidance for organizations that do not meet the financial accountability criteria for inclusion as component units but that nevertheless should be included because the primary government's management determines that it would be misleading to exclude them. GASB-61 clarifies the manner in which that determination should be made and the types of relationships that generally should be considered in making the determination. Under GASB-61, par. 4 [GASB Cod. Secs. 2100.111 and 2600.102], a primary government may determine, through exercise of management's professional judgment, that an organization that does not meet the specific financial accountability criteria should be included as a component unit to prevent the reporting entity's financial statements from being misleading. This determination should be based on the nature and significance of the organization's relationship with the primary government. In addition, other organizations should be evaluated as potential component units if they are closely related to, or financially integrated with, the primary government. GASB-61 states that it is a matter of professional judgment to determine whether the nature and the significance of a potential component unit's relationship with the primary government warrant inclusion in the reporting entity.

Although the financial reporting entity standards are written from the perspective of a primary government, the standards established should be used to prepare the financial statements of governmental entities that are not primary governments. Thus, an entity that is not a primary government must assess its relationships with other entities to determine whether it is financially accountable for those entities. If financial accountability exists, a financial reporting entity should be constructed that includes the governmental entity and its component units.

In addition to establishing criteria for determining the scope of the financial reporting entity, GASB-14, as amended, addresses accounting and reporting standards for entities that are not component units. These entities include governmental joint ventures, jointly governed organizations, pools, and certain stand-alone governmental organizations.

GASB-14, as amended, applies to financial reporting by all state and local governments. However, the basis for reporting is not necessarily the narrowly defined state or local government, but rather is the "financial reporting entity," as defined below (GASB-14, par. 9, and Glossary) [GASB Cod. Secs. 2100.109–.111, .511, 2600.101]:

> A primary government, organizations for which the primary government is financially accountable, and other organizations for which the nature and significance of their relationships with the primary government are such that exclusion would cause the reporting entity's financial statements to be misleading or incomplete. The nucleus of a financial reporting entity usually is a primary government. However, a governmental organization other than a primary government (such as a component unit, a joint venture, a jointly governed organization, or another stand-alone government) serves as the nucleus for its own reporting entity when it issues separate financial statements [see later discussion in the section titled "The Financial Reporting Entity Concept"].

The focal point for defining the financial reporting entity begins with a "primary government," which is defined as follows:

> A state government or general-purpose local government. Also, a special-purpose government that has a separately elected governing body, is legally separate, and is *fiscally independent* of other state or local governments.

Thus, states, counties, cities, towns, other municipalities, and similar general-purpose local governments, as well as certain special-purpose governmental entities, are primary governments (GASB-14, par. 131, Glossary) [GASB Cod. Sec. 2100.521].

To prepare the financial statements of the financial reporting entity, the financial statements of a primary government are combined with the financial statements of its component units. "Component units" are defined as follows:

> Legally separate organizations for which the elected officials of the primary government are financially accountable. In addition, a component unit can be another organization for which the nature and significance of its relationship with a primary government is such that exclusion would cause the reporting entity's financial statements to be misleading or incomplete [see later discussion in section titled "Component Units"] (GASB 14, par. 131) [GASB Cod. Secs. 2100.119, .505].

Footnote 4 to GASB-61, paragraph 4b (amending GASB-14, par. 20) [GASB Cod. Sec. 2600 fn. 2], states component units may be a not-for-profit or a for-profit corporation or another government.

Although the financial reporting entity standards are discussed in the context of a primary government, GASB-14 recognizes that the focal point for defining a financial reporting entity may start with one of the following entities, rather than a primary government (GASB-14, par. 131, Glossary) [GASB Cod. Secs. 2100.514–.515, .520]:

Type of Entity	Definition
Joint venture (governmental)	A legal entity or other organization that results from a contractual arrangement and that is owned, operated, or governed by two or more participants as a separate and specific activity subject to joint control, in which the participants retain (*a*) an ongoing financial interest or (*b*) an ongoing financial responsibility [see later discussion in section titled "Joint Ventures"].
Jointly governed organization	A regional government or other multi-governmental arrangement that is governed by representatives from each of the governments that create the organization, but that is not a joint venture because the participants do not retain an ongoing financial interest or responsibility [see later discussion in section titled "Jointly Governed Organizations"]. This entity may also be known as a "joint powers authority."
Other stand-alone government	A legally separate governmental organization that (*a*) does not have a separately elected governing body and (*b*) does not meet the definition of a component unit. Other stand-alone governments include some special-purpose governments, joint ventures, jointly governed organizations, and pools [see later discussion in section titled "Other Stand-Alone Government Financial Statements"].

In some instances, the focal point for preparing a financial reporting entity's financial statements could be a component unit, particularly when the component unit issues separate financial statements.

OBSERVATION: The standards established in GASB-14, as amended, are based on the philosophy of building from the "bottom up" when preparing financial statements. This concept is discussed later in this chapter under the heading "Reporting Component Units."

GASB-61 amended the requirements of GASB-14 and GASB-39 for reporting joint ventures, equity interests, and additional criteria for blending component units. The major changes included:

- If component units are currently included because they have a fiscal dependency on a primary government, a component unit would require a financial benefit or burden between the primary government and the component unit.

- As previously discussed, if financial accountability is not present, the standard clarifies when potential component units should be included as part of the reporting entity.

- The definition of what is a "blended" component unit is expanded to include component units that have issued debt that is paid entirely or almost entirely by primary government resources.

- Additional reporting guidance is included on blending component units into single-column business-type activity governments.

- Equity interests in an entity require analysis and potentially blending if certain criteria are met.

The following are some examples of governmental entities, in addition to primary governments, that must follow the standards established by GASB-14, as amended (GASB-14, par. 9) [GASB Cod. Sec. 2600.101]:

- Commissions;

- Districts;

- Governmental enterprises;

- Public authorities;

- Public benefit corporations;

- Public employee retirement systems;

- Publicly owned utilities;

- Public owned hospitals and other health care providers; and

- Public colleges and universities.

NOTE: Some commissions, districts, trusts, authorities, and so on are not separate legal entities. Rather, they are ministerial or administrative bodies. Care must be taken to gather an understanding of an entity's legal status before making any judgment under the provisions of GASB-14, as amended.

The standards established by GASB-14, as amended, should be applied to all component units, both governmental and non-governmental, when those units are part of the financial reporting entity (GASB-14, par. 9) [GASB Cod. Sec. 2600.101].

Non-governmental entities *may* be included in the definition of a governmental financial reporting entity. For example, a tribal government that applies U.S. GAAP established by the GASB may own and operate a commercial concrete manufacturer. When the non-governmental entity's financial information is included in a governmental financial reporting entity, the reporting standards established by GASB-14 should be observed. The government's intent (operational or investment) has an impact on the accounting and financial reporting treatment of the non-governmental entity within the government's financial statements.

One of the elements of the debate on the reporting entity that was not included GASB-61 was how to report so-called "sub-government" entities such as departments and agencies that are frequently audited for operational and managerial purposes. No U.S. GAAP exists for sub-government entities that are part of the reporting entity of a government. The AICPA Audit and Accounting

Guide *State and Local Governments* contains guidance on the potential audit reports for sub-units of governments. Unless the sub-unit reports use a special-purpose framework, U.S. GAAP generally must be followed as if the sub-unit was an entire reporting entity.

THE FINANCIAL REPORTING ENTITY CONCEPT

GASB Concepts Statement No. 1 (GASB:CS-1) (*Objectives of Financial Reporting*) states that the basic foundation for governmental financial reporting is accountability. The Concepts Statement asserts that accountability "requires governments to answer to the citizenry—to justify the raising of public resources and the purposes for which they are used." In turn, the concept of accountability becomes the basis for defining the financial reporting entity. However, GASB-14 establishes a more operational definition by describing "accountability" (or accountable) as "the relationship that results from the appointment of a voting majority of an organization's governing board."

At every level of government (local, state, and federal), all public resources are the responsibility of elected officials. In the context of financial reporting, once public officials are elected, the citizenry has a right to be informed as to how public resources were used during a period. To hold public officials responsible for an entity's financial affairs, care must be taken in defining the financial reporting entity. If the financial reporting entity is defined in a manner that does not represent the authority empowered in public officials, the objective of accountability cannot be achieved. Fundamentally, GASB-14, as amended, attempts to follow a basic rule of responsibility accounting, which reasons that one should not be held accountable for something that one cannot influence (GASB-14, pars. 10–11) [GASB Cod. Sec. 2600.101].

The reporting entity's financial statements should be structured so that a reader can differentiate between the primary government, including its blended component units, and its discretely presented component units. This is accomplished by formatting the government-wide financial statements so that balances and transactions of the primary government are presented separately from those of its discretely presented component units. In addition, the reporting entity's fund financial statements should include only the primary government's governmental, proprietary, and fiduciary funds, and the first two fund categories should be presented by major fund, with nonmajor funds being aggregated and presented in a single column.

The two methods used to integrate the financial information of component units into the financial statements of the reporting entity are "discrete presentation" and "blending." GASB-14 defines these methods as follows (GASB-14, par. 11; GASB-34, pars. 6, 13–15, and 125–126) [GASB Cod. Sec. 2600.101]:

Discrete presentation method—The method of reporting financial data of component units in a column(s) separate from the financial data of the primary government. An integral part of this method of presentation is that major component unit supporting information is required to be provided in the reporting entity's basic financial statements by:

- Presenting each major component unit in a separate column in the reporting entity's statements of net position and activities,

- Including combining statements of major component units in the reporting entity's basic statements after the fund financial statements, or

- Presenting condensed financial statements in the notes to the reporting entity's basic financial statements.

For component units that are fiduciary in nature, financial information is reported only in the fund financial statements in the primary government's statements of fiduciary net position and changes in fiduciary net position. The same basis of accounting for fiduciary funds is used. (GASB-14, pars. 44 and 51, as amended by GASB-35, par. 5, GASB-34, pars. 14, 106–117, 125–127 and fns. 49–50, as amended by GASB-61, par. 8, and GASB-63, par. 8) [GASB Cod. Secs. 2600.107–.108].

Blending method—The method of reporting the financial data of a component unit that presents the component unit's balances and transactions in a manner similar to the presentation of the balances and transactions of the primary government's funds. Despite legal separation, such entities are so interrelated to the primary government that they are, in essence, a part of the primary government. Therefore, the balances and results of operations are reported similarly to other funds [See later discussion in section titled "Blending Component Units"] (GASB-14, par. 52, GASB-34, pars. 6 and 125) [GASB Cod. Sec. 2600.112].

DEFINITION OF THE FINANCIAL REPORTING ENTITY

The financial reporting entity consists of the following:

- The primary government;

- Organizations for which the primary government is financially accountable; and

- In addition, the primary government may determine, through exercise of management's professional judgment, that the inclusion of an organization that does not meet the financial accountability criteria is necessary in order to prevent the reporting entity's financial statements from being misleading. In such instances, that organization should be included as a component unit.

The paragraph further explains:

> The nucleus of a financial reporting entity usually is a primary government. However, a governmental organization other than a primary government (such as a component unit, a joint venture, a jointly governed organization, or another stand-alone government) serves as the nucleus for its own reporting entity when it issues separate financial statements. [The requirements of GASB-61] apply to the separately issued basic financial statements of governmental component units, joint ventures, jointly governed organizations, and other stand-alone governments (GASB-14, pars. 12 and 20, as amended by GASB-61, par. 4) [GASB Cod. Secs. 2100.111, 2600.102].

GASB-14 defines "financial accountability" as follows:

> The level of accountability that exists if a primary government appoints a voting majority of an organization's governing board and is either able to

impose its will on that organization or there is a potential for the organization to provide specific financial benefits to, or impose specific financial burdens on, the primary government. A primary government may also be financially accountable for governmental organizations with a separately elected governing board, a governing board appointed by another government, or a jointly appointed board that is fiscally dependent on the primary government [see later discussion in section titled "Financial Accountability"] (GASB-14, par. 21, as amended by GASB-61, par. 6) [GASB Cod. Sec. 2100.120].

The core of a financial reporting entity usually is a primary government. However, a governmental organization other than a primary government (such as a component unit, a joint venture, a jointly governed organization, or another stand-alone government) serves as the core for *its own reporting entity* when it issues separate financial statements. In those cases of entities other than a primary government having component units, provisions of U.S. GAAP also apply to their separately issued basic financial statements for those governmental component units, joint ventures, jointly governed organizations, and other stand-alone governments and, therefore, those entities may present financial reports similarly to a primary government.

PRIMARY GOVERNMENTS

Definition of a Primary Government

The focal point in defining a financial reporting entity is the identification of a primary government. GASB-14 states that a primary government must have a separately elected governing body. States, including tribal governments, and general-purpose local governmental entities, such as counties and municipalities, are primary governments (GASB-14, Glossary).

In addition to states, tribal governments, and general-purpose local governmental entities, special-purpose governmental entities are considered primary governments if they satisfy *all* of the following criteria (GASB-14, par. 15) [GABS Cod. Sec. 2100.114]:

- The entity has a separately elected governing body, elected by the citizenry in a general, popular election.

- The entity is legally separate from other entities, including the possession of "corporate powers." Such powers include the right to have a name, the right to sue or be sued in its own name without recourse to any other governmental unit, and the right to buy, sell, lease, or incur debt in its own name. Such powers are enumerated in enabling statutes, charters, and similar, depending upon state laws or constitution (see later discussion in section titled "Determining Separate Legal Standing").

- The entity is fiscally independent of other state and local governmental entities (see later discussion in section titled "Determining Fiscal Independence or Dependence").

All governmental entities that are not legally separate from the primary government are considered part of the primary government. Thus, the primary government is composed of various funds, departments, institutions, offices, and other governmental entities that do not have separate legal status. If a governmental entity is not legally separate from the primary government, its financial data should be merged with the financial data of the primary government (GASB-14, par. 14) [GASB Cod. Sec. 2100.113].

Determining Separate Legal Standing

GASB-14 provides the following definition of "separate legal standing":

> An organization created as a body corporate or a body corporate and politic or otherwise possessing similar corporate powers. An organization that has separate legal standing has an identity of its own as an "artificial person" with a personality and existence distinct from that of its creator and others.

An entity is a legally separate organization if it is given the powers that are generally held by an individual. In effect, a separate legal entity is an artificial person having such powers as a distinct separate name, the right to be a party in litigation, and the right to enter into legal contracts. This concept is also known as the "body politic." It may also have the right to buy or sell property, have a corporate seal, establish a budget, issue debt, or set rates and charges.

For a special-purpose government to be a primary government, it must have separate legal standing. If it does not have such standing, it is part of the primary government that exercises the corporate powers related to its activities (GASB-14, par. 15) [GASB Cod. Sec. 2100.114].

Determining Fiscal Independence or Dependence

The third criterion that must be satisfied for a special-purpose government to be considered a primary government is fiscal independence. For an entity to be considered fiscally independent, it must have the authority, without *substantive approval* or modification of another government, to do all three of the following (GASB-14, par. 16) [GASB Cod. Sec. 2100.115]:

1. Establish a budget.
2. Either levy taxes or set rates or charges.
3. Issue bonded debt.

If a special-purpose government does not satisfy all three criteria, the entity is fiscally dependent on the primary government that holds the power of approval or modification.

Footnote 3 to GASB-14 [GASB Cod. Sec. 2100 fn. 2] acknowledges that a primary government may be temporarily subject to the financial control of another government. Usually this involves a state government taking control or providing oversight of a municipal government or a school district because of financial difficulties. When the financial control is temporary, the governmental entity subject to the control is considered fiscally independent for purposes of GASB-14. Of course, the government under fiscal control may also have to implement GASB-58, if Chapter 9 bankruptcy is available in the jurisdiction.

In some cases, a law contains a formal agreement that establishes a temporary financial burden. *Implementation Guide 2015-1*, question 4.22.3 [GASB Cod. Sec. 2100.715-8], explains how GASB-14 *does not require* a legally binding financial burden relationship for a potential component unit to meet the criteria for inclusion in the reporting entity. GASB-14, as amended only requires *the potential for an organization to impose financial burdens on the primary government.* For example, in the discussion of financial burden as a result of a primary government's obligation in some manner for the debt of an organization, GASB-14, par. 33(g) [GASB Cod. Sec. 2100.132(g)] states that financial burden exists when *"previous actions by the primary government related to actual or potential defaults on another organization's debt make it probable that the primary government will assume responsibility for the debt in the event of default."* The fact that the primary government has entered into an agreement that creates a financial burden may indicate that it would do so again in the future, which would create the potential for financial burden and meet the criteria for inclusion. Professional judgment should be used to determine whether the facts in a given situation manifest financial accountability.

In practice, if the government is expected to exit fiscal oversight in this case, it is unlikely that a continuing component unit relationship may exist with the overseeing government. However, disclosure of the relationship may be warranted.

PRACTICE ALERT: GASB is in the midst of performing research in this area of practice and going concern in general. GASB staff are gathering information if additional disclosures may be warranted when a government is in the midst of fiscal oversight.

Fiscal dependency does not require that the special-purpose government receive financial assistance from the primary government. Thus, a fiscally dependent relationship is not based on the existence of either a financial burden on or a financial benefit for the primary government. These terms are defined as follows (GASB-14, par. 131) [GASB Cod. Secs. 2100.128–.129, .130–,132, .509–.510]:

Financial burden	An obligation, legal or otherwise, to finance the deficits of, or provide financial support to, an organization; or an obligation in some manner for the debt of an organization [see later discussion in section titled "Financial Benefit to or Burden on a Primary Government"].
Financial benefit	Legal entitlement to, or the ability to otherwise access, the resources of an organization [see later discussion in section titled "Financial Benefit to or Burden on a Primary Government"].

The authority of a primary government to approve or modify actions taken by a special-purpose government should be examined to determine whether that authority is procedural in nature or one of substantive evaluation. In many instances, a primary government has general oversight responsibility with respect to a special-purpose government, but that oversight is exercised within specific parameters that have been established. That is, the actions taken by the special-purpose government must comply with pre-established guidelines, limits, standards, or other parameters. Under this circumstance, the authority held by the primary government is considered procedural and not substantive. The following are some examples of authority that is procedural rather than substantive:

- State agency approves the issuance of debt based on a review to determine whether total debt issued by the special-purpose government does not exceed an established percentage of assessed property valuation.

- State department of education reviews a special-purpose government's budget to determine whether the special-purpose government qualifies for state funding based on pre-established conditions set by the state.

- County clerk approves a special-purpose government's tax rate or levy to determine whether the rate or levy exceeds pre-established limits.

On the other hand, if a special-purpose government's actions are subject to substantive approval or modification, the special-purpose government cannot be considered a primary government. For example, if a municipal government can review its public utility authority's budget and, based on that review, reduce the level of spending or require a change in rates, the special-purpose government (the utility authority) is not a primary government with respect to the definition of a financial reporting entity (GASB-14, par. 17) [GASB Cod. Sec. 2100.116].

Some special-purpose governments may be prohibited by law from issuing debt. Such prohibition in itself does not mean that a special-purpose government cannot be a primary government. The rationale for this conclusion is that another governmental entity cannot approve or modify the special-purpose government's ability to issue debt, because the ability does not exist (GASB-14, par. 18) [GASB Cod. Sec. 2100.117].

The financial statements of the primary government and its blended component units are reported in accordance with the provisions of GASB-14 and GASB-34, both as amended, including fiduciary funds. For certain types of fiduciary activities, they may or may not meet the definition for inclusion in the financial reporting entity. They should however, be reported as a fiduciary fund of the primary government *if the primary government has a fiduciary responsibility for them* (GASB-14, par. 19, as amended by GASB 35, par. 5) [GASB Cod. Sec. 2100.118].

PRACTICE ALERT: GASB Statement No. 32 (*Accounting and Financial Reporting for Internal Revenue Code Section 457 Deferred Compensation Plans*) references paragraph 19 of GASB-14. In the deliberations of the GASB to what has become GASB-84, the GASB noted that paragraph 19 may not be sufficiently descriptive to assist governments in determining whether an activity should be reported as a fiduciary activity. GASB-84 clarifies those situations. (See **PRACTICE ALERT** on GASB-84 later in this chapter.) As part of the implementation of GASB-84, GASB-32 will be rescinded. GASB-84 may also clarify the relationship of an Internal Revenue Code Section 529 plan to a primary government.

COMPONENT UNITS

Definition of Component Units

GASB-14, par. 20, as amended, describes component units as legally separate organizations for which the elected officials of the primary government are financially accountable. In addition, component units can be other organizations for which the nature and significance of their relationship with a primary government are such that exclusion would cause the reporting entity's financial statements to be misleading. Component units can be governmental organizations, not-for-profit corporations, or even for-profit corporations. A component unit cannot be a primary government. GASB-14, as amended by GASB-61, requires that three separate criteria be applied to an organization to determine whether it is a component unit of the primary government. These three criteria are summarized as follows and in Exhibit 4-1:

1. Financial accountability;
2. Nature and significance of relationship; and
3. How closely the entities are related or financially integrated.

Component units, therefore, are legally separate organizations for which the elected officials of the primary government are financially accountable. In addition, component units can be other organizations for which the nature and significance of their relationship with a primary government are such that exclusion would cause the reporting entity's financial statements to be misleading.

GASB-61 further discusses the concept of accountability. Accountability is not only financial in nature but also operational. The statement discusses in an amendment to GASB-14, par. 21, as amended by GASB-61, par. 6 [GASB Cod. Sec. 2100.120], that accountability flows from the notion that individuals are obliged to account for their acts, including the acts of the officials they appoint to operate governmental agencies. Thus, elected officials are accountable for an organization if they appoint a voting majority of the organization's governing board. Sometimes, however, appointments are not substantive; other governments (usually at a lower level) may have oversight responsibility for those officials.

Financial Accountability

A primary government that is financially accountable for a legally separate entity should include the financial information of that entity with its own financial statements to form the financial reporting entity. Financial accountability exists if the primary government appoints a voting majority of the entity's governing body and if either one of the following conditions exists:

- It is able to impose its will on that organization *or*
- There is a potential for the organization to provide specific financial benefits to, or impose specific financial burdens on, the primary government, regardless of whether the organization has

— a separately elected governing board,

— governing board appointed by a higher level of government, or

— a jointly appointed board.

Accountability is primarily demonstrated when individuals are obliged to account for their acts, including the acts of the officials they appoint to operate governmental agencies. Therefore, elected officials are accountable for an organization if they appoint a voting majority of the organization's governing board. Sometimes, however, appointments are more ministerial than substantive. In these cases, other governments (usually at a lower level) may have oversight responsibility for those officials (GASB-14, par. 21, fn. 5, as amended by GASB 61, par. 6) [GASB Cod. Sec. 2100.120, fns. 4–5].

OBSERVATION: The first criterion, financial accountability, is the primary objective benchmark that determines whether an entity is a component unit of the financial reporting entity. However, the other two criteria were added to allow for a greater degree of professional judgment in determining which entities are component units.

EXHIBIT 4-1
DETERMINING WHETHER AN ORGANIZATION IS A COMPONENT UNIT OF A PRIMARY GOVERNMENT

Criterion	Methods of Integration	GASB Statement References
The primary government appoints the voting majority of the Board	Blended *or* discrete presentation	GASB-14, pars. 22–24 (as amended) [GASB Cod. Secs. 2100.121–.123]
The primary government is financially accountable for the other organization through financial benefits/burdens *or* imposition of will	Blended *or* discrete presentation	GASB-14, pars. 25–33 (as amended by GASB-61) [GASB Cod. Secs. 2100.124–.132]
The primary government may be financially accountable for a fiscally dependent government, inclusive of the potential to provide a financial benefit to/burden on the primary government. This may include special-purpose governments with separately elected governing boards, governmental organizations with boards appointed by another government or governmental organizations with jointly approved boards.	Blended *or* discrete presentation	GASB-14, pars. 34–37, as amended by GASB-61, par. 6 [GASB Cod. Secs. 2100.133–.136].

Criterion	Methods of Integration	GASB Statement References
The nature and significance of the relationship between the primary government and the other organization.	Blended *or* discrete presentation	GASB-14, par. 39 (as amended by GASB-39, par. 5, and GASB-61, par. 4) [GASB Cod. Sec. 2100.138]
The other organization is a not-for-profit corporation in which the primary government is the sole corporate member as identified in the articles of incorporation or by-laws.	Blended	GASB-80 [GASB Cod. Sec. 2600.113] (see **PRACTICE ALERTS** herein).

In addition, financial accountability may exist when another entity is fiscally dependent (see the earlier discussion in the section titled "Determining Fiscal Independence or Dependence") on the primary government, even if the primary government does not appoint a voting majority of the entity's governing body. Therefore, fiscal accountability could exist even when the entity's governing board is separately elected, appointed by a government higher than the primary government, or jointly appointed (see the later discussion in the section titled "Financial Accountability as a Result of Fiscal Dependency") (GASB-14, par. 21, as amended by GASB-61, par. 6) [GASB Cod. Sec. 2100.120].

Appointment of a Voting Majority

Financial accountability is dependent on whether a primary government appoints a voting majority of another entity's governing body. In most instances, the appointment of a simple majority is equivalent to a voting majority because the approval of financial issues is based on a simple majority vote. However, if more than a simple majority is required to approve financial issues, the appointment of a simple majority does not result in the primary government being financially accountable for the other entity.

OBSERVATION: Footnote 5 to GASB-14 [GASB Cod. Sec. 2100 fn. 5] states that in determining whether a majority of the entity's governing body has been appointed, the number of appointments by the primary government would include primary government officials who are serving on the entity's governing board as required by law (also known as "ex-officio").

GASB-14, par. 131 [GASB Cod. Secs. 2100.121–.123, .503] defines "appoint" as follows:

> To select members of a governing board (as long as the ability to do so is not severely limited by a nomination process) or confirm appointments made by others (provided that the confirmation is more than a formality or part of a ministerial responsibility).

The above definition recognizes that the appointment process must be more than perfunctory in that the process must demonstrate substance rather than form. In determining whether the appointment process is *substantive*, the nomination and confirmation processes should be examined.

Nomination process. The appointment process should not be significantly restricted by the nomination process. If the primary government must appoint members of the other entity's governing body who are nominated by another entity or entities, financial accountability cannot exist. What constitutes substantive appointment authority by the primary government is subjective. However, in one example, GASB-14 characterizes a limiting nomination process as one where the primary government must select three appointees from a slate of five candidates. In practice, the nomination process should be carefully examined to determine the degree of substantive involvement of the primary government in the nomination process.

Confirmation process. GASB-14 takes the position that the confirmation process is not a substitute for the appointment process. Thus, if prospective members of the other entity's governing body are nominated or appointed by parties other than the primary government's officials or appointees, the primary government's right to confirm the nomination or appointment may suggest the appointment process is not substantive (GASB-14, par. 23) [GASB Cod. Sec. 2100.122].

OBSERVATION: Based on the language of GASB-14, the appointment process could still be substantive even if the primary government's role in the appointment process is limited to confirmation. Although GASB-14 does not elaborate on this possibility, presumably the appointment process would be considered substantive if the primary government has the necessary prerequisites to conduct an effective confirmation hearing. These prerequisites could include the necessary legislative authority, sufficient staff to research issues, and a time frame that allows for sufficient investigation before nominations become effective.

Appointment authority is usually continuing and not limited to an initial appointment. Thus, the primary government may have the authority to make appointments as vacancies arise. In those circumstances where continuing authority for appointment does not exist, financial accountability between the primary government and the other entity will exist if the primary government has created the other entity (equivalent to appointing the governing body) and can unilaterally abolish the other entity (GASB-14, par. 24) [GASB Cod. Sec. 2100.123].

OBSERVATION: Substantive versus ministerial appointment authority is addressed in the GASB *Implementation Guide 2015-1*. Question 4.19.1 [GASB Cod. Sec. 2100.713-7]defines a "substantive appointment" as not based on *ceremony* or *formality*. Generally, a substantive appointment is a selection that is *not significantly encumbered by a limited field of preselected candidates* (known as a "slate" in some instances.) Professional judgment should be used to determine whether the role of the primary government is substantive based on all of the relevant information available about the appointment process. Question

4.19.2 [GASB Cod. Sec. 2100.713-8]shows the opposite effect. If the appointing official may reject all nominees, the process would not limit the primary government's appointment authority and its authority *would be considered substantive.* There's no provision in U.S. GAAP specifying the number of nominees that could be rejected before the appointment would be considered substantive.

Imposition of Will

Imposition of will is evidenced by the primary government's ability to affect the day-to-day operations of the other entity. GASB-14 refers to this capability as "imposition of will," which is defined as:

> The ability to significantly influence the programs, projects, activities, or level of services performed or provided by an organization.

The determination of whether imposition of will takes place is a matter of judgment, and the specific circumstances of each relationship must be carefully evaluated. In evaluating the imposition of will, the ability to affect day-to-day operations must be substantive and not merely procedural (see earlier discussion in the section titled "Determining Fiscal Independence or Dependence"). Although the determination of whether imposition of will takes place is a matter of judgment, GASB-14 states that existence of *any* of the following is a clear indication of the ability of the primary government to affect the day-to-day operations of another entity:

- Appointed members can be removed at will by the primary government.

- The budget can be modified or approved by the primary government.

- Rate or fee changes that affect revenues can be modified or approved by the primary government.

- Decisions other than those related to the budget, rates, or fees may be vetoed, overruled, or modified by the primary government.

- Management personnel may be appointed, hired, reassigned, or dismissed by the primary government (GASB-14, pars. 25–26) [GASB Cod. Secs. 2100.124–.125].

OBSERVATION: Many enabling statutes contain "sunset" legislation or provisions, which are dates in which the statute is no longer law. The GASB *Implementation Guide 2015-1*, question 4.20.3 [GASB Cod. Sec. 2100.714-4], addresses sunsets. *In general*, sunsets do not give the ability to impose will as defined in GASB-14. A legislative body's ability to terminate agencies, programs, or organizations generally involves a formal system of due process. The ability to *unilaterally* abolish is similar to the ability to remove an appointed board member at *will*. Otherwise, *sunset review process* is similar to *removal for cause.* The GASB notes the former is the ability to impose will, while the latter is not.

Financial Benefit to or Burden on a Primary Government

GASB-14, as amended, states that financial benefit or financial burden is created if *any* of the following relationships exists:

- The primary government is legally entitled to or can otherwise access the organization's resources.

- The primary government is legally obligated or has otherwise assumed the obligation to finance the deficits of, or provide financial support to, the organization.

- The primary government is obligated in some manner for the debt of the organization.

GASB-14 also states that if there are exchange transactions between a primary government and a potential component unit, the transactions are *not necessarily* indicative of a financial benefit or burden. Exchange transactions are value for value. In a government, exchange transactions may appear to be funding for clean water infrastructure in exchange for clean water. But GASB-61 discloses that the funding aspect is not a purchase of services. Rather, it is a grant or a subsidy that usually benefits the general public, not just the primary government (GASB-14, par. 27, as amended by GASB-61, par. 6) [GASB Cod. Sec. 2100.126].

In identifying financial benefits or financial burdens that create financial accountability, the benefits to or the burdens on the primary government can be either direct or indirect. For example, if the primary government is entitled to any surplus of another governmental entity, the effect is direct. On the other hand, if a component unit of the primary government is entitled to its own surplus, the effect is indirect with respect to the primary government. Either direct or indirect financial burden or benefit implies financial accountability between a primary government and another entity.

As discussed, governmental entities will enter into a variety of exchange transactions with other parties. Exchange transactions are characterized by each party giving up goods or services of approximately equivalent value. For example, a primary government may purchase used computer equipment from another governmental entity or a commercial enterprise. An exchange transaction does not create a financial benefit or financial burden relationship and therefore is not relevant in determining whether a primary government is financially accountable for another entity (GASB-14, par. 28) [GASB Cod. Sec. 2100.127].

Access to the other entity's resources. Financial benefits arise when the primary government has the ability to use the resources of another entity. The ability need only exist—there need not be an actual transaction that has occurred during the period or during previous periods to demonstrate that the primary government has received assets from the other entity.

A primary government may have a right to the residual assets of another entity if the other entity is liquidated or otherwise dissolved. An interest in the residual assets of another entity is not considered equivalent to access to the other entity's resources and therefore is not considered a benefit to the primary government for the purposes of determining financial accountability.

Access to an entity's resources may be obvious because of the relationship between the primary government and the other entity. For example, an entity may be organized specifically to collect revenue that will be remitted to the primary government (e.g., a state lottery) (GASB-14, par. 29) [GASB Cod. Sec. 2100.128].

Alternatively, access to an entity's resources may be based on a strategy that enables the other entity to charge a fee for its services that exceeds the amount needed to maintain its own capital, and then remit the excess to the primary government. Irrespective of the name used for such a remittance (payments in lieu of taxes, contributions, or amounts due the primary government), the relationship demonstrates that the primary government has access to the other entity's resources (GASB-14, par. 30) [GASB Cod. Sec. 2100.129].

Responsibility for deficits or support. Specific financial burdens arise when the primary government is legally obligated or has assumed the responsibility to (1) finance an entity's deficit or (2) provide financial support to the entity. GASB-14 provides the following examples of this type of specific financial burden:

- An entity charges an amount for its services that will not be sufficient to cover the total cost of providing such services, and a primary government, either by law or by public policy, assumes the responsibility for any deficit that may arise. Examples of this include operating subsidies for a public college or university and capital grants for urban mass transit systems.

- A primary government assumes the responsibility for any deficit that another entity may incur even though a deficit has never arisen and there is no expectation that one will arise (GASB-14, par. 31) [GASB Cod. Sec. 2100.130].

A special arrangement may exist whereby an entity may be fully or partially funded through tax increment financing. For example, a tax rate may be established at 7% by a primary government but another entity may receive 1% of the revenue raised to finance its operations. Tax increment financing is considered a form of financial burden irrespective of whether the incremental amount is collected by the primary government or directly by the other entity (GASB-14, par. 32) [GASB Cod. Sec. 2100.131].

Responsibility for debt. The primary government may accept an obligation for the debt of another entity. The obligation may be expressed or implied. For example, an expressed obligation could arise from legislation that specifically makes a state liable for another entity's debt, or covenants contained in a bond agreement that obligate the state in case of default by the other entity. In addition, the primary government may take explicit action by assuming responsibility for the debt of another entity. An implied obligation could be based on relevant legal precedents that have occurred in a particular state.

GASB-14 lists the following as example conditions any one of which would obligate the primary government for the debt of another entity:

1. The primary government is legally responsible for debt that is not paid after other default remedies have been pursued.

2. The primary government is required to provide funds to cover temporary deficiencies that will eventually be paid by primary repayment sources or by other default remedies.

3. The primary government is required either to fund reserves maintained by the other entity or to create its own reserve fund.

4. The primary government is authorized either to fund reserves maintained by the other entity or to create its own reserve fund and has established such a fund (see 6 and 7 below for guidance that is relevant when the primary entity has not established a fund).

5. The primary government is authorized either to provide financing for a reserve fund maintained by the other entity for the purpose of repurchasing outstanding debt or to create its own reserve fund and has established such a fund (see 6 and 7 below for guidance that is relevant when the primary entity has not established a fund).

6. The debt contract states that the primary government may cover defaults, although it is not required to do so.

7. Legal precedents within a state, or actions taken by a primary government, related to actual or potential defaults make it probable that the primary government will be responsible for the other entity's defaulted debt (GASB-14, par. 33) [GASB Cod. Sec. 2100.132].

GASB-14 does not define the term "probable," but the term is defined in U.S. GAAP (notably GASB-10, Glossary, and GASB-62, par. 100(a)) [GASB Cod. Sec. C50.155] as "the future event or events are likely to occur."

GASB-70 (*Accounting and Financial Reporting for Nonexchange Financial Guarantee Transactions*) changes the accounting and financial reporting of contracts and other liabilities that are guaranteed by governments (primarily in the form of debt guarantees). GASB-70 is only for *nonexchange* transactions, where one government is providing the guarantee to another (or a private entity). Governments have to consider qualitative as well as historical or quantitative factors regarding whether a liability exists at the guarantor government to provide for payment of the debts of the guaranteed government. The GASB uses a threshold of "more likely than not," or surmised to be more than 50% of a likelihood that a guarantee will be exercised considering qualitative as well as quantitative aspects. If a range of probabilities of exercise is known and no amount is better than another to establish whether the more-likely-than-not standard is met, then the minimum amount will be used to measure the likelihood that a guarantee will be exercised. Since a guarantee may be provided between a primary government and a component unit. In circumstances in which a government has issued an obligation guaranteed in a nonexchange transaction by its primary government (and the government is a blended component unit of the primary government), by one of its blended component units, or by another blended component unit of the same primary government of which the government is a blended component unit, GASB-70 requires the government to recognize a receivable in the amount of any guarantee liability recognized by the guarantor.

By excluding guarantees from receivable recognition between primary governments and discretely presented component units, in the basis for conclusions (par. 52 of GASB-70), the GASB recognizes that the net position of a primary government will decrease in circumstances in which a liability has been recognized for a guarantee extended *prior to the guarantee payment being made* when (*a*) the guarantor is a primary government and the government issuing the guaranteed debt is one of its blended component units, (*b*) the government issuing the guaranteed debt is a primary government and the debt is guaranteed by one of its blended component units, or (*c*) the guarantor and the government issuing the guaranteed debt are both blended component units of the same primary government. After considering the comments made by respondents, the GASB determined that in these specific circumstances the government that issued the guaranteed obligation should recognize a receivable in the amount of the liability recognized by the guarantor. This provides a mechanism by which the guarantee liability could be eliminated when the financial statements of the components are aggregated. The GASB concluded that this elimination *would not be necessary for a guarantee involving a discretely presented component unit* and, therefore, did not include a provision for a receivable to be recorded in that circumstance.

PRACTICE POINT: Additional discussions on nonexchange financial guarantees are contained in Chapters 12 (for long-term debt), 16 (for the potential of a liability at the guarantor), and 17 (for revenue recognition at a debtor).

Financial Accountability as a Result of Fiscal Dependency

A primary government is financially accountable for another entity when the other entity is fiscally dependent on the primary government. There is no difference if the entity has a separately elected governing board, a board appointed by another government, or a jointly appointed board (GASB-14, par. 34, as amended by GASB-61, par. 6) [GASB Cod. Sec. 2100.133].

Fiscal independence was discussed earlier in this chapter in the context of a special-purpose government considered a primary government for financial reporting purposes. An entity that is *not fiscally independent* must be considered fiscally dependent. More specifically, fiscal dependency arises if one or more of the following activities cannot be performed by the entity without substantive approval or modification by a primary government:

- Establish a budget.
- Either levy taxes or set rates or charges.
- Issue bonded debt.

Special-purpose governments with separately elected governing boards. Numerous governmental entities that have been established for special purposes and have separately elected governing boards are fiscally dependent on a primary government. For example, school districts often have separately elected boards, but their fiscal activities are subject to approval or modification by the municipality or county in which they serve. Entities of this nature should be presented as component units of the primary government on which they are fiscally dependent if a financial benefit or burden relationship also exists (GASB-14, par. 35, as amended by GASB-61, par. 6) [GASB Cod. Sec. 2100.134].

PRACTICE POINT: School boards especially may believe they are autonomous from the municipalities they may be geographically part of. The legal facts and circumstances must be analysed to determine if the school district has some form of fiscal accountability to the municipality. Each jurisdiction may be different due to state statutes. A common example may be in how charter schools are structured in a particular jurisdiction. In GASB *Implementation Guide* question 4.11.6 [GASB Cod. Sec. 2100.716-8], a charter school does not have the constitutional or statutory authority to levy property taxes. Funding is provided by an enrollment-based formula similar to the formula used for public schools in the state. One component of the formula for charter schools is an allocation of the sponsoring school district's property tax levy, based on a per-student metric. In this case, the charter school *would* be fiscally dependent on the school district (or municipality), if the charter school could not levy taxes without the approval of the sponsoring district. But since the school has no tax levy of its own that would be subject to the approval of the sponsoring district, a financial burden *is* on the sponsoring school district due to the allocation formula. However, it is not necessarily an indication of fiscal dependency.

Governmental organizations with boards appointed by another government. More than one primary government may control to some degree the activities of another governmental entity. Specifically, the governing board of a governmental entity may be appointed by the state (a higher-level government) while a local government (lower-level government) is financially accountable for the governmental entity. GASB-14 takes the position that even though the local government does not appoint the voting majority or any of the entity's governing body, that governmental entity should be considered a component unit of the local government and not the state government. In this instance, the fiscal dependency factor is considered more relevant in defining the financial reporting entity than the appointment power (GASB-14, par. 36, as amended by GASB-61, par. 6) [GASB Cod. Sec. 2100.135]. (See also the later discussion in the section titled "Potential for Dual Inclusion.")

Governing entities with jointly appointed boards. Various primary governments may participate jointly in the appointment of the governing boards of a governmental entity. For example, two or more states may agree to create a port authority, or a state and several local communities may agree to create a mass transit authority. In these circumstances, no one primary government may have the authority to appoint a voting majority of the entity's governing body. When this occurs, the entity should be considered a component unit of the primary government to which it is fiscally dependent, unless the entity meets the criteria to be reported as a joint venture (discussed later in this chapter). An example would be where an entity may not issue debt without a state's approval. In this case, a financial benefit or burden relationship exists between the state and the entity and the entity should be included within the state's reporting entity (GASB-14, par. 37, as amended by GASB-61, par. 6) [GASB Cod. Sec. 2100.136].

PRACTICE POINT: Common examples of jointly appointed boards usually related to large infrastructure entities. Ports, airports, public transportation systems, councils of governments that are used to fund multi-jurisdiction highway and utility projects all have the potential for jointly appointed boards. Jointly appointed boards may also be at different levels of government. For example, a state, counties within the state, and cities within a state may all appoint members of a governing board of a water irrigation entity that spans multiple jurisdictions.

Potential for Dual Inclusion

It is possible that an entity could satisfy the GASB-14 criteria in a manner that would suggest that it is a component unit of more than one primary government. GASB-14 recognizes the anomaly but states that an entity can be a component unit for only one primary government. Professional judgment should be exercised to determine which primary government should report the entity as a component unit. However, that judgment should focus on fiscal dependency rather than any other factor.

The potential for dual inclusion generally occurs when (1) one government appoints the governing board of an entity and (2) the appointing government and another government provide funding for the entity. If the funding by the appointing government is based on legislation that directs resources to the governmental entity using various formulas, it is likely that the governmental entity is a component unit of the funding government and not the appointing government. For example, most state governments mandate programs and services to be provided by local governments and in return present fiscal aid to fund these expenditures. This funding does not mean that all local governments have to be reported as part of the state's reporting entity, because the state doesn't appoint the governing board of the entity.

Elementary and secondary education is typically financed through a combination of local taxation and state aid distributed in accordance with legislatively established formulas. In most such instances, the entity status of a school district will be readily apparent as either a primary government or a component unit of a local government because either its governing board is separately elected or a voting majority is appointed by the local government. In some instances, however, school district governing boards are appointed by state officials, and the state may appear to be financially accountable for the district because of the state aid distribution. Judgment needs to be exercised as to whether the district should be considered a component unit of the state or of a local government. Usually, fiscal dependency on a local government should govern in determining the appropriate reporting entity of such school districts.

In those situations where state funding is more discretionary (not based on predetermined formulas) the question of which government, state government or local government, is financially accountable for the other entity becomes more difficult. The state and local governments should communicate with one another to determine which one of them is the most appropriate primary government for the entity (GASB-14, par. 38, as amended by GASB-61) [GASB Cod. Sec. 2100.137].

> **PRACTICE POINT:** Making this determination of the appropriate primary government to report the entity may be arrived at through professional judgment (or negotiation). GASB *Implementation Guide* question 4.24.1 [GASB Cod. Sec. 2100.717-1] discusses a potential situation for dual inclusion by more than one reporting entity. GASB-14 does not suggest the level of government should be the deciding factor. Professional judgement is required to determine whether the significance of the combined fiscal dependency and financial benefit or burden relationship outweighs the financial accountability. In some cases, this judgment may be at a lower level of government than another (a city versus a state for example). Communication of this judgment may be needed with the other entity (or entities) that may be making the same decision to include to lower the risk of dual inclusion.

Nature and Significance of Relationship

GASB-14 states that the financial statements of governmental and nongovernmental organizations for which a primary government (or the primary government's component units) is not financially accountable should still, under certain circumstances, be included in the primary government's financial statements (GASB-14, par. 39, as amended by GASB-39, par. 5, and GASB-61, par. 4) [GASB Cod. Sec. 2100.138].

This determination is based on "the nature and significance of the relationship between the primary government and the potential component unit, including the latter's ongoing financial support of the primary government and its other component units." While that concept is broad, GASB-39 states that a legally separate, tax-exempt organization's financial statements are included in the primary government's financial statements if *all* of the following conditions exist:

- The economic resources received or held by the separate organization are entirely or almost entirely for the direct benefit of the primary government, its component units, or its constituents.

- The primary government or its component units is entitled to, or has the ability to otherwise access, a majority of the economic resources received or held by the separate organization.

- The economic resources received or held by an individual organization that the specific primary government, or its component units, is entitled to, or has the ability to otherwise access, are significant to that primary government (GASB-39, par. 5) [GASB Cod. Sec. 2100.140].

When these conditions are satisfied, the other organization's financial statements are presented as a (discrete) component unit in the primary government's external financial statements.

Direct Benefit of Economic Resources

There is direct economic benefit when the other organization "obtains, seeks to obtain, or holds and invests resources that will benefit the primary government, its component units, or its constituents." This condition does not imply that there must be an actual transfer from the other organization during the year but rather that "the resources obtained or held are required to ultimately be used for the benefit of a specific primary government, its component units, or its constituents."

The first condition generally means that an organization that provides resources to multiple constituent groups, for example a federated fund-raising organization, would not be considered a component unit of a primary government. Under this circumstance it is possible that a significant amount of resources may be provided to the primary government (or its component units or constituents) in one year but in other years other governmental or nongovernmental entities may receive a significant portion of the other organization's resources. This situation would not satisfy the requirement that all or almost all of the resources be available to the primary government.

However, a common example involves a university fund-raising foundation as detailed in GASB Cod. Sec. 2100.902, example 40. In the GASB's *nonauthoritative* example, a University Foundation is a legally separate, tax-exempt organization whose bylaws state that it exists solely to provide financial support to a University. The foundation regularly makes distributions directly to the university and pays for the maintenance of the university's football stadium and auditorium (by making payments directly to vendors and contractors rather than the university). Separately, the direct cash payments to the university and the maintenance expenses of the university paid by the foundation are not significant to the university—combined, however, they are significant. The economic resources of the foundation that are restricted for the benefit of the university are significant. In this case, the University Foundation *is a component unit* of the university and should be discretely presented. This is based on the language in the bylaws satisfying the "direct benefit" criterion and the "entitlement/ability to access" criterion as well. The funding is significant, regardless of the "in-kind" assistance to the university.

Access to Economic Resources

The second condition requires that the primary government either (1) be entitled to a majority of the economic resources received or held by the separate organization or (2) have the ability to otherwise access those resources. There is no difficulty in applying this condition when the primary government is entitled to the resources. For example, that entitlement may be based on the legal relationship between the primary government and the separate organization or the donations made to the separate organization may be legally restricted by donors to the benefit of the primary government.

Difficulties arise when the criterion is based on the ability to otherwise access the resources of the other organization. The concept "ability to otherwise access" is broad and is not based on the narrow idea of control. GASB-39, pars. 5–6, as amended by GASB-61, par. 5 [GASB Cod. Secs. 2100.140–.141], state that this broad concept can be demonstrated in several ways, including the following:

- The primary government or its component units in the past have received, directly or indirectly, a majority of the economic resources provided by the organization.

- The organization previously has received and honored requests to provide resources to the primary government.

- The other organization is financially interrelated with the primary government.

GASB-39 notes that "this criterion (access to economic resources) will further limit inclusion to organizations such as entity-specific fund-raising foundations" because these foundations (1) have a history of providing economic resources to the primary government or (2) honor requests for economic resources initiated by the primary government.

The third example (financially interrelated) is based on the belief that most of the "other organizations" that are evaluated in the context of the criteria established by GASB-39 are nongovernmental entities that follow the financial and accounting standards established fundamentally by the FASB's Accounting Standards Codification® (ASC) Topic 958 (*Financial Statements of Not-for-Profit Organizations*). GASB-39, as amended, uses the guidance in FASB ASC® Topic 958 by stating that the two parties are "financially interrelated" when *both* of the following two conditions exist:

1. One organization has the ability to influence the operating and financial decisions of the other. The ability to exercise that influence may be demonstrated in several ways:

   a. The organizations are affiliates;

   b. One organization has considerable representation on the governing board of the other organization;

   c. The charter or bylaws of one organization limit its activities to those that are beneficial to the other organization; or

   d. An agreement between the organizations allows one organization to actively participate in policy-making processes of the other, such as setting organizational priorities, budgets, and management compensation.

2. One organization has an ongoing economic interest in the net position of the other. If the specified beneficiary has an ongoing economic interest in the net position of the recipient organization, the beneficiary's rights to the assets held by the recipient organization are residual rights; that is, the value of those rights increases or decreases as a result of the investment, fund-raising, operating, and other activities of the recipient organization. Alternatively, but less commonly, a recipient organization may have an ongoing economic interest in the net position of the specified beneficiary. If so, the recipient organization's rights are residual rights, and their value changes as a result of the operations of the beneficiary.

An example of this access to the resources of another organization for financial benefit is contained in GASB Cod. Sec. 2100.902, examples 4 and 4a. In part of the examples, a city is allowed to impose a payment "in lieu of taxes" (PILOT) on certain municipal corporations, including an airport, to recover the cost of providing governmental services to public entities that are exempt from property taxes. The payment is not required to be directly related to the costs of providing specific services and the city has not assessed a payment on the airport. The airport is a discretely presented component unit. Due to the legal entitlement to the PILOT, the city has access to airport resources, despite not exercising this ability.

The opposite would be in example 8 in the same codification section. In this example, a state electric utility is a fiscally independent public benefit corporation with specific duties and powers benefitting the state's citizens. The utility determines its own budget and sets its own rates. It also issues debt in its own name. The state is not obligated in any manner for the debt of the utility. The state also has no obligation to provide financial support to the utility and it does not have access to the utility's resources. The enabling legislation requires that certain contracts for power sales be approved by the governor. However, these contracts represent only a small fraction of the utility's outstanding contracts and the governor's approval authority is limited by financing provisions within the enabling legislation and the utility's bond covenants. In this example, the utility is *not* a component unit. However, the utility's board is appointed by the governor. As such, it is a related organization. There is no imposition of will as the board members can only be removed based on formal charges and a public hearing. There is also no financial benefit or burden relationship between the entities.

Significant Economic Support

The final condition recognizes that some governmental entities receive resources from various support groups that are clearly component units, but the GASB does not intend to require support that is insignificant to trigger the inclusion of such groups in the primary government's financial statements. This criterion is a materiality threshold. The GASB concedes that this materiality threshold is higher than that used for component units that are included in the reporting entity based on the financial accountability established by GASB-14 for the following reasons:

- The importance of the financial support is relative to the entire primary government rather than an individual reporting unit.

- The criteria are applied to an individual organization rather than all organizations of a similar type (e.g., parent-teacher associations).

For example, many public school athletic programs have separate support organizations that may pay for team trips and banquets, additional compensation for coaches, and similar items. Generally these support groups would not be presented as component units of the public school district because the economic support to the school (not to the specific program or activity) is insignificant.

The financial statements of other organizations that are considered to be component units because of the nature and significance of their relationship to the primary government are to be discretely presented (not blended) in the primary government's financial statements.

Closely Related or Financially Integrated

The GASB recognizes that the three conditions listed above may be too constricting in that certain organizations that might not satisfy the three conditions listed can nonetheless be important component units of a primary government. For this reason, GASB-39 and GASB-61 state that if the professional judgment primary government determines that the nature and the significance of a potential component unit's relationship with the primary government warrants inclusion in the reporting entity, then those organizations should also be reported as component units by the primary government (GASB-14, par. 41, as amended by both GASB-39, par. 6, and GASB-61, par. 5) [GASB Cod. Sec. 2100.141].

GASB-39 points out that financial integration may be exhibited and documented through the policies, practices, or organizational documents of either the primary government or the organization being evaluated as a potential component unit. Financial integration could be demonstrated in a number of ways, including the following:

- Descriptions in charters and bylaws of the primary government or the other organizations (e.g., the charter might state that the organization will lose its tax-exempt status if it fails to distribute its resources to the primary government).

- Participation by the other organization's employees in a primary government's programs or activities.

- Representation in financial aid accountability systems of work-study fellowship grants to students of a primary government for work performed for the other organization.

- Participation by the primary government's employees in the other organization's research activities and inclusion of those activities in the service effort report of the primary government.

- Sharing of office space and administrative services by the primary government and the other organization.

OBSERVATION: The GASB emphasizes that the above list is not all-inclusive and that professional judgment rather than a list of relationships is the basis for determining whether the exclusion of a potential component unit's financial statements might result in the primary government's financial statements being misleading or incomplete.

The financial statements of other organizations that are considered to be component units because they are closely related to or financially integrated with the primary government may be presented in the primary government's financial statements by either blending or discrete presentation. If the organization is fiduciary in nature and is identified as a component unit in accordance with the provisions of GASB-14, as amended, the organization is included only in the fund financial statements with the primary government's other fiduciary funds. If a discretely presented component unit is not fiduciary in nature, but has fiduciary funds, such funds are *not* reported in the primary government's financial statements. GASB-34, par. 126, as amended [GASB Cod. Secs. 2200.101, .209, .215, 2600.107–.108, .111], requires presentation of an aggregated total of financial information. Paragraph 13, as amended, of GASB-34 (referenced in many sections of the *Codification*) excludes fiduciary funds. This has led to some confusion among preparers as to how a component unit that is fiduciary in nature should be reported.

PRACTICE ALERT: GASB Statement No. 84 (*Fiduciary Activities*) will redefine those activities and funds upon implementation for reporting periods beginning after December 15, 2018. For June 30th governments, the transition will take place on July 1, 2019. The basis of accounting and measurement focus for fiduciary funds will not change. However, the fund types and recognition as a fiduciary activity may change.

Fiduciary component units, in accordance with the provisions of GASB-84 are an organization that meets the component unit criteria of GASB-14, as amended and is a fiduciary activity if it meets *one* of the following arrangements:

- The organization is a pension plan that is administered through a trust that meets the criteria of GASB Statement No. 67 (*Financial Reporting for Pension Plans*), paragraph 3, or

- The organization is an OPEB plan that is administered through a trust that meets the criteria of GASB Statement No. 74 (*Financial Reporting for Postemployment Benefit Plans Other Than Pension Plans*), paragraph 3, or

- A circumstance in which assets from entities that are *not* part of the reporting entity are accumulated for pensions as described in paragraph 113 of GASB Statement No. 73 (*Accounting and Financial Reporting for Pensions and Related Assets That Are Not within the Scope of GASB Statement 68, and Amendments to Certain Provisions of GASB Statements 67 and 68*), or finally,

- A circumstance in which assets from entities that are *not* part of the reporting entity are accumulated for OPEB as described in paragraph 59 of GASB-74.

In many cases, pension plans or OPEB plans that meet either of the previous two criteria are legally separate entities. GASB-84 presents guidance in determining whether those entities are component units. A primary government is considered to have a financial burden if it is legally obligated or has otherwise assumed the obligation to make contributions to the pension or OPEB plan.

Fiduciary component units may also be present in accordance with the provisions of GASB-84, even if they are not pension or OPEB arrangement, if the assets associated with the activity have *one or more* of the following characteristics:

- The assets are:

  — Administered through a trust agreement or equivalent arrangement in which the government itself is *not* a beneficiary,

— Dedicated to providing benefits to recipients in accordance with the benefit terms, and

— Legally protected from the creditors of the government.

- The assets are for the benefit of individuals and the government *does not* have administrative involvement with the assets or direct financial involvement with the assets. In addition, the assets are not derived from the government's provision of goods or services to those organizations, other governments or individuals.

- The assets are for the benefit of organizations or other governments that are not part of the reporting entity. Similarly to the previous point, the assets are also not derived from the government's provision of goods or services to those organizations, other governments or individuals.

Control of the assets is *not* a factor to consider a fiduciary component unit relationship. One of the criteria in the definition introduces the phrases "administrative involvement" and "direct financial involvement." GASB-84, footnote 1, describes how a government has administrative involvement with the assets if, for example, it (*a*) monitors compliance with the requirements of the activity that are established by the government or by a resource provider that does not receive the direct benefits of the activity, (*b*) determines eligible expenditures that are established by the government or by a resource provider that does not receive the direct benefits of the activity, or (*c*) has the ability to exercise discretion in how assets are allocated. A government has direct financial involvement with the assets if, for example, it provides matching resources for the activities. These activities are common in subrecipient relationships with federal grant awards.

As part of the implementation of GASB-84, GASB Statement No. 32 (*Accounting and Financial Reporting for Internal Revenue Code Section 457 Deferred Compensation Plans*) is rescinded as the relationship of such plans to a primary government will be clarified.

REPORTING COMPONENT UNITS

When an entity is considered a component unit, its financial information and the financial information of its primary government should be presented in the financial statements of the financial reporting entity. The presentation of the financial information is accomplished by use of either:

- The discrete presentation method or
- The blending method.

The presentation in the reporting entity's financial statements should be formatted so that a reader can distinguish between the financial position and financial activities of the primary government, including its blended component units, and those of its discretely presented component units.

It is possible that a component unit (CU #1) of a primary government may have its own component units (CU #2 and CU #3). Under this circumstance, the financial statements should be built from the bottom up. CU #1 should include in its financial statements, through either blending or discrete presentation, or combination of the two, the financial statements of its component units (CU #2 and CU #3). In turn, the primary government would create its reporting entity by combining the financial statements of the CU #1 financial reporting entity with its own financial statements through blending or discrete presentation. Although CU #2 and CU #3 are not technically component units of the primary government, their financial information is nonetheless incorporated into the higher-level financial report of the primary government as part of CU #1 (GASB-14, par. 43) [GASB Cod. Sec. 2100.143].

Discrete Presentation of Component Units

GASB-34 (*Basic Financial Statements—and Management's Discussion and Analysis—for State and Local Governments*) was written in a manner that satisfies the financial reporting entity standards originally established by GASB-14 with respect to component units. Relevant guidance established by GASB-14 in this regard is reproduced below (GASB-34, par. 124) [GASB Cod. Sec. 2200.213]:

> The financial statements of the reporting entity should allow users to distinguish between the primary government and its component units by communicating information about the component units and their relationships with the primary government rather than creating the perception that the primary government and all of its component units are one legal entity.

In addition, GASB-14, par. 51 [GASB Cod. Sec. 2600.108], requires that information related to each major discretely presented component unit be presented in the reporting entity's basic financial statements. To satisfy this standard, any one of the following three approaches can be used (GASB-34, par. 126) [GASB Cod. Secs. 2200.101, .209, .215, 2600.107–.108, .111]:

1. Present each major discretely presented component unit in a separate column in the government-wide financial statements;

2. Present combining statements within the basic financial statements; or

3. Present condensed financial statements in a note to the financial statements.

PRACTICE POINT: Many preparers use the same methodology of determining major component units as they do major funds. This may not always be the proper method as the major fund calculation does not include qualitative aspects. GASB-61 clarifies the concept of what a major component unit is. Major component units are determined based on the nature and significance of their relationship to the primary government. This based on any of the following factors:

1. The services provided by the component unit to the citizenry are such that separate reporting as a major component unit is considered to be essential to financial statement users,

2. There are significant transactions with the primary government, or

3. There is a significant financial benefit or burden relationship with the primary government.

Major component unit reporting requirements are satisfied by any one of the following:

1. Presenting each major component unit in a separate column in the reporting entity's statements of net position and activities,

2. Including combining statements of major component units in the reporting entity's basic financial statements after the fund financial statements, or

3. Presenting condensed financial statements in the notes to the reporting entity's financial statements.

Non-major component units should be aggregated in a single column. A combining statement for the non-major component units is not required but may be presented as supplementary information.

Each of these three presentation approaches creates information that is part of the basic financial statements.

As a reminder, the requirement for major component unit information does not apply to component units that are fiduciary in nature.

In addition, the *GASB Implementation Guide 2015-1*, question 7.7.3 [GASB Cod. Sec. 2600.704-16], reminds practitioners the reporting governmental entity cannot combine as a single function (e.g., higher education) related information of the primary government and a higher education discretely presented component unit, because GASB-14 requires that the financial statements of the reporting entity distinguish between the accounts and transactions of the primary government and its discretely presented component units.

Separate Column(s) in Government-Wide Financial Statements

Under the presentation format using separate columns, the government-wide financial statements (statement of net position and statement of activities) have columns for (1) governmental activities of the primary government, including blended component units, (2) business-type activities of the primary government, including blended component units, and (3) major discretely presented component units. These financial statements should provide a total column for governmental activities and business-type activities (the primary government), but a total column for the reporting entity is optional.

Combining Statements

Rather than presenting a separate column in the government-wide financial statements for each major discretely presented component unit, combining statements for component units may be presented. The combining financial statements should be based on the accrual basis of accounting and economic resources measurement focus (as discussed in Chapter 3, "Basis of Accounting and Measurement Focus") and should include a statement of net position and a statement of activities. A separate column should be used for each major discretely presented component unit, and all nonmajor component units should be aggregated into a single column. A total column for all discretely presented component units should be presented, and those totals should be traceable to the component unit's column in the government-wide financial statements. The combining statements should be placed after the fund financial statements.

OBSERVATION: If the combining-statement method is used, a combining statement for nonmajor discretely presented component units may be presented as supplementary information (but this is not a requirement).

However, if the combining-statement approach is used, GASB-34, par. 126 (as referenced above), requires that the aggregated total component unit information, as discussed in GASB-14, be the total for the component unit and all of its own component units, even if the component unit does not present a total column for its reporting entity as a whole within its stand-alone financial statements (GASB-37, par. 18) [GASB Cod. Secs. 2200.209, 2200.215, 2600.111].

Condensed Financial Statements in Notes

If the note-disclosure method is used, the following disclosures must be made (GASB-34, par. 127) [GASB Cod. Secs. 2200.216, 2600.109]:

- Condensed statement of net position
  - *Total assets*—Distinguishing between capital assets and other assets. Amounts receivable from the primary government or from other component units of the same reporting entity should be reported separately.
  - *Total deferred outflows of resources* (if any).
  - *Total liabilities*—Distinguishing between long-term debts outstanding and other liabilities. Amounts payable to the primary government or to other component units of the same reporting entity should be reported separately.
  - *Total deferred inflows of resources* (if any).
  - *Total net position*—Distinguishing between restricted, unrestricted, and net investment in capital assets.
- Condensed statement of activities
  - Expenses, with separate identification of depreciation expense and amortizations of long-lived assets
  - Program revenues (by type)
  - Net program (expense) revenue
  - Tax revenues
  - Other nontax general revenues
  - Contributions to endowments and permanent fund principal
  - Extraordinary and special items
  - Change in net position
  - Beginning and ending net position.

The notes to the financial statements should also describe the nature and amount of significant transactions between major discretely presented component units and the primary government and other component units (GASB-34, par. 128) [GASB Cod. Secs. 2200.217, 2600.110].

PRACTICE POINT: In practice, few governments take advantage of presenting condensed component unit information in the notes. For some governments, the length of the disclosure may be less in the notes than on the face of the basic financial statements and (if needed) in combining statements.

OBSERVATION: GASB-14 states that if a discretely presented component unit does not issue a separate financial report, the primary government reporting entity's CAFR, if one is issued, must include fund financial statements for the component unit (major fund reporting format). This information is presented as required supplementary information. This requirement is based on GASB-14 (par. 50) [GASB Cod. Sec. 2600.111], except GASB-34 requires that the fund financial statements be focused on major funds of the component unit rather than its fund types. Presentation of the fund financial statements of the individual component units is not required unless such information is not available in separately issued financial statements of the component unit. Combining financial statements for nonmajor discretely presented component units should be included in the reporting entity's CAFR using the same methodology as combining (and individual fund) statements of the nonmajor funds of the primary government.

Blending Component Units

A basic strategy of GASB-14 is to present financial information for component units separately from the financial information for the primary government. This strategy is achieved through the use of the discrete-presentation method. However, in some circumstances the GASB believes that although a component unit is legally separate from the primary government it may simply be an extension of the primary government. Under this condition, it is more appropriate to use the blending method to incorporate the financial information of a component unit into the reporting entity's financial statements (GASB-14, par. 52, GASB-34, pars. 6 and 125) [GASB Cod. Sec. 2600.112].

When the blending method is used, transactions of a component unit are presented as if they were executed directly by the primary government, normally through presentation as one or more funds within the primary government's fund financial statements. In a similar manner, balances in a blended component unit's financial statements are merged with similar balances of the primary government in the preparation of the government-wide financial statements as either governmental activities or business-type activities so that there is no way to identify which balances relate to a blended component unit and which relate to the primary government (GASB-14, par. 52).

The only two circumstances that require the blending of a component unit's financial statements with those of the primary government relate to

- Similar governing bodies and
- Scope of services.

Similar Governing Bodies

If the component unit's governing body is substantively the same as the primary government's, then a component unit's financial statements should be blended with the primary government. The blending of financial statements should also occur when the governing body of the primary government has sufficient membership on the component unit's government body that the primary government controls the component unit's activities, because the two bodies are considered substantively the same. The term "substantively the same" is not defined in GASB-14, but in footnote 7 in GASB-14 the following examples are offered (GASB-14, par. 53, fn. 7, as amended by GASB-61, par. 8) [GASB Cod. Sec. 2600 fn. 5]:

- When a municipal component unit's governing body is composed of *all* city council members, along with the mayor serving ex officio, the two governing bodies are considered substantively the same.

- When a municipal component unit's governing body is composed of the mayor and only two of the 10 members of the city council, the two governing bodies are *not* considered substantively the same.

Because of the relatively large number of members of the governing body of a state government, it is unlikely that a state government would meet the "substantively the same criterion". The concept of being "substantively the same" includes two elements. First, a majority of the members of the governing body of the primary government must serve on the governing body of the component unit. Second, the number of primary government members on the component unit's board must be a voting majority. Thus, a situation could arise where all of the members of a city council serve on the board of a component unit but their numbers are less than half (or whatever it takes to represent a voting majority) and therefore the primary government does not control the component unit's activities.

GASB-61 clarified the blending criterion so that it applies when *any* of the following elements exist:

1. The component unit's government body is substantively the same as the governing body of the primary government and

2. Either

   a. There is a financial benefit or burden between the primary government and the component unit, such as the payment of debt service of the component unit by the primary government; *or*

   b. Management of the primary government has operational responsibility for the component unit, which occurs when management runs the component unit in the same manner as other programs. For example, management of a department of transportation keeps all the records and finances of a partnership to build a road, *and*

3. Either

   a. The component unit provides services to the primary government in a scope of services arrangement; or

b. The component unit's total debt outstanding including leases or any other types of debt, is to be repaid entirely or almost entirely by the primary government. This would include an irrevocable or general obligation pledge and appropriation to the component unit that the component unit, in turn, pledges to bondholders or lessors.

The effect of the provisions of GASB-61 is that many entities created solely to finance the debts of a primary government in a form of "off-balance-sheet financing" with security consisting of an inter-entity lease are not discretely presented component units. They are required to be blended component units. This may be counter to what budgeting or other officials charged with governance intended for these transactions.

PRACTICE ALERT: As discussed summarily above, GASB-80 adds another blending criteria to paragraph 53 of GASB-14 [GASB Cod. Sec. 2600.113]. A component unit should be included in the reporting entity financial statements using the blending method if the component unit is organized as a not-for-profit corporation in which the primary government is the sole corporate member as identified in the component unit's articles of incorporation or bylaws, and the component unit is included in the financial reporting entity pursuant to the provisions in paragraphs 21–37 of GASB-14, as amended (and discussed previously in this chapter) [GASB Cod. Secs. 2100.120–.136]. The sole corporate member requirement in this GASB-80 should not be analogized to any other situations that may be considered similar to those in which the primary government is the sole corporate member, such as situations in which the primary government is the residual equity interest owner.

Scope of Services

The second circumstance that requires the blending of a component unit's financial statements depends on the scope of the services provided by the unit. If the component unit provides, either directly or indirectly, services or benefits exclusively or almost exclusively to the primary government, then blending should be used. The idea of exclusive services to or benefits for the primary government is similar to the purpose of an Internal Service Fund. Thus, the component unit is created to provide services or benefits not to external parties but to the primary government as the recipient of the services or benefits.

The component unit may provide similar services or benefits to governmental entities other than the primary government. If the services or benefits provided to the other entities are insignificant, the component unit's financial statements should be blended with those of the primary government.

The services or benefits provided to the primary government by the component entity may be direct or indirect. In a direct relationship, the services or benefits are provided to the primary government. For example, a component unit may be created to finance the construction of buildings for various departments or agencies of the primary government. In an indirect relationship, the services or benefits are provided to employees of the primary government. For example, a component unit may be created to administer employee benefit programs (filing claims under health insurance contracts, approving health care providers, etc.) for the primary government.

GASB-61 also discusses the situation in which the primary government is a business-type activity that reports in a single column. For governmental entities, if a component unit is blended, the funds of the component unit are subject to the same financial reporting requirements as the primary government's own funds. The funds of a blended component unit should be presented by including them with the primary government's other funds in the appropriate fund financial statements and combining statements, if presented. However, because the primary government's general fund is usually the main operating fund of the reporting entity and is often a focal point for report users, its general fund should be the only general fund for the reporting entity. The general fund of a blended component unit should be reported as a special revenue fund. For governments engaged only in business-type activities that use a single column for financial statement presentation, a component unit may be blended by consolidating its financial statement data within the single column of the primary government and presenting condensed combining information in the notes to the financial statements. The condensed combining information should include the details described in the following—and at a minimum the elements discussed above when condensed financial statements are presented in the notes to the basic financial statements.

Debt Outstanding (of All Types) Is Paid for Entirely or Almost Entirely by the Primary Government

There are many transactions that include debt issuances supported entirely or almost entirely by a lease document from a primary government. The debt issuances can be the form of any type of debt, including another lease. Repayment generally occurs from this continuing pledge. In this situation, a blended component unit automatically exists, especially if the payments from the primary government are for similar amounts, with similar dates and credit aspects. If this occurs, the component unit will appear like a fund in the primary government's basic financial statements.

PRACTICE ALERT: As discussed previously, GASB-80 adds a criterion for blending. Component units that are organized as not-for-profit corporations in which the primary government is the sole corporate member as identified in the component unit's articles of incorporation or bylaws and the component unit is included in the financial reporting entity will be required to be blended.

NONGOVERNMENTAL COMPONENT UNITS

Some component units, especially those meeting the amended criteria as a component unit of a primary government to be reported as a discretely presented component unit, may be a nongovernmental entity (e.g., a nonprofit organization) and follow FASB standards in their separately issued financial statements.

When nongovernmental entities are reported as discretely presented component units, they should be incorporated into the reporting entity's financial statements generally in the same manner as governmental component units. There is no requirement to change the recognition, measurement, or disclosure standards applied in the nongovernmental component unit's separate financial statements. However, the financial statements of the nongovernmental component unit may need to be reformatted to comply with the classification and display requirements of GASB-34. The GASB *Implementation Guide,* question 4.33.1 [GASB Cod. Sec. 2600.704-12], discusses how to present nongovernmental component units as part of the primary government's basic financial statements. In essence, all component units are required to apply the *definition and display* provisions of GASB-14, as amended, before they are combined with the primary government. For the reporting entity's statement of net position, a discretely presented component unit's financial data may be presented in a separate discrete column or combined with the financial data of other discretely presented component units. Similar treatment is afforded in the statement of activities. If it is impractical to reformat the nongovernmental component unit's change statement data, question 4.33.1 allows the component unit to be presented on a separate following page.

Question 4.33.4 [GASB Cod. Sec. 2600.704-14] further discusses the potential reformatting. If the component unit's statement of net assets (position) is not presented in a classified format, reclassification may be required to present current and noncurrent components based on the definitions in GASB-62. The net assets may need to be redistributed in accordance with GASB-63 (net investment in capital assets, restricted expendable and restricted nonexpendable net position and unrestricted net position). The statement of activities may need to be realigned between operating and nonoperating income to conform to the approach used by the primary government. Finally, there may be different revenue and expense recognition provisions between the component unit and the primary government that may cause realignment.

Investments in For-Profit Corporations

A primary government may own voting stock in a variety of for-profit entities. The intent of the primary government determines how the ownership interest will be presented in the financial reporting entity. If ownership interest was purchased for investment purposes, the interest should be accounted for as an investment. On the other hand, if the purpose of the ownership interest is to enhance or facilitate the primary government's ability to deliver services to its citizens, the interest should be accounted for as a component unit (GASB-14, par. 55, as amended most recently by GASB-72, par. 64) [GASB Cod. Sec. 2600.116].

For example, if a primary government purchases common stock of a corporation to obtain a return on excess resources, the interest in the corporation should be accounted for as an investment. Alternatively, if a primary government purchases all of the common stock of a landscaping company to maintain and care for its buildings and open spaces, the interest should be accounted for as a component unit. If the component unit is discretely presented, the equity interest should be reported as an asset of the fund that has the equity interest. Changes in the equity interest should be reported in governmental funds to the extent that amounts are received or paid. For proprietary funds, adjustments are made based on the amounts earned or expensed whether or not received. If the component unit is blended, in the period of acquisition the purchase should typically be reported as an outflow of the fund that provided the resources for the acquisition and, in that and subsequent reporting periods the component unit should be reported pursuant to the blending requirements of GASB-14, as amended. If, however, the government owns the equity interest for the purpose of obtaining income or profit rather than to directly enhance its ability to provide governmental services, it should report its equity interest as an investment, regardless of the extent of its ownership.

PRACTICE ALERT: GASB Statement No. 90 (*Accounting and Financial Reporting for Majority Equity Interests*) was issued in 2018 with a goal of improving the consistency of reporting a government's majority equity interest in a legally separate organization. If the holding of the interest meets the definition of an investment, the interest should be reported as an investment. For a majority equity interest that is reported as an investment, the accounting and financial reporting should utilize the equity method unless it is held by a special-purpose government engaged only in fiduciary activities, a fiduciary fund, or an endowment (including permanent and term endowments) or a permanent fund, which would measure the majority equity interest at fair value. All other majority equity interest holdings are reported as component units. The government or fund holding the equity interest should report an asset related to the interest using the equity method. GASB-90's implementation date is for periods beginning after December 15, 2018. Some requirements are required to be implemented retroactively. Reporting a majority equity interest in a component unit and reporting a component unit that is acquired through a 100% equity interest is to be implemented prospectively.

DIFFERENT REPORTING PERIODS

The fiscal year of the financial reporting entity's financial statements should be the same as the fiscal year of the primary government. Ideally, the primary government and its component units should have the same fiscal years, and the GASB encourages the adoption of the same fiscal year by all of the units that compose the financial reporting entity.

If it is impractical for a component unit to have the same fiscal year as the primary government, a component unit's financial statements that have an ending date that occurs during the primary government's fiscal year should be incorporated into the financial statements of the reporting entity. For example, if the primary government's fiscal year ends on June 30 and a component unit's fiscal year ends on December 31, for the fiscal year ended June 30, 20X8, the financial reporting entity should include the component unit's financial statements ended December 31, 20X7.

GASB-14 does allow one exception to the inclusion of a component unit that has a fiscal year different from, or that does not end within, that of the primary government. If a component unit's fiscal year ends *within the first quarter after* the end of the primary government's fiscal year, then the component unit's financial statements subsequent to the primary government's fiscal year financial statements may be included in the statements of the financial reporting entity. For example, if the primary government's fiscal year ends on June 30, and a component unit's fiscal year ends on August 31, for the fiscal year ended June 30, 20X8, the financial reporting entity could include the component unit's financial statements ended August 31, 20X8 (GASB-14, par. 59) [GASB Cod. Sec. 2600.119].

When the financial statements of a component unit have a fiscal year different from that of the primary government, it is likely that intra-entity transactions and related balances will differ, resulting in receivables or payables that may not articulate between the statements. When the amounts differ, the nature and amount of the intra-entity transactions and related balances should be disclosed in a note to the financial statements.

Once a component unit adopts a fiscal year, that date should be used consistently from year to year. If the fiscal year-end changes, the change should be disclosed in a note to the financial statements (GASB-14, par. 60) [GASB Cod. Sec. 2600.120].

Although a reporting entity's financial statements may contain financial information for component units with periods different from that of the primary government, there is no need to change the title of the reporting entity's financial statements to indicate the different dates. The financial statement titles should reflect the primary government's reporting date and period. The notes to the financial statements should disclose the fiscal period reported for component units if it is different from that of the primary government.

NOTE DISCLOSURES

The following should be disclosed in a note to the reporting entity's financial statements (GASB-14, par. 61, GASB-61, par. 11) [GASB Cod. Sec. 2600.121]:

- *Brief* description of the component units.
- Relationship of the primary government with each component unit.
- Discussion of criteria or rationale used for including each component unit.
- Identification of method(s) used (discrete presentation, blending or included in the fiduciary fund financial statements) to incorporate the component unit in the financial reporting entity's financial statements. Component units may be disclosed together if they have common characteristics, as long as each component unit is separately identified. As an example, a state department of transportation with 15 intercity bus component units that are only separated by geography and subject to the same statutes would likely be disclosed together as a combined "regional transportation authorities" (or similar).
- Identification of how financial statements of each component unit may be obtained.

> **OBSERVATION:** Disclosure in this area in practice differs based on the number of component units and their operations. Some states disclose this information in a table, inclusive of fiscal year-end, the nature of transactions between the primary government and the component unit(s), rationale, links to the component unit's website to obtain information, and even whether the component unit was audited by the primary government's auditor or a separate auditor and whether the audit was performed in accordance with generally accepted government auditing standards (GAGAS).

GASB-14 adopts the basic philosophy that the financial information pertaining to the primary government, including blended component units, and similar information pertaining to discretely presented component units should be distinguishable. This philosophy is extended to disclosures in notes and the presentation of required supplementary information in the financial statements of the financial reporting entity.

Determining what should be disclosed in notes to the financial statements *is a matter of professional judgment.* The professional accountant must consider what disclosures are essential to the fair presentation of the basic financial statements. Because the financial reporting entity includes the primary government, including its blended component units, and perhaps one or more discretely presented component units, an additional dimension of professional judgment arises with regard to whether the notes related to the primary government should include relevant information from some of the discretely presented component units, all of the discretely presented component units, or none of the discretely presented component units presented in the reporting entity's financial statements (GASB-14, par. 62) [GASB Cod. Sec. 2600.122].

Notes Related to the Primary Government

Chapter 20, "Comprehensive Annual Financial Report," identifies numerous types of disclosures that may be made in notes to the financial statements and provides a comprehensive disclosure checklist. The list of disclosures in that chapter is not meant to be all-inclusive. Determining the need for a note disclosure should be based on the primary government's (1) governmental and business-type activities as presented in the government-wide financial statements and (2) individually presented major funds and aggregated nonmajor funds as presented in the fund financial statements (GASB-14, par. 63 as most recently amended by GASB-73, par. 24) [GASB Cod. Sec. 2600.123].

For certain pension activities, if a primary government and its component units provide pensions through the same single-employer or agent pension plan, the note disclosure requirements of GASB-68, pars. 37–47 apply (GASB-68, pars. 18, 37–47, as amended by GASB-73, par. 117) [GASB Cod. Secs. P20.117, .136–.146]. In stand-alone financial statements, each government accounts for and reports its participation in the single or agent pension plan as if it was a cost-sharing employer and should apply the requirements of the related paragraphs in GASB-68 (pars. 48–82, as amended by GASB-73, pars. 117–118) [GASB Cod. Sec. P20.147–.182]. Similar provisions also are in place for Other Post-Employment Benefits (OPEB).

Notes Related to Discretely Presented Component Units

GASB-14 states that *only some* of the disclosures related to discretely presented component units need be presented in the reporting entity's financial statements. The specific disclosures to be made should be based on:

- A component entity's significance in relationship to all discretely presented component units; and

- The nature and significance of a discretely presented component's relationship with the primary government.

Thus, each discretely presented component unit must be evaluated separately to determine its relative importance.

Identification of a discretely presented component unit as significant does not mean that all of the notes relative to that component unit must be presented in the financial statements of the reporting entity. Only the notes that relate to the basis used to justify a significant relationship should be presented. Thus, two component units could be classified as significant, but the specific disclosures made for each component unit could be different because the basis for determining significance is different (GASB-14, pars. 62–63, as amended by GASB-34, par. 6, GASB-61, par. 11, GASB-68, par. 18, GASB-73, par. 24, and GASB-34, par. 113) [GASB Cod. Secs. 2600.122–.123].

The following are two examples of how the significance of a component unit may be identified:

1. *Considered significant relative to all discretely presented component units*— The debt of one component unit represents 80% of the debt of all component units and thus a summary of debt service requirements to maturity for that component unit should be disclosed.

2. *Considered significant based on the relationship to the primary government*— The primary government is obligated for the debt of a component unit and thus a summary of debt service requirements to maturity for the component unit should be disclosed.

GASB-61 added that notes relating to component units presented in primary government basic financial statements *should only be those notes essential to fair presentation in the notes to the basic financial statements.* These may include the following:

- Governmental and business-type activities, major funds individually, and non-major funds in the aggregate of the primary government (including its blended component units).

- Major discretely presented component units considering the nature and significance of each component unit's relationship to the primary government.

Determining which discretely presented component unit disclosures are *essential* to fair presentation is a matter of professional judgment and should be done on a component unit–by–component unit basis. A specific type of disclosure might be essential for one component unit but not for another depending on the individual component unit's relationship with the primary government. For example, if a primary government is obligated in some manner for the debt of a particular component unit, it is likely that debt-related disclosures should be made for that component unit.

A way to present information on component units could be as a separate note on component units (or any other entity within the reporting government) that is separately audited. Within the note, the nature of the relationship and transactions between the component unit and the primary government could be listed, along with information if the entity was audited in accordance with Government Auditing Standards. Information should be included on how to obtain publicly available audited financial statements of the component unit, or if the statements are not publicly available. Finally, it should be noted if the fiscal year of the component unit is different from that of the primary government.

Many practitioners believe erroneously that every note disclosure from every discretely presented component unit should be copied and included in the primary government's notes to the basic financial statements. In summation, this could not be further from the truth. As discussed in *Implementation Guide 2015-1,* question 4.39.1 [GASB Cod. Sec. 2600.711-1], to the extent that the disclosures are *essential to the fair presentation* of the financial reporting entity's basic financial statement, they are required. Clearly, many notes to the basic financial statements of government are too long and contain redundant language that is carried forward from year to year. Therefore, a best practice is to annually edit the notes to the basic financial statements *prior to the start* of the annual financial audit. This editing should be based on new standards being implemented and any changes in the relationship between the primary government and its discretely presented component units with a goal of only including information from discretely presented component units that is *essential to the fair presentation* of the financial reporting entity's basic financial statements.

PRACTICE ALERT: The GASB has begun reexamining the effectiveness of note disclosures with a primary focus on:

- Note disclosures required by pronouncements that have not been effective for at least three years.

- Note disclosures added more recently (mainly relating to *Certain Disclosures Related to Debt, Including Direct Borrowings and Direct Placements, Leases* and *Certain Debt Extinguishments*) [GASB-88, GASB-87, and GASB-86, respectively].

- Note disclosures that are the subject of other pre-agenda research projects on going concern disclosures and conduit debt.

It is estimated that an initial due process document on this project may be released in 2019.

PRIMARY GOVERNMENT SEPARATE FINANCIAL STATEMENTS

A primary government may request (or be required) to issue separate financial statements that do not include financial information of component units. GASB-14 does not prohibit the issuance of separate financial statements by the primary government. However, such statements should acknowledge that the financial statements do not include financial information of component units necessary for reporting in conformity with U.S. GAAP (GASB-14, par. 64) [GASB Cod. Sec. 2600.124].

The GASB does not specify a generally accepted practice for reporting the primary government only. The AICPA's Audit and Accounting Guide *State and Local Governments* states that the notes to the financial statements and auditor's report should clearly disclose that the presentation is that of only the primary government and does not include any component units.

COMPONENT UNIT SEPARATE FINANCIAL STATEMENTS

GASB-14 is written from the perspective of a primary government in that it considers the focal point for the preparation of the financial statements of a financial reporting entity to be a primary government. However, component units may be requested or required to distribute separate financial statements, and the guidance in GASB-14 should also be used to prepare those statements. In effect, the focal point for the preparation of a component unit's separate financial statements is the component unit. For example, to determine whether a component unit itself has component units, standards established in paragraphs 21 through 41 of that GASB Statement, as amended, should be applied to the entity.

As discussed in the section titled "Reporting Component Units," governmental financial statements should be built in layers from the lowest-level component unit to the highest-level component unit. The bottom-up concept is important in determining which component units at which levels should be included in separately issued financial statements. From a practical perspective, if one visualizes looking down from each level or layer, then every component unit under a particular level should be included in the separately issued financial statements of the component unit at that level. Thus, a primary government should include all levels of component units in its separately issued financial statements, while the lowest-level component unit should present only its own financial statements because there are no component units below it.

When a component unit issues separate financial statements, there should be an acknowledgment that the governmental entity (the issuing component unit) is a component unit of another government. The other governmental entity could be a primary government or another component unit that is the focal point of separately issued financial statements. In addition, the following disclosures should be made in a note to the component unit's separately issued financial statements:

- Identify the other (higher-level) governmental entity.
- Describe the relationship with the (higher-level) governmental entity.

The GASB does not specify a generally accepted practice for reporting a component unit only. The AICPA's *State and Local Governments* Guide states that the notes to the financial statements and auditor's report should clearly disclose that the presentation is that of a component unit of another primary government (GASB-14, par. 65) [GASB Cod. Secs. 1100.114, 2600.125, C50.147, Ca5.108, Co5.107, Ho5.108, In3.108, Sp20.112, Ut5.108].

REPORTING RELATIONSHIPS WITH ORGANIZATIONS OTHER THAN COMPONENT UNITS

A primary government may appoint all or some of the members of the governing board of an entity that is not a component unit because it does not satisfy the criteria established in paragraphs 21 through 41 of GASB-14 as amended by GASB-39. These organizations are broadly classified by GASB-14 as (1) related organizations, (2) joint ventures and jointly governed organizations, (3) component units of another government with the characteristics of a joint venture or jointly governed organization, (4) pools, (5) undivided interests, and (6) cost-sharing arrangements (GASB-14, par. 67) [GASB Cod. Secs. 2600.127, J50.101].

Related Organizations

A "related organization" is defined as follows:

> An organization for which a primary government is not financially accountable (because it does not impose will or have a financial benefit or burden relationship) even though the primary government appoints a voting majority of the organization's governing board.

Thus, related organizations are not component units, yet there is some form of accountability, other than financial accountability, that exists between the primary government and the related organization because of the appointment authority. For this reason, the primary government should disclose in a note to the financial statements the nature of its relationship to the related organizations.

Some primary governments, especially states, have a common relationship with a number of related organizations. Rather than identify each related organization, related organizations with a common relationship can be grouped together for disclosure purposes. For example, if a state government appoints all of the members of 20 local governing boards for highway beautification and there is no other relationship with the boards, a single disclosure could be made without specifically naming the 20 boards (GASB-14, par. 67).

Due to the nature of the relationship between the primary government and related organizations, the primary government should consider whether related party transactions should be disclosed in the financial statements of the reporting entity.

Financial statements issued by a related organization should disclose the related primary government and describe the relationship between the two (GASB-14, par. 68) [GASB Cod. Sec. 2600.128].

Joint Ventures

Governments may enter into a joint venture agreement or arrangement to create a separate entity to provide a service directly to the individual governments involved or the citizens served by the governments. For example, two municipalities may enter into a joint venture and create a separate entity to operate a landfill. The creation of a joint venture entity rather than a sole venture may be based on a number of reasons, ranging from economies of scale to effective risk management.

GASB-14 provides the following definition of a "joint venture":

> A legal entity or other organization that results from a contractual arrangement and that is owned, operated, or governed by two or more participants as a separate and specific activity subject to joint control in which the participants retain (*a*) an ongoing financial interest or (*b*) an ongoing financial responsibility.

OBSERVATION: If the agreement to jointly provide services or operate certain facilities or functions does not involve the creation of a separate legal entity or organization, the arrangement is not considered a joint venture. However, it may meet the criteria to be considered a jointly governed organization, pool, undivided interest, or cost-sharing arrangement as discussed later in this chapter.

Joint Control

One condition for a joint venture is that no one entity can unilaterally control the operational and financial policies of the commonly controlled entity. Thus, if two or more participating governments have created an entity, and each of those governments has an equal influence on it, the prerequisite condition for a joint venture exists. However, if the two or more governments do not have equal control or voting influence, then the entity is not a joint venture and may be either a component unit or some other related organization.

If the joint control criterion is satisfied, but there is no ongoing financial interest or ongoing financial responsibility, the entity is a jointly governed organization and not a joint venture (see section titled "Jointly Governed Organizations") (GASB-14, par. 69) [GASB Cod. Sec. J50.102].

Ongoing Financial Interest

GASB-14 defines the term "ongoing financial interest" as follows:

> An equity interest or any other arrangement that allows a participating government to have access to a joint venture's resources.

In addition, the term "equity interest" is defined as follows:

> A financial interest in a joint venture evidenced by the ownership of shares of the joint venture's stock or by otherwise having an explicit, measurable right to the net resources of the joint venture that is usually based on an investment of financial or capital resources by a participating government.

The concept of ongoing financial interest is not limited to an existing equity interest (holding voting stock of the entity). There may be an arrangement represented by a separate contract, letter of agreement, or other document that specifically describes a participating government's right of access to the joint venture's resources.

Access to the joint venture's resources may be direct or indirect. Direct access to resources would include the participating government's right to a share of profits or surpluses earned by the joint venture or to participate in gains realized through the disposition of operating assets. Indirect access to resources enables participating governments to persuade the joint venture to use its surplus resources so that citizens are benefited directly rather than through their participating governments. For example, a regional recreation joint venture may be persuaded to build tennis courts at participating governments' playgrounds (GASB-14, par. 70) [GASB Cod. Sec. J50.103].

Ongoing Financial Responsibility

GASB-14 defines the term "ongoing financial responsibility" as follows:

1. When a participating government is obligated in some manner for the debts of a joint venture or

2. When the joint venture's existence depends on continued funding by the participating government.

For an analysis of what constitutes "obligated in some manner," see the discussion in the section (above) titled "Financial Benefit to or Burden on a Primary Government." The other component of ongoing financial responsibility deals with a participating government's financial responsibility for the continued existence of the joint venture.

In most instances, the continued existence of the joint venture is dependent on the participating governments because they or their citizens have agreed to pay for the goods used or services provided by the joint venture. However, GASB-14 relates responsibility for continued existence to a single participating government. If the number of participating governments is small (two or three), the withdrawal of any one of the three participating governments could mean the end for the joint venture. As the number of participating governments increases, it becomes more likely that no one participating government's action would mean the end of the joint venture. Of course, there is no specific guidance as to which number of participants would invalidate the continued existence concept. For this reason, professional judgment must be exercised (GASB-14, par. 71) [GASB Cod. Sec. J50.104].

Reporting Joint Ventures with Equity Interest

Financial reporting standards for joint ventures depend on whether the joint venture is represented by a specified equity interest. If a joint venture is represented by an equity interest, a participating government should show the interest as an asset. If an equity interest is not apparent, only certain disclosures concerning the joint venture should be made in the participating government's financial statements.

A joint venture with an equity interest is demonstrated by a participating government's interest in the resources of the joint venture that is explicit and measurable. The equity interest is usually based on the contribution of resources, either financial assets or capital assets, by the participating government.

The most obvious demonstration of an explicit and measurable interest in a joint venture would be the ownership of voting stock by a participating government. For example, a participating government that has a 25% interest in a joint venture generally has a proportional interest in the net resources of the joint venture. However, the demonstration of an equity interest in a joint venture can also be based on an arrangement other than that represented by voting stock ownership. For example, the participating governments can enter into a contract whereby the joint venture is created. The contract must be written in such a manner that the participant's interest in the joint venture's net resources is explicit and measurable. A residual interest in the net resources of a joint venture upon dissolution, because there is no other equitable claimant, is not equivalent to an equity interest (GASB-14, par. 72) [GASB Cod. Sec. J50.105].

If the reporting entity's participation in a joint venture is represented by an equity interest in the net resources of the joint venture, an asset should be reported in the financial statements of the participating government. The manner of presenting the asset, which represents the net equity in the joint venture's net position, depends on whether the participating government accounts for the investment in a proprietary fund or a governmental fund.

Proprietary funds. The initial investment of financial and/or capital resources in the joint venture should be recorded at cost. Whether the initial investment should be increased or decreased depends on the joint venture agreement. If the joint venture agreement states that a participating government is to share in the profits and losses of the joint venture, the investment account should be adjusted to reflect the joint venture's results of operations.

The recognition of a proportional share of the joint venture's results of operations is not dependent on whether there is an actual remittance between the joint venture and a participating government. In determining the joint venture's results of operations for a period, profits or losses on transactions with the proprietary fund should be eliminated. Non-operating transactions, such as additional equity contributions, loans, and dividends, should be reflected as an addition or decrease to the carrying amount of the net investment in the joint venture.

The interest in the net position of the joint venture should be reported as a single asset (account) in the proprietary fund. There should be no attempt to present on a participating government's balance sheet a proportional interest in the various assets and liabilities of the joint venture. In addition, the proportional shares of the joint venture's results of operations should be presented as a single operating account on the proprietary fund's operating statement. There should be no attempt to present a proportional interest in the various operating accounts of the joint venture.

To illustrate the accounting for a joint venture in which there is an equity interest, assume that the County of Castle Rock enters into a joint venture agreement with two other municipalities. In the terms of the agreement, each municipality has a one-third interest in the net position and profits/losses of the joint venture. If Castle Rock contributes $100,000 in cash and $200,000 in equipment, the following entry would be made (all entries are made in an Enterprise Fund):

	Debit	Credit
Equity Interest in Joint Venture	300,000	
Cash		100,000
Equipment		200,000
To record contribution to joint venture.		

If after the first year of operations, the joint venture incurs an operating loss of $90,000, the following entry would be made:

	Debit	Credit
Equity Interest in Joint Venture Operating Losses	30,000	
Equity Interest in Joint Venture		30,000
To record equity share of operating loss for the *year. ($90,000 × 1/3)*		

GASB-61 changed the caption "investment in joint venture" to "equity interest in joint venture" for financial reporting purposes. However, many systems may have the prior name coded into their chart of accounts and changing may be difficult.

(GASB-14, par. 73, as amended by GASB-61, par. 10, GASB-63, par. 8, GASB-34, par. 91) [GASB Cod. Sec. J50.106].

(See previous **PRACTICE ALERT** on GASB-90 (*Accounting and Financial Reporting for Majority Equity Interests*)).

Governmental funds. The initial investment of financial and/or capital resources in the joint venture should be recorded at cost, but only to the extent the investment is evidenced by current financial resources (as defined in Chapter 3, "Basis of Accounting and Measurement Focus"). When the investment in the joint venture is recorded in a governmental fund, only the portion of the investment considered available and expendable should be recorded on the balance sheet. Usually this portion of the investment is limited to amounts due to and from the joint venture. The remaining investment or payments made to the joint venture should be reported as expenditures of the governmental fund (GASB-14, par. 74, as amended by GASB-34, par. 6, and GASB-61, par. 10, GASB-34, pars. 78–80, 82, as amended by GASB-63, par. 8) [GASB Cod. Sec. J50.107].

Government-wide financial statements. Joint ventures that are presented in proprietary funds and governmental funds should also be presented in the government-wide financial statements and should be accounted for at this level using the method described earlier for proprietary funds.

Disclosure Requirements for Joint Venture Participants

For all joint ventures (with or without equity interest), a participating government should disclose in a note to its financial statements a general description of the joint venture, including the following:

- Description of ongoing financial interest, including equity interest, if applicable, or ongoing financial responsibility; and

- Information that enables a reader to determine whether the joint venture is accumulating assets that may result in a financial benefit to the participating government or experiencing fiscal stress that may result in a financial burden on the participating government.

In addition, a participating government should disclose information about the availability of the joint venture's separate financial statements.

Finally, a participating government should disclose information concerning related party transactions between the participating governments and the joint venture (GASB-14, par. 75) [GASB Cod. Sec. J50.109].

Joint Building or Finance Authorities

Participating governments may enter into a relationship whereby there is a formal joint venture but the substance of the relationship is an undivided-interest arrangement. An undivided-interest arrangement is "an ownership arrangement in which two or more parties own property in which title is held individually to the extent of each party's interest." Thus, for accounting purposes, even though a joint venture exists, the undivided interest in property acquired through the joint venture is recorded directly by each participating government.

A joint building authority and a finance authority are examples of this type of arrangement. A joint building authority may be created to construct or acquire capital assets and in turn to lease the assets to a participating government. Under this arrangement, a participating government would have capitalized the lease based on standards discussed in Chapter 14, "Leases and Service Concession Arrangements." For this reason, a participating government would reflect the effects of the lease on its financial statements (GASB-14, par. 76) [GASB Cod. Sec. J50.110].

Jointly Governed Organizations or Joint Powers Authorities

A state may allow local governments to form regional governments or similar entities to provide goods or services to the citizens served by the local governments. For example, a state may provide for the creation of a municipal power authority that acquires, generates, and provides electrical power to participating local governments or utility districts. Such arrangements should be evaluated to determine whether they meet the definition of a joint venture. If an arrangement of this type does meet the criteria to be reported as a joint venture, the only disclosures that need to be made in a participating government's financial statements are those concerning its participation in the jointly governed organization and its related-party transactions (GASB-14, par. 77) [GASB Cod. Sec. J50.111].

Component Units and Related Organizations with Joint Venture Characteristics

The third type of reporting relationship with organizations other than component units concerns component units and related organizations with joint venture characteristics. A government may participate with other governments to create an organization that is either a component unit or a related organization of another government. For example, governments #1, #2, and #3 create an organization, and assume that the organization is either a component unit or a related organization of government #1. Thus, the majority participating government (government #1) reports the organization in a manner consistent with the standards applicable to component units or related organizations. The minority participating governments (governments #2 and #3) should report their relationships with the organization based on the standards discussed in the previous sections titled "Joint Ventures" and "Jointly Governed Organizations."

The organization reported as a component unit in the statements of the reporting entity that includes the financial statements of the majority participating government should present any equity interest of the minority participating governments as part of its equity section.

OBSERVATION: GASB-61 changed the nomenclature of a minority interest to "restricted net position, nonexpendable." GASB-54 requires the minority interest to be a nonexpendable fund balance if the investment was reported in a governmental fund.

When participating governments jointly control an organization and it is fiscally dependent on one of the participating governments, the majority participating government should report the organization either as a component unit or as a related organization. The minority participating governments should report the jointly controlled organization in accordance with the standards discussed in the previous sections titled "Joint Ventures" and "Jointly Governed Organizations" (GASB-14, par. 78, as amended by GASB-34, pars. 32, 98, GASB-61, par. 12, GASB-63, par. 8) [GASB Cod. Sec. J50.112].

Pools

Although a pool is another example of an arrangement in which a number of governments jointly participate in a venture, GASB-14 states that a pool is different from a joint venture. Pools are characterized by the following:

- Membership is open (participants are free to join, resign, or alter their level of participation at will).
- Equity interest is recognized in participant's financial statements.
- Limited disclosures are required.

An investment pool would likely give participants a higher degree of flexibility in determining to what extent each participant wants to participate in the venture. In addition, a pool arrangement results in an investment being presented directly in the financial statements of a participating government, and therefore there is no need to compute and present a separate equity interest in the pool. Furthermore, because of the flexibility that characterizes each pool, it is not necessary to make the type of disclosures required for joint venture participants (as discussed in paragraph 75) (GASB-14, par. 79, GASB-31, par. 2, GASBI-4, par. 3) [GASB Cod. Sec. J50.113].

Governmental entities that participate in an external investment pool should observe the standards established by GASB-31 (*Accounting and Financial Reporting for Certain Investments and for External Investment Pools*).

OBSERVATION: The GASB recently released GASB Statement No. 79 (GASB-79) (*Certain External Investment Pools and Pool Participants*). State and local government treasurers that manage investment pools or participate in external investment pools should review GASB-79 carefully. Further discussion of GASB-79 is presented in Chapter 9, "Deposits, Investments, and Derivative Instruments."

GASBI-4 (*Accounting and Financial Reporting for Capitalization Contributions to Public Entity Risk Pools*) states that governmental entities that make capital contributions to or participate in the activities of a public entity risk pool should *not* account for the investment and subsequent results of operations of the pool as a joint venture. This prohibition applies to contributions to public entity pools where risk is transferred as well as where risk is not transferred. In addition, if under a retrospectively rated policy the governmental entity's ultimate premium payments are based on the experience of the public entity risk pool, GASBI-4 states that this relationship does not create a joint venture relationship for financial reporting purposes (GASBI-4, par. 3) [GASB Cod. Sec. J50.113].

Undivided Interests

Participating governments may join with one another in a type of joint venture in which no new joint entity is created. Such an arrangement results in an undivided interest (joint operation). An undivided interest arises when two or more parties own property that is held individually on the basis of each party's interest in the property. In addition, liabilities related to the operation of the undivided interest are obligations of each participating government.

In an undivided interest, no separate entity is created and, therefore, accounts and transactions related to the operations of the undivided interest must be recorded in the records of the participating governments. For this reason, there is no requirement to make disclosures similar to those described in the section titled "Disclosure Requirements for Joint Venture Participants."

Governments may participate in arrangements that have characteristics of both a joint venture (separate entity) and an undivided interest. Under this arrangement, the undivided interest should be accounted for as described in the previous paragraph and the equity interest related to the joint venture should be accounted for as described in the section titled "Reporting Participation in Joint Ventures in Which There Is an Equity Interest" (GASB-14, par. 80) [GASB Cod. Sec. J50.114].

Cost-Sharing Arrangements

GASB-14 states that cost-sharing projects, such as the financing of highway construction by the federal, state, and local governments, are not joint ventures, because there is no ongoing financial interest or responsibility by the participating governmental entities.

In addition, joint purchasing agreements or shared-services arrangements that commit participating governments to purchase a stated quantity of goods or services for a specified period of time are not joint ventures (GASB-14, par. 81, as amended by GASB-62, pars. 13–46, GASB-73, pars. 115–116, GASB-74, pars. 9–36 and 38–57) [GASB Cod. Sec. J50.115].

There are no specific financial reporting or disclosure requirements related to a government's participation in a cost-sharing arrangement.

OTHER STAND-ALONE GOVERNMENT FINANCIAL STATEMENTS

Other stand-alone governmental entities are legally separate governmental entities (see the section titled "Determining Separate Legal Standing") that have the following characteristics:

- They do not have a separately elected governing body; and
- They are not component units of another governmental entity (see section titled "Financial Accountability").

As previously discussed, examples of other stand-alone governmental entities include the following:

- Certain special-purpose governments;
- Joint ventures;
- Jointly governed organizations; and
- External investment or risk pools.

When a stand-alone governmental entity issues financial statements, the standards established by GASB-14 should be observed. Thus, the other stand-alone governmental entity becomes the focal point for preparing the financial statements of the financial reporting entity. For example, the other stand-alone governmental entity should follow standards established in the sections titled "Financial Accountability" and "Nature and Significance of Relationship" to determine whether it has component units for which financial statements should be incorporated into the standards of the financial reporting entity.

Other stand-alone governmental entities for which the governing board's voting majority is appointed by a primary government should disclose the accountability relationship in their separately issued financial statements (see the section titled "Related Organizations") (GASB-14, par. 66, as amended by GASB-61, par. 4) [GASB Cod. Sec. 2600.126].

The description of the relationship between the stand-alone governmental entity and the primary government should emphasize the general concept of accountability rather than the specific criteria for financial accountability. There can be no financial accountability, as defined by GASB-14, for a stand-alone governmental entity or, by definition, it would be a component unit.

GOVERNMENT COMBINATIONS AND DISPOSALS OF GOVERNMENT OPERATIONS (GASB-69)

GASB-69 discusses a variety of transactions referred to as mergers, acquisitions and transfers of operations. The GASB distinguishes between mergers and acquisitions by the degree of "consideration" that is exchanged in conjunction with the transaction. Assets and liabilities that are involved in the combination are measured at carrying value when involved in a merger. However, in an acquisition, assets and liabilities are measured at their acquired value with certain exceptions.

The accounting and financial reporting guidance previous to GASB-69 addressing disposals of components for nongovernmental entities also conflicts with the financial statement presentation requirements in paragraphs 100 and 101 of GASB-34 (*Basic Financial Statements—and Management's Discussion and Analysis—for State and Local Governments*). These holes in standards and the FASB Codification project hastened the need for change.

GASB-69 also discusses the transfer or disposal of operations. Disposals of operations occur when a government discontinues or transfers specific activities.

GASB-69's scope involves combinations of legally separate entities, such as a governmental entity with other governmental entities. Combinations may also occur between a governmental entity and a not-for-profit or for-profit entity if the new or continuing organization is a government. Government combinations also include mergers and acquisitions of activities that comprise less than an entire legally separate entity and involve only the assets and liabilities previously used by an entity to provide specific goods or services (GASB-69, par. 3) [GASB Cod. Sec. Co10.101].

GASB-69 refers to portions of governments as "operations." The GASB describes an "operation" as an integrated set of activities conducted and managed for the purpose of providing identifiable services with associated assets or liabilities. For example, GASB-69 describes an operation as possibly including the assets and liabilities specifically associated with the activities conducted and managed by the fire department in a city. Conversely, fire engines donated to or acquired by a fire department would comprise only a portion of that activity and, therefore, would not constitute an operation. Anything that constitutes less than an operation (e.g., a process) is out of scope of the standard.

Government combinations must result in a continuation of a large portion of the services provided by the previously separate entities or operations after the transaction. The legal instrument (law, ordinance, contract, etc.) that provides the basis for the combination will contain information, including whether services should be continued after the combination or whether assets (and/or liabilities) have been acquired. If the legal instrument is not specific with regard to the continuation of services, GASB-69 allows for professional judgment to determine whether a combination has occurred (GASB-69, par. 9) [GASB Cod. Sec. Co10.106].

Types of Combinations

GASB-69 discusses three types of combinations: "government mergers," "government acquisitions," and "transfers of operations." Government mergers occur when legally separate entities combine in which no significant consideration is exchanged and *either* one or more governments or non-governmental entities cease to exist or one or more legally separate governments or non-governmental entities cease to exist and their operations are absorbed into, and continue to be provided by, one or more continuing governments. In other words, government A plus government B can equal the new government C or government A absorbs government B and government A remains intact (GASB-69, par. 10) [GASB Cod. Sec. Co10.107].

A "government acquisition" occurs when a government acquires another entity, or the operations of another entity, in exchange for significant consideration. The consideration provided should be significant in relation to the assets and liabilities acquired (namely more than $1). The acquired entity or operation becomes part of the acquiring government's legally separate entity (GASB-69, par. 11) [GASB Cod. Sec. Co10.108].

A "transfer of operations" occurs when a government takes a function and transfers it to another function. GASB-69 notes that this may result from reorganizations, redistricting, annexation, or jurisdictional changes in boundaries. However, the standard also notes that a transfer may be present in shared service arrangements where governments agree to combine operations. Transfers of operations may occur when a particular function is "spun off" to create a new government (GASB-69, par. 12) [GASB Cod. Sec. Co10.109].

OBSERVATION: Transfers of operations may also occur due to economic conditions or other factors. For example, assume that two adjoining cities have shared a common police department. During the year, one of the cities voted to end the contract with the adjoining city. The leaving city then issued a procurement, approving a bid by the county sheriff to provide services through a competitive process. The sheriff submitted a lower bid than a number of other cities that also adjoin the government. This activity is a transfer of operations.

Accounting and Financial Reporting for Various Combinations

Mergers Where Two or More Governments Combine to Form a New Government

For mergers where two or more governments combine to form a new government, the transaction date is the date on which the combination becomes effective. The initial reporting period of the new government begins on the merger date. The combined assets, deferred outflows of resources, liabilities, and deferred inflows of resources of the merging entities is recognized and measured in the statement of net position as of *the beginning* of that initial reporting period. The combination presumes that the former government followed generally accepted accounting principles. If U.S. GAAP was not followed, adjustments will be necessary to make the combination effective (GASB-69, par. 13) [GASB Cod. Sec. Co10.110].

The new government measures the various accounting elements as of the merger date at the *carrying values* as reported on the separate financial statements of the merging entities. If there are no financial statements as of the date of the merger, GASB-69 allows for usage of the most recent financial statements, as long as they were prepared in accordance with U.S. GAAP (GASB-69, pars. 14–19) [GASB Cod. Secs. Co10.111–.116].

> **OBSERVATION:** Allowing for the usage of the most recent financial statements in a merger that is between fiscal year-ends is a large relief in many government combinations. It is very difficult for many governments to project assets and liabilities in between fiscal year-ends and therefore from an audit and an operational standpoint, the allowance eases the transition.

However, adjustments may be needed in a merger where different but acceptable bases of accounting may have been used in the various accounting elements. For example, depreciation periods may be different on similar assets. Furthermore, asset impairments may exist. For example, two city halls may no longer be needed if a single city remains.

> **OBSERVATION:** Assume that a city was spun off from a county due to a citizens' referendum. However, assume that funds were due to the new city when it formed, to be paid from a state, were never paid due to a change in a law, leaving the new city insolvent. In this very real example, the same citizens held another referendum, voting to dissolve and rejoin the county. This activity is a combination, but in reverse, as the city has voted to dissolve and rejoin the county.

Mergers Where Two or More Governments Combine and One Government Continues

In continuing governments (where one government absorbs one or more governments) the merger date is the beginning of the reporting period in which the combination occurs, regardless of the actual date of the merger. Continuing governments recognize and measure the various accounting elements of the merging entities for the reporting period in which the combination occurs as though the entities had been combined at the beginning of the continuing government's reporting period. However, the same relief is available if there are no financial statements as of the date of the merger. Similarly, adjustments and impairments may occur because of the combination. Furthermore, there may be eliminations similar to those that commonly occur between governments. These may involve loans between governments and other transfers. Should one of the parties no longer exist, then the loan or transfer may have to be eliminated in accordance with the provisions of GASB-34, paragraph 58 (GASB-69, par. 20) [GASB Cod. Sec. Co10.118].

> **OBSERVATION:** Mergers may also affect the balances and results of operations in governmental funds. Fund statements may have to be adjusted and combined in those instances.

Acquisitions

In the rare instance that a government acquisition occurs, GASB-69 recognizes the acquisition as of the date on which the acquiring government obtains control of the assets and becomes obligated for the liabilities of an entity or its operations. Generally, the acquisition date coincides with the "closing" date because consideration is paid at that time. However, the parties may have designated another date at which the acquiring government obtains control of assets and becomes obligated for the liabilities of the former government (GASB-69, par. 29) [GASB Cod. Sec. Co10.126].

The value of the various elements involved in an acquisition is the "acquisition value" or "market price" as of the date of the acquisition. However, employee benefits, including pensions, compensated absences, other postemployment benefits, landfill post-closure care, and similar items remain measured at current U.S. GAAP (carrying value). Deferred positions related to derivatives should be adjusted to reflect the difference between the acquisition value and the carrying value of acquired hedged items (GASB-69, pars. 30–32) [GASB Cod. Secs. Co10.127–.129].

> **PRACTICE ALERT:** As introduced previously, GASB-90 (*Accounting and Financial Reporting for Majority Equity Interests—an amendment of GASB Statement No. 14*) contemplates acquisition of a 100% equity interest. If a primary government acquires a 100% equity interest in a legally separate organization that is reported as a component unit, the component unit should measure its assets, deferred outflows of resources, liabilities, and deferred inflows of resources in accordance with the provisions of GASB-69 (*Government Combinations and Disposals of Government Operations*), as amended, at the date on which the primary government acquired the 100% equity interest. In applying those measurement provisions, consideration provided (see next section) should include the net resources exchanged to complete the acquisition of the 100% equity interest *plus* any majority equity interest asset recognized prior to the completion of the acquisition. In addition, the net position acquired should be equal to the net position of the component unit after measuring assets, deferred outflows of resources, liabilities, and deferred inflows of resources in accordance with the provisions of GASB-69. The flows statements of the component unit should include only those transactions that occurred subsequent to the acquisition of the 100% equity interest (GASB-90, par. 7) [GASB Cod. Sec. 2600.128].

What is Consideration?

Consideration may include financial and nonfinancial assets. Cash, investments, or capital assets are likely forms of consideration. In addition, a liability incurred may represent an obligation to provide consideration to the former owners of the acquired entity. GASB-69 uses an example where a government issues a note payable in addition to, or in lieu of, cash to the former owners of an organization in exchange for the net position of that organization. In governments that are acquired with a negative net position, GASB-69 notes that relief of the negative net position is not consideration. GASB-69 also supposes that contingencies may be involved in consideration based on future events. If this does occur, GASB-62, paragraphs 96–112, contain guidance for the accounting and financial reporting of this contingency.

Since there is no element of "goodwill" in a governmental acquisition, if the consideration exceeds the various values acquired from the former government, a deferred outflow of resources is created. The deferred outflow of resources position is amortized using a number of possible factors largely based on the remaining estimated service lives of capital or similar long-lived assets or liabilities acquired. If the consideration is less than the various values acquired from the former government, the various values are adjusted ratably to equal the consideration. There is no provision for "bad-will." In the case where consideration is in the form of economic aid, a contribution is recognized (GASB-69, pars. 37–41) [GASB Cod. Secs. Co10.134–.138].

PRACTICE POINT: GASB Statement No. 85 (*Omnibus 2017*), paragraph 5, amends paragraph 39 of GASB-69. For acquisitions that occurred prior to the effective date of GASB-69, paragraph 39 of GASB-69 applies. For circumstances in which the consideration provided exceeds the net position acquired, the acquiring government should report the difference as a deferred outflow of resources. The deferred outflow of resources should be attributed to future periods in a systematic and rational manner, based on professional judgment, considering the relevant circumstances of the acquisition. The length of the attribution period may be determined by considering such factors as the following:

- The estimated service lives of capital assets acquired, when acquisitions are largely based on the expected use of those capital assets;

- The estimated remaining service life for acquisitions of landfills that are capacity-driven;

- The expected length of contracts acquired; or

- The estimated remaining service life of technology acquired, if the acquisition is based on the expected efficiencies of a technology system.

A government should periodically review and revise its estimate of the attribution period in subsequent reporting periods.

GASB-85 does not allow reporting of "negative" goodwill. The provisions became effective for reporting periods beginning after June 15, 2017 with earlier application encouraged. Implementation of the provisions require a retroactive restatement of all prior periods presented, if practicable. In the first period of implementation of GASB-85, amounts reported as goodwill resulting from acquisitions prior to the effective date of GASB-69, should be reclassified as deferred outflows of resources and amounts reported as negative goodwill should be included as part of the restatement of net position.

Other Items in Acquisitions

The costs of the transaction should be expensed during the current period. Also, if the acquisition occurs within the same reporting entity, the acquiring government recognizes the various accounting elements at the carrying values of the selling entity. The difference between the acquisition price and the carrying value of the net position acquired is reported as a special item by the acquiring government in its separately issued statements and reclassified as transfers or subsidies, as appropriate, in the financial statements of the reporting entity (GASB-69, par. 42) [GASB Cod. Sec. Co10.139].

For acquisitions that are announced but not finalized as of the end of the fiscal year, estimated amounts are recognized for the items for which measurement is not complete. Once the acquisition is completed, the acquiring government should prospectively update the estimated amounts reported as of the acquisition date to reflect new information obtained about facts and circumstances that existed as of the acquisition date that, if known, would have affected the measurement of amounts recognized as of that date (GASB-69, par. 44) [GASB Cod. Sec. Co10.141].

Transfers and Disposals of Operations

The effective date of a transfer of operations is the date the transferee government obtains control of the assets and becomes obligated for the liabilities of the operation transferred. A continuing government should report a transfer of operations as a transaction in the financial statements for the reporting period in which it occurs. Alternatively, if a transfer of operations results in the formation of a new government, the new government's initial reporting period begins at the effective transfer date. In the Planning Point, above, with regard to a police department, the county sheriff and the city would recognize the transfers as of the effective transfer date. U.S. GAAP is presumed in calculating the carrying values of the various accounting elements. However, as stated previously, adjustments and impairment testing may be needed.

In a disposal, the disposing government recognizes a gain or loss on the disposal of operations. Gains or losses on the disposal of operations are reported as a special item in the period in which the disposal occurs, based on either the effective transfer date of a transfer of operations or the date of sale for operations that are sold. The disposing government should include only those costs that are directly associated with the disposal of operations when determining the amount of the gain or loss to report. These costs may include employee termination costs calculated in accordance with GASB-47 (*Accounting for Termination Benefits*). Other contingencies may be present, including legal claims, and those should be accounted for in accordance with GASB-62, paragraphs 96–113 (GASB-69, pars. 46–54) [GASB Cod. Secs. Co10.143–.151].

Note Disclosure

GASB-69 requires note disclosure similar to other GASB standards. The disclosure includes a brief description of the combination, dates, and legal reason for the combination. Mergers and acquisitions will include greatly condensed financial statements of the combination, the nature of adjustments made and the new initial amounts. It is envisioned that this disclosure would be in a table. Any consideration should be described, along with any contingencies. Disposals should disclose similar items (GASB-69, pars. 55–58) [GASB Cod. Secs. Co10.152–.155].

QUESTIONS

1. Which GASB standard(s) establish(es) or amend(s) criteria for determining which and by what method organizations should be included in a governmental financial reporting entity?

   a. GASB-3, GASB-40, and GASB-59.

   b. GASB-34, GASB-35, and GASB-37.

   c. GASB-25, GASB-27, GASB-67, and GASB-68.

   d. GASB-14, GASB-39, GASB-61, and GASB-80.

2. The AICPA Audit and Accounting Guide *State and Local Governments* contains a framework for defining a government that is agreed upon by GASB. As stated in paragraph 1.01 of the AICPA's guide, which of the following characteristics *is not necessary* to be recognized as a governmental organization?

   a. Adoption of a charter.

   b. Popular election of officers or appointment (or approval) of a controlling majority of the members of the organization's governing body by officials of one or more state or local governments.

   c. The potential for unilateral dissolution by a government with the net position reverting to a government.

   d. The power to enact and enforce a tax levy.

3. According to GASB-14, as amended, what is the nucleus of a financial reporting entity?

   a. People.

   b. The primary government.

   c. Component units.

   d. Accountability.

4. According to GASB-14, as amended, what *is not included* as part of the financial reporting entity?

   a. The primary government.

   b. Organizations for which the primary government is financially accountable.

   c. Corporate entities that in an auditor's judgment merit inclusion.

   d. Entities, through exercise of the primary government management's professional judgment, that do not meet the financial accountability criteria but are necessary in order to prevent the reporting entity's financial statements from being misleading.

5. GASB-14 (as amended), par. 21 [GASB Cod. Sec. 2100.120], discusses financial accountability. Financial accountability does *not* include which one of the three following possibilities:

   a. Imposition of will from the component unit to the primary government.

   b. Imposition of will from the primary government to the component unit.

   c. Providing specific financial benefits to or imposing specific financial burdens on the primary government, regardless of whether the organization has a separately elected board, a governing board appointed by a higher level of government, or a jointly appointed board.

6. GASB-14, as amended, states that financial benefit or burden is created if *any* of the following relationships exist *except for*:

   a. The primary government is legally entitled to or can otherwise access the organization's resources.

   b. The component unit was established by the primary government.

   c. The primary government is legally obligated or has otherwise assumed the obligation to finance the deficits of, or provide financial support to, the organization.

   d. The primary government is obligated in some manner for the debt of the organization.

7. GASB-14, as amended by GASB-34, requires that information related to each major discretely presented component unit be presented in the reporting entity's basic financial statements. To satisfy this standard, which one of the following approaches *cannot* be used?

   a. Present each major discretely presented component unit in a separate column in the government-wide financial statements.

   b. Present combining statements within the basic financial statements.

   c. Present condensed financial statements in a note to the financial statements.

   d. Incorporate by reference if the report is publicly available.

8. GASB-14, as amended, defines what type of organization for which a primary government is not financially accountable (because it does not impose will or have a financial benefit or burden relationship) even though the primary government appoints a voting majority of the organization's governing board?

   a. A joint venture.

   b. A jointly governed organization.

   c. A related organization.

   d. A component unit.

9. GASB-14, as amended, defines what type of organization that results from a contractual arrangement and is owned, operated, or governed by two or more participants as a separate and specific activity subject to joint control in which the participants retain (*a*) an ongoing financial interest or (*b*) an ongoing financial responsibility?

 a. A joint venture.

 b. A jointly governed organization.

 c. A related organization.

 d. A component unit.

10. GASB-69 defines a governmental combination with significant consideration as:

 a. An annexation.

 b. A governmental acquisition.

 c. A governmental merger.

 d. A transfer of operations.

Practice Case (adapted from the GASB's *Implementation Guide 2015-1*):

An entity was created by a City as a body corporate and politic and is governed by a commission of five members appointed to staggered terms by the mayor of the City. Members of the board may be removed only for cause. The authority's purpose is to provide safe, decent, and affordable housing to the residents of the City. Operations of the authority are subsidized by the federal government and other grantors. The housing authority determines its own budget, subject to federal approval, sets rental rates, and may issue debt in its own name. The City is not responsible for deficits or liabilities of the authority.

 a. Is this entity a component unit of the City?

 b. If the answer is that it is not a component unit, what sort of entity should this be referred to as in the City's notes to its basic financial statements?

 c. Is this entity a component unit of the City if the City provides services at no charge to the entity?

 d. Is this entity a component unit of the City if the City and the entity agree that the entity will make annual payments in lieu of taxes established by the City?

ANSWERS

1. Which GASB standard(s) establish(es) criteria for determining which organizations should be included in a governmental financial reporting entity?

   Answer – D: GASB-14, GASB-39, GASB-61, and GASB-80 all set or amend standards on the financial reporting entity. GASB-3, GASB-40, and GASB-59 deal with financial instruments and risk. GASB-34, GASB-35, and GASB-37 all set standards on the reporting model. GASB-25, GASB-27, GASB-67, and GASB-68 set standards on pensions and pension plans.

2. The AICPA Audit and Accounting Guide *State and Local Governments* contains a framework for defining a government that is agreed upon by GASB. As stated in paragraph 1.01 of the AICPA's Guide, which of the following characteristics *is not necessary to* be recognized as a governmental organization?

   Answer – A: Adoption of a charter is not necessary to be recognized as a governmental organization. Popular election of officers or appointment (or approval) of a controlling majority of the members of the organization's governing body by officials of one or more state or local governments, the potential for unilateral dissolution by a government with the net position reverting to a government, or the power to enact and enforce a tax levy all may signify a governmental entity.

3. According to GASB-14, as amended, what is the nucleus of a financial reporting entity?

   Answer – B: The primary government is the nucleus of a financial reporting entity, even though people, component units, and accountability are important.

4. According to GASB-14, as amended, what *is not included* as part of the financial reporting entity?

   Answer – C: The AICPA's *Code of Professional Conduct* precludes auditors from making decisions that should be made by management. Management is responsible for determining and disclosing the financial reporting entity.

5. GASB-14 (as amended), par. 21 [GASB Cod. Sec. 2100.120], discusses financial accountability. Financial accountability does not include which one of the three following possibilities:

   Answer – A: Imposition of will from the component unit to the primary government indicates that the component unit is likely the primary government and vice versa.

6. GASB-14, as amended, states that financial benefit or burden is created if any of the following relationships *exist except for*:

   Answer – B: Establishment by the primary government does not indicate financial benefit or burden in and of itself. The other answers are all indicators of financial benefit or burden.

7. GASB-14, as amended by GASB-34, requires that information related to each major discretely presented component unit be presented in the reporting entity's basic financial statements. To satisfy this standard, which one of the following approaches *cannot be* used?

   Answer – D: U.S. GAAP *currently* does not allow incorporation by reference to present major discretely presented component unit information in the reporting entity's basic financial statements.

8. GASB-14, as amended, defines what type of organization for which a primary government is not financially accountable (because it does not impose will or have a financial benefit or burden relationship) even though the primary government appoints a voting majority of the organization's governing board?

   Answer – C: This is the definition of a related organization.

9. GASB-14, as amended, defines what type of organization that results from a contractual arrangement and is owned, operated, or governed by two or more participants as a separate and specific activity subject to joint control in which the participants retain (*a*) an ongoing financial interest or (*b*) an ongoing financial responsibility?

   Answer – A: This is the definition of a joint venture.

10. GASB-69 defines a governmental combination with significant consideration as:

    Answer – B: This is a governmental acquisition.

Practice Case (adapted from the GASB's *Implementation Guide 2015-1*):

An entity was created by a City as a body corporate and politic and is governed by a commission of five members appointed to staggered terms by the mayor of the City. Members of the board may be removed only for cause. The authority's purpose is to provide safe, decent, and affordable housing to the residents of the City. Operations of the authority are subsidized by the federal government and other grantors. The housing authority determines its own budget, subject to federal approval, sets rental rates, and may issue debt in its own name. The City is not responsible for deficits or liabilities of the authority.

   a. The entity is not a component unit of the City.

   b. The City should disclose the authority as a related organization. The governing board of the authority is appointed by a City official, but the City is not able to impose its will on the authority and there is no financial burden or benefit relationship between the City and the authority.

c. The entity becomes a component unit of the City and should be discretely presented. The governing board of the authority is appointed by a City official. The City is not able to impose its will on the authority, because the board members may be removed only for cause. However, the services provided by the City to the authority impose a financial burden on the city. Therefore, the City is financially accountable for the housing authority. The two boards are not substantively the same and the services of the authority are provided to the residents of the City rather than to the City itself; therefore, the authority would not meet the criteria for blending and should be discretely presented.

d. The entity is a component unit of the City and should be discretely presented. The governing board of the authority is appointed by a City official. The City is not able to impose its will on the authority, because the board members may be removed only for cause. However, the requirement that the authority make payments in lieu of taxes provides a financial benefit to the City because there is no indication that there is a direct relationship between the payments made and the cost of specific services provided to the authority by the City. Therefore, the City is financially accountable for the authority. The two boards are not substantively the same and the services of the authority are provided to the residents of the City rather than to the City itself; therefore, the authority would not meet the criteria for blending and should be discretely presented.

CHAPTER 5
TERMINOLOGY AND CLASSIFICATION

CONTENTS

INTRODUCTION

A governmental reporting entity should use consistent terminology and classifications in its accounting system. From an internal perspective, the use of a
common language and classification scheme enhances management's ability to
evaluate and control operations. For financial reporting purposes, the consistent
use of terms and classifications in the budgeting, accounting, and reporting
systems facilitates the preparation of financial statements and makes those
financial statements more understandable to user groups (NCGA-1, pars. 124
and 126) [GASB Cod. Secs. 1800.124, .126].

This chapter discusses terminology and classification standards for governmental financial statements as set out in NCGA-1 (*Governmental Accounting and
Financial Reporting Principles*), as amended by GASB-34 (*Basic Financial Statements—and Management's Discussion and Analysis—for State and Local
Governments*).

TERMINOLOGY AND CLASSIFICATION IN REPORTING INTERFUND ACTIVITY

Reporting Interfund Activity in Fund Financial Statements

In order to determine how interfund transfers within and among governmental
funds, proprietary funds, and fiduciary funds should be presented in the fund
financial statements, transfers must be categorized as follows:

- Reciprocal interfund activity
  - Interfund loans
  - Interfund services provided and used

- Nonreciprocal interfund activity
  — Interfund transfers
  — Interfund reimbursements.

"Reciprocal interfund activities" are interfund activities that have many of the same characteristics of exchange and exchange-like transactions that occur with external parties, meaning that equal value is exchanged simultaneously or near simultaneously. "Nonreciprocal interfund activities" are interfund activities that have many of the same characteristics of nonexchange transactions that occur with external parties, meaning that non-equal-value exchanges occur or only a "one way" transaction occurs (GASB-34, par. 112, as amended by GASB-63, par. 8) [GASB Cod. Sec. 1800.102].

Interfund Loans (Reciprocal Interfund Activity)

Many governments initiate advances or loans between funds. These are different from short-term amounts due to and due from funds based upon the notion that amounts due to and due from would be "repaid within a reasonable time." The concept of a loan as envisioned by GASB-34 is based on the expectation that the loan will be repaid at some point. Loans should be reported as interfund receivables by the lender fund and interfund payables by the borrower fund. That is, the interfund loan should not be eliminated in the preparation of financial statements at the fund level. Thus, the proceeds from interfund loans should not be reported as "other financing sources or uses" in the operating statements in the fund financial statements. If a loan or a portion of a loan is not expected to be repaid *within a reasonable time*, the interfund receivable / payable should be reduced by the amount not expected to be repaid and that amount should be reported as an interfund transfer by both funds that are a party to the transfer.

The *GASB Implementation Guide 2015-1* addresses the question of what is meant by "repaid within a reasonable time." The *Guide's* answer in question 7.82.1 [GASB Cod. Sec. 1800.702-8] is as follows:

> There is no precise definition of the provision. Professional judgment should be exercised in determining whether an interfund loan should be reclassified. The *expectation* aspect of the phrase means that the government intends to, and has the ability to, repay the amount loaned. For example, recurring payments made to reduce the interfund loan balance may provide evidence that "repayment is expected." What constitutes a *reasonable time* for repayment is again a matter of professional judgment, but the notion is not without precedent in financial reporting standards. GASB-10 invokes a "reasonable time" consideration in paragraphs 66(b) and 68, as amended, [GASB Cod. Secs. C50.128(b), .130] with regard to recovery of the full cost of internal service fund expenses.

If there is some doubt about repayment, a government may tend to want to use an allowance account against a receivable. However, the receivables, net of allowances for doubtful accounts will not balance against the offsetting payable account in the paying fund. If there is any doubt about repayment, a government should use transfers, rather than interfund loans.

Interfund Services Provided and Used (Reciprocal Interfund Activity)

Interfund receivables/payables may arise from an operating activity (i.e., the sale of goods and services) between funds rather than in the form of a loan arrangement. If the interfund operating activity is recorded at an amount that approximates the fair value of the goods or services exchanged, the provider / seller fund should record the activity as revenue and the user/purchaser fund should record an expenditure / expense, not an interfund transfer. Any unpaid balance at the end of the period should be reported as an interfund receivable/payable in the fund balance sheet or statement of net position.

OBSERVATION: GASB-34 (par. 112, footnote 45) [GASB Cod. Sec. 1800.102, fn. 1] points out that GASB-10 (*Accounting and Financial Reporting for Risk Financing and Related Insurance Issues*), paragraph 64 [GASB Cod. Sec. C50.126], requires that when the General Fund is used to account for risk-financing activities, interfund charges to other funds must be accounted for as interfund reimbursements.

Interfund Transfers (Nonreciprocal Interfund Activity)

This type of nonreciprocal transaction represents interfund activities whereby the two parties to the events do not receive equivalent cash, goods, or services. Governmental funds should report transfers of this nature in their activity statements as other financing uses and other financial sources of funds. Proprietary funds should report this type of transfer in their activity statements following net income (loss) before transfers.

Based on the standards established by GASB-34, there is no differentiation between operating transfers and residual equity transfers. Thus, equity-type transfers should not be reported as adjustments to a fund's beginning equity balance.

GASB-34 contains guidance on payments *in lieu of taxes* from other enterprise funds to governmental funds. These payments should be reported as interfund transfers, *unless the payments and services received are equivalent in value based on the exchange of specific services or goods*. If the two are equivalent in value, the disbursing fund may treat the payment as an expenditure (expense) and the receiving fund may record revenue.

Interfund Reimbursements (Nonreciprocal Interfund Activity)

A fund may incur expenditures or expenses that will subsequently be reimbursed by another fund. Reimbursements should not be reported in the governmental entity's financial statements in order to avoid "double counting" revenues and expense / expenditure items. To illustrate, assume that the General Fund pays a utility bill of $50,000 for an Enterprise Fund. The initial payment is recorded as follows in the General Fund:

	Debit	Credit
Expenditures—Utilities	50,000	
Cash		50,000

When the Enterprise Fund reimburses the General Fund at a later date, the General Fund reverses its original entry:

	Debit	Credit
Cash	50,000	
Expenditures—Utilities		50,000

Reporting Eliminations and Reclassifications in Government-Wide Financial Statements

The preparation of government-wide financial statements is based on a consolidating process (similar to corporate consolidations) rather than a combining process. These eliminations and reclassifications related to the consolidation process are based on (1) internal balances (statement of net position), (2) internal activities (statement of activities), (3) intra-entity activity, and (4) Internal Service Fund balances.

Internal Balances (Statement of Net Position)

The government-wide financial statements present the governmental entity and its blended component units as a single reporting entity. Based on this philosophy, most balances between funds that are initially recorded as interfund receivables and payables at the individual fund level should be eliminated in the preparation of the statement of net position within each of the two major reporting groups of the primary government (the government activities and business-type activities). The purpose of the elimination is to avoid the "grossing-up" effect on assets and liabilities presented on the statement of net position within the governmental and business-type activities columns.

For example, if there is an interfund receivable / payable between the General Fund and a Special Revenue Fund, those amounts would be eliminated in order to determine the balances that would appear in the governmental activities column. Likewise, if there is an interfund receivable/payable between two proprietary funds of the primary government, those amounts would also be eliminated in the business-type activities column. However, the net residual interfund receivable/payable between governmental and business-type activities should not be eliminated but should be presented in each column (government activities and business- type activities) and labeled as "internal balances" or a similar description. These amounts will be the same and, therefore, will cancel out when they are combined (horizontally) in the statement of net position in order to form the column for total primary government activities.

OBSERVATION: Generally, a governmental entity will maintain its accounting transactions using the conventional-fund approach and convert this information to a government-wide basis using the flow of economic resources and accrual basis of accounting at the time the government-wide financial statements are prepared. Thus, at the fund level the internal balance between a governmental fund (reported on the modified accrual basis) may not equal the related balance with a proprietary fund (reported on the accrual basis); however, once the governmental fund activity is adjusted to the government-wide presentation, those adjusted amounts will equal the amounts presented in the proprietary funds.

> **PRACTICE POINT:** Transfers between a primary government and a blended component unit are common. Some of these component units may have a different fiscal year, resulting in an out of balance condition due to the timing of the reporting dates. As explained in the GASB *Implementation Guide 2015-1*, question 7.22.10 [GASB Cod. Sec. 1800.703-1], this situation is allowable, as long as GASB-14 (*The Financial Reporting Entity*), paragraph 60 [GASB Cod. Sec. 2600.120], is followed, stating the reason for the imbalance in the notes. Some practitioners provide a reconciliation of net position changes rather than just disclosing the imbalance due to "timing."

There also may be interfund receivables/payables that arise because of transactions between the primary government and its fiduciary funds. These amounts should not be eliminated, but rather should be reported on the statement of net position similar to receivables from and payables to external parties (GASB-34, par. 58, as amended by GASB-63, par. 8 and GASB-65, par. 13) [GASB Cod. Sec. 1800.103].

> **NOTE:** The financial statements of fiduciary funds are not consolidated as part of the government-wide financial statements.

Interfund balances between fiduciary funds and other funds (governmental and proprietary funds) are reported in fund financial statements but, as noted above, are not part of the internal balance amount reported on the statement of net position (government-wide financial statement). The *GASB Implementation Guide 2015-1*, in question 7.52.1 [GASB Cod. Sec. 2300.710-1], reminds practitioners that there is no need to explain in a note to the financial statement that internal balances with fiduciary funds are not reported as part of the internal balance. However, a governmental entity may (but is not required to) add some clarity to this difference by using one or both of the following approaches:

- Include an explanation in the note required by GASB-38, paragraph 14 [GASB Cod. Secs. 2300.106, .126], with respect to the identification of the amounts due from other funds by (1) individual major funds, (2) aggregated non-major governmental funds, (3) aggregated non-major Enterprise Funds, (4) aggregated Internal Service Funds, and (5) fiduciary fund types.

- Separately present in the fund financial statements the amounts due to / from fiduciary funds from amounts due to/from other funds.

Internal Activities (Statement of Activities)

In order to avoid the "doubling-up" effect of internal activities among funds, interfund transactions should be eliminated so that expenses and revenues are recorded only once. For example, a fund (generally the General Fund or an Internal Service Fund) may charge other funds for services provided (such as insurance coverage or allocation of overhead expenses) on an internal basis. When these funds are consolidated in order to present the functional expenses of governmental activities in the statement of activities, the double counting of the expense (with an offset to revenue recorded by the provider fund) should be eliminated in a manner so that "the allocated expenses are reported only by the function to which they were allocated" (GASB-34, par. 59) [GASB Cod. Sec. 1800.104].

Internal activities should not be eliminated when they are classified as "interfund services provided and used." For example, when a municipal water company charges a fee for services provided to the general government, the expense and revenues related to those activities should not be eliminated (GASB-34, par. 60) [GASB Cod. Sec. 1800.105]. (This type of internal activity is further discussed in Chapter 20, "Comprehensive Annual Financial Report.")

Intra-Entity Activity

Transactions (and related balances) between the primary government and its blended component units should be reclassified based on the guidance discussed in Chapter 20, "Comprehensive Annual Financial Report." Transactions (and related balances) between the primary government and its discretely presented component units should not be eliminated in the government-wide financial statements. That is, the two parties to the transactions should report revenue and expense accounts as originally recorded in those respective funds. Amounts payable and receivable between the primary government and its discretely presented component units should be reported as separate line items on the statement of net position. Likewise, payables and receivables between discretely presented component units must also be reported separately (GASB-34, par. 61, as amended by GASB-63, par. 8 and GASB-65, par. 13) [GASB Cod. Sec. 1800.106].

GASB-48 provides financial statement users with consistent measurement, recognition, and disclosure across governments and within individual governments relating to the accounting for sales and pledges of receivables and future revenues and intra-entity transfers of assets and future revenues. See further discussion of accounting and reporting treatment for intra-entity transfers of assets and future revenues in Chapter 17, "Revenues: Nonexchange and Exchange Transactions."

Internal Service Fund Balances

As described above, internal services and similar activities should be eliminated to avoid doubling-up expenses and revenues when preparing the governmental-activities column of the statement of activities. The effect of this approach is to adjust activities in an Internal Service Fund to a "break-even" balance. That is, if the Internal Service Fund had a "net profit" for the year, there should be a pro rata reduction in the charges made to the funds that used the Internal Service Fund's services for the year. Likewise, a net loss would require a pro rata adjustment that would increase the charges made to the various participating funds. After making these eliminations, any residual balances related to the Internal Service Fund's assets and liabilities should be reported in the governmental activities column in the government-wide statement of net position (GASB-34, par. 62, as amended by GASB-63, pars. 7–8) [GASB Cod. Sec. 1800.107].

In some instances, an internal service may not be accounted for in an Internal Service Fund but rather accounted for in another governmental fund (generally the General Fund or a Special Revenue Fund). Furthermore, the internal-service transaction may not cut across functional expense categories. That is, there is a "billing" between different departments, but the expenses of those departments are all included in the same functional expenses. Conceptually, the same break-even approach as described above should be applied so as not to gross-up expenses and program revenues of a particular functional expense; however, the GASB does not require that an elimination be made (unless the amounts are material) because the result of this non-elimination is that direct expenses and program revenues are overstated by equal amounts but net (expense) revenue related to the function is not overstated.

The GASB takes the position that activities conducted with an Internal Service Fund are generally reported as government activities rather than business-type activities, even though an Internal Service Fund uses the flow of economic resources and the accrual basis of accounting. However, when Enterprise Funds account for all or the predominant activities of an Internal Service Fund, the Internal Service Fund's residual assets and liabilities should be reported in the business-type activities column of the statement of net position.

OBSERVATION: For internal service fund activities that are reimbursed out of federal funds, the *Uniform Administrative Requirements, Cost Principles and Audit Requirements for Federal Awards* subpart E places stringent requirements on what can be charged as an "allowable cost," with an emphasis on consistent accounting no matter what the source of funds is. Complete coverage of the updated provisions from an auditing perspective is found in CCH's *Knowledge-Based Audits*™ *of State and Local Governments with Single Audits.*

TERMINOLOGY AND CLASSIFICATION IN GOVERNMENTAL FUND FINANCIAL STATEMENTS

Debt Issuance Proceeds

In governmental funds the proceeds from the issuance of long-term debt are recorded not as a liability but as an "other financing source" on the statement of revenues, expenditures, and changes in fund balances, using such captions as "bond issue proceeds" and "proceeds from the issuance of long-term notes (or debt)." This is due to the emphasis on the current financial resources of the governmental funds. Discounts and premiums and certain payments to escrow agents for bond refundings should also be reported as other financing sources and uses. Proceeds from the issuance of special assessment debt for which a government entity is "not obligated in any manner" should not be referred to as bond proceeds but instead titled as "contributions from property owners"

(NCGA-1, par. 108; GASB-6, par. 19; and GASB-34, par. 88, as amended by GASB-37, par. 16) [GASB Cod. Secs. 1800.124, S40.119].

PRACTICE POINT: The treatment of debt issuance proceeds is one of the challenges that governmental funds have in the measurement focus and basis of accounting. Given the short-term focus of many governments, some believe it is understandable that debt issuance proceeds is an inflow (revenue). But in theory, a liability is created, even though it may not be due for a year or more. In the deliberations to the GASB's *Financial Reporting Model—Reexamination* project, the GASB has preliminarily concluded that tax and revenue anticipation notes in advance of such inflows would be liabilities of governmental funds. This is due to the GASB's preliminary view resulting in a longer period of availability.

Resources received based on current and advance refundings related to the defeasance of general long-term debt should be reported as an "other financing source" and given a label similar to "proceeds of refunding bonds" to describe the transaction. Related payments to the escrow agent should be reported as an "other financing use" and identified as "payments to refunded bond escrow agent." However, when the payments are made to an escrow agent using funds other than those related to the refunding, the repayment should be reported as debt service expenditures (GASB-7, par. 8; GASB-34, pars. 82 and 88, GASB-37, par. 16) [GASB Cod. Sec. 1800.125].

PRACTICE ALERT: The federal Tax Cuts and Jobs Act of 2017, Section 13532, repeals the ability for states and local governments to advance refund bonds after December 31, 2017 and remaining tax exempt. It is unclear as of the date of publication if the GASB will amend GASB-related provisions Statements 7, 34, 37, and 23 to reflect this repeal.

Other Debt Issuance Transactions

GASB-65 (*Items Previously Reported as Assets and Liabilities*), paragraph 15, requires debt issuance costs to be reported as outlays for all types of funds, not just governmental funds. Debt issuance costs do not include prepaid insurance costs. Prepaid insurance costs are reported as an asset and amortized systematically and rationally over the duration of the related debt, except such costs are expended when incurred in governmental funds (GASB-62, par. 187, as amended by GASB-65, par. 15) [GASB Cod. Sec. I30.115].

PRACTICE ALERT: As part of the GASB's *Financial Reporting Model— Reexamination* project, the effect of prepaid insurance costs on governmental funds was deliberated. As the GASB's preliminary view is to extend the period of availability for governmental funds to one year, prepaid items such as insurance would be recognized as assets, unless beyond one year.

Demand Bonds

Demand bonds may be reported as long-term debt of the government when all of the following criteria are met:

- Before the financial statements are issued, the issuer has entered into an arm's-length financing (takeout) agreement to convert bonds "put" but not resold into some other form of long-term obligation.

- The takeout agreement does not expire within one year from the date of the issuer's balance sheet.

- The takeout agreement is not cancelable by the lender or the prospective lender during that year, and obligations incurred under the takeout agreement are not callable by the lender during that year.

- The lender or the prospective lender or investor is expected to be financially capable of honoring the takeout agreement.

When the conditions of GASB Interpretation No. 1 (GASBI-1) (Demand Bonds Issued by State and Local Governmental Entities) have not been met, demand bonds must be presented as a liability of the fund that received the proceeds from the issuance of the bonds, or as a current liability if the proceeds were received by a proprietary fund. If demand bonds are issued and no takeout agreement has been executed at their issuance date or at the balance sheet date, the bonds cannot be considered a long-term liability.

If the demand bonds are presented for redemption, the redemption should be recorded as a reduction of bonds payable.

Demand bonds that were originally classified as general long-term debt because a take-out agreement existed at the issuance date of the bonds would have to be reclassified if the original takeout agreement expires. Under this circumstance, it would be necessary to establish a liability in the fund that originally recorded the demand bond proceeds. Any actual bond redemption occurring after the debt is reclassified as the liability of a specific governmental fund should be recorded as an expenditure of the fund that accounts for the servicing of the debt (GASBI-1, pars. 10 and 13, as amended by GASB-63, par. 8, GASB-34, pars. 12, 82, 91, and 97, as amended by GASB-62, pars. 29–43) [GASB Cod. Secs. 1800.127, D30.108-109].

A full discussion on debt transactions and disclosures is contained in Chapter 12, "Long-Term Debt."

Capital Lease Transactions

Because general capital assets of a governmental fund do not represent current financial resources available for appropriation and expenditure, a capital lease transaction should not be reported as a capital asset and a liability of a governmental fund. GASB-62, paragraphs 211-271 [GASB Cod. Sec. L20], contain an extensive discussion of leases. When a capitalized lease represents the purchase or construction of general capital assets, the transaction should be shown as a capital outlay expenditure and other financing sources in a governmental fund.

However, it is converted to an increase in capital assets and capitalized leases (a liability) on the statement of net position.

PRACTICE ALERT: In June 2017, the GASB released Statement No. 87 (*Leases*). A lease will be defined as a contract that conveys the right to use a nonfinancial asset (the underlying asset) for a period of time in an exchange or exchange-like transaction. Examples of nonfinancial assets include buildings, land, vehicles, and equipment. Any contract that meets this definition will be accounted for under the updated leases guidance upon implementation, unless specifically excluded. GASB-87 has an effective date of a final standard for reporting periods beginning after December 15, 2019. For June 30th governments, the effective date would be for periods beginning after July 1, 2020. Leases will be recognized and measured using the facts and circumstances that exist at the beginning of the period of implementation (or, if applied to earlier periods, the beginning of the earliest period restated).

A more thorough discussion of GASB-87 is contained in Chapter 14, "Leases and Service Concession Arrangements."

Capital Asset Sales

When a governmental entity sells a capital asset of a governmental fund, the proceeds from the sale should be reported as an other financing source, unless the transactions meets the definition of a special item (events within the control of management that are either unusual in nature or infrequent in occurrence—discussed later in this chapter) as defined by GASB-34 (GASB-34, pars. 56 and 88) [GASB Cod. Sec. 1800.126].

Revenue and Expenditure Classification

A governmental fund's results of operations are presented in a statement of revenues and expenditures and changes in fund balances. This statement should reflect the all-inclusive concept, and all financial transactions and events that affect the fund's operations for the period should be presented in the activity statement. A governmental fund's activity statement is *not* referred to as an income statement because the accounting basis for its preparation is the modified accrual basis, not the accrual basis. Similarly, net income is *not* an element presented in a governmental fund's activity statement for the same reason and also because the statement does not reflect allocations of various economic resources, such as the depreciation of capital assets (NCGA-1, par. 57) [GASB Cod. Secs. 1100.110, 1600 et seq.].

Revenues

For governmental funds, NCGA-1 defines "revenues" as an "increase in (sources of) fund financial resources other than from interfund transfers and debt issue proceeds." Revenues should be classified by fund and source. Revenues applicable to a particular fund should be reflected in the fund's activity statement and should not be attributed to another fund. NCGA-1 notes that major revenue sources include taxes, licenses and permits, intergovernmental revenues, charges for services, fines and forfeits, and miscellaneous items. More generically, revenues are a form of inflows of resources, which are defined in GASB:CS-4, pars. 28–31: "An *inflow of resources* is an acquisition of (net position) by the government that is applicable to the reporting period."

As a supplement to the accumulation of revenues by fund and source, revenues may be classified in various ways to facilitate management evaluation and preparation of special reports or analyses, or to aid in the audit or review of accounts. For example, revenues may be classified by the operating division or branch responsible for their actual collection (NCGA-1, par. 110) [GASB Cod. Sec. 1800.131].

Expenditures

Governmental fund expenditures represent decreases in or uses of fund financial resources, except for those transactions that result in transfers to other funds. Initially, expenditures should be classified according to the fund accountable for the disbursement. To facilitate both internal and external analysis and reporting, expenditures may be classified further by (1) function (or program), (2) organizational unit, (3) activity, (4) character, and (5) object class (NCGA-1, par. 109, as amended by GASB-6, par. 9, GASB-7, par. 8 and GASBI-1, par. 13 and NCGA-1, par. 111) [GASB Cod. Secs. 1800.130, .132].

More generically, expenditures and expenses are forms of *outflows of resources*, also defined in GASB:CS-4 (pars. 24–27): "An outflow of resources is a consumption of (net position) by the government that is applicable to the reporting period."

Function (or program) classification. Functions refer to major services provided by the governmental unit or responsibilities established by specific laws or regulations. Classifications included as functions are, for example, public safety, highways and streets, general governmental services, education, and health and welfare. Rather than use a functional classification, a governmental unit that employs program budgeting may group its expenditures by program classifications and sub-classifications. A program classification scheme groups activities related to the achievement of a specific purpose or objective. Program groupings would include activities such as programs for the elderly, drug addiction, and adult education (NCGA-1, par. 112) [GASB Cod. Sec. 1800.133].

Organizational unit classification. An accounting system should incorporate the concept of "responsibility accounting" so that information reflecting a unit's responsibility for activities and expenditures will be present in the system. When an organization is responsible for certain expenditures, but the expenditures are not coded so the disbursements can be associated with the organization, it becomes difficult to hold the organizational unit responsible for the activity. Organizational unit classification generally groups expenditures based on the operational structure (department, agencies, etc.) of the governmental unit. Often, functions or programs are administered by two or more organizational units; for example, if the responsibility for the public safety function is shared by the police and fire departments (NCGA-1, par. 113) [GASB Cod. Sec. 1800.134].

Activity Classification. Function or program classifications are broad in nature and often do not provide a basis for adequately analyzing governmental operations. For this reason, expenditures may be associated with specific activities, thus allowing measurement standards to be established. These standards can be used (1) as a basis for evaluating the economy and efficiency of operations and (2) as a basis for budget preparation. Also, grouping expenditures by activity is an important part of management accounting in which decisions may require the development of accounting data different from the information presented in the external financial reports. For example, in a make-or-buy decision, it may be necessary to consider a depreciation factor in computing a per unit cost figure (for external reporting purposes, depreciation is not generally presented) (NCGA-1, par. 114, as amended by GASB-34, pars. 22, 38, and 80) [GASB Cod. Sec. 1800.135].

Character classification. Categorizing expenditures by character refers to the fiscal year that will benefit from the expenditure. Character classifications include the following (NCGA-1, par. 115) [GASB Cod. Sec. 1800.136]:

Character	Period(s) Benefited
Current expenditures	Current period
Capital outlays	Current and future periods
Debt service	Current, future, and prior periods
Intergovernmental	Depends on the nature of the programs financed by the revenue

As discussed in the following section, object classes are subdivisions of expenditure character groupings.

Object classification. Object classes represent the specific items purchased or services acquired within the overall character classifications. For example, debt service expenditures can be further classified as payments for principal and interest, while current expenditures by object class may include the purchase of supplies and disbursements for payroll.

NCGA-1 recognizes that external reporting of expenditures by object class should be restrained because the user, on both an internal and an external basis, could be overwhelmed by voluminous information that does not enhance the decision-making process (NCGA-1, par. 116) [GASB Cod. Sec. 1800.137].

PRACTICE ALERT: Chapter 3 of the Invitation to Comment (ITC), *Financial Reporting Model Improvements—Governmental Funds* partially focused on the format and content of the Governmental Funds Statement of Revenues, Expenditures and Changes in Fund Balances (also known as the Resource Flows Statement). Two formats were offered by GASB staff as alternatives: (1) retain the existing statement of revenues, expenditures and changes in fund balance format or (2) separating current and long-term activities. Even though the existing format continues traditional financial reporting of governmental funds, other financing sources and uses are inconsistent. Debt service is reported as expenditures rather than other financing uses. Proceeds from debt issuance is still considered an other financing source. Resources received from capital asset sales are other financing sources. Although purchases of capital assets are expenditures, rather than other financing uses. The current and long-term format would present flows for the period that correspond to long-term assets or liabilities that are not presented in the governmental fund balance sheet in the long-term portion of the Resource Flows statement. A potential benefit of this is internal consistency.

However, as of the date of publication, it is unclear if the existing format will change. Most notably is the GASB's preliminary view that if the government-wide Statement of Activities is presented by function (general government, public safety, education, etc.), then a schedule may be required presenting expenditures in the natural classification format or by object (payroll, employee benefits, travel, etc.). Most modern accounting systems capture this information in order to provide internal reporting, grant compliance and potentially payroll tax filings.

PRACTICE POINT: Many governments are subject to a uniform accounting system typically established by a state auditor, revenue department, or comptroller in order to facilitate reporting to a legislative body. Each fund authorized by legislation may have its own numbering system solely for the purpose of a consistent chart of accounts. A typical chart of accounts could be as follows for a fund:

Chart Element	Information
Fund number	100
Fund name	General Fund
Account Type Code (drop down box)	Asset (A), Deferred Outflow (DO), Liability (L), Deferred Inflow (DI), Fund Balance or Net Position (FB), Revenues and Other Financing Sources, (R), Expenditures and Other Financing Uses (E)
Account Number	5 digit numeric (example—10000)
Account Name	Text—(example—Cash)
Subaccount type	Specific digits (example—2 alphanumeric)
Subaccount name	Restricted (drop down for R)
Function	Text—(example City versus Component Unit) (to delineate areas of the reporting entity)
Subfunction	Text—(example areas of operations—general government, public safety, debt service, education, etc.)
Subfunction number	5 digit numeric (example—40000)
Subfunction name	40000 General Government
Character (expenditures)	Drop down text (Current operating expenditures, capital outlay, debt service, intergovernmental, others)
Object Class	Drop down text (Personnel, benefits, supplies, contractor charges, capital outlay, interest, transfers, others)
Object Code	Specific digits (example—3 numeric)
Object Code Name	100 Wages
Subobject Code	Specific digits (example—3 numeric)
Subobject name	103 Temporary employees (less than 400 hours)

Charts of accounts can be as simple or as complex based on the government's operations. In some cases, defining a new chart of accounts may take months or longer just to agree on responsibilities, security, and what reporting should look like. A best practice is to have a chart maintained centrally with clear lines of decision-making for effective internal controls and security.

TERMINOLOGY AND CLASSIFICATION IN PROPRIETARY FUND FINANCIAL STATEMENTS

Assets, deferred outflows of resources, liabilities, deferred inflows of resources, and net position are presented on the statement of net position of a proprietary fund and should be classified as current and long-term, based on the guidance established in GASB-62, pars. 30–44, and GASB-63 [GASB Cod. Secs. 1800.109–.123 with related sections in 1500, 2200, 2300]. The statement of net position may be presented in either one of the following formats:

- *Net position format:* Assets + Deferred outflows of resources – Liabilities – Deferred inflows of resources = Net Position.

- *Balance sheet format:* Assets + Deferred outflows of resources = Liabilities + Deferred inflows of resources + Net position.

Net position should be identified as (1) net investment in capital assets, (2) restricted, and (3) unrestricted. The guidance discussed earlier (in the context of government-wide financial statements) should be used to determine what amounts should be related to these three categories of net position. GASB-34 notes that capital contributions should not be presented as a separate component of net position. Also, similar to the guidance for government-wide financial statements, designations of net position cannot be identified on the face of the proprietary fund statement of net position (GASB-34, pars. 97–98) [GASB Cod. Secs. 1400.115, 2200.172, D30.108, P80.110, 1800.164, 2200.173, C50.129].

GASB-34 did not change the previous standards used to account for capital assets of a proprietary fund; however, the modified approach to reporting infrastructure asset systems (as described in Chapter 10, "Capital Assets") can also be used to account for these capital assets when they are presented in a proprietary fund. For example, a highway reported under the modified approach that is part of a toll road system could be accounted for in an Enterprise Fund.

Revenues of a proprietary fund should be reported by major sources, and expenses should be classified in a manner similar to a business entity that is involved in the same activities as the proprietary fund. However, the presentation of information in a proprietary fund's financial statements cannot be inconsistent with guidance provided by the GASB, including pronouncements issued by its predecessor (NCGA-1, par. 117; GASB-34, par. 100, and GASB-63, par. 8) [GASB Cod. Secs. 1100.112, 1800.101, .138, .152, 2200.190, 2450 fn5, P80.113, P80.116 and S40.122).

PRACTICE ALERT: A major portion of the second phase of the GASB's *Financial Reporting Model—Reexamination* project may result in a clearer definition of operating versus nonoperating revenues and expenses of proprietary funds. Some practitioners desire revenue and expense reporting aligned to an entity's mission. The GASB's preliminary view may focus on whether an operation is self-sustaining (where revenues provide for expenses) or subsidies are needed to fund expenses. The subsidies may be a defining point of what is nonoperating revenues and expenses. Proprietary activities ranging from airports to zoos are closely following this deliberation as the result may have a major impact on their financial operations and debt compliance measures.

For a discussion of the reporting standards that apply to proprietary fund activities see the Enterprise Funds section of Chapter 7, "Proprietary Funds."

TERMINOLOGY AND CLASSIFICATION IN GOVERNMENT-WIDE FINANCIAL STATEMENTS

Statement of Activities

The format for the government-wide statement of activities is significantly different from any operating statement used in fund financial reporting. The focus of the statement of activities is on the *net cost* of various activities provided by the governmental entity. The statement begins with a column that identifies the cost of each governmental activity. Another column identifies the revenues that are specifically related to the classified activities. The difference between the expenses and revenues related to specific activities computes the net cost or benefits of the activities, which "identifies the extent to which each function of the government draws from the general revenues of the government or is self-financing through fees and intergovernmental aid" (GASB-34, pars. 38–40).

The GASB established the unique presentation format for the statement of activities in part because it believes that format provides an opportunity to provide feedback on a typical economic question that is asked when a program is adopted; namely, "What will the program cost and how will it be financed?"

The governmental entity must determine the level at which governmental activities are to be presented; however, the level of detail must be at least as detailed as that provided in the governmental fund financial statements (which are discussed later). Generally, activities would be aggregated and presented at the functional category level; however, entities are encouraged to present activities at a more detailed level, such as by programs.

Due to the size and complexities of some governmental entities, it may be impractical to expand the level of detail beyond that of functional categories. The minimum level of detail at which governmental activities can be presented is discussed in paragraphs 111–116 of NCGA-1 [GASB Cod. Secs. 1800.132–.137]. Business-type activities should be reported at the level of segments, which is defined later in this chapter. The GASB encourages governmental entities to expand the detail level from functions (which is very broad) to more specific levels, such as programs and services. However, the GASB was concerned about requiring a more detailed expense format presentation than was required by then current standards.

Once the level of detail is determined, the primary government's expenses for each governmental activity should be presented. It should be noted that these are expenses and not expenditures and are based on the concept of the flow of economic resources, which includes depreciation expense. As noted earlier, the minimum level of detail allowed by GASB-34 is functional program categories, such as general government, public safety, parks and recreation, and public works. At a minimum, each functional program should include direct expenses, which are defined as "those that are specifically associated with a service, program, or department and, thus, are clearly identifiable to a particular function" (GASB-34, par. 41) [GASB Cod. Secs. 1800.141, 2200.129, C50.121].

PRACTICE ALERT: The aforementioned preliminary views document as part of the next phase of the GASB's *Financial Reporting Model—Reexamination* project considers alternatives for the format of the Statement of Activities. Many stakeholders have voiced their opinion desiring a more traditional revenue and expense format for a Statement with revenues above expenses, rather than expenses offset by revenues. Should the format change to a more traditional revenue and expense format, one of the provisions as a result of the change is a schedule in the notes to the basic financial statements or in required supplementary (or supplementary information) showing expenses based on object classification in a similar manner to what is required for not-for-profit entities and what is commonly presented by public institutions of higher education.

Revenues and Other Resource Inflows

A fundamental concept in the formatting of the statement of activities, as described above, is the identification of resource inflows to the governmental entities that are related to specific programs and those that are general in nature. GASB-34 notes that specific governmental activities are generally financed from the following sources of resource inflows:

- Parties who purchase, use, or directly benefit from goods and services provided through the program (e.g., fees for public transportation and licenses);
- Outside parties (other governments and nongovernmental entities or individuals) who provide resources to the governmental entity (e.g., a grant to a local government from a state government);
- The reporting government's constituencies (e.g., property taxes); and
- The governmental entity (e.g., investment income).

The first source of the resources listed above is always program revenue. The second source is program revenue if it is restricted to a specific program, otherwise the item is considered general revenue. The third source is always general revenue, even when restricted. The fourth source of resources is usually general revenue.

Using this classification scheme the governmental entity should format its statement of activities based on the following broad categories of resource inflows (GASB-34, par. 47) [GASB Cod. Sec. 2200.135]:

- Program revenues
  - Charges for services
  - Operating grants and contributions
  - Capital grants and contributions

- General revenues
- Contributions to permanent funds
- Extraordinary items
- Special items
- Transfers.

Program revenues. These revenues arise because the specific program with which they are identified exists, otherwise the revenues would not flow to the governmental entity. Program revenues are presented on the statement of activities as a subtraction from the related program expense in order to identify the net cost (or benefit) of a particular program. This formatting scheme enables a reader of a governmental entity's statements to identify those programs that are providing resources that may be used for other governmental functions or those that are being financed from general revenues and other resources. Program revenues should be segregated into (1) charges for services, (2) operating grants and contributions, and (3) capital grants and contributions (GASB-34, par. 48) [GASB Cod. Secs. 1800.142, 2200.136].

Identifying revenues with a particular function does not mean that revenues must be allocated to a function. Revenues are related to a function only when they are directly related to the function. If no direct relationship is obvious, the revenue is a general revenue, not a program revenue.

Charges for services. Revenues that are characterized as charges for services are based on exchange or exchange-like transactions and arise from charges for providing goods, services, and privileges to customers or applicants who acquire goods, services, or privileges directly from a governmental entity. Generally, these and similar charges are intended to cover, at least to some extent, the cost of goods and services provided to various parties. GASB-37 lists the following as examples of charges-for-services revenue (GASB-37, par. 13) [GASB Cod. Sec. 2200.137]:

Type of Charge for Service	Common Examples
Service Charges	Water usage fees, garbage collection fees, any other "fee for service"
License and permit fees	Dog licenses, liquor licenses, building permits
Operating special assessments	Street cleaning, special-street lighting, other direct to taxpayer assessments for a specific area or jurisdiction
Intergovernmental charges based on exchange transactions	A County charging a City for housing of short-term jailed prisoners

Program-specific grants and contributions (operating and capital). Governmental entities may receive mandatory and voluntary grants or contributions (nonexchange transactions) from other governments or individuals that must be used for a particular governmental activity. For example, a state government may provide grants to localities that are to be used to reimburse costs related to adult literacy programs. These and other similar sources of assets should be reported as program-specific grants and contributions in the statement of activities but they must be separated into those that are for operating purposes and those that are for capital purposes. If a grant or contribution can be used either for operating or capital purposes, at the discretion of the governmental entity, it should be reported as an operating contribution (GASB-34, par. 50) [GASB Cod. Secs. 1400.154–.155, 2200.138, S40.125].

NOTE: Mandatory and voluntary nonexchange transactions are defined in GASB-33 (*Accounting and Financial Reporting for Nonexchange Transactions*) as amended by GASB-65 (see Chapter 17, "Revenues: Nonexchange and Exchange Transactions").

Grants and contributions that are provided to finance more than one program (multipurpose grants) should be reported as program-specific grants "if the amounts restricted to each program are specifically identified in either the grant award or the grant application." (The grant application should be used in this manner only if the grant was based on the application.) If the amount of the multipurpose grants cannot be identified with particular programs, the revenue should be reported as general revenues rather than program-specific grants and contributions.

OBSERVATION: If a government uses a cost allocation plan (typically federal or state approved), certain costs such as general government, support services, and administration might be allocated to functions before revenues are shown in the statement of activities. Although there is no requirement to allocate these indirect costs, posting this cost allocation plan is more of a full-costing approach to expenses. These allocated costs should be shown in a separate column from the "direct" program expenses. However, in practice, this portrayal is rarely used. If it is used, a subtotal column showing total expenses is not required (GASB-34, par. 42) [GASB Cod. Sec. 2200.130].

Investment earnings. Earnings related to endowments or permanent fund investments are considered program revenues if those are restricted to a specific program use; however, the restriction must be based on either an explicit clause in the endowment agreement or contract. Likewise, earnings on investments that do not represent endowments or permanent fund arrangements are considered program revenues if they are legally restricted to a specific program. Investment earnings on endowments or permanent fund investments that are not restricted, and therefore are available for general operating expenses, are not program revenues but rather should be reported as general revenues in the statement of activities.

Earnings on investments *not related to permanent funds* that are legally restricted for a particular purpose should be reported as program revenues. Also, earnings on "invested accumulated resources" of a specific program that are legally restricted to the specific program should be reported as program revenues (GASB-34, par. 51) [GASB Cod. Sec. 2200.139].

> **PRACTICE POINT:** Understandably, investment earnings and related expenses are a prime focus area for fiduciary activities. A slightly different presentation of investment earnings occurs in fiduciary funds. This is further discussed in Chapter 8, "Fiduciary Funds," and Chapter 9, "Deposits, Investments, and Derivative Instruments."

General revenues. General revenue should be reported in the lower portion of the statement of activities. Such revenues include resource flows related to income taxes, sales taxes, franchise taxes, and property taxes, and they should be separately identified in the statement. Nontax sources of resources that are not reported as program revenues must be reported as general revenues. This latter group includes unrestricted grants, unrestricted contributions, and investment income (GASB-34, par. 52) [GASB Cod. Secs. 1400.154–.55, 1800.143, 2200.140].

General revenues are used to offset the net (expense) revenue amounts computed in the upper portion of the presentation, and the resulting amounts are labeled as excess (deficiency) of revenues over expenses before extraordinary items and special items.

> **OBSERVATION:** All taxes, including dedicated taxes (e.g., motor fuel taxes) are considered general revenues rather than program revenues. The GASB takes the position that only charges to program customers or program-specific grants and contributions should be characterized as reducing the net cost of a particular governmental activity.

Contributions to permanent funds. When a governmental entity receives contributions to its term and permanent endowments or to permanent fund principal, those contributions should be reported as separate items in the lower portion of the statement of activities. These receipts are not considered to be program revenues (such as program-specific grants) because, as in the case of term endowments, there is an uncertainty of the timing of the release of the resources from the term restriction and, as in the case of permanent contributions, the principal can never be expended (GASB-34, par. 53) [GASB Cod. Secs. 1100.112, 1800, 2200.141].

> **PRACTICE ALERT:** The status of permanent funds is part of the GASB's *Financial Reporting Model—Reexamination* project.

Extraordinary items. The next section of the statement of activities includes the category where extraordinary items (gains or losses) are presented. GASB-34 defines "extraordinary items" as both unusual in nature and infrequent in occurrence (GASB-34, par. 55) [GASB Cod. Secs. 1800.145, 2200.143, C50.121]. This definition was reiterated in GASB-62, pars. 46–50 [GASB Cod. Secs. 1800.148–.151, 2200.145–.150, 2300.107]. The GASB explained the difference between "extraordinary items" and "special items" (see next section) in GASB-62, par. 563, and GASB-34, par. 56. Because special items are "significant transactions or other events *within the control of management* that are either unusual in nature or infrequent in occurrence," extraordinary items are out of the control of management, while remaining unusual in nature or infrequent in occurrence.

Special items. As previously discussed, "special items" are described as "significant transactions or other events within the control of management that are either unusual in nature or infrequent in occurrence." Special items should be reported separately and before extraordinary items. If a significant transaction or other event occurs but is not within the control of management and that item is either unusual or infrequent, the item is not reported as a special item but the nature of the item must be described in a note to the financial statements (GASB-34, par. 56) [GASB Cod. Secs. 1800.146, 2200.144, 2300.107, C50.121].

Transfers. Transfers should be reported in the lower portion of the statement of activities (GASB-34, par. 53) GASB Cod. Secs. 1100.112, 1800, 2200.141]. (The standards that determine how transfers should be reported in the statement of activities were discussed earlier in this chapter.)

TERMINOLOGY AND CLASSIFICATION IN REPORTING EXTRAORDINARY AND SPECIAL ITEMS

Special and Extraordinary Items

Special items and extraordinary items, are presented after the category titled "other financing sources and uses." If a governmental entity has both special items and extraordinary items, they should be reported under a single heading labeled "special and extraordinary items." That is, there should not be separate broad headings for each type of item (GASB-34, par. 89) [GASB Cod. Secs. 1100.112, 1800, 2200.168, 2300.107]. (See Chapter 20, "Comprehensive Annual Financial Report," for further discussion of special and extraordinary items.)

When a significant transaction or other event occurs that is either unusual or infrequent but not both and is not under the control of management, that item should be reported in one of the following ways:

- Presented and identified as a separate line item in either the revenue or expenditures category; or
- Presented but not identified as a separate line item in either the revenue or expenditures category, and described in a note to the financial statements.

An extraordinary gain or loss related to the early extinguishment of debt cannot occur on a statement of revenues, expenditures, and changes in fund balances because this type of statement presents only the changes in current financial resources (as part of other financing sources and uses on the current financial resources measurement focus) and not gains and losses from economic events and transactions.

PRACTICE ALERT: Part of the third phase of the GASB's *Financial Reporting Model—Reexamination* project is expected to include the Board's consideration of alternatives to improve the consistency of application of the guidance for reporting extraordinary and special items. The FASB has recently updated its guidance on extraordinary and unusual items (the FASB version of special items) contained within Accounting Standards Update 2015-1. Unusual items have changed to "infrequently occurring items." The update became effective for annual periods and interim periods within those annual periods that began after December 15, 2015.

GASB-34 mandates that the following format be used for governmental funds (GASB-34, par. 86) [GASB Cod. Sec. 2200.165] for inserting information on special and extraordinary funds:

	Major Fund 1	Major Fund 2	Nonmajor Funds	Total
Revenues (detailed)	$XXX	$XXX	$XXX	$XXX
Expenditures (detailed)	XXX	XXX	XXX	XXX
Excess (deficiency) of revenues over (under) expenditures	XXX	XXX	XXX	XXX
Other financing sources and uses, including transfers (detailed)	XXX	XXX	XXX	XXX
Special and extraordinary items (detailed)	XXX	XXX	XXX	XXX
Net change in fund balance	XXX	XXX	XXX	XXX
Fund balances—beginning of period	XXX	XXX	XXX	XXX
Fund balances—end of period	$XXX	$XXX	$XXX	$XXX

For proprietary funds, special and extraordinary items are reported in the Statement of Revenues, Expenses and Changes in Net Position after all operating and non-operating revenues and expenses, capital contributions and additions to term and permanent endowments, as well as transfers.

TERMINOLOGY AND CLASSIFICATION IN REPORTING NET POSITION AND FUND BALANCES

Reporting Net Position in Proprietary Funds and Government-Wide Financial Statements

The provisions of GASB-63 (*Financial Reporting of Deferred Outflows of Resources, Deferred Inflows of Resources, and Net Position*) require a Statement of Net Position, incorporating Deferred Outflows and Inflows of Resources as applicable. Net position includes three elements: (1) net investment in capital assets, (2) restricted net position, and (3) unrestricted net position. Net Position is the sum of assets and deferred outflows of resources reduced by liabilities and deferred inflows of resources (deferred positions presented separately from assets and liabilities).

Net position represents the difference between a governmental entity's total assets and deferred outflows of resources and its total liabilities and deferred inflows of resources. The net position Statement of Net Position must identify the components of net position as follows (GASB-63, pars. 8–11) [GASB Cod. Secs. 1800.155–.156, .162, 2200.109, .117–.119, .124]:

- Net investment in capital assets;
- Restricted net position; and
- Unrestricted net position.

Net Investment in Capital Assets

In a statement of net position, the net investment in capital assets consists of the capital assets, net of accumulated depreciation, reduced by

- The outstanding balances of bonds, mortgages, notes, or other borrowings (including leases) attributable to the acquisition, construction, or improvement of those assets.

- Deferred outflows of resources and deferred inflows of resources that are attributable to the acquisition, construction, or improvement of those assets or related debt are also included.

When debt has been used to finance the acquisition, construction, or improvement of capital assets but all or part of the cash has not been spent by the end of the fiscal year, the unspent portion of the debt should not be used to determine the amount of invested capital assets (net of related debt) amount. The portion of the unspent debt "should be included in the same net assets component as the unspent proceeds—for example, *restricted for capital projects*."

In GASB-63, the GASB concluded that if the unspent portion of the capital related debt was considered "capital related," the net investment in capital assets component of net position (net position) would be understated because there would be no capital assets to offset the debt. On the other hand, including the unspent proceeds with capital assets would not be appropriate. Under GASB-63, if the amounts are significant, they are excluded.

OBSERVATION: In addition, many large general-purpose governments such as states construct assets and issue debt for municipalities or entities that are not part of the government's reporting entity. The GASB's *Implementation Guide 2015-1*, question 7.23.10 [GASB Cod. Sec. 2200.708-12], addresses the situation where debt is issued but assets are not present. The issuing government acquires no capital assets; therefore, the debt is not "capital-related." The effect of the noncapital debt should be reflected in the unrestricted component of the government's net position. The fact that the bonds are related to capital assets of another entity does not make the debt "capital" debt of the issuing government—even though the assets acquired may benefit its residents in the case of a special district within a city. The government has incurred a liability, decreasing its net position, with no corresponding increase in its capital or financial assets. The effect on the government's total net position should be the same regardless of whether it (1) gave the special district cash from existing resources, (2) constructed or acquired assets and donated them to the district, or (3) issued debt to finance the construction or acquisition. In all three instances, the government has decreased its net position. If the effect on unrestricted net position is significant, the government may disclose additional details of unrestricted net position in the notes to the financial statements to isolate the effect of debt issued for others. The government may also address these circumstances in the Management's Discussion and Analysis as part of either the net position or debt discussions.

Common errors made by financial statement preparers when calculating this net position component include the following:

- Failure to properly reduce the "related debt" amount by the balance of unspent capital debt proceeds before it is netted against capital assets;

- Failure to include capital debt related accounts such as bond premiums and discounts in the computation;

- Failure to exclude issued debt (including leases) for noncapital assets; and

- Improper inclusion of net position restricted for capital related debt service (future debt service is not used for capital asset acquisition or construction).

In determining capital-related debt, governments are not expected to categorize all uses of bond proceeds to determine how much of the debt actually relates to assets that have been capitalized. Unless a significant portion of the debt proceeds is spent for non-capitalized purposes, the entire amount could be considered "capital-related." In addition, if debt is issued to refund existing capital-related debt, the new debt is also considered capital-related because the replacement debt assumes the capital characteristics of the original issue.

Unamortized bond premiums and discounts, and deferred amounts from debt refunding should "follow the debt" in calculating net asset components for the statement of net position. That is, if debt is capital-related, the deferred amounts would be included in the calculation of net investments in capital assets. If the debt is restricted for a specific purpose and the proceeds are unspent, the net proceeds would affect restricted net position. Reporting both within the same element of net position prevents one classification from being overstated while another is understated by the same amount. If the debt proceeds are not restricted for capital or other purposes, the unamortized costs would be included in the calculation of unrestricted net position.

Retainage

States and local governments commonly incorporate retainage clauses as part of long-term contracts for construction or similar acquisitions that are capital-related. In many cases, the projects are funded by capital-related debt. GASB *Implementation Guide 2015-1*, questions 7.23.13-14 [GASB Cod. Secs. 2200.709-12–13] address the issue of retainage and the net investment in capital assets calculation component of net position. As a retainage payable represents a liability usually attributable to the acquisition, construction, or improvement of capital assets and likely with a debit recognized as construction in progress, any retainage liability should be included in the calculation of the net investment in capital assets. If unspent bond proceeds are involved, the calculation of capital-related debt is adjusted including the portion of bonds payable that has been spent on capital construction, plus retainages and accounts payable attributable to that construction.

PRACTICE POINT: In some cases, retainage is required to be accounted for in a separate fund or held in escrow with specific investments. Upon completion of the contract, the retainage and related investment earnings are released to the contractor. In such cases, the separate fund is a private purpose trust fund or an agency fund (until the implementation of GASB Statement No. 84 (*Fiduciary Activities*)). The investments would be valued at fair value and no net investment in capital assets calculation would be presented in the retainage fund as it only holds the investment escrow. (GASB *Implementation Guide 2016-1*, 4.26) [GASB Cod. Sec. I50.701-6].

Example 5-1 *Net Investment in Capital Assets Calculation*

Assume a local government has the following balances within its governmental activities' assets and liabilities:

- *Restricted Cash for Debt Service* $800,000 (debit balance that represents cash accumulated from property tax levies legally restricted for the debt service payments on capital-related general obligation bonds)
- *Restricted Cash for Capital Projects* $1,200,000 (debit balance that represents unspent proceeds from general obligation bonds to be used for capital projects)
- *Restricted Cash for Capital Replacement* $2,500,000 (debit balance that represents cash set aside from excess net revenues of years that is restricted by ordinance for use in replacing capital assets)
- *Capital Assets* $34,500,000 (debit balance that represents the historical cost of governmental activities capital assets including infrastructure)
- *Accumulated Depreciation* $9,500,000 (credit balance that represents the accumulated depreciation on depreciable capital assets)
- *Bond Issuance* Costs $500,000 (debit balance that represents the issuance expense associated with capital-related debt)
- *General Obligation Bonds* $10,200,000 (credit balance that represents outstanding principal balance of capital-related general obligation bonds)
- *Capital Lease Obligations Payable* $1,000,000 (credit balance that represents outstanding principal balance of capital lease obligations)

Based on the above assumptions, the calculation of net position invested in capital assets, net of related debt should be as follows:

Element	Amount	
Capital-Related Assets:		
Capital assets	$34,500,000	
Accumulated depreciation	(9,500,000)	
Subtotal—capital-related assets		25,000,000
Capital-Related Debt:		
General obligation bonds	10,200,000	

Element	Amount
Capital lease obligations	1,000,000
Restricted cash for capital projects—unspent bond proceeds	(1,200,000)
Subtotal—capital-related debt	10,000,000
Net Investment in Capital Assets	$15,000,000

Note that in the above calculation the following account balances are not included:

- *Restricted Cash for Debt Service* $800,000: Excluded because the restricted cash is to be used for debt service on capital debt as opposed to the acquisition or construction of capital assets and does not represent unspent bond proceeds.
- *Restricted Cash for Capital Replacement* $2,500,000: Excluded because the restricted cash has been accumulated for net resources of the entities' operations and does not represent unspent bond proceeds.
- *Bond Issuance Costs* $500,000: Excluded because they are outlays that do not acquire, construct, or improve capital assets. This amount is expensed in accordance with the provisions of GASB-65, pars. 14–15 [GASB Cod. Sec I30.115].

The GASB *Implementation Guide 2015-1*, question 7.23.9 [GASB Cod. Sec. 2200.709-9], states that if the outstanding capital debt *exceeds* the carrying value of capital assets, the caption "net investment in capital assets" should still be used and a negative amount reported. In the *Guide* (question 7.23.7) [GASB Cod. Sec. 2200.709-7], the GASB also states that if a government has capital assets but no related debt, the net position component should be titled simply "invested in capital assets" because there is no capital debt. Additionally, question 7.22.9 [GASB Cod. Sec. 708-7] excludes accrued interest on any capital-related debt, including deep-discount debt from the computation of the net investment in capital assets component. The GASB concluded that the amount of the "borrowing attributable to the acquisition, construction, or improvement" of a capital asset is the proceeds, rather than the total amount, including interest, that will be paid at maturity. Generally, an accrued interest liability would be included in unrestricted net position. However, if the government has established a "sinking" fund to accumulate cash to pay off the debt at maturity, accrued interest would be included in (reduce) the same component of net position as the sinking fund resources.

Restricted Net Position

Restricted net position arises if either of the following conditions exists (GASB-34, par. 34) [GASB Cod. Secs. 1800.157, 2200.119, Po20.118]:

- Restrictions are externally imposed by creditor (such as through debt covenants), grantors, contributors, or laws or regulations of other governments; or
- Restrictions are imposed by law through constitutional provisions or enabling legislation.

> **OBSERVATION:** GASB-61 added a further category of restricted net position for component units with joint venture characteristics. The organization itself, when included as a component unit in the majority participant's financial reporting entity, should report any equity interests of the minority participants as "restricted net position, nonexpendable."

GASB-34 points out that enabling legislation "authorizes the government to assess, levy, charge, or otherwise mandate payment of resources (from external resource providers)" and includes a legally enforceable requirement that those resources be used only for the specific purposes stipulated in the legislation.

In its definition of "legal enforceability," GASB-46 (*Net Assets Restricted by Enabling Legislation—an amendment of GASB Statement No. 34*) states that a government can be compelled by an external party (citizens, public interest groups, or the judiciary) to use resources created by enabling legislation only for the purposes specified by the legislation. However, enforceability cannot ultimately be proven unless it is tested through the judicial process; therefore professional judgment must be exercised. This definition also carries forward to GASB-54 for restricted fund balances.

GASB-33 (*Accounting and Financial Reporting for Nonexchange Transactions*) describes enabling legislation as a law that authorizes a government to assess, levy, charge, or otherwise mandate payment of resources (from external resource providers). It also describes the manner in which those resources are used. GASB-46 further clarifies that if a government passes new enabling legislation that replaces the original enabling legislation by establishing a new legally enforceable restriction on the resources raised by the original enabling legislation, then from the effective date of the legislation, the resources accumulated under the new enabling legislation should be reported as restricted to the purpose specified by the new enabling legislation. Professional judgment should be used to determine if remaining balances accumulated under the original enabling legislation should continue to be reported as restricted for the original purpose, restricted to the purpose specified in the new legislation, or unrestricted. If resources are used for a purpose other than those stipulated in the enabling legislation or if there is other cause for reconsideration, governments should reevaluate the legal enforceability of the restrictions to determine if the resources should continue to be reported as restricted. If reevaluation results in a determination that a particular restriction is no longer legally enforceable, then for all periods of that year, the amounts are unrestricted. If it is determined that the restrictions continue to be legally enforceable, then for the purposes of financial reporting, the restricted net position should not reflect any reduction for resources used for purposes not stipulated by the enabling legislation.

Restricted net position should be identified based on major categories that make up the restricted balance. These categories could include items such as net position restricted for capital projects and net position restricted for debt service.

In some instances net position may be restricted on a permanent basis (in perpetuity). Under this circumstance, the restricted net position must be subdivided into expendable and nonexpendable restricted net position (GASB-34, par. 35) [GASB Cod. Secs. 1800.161, 2200.123].

GASB-34 discusses that, generally, the amount of net position identified as restricted on the statement of net position will not be the same as the amount of fund balance or restricted net position presented on the governmental funds balance sheet/statement of net position because (1) the financial statements are based on different measurement focuses and bases of accounting and (2) there are different definitions for restricted net position and reserved fund balance. (Fund financial statements are discussed later.)

The basic concept of restricted net position is that the restrictions are not unilaterally established by the reporting government itself and cannot be removed without consent of those imposing the restrictions (externally imposed restrictions) or through formal due process (internally imposed restrictions).

"Externally imposed restrictions" are commonly found in the form of:

- Laws and regulations of another government that has jurisdiction over the reporting government;
- Debt covenants of the government's creditors;
- Requirements contained in grant agreements with grantors; and
- Contractual agreements with donors or other contributors.

"Legally imposed restrictions" are commonly found in the form of:

- The reporting government's constitution or similar document (such as a municipal charter); and
- Enabling legislation (such as state laws for a state and municipal ordinances for a municipality) that creates a new resource and imposes legally enforceable restrictions on the use of the new resource.

It is important to note that the earmarking of an existing resource or revenue for a specific use by the reporting government does not result in the reporting of restricted net position from the earmarking. The GASB *Implementation Guide 2015-1*, question 7.24.11 [GASB Cod. Sec. 2200.710-8], states that "earmarking existing revenue is not equivalent to enabling legislation." The earmarking of an existing resource is similar to what may be called a designation of the management of the government's intent and is not the same as a legal restriction established at the time the revenue was created.

Common errors made by financial statement preparers related to reporting restricted net position include the following:

- Inappropriately classifying all restricted fund balances of governmental funds as restricted net position of governmental activities;
- Inappropriately believing that all assets reported as restricted will also be reported as restricted net position; and

- Failing to reduce restricted assets by the liabilities payable from those restricted assets or the liabilities that were incurred to generate the restricted assets.

Example 5-2 *Restricted Net Position*

Assume a local government has the following balances within its governmental activities' assets and liabilities:

- *Restricted Cash for Street Improvements* $500,000 (debit balance that represents the unspent portion of a state gas tax shared with the local government and restricted for street improvements pursuant to the state's enabling legislation)

- *Restricted Cash for Debt Service* $800,000 (debit balance that represents cash accumulated from property tax levies legally restricted for the debt service payments on capital-related general obligation bonds)

- *Restricted Cash for Bond Issue Capital Projects* $1,200,000 (debit balance that represents unspent proceeds from general obligation bonds to be used for capital projects)

- *Restricted Cash for Capital Replacement* $2,500,000 (debit balance that represents cash set aside and transferred to a capital replacement fund by the local government in the amount of 2% of annual revenues of each year that is restricted by local ordinance for use in replacing capital assets)

- *Restricted Investments for Museum* $1,000,000 (debit balance that represents the principal amount of a museum endowment that cannot be spent: only the interest earnings may be used for museum purposes)

- *Investment in Joint Venture* $1,200,000 (debit balance representing the carrying value of an investment in a joint venture with equity interest)

- *Accounts Payable from Restricted Assets—Streets* $200,000 (credit balance that represents the amount of open invoices to be paid from cash restricted for street improvements as noted above)

- *Accounts Payable from Restricted Assets—Bond Issue Capital Projects* $500,000 (credit balance that represents the amount of open invoices to be paid from cash restricted for the unspent proceeds of the capital general obligation bonds as noted above)

- *Accounts Payable from Restricted Assets—Capital Replacement* $700,000 (credit balance that represents the amount of open invoices to be paid from cash restricted for capital replacement as noted above)

- *Accrued Interest Payable on Bonds* $300,000 (credit balance that represents the amount of accrued but unpaid interest on capital-related general obligation bonds)

- *General Obligation Bonds Payable* $10,200,000 (credit balance that represents outstanding principal balance of capital-related general obligation bonds)

Based on the above assumptions, the calculation of restricted net position should be as follows:

Element	Amount
Assets:	
Restricted Cash for Street Improvements	$500,000
Restricted Cash for Debt Service	800,000
Restricted Cash for Bond Issue Capital Projects	1,200,000
Restricted Investments for Museum	1,000,000
Subtotal—Restricted Assets	3,500,000
Less Related Liabilities:	
Accounts Payable from Restricted Assets—Streets	200,000
Accrued Interest Payable on Bonds	300,000
General Obligation Bonds Payable (unspent proceeds portion)	1,200,000
Subtotal—related liabilities	1,700,000
Restricted Net Position	$1,800,000

Note that in the above calculation the following account balances are not included:

- *Restricted Cash for Capital Replacement* $2,500,000: Excluded because the restricted cash is essentially the earmarking of existing resources and not the result of externally imposed restrictions or legal restrictions from constitutional law or enabling legislation.

- *Investment in Joint Venture* $1,200,000: Question 7.25.1 [GASB Cod. Sec. 2200.708-13] of the *GASB Implementation Guide 2015-1* states that an equity interest in a joint venture is generally not restricted (even though it may be comprised of equity in capital assets) and should be included in the computation of unrestricted net position. However, GASB-61 slightly amended this in paragraph 12a, which stipulates that the organization itself, when included as a component unit in the majority participant's financial reporting entity, should report any equity interests of the minority participants as "restricted net position, nonexpendable." The example is not for the joint venture but for *the investment* in the joint venture.

- *Accounts Payable from Restricted Assets—Bond Issue Capital Projects* $500,000: Although these are liabilities payable from restricted cash, the restricted cash has already been reduced to zero by netting the portion of the bonds representing unspent proceeds against the restricted asset; further reduction would result in the reporting of negative net position for this category.

The *GASB Implementation Guide 2015-1*, question 7.24.13 [GASB Cod. Sec. 2200.710-9], states that negative amounts should not be reported for any category of restricted net position. Restricted net position is intended to portray, as of a point in time, the extent to which the government has assets that can only be used for specific purposes. If liabilities that relate to specific restricted net position exceed those assets, the net negative amount should reduce unrestricted net positions.

- *Accounts Payable from Restricted Assets—Capital Replacement* $700,000: Excluded because the related asset is the result of an earmarking and is not included in the computation of restricted net position.

- *General Obligation Bonds Payable* $9,000,000 ($10,200,000 less the portion related to unspent bond proceeds in restricted cash): Excluded because this remaining long-term debt balance is considered in the computation of net position, net investment in capital assets.

The $1,800,000 of restricted net position as determined in the above example should be displayed on the face of the statement of net position in the following manner by category of restriction:

Restricted Net Position

Restricted for street improvements	$ 300,000
Restricted for debt service	500,000
Restricted for permanent endowment—museum	1,000,000

Note that none of the above restricted net position is required to be disclosed in the notes to the financial statements as being restricted by enabling legislation. Although the net position restricted for street improvements represent the net position resulting from resources restricted by the state's enabling legislation, it is not restricted by the enabling legislation of the reporting government, which would require note disclosure.

Unrestricted Net Position

Unrestricted net position is the residual amount that is classified neither as net investment in capital assets nor as restricted net position. Portions of the entity's net position may be identified by management to reflect tentative plans or commitments of governmental resources. The *tentative* plans or commitments may be related to items such as plans to retire debt at some future date or to replace infrastructure or specified capital assets. Designated amounts *are not* the same as restricted amounts because designations represent planned actions, not actual commitments. For this reason, designated amounts should not be classified with restricted net position but rather should be reported as part of the unrestricted net asset component. In addition, designations cannot be disclosed as such on the face of the statement of net position (GASB-63, par. 11, GASB-34, par. 37, as amended by GASB-54, pars. 10–16, GASB-63, par. 8) [GASB Cod. Secs. 1800.163, 2200.125].

Reservations and Designations in Governmental Funds in Accordance with GASB-54

Due to the implementation of GASB-54, the term "reserve" and its many variants have been eliminated for general purpose external financial reporting purposes, but may be utilized for *internal management purposes*. Valuation accounts, such as the allowance for uncollectible property taxes, should not be referred to in the financial statements as a reserve. Likewise, estimated liabilities or unearned revenues should not be classified as reserves.

The AICPA's Audit and Accounting Guide *State and Local Governments* reminds practitioners that a statutory requirement or contractual commitment to a third party that is not reported as a liability is an example of an amount that is legally segregated for a specific purpose and that non-appropriable amounts include balances related to "inventories, prepaid items, noncurrent receivables that are not offset by deferred revenue, and the noncurrent portion of interfund receivables."

OBSERVATION: For fiduciary entities, reserves for different operating purposes are commonplace. However, care must be taken that the reserves in the aggregate agree with net position available to pay plan benefits and that the reserves are not reported on the face of any fiduciary statement.

Designations

Portions of the fund balance may be identified by management to reflect tentative plans or commitments of governmental resources. The tentative plans or commitments may be related to items such as debt retirement. Designated amounts are not the same as fund balance amounts that are restricted, committed, assigned, or unassigned because they represent planned actions, not actual commitments. For this reason, designated amounts should not be presented as a separate element of fund balance but rather included as part of the unassigned fund balance of the General Fund or assigned fund balance of other governmental funds. The amount and nature of the designated amount may be explained in a note to the financial statements.

Reporting Fund Balances under GASB-54

GASB issued GASB-54 (*Fund Balance Reporting and Governmental Fund Type Definitions*) in an effort to improve the consistency in reporting fund balance components, enhance fund balance presentation, improve the usefulness of fund balance information, and clarify the definitions of the governmental fund types. The GASB project research revealed that fund balance was one of the most widely used elements of financial information in state and local government financial statements but at the same time was one of the most misunderstood and misapplied elements.

Why did GASB change the presentation of fund balance? Fund balance information is used by taxpayers, bond analysts, research groups, oversight agencies, and government managers and legislators in key decision-making regarding a government's available liquid resources for repaying debt, reducing taxes, adding or expanding programs or projects, and enhancing financial position. The GASB research began when concerns were raised by certain financial statement users that there was substantial variation in the information that governments were reporting about fund balance in their governmental funds, resulting primarily from differences in understanding among financial statement preparers as to the definitions of reserved and unreserved fund balances and confusion over the difference between reserved fund balances and restricted net position.

The classification requirements in GASB-54 improved financial reporting by providing fund balance categories and classifications that are more easily understood. For example, elimination of the reserved component of fund balance in favor of a restricted classification seemingly has improved consistency between information reported in the government-wide statements and the governmental fund financial statements and reduced some of the confusion about the relationship between the now-obsolete term "reserved fund balance" and restricted net position. Also, user understanding should be enhanced through the consistent classification of the spendable portion of fund balance based on the relative strength of the constraints that control the purposes for which specific amounts can be spent, including amounts that are restricted, committed, assigned, and unassigned.

Fund Balance Classifications

In addition to identifying the portion of fund balance that is not spendable, GASB-54 established a hierarchy of fund balance classifications based primarily on the extent to which a government is bound to observe spending constraints imposed upon how resources reported in governmental funds may be used. For example, GASB-54 distinguishes fund balance between

1. Amounts that are considered non-spendable because they are not available for current use (such as fund balance associated with inventories, long-term receivables, and permanent fund principal), and

2. Amounts that are available for use but are classified based on the relative strength of the constraints that control the purposes for which specific amounts can be spent. Beginning with the most binding constraints, these classifications are:

   a. Restricted;

   b. Committed;

   c. Assigned; and

   d. Unassigned.

Non-Spendable Fund Balance

Amounts that *cannot be spent* because they are either (1) not in spendable form (i.e., inventories, prepaid amounts, long-term loans and notes receivables, property held for resale) or (2) legally or contractually required to be maintained intact (e.g., the corpus or principal of a permanent fund.)

Although long-term loans and notes receivables and property held for resale are generally reported as part of non-spendable fund balance, if the use of the proceeds from collection of the receivables or sale of the properties is restricted, committed, or assigned, then they should be included in those appropriate fund balance classifications rather than the non-spendable classification.

The amount that should be reported as non-spendable fund balance must be determined first before classifying any remaining amounts by level of constraint (i.e., restricted, committed, or assigned).

GASB-54 states that amounts for the two categories of nonspendable fund balance [i.e., (1) the not in spendable form and (2) legally or contractually to be retained intact] may be presented separately or in the aggregate on the face of the governmental fund's balance sheet. If the amounts are displayed in the aggregate, the notes to the financial statement should present the separate amounts. See Exhibit 5-1 for an example of separate display, and Exhibit 5-2 for an example of aggregate display.

Although GASB-54 does bring consistency between reporting restricted fund balance in governmental funds and restricted net position for governmental activities in the government-wide statement of net position pursuant to GASB-34, there are still some differences. For example, GASB-34 requires net position required to be held in perpetuity (i.e., permanent fund principal) to be reported as part of "restricted net position." However, under GASB-54, such amounts are classified as "non-spendable" fund balance.

Items that may result in nonspendable fund balances include:

- Long-term receivables that are in governmental funds if the proceeds from their collection are not restricted, committed, or assigned;

- Property held for resale if the proceeds from the sale are not to be restricted, committed or assigned;

- Inventories and prepaid amounts as their ultimate use is not to be converted to cash;

- The corpus of a permanent fund even if used to make loans (loans made is not considered "spending" for financial reporting purposes per the *GASB Implementation Guide 2015-1*, question Z.54.48) [GASB Cod. Sec. 1800.741-7];

- Nonspendable trust funds, even for capital appreciation; and

- A minimum balance in a fund for financial resources restricted by enabling legislation and inclusive of language in the legislation that limits the fund's expenditures so that a minimum fund balance (determined by formula) is maintained (GASB-54, pars. 6–7, as amended by GASB-63, par. 8) [GASB Cod. Secs. 1800.166–.167].

Restricted Fund Balance

Restricted fund balances represent amounts that are constrained for a specific purpose through restrictions of external parties (i.e., creditors, grantors, contributors, or laws or regulations of other governments), or by constitutional provision or enabling legislation, pursuant to the definition of "restricted" in paragraph 34 of GASB-34, as amended by GASB-46 (*Net Assets Restricted by Enabling Legislation*).

The term "enabling legislation" as used in GASB-54 means legislation that authorizes a government to assess, levy, charge, or otherwise mandate payment of resources from external resource providers and that includes a legally enforceable requirement that the resources be used only for the specific purposes defined in the legislation. Similarly to nonspendable fund balance, see Exhibit 5-1 for an example of separate display, and Exhibit 5-2 for an example of aggregate display of restricted fund balance.

Items that may result in restricted fund balance are similar to restricted net position, but different amounts usually result between the two due to the different measurement focuses and bases of accounting between a governmental fund balance sheet and a statement of net position. Commonly found restricted fund balances include:

- A balance in a fund for financial resources above a minimum fund balance, that is otherwise restricted by enabling legislation and inclusive of language in the legislation that limits the fund's expenditures so that a minimum fund balance (determined by formula) is maintained (*GASB Implementation Guide 2015-1*, question 7.49.1) [GASB Cod. Sec. 1300.704-1].
- Proceeds of a grant and required matching funds (GASB-54, pars. 8–9) [GASB Cod. Secs. 1800.168–.169].

Committed Fund Balance

Committed amounts are constrained for specific purposes imposed by *formal action* of the government's highest level of decision-making authority (i.e., amounts that have been committed by a governing body legislation, ordinance, or resolution for a specific purpose, such as an amount from specific park and recreation revenues committed by governing body resolution to be used only for park maintenance).

Committed fund balances cannot be used for other purposes unless the government uses the same action (i.e., legislation, ordinance, or resolution) that it took to originally commit the amounts. The authorization containing the specific purposes of the committed amounts should have the consent of both the legislative and executive branches of the government. Also, the formal action to commit resources by the government's highest level of decision-making authority should occur prior to the end of the reporting period—and the actual amount committed may be determined in a subsequent period.

Fund balance "committed" by legislation is distinguished from fund balance "restricted" by enabling legislation by the fact that amounts committed by legislation may be deployed for other purposes with appropriate due process by the government, such as through changes in legislation, ordinance, or resolution. In addition, constraints imposed on the use of committed fund balances are imposed by the government "separate" from the enabling legislation that authorized the raising of the underlying revenue. Therefore, compliance with the constraints on the resources that commit the government to spend the amounts for specific purposes is not considered "legally enforceable."

Similarly to nonspendable and restricted fund balance, GASB-54 states that committed fund balance may be displayed on the face of the governmental fund's balance sheet in the aggregate or in a manner that distinguishes between the major commitments. If the amounts are displayed in the aggregate, the notes to the financial statement should present the separate amounts for specific purposes. Exhibit 5-1 is an example of separate display and Exhibit 5-2 is an example of aggregate display.

Commonly found committed fund balances include (GASB-54, pars. 10–12) [GASB Cod. Secs. 1800.170–.172]:

- Resources specifically committed for satisfying contractual obligations including leases or settlement awards.

- By exercising its highest level of decision-making authority, when a government has established a budgetary stabilization fund and imposed a requirement that 15% of certain mineral rights royalties received should be set aside to provide for budgetary imbalances. That decision can only be reversed or modified by the government taking the same action (*GASB Implementation Guide 2015-1*, question Z.54.26) [GASB Cod. Sec. 1300.704-6].

- When a county board of supervisors, the highest level of decision-making authority for the county, passes resolutions to commit estimated amounts to long-term construction projects. The resolution, also the highest form of decision-making authority, commits the amount as the maximum and acknowledges that unneeded resources at the end of the project will be returned to the general fund or transferred to other construction projects (*GASB Implementation Guide 2015-1*, question Z.54.52) [GASB Cod. Sec. 1800.743-4].

Assigned Fund Balance

Assigned fund balance consists of amounts that are constrained by the government's intent to be used for a specific purpose but are neither restricted nor committed. Intent should be expressed by (1) the governing body itself or (2) a body (e.g., a budget or finance committee) or official to which the governing body has delegated the authority to assign amounts to be used for specific purposes (i.e., the amounts are intended to be used by government for specific purposes but do not meet the criteria to be classified as restricted or committed, such as an amount set aside by management to fund a projected budgetary deficit in a subsequent year's budget).

"Assigned" fund balance is distinguished from "committed" fund balance by the fact that amounts committed must be constrained by the government's highest level of decision-making authority, whereas assigned amounts do not require this level of authority to place the assignment or remove it. For example, management of a government may be authorized by the governing body to designate fund balances for a specific purpose, such as an amount set aside to fund accrued compensated absences for terminated employees, without formal action by the governing body itself. The amounts associated with this designation by management would meet the criteria to be reported as assigned fund balances. Assigned fund balances are similar to the unreserved—designated fund balances reported prior to GASB-54.

Assigned fund balances include all remaining amounts not reported as nonspendable, restricted, or committed in all governmental funds other than the general fund (i.e., special revenue, capital project, debt service, and permanent funds). By reporting particular amounts that are not restricted or committed in a special revenue, capital projects, or debt service fund, the government has in essence assigned those amounts to the purposes of the respective funds. Assignment within the general fund conveys that those amounts are intended for a specific purpose that is narrower than the general purposes of the government itself. However, governments should not report an assignment for an amount to a specific purpose if the assignment would result in a deficit in unassigned fund balance.

Similarly to other forms of fund balance, GASB-54 states that assigned fund balance may be displayed on the face of the governmental fund's balance sheet in the aggregate or in a manner that distinguishes between the major assignments. If the amounts are displayed in the aggregate, the notes to the financial statement should present the separate amounts for specific purposes. Exhibit 5-1 is an example of separate display and Exhibit 5-2 is an example of aggregate display.

Commonly found assigned fund balances include (GASB-54, pars. 13–16) [GASB Cod. Secs. 1800.173–.176]:

- Encumbrances (based on an executed purchase order) (unless the purchase order relates to restricted or committed resources), but *not* displayed separately on the face of the financial statements (*GASB Implementation Guide 2015-1*, question Z.54.27) [GASB Cod. Sec. 1800.751-1];

- When a government passes a budget for the next year reflecting an excess of appropriations over revenues and the government has appropriated a portion of fund balance to eliminate the excess (*GASB Implementation Guide 2015-1*, question Z.54.56) [GASB Cod. Sec. 1800.744-5]; and

- The residual of any *non-General Fund* governmental fund.

Unassigned Fund Balance

Unassigned fund balance is the residual classification for a government's general fund; it includes all amounts that are not constrained as reported in the other classifications.

Although any governmental fund may report amounts that are nonspendable, restricted, committed, or assigned, or any combination of these four classifications, only the general fund can report a positive unassigned amount. In other governmental funds, if expenditures incurred for specific purposes exceed the amounts restricted, committed, or assigned to those purposes, the government should first reduce any assigned amounts within the fund and then, if there are no further assigned amounts to reduce, the government should report the negative residual amount as "negative unassigned" fund balances. This means that a negative residual amount *should not be reported* for restricted, committed, or assigned balances in any fund.

Similar to GASB-34's treatment of net position, governments should develop and apply an accounting policy that determines the order of fund balance reduction for committed, assigned, or unassigned fund balances when amounts are expended for purposes for which funds in any of these unrestricted classifications could be used. GASB-54 states that if a government does not establish such a policy, it should consider that committed amounts are reduced first, followed by assigned amounts, and then unassigned amounts.

Exhibit 5-1 illustrates the fund balance classifications displayed on the face of the governmental fund type balance sheets (GASB-54, par. 17) [GASB Cod. Sec. 1800.177].

Disclosure Requirements

GASB-54 requires that governments disclose in the notes to the financial statements the following information about their fund balance classification policies and procedures and other related information (GASB-54, pars. 18–19) [GASB Cod. Secs. 1800.178–.179]:

- For committed fund balance: (1) the government's highest level of decision-making authority and (2) the formal action that is required to be taken to establish (and modify or rescind) a fund balance commitment.

- For assigned fund balance: (1) the body or official authorized to assign amounts to a specific purpose and (2) the policy established by the governing body granting that authorization.

- For all the classification of fund balances (1) whether the government considers restricted or unrestricted amounts to have been spent when an expenditure is incurred for purposes for which both restricted and unrestricted fund balance is available and (2) whether committed, assigned, or unassigned amounts are considered to have been spent when an expenditure is incurred for purposes for which amounts in any of those unrestricted fund balance classifications could be used.

- For nonspendable fund balance displayed in the aggregate on the face of the balance sheet, the notes should disclose amounts for the two nonspendable components, if applicable. If restricted, committed, or assigned fund balances are displayed in the aggregate, specific purposes information not portrayed on the face of the balance sheet should be disclosed.

- For established stabilization arrangements (see next section), even if an arrangement does not meet the criteria to be classified as restricted or committed, the government should disclose the following information in the notes to the financial statements:

  — The authority for establishing stabilization arrangements (e.g., by statute or ordinance);

  — The requirements for additions to the stabilization amount;

  — The conditions under which stabilization amounts may be spent; and

  — The stabilization balance, if it is not apparent on the face of the financial statements.

- A governing body that has formally adopted a minimum fund balance policy (e.g., specifying a percentage of annual revenue or some other amount in lieu of separately setting aside stabilization amounts) should describe it in the notes to its financial statements.

- Encumbrances should be disclosed *in the notes to the financial statements* as commitments of government by major funds and nonmajor funds in the aggregate for funds that use encumbrance accounting, but not on the face of the financial statements.

Stabilization Arrangements

Many state and local governments have established and reported "rainy day," "budget or revenue stabilization," "working capital needs," or "contingencies or emergencies" and similar amounts within fund balances as reserves or designations. Such amounts are generally restricted or committed as to use for meeting emergency needs, stabilizing financial position when revenue shortfalls are experienced or for other, similar purposes. The GASB recognized that there existed considerable diversity in current practice as to how these amounts were reported. The GASB addressed this diversity in GASB-54.

GASB-54 states that the authority to establish stabilization arrangements and set aside such resources should come from constitution, charter, statute, ordinance, or resolution provisions stating that the resources may be expended only when certain circumstances exist as defined in the formal action document. The formal action that imposes the spending parameters or criteria should identify and describe the circumstances that qualify as an appropriate use of the stabilization resources, and the circumstances should be such that they would not be expected to occur routinely.

OBSERVATION: GASB-54 discusses how a stabilization amount that can be accessed "in the case of emergency" would not qualify to be classified within the committed category because the circumstances or conditions that prescribe its use (i.e., what exactly constitutes an emergency) are not sufficiently detailed. Similarly, an amount set aside to "offset an anticipated revenue shortfall" would not qualify as a restricted or committed fund balance stabilization arrangement unless the shortfall was quantified and was of such magnitude to distinguish it from other revenue shortfalls that routinely occur.

GASB-54, paragraphs 20–21 [GASB Cod. Secs. 1800.180–.181], treat a qualifying stabilization reserve as a specific purpose, allowing the amounts constrained to be reported as a restricted or committed fund balance in the general fund if they meet certain criteria for such classification, based on the source of the constraint on their use. "Stabilization" is regarded as a specific purpose only if circumstances or conditions that signal the need for stabilization are identified in sufficient detail and are not expected to occur routinely. Amounts related to stabilization arrangements that do not meet the criteria to be reported as restricted or committed fund balances should be reported as unassigned fund balance within the general fund.

If a government has not established a stabilization amount pursuant to the proposed criteria but has formally established a minimum fund balance requirement, then the minimum fund balance requirement is reported as unassigned fund balance in the general fund and is required to be disclosed in the notes to the financial statements.

GASB-54 defines special revenue funds as those funds used to account for and report the proceeds of specific revenue sources that are restricted or committed to expenditure for specified purposes other than debt service or capital projects. Therefore, a stabilization arrangement would meet the criteria to be reported as a separate special revenue fund only if the fund's resources are derived from a specific revenue source that is specifically restricted or committed for that stabilization purpose.

PRACTICE POINT: The government that is utilized as a model for Exhibit 5-1 does not have committed fund balances. However, they would be shown in this exhibit if applicable.

EXHIBIT 5-1
ILLUSTRATIVE GASB-54 FUND BALANCE PRESENTATION: SEPARATE DISPLAY APPROACH

	General Fund	Road and Bridge	Social Services	Capital Expenditures	Other Governmental	Total
Fund Balances:						
Nonspendable:						
Inventory	$ 382,497	$ -	$ 1,899	$ -	$ -	$ 384,396
Prepaid expenses	1,311,925	-	-	-	-	1,311,925
Long-term receivables	1,832,008	-	-	-	-	1,832,008
Subtotal – Nonspendable	**3,526,430**	**-**	**1,899**	**-**	**-**	**3,528,329**
Restricted:						
Federal grants	1,621,474	-	5,093,678	-	44,370	6,759,522
Debt service	-	-	-	14,505,582	12,315,490	26,821,072
Constitutional provisions	5,756,647	-	-	-	2,750,051	8,506,698
Open space	-	-	-	-	32,917,103	32,917,103
Highway Construction	-	10,078,146	-	-	14,240,403	24,318,549
Law enforcement	-	-	-	-	1,996,582	1,996,582
Conservation trust funds	-	-	-	-	1,781,691	1,781,691
Developmental disabilities	-	-	-	-	400,918	400,918
Wildfire fire training	-	-	-	-	136,319	136,319
Sanitation	-	-	-	-	952,171	952,171
Subtotal – Restricted	**7,328,121**	**10,078,146**	**5,093,678**	**14,505,582**	**67,535,098**	**104,590,625**
Assigned:						
Budgetary appropriations	25,079,639	-	-	-	-	25,079,639
Unassigned:	40,505,065	-	-	-	-	40,505,065
Total Fund Balances	**$76,489,255**	**$10,078,146**	**$5,095,577**	**$14,505,582**	**$67,535,098**	**$173,703,658**

EXHIBIT 5-2

ILLUSTRATIVE GASB-54 FUND BALANCE PRESENTATION: AGGREGATE DISPLAY APPROACH

	General Fund	Road and Bridge	Social Services	Capital Expenditures	Other Governmental	Total
Fund Balances:						
Nonspendable	$3,526,430	$-	$1,899	$-	$-	$3,528,329
Restricted	7,328,121	10,078,146	5,093,678	14,505,582	67,535,098	104,590,625
Assigned	25,079,639	-	-	-	-	25,079,639
Unassigned	40,505,065	-	-	-	-	40,505,065
Total Fund Balances	**$76,489,255**	**$10,078,146**	**$5,095,577**	**$14,505,582**	**$67,535,098**	**$173,703,658**

QUESTIONS

1. According to GASB-34, as amended by GASB-63, how are transfers categorized within and among governmental funds, proprietary funds, and fiduciary funds in the fund financial statements?

    a. Reciprocal interfund activity and nonreciprocal interfund activity.

    b. Deferred inflows of resources and deferred outflows of resources.

    c. Allowances and bad debts.

    d. Forms and substances.

2. GASB-34 requires that the preparation of government-wide financial statements be based on a consolidating process (similar to corporate consolidations) rather than a combining process. Which of the following entries are *not related* to the consolidation process?

    a. Internal balances (statement of net position).

    b. Internal activities (statement of activities).

    c. Allowance accounts (statement of net position).

    d. Intra-entity activity and internal service fund balances.

3. In accordance with GASB-65, how should the costs of issuing bonds (except for insurance costs in certain circumstances) be treated in the basic financial statements?

    a. As assets.

    b. As expenses/expenditures.

    c. As deferred outflows of resources.

    d. As deferred inflows of resources.

4. Which of the following is *not* required to record demand bonds as a long-term debt of the government in accordance with GASBI-1:

    a. Before the financial statements are issued, the issuer has entered into an arm's-length financing (takeout) agreement to convert bonds "put" but not resold into some other form of long-term obligation.

    b. The takeout agreement does not expire within one year from the date of the issuer's balance sheet.

    c. The takeout agreement is not cancelable by the lender or the prospective lender during that year, and obligations incurred under the takeout agreement are not callable by the lender during that year.

    d. The lender has gone into bankruptcy.

5. According to GASB-34, what is the focus of the statement of activities?

    a. Presentation of revenues and expenses in a single column.

    b. Presentation of current and noncurrent assets and liabilities.

    c. Presentation of the net cost of various activities provided by the governmental entity.

    d. Presentation of deferred inflows and outflows of resources.

6. According to GASB-63, what is the element that is presented that equates to the sum of capital assets, net of accumulated depreciation, reduced by the outstanding balances of bonds, mortgages, notes, or other borrowings (including leases) that are attributable to the acquisition, construction, or improvement of those assets and deferred outflows of resources and deferred inflows of resources that are attributable to the acquisition, construction, or improvement of those assets or related debt are also included?

   a. Net investment in capital assets.

   b. Restricted net capital assets.

   c. Investment in capital assets, net of related debt.

   d. Unrestricted net position.

7. According to GASB-34, as amended, which of the following *is not likely* to result in restricted net position in and of itself?

   a. Receipt of bond proceeds with debt covenants to be met as security.

   b. Receipt of municipal aid from a state government.

   c. Receipt of taxation subject to a constitutional provision.

   d. Receipt of a donation as a bequest to provide education in the arts in an elementary school.

8. According to GASB-54, which of the following classifications of fund balance *is not* allowed for general-purpose external financial reporting?

   a. Restricted.

   b. Committed.

   c. Reserved.

   d. Assigned.

9. How can an entity designated as the government's highest level of decision-making authority remove a commitment of fund balance?

   a. Using the same action (i.e., legislation, ordinance, or resolution) that it took to originally commit the amounts. The authorization containing the specific purposes of the committed amounts should have the consent of both the legislative and executive branches of the government and occur before the end of the reporting period.

   b. Using an executive order, signed by the chief executive, to remove the commitment and reserving it for other purposes.

   c. Using a memorandum to all government employees drafted by the department or agency heads that they are no longer committed to the balance.

   d. Using guidance from the government's external auditors that they can spend the funds as long as they follow state law.

10. In special revenue, capital projects, debt service, or permanent funds, if expenditures incurred for specific purposes exceed the amounts restricted, committed, or assigned to those purposes, what should a government report for a fund balance?

    a. Report a nonspendable fund balance.

    b. Transfer amounts between funds until expenditures are reported equal to revenues.

    c. Reduce any assigned amounts within the fund and then, if there are no further assigned amounts to reduce, report "negative unassigned" fund balances.

    d. Bill the federal government for the excess expenditures.

Practice Case (*Adapted from GASB Standards*)

Castle Rock County is in the process of preparing the governmental fund financial statements for the fiscal year. The following fund balances were noted by the auditor/controller, irrespective of fund:

1. Inventory had a balance of $249,000.

2. Trust funds where the balance cannot be spent, but investment earnings that can be spent had a principal of $164,000.

3. Social services grants from the federal government had an unspent balance of $240,000.

4. Parks and recreations donations from citizens were $80,000.

5. Education grants from the federal government were $55,000.

6. Highway planning and construction federal grant funds had balances of $444,000.

7. Amounts from gas taxes imposed in the constitution of the state for road surface repairs were $24,000.

8. Amounts held aside in reserve from property taxes to pay for debt service were $206,000.

9. Amounts charged as assessments in a subdivision for school construction were $301,000.

10. Amounts received from the United States Department of Justice for community policing funds for the next year were $214,000.

11. Amounts held aside required by a bond indenture for renewal and replacement of capital facilities were $81,000.

12. Amounts from prior encumbrances due to contracts approved by the county board of supervisors already included in the next year's budget for the zoning board, justice, education, health and welfare were $574,000.

13. Amounts from approved budgets identified by management of 15 departments for various operations amounting to $1,855,400.

14. The residual of all other cumulative revenues over expenditures added to the prior fiscal year balance was $525,000.

How should these amounts be reported in accordance with GASB-54?

ANSWERS

1. According to GASB-34, as amended by GASB-63, how are transfers categorized within and among governmental funds, proprietary funds, and fiduciary funds in the fund financial statements?

   Answer – A: Reciprocal interfund activity and nonreciprocal interfund activity includes loans, transfers and related balances.

2. GASB-34 requires that the preparation of government-wide financial statements be based on a consolidating process (similar to corporate consolidations) rather than a combining process. Which of the following entries are *not related* to the consolidation process?

   Answer – C: Allowance accounts are not related to the consolidation as they are either presented on the face of the statement of net position or in the notes to the basic financial statements when discussing receivables and similar. All other internal balances and activity are eliminated as part of the consolidation.

3. In accordance with GASB-65, how should the costs of issuing bonds (except for certain insurance costs) be treated in the basic financial statements?

   Answer – B: GASB-65 eliminated the deferred charge and amortization of bond issuance costs.

4. Which of the following is *not* required to record demand bonds as a long-term debt of the government in accordance with GASBI-1:

   Answer – D: Bankruptcy by the lender will have a minimal effect on the recording of demand bonds as a debt of the government.

5. According to GASB-34, what is the focus of the statement of activities?

   Answer – C: The statement of activities is unique in financial reporting because it presents the net cost of activities of government after funding by various forms of grants and revenues.

6. According to GASB-63, what is the element that is presented that equates to the sum of capital assets, net of accumulated depreciation, reduced by the outstanding balances of bonds, mortgages, notes, or other borrowings (including leases) that are attributable to the acquisition, construction, or improvement of those assets and deferred outflows of resources and deferred inflows of resources that are attributable to the acquisition, construction, or improvement of those assets or related debt are also included?

   Answer – A: Net investment in capital assets.

7. According to GASB-34, as amended, which of the following *is not likely* to result in restricted net position in and of itself?

   Answer – B: Receipt of municipal aid is of a general nature in most cases. All other items are external restrictions. In certain circumstances dictated in law or debt covenants, municipal aid may be restricted in some way. However, the majority is usually unrestricted aid.

8. According to GASB-54, which of the following classifications of fund balance are *not* allowed for general-purpose external financial reporting?

   Answer – C: GASB-54 eliminated the presentation of reserves for general purpose external financial reporting. However, they are still used for internal operations and decision-making.

9. How can an entity designated as the government's highest level of decision-making authority remove a commitment of fund balance?

   Answer – A: GASB-54 requires that the action that committed a balance be used to remove a balance.

10. In special revenue, capital projects, debt service, or permanent funds, if expenditures incurred for specific purposes exceed the amounts restricted, committed, or assigned to those purposes, what should a government report for a fund balance?

    Answer – C: Negative balances should first reduce assigned and then report negative unassigned balances in nongeneral fund governmental funds. The general fund would report a negative unassigned balance if the same were true in the general fund, but it is a sure sign of fiscal distress.

Practice Case (*Adapted from GASB Standards*)

Castle Rock County is in the process of preparing the governmental fund financial statements for the fiscal year. How should these amounts be reported in accordance with GASB-54?

Nonspendable fund balances:

- Inventory had a balance of $249,000.
- Trust funds where the balance cannot be spent but investment earnings can be spent had a principal of $164,000.

Restricted fund balances:

- Social services grants from the federal government had an unspent balance of $240,000.
- Parks and recreations donations from citizens were $80,000.
- Education grants from the federal government were $55,000.
- Highway planning and construction federal grant funds had balances of $444,000.
- Amounts from gas taxes imposed in the constitution of the state for road surface repairs were $24,000.
- Amounts held aside in reserve from property taxes to pay for debt service were $206,000.
- Amounts charged as assessments in a subdivision for school construction were $301,000.
- Amounts received from the United States Department of Justice for community policing funds for the next year were $214,000.

- Amounts held aside required by a bond indenture for renewal and replacement of capital facilities were $81,000.

Committed fund balances:

- Amounts from prior encumbrances due to contracts approved by the county board of supervisors already included in the next year's budget for the zoning board, justice, education, health and welfare were $574,000.

Assigned fund balances:

- Amounts from approved budgets identified by management of 15 departments for various operations amounting to $1,855,400.

Unassigned fund balances:

- The residual of all other cumulative revenues over expenditures added to the prior fiscal year balance was $525,000.

II. FUND ACCOUNTING

CHAPTER 6
GOVERNMENTAL FUNDS

CONTENTS

INTRODUCTION

This chapter discusses the financial accounting and reporting standards that apply to governmental funds, which comprise the following "fund" types:

- The General Fund;
- Special Revenue Funds;
- Capital Projects Funds;
- Debt Service Funds; and
- Permanent Funds.

Governmental funds primarily are used to account for the sources, uses, and balances of current financial resources and often have a budgetary orientation. Current financial resources are those assets that are expendable during a budgetary period and they are often segregated into a specific governmental fund based on restrictions imposed by outside authorities or parties, or strategies established by internal management. Liabilities of a governmental fund are obligations that will be paid from resources held by that particular fund.

The difference between a fund's assets and a fund's liabilities is the fund balance (colloquially known as the "fund's equity"). Chapter 5, "Terminology and Classification," discusses the reporting of fund balances in governmental funds and fund balance classifications in accordance with GASB-54 (*Fund Balance Reporting and Governmental Fund Type Definitions*).

PRACTICE ALERT: The GASB is in the midst of a wide-ranging multiple-year project reexamining the financial reporting model, a related project reexamining revenue and expense recognition principles and note disclosure. In late 2016, the GASB issued an Invitation to Comment, *Financial Reporting Model Improvements—Governmental Funds*. The release represented the first due process document and asked respondents for comment on a large portion of the current financial reporting model. An Invitation to Comment is a GASB staff document, asking for comments at a relatively early stage of a project prior to the GASB Board reaching a consensus view. The topics considered in this initial phase included:

- Recognition approaches (measurement focus and basis of accounting) for governmental funds,
- The format of the governmental funds statement of resource flows (also known as the statement of revenues, expenditures, and changes in fund balances),
- Specific terminology,

- Reconciliation of the governmental fund statements to the government-wide statements, and

- For certain recognition approaches, a statement of cash flows.

In September 2018, the GASB released a second due process document consisting of the Board's Preliminary Views on the *Financial Reporting Model—Reexamination* project. Most notably, the GASB is focusing on a proposed one-year (operating cycle) period of availability for governmental funds with a goal of resolving inconsistencies in the recognition of prepaid items, inventory, tax and revenue anticipation notes, and grant receivables. Topics considered included:

- Refinement of the management's discussion and analysis

- The format of the government-wide statement of activities, including whether additional information should be presented in a "natural classification" (salaries, employee benefits, etc.) schedule in the notes

- Debt service fund presentations, potentially elevating them to major fund status, similarly to the general fund

- The status and reporting of permanent funds

- Proprietary fund and business-type activity financial statements, especially the presentation of operating and non-operating revenues and expenses

- The presentation of fiduciary fund financial statements and whether the statements should be presented in the basic financial statements

- Consistency of presentation of budgetary comparisons within required supplementary information.

Additional related projects include a reexamination of the current revenue and expense/expenditure recognition model (primarily contained in GASB-33 and GASB-36, as amended); a potential project reexamining note disclosure issued prior to the issuance of GASB Statement No. 72 (*Fair Value Measurement and Application*); and a potential GASB Concepts Statement related to the Conceptual Framework for recognizing transactions (which was started in 2010, but stalled in 2011). These projects may not finalize until at least 2023.

THE GENERAL FUND

Every general-purpose state and local government must have a General Fund to account for all of the unit's financial resources except for those resources not accounted for and reported in another fund. The General Fund is the primary fund used to account for the governmental unit's current operations by recording inflows and outflows of financial resources. Current inflows typically are from revenue sources such as property taxes, income taxes, sales taxes, grants and contributions, fines, penalties, and other general revenues. Current outflows are usually related to the unit's provision for various governmental services such as health and welfare, streets, public safety, and general governmental administration. In addition to accounting for current operating revenues and expenditures, the General Fund accounts for other sources of financial resources, such as the issuance of long-term debt and transfers from other funds, and uses of financial resources such as transfers to other funds. Although a state or local government can maintain more than one fund in each fund type, it can report only one General Fund (GASB-54, par. 29) [GASB Cod. Sec. 1300.104].

When a governmental entity has a general-purpose component unit that is blended into its financial statements, the General Fund of the component unit must be reported as a Special Revenue Fund.

SPECIAL REVENUE FUNDS

GASB-54, par. 30 [GASB Cod. Sec. 1300.105]states that:

> Special revenue funds are used to account for and report the proceeds of specific revenue sources that are restricted or committed to expenditure for specified purposes other than debt service or capital projects.

An example of a Special Revenue Fund is a fund that accounts for a state gasoline tax for which distributions are made to local governments. The expenditures from the Fund are restricted by state law to the maintenance of the local highway system. Prior to the issuance of GASB-54, Special Revenue Funds should have been used only when they were legally mandated. However, in practice, many governments had established special revenue funds to account for resources that were not legally restricted or where the proceeds were not derived from specific revenue sources. In many instances, it may be possible to account for restricted resources directly in the General Fund if these restricted resources are used to support expenditures that are usually made from the General Fund. Special revenue funds are not used to account for resources that may be restricted or committed but are held in trust for individuals, private organizations, or other governments. These resources are to be accounted for in fiduciary type funds, as discussed in Chapter 8, "Fiduciary Funds."

The restrictions as described in GASB-54 for special revenue funds are similar in operations to other restrictions throughout the governmental funds that were introduced in GASB-46 (*Net Assets Restricted by Enabling Legislation (an amendment of GASB Statement No. 34)*).

After conducting its GASB-54 project research, the GASB acknowledged the diversity in practice regarding the reporting of special revenue funds that has resulted from the confusion over its current definition. Many governments believed that special revenue funds should be used narrowly, to only report the use and availability of specific revenues (such as a legally restricted motor fuel tax), while other governments believed that special revenue funds are broader in definition and may also be used to report the revenues and expenditures of specific programs or activities (such as a special library fund even though a restricted revenue was not involved). GASB-54 clarified the definition of special revenue funds to state that they are to be used "to account for and report the proceeds of specific revenue sources that are restricted or committed to expenditure for specified purposes other than debt service or capital projects." By making this definition change, the GASB has elected to develop a solution that combines the two perspectives and goes on to state that special revenue funds can be used to report the use and availability of a specific program or activity but that a specific restricted or committed revenue source must serve as the foundation of the fund and continue to comprise a substantial portion of the inflows reported in the fund. However, the GASB-54 definition removed the term "legally" from the current definition, opening up the use of special revenue funds for activities and programs that are funded primarily by a restricted or committed revenue source.

NOTE: GASB-54, par. 31 states that governments should discontinue reporting a special revenue fund and instead report the fund's remaining resources in the general fund if the government no longer expects that a substantial portion of the inflows will be derived from restricted or committed revenue sources.

GASB-54 provides that specific restricted or committed revenues to be expended in a special revenue fund may be initially received in another fund, such as the general fund, and subsequently distributed to the special revenue fund. In these circumstances, the amounts should not be recognized as revenue in the fund initially receiving them but instead be recognized as revenues in the special revenue fund where they will be expended in accordance with the specified purposes.

OBSERVATION: Some legislative bodies may call what in reality is a special revenue fund a "trust" within legislation and vice versa. Care must be taken to delineate between funds with trust documents and funds with enabling legislation that meets the definition of a special revenue fund in GASB-54. Because of the variability in the way that Special Revenue Funds have been established by governments, there could be some instances of where Special Revenue Funds in current practice do not meet the definition under GASB-54. Should this occur, then the fund's balances and operations should be reclassified to the General Fund.

CAPITAL PROJECTS FUNDS

A governmental entity may be involved in a number of capital projects, ranging from the construction of schools and libraries to the construction of storm sewers and highways. Prior to GASB-54, it was intended that the acquisition or construction of capital facilities other than those financed by proprietary fund activities may be accounted for in a Capital Projects Fund. A Capital Projects Fund would be used to account for major capital expenditures, such as the construction of civic centers, libraries, and general administrative services buildings, which are quite often financed with the proceeds of governmental bond issues. The acquisition of other capital assets, such as machinery, furniture, and vehicles, is usually accounted for in the fund responsible for the financing of the expenditure. The purpose of a Capital Projects Fund, as defined by GASB-54 is as follows (GASB-54, par. 33) [GASB Cod. Sec. 1300.106]:

> To account for and report financial resources that are restricted, committed, or assigned to expenditure for capital outlays, including the acquisition or construction of capital facilities and other capital assets.

Capital project funds exclude those types of capital-related outflows financed by proprietary funds or assets that will be held in trust for individuals, private organizations, or other governments (see Chapter 8, "Fiduciary Funds").

In practice, a separate Capital Projects Fund is often established when the acquisition or construction of a capital project extends beyond a single fiscal year and the financing sources are provided by more than one fund, or a capital asset is financed by specifically designated resources. Specifically designated resources may arise from the issuance of general obligation bonds, receipts of grants from other governmental units, designation of a portion of tax receipts, or a combination of these and other financing sources. A Capital Projects Fund must be used when mandated by law or stipulated by regulations or covenants related to the financing source. For control purposes, it can also be advantageous to use a separate Capital Projects Fund for major capital facilities even though one is not legally required. As with all funds in a governmental entity, the purpose of establishing a specific fund is to establish a basis of accountability for resources provided for a particular purpose.

In its basis for conclusions in GASB-54, the GASB acknowledged the diversity in practice regarding the reporting of capital project funds. Some governments believed that capital project funds could only be narrowly used for project-oriented capital activities funded from restricted or committed revenues (such as a road construction project financed with voter-approved bond proceeds), while other governments believed that capital project funds may be used in a broader sense to account for the acquisition of any capital asset (whether owned by the government or transferred to another government) and financed by any source of revenue (such as an equipment replacement fund funded from interfund transfers). GASB-54 redefined capital project funds by combining various aspects of these competing perspectives. The GASB has now defined capital project funds as those funds using restricted or committed revenues for the acquisition or construction of capital assets that clearly comprise capital facilities (such as buildings, building improvements, and infrastructure, including ancillary items) and those related to other capital assets (such as vehicles, machinery, and equipment).

OBSERVATION: There is an uncertainty as to what type of fund would be used for projects that are capital in nature, financed by bonds, but not ultimately owned by a government (e.g., construction of a municipal school by a state authority that is a governmental activity). GASB-54, par. 33 [GASB Cod. Sec. 1300.106], specifically excludes capital projects funds for capital-related outflows financed by proprietary funds or for assets that will be held in trust for individuals, private organizations, or other governments. It is the author's opinion that those sorts of projects could be accounted for in a Special Revenue Fund or an Agency Fund. For acquisition of items that do not meet a government's capitalization threshold, the GASB *Implementation Guide 2015-1*, question Z.54.42 [GASB Cod. Sec. 1300.704-18], does allow use of a capital projects fund to account and report the expenditures.

However, question Z.54.43 [GASB Cod. Sec. 1300.704-19] discusses when a state law allows school districts to establish a "Capital Reserve Fund" into which amounts of unused appropriations (for other purposes) at year-end and unassigned amounts in the general fund may be transferred. The resources in the fund can only be used for capital improvements, the replacement of and additions to public works, and the acquisition of major equipment items. In this case, a reserve does not meet the criteria to be reported as a special revenue fund because the transfers do not represent restricted or committed revenues and the resources are restricted by state law for capital projects. A separate capital projects fund may be reported, but it is not required.

DEBT SERVICE FUNDS

A Debt Service Fund is created to account for resources that will be accumulated and used to service general long-term debt. General long-term debt can include noncurrent bonds and notes, as well as other noncurrent liabilities that might arise from capitalized lease agreements and other long-term liabilities not created by the issuance of a specific debt instrument. The purpose of a Debt Service Fund, as defined by GASB-54, par. 34 [GASB Cod. Sec. 1300.107] is as follows:

> Funds that are used to account for and report financial resources that are restricted, committed, or assigned to expenditure for principal and interest. Debt service funds *should* be used to report resources if doing so is legally mandated, and when financial resources are being accumulated for principal and interest maturing in future years.

A Debt Service Fund is somewhat similar to a sinking fund used by a commercial enterprise in that resources are accumulated for the purpose of eventually retiring long-term obligations.

Although separate Debt Service Funds can be established for long-term obligations that are not based on an outstanding debt instrument (such as compensated absences and special termination benefits), these obligations are generally accounted for in other funds such as the General Fund or Special Revenue Funds.

PERMANENT FUNDS

GASB-54 stipulates that permanent funds are to be used when governmental entities receive resources from other parties, including individuals, private organizations, and other governments, whereby the use of the resources is restricted to the extent that only earnings, and not principal, may be used for purposes that support the reporting government's programs—that is, for the benefit of the government and its citizenry (GASB-54, par. 35) [GASB Cod. Sec. 1300.108].

For example, a cemetery perpetual-care fund should be created when the earnings of the dedicated resources can be used only for the maintenance of a public cemetery and the principal of the fund is to remain intact. GASB-34 (*Basic Financial Statements—and Management's Discussion and Analysis—for State and Local Governments*) requires that a Permanent Fund be used to report this type of resource restriction.

Permanent funds do not include private-purpose trust funds where the government is required to use the principal or earnings for the benefit of individuals, private organizations, or other governments (see Chapter 8, "Fiduciary Funds").

Based on the standards established by GASB-34, public-purpose trust funds previously presented as Nonexpendable Trust Funds are to be presented as

Permanent Funds. A Permanent Fund is a governmental fund and therefore is accounted for under the modified accrual basis of accounting. The GASB believes that even though a public-purpose trust fund might initially appear to be appropriately classified in the fiduciary fund category, these funds are created for the benefit of the governmental entity rather than for external parties. Thus, it is more appropriate for them to be considered governmental funds (at the fund financial statement reporting level) and governmental activities (at the government-wide financial statement reporting level).

PRACTICE ALERT: The GASB's *Financial Reporting Model—Reexamination* project includes deliberations on the status of permanent funds. Frequently, permanent funds are mischaracterized as fiduciary activities. With the release of GASB Statement No. 84 (*Fiduciary Activities*), coupled with the GASB's reexamination, the status of permanent funds may change in the future.

In some instances, the mandated purpose of specific resources to be accounted for in a separate fund may be such that it is not readily apparent which fund type should be used for financial reporting purposes. For example, the *GASB Implementation Guide 2015-1*, question 7.49-1 [GASB Cod. Sec. 1300.704-1] notes that a governmental entity may need to account for financial resources that are legally restricted by enabling legislation, but a minimum balance (nonspendable) is defined by the legislation and that balance must be maintained in the fund. The nonspendable portion of the fund description would suggest that a Permanent Fund should be used while the legal restriction characteristic would suggest that a Special Revenue Fund could be appropriate. The GASB's Guide notes that either fund type could be used under this circumstance. If a Permanent Fund is used, the portion of the fund that is expendable should be identified as a restricted, committed, or assigned fund balance depending upon the nature of the ability to spend and if the fund was created due to the implementation of an external restriction. If a special revenue fund is to be used, similar reporting may result.

ACCOUNTING AND REPORTING FOR GOVERNMENTAL FUNDS

Basis of Accounting and Measurement Focus

The modified accrual basis of accounting and flow of current financial resources measurement focus are used to prepare the financial statements of governmental funds. These concepts are discussed in Chapter 3, "Basis of Accounting and Measurement Focus."

Budgetary System and Accounts

The General Fund and Special Revenue Funds often have an annual budget that serves as the plan of financial operations and establishes the basis for the financial and legal control and evaluation of activities financed through these Funds. The budgetary control process is most effective when a budgetary accounting system, including the use of budgetary accounts, is employed. GASB-34 requires that a budgetary comparison schedule be presented for the General Fund and each "major" Special Revenue Fund that has a legally adopted annual budget. The budgetary process is illustrated in Chapter 2, "Budgetary Accounting."

The *GASB Implementation Guide 2015-1*, question 7.91.2 [GASB Cod. Sec. 2200.763-4], raises the question of whether a Special Revenue Fund that does not meet the percentage criteria in paragraph 76a and 76b of GASB-34 (as amended by GASB-65, par. 33) [GASB Cod. Secs. 2200.159, P80.106] but is nonetheless considered a major fund is required to present a budgetary comparison schedule. The GASB's *Implementation Guide* discusses that if a fund is considered a major fund (for whatever reason), then all of the major fund reporting requirements must be satisfied, including those related to budgetary information. In order for the budgetary information to apply to a major Special Revenue Fund, that fund must have a legally adopted annual budget.

Unlike some governmental funds, a Capital Projects Fund is project-oriented rather than period-oriented, and for this reason it is often not necessary to record the fund's budget for control purposes. For example, the authorization of a bond ordinance by the legislature or the public will identify the specific purpose of the fund as well as the amount of resources that can be used to construct or purchase the capital asset. Subsequent action by the legislature will generally not be necessary.

Unless a Debt Service Fund budget is legally adopted, there is no requirement to record the fund's budget or to prepare financial statements that compare the results of operations for the period on a budget basis with those on an actual basis. Usually the loan or bond indenture provision that requires the establishment of a Debt Service Fund also controls expenditures to be made from the fund. NCGA-1 states that it is unlikely that budgetary accounts should be integrated into the financial accounting system of a Debt Service Fund when the receipts and expenditures (1) are controlled by bond indenture or sinking fund provisions and (2) occur infrequently during the budgetary period.

Revenues and Other Financing Sources

GASB:CS-4 (*Elements of Financial Statements*) defines the elements of the "resource flows (change) statements" involving revenue and other financing sources, and indicates that an "inflow of resources" is an acquisition of net position by the entity that is applicable to the reporting period.

The acquisition of fund balance (inflow) in governmental funds is defined as net financial assets coming under the control of the entity or net financial assets becoming newly available to the entity even if the resources are consumed directly when acquired. An acquisition of net financial assets results in (1) an increase in financial assets in excess of any related increase in fund liabilities or (2) a decrease in fund liabilities in excess of any related decrease in financial assets. Examples of acquisition of fund balance in governmental funds include (1) imposing a tax (because the resources have newly come under the control of the entity) and (2) receiving the proceeds of a bond issue (because no fund liability has been created but cash has been received, thereby increasing the entity's net position).

Revenues

Revenues represent increases in current financial resources other than increases caused by the issuance of long-term debt or the receipt of transfers from other funds. Governmental Fund revenues are recorded when they are susceptible to accrual, which means that the revenues must be both measurable and available in accordance with the modified accrual basis of accounting (NCGA-1, par. 62, GASB-38, par. 7) [GASB Cod. Sec. 1600.106]. GASB-65, par. 30 [GASB Cod. Sec. 1600.115], also stipulates that a government should report a deferred inflow of resources is assets are recorded but revenue is not available. This is common for taxation that is levied in one year, but legislation does not allow for recognition until a subsequent year. Such amounts are declared receivable where taxpayer liability has been established, with collectability assured or losses can be estimated. However, as recognition does not occur until a subsequent year, a deferred inflow of resources is recognized. As part of the opening of the subsequent year, the deferred inflow of resources is negated and revenue recognized.

Other Financing Sources

"Other financing sources" is a classification of governmental fund resources other than those defined as "revenues." For example, when long-term debt is issued and the proceeds are available to a governmental fund, the proceeds are recorded as other financing sources. The long-term debt is not recorded as a liability in the governmental fund but, rather, is reported as a liability only in the entity's statement of net position (government-wide financial statement). Interfund transfers from other funds are also reported as "other financing sources." (GASB-34, par. 88, as amended by GASB-37, par. 16) [GASB Cod. Secs. 1100.112, 1500.121, 1800.101, .124, .129, 2200.167, D20.109].

OBSERVATION: The face amount of the long-term debt and related discount or premium and debt-issuance costs should be separately reported in the governmental fund operating statement. The debt-issuance costs should be presented as expenditures and the other items should be presented as other financing sources and uses. U.S. GAAP requires that the "face amount," and not the proceeds (net of any discount or premium) from the issuance of the debt, be presented as other financing sources.

Classification and Disclosure

Revenues should be presented in the governmental funds' statement of revenues and expenditures and identified by major source, such as property taxes, income taxes, and so on (see Chapter 5, "Terminology and Classification"). The revenue recognition methods used by the governmental funds should be explained in the summary of significant accounting policies.

Expenditures and Other Financing Uses

GASB:CS-4 (*Elements of Financial Statements*) defines the elements of the "resource flows (change) statements" involving expenditures and other financing uses, and indicates that an "outflow of resources" is a consumption of fund balance by the entity that is applicable to the reporting period.

The consumption of fund balance (outflow) in governmental funds is defined as the using up of net financial assets that results in (1) a decrease in financial assets in excess of any related decrease in fund liabilities or (2) an increase in fund liabilities in excess of any related increase in financial assets. Examples of consumption of financial resources in governmental funds include (1) using financial resources to acquire capital assets (because existing cash resources of the entity have been consumed) and (2) using the labor of employees to provide government services for which payment will be made in the next reporting period (because the entity has consumed employee labor resources that were directly acquired from the employees).

Expenditures

NCGA-1, par. 109, as amended by GASB-6, par. 19, GASB-7, par. 8, and GASBI-1, par. 13 [GASB Cod. Sec. 1800.130] describe expenditures as decreases in fund financial resources other than through interfund transfers. Events that represent (1) a reduction of a governmental fund's expendable financial resources or (2) a claim at the end of the period that is normally expected to be liquidated by using current expendable financial resources are recorded as expenditures. Expenditures are accrued when incurred if the event or transaction results in a reduction of the governmental fund's current financial resources. If there is no reduction in the fund's net *current financial resources*, no expenditure is recorded. For example, a governmental unit may incur an estimated liability for compensated absences, but if the actual payments to employees are not due at period end, the expenditure would not be reflected in the governmental fund. Instead, it is reported as a liability in the entity's statement of net position (a government-wide financial statement).

PRACTICE ALERT: Part of the GASB's *Financial Reporting Model—Reex amination Project* includes a potential clarification of "financial resources." The GASB has a preliminary view that the term "financial resources" means cash, resources that are expected to be converted to cash, and resources that are consumable in lieu of cash. Whatever final definition of "financial resources" is used will determine what are revenues, other financing sources, expenditures, and other financing uses in governmental funds.

Other Financing Uses

Other financing uses may consist of transfers to other funds and expenditures related to the issuance of general obligation debt (GASB-34, pars. 88, 112, as amended by GASB-37, par. 16) [GASB Cod. Sec. 2200.167].

Classification and Disclosure

For internal and external analysis and reporting, governmental fund expenditures may be classified by (1) function or program, (2) organizational unit, (3) activity, (4) character, and (5) object class (see Chapter 5, "Terminology and Classification").

GASB Concepts Statement 6 (GASB:CS-6) (*Measurement of Elements of Financial Statements*) addresses both measurement approaches and measurement attributes. A measurement approach determines whether an asset or liability presented in a financial statement should be (1) reported at an amount that reflects a value at the date that the asset was acquired or the liability was incurred or (2) remeasured and reported at an amount that reflects a value at the date of the financial statements. A measurement attribute is the feature or characteristic of the asset or liability that is measured. GASB:CS-6 establishes two measurement approaches that would be used in financial statements, as follows:

1. *Initial-Transaction-Date-Based Measurement (Initial Amount)*—The transaction price or amount assigned when an asset was acquired or a liability was incurred, including subsequent modifications to that price or amount, such as through depreciation or impairment.

2. *Current-Financial-Statement-Date-Based Measurement (Remeasured Amount)*—The amount assigned when an asset or liability is remeasured as of the financial statement date.

GASB:CS-6 also establishes the four measurement attributes that would be used in financial statements, as follows:

1. *Historical cost* is the price paid to acquire an asset or the amount received pursuant to the incurrence of a liability in an actual exchange transaction.

2. *Fair value* is the price that would be received to sell an asset or paid to transfer a liability in an orderly transaction between market participants at the measurement date.

3. *Replacement cost* is the price that would be paid to acquire an asset with equivalent service potential in an orderly market transaction at the measurement date.

4. *Settlement amount* is the amount at which an asset could be realized or a liability could be liquidated with the counterparty other than in an active market.

OBSERVATION: GASB Statement No. 72 (*Fair Value Measurement and Application*) introduced a concept that is not contained within GASB:CS-6. Consistent with Concepts Statement 6, many assets are measured based on measurement attributes other than fair value. In its deliberations, the GASB agreed that fair value should be replaced by **acquisition value** for *certain transactions*.

Acquisition value is the price that would be paid to acquire an asset with equivalent service potential in an orderly market transaction at the acquisition date, or the amount at which a liability could be liquidated with the counterparty at the acquisition date. It is a market-based entry price. Fair value, on the other hand, is an exit price—the price that would be received to sell an asset or paid to transfer a liability. Acquisition value is a measurement at the initial transaction date using the replacement cost or the settlement amount measurement attribute. The GASB believes that an entry price measurement is more appropriate than an exit price because (*a*) the transaction represents the government acquiring the asset and (*b*) it would result in a similar measurement as if the government had purchased the asset. Based on this conclusion, acquisition value should be used for the following assets *only*:

- Donated capital assets;
- Donated works of art, historical treasures, and similar assets; and
- Capital assets that a government receives in a service concession arrangement.

The notion of an acquisition price is further supported by the view that those assets generally will be used in providing services, rather than converted to cash.

Assets

"Assets," as defined in GASB:CS-4, are:

Resources with a present service capacity that the entity presently controls.

Assets of governmental funds include resources that are considered current expendable financial resources available for subsequent appropriation and expenditure. Assets other than those that are currently expendable, such as capital assets, are indeed assets, but they are not available to finance future expenditures that will be made from the governmental funds.

Current Assets

The governmental funds' balance sheet is unclassified in that current and noncurrent categories are not presented. Assets of the governmental funds are primarily current assets, including cash, cash equivalents, marketable investments, inventories, various receivables, and amounts due from other funds.

Certain noncurrent assets (not currently expendable) may be reported in governmental funds, but these assets result in a restricted or non-spendable fund balance. For example, if a long-term note receivable is reported in the General Fund, the General Fund's fund balance should be reported as a nonspendable.

Investments

The standards established by GASB-31 (*Accounting and Financial Reporting for Certain Investments and for External Investment Pools*) apply to most governmental fund investments. The accounting standards for investments are discussed in Chapter 9, "Deposits, Investments, and Derivative Instruments."

OBSERVATION: GASB Statement No. 72 redefines "investments." In the updated standard, an investment is a security or other asset that (*a*) a government holds primarily for the purpose of income or profit and (*b*) has a present service capacity based solely on its ability to generate cash or to be sold to generate cash. A further discussion on GASB-72 is contained in Chapter 9, "Deposits, Investments, and Derivative Instruments."

Long-Term Receivables

Governmental funds generally reflect assets that are available to finance current expenditures. However, noncurrent financial assets, such as long-term receivables, should also be presented in the governmental funds' balance sheets, along with a fund balance assigned by an equal amount. Note that management has negotiated the loan under terms delegated by the government's highest level of decision making authority. To illustrate, if a $100,000 advance to a Special Revenue Fund will not be repaid during the subsequent budgetary period, the transaction would be recorded as follows in the General Fund:

GENERAL FUND	Debit	Credit
Interfund Loans Receivable—	100,000	
General Fund Cash		100,000
Fund Balance—Unassigned	100,000	
Fund Balance—Nonspendable-Interfund Loan		100,000
To record long-term loans to Special Revenue Fund.		

Capital Assets

General capital assets, such as land, buildings, infrastructure and equipment, purchased and used by governmental funds should be recorded as a capital outlay expenditure in the governmental funds and not reported as a fund asset. However, the capital asset is reported in the entity's statement of net position (a government-wide financial statement).

The accounting for governmental funds' expenditures associated with the acquisition or construction of a capital asset is illustrated by the following transactions:

Transaction: Purchase orders and contracts of $400,000 related to the construction of an addition to a building are signed and the project is to be funded from a Capital Projects Fund:

CAPITAL PROJECTS FUND	Debit	Credit
Encumbrances	400,000	
Reserve for Encumbrances		400,000

NOTE: This transaction will only be carried in the ledgers during the year. For financial reporting purposes, encumbrances and reserves for encumbrances are not presented.

Transaction: Purchase orders and contracts that were encumbered for $150,000 are vouchered for $157,000 and paid:

CAPITAL PROJECTS FUND	Debit	Credit
Reserve for Encumbrances	150,000	
Encumbrances		150,000
Expenditures—Capital Outlays	157,000	
Vouchers Payable/Cash		157,000

NOTE: This transaction will only be carried in the ledgers during the year. For financial reporting purposes, encumbrances and reserves for encumbrances are not presented.

Transaction: Construction is completed and the remaining purchase orders and contracts are vouchered for $245,000 and paid:

CAPITAL PROJECTS FUND	Debit	Credit
Reserve for Encumbrances	250,000	
Encumbrances		250,000
Expenditures—Capital Outlays	245,000	
Vouchers Payable/Cash		245,000

Classification and Disclosure

With respect to governmental funds' assets, the following disclosures should be made:

- Disclose valuation bases and significant or unusual accounting treatment for material account balances or transactions. (Disclosures should be described in the order of appearance in the balance sheet.)
- Disclose detail notes on the following, if appropriate:
  - Pooling of cash and investments;
  - Investments by type; and
  - Disaggregation of receivables by type of receivable, if not presented on the face of the balance sheet.

The assets that appear on the governmental funds' balance sheet are presented in an unclassified format.

Liabilities

GASB:CS-4 defines "liabilities" as:

> Present obligations to sacrifice resources that the entity has little or no discretion to avoid.

Governmental fund liabilities are debts or obligations of the governmental unit that are to be met by using the governmental fund's current expendable financial resources. Liabilities that do not require the use of current expendable financial resources but will be retired at a later date by resources made available through governmental funds, are reported as an obligation on the statement of net position. As previously discussed in this chapter, the definition of a "liability" is also somewhat unclear when considering what a "matured liability," an "obligation," and a "commitment" are due to the lack of uniformity in a definition of "current expendable financial resources."

OBSERVATION: The definition of a "liability" has become extraordinarily important. As liabilities are present obligations to sacrifice resources that the entity has little or no discretion to avoid, the GASB reasoned in GASB-67 (*Financial Reporting for Pension Plans—an amendment of GASB Statement No. 25*) and GASB-68 (*Accounting and Financial Reporting for Pensions—an amendment of GASB Statement No. 27*) that the employer-employee nexus occurs at an employer level. Due to the interaction, employers should carry a liability for the present value of unfunded accrued postemployment benefits. Chapter 13, "Pension, Postemployment, and Other Employee Benefit Liabilities," includes a complete discussion of the standards and their implications.

Current Liabilities

Although the governmental funds' balance sheet is unclassified, a liability presented on the financial statement is generally considered to be a current liability. Current liabilities of governmental funds include items such as accounts and vouchers payable, short-term notes payable, accrued liabilities, interest due and payable, and payroll withholdings. These liabilities represent debts that will be paid within a relatively short period (i.e. a few months) after the close of the state or local government's fiscal year and are generally easy to identify as current rather than noncurrent liabilities. Liabilities must be evaluated to determine whether they are debts of governmental funds or are more appropriately reported only on the entity's statement of net position.

GASB Statement No. 65 (Items Previously Reported as Assets and Liabilities) and Deferred Inflows of Resources in Governmental Funds

GASB-65, par. 30 [GASB Cod. Sec. 1600.115], requires that when an asset is recorded in governmental fund financial statements but the revenue is not available, the government should report a deferred inflow of resources until such time as the revenue becomes available. Furthermore, in GASB-65, par. 31 [GASB Cod. Sec. 1600.114], the GASB has limited the use of the term "deferred" except when declaring either deferred inflows of resources or deferred outflows of resources. Some governments use the term "unearned revenue." However, this has never been allowable in governmental U.S. GAAP except for certain types of insurance transactions. The use of the term "deferred revenue" is no longer allowed. Instead, when assets are provided and revenue is available to declare but there is an uncertainty as to allowability of recognition, the term *advance* should be used. For example, "advances from grantors" is perfectly acceptable.

As previously discussed in Chapter 1, "Foundation and Overview of Governmental Generally Accepted Accounting Principles," the term "liability" is often misunderstood because contained within it are the concepts of obligations and, to some extent, time. An obligation is a social, legal, or moral requirement, such as a duty, contract, or promise that compels one to follow or avoid a particular course of action. Obligations can be legally enforceable as exemplified when a court compels the government to fulfill its obligation. Obligations could arise from legislation or contractual obligations; however, they may differ based on whether exchange transactions (value for value) or nonexchange transactions take place. Constructive liabilities may occur in exchange transactions when resources are transferred to a government. In such a case, the government must fulfill its obligations. The concept of "little or no discretion to avoid" arises when no power exists to decline sacrificing of resources or penalty/consequences of not doing the action is more than minor. One of the consistent themes in all of these nuances is that the parties to an obligation that may be a liability are usually external to the government.

The language contained in GASB Interpretation 6 (GASBI-6), *Recognition and Measurement of Certain Liabilities and Expenditures in Governmental Fund Financial Statements*, was one of the reasons why the clarification of the concepts of the terms "liability" and "obligation" needed to be released. GASBI-6, par. 10, describes "matured liabilities" in governmental funds (not associated with proprietary funds) as only those that are normally due and payable in full when incurred or the matured portion of general long-term indebtedness (the portion that has come due for payment). In GASBI-6, par. 11, the GASB also interprets matured liabilities to include debt service on formal debt issued when due (matured) and compensated absences, claims and judgments, special termination benefits, and landfill closure and postclosure care costs. All of these should be recognized as governmental fund liabilities and expenditures to the extent the liabilities are "normally expected to be liquidated with expendable available financial resources." In its basis for conclusions, the GASB considered but rejected an alternative interpretation that "other commitments" are the long-term portion of any other liabilities, provided that the government has entered into a multilateral agreement to defer payment to a future period. The GASB concluded that there is no accrual modification that would permit deferring to a future period the recognition of fund liabilities (such as salaries and utilities) that normally are paid in a timely manner and in full from current financial resources when incurred. Rather, the GASB proposed that such transactions be reported as governmental fund liabilities and expenditures when incurred (GASBI-6, pars. 10–11) [GASB Cod. Secs. 1500.103, .118–.119].

OBSERVATION: With the implementation of GASB-76 (*The Hierarchy of Generally Accepted Accounting Principles for State and Local Governments*) and the related *Implementation Guide 2015-1*, GASB Interpretations are no longer authoritative and have largely been incorporated into other standards. The *GASB Implementation Guide* is authoritative, but not as authoritative as a GASB Statement. Chapter Z of the *Comprehensive Implementation Guide 2015-1*, Q&A 16.1, as amended and 16.2 [GASB Cod. Secs. C60.707-2 and 710-1, respectively], address the issues of liabilities in governmental funds and is authoritative.

Bond, Tax, and Revenue Anticipation Notes

Governments may issue bond, tax, or revenue anticipation notes that will be retired when specific taxes or other specified revenues are collected by the governments. For example, a local government may issue property tax anticipation notes a few weeks or months before the anticipated receipt of property tax installments are to be paid by taxpayers. Bond, tax, and revenue anticipation notes and whether they are reported as governmental fund liabilities or only as general long-term liabilities are discussed in Chapter 12, "Long-Term Debt."

PRACTICE ALERT: The status of tax and revenue anticipation notes may change as a result of the GASB's *Financial Reporting Model—Reexamination* project. Such notes may become a fund liability if the GASB adopts changes to the definition of "financial resources" and the period of availability for governmental funds.

Demand Bonds

A bond agreement may contain a clause that allows bondholders to require a governmental unit to redeem the debt during a specified period of time. The demand feature, or put, and related circumstances must be evaluated to determine whether the demand bonds should be reported as a debt obligation only in the statement of net position (a government-wide liability) or also as a short-term debt (a governmental fund liability). This topic is discussed in Chapter 12, "Long-Term Debt." (GASBI-1) [GASB Cod. Sec. D30.101].

Arbitrage

Arbitrage involves the simultaneous purchase and sale of the same or essentially the same securities with the objective of making a profit on the spread between the two markets. In the context of governmental finance, this practice often occurs when a governmental entity issues tax-exempt debt and uses the proceeds to invest in debt securities that have a higher rate of return. Because of the spread between the debt securities interest rates and the tax-exempt interest rate, an entity can more effectively manage its financial resources. However, state and local governments must cautiously apply this indirect federal tax subsidy because the federal government has established arbitrage restrictions (requirements for how long the funds can be invested) and arbitrage rebate rules (the amount of arbitrage earnings that must be paid to the federal government).

The governmental entity must apply the rules and regulations established by the federal government in order to determine whether the entity has a liability that it should record in its financial statements. Such liabilities should be recorded using the general guidance contained in GASB-62, pars. 96–113 [GASB Cod. Secs. C50.151–.168, 2300.106]. If the governmental entity should accrue a liability, it should record the portion that represents the use of current financial resources as expenditures (although some governmental entities offset the amount against interest income) and also the balance of the liability as a liability in its government-wide financial statements.

Capital Leases

Rather than acquire capital assets by making current payments or issuing bonds or notes to finance the acquisition, a governmental unit may enter into a long-term lease agreement. Accounting for lease agreements in a governmental fund is based on whether the agreement is classified as a capital lease or operating lease. GASB-62, pars. 211–271 [GASB Cod. Secs. L20.103-501–515], contains the former standards established by FAS-13 (*Accounting for Leases*), as amended and codified in FASB Accounting Standards Codification® (ASC) Topic 840 (*Leases*), with appropriate modifications to reflect the measurement focus of government funds. Accounting for lease agreements is discussed in Chapter 14, "Leases and Service Concession Arrangements," along with a discussion of the wide-ranging GASB Statement No. 87 (*Leases*).

Long-Term Debt

The proceeds from the issuance of long-term debt are recorded in the governmental funds as other financing sources; and the liability itself is not reported as debt of the governmental funds but, rather, is reported as an obligation in the government-wide financial statements. For example, the issuance of general obligation serial bonds of $10,000,000 would be recorded as follows:

CAPITAL PROJECTS FUND	Debit	Credit
Cash	10,000,000	
Other Financing Sources—Proceeds from Issuance of Serial Bonds		10,000,000
To record the issuance of general obligation serial bonds series 201Z-A.		

Bonds Issued Between Interest Payment Dates

Long-term bonds may be issued on a date that does not coincide with an interest payment date. When this occurs, the proceeds from the bond issuance include an amount of accrued interest. The accrued interest does not represent other financing sources of a governmental fund, and it should be recorded as a payable to the governmental fund responsible for servicing the long-term debt. For example, assume that $10,000,000 of bonds carrying a 6% interest rate are issued for $10,100,000, including two months of interest ($100,000) and the proceeds are recorded in a Capital Projects Fund. The issuance of the bonds between interest payment dates would be recorded as follows, assuming a Debt Service Fund will accumulate resources to make interest and principal payments over the life of the bonds:

CAPITAL PROJECTS FUND	Debit	Credit
Cash	10,100,000	
Proceeds from Long-Term Debt Issued		10,000,000
Due to Debt Service Fund		100,000
DEBT SERVICE FUND		
Due from Capital Projects Fund	100,000	
Interest Payable		100,000
To record the issuance of general obligation serial bonds series 201Z-B and related payable amounts for days between interest payments.		

Alternatively, the portion of the proceeds that represents the interest that will be payable at the next interest payment date may be recorded directly in the fund responsible for servicing the debt. If this approach were chosen, the previous illustration would be recorded as follows:

CAPITAL PROJECTS FUND	Debit	Credit
Cash	10,000,000	
Proceeds from Long-Term Debt Issued		10,000,000
DEBT SERVICE FUND		
Cash	100,000	
Interest Payable		100,000
To record the issuance of general obligation serial bonds series 201Z-B and related payable amounts for days between interest payments.		

Bond Premium, Discount, and Bond Issuance Costs

The face amount of the long-term debt, any related discount or premiums, and debt issuance costs should be reported separately. The debt proceeds (based on the face amount of the debt), discount, and premium must be presented as other financing sources and uses. The debt issuance costs should be presented as expenditures in accordance with the provisions of GASB-65 (*Items Previously Reported as Assets and Liabilities*).

Unmatured Principal and Interest

Under the modified accrual basis, expenditures of a governmental fund are recognized when the related liability is incurred. The one significant exception to this fundamental concept is the accounting treatment for unmatured principal and accrued interest. Unmatured principal and accrued interest are not recognized as a liability of a governmental fund until the amounts are due to be paid.

For example, if long-term debt was issued on October 1, 20X8, and the first interest payment was due on April 1, 20X9, there would be no accrual of interest as of December 31, 20X8 (end of fiscal year). Likewise, if a serial bond repayment was due on April 1, 20X9, the liability would not be required to be recorded in the Debt Service Fund's balance sheet as of March 31, 20X9, even though the amount would be due the next day.

PRACTICE ALERT: The GASB's *Financial Reporting Model—Reexamination* project may clarify this inconsistency between governmental fund reporting of debts and debts presented on the government-wide financial statements. The clarification may occur with adjustments in the period of availability and a clarified definition of "financial resources."

Current accounting standards provide for an exception to the basic concept that general long-term indebtedness is not reported as expenditures until the amount becomes due and payable. When funds have been transferred to the Debt Service Fund during the fiscal year in anticipation of making debt service payments "shortly" after the end of the period, it is acceptable to accrue interest and debt in the Debt Service Fund as an expenditure in the year the transfer is made This period is also known as "the period of availability."

Prior to the issuance of GASBI-6 (*Recognition and Measurement of Certain Liabilities and Expenditures in Governmental Fund Financial Statements*) there was a considerable amount of confusion about what was meant by "shortly." The Interpretation states that "shortly" means "early in the following year." However, the period of time after the end of the year cannot be greater than one month (GASBI-6, par. 9, as amended by GASB-47, par. 3, and GASB-49, pars. 9 and 24, GASBI-6, par. 13) [GASB Cod. Secs. 1500.117, .122].

PRACTICE ALERT: In the GASB's *Financial Reporting Model—Reexamination* project, this generalization may be resolved with a clarified definition of financial resources and adjustments to the period of availability.

Debt Extinguishments

Scheduled debt retirements are accounted for as just described. In addition to scheduled retirements, general obligations of a governmental unit may be extinguished by (1) legal defeasance or (2) in-substance defeasance or debt refunding. These transactions require special accounting treatment in governmental funds and are discussed in Chapter 12, "Long-Term Debt."

PRACTICE POINT: GASB Statement No. 86 (*Certain Debt Extinguishment Issues*) was issued during 2017. For governmental funds, payments to the escrow agent made from existing resources (not from issuing any form of new debt) should be reported as debt service expenditures. Note disclosure includes: (1) a description of the transaction; (2) the amount of the debt involved; (2) the amount of existing resources placed with the escrow agent; (3) the reasons for the defeasance; and (4) the cash flows required to service the debt. GASB-86 became effective for periods beginning after June 15, 2017. Changes to conform to the provisions of GASB-86 are applied retroactively by restating financial statements, if practicable for all prior periods presented. Further information on GASB-86 is also contained in Chapter 12, "Long-Term Debt."

Zero-Interest-Rate Bonds

Zero-interest-rate bonds (often referred to as zero-coupon bonds) are issued at a deep discount, and the difference between the initial price of the bonds and their maturity value represents interest. Interest is not accrued but, rather, is recognized as an expenditure when due and payable. The interest expenditure for zero-interest-rate bonds is recorded when the bonds mature. However, the accrued interest must be recognized as part of the general debt in the governmental entity's government-wide statement of net position.

To illustrate the accounting for zero-interest-rate bonds, assume that $3,000,000 (maturity value) of non-interest-bearing term bonds are issued to yield a rate of return of 5%. The bonds mature in 10 years and are issued for $1,841,730

($3,000,000 × 0.61391, where $i = 5\%$, $n = 10$ for the present value of an amount). The equation is as follows:

$$\text{Price} = [\text{Maturity Value} \div (1 + \text{interest rate})^{\text{number of periods}}]$$
$$\text{Price} = [\$3,000,000 \div (1 + 5\%)^{10}]$$
$$\text{Price} = \$1,841,730$$

The issuance of the bonds, assuming the proceeds are made available to the General Fund, is recorded as follows:

GENERAL FUND	Debit	Credit
Cash	1,841,730	
Other Financing Uses—Discount on Long-Term Debt Issued	1,158,270	
Other Financing Sources—Long-Term Debt Issued		3,000,000
To record the issuance of discount bonds Series 201Z-A at 5%.		

At the end of the first fiscal year, the amount of accrued interest earned by investors on the bonds is $92,087 calculated as ($1,841,730 × 5%). Because the interest will not be paid by the Debt Service Fund until the bonds mature, the accrued interest is not recognized as expenditures. However, the accrued interest must be included as part of general long-term debt in the government-wide statement of net position.

When the bonds mature in 10 years, assuming that sufficient funds have been accumulated in the Debt Service Fund, the following entries are made:

DEBT SERVICE FUND	Debit	Credit
Expenditures—Principal	1,841,730	
Expenditures—Interest	1,158,270	
Cash		3,000,000
To record the maturity of discount bonds Series 201Z-A.		

Classification and Disclosure

With respect to fund and long-term liabilities payable from governmental funds, the following disclosures should be made:

- Description of long-term debt and other obligations;
- Changes in long-term debt balances;
- Changes in short-term loan balances;
- Disaggregation of payables by type, if not on the face of the balance sheet;
- Debt service requirements to maturity, separated by principal and interest components (for debt serviced from the governmental funds); and

- The amount of outstanding debt considered retired resulting from debt refunding or in-substance defeasance transactions and the cash flow and economic gains or losses from the transactions in the current period.

OBSERVATION: The implementation of GASB-68 (*Accounting and Financial Reporting for Pensions*) has generated a number of questions as to what to record in the funds, if anything. The *Guide to Implementation of GASB Statement 68 on Accounting and Financial Reporting for Pensions—Questions and Answers* includes a question on the guidance for recognizing a portion of the net pension liability in fund statements if a portion of the net pension liability will be paid from an *enterprise, internal service, or fiduciary fund*. The GASB notes that GASB-68 does not establish specific requirements for allocation of the net pension liability or other pension-related measures to individual funds. However, for proprietary and fiduciary funds, consideration should be given to NCGA-1 (par. 42, as amended) [GASB Cod. Secs. 1100.108, 1500.102, C60.110], *Governmental Accounting and Financial Reporting Principles*, which requires that long-term liabilities that are "directly related to and expected to be paid from" those funds be reported in the statement of net position or statement of fiduciary net position, respectively. Therefore, for a governmental fund, the only likely liability would be for amounts that are owed to the plan but unpaid at the end of a period. Pension expenditures may be declared for outflows that meet the definition of a "governmental expenditure." However, it is unlikely that a deferred inflow of resources or a deferred outflow of resources would be declared in a governmental fund due to activity related to pensions in accordance with GASB-68. Similar provisions may also occur with regard to GASB-75 (*Accounting and Financial Reporting for Postemployment Benefits Other than Pensions*).

Fund Equity or Net Position

GASB:CS-4 defines "Net Position" as the residual of all other elements presented in a statement of financial position. In governmental funds, this net position (the difference between "fund assets—current financial resources" and "fund liabilities—obligations normally payable from current financial resources") is referred to as "fund balance." Deferred inflows of resources may also be present; however, it would be rare for deferred outflows of resources to be present in a governmental fund.

Reporting Fund Balance of a Special Revenue Fund in the Government-Wide Financial Statements

In practice, Special Revenue Funds have been established for purposes other than that stipulated by GASB-54. Many state and local governments have established special revenue funds in various legal acts that do not necessarily conform to the definitions contained in GASB-54. Thus, the nature of each Special Revenue Fund must be evaluated to determine how its net position should be presented on the statement of net position.

If a special revenue fund has been established by the governing body to earmark a percentage of its sales tax revenue to be used for a specific purpose, the net position reported at the government-wide level related to the fund would not be reported as restricted net position. This is because the earmarking of existing revenue is not equivalent to a "restriction by enabling legislation" as defined in GASB-34 needed for these amounts to be reported as restricted net position. Essentially, the governing body could un-earmark the revenue relatively easily, thereby in substance, unrestricting the revenue at the government-wide level for reporting purposes.

FUND FINANCIAL STATEMENTS

GASB-34 requires that the following financial statements be presented for governmental funds:

- Balance sheet; and
- Statement of revenues, expenditures, and changes in fund balances.

Reporting standards require that a governmental fund be presented in a separate column in the fund financial statements if the fund is considered a major fund. All other governmental funds are considered nonmajor and are aggregated in a single column in the fund financial statements. See Chapter 1, "Foundation and Overview of Governmental Generally Accepted Accounting Principles," for discussion of the definition of "major funds."

(Exhibit 20-4 in Chapter 20, "Comprehensive Annual Financial Report," is an illustration of a balance sheet for governmental funds. Exhibit 20-5 is an illustration of a statement of revenues, expenditures, and changes in fund balances for governmental funds.)

GOVERNMENT-WIDE FINANCIAL STATEMENTS

The information developed for the preparation of the fund statements for the five governmental fund types (on the modified accrual basis and current financial resources focus) is the starting point for converting the information in preparing the governmental activities column of the government-wide financial statements (on the accrual basis and economic resources focus). Government-wide financial statements are more fully discussed and illustrated in Chapter 20, "Comprehensive Annual Financial Report."

NOTE: The process by which fund financial statements are converted to government-wide financial statements is comprehensively illustrated in Appendix 20A of this guide and in CCH's *Governmental GAAP Practice Manual.*

QUESTIONS

1. A governmental fund that accounts for all of the unit's financial resources except for those resources not accounted for and reported in another fund is referred to as:

   a. Special revenue fund.

   b. Permanent fund.

   c. Capital projects fund.

   d. General fund.

2. A governmental fund that accounts for and reports financial resources that are restricted, committed, or assigned to expenditure for principal and interest is known as a:

   a. Special revenue fund.

   b. Permanent fund.

   c. Debt service fund.

   d. Capital projects fund.

3. For the general fund and similar governmental funds, revenues are recognized when:

   a. They are susceptible to accrual, which means that the revenues must be both measurable and available.

   b. They are received because they are both measurable and not necessarily available.

   c. They are recorded upon being available but are not necessarily measurable.

   d. They can be converted to cash.

4. In a governmental fund, when assets are received but revenue is not available, what should be recorded?

   a. An advance.

   b. Deferred inflows of resources.

   c. Unearned revenue.

   d. Deferred revenue.

5. In a governmental fund, when are expenditures recorded?

   a. When cash is paid.

   b. When deferred outflows of resources are recorded.

   c. When incurred if the event or transaction results in a reduction of the governmental fund's current financial resources.

   d. When an advance is recorded.

Practice Case (*Adapted from the GASB Implementation Guide 2015-1*)

Castle Rock County has a blended component unit, the Castle Rock Public Facility Corporation. The fund that accumulates revenues and transfers for the payment of principal and interest for the Public Facility Corporation is included as a major fund. All other funds of the Public Facility Corporation are reported as part of aggregated other governmental funds on Castle Rock County's basic financial statements. The adjusted trial balance for the fund includes $11,343,051 of investments, plus accrued interest, and $7,250 of accounts receivable, with the only other entry being to fund balance.

1. What type of fund would be declared for this activity?
2. What type of accounting elements would be declared for the $11,343,051 and the $7,250 (assets, liabilities, revenues, expenditures, or deferred inflows of resources)?
3. What type of fund balance would be declared for the entries above?
4. Would the entries for the fund be declared current or long-term?
5. If proceeds were received from bond sales, in your best judgment would they be recorded in this fund? (Justify your answer.)

ANSWERS

1. A governmental fund that accounts for all of the unit's financial resources except for those resources not accounted for and reported in another fund is referred to as:

   Answer – D: General Fund. Special revenue funds account for and report the proceeds of specific revenue sources that are restricted or committed to expenditure for specified purposes other than debt service or capital projects. Permanent funds are to be used when governmental entities receive resources from other parties, including individuals, private organizations, and other governments, whereby the use of the resources are restricted to the extent that only earnings, and not principal, may be used for purposes that support the reporting government's programs—that is, for the benefit of the government and its citizenry. Capital projects funds account for and report financial resources that are restricted, committed, or assigned to expenditure for capital outlays, including the acquisition or construction of capital facilities and other capital assets.

2. A governmental fund that accounts for and report financial resources that are restricted, committed, or assigned to expenditure for principal and interest is known as a:

   Answer – C: Debt service funds as they are used to account for and report financial resources that are restricted, committed, or assigned to expenditure for principal and interest. Debt service funds *should* be used to report resources if doing so is legally mandated, and when financial resources are being accumulated for principal and interest maturing in future years. All other types of funds in A, B, and D are discussed in the answer to question 1.

3. For the general fund and similar governmental funds, revenues are recognized when:

   Answer – A: They are susceptible to accrual, which means that the revenues must be both measurable and available. Answers B, C, and D are not U.S. GAAP.

4. In a governmental fund, when assets are received but revenue is not available, what should be recorded?

   Answer – B: In accordance with GASB-65, par. 30 [GASB Cod. Sec. 1300.105]. Answer A would only be acceptable if revenue is not available and if there is a possibility that the assets declared do not meet the definition of "allowable costs." C and D are not U.S. GAAP in accordance with GASB-65.

5. In a governmental fund, when are expenditures recorded?

   Answer – C: When incurred if the event or transaction results in a reduction of the governmental fund's current financial resources. All others are not U.S. GAAP.

Practice Case (*Adapted from GASB Implementation Guide 2015-1*)

Castle Rock County has a blended component unit, the Castle Rock Public Facility Corporation. The fund that accumulates revenues and transfers for the payment of principal and interest for the Public Facility Corporation is included as a major fund. All other funds of the Public Facility Corporation are reported as part of aggregated other governmental funds on Castle Rock County's basic financial statements. The adjusted trial balance for the fund includes $11,343,051 of investments, plus accrued interest, and $7,250 of accounts receivable, with the only other entry being to fund balance.

1. What type of fund would be declared for this activity?

   Answer – A debt service fund, even though they may be accumulating resources for future debt service payments.

2. What type of accounting elements would be declared for the $11,343,051 and the $7,250 (assets, liabilities, revenues, expenditures, or deferred inflows of resources)?

   Answer – Assets.

3. What type of fund balance would be declared for the entries above?

   Answer – Restricted Fund Balance for Debt Service.

4. Would the entries for the fund be declared current or long-term?

   Answer – No. U.S. GAAP does not allow presentation of current assets and liabilities apart from long-term assets and liabilities in governmental funds.

5. If proceeds were received from bond sales, in your best judgment would they be recorded in this fund? (Justify your answer.)

   Answer – No. GASB-54 and NCGA-1 would require the proceeds of long-term debt to be recorded in either a capital projects fund if constructing or acquiring a capital asset or a special revenue or an agency fund if received to construct or acquire an asset for another entity. Conceivably, if the proceeds were for cash flow purposes of the government, the general fund could also be used to record the proceeds, but care must be taken that the proceeds are used for tax-exempt purposes if the bonds are to be tax-exempt.

CHAPTER 7
PROPRIETARY FUNDS

CONTENTS

INTRODUCTION

A proprietary fund is used to account for a state or local government's activities that are similar to activities that may be performed by a commercial enterprise. For example, a hospital may be operated by a governmental unit, such as a city, or by a profit-oriented corporation. The accounting and reporting standards used by a proprietary fund and a business enterprise are similar because the activities performed are basically the same.

Although a proprietary fund is accounted for in much the same manner as a commercial enterprise, a proprietary fund is nonetheless a fund used by governmental entities. NCGA-1, par. 2 [GASB Cod. Secs. 1100.101, 1200] *Governmental Accounting and Financial Reporting Principles* defines a "fund" as

A fiscal and accounting entity with a self-balancing set of accounts recording cash and other financial resources, together with all related liabilities and residual equities or balances, and changes therein, which are segregated for the purpose of carrying on specific activities or attaining certain objectives in accordance with special regulations, restrictions, or limitations.

The basic objective of a proprietary fund, as alluded to in the NCGA's definition, is different from the fundamental purpose of a commercial enterprise. The purpose of a proprietary fund is not to maximize its return on invested capital. Generally, the purpose of a proprietary fund is to provide a service or product to the public or other governmental entities at a reasonable cost. The objective is achieved by creating one of the following two types of proprietary funds: an Enterprise Fund or an Internal Service Fund.

ENTERPRISE FUNDS

An Enterprise Fund may be used to "report any activity for which a fee is charged to external users for goods or services." GASB-34 (*Basic Financial State-*

ments—and Management's Discussion and Analysis—for State and Local Governments) states that an Enterprise Fund *must* be used to account for an activity if any one of the following three criteria is satisfied, applying the criteria in the context of the activity's *principal revenue sources* (GASB-34, par. 67) [GASB Cod. Secs. 1300.109, Ca5.103, Ho5.103, In3.103, Sp20.103, Ut5.103]:

1. The activity is financed with debt that is secured *solely* by a pledge of the net revenues from fees and charges of the activity. However, debt that is secured by a pledge of net revenues from fees and charges *as well as* the full faith and credit of a related primary government or component unit, even if that government is not expected to make any payments, is *not* payable *solely* from fees and charges of the activity.

> **OBSERVATION:** Many activities that are financed by debt are denominated as "revenue credits" or similar. As revenue credits, they are paid by a pledge of the net revenues from applicable fees and charges securing the debt. Therefore, to increase the marketability or security of the pledge, many governments place an additional pledge of the full faith and credit of the government. Therefore, the criteria may be difficult to attain in some circumstances.

2. Laws or regulations require that the activity's costs of providing services, including capital costs (such as depreciation or capital debt service), be recovered with fees and charges, rather than with taxes or similar revenues.

> **OBSERVATION:** Footnote 34 for GASB-34 [GASB Cod. Secs. 1300.fn7, U50.101] specifically requires state unemployment compensation funds to be reported in enterprise funds due to this criterion.

3. The pricing policies of the activity establish fees and charges designed to recover its costs, including capital costs (such as depreciation or debt service).

Some financial statement preparers raised the question about whether the three criteria listed above apply to activities that are currently accounted for in Internal Service Funds. GASB-34 takes the position that an Enterprise Fund, not an Internal Service Fund, must be used when external users are the predominant participants in the fund. GASB-37 reemphasizes this point by adding a footnote to paragraph 67 that states, "the focus of these criteria is on fees charged to external users" (GASB-37, par. 14) [GASB Cod. Secs. 1300.fn8, Ca5.fn6, Ho5.fn6, In3.fn6, Ut5.fn6].

The first criterion refers to debt secured solely by fees and charges. If that debt is secured by a pledge of fees and charges from the activity and the full faith and credit of the primary government or component unit, this arrangement does not satisfy the "sole source of debt security" and the activity does not have to be accounted for (assuming the other two criteria are not satisfied) in an Enterprise Fund. This conclusion is not changed even if it is anticipated that the primary government or component unit is not expected to make debt payments under the arrangement. On the other hand, debt that is secured partially by a portion of its own proceeds does satisfy the "sole source of debt security" criterion.

The second and third criteria refer to the establishment of a pricing policy that recovers costs, including depreciation expense or debt service. In some situations, the activity might be responsible for little or no debt. The *GASB Implementation Guide 2015-1*, question 7.50.4 [GASB Cod. Sec. 1300.705-5], states that in this circumstance, the criteria are still met if the pricing policy is designed to recover *either* depreciation or debt service requirements (principal and interest). There is no assumption that there is equality between the depreciation expense and the debt service on capital debt for a particular activity.

OBSERVATION: If the enterprise fund also receives revenue from federal sources, they may have special guidelines about the level of non-federal revenue that is needed to be raised from non-federal sources to be in compliance with the federal grant conditions. This is typically found in public transportation grants. If pension or other post-employment benefit (OPEB) contributions are made from enterprise funds, the combination of the provisions of GASB-68, GASB-75 and the provisions of NCGA-1 defining an "enterprise fund" may cause allocation of pension expense to enterprise funds in a systematic and rational manner to fully recognize costs to be recovered. Furthermore, federal awards are subject to the provisions of the *Uniform Administrative Requirements, Cost Principles, and Audit Requirements of Federal Awards* (Title 2 Code of Federal Regulations, Part 200). Paragraph 200.431 is of particular interest as it allows federal cost recovery for employee benefits at the lower of the cash outflow or the accrued expense. This becomes extremely important in the implementation of GASB-68 with net pension asset or nearly net pension asset positions that also fund pension expense. Should the pension expense for a year be less than a cash outflow (which may be statutorily based), the federal agency may question the cost. See the additional **OBSERVATION** in the expenses section herein.

The third criterion is similar to the previous standard for determining when an Enterprise Fund should be used to account for an activity except that the principles contained in GASB-34 are based on "established policies" rather than management's intent.

The criteria established by GASB-34 are different from those established by NCGA-1. The GASB believes that the establishment of the three criteria listed above will reduce the degree of subjectivity that is now used by governmental entities in determining when an Enterprise Fund should be used.

The three criteria should be applied to a governmental entity's principal revenue sources; however, the criteria do not have to be applied to "insignificant activities" of a governmental entity. If none of the criteria apply, the activity can be accounted for in a governmental fund.

It should be noted that GASB-34 states that a fee-based activity can be accounted for in an Enterprise Fund even if the three criteria described above do not exist. The three criteria apply to fee-based activities that must be accounted for in an Enterprise Fund.

Activities commonly reported as Enterprise Funds of state and local governments include the following:

- Airports;
- Electric, gas, water, wastewater, and sanitation/landfills and similar utilities (see **OBSERVATION** on regulated operations discussing GASB-62, pars. 476–500 [GASB Cod. Sec. Re10], later in the chapter);
- Golf courses;
- Hospital or other health care services;
- Institutions of higher education that do not have the power to tax separately;
- Lotteries and gaming;
- Parking and transit; and
- Unemployment insurance (States only).

Note that some lotteries are accounted for as governmental funds, following a rationale that they are mainly cash flow mechanisms for the government rather than entities that meet the aforementioned criteria for an enterprise fund.

INTERNAL SERVICE FUNDS

GASB-34 describes an Internal Service Fund as a proprietary fund that may be used to report "any activity that provides goods or services to other funds, departments, or agencies of the primary government and its component units, or to other governments, on a cost reimbursement basis." An Internal Service Fund should be used only when the reporting government itself is the predominant participant in the fund. When the transactions with the other governmental entities represent the predominant portion of the activity, an Enterprise Fund must be used.

There is no circumstance under which an Internal Service Fund *must* be used. For example, an activity may be centralized by a governmental entity whereby all departments, programs, and so forth within the reporting entity must use the centralized activity and be billed for the service provided. That activity could be accounted for in an Internal Service Fund, but it could also be accounted for in another governmental fund (probably the General Fund).

Activities commonly reported as Internal Service Funds of state and local governments include the following:

- Central services, such as purchasing, warehousing, information systems, and similar processes that are allocable and applicable to multiple areas of a government;
- Risk management/self-insurance; and
- Vehicle and equipment maintenance.

OBSERVATION: For internal service fund activities that are reimbursed from federal funds, the *Uniform Administrative Requirements, Cost Principles, and Audit Requirements for Federal Awards*, Subpart E places stringent requirements on what can be charged as an "allowable cost," with an emphasis on consistent accounting no matter what the source of funds is. Budgeted allocations from internal service funds are usually regularly reviewed and approved by a federal agency as part of the setting of rates and charges in accordance with an indirect (overhead) rate. Complete coverage of the *Uniform Administrative Requirements, Cost Principles, and Audit Requirements for Federal Awards* from an auditing perspective is found in CCH's *Knowledge-Based Audits™ of State and Local Governments with Single Audits.*

ACCOUNTING AND REPORTING

Basis of Accounting and Measurement Focus

The accrual basis of accounting and the flow of economic resources are used to prepare the financial statements of a proprietary fund. These concepts are discussed in Chapter 3, "Basis of Accounting and Measurement Focus."

GASB-62 (*Codification of Accounting and Financial Reporting Guidance Contained in Pre-November 30, 1989 FASB and AICPA Pronouncements*) contains the provisions previously contained in incorporating into the GASB's literature all FASB Statements and Interpretations, APB Opinions, and ARBs no matter when issued that did not conflict with a GASB pronouncement and are applicable to government operations. GASB-62 also incorporates all applicable AICPA pronouncements.

Budgetary System and Accounts

Although the National Council on Governmental Accounting recommended that all funds adopt a budget for control purposes, it recognized that the nature of budgeting is different for governmental funds and proprietary funds. Generally, a proprietary fund should prepare a flexible budget, which reflects changes in the activity level. A fixed budget is inappropriate for proprietary funds because, in a fixed budget, overall activity is measured in terms of revenues and expenses and will fluctuate, in part, depending on the demand for goods and services by the public or governmental agencies. The flexible budget does not provide a basis for appropriations. Rather it serves as an approved financial plan that can facilitate budgetary control and operational evaluations. A flexible budget approach allows the governmental unit to prepare several budgets at different activity levels to establish an acceptable comparative basis for planned activity and actual results.

The basis of accounting used to prepare a budget for a proprietary fund should be the same as the basis used to record the results of actual transactions. It is not appropriate to integrate the budgetary accounts into the proprietary fund's accounting system.

Because a proprietary fund is generally not subject to a legislatively adopted budget, governmental entities are normally not required to use an encumbrance system to control executory contracts and other commitments for such funds.

Revenues

GASB:CS-4 (*Elements of Financial Statements*) defines the elements of the "resource flows (change) statements" involving revenue, and indicates that an "inflow of resources" is an acquisition of net position by the entity that is applicable to the reporting period.

The acquisition of net position (inflow) is defined as net position coming under the control of the entity or becoming newly available to the entity even if the resources are consumed directly when acquired. An acquisition of net position results in:

- An increase in assets in excess of any related increase in liabilities, or
- A decrease in liabilities in excess of any related decrease in assets.

Examples of acquisition of net position in proprietary funds include:

- Imposing a charge for services rendered (because the resources have newly come under the control of the entity), and
- Performing under the conditions of an operating grant received in advance (because liabilities in the form of deferred revenues of the entity have been satisfied, thereby increasing the entity's net position).

A proprietary fund should recognize revenue on an accrual basis, meaning that revenue is considered realized when (1) the earning process is complete or virtually complete and (2) an exchange has taken place.

Proprietary funds, such as water and sewer Enterprise Funds, have unbilled revenue at the end of an accounting period. Whether revenue is billed or unbilled is not the critical issue in the recognition of revenue in a proprietary fund. When a service has been provided (e.g., the consumption of a service by a customer), the related revenue should be recognized.

Accounting and Reporting Issues

Uncollectible accounts related to revenue. GASB-34, footnote 41 [GASB Cod. Secs. 2200.fn44, 2300.107, P80.fn6], requires that revenues be reported net of related discounts or allowances. The amount of the discounts or allowances must be presented on the operating statement (either parenthetically or as a subtraction from gross revenues) or in a note to the financial statements. GASB-34 does not require that estimates of bad debt expenses be reported as an offset to revenues, but the *GASB Implementation Guide 2015-1*, question 7.72.2 [GASB Cod. Sec 2200.751-2] states that estimates of uncollectible accounts should be presented in a manner similar to discounts and allowances. That is, revenues should be reported net of the increase or decrease of the estimate of uncollectible accounts.

Capital contributions from governmental funds. A proprietary fund must take into consideration the nature of a capital contribution received from another fund. For example, question 7.74.4 in the *GASB Implementation Guide 2015-1* [GASB Cod. Sec. 2200.739-1] discusses the reassignment of a capital asset between an enterprise fund and governmental activities. If the assets reassigned from governmental activities to an enterprise fund are capital assets, the transaction is not "interfund" because it involves only one fund; consequently, the enterprise fund would report the receipt of the capital assets as a capital contribution from governmental activities (in the last section of the statement of revenues, expenses, and changes in net position).

In the reverse situation, in which a capital asset is reassigned from an enterprise fund to governmental activities, the disposal of the capital asset would be reported by the enterprise fund as a nonoperating expense. In either case, governmental funds would not report the event because there has been no flow of current financial resources. In the statement of activities, the reassignment of the capital asset between governmental activities and business-type activities would be reported as a transfer, requiring a reconciling item in the governmental funds' reconciliation because a difference is created between the change in fund balances and the change in total net position.

In both cases, since the transfer consists of nonfinancial resources (a capital asset), *the governmental fund will not record the transfer* (because only financial resources are accounted for in a governmental fund); *however, the proprietary fund will record the transaction not as a transfer but as capital contribution revenue in the lower portion of its operating statement.* Even though the transfer is not presented in the governmental fund it must be presented as a transfer in the governmental activities column in the statement of activities; however, the inconsistency between the treatment of the transfer at the fund financial statement level and the government-wide financial statement level would generate a reconciling item for the governmental fund's operating statement and a related note disclosure.

Expenses

GASB:CS-4 defines the elements of the "resource flows (change) statements" involving expenses, and indicates that an "outflow of resources" is a consumption of net position by the entity that is applicable to the reporting period.

The consumption of net position (outflow) is defined as the using up of net position that results in (1) a decrease in assets in excess of any related decrease in liabilities or (2) an increase in liabilities in excess of any related increase in assets.

Unlike governmental funds that report expenditures related to the use of financial resources, proprietary funds report *expenses* related to the use of economic resources. For example, a proprietary fund would record a loss contingency as an expense irrespective of when the related liability is expected to be paid or financial resource used.

Accounting and Reporting Issues

Depreciation expense. All depreciable capital assets of a proprietary fund must be depreciated in accordance with generally accepted accounting principles as applied by a commercial enterprise.

OBSERVATION: GASB-34, as amended, discusses how any established depreciation method is acceptable as long as it is rational and systematic. The *GASB Implementation Guide 2015-1*, question 7.13.2 [GASB Cod. Sec. 1400.739-1], lists possible methods including:

- The straight-line method;

- Decreasing-charge methods, which include declining-balance, double-declining- balance, and sum-of-the-years' digits, among others;

- Increasing-charge methods; and

- Unit-of-production/service methods, which allocate the depreciable cost of an asset over its expected output.

In practice, the straight-line method is most common as the other methods may provide taxation advantages, which are not applicable to governments. A further discussion on capital assets is contained in Chapter 10, "Capital Assets."

Uncollectible accounts related to nonrevenue transactions. A governmental entity may make loans to other parties and subsequently have to write off those loans as uncollectible. A change in the allowance for uncollectible accounts not related to revenue transactions must be presented as an expense rather than netted against revenue, because there is no related revenue account.

Payments in lieu of taxes (or PILOT payments). An Enterprise Fund, such as a housing authority fund or a transportation entity, may make a payment to a local government in lieu of the payment of property taxes. In order for a transaction to be presented as an expense by an Enterprise Fund, it must be considered an exchange or exchange-like transaction. An exchange transaction occurs when two parties exchange assets or commitments of approximate equal value. The GASB defines an exchange-like transaction as being "an identifiable exchange between the reporting government and another party, but the values exchanged may not be quite equal or the direct benefits of the exchange may not be exclusively for the parties to the exchange." Payments in lieu of taxes should be reported as expenses because they can be considered exchange-like transactions.

PRACTICE ALERT: The GASB staff's Invitation to Comment *Revenue and Expense Recognition* presents two potential models that may become the components of a comprehensive revenue and expense model. The initial model focuses on exchange/nonexchange transactions which is primarily based on existing standards contained in GASB Statement No. 33 (*Accounting and Financial Reporting for Nonexchange Revenues*) and GASB Statement No. 36 (*Recipient Reporting for Certain Shared Nonexchange Transactions*), both as amended. The second model is similar to the newly updated Financial Accounting Standards Board (FASB) revenue recognition model which is based on whether or not a performance obligation is present. GASB staff also asked for alternatives to the two models presented. Comments were due in April 2018 with public hearings held in May 2018. A further due process document is not expected until 2020.

A summary comparison of both models is as follows:

	Exchange/Nonexchange Model	Performance Obligation/No Performance Obligation Model
Classification	Is the transaction an exchange or nonexchange transaction?	Does the transaction contain a performance obligation? (Example —does the government's ambulance service have to transport a patient prior to revenue recognition)?
Recognition	*Exchange Transaction*—recognize based on earnings approach, where the government controls the asset (or incurs a liability) *and* an inflow of resources (or outflow of resources) is applicable to the period. *Nonexchange Transaction*—recognize based on GASB-33 provisions for derived tax revenues, imposed nonexchange revenues, government-mandated nonexchange transactions or voluntary nonexchange transactions. (See Chapter 17, "Revenues: Nonexchange and Exchange Transactions," and 18, "Expenses/Expenditures: Nonexchange and Exchange Transactions.")	*Transaction Contains a Performance Obligation* (*or obligations*)—recognize based on performing the service or delivery. Determine consideration, allocate the consideration to the performance obligation and recognize revenue or expense as obligation is satisfied. *Transaction does not contain a performance obligation*—recognized based on GASB-33 provisions.
Measurement	To be determined for both models as a result of further due process.	

Pension (and other Employee Benefits). Conceivably, if compensation is paid from a proprietary fund, then employee benefits would also be declared as an expense, even if allocated.

OBSERVATION: The implementation of GASB-68 (*Accounting and Financial Reporting for Pensions*) and GASB-75 (*Accounting and Financial Reporting for Postemployment Benefits Other than Pensions*) (OPEB), both as amended, have generated a number of questions about what to record in the funds, if anything. Each standard also resulted in implementation guidance released from GASB, including questions on the guidance for recognizing a portion of the net pension or OPEB liability in fund statements if a portion of the net pension or OPEB liability will be paid from an *enterprise, internal service, or fiduciary fund.* The GASB notes that neither GASB-68 nor GASB-75 establishes specific requirements for allocation of the net pension or OPEB liability or other related measures to individual funds. However, for proprietary and fiduciary funds, consideration should be given to NCGA-1 (par. 42, as amended), *Governmental Accounting and Financial Reporting Principles,* which requires that long-term liabilities that are "directly related to and expected to be paid from" those funds be reported in the statement of net position or statement of fiduciary net position, respectively. Conceivably, a deferred inflow of resources or a deferred outflow of resources may also be declared in a proprietary or fiduciary fund based upon an allocation discussed later in this chapter and in more detail in Chapter 13, "Pension, Postemployment, and Other Employee Benefit Liabilities."

Assets

"Assets," as defined in GASB:CS-4, are:

> Resources with a present service capacity that the entity presently controls.

Governmental funds, in contrast to proprietary funds, report only those assets available to finance current operations. For example, a General Fund could not accrue a gain arising from a settled lawsuit, even though the amount is known with certainty, if payments from the other party are to be received over several years. A proprietary fund's financial statements would reflect all assets related to the operations of the fund irrespective of when the asset is expected to be realized.

Accounting and Reporting Issues

Reporting restrictions on asset use. In a proprietary fund it is assumed that assets (especially current assets) are unrestricted in that there are no conditions that would prevent the governmental entity from using the resources to pay existing liabilities. If the name of the asset account does not adequately explain the normally perceived availability of that asset, the item should be identified as a restricted asset on the statement of net position. For example, an amount of cash may be restricted to a specific type of expenditure (e.g., debt service) and therefore it would be misleading to report the restricted cash with all other unrestricted cash (classified as current assets). Under this circumstance, the cash should be reported as restricted cash in the financial statement category labeled noncurrent assets. On the other hand, cash that is restricted for purposes related to current operations (such as cash restricted for repairs and maintenance) should be labeled as restricted cash but be reported as current assets. Equipment and other capital assets are not available to pay liabilities, but the title of the account adequately describes the availability (or lack of liquidity) of the asset and therefore there is no need to identify the asset as restricted (GASB-34, par. 99) [GASB Cod. Secs. 2200.179, P80.112].

According to GASB-62 (par. 31) [GASB Cod. Secs. 1800.110, 2200.176], current assets *should exclude*:

- Cash and claims to cash that cannot be used for current operations and that are to be disbursed to acquire or construct noncurrent assets or that are segregated for the liquidation of long-term debts;

- Receivables arising from unusual transactions (such as the sale of capital assets) that are not expected to be collected within 12 months;

- Cash surrender value of life insurance policies;

- Land and other natural resources;

- Depreciable assets; and

- Long-term prepayments that are applicable to the operations of several years or are deferred outflows of resources such as prepayments under a long-term lease.

Many governmental entities have assets that are restricted to specific purposes, but if those purposes are related to current operations, they should be reported as current assets.

Interest capitalization. (See following **PRACTICE ALERT**). Paragraphs 5–22 of GASB-62 [GASB Cod. Secs. 1400.120–.137] describe the capitalization of interest in proprietary funds. Interest cost incurred during the construction of the following assets of a proprietary fund should be capitalized when:

- Assets are constructed or otherwise produced for an enterprise's own use (including assets constructed or produced by others for the enterprise for which deposits or progress payments have been made).

- Assets intended for sale or lease are constructed or otherwise produced as discrete projects (e.g., real estate developments).

- Investments (equity, loans, and advances) accounted for by the equity method while the investee has activities in progress necessary to commence its planned principal operations provided that the investee's activities include the use of funds to acquire qualifying assets for its operations.

On the other hand, the construction cost of the following assets related to a proprietary fund should not include an interest cost element:

- Inventories that are routinely manufactured or otherwise produced in large quantities on a repetitive basis.

- Assets that are in use or ready for their intended use in the earning activities of the enterprise.

- Investments accounted for by the equity method after the planned principal operations of the investee begin.

- Investments in regulated investees that are capitalizing both the cost of debt and equity capital.

- Assets acquired with gifts and grants that are restricted by the donor or grantor to acquisition of those assets to the extent that funds are available from such gifts and grants (interest earned from temporary investment of those funds that is similarly restricted shall be considered in addition to the gift or grant for this purpose).

The interest capitalization period begins when the following conditions are present:

- Outflows of resources for the capital asset have been made (cash or accrued).

- Activities that are necessary to get the capital asset ready for its intended use are in progress.

- Interest cost is being incurred.

To determine the amount of interest cost to be capitalized, the weighted-average amount of accumulated outflows for the period is multiplied by the proprietary fund's average borrowing rate for the period. Rather than use the overall average borrowing rate, the following approach can be employed:

- The interest rate for the obligation incurred specifically to finance the construction of the capital asset may be used.

- The overall average borrowing rate of the proprietary fund would be used for any accumulated expenditures in excess of specific borrowings.

The amount of interest cost to be capitalized is limited to the actual amount of interest expense recognized for the period.

The *GASB Implementation Guide 2015-1,* in part of the answer to question 7.10.3 [GASB Cod. Sec. 1400.713-1], clarifies the guidance in GASB-62, paragraphs 11–20 [GASB Cod. Secs. 1400.126–.135], on construction period interest on assets. The interest capitalization requirement in GASB-62 does not require or anticipate matching specific debt to specific assets. In general, GASB-62 requires a portion of all interest expense to be allocated to the costs of all assets under construction during the period. Therefore, if the enterprise fund has any type of debt, the portion of the interest expense that theoretically could have been avoided generally should be capitalized as part of the cost of assets constructed during the period.

Paragraphs 19–20 of GASB-62 discuss that the amount of interest cost to be capitalized for assets constructed with tax-exempt borrowings is equal to the cost of the borrowing, less interest earned on related interest-bearing investments acquired with proceeds of the related tax-exempt borrowings. An additional question in the *GASB Implementation Guide 2015-1* (question 7.10.7) [GASB Cod. Sec. 1400.715-1] discusses Build America Bonds and similar bonds subsidized by the federal government. Such bonds are taxable and for the purpose of determining capitalized interest, amounts should not be counted. In accordance with further guidance in question Z.33.25 [GASB Cod. Sec. N50.710-3], the federal reimbursement is a separate nonexchange transaction and should be recognized as nonexchange revenue when all eligibility requirements are met. Thus, the payment of interest on the qualifying bonds is reported gross, not netted with the federal reimbursement. See Chapter 17, "Revenues: Nonexchange and Exchange Transactions," for a discussion of nonexchange revenues.

PRACTICE ALERT: GASB Statement No. 89 (*Accounting for Interest Cost Incurred before the end of a Construction Period*) supersedes these provisions upon implementation for periods beginning after December 15, 2019. Upon implementation, interest cost incurred during the period of construction will be a period expense for financial statements prepared under the economic resources measurement focus (including proprietary funds, internal service funds and the government-wide financial statements). Interest cost will no longer be included in the historical cost of a capital asset. For construction-in-progress, interest cost incurred after the beginning of the first reporting period for which GASB-89 will now apply should not be capitalized. For regulated operations that require capitalization of interest, no change would occur upon implementation of GASB-89.

OBSERVATION: Many governments sell debt in a consolidated fashion - meaning that more than one authorization is funded from a particular bond issuance. If consolidated sales are made, care must be taken in allocating proceeds between governmental and business-type activities for the purposes of allocating interest costs for capitalization. Amounts that are allocated to business-type activities may not be in a range of maturities and may be scattered based on bond authorization language. If at all possible, it is practical to have a second series of bonds for business-type activities as they may be secured by fees and charges, rather than general tax revenues. By having a second series, interest capitalization is much easier to calculate.

Infrastructure assets. The *GASB Implementation Guide 2015-1,* question 7.16.4 [GASB Cod. Sec. 1400.703-5], discusses how the modified approach may be applied to eligible infrastructure assets accounted for as either governmental activities or business-type activities. For example, an Enterprise Fund that owns a toll road (which is an infrastructure asset) could use the modified approach. If the Enterprise Fund uses the modified approach, it should be used in the preparation of both the government-wide and proprietary fund financial statements. See Chapter 10, "Capital Assets," for further discussion of infrastructure assets and the modified approach.

OBSERVATION: GASB-62, pars. 476–500 [GASB Cod. Sec. Re10], discuss regulatory operations. Utility services such as electric, water, sewer, and gas may use regulatory accounting. Regulatory accounting may be applied if *all of the following criteria are met:*

- The regulated business-type activity's rates for regulated services provided to its customers are established by or are subject to approval by an independent, third-party regulator or by its own governing board empowered by statute or contract to establish rates that bind customers;

- The regulated rates are designed to recover the specific regulated business-type activity's costs of providing the regulated services; and

- In view of the demand for the regulated services or products and the level of competition, direct and indirect, it is reasonable to assume that rates set at levels that will recover the regulated business-type activity's costs can be charged to and collected from customers. This criterion requires consideration of anticipated changes in levels of demand or competition during the recovery period for any capitalized costs.

The section of GASB-62 includes subsections for general standards of accounting for the effects of regulation, allowances for resources used during construction, intra-entity profit, accounting for impairment of regulatory assets, disallowed costs of recently completed plants, refunds, recovery without return on investment, and discontinuance of regulatory accounting. GASB-62 should be reviewed first for guidance in cases of regulatory accounting and then the AICPA Audit and Accounting Guide *State and Local Governments.*

Customer deposits for utility services. Governmental entities that provide utility services, such as electric, water, sewer, and gas, may require deposits from customers, or a governmental entity may charge developers and/or customers system development fees (tap fees). A customer deposit is generally required to be paid before a service is turned on, and when the service is terminated, the deposit is returned to the customer. Utility services are generally accounted for as Enterprise Funds, and the AICPA's Audit and Accounting Guide *State and Local Governments* points out that receipts of customer deposits should be recorded as a liability and continue to be reported as such until they are "applied against unpaid billings or refunded to customers." Generally, these customer deposits are reported as restricted assets and offset with a corresponding liability payable from restricted assets.

Customer system development fees. The AICPA's *State and Local Governments* Guide also notes that the initial receipt of a customer system development fee should be recorded as a liability and recognized as revenue using the general guidance related to either an exchange transaction or a nonexchange transaction. In an exchange transaction the governmental entity and the other party to the transaction exchange cash, goods, or services that are essentially of the same value.

A nonexchange transaction arises when the transfer of goods or services between two parties is not of equal value. When a customer system development fee is considered to be a nonexchange transaction, it must be accounted for based on the guidance established by GASB-33. See Chapter 17, "Revenues: Nonexchange and Exchange Transactions," for a discussion of nonexchange revenues.

Liabilities

GASB:CS-4 defines "liabilities" as:

> Present obligations to sacrifice resources that the entity has little or no discretion to avoid.

Unlike governmental funds, a proprietary fund reports both current and noncurrent liabilities expected to be paid from the fund. A proprietary fund may receive the proceeds from the issuance of either general obligation bonds or revenue bonds, but in either circumstance the receipt of the proceeds coupled with the requirement to repay such debt results in a proprietary fund liability.

Accounting and Reporting Issues

General obligation bonds. A governmental entity may issue general obligation bonds whereby the proceeds are used to construct capital assets reported in a proprietary fund. If the debt is directly related to and expected to be paid from the proprietary fund, both the capital asset and the debt are reported in the proprietary fund financial statements and the business-type activities column of the government-wide statement of net position.

Revenue bonds. Principal and interest on revenue bonds are paid exclusively from the earnings of a proprietary fund. If the debt is also secured by specific fixed assets of the proprietary fund, they are referred to as mortgage revenue bonds. Revenue bonds, both current and long-term portion, are recorded as a liability of the Enterprise Fund.

A proprietary fund's long-term liabilities may include obligations other than those that arise from the issuance of a security debt instrument. These other obligations may be created from capitalized leases, claims and judgments, land-fill closure and postclosure care, pollution remediation, employee termination benefits and OPEB obligations. These, as well as other liabilities of a proprietary fund, should be accounted for in a manner similar to the accounting and reporting standards applicable to them in U.S. GAAP.

Fund Net Position

GASB:CS-4 defines "Net Position" as:

> The residual of all other elements presented in a statement of financial position.

Proprietary fund equity or net position is referred to as "net position." Proprietary fund net position should be identified similarly to the government-wide statements:

- Net investment in capital assets,
- Restricted, and
- Unrestricted.

GASB-34 notes that capital contributions should not be presented as a separate component of net position. Also, similar to the guidance for government-wide financial statements, designations of net position cannot be identified on the face of the proprietary fund statement of net position. See Chapter 5, "Terminology and Classification," for discussion of the net position components.

Restricted net position arises only when they are (1) externally imposed by creditors (such as through debt covenants), grantors, contributors, or laws or regulations of other governments or (2) imposed by law through constitutional provisions or enabling legislation.

Also, similarly to the government-wide statements, net position is the sum of assets and deferred outflows of resources reduced by liabilities and deferred inflows of resources (deferred positions presented separately from assets and liabilities).

FUND FINANCIAL STATEMENTS

Based on the fundamental concepts discussed above, the following financial statements must be prepared for Enterprise Funds and Internal Service Funds (GASB-34, par. 91, as amended by GASB-63) [GASB Cod. Secs. 1300.102, 2200.105, 2200.170, 2450.103, C20 fn2, C60 fn5, D30.108, I50 fn10, I50 fn18, I55 fn4, I55 fn5, I60 fn3, I60 fn6, J50.106, L10 fn5, P21 fn6, P80.104]. The financial statements in accordance with GASB-63 are as follows:

- Statement of net position;
- Statement of revenues, expenses, and changes in net position; and
- Statement of cash flows.

Statement of Net Position

Assets and liabilities presented on the statement of net position of a proprietary fund should be classified as current and noncurrent, based on the guidance established in GASB-62, paragraphs 30–44 [GASB Cod. Secs. 1500.107–.115, 1800.109–.123, 2200.175–.189, 2300.107, .116]. The statement of net position may be presented in either one of the following formats (GASB-34, pars. 97–98, as amended by GASB-63) [GASB Cod. Secs. 1400.115, 2200.172–.173, 1800.164, D30.108, P80.110, C50.129]:

- Net position format: assets plus deferred outflows of resources less liabilities less deferred inflows of resources equals net position; or

- Balance sheet format: assets plus deferred outflows of resources equals liabilities plus deferred outflows of resources plus net position.

(Exhibit 20-5, "Castle Rock County Statement of Net Position Proprietary Fund" in Chapter 20, "Comprehensive Annual Financial Report," illustrates a statement of net position for proprietary funds using the net position format that is consistent with the standards established by GASB-34.)

Statement of Revenues, Expenses and Changes in Net Position

The operating statement of a proprietary fund is the statement of revenues, expenses, and changes in fund net position. In preparing this statement, the following standards should be observed (GASB-34, par. 100) [GASB Cod. Secs. 1100.112, 1800, 2200.190, 2450 fn5, P80.113, P80.116, S40.122]:

- Revenues should be reported by major source; and

- Revenues that are restricted for the payment of revenue bonds should be identified.

Paragraph 100 also requires the following categories (as applicable to the Fund's operations) in the Statement of Revenues, Expenses and Changes in Net Position:

- Operating revenues (detailed)
- Total operating revenues
- Operating expenses (detailed)
- Total operating expenses
- Operating income (loss)
- Nonoperating revenues and expenses (detailed)
- Subtotal (optional)
- Income before other revenues, expenses, gains, losses, and transfers
- Capital contributions (grant, developer, and other), additions to permanent and term endowments, special and extraordinary items (detailed), and transfers
- Increase (decrease) in net position
- Net position—beginning of period
- Net position—end of period

Footnote 41 to GASB-34 [GASB Cod. Sec. 2200.fn44, 2300.107, P80.fn6] requires revenues to be reported net of discounts and allowances, with the discount disclosed in a parentheses on the face of the statement of revenues, expenses and changes in net position or in a note to the basic financial statements. Many governments report gross revenues with the related discount and/or allowances reported directly beneath the gross revenue amount.

Operating Revenues and Expenses

Operating revenues and expenses differ from government to government in a similar fashion to other organizations. GASB-34, paragraph 102, [GASB Cod. Secs. 2200.192, 2450.fn5, P80.115] requires a policy defining operating revenues and expenses that is "appropriate to the nature of the activity being reported." This policy needs to be consistently applied.

PRACTICE ALERT: A major portion of the second phase of the GASB's *Financial Reporting Model—Reexamination* project may result in a clearer definition of operating versus nonoperating revenues and expenses of proprietary funds. Some practitioners desire revenue and expense reporting aligned to an entity's mission. The GASB's preliminary view may focus on whether an operation is self-sustaining (where revenues provide for expenses) or subsidies are needed to fund expenses. The subsidies may be a defining point of what is nonoperating revenues and expenses. Proprietary activities ranging from airports to zoos are closely following this deliberation as the result may have a major impact on their financial operations and debt compliance measures.

Exhibit 20-6, "Statement of Revenues, Expenses, and Changes in Net Position: Proprietary Funds," in Chapter 20, "Comprehensive Annual Financial Report," illustrates a statement of revenues, expenses, and changes in net position for proprietary funds that is consistent with the standards established by GASB-34.

Reconciliations

Although there must be a reconciliation between the government-wide financial statements (statement of net position and statement of changes in net position) and the governmental funds, generally there is no need for a similar reconciliation between the government-wide financial statements and proprietary fund financial statements because both sets of financial statements are based on the same measurement focus and basis of accounting. However, there could be governmental activities reported in proprietary funds or business-type activities reported in governmental funds. In these circumstances, a reconciliation is required (GASB-34, par. 104) [GASB Cod. Secs. 2200.194, P80.108].

In a circumstance where there are differences between the two sets of financial statements, the differences must be reconciled on the face of the proprietary fund financial statements. GASB-34 notes that a reconciling item could arise when the residual assets and liabilities of an Internal Service Fund is presented as part of the business-type activities column in the statement of net position (a government-wide financial statement). This circumstance can arise only when "enterprise funds are the predominant or only participants in an Internal Service Fund."

Statement of Cash Flows

Proprietary funds should prepare a statement of cash flows based on the guidance established by GASB-9, as amended by GASB-34, formatted based on the *direct method* in computing cash flows from operating activities. The statement of cash flows would be supplemented with a reconciliation of operating cash flows and operating income (the indirect method) (GASB-34, par. 105) [GASB Cod. Secs. 2200.195, 2450.128, P80.117].

(Exhibit 20-7, "Statement of Cash Flows: Proprietary Funds," in Chapter 20, "Comprehensive Annual Financial Report," illustrates a statement of cash flows for enterprise funds that is consistent with the standards established by GASB-9, as amended by GASB-34.)

Segment Information: Enterprise Funds

Segment disclosures must be made by governmental entities that report Enterprise Funds or that use enterprise fund accounting and reporting standards to report activities. A segment is defined as follows (GASB-34, par. 122, as amended) [GASB Cod. Secs. 2300.106, 2500.101]:

> . . . an identifiable activity (or grouping of activities) reported as or within an Enterprise Fund or an other stand-alone entity that has one or more bonds or other debt instruments (such as certificates of participation) outstanding, with a revenue stream pledged in support of that debt. In addition, the activity's revenues, expenses, gains and losses, assets and liabilities are required to be accounted for separately.

The *GASB Implementation Guide 2015-1,* questions 7.86.1 through 7.86.6, [GASB Cod. Secs. 2200.768-4, 2500.701-2–6], emphasize in various examples that paragraph 122 of GASB-34 does not require that the pledged revenue stream be the only backing for the debt in order for the activity to be considered a segment. For example, the debt could also be backed by the full faith and credit of the governmental entity.

The original language used in GASB-34 was interpreted by some financial statement preparers as requiring disclosures for activities that were not intended to be covered by the GASB. The purpose of GASB-34 was to "provide separate financial statement information for *identifiable activities* that were combined in a single major Enterprise Fund or included in the nonmajor fund aggregation." In order to clarify this objective, GASB-37 revised paragraph 122 of GASB-34 by adding the following points: (1) A segment is an identifiable activity (or grouping of activities), as discussed in paragraph 39b, footnote c, of GASB-34, reported by, as, or within an Enterprise Fund (or another stand-alone entity) that has one or more bonds or other debt instruments (such as certificates of participation) outstanding, with a revenue stream pledged in support of that debt, and (2) based on the agreement between the governmental entity and an external party, there is a requirement that related revenues, expenses, gains and losses, assets, and liabilities be accounted for separately.

Segment disclosures do not apply to an activity that is solely related to conduit debt "for which the government has no obligation beyond the resources provided by related leases or loans." Also, segment disclosures do not apply when an activity is reported as a major fund.

The following segment disclosures should be made by providing condensed financial statements in a note(s) to the financial statements:

- A description of the goods or services provided by the segment.
- Condensed statement of net position that includes the following:
  — Total assets: Distinguishing between current assets, capital assets, and other assets (Amounts receivable from other funds or component units should be reported separately.)
  — Total Deferred Outflows of Resources
  — Total liabilities: Distinguishing between current and long-term amounts (Amounts payable to other funds or component units should be reported separately.)
  — Total Deferred Inflows of Resources
  — Total fund net position: Distinguishing between restricted, unrestricted, and amounts invested in capital assets (net of related debt), with separate identification of expendable and nonexpendable components for restricted net position, if appropriate.
- Condensed statement of revenues, expenses, and changes in net position:
  — Operating revenues by major sources
  — Operating expenses, with separate identification of depreciation expense and amortizations of long-lived assets
  — Operating income (loss)
  — Nonoperating revenues (expenses), with separate reporting of major revenues and expenses
  — Capital contributions and additions to permanent and term endowments
  — Extraordinary and special items
  — Transfers
  — Changes in net position
  — Beginning and ending net position.
- Condensed statement of cash flows:
  — Net cash provided (used by):
    - Operating activities
    - Noncapital financing activities
    - Capital and related financing activities
    - Investing activities
  — Beginning and ending balances of cash (or cash and cash equivalent balances).

The *GASB Implementation Guide 2015-1,* questions 7.86.1 through 7.86.5 [GASB Cod. Secs. 2500.701-2–6], provide the following examples for determining when segment information is presented in a governmental entity's financial statements:

Fact Pattern	Suggested Guidance
A City uses a single Enterprise Fund to account for its water and sewer operations. Although both operations are accounted for in a single fund, the city maintains separate asset, liability, revenue and expense accounts for each. There are outstanding revenue bonds that pertain to the water reservoir and distribution lines. The sewer operation has no long-term debt attributable to it. What are the segment reporting requirements for the Water and Sewer Fund?	Segment information for the water activity must be disclosed in the notes to the financial statements because that activity has "one or more revenue bonds or other revenue-backed debt instruments" outstanding. The sewer activity has no such debt and therefore segment information related to this activity does not have to be presented.
A public university has fifteen residence halls on its campus, 10 of which have individual bond debt secured by the room fee revenues of the specific dorm. Is the "identifiable activity" the entire group of fifteen residence halls, or only those with revenue bonds outstanding?	As defined earlier, a segment is an activity that has an identifiable revenue stream that is dedicated to support revenue bonds or other revenue-backed debt and has identifiable expenses, gains and losses, assets, and liabilities that are related to its activities. Whether each dorm or the dorm system constitutes the segment depends on the breadth of the pledged revenue. If the pledged revenue of a specific dorm applies only to the debt of that particular dorm then each dorm is considered a separate segment (ten segments). On the other hand, if the pledged revenues from all of the 10 dorms apply to the dorm debt as a whole, then there is one segment (the dorm segment).

Professional judgment must be used to determine whether segment information for discretely presented component units must be made in the notes to the financial statements. GASB-34 states that the decision should be based on the following factors:

- The significance of the individual component unit to all component units presented on a discrete basis; and

- The relationship between the individual component unit and the primary government.

The *GASB Implementation Guide 2015-1* states that a condensed statement of cash flows is not required when segment disclosures are made for major discretely presented component units.

PRACTICE POINT: Recognition of the existence of a segment and presenting the required disclosures are a common problem for preparers. The release of required note disclosure information for pledged revenues contained in GASB-48 did not update segment disclosures even though the pledge of receivables and future revenues to securitize bonds is closely related to the provisions of a segment. Practitioners that have activities that align with the criteria contained in GASB-34, par. 122, as amended [GASB Cod. Secs. 2300.106, 2500.101], should incorporate segment disclosures into the notes to the basic financial statements.

Rate Setting and Enterprise Funds (or Internal Service Funds)

Most Enterprise Funds and Internal Service Funds base their operations on a rate setting process. The goal of the process is to provide enough revenues to support the full cost of operations in order to substantiate the operations of the fund. Determining the full cost of operations is an iterative process and in some cases is more dependent on estimations than on facts. If costs exceed budgeted amounts, a deficit may be in place and may either be carried forward and absorbed as part of the next iteration of rate setting, or a transfer occurs from the General Fund to fund the deficit. In many cases, estimated rates must be approved by a governing body prior to implementation. For example, transportation fares (a rate) may need to be approved by not only a local board, but also a state or even a federal board.

To establish a rate, a budget must be developed with the following inputs:

- Direct salaries and wages, including overtime and other adjustments to salaries as applicable,
- Direct employee expenses that are paid from rates and charges, including pensions, OPEB and similar,
- Capital outlay applicable to the rate,
- Maintenance and supplies applicable to the rate,
- Debt service applicable to the rate,
- Allocated indirect charges (overhead) from other funds and operations, including legal, utilities, insurance, accounting, auditing, office space, and similar.

Upon development of the estimated budget, the prior year rate is analysed. Any estimated surplus or deficit that is not transferred to or from other funds is then carried forward into the new rate.

The budgeted amount is then compared to an allowable or meaningful denominator based on operations of the fund. The following could be denominators based on common enterprise or internal service funds:

Fund Operation	Denominator
Water and Sewer	Gallons of flow per household per year
Airport	Parking facilities—estimated car usage in garages, takeoffs and landings, cargo tonnage, cost per square foot
Public transit	Estimated fare paying passengers (with a rate set usually at a federal minimum of 20% of total costs)
Landfill	Estimated tons per load

Fund Operation	Denominator
Dormitory	Square footage per student
Print shop	Estimated cost per page
Legal Department	Estimated claims for torts
Insurance	Budgetary line item for department/agency
Information technology	Bytes of storage (or throughput for cloud services)

Therefore, if $3,134,222 is estimated to be the full cost budget of a water and sewer operation and 1,970,334 gallons of flow per household is estimated for the year, then the rate would be approximately $1.59 per gallon for the year. Each billing cycle would then be based on meter readings multiplied by the $1.59 per gallon.

Presentation of Internal Service Funds in the Fund Financial Statements

The major fund reporting requirement does not apply to Internal Service Funds even though they are proprietary funds. Instead, all Internal Service Funds should be combined into a single column and presented on the face of the proprietary funds' financial statements. This column must be presented to the right of the total column for all Enterprise Funds. The Internal Service Funds column and the Enterprise Funds total column should not be added together.

(An example of the presentation of the financial statements of Internal Service Funds can be found in Exhibit 20-6, Exhibit 20-7, and Exhibit 20-8, in Chapter 20, "Comprehensive Annual Financial Report.")

Integrating Internal Service Funds into Government-Wide Financial Statements

Internal Service Funds and similar activities should be eliminated to avoid doubling-up expenses and revenues in preparing the government activities column of the statement of activities. The effect of this approach is to adjust activities in an Internal Service Fund to a breakeven balance. That is, if the Internal Service Fund had a "net profit" for the year there should be a pro rata reduction in the charges made to the funds that used the Internal Service Fund's services for the year. Likewise, a net loss would require a pro rata adjustment that would increase the charges made to the various participating funds. After making these eliminations, any residual balances related to the Internal Service Fund's assets, liabilities, and net position should generally be reported in the governmental activities column in the statement of net position.

To illustrate the merging of an Internal Service Fund's accounts in the government-wide financial statements, assume the following pre-closing trial balances exist at the end of a governmental entity's fiscal year:

The following is a pre-closing Trial Balance for *Governmental Activities*:

	Debit	Credit
Assets	$16,000	$—
Liabilities	—	6,000
Program Revenues	—	39,000
Program A Expenses	10,000	—
Program B Expenses	20,000	—
Interest Expense	4,000	—
Investment Income	—	1,000
Net Position	—	4,000
Totals	$50,000	$50,000

Note: These amounts include all governmental funds (General Fund, Special Revenue Funds, Capital Projects Funds, Debt Service Funds, and Permanent Funds) adjusted from a modified accrual basis (as presented in the fund-level financial statements) to an accrual basis (which is the basis required in the government-wide financial statements).

The following is a pre-closing Trial Balance for the *Internal Service Fund*:

	Debit	Credit
Assets	$4,000	$—
Liabilities	—	2,000
Revenues	—	5,000
Expenses	4,500	—
Net Position	—	1,500
Totals	$8,500	$8,500

Note: The Internal Service Fund balances are reported on an accrual basis at the fund financial statement level.

The activities accounted for in the Internal Service Fund resulted in a "net profit" of $500 ($5,000 of revenues – $4,500 of expenses), which means that the operating expenses listed in the pre-closing trial balance of government activities are overstated by $500. In order to merge the residual amounts of the Internal Service Fund into the government-activities column of the reporting entity, the following worksheet adjustments are made:

	Pre-closing Trial Balance for Governmental Activities		Eliminations Based on Internal Service Residual Balances		Pre-closing Trial Balance for Governmental Activities Including Internal Service Residual Balances (Pre-closing consolidating eliminations)	
	Debit	Credit	Debit	Credit	Debit	Credit
Assets	$16,000	$—	$4,000	$—	$20,000	$—
Liabilities	—	6,000	—	2,000	—	8,000
Program Revenues	—	39,000	—	—	—	39,000
Program A Expenses	10,000	—	—	300	9,700	—
Program B Expenses	20,000	—	—	200	19,800	—
Interest Expense	4,000	—	—	—	4,000	—
Investment Income	—	1,000	—	—	—	1,000
Net Position	—	4,000	—	1,500	—	5,500
Totals	$50,000	$50,000	$4,000	$4,000	$53,500	$53,500

Note: For illustrative purposes only, it is assumed that during the year the Internal Service Funds activities were provided to Program A (60%) and Program B (40%), which were reported in governmental funds. For this reason, $300 of the $500 Internal Service Fund "net profit" (surplus) is reported as a reduction of Program A expenses, while the remaining 40%, or $200, results in a reduction of Program B expenses. (The $500 is derived from $5,000 in revenues and $4,500 in expenses in the second table in this section.)

Once the government activities have been adjusted to include residual values (including assets, liabilities, net position, and operating activities), the statement of net position and statement of activities must be formatted to reflect the standards established by GASB-34.

The government-wide financial statements are divided into governmental activities and business-type activities. Generally, as illustrated above, the activities conducted by an Internal Service Fund are related to government activities and therefore the residual amounts of the Internal Service Fund should be consolidated with other governmental funds and presented in the governmental activities column of the government-wide financial statements. However, the activities of an Internal Service Fund must be analyzed to determine whether they are governmental or business-type in nature, or both. If the activities are business-type in nature, the residual amounts must be consolidated with the business-type activities in the government-wide financial statements. In addition, the operating accounts reported by the Internal Service Fund must be analyzed to determine whether they should be used to compute the "net profit or loss" that is the basis for allocation to the governmental or business-type activities.

NOTE: For a discussion of government-wide financial statements see Chapter 20, "Comprehensive Annual Financial Report."

Activities That Are Exclusively Government Activities

When the activities conducted by an Internal Service Fund are related to governmental activities rather than business-type activities, the residual balances of the fund are allocated to the government activities columns in the government-wide financial statements. However, several accounts may appear on the Internal Service Fund's operating statement (namely, interest expense, investment income, depreciation expense, and interfund transfers in/out) that must be considered before the residual amounts of the Internal Service Fund are allocated to the governmental activities column that appears in the government-wide financial statements.

Interest Expense

Generally, interest expense on debt issued by an Internal Service Fund is considered an *indirect expense* and should not be allocated as a direct expense to specific functional categories that appear on the statement of activities; rather, it should be presented as a single line item, appropriately labeled. For this reason, when an Internal Service Fund has interest expense, only the profit or loss before interest charges should be allocated to the governmental operating programs. The interest expense should be combined with other interest expense related to governmental activities and the single amount should be presented on the statement of activities.

To illustrate the allocation of Internal Service Fund accounts when interest expense exists for the fund, assume that in the previous example the pre-closing trial balance for the Internal Service Fund is as follows with interest expense separated from other expenses of the fund:

	Debit	Credit
Assets	$4,000	$—
Liabilities	—	2,000
Revenues	—	5,000
Expenses	4,400	—
Interest Expense	100	—
Net Position	—	1,500
Totals	$8,500	$8,500

The activities accounted for in the Internal Service Fund result in a "net profit before interest expense" (or surplus) of $600 ($5,000 – $4,400). The net profit or surplus amount is the basis for allocation to the program expenses reported in the governmental activities column of the statement of activities. The interest expense of $100 is directly allocated to the interest expense row that appears in the statement. The eliminating entry under this circumstance is illustrated as follows:

	Pre-closing Trial Balance for Governmental Activities		Eliminations Based on Internal Service Residual Balances		Pre-closing Trial Balance for Governmental Activities Including Internal Service Residual Balances	
	Debit	Credit	Debit	Credit	Debit	Credit
Assets	$16,000	$—	$4,000	$—	$20,000	$—
Liabilities	—	6,000	—	2,000	—	8,000
Program Revenues	—	39,000	—	—	—	39,000
Program A Expenses	10,000	—	—	360	9,640	—
Program B Expenses	20,000	—	—	240	19,760	—
Interest Expense	4,000	—	100	—	4,100	—
Investment Income	—	1,000	—	—	—	1,000
Net Position	—	4,000	—	1,500	—	5,500
Totals	$50,000	$50,000	$4,100	$4,100	$53,500	$53,500

Investment Income

A fundamental concept in the formatting of the statement of activities is the identification of resource inflows to the governmental entities that are related to specific programs and those that are general in nature.

Based on the nature of an Internal Service Fund, investment income will usually be considered general revenue and reported in the lower section of the statement of activities. Therefore, when an Internal Service Fund has investment income, only the net profit or loss before investment income should be allocated to the operating programs. The investment income should be combined with other unrestricted income and presented as a separate line item in the statement of activities.

To illustrate the allocation of Internal Service Fund accounts when investment income exists for the fund, assume that in the previous example the pre-closing trial balance for the Internal Service Fund is as follows:

	Debit	Credit
Assets	$4,000	$—
Liabilities	—	2,000
Revenues	—	4,800
Expenses	4,400	—
Interest Expense	100	—
Investment Income	—	200
Net Position	—	1,500
Totals	$8,500	$8,500

The activities accounted for in the Internal Service Fund result in a "net profit before interest expense and investment income" (net surplus) of $400 ($4,800 of revenues – $4,400 of expenses). The $400 amount is the basis for allocation to the program expenses, including the investment income of $200, as illustrated below and is combined with the investment income of the other governmental funds and presented as a single amount, as follows:

	Pre-closing Trial Balance for Governmental Activities		Eliminations Based on Internal Service Residual Balances		Pre-closing Trial Balance for Governmental Activities Including Internal Service Residual Balances	
	Debit	Credit	Debit	Credit	Debit	Credit
Assets	$16,000	$—	$4,000	$—	$20,000	$—
Liabilities	—	6,000	—	2,000	—	8,000
Program Revenues	—	39,000	—	—	—	39,000
Program A Expenses	10,000	—	—	240	9,760	—
Program B Expenses	20,000	—	—	160	19,840	—
Interest Expense	4,000	—	100	—	4,100	—
Investment Income	—	1,000	—	200	—	1,200
Net Position	—	4,000	—	1,500	—	5,500
Totals	$50,000	$50,000	$4,100	$4,100	$53,700	$53,700

Depreciation Expense

GASB-34 requires that depreciation expense be reported on the statement of activities as a direct expense of specific functional categories if the related capital asset can be identified with the functional or program activities. Because an Internal Service Fund bills various operating departments, depreciation expenses on capital assets held by the fund are directly related to the functional categories (public safety, health and sanitation, etc.) that use the services of the Internal Service Fund. For this reason, depreciation expense should be included in the computation of the net profit or loss allocated to the various programs presented in the statement of activities.

Depreciation expense related to capital assets *that are not identified with a particular functional category (such as the depreciation on city hall) does not have to be reported as a direct expense of specific functions.* Rather, the depreciation expense may be presented as a separate line item in the statement of activities or included in the general governmental functional category. However, when unallocated depreciation expense is reported as a separate line in the statement of activities it should be indicated on the face of the statement that the amount reported as depreciation expense represents only unallocated depreciation expense and not total depreciation expense.

Interfund Transfers

GASB-34 states that interfund transfers are a type of nonreciprocal transaction that represents interfund activities where the two parties to the events do not receive equivalent cash, goods, or services. Governmental funds should report transfers of this nature in their fund operating statements as other financing uses and other financial sources of funds. Proprietary funds should report this type of transfer in their activity statements after nonoperating revenues and nonoperating expenses.

Based on the nature of transfers in/out as defined in GASB-34, these transfers should not be considered when determining the amount of net profit or loss that must be allocated back to the various programs reported on the statement of activities.

Activities That Are Exclusively Business-Type Activities

When activities conducted by an Internal Service Fund are related to business-type activities rather than governmental activities, the residual balances of the fund are allocated to the business-type activities column in the government-wide financial statements.

To illustrate the consolidation of an Internal Service Fund's accounts in the government-wide financial statements when its activities are exclusively related to business-type activities, assume the following pre-closing trial balances exist at the end of the fiscal year:

The following is a pre-closing Trial Balance for Business-Type Activities:

	Debit	Credit
Assets	$20,000	$—
Liabilities	—	5,000
Operating Revenues	—	47,000
Operating Expenses	40,000	—
Nonoperating Revenues	—	10,000
Nonoperating Expenses	5,000	—
Interest Expense	2,000	—
Investment Income	—	1,000
Net Position	—	4,000
Totals	$67,000	$67,000

Note: These amounts include all Enterprise Funds. Because Enterprise Funds are presented at the fund financial statement level using the accrual basis of accounting, these totals are the basis for preparing the business-type activities columns in the government-wide financial statements.

The following is a pre-closing Trial Balance for the Internal Service Fund:

	Debit	Credit
Assets	$1,500	$—
Liabilities	—	2,000
Revenues	—	5,000
Expenses	7,000	—
Net Position	—	1,500
Totals	$8,500	$8,500

The activities accounted for in the Internal Service Fund resulted in a "net loss" of $2,000 ($5,000 of revenues −$7,000 of expenses), which means that the expenses listed in the pre-closing trial balance of business-type activities are understated by $2,000. In order to merge the residual amounts of the Internal Service Fund into the business-type activities column of the reporting entity, the following worksheet adjustments are made:

	Pre-closing Trial Balance for Business-Type Activities		Eliminations Based on Internal Service Residual Balances		Pre-closing Trial Balance for Business-Type Activities Including Internal Service Residual Balances	
	Debit	Credit	Debit	Credit	Debit	Credit
Assets	$20,000	$—	$1,500	$—	$21,500	$—
Liabilities	—	5,000	—	2,000	—	7,000
Operating Revenues	—	47,000	—	—	—	47,000
Operating Expenses	40,000	—	2,000	—	42,000	—
Nonoperating Revenues	—	10,000	—	—	—	10,000
Nonoperating Expenses	5,000	—	—	—	5,000	—
Interest Expense	2,000	—	—	—	2,000	—
Investment Income	—	1,000	—	—	—	1,000
Net Position	—	4,000	—	1,500	—	5,500
Totals	$67,000	$67,000	$3,500	$3,500	$70,500	$70,500

Because the Internal Service Fund's activities exclusively support business-type activities, the results of the Internal Service Fund are presented as part in the business-type activities column of the statement of net position and the additional expense (the net loss of $2,000 incurred in the Internal Service Fund) increases the operating expenses reported in the statement of activities, exclusively for the business-type activities and not the governmental activities.

Interest Expense

When interest expense is incurred by an Internal Service Fund that services only Enterprise Funds, the interest is directly related to business-type activities. That is, the funds could have been borrowed by the Internal Service Fund or directly by the Enterprise Funds. For this reason, interest expense under this circumstance should be used in determining the amount of net profit or loss incurred by the Internal Service Fund that should be allocated to business-type activities.

Investment Income

As explained earlier, investment income earned by an Internal Service Fund would generally not be considered in determining the amount of net income or net loss to be allocated to governmental activities. This concept also applies to Internal Service Funds that exclusively service Enterprise Funds except the investment income is presented in the statement of activities as a business-type activity.

Depreciation Expense

Depreciation expense of an Internal Service Fund that exclusively services Enterprise Funds is directly related to the activities of the Enterprise Funds. For this reason the net profit or loss incurred by an Internal Service Fund under this circumstance should include the charge for depreciation.

Interfund Transfers

Based on the nature of transfers in/out as defined in GASB-34, these transfers should not be considered when determining the amount of net profit or loss that must be allocated back to business-type activities when an Internal Service Fund provides services only to Enterprise Funds. Transfers in/out by the Internal Service Fund are reported as a business-type activity in the lower section of the statement of activities.

Activities That Support Predominantly Governmental Funds

When activities conducted by an Internal Service Fund predominantly support governmental activities but also support Enterprise Funds, the residual balances of the Internal Service Funds are for the most part allocated to the governmental activities column of the government-wide financial statements. However, a portion of the net income or loss related to services provided to the Enterprise Funds is allocated to business-type activities.

To illustrate the consolidation of an Internal Service Fund's accounts in the government-wide financial statements when its activities are predominantly related to governmental activities, assume the following pre-closing trial balances exist at the end of the fiscal year:

The following is a pre-closing Trial Balance for Governmental Activities:

	Debit	Credit
Assets	$16,000	$—
Liabilities	—	6,000
Program Revenues	—	39,000
Program A Expenses	10,000	—
Program B Expenses	20,000	—
Interest Expense	4,000	—

	Debit	Credit
Investment Income	—	1,000
Net Position	—	4,000
Totals	$50,000	$50,000

The following is a pre-closing Trial Balance for Business-Type Activities:

	Debit	Credit
Assets	$20,000	$—
Liabilities	—	5,000
Operating Revenues	—	47,000
Operating Expenses	40,000	—
Nonoperating Revenues	—	10,000
Nonoperating Expenses	5,000	—
Interest Expense	2,000	—
Investment Income	—	1,000
Net Position	—	4,000
Totals	$67,000	$67,000

The following is a pre-closing Trial Balance for the Internal Service Fund:

	Debit	Credit
Assets	$1,500	$—
Liabilities	—	2,000
Revenues	—	5,000
Expenses	7,000	—
Net Position	—	1,500
Totals	$8,500	$8,500

During the year the Internal Service Fund billed the operating department of the General Fund for 80% (Programs A and B) of its activities and the balance was billed to Enterprise Funds. The activities accounted for in the Internal Service Fund resulted in a *net loss* of $2,000 ($5,000 of revenues – $7,000 of expenses), which means that the expenses listed in the pre-closing trial balance of governmental activities and business-type activities are understated. In order to consolidate the residual amounts of the Internal Service Fund into the governmental activities and business-type activities columns of the government-wide financial statements, the following worksheet adjustments are made:

	Pre-closing Trial Balance for Governmental Activities		Eliminations Based on Internal Service Residual Balances		Pre-closing Trial Balance for Governmental Activities Including Internal Service Residual Balances	
	Debit	Credit	Debit	Credit	Debit	Credit
Governmental Activities:						
			(a)			
Assets	$16,000	$—	$1,500	$—	$17,500	$—
Internal Balances	—	—	(b) 400	—	400	—
Liabilities	—	6,000	—	(a) 2,000	—	8,000
Program Revenues	—	39,000	—	—	—	39,000
Program A Expenses	10,000	—	(a) 960	—	10,960	—
Program B Expenses	20,000	—	(a) 640	—	20,640	—
Interest Expense	4,000	—	—	—	4,000	—
Investment Income	—	1,000	—	—	—	1,000
Net Position	—	4,000	—	(a) 1,500	—	5,500
Totals	$50,000	$50,000	$3,500	$3,500	$53,500	$53,500

	Pre-closing Trial Balance for Business-Type Activities		Eliminations Based on Internal Service Residual Balances		Pre-closing Trial Balance for Business-Type Activities Including Internal Service Residual Balances	
	Debit	Credit	Debit	Credit	Debit	Credit
Business-Type Activities:						
Assets	$20,000	$—	$—	$—	$20,000	$—
Liabilities	—	5,000	—	—	—	5,000
Internal Balances	—	—	—	(b) 400	—	400
Operating Revenues	—	47,000	—	—	—	47,000
Operating Expenses	40,000	—	(a) 400	—	40,400	—
Nonoperating Revenues	—	10,000	—	—	—	10,000
Nonoperating Expenses	5,000	—	—	—	5,000	—
Interest Expense	2,000	—	—	—	2,000	—
Investment Income	—	1,000	—	—	—	1,000
Net Position	—	4,000	—	—	—	4,000
Totals	$67,000	$67,000	$400	$400	$67,400	$67,400

The first entry, (a), allocates the net loss back to the funds that used the services during the period in a manner similar to entries discussed earlier in this section. The second entry, (b), arises because the governmental activities subsidized business-type activities through a deficit incurred in the Internal Service

Fund. In effect, the governmental activities paid some of the expenses for the Enterprise Fund. This is treated as an internal transaction and a "receivable" is created for the governmental activities column and a "payable" is created for the business-type activities column of the government-wide financial statements. Internal balances are presented on the face of the statement of net position for both the governmental activities and the business-type activities, but they offset (net to zero) when totals are extended to the "reporting entity column" on the statement.

Differentiating between Governmental and Business-Type Activities

The activities of an Internal Service Fund must be analyzed to determine whether account balances and transactions of the fund must be reported as a governmental activity or a business-type activity on the government-wide financial statements. The *GASB Implementation Guide 2015-1,* question 7.47.19 [GASB Cod. Sec. 2200.727-3], raises the issue of how the activities of a state investment board (accounted for as an Internal Service Fund) that manages investments for several state funds (Pension Trust Funds, Internal Service Funds, Enterprise Funds, and various governmental funds) should be reported in the government-wide financial statements. The state board's activities are financed exclusively by a fee that is charged to each participant. The GASB responded that the activities of the state board should be reported in the governmental activities column in the government-wide financial statements. The fact that a high percentage of the state board's activity involved pension funds is irrelevant even though fiduciary fund financial statements are not presented at the government-wide financial statement level. The criterion to determine where to include an Internal Service Fund's balances is based on whether the fund services governmental funds or Enterprise Funds. Only if Enterprise Funds are the predominant or only participants in the state board's activities should the balances be presented in the business-type activities column.

Activities with External Parties

GASB-34 states that an "Internal Service Fund should be used only if the reporting government is the predominant participant in the activity." When external parties are the predominant participants in the services offered by a governmental entity, an Enterprise Fund should be used.

A governmental entity may establish an Internal Service Fund that has its predominant activities with other units of the reporting entity but for simplicity purposes also makes sales (of a non-predominant amount) to external parties. Under this circumstance, the external sales and related cost of sales should not be used to determine the net profit or loss amount that is the basis for adjusting the expenses incurred in the governmental column of the statement of activities.

To illustrate the consolidation of an Internal Service Fund's accounts in the government-wide financial statements when sales are made to an external party and the activities of the fund are predominantly governmental activities, assume the following pre-closing trial balances exist at the end of the fiscal year:

The following is a pre-closing Trial Balance for Governmental Activities:

	Debit	Credit
Assets	$16,000	$—
Liabilities	—	6,000
Program Revenues—General Government	—	29,000
Program Expenses—General Government	21,000	—
Program Revenues—Other	—	10,000
Program Expenses—Other	9,000	—
Interest Expense	4,000	—
Investment Income	—	1,000
Net Position	—	4,000
Totals	$50,000	$50,000

The following is a pre-closing Trial Balance for the Internal Service Fund:

	Debit	Credit
Assets	$1,500	$—
Liabilities	—	2,000
Revenues	—	4,520
Revenues—External Parties	—	480
Expenses	7,000	—
Net Position	—	1,500
Totals	$8,500	$8,500

The sales to external parties are billed at approximately 20% above the direct cost incurred by the Internal Service Fund.

The activities accounted for in the Internal Service Fund resulted in a net loss of $2,000 ($5,000 of revenues including revenues from external parties – $7,000 expenses); however, the revenue from external parties and the related cost ($400) is not part of the basis used to allocate the results of operations to governmental activities.

The net loss to be allocated to governmental activities is computed as follows:

	Total	Related to External Activities	Related to Internal Activities
Revenues	$5,000	($480)	$4,520
Expenses	7,000	(400)	6,600
Net loss to be allocated			$2,080

In order to consolidate the residual amounts of the Internal Service Fund into the governmental activities columns of the government-wide financial statements, the following worksheet adjustments are made:

	Pre-closing Trial Balance for Governmental Activities		Eliminations Based on Internal Service Residual Balances		Pre-closing Trial Balance for Governmental Activities Including Internal Service Residual Balances	
	Debit	Credit	Debit	Credit	Debit	Credit
Assets	$16,000	$—	$1,500	$—	$17,500	$—
Liabilities	—	6,000	—	2,000	—	8,000
Program Revenues—General Government	—	29,000	—	480	—	29,480
Program Expenses—General Government	21,000	—	400	—	21,400	—
Program Revenues—Other	—	10,000	—	—	—	10,000
Program Expenses—Other	9,000	—	2,080	—	11,080	—
Interest Expense	4,000	—	—	—	4,000	—
Investment Income	—	1,000	—	—	—	1,000
Net Position	—	4,000	—	1,500	—	5,500
Totals	$50,000	$50,000	$3,980	$3,980	$53,980	$53,980

In the above example, it is assumed that the activity performed by the Internal Service Fund should be classified as general governmental expenses. For example, the activity could be data processing. For this reason, the amount of revenue related to external sales ($480) is classified as program revenues from general government activities and the related expense ($400) is classified as general government expenses in the statement of activities. The balance of the adjustment ($2,080) is allocated to specific programs (e.g., public safety), which for simplicity are identified as "other program expenses." If the activity of the Internal Service Fund were predominantly related to business-type activities rather than governmental activities, the residual balances of the Internal Service Fund would be merged with other business-type activities.

Activities with Fiduciary Funds

In some instances, an Internal Service Fund provides services or goods to fiduciary funds. The *GASB Implementation Guide 2015-1*, question 7.47.20 [GASB Cod. Sec. 2200.725-14], states that in determining whether the services are predominantly provided to internal parties (therefore an Internal Service Fund is appropriate) or predominantly provided to external parties (therefore an Enterprise Fund is appropriate), the activities with fiduciary funds should be considered internal. However, in folding the activities into the government-wide financial statements, activities with fiduciary funds should be treated as external transactions. In this circumstance, the external sales and related cost of sales should not be used to determine the net profit or loss amount (the look-back adjustment) that is the basis for adjusting the expenses incurred in the governmental column of the statement of activities.

GOVERNMENT-WIDE FINANCIAL STATEMENTS

Enterprise fund financial statements generally serve as the basis for the business-type activities column presentation in the government-wide financial statements. There is usually no need for reconciliation between the government-wide financial statements and proprietary fund financial statements, because both sets of financial statements are based on the same measurement focus and basis of accounting (GASB-34, par. 104) [GASB Cod. Secs. 2200.194, P80.108]. However, the treatment of internal service fund activity within the government-wide financial statements does require additional consideration.

REPORTING CASH FLOWS OF PROPRIETARY FUNDS

GASB-9 (*Reporting Cash Flows of Proprietary and Nonexpendable Trust Funds and Governmental Entities That Use Proprietary Fund Accounting*) provides authoritative guidance in the preparation of cash flow statements for proprietary fund types. Proprietary funds cannot use the standards contained in FASB Accounting Standards Codification™ (ASC) Topic 230 to prepare their cash flow statements.

GASB-9 essentially adopted the fundamental concepts contained at the time of issuance in FASB standards. The fundamental differences between GASB-9 and FASB standards are as follows:

- GASB-9 requires the use of four categories, rather than three, to summarize cash activity of proprietary fund types.

- In GASB-9, cash flows from operating activities are more narrowly defined for proprietary fund types.

The GASB did not wish to create a comparability issue by having two separate sets of reporting standards with respect to the preparation of the statement of cash flows: a set of standards for commercial enterprises and a set of standards for proprietary fund types. GASB-9 did not address all of the issues addressed in FASB ASC™ 230-10-45 because the GASB believed that such issues seldom would be encountered in the governmental sector. When preparing the financial statements for a proprietary fund type, if the accountant encounters an accounting issue that is not addressed in GASB-9 but is addressed in FASB ASC™ 230-10-45, the guidance established by ASC™ 230-10-45 as well as amendments to GASB-9, may be used.

GASB-9, as amended by GASB-34, establishes the requirement for presentation of a statement of cash flows for the following entities:

- Proprietary funds; and

- All governmental entities that follow proprietary fund accounting standards.

The second category of entities includes public benefit corporations and authorities, governmental utilities, and governmental hospitals. The category also includes governmental colleges and universities that follow accounting and reporting standards established by NCGA-1 (*Governmental Accounting and Financial Reporting Principles*), as amended by GASB-35. Thus, statements of cash flows must be presented for proprietary funds of governmental colleges and universities that follow standards established by NCGA-1, as amended by GASB-35.

The following entities are exempt from the standards established by GASB-9 (GASB-9, par. 5) [GASB Cod. Secs. 2450.101–.102]:

- Public employee retirement systems (PERS);

- Pension and OPEB Trust Funds; and

- Investment Trust Funds.

PRACTICE ALERT: The GASB's *Financial Reporting Model—Reexamination* project includes the possibility of enhancements to or expansion of the statement of cash flows to the governmental activities or to the government as a whole. It is unclear at the time of publication which direction the GASB may ultimately decide.

Basic Requirement and Purpose

GASB-9 establishes the statement of cash flows as a basic financial statement for proprietary fund types (GASB-9, par. 6) [GASB Cod. Secs. 2200.208, 2450.103].

A core purpose of a statement of cash flows is to identify cash inflows and cash outflows, enhancing the user's understanding that the inflows and outflows presented in the statement of revenues, expenses and changes in net position *do not* equate to cash flows. Specifically, GASB-9 notes that the statement of cash flows, along with related disclosures and information in other financial statements, can be useful in assessing the following:

- Ability of an entity to generate future cash flows;

- Ability of an entity to pay its debt as the debt matures;

- Need to seek outside financing;

- Reasons for differences between cash flows from operations and operating income (or net income if operating income is not separately presented in the entity's statement of operations); and

- Effect on an entity's financial position of cash and noncash transactions from investing, capital, and financing activities.

These assessments can be made when a statement of cash flows is prepared in a manner that summarizes:

- Cash flows from operations;

- Noncapital financing activities;

- Capital and related financing activities; and
- Investing activities.

In addition, noncash transactions that have an effect on the entity's financial position should be presented. Finally, there should be a reconciliation between operating income (or net income if operating income is not presented) and net cash flow from operating activities (GASB-9, pars. 6–7) [GASB Cod. Secs. 2200.208, 2450.103–.104].

GASB-9 requires that the amounts per the statement of cash flows "be easily traceable to similarly titled line items or subtotals shown in the statement of financial position"; however, there is no requirement that a single amount identified on the statement of cash flows be exactly the same as a single amount on the statement of financial position. For example, the ending balance of cash and cash equivalents on the statement of cash flows could be traceable to two balances on the statement of financial position (unrestricted and restricted cash and cash equivalents). Because it is obvious to a reader that cash amounts include both restricted and unrestricted amounts, the requirements of GASB-9 are satisfied. It is, of course, a matter of professional judgment to determine what is "easily traceable" from one financial statement to another. If it is concluded that the information is not easily traceable, one option could be to include a reconciliation at the bottom of either financial statement that would easily tie the two financial statements together and therefore satisfy the reporting requirement established by GASB-9.

Focus of Statement

The statement of cash flows in a proprietary fund focuses on summarizing activities that have an effect on cash, or cash and cash equivalents. GASB-9 uses the same focal point as FASB ASC™ 230-10-45.

In addition to selecting a more definite focal point, the GASB requires that the information on the statement of cash flows be easily traceable to the information on the balance sheet or statement of net position. For example, if an entity selects cash and cash equivalents as the focal point of the statement of cash flows (GASB-9, par. 8) [GASB Cod. Sec. 2450.105]:

- The statement of cash flows should show a reconciliation between the beginning and ending balances of cash and cash equivalents; and
- The same beginning and ending balances of cash and cash equivalents should be presented in the entity's balance sheets or statements of net position.

"Cash" includes amounts that are subject to immediate use by the entity. Examples are:

- Cash on hand;
- Cash on (demand) deposit with financial institutions that can be withdrawn without prior notice or penalty; and
- Other deposits or cash management pools that have characteristics similar to demand deposit accounts (e.g., additional funds may be deposited to the account at any time and withdrawals can be made at any time without prior notice or penalty).

"Cash equivalents" are short-term, highly liquid investments that have both of the following characteristics:

- Readily convertible to known amounts of cash; and

- Mature in such a short period of time that their values are effectively immune from changes in interest rates.

The GASB *Implementation Guide Update 2016-1,* question 4.3 [GASB Cod. Sec. I50.728-4], discusses how generally, cash equivalents are measured at other than fair value (including amortized cost). They are not subjected to fair value disclosures similarly to investments. If a government has a policy of reporting a particular investment as a cash equivalent, including positions in external investment pools, then such investments are part of a statement of cash flows.

Examples of cash equivalents provided by GASB-9 include treasury bills, commercial paper, certificates of deposit and money market funds.

The GASB allows the focal point of the statement of cash flows to include cash equivalents because cash equivalents generally are acquired as part of a governmental entity's cash management strategy. Excess cash is invested because it is available, not because the strategy is part of the entity's investment or financing strategy.

If an entity believes that cash equivalents are acquired for reasons other than cash management, cash equivalents (all or some of the cash equivalents) do not have to be part of the focus (analyzing the effect of activities on cash and cash equivalents) of the preparation of the statement of cash flows (GASB-9, par. 10) [GASB Cod. Sec. 2450.107].

An entity should establish and disclose its treatment of cash equivalents in the preparation of the statement of cash flows. The policy should be disclosed in the entity's summary of significant accounting policies. If the policy is subsequently altered, the alteration is considered a change in an accounting principle that must be accounted for by restating prior years' financial statements presented on a comparative basis (GASB-9, par. 11) [GASB Cod. Sec. 2450.108].

Some proprietary fund types have restricted assets that include cash and cash equivalents. For cash flow reporting purposes, unrestricted cash and unrestricted cash equivalents should be included with restricted cash and restricted cash equivalents. As noted in GASB-9, a governmental entity may elect to treat its unrestricted cash equivalents as investments. The same election can be made for restricted cash equivalents. The method of defining cash equivalents should be disclosed in the entity's summary of significant accounting policies.

Cash Flow Amounts

A fundamental rule in financial reporting is that amounts and accounts should not be netted. For example, an amount due to a proprietary fund from a vendor and an amount due from the proprietary fund to the same vendor should not be netted for financial reporting purposes. This concept is maintained for the preparation of the statement of cash flows, except as explained in this section (GASB-9, par. 12) [GASB Cod. Sec. 2450.109].

GASB-9 states that gross amounts of related receipts and payments that have the following characteristics *may be* netted:

- Transactions have a quick turnover rate. Footnote 7 to paragraph 13 [GASB Cod. Sec. 2450.fn4] notes that most repurchase agreements (assuming the entity chooses not to include them as cash equivalents) and loans to and from other funds to cover temporary (three months or less) cash needs would be deemed to have a quick turnover rate.

- Transactions result in instruments with short maturities. (The instruments mature no more than three months after the date of purchase or are due on demand.)

Such transactions include investments (other than cash equivalents), loans receivable, and debt (GASB-9, par. 13) [GASB Cod. Sec. 2450.110].

For example, if a proprietary fund type entered into transactions during the year that resulted in the (nonoperating) borrowing of $10,000,000 from other funds and the loaning of $12,000,000 to other funds, the net amount of $2,000,000 could be presented in the statement of cash flows for the year.

GASB-9 provides one other set of transactions that may be netted. Net purchases and sales of a governmental entity's highly liquid investments may be reported on a net basis under the following circumstances (GASB-9, par. 14) [GASB Cod. Sec. 2450.111]:

- During the year, substantially all of the entity's assets consisted of highly liquid investments or other assets that are readily marketable.

- During the year, the entity had relatively no debt. "Relativity" is defined as the amount of average debt to the amount of average assets during the year.

Entities that would qualify for netting based on the previously listed criteria would function as investment accounts because there would be substantially no operating assets or debt.

FASB ASC™ 230 exempts certain common trust funds from the requirement to prepare a statement of cash flows. Some governmental entities are similar to the common trust funds exempted by FASB ASC™ 230. However, the GASB stated that such governmental entities must prepare a statement of cash flows. GASB-9 does not allow such governmental entities to substitute a statement of changes in net position for a statement of cash flows, but they may net the purchases and sales of highly liquid investments.

Classification of Cash Flows

The format of the statement of cash flows adopted by GASB-9 provides for four main categories, or classifications, of cash flows, unlike FASB standards, which require three main categories. The categories to be used by a proprietary fund type are:

1. Cash flows from operating activities;
2. Cash flows from noncapital financing activities;
3. Cash flows from capital and related financing activities; and
4. Cash flows from investing activities.

Thus, the general format of a statement of cash flows for a proprietary fund type would appear as follows (assuming a June 30 year-end):

	Amount
Cash flows from operating activities	$X
Cash flows from noncapital financing activities	X
Cash flows from capital and related financing activities	X
Cash flows from investing activities	X
Net increase in cash (or cash and cash equivalents)	X
Cash (or cash and cash equivalents) at 6/30/X-PY	X
Cash (or cash and cash equivalents) at 6/30/X-CY	$X

The amount of cash related to each of the four categories includes transactions that increase cash as well as those that decrease cash. The net increase in cash adjusts the beginning cash (or cash and cash equivalents), which should equal to or reconcile the amount reported in the statement of net position (GASB-9, par. 15) [GASB Cod. Sec. 2450.112].

Operating Cash Flows

The "cash flows from operating activities" is a residual classification category. In other words, all transactions that are not classified as capital and related financing activities, noncapital financing activities, or investing activities are classified as operating activities. Thus, operating activities are related to the governmental entity's delivery of its goods and/or services to its customers (operating revenues) and the use of resources related to the delivery of its goods and/or services (operating expenses). Cash flows related to these activities should be used to compute net cash flows from operations (GASB-9, par. 16) [GASB Cod. Sec. 2450.113].

The specific types of cash inflows and outflows from operations are presented in the summary below. Related cash inflows and outflows are paired (GASB-9, pars. 17–18, GASB-34, par. 112) [GASB Cod. Secs. 2450.114–.115].

Cash Inflows: Operating Activities	Cash Outflows: Operating Activities
Receipts from the sale of goods or services, including collections on trade accounts and short-term and long-term trade notes receivable	Payments for services and goods held for resale, including payments on trade accounts and short-term and long-term trade notes payable
	Payments for other goods or services
	Payments for employees services

Cash Inflows: Operating Activities	Cash Outflows: Operating Activities
Receipts from interfund services provided	Payments for interfund services used, including payments in lieu of taxes that are payments for, and reasonably equivalent in value to, service provided
Receipts from grants for specific activities that would be considered operating activities of the entity making the grant	Payments of grants for specific activities to other governmental entities or organizations that would be considered operating activities of the entity making the grant
Receipts from interfund reimbursements	Payments for taxes, duties, fines, and other fees or penalties
All other receipts that cannot be classified as capital and related financing, noncapital financing, or investing activities	All other payments that cannot be classified as capital and related financing, noncapital financing, or investing activities

In addition to the categories listed, GASB-9 identifies transactions related to *certain* loan programs that should be used to determine the net cash flows from operations. Conceptually, cash flows related to loans would be considered investing activities. However, some loan programs are established as part of the strategy to achieve social and educational goals of the governmental entity and should therefore be considered operating activities. For example, cash flows from student loan programs would be considered part of a governmental college or university's operating activities and would be used to determine cash flows from operations for the year.

Operating cash flows would include both cash payments to the recipients of these certain loan programs and repayments, including interest, from the recipients (GASB-9, par. 19) [GASB Cod. Sec. 2450.116].

If a governmental entity issues bonds to finance these certain loan programs, the proceeds and repayments, including interest, would be classified as noncapital financing activities.

The decoupling of the issuance of bonds to finance these loan programs as noncapital financing activities with the issuance of the loans financed by those bonds as operating activities has caused a large amount of discussion within the public institutions of higher education. Many private institutions categorize them as investing or operating activities. According to the GASB's *Implementation Guide 2015-1*, question 2.25.1 [GASB Cod. Sec. 2450.708-3], only low-income housing mortgage programs and student loan programs directly qualify for the treatment established in GASB-9, par. 19. In deliberating paragraph 19, the GASB concluded that it would be inappropriate in some circumstances to classify loan activities as investing activities, basing its decision on the characteristics of governmental loan programs. The key element is that loans are not typical investments, because they are not necessarily intended to earn a profit and they are distinguished from other loan programs because they are undertaken to provide a direct benefit for constituents. However, the GASB did not intend for all loan programs to be classified as operating activities. There are no specific criteria in GASB-9, par. 19, for determining which loan activities should be classified as operating rather than investing activities, nor is there an explanation of "direct benefits" being provided to "individual constituents." Even for financing authorities, paragraph 19 applies as making and collecting loans are the primary operations of the enterprise. A finance authority that facilitates financing by serving as an intermediary or conduit generally would not qualify even if the project to be financed indirectly benefits the government or its constituents. The GASB gives examples of an authority created to finance government building projects (such as state office buildings or public university dormitories) as not qualifying because the direct beneficiary is the government rather than individual constituents. A second example of a public university dormitory authority that is also not qualifying because debt is issued by the authority and the proceeds are loaned to universities for their dormitory construction projects. Although the students who eventually live in the dorms will benefit from the activity, the direct beneficiary of the dormitory authority is the university itself, which is part of the governmental financial reporting entity. Such an arrangement merely facilitates the government's financing process. The substance of the arrangement is that the government issued bonds to serve its own needs.

Cash flows from operations do not include some transactions and events, even though these transactions and events may be cash flows and may appear on the entity's statement of operations. These transactions and events include the following (the parenthetical comment describes where the item would be presented in the statement of cash flows):

- Interest payments on capital debt (cash flows from capital and related financing activities);

- Interest payments on noncapital debt (cash flows from noncapital financing activities);

- Interest receipts from investments (cash flows from investing activities); and

- Subsidies to finance operating deficits (cash flows from noncapital financing activities).

Under FASB ASC™ 230-10-45, the elements previously listed would be used to compute cash flows from operations. However, GASB-9 states that these activities should not be classified as operational cash flows.

The cash flows from operating activities is a residual category. That is, if a transaction cannot be classified into one of the other three categories discussed in the following section, the transaction is placed in the operating activities category by default.

GASB-9 requires that the direct method be used in formatting the cash flows from operating activities category and that there be a separate reporting of cash flows from interfund services provided and used. However, there is no requirement that there be a separate reporting for cash transactions with component units. The *GASB Implementation Guide*, question 2.29.6 [GASB Cod. Sec. 2450.713-6], discusses while the latter category is not mandated, a governmental entity may, if it so desires, present such transactions in its operating activities section.

> **OBSERVATION:** GASB-34, par. 128 [GASB Cod. Secs. 2200.217, 2600.110], require that the notes to the financial statements also describe the nature and amount of significant transactions between major component units and the primary government and other component units.

Noncapital Financing Cash Flows

GASB-9 created a classification of cash flows that is not contained in FASB ASC™ 230-10-45. Cash flows related to noncapital financing activities must be presented separately on a proprietary fund type's statement of cash flows. The noncapital financing category comprises transactions related to operating debt and subsidies. For example, borrowing and repaying funds (including interest) for purposes other than acquiring, constructing, or improving capital assets would be considered a noncapital financing activity (GASB-9, par. 20) [GASB Cod. Sec. 2450.117].

The specific types of cash inflows and outflows from noncapital financing activities are presented in the following summary. Where appropriate, related cash inflows and outflows are paired (GASB-9, pars. 21–22, GASB-34, par. 112) [GASB Cod. Secs. 2450.118–.119]:

Cash Inflows: Noncapital Financing Activities	Cash Outflows: Noncapital Financing Activities
Receipts from issuing bonds, notes, and other instruments not related to the acquisition, construction, or improvement of capital assets	Repayments of funds borrowed not related to the acquisition, construction, or improvement of capital assets
	Payments of interest on liabilities incurred for purposes other than acquiring, constructing, or improving capital assets
Receipts from grants or subsidies *except*: (1) amounts restricted for capital purposes and (2) amounts considered to be operating activities by the governmental unit	Payments of grants or subsidies to other governmental entities or organizations except those allocated for activities that are considered operating unit activities by the governmental unit making the grant or providing the subsidy
Receipts from other funds except (1) those amounts that are clearly attributable to acquisition, construction, or improvement of capital assets, (2) interfund service provided, and (3) reimbursement for operating transactions	Payments to other funds, except for interfund services used
Receipts from property and other taxes collected for the entity and not restricted to capital purposes	

GASB-9 notes that in the previous classification, cash payments of grants to another government or organization are not considered to be noncapital financing activities when the specific activity that the grant is to be used for is considered to be an operating activity by the grantor. As noted in footnote 10, it is irrelevant whether the grantee actually uses the grant as an operating subsidy or for capital purposes.

Capital and Related Financing Cash Flows

Cash flow expenditures for the acquisition of capital assets used in the entity's operations and the financing of those activities should be classified as cash flows from capital and related financing activities on the statement of cash flows. Also, repayments on debt issued to finance the acquisition, construction, or improvement of capital assets are included in this category. Finally, the category includes payments for capital assets acquired from vendors on credit (GASB-9, par. 23) [GASB Cod. Sec. 2450.120].

The specific types of cash inflows and outflows from capital and related financing activities are presented in the following summary. Where appropriate, related cash inflows and outflows are paired (GASB-9, pars. 24–25) [GASB Cod. Secs. 2450.121–.122].

Cash Inflows: Capital and Related Financing Activities	Cash Outflows: Capital and Related Financing Activities
Receipts from the issuance or refunding of bonds, mortgages, notes, and other (short-term or long-term) borrowings that are clearly related to the acquisition, construction, or improvement of capital assets	Payments to retire or refunding obligations specifically used to acquire, construct, or improve capital assets
Receipts from capital grants	Payments to vendors who provided the financing for the acquisition, construction, or improvement of capital assets
Receipts from other funds, other governments, and other organizations or individuals that are for the specific purpose of defraying the cost of acquiring, constructing, or improving capital assets	Payments for interest on obligations that were used to acquire, construct, or improve capital assets
Receipts from the sale of capital assets	Payments to acquire, construct, or improve capital assets
Receipts from an insurance policy that provides coverage against the theft or destruction of capital assets	
Receipts from special assessments, property taxes, or other taxes levied to specifically finance the acquisition, construction, or improvement of capital assets	

FASB ASC™ 230-10-45 classifies the construction, acquisition, and improvement of capital assets as investing activities, while GASB-9 classifies them as capital and related financing cash flows activities. FASB ASC™ 230-10-45 classifies all financing, capital and noncapital, as financing activities, while GASB-9 classifies them as capital and related financing cash flows activities or noncapital financing activities, depending on their character. Finally, FASB ASC™ 230-10-45 classifies cash payments for interest expense as operating activities, while

GASB-9 classifies (1) interest payments on capital debt as part of capital and related financing cash flows activities and (2) interest payments on noncapital debt as part of noncapital financing activities.

Investing Cash Flows

The fourth category of transactions on the statement of cash flows relates to investing activities. This category is narrowly defined and is limited to cash received as investment income, cash payments for other loans and the collection of cash receipts for those loans, and payments for acquiring debt and equity instruments and proceeds from the liquidation of debt and equity investments. The exception for the payment and subsequent receipt of loans in this category is that program loans are considered operating activities (GASB-9, par. 26) [GASB Cod. Sec. 2450.123].

The specific types of cash inflows and outflows from investing activities are presented in the following summary. Where appropriate, related cash inflows and outflows are paired (GASB-9, pars. 27–28) [GASB Cod. Secs. 2450.124–.125].

Cash Inflows: Investing Activities	Cash Outflows: Investing Activities
Receipts from loan collections, with the exception of program loans	Loans made to other parties, with the exception of program loans
Receipts from the sale of investments in debt instruments issued by other entities except for the sale of investments that are within the reporting entity of the primary government	Payments for investing in debt instruments issued by other entities except for purchases of investments that are considered to be cash equivalents
Receipts from the sale of investments in equity instruments	Payments for investments in equity instruments
Receipts that represent the return of investments in equity instruments	
Receipts of interest and dividends on investments and loans, except for program loans	
Withdrawals from investment pools that are not used as demand deposits	Deposits to investment pools that are not used as demand deposits

As a contrast, FASB ASC™ 230-10-45 classifies cash received from investment earnings (dividends and interest) as an operating activity, whereas GASB-9 classifies such cash earnings as an investing activity.

Capital Distinguished from Noncapital Financing

In most debt transactions, it is apparent whether the debt has been issued to construct, acquire, or improve capital assets and therefore the proceeds and subsequent repayments of the principal and interest related to the debt should be classified as capital financing activities on the statement of cash flows.

The GASB did recognize, however, that in some instances distinguishing capital financing from noncapital financing may not be obvious. Therefore, GASB-9 provides the following additional guidance:

- When debt is issued and it is not clear that the purpose of issuing the debt was to construct, acquire, or improve capital assets, the issuance of the debt and the subsequent debt service payments (principal and interest) should be classified as noncapital financing activities on the statement of cash flows.

- When capital debt has been issued but the related capital asset has been sold, abandoned, etc., the debt service payments on the original capital debt should continue to be classified as capital financing activities on the statement of cash flows.

- When capital debt is decreased through a refunding, the proceeds from the new debt and the payment to retire the old debt should be classified as capital financing activities. In addition, subsequent debt service payments on the new debt should be classified as capital financing activities on the statement of cash flows.

In the final guideline, debt may be issued to decrease capital debt but the proceeds from the refunding may exceed the amount needed to retire the capital debt. Under this circumstance, the use of the excess funds determines how the proceeds from the issuance of the debt and subsequent debt service payments should be classified. For example, assume that $1,000,000 of new debt (5-year, 10%, serial bonds) is issued to refund $980,000 of capital debt and the excess ($20,000) is used for operating purposes. The following example describes how the transaction would affect the statement of cash flows, assuming the transaction occurred on the last day of the governmental entity's fiscal year (GASB-9, par. 29) [GASB Cod. Sec. 2450.129]:

	Year of Refunding	Subsequent Years
Cash flows from operating activities:		
Operating payments	$ (20,000)	
Cash flows from capital and related financing activities:		
Issuance of debt	980,000	
Retirement of debt	(980,000)	
Retirement of serial debt ($980,000/5 years)		$ (196,000)
Interest on serial debt ($980,000 × 10%)		(98,000)
Cash flows from noncapital financing activities:		
Issuance of operating debt	20,000	
Retirement of serial debt ($20,000/5 years)		(4,000)
Interest on serial debt ($20,000 × 10%)		(2,000)

The classification of capital and related financing activities is dependent on the definition of a capital asset. While GASB-9 does not attempt to define a capital asset, it is noted in Appendix A to GASB-9 that the accounting treatment for a particular transaction would provide guidance in determining whether an asset is a capital asset. For example, if a lease agreement is capitalized based on the guidelines incorporated in GASB-62, pars. 211–271 [GASB Cod. Sec. L20] for leases, cash flows related to the transaction would be classified as a cash flow from capital and related financing activities. In addition, transactions related to both tangible and intangible assets, as defined in GASB-51 should be included in the capital and related financing activities grouping. For example, the acquisition of water rights would be considered a capital transaction because such an asset is considered a capital asset in accordance with GASB-51.

PRACTICE ALERT: See Chapter 14, "Leases and Service Concession Arrangements," for a discussion of GASB Statement No. 87 (*Leases*). Upon implementation, nearly all leases would be classified as a cash flow from capital and related financing activities.

Formatting the Statement of Cash Flows

The net amount of cash flows from each of the four categories should be shown on the statement of cash flows. In addition, the effects of those net amounts should be shown in a manner that reconciles the beginning balance of cash, or cash and cash equivalents, to the ending balance of cash, or cash and cash equivalents.

Proprietary funds should prepare a statement of cash flows based on the guidance established by GASB-9, as amended by GASB-34, formatted based on the *direct method* in computing cash flows from operating activities. The statement of cash flows is supplemented with a reconciliation of operating cash flows and operating income (the indirect method) (GASB-9, par. 30; GASB-34, par. 105) [GASB Cod. Sec. 2450.127].

Under the direct method, cash flows from operating activities are presented by major categories. At a minimum, the following categories must be presented:

- Receipts from customers;
- Receipts from interfund services provided;
- Receipts from other operating activities;
- Payments to other suppliers of goods and/or services;
- Payments to employees;
- Payments for interfund services used, including payments in lieu of taxes that are payments for, and reasonably equivalent in value to, services provided; and
- Payments for other operating activities.

The governmental entity is not limited to the categories listed, and additional categories should be used if the usefulness of the financial statements is enhanced (GASB-9, par. 31, GASB 34, pars. 105, 112) [GASB Cod. Sec. 2450.128].

In computing amounts for operating activities under the direct method, the accrual amount on the statement of operations is converted to a cash amount by taking into consideration related accruals and deferrals on the balance sheet or statement of net position. For example, to compute cash receipts from customers, the accrual sales figure would be adjusted by the net change for the year in customer receivables.

The reconciliation should include all major classes of reconciling items, including, at a minimum, the following:

- Net change in receivables related to operations;
- Net change in inventories; and
- Net change in payables related to operations.

The governmental entity is not limited to the three categories, and additional categories should be used if the usefulness of the financial statements is enhanced (GASB-9, pars. 32–34, as amended by GASB-34, pars. 100 and 105, GASB-65, par. 31).

Except for the netting convention allowed, cash inflows and cash outflows in each major section of the statement of cash flows should be shown at gross amounts. For example, assume a governmental entity has borrowed $10,000,000 for capital expenditures during the year and has repaid $8,000,000 to reduce capital debt during the same year. In the section titled "Cash Flows from Capital and Related Financing Activities," an inflow of $10,000,000 and an outflow of $8,000,000 would be disclosed separately, rather than a single net cash inflow of $2,000,000 (GASB-9, par. 35) [GASB Cod. Sec. 2450.130].

In preparing a statement of cash flows for an individual proprietary fund type, the gross amounts of interfund cash transfers should be presented in the appropriate category. In preparing combined and combining statements of cash flows for all proprietary funds, interfund transfers may be eliminated under the following conditions (GASB-9, par. 36, as amended by GASB-34, pars. 6 and 105) [GASB Cod. Sec. 2450.131]:

- Interfund transfers are eliminated in preparing other combined and combining financial statements.
- Interfund eliminations made as part of preparing combined or combining statements of cash flows should be apparent from the headings or disclosed in a note.

Combined or combining statements of cash flows should be prepared using only the direct method of presenting cash flows from operations.

Noncash Investing, Capital, and Financing Activities

Certain transactions may have a significant impact on the financial position of a governmental entity but may not affect, or may only partially affect, the entity's cash position. For example, a governmental entity may acquire equipment by issuing a long-term note. While the transaction does not affect cash, it does have an effect on the entity's balance sheet.

GASB-9 states that such transactions should be adequately described in a separate schedule. The format of the schedule may be narrative or tabular. In addition, the schedule may be presented on the same page as the entity's statement of cash flows.

Examples of transactions that should be presented in a governmental entity's schedule of noncash investing, capital, and financing activities include the following:

- Acquiring capital assets through deferred payment plans;
- Acquiring property rights through lease contracts that must be capitalized as required by GASB-62 (see also **PRACTICE ALERT** on GASB-87 in this chapter and in Chapter 14, "Leases and Service Concession Arrangements");
- Acquiring property through an exchange of property;
- Retiring debt through the issuance of other debt; and
- Retiring debt by giving property to a debtor.

The concept of reporting noncash investing, capital, and financing activities, commonly referred to as "the all financial resources approach," was originally established by APB-19.

Some transactions will have both a cash and a noncash component. Under this circumstance, only the cash portion of the transactions is displayed in the statement of cash flows, and the noncash portion is presented in the schedule of noncash investing, capital, and financing activities. For example, assume that an entity purchases $100,000 of equipment by making a down payment of $20,000 and signing a note for the balance. The $20,000 cash payment is classified on the statement of cash flows as a cash outflow in the capital and related financing activities category, and the long-term financing of $80,000 is presented in the schedule supporting the statement of cash flows (GASB-9, par. 37) [GASB Cod. Sec. 2450.132].

OBSERVATION: The *GASB Implementation Guide 2015-1*, questions 2.24.3 [GASB Cod. Sec. 2450.707-11] and 2.32.1–.2 [GASB Cod. Secs. 2450.714-2-3], all discuss how noncash transactions (and transactions that involve both cash and noncash elements) must be reported in a schedule that "clearly describes the cash and noncash aspects of transactions involving similar items" and that schedule may be reported on the face of the statement or on a separate page that references the statement. The schedule may be set up as a narrative format or a tabular format. Noncash transactions should not be reported only in a note to the financial statements as a substitute for financial statement display.

Cash Overdraft Position

An overdraft position creates a presentation problem on the statement of cash flows because of the treatment of a negative cash position on an entity's balance sheet or statement of net position. On the balance sheet or statement of net position the cash overdraft must be presented as a current liability rather than as negative asset, because the negative asset concept has no meaning in financial reporting. That means that the change in cash for the period is determined by the difference between the beginning balance of cash and an assumed zero balance in cash at the end of the period. Unless there is an adjustment to the statement of cash flows, the net change (decrease) in cash for the period will be greater on the statement of cash flows than the implied change as interpreted on the comparative balance sheet.

This difference can be removed by making an adjustment (increase) to the noncapital financing activities on the statement of cash flows. The adjustment is based on the assumption that the cash overdraft is covered by the bank through an in-substance loan to the entity. The adjustment shown in the "cash flows from noncapital financing activities" category on the statement of cash flows should clearly explain the nature of the assumption. For example, the line item could be labeled "cash overdraft position assumed to be financed" or the adjustment could be cross-referenced to a note that would explain the entity's (negative) cash position and the nature of the financing assumption. In the following period, it would be assumed that the "loan" from the bank is repaid by showing an assumed loan repayment as a noncapital financing activity.

Illustration. Exhibit 7-1 is an example of a statement of cash flows based on the requirements established by GASB-9, as amended. As required by GASB-34, the direct method is used to determine cash flows from operating activities.

EXHIBIT 7-1
ILLUSTRATION: ENTERPRISE FUND—AIRPORT
Statement of Cash Flows for Year Ended June 30, 20X8

	Increase/(Decrease) in Cash and Cash Equivalents
Cash flows from operating activities:	
Cash received from rental income	$2,846,983
Cash received from other activities	372,489
Cash payments to employees	(1,434,641)
Cash payments to suppliers	(381,868)
Cash payments to others	(877,909)
Net cash provided by operating activities	**$ 525,054**
Cash flows from noncapital financing activities:	
Fuel taxes	289,346
Net cash provided by noncapital financing activities	**289,346**
Cash flows from capital and related financing activities:	
Proceeds from the sale of capital assets	1,893
Cash paid for acquisition of capital assets	(14,879,152)
Payment to the General Fund for capital loan	(209,582)
Capital grants received	15,142,007
Interest payments	(111,657)
Loan payments	(212,361)
Net cash used for capital and related financing activities	**(268,852)**

	Increase/(Decrease) in Cash and Cash Equivalents
Cash flows from investing activities:	
Receipts of interest and dividends	33,769
Net cash provided from investing activities	**33,769**
Net increase in cash and cash equivalents	**579,328**
Cash and cash equivalents 6/30/X7	2,087,155
Cash and cash equivalents 6/30/X8	$2,666,483

Reconciliation of operating income to net cash provided by operating activities:

Operating income (loss)		**$(2,148,087)**
Adjustments to reconcile operating income to net cash provided by operating activities:		
Depreciation expense	$2,335,060	
(Increase) decrease of assets:		
Receivables	189,009	
Other	(51)	
Increase (decrease) of liabilities:		
Accounts payable	156,632	
Accrued salaries and benefits	881	
Other accrued liabilities	(8,390)	
Total adjustments		2,673,141
Net cash provided by operating activities		**$ 525,054**

Noncash investing, capital, and financing activities:

The airport reported transactions that were noncash as follows:

- Acquisition of capital assets in accounts payable balances $ 838,676
- Capital grants in due from other governments balances $ 2,608,200

QUESTIONS

1. Enterprise funds *must* be used to account for an activity if any one of the following criteria is satisfied *except for:*

   a. The activity is financed with debt that is secured *solely* by a pledge of the net revenues from fees and charges of the activity.

   b. Taxes from hotel room stays are deposited in the activity.

   c. Laws or regulations require that the activity's costs of providing services, including capital costs (such as depreciation or capital debt service), be recovered with fees and charges rather than with taxes or similar revenues.

   d. The pricing policies of the activity establish fees and charges designed to recover its costs, including capital costs (such as depreciation or debt service).

2. Internal service funds are required *except for* when:

   a. Central services, such as purchasing, warehousing, and information systems costs, are allocated to other funds.

   b. Risk management and self-insurance expenses are allocated to other funds.

   c. Vehicle and equipment maintenance expenses are allocated to other funds.

   d. U.S. GAAP does not require internal service funds in any particular circumstance.

3. Interest incurred by a proprietary fund should be capitalized *except for* when:

   a. Bonds are sold to finance capital projects in capital projects funds for the government's own use.

   b. Assets are constructed or otherwise produced for an enterprise's own use (including assets constructed or produced by others for the enterprise for which deposits or progress payments have been made).

   c. Assets intended for sale or lease are constructed or otherwise produced as discrete projects (e.g., real estate developments).

   d. Investments (equity, loans, and advances) accounted for by the equity method while the investee has activities in progress necessary to commence its planned principal operations provided that the investee's activities include the use of funds to acquire qualifying assets for its operations.

4. Interest capitalization in a proprietary fund begins when the following conditions are present *except for:*

   a. Expenditures for the capital asset have been made.

   b. Activities that are necessary to get the capital asset ready for its intended use are in progress.

   c. The bonds are sold to finance the project.

   d. Interest cost is being incurred.

5. GASB-9 requires the following categories of cash flows to be displayed using the direct method *except for:*

   a. Operating activities.

   b. Noncapital financing activities.

   c. Cash equivalent activities.

   d. Investing activities.

Practice Case (*Adapted from the GASB Implementation Guide 2015-1*)

Castle Rock County's Water and Sewer Utility Fund reports the following activities as part of preparing a direct method statement of cash flows. Indicate whether the activity is an operating, noncapital financing, or investing activity:

1. Interest and dividends from investments

2. Proceeds from sales and maturities of investments

3. Transfers from General Fund

4. Cash received from utility customers

5. Cash paid to General Fund for supplies

6. Utility customer deposits received

7. Cash payments to employees for services

8. Cash payments to suppliers for goods and services

9. Purchases of investments

10. Utility customer deposits returned

ANSWERS

1. Enterprise funds *must* be used to account for an activity if any one of the following criteria is satisfied *except for:*

   Answer – B: Taxes from hotel room stays are sometimes general fund activities, sometimes enterprise fund activities, depending on laws or regulations. A, C, and D are standard criteria for enterprise funds in accordance with GASB-34.

2. Internal service funds are required *except for* when:

   Answer – D: There is no specific requirement for an internal service fund in U.S. GAAP in accordance with GASB-34. However, activities in A, B, and C are commonly found in internal service funds.

3. Interest incurred by a proprietary fund should be capitalized *except for* when:

   Answer – A: If bond proceeds are deposited into a capital projects fund, it's a governmental activity, not a proprietary fund activity. Otherwise, B, C, and D are capitalization triggers.

4. Interest capitalization in a proprietary fund begins when the following conditions are present *except for:*

   Answer – C: The bond sale does not signify the beginning of capitalization in a proprietary fund. In accordance with GASB-62, answers, A, B, and D are the conditions when to begin capitalization. When the asset is ready for its intended use, capitalization of interest ends.

5. GASB-9 requires the following categories of cash flows to be displayed using the direct method *except for:*

   Answer – C: Cash equivalent activities are not a category of cash flows to be displayed using the direct method in accordance with GASB-9 (as amended by GASB-34). A, B, and D are categories, along with investing activities.

Practice Case (*Adapted from the GASB Implementation Guide 2015-1*)

Castle Rock County's Water and Sewer Utility Fund reports the following activities as part of preparing a direct method statement of cash flows. Indicate whether the activity is an operating, noncapital financing, or investing activity:

Item Number	Element	Treatment
1.	Interest and dividends from investments	Investing activities
2.	Proceeds from sales and maturities of investments	Investing activities
3.	Transfers from General Fund	Noncapital financing activities
4.	Cash received from utility customers	Operating activities
5.	Cash paid to General Fund for supplies	Operating activities
6.	Utility customer deposits received	Operating activities
7.	Cash payments to employees for services	Operating activities

Item Number	Element	Treatment
8.	Cash payments to suppliers for goods and services	Operating activities
9.	Purchases of investments	Investing activities
10.	Utility customer deposits returned	Operating activities

CHAPTER 8
FIDUCIARY FUNDS

CONTENTS

INTRODUCTION

Fiduciary funds are used to account for assets held by a governmental entity for other parties (either as a trustee or as an agent) and that cannot be used to finance the governmental entity's own operating programs, which includes:

- Pension (and other employee benefit) Trust Funds;

- Investment Trust Funds;

- Private-Purpose Trust Funds; and

- Until the implementation of GASB Statement No. 84 (*Fiduciary Activities*), Agency Funds (see **PRACTICE ALERTS** on GASB-84 and the **Appendix** to this chapter).

Until the implementation of GASB Statement No. 84 (*Fiduciary Activities*), current standards of fiduciary reporting stem from GASB-14, par. 19, as amended by GASB-34 and GASB-61 [GASB Cod. Secs. 1100.101, 2100.118, 2200.101, 105, 196–.200, 2600.104]. However, those standards primarily focus on fiduciary reporting, including when a fiduciary component unit should be reported with a primary government, rather than what a fiduciary activity *is*. Not fully defining what a fiduciary activity entails and therefore is required to be reported has led to inconsistent presentation of fiduciary funds. As explained in the background information for GASB-84, par. A1:

> Existing standards do not provide guidance regarding characteristics that should be considered in deciding whether a government has a fiduciary responsibility. Thus, governments have interpreted differently which activities should be reported as fiduciary activities, resulting in a lack of comparability between governments.

Currently, three types of trust funds are used to report resources and activities when the governmental entity is acting as a trustee (i.e., in a fiduciary capacity) for individuals, private organizations, and other governments. GASB-34 (*Basic Financial Statements—and Management's Discussion and Analysis— for State and Local Governments*) states that the three trust funds are distinguished from an Agency Fund in that the trust funds are generally characterized "by the existence of a trust agreement that affects the degree of management involvement and the length of time that the resources are held" (GASB-34, par. 69) [GASB Cod. Sec. 1300.102(c)].

A common financial reporting deficiency related to fiduciary funds involves the reporting of a fiduciary fund for assets held on behalf of other funds of the government or for the benefit of the primary government's operations or activities. GASB-34, par. 69 states, in part, that fiduciary funds are used to account for assets held in a trustee or fiduciary capacity for "individuals, private organizations, or *other* governments." For example, it would be inappropriate to use a private-purpose trust fund to report a county sheriff office's activities related to telephone commission revenues earned from inmate use that are to be expended for inmate care purposes. While these revenues are for the ultimate benefit of individuals, the county is receiving and expending these resources in the context of their county responsibilities to provide inmate care and welfare, and not within the context of holding individual inmate resources in a fiduciary capacity.

PENSION (AND OTHER EMPLOYEE BENEFIT) TRUST FUNDS

Currently, Pension (and other employee benefit-OPEB) Trust Funds are used to account for resources held in trust for employees and their beneficiaries based on defined benefit pension agreements, defined contribution agreements, other postemployment benefit agreements, and other employee benefit arrangements (GASB-34, par. 70) [GASB Cod. Sec. 1300.111].

A "trust" or "equivalent arrangement" is defined in the various Pension and OPEB standards, with certain word changes for clarity as having *all* of the following characteristics:

1. Contributions from employers and nonemployer contributing entities to the plan and earnings on those contributions are irrevocable;

2. Plan assets are dedicated to providing (pensions or OPEB) to plan members in accordance with benefit terms; and

3. Plan assets are legally protected from the creditors of employers, nonemployer contributing entities and the plan administrator. If the plan is a defined benefit pension or OPEB plan, plan assets are also legally protected from the creditors of plan members.

In some circumstances, contributions are made by the employer to satisfy plan member contribution requirements. If the contribution amounts are recognized by the employer as salary expense, those contributions should be classified as plan member contributions. (See Chapter 13, "Pension, Postemployment and Other Employee Benefit Liabilities," **PRACTICE POINT** on GASB Statement No. 82 (*Pension Issues—an Amendment of GASB Statements No. 67, No. 68, and No. 73*), specifically regarding employer paid member contributions.) Refunds to an employer or nonemployer contributing entity of the noninvested portion of contributions that are forfeited by plan members in a defined contribution *do not* change the irrevocable status of a trust. Furthermore, the use of plan assets to pay plan administrative costs also *does not* change the irrevocable status of a trust.

OBSERVATION: If a trust or equivalent arrangement is *not present*, provisions of GASB-73 (for pensions) and 74 (for OPEB) apply. Until the implementation of GASB-84, agency funds are used to report assets *not* held in trust for plan benefits as assets accumulated for these purposes are required to be reported as assets of the employer or nonemployer contributing entity.

A common misunderstanding with regard to pension (and other employee benefit) trust funds is that a trust fund is indeed required, usually irrevocable in nature and created by either force of law or a trust document. This is false as a governing body usually needs to approve of a trust fund in accordance with the three criteria contained in U.S. GAAP and in accordance with statutory authority. In absence of a valid trust fund, an agency fund is currently used to account for and report the activities of pensions and other employee benefits until the implementation of GASB-84.

OBSERVATION: A second common misunderstanding is with statewide plans that are legally separate from states. On the one hand, only the elements of the plan that are truly for the benefit of the beneficiaries of the plan of the state should be reported. For example, if a state is a member of a statewide cost-sharing multiple employer plan, the fiduciary fund reporting may be minimal if the state does not administer, or is not the trustee of the plan. However, if the plan is a component unit, as used in paragraph 19 of GASB-14 [GASB Cod. Sec. 2600.104], the term "fiduciary responsibility" encompasses all transactions and balances that would be accounted for in fiduciary funds if the primary government has a fiduciary responsibility for them. "Fiduciary responsibility" is currently defined in GASB-34, paragraph 69 [GASB Cod. Sec. 1300.102(c)], and it refers assets held in a trustee or agency capacity for others and therefore cannot be used to support the government's own programs. Therefore, component units that are fiduciary in nature are included in the fiduciary fund financial statements, *if the government has fiduciary responsibility.* A further discussion on this is contained in the **Appendix** to this chapter.

Other postemployment benefit (OPEB) plan accounting and financial reporting is subject to the standards most recently contained by GASB Statement No. 74 (*Financial Reporting for Postemployment Benefit Plans Other Than Pension Plans*) and GASB Statement No. 75 (*Accounting and Financial Reporting for Postemployement Benefits Other than Pensions*) and amended by GASB Statement No. 85 (*Omnibus 2017*) (see **PRACTICE POINT** following). The following table details which standards apply to which pension and other employee benefit trust fund activities:

GASB Standard	Pensions		OPEB	
	Employers	Plans	Employers	Plans
GASB Statement No. 67, *Financial Reporting for Pension Plans*		✓		
GASB Statement No. 68, *Accounting and Financial Reporting for Pensions*	✓			
GASB Statement No. 71, *Pension Transition for Contributions Made Subsequent to the Measurement Date – An Amendment of GASB Statement No. 68*	✓			
GASB Statement No. 73, *Accounting and Financial Reporting for Pensions and Related Assets That Are Not Within the Scope of GASB Statement 68, and Amendments to Certain Provisions of GASB Statements 67 and 68.*	✓	✓		
GASB Statement No. 74, *Financial Reporting for Postemployment Benefits Plans Other Than Pension Plans*				✓
GASB Statement No. 75, *Accounting and Financial Reporting for Postemployment Benefits Other Than Pensions*			✓	
GASB Statement No. 78, *Pensions Provided through Certain Multiple-Employer Defined Benefit Pension Plans*	✓			
GASB Statement No. 82, *Pension Issues—An Amendment of GASB Statements No. 67, No. 68, and No. 73*	✓	✓		
GASB Statement No. 85, *Omnibus 2017—* (applicable parts)			✓	✓

A government's pension or other postemployment benefit plan should be presented as Pension (or Other Benefit) Trust Funds within the government's financial statements *if* the government *has the fiduciary responsibility for administering the plan*. For example, a local government that maintains and administers its own sole-employer defined-benefit pension or OPEB plan should report the plan as a Pension Trust Fund within its fiduciary fund financial statements. For a member of an agent multiple-employer plan, the balances that would be reported in a statement of fiduciary net position in the fiduciary funds may be minimal and only contain balances held in trust, but not transferred to the plan due to timing, *as they may not have any responsibility* for administering the plan. If a governmental nonemployer contributes to the pension plan on behalf of the government, then that activity may also be reported in a Pension Trust Fund.

Assets held and benefits paid by pension and OPEB plans are generally administered by a public employee retirement system (PERS) or a trust fund established by a governmental employer or the plan sponsor. (In practice, the terms "PERS" and "Pension or OPEB Trust Funds" are used interchangeably along with defined benefit pension or OPEB plans.) A PERS often administers several pension or OPEB funds for various governmental entities located within a particular state. In addition, a PERS may administer defined contribution plans, deferred compensation plans, and other employee benefit plans. GASB-67 and GASB-74 describe a PERS as "a state or local governmental fiduciary entity entrusted with administering a plan (or plans) and not to the plan itself." Thus, the standards contained in GASB-67 and GASB-74 do not address directly the financial reports prepared by a PERS but rather apply to the individual plans administered by the PERS. Thus, the standards must be applied to the PERS's combining financial statements on an individual plan basis.

The standards within GASB-67 and GASB-74 apply to all state and local governmental plans. They address measurement and reporting guidance for defined benefit pension plans and disclosure requirements for defined contribution plans. These plans are defined in GASB-67 and GASB-74 as follows:

Defined benefit plan—A plan having terms that specify the amount of pension or other postemployment benefits to be provided at a future date or after a certain period of time; the amount specified usually is a function of one or more factors such as age, years of service, and compensation.

Defined contribution plan—A plan having terms that specify how contributions to a plan member's account are to be determined, rather than the amount of retirement income or other postemployment benefits the member is to receive. The amounts received by a member will depend *only* on the amount contributed to the member's account, earnings on investments of those contributions, and forfeitures of contributions made for other members that may be allocated to the member's account.

In some instances, pension and OPEB plans have characteristics of *both* defined benefit pension plans and defined contribution plans. Such plans are commonly referred to as *hybrid* plans. The applicable standards refer to similar provisions that discuss if the substance of the plan is to provide a defined benefit in some form, the provisions of (the applicable standards) for defined benefit pension and OPEB plans apply.

The standards within the various standards apply to defined pension benefit and defined contribution plans irrespective of how they are funded. The following defined benefit pension plans are included:

Single-employer plan—A plan that covers the current and former employees, including beneficiaries, of only one employer.

Agent multiple-employer plan—An aggregation of single-employer plans, with pooled administrative and investment functions. Separate accounts are maintained for each employer so that the employer's contributions provide benefits only for employees of that employer. A separate actuarial valuation is performed for each individual employer's plan to determine the employer's periodic contribution rate and other information for the individual plan, based on the benefit formula selected by the employer and the individual plan's proportionate share of the pooled assets. The results of the individual valuations are aggregated at the administrative level.

Cost-sharing multiple-employer plan—A single plan with pooling (cost-sharing) arrangements for the participating employers. All risks, rewards, and costs, including benefit costs, are shared and are not attributed individually to the employers. A single actuarial valuation covers all plan members and the same contribution rate(s) applies for each employer.

Defined contribution plans also have variants, including, but not limited to:

Cash Balance Plan—A plan with hypothetical accounts maintained for participants. The employer credits participants' accounts with funds annually and promises earnings at a specified rate. However, the rate may be different from actual earnings. Therefore, the risk is largely on the employer, unless the employer changes the formula for posting earnings.

Money Purchase Plan—A plan where employers make contributions determined for and allocated to specific individuals as a percentage of compensation based on a formula.

Target Benefit Plan—A plan where employees make contributions on an actuarial basis knowing a certain date of retirement in the future. There are no guarantees of balance or return.

Internal Revenue Code (IRC) 403(b) Plan—A plan that includes tax-deferred annuities funded by salary reductions. 403(b) plans are prevalent in public school systems, public institutions of higher education, and public hospitals. However, certain governments are also using them to transfer lump sums from defined benefit plans at retirement into these plans managed by the new retiree. Therefore, the risk of loss shifts to the retiree.

IRC 457 Plan—This plan is common in state and local governments. A plan administrator invests plan assets at the direction of plan participants. The participant has a risk of loss of value and there is not a requirement for the employer to match or contribute to the plan.

The GASB-67, and GASB-74 standards apply to plans reported as (1) stand-alone plans (the plan's financial statements are presented as separate reports by the plan or by a PERS) and (2) Pension (or OPEB) Trust Funds or fiduciary component units in the statement of fiduciary net position and statement of changes in fiduciary net position of the plan sponsor or employer (GASB-67, par. 5, GASB-74, par. 5) [GASB Cod. Secs. Pe5.104, Po50.104].

The accounting and reporting requirements for stand-alone pension and other postemployment benefit plan financial statements are discussed in Chapter 22, "Pension and Other Postemployment Benefit Plans."

PRACTICE POINT: It is a common practice for a PERS to collect a single stream of payments from an employer (or employers) and administer *both* defined benefit pensions and defined benefit OPEB within one trust. Absent IRC Section 401(h) provisions discussed in the following paragraph, if a PERS collects from employers and remits to a separate entity contributions for postemployment healthcare benefits administered by that separate entity, the PERS is serving as a cash conduit if it has no administrative authority for OPEB benefits. Therefore the PERS should not follow the OPEB standards contained in GASB-74 [GASB Cod. Sec. Po50]. Instead, the separate entity would follow the

OPEB standards (if they are a governmental entity). (GASB *Implementation Guide* 2016-1 Q5.8) [GASB Cod. Sec. Pe5.701-19]. However, if the PERS *is an administrator* for *both* pensions and OPEB held under a common trust, two separate plans exist for reporting purposes. Either may or may not be held in trust and should use the provisions of GASB-67, GASB-73, and GASB-74, as applicable (GASB *Implementation Guide 2016-1* Q. 4.65) [GASB Cod. Sec. Pe5.701-20]. The PERS will allocate the assets between the pension and the OPEB plan based on specific circumstances, including the benefit structure and the terms and the method(s) of financing the pension and OPEB benefits. Therefore, the PERS should have an accounting policy adopted and consistently applied from period to period. (GASB *Implementation Guide 2017-2* Q.4.18) [GASB Cod. Sec. Po50.701-18].

PRACTICE POINT: Internal Revenue Code (IRC) Section 401(h) accounts are used to pay current retiree health benefits which are obligations of a separate plan. Although the assets may be invested together with assets that are available to pay pension benefits, separate accounting must be maintained for all flows and balances. Stringent provisions are in place within the IRC regarding transfers of pension assets to fund 401(h) accounts and ongoing contribution and benefit provisions. Tax advice should be sought from counsel as 401(h) accounts are beyond the scope of this *Guide*.

PRACTICE POINT: GASB-85 contains various sections that apply applicable provisions of GASB-78 and GASB-82 to GASB-74 and GASB-75. The provisions include:

- Timing of the measurement of pension or OPEB liabilities and expenditures recognized in financial statements prepared using the current financial resources measurement focus,

- Recognizing on-behalf payments for pensions or OPEB in employer financial statements,

- Presenting payroll-related measures in required supplementary information for purposes of reporting by OPEB plans and employers that provide OPEB,

- Classifying employer-paid member contributions for OPEB,

- Simplifying certain aspects of the alternative measurement method for OPEB,

- Accounting and financial reporting for OPEB provided through certain multiple-employer defined benefit OPEB plans.

Changes necessary to conform to the provisions of GASB-85 requires a restatement of all prior periods presented, if practicable. If restatement for prior periods is not practicable, the cumulative effect, if any, of applying GASB-85 should be reported as a restatement of beginning net position (or fund balance or fund net position, as applicable) for the earliest period restated.

INVESTMENT TRUST FUNDS

Investment Trust Funds are used by a governmental entity to report the external portion of an investment pool as defined in GASB-31 (*Accounting and Financial Reporting for Certain Investments and for External Investment Pools*). Governmental entities often pool resources for investment purposes.

In some investment arrangements the participants in the pool may be restricted to only governmental units and departments that are part of a single governmental entity, therefore internal to the government. This investment pooling strategy is referred to by GASB-31 (*Accounting and Financial Reporting for Certain Investments and for External Investment Pools*) as an "*internal* investment pool" and is described as follows:

> An arrangement that commingles (pools) the moneys of more than one fund or component unit of a reporting entity. (Investment pools that include participation by legally separate entities that are not part of the same reporting entity as the pool sponsor are not internal investments pools but rather are external investment pools).

As suggested in the above description, the pooling participants may include external parties, in which case the strategy creates an "*external* investment pool," which is described as follows (GASB-31, par. 22) [GASB Cod. Secs. I50.522, .533]:

> An arrangement that commingles (pools) the moneys of more than one legally separate entity and invests, on the participant's behalf, in an investment portfolio; in addition, one or more of the participants is not part of the sponsor's reporting entity. An external investment pool can be sponsored by an individual government, jointly by more than one government, or by a nongovernmental entity. An investment pool that is sponsored by an individual state or local government is an external investment pool if it includes participation by a legally separate entity that is not part of the same reporting entity as the sponsoring government. If a government-sponsored pool includes only the primary government and its component units, it is an internal investment pool and not an external investment pool.

OBSERVATION: GASB Statement No. 79 (*Certain External Investment Pools and Pool Participants*) may affect many external investment pool investments, as well as the external investment pool operations. The provisions of GASB-79 address the regulatory amendments to Rule 2a7 of the Investment Company Act of 1940 issued by the Securities and Exchange Commission (SEC) to money market funds that took effect in 2016. Further discussion of this issue is presented in Chapter 9, "Deposits, Investments, and Derivative Instruments."

The primary activity of an Investment Trust Fund involves investing its resources in a variety of assets for the purpose of generating current income and capital appreciation. These investments may include investments in securities as well as other investments, such as real estate or limited partnerships. All investments held by Investment Trust Funds must observe the standards established by GASB-31, paragraph 7 (fair value), paragraph 8 (investment contracts), paragraph 10 (open-end mutual funds), paragraph 11 (non-SEC-registered pools), paragraph 12 (2a7-like pools), paragraph 13 and paragraph 14 (recognition and reporting), and paragraph 15 (disclosures); and GASB-52 (*Land and Other Real Estate Held as Investments by Endowments*) [GASB Cod. Secs. In5.108, .117, .121, .123–.124, .131–.132].

GASB-59 (*Financial Instruments Omnibus*), among other things, clarified issues in investment trust fund operations. With respect to GASB-31, paragraph 12 (2a7-like pools), many state and municipal treasurers serve as trustees of such pools. GASB-59 amended GASB-31, paragraph 12, to clarify current practices. Measurement at net asset value per share is a requirement. The net asset value is generally calculated on a basis other than fair value, such as using an "amortized cost" method. GASB-59 added a condition that allows pools to be considered "2a7 like" that stipulates that the principal executive officer of the pool, who can be an elected official, has the power to operate the pool (e.g., contractual and hiring authority). However, investment policies must still rest with a group of individuals who function as a board of directors. (See **PRACTICE ALERT** on GASB-79 above and Chapter 9, "Deposits, Investments, and Derivative Instruments.")

Sponsoring Governments

GASB-34 states that the fiduciary fund category should be used to account for "assets held in a trustee or agency capacity for others and therefore cannot be used to support the government's own programs." When an external investment pool is created, a trustee or fiduciary relationship is created between the sponsoring government and the external parties that participate in the pool. An Investment Trust Fund (a fiduciary fund) is used when a governmental entity has an external investment pool.

Sponsoring governments may pool funds from governmental units that make up its financial reporting entity (internal portion of the pool) and from governmental units that are not part of its financial reporting entity (external portion of the pool). The internal portion of each governmental external investment pool should be allocated to the various funds and component units that make up the financial reporting entity, based on each fund's or component unit's equity interest in the investment pool.

A "sponsoring government" is defined as "a governmental entity that provides investment services—whether an external investment pool or individual investment accounts—to other entities and that therefore has a fiduciary responsibility for those investments."

A sponsoring government should report the external portion of each investment pool in an Investment Trust Fund. In the statement of fiduciary net position, the difference between the fund's assets and its liabilities should be labeled as "net position held in trust for pool participants."

When the governmental investment pool issues a separate financial report, the sponsoring government should describe in a note to its financial statements how to obtain the investment pool's annual report. When the governmental investment pool does not issue a separate financial report, the sponsoring government should make the following disclosures in its financial statements:

- The basic disclosures required for governmental investment pools (as described earlier);

- For each pool, separate presentation of disclosures required by GASB-3, GASB-28, and GASB-40 and "other cash and investment standards"; and

- Condensed statements of net position and changes in net position for each pool (if the pool includes participation by internal and external governmental entities, the condensed information should include totals for the combined internal and external portions; however, net equity of the pool should be apportioned between the amounts applicable to internal and external participants).

Individual Investment Accounts

In addition to organizing external investment pools, a governmental entity may create "individual investment accounts," which are defined as follows:

> An investment service provided by a governmental entity for other, legally separate entities that are not part of the same reporting entity. With individual investment accounts, specific investments are acquired for individual entities and the income from and changes in the value of those investments affect only the entity for which they were acquired.

Governmental entities that provide individual investment accounts should report those accounts in a separate Investment Trust Fund(s) in a manner similar to the presentation of the external portion of an investment pool as described earlier. However, note disclosures that apply to external investment pools do not apply to individual investment accounts.

When a governmental entity offers an entity an individual investment account service as an alternative (or supplement) to participation in an external investment pool, the individual investment account should be reported in a trust fund, separate from that used to report the investment pool (GASB-31, par. 22) [GASB Cod. Sec. I50.529].

PRIVATE-PURPOSE TRUST FUNDS

Private-Purpose Trust Funds are used to account for the principal and income for all other trust arrangements that benefit individuals, private organizations, or other governments. A valid trust document is not necessarily required if the activities are of a nature of a trust.

When a fiduciary relationship between a governmental entity and another party is created and it is not appropriate to account for the related transactions in a Pension Trust Fund or Investment Trust Fund, a Private-Purpose Trust Fund should be used to account for the principal and income for all other trust arrangements that benefit individuals, private organizations, or other governments. For example, a Private-Purpose Trust Fund may be used to account for escheat property as described in GASB-21 (*Accounting for Escheat Property*).

The *GASB Implementation Guide 2015-1*, question 7.52.7 [GASB Cod. Sec. E70.702-2], explains that it is optional to use a private-purpose trust fund for escheat funds, not a requirement. Alternatives would be an agency fund (as appropriate) or in the governmental or proprietary fund in which the escheat property is otherwise reported. The reason for the variability is primarily due to the potential outcomes of the property that escheats. As included in question 7.52.8 [GASB Cod. Sec. E70.702-3], the following alternatives may result in different funds:

Escheat Property is Held For	Type of Fund
Heirs or beneficiaries	Private-Purpose Trust Fund
Ultimately will revert to the reporting government	Governmental or Proprietary Fund (or both if split by law)
Other governments	Agency Fund (see **APPENDIX** on GASB-84)

A common financial reporting deficiency is the use of a Private-Purpose Trust Fund to account for the receipts and the expenditures of resources that may benefit private parties but are nonetheless resources that are merely restricted for use by the government to meet its public service responsibilities. For example, if the receipt and use of inmate telephone charge commissions is restricted for use in inmate welfare and a separate fund is used for these activities, it should be a Special Revenue Fund.

The *GASB Implementation Guide 2015-1*, question 7.52.5 [GASB Cod. Sec. 1300.704-4], states that when resources or an activity benefits both the government and private parties, two separate funds (Special Revenue Fund and Private-Purpose Trust Fund) may be used or a special revenue fund may be used. If a single special revenue fund is used, the resources held by the government for the "private purpose" should be reported as a liability. The remaining fund balance should be classified as restricted.

In some circumstances, a fund's principal or income may benefit a discretely presented component unit. The *GASB Implementation Guide 2015-1*, question 7.52.6 [GASB Cod. Sec. E70.702-1], discusses the situation when a discretely presented component unit is part of the financial reporting entity, so it is not an "individual, private organization or other government." GASB-34 requires fiduciary funds to be used to report assets held in a trustee or agency capacity for others and therefore cannot be used to support the government's own programs. For the purposes of the definition, the phrase *government's own programs* includes its discretely presented component units as they are part of the reporting entity. Therefore, a special revenue fund should be used if it meets the criteria in GASB-54 (*Fund Balance Reporting and Governmental Fund Type Definitions*), or the General Fund.

AGENCY FUNDS

Assets held by a governmental entity (either as a trustee or as an agent) for other parties and that cannot be used to finance the governmental entity's own operating programs should be reported in the entity's fiduciary fund financial statements as an Agency Fund under current standards. (See **APPENDIX** on GASB-84 and the major changes discussed on Agency Fund accounting and financial reporting.)

Generally, an Agency Fund is created to act as a custodian for other governmental entities or private individuals or entities. Assets are recorded by the Agency Fund, held for a period of time as determined by a legal contract or circumstances, and then returned to their owners.

A common financial reporting deficiency related to agency fund involves the use and reporting of an agency fund for assets held on behalf of other funds of the government, such as a fund to temporarily hold county taxes awaiting apportionment to various county agencies. These assets are being held for the ultimate use of the county government's operations or activities. GASB-34 states that agency funds are used to account for assets held in an agent capacity for "individuals, private organizations, or other governments." However, an agency fund would be appropriate for reporting assets held in an agent capacity resulting from taxes collected by a county awaiting distribution to other taxing governments within the county such as municipalities and school districts.

For example, an Agency Fund may be used to account for taxes collected by one governmental entity (county) for another governmental entity (municipality or school district). When one entity collects taxes for the other governmental entity, the collecting entity would make the following entry in the Agency Fund:

	Debit	Credit
Cash	xxx	
Due to Other Governmental Unit		xxx

When the taxes are remitted to the other governmental unit as determined by state law or local ordinance, the collecting entity would make the following entry in the Agency Fund:

	Debit	Credit
Due to Other Governmental Unit	xxx	
Cash		xxx

Thus, the basic accounting procedures for an Agency Fund are simple.

In an Agency Fund, the measurement focus is custodial, because the fund is not involved with the performance of governmental services. An Agency Fund has no revenues or expenditures and, therefore, no fund equity or need to measure the results of operations for a period. The custodial nature of an Agency Fund means that there is no need to adopt a budgetary accounting system.

An Agency Fund should be established only when it is legally mandated or when the creation of the fund enhances the operational efficiency or effectiveness of the governmental entity. For example, payroll deductions from gross earnings of governmental employees may be accounted for in an Agency Fund, but unless legally prohibited, the withholdings may be shown as a liability of the fund that incurred the payroll expenditure.

A governmental entity may issue bonds that it is responsible to repay, but the proceeds are to be used to finance the construction of a capital asset for a component unit. If at the end of the accounting period there are unspent bond proceeds that will subsequently be transferred to the component unit to pay future construction costs, the unspent amount should not be reported in an Agency Fund. The *GASB Implementation Guide 2015-1*, question 7.52.3 [GASB Cod. Sec. 1300.706-2], states that this financial arrangement between the governmental entity and its component unit is similar to an expenditure-driven grant whereby the amounts transferred during the year and the unreimbursed costs at the end of the year represent the amount of the grant for the year, whereas the unspent portion is the "advanced portion" of the grant and therefore should be reported as an asset of the governmental entity.

The expenditures for construction of a capital asset that will ultimately be owned by a component unit would be accounted for either in an Agency Fund or a Special Revenue Fund. If an Agency Fund is used, only cash, receivables, and accounts payable will likely be present in an Agency Fund Statement of Net position. If a Special Revenue Fund is used, conceivably construction in process may be present, along with a payable to the component unit. Either fund type could be used depending on the facts and circumstances.

The *GASB Implementation Guide 2015-1*, in questions 7.81.1-2 [GASB Cod. Sec. 2200.759-1-2], provides the following examples for determining when an Agency Fund should be used (until the implementation of GASB-84):

Fact Pattern	Suggested Guidance
A county tax collector collects property taxes for all taxing bodies in the county, including the tax-levying funds of the county. The county uses an Agency Fund as a distribution mechanism for the taxes. At year-end, the collector is holding $3,450,000 in the tax distribution account.	The $750,000 held for county funds must be allocated to the appropriate funds. That is, the reported cash balance (not the actual cash balance) in the Agency Fund must be reduced by $750,000 and the cash balances of other funds should be increased by the appropriate amounts.
Of that total, $750,000 will be distributed to the county funds, and the remaining $2,700,000 represents taxes collected for the other taxing bodies in the county. How does the county apply the "clearing account" provision in paragraph 111 of GASB-34 [GASB Cod. Sec. 2200.200] for Agency Funds?	The amounts due to other funds should not be reported as receivable/payables in the county's financial statements. The $2,700,000 should continue to be reported in the Agency Fund since that amount is held in trust for amount is taxing bodies in the county.

Fact Pattern	Suggested Guidance
If a government uses a central payroll system and reports all payroll deductions in an Agency Fund, should the unremitted balances in the Agency Fund at year-end be reclassified to the funds from which the payroll deductions arose?	*No.* The assets held by this clearing account reported as an Agency Fund will be distributed to outside parties, not to the government's funds. Therefore, Agency Fund reporting of these assets and liabilities is allowable because the funds reporting the payroll costs have no further liability. (Note: There is no requirement to use an Agency Fund for these liabilities. They may merely be reported as liabilities of the funds reporting the payroll costs if a clearing account is not used.)

Sometimes an Agency Fund distributes more cash than it has, or it has more liabilities than assets. The AICPA *State and Local Governments* Guide notes that if the governmental entity that reports the Agency Fund in its fund financial statements is responsible for the shortfall, an interfund payable should be established by the fund responsible for the shortfall and the Agency Fund should report an interfund receivable.

For example, assume that an Agency Fund is used to report a share of pooled cash held as municipal court bonds that may be refunded to defendants after a court hearing or converted to fines and paid to the General Fund if found guilty. At period end, the Agency Fund has a cash position in the pool of $20,000 but owes $25,000 as refundable court bonds (a negative cash position) because the fund paid $5,000 in error to the General Fund for converted fines. To correct this error, the following entries would be made by the two funds:

	Debit	Credit
AGENCY FUND		
Due from General Fund	5,000	
Amounts due to Other Parties		5,000
GENERAL FUND		
Fine and Forfeiture Revenues	5,000	
Due to Agency Fund		5,000

Note: The charge in the General Fund is reported as a reduction to revenue because revenue was overstated for fines received that still represented refundable court bonds.

The interfund loan would not be eliminated in the preparation of the fund financial statements and the government-wide financial statements because Agency Funds financial information is not incorporated into the government-wide financial statements.

ACCOUNTING AND REPORTING

Basis of Accounting and Measurement Focus

The accrual basis of accounting and the flow of economic resources are used to prepare the financial statements of fiduciary funds. These concepts are discussed in Chapter 3, "Basis of Accounting and Measurement Focus."

Budgetary System and Accounting

Pension Trust Funds (and similar employment or postemployment benefit trust funds), Investment Trust Funds, and Private-Purpose Trust Funds are accounted for in a manner similar to proprietary funds and may use budgetary controls. Budgets are not appropriate for Agency Funds, because the government entity functions only as a custodial agent and such funds do not record revenues or expenditures.

FUND FINANCIAL STATEMENTS

The following financial statements should be prepared for Fiduciary Funds (except for Agency Funds, which do not report a statement of changes in fiduciary net position):

- Statement of fiduciary net position; and
- Statement of changes in fiduciary net position.

Fiduciary fund financial statements are not reported by major fund (which is required for governmental funds and proprietary funds) but must be separately reported based on the following fund types:

- Pension (and other employee benefit) Trust Funds;
- Investment Trust Funds;
- Private-Purpose Trust Funds; and
- Agency Funds.

Statement of Fiduciary Net Position

The assets, liabilities, and net position of Fiduciary Funds should be presented in the statement of fiduciary net position by type of fiduciary fund. There is no need to divide net position into the three categories (invested in capital assets [net of related debt], restricted net position, and unrestricted net position) that must be used when preparing government-wide financial statements as described in GASB-34.

(Exhibit 20-8, in Chapter 20, "Comprehensive Annual Financial Report," is an illustration of a statement of fiduciary net position.)

Statement of Changes in Fiduciary Net Position

The statement of changes in fiduciary net position should summarize the additions to, deductions from, and net increase or decrease in net position for the year. In addition, GASB-34 requires that the statement provide information "about significant year-to-year changes in net position."

(Exhibit 20-9, in Chapter 20, "Comprehensive Annual Financial Report," is an illustration of a statement of changes in fiduciary net position.)

Agency funds are not included in the Statement of Changes in Fiduciary Net position, because they do not report revenues, expenditures/expenses, or net position.

OBSERVATION: For plans, the net of assets and liabilities is "net position restricted for pensions" or "net position restricted for other postemployment benefits" (or OPEB). For fiduciary funds in a set of basic financial statements, the net of assets and liabilities is "plan fiduciary net position." The net of revenues and expenses is a change in fiduciary net position. However, if assets *are not held in trust*, plan fiduciary net position is absent per GASB-73. Therefore, until, if and when the GASB-84 is implemented, per GASB-73, paragraph 116 [GASB Cod. Secs. 2200.199, P23.106], an Agency Fund would be used to report assets accumulated for pension or OPEB purposes in a fiduciary capacity.

REQUIRED SUPPLEMENTARY INFORMATION

Supplementary schedules are required to be presented in the *employer* government's financial statements for single- or multiple-employer defined benefit pension or OPEB plans that are included as fiduciary funds of fiduciary component units within the government's financial statements as follows utilizing 10-year schedules (GASB-68, pars. 46–47, 81–82, 114–115, 117, as amended by GASB-73, pars. 45–46, 66–67, 93–94, 96, 117, 119, GASB-75, pars. 57–58, 97–98, 134–135, 137, 170–171, 191–192, 218–219, 221, GASB-78, pars. 9–10, and GASB-82, par. 6, GASB-85, par. 14 [GASB Cod. Secs. P20.145–.146, 181–.182, 216–.217, 219, 229–.230, P22.136–.137, 157–.158, 184–.185, 187, P50] (See Chapter 22, "Pension and Other Postemployment Benefit Plans," for plan reporting):

	Pensions		OPEB	
	With an Irrevocable Trust	*Without an Irrevocable Trust*	*With an Irrevocable Trust*	*Without an Irrevocable Trust*
Single and Agent Employers	Schedule of Changes in the Net Pension Liability (10 years) along with various ratios.	Schedule of Changes in the Total Pension Liability (10 years) along with various ratios.	Schedule of Changes in the Net OPEB Liability (10 years) along with various ratios.	Schedule of Changes in Total OPEB Liability (10 years) along with various ratios.
Single and Agent Employers	Schedule of Employer Contributions (Actuarially, Statutorily or Contractually Required Contributions) and Contributions Made (10 years) along with various ratios.	Not applicable.	Schedule of Employer Contributions (Actuarially, Statutorily or Contractually Required Contributions) and Contributions Made (10 years) along with various ratios.	Not applicable.
	Notes to the Required Schedules.		Notes to the Required Schedules.	
Cost Sharing Employers	Schedule of the Employer's Proportionate Share of the Net Pension Liability (10 years) along with various ratios.	Schedule of the Employer's Proportionate Share of the Total Pension Liability (10 years) along with various ratios.	Schedule of the Employer's Proportionate Share of the Net OPEB Liability (10 years) along with various ratios.	Would be unlikely in practice.
Cost Sharing Employers	Schedule of Employer Contributions (10 years) along with various ratios.	Not applicable.	Schedule of Employer Contributions (10 years) along with various ratios.	Not applicable.
	Notes to the Required Schedules.		Notes to the Required Schedules.	Not applicable.

	Pensions		OPEB	
	With an Irrevocable Trust	*Without an Irrevocable Trust*	*With an Irrevocable Trust*	*Without an Irrevocable Trust*
Special Funding Situations (Nonemployer contributing entity) (separate guidance for substantial amounts and less than substantial amounts)	Schedule of Nonemployer Contributing Entity's Proportionate Share of Net Pension Liability (10 years) along with various ratios.	Schedule of Nonemployer Contributing Entity's Proportionate Share of the Total Pension Liability (10 years) along with various ratios.	Schedule of Nonemployer Contributing Entity's Proportionate Share of Net OPEB Liability (10 years) along with various ratios.	Would be unlikely in practice.
Special Funding Situations (Nonemployer contributing entity) (separate guidance for substantial amounts and less than substantial amounts)	Schedule of Nonemployer Contributing Entity's Contributions (10 years) along with various ratios.	Not applicable.	Schedule of Nonemployer Contributing Entity's Contributions (10 years) along with various ratios.	Not applicable.
	Notes to the Required Schedules.		Notes to the Required Schedules.	Not applicable.

This required supplementary information should be presented immediately after the notes to the financial statements.

With regard to the notes to the required schedules, GASB-73 amended the provisions of GASB-67 and GASB-68. Paragraph 117 [GASB Cod. Sec. P20.146] limits information about investment-related factors that significantly affect trends in the amounts reported, which should be limited to those factors over which the pension plan or participating governments have influence (e.g., changes in investment policies). Information about external, economic factors (e.g., changes in market prices) should not be presented. Similar provisions are present in GASB-74 and GASB-75 [GASB Cod. Sec. P22].

For defined benefit plan information for both pensions and OPEB, required supplementary information will differ slightly depending on the type of plan that the employer is involved with. If the employer is part of a single or agent multiple employer plan, the following required supplementary information is presented and determined as of the measurement date, for each of the 10 most recent fiscal years:

- Sources of changes in the net pension liability; and
- The components of the net pension liability and related ratios, including the pension plan's fiduciary net position as a percentage of the total pension liability, and the net pension liability as a percentage of covered-employee payroll.

If the contributions of a single or agent employer are actuarially determined, the employer would present in required supplementary information a schedule covering each of the 10 most recent fiscal years. This would include information about the actuarially determined contribution, contributions to the pension plan, and related ratios. If the contributions of a single or agent employer are not actuarially determined but are established in statute or by contract, the employer should present a schedule covering each of the 10 most recent fiscal years that includes information about the statutorily or contractually required contribution rates, contributions to the pension plan, and related ratios.

Significant methods and assumptions used in calculating the actuarially determined contributions, if applicable, should be presented as notes to required supplementary information. In addition, the employer should explain factors that significantly affect trends in the amounts reported in the schedules, such as changes of benefit terms, changes in the size or composition of the population covered by the benefit terms, or the use of different assumptions.

If the employer is part of a cost-sharing multiple employer plan, the employer will present 10-year schedules containing (1) the net pension liability and certain related ratios and, if applicable, (2) information about statutorily or contractually required contributions, contributions to the pension plan, and related ratios.

If the government participates in a special funding situation (like most school districts and states that contribute to municipal school district pensions), the information that would be disclosed in required supplementary information of a governmental nonemployer contributing entity (e.g., a state to a school district) in a special funding situation depends on the proportion of the collective net pension liability that it recognizes. If the governmental nonemployer contributing entity recognizes a substantial proportion of the collective net pension liability, it should disclose in a schedule of required supplementary information similar to those required of a cost-sharing employer. Reduced required supplementary information is required for governmental nonemployer contributing entities that recognize a less-than-substantial portion of the collective net pension liability.

GASB Statement No. 82 (*Pension Issues*) changed the ratios in required supplementary information for pension plans. GASB-67 and GASB-68 originally required ratios to be measured using *covered employee payroll* which is different from *covered payroll*. Similar provisions were adopted in GASB Statement No. 85 (*Omnibus 2017*), but applicable to OPEB. Care must be taken in both accounts about choice of measure to use, even though differences between them may be immaterial.

- *Covered Payroll* is the portion of compensation paid to *active employees* on which contributions to a pension or OPEB plan are based.
- *Covered Employee Payroll* is the payroll of employees that are paid through the plan.

For employers that provide pensions through pension plans that are administered through trusts, the measure of payroll is covered payroll.

If contributions to a Single Employer OPEB plan (*only*) are not based on a measure of pay, GASB-85 requires no measure of payroll to be presented. This scenario is common in OPEB funding. Other types of OPEB plans would present covered-employee payroll if the contributions *are not* based on a measure of pay. Otherwise, covered payroll is used when contributions *are* based on a measure of pay. Changes to conform to this presentation would require a retroactive restatement of prior balances.

GOVERNMENT-WIDE FINANCIAL STATEMENTS

The focus of government-wide financial statements is on the overall financial position and activities of the government as a whole. These financial statements are constructed around the concept of a primary government as defined by GASB-14 (*The Financial Reporting Entity*) (as amended by GASB-39 and GASB-69) and therefore encompass the primary government and its component units except for fiduciary funds of the primary government and component units that are fiduciary in nature. Financial statements of fiduciary funds are not presented in the government-wide financial statements but are included in the fund financial statements.

The financial statements of Fiduciary Funds are excluded from government-wide financial statements because resources of these funds cannot be used to finance a governmental entity's activities. The financial statements are included in the fund financial statements because a governmental entity is financially accountable for those resources even though they belong to other parties.

QUESTIONS

1. Fiduciary funds, which are used to account for assets held by a governmental entity for other parties (either as a trustee or as an agent) and cannot be used to finance the governmental entity's own operating programs, *do not include* which of the following funds?

   a. Pension (and other employee benefit) Trust Funds

   b. Investment Trust Funds

   c. Special Revenue Funds

   d. Private-Purpose Trust Funds

2. In an Agency Fund, the *current* measurement focus is custodial, because the fund is not involved with the performance of governmental services. Therefore, which of the following accounting elements are not reported?

   a. Expenditures

   b. Assets

   c. Liabilities

3. GASB-31 (*Accounting and Financial Reporting for Certain Investments and for External Investment Pools*) sets the standards for investment pools. Governmental entities often pool resources for investment purposes. The main difference between an internal investment pool and an external investment pool is the following:

   a. Assets (and liabilities) are at fair value in internal investment pools but not in external investment pools.

   b. Both types of investment pools are required to report a $1 net asset value.

   c. Both types of investment pools have limited authorization of what to invest in from either the government or a higher level of government (e.g., a state).

   d. Legal separation between the participants and the pool invests on the participant's behalf in an investment portfolio; in addition, one or more of the participants is not part of the sponsor's reporting entity.

4. The types of financial statements for fiduciary funds include which of the following:

   a. Statement of fiduciary net position and statement of changes in fiduciary net position.

   b. Statement of net position, statement of changes in net position, and statement of cash flows.

   c. Balance sheet and statement of revenues, expenditures, and changes in fund balance.

   d. Reconciliation schedules between fund balance and net position.

5. The types of defined contribution plans do not include:
   a. IRC 457 plans
   b. IRC 403(b) plans
   c. Defined benefit plans
   d. Money purchase plans

ANSWERS

1. Fiduciary funds, which are used to account for assets held by a governmental entity for other parties (either as a trustee or as an agent) and cannot be used to finance the governmental entity's own operating programs, *do not include* which of the following funds?

   Answer – C: Special Revenue Funds. All other funds are fiduciary funds.

2. In an Agency Fund, the *current* measurement focus is custodial, because the fund is not involved with the performance of governmental services. Therefore, which of the following accounting elements are not reported?

   Answer – A: Expenditures. Only assets and liabilities are *currently* reported.

3. GASB-31 (*Accounting and Financial Reporting for Certain Investments and for External Investment Pools*) sets the standards for investment pools. Governmental entities often pool resources for investment purposes. The main difference between an internal investment pool and an external investment pool is the following:

   Answer – D: Legal separation is the main difference between the participants. Assets (and liabilities) currently are at *fair value* for both types. The net asset value of a money market fund is generally calculated on a basis other than fair value, such as using an "amortized cost" method. The pools may or may not report a $1 net asset value and investments are sometimes regulated by the government or a higher level of government.

4. The types of financial statements for fiduciary funds include which of the following:

   Answer – A: B is for proprietary funds, C for governmental funds, and D for reconciling between the governmental funds balance sheets and the statement of net position.

5. The types of defined contribution plans do not include:

   Answer – C: Defined benefit plans. All others are defined contribution plans.

APPENDIX—GASB STATEMENT NO. 84 (*Fiduciary Activities*)

PRACTICE ALERT: GASB Statement No. 84 (*Fiduciary Activities*) updates and clarifies many of the provisions for fiduciary activities. A fiduciary activity that is *not a component unit* is present if the government controls the assets of the arrangement (described herein) *and* is any of the following:

- A pension plan that is administered through a trust in accordance with the provisions of GASB Statement No. 67 (*Financial Reporting for Pension Plans*) (see Chapter 22, "Pension and Other Postemployment Benefit Plans");

- An other postemployment benefits (OPEB) plan administered through a trust in accordance with the provisions of GASB Statement No. 74 (*Financial Reporting for Postemployment Benefit Plans Other than Pension Plans*) (also see Chapter 22); or

- A circumstance in which assets from entities that are *not* part of the reporting entity are accumulated for pensions as described in GASB Statement No. 73 (*Accounting and Financial Reporting for Pensions and Related Assets That Are Not within the Scope of GASB Statement 68, and Amendments to GASB Statements 67 and 68*) or OPEB as described in GASB-74 (see Chapter 13, "Pension, Postemployment, and Other Employee Benefit Liabilities"). (GASB-84, par. 10).

If the activity is not a pension or OPEB plan or where assets are accumulated for pensions or OPEB as described, the activity is a fiduciary activity if *all of the following criteria are met*:

1. The assets associated with the activity are controlled by the government;

2. The assets associated with the activity are *not* derived either:

    a. Solely from the government's *own—source revenues*, or

    b. From government-mandated nonexchange transactions or voluntary nonexchange transactions with the exception of pass-through grants for which the government does *not* have administrative or direct financial involvement (see Chapter 17, "Revenues: Nonexchange and Exchange Transactions");

3. The assets associated with the activity have *one or more* of the following characteristics:

    a. The assets are (like many trusts or benefit plans):

        (1) Administered through a trust agreement or equivalent arrangement in which the government *itself* is not a beneficiary;

        (2) Dedicated to providing benefits to recipients in accordance with the benefit terms; and

        (3) Legally protected from the creditors of the government.

    b. The assets are for the benefit of individuals and the government does *not* have administrative involvement with the assets or direct financial involvement over the assets. In addition, the assets are *not* derived from the government's provision of goods or services to those individuals (situations where governments may serve as a custodian of funds).

    c. The assets are for the benefit of organizations or other governments that *are not* part of the financial reporting entity. In addition, the assets are *not* derived from the government's provisions of goods or services to those organizations or other governments (e.g., Internal Revenue Code Section 529 plans) (GASB-84, par. 11).

A government *controls* the assets of an activity if the government (*a*) holds the assets *or* (*b*) has the ability to direct the use, exchange or employment of the assets in a manner that provides benefits to the specified or intended recipients. Restrictions from legal or other external constraints that stipulate the assets can be used only for a specific purpose do not negate control. (GASB-84, par. 12).

Own-source revenues are revenues generated by the government itself like water and sewer charges, investment earnings, sales and income taxes, property taxes and other inflows (GASB-84, par. 13).

Types of Fiduciary Funds

The types of fiduciary funds that will be reported in the basic financial statements include:

- *Pension (and Other Employee Benefit) Trust Funds*—similar to current reporting, including pension and OPEB plans administered through trusts;

- *Investment Trust Funds*—similar to current reporting, including the external portion of investment pools and individual investment accounts that are held in trust;

- *Private-Purpose Trust Funds*—similar to current reporting of all fiduciary activities that are *not* pension arrangements, OPEB arrangements, or activities required to be reported in investment trust funds and are held in trust;

- *Custodial Funds*—a new category to report fiduciary activities that are *not required to be reported* in the previous types of funds. A subcategory of custodial funds would report those few situations where an external investment pool does not have a trust or equivalent arrangement.

Upon implementation, agency fund reporting will be discontinued and likely presented in custodial funds. Statements of Fiduciary Net Position and Statements of Changes in Fiduciary Net Position will continue to be used to report fiduciary activities (GASB-84, pars. 14–25).

Implementation of GASB-84 will be for periods beginning after December 15, 2018. For June 30th governments, implementation will begin for the period beginning on July 1, 2019. Earlier application is encouraged. Changes adopted to conform to the provisions of GASB-84 should be applied retroactively by restating financial statements, if practicable, for all prior periods presented. If restatement for prior periods is not practicable, the cumulative effect, if any, of applying GASB-84 should be reported as a restatement of beginning net position (or fund balance or fund net position, as applicable) for the earliest period restated. In the first period that this Statement is applied, the notes to the financial statements should disclose the nature of the restatement and its effect. Also, the reason for not restating prior periods presented should be disclosed.

PRACTICE POINT: The effect of GASB-84's implementation may be pervasive for many governments. Agency fund activity will now be converted to custodial funds. Business-type activities that hold resources with a corresponding liability that should be reported in a custodial fund will report such activity that will be held for three months or less as a liability and not as a separate custodial fund. The presentation of a statement of fiduciary net position and a statement of changes in fiduciary net position will be clarified. The recognition of fiduciary component units are expected to also be more standardized.

The GASB has afforded governments a lengthy implementation period due to these changes that may occur in operations.

Fiduciary Component Units

For an entity to be a fiduciary component unit, the criteria in GASB-14, as amended, must be met prior to determining if a fiduciary activity is present. (See Chapter 4, "Governmental Financial Reporting Entity.") Upon determination as a component unit, a fiduciary activity is present if it is one of the following arrangements:

1. A pension plan that is administered through a trust in accordance with GASB-67.

2. An other postemployment benefit (OPEB) plan that is administered in accordance with GASB-74.

3. A circumstance in which assets from entities that are not part of the reporting entity are accumulated for pensions as described (GASB-73, par. 116).

4. A circumstance in which assets from entities that are not part of the reporting entity are accumulated for OPEB as described in GASB-74, par. 59 (GASB-84, par. 6).

Generally, if a trust is present, such entities are legally separate. A financial burden exists if there is some form of legal obligation to the plan or the government has otherwise assumed the obligation to make contributions to the plan (GASB-84, par. 7).

Non-Pension or OPEB Fiduciary Component Units

A similar situation may exist for non-pension or OPEB fiduciary component units. Typically such entities are external investment pools. As long as the assets are:

1. Administered through a trust agreement or equivalent arrangement (hereafter jointly referred to as a trust) in which the government itself is not a beneficiary,

2. Dedicated to providing benefits to recipients in accordance with the benefit terms, and

3. Legally protected from the creditors of the government, a fiduciary component unit could exist.

A fiduciary component unit could also exist if the assets are for the benefit of individuals and the government does *not* have administrative involvement with the assets or direct financial involvement with the assets. In addition, the assets are *not* derived from the government's provision of goods or services to those individuals.

A fiduciary component unit may also exist if the assets are for the benefit of organizations or other governments that are not part of the financial reporting entity. In addition, the assets are *not* derived from the government's provision of goods or services to those organizations or other governments (GASB-84, par. 8).

Governments will need to make a determination on whether a component unit relationship exists and then if a fiduciary activity exists. Control aspects are not considered in this determination (GASB-84, par. 9).

Reporting Fiduciary Component Units

Similarly to current reporting, when reported in the fiduciary fund financial statements of the primary government, a fiduciary component unit is combined with the primary government's fiduciary funds (GASB-84, par. 26).

Student Activity, Patient and Inmate Funds, and GASB-84

Many of the respondents to what became GASB-84 were concerned with the effect of the eventual statement on student activity funds, many of which are statutorily regulated. As discussed in the Basis for Conclusions for GASB-84, some respondents to the Exposure Draft either disagreed or had questions regarding the intent of the criterion related to assets held for the benefit of individuals that are not required to be residents or recipients of the government's goods and services as a condition of being a beneficiary. Some of those respondents believed that the criterion excluded certain activities that should be reported as fiduciary activities. Examples of such activities include holding resources (that do not arise from the provision of services) for the benefit of students in educational institutions such as student activity funds, patients in health-care facilities, and inmates in correctional institutions. The GASB recognized that there may be situations in which the government serves only as a custodian for the resources. In many of these cases, the government (school district, hospital, facility) may serve as an administrator, but utilize a trustee to account for the flows and balances.

Some respondents also requested that the GASB specifically require that student activity resources be reported as fiduciary funds. However, the GASB believes that some of those activities are part of the government's provision of goods or services. For example, student activity funds may purchase inventory, equipment, fund positions, or capital projects. The GASB noted that the administration of those activities may vary across governments, with some governments assessing fees to pay for certain activities and other governments using other resources available to pay for certain activities. As a result, the GASB concluded that a specific requirement addressing all student activity resources is not appropriate.

If the fund is utilized for providing goods or services, a special revenue fund or capital projects fund (or even the General Fund) may be more appropriate than a fiduciary fund.

PRACTICE POINT: The GASB *Codification* references for the elements of GASB-84 will primarily replace paragraphs in GASB Cod. Secs. 1300, 1600, 2100, and 2200. A separate *Implementation Guide* for GASB-84 is expected to be released in 2019 with any final questions codified in 2020.

III. SPECIFIC ACCOUNTING AND REPORTING ISSUES

CHAPTER 9
DEPOSITS, INVESTMENTS, AND DERIVATIVE INSTRUMENTS

CONTENTS

INTRODUCTION

The accounting treatment of governmental deposits with financial institutions is essentially the same as accounting for deposits by private-sector businesses, with certain exceptions for unique considerations involving fund accounting. Guidance for most investments held by governmental entities is found in GASB-31 (*Accounting and Financial Reporting for Certain Investments and for External Investment Pools*) and most recently GASB-72 (*Fair Value Measurement and Application*) and GASB-79 (*Certain External Investment Pools and Pool Participants*). That said, the accounting and financial reporting for investments and investment pools is among the more complex in governmental GAAP due to the interaction of for-profit standards, governmental standards, and Securities and Exchange Commission (SEC) regulations.

GASB-31 originally defined an "investment" as a security or other asset acquired primarily for the purpose of obtaining income or profit. GASB-72 clarifies the definition of an "investment" as follows (GASB-72, par. 64) [GASB Cod. Sec. I50.103]:

> An "investment" is defined as a security or other asset (*a*) that a government holds primarily for the purpose of income or profit and (*b*) with a present service capacity that is based solely on its ability to generate cash or to be sold to generate cash.

Deposits, investments and derivative instrument disclosures are pervasive through GASB standards and originally issued standards have been amended or superseded several times throughout the course of GASB's history in a continuously evolving process as banking practices and markets change. This can plainly be seen when reviewing what is authoritative versus what is no longer authoritative is contained in Appendix A to this chapter.

External Investment Pools and GASB-79

Many governments belong to external investment pools (commonly known as "2a7-like") that are structured like money market funds. A "2a7-like" pool is not registered with SEC as an investment company, but nevertheless has a policy that it will, and does, operate in a manner consistent with the SEC's Rule 2a-7 of the Investment Company Act of 1940. Governmental external investment pools that are 2a7-like pools are permitted to report their investments at amortized cost. Otherwise, external investment pools should report their investments in open-end mutual funds and other external investment pools at fair value.

The net asset value (NAV) per share generally is calculated on a basis other than fair value, such as by the "amortized cost" method that provides a NAV per share that approximates fair value.

OBSERVATION: GASB-79 realigned the provisions relating to external investment pools for both pool administrators and participants to those contained within GASB-72 (further discussed in the next section) and other standards. GASB-79 established the criteria for an external investment pool to qualify for making *an election* to measure all of its investments at *amortized cost* for financial reporting purposes.

An external investment pool qualifies for that reporting if it meets *all* of the applicable criteria established in GASB-79. If an external investment pool *does not* meet the criteria established by GASB-79, or becomes noncompliant with the election to do so, or fails to correct the noncompliance during the reporting period, the value of the pool is at fair value and would apply the existing provisions of GASB-31, as amended.

The criteria for the external investment pool to use amortized cost in accordance with GASB-79 are as follows (GASB-79, par. 4) [GASB Cod. Sec. In5.104(a)]:

1. The pool must transact with its participants at a stable net asset value per share (e.g., all contributions and redemptions are transacted at $1.00 NAV).

Transacting at a stable net asset value per share does not necessarily mean an external investment pool can measure all of its investments on an amortized cost basis. For example, many external investment pools currently transact with participants at a stable NAV but measure investments in their financial statements at fair value. On the other hand, many money market funds are required by the amended SEC rules to transact at a floating net asset value per share. Although there is no direct correlation between operational transactions and the measurement of an external investment pool's investments, the GASB believes that the measurement basis should provide the most relevant reflection possible of operations. If an external investment pool is measuring all of its investments at amortized cost and transacting at a floating net asset value per share, financial reporting using amortized cost would not properly reflect the amounts that participants would receive. Additionally, if an external investment pool transacted with participants at a floating net asset value per share, the participants would be participating in the fair value gains and losses of the external investment pool, which suggests that fair value would be the more appropriate measure for such situations.

2. The pool portfolio must meet stringent maturity requirements.

The underlying investments should contain securities or other investments only if the investment has a remaining maturity of 397 calendar days or less. The maturity of the investment should be the period remaining until the date on which the total or remaining principal amount is required to be unconditionally repaid in accordance with the terms of the investment, with a number of exceptions. If the investment has a demand feature and the pool is *not relying* on that demand feature, then the demand feature is disregarded. The exceptions are as follows (GASB-79, pars. 4(b), 8–16 [GASB Cod. Secs. In5.104(b), .108–.116]:

Type of Investment	U.S. Government Securities and Similar	Non-U.S. Government Securities	
		397 Days or Less	*More than 397 Days*
Variable interest rate investments	Measurement period is to the next readjustment of interest rate	The shorter of the period to the next readjustment of the interest rate or the date when the principal can be recovered through demand.	The *longer* length to the next readjustment of the interest rate or the date when the principal can be recovered through demand.
Floating interest rate investments based on an index or market changes	Deemed to be daily by GASB-79.	The remaining maturity is the shorter of the period until the interest rate resets or the maturity date of the investment.	Period remaining until the principal amount can be recovered through demand.
Repurchase agreements	Not specified in GASB-79.	Should be either (*a*) the period remaining until the date on which the repurchase (or return) of the underlying securities is scheduled to occur or (*b*) the duration of the notice period applicable to a demand for the repurchase (or return) of the securities, such as a put option.	Not likely in practice.

	Non-U.S. Government Securities	
Type of Investment	U.S. Government Securities and Similar	397 Days or Less	More than 397 Days
Investment in a money market fund or another external investment pool.		The period within which the fund or the pool is required to make a payment upon redemption.	Not likely in practice.

The weighted average *maturity* of the portfolio must be 60 days or less. A weighted average maturity measure expresses investment time horizons—the time when investments become due and payable—in this case, days weighted to reflect the dollar size of individual investments. In essence, weighted average maturity includes "call features" and investment size. If a larger investment has a call feature every seven days, it would have a lower weighted average maturity than a smaller investment that did not have a call feature, but matured in 30 days. Certain maturity shortening features, such as interest rate resets, should be taken into account, such as the variable rate securities described in the table above.

The weighted average *life* of the portfolio must be 120 days or less. A weighted average life measure expresses the average length of time that each dollar of principal remains unpaid without taking into account the maturity shortening features used in calculating the weighted average maturity. Therefore, no call features are used in making this calculation—only the ultimate maturity when the principal is redeemed.

3. The pool portfolio must meet investment quality requirements.

To make the election to use amortized cost in accordance with GASB-79, the underlying investments must be rated by a nationally recognized statistical rating organization (NRSRO), is denominated in U.S. dollars, and has a credit rating within the highest category of short-term credit ratings (or its long-term equivalent category) or if unrated, is of similar credit quality. The Securities and Exchange Commission registers the NRSROs. As of the date of this publication, they include firms such as A.M. Best, Fitch, Inc., Moody's Investors Service, Inc. and Standard & Poor's Ratings Services, among others.

The highest category of short-term credit ratings (or its long-term equivalent category) as established by an NRSRO may have multiple sub-categories or gradations indicating relative standing (i.e., several different ratings may constitute the single highest category). If an external investment pool is aware that a security has multiple ratings and the rating categories conflict, the following provisions apply in accordance with GASB-79:

- If a security has two ratings, the security should be considered to be in the lower category.
- If a security has more than two ratings, the security should be considered to be in the highest category of ratings as determined by at least two ratings.
- For unrated securities, they must be denominated in U.S. dollars. The pool would then determine if the investment is of comparable credit quality to securities that have been rated within the highest category of short-term credit ratings (or its long-term equivalent category) (GASB-79, pars. 17–19) [GASB Cod. Secs. In5.117–.119].

Declines in Credit Quality

Investments may be acquired that are of the highest rating. However, they may decline in quality during the time they are held by the pool. At the reporting date, the pool would still be incompliance as long as the pool holds no more than 3% of its total assets in:

- Securities that have credit ratings within the second-highest category of short-term credit ratings (or its long-term equivalent category); and
- Securities that are not rated but are determined to be of comparable credit quality to securities that have been rated within the second-highest category of short-term credit ratings (or its long-term equivalent category).

As of any reporting date, the pool should not hold any security that has a credit rating below the second-highest category of short term credit ratings or its equivalent long-term category or comparable if non-rated (GASB-79, par. 20) [GASB Cod. Sec. In50.120].

Guaranteed Securities

Securities that are guaranteed may meet the rating requirements to be qualified as securities that can be held by the pool. One of the two following criteria must be met for a guaranteed security to be allowable:

- The guarantee has received a credit rating within the highest category of short-term credit ratings (or its long-term equivalent category) or, if no credit rating is available, is determined (based upon the qualifying external investment pool's analysis) to be of comparable quality.
- The guarantor has obtained a credit rating within the highest category of short-term credit ratings (or its long-term equivalent category) or, if no credit rating is available, is determined (based upon the qualifying external investment pool's analysis) to be of comparable quality (GASB-79, par. 21) [GASB Cod. Sec. In5.121].

Other Features of Credit Quality

Demand features may also be present. The demand feature may have its own credit rating and should be taken into consideration. Securities should not be exposed to custodial credit risk as further described in this chapter. Therefore, the pool should consider the credit quality of the institution issuing or holding the security. The security may have an increase in credit quality if it is insured or collateralized to minimize or eliminate custodial credit risk.

For repurchase agreements, the credit quality of the counterparty must be analyzed. GASB-79 includes a criteria for the counterparty of a repurchase agreement to be a primary dealer as defined by the Federal Reserve Bank of New York, in addition to credit quality. Underlying collateral of repurchase agreements must be valued at fair value and not exposed to custodial credit risk (GASB-79, pars. 22–26) [GASB Cod. Secs. In5.122–.126].

4. The pool portfolio must be diverse.

To qualify, the external investment pool should acquire a security or other investment only if, after acquisition, the external investment pool would hold no more than 5% of its total assets in investments of any one issuer of securities. Some securities have some form of credit support through a guarantee or demand feature. If there is credit support, or if the pool purchases an investment directly of the entity providing the support, the threshold raises to 10% of total assets.

Similarly to the third criteria above, if the security has a credit rating of other than the highest ratings, any one issuer is limited to 1% of total assets. If there are demand features or guarantees, the limit is 2.5% of total assets in any one issuer. U.S. government securities are exempt from these provisions (GASB-79, pars. 27–30) [GASB Cod. Secs. In5.127–.130].

Common Control Issuers

Many issuers of securities are of similar parent companies. For example, securities may be from Megabank NA, Megabank of Delaware, Megabank of New York etc. These are often found in asset-backed securities due to the need to spread risk and local laws. GASB-79 requires additional analysis of commonly controlled securities as follows:

1. Two or more issuers of securities should be considered to be a single issuer if one issuer controls the other or the two issuers *are under common control*. Control is assumed to be present if one entity owns more than 50% of the issuer's voting securities.

2. The acquisition of a repurchase agreement should be considered to be the acquisition of the underlying securities if the repurchase obligation is collateralized fully without regard to maturity date.

3. The acquisition of a refunded security should be considered to be the acquisition of the escrowed securities.

4. A conduit debt obligation should be considered to be issued by the entity responsible for the payments related to the obligation rather than the governmental issuer.

5. An asset-backed security should be considered to be issued by the entity that issued the security *except* when the obligations of a single entity constitute 10% or more of the assets that back the security, that entity itself should be considered to be the issuer of that portion of the asset-backed security.

Example 1: An external investment pool holds asset-backed commercial paper that is 3% of the external investment pool's total assets. 15% of the assets that back the commercial paper are receivables from a single bank. For purposes of the diversification calculation, 0.45% of the pool's total assets are considered to be issued by that bank. [0.45% = 3% × 15%].

6. If some or all of the assets that back the security *are themselves asset-backed securities* (secondary asset-backed securities), any entity that issues obligations constituting 10% or more of the assets that back the secondary securities should be considered to be the issuer of that portion of the asset-backed security.

Example 2: An external investment pool holds asset-backed commercial paper that is 3% of the pool's total assets. 20% of the assets that back the commercial paper are other asset-backed securities (secondary securities). 15% of the assets that back the secondary securities are receivables from a single bank. For purposes of the diversification calculation, 0.09% of the pool's total assets are considered to be issued by that bank.

[0.09% = 3% × 20% × 15%]

Example 3: A local government external investment pool sponsored by a county treasurer has investments in a publicly available money market mutual fund *and* a state-sponsored external investment pool. The local government external investment pool is compliant with GASB-79, par. 4, and makes the election. The state-sponsored external investment pool also is compliant with the same provisions. The 5% limit does not apply to either of the investments. The 5% limit does not apply to the qualifying local government external investment pool's investments in a publicly available money market mutual fund because a money market mutual fund is subject to the Securities and Exchange Commission's money market fund requirements, including portfolio diversification requirements. The 5% limit also does not apply to the qualifying local government external investment pool's investments in the state-sponsored external investment pool in this circumstance. Given the state-sponsored pool is compliant with GASB-79, par. 4, including the portfolio diversification requirements, the pooled investments held by the state-sponsored pool are sufficiently diversified for application of the 5% limit by the local government external investment pool to be unnecessary (GASB-79, par. 31) [GASB Cod. Sec. In5.131].

5. The portfolio must be liquid.

Liquidity is vital in an external investment pool. There must be liquid assets sufficient to support reasonably foreseeable redemptions. The following are the GASB-79 provisions for liquidity in a qualifying external investment pool (GASB-79, pars. 32–38) [GASB Cod. Secs. In5.132–.138]:

Element	Daily Liquid Assets	Weekly Liquid Assets	Illiquid Assets
Limitation	>= 10% of Total Assets	>= 30% of Total Assets	<= 5% of Total Assets
Definition	Assets that mature within one business day.	Assets that mature within five business days.	Those that cannot be sold or disposed of in the ordinary course of business at its amortized cost value within five business days.
Example(s)	• Cash, including demand deposits and certificates of deposit that mature within one business day.	• Cash, including demand deposits and certificates of deposit that mature within five business days and are expected to be held to maturity.	• A nonnegotiable certificate of deposit that does not mature within five business days.
	• US Government securities that are direct obligations.	• US Government securities that are direct obligations.	
	• Securities that will mature within one business day, without taking into account interest rate resets or call features.	• US Government securities that are *not* direct obligations but issued at a discount without provision for the payment of interest and have a remaining maturity of 60 days or less.	
	• Securities that are subject to demand features that are exercisable and payable within one business day.	• Securities that will mature within five business days, without taking into account interest rate resets or call features.	
Example(s) (continued)	• Amounts receivable and due unconditionally within one business day on pending sales of portfolio securities.	• Securities that are subject to demand features that are exercisable and payable within five business days.	

Element	Daily Liquid Assets	Weekly Liquid Assets	Illiquid Assets
Limitation	>= 10% of Total Assets	>= 30% of Total Assets	<= 5% of Total Assets
		• Amounts receivable and due unconditionally within five business days on pending sales of portfolio securities.	

6. The pool must be transparent through the publication of a "shadow price."

The updated SEC regulations include provisions for a "shadow price." The shadow price is the NAV per share of a qualifying external investment pool, calculated using total investments measured at fair value at the calculation date. The calculation should be performed monthly no earlier than five business days prior to and no later than the end of the month. At each date, the pool must have a shadow price within $1/2$ of 1% (0.5%) of the NAV at amortized cost.

If the external investment pool does not adhere to these provisions, it must be reported at fair value (GASB-79, pars. 39–40) [GASB Cod. Secs. In5.139–.140].

PRACTICE POINT: A further discussion of a participating government's disclosures for positions in an external investment pool is contained in this chapter.

GASB-72, *FAIR VALUE MEASUREMENT AND APPLICATION*

PRACTICE POINT: GASB-72 (*Fair Value Measurement and Application*) addresses accounting and financial reporting issues related to fair value measurements and how to apply those measurements in different situations.

The definition of "fair value" is the price that may be received to sell an asset or paid to transfer a liability in an orderly transaction between market participants at the measurement date. In other words, fair value is described as an *exit* price. Fair value measurements assume a transaction takes place in a government's principal market. This assumes that the participants in the general market would act in their economic best interest—meaning the price that is most advantageous to them at a given point in time. Some call the differential between the economic best interests "bid" and "ask" with a final exit price or fair value, somewhere in the middle of the bid and ask. Fair value should not be adjusted for transaction costs (GASB-72, par. 5) [GASB Cod. Sec. 3100.102].

Guidance is provided for determining a fair value measurement for financial reporting purposes along with application guidance for certain investments and related disclosures. To determine a fair value measurement, a government should consider the *unit of account* of the asset or liability. *The unit of account* refers to the level at which an asset or a liability is aggregated or disaggregated for recognition and disclosure purposes as provided by the accounting standards. For example, the unit of account for investments held in a brokerage account is each individual security, whereas the unit of account for an investment in a mutual fund is each share in the mutual fund held by a government. Examples of a unit of account include, but are not limited to the following (GASB-72, pars. 7–8, C1) [GASB Cod. Secs. 3100.104–.105, .901]:

Investment Type	Potential Unit of Account
Multiple investments	• Multiple investments may be held in one brokerage account, but the unit of account would be each individual security rather than the account as a whole.
External investment pool	• A government holds a position in an external investment pool that is not a 2a7-like external investment pool (has not made the GASB-79 qualifying election and continues to follow GASB-31). The unit of account is each share held, and the value of the position would be the fair value of the pool's share price multiplied by the number of shares held. The government-investor does not "look through" the pool to report a pro rata share of the pool's investments, receivables, and payables (see additional discussion on disclosures of positions in external investment pools later in this chapter).
Mutual fund	• A government holds a position in a mutual fund. The unit of account is each share held, and the value of the position would be the stated price of the mutual fund multiplied by the number of shares held.
Limited partnership	• A government owns an interest in a hedge fund organized as a limited partnership. The limited partnership owns investment assets, but the government owns an interest in the partnership itself rather than an interest in each underlying asset and liability. Therefore, the unit of account is the government's ownership interest in the limited partnership, rather than the percentage in individual assets and liabilities held by the partnership.
Government acquisition	• A government acquires another government in an acquisition. The units of account to the acquiring government are the same as they were to the acquired government, but the measurement attributes for the acquisition are prescribed by GASB-69 (*Government Combinations and Disposals of Government Operations*). Acquired assets, deferred outflows of resources, liabilities, and deferred inflows of resources are measured at acquisition value, fair value, or carrying value.

Fair value should be determined using one or more of the following widely used approaches or techniques: (*a*) the market approach, (*b*) the cost approach, or (*c*) the income approach.

- The market approach uses prices and other relevant information generated by market transactions involving identical or comparable assets, liabilities, or a group of assets and liabilities.

- The cost approach reflects the amount that would be required currently to replace the service capacity of an asset.

- The income approach converts future amounts (such as cash flows or income and expenses) to a single current (discounted) amount.

Valuation techniques should be applied consistently, although a change may be appropriate in certain circumstances. Valuation techniques should maximize the use of relevant observable inputs and minimize the use of unobservable inputs (GASB-72, pars. 23–27) [GASB Cod. Secs. 3100.120–.124].

A hierarchy of inputs to valuation techniques is established to measure fair value. The hierarchy has three levels as follows:

- Level 1 is quoted prices (unadjusted) in active markets for identical assets or liabilities;

- Level 2 is inputs other than quoted prices included within Level 1 that are observable for the asset or liability, either directly or indirectly; and

- Level 3 is unobservable inputs, which may assume for example an assumed rate of default on a private loan (GASB-72, par. 32) [GASB Cod. Sec. 3100.129].

Examples of Level 2 and Level 3 inputs include, but are not limited to (GASB-72, pars. 40–44, C1) [GASB Cod. Secs. 3100.137–.141, .901]:

Example	Potential Inputs Used
Bond valued by a pricing service that uses matrix pricing	• A level 2 input is a price or yield of a similar bond.
Pay-fixed, receive-variable interest rate swap based on the London Interbank Offered Rate (LIBOR) swap rate	• A level 2 input is the LIBOR swap rate if that rate is observable at commonly quoted intervals for substantially the full term of the swap.
Three-year option on exchange-traded shares	• A level 2 input is the implied volatility for the shares derived through extrapolation to Year 3 if *both* of the following conditions exist: — Prices for one-year and two-year options on the shares are observable. — The extrapolated implied volatility of a three-year option is corroborated by observable market data for substantially the full term of the option. In that case, the implied volatility could be derived by extrapolating from the implied volatility of the one-year and two-year options on the shares and corroborated by the implied volatility for three-year options on comparable entities' shares, provided that correlation with the one-year and two-year implied volatilities is established.

Example	Potential Inputs Used
Valuation Multiple	• A level 2 input is a multiple of earnings or revenue or a similar performance measure derived from observable market data—for example, multiples derived from prices in observed transactions involving comparable (similar) businesses, taking into account operational, market, financial, and nonfinancial factors.
Long-dated currency swap	• A level 3 input is an interest rate in a specified currency that is not observable and cannot be corroborated by observable market data at commonly quoted intervals or otherwise for substantially the full term of the currency swap. The interest rates in a currency swap are the swap rates calculated from the respective countries' yield curves.
Three-year option on exchange-traded shares	• A level 3 input is historical volatility, that is, the volatility for the shares derived from the share's historical prices. Historical volatility does not represent current market participants' expectations about future volatility, even if it is the only information available to price an option.
Interest rate swap	• A level 3 input is an adjustment to a midmarket consensus (nonbinding) price for a swap developed using data that are not directly observable and cannot otherwise be corroborated by observable market data.
Commercial real estate	• A level 3 input is a financial forecast (e.g., of cash flows or earnings) developed using a government's own data if there is no reasonably available information that indicates that market participants would use different assumptions.

Fair value measurement assumes the highest and best use for a nonfinancial asset. GASB-72 discusses the concept of highest and best use by taking into account the use of the asset that is physically possible, legally permissible and financially feasible such as when dealing with the value of a piece of commercial property:

- The location and size of the property makes it advantageous to buyers, increasing the price (physical possibility).

- The zoning of the property allows for commercially viable and robust tenants (legal permissibility).

- Taking into account the location and the zoning derives a financially feasible property, producing an investment return that the buyers require.

A government's current use of a nonfinancial asset is assumed to be its highest and best use, unless there are other market forces. For example, a developer may approach a City desiring to redevelop a City building, inclusive of condominiums. Therefore, the developer sees a value higher than the City does.

A fair value measurement of a liability assumes that the liability would be transferred to a market participant and not settled with the counterparty. So for example, to value a liability, one would assume it would be sold to a third party that is completely separate from the entity receiving the payment on the liability. In the absence of a quoted price for the transfer of an identical or similar liability and when another party holds an identical item as an asset, a government should be able to use the fair value of that asset to measure the fair value of the liability (GASB-72, pars. 55–58) [GASB Cod. Secs. 3100.152–.155].

Additional analysis may be required when the volume or level of activity for an asset or liability has significantly decreased. For example, if an investment is not publicly traded, it is far harder to value than one that has a higher volume or is publicly traded. It also requires identification of transactions that are not orderly. Non-orderly transactions are unusual or in illiquid markets (GASB-72, pars. 45–46) [GASB Cod. Secs. 3100.142–.143].

As discussed previously, GASB-72 also clarifies the definition of an "investment." An "investment" is defined as a security or other asset (*a*) that a government holds primarily for the purpose of income or profit and (*b*) with a present service capacity that is based solely on its ability to generate cash or to be sold to generate cash. Investments not measured at fair value continues to include, for example, money market investments, 2a7-like external investment pools (until an external investment pool sponsor decides to either report at amortized cost or report at fair value in accordance with GASB-79), investments in life insurance contracts, common stock meeting the criteria for applying the equity method, unallocated insurance contracts, and synthetic guaranteed investment contracts.

Acquisition value is to be used for donated capital assets, works of art, historical treasures and similar assets, and capital assets received in a service concession arrangement. Other than assets received in a service concession arrangements, prior to GASB-72, they were required to be valued at fair value (an exit price) (GASB-34, pars. 18, as amended by GASB-72, par. 79, GASB-37, par. 6, and GASB-72, par. 68) [GASB Cod. Sec. 1400.102].

Fair value disclosures require the level of fair value hierarchy, and valuation techniques. Governments should organize these disclosures by type or class of asset or liability reported at fair value. It also requires additional disclosures regarding investments in certain entities that calculate NAV per share (or its equivalent) (GASB-72, par. 81) [GASB Cod. Sec. I50.141].

The basis for conclusions of GASB-72 in discussing measurement focus and basis of accounting, makes no distinction between the bases of accounting in recognizing the fair value of investments. Investments reported in governmental fund financial statements, prepared using the current financial resources measurement focus and modified accrual basis of accounting, should be measured at fair value. The GASB also believes that gains and losses from the changes in fair value cannot be separately realized from the underlying investment and, therefore, the changes in fair value are a faithful reflection of the increase or decrease in the financial resources available to the government to fund its activities.

ACCOUNTING AND FINANCIAL REPORTING FOR DEPOSITS AND INVESTMENTS

Accounting Basis and Measurement Focus

The standards established by GASB-31 apply to governmental funds, proprietary funds, government-wide financial statements, and fiduciary funds. That is, an entity must use fair value as the basis to present investments and changes in fair value of the investments identified in GASB-31 in its various financial statements, no matter what type of fund as well as the government-wide financial statements.

Pooled Cash and Investments

Amounts of cash deposits and temporary investments belonging to various funds of the government entity may be in the form of separate accounts for each fund or may be pooled with similar assets of other funds to maximize the return on invested resources. For pooled cash and investments, adequate records must be maintained to provide a basis for identifying each fund's share of the pooled assets, including interest earned and receivable at the end of the period. Each fund's portion of the pooled assets may be designated "equity in pooled cash and temporary investments" or some other, similar designation. The method of allocating interest on pooled resources to each fund should be disclosed in the financial statements.

Pooled cash and investments may be in the form of internal or external investment pools. As discussed in Chapter 8, "Fiduciary Funds," internal pools benefit solely the government, its funds, its component units, and its agencies. External investment pools are discussed in the scope of standards established by GASB-31 section and the previous section on GASB-79.

Certain pools may solely comprise deposits and short-term investments, such as those defined by GASB-9 as cash and cash equivalents, and other pools may solely comprise longer-term marketable investments. When reporting positions held in these cash and investment pools, a government should consider separately reporting the positions held in these different types of pools in the balance sheet or statement of net position, such as "equity in state treasurer cash and cash equivalent pool" and "equity in state treasurer investment pool."

Scope of the Standards Established by GASB-31

The standards established by GASB-31 address the following (GASB-31, par. 22, as amended) [GASB Cod. Secs. I50.506, .515, .520, .522, .531, .546–.547]:

- *Interest-earning investment contracts* A direct contract, other than a mortgage or other loan, that a government enters into as a creditor of a financial institution, broker-dealer, investment entity, insurance company, or other financial services company and for which it receives, directly or indirectly, interest payments. Interest-earning investment contracts include time deposits with financial institutions (such as certificates of deposit), repurchase agreements, and guaranteed and bank investment contracts (GICs and BICs, respectively).

- *External investment pools* An "external investment pool" is defined as an arrangement that commingles (pools) the moneys of more than one legally separate entity and invests, on the participants' behalf, in an investment portfolio; one or more of the participants is not part of the sponsor's reporting entity. An external investment pool can be sponsored by an individual government, jointly by more than one government, or by a nongovernmental entity. An investment pool that is sponsored by an individual state or local government is an external investment pool if it includes participation by a legally separate entity that is not part of the same reporting entity as the sponsoring government. If a government-sponsored pool includes only the primary government and its component units, it is an internal investment pool and not an external investment pool. (See previous section on GASB-79.)

- *Open-end mutual fund* An SEC-registered investment company that issues shares of its stock to investors, invests in an investment portfolio on the shareholders' behalf, and stands ready to redeem its shares for an amount based on its current share price. An open-end mutual fund creates new shares to meet investor demand, and the value of an investment in the fund depends directly on the value of the underlying portfolio. Open-end mutual funds include governmental external investment pools that are registered as investment companies with the SEC and that operate as open-end funds. Open-end mutual funds are the most common mutual funds that are traded.

- *Debt securities* Any security representing a creditor relationship with an entity. It also includes (*a*) preferred stock that either is required to be redeemed by the issuing entity or is redeemable at the option of the investor and (*b*) a collateralized mortgage obligation (CMO) or other instrument that is issued in equity form but is accounted for as a non-equity (non-ownership) instrument. However, it excludes option contracts, financial futures contracts, and forward contracts. Thus, the term debt security includes, among other items, U.S. Treasury securities, U.S. government agency securities, municipal securities, corporate bonds, convertible debt, commercial paper, negotiable certificates of deposit, securitized debt instruments [such as CMOs and real estate mortgage investment conduits (REMICs)], and interest-only and principal-only strips. Trade accounts receivable arising from sales on credit and loans receivable arising from real estate lending activities of proprietary activities are examples of receivables that do not meet the definition of a security; thus, those receivables are not debt securities. (However, if they have been securitized, they would then meet the definition.)

OBSERVATION: The GASB *Implementation Guide Update* 2016-1, question 4.6 [GASB Cod. Sec. I50.737-2], describes negotiable CDs as a form of participating interest-earning investment contract whose value generally is affected by market (interest-rate) changes. For a negotiable CD at fair value, the investment risk disclosures and the fair value disclosures described in this chapter should be made (in accordance with GASB Statement No. 40 (*Deposit and Investment Risk Disclosures—an Amendment of GASB Statement No. 3*) and GASB-72, respectively). For a negotiable CD that is measured at amortized cost, the investment risk disclosures of GASB-40 only should be made.

- *Equity securities (including unit investment trusts)* Any security that represents an ownership interest in an entity, including common, preferred, or other capital stock. However, the term equity security does not include convertible debt or preferred stock that either is required to be redeemed by the issuing entity or is redeemable at the option of the investor. (Applies only when the instrument has a readily determinable fair value.)

- *Closed-end mutual funds* An SEC-registered investment entity that issues a limited number of shares to investors that are then traded as an equity security on a stock exchange. (Applies only when the instrument has a readily determinable fair value.)

- *Options contracts* A contract giving the buyer (owner) the right, but not the obligation, to purchase from (call option) or sell to (put option) the seller (writer) of the contract a fixed number of items (such as shares of equity securities) at a fixed or determinable strike price on a given date or at any time on or before a given date. (Applies only when the instrument has a readily determinable fair value.)

- *Stock warrants* Certificates entitling the holder to acquire shares of stock at a certain price within a stated period. Warrants often are made part of the issuance of bonds or preferred or common stock. (Applies only when the instrument has a readily determinable fair value.)

- *Stock rights* Abilities given to existing stockholders to purchase newly issued shares in proportion to their holdings at a specific date. (Applies only when the instrument has a readily determinable fair value.)

GASB-31 applies to purchased put and call option contracts, but not to written option contracts. Written option contracts are not investments but rather obligations of the option writer.

The investments listed above (and all investments held by governmental external investment pools) should be accounted for at fair value, as previously described in the section on GASB-72.

The GASB notes that quoted market prices are the most reliable and verifiable sources of measuring investments at fair value. For certain investments (such as debt instruments and participating interest-earning investment contracts), however, quoted market prices are not available and the governmental entity will need to estimate fair value based on techniques such as discounted future cash flows, fundamental analysis, and matrix pricing.

GASB-31 does not apply to an equity interest in a component unit; however, an equity interest in a for-profit corporation may be considered an investment if the purpose of the acquisition *is not* to provide governmental services [see paragraph 55 of GASB-14 (*The Financial Reporting Entity*), as amended by GASB-61, par. 10(a)]. If the acquisition is to provide governmental services, the organization is reported as a component unit in accordance with GASB-14, as amended by GASB-61 [GASB Cod. Sec. 2600.116].

PRACTICE ALERT: GASB Statement No. 90 (*Accounting and Financial Reporting for Majority Equity Interests—an amendment of GASB Statement No. 14*), amends these provisions on equity interests. GASB-90 improves the consistency of reporting a government's majority equity interest in a legally separate organization. If the definition of an investment is met, the majority equity interest is reported using the equity method, unless the interest is engaged only in fiduciary activities, or a permanent fund (a governmental fund). In such cases, the interest is reported at fair value. Any other holding would be reported as a component unit. The asset related to the majority equity interest is reported by the fund that holds the interest. If a 100% equity interest is acquired, acquisition value is used to measure the various accounting elements of the acquired entity, similarly to the provisions contained in GASB Statement No. 69 (*Government Combinations and Disposals of Government Operations*) [GASB Cod. Sec. Co10].

The effective date of GASB-90 is for periods beginning after December 15, 2018. For June 30th governments, the period begins on July 1, 2019. The requirements are applied retroactively, except for the provisions related to (1) reporting a majority equity interest in a component unit and (2) reporting a component unit in which the primary government acquired a 100% equity interest. Those provisions are applied on a prospective basis.

GASB-31 states that the value of restricted stock is not readily determinable. "Restricted stock" is defined as

> Equity securities whose sale is restricted at acquisition by legal or contractual provisions (other than in connection with being pledged as collateral) except if that restriction terminates within one year or if the holder has the power by contract or otherwise to cause the requirement to be met within one year. Any portion of the security that can reasonably be expected to qualify for sale within one year, such as may be the case under SEC Rule 144 (17 Code of Federal Regulations § 230.144) or similar rules of the SEC, is not considered restricted (GASB-31, par. 22) [GASB Cod. Sec. I50.560].

"Market value" implies that an asset can be measured on that basis only if there is an active market. "Fair value," which is a much broader concept, encompasses a variety of measurement techniques, including appraisal value and present value of net future cash flows as well as market value.

While the standards originally established by GASB-31 are similar to the accounting standards for investments established by the FASB for nongovernmental entities, there are significant differences. GASB-31 standards require that investments in debt instruments be reported at fair value in the governmental entity's statement of financial position and that unrealized gains and losses related to the valuation be reported on the entity's activity statement. FASB ASC™ 320 requires that investments in debt instruments be classified as part of (1) the held-to-maturity portfolio, (2) the trading portfolio, or (3) the available-for-sale portfolio. Investments included in the held-to-maturity portfolio are reported at amortized cost, while investments in the trading and available-for-sale portfolios are reported at fair value, with unrealized gains or losses for the available-for-sale portfolio reported as an equity component and gains or losses for the trading portfolio reported on the commercial enterprise's statement of income. ASC™ 958 requires that investments in debt securities be reported at fair value and unrealized gains and losses be reported on the entity's not-for-profit activity statement.

The standards originally established by GASB-31 *do not apply uniformly to all governmental entities.* The fair value approach applies only to investments in certain securities held by most governmental entities; however, the fair value approach applies to all investments held by governmental external investment pools. Thus, governmental external investment pools must apply fair value to investments such as real estate interests, loans, limited partnerships, and futures contracts, unless they elect in accordance with GASB-79 to use amortized cost in accordance with the criteria stated previously.

Valuation

Investments held by governmental entities, including governmental external investment pools, should be reported at fair value, except in the following situations (which are discussed later in this section):

- Non-participating interest-earning investment contracts; and

- Money market investments and certain participating interest-earning investment contracts (GASB-31, pars. 8–9, as amended by GASB-67, par. 18, GASB-72, pars. 64, 69) [GASB Cod. Secs. I50.121, .123].

Ideally, the governmental entity's determination of fair value should be based on quoted market prices. When a governmental entity does not report an investment in a security at fair value (because market information is lacking) and the entity has invested in put option contracts or has written call option contracts on the same security, the put and call option contracts should be taken into consideration in determining the amount at which the investment in the security should be presented. For example, the GASB drew the following conclusions with respect to this issue (GASB-31, par. 7) [GASB Cod. Sec. I50.108]:

- If an entity has the right to sell securities under a put option, the combined measures of the security and the option contract should approximate the strike price if that price is above the security's market price. If the put option contract is not reported at fair value, the entity should consider the unrecorded value of the option contract in measuring the underlying security at fair value.

- If the strike price is less than the security's market price, the combined value of a security subject to sale under a call option and the call option liability should approximate the strike price. If the call option contract is not reported as a liability and is not reported at fair value, the quoted market price of the underlying security would need to be adjusted in order for the security's fair value to be properly reported.

Investments in open-end mutual funds should be reported at fair value, based on the fund's current share price (GASB-31, par. 10, GASB-67, par. 18) [GASB Cod. Sec. I50.120].

Participating Interest-Earning Investment Contracts

Interest-earning investment contracts include time deposits with financial institutions (such as certificates of deposit), repurchase agreements, and guaranteed and bank investment contracts. These contracts are considered participation contracts when they enable the investor to "capture market (interest rate) changes through the investment's negotiability or transferability, or redemption terms that consider market rates." Participating interest-earning investment contracts should be reported at fair value (except as explained in the following section).

When an interest-earning investment contract is not participating, the investor is exposed to interest rate risk (i.e., a change in the market interest rate will result in a change in the value of the investment). However, the GASB points out that while the non-participating contract can result in changes in the value of the investment, the holder of the investment is unlikely to eventually realize any interim gain or loss. For example, if interest rates fall, the holder of a non-participating contract has an unrealized gain in the valuation of the investment, but in order to realize the gain, the holder would have to redeem the contract early and pay an early-redemption penalty and in fact may incur a realized loss from the redemption. For this reason, the GASB states that non-participating contracts (e.g., certificates of deposit) should not be reported at fair value but rather should be reported at cost, assuming that the value of the investment is not affected by the financial institution's credit standing or other relevant factors (GASB-31, par. 8, GASB-67, par. 18, GASB-72, pars. 64, 69) [GASB Cod. Sec. I50.121].

Money Market Investments and Certain Participating Interest-Earning Investment Contracts

A "money market investment" is defined by GASB-31 as "a short-term, highly liquid debt instrument, including commercial paper, banker's acceptances, and U.S. Treasury and agency obligations." Money market investments and participating interest-earning investment contracts that mature within one year or less of the date of their acquisition may be reported at amortized cost, assuming that the investment is not affected by the financial institution's credit standing or other relevant factors. The relevant date for determining the time period to maturity ("one year or less" criterion) is the date the investment was acquired rather than the date the investment was originally issued (GASB-31, par. 9, GASB-67, par. 18, GASB-72, par. 69) [GASB Cod. Sec. I50.123].

Based on a cost-benefit consideration, GASB-31 allows for money market investments to be reported at amortized cost rather than fair value. The GASB believes that reporting such investments at amortized cost will reasonably approximate fair value.

Asset-backed securities, derivatives, and structured notes are not considered money market investments. "Asset-backed securities" are defined as "assets that are composed of, or collateralized by, loans or receivables." The collateralization can be based on "liens on real property, leases, or credit card debt." "Structured notes" are defined as "debt securities whose cash flow characteristics (coupon, redemption amount, or stated maturity) depend on one or more indexes, or that have embedded forwards or options."

GASB-31 notes that investments in money market investments and participating interest-earning investment contracts may be based on commingled funds from internal and external pool participants. In this circumstance, the investment should be reported based on the guidance for Investment Trust Funds discussed in Chapter 8, "Fiduciary Funds."

Investments in External Investment Pools

If an external investment pool does not make the election to use amortized cost or does not meet the criteria to use amortized cost in accordance with the provisions of GASB-79, the governments in the pool should measure their investments in the pool at fair value (GASB-31, par. 11, as amended by GASB-79, pars. 4 and 41, GASB-67, par. 18) [GASB Cod. Sec. I50.117].

PRACTICE POINT: For custodians/administrators of external investment pools, the allocation of investment income and pool administrative costs between accounts is especially important for audit purposes. Allocations should be performed in conjunction with applicable laws, regulations, and pool provisions. If there are no pertinent laws, regulations, or pool provisions, allocations should be performed systematically and rationally without unfairly benefiting or burdening any one or group of accounts. If accounts contain proceeds from federal awards, systematic and rational allocation is required so that program income be recognized in accordance with the federal award provisions.

Investments in Internal Investment Pools

Some governmental entities combine resources from various funds and component units into one or more "internal investment pools," which GASB-31 defines as follows (GASB-31, par. 14, as amended by GASB-34, pars. 3, 112, GASB-35, par. 5, GASB-31, par. 22) [GASB Cod. Secs. I50.132, .533]:

> An arrangement that commingles (pools) the moneys of more than one fund or component unit of a reporting entity. Investment pools that include participation by legally separate entities that are not part of the same reporting entity as the pool sponsor are not internal investment pools, but rather are external investment pools.

Under this arrangement, for external financial reporting purposes the internal investment pool must allocate its investments to the various funds and component units based on the equity interest that each fund or component unit holds in the internal investment pool. Also, investment income and losses that the internal investment pool incurs must be allocated to the participating funds and component units based on their respective equity interests in the pool.

In some circumstances, one fund (the investing fund) may have an equity interest in an internal investment pool, while another fund (the income recipient fund) may receive the investment income from the pool. When the recipient fund's right to the investment income is based on "legal or contractual provisions," that language must be used as a basis for determining how each fund should record the allocation of investment income. If, based on the specific language in the provision, the investment income is considered to belong to the recipient fund, then the recipient fund should record the investment income. However, if the specific language is interpreted to mean that the investment income belongs to the investing fund, the investment income should be recorded in the investing fund—and subsequently (or perhaps concurrently) recorded as a transfer by the investing fund (transfers out) and by the recipient fund (transfers in). On the other hand, when a recipient fund's right to the investment income is based on other than "legal or contractual provisions" (i.e., management's discretion), the investment income should be recorded in the investing fund, with each of the funds involved in the transfer subsequently recording an interfund transfer.

OBSERVATION: As introduced above, a component unit may have a position in an internal investment pool of a primary government. The GASB *Implementation Guide Update 2016-* 1, question 4.4, [GASB Cod. Sec. I50.734-7] describes the disclosure of an internal investment pool position by a component unit as being similar to other investments. "Looking through" to the underlying investments of the pool is *not appropriate* in *separately issued* component unit financial statements. Therefore, the component unit disclosures are limited to the position in the investment pool and not the underlying investments.

Investments in Land and Other Real Estate Held by Endowments

A government may acquire or receive from a donor income-producing real estate (or a partial interest in income-producing real estate) as a permanent or term endowment for the benefit of an individual, private organization, or other government and report it in a Private-Purpose Trust Fund (or for the benefit of the government itself and reported in a Permanent Fund).

GASB-52 (*Land and Other Real Estate Held as Investments by Endowments*) requires that land and other real estate held as investments by endowments be reported at fair value at the reporting date. Any changes in fair value during the period should be reported as investment income. GASB-52 applies to all state and local governments (GASB-52, par. 4, GASB-72, pars. 64 and 75) [GASB Cod. Sec. I50.124].

In promulgating what became GASB-52, the GASB discussed (1) real estate that cannot be sold, (2) lands granted by the federal government in connection with a state being admitted to the United States, (3) investments in real estate investment trusts (REITs), and (4) investments in real estate limited partnerships. The GASB concluded that real estate that cannot be sold should remain within the scope of GASB-52. However, with regard to the federal land grants, the GASB acknowledged that the technical agenda project was not designed to address this issue. Accordingly, it excluded these lands from the scope of GASB-52. Similarly, investments in Real Estate Investment Trusts (REITs) and investments in real estate limited partnerships were decided to be beyond the project's scope and no guidance was provided in GASB-52 for those investments. The GASB has said that further guidance for federal land grants and investments in real estate limited partnerships will be more appropriately addressed in another investment project currently on the GASB research agenda.

GASB-52 amended paragraph 2 of GASB-31 to require that investments in land and other real estate held by endowments be added to the disclosure provisions in paragraph 15 of GASB-31 and as further amended by GASB-72. Land and other real estate mostly held by endowments and post-employment benefits plans tends to be termed "hard to value" and may use an expected cash flow technique or royalty technique to value the asset. Accordingly, disclosures should include the methods and significant assumptions used to determine the fair value of such investments and provide other information that is currently presented for other investments reported at fair value (GASB-52, par. 5) [GASB Cod. Sec. I50.101].

Governments That Are Beneficiaries of Irrevocable Split-Interest Agreements

---

PRACTICE POINT: The GASB has issued Statement No. 81 (GASB-81) *Accounting and Financial Reporting for Irrevocable Split-Interest Agreements* [GASB Cod. Sec. I70]. Split-interest agreements are structured in a number of different forms, including:

- When the government may be a full beneficiary of a donation;
- When the government's interest is split with the donor (i.e., split-interest);
- When the government may receive what is left after the donor dies (i.e., a charitable remainder unitrust or annuity trust);
- When a government may receive funds first for a specific time period;
- Before another beneficiary receives the remainder of the funds (i.e., a charitable lead trust); or
- A number of similar annuities, interests, or income funds.

Public colleges, universities, and health care facilities are the primary recipients of one or more types of donations that are split-interest arrangements. Because these trusts are usually held by third-party trustees or by foundations that are component units of the institution, information about the beneficial interests in the assets held by the trustees generally does not appear in the financial statements of the trustee or the foundation. This has resulted in inconsistent reporting or no reporting of the donation.

GASB-81 considers (*a*) recognition, measurement, and disclosure of beneficial interests in resources held by third parties that are outside the reporting entity and (*b*) expanded guidance on recognition, measurement, and disclosure for split-interest agreements for which the government or its component units administer the assets.

Until the implementation of GASB-81, U.S. GAAP for donations to a government was primarily contained in GASB-33 (*Accounting and Financial Reporting for Nonexchange Transactions*). However, the guidance was only for when the government is the recipient of the donated asset and the sole beneficiary of the donated asset. GASB-33 established the concept of revenue recognition when all the eligibility requirements are met by the beneficiary government, regardless of the timing of the transfer of the donated asset. Paragraph 22 of GASB-33 also directed governments to recognize revenue when the resources received are constrained by time requirements, such as "the asset cannot be sold, disbursed, or consumed until after a specific event has occurred if ever" (provided that all other eligibility requirements are met). The reason for this guidance, discussed in footnote 12, is that the government would be complying with the time eligibility requirements by honoring the donor's stipulations. These concepts are somewhat clarified with regard to split-interest arrangements in Question 7.72.11 of the *GASB Implementation Guide 2015-1*. The answer to the question directs the recipient government to recognize the related liability to other beneficiaries of a split-interest agreement for which the government is the remainder beneficiary, stating:

Split-interest agreements provide that the public institution acts as trustee for the gift assets, with the requirement that an annual distribution be made to a specified beneficiary. Normally, these distributions are for a fixed dollar amount (annuity trust) or a fixed percentage of the trust's fair market value (unitrust). The more common types of split-interest agreements operate similarly.

The public institutions should recognize an asset for the fair value of the trust assets and a liability for the obligation to the beneficiary, with the difference between the asset and liability recognized as gift revenue. Question 7.72.11 is rescinded upon the implementation of GASB-81.

Recognition of revenue on donated assets in a split-interest arrangement may be complex. Donated assets related to a split-interest agreement are proposed to be recognized at fair value and remeasured at each financial reporting date similar to other investments. Because there is an income stream and an asset that may involve a third party, a derivative-like or a similar aspect of a service concession arrangement may exist. There may even be an obligation attached to the agreement in which the government may have to perform some service or duty in order to receive the funds in the future. GASB-81 requires that the initial recognition of this obligation would result in a liability measured at a settlement amount. Therefore, in a remainder trust in which the government would receive what is left of the assets after income is paid to a third party, the GASB has concluded that the initial value of the governmental remainder beneficiary would be the fair value of the assets, less the value of the liability. This would result in an asset to the government measured at fair value, a liability of the income stream (or the remainder amount) to the income donor at a settlement amount, and a deferred inflow of resources for the remainder (or the income benefit).

Recognition and Reporting—Irrevocable Split-Interest Agreements

Accounting and financial reporting for irrevocable split-interest agreements is dependent upon the facts and circumstances of the agreement.

Scenario 1: A government is the intermediary (trustee, fiscal agent, etc., holding and administering the donated assets) and the *remainder interest* beneficiary (has the right to receive all or a portion of the resources remaining at the end of a split-interest agreement's term) (GASB-81, par. 10) [GASB Cod. Sec. I70.107]:

	Debits	Credits
At the Date of the Irrevocable Split-Interest Agreement		
Resources received or receivable (assets)	XX	
Lead interest assigned to other beneficiaries (liability)		XX
Deferred inflow of resources representing the government's unconditional remainder interest		XX

The asset balance will change based on interest, dividends and changes in fair value. As the assets change, the deferred inflow of resources changes. The liability is measured based on a settlement amount (the stream of payments expected to be provided to other beneficiaries). To develop the liability, assumptions may include the payment provisions in the contract, the estimated rate of return on the assets, the mortality rate (if the term of the agreement is contingent on the life of the beneficiary) and the discount rate if a present value technique is used. Disbursements to the beneficiaries lower the liability. Upon termination of the agreement, the amount reported as a deferred inflow of resources is recognized as revenue and any remaining liability that no longer needs to be disbursed is a gain (GASB-81, pars. 11–15) [GASB Cod. Secs. I70.108–.112].

> *Scenario 2:* A government is the intermediary (trustee, fiscal agent, etc., holding and administering the donated assets) and the *lead interest* beneficiary (has the right to receive all or a portion of the resources at the beginning of a split-interest agreement's term with the remainder to the beneficiaries) (GASB-81, par. 16) [GASB Cod. Sec. I70.113]:

	Debits	Credits
At the Date of the Irrevocable Split-Interest Agreement		
Resources received or receivable (assets)	XX	
Lead interest assigned to other beneficiaries (liability)		XX
Revenue from Irrevocable Split-Interest Agreement		XX
Deferred inflow of resources representing the government's unconditional remainder interest (i.e., due in future periods)		X

Similar accounting and financial reporting would exist. However, the liability would be much less. Revenue would be declared for any benefit received in the initial period (GASB-81, pars. 16–21) [GASB Cod. Secs. I70.113–.118].

> *Scenario 3A:* A government is party to a life-interest in real estate that is recognized as an investment by the government in accordance with the definition of an investment in GASB-72 (see above). The donor retains the right to use the asset (a residence). As an investment, the residence is recognized at fair value at the date of the agreement (GASB-81, par. 22) [GASB Cod. Sec. I70.119].

	Debits	Credits
At the Date of the Irrevocable Split-Interest Agreement		
Resources received or receivable at fair value (asset)	XX	
Various liabilities related to the residence		XX
Deferred inflow of resources representing the difference		X

Liabilities related to the life-interest are dependent upon the agreement. For example, insurance, maintenance, repairs or an outstanding mortgage may be assumed by the government. An additional receivable may be present if the donor is paying the government rent. Changes in fair value will increase or decrease the related deferred inflow of resources. At the termination of the agreement (typically at the date of the donor's death or vacating of property), revenue is recognized for any remaining portion of the deferred inflow of resources and liabilities that are no longer needed to be recognized (GASB-81, par. 23) [GASB Cod. Sec. I70.120].

> *Scenario 3B*: A government is party to a life-interest in real estate that is recognized as a capital asset as it will be used for the government's programs and services. The donor retains the right to use the asset (a residence). As a capital asset, the residence is valued at acquisition value in accordance with GASB-72.

	Debits	Credits
At the Date of the Irrevocable Split-Interest Agreement		
Resources received or receivable at *acquisition* value (asset)	XX	
Various liabilities related to the residence		XX
Deferred inflow of resources representing the difference		X

Since the asset is recognized at acquisition value, depreciation will now occur systematically and rationally over the remaining service life of the residence (GASB-81, pars. 24–28) [GASB Cod. Secs. I70.121–.125].

> *Scenario 4*: A third party is the intermediary (trustee) where a government has an interest in an irrevocable split-interest agreement.

	Debits	Credits
At the Date of the Irrevocable Split-Interest Agreement		
Resources received or receivable at *acquisition* value (asset)	XX	
Deferred inflow of resources representing the difference		XX

To recognize assets, *all* of the following must be met:

1. The government is specified by name as beneficiary in the legal document underlying the donation;
2. The donation agreement is irrevocable;
3. The donor has not granted variance power to the intermediary with respect to the donated resources (Variance power is the unilateral power

to redirect the benefit of the transferred resources to another beneficiary, overriding the donor's instructions.);

4. The donor does not control the intermediary, such that the actions of the intermediary are not influenced by the donor beyond the specified stipulations of the agreement; and

5. The irrevocable split-interest agreement establishes a legally enforceable right for the government's benefit (an unconditional beneficial interest).

The assets would be recognized at fair value as of the date of the agreement and remeasured each reporting date. Changes in fair value increase or decrease the deferred inflow of resources. Revenue may be recognized initially if the government is the lead interest, reducing the beneficial interest asset to be received in the future.

If the government is the remainder interest beneficiary, the government will recognize revenue for the beneficial interest at the termination of the agreement (GASB-81, pars. 29–34) [GASB Cod. Secs. I70.126–.131].

Recognition and Reporting—Other Investments

All investment income, including changes in the fair value of investments, must be reported as revenue on the governmental entity's operating statement. Investment income includes interest and dividend income, realized gains and losses on the sale of investments, and changes in the fair value of investments the governmental entity holds, inclusive of irrevocable split-interest agreements as discussed in the previous section. If the governmental entity elects to separately identify the change in the fair value of its investments, the change should be labeled as "net increase (decrease) in the fair value of investments," which is defined as "the difference between the fair value of investments at the beginning of the year and at the end of the year, taking into consideration investment purchases, sales, and redemptions".

Unrealized Gains and Losses

Unrealized gains and losses (from the valuation of investments at the end of the period) and *realized* gains and losses (from the sale of investments during the period) must not be reported separately on the operating statement. Realized gains and losses may be presented separately in a note to the financial statements of the governmental entity if such gains and losses are measured as the difference between the sales price of the investment and the original cost of the investment. However, governmental external investment pools that prepare separate financial reports may report realized gains and losses separately from the net increase or decrease in the fair value of investments on the face of their operating statements. If a governmental external investment pool elects this option, the unrealized gains and losses should be labeled as net increase (decrease) in the fair value of investments, as noted in the previous paragraph (GASB-31, par. 13, and GASB-67, par. 24, as amended by GASB-81, pars. 12 and 18) [GASB Cod. Sec. I50.131].

Foreign Currency Gain and Loss Transactions

GASB-62 (*Codification of Accounting and Financial Reporting Guidance Contained in Pre-November 30, 1989 FASB and AICPA Pronouncements*), pars. 165–172 [GASB Cod. Secs. F70.101–.105], contains guidance on foreign currency translation adjustments, which are usually extremely rare for general purpose governments. Should a foreign currency translation adjustment be required, at the date the transaction is recognized each asset, liability, revenue, expense, gain, or loss arising from the transaction should be measured and recorded in U.S. dollars by use of the exchange rate in effect at the date of transaction. At each financial statement date, recorded balances that are denominated in a currency other than the U.S. dollar should be adjusted to reflect the current exchange rate. Exchange rates are the ratios of a unit of one currency to the amount of another currency for which that unit can be exchanged at a particular time. The exchange rate to be used to translate and record foreign currency transactions is the applicable rate at which a particular transaction could be settled at the transaction date. At subsequent financial statement dates, the current rate is that rate at which the related receivable or payable could be settled at that date. The aggregate transaction gain or loss recognized in the period should be disclosed in the notes to financial statements.

The calculation of the increase or decrease in the fair value of investments is illustrated in Appendix C of GASB-31 [GASB Cod. Sec. I50.914], part of which is reproduced in Exhibit 9-1.

EXHIBIT 9-1
CALCULATION OF CHANGE IN FAIR VALUE OF INVESTMENTS

Year 1

Specific Identification Method

	Cost	A Beginning fair value	B Purchases	C Sales	D Subtotal*	E Ending fair value	F Change in fair value**
Security 1	$100	$100	—	—	$100	$120	$20
Security 2	520	540	—	—	540	510	(30)
Security 3	200	240	—	$250	(10)	—	10
Security 4	330	—	$330	—	330	315	(15)
Totals		$880	$330	$250	$960	$945	$(15)

* Column D = Columns A+B *less* Column C.

** Column F = Column E *less* Column D.

Aggregate Method	Amounts
Fair value at December 31, 20X8	$945
Add: Proceeds of investments sold in year 20X8	250
Less: Cost of investments purchased in year 20X8	(330)
Less: Fair value at December 31, 20X7	(880)
Change in fair value of investments	$ (15)

Year 2

Specific Identification Method

	Cost	A Beginning fair value	B Purchases	C Sales	D Subtotal*	E Ending fair value	F Change in fair value**
Security 1	$100	$120	—	$110	$10	$—	$(10)
Security 2	520	510	—	—	510	550	40
Security 3	330	315	—	330	(15)	—	15
Security 4	310	—	310	—	310	300	(10)
Total		$945	$310	$440	$815	$850	$35

* Column D = Columns A + B *less* Column C.
** Column F = Column E *less* Column D.

Aggregate Method	*Amounts*
Fair value at December 31, 20X9	$850
Add: Proceeds of investments sold in year 20X9	440
Less: Cost of investments purchased in year 20X9	(310)
Less: Fair value at December 31, 20X8	(945)
Change in fair value of investments	$35

The calculation of the change in the fair value of investments simplifies a difficult presentation problem that arises when assets are presented at fair value and some of the assets are held for more than two accounting periods before they are sold. Specifically, the question is how to present realized and unrealized gains and losses for the same investment. For example, assume that an investment purchased for $100 has a value of $150 at the end of the first year and is sold for $180 during the second year. The governmental entity has a $50 unrealized gain in year 1 ($150 − $100) and an $80 realized gain in year 2 ($180 − $100); however, the maximum amount of (economic) gain that can be reported on operating statements for the two years is $80. For this reason, the effect on the operating statement in the second year is $30, because the $50 unrealized gain must be netted against the $80 realized gain. The illustrated calculation of the net change in investments simplifies the computation by not separating unrealized and realized gains and losses. The standard prohibits the presentation of realized gains and losses on the income statement, because the presentation may detract from the reporting of the change in the fair value of investments and could be misinterpreted if the reader does not understand how a realized gain may not be an economic gain in the year the investment is sold if the investment had an unrealized gain (that was equal to the realized gain in the current period) in the previous period.

Investments Not Subject to GASB-31

GASB-31 does not establish accounting standards for investments in securities not specifically listed in the Statement. The AICPA's *State and Local Governments* Guide states that generally those investments should be reported "at original cost when acquired and that any purchased discount or premium from the investment's face or maturity value [be] accreted or amortized to investment income over the life of the investment in a systematic and rational manner." For example, if a governmental entity acquires nonmarketable equity securities, the investment is recorded at cost in subsequent periods (irrespective of its change in fair value) unless there is a decline in its fair value that is other than temporary.

Investments that are not subject to the fair value standards established by GASB-31 should generally be accounted for based on the historical cost concept. Investments not subject to GASB-31 standards include the following:

- Investment in equity securities (equity method);
- Investments in nonpublic equity securities (cost method); and
- Escheat property (GASB-31, par. 5, as amended by GASB-61, par. 10, GASB-62, pars. 202–210, GASB-72, pars. 2, 64, and 78) [GASB Cod. Sec. I50.102].

Investments in Equity Securities (Equity Method)

In some instances a governmental entity may be named as the trustee of an equity interest in a company where the interest represents 20% or more of the voting stock of a company. In accordance with GASB-62, pars. 202–210 [GASB Cod. Secs. I50.101, .109, .111–.116, .145, 2300.107], an asset should be reported in the financial statements of a Private-Purpose Trust Fund. The initial receipt of the securities from the donor should be recorded at fair value. The recognition of a proportional share of the investee company's results of operations is not dependent on whether there is an actual remittance between the investee and the Private-Purpose Trust Fund.

GASB-61 (*The Financial Reporting Entity: Omnibus—an amendment of GASB Statements No. 14 and No. 34*) amended the guidance on equity interests in joint ventures by stipulating that if the *government's intent* for owning a majority equity interest is to directly enhance its ability to provide governmental services, the organization should be reported as a component unit. For example, a government that purchases 100% of the stock of a manufacturer to provide a controlled source of materials for its capital projects should report the company as a component unit. When such a component unit is discretely presented, the equity interest should be reported as an asset of the fund that has the equity interest. When such a component is blended, in the period of acquisition the purchase typically should be reported as an outflow of the fund that provided the resources for the acquisition and, in that and subsequent reporting periods, the component unit should be reported as a blended component unit. If, however, the government owns the equity interest for the purpose of obtaining income or profit rather than to directly enhance its ability to provide governmental services, it should report its equity interest as an investment regardless of the extent of its ownership. (See previous **PRACTICE ALERT** on GASB-90.)

The interest in the net position of the investee company should be reported as a single asset (account) in a Private-Purpose Trust Fund. There should be no attempt to present on the Private-Purpose Trust Fund's balance sheet a proportional interest in the various assets and liabilities of the investee company. In addition, the proportional share of the investee company's results of operations should be presented as a single operating account on the Private-Purpose Trust

Fund's statement of changes in fiduciary net position. Finally, a proportional interest in the various operating accounts of the investee company should not be presented.

In determining the investee company's results of operations for a period, profits on transactions (if any) with a Private-Purpose Trust Fund should be eliminated. Non-operating transactions, such as additional equity contributions, loans, and dividends, should be reflected as an addition or decrease to the carrying amount of the net investment in the investee company.

GASB-72 excludes the following types of activities from using the equity method of accounting (GASB-72, par. 77) [GASB Cod. Secs. C55.101, I50.109–.110]:

- Common stock held by:
  - External investment pools;
  - Pension or other postemployment benefit plans;
  - Internal Revenue Code Section 457 deferred compensation plans; and
  - Endowments (including permanent and term endowments) or permanent funds.
- Investments in certain entities that calculate the NAV per share (or its equivalent) (mainly "private equity" or nonpublic equity securities); and
- Equity interests in joint ventures or component units.

Equity interests in common stock that do not meet *both* the definition of an investment *and* the criteria for using the equity method should be accounted for using the cost method.

Investments in Nonpublic Equity Securities (Cost Method) or in Certain Entities That Calculate Net Asset Value per Share (or Its Equivalent)

When a donor transfers equity securities (where the fair value is not readily determinable) to a governmental entity to be used to benefit individuals, private organizations, or other governments, the securities should be recorded at fair value. However, once the investment is recorded, it should be accounted for based on the historical cost principle. Thus, a Private-Purpose Trust Fund would record dividend income (a receipt of resources) when the board of directors of the investee company declares the dividend.

If the securities calculate value by using a net asset value (NAV) per share or its equivalent, GASB-72, pars. 71–74 [GASB Cod. Secs. I50.101, .127–.130, In5.102] allow a government to establish the fair value of an investment. These types of investments calculate NAV based on member units or an ownership interest in partners' capital, to which a proportionate share of net assets is attributed. The NAV is calculated as of the government's measurement date in a manner consistent with FASB standards.

There may be many instances where the NAV of an investment is not determined as of a government's measurement date or is not calculated in manner consistent with FASB standards. In such an event, the government may need to adjust to the most recent NAV per share. The government may determine that fair value should be applied. The method of determining fair value should be applied consistently to the fair value measurement of the government's entire position in a particular investment, *unless it is probable* at the measurement date that the government will sell a portion of an investment at an amount different from the NAV per share (or its equivalent) In those situations, the government should account for the portion of the investment that is being sold at fair value in accordance with GASB-72.

A sale is considered probable only if all of the following criteria have been met as of the government's measurement date:

- The government, having the authority to approve the action, commits to a plan to sell the investment;

- An active program to locate a buyer and other actions required to complete the plan to sell the investment have been initiated;

- The investment is available for immediate sale subject only to terms that are usual and customary for sales of such investments (e.g., a requirement to obtain approval of the sale from the investee, or a buyer's due diligence procedures); and

- Actions required to complete the plan indicate that it is unlikely that significant changes to the plan will be made or that the plan will be withdrawn.

Escheat Property

GASB-21 defines the "escheat process" as "the reversion of property to a governmental entity in the absence of legal claimants or heirs." Governmental entities that receive escheat property may manage the receipts in a number of ways, including using the funds to finance current operations or investing the funds and using only the investment income to finance governmental activities. GASB-37 requires that escheat property generally be reported in the governmental or proprietary fund that ultimately will receive the escheat property. Escheat property that is held for individuals, private organizations, or another government is reported either in (1) a Private-Purpose Trust Fund, (2) an Agency Fund, or (3) in the governmental or proprietary fund that reports escheat property. In the last case, the portion of the escheat property that is expected (likely to occur) to revert to an external party is reported as a liability (GASB-21, pars. 3, 5) [GASB Cod. Secs. E70.101, .103].

The *GASB Implementation Guide 2015-1*, question 7.52.8 [GASB Cod. Sec. E70.702-3], provides additional insight into the issue by classifying escheat property in the following categories:

- Property that will be paid to heirs or beneficiaries;
- Property temporarily held for other governments; and
- Property that will revert to the government itself in the absence of rightful heirs or claimants.

The question identifies two alternatives that could be used to account for escheat property. Under Alternative 1, all three categories of escheat property are accounted for in either a governmental fund or a proprietary fund and all estimated amounts due to other parties (other governments or claimants) are reported as a liability of the fund. Under Alternative 2, (1) the estimated portion of the amount of escheat property for all three categories that is expected to revert to the governmental entity is accounted for in either a governmental fund or a property fund and (2) the balance of the amount of the escheat property that is expected to be distributed to external parties is accounted for in an Agency Fund (for property temporarily held for other governments) or a Private-Purpose Trust Fund (for property expected to be distributed to claimants).

Escheat property that is reported in a Private-Purpose Trust Fund is reported as an "addition" in the statement of changes in fiduciary net position and any balance remaining at the end of the accounting period is reported as "held in trust for trust beneficiaries" in the statement of fiduciary net position. When the escheat property is reported in an Agency Fund only a statement of fiduciary net position is prepared. Consistent with the basic standards established by GASB-34, escheat property reported in a Private-Purpose Trust Fund or an Agency Fund is not reported in the entity's government-wide financial statements. (See additional discussion and **Appendix** on GASB Statement No. 84 (*Fiduciary Activities*) in Chapter 8, "Fiduciary Funds.")

When escheat property is reported in a governmental or proprietary fund, the total amount of escheat property received during the year is apportioned between an escheat liability account and an escheat revenue account. The amount of the liability recorded is the estimated amount expected to be paid to claimants, and the balance is recorded as revenue. Again, based on the standards originally established by GASB-34, escheat property reported in a governmental or proprietary fund is reported in the government-wide financial statements based on accrual accounting principles. Escheat property reported as revenue in a governmental fund must satisfy the criteria of measurability and availability.

Summary of Investment Measurement Standards

Exhibit 9-2 summarizes the measurement standards established by GASB-31, as amended, for governmental entities (except external investment pools, defined benefit pension plans, and Internal Revenue Code (IRC) § 457 deferred compensation plans).

EXHIBIT 9-2
SUMMARY OF MEASUREMENT STANDARDS FOR INVESTMENT SPECIFIED IN GASB-31, GASB-72, and GASB-79

Investments held by governmental entities (except external investment pools, defined benefit pension and OPEB plans, and IRC § 457 deferred compensation plans)	*Appropriate accounting method*
• Marketable equity securities (including unit investment trusts and closed-end mutual funds) • Marketable option contracts • Marketable stock warrants • Marketable stock rights	Report at fair value (GASB-31, par. 3) and GASB-72.
• Interest-earning investment contracts	Non-participating contracts (e.g., certificates of deposits) should be reported at cost rather than fair value, assuming the value of the investment is not affected by the financial institution's credit standing, market rate changes or other relevant factors (GASB-31, par. 8) (as well as GASB-72, par. 69(a)). Participating interest-earning investment contracts including negotiable certificates of deposit that mature beyond one year of their acquisition date should be reported at fair value (GASB-31, par. 8). Participating interest-earning investment contracts including negotiable certificates of deposit that mature within one year or less at the date of their acquisition may be reported at amortized cost, assuming the investment is not affected by the financial institution's credit standing, changes in market rates or other relevant factors (GASB-31, par. 9) (as well as GASB-72, par. 69(c)).
• Debt securities	Report at fair value (GASB-72, par. 76). **Exception:** Money market investments that mature within one year or less at the date of their acquisition may be reported at amortized cost, assuming the investment is not affected by the financial institution's credit standing or other relevant factors (GASB-31, par. 9).
• Open-end mutual fund	Report at fair value based on the fund's current share price (GASB-31, par. 10).

Investments held by governmental entities (except external investment pools, defined benefit pension and OPEB plans, and IRC § 457 deferred compensation plans)	Appropriate accounting method
• External investment pools that are not SEC registered non-governmental pools, except 2a7-like pools)	Report at fair value based on the fair value per share of the pool's underlying portfolio. If the governmental entity cannot obtain sufficient information from the pool sponsor to determine the fair value of the investment in the pool, the best estimate of its fair value should be made and the basis for the estimate should be disclosed in a note to the financial statements (NAV or equivalent) (GASB-31, pars. 11 and 15e) (as well as GASB-59, par. 5).
• Governmental external investment pools	Report the investment based on the pool's share price (NAV) if at floating value or fixed net asset value per share (example $1.00) or at amortized cost, depending upon the election of the pool in accordance with GASB-79. (If at amortized cost, position is not characterized in the fair value hierarchy.)
• Unallocated insurance contracts (not in a beneficiary's name)	Similarly to interest-earning investment contracts above.
• Life insurance contracts	Cash surrender value (GASB-72, par. 69(g)).
• Life settlement contracts	Fair value (GASB-72, par. 70) assuming the government does not have an insurable interest, the government provides consideration to the policy owner of an amount in excess of the cash surrender value, the contract pays the government the face value of the policy when the insured dies and the government is the policyholder.
• Synthetic guaranteed investment contracts that are fully benefit responsive	Contract value in accordance with GASB-53, paragraph 67 (see following on derivatives) (as well as GASB-72, par. 69e).

DISCLOSURE REQUIREMENTS FOR DEPOSITS AND INVESTMENTS

Guidance for disclosures related to deposits and investments is established in GASB-31, GASB-3, GASB-40, and GASB-72.

Disclosures of all three standards apply in most instances, except for certain component unit presentations. As discussed in the GASB *Implementation Guide Update 2016-1*, question 4.2 [GASB Cod. Sec. I50.701-2], GASB-3 and GASB-40, disclosures apply to all deposits with financial institutions and investments that are reported on the face of a governmental reporting entity's financial statements. GASB-72 applies to all deposits and investments that should be reported at fair value. In addition, GASB-72 also provides for measurement of certain investments at other than fair value. Therefore, all apply to deposit and investment transactions of all funds, including those for which the reporting entity is a custodian and that are reported in an agency, trust, or other fund—such as deferred compensation plan assets and pooled amounts invested by a state treasurer on behalf of local governments. The same disclosure applies despite whether they are titled cash and cash equivalents (if they are deposits) or investments.

For annuity contracts that are in the name of lottery prize winners, the disclosure requirements of GASB-3, 40, and 72 also apply, if they are reported in the government's financial statements. The requirements also apply to deposits and investments held by another entity for a government—for example, amounts held by fiscal agents for bond payments and reserves—if they are reported on the face of the government's financial statements.

Disclosure requirements do not apply to deposits and investments that are not reported in the statement of net position/balance sheet—for example, amounts held by escrow agents on debt that is reported as defeased in substance in accordance with GASB-7 (*Advance Refundings Resulting in Defeasance of Debt*) and GASB-23 (*Accounting and Financial Reporting for Refundings of Debt Reported by Proprietary Activities*) as amended.

Question 4.3 of 2016-1 [GASB Cod. Sec. I50.728-4] continues discussion of disclosure requirements, excepting certain disclosures for cash equivalents as they are highly liquid and close to maturity. Generally, they are not subject to the disclosures in GASB-72. However, they may be subject to disclosures required by GASB-3, 31, and 40.

APPENDIX B includes a comprehensive illustration of investment disclosures for a State.

PRACTICE POINT: CCH's *2018 Governmental GAAP Disclosure Manual*, Chapter 16 contains comprehensive illustrations of investment disclosures for small and large governments, a statewide defined benefit plan, a public college and a State lottery.

Beyond the comprehensive illustration in Chapter 16 of the *2018 Governmental GAAP Disclosure Manual*, the following chapters in the *Manual* contain various aspects of the disclosure requirements contained in the following sections:

Chapter	Required Disclosure
15	Cash Deposits with Financial Institutions
48	Reverse Repurchase and Dollar Reverse Repurchase Agreements
49	Securities Lending Transactions
56	Sponsoring Government Disclosures About External Investment Pools Reported As Investment Trust Funds
66	Derivative Instruments

Chapter	Required Disclosure
78	Investments in Common Stock
81	Foreign Currency Transactions
91	Fair Value Measurement

GASB-31 Disclosure Requirements

GASB-31 establishes that a governmental entity must disclose in notes to the financial statements the following information about its investments, which were unchanged by the issuance of GASB-72:

- The methods and significant assumptions used to estimate the fair value of an investment, when fair value is not based on a quoted market price;
- The policy used to identify investments that are reported at amortized cost;
- For investments in external investment pools that are not SEC-registered, a description of regulatory oversight, if any, and a statement as to whether the fair value of the investment is the same as the value of the pool shares;
- Description of involuntary participation (i.e., participation required by law) in an external investment pool;
- For positions in external investment pools for which fair value information cannot be obtained from the pool sponsor, the methods and significant assumptions used to estimate the fair value and the reasons for having to use such an estimate;
- For investments in external investment pools that report their investments at amortized cost, the presence of any limitations or restrictions on withdrawals (These may include notice periods, maximum transaction amounts and the qualifying external investment pool's authority to impose liquidity fees or redemption gates.); and
- Income from investments whereby the income from one fund has been assigned to another fund (GASB-31, par. 15, as amended by GASB-72, par. 81, and GASB-79, par. 43) [GASB Cod. Sec. I50.143].

In some instances, external investment pools do not provide fair value information or timely information to participants in the pool. For example, the year-end date for the external investment pool might not be the same as the year-end date for the participant. Under these circumstances, the participant must estimate its fair value position in the pool, disclose the methods and significant assumptions used to compute the estimate, and disclose why an estimate must be made.

In addition, if (1) a governmental entity elects to disclose in its notes any realized gains and losses from investments or (2) an external investment pool elects to report on its operating statement any realized gains and losses from investments, the following must be disclosed:

- That the determination of realized gains and losses is independent of the determination of the net change in the fair value of investments;
- That realized gains and losses on investments that were held by the governmental entity during a previous accounting period(s) but sold during the current period were used to compute the change in the fair value of investments for the previous year(s) as well as the current year. (GASB-31, par. 15, GASB-67, par. 24) [GASB Cod. Sec. I50.144].

GASB-31 requires that investments in (1) interest-earning investment contracts, (2) external investment pools, (3) open-end mutual funds, (4) debt securities, and (5) equity securities be reported at fair value; furthermore, any embedded derivatives in these investments must also be reported at fair value. GASB-67 and GASB-74 requires that all investments (excluding insurance contracts) held by defined benefit plans be reported at fair value.

GASB-59 amended GASB-25 and GASB-43 with regard to *unallocated* insurance contracts. There are two types of insurance contracts: (1) unallocated (with no beneficiary) and (2) allocated (with a beneficiary). Unallocated insurance contract investments should be reported as interest-earning investment contracts in a similar manner to the provisions of GASB-31, par. 8 [GASB Cod. Sec. I50.121]. Fair value is measured by the market price if there is an active market for the contract. Fair value is estimated if there is no market. Allocated insurance contracts should be excluded from plan assets (GASB-59, par. 4, as amended by GASB-73, pars. 115–116, GASB-67, par 18, GASB-72, par. 69) [GASB Cod. Sec. I50.122].

Deposit and Investment Risk Disclosures

Guidance for disclosures related to deposits and investment risks is established in GASB-3, as amended by GASB-40 and GASB-72.

The purpose of GASB-3, GASB-40, and GASB-72 is to provide users of financial statements with information to assess the risk related to a governmental entity's investments, including repurchase agreements, deposits with financial institutions, and reverse repurchase agreements. GASB-3 requires that the following disclosures related to investment risk be made in notes to the governmental entity's financial statements (GASB-3, par. 63) [GASB Cod. Sec. C20.103, I50.146, I55.106]:

- Legal or contractual provisions for deposits and investments, including repurchase agreements;
- Deposits and investments, including repurchase agreements, as of the balance sheet date;
- Legal or contractual provisions for reverse repurchase agreements; and
- Reverse repurchase agreements as of the balance sheet date.

GASB-40 amends GASB-3 to require the following additional disclosures related to deposit and investment risks:

- Credit risk, including custodial credit risk and concentrations of credit risk;
- Interest rate risk;

- Foreign currency risk; and
- Deposit and investment policies related to the applicable risks.

The additional risk disclosures required by GASB-40 should generally be made for the primary government, including its blended component units. The disclosures should be made for the governmental activities, business-type activities, individual major funds, non-major funds in the aggregate, and fiduciary fund types when the risk exposures are significantly greater for these units than for the primary government as a whole.

GASB-59 further amended GASB-40, affording some relief to investments in mutual funds, external investment pools, and other pooled investments. Interest rate risk disclosure in these types of investments is limited to investments in *debt* mutual funds, external *debt* investment pools, and other pooled *debt* instruments, which firmly relieves pressure on preparers to "look through" most mutual funds and investment pools.

Legal or Contractual Provisions for Deposits and Investments

The governmental entity should disclose the types of investments that can be acquired by the primary government based on legal and contractual restrictions. There may be significantly different restrictions for component units, or the restrictions may vary significantly among funds or fund types. Under both of these circumstances, the different investment restrictions should be disclosed when investment activities for the component unit's individual funds or individual fund types are material in relationship to the reporting entity's investment activities. Violation of these and other investment restrictions should be disclosed in notes to the financial statements (GASB-3, pars. 65–66) [GASB Cod. Secs. I50.149–.150, C20.106].

Disclosures Related to Cash Deposits with Financial Institutions

When deposits with financial institutions are fully insured or collateralized by securities held by the governmental entity or its agent in the governmental entity's name, the only disclosure necessary is a statement that deposits with financial institutions are fully insured or collateralized by securities held in the government's name. On the other hand, when deposits are not fully insured or collateralized, the governmental entity is exposed to "custodial credit risk," which is defined as "the risk that a government will not be able to recover deposits if the depository financial institution fails or will not be able to recover collateral securities that are in the possession of an outside party."

Specifically, deposits with financial institutions are subject to custodial credit risk (and must be disclosed) when they are not covered by depository insurance and have one of the three following characteristics (GASB-40, par. 8) [GASB Cod. Sec. C20.107]:

1. Uncollateralized (no securities are pledged to the depositor government);
2. Collateralized with securities held by the pledging financial institution in the depositor government's name; or

3. Collateralized with securities held by the pledging financial institution, or by its trust department or agent, but not in the depositor government's name.

Depository insurance includes the following:

- Federal depository insurance funds, such as those maintained by the Federal Deposit Insurance Corporation (FDIC);

- State depository insurance funds; and

- Multiple financial institution collateral pools that insure public deposits. (In such a pool, a group of financial institutions holding public funds pledge collateral to a common pool.)

When a governmental entity has deposits in financial institutions at the end of the year that are subject to any one of the three custodial risks described above, the disclosure should include (1) the amount of the bank balance, (2) a statement that the balance is uninsured, and (3) the nature of the custodial credit risk for each uninsured deposit (category 1, 2, or 3, as listed above).

In addition, the governmental entity should disclose deposit policies that are related to custodial credit risks. If a governmental entity has no deposit policy that addresses custodial credit risk to which it is exposed, that fact must nonetheless be disclosed (GASB-40, par. 6) [GASB Cod. Secs. C20.109, I50.151].

The disclosure is based on the deposited amount as reported by the bank rather than the amount reported in the financial statements because the former identifies the amount of the deposit subject to custodial credit risk.

Deposits in foreign financial institutions denominated in a foreign currency are subject to foreign currency risk (the risk that changes in exchange rates will adversely affect the fair value of a deposit). When a governmental entity is exposed to foreign currency risk, GASB-40 requires that the U.S. dollar amount of the deposit and the currency used to denominate the deposit be disclosed (GASB-40, par. 17) [GASB Cod. Secs. C20.108, I50.158].

If the governmental entity has suffered losses from defaults by counterparties to deposit transactions or has recovered amounts reported as losses in previous years, those amounts should be disclosed in the financial statements (GASB-3, par. 75) [GASB Cod. Secs. C20.110, I50.160].

Level of Detail

Disclosure requirements for deposits with financial institutions focus on the primary government (including blended component units) and also on deposits reflected in (1) governmental activities, (2) business-type activities, (3) major funds, (4) non-major governmental funds and enterprise funds in the aggregate, and (5) fiduciary fund types (GASB-40, par. 5) [GASB Cod. Secs. C20.104, I50.147, I55.107].

The various investment note disclosure standards are also applicable for stand-alone financial reports of component units.

Disclosures Related to Investments

Deposits and investments generally are two of the largest asset classifications reported in a governmental entity's financial statements. Their importance was emphasized by the issuance of GASB-3 to provide users of financial statements with disclosures sufficient to assess risks related to a governmental entity's investments, including repurchase agreements, deposits with financial institutions, and reverse repurchase agreements. The disclosures in GASB-3 concentrated on describing credit risk and especially custodial credit risk, which were clarified in GASB-40 and are currently defined as follows (GASB 40, par. 19, and GASB-72, par. 86) [GASB Cod. Secs. I50.512, .514]:

Risk	Definition
• *Credit risk*	The risk that an issuer or other counterparty to an investment will not fulfill its obligations.
• *Custodial credit risk*	The custodial credit risk for investments is the risk that a government will not be able to recover the value of investment or collateral securities that are in the possession of an outside party if the counterparty to the transaction fails.

GASB-40 was issued in order to modify custodial credit risk disclosures and to "establish more comprehensive disclosure requirements addressing other common risks of the deposits and investments of state and local governments."

GASB-40 focuses on what the GASB considers to be the most common risks related to deposits and investments; however, the GASB encourages preparers of governmental financial statements to disclose other risks that are not specifically mandated in GASB-40.

Investment Types

Generally, disclosures related to investments should be formatted based on investment types, such as investments in U.S. treasuries, corporate bonds, and equities. Professional judgment must be used in order not to aggregate dissimilar investments for disclosure purposes. For example (for disclosure purposes), investments in mutual funds that predominantly invest in equities should generally not be aggregated with direct equity securities held by the governmental entity (GASB-40, par. 4) [GASB Cod. Sec. I50.148].

Level of Disclosure

Investment disclosures should focus separately on (1) governmental activities, (2) business-type activities, (3) individual major funds, (4) aggregated nonmajor funds, and (5) fiduciary fund types of the primary government when the risk is significantly greater for one of the five categories than for the primary government as a whole. For example, GASB-40 points out that concentration of credit risk may not be great for the overall primary government but it could be for an individual major fund because that particular fund invests most of its resources in the securities of a single issuer (GASB-40, par. 5) [GASB Cod. Secs. C20.104, I50.147, I55.107].

Investment Policies

GASB-40 requires that a governmental entity disclose investment policies that are related to investment risks. For example, if the entity holds investments denominated in a foreign currency, it should disclose its investment policy with respect to foreign currency risk. For example, a governmental entity may have an investment policy that limits investments denominated in foreign currencies to 5% of total investments. If the entity has adopted no policy with respect to a particular risk, that fact should be part of the disclosure (GASB-40, par. 6) [GASB Cod. Secs. C20.109, I50.151]. Specifically, GASB-40 addresses disclosure issues related to the following investment risks:

- Credit risk;
- Custodial credit risk;
- Concentration of credit risk;
- Interest rate risk; and
- Foreign currency risk.

Credit Risk

GASB-40 requires a governmental entity to make disclosures related to investments in debt instruments about the credit risk (the risk that an issuer or other counterparty to an investment will not fulfill its obligations). Credit risk disclosure is accomplished by classifying debt investments as of the entity's balance sheet date by debt type and by credit quality ratings assigned by nationally recognized rating agencies (Standard & Poor's, Moody's Investors Service, and Fitch). For example, investments in commercial paper could be rated as A1 by Standard & Poor's, Aaa by Moody's Investors Service, and F-1 by Fitch. If the investment grade of a governmental entity's investment in commercial paper varies, the investment categories must be expanded to disclose the different quality of ratings by dollar amount (GASB-40, par. 7) [GASB Cod. Sec. I50.152].

The disclosure for debt investments applies to external investment pools, money market funds, bond mutual funds, and other pooled investments for fixed-income securities. If credit ratings for any of these investments are not available, the disclosure should indicate which investments are unrated.

Unless there is evidence to the contrary, investments in U.S. government debt or debt guaranteed by the U.S. government is considered to have no credit risk and therefore the credit rating for these investments does not have to be disclosed.

In the *GASB Implementation Guide 2015-1*, question 1.9.7 [GASB Cod. Sec. I50.738-8], there is guidance when a debt security issued by a federal government-sponsored enterprise (GSE) that has only the implicit guarantee of the federal government and is held by a state or local government is subject to credit risk disclosures. The guarantee must only be an implicit guarantee. However, GASB also notes if the structures of financial markets change, whether a GSE has an implicit or an explicit guarantee may change. A credit risk disclosure is based on the status of a federal guarantee as of the date of the financial statements.

Custodial Credit Risk

GASB-40 points out that a governmental entity's investments are exposed to custodial credit risk when they are uninsured, unregistered, and are held by either (1) the counterparty or (2) the counterparty's trust department or agent, but not in the government's name. When investments held as of the date of the balance sheet are exposed to custodial credit risk the following proposed disclosures should be made:

- The type of investment;
- The reported amount; and
- How the investments are held.

The GASB reiterates the point made in GASB-3 (par. 69) that generally, investments in external investment pools and in open-end mutual funds are not subject to custodial credit risk because "their existence is not evidenced by securities that exist in physical or book entry form." Also, securities for reverse repurchase agreements are not exposed to custodial credit risk, because those securities are held by the buyer-lender.

Concentration of Credit Risk

GASB-40 recognizes that there is an additional dimension to credit risk that relates to the amount of investment in any one entity. For this reason GASB-40 requires that a governmental entity disclose the amount invested in a separate issuer (except investments held in the U.S. government or investments guaranteed by the U.S. government) when that amount is at least 5% of total investments. The base (total investments) to be used to determine the 5% threshold must be selected consistent with the "level of disclosure criterion" required by GASB-40 (the level of disclosure was discussed earlier) (GASB-40, par. 11) [GASB Cod. Sec. I50.154].

Interest Rate Risk

Interest rate risk arises from investments in debt instruments and is defined as "the risk that changes in interest rates will adversely affect the fair value of an investment." The amount of loss in the fair value of a fixed-income security increases as the current market interest rate related to the investment rises (GASB-40, pars. 14–16) [GASB Cod. Secs. I50.155–.157].

GASB-40 requires that a governmental entity provide information about debt investments so that a reader can assess to some degree the entity's exposure to interest rate risk. This disclosure is achieved by grouping investments into investment types and using one of the following methods to inform users of the level of interest rate sensitivity for debt investments:

- Segmented time distributions;
- Specific identification;
- Weighted average maturity;
- Duration; and
- Simulation model.

The disclosure method selected to demonstrate interest rate risk should be the one that the governmental entity uses to identify and manage its interest rate risk. Assumptions that are necessary to describe interest rate risk, such as the timing of cash flows (e.g., when an investment has a call provision) and changes in interest rates, should also be disclosed.

GASB-40 requires additional disclosures for investments in debt instruments whose fair values are "highly sensitive" to changes in interest rates. For example, a debt investment may have a variable interest rate that is 1.3 times the three-month London Interbank Offered Rate (LIBOR). For debt investments that are highly sensitive to changes in interest rates, the governmental entity must provide (1) a description of the interest rate sensitivity and (2) contract terms (such as multipliers and benchmark indexes).

Segmented Time Distributions

The segmented time distributions method of disclosing interest rate risk is simple because it groups "investment cash flows into sequential time periods in tabular form." For example, investment types could be categorized as those that mature in less than one year, between one and five years, and so on.

Specific Identification

The specific identification method does not compute a disclosure measure but presents a list of the individual investments, their carrying amounts, maturity dates, and any call options.

Weighted Average Maturity

When the weighted average maturity method is used to describe a governmental entity's exposure to interest rate risk, the disclosure "expresses investment time horizons—the time when investments become due and payable—in years or months, weighted to reflect the dollar size of individual investments." For example, assume that a debt investment type comprises the following two specific investments (A and B):

Investment	Months to Maturity	Maturity Amount	Weighted Months
A	50	$100,000	16.7*
B	90	200,000	60.0
Total	140	$300,000	76.7

* 50 × ($100,000 / $300,000) = 16.7 months

Based on the above facts, the governmental entity would disclose (in tabular form, along with similar information for other investment types) that this particular investment type had a fair value of $300,000 and a weighted average maturity of 76.7 months.

Duration

GASB-40, par. 19 [GASB Cod. Sec. I50.518] defines "duration" as follows:

> A measure of a debt investment's exposure to fair value changes arising from changing interest rates. It uses the present value of cash flows, weighted for those cash flows as a percentage of the investment's full price.

Effective duration makes assumptions regarding the most likely timing and amounts of variable cash flows arising from such investments as callable bonds, prepayments, and variable-rate debt.

A variety of methods can be used to compute the effective duration of an investment. GASB-40 does not mandate the use of a specific technique. The following example is based on the Macaulay duration approach that is illustrated in an illustration in the *GASB Implementation Guide 2015-1 Appendix B-1-2* [GASB Cod. Sec. I50.908]. To illustrate this approach, assume that a governmental entity as of December 31, 20X6 has an investment in a $100 bond that has a 7.5% coupon rate (semiannual payments) and has a yield to maturity of 7.5% that matures on December 31, 20X8. The cash flows from the investments are summarized as follows:

					(A)	(B)	(C)
				Present Value Factor @4%	Present Value @ 12/31/X6	Periods Before Cash Flows	(A) X (B)
		CASH FLOWS					
6/30/X7	12/31/X7	6/30/X8	12/31/X8				
3.75	—	—	—	.96154	$3.61	.5	1.81
—	3.75	—	—	.92456	3.48	1.0	3.48
—	—	3.75	—	.88900	3.36	1.5	5.04
—	—	—	103.75	.85480	89.54	2.0	179.09
					$100.00		$189.41

The Macaulay duration is computed by dividing the total present values (column C) by the bond price, as follows:

$$\$189.41 \div \$100 = 1.8941 \text{ years}$$

Next, the effective duration is computed by dividing the Macaulay duration (as computed above) by 1 + the coupon rate (7.5% or 0.075) per payment period (2 per year). Thus, the effective duration, which is to be disclosed by investment type, is 1.83 years (rounded), as follows:

$$1.8941 \div [(1+.075 /2)] = 1.83 \text{ years}$$

Simulation Model

Finally, a governmental entity can use various simulation models to describe its exposure to interest rate risk, which "estimate changes in an investment's or a portfolio's fair value, given hypothetical changes in interest rates." For example, an investment type's fair value could be presented as of the balance sheet date along with estimated fair values of the same investments assuming that there is a 100-point, 200-point, and so forth increase in the current market interest rate.

Foreign Currency Risk

Investments (as well as deposits in foreign financial institutions) denominated in a foreign currency are subject to "the risk that changes in exchange rates will adversely affect the fair value of an investment." When a governmental entity is exposed to foreign currency risk, GASB-40 requires that the U.S. dollar amount of the investment (classified by investment type) and the currency used to denominate the investment be disclosed (GASB-40, par. 17) [GASB Cod. Secs. C20.108, I50.158].

If the governmental entity has suffered losses from defaults by counterparties to investments or has recovered amounts reported as losses in previous years, those amounts should also be disclosed in the financial statements (GASB-3, par. 75) [GASB Cod. Secs. C2w0.110, I50.160].

Disclosures Related to Fair Value (GASB-72)

Paragraph 80 of GASB-72 outlines additional required disclosures of the fair value of investments. Disclosures of the fair value of investments are now to be organized by type or class of asset or liability. The level of detail and how much emphasis to place on each disclosure requirement needs to consider:

- The nature, characteristics, and risks of the asset or liability. For example, GASB-72 disaggregates U.S. Treasury notes from U.S. Treasury separate trading of registered interest and principal securities (STRIPS).

- The level of the fair value hierarchy within which the fair value measurement is categorized. For example, a greater degree of uncertainty and subjectivity may require more investments to be categorized as Level 3 of the fair value hierarchy.

- Whether a specific type or class of an asset or liability is required by another GASB statement. GASB-72 notes that GASB-53 requires derivative instrument disclosures by hedging derivative instruments and investment derivative instruments. Those disclosures are unchanged by GASB-72.

- The objective or the mission of the government may yield increased or decreased disclosures. For example, the objective of an external investment pool to achieve income or profit suggests greater disaggregation compared to a general purpose government. Many general purpose governments are constrained by investments due to laws, regulations and operational practices and therefore would have minimal changes to disclosure upon implementation of GASB-72.

- A government may be composed of governmental and business-type activities, individual major funds, non-major funds in the aggregate, or fiduciary fund types and component units. Additional disclosures may be appropriate when the risk exposures are significantly greater than the deposit and investment risks of the primary government. For example, a primary government's total investments may not be exposed to concentration risk. However, if the government's capital projects fund has all of its investments in one issuer of corporate bonds, disclosure should be made for the capital projects fund's exposure to a concentration of credit risk.

- The relative significance of assets and liabilities measured at fair value compared to total assets and liabilities should be evaluated in terms of the government structure. If investments are immaterial, then additional disclosure may not be necessary (GASB-72, par. 80) [GASB Cod. Secs. 1400.196, 2300.107, 3100.161, D40.166, I50.140, L30.137, In3.137, In5.103, Po20.146, Po50.126].

Recurring fair value measurements are assets or liabilities that are revalued and presented in the statement of net position at the end of each reporting period. *Nonrecurring fair value measurements* are those that are permitted to be presented in the statement of net position in particular circumstances. For example, GASB-62, par. 453 [GASB Cod. Sec. L30.123], requires measurement of a mortgage loan held for sale at the lower of carrying value or fair value at each reporting date.

If the fair value of investments is to be disclosed after consideration of the aforementioned provisions, then for both recurring and nonrecurring measurements, the following is disclosed:

- The fair value measurement at the end of the reporting period.
- The level of the fair value hierarchy within which the fair value measurements are categorized in their entirety (Level 1, 2, or 3).
- A description of the valuation techniques used in the fair value measurement.
- If there has been a change in valuation technique that has a significant impact on the result (e.g., changing from an expected cash flow technique to a relief from royalty technique or the use of an additional valuation technique), that change and the reason(s) for making it.

For nonrecurring fair value measurements, the reason(s) for the measurement would be disclosed (GASB-72, par. 81) [GASB Cod. Secs. 1400.196, 2300.107, 3100.162, D40.166, I50.141, L30.137, In3.138, In5.103, Po20.146, Po50.126].

GASB-72, par. 82 [GASB Cod. Secs. 2300.107, 3100.163, I50.142, In3.138, In5.103, Po20.146, and Po50.146], requires additional disclosures to investments in entities that:

- Calculate a NAV per share (or its equivalent), regardless of whether any other method of determining fair value has been applied;
- Do not have a readily determinable fair value; and
- Are measured at fair value on a recurring or nonrecurring basis during the period.

A government would disclose information that addresses the nature and the risks of the investments and whether the investments are probable of being sold at amounts *different from the NAV* per share. Therefore, for each type of investment that are valued at NAV per share, the following additional disclosures are now required:

- The fair value measurement of the investment type at the measurement date and a description of the significant investment strategies of the investee(s) in that type.
- For each type of investment that includes investments that can never be redeemed with the investees, but the government receives distributions through the liquidation of the underlying assets of the investees, the government's estimate of the period over which the underlying assets are expected to be liquidated by the investees.

- The amount of the government's unfunded commitments related to that investment type.

- A general description of the terms and conditions upon which the government may redeem investments in the type (e.g., quarterly redemption with 60 days' notice).

- The circumstances in which an otherwise redeemable investment in the type (or a portion thereof) might not be redeemable (e.g., investments subject to a redemption restriction, such as a lockup or gate). Also, for those otherwise redeemable investments that are restricted from redemption as of the government's measurement date, the estimate of when the restriction from redemption might lapse should be disclosed. If an estimate cannot be made, that fact and how long the restriction has been in effect should be disclosed.

- Any other significant restriction on the ability to sell investments in the type at the measurement date.

- If a government determines that it is probable that it will sell an investment(s) for an amount different from NAV per share, the total fair value of all investments that would be sold at an amount different from NAV per share and any remaining actions required to complete the sale.

- If a group of investments would otherwise be valued at NAV, but the individual investments to be sold have not been identified (e.g., if a government decides to sell 20% of its investments in private equity funds but the individual investments to be sold have not been identified), such that the investments continue to qualify for the method of estimating fair value at NAV, the government's plans to sell and any remaining actions required to complete the sale(s).

- If a separately issued financial statement is available, disclosures may be incorporated by reference. For example, a state government may consider reduced disclosures of fair value measurements of investments in certain entities that calculate NAV per share (or its equivalent) if the financial statements of the state's pension plan includes that information.

Defined benefit plans and endowments have broader disclosure due to the considerations discussed previously. The additional disclosure is detailed in Chapter 22, "Pension and Other Postemployment Benefit Plans."

Disclosures for Qualifying External Investment Pools (at Amortized Cost)

GASB-79 requires qualifying external investment pools that have elected to report at amortized cost the following in the notes to the pool's basic financial statements:

- Fair value measurements, including a summary of the fair value, the carrying amount (if different from fair value), the number of shares or the principal amount, ranges of interest rates, and maturity dates of each major investment classification (as referenced in the previous section. The fair value measurement would be at the end of the reporting period and separated by recurring and nonrecurring fair value measurements.

- Except for investments that are measured at net asset value (NAV) per share or its equivalent, the level of the fair value hierarchy within which the fair value measurements are categorized in their entirety (Level 1, Level 2, or Level 3).

- A description of the valuation techniques used in the fair value measurement.

- If there has been a change in the valuation technique from previous periods that has a significant impact on the result and the reasons for making the change.

- For nonrecurring fair value measurements, the reasons for the measurement.

- For investments that calculate NAV or its equivalent, the elements of disclosure discussed previously in this chapter on NAV disclosure.

- The presence of any limitations or restrictions on participant withdrawals such as redemption notice periods, maximum transaction amounts and the authority to impose liquidity fees or redemption gates.

Disclosures for Participating Governments in Qualifying External Investment Pools (at Amortized Cost)

For participating governments in qualifying external investment pools at amortized cost, disclosure is limited to the presence of any limitations or restrictions on withdrawals such as redemption notice periods, maximum transaction amounts and the authority to impose liquidity fees or redemption gates. This is in addition to the government's investment balance in the external investment pool as of the reporting date.

OBSERVATION: This disclosure appears not to agree with the provisions of GASB-72. The GASB clarifies this disclosure in the GASB *Implementation Guide Update* 2017-1, question 4.36 [GASB Cod. Sec. I50.713-9]. If the external investment pool is compliant with GASB-79, paragraph 4, and for financial reporting purposes elects to measure all of its investments at amortized cost, then the investment position of a participating government is NOT at fair value. Therefore, it is not categorized as a level 1, 2, or 3 investment in the fair value hierarchy required by GASB-72. Participating governments in this situation should first review their policy if indeed the position is really a cash equivalent. If it is not a cash equivalent, the position becomes a reconciling item to investments. In practice, the government would disclose investments as follows in accordance with GASB-72:

	Fiscal Year-End 6/30/X8	Fair Value Measurements Using		
		Quoted Prices in Active Markets for Identical Assets (Level 1)	Significant Other Observable Inputs (Level 2)	Significant Unobservable Inputs (Level 3)
Investments by fair value level				
Descriptions of various types of securities held at the reporting date	$XX	$XX	$XX	$XX
Total investments by fair value level	XX	$XX	$XX	$XX
Investments measured at the net asset value (NAV)				
Descriptions of various types of securities held at the reporting date	XX			
Total investments at the NAV	XX			
Total investments at fair value	**XX**			
Investment Derivative Instruments	XX			
Investment in External Investment Pool	XXX			
Total Investments in Statement of Net Position	**$ X,XXX**			

If participating governments have restricted investments, a further reconciliation below this table may be warranted to reconcile to the amounts in the Statement of Net Position, especially if investments are contained in a number of categories such as restricted and unrestricted.

If the external investment pool generally measures its investments at *fair value* instead of at amortized cost, in accordance with GASB-79, par. 5 or GASB-31, par. 16 [GASB Cod. Secs. In5.102, 105], the local government's position is measured at fair value, regardless if the pool transacts with participants at a floating net asset value per share or a fixed net asset value per share (e.g., $1.00). This position should not be categorized in the hierarchy, but instead would be characterized as an NAV investment and shown in the NAV section of the above table.

ACCOUNTING AND REPORTING FOR REPURCHASE/ REVERSE REPURCHASE AGREEMENTS

In addition to requiring certain disclosures for investments, and deposits with financial institutions, GASB-3 established accounting, reporting, and disclosure guidelines for repurchase and reverse repurchase agreements. Descriptions of the accounting and reporting standards follow for each specific type of agreement (GASB-3, pars. 78–83) [GASB Cod. Secs. I55.111–.119, I50.133–.134].

Repurchase Agreements

In a repurchase agreement transaction, the governmental entity (buyer-lender) transfers cash to a broker-dealer or financial institution (seller-borrower); the broker-dealer or financial institution transfers securities to the governmental entity and promises to repay the cash plus interest in exchange for the return of the *same* securities. The governmental entity should report income from repurchase agreements as interest income (GASB-3, par. 82) [GASB Cod. Secs. I50.133, I55.116].

Dollar Fixed Coupon Repurchase Agreements

These are agreements to sell and repurchase similar but not identical securities. The governmental entity should report income from dollar fixed coupon repurchase agreements as interest income (GASB-3, par. 81) [GASB Cod. Sec. I55.115].

Dollar Yield Maintenance Repurchase Agreements

These are transactions involving the sale of securities by one party to another, subject to an agreement that at a specified date or in specified circumstances the purchaser will deliver securities for repurchase by the seller that may bear a different contract interest rate than the securities sold but that will provide the selling institution with a yield similar to the yield on the securities sold. When a governmental entity enters into a dollar yield maintenance repurchase agreement, the transaction should be accounted for as a purchase and sale of securities with an appropriate recognition of a gain or loss at the time of the sale of the securities (GASB-3, par. 83) [GASB Cod. Secs. I50.134, I55.119].

Dollar Fixed Coupon Reverse Repurchase Agreements

The governmental entity should report assets and liabilities arising from dollar fixed coupon reverse repurchase agreements as separate line items in its balance sheet. The liability account should be reported as a debt of a governmental fund and identified as obligations under reverse repurchase agreements. The assets should be reported as investments (GASB-3, par. 82) [GASB Cod. Secs. I50.133, I55.116].

Dollar Yield Maintenance Reverse Repurchase Agreements

When a governmental entity enters into a dollar yield maintenance reverse repurchase agreement, the transaction should be accounted for as a sale and purchase of securities with an appropriate recognition of a gain or loss at the time of the sale of the securities (GASB-3, par. 83) [GASB Cod. Secs. I50.134, I55.119].

Reverse Repurchase Agreements

Governmental entities sometimes enter into reverse repurchase agreements when they want to temporarily convert securities in their portfolios to cash. In these transactions, the governmental entity is a seller-borrower who transfers securities to the buyer-lender for cash, and promises to repay cash plus interest in exchange for the return of the same securities. The cash obtained in these transactions is often used for operating or capital purposes or is invested in other securities to improve yield.

The governmental entity should report assets and liabilities arising from reverse repurchase agreements as separate line items in its balance sheet. The liability account should be reported as a debt of a governmental fund and identified as "obligations under reverse repurchase agreements." The assets should be reported as investments (GASB-3, par. 81) [GASB Cod. Sec. I55.115].

Disclosures for reverse repurchase agreements as of the balance sheet date depend on whether the transaction is based on a yield maintenance agreement (GASB-3, pars. 78–79) [GASB Cod. Secs. I55.111–.112].

Yield Maintenance Agreement

In a yield maintenance agreement, the securities to be returned to the governmental entity provide a yield specified in the agreement. The following disclosures should be made for commitments to repurchase securities based on yield maintenance reverse repurchase agreements as of the balance sheet date (GASB-3, par. 79) [GASB Cod. Sec. I55.112]:

- The fair value of securities to be repurchased at the balance sheet date; and
- A description of the terms of the agreement.

Other Agreements

For all reverse repurchase agreements outstanding as of the balance sheet date, other than yield maintenance agreements, the total amounts of the obligation under the agreements (including accrued interest) and the total fair value of the securities related to the agreements should be disclosed. The difference between the two amounts is a measure of the credit risk exposure for the governmental entity in reverse repurchase agreements (GASB-3, pars. 78–79) [GASB Cod. Secs. I55.111–.112].

Losses from reverse repurchase agreements because of defaults by counterparties, and subsequent recovery of such losses, should be disclosed either in the governmental entity's operating statement or in notes to the financial statements (GASB-3, par. 80) [GASB Cod. Sec. I55.113].

GASBI-3 requires that a governmental entity disclose whether the maturity dates of investments made with proceeds from reverse repurchase agreements are generally matched with the maturity dates of the related reverse repurchase agreements during the accounting period. The degree to which such matching occurs as of the balance sheet date also must be disclosed (GASBI-3, par. 6) [GASB Cod. Sec. I55.114].

Also, GASBI-3 notes that disclosures made by pension plans relative to paragraph 80 of GASB-3 are no substitute for the disclosure requirements established by paragraph 29 of GASB-25 (GASBI-3, par. 5) [GASB Cod. Sec. I55.113].

Legal or Contractual Provisions for Reverse Repurchase Agreements

If reverse repurchase agreements were used during the period, the governmental entity should disclose the source of legal or contractual authorization for the transactions. Also, significant violations of restrictions related to reverse repurchase agreements should be disclosed (GASB-3, pars. 76–77) [GASB Cod. Secs. I55.109–.110].

Reverse Repurchase Agreements and Investment Pools

Some governmental entities may combine their resources from various funds into one investment pool, and that investment pool in turn may enter into reverse repurchase agreements. Under this circumstance, the investment pool must allocate the assets and liabilities that arise from the reverse repurchase agreement to the individual funds based on each fund's equity in the pool. In addition, cost incurred and income earned based on reverse repurchase agreements made by the investment pool should be allocated to the participating funds' operating statements based on their respective equity interest in the investment pool.

ACCOUNTING AND REPORTING FOR SECURITIES LENDING TRANSACTIONS

As part of the management of its cash and investments, a governmental entity may enter into a "securities lending transaction," which the GASB defines as follows:

> Transactions in which governmental entities transfer their securities to broker-dealers and other entities for collateral—which may be cash, securities, or letters of credit—and simultaneously agree to return the collateral for the same securities in the future (GASB-28, par. 18) [GASB Cod. Sec. I60.513].

The accounting standards for securities lending transactions apply to all funds and the government-wide financial statements. The standards established by GASB-28 apply to all governmental entities that have entered into securities lending transactions during the accounting period for which financial statements are being prepared.

Securities lending transactions are generally entered into by large governmental entities, such as pension funds and investment pools that have significant resources to invest for extended periods. Due to the risk and the administration of securities lending transactions, many smaller governmental entities are precluded by law from consummating such transactions.

In a securities lending transaction, the governmental entity (lender) transfers its investments in securities, referred to as the underlying securities, to a broker-dealer (borrower), and the entity receives cash, other securities, or letters of credit. The purpose of the transaction is to enhance the return on the governmental entity's portfolio. For example, cash collateral may be received by the entity and subsequently invested. If the investment income exceeds the amount paid (interest) to the broker-dealer, the governmental entity will earn a net profit on the transaction; however, if the return is less than the amount paid, a net loss will occur. From the broker-dealer perspective, the securities are borrowed to cover short positions in specific securities.

At the end of the securities lending transaction, the governmental entity will return the collateral (the cash, securities or similar securities, or letter of credit) to the broker-dealer, and the broker-dealer will return the underlying securities (or similar securities) to the entity. Although the governmental entity can deal directly with a broker-dealer, securities lending transactions are usually executed through a "securities lending agent," which GASB-28 (*Accounting and Financial Reporting for Securities Lending Transactions*) defines as "an entity that arranges the terms and conditions of loans, monitors the fair values of the securities lent and the collateral received, and often directs the investment of cash collateral." (GASB-28, par. 18, as amended by GASB-31, par. 6) [GASB Cod. Sec. I60.512].

Securities lending transactions raise the fundamental question of whether the governmental entity has incurred a liability that should be presented on its balance sheet or statement of net position. GASB-28 addresses that fundamental question, along with disclosure requirements.

The disclosure requirements established by GASB-28 apply to the primary government and its blended component units. For component units that are discretely presented, the disclosure guidance established by GASB-14, as amended must be observed (GASB-28, par. 4, as amended by GASB-34, par. 6) [GASB Cod. Sec. I60.102]. For component unit disclosures presented as part of the primary government's notes to the basic financial statements, care must be taken by the preparer to determine which disclosures are *essential*. In some cases, professional judgment may determine that such component unit disclosures are not essential (GASB-28, fn. 2) [GASB Cod. Sec. I60.fn2].

Accounting and Reporting Standards

For all securities lending transactions, the governmental entity should report the underlying securities (the securities loaned to the broker-dealer) as assets in its balance sheet. Although the underlying securities are transferred to the broker-dealer, they are nonetheless reported as an asset of the governmental entity. Additional accounting treatment for the transaction depends on whether the governmental entity receives (1) cash, (2) securities that can be pledged or sold, (3) securities that cannot be pledged or sold, or (4) letters of credit (GASB-28, par. 5) [GASB Cod. Sec. I60.103].

Receipt of Cash

When a governmental entity transfers securities to a broker-dealer or other entity and receives cash as collateral, the securities lending transaction should be recorded as a secured loan. A liability should be recognized, and the transferred securities should not be removed from the governmental entity's balance sheet and/or statement of net position (GASB-28, par. 6, GASB-72, par. 64) [GASB Cod. Sec. I60.104].

In transactions that involve cash collateral, the broker-dealer is paid interest (borrower rebate) on the amount it advances to the governmental entity. The government uses the cash to earn investment income by depositing the funds with a financial institution or by purchasing securities. The profitability of the transaction from the governmental entity's perspective depends on the rate of return on the collateral invested and the interest paid to the broker-dealer.

GASB-3 defines a "reverse repurchase agreement" as "an agreement in which a broker-dealer or financial institution (buyer/lender) transfers cash to a governmental entity (seller/borrower); the entity transfers securities to the broker-dealer or financial institution and promises to repay the cash plus interest in exchange for the same securities" (GASB-3, par. 116) [GASB Cod. Sec. I50.561]. On the basis of this definition, the GASB states that a reverse repurchase agreement is essentially the same (from an economic perspective, not a legal and tax perspective) as a securities lending transaction in which cash collateral is received by the governmental entity. GASB-3 requires that reverse repurchase agreements be accounted for as secured loans and not as sales of the securities that are the basis for the transaction. Thus, the accounting and disclosure standards established by GASB-28 for securities lending transactions involving cash collateral are similar to those established by GASB-3 for reverse repurchase agreement transactions.

To illustrate securities lending transactions that involve cash collateral, assume a governmental entity holds investments in U.S. governmental securities that have a cost and fair value basis of $900,000. These securities are transferred to a broker-dealer for cash of $927,000, with the requirement that the securities be returned to the governmental entity at the end of five days. The entity would make the following entry to record the securities lending transaction:

	Debit	Credit
Cash	927,000	—
Liability under Securities Lending Transaction	—	927,000

The securities transferred to the broker-dealer remain on the statement of net position or the balance sheet of the governmental entity. As illustrated in the example, the governmental entity records the cash collateral received from the broker-dealer and will subsequently record any securities or deposits acquired or made using the cash collateral as an asset.

GASB-28 points out that the governmental entity may receive cash (collateral) from a broker-dealer that cannot be invested in securities (only deposited). When this restriction is imposed, the securities lending transactions "should be accounted for as involving securities collateral rather than cash collateral." Accounting for the receipt of securities collateral is discussed in the following section (GASB-28, fn. 4) [GASB Cod. Sec. I60.fn4].

Receipt of Securities That Can Be Pledged or Sold

When a governmental entity transfers securities to a broker-dealer and receives securities that can be pledged or sold, even if the borrower has not defaulted on the transaction, the securities lending transaction should be recorded as a secured loan in a manner similar to a collateral transaction previously illustrated (asset and liability accounts are created). The broker-dealer pays the governmental entity a loan premium or fee for the loan of the securities (GASB-28, par. 6, GASB-72, par. 64) [GASB Cod. Sec. I60.104].

GASB-28 states that the right to pledge or sell collateral securities without a borrower default must be stated in the securities lending transaction. However, that right could exist for purposes of GASB-28, if the right has been previously demonstrated by pledging or selling securities under a previous contract that did not contain the explicit right. Also, the right could exist if "there is some other indication of the ability to pledge or sell the collateral securities." A borrower default would include failure to return underlying securities, pay income distributions, or make margin calls; acts of insolvency; and suspension by the Securities and Exchange Commission, an exchange, or a self-regulatory association (GASB-28, fn.5) [GASB Cod. Sec. I60.fn5].

In a securities lending transaction that involves securities as collateral, the broker-dealer receives certain incidents of ownership over the underlying securities during the term of the transaction, including the right to sell or pledge the securities. The governmental entity also receives certain incidents of ownership over the collateral securities. Although both parties have certain ownership rights over the securities they hold (the underlying securities and the collateral securities), each has income distribution rights as described by GASB-28 as follows (GASB-28, par. 18) [GASB Cod. Sec. I60.508]:

> Interest, dividends, stock splits, and other distributions made by an issuer of securities. Income distributions on underlying securities are payable from the borrower to the lender, and income distributions on collateral securities are payable from the lender to the borrower.

Thus, the governmental entity has distribution rights on the underlying securities and the broker-dealer has distribution rights on the collateral securities.

To illustrate this type of securities lending transaction, assume that in the previous example the governmental entity received investments in corporate fixed-income securities that have a fair value of $927,000, with the requirement that the underlying securities be returned to the governmental entity at the end of five days. The governmental entity would make the following entry to record the securities lending transaction:

	Debit	Credit
Investments in Corporate Fixed-Income Securities	927,000	—
Liability under Securities Lending Transaction	—	927,000

Both the securities transferred to the broker-dealer (underlying securities) and the securities received from the broker-dealer (collateral securities) are reported on the statement of net position and balance sheet of the governmental entity. The reporting of underlying securities on the balance sheet of the governmental entity is necessary because the securities lending transaction is considered to be a loan of securities and not a sale. At the termination date of the transaction, the governmental entity receives the same or similar securities from the broker-dealer. The reporting of the collateral securities is necessary because the governmental entity is entitled to the risk and rewards of these securities during the term of the contract. The governmental entity can sell or pledge the securities, but at the end of the transaction it must return similar securities to the broker-dealer. If, for example, the collateral securities are sold at one price and their value rises before the governmental entity must return similar securities to the broker-dealer, the governmental entity will have an economic loss on the investment.

Receipt of Securities That Cannot Be Pledged or Sold

When a governmental entity transfers securities to a broker-dealer and receives securities that cannot be pledged or sold unless the borrower defaults, the securities lending transaction is not recorded in the general ledger by the governmental entity. Thus, investment and liability accounts are not created by the transaction. In this type of securities lending transaction, the GASB has concluded that the government's control over the collateral securities is so limited that it would be inappropriate to record the transaction as a secured loan.

Receipt of Letters of Credit

In a letter of credit, a financial institution guarantees specified payments of a customer's draft for a designated period of time. When a governmental entity transfers securities to a broker-dealer and receives a letter of credit, the securities lending transaction is not recorded by the governmental entity (GASB-28, par. 7) [GASB Cod. Sec. I60.105].

Transaction Costs

Costs incurred by a governmental entity in executing a securities lending transaction should be reported as an expenditure/expense in the governmental entity's operating statement (statement of revenues, expenditures and changes in fund balances, statement of activities, etc.). GASB-28 states that such costs include the following (GASB-28, par. 8) [GASB Cod. Sec. I60.106]:

- *Borrower rebates* Payments from the lender to the borrower as compensation for the use of the cash collateral provided by the borrower. [Borrower rebates are to be reported as interest expenditure/expense.]

- *Agent fees* Amounts paid by a lender to its securities lending agent as compensation for managing its securities lending transactions.

Transaction costs should not be netted against income (interest income, investment income, loan premiums or fees, or any other income that arises from the securities lending transaction). GASB-28 provides the following definition of "loan premiums or fees" (GASB-28, par. 18) [GASB Cod. Sec. I60.511]:

Payments from the borrower to the lender as compensation for the use of the underlying securities when the borrower provides securities or letters of credit as collateral.

GASB-28 requires investment expenses to be reported in the additions section (as a reduction to the total of investment income) of the statement of changes in fiduciary net position of a defined benefit plan (GASB-28, fn. 7, as amended by GASB-63, par. 8, GASB-67, par. 26, and GASB-73, pars. 115–116) [GASB Cod. Sec. I60.fn7].

Governmental Investment Pools and Securities Lending Transactions

Some governmental entities combine resources from their various funds into an investment pool, and the investment pool in turn may enter into securities lending transactions as defined by GASB-28. Thus, such transactions may create assets and liabilities that must be reported by the governmental entity (when cash or securities that may be sold or pledged with a borrower default are received as collateral). Under this circumstance, the investment pool must allocate the assets and liabilities that arise from the securities lending transactions to the individual funds based on each fund's equity in the pool (GASB-28, par. 9, as amended by GASB-34, par. 15) [GASB Cod. Sec. I60.107].

GASB-28 requires such an allocation because an internal investment pool usually is not reported as a separate fund in a governmental entity's financial statements. Thus, the investment pool must observe the standards established by GASB-28 so that it has sufficient information to make the allocation to the various funds based on the relative equity position of each participating fund. Under this approach, the fund "that has the risk of loss on the collateral assets" will report its appropriate share of assets and liabilities related to securities lending transactions entered into by the governmental investment pool.

Costs incurred and income earned based on securities lending transactions made by the investment pool should be recorded by the investment pool based on the standards established by GASB-28. In turn, those cost and income amounts should be allocated to the participating funds based on their respective equity interest in the investment pool (GASB-28, par. 10, as amended by GASB-34, pars. 15 and 112) [GASB Cod. Sec. I60.108].

The standards established by GASB-28 apply only to the entities that make up the governmental reporting entity (the primary government and its components) and not to legally separate (outside) entities that participate in the investment pool.

Disclosure Standards

Generally, governmental entities are restricted as to how resources may be invested. Restrictions may be based on legal or contractual provisions. GASB-28 requires that the following be disclosed with respect to securities lending transactions (GASB-28, pars. 11–15, GASB-40, pars. 9–10, as amended by GASB-63, par. 8):

- Basis of authorization (legal or contractual authorization) for entering into securities lending transactions;
- Significant violations of the basis of authorization because securities lending transactions were executed during the accounting period;
- General description of securities lending transactions including:
    - Types of securities loaned by the governmental entity;
    - Types of collateral received by the governmental entity;

— Whether the governmental entity has the right to sell or pledge securities received as collateral without a borrower default;

— Amount by which the value of the securities received as collateral exceeds the value of the securities loaned by the governmental entity;

— Restrictions on the amount of securities that can be loaned; and

— Carrying value and fair value of the underlying securities (the securities loaned by the governmental entity to the broker-dealer) at the balance sheet date;

• Description of loss indemnification (a securities lending agent's guarantee that it will protect the lender from certain losses) provided by the securities lending agent (an entity that arranges the terms and conditions of loans, monitors the fair value of the securities lent and the collateral received, and often directs the invest of cash collateral);

• Statement of whether the maturity dates of investments made with cash collateral received from broker-dealers match the maturity dates of the related securities loans;

• The extent to which maturity dates of investments made with cash collateral received from broker-dealers match the maturity date of the related securities loans as of the balance sheet date;

• Amount of losses from default of a borrower or lending agent for the year related to securities lending transactions;

• Amount of losses recovered from defaults in previous periods; and

• Amount of credit risk (if any) as of the date of the balance sheet (if no credit risk exists, that fact should be stated in the disclosure).

The disclosure requirement relating to the matching of maturing dates can be a general description rather than a detailed listing of maturity dates. The following are three illustrative general descriptions provided in GASB-28:

1. The policy is to match the maturities of the collateral investments and the securities loans and that at year-end all securities loans could be terminated on demand by either the entity or the borrower and that substantially all cash collateral was invested in overnight or on-demand investments. (Disclosure explains how maturities are matched.)

2. Substantially all securities loans can be terminated on demand either by the entity or by the borrower, although generally the average term of these loans is one week; cash collateral is invested in securities of a longer term, generally with maturities between one week and three months. (Disclosure explains how maturities are not matched.)

3. At year-end, 50% of the collateral investments were in maturities of less than one week, and the weighted-average term to maturity of all collateral investments was 35 days. (Disclosure explains how maturities are not matched.)

GASB-28, as amended by GASB-40, defines "credit risk" as "the risk that an insurer or other counter party to an investment will not fill its obligations." (GASB-28, par. 18, GASB-40, par. 19) [GASB Cod. Sec. I60.507]. For securities lending, credit risk is the aggregate of the lender's exposures to the borrowers of its securities. Thus, the governmental entity has credit risk with respect to the broker-dealer when the amount the broker-dealer owes the governmental entity exceeds the amount the governmental entity owes the broker-dealer. To calculate credit risk, the governmental entity must consider the extent, if any, to which the right of offset exists in the case of the broker-dealer, where "offset" refers to the legal right a party has to offset amounts due to and due from another party in the case of default.

To compute the amount owed to the governmental entity, the following must be considered:

1. the fair value of the underlying securities (including accrued interest),
2. unpaid income distributions on the underlying securities, and
3. accrued loan premiums or fees due from the broker-dealer.

To compute the amount owed the broker-dealer, the following must be considered:

1. the cash collateral received,
2. the fair value of collateral securities received (including accrued interest),
3. the face value of letters of credit,
4. unpaid income distributions on collateral securities held by the governmental entity, and
5. accrued borrower rebates payable to the broker-dealer.

Generally, the governmental entity initially does not have a credit risk because the fair value of collateral received from the broker-dealer is usually a few percentage points greater than the value of the underlying securities loaned to the broker-dealer. For purposes of the transaction (not for financial reporting), the underlying securities and the collateral securities (but not the securities purchased by cash collateral) are marked-to-market each day and the agreement may require that the broker-dealer provide additional collateral if the fair value of the collateral falls below the fair value of the underlying securities.

Collateral Securities and Underlying Securities

The carrying amounts and fair values of both collateral securities reported on the governmental entity's balance sheet and underlying securities that are the basis for securities lending transactions should be disclosed (based on the requirements of paragraph 9 of GASB-40). Also, collateral securities reported on the governmental entity's balance sheet should be classified, as required by GASB-3, as amended by GASB-40, par. 9.

Collateral securities arising from securities lending transactions should be classified according to the current scheme, unless the collateral securities are part of a "collateral investment pool," which is defined as follows by GASB-28 (GASB-28, par. 18) [GASB Cod. Sec. I60.506]:

> An agent-managed pool that for investment purposes commingles the cash collateral provided on the securities lending transactions of more than one lender.

Underlying securities are not subject to custodial credit risk if the related custodial securities are presented in the governmental entity's balance sheet (and therefore the related custodial securities are evaluated to determine whether they are subject to custodial credit risk as defined in GASB-40). However, underlying securities are subject to custodial risk when the related custodial securities are not presented in the governmental entity's balance sheet (and therefore are not subject to custodial risk disclosures), in which case the determination of whether they are subject to custodial risk is based on the type of collateral that supports the underlying securities.

Cash Collateral Held as Deposits

Deposits with financial institutions (including cash collateral held as deposits) must be evaluated for the possible need for custodial credit risk disclosures based on the guidance established by paragraph 8 of GASB-40.

ACCOUNTING AND REPORTING FOR DERIVATIVE INSTRUMENTS

For many state and local government financial statement preparers, auditors, and users, the concepts and terminology associated with derivative instruments is relatively unfamiliar and difficult to fully understand.

Definition of Derivative Instruments

A derivative is a financial instrument or arrangement, often complex in nature, whereby two parties agree to make payments to each other under different obligation scenarios (e.g., by utilizing an "interest rate swap"). Governments normally enter into derivatives for the following reasons:

- To generate additional investment income (mainly with postemployment benefit plans);
- To fix prices to better manage cash flows;
- To lower borrowing costs; and
- To potentially minimize or mitigate a certain risk.

GASB-53 (*Accounting and Financial Reporting for Derivative Instruments*) states that for the purposes of state and local government accounting and financial reporting, its derivative standards apply to financial arrangements that have values or cash payments based on what happens in separate transactions, agreements, or rates and that has *all* three of the following characteristics:

1. The financial arrangement contains settlement factors that determine the amount of the settlement, and, in some cases, whether or not a settlement is required. Settlement factors include the reference rate (e.g., rate and swap indexes), the notional amount (e.g., number of currency units, shares, pounds), and a payment provision (e.g., a provision for a payment to be made if a reference rate behaves in a certain manner).

2. The financial arrangements are leveraged (i.e., they require no initial investment on the part of the government or an initial investment that is

small relative to what would otherwise be required to obtain the same results in the market).

3. The financial arrangements have net settlement terms whereby the arrangements can be or are required to be settled net by means outside the contract such as by cash payment, or it provides for delivery of an asset that puts the recipient in a position not substantially different from net settlement (GASB-53, par. 7) [GASB Cod. Sec. D40.103].

The scope of GASB-53 excludes the following types of financial instruments:

• Derivative instruments that represent normal purchases and sales contracts (e.g., commodity purchases where it is probable the government will take or make delivery of the commodity);

• Nonperformance guarantees on contracts that are dependent on the failure of a counterparty to fulfill the contract terms;

• Insurance contracts accounted for in accordance with GASB-10 (*Accounting and Financial Reporting for Risk Financing and Related Insurance Issues*) or that are similar to contracts in accordance with a claim or a judgment;

• Certain financial guarantee contracts, *unless they are entered into as an investment derivative instrument.* (Guarantees, for example, may be a loan guarantee that provides for the government to make payments if the debtor defaults or fails to meet a debt covenant. They could also include a federal guarantee that protects a university from loss in its student loans, a guarantee that a state provides for the nonpayment of debt of a private corporation or bond insurance where the government pays the premium, the bond insurance is associated with the government's debt, and the debt holder is the beneficiary.);

• Certain contracts that are not exchange-traded (e.g., contracts that provide for the payment of liquidated damages if a party fails to perform under the contract);

• Revenue-based contracts that are not exchange-traded and have reference rates based on sales or service levels or volumes; and

• Loan commitments (e.g., a loan commitment extended by a government housing finance authority to potential home buyers meeting specific criteria) (GASB-53, par. 4) [GASB Cod. Sec. D40.101].

IMPORTANT NOTE: These exclusions are often confused with *investment derivative instruments*, which are derivatives entered into for the purpose of income or profit and are potentially part of the scope of GASB-53.

To understand what a normal purchases and sales contract is, GASB's *Implementation Guide 2015-1*, question 10.3.4 [GASB Cod. Sec. D40.702-4], provides the following example that would meet the normal purchases and normal sales scope exception: A government enters into a take-or-pay contract for a commodity (e.g., a utility contract for an amount of electricity). Under this contract, the government agrees to pay a specified price for a specified quantity of the commodity (the electricity), whether or not it takes delivery. The government uses the commodity in its operations, and the quantity specified in the contract is consistent with the government's activities. It is probable that the government will take delivery of the commodity specified in the contract. This form of take-or-pay contract generally meets the definition of a derivative instrument. However, as long as the government plans on taking delivery and the quantity specified is consistent with what is used in the government's operations, for example when the government is a public utility, the contract qualifies for the normal purchases and sales scope exception and should not be reported according to the requirements of GASB-53.

Types of Derivative Instruments

A typical derivative instrument is leveraged in that it is entered into with little or no initial payment, contains settlement factors that determine the amount of settlement, can be settled with a cash payment or the transfer of an equivalent asset, and has a value based on a separate transaction or agreement. In other words, the cash flows and fair values of derivative instruments are determined by changing market prices, such as bond or commodity prices or indexes. Some derivative instruments may even provide an up-front cash payment to a government. Common types of derivative instruments used by governments include interest rate and commodity swaps, interest rate locks, options, swaptions, forward contracts, and futures contracts. Examples of derivative instruments are as follows (GASB-53, par. 82) [GASB Cod. Secs. D40.501–.561]:

Type of Derivative	Description of the Derivative
Commodity swaps	Commodity swaps are contracts that have a variable payment based on the price or index of an underlying commodity.
Forward contracts	Forward contracts are agreements to buy or sell a security, commodity, foreign currency, or other financial instrument at a certain future date for a specific price. An agreement with a supplier to purchase a quantity of heating oil at a certain future time, for a certain price, and a certain quantity is an example of a forward contract. Forward contracts are not securities and are not exchange-traded. Some forward contracts may be settled by a cash payment that is equal to the fair value of the contract rather than delivery of a commodity or financial instrument.
Futures contract	A government could enter into an agreement to buy or sell an actively traded product or commodity (e.g., fuel) for a specified price on a specific future date in order to protect against future increases in the commodity prices. For example, a government-owned utility might enter into a futures contract to lock in a price for the purchase of energy (e.g., electricity or natural gas) without ever having to buy the energy.

Type of Derivative	Description of the Derivative
Interest rate swap	A government may enter into an agreement to attempt to lower its borrowing costs. In this type of derivative, a government that has issued variable-rate debt also enters into an interest rate swap in which it agrees to pay a steady interest rate to a financial firm (usually a higher rate of interest than it currently pays on the variable-rate debt). In return, the financial firm agrees to pay the government an amount (that changes as market interest rates change), which is expected to offset the government's interest payments due to the bond or debt holders. Not only are the cash flows of an interest rate swap (i.e., the payments between the government and the financial firm) determined by changing market interest rates, but the value of the derivative also changes.
Interest rate lock	An agreement could be entered into between a government and a lender to lock interest rates to protect from rising interest rates between the time of the agreement and the time of actual debt issuance. (This is used similarly in rate locks for home mortgages.)
Options (such as calls, puts, collars, floors, and swaptions)	Options are contracts or securities that give their holders the right but not the obligation to buy or sell a financial instrument or commodity at a certain price for a certain period of time.

GASB's *Implementation Guide 2015-1,* question 10.9.1 [GASB Cod. Sec. D40.706-9], distinguishes insurance contracts from derivative instruments. Insurance contracts may resemble derivative instruments because they are entered to manage risk, payments are based on the occurrence of specific events, and casualty payments may be significant compared to the initial net investment (the insurance premium). An insurance contract is not a derivative instrument if it entitles the holder to be compensated only if as a result of an identifiable insurable event (other than a change in price) the holder incurs a liability or there is an adverse change in the value of a specific asset or liability for which the holder is at risk. For example, the following types of contracts written by insurance enterprises, including public-entity risk pools, or held by the insured parties are not within the scope of GASB-53:

- Traditional life insurance contracts (the payment of death benefits is the result of an identifiable insurable event (death of the insured) instead of changes in a variable); and

- Traditional property and casualty contracts (the payment of benefits is the result of an identifiable insurable event (e.g., theft or fire) instead of changes in a variable.

Derivative instruments can generally be classified by their primary objectives into one of the following two categories:

1. *Hedging derivative instrument* - A derivative instrument associated with a hedgeable item that is effective by significantly reducing an identified financial risk by substantially offsetting changes in cash flows or fair values of the hedgeable item (e.g., an interest rate swap).

2. *Investment derivative instrument* - A derivative instrument that is entered into primarily for the purpose of obtaining income or profit or that does not meet the criteria of a hedging derivative. These are sometimes classified as part of *alternative investments*, which may include private equity funds or similar funds (GASB-53, par. 82, as amended by GASB-72, par. 64) [GASB Cod. Secs. D40.526, .534].

Risks Associated with Hedging Derivative Instruments

Although hedging derivative instruments can be a valuable component of the financial management of an entity and can help a government manage or hedge a specific risk, they can also present significant other risks to the government that could affect its liquidity and investment performance. A hedging derivative instrument significantly reduces financial risk by substantially offsetting changes in the cash flows (a cash flow hedge) or fair values (a fair value hedge) of an associated item that is eligible to be hedged. GASB-53 provides guidance in applying acceptable methods for testing whether a derivative instrument meets this effectively hedged definition. GASB-53 provides for the deferring of changes in the fair value of the hedged derivative instrument if it is effectively hedged.

Risks associated with hedging derivative instruments include:

Risks Associated with Hedging Derivative Instruments	Explanation of Risks
Credit risk	The risk that the counterparty to the agreement will not fulfill its terms. For example, a failure to meet a promise to pay the government when required.
Interest rate risk	The risk that changes in interest rates will adversely affect the fair value of the government's financial instrument or its cash flows. For example, the longer the term of the derivative, the greater the chance of a decline in the value of the derivative due to changing interest rates.
Termination risk	The risk that a derivative may end earlier than originally expected, resulting in a potential termination payment requirement by the government or its asset or liability management strategy. For example, the unscheduled termination of an interest rate swap may subject the government to increasing interest rate payments.
Basis risk	The risk that arises when variable rates or prices of the hedging derivative instrument and the hedged item are based on different reference rates. For example, the risk that the basis for the government's payment (generally from an international rate index, such as the London Interbank Offered Rate [LIBOR]) may cause the government's payment out to be in excess of its received payments from the counterparty.
Rollover risk	The risk that the derivative instrument term does not last as long as the maturity of the associated hedged item, thereby ending the government's risk protection when the derivative ends. For example, an interest rate swap agreement term may be 15 years and the term of the hedged debt is 30 years.

Risks Associated with Hedging Derivative Instruments	Explanation of Risks
Market-access risk	The risk that a government will not be able to enter the credit markets or do so in a cost-effective manner. For example, a derivative instrument may involve the planned issuance of debt (e.g., a debt refunding) by the government at a certain time in the future; however, the government may be unable to issue the debt or doing so will become more expensive than when it was planned.
Foreign currency risk	The risk that changes in exchange rates would adversely affect the fair value of a derivative or cash flows of the government.

Risks Associated with Investment Derivative Instruments

Investment derivative instruments can be effective in generating income or profit for the government; however, they also carry certain risks of loss, including credit risk, interest rate risk, and foreign currency risk, as discussed above.

Accounting and Reporting Standards Overview

With certain exceptions, GASB-53 generally requires that derivatives covered by its scope be reported in the government's accrual-based financial statements at fair value. The fair value of a derivative instrument as of the end of the period is to be reported in the statement of net position of the government-wide financial statements and the proprietary and fiduciary fund financial statements. Changes in fair value should be reported in the flow of resources statements (such as the statement of activities; statement of revenues, expenses, and changes in net position; or statement of changes in fiduciary net position) as investment gains or losses except for the annual changes in the fair value of a hedging derivative instrument that *is effective*. Fair value changes associated with *effective hedges* should be reported as deferred inflows or outflows on the statements of net position (GASB-53, pars. 19–20, as amended by GASB-63, par. 8) [GASB Cod. Secs. D40.115–.116].

The GASB provided for reporting of fair value and changes in fair value for derivative instruments only in accrual-based financial statements (government-wide, proprietary and fiduciary funds), and not in governmental funds that are reported on the modified accrual basis of accounting and current financial resources measurement focus.

Except in governmental funds, GASB-53 requires derivative instruments (both those resulting in assets and those resulting in liabilities) to be reported on the statement of net position at fair value. The key to understanding the recognition and measurement of changes in fair value of a derivative instrument is determining whether the instrument is an *effectively hedged* derivative and therefore subject to hedge accounting. Hedge accounting involves the deferral of changes in fair value in the statement of net position as deferred inflows or outflows. If a derivative instrument is an investment derivative instrument or not an effectively hedged derivative instrument, then changes in fair value should be reported within the investment revenue or income classification in the flow-of resources statement.

GASB Implementation Guide 2016-1, question 4.67 [GASB Cod. Sec. D40.708-2], discusses the accounting and financial reporting treatment when a derivative instrument that ceases to meet the criteria of a hedging derivative instrument becomes an investment derivative instrument and, as such, falls under investment derivative instrument disclosure requirements. In addition to the disclosure requirements of GASB-40 the investment derivative disclosure requirements of GASB-53 should be applied. GASB-72, paragraph 80c, refers back to GASB-53 for the fair value disclosure elements of investment derivative instruments.

Hedge Accounting

When a derivative instrument significantly reduces financial risk by substantially offsetting the changes in the cash flows (a cash flow hedge) or fair values (a fair value hedge) of an associated item (hedgeable item) that is eligible to be hedged, the hedge is considered effective and hedge accounting should be applied. GASB-53 provides guidance in applying acceptable methods for testing whether a derivative instrument meets this definition of effectively hedged. The GASB states that for a derivative to be considered effectively hedged (i.e., a hedging derivative instrument), both of the following criteria must be met:

1. The derivative is associated with an item that is eligible to be hedged (e.g., a hedgeable item). Association involves:

   a. A notional amount of the derivative instrument that is consistent with the principal amount or quantity of the hedgeable item.

   b. Reporting the derivative instrument in the same fund as the hedgeable item.

   c. A term or time period of the derivative instrument is consistent with the term or time period of the hedgeable item.

   d. A hedgeable item that is not reported in the financial statements at fair value.

2. The government demonstrates the potential hedging derivative's effectiveness using one of three approaches: (1) consistent critical terms, (2) synthetic instruments, or (3) quantitative techniques. In other words, the changes in cash flows or fair values of the potential hedging derivative substantially offset the changes in cash flows or fair values of the hedgeable item (GASB-53, par. 27) [GASB Cod. Sec. D40.123].

GASB-53 states that a government should evaluate the effectiveness of a potential hedging derivative instrument as of "the end of each reporting period." *GASB Implementation Guide 2015-1, question 10.20.1* [GASB Cod. Sec. 711-1], clarifies how effectiveness should be evaluated at the end of each reporting period for which financial statements are prepared in conformity with U.S. generally accepted accounting principles (U.S. GAAP). For example, if a government issues annual U.S. GAAP financial statements, the evaluation should be performed as of the end of the year.

Four methods are available for determining if a hedge is effective. The *consistent critical terms method* utilizes mainly *qualitative* analysis, allowing the practitioner to easily understand the terms and conditions of the hedgeable item (e.g., a variable rate debt issue) and the terms and conditions of the potential hedging derivative.

In the consistent critical terms method, the terms and conditions of the hedgeable item and the potential hedging derivative instrument are the same, *or similar* in such a way that the changes in cash flows or fair values will offset. This method is commonly used for *interest rate swaps—cash flow hedges, interest rate swaps—fair value hedges* and *forward contracts*.

1. *Interest Rate Swaps—Cash Flow Hedges*—to be effective under the consistent critical terms method, all the following must be met:

   a. The notional amount of the derivative is the same as the principal amount of the hedgeable item throughout the life of the item, even if it amortizes.

   b. The swap must have a zero fair value upon association.

   c. The formula for computing net settlements is the same throughout the swap.

   d. The reference rate is consistent with either a reference rate or payment of the hedgeable item (such as a cost of funds swap) or a benchmark rate (such as a percentage of LIBOR).

   e. The interest flows (receipts or payments) occur during the term of the hedgeable item and not after.

   f. There are no floors or caps for the swap unless the hedgeable item has a floor or cap.

   g. The maturity or time interval of the swap is the same as the hedgeable item (e.g., a variable rate debt that resets interest rates every seven days according to a seven-day swap index).

   h. The frequency of the rate rests are the same (e.g., every seven days).

   i. Swap payments settle within 15 days of the payments of the hedgeable item. (GASB-53, par. 37) [GASB Cod. Sec. D40.133].

2. *Interest Rate Swaps—Fair Value Hedges*—To be effective under the consistent critical terms method, all must be present:

   a. Items a.-d. above for cash flow hedges must be present.

   b. The hedgeable item is not prepayable prior to its scheduled maturity. (This does not apply to debts with call options as long as the derivative has a call option.)

   c. The expiration date of the interest rate swap is on or about the maturity date of the hedgeable item to mitigate interest rate or market risk.

   d. No floors or caps must be present.

e. The reference rate on the interest rate swap resets at least every 90 days to minimize interest rate risk (GASB-53, par. 38) [GASB Cod. Sec. D40.134].

3. *Forward Contracts*—A forward contract is effective utilizing the consistent critical terms method if all the following are met:

   a. The purchase or sale are for the same quantities between the notional item and the derivative.

   b. A zero fair value is at the point of association.

   c. The reference rate is consistent.

Any changes in discounts or premiums in forward contracts are excluded from the assessment of effectiveness. Such changes become part of investment revenue (GASB-53, par. 39) [GASB Cod. Sec. D40.135].

If the consistent critical terms method provisions cannot be met, one of three quantitative methods may be used to evaluate effectiveness. They are the *synthetic instrument method, the dollar-offset method*, and the *regression analysis method*. Other methods may be available, as long as they meet certain criteria (GASB-53, par. 40) [GASB Cod. Sec. D40.136]. In many circumstances, if the consistent critical terms method is not available, the synthetic instrument method is commonly used given its easily understood parameters and fairly wide latitude to judge effectiveness.

The *synthetic instrument method* relies on a combination of cash flows and the analysis of the cash flows to determine if the flows offset the potential hedging derivative flows. As such, all of the following must be present to be effective:

1. The notional amount of the derivative is the same as the principal amount of the hedgeable item throughout the life of the item, even if it amortizes.

2. Upon association, the hedging derivative instrument has a zero fair value, *or the forward price is "at the market."*

3. The formula for computing net settlements is the same throughout the swap.

4. The interest flows (receipts or payments) occur during the term of the hedgeable item and not after (GASB-53, par. 42) [GASB Cod. Sec. D40.138].

To accomplish this method, an interest rate must also be substantially fixed (called the *actual synthetic rate*). However, interest rates are never truly fixed. Therefore, U.S. GAAP allows the variable rate debt to adjust within a "corridor" of 90% to 111% of the fixed rate of potential hedging derivative instrument to be substantially fixed (GASB-53, par. 43) [GASB Cod. Sec. D40.139].

The *dollar-offset method* also utilizes changes in cash flows, but allows either the current period to measure changes or life-to-date. It is a similar method to the *synthetic instrument method* but allows a corridor of 80% to 125% in absolute terms of cash flows in dollars, rather than interest rates (GASB-53, par. 44) [GASB Cod. Sec. D40.140].

The *regression analysis method* considers the statistical relationship between the potential hedging derivative and the hedgeable item by comparing changes in cash flows *or* fair values and whether they offset. To be effective, a sufficient amount of data must be analysed and in many cases, sophisticated software or macros are utilized to determine the effectiveness (GASB-53, par. 45) [GASB Cod. Sec. D40.141]. In practice, the regression analysis method may require a specialist to perform the calculations.

As introduced previously, other quantitative methods are allowable by GASB-53 as long as the method demonstrates that the changes in cash flows or fair values substantially offset, the evaluation of effectiveness are complete and documented, and substantive characteristics of the hedgeable item and potential derivative are considered (GASB-53, par. 48) [GASB Cod. Sec. D40.144].

GASB-53 requires hedge accounting if a derivative instrument is effective in significantly reducing an identified financial risk. In other words, applying hedge accounting is not optional.

The GASB provided for the deferral of changes in fair value for effectively hedged derivatives (and, therefore, recognizing deferred inflows of resources or deferred outflows of resources). This is because the GASB believes it provides a better measure of interperiod equity (taxpayer benefit/burden measurement) than recognizing the fair value changes as gains or losses in the current period. The deferral of changes in fair value begins in the period that a hedging derivative instrument is established and continues until a hedging termination event occurs, at which time the deferred gains or losses are to be reported as part of investment income in that period.

The following is an illustration of hedge accounting according to the measurement and recognition requirements of GASB-53. This illustration (based upon the *Comprehensive Implementation Guide*) deals with an interest rate swap hedging derivative instrument accounted for in a proprietary fund, and it comprises example assumptions (Exhibit 9-3), example journal entries for the related transactions or events (Exhibit 9-4), and pro-forma financial statement amounts for related accounts (Exhibit 9-5) (GASB-53, Illustrations) [GASB Cod. Sec. D40.901].

EXHIBIT 9-3
DERIVATIVE ILLUSTRATION: ASSUMPTIONS

Assumptions

Objective	To hedge interest rate risks that could adversely affect cash flows on variable rate demand bonds issued by the government.
Hedged item	Variable rate demand bonds issued for $100,000,000 par amount, dated 7/1/X6 with a maturity in 6/18/Y0, variable rate index is the Securities Industry and Financial Markets Association (SIFMA) swap index, plus a state tax difference 10 basis points.

Assumptions	
Derivative instrument	Pay-fixed, receive-variable interest rate swap, with a $100,000,000 notional amount, dated 7/1/X6 with a termination date of 6/11/Y0, and pay-fixed rate of 3.807160% and variable payment based on SIFMA swap index.
Interest rate changes	From the point in time when the bonds were issued in 7/1/X6, the interest rates fell during the years the bonds were outstanding. Therefore, the fixed interest payments due to the counterparty from the government each year (3.807160%) were in excess of the variable payments (at the lower rates) due from the counterparty to the government.

Table of Payments and Receipts Counterparty Swap Payment

Fiscal Year Ended June 30,	Counterparty Swap Payment To	Counterparty Swap Payment From	Net	Interest Payments To Bondholders	Total Payments
20X7	$(3,807,160)	$1,689,314	$(2,117,846)	$(1,789,314)	$(3,907,160)
20X8	(3,807,160)	1,259,205	(2,547,955)	(1,359,205)	(3,907,160)
20X9	(3,807,160)	978,661	(2,828,499)	(1,078,661)	(3,907,160)
20Y0	(3,807,160)	1,830,405	(1,976,755)	(1,930,405)	(3,907,160)
Total	**$(15,228,640)**	**$5,757,585**	**$(9,471,055)**	**$(6,157,585)**	**$(15,628,640)**

Fair value of swap: The fair value and changes in fair value for each of the years of the swap as determined by discounted formula-based cash flow estimates were as follows:

	Fair Value Change	Fair Value at Fiscal Year-End
Fair value at 7/1/X6		$0
Decrease in fair value in X7	(2,984,833)	
Fair value at 6/30/X7		(2,984,833)
Decrease in fair value in X8	(1,801,798)	
Fair value at 6/30/X8		(4,786,631)
Increase in fair value in X9	2,877,893	
Fair value at 6/30/X9		(1,908,738)
Increase in fair value in Y0	1,908,738	
Fair value at 6/11/Y0 (termination)		$0

Hedge effectiveness: The terms of the bonds and interest rate swap **are consistent**, and the government used the consistent critical terms method to evaluate hedge effectiveness. Because the critical terms are consistent, the hedge is effective in each year. The swap agreement is not terminated early and reaches its planned termination date.

EXHIBIT 9-4
DERIVATIVE ILLUSTRATION: EXAMPLE JOURNAL ENTRIES

Example Journal Entries

PROPRIETARY FUND:	Debit	Credit
7/1/X6		
Cash	100,000,000	
Bonds Payable		100,000,000
To record sale of bonds at par value. No up-front payment received related to derivative instrument, therefore the fair value of the swap is zero at 7/1/X6.		
6/30/X7		
Interest Expense—Bondholders	1,789,314	
Interest Expense—Swap Counterparty	2,117,846	
Cash or Interest Payable		3,907,160
To record interest expense on the bonds in 20X7, including amounts due bondholders and the net amount resulting from the swap.		
Deferred Outflow of Resources—Interest Rate Swap	2,984,833	
Derivative Instrument Liability—Interest Rate Swap		2,984,833
To record the fair value changes in the swap during 20X7.		
6/30/X8		
Interest Expense—Bondholders	1,359,205	
Interest Expense—Swap Counterparty	2,547,955	
Cash or Interest Payable		3,907,160
To record interest expense on the bonds in 20X8, including amounts due bondholders and the net amount resulting from the swap.		
Deferred Outflow of Resources—Interest Rate Swap	1,801,798	
Derivative Instrument Liability—Interest Rate Swap		1,801,798
To record the fair value changes in the swap during 20X8.		
6/30/X9		
Interest Expense—Bondholders	1,078,661	
Interest Expense—Swap Counterparty	2,828,499	
Cash or Interest Payable		3,907,160
To record interest expense on the bonds in 20X9, including amounts due bondholders and the net amount resulting from the swap.		
Derivative Instrument Liability—Interest Rate Swap	2,877,893	
Deferred Outflow of Resources—Interest Rate Swap		2,877,893
To record the fair value changes in the swap during 20X9.		

Example Journal Entries

PROPRIETARY FUND:	Debit	Credit
6/30/Y0		
Interest Expense—Bondholders	1,930,405	
Interest Expense—Swap Counterparty	1,976,755	
Cash or Interest Payable		3,907,160

To record interest expense on the bonds in 20Y0, including amounts due bondholders and the net amount resulting from the swap.

Derivative Instrument Liability—Interest Rate Swap	1,908,738	
Deferred Outflow of Resources—Interest Rate Swap		1,908,738

To record the fair value changes in the swap during 20Y0. [The swap would have a $0 value as of maturity at 6/11/Y0].

Bonds Payable	100,000,000	
Cash		100,000,000

To record retirement of outstanding bonds payable on maturity date of 6/18/Y0.

OBSERVATION: Notice how the inflows to and outflows from the counterparty are netted, which exemplifies the net settlement nature of derivative contracts. Some preparers may want to account for the net flows on a disaggregate basis to prepare an investment section or financing section of a direct method statement of cash flows. However, the disaggregation is not GAAP.

EXHIBIT 9-5
DERIVATIVE ILLUSTRATION: PRO-FORMA FINANCIAL STATEMENT BALANCES

Proprietary Fund:	Assets	Deferred Outflow of Resources	Liabilities	Income	Deferred Inflow of Resources	Expense
6/30/X7:						
Cash	$96,092,840	—	—	—	—	—
Deferred Outflow Interest Rate Swap	—	$2,984,833	—	—	—	—
Derivative Instrument Liability—Interest Rate Swap	—	—	$2,984,833	—	—	—
Bonds Payable	—	—	$100,000,000	—	—	—
Investment Income (Loss)	—	—	—	—	$0	—
Interest Expense	—	—	—	—	—	$3,907,160
6/30/X8:						
Cash	92,185,680	—	—	—	—	—
Deferred Outflow Interest Rate Swap	—	$4,786,631	—	—	—	—
Derivative Instrument Liability—Interest Rate Swap	—	—	$4,786,631	—	—	—
Bonds Payable	—	—	$100,000,000	—	—	—
Investment Income (Loss)	—	—	—	—	$0	—
Interest Expense	—	—	—	—	—	$3,907,160
6/30/X9:						
Cash	$88,278,520	—	—	—	—	—

		Pro-Forma Financial Statement Balances				
Proprietary Fund:	Assets	Deferred Outflow of Resources	Liabilities	Income	Deferred Inflow of Resources	Expense
Deferred Outflow Interest Rate Swap	—	$1,908,738	—	—	—	—
Derivative Instrument Liability—Interest Rate Swap	—	—	$1,908,738	—	—	—
Bonds Payable	—	—	— $100,000,000	—	—	—
Investment Income (Loss)	—	—	—	—	$0	—
Interest Expense	—	—	—	—	—	$3,907,160
6/30/Y0:						
Cash	$(15,628,640)	—	—	—	—	—
Deferred Outflow Interest Rate Swap	—	$0	—	—	—	—
Derivative Instrument Liability—Interest Rate Swap	—	—	$0	—	—	—
Bonds Payable	—	—	$0	—	—	—
Investment Income (Loss)	—	—	—	—	$0	—
Interest Expense	—	—	—	—	—	$3,907,160

Note: For the purposes of this illustration, only the journal entries and pro-forma financial information for the proprietary fund are shown. The presentation in the business-type activities column in the government-wide financial statements is not included.

Hedge Termination Events

If a derivative instrument is effectively hedged, GASB-53 provides for the deferring of changes in its fair value. If the derivative is terminated or ceases to be effective prior to its expected ending date, the accumulated deferrals are eliminated from the statement of net position and reported as gains or losses in investment revenue or income in the resource-flow statements. Termination events include the following:

- The hedging derivative instrument is no longer effective.
- The hedged expected transaction occurs (such as commodities are purchased or bonds are sold).
- It is no longer probable that the hedged expected transaction will occur.
- The hedged asset or liability is sold or retired but not reported as a debt refunding resulting in defeasance.
- A current or advanced refunding that results in defeasance is executed.
- The hedging derivative instrument is terminated.

PRACTICE ALERT: The recently enacted Tax Cuts and Jobs Act of 2017 eliminated the ability for states and local governments to legally perform advance refunding of debt. At the time of publication, it is unclear if any changes in GASB pronouncements will need to occur. Existing refunding debt issued prior to December 31, 2017 are not affected by the provisions of the Act.

The accounting treatment for the deferred inflows or outflows at the time a terminating event occurs depends on the type of terminating event. Generally, the treatment involves eliminating the deferred amount from the statement of net position and reporting it as gains or losses in investment revenue or income in the resource-flow statements.

Many different types of derivatives terminations may occur depending on the facts and circumstances of the transaction. Should a current refunding occur, the GASB's *Implementation Guide 2015-1* in illustration 5.4 (nonauthoritative) [GASB Cod. Sec. D40.901] and in question 10.15.4 [GASB Cod. Sec. D40.708-4] show when a fair value of a swap is a liability at a point of a refunding and requires a termination payment, then the amount of the payment needs to be included as part of the calculation of the deferred amount on refunding as an offset to the net carrying amount. Therefore, the deferred amount on refunding would be lowered because of the termination payment.

GASB-64 (*Derivative Instruments: Application of Hedge Accounting Termination Provisions—an amendment of GASB Statement No. 53*) specifically addresses when a government enters into interest rate swap agreements and commodity swap agreements in which a swap counterparty, or the swap counterparty's credit support provider, commits or experiences either an act of default or a termination event as both are described in the swap agreement. Governments then replace their swap counterparty, or swap counterparty's credit support provider, either by amending existing swap agreements or by entering into new swap agreements. Previous to the issuance of GASB-64, certain provisions of GASB-53 required a government to cease hedge accounting upon the termination of the hedging derivative instrument, resulting in the immediate recognition of the deferred outflows of resources or deferred inflows of resources as a component of investment income.

GASB-64 amends the accounting and financial reporting for terminations of hedges if certain conditions exist. The hedging derivative instrument is terminated unless an effective hedging relationship continues. An effective hedging relationship continues when *all of the following* criteria are met:

- Collectability of swap payments is considered to be probable.
- The swap counterparty of the interest rate swap or commodity swap, or the swap counterparty's credit support provider, is replaced with an assignment or in-substance assignment.
- The government enters into the assignment or in-substance assignment in response to the swap counterparty, or the swap counterparty's credit support provider, either committing or experiencing an act of default or a termination event as both are described in the swap agreement.

GASB-64 also amends the terminology in terminations. An assignment occurs when a swap agreement is amended to replace an original swap counterparty, or the swap counterparty's credit support provider, but all of the other terms of the swap agreement remain unchanged. An in-substance assignment occurs when all of the following criteria are met:

- The original swap counterparty, or the swap counterparty's credit support provider, is replaced.
- The original swap agreement is ended, and the replacement swap agreement is entered into on the same date.

- The terms that affect changes in fair values and cash flows in the original and replacement swap agreements are identical. These terms include, but are not limited to, notional amounts, terms to maturity, variable payment terms, reference rates, time intervals, fixed-rate payments, frequencies of rate resets, payment dates, and options, such as floors and caps.

- Any difference between the original swap agreement's exit price and the replacement swap's entry price is attributable to the original swap agreement's exit price being based on a computation specifically permitted under the original swap agreement. Exit price represents the payment made or received as a result of terminating the original swap. Entry price represents the payment made or received as a result of entering into a replacement swap.

The requirement of GASB-53 that the differential between the exit price and the entrance price be deferred and amortized was not changed due to GASB-64 (GASB-53, pars. 22–25, as amended by GASB-63, par. 8, and GASB-64, par. 4) [GASB Cod. Secs. D40.118–.121].

An example of a terminating event is as follows: Assume the cash flow hedge, pay-fixed interest rate swap illustrated in Exhibit 9-5 is terminated on 12/31/X8 because the derivative no longer meets the effectiveness criteria of GASB-53. As a result of this early termination, the journal entry presented in Exhibit 9-6 would be recorded.

EXHIBIT 9-6
DERIVATIVE ILLUSTRATION: EXAMPLE EARLY TERMINATION
JOURNAL ENTRY

	Debit	Credit
PROPRIETARY FUND:		
12/31/X8:		
Investment Income (Loss)	$1,908,738	
Deferred Outflow of Resources—Interest Rate Swap		$1,908,738
To reclassify the deferred outflow balance as an investment loss at the time the hedge is no longer considered effective.		

After the early termination and the reclassification, all further changes in fair value to the derivative would be recorded as investment income or loss.

Determining Fair Value of Derivatives

GASB-53 provides that fair value should be measured by the market price when there is an active market for a derivative instrument. When an active market price is unavailable, the fair value may be estimated through an acceptable method of forecasting expected cash flows that are discounted. GASB-53 identifies a number of acceptable formula-based and mathematics-based methods, including matrix pricing, the zero-coupon method, and the par value method. For options, fair value may be based on a recognized option pricing model. Fair values may also be developed by pricing services, provided they are developed under the aforementioned acceptable methods.

Appendix C to GASB-53 and the *GASB Implementation Guide 2015-1* Chapter 10 [GASB Cod. Sec. D40.901] provide a number of illustrative examples of the application of the accounting and financial reporting treatment for different types of derivative instruments. Financial statement preparers, auditors, and users will find these illustrations very helpful in understanding the complexities of accounting and financial reporting for derivative instruments.

Disclosure Requirements

GASB-53 requires the objectives, terms, and risks of hedging derivative instruments to be disclosed, in addition to a summary of derivative instrument activity that provides the location of fair value amounts reported on the financial statements. The disclosures for investment derivative instruments are similar to the disclosures of other investments.

The disclosure requirements for derivative instrument activities, balances, and their related risks are quite extensive and vary depending on the different types of derivative instruments that a government is party to. If the government is involved in significant derivative activity and has a number of different types of derivative instruments, many of the required disclosures will likely be better presented in a tabular or columnar display. However, GASB-53 states that the disclosures may be in a columnar display, narrative form, or a combination of both methods. To assist financial statement preparers, Appendix C to GASB-53 provides a number of illustrated example disclosures.

In addition to providing summary disclosures regarding the government's derivative instrument activities and balances (General Disclosures), there are more specific disclosure requirements that depend on the type of derivative instrument.

General Disclosures for Derivative Instruments

GASB-53 requires certain general disclosures that provide a summary of the government's derivatives activities and balances. These general disclosures include a summary of the government's derivative instrument activity during the period and related balances at period end that are:

- Organized by governmental activities, business-type activities, and fiduciary funds to the extent applicable; and

- Separated into categories for hedging derivative instruments and investment derivative instruments; and, within each category, aggregated by type of derivative (e.g., receive-fixed swaps, pay-fixed swaps, swaptions, and futures contracts).

The summary information about the derivative instruments should include:

- Notional or face amount of the derivative instrument;

- Fair value changes during the period and the location in the financial statements where the changes in fair values are reported;

- Fair values at period end and the location in the financial statements where the fair values are reported;

- If the fair value of any derivative is based on other than quoted market prices, the method and assumptions used to estimate fair value; and

- Fair values of any hedging derivative instruments that have been reclassified to an investment derivative during the period and the deferral amount that was reported within investment income upon reclassification.

GASB-53 does not require a government to disclose the identities of the counterparties to the government's derivative instruments. In addition, the credit quality rating of derivative instruments does not need to be separately disclosed and may be aggregated by derivative instrument type or by credit quality rating. A portfolio, for example, consisting of swaps and forward contracts with differing credit quality ratings may be aggregated and displayed by credit quality.

For investment derivatives (mainly held by post-employment benefit plans), the disclosure is similar to what is required by GASB-40. Investment derivatives should disclose credit risk, interest rate risk, and foreign currency risk at a minimum, as applicable. Credit risk disclosures should include the credit quality ratings of counterparties as described by nationally recognized statistical rating organizations (rating agencies) as of the end of the reporting period. If the counterparty is not rated, the disclosure should state that fact. They should also include the maximum amount of loss due to credit risk, based on the fair value of the hedging derivative instrument as of the end of the reporting period, that the government would incur if the counterparties to the hedging derivative instrument failed to perform according to the terms of the contract, without respect to any collateral or other security or netting arrangement.

Should the government have a policy requiring collateral or other security to support hedging derivative instruments subject to credit risk, a summary description and the aggregate amount of the collateral or other security that reduces credit risk exposure, and information about the government's access to that collateral or other security should also be included.

If the government has a policy of entering into master netting arrangements, included should be a summary description and the aggregate amount of liabilities included in those arrangements. (Master netting arrangements are established when (a) each party owes the other determinable amounts, (b) the government has the right to set off the amount owed with the amount owed by the counterparty, and (c) the right of setoff is legally enforceable.)

Finally, significant concentrations of net exposure to credit risk (gross credit risk reduced by collateral, other security, and setoff) with individual counterparties and groups of counterparties should also be disclosed. A concentration of credit risk exposure to an individual counterparty may not require disclosure if its existence is apparent from the required disclosures described here; for example, a government has entered into only one interest rate swap. Group concentrations of credit risk exist if a number of counterparties are engaged in similar activities and have similar economic characteristics that would cause their ability to meet contractual obligations to be similarly affected by changes in economic or other conditions. Interest rate risk is disclosed similarly to other existing debt instrument disclosure, including one of the five approved methods within GASB-40. Furthermore, swaps are added to the list of highly sensitive instruments and should be disclosed similarly to other interest rate sensitive investments.

Specific Disclosures for Hedging Derivative Instruments

Although hedging derivative instruments can be a valuable component of the financial management of an entity and can help a government manage or hedge a specific risk, they can also present significant other risks to the government that could affect the entity's liquidity and investment performance. GASB-53 requires a number of disclosures about a government's use of hedging derivative instruments. The disclosures for each type of derivative instrument outstanding at period end should include:

- The government's objective for entering into the derivative instrument; and

- The significant terms of the derivative instrument.

GASB-53 also requires that the following risks associated with hedging derivative instruments be disclosed to the extent the government has exposure to those risks as previously described (*credit risk, interest rate risk, termination risk, basis risk, rollover risk, market access risk, and foreign currency risk*).

Specific Disclosures for Investment Derivative Instruments

Rather than apply the hedging derivative instrument disclosures, derivative instruments that are considered investments (including derivatives originally intended to be hedged but that do not meet the hedge effectiveness criteria) are disclosed according to the requirements set forth in GASB-40. Therefore, the following GASB-40 investment-risk disclosures for investment derivative instruments for credit risk, interest rate risk, and foreign currency risk should be included to the extent the government is exposed to such risk.

This disclosure of risks related to investment derivatives should be included in the investment-related footnotes of the government's financial statements.

Other Derivative-Related Disclosures

GASB-53 also requires certain other disclosures when specific circumstances are met. These include (1) disclosure of contingent features that are included in derivative instruments held at period end (such as a government's obligation to post collateral if credit quality declines), (2) the net debt service requirements of the hedged debt considering the hedging derivative instrument, (3) disclosure of embedded derivatives or other hybrid instruments (such as an interest rate swap embedded in a borrowing), and (4) disclosure of descriptive and fair value information about any synthetic guaranteed investment contracts the government is a party to (GASB-53, pars. 68–79, as amended by GASB-72, pars. 80–81) [GASB Cod. Secs. D40.164–.176].

PRACTICE POINT: A comprehensive example of derivatives note disclosure is presented in Chapter 66 of the 2018 *Governmental GAAP Disclosures Manual.*

QUESTIONS

1. Under guidance contained in GASB-72, an investment is defined as:

   a. An asset primarily used to provide governmental services.

   b. Assets that are not capital assets.

   c. Securities or other assets acquired primarily for the purpose of obtaining income or profit and with a present service capacity that is based solely on its ability to generate cash or to be sold to generate cash.

   d. Securities or other assets acquired primarily for the purpose of maintaining fiscal balance.

2. Which of the following types of assets are not addressed by GASB-31?

   a. Escheat property

   b. Interest-earning investment contracts

   c. External investment pools

   d. Debt securities

3. Which of the following investments held by governmental entities, including external investment pools, *should be* reported at fair value?

   a. Non-participating interest-earning investment contracts.

   b. Money market investments and certain participating interest-earning investment contracts.

   c. Investment positions in SEC 2a7-like pools.

   d. Investments in common stock.

4. The risk that an issuer or other counterparty to an investment will not fulfill its obligations is an example of:

   a. Custodial credit risk

   b. Credit risk

   c. Interest rate risk

   d. Market-access risk

5. The risk that a government will not be able to recover the value of investment or collateral securities that are in the possession of an outside party if the counterparty to the transaction fails is an example of:

   a. Custodial credit risk

   b. Credit risk

   c. Interest rate risk

   d. Market-access risk

6. Which of the following methods to inform users of the level of interest rate sensitivity for debt investments is not approved by GASB-40?

    a. Segmented time distributions

    b. Specific identification

    c. Consistent critical terms

    d. Duration

7. When a governmental entity transfers cash to a broker-dealer or financial institution and the broker-dealer or financial institution transfers securities to the governmental entity and promises to pay cash plus interest for the return of the same securities is an example of:

    a. Reverse repurchase agreement

    b. Derivative

    c. Securities lending

    d. Repurchase agreement

8. Transactions in which governmental entities transfer their securities to broker-dealers and other entities for collateral and simultaneously agree to return the collateral for the same securities in the future is an example of:

    a. Reverse repurchase agreement

    b. Derivative

    c. Securities lending

    d. Repurchase agreement

9. Which of the following reasons would a government not likely enter into a hedging derivative?

    a. To generate additional investment income.

    b. To fix prices to better manage cash flows.

    c. To lower borrowing costs.

    d. To potentially minimize or mitigate a certain risk.

10. Which of the following is *not* a hedge termination event?

    a. The hedging derivative is no longer effective.

    b. The fair value of the derivative changed.

    c. A current or advanced refunding that results in defeasance is executed.

    d. It is no longer probable that the hedged expected transaction will occur.

PRACTICE CASE (Adapted from the *GASB Implementation Guide*)
Assumptions

A special-purpose government had the following depository accounts. All deposits are carried at cost plus accrued interest. The government does not have a deposit policy.

Depository Account	Bank Balance
Insured	$ 200,000
Collateralized:	
Collateral held by city's agent in the city's name	3,015,000
Collateral held by pledging bank's trust department in the city's name	4,380,000
Collateral held by pledging bank's trust department not in the city's name	500,000
Uninsured and uncollateralized	1,683,000
Total deposits	**$9,778,000**

The bank balance is at fair value and all securities are valued using quoted prices for identical assets in active markets. The FDIC limit on deposits is $500,000. There is no state depositor's insurance fund. What amount of deposits is exposed to custodial credit risk? Insert a paragraph describing the custodial credit risks on deposits for the City and the amounts exposed by their categories.

ANSWERS

1. Under guidance contained in GASB-72, an investment is defined as:

   Answer – C: Securities or other assets acquired primarily for the purpose of obtaining income or profit and with a present service capacity that is based solely on its ability to generate cash or to be sold to generate cash. All others are not investments.

2. Which of the following types of assets are not addressed by GASB-31?

   Answer – A: Escheat property is addressed by GASB-21. All others are discussed in GASB-31.

3. Which of the following investments held by governmental entities, including external investment pools, *should be* reported at fair value?

   Answer – D: Investments in common stock. All others are reported at cost or carrying value.

4. The risk that an issuer or other counterparty to an investment will not fulfill its obligations is an example of:

   Answer – B: Credit risk. Custodial credit risk is explained in question 5. Interest rate risk is the risk that changes in interest rates will adversely affect the fair value of the government's financial instrument or its cash flows and market-access risk is the risk that a government will not be able to enter the credit markets or do so in a cost-effective manner.

5. The risk that a government will not be able to recover the value of investment or collateral securities that are in the possession of an outside party if the counterparty to the transaction fails is an example of:

   Answer – A: Custodial credit risk. The other risks are discussed in the answer to question 4.

6. Which of the following methods to inform users of the level of interest rate sensitivity for debt investments is not approved by GASB-40?

   Answer – C: Consistent critical terms has to do with hedging derivatives. All others are approved.

7. When a governmental entity transfers cash to a broker-dealer or financial institution and the broker-dealer or financial institution transfers securities to the governmental entity and promises to pay cash plus interest for the return of the same securities is an example of:

   Answer – D: Repurchase agreement. The other answers do not apply.

8. Transactions in which governmental entities transfer their securities to broker-dealers and other entities for collateral and simultaneously agree to return the collateral for the same securities in the future is an example of:

   Answer – C: Securities lending. The other answers do not apply.

9. Which of the following reasons would a government not likely enter into a hedging derivative?

   Answer – A: Generating additional investment income is an example of an investment derivative not a hedging derivative. Answers b through d are common reasons why hedging derivatives are used.

10. Which of the following is *not* a hedge termination event?

    Answer – B: Change in fair value is a normal occurrence. The remaining answers are common termination events.

PRACTICE CASE (Adapted from the *GASB Implementation Guide*)
Assumptions

A special-purpose government had the following depository accounts. All deposits are carried at cost plus accrued interest. The government does not have a deposit policy.

Depository Account	Bank Balance
Insured	$ 200,000
Collateralized:	
Collateral held by city's agent in the city's name	3,015,000
Collateral held by pledging bank's trust department in the city's name	4,380,000
Collateral held by pledging bank's trust department not in the city's name	500,000
Uninsured and uncollateralized	1,683,000
Total deposits	**$9,778,000**

The bank balance is at fair value and all securities are valued using quoted prices for identical assets in active markets. The FDIC limit on deposits is $500,000. There is no state depositor's insurance fund. What amount of deposits was exposed to custodial credit risk? Insert a paragraph describing the custodial credit risks on deposits for the City and the amounts exposed by their categories.

Answer

Disclosure

a. $9,778,000 was exposed to custodial credit risk because it was held by an outside party to the City.

b. Custodial Credit Risk—Deposits. Custodial credit risk is the risk that in the event of a bank failure, the government's deposits may not be returned to it. The government does not have a deposit policy for custodial credit risk. As of December 31, 20X5, $2,183,000 of the government's bank balance of $9,778,000 was exposed to custodial credit risk as follows:

Uninsured and uncollateralized	$1,683,000
Uninsured and collateral held by pledging bank's trust department not in the city's name	500,000
Total	**$2,183,000**

All securities would be valued at fair value with level 1 inputs for measurement. The City would have simplified disclosure in accordance with the provisions of paragraphs 79 to 81 of GASB-72.

APPENDIX A

Authoritative Status of Deposits, Investments, and Derivative Instruments Principles

GASB Statement	Year Issued	Title	Status – Portions have been amended or superseded by (or it has been superseded by)
3	1986	Deposits with Financial Institutions, Investments (including Repurchase Agreements), and Reverse Repurchase Agreements	• GASB-14, 31, 34, 40, and 72.
9	1989	Reporting Cash Flows of Proprietary and Nonexpendable Trust Funds and Governmental Entities That Use Proprietary Fund Accounting	• GASB-34.
10	1989	Accounting and Financial Reporting for Risk Financing and Related Insurance Issues	• GASB-14, 30, 31, 34, 49, 62, 63, 65, and 72.
25	1994	Financial Reporting for Defined Benefit Plans and Note Disclosures for Defined Contribution Plans	• Many statements, to be rescinded by GASB-73 and 74.
28	1995	Accounting and Financial Reporting for Securities Lending Transactions	• GASB-31, 34, and 63.
31	1997	Accounting and Financial Reporting for Certain Investments and Investment Pools	• GASB-32, 34, 43, 53, 59, 62, 63, 72, and 79.
32	1997	Accounting and Financial Reporting for Internal Revenue Code Section 457 Deferred Compensation Plans	• GASB-34. To be rescinded upon implementation of GASB-84 for periods beginning after December 15, 2018.
40	2003	Deposits and Investments Risks Disclosures	• GASB-53, 59, 63, and 79.
43	2004	Financial Reporting for Postemployment Benefit Plans, Other Than Pension Plans	• GASB-47, 53, 54, 57, 59, 63, and 72. To be rescinded by GASB-74.

GASB Statement	Year Issued	Title	Status – Portions have been amended or superseded by (or it has been superseded by)
52	2007	Land and Other Real Estate Held as Investments by Endowments	• GASB-72.
53	2008	Accounting and Financial Reporting for Derivative Instruments	• GASB-59, 62, 63, 64, and 72.
59	2010	Financial Instruments Omnibus	• None.
62	2010	Codification of Accounting and Financial Reporting Guidance Contained in Pre-November 30, 1989 FASB and AICPA Pronouncements	• GASB-63 and 72.
64	2011	Derivative Instruments: Application of Hedge Accounting Termination Provisions	• None.
67	2012	Financial Reporting for Pension Plans	• GASB-72 and 73.
72	2015	Fair Value Measurement and Application	• GASB-79.
74	2015	Financial Reporting for Postemployment Benefit Plans Other than Pension Plans	• None. Certain portions amended by GASB Statement No. 86 (Omnibus 2017) upon implementation.
79	2015	Certain External Investment Pools and Pool Participants	• None.
81	2016	Irrevocable Split-Interest Agreements	• None.

APPENDIX B

Comprehensive Illustration of Investment Disclosures For A State

Source – State of Nevada

PRACTICE POINT: This includes the most common disclosures as of the fiscal year ended June 30, 201X. It is not authoritative. Disclosures will differ from government to government based on the nature and extent of investments. The information on determining fair value is not contained herein as it is in the summary of significant accounting policies. Component units are excluded for the purposes of this illustration.

NOTE 3 – Deposits and Investments

The Revised Statutes (RS) and Administrative Code, as well as procedures approved by the State Board of Finance, govern deposits and investing activities for the primary government and its discretely presented component units which are not expressly required by law to be received and kept by another party. RS

226.110(3) further requires that the Office of the State Treasurer shall establish the policies to be followed in the investment of money of the State.

A. Deposits

Primary Government, Private Purpose Trust, Pension and Other Employee Benefit Trust, and Investment Trust Funds—

The State minimizes its custodial credit risk by legislation establishing a program to monitor a collateral pool for public deposits. Custodial credit risk for deposits is the risk that in the event of a bank failure, the State's deposits may not be recovered. The RS directs the Office of the State Treasurer to deposit funds into any state, or national bank, credit union or savings and loan association covered by federal depository insurance. For those deposits over and above the federal depository insurance maximum balance, sufficient collateral must be held by the financial institution to protect the State against loss. The pooled collateral for deposits program maintains a 102% pledged collateral for all public deposits. As of June 30, 201X, the bank balance of the primary government, private-purpose trust, pension and other employee benefit trust, and investment trust funds totaled $747,559,255, of which $48,809,712 was uncollateralized and uninsured.

B. Investments

RS 355.140 details the types of securities in which the State may invest. In general, authorized investments include: certificates of deposit, asset-backed securities, bankers' acceptances and commercial paper, collateralized mortgage obligations, corporate notes, municipal bonds, money market mutual funds whose policies meet the criteria set forth in the statute, United States treasury securities, and specific securities implicitly guaranteed by the federal government. Additionally, the State may invest in limited types of repurchase agreements; however, statutes generally prohibit the State from entering into reverse-repurchase agreements. The State's Permanent School Fund is further limited by statute as to the types of investments in which it may invest (RS 355.060). Cash and Investments are also discussed in Note 1 under Assets, Liabilities, Deferred Outflows/Inflows of Resources and Net Position/Fund Balance.

The State Board of Finance reviews the State's investment policies at least every four months. The Board is comprised of the Governor, the State Controller, the State Treasurer and two members appointed by the Governor, one of whom must be actively engaged in commercial banking in the State.

Investments held in the Local Government Investment Pool (LGIP), Retirement Benefits Investment Fund (RBIF), and Enhanced Savings Term (EST) are specifically identifiable investment securities and are included in the following tables. LGIP, RBIF, and EST are investment trust funds and discussed further in Note 1, Assets, Liabilities, Deferred Outflows/Inflows of Resources and Net Position/Fund Balance. LGIP and NVEST are governed by the State Board of Finance and administered by the State Treasurer. Complete financial statements for LGIP and EST may be obtained from the State Treasurer's Office, 101 N. Kit Street, Suite 8, Capital City, ZZ 98765. RBIF is administered by the Retirement Benefits Investment Board. The audited financial statements of RBIF may be obtained from the Public Employees' Retirement System, 693 West Lilly Lane, Capital City, ZZ 98765.

Interest Rate Risk: Interest rate risk is the risk that changes in interest rates will adversely affect the fair value of an investment.

Primary Government, Private Purpose Trust, Pension and Other Employee Benefit Trust, and Investment Trust Funds—

The State minimizes interest rate risk by maintaining an effective duration of less than 1.5 years and holding at least 25% of the portfolio's total market value in securities with a maturity of 12 months or less. However, the benchmark used by the State Treasurer to determine whether competitive market yields are being achieved is the 90 day U.S. Treasury Bill's average over the previous three month period (Rolling 90 day T-Bill). Investment policies for the pension and other employee benefit trust funds authorize all securities within the Barclays Aggregate Index benchmark. If securities are purchased outside the Barclays U.S. Treasury Index, they must be of investment grade rating by at least two of the following: Moody's, Standard & Poor's or Fitch (BBB- or better by Standard & Poor's/Fitch, Baa3 or better by Moody's) except those issued or guaranteed by the U.S. Government or its agencies. The following table provides information about the interest rate risks associated with the State's investments as of June 30, 201X (expressed in thousands):

		Maturities in Years			
	Fair Value	Less than 1	1-5	6-10	More than 10
US. Treasury Securities	$768,764	$146,977	$457,358	$132,267	$32,162
Negotiable certificates of deposit	487,544	485,085	2,459	—	—
US Agencies	10,751,086	532,249	6,529,208	1,892,353	1,797,276
Mutual Funds	121,479	121,479	—	—	—
Repurchase agreements	358,006	358,006	—	—	—
Asset backed corporate securities	97,680	227	71,730	19,079	6,647
Corporate bonds and notes	340,113	138,595	178,130	11,371	12,017
Commercial paper	374,446	374,446	—	—	—
Fixed income securities	794	794	—	—	—
Municipal bonds	10,792	7,708	3,084	—	—
Investment agreements	175	—	—	—	175
Other short—term investments	294,015	294,015	—	—	—
Other investments	17,162	15,105	2,057	—	—
Total	$13,622,056	$2,474,686	$7,244,026	$2,055,067	$1,848,277

The State College Savings Plan, a private-purpose trust, currently has no formal investment policy with regard to interest rate risk for the investments.

The mutual funds held by various mutual funds have various maturities from 28 days to 13.9 years and are not included in the table above.

Credit Risk: Credit risk is the risk that an issuer or other counterparty to an investment will not fulfill its obligations to the State.

Primary Government, Private Purpose Trust, Pension and Other Employee Benefit Trust, and Investment Trust Funds—

RS 355.140, the State Treasurer's investment policy, and investment policies of the pension and other employee benefit trust and investment trust funds all address credit risk. A summary of the policies is presented as follows:

- Commercial paper, Negotiable Certificates of Deposit, and Bankers' Acceptances are rated by a nationally recognized rating service as "A-1," "P-1" or its equivalent, or better,

- Notes, bonds and other unconditional obligations issued by corporations in the U.S. and municipal bonds (effective September 201X) are rated by a nationally recognized rating service as "A" or its equivalent, or better,

- Money market mutual funds are SEC registered 2(a)7 and rated by a nationally recognized rating service as "AAA" or its equivalent,

- Collateralized mortgage obligations and asset-backed securities are rated by a nationally recognized rating service as "AAA" or its equivalent,

- Repurchase agreements with banks or registered broker dealers provided the agreement is collateralized by 102% with U.S. Treasuries or U.S. government agency securities on a delivery basis.

In addition to the above provisions, investment policies for the pension and other employee benefit trust funds allow investment in corporate bonds, assets related instruments, and foreign debt issued in the U.S. rated by *at least two* of the following:

Moody's, Standard & Poor's, or Fitch (BBB—or better by Standard & Poor's/ Fitch, Baa3 or better by Moody's).

The State College Savings Plan, a private-purpose trust, currently has no formal investment policy with regard to credit risk for the investments. Investments having credit risk are included in the table below.

The State's investments as of June 30, 201X were rated by Standard & Poor's and/or an equivalent national rating organization, and the ratings are presented below using the Standard & Poor's rating scale (at fair value, expressed in thousands):

	Quality Rating						
	AAA	AA	A	BBB	BB	B	Unrated
Negotiable certificates of deposit	$2,307	$10,007	$172,048	$—	$—	$—	$—
US Agencies	54,481	700,283	—	—	—	—	—
Mutual Funds	1,923	—	—	—	—	—	10.955.948

	Quality Rating						
	AAA	AA	A	BBB	BB	B	Unrated
Repurchase agreements	—	5,006	—	—	—	—	—
Asset backed corporate securities	18,899	69,401	434	646	874	363	—
Corporate bonds and notes	9,835	75,910	147,447	28,453	2,961	446	9,419
Commercial paper	—	—	242,552	—	—	—	—
Fixed income securities	—	—	—	—	—	—	126
Municipal bonds	—	10,791	—	—	—	—	—
Investment agreements	—	—	183	12	—	—	—
Other short-term investments	94,481	203	108,350	—	—	—	182,963
Other investments	—	6,039	10,089	—	—	—	—
Total	$179,926	$877,640	$681,083	$29,111	$3,835	$809	$17,148,456

Concentration of Credit Risk: Concentration of credit risk is the risk of loss that may be attributed to the magnitude of a government's investment in a single issuer. The RS 355.140, 355.060, and the State Treasurer's investment policy limit the investing in any one issuer to 5% of the total par value of the portfolio. At June 30, 201X, no individual investment exceeded 5% of the total portfolio of the Primary Government.

At June 30, 201X, the following investments exceeded 5% of the Higher Education Tuition Trust's total investments—Federal Home Loan Mortgage Corporation—Asset—Backed Mortgage Security with a fair value of $16,618,000 comprising 7.42% of the Trust's portfolio.

The State's Housing Division currently places no limit on the amount it may invest in any one issuer provided their ratings are in the highest two general rating categories. However, the Housing Division monitors rating changes on all issuers. If warranted, more concentrated investments may have to be diluted to alternative investment providers. As of June 30, 201X, the Housing Division's investments in Fannie Mae and Ginnie Mae are 3.94% and 42.04% respectively, of the Housing Division's total investments. The Fannie Mae and Ginnie Mae investments are in mortgage backed securities matched to the interest rate and maturity of the underlying bonds. Because such investments are matched to concomitant liabilities, the Housing Division is less concerned about a concentration risk on these investments.

Foreign Currency Risk: Foreign currency risk is the risk that changes in exchange rates will adversely affect the fair value of an investment or deposit.

Primary Government, Pension and Other Employee Benefit Trust Funds, and Investment Trust Funds—The primary government does not have a policy regarding foreign currency risk; however, the State Treasurer's office does not have any deposits or investments in foreign currency. The Public Employee Retirement System (PERS), Legislative Retirement System (LRS), Judges Retirement System (JRS) and RBIF do have foreign currency policies for deposit and investments, which may be used for portfolio diversification and hedging. Highly speculative positions in currency are not permitted. LRS and JRS had no exposure to foreign currency risk as of June 30, 201X. The following table summarizes the pension and investment trust funds' exposure to foreign currency risk in U.S. dollars as of June 30, 201X (expressed in thousands):

| | Currency by Investment and Fair Value | | | |
	Equity	Pending Transactions	Cash	Total
Australian Dollar	$433,885	$(200)	$401	$434,086
British Pound Sterling	1,174,188	(400)	1,518	1,175,306
Danish Krone	118,547	—	—	118,547
Euro	1,782,991	(800)	(169)	1,782,022
Hong Kong Dollar	186,619	(100)	1,009	187,528
Israeli Shekel	35,700	—	203	35,903
Japanese Yen	1,395,662	(3,400)	4,370	1,396,632
Norwegian Krone	11,322	—	100	11,422
Polish Zloty	38,633	—	101	38,734
Singapore Dollar	80,370	—	622	80,892
Swedish Krona	166,061	—	103	166,164
Swiss Franc	555,155	—	3	555,158
Total	$5,979,133	$(4,900)	$8,261	$5,982,394

Private Purpose Trust Fund—The State College Savings Plan, a private-purpose trust, currently has no formal investment policy with regard to foreign currency risk for the investments. The Plan consists of various mutual funds which all state that there are certain inherent risks involved when investing in international securities through mutual funds that are not present with investments in domestic securities, such as foreign currency exchange rate fluctuations, adverse political and economic developments, natural disasters and possible prevention or delay of currency exchange due to foreign governmental laws or restrictions. The Plan held approximately $166,000 in various currencies at year end.

Fair Value of Investments: The State categorizes the fair value measurements of its investments based on the hierarchy established by generally accepted accounting principles. The fair value hierarchy, which has three levels, is based on the valuation inputs used to measure an asset's fair value: Level 1 inputs are quoted prices in active markets for identical assets; Level 2 inputs are significant other observable inputs; Level 3 inputs are significant unobservable inputs. The State had no Level 3 inputs for the fiscal year ended June 30, 201X. The following table summarizes the fair value measurements of the primary government as of June 30, 201X (expressed in thousands):

| | | Fair Value Measurements Using | |
	Fair Value	Level 1 Inputs	Level 2 Inputs
Investments by fair value level:			
Debt securities			
US. Treasury Securities	$600,043	$541,818	$58,225
Negotiable certificates of deposit	462,391	—	462,391
US Agencies	526,540	27,964	498,576

| | Fair Value | Fair Value Measurements Using | |
		Level 1 Inputs	Level 2 Inputs
Mutual Funds	198,077	198,077	—
Repurchase agreements	353,000	—	353,000
Asset backed corporate securities	68,593		68,593
Corporate bonds and notes	166,927	14,666	152,261
Commercial paper	267,966	—	267,996
Fixed income securities	10,791	—	10,791
Municipal bonds	20,948	710	20,238
Collateralized Mortgage Obligations	24,057	14,103	9,954
Federal National Mortgage Association	12,558	10,501	2,057
Other investments	17,162	15,105	2,057
Total debt securities	$2,711,921	$807,839	$1,904,082
Equity Securities			
Financial services industry	1,691	—	1,691
Total investments by fair value level	**$2,713,612**	**$807,839**	**$1,905,773**

C. Securities Lending

Primary Government and Investment Trust Funds—RS 355.135 authorizes the State Treasurer to lend securities from the investment portfolio of the State if collateral received from the borrower is at least 102% of fair value of the underlying securities and the value of the securities borrowed is determined on a daily basis. There were no securities on loan at June 30, 201X (excluding PERS).

PERS maintains a securities lending program under the authority of the "prudent person" standard of RS 286.682. Securities loaned under this program consist of U.S. Treasury Obligations, corporate fixed income securities, international fixed income securities, equity securities, and international equity securities. Collateral received consists of cash and securities issued by the U.S. Government, its agencies or instrumentalities. Collateral received for the lending of U.S. securities must equal at least 102% of fair value, plus accrued interest in the case of fixed income securities. Collateral received for the lending of international securities must equal at least 105% of fair value, plus accrued interest in the case of fixed income securities.

At year-end, PERS has no credit risk exposure to borrowers because the associated value of the collateral held exceeds the value of the securities borrowed. PERS has no discretionary authority to sell or pledge collateral received or securities loaned. The contract with the securities lending agent requires the agent to indemnify PERS for all losses relating to securities lending transactions. There were no losses resulting from borrower default during the period nor were there any recoveries of prior period losses.

PERS may only loan up to 33 1/3% of its total portfolio. Either PERS or the borrower can terminate all securities loans on demand. The PERS Board allows only overnight repurchase agreements collateralized by U.S. government obligations issued or guaranteed by the U.S. Government, its agencies or instrumentalities within the reinvestment portfolio. This action effectively eliminated risk in securities lending collateral reinvestment portfolio since securities issued or guaranteed by the U.S. Government are considered to be free of credit risk. The maturities of the investments made with cash collateral generally do not match the maturities of the securities loaned because securities lending transactions can be terminated at will.

The fair value of underlying securities on loan at June 30, 201X is $3,954,057,876. Collateral received for outstanding securities lending arrangements consisted of cash in the amount of $411,128,913 and non-cash in the amount of $3,635,396,664. The cash collateral is reported on the Statement of Fiduciary Net Position as an asset with a related liability. At June 30, 201X, PERS has collateral consisting of cash and securities issued by the U.S. Government, its agencies or instrumentalities, in excess of the fair value of investments held by brokers/dealers under a securities lending agreement.

D. Investment Derivatives

Primary Government—The Office of the State Treasurer's investment policies do not contain any specific language regarding derivatives other than prohibiting certain types of derivatives such as option contracts, futures contracts, and swaps in the General Portfolios and the Local Government Investment Pool. The primary government has no exposure to derivatives as of June 30, 201X.

Private Purpose Trust Fund—Certain investments in the State College Savings Plan are managed by the various mutual funds. The Portfolios use six types of derivatives: options, futures contracts, forward currency contracts, total return swap contracts, interest rate swap contracts, and credit default contracts. Currently, there is no written investment policy with regard to derivatives for the Portfolios. All six types of derivatives are considered investments. The fair value amount in the table below represents the unrealized appreciation (depreciation) from derivative instruments and is reported in the Statement of Fiduciary Net Position. The net increase (decrease) in fair value is reported as investment income on the Statement of Changes in Fiduciary Net Position. The Portfolios' investment derivative instruments as of June 30, 201X, and changes in fair value for the year then ended had a fair value of approximately $375,000 and an annual change in fair value of a positive $425,000. Detailed information on the portfolios is available from the State College Savings Plan obtained from the State Treasurer's Office, 101 N. Kit Street, Suite 8, Capital City, ZZ 98765.

CHAPTER 10
CAPITAL ASSETS

CONTENTS

INTRODUCTION

Capital assets include the following items that have initial useful lives extending beyond a single reporting period (GASB-34, par. 19) [GASB Cod. Sec. 1400.103]:

- Land and land improvements;
- Easements;
- Buildings and building improvements;
- Vehicles;
- Equipment;
- Property rights related to capitalized leases;
- Works of art, historical treasures, and other similar assets;
- Infrastructure assets; and
- All other tangible or intangible assets used in operations.

PRACTICE ALERT: GASB Statement No. 87 (*Leases*) focuses on a "right-to-use" model for recognition of an asset by a lessee, without derecognition of a leased asset by a lessor. The asset of a lease will then be an intangible capital asset for the lessee which at inception will equate to the present value of the lease payments plus any up-front payments or deposits. GASB-87 will be implemented for periods beginning after December 15, 2019, and will require a restatement of prior periods. See Chapter 14, "Leases and Service Concession Arrangements," for a more complete discussion of GASB-87.

GASB Implementation Guide 2015-1, question 7.9.1 [GASB Cod. Sec. 1400.702-1], defines land improvements as "betterments, other than buildings, that ready land for its intended use." Examples include the excavation of the land, utility installations, parking lots, and landscaping.

OBSERVATION: Capital assets are sometimes termed colloquially as "fixed assets." Using the term "fixed assets" in a set of financial statements is not proper, because capital assets may include movable assets and intangible assets. Statements of Net Position should only use the term "capital assets."

The accounting standards that are used to determine which assets should be presented in a governmental entity's financial statements vary depending on whether an asset is presented in (1) governmental funds, (2) proprietary and fiduciary funds, (3) the government-wide financial statements.

GOVERNMENTAL FUNDS

The modified accrual basis of accounting and the current financial resources measurement focus should be used in accounting for assets within governmental funds. On the balance sheet of a governmental fund, in accordance with the modified accrual basis of accounting and the current financial resources measurement focus, assets are not classified as current or noncurrent.

However, when assets are presented on a governmental fund's balance sheet, it is implied that they are current. In governmental accounting, current assets represent current financial resources that are available for appropriation and expenditure. Financial resources are considered current when they are available for subsequent appropriation and expenditure. Examples of current financial resources include cash, various receivables, and short-term investments.

Capital assets represent past expenditures, not financial resources available to finance current governmental activities. For this reason, general capital assets (assets not related to a proprietary fund or fiduciary fund) of a governmental entity are not presented in a specific governmental fund but, rather, are reported in the entity's government-wide financial statements (as discussed later in this chapter). Capital assets that are acquired through the use of resources from a governmental fund should be recorded as expenditures for the period. For example, if a governmental entity uses resources from the General Fund to purchase equipment that has a cost of $10,000, the following entry would be made.

	Debit	Credit
GENERAL FUND		
Expenditures—Capital Outlays	10,000	
Cash		10,000

PRACTICE ALERT: The status of capital asset transactions in governmental funds was part of the GASB's initial deliberations in the *Financial Reporting Model—Reexamination* project. The GASB has tentatively concluded that the current model for capital outlay transactions in governmental funds will not change as the result of the reexamination.

PROPRIETARY AND FIDUCIARY FUNDS AND THE GOVERNMENT-WIDE FINANCIAL STATEMENTS

The accrual basis of accounting and economic resources measurement focus should be used to determine which assets should be presented in the proprietary and fiduciary funds and the government-wide entity's statement of net position.

Inexhaustible capital assets should be presented in the proprietary and fiduciary funds and government-wide statements of net position at historical cost. GASB's *Implementation Guide 2015-1*, question 7.9.3 [GASB Cod. Sec. 1400.702-3], defines an inexhaustible capital asset as one "whose economic benefit or service potential is used up so slowly that its estimated useful life is extraordinarily long." Examples of inexhaustible capital assets are land and some land improvements (e.g., fortifying hillsides against erosion by infusing concrete). Capital assets that are inexhaustible and not subject to depreciation (such as land, construction in progress, and certain infrastructure assets and intangible assets, described below) must be presented as a separate line item on the face of the statement of net position if these assets are significant (GASB-34, par. 20, as amended by GASB-63, par. 8) [GASB Cod. Sec. 1400.112].

For depreciable capital assets, a single amount (net of accumulated depreciation) may be presented on the face of the financial statements, in which case accumulated depreciation and the major categories of capital assets (land, buildings, equipment, infrastructure, etc.) must be reported in a note.

The GASB's *Implementation Guide 2015-1*, question 7.11.1 [GASB Cod. Sec. 1400.702-10], notes that construction in progress is a capital asset and should be reported in the statement of net position with other assets that are not depreciated, such as land. The *Guide* also points out that land improvements must be evaluated to determine whether they are subject to depreciation. That is, costs that are permanent in nature are not subject to depreciation. For example, grading cost incurred to prepare a site for the construction of a building is generally considered a permanent improvement and is reported as part of the carrying value (historical cost) of the land and, therefore, is not depreciated. Costs that are not permanent should be depreciated. For example, paving a parking lot is not permanent and is reported as a land improvement subject to depreciation.

ACCOUNTING AND FINANCIAL REPORTING FOR CAPITAL ASSETS

Capitalization Policies

A governmental entity may establish a policy whereby capital acquisitions that are less than an established amount are expensed rather than capitalized. GASB's *Implementation Guide 2015-1*, question 7.9.5 [GASB Cod. Sec. 1400.702-5], addresses the issue of whether the threshold amount applies to the purchase of a group of assets (such as the acquisition of 100 computers) as well as to an individual asset (such as the acquisition of a single computer). There is no pronouncement that addresses this issue, but the general rule of materiality should apply. That is, it is acceptable to expense capital assets acquired as a group as long as the financial statements are not materially misstated and any policy established is applied in a consistent manner.

PRACTICE ALERT: In the basis for conclusions to GASB-87, the GASB explains a struggle in deliberations pointing to thresholds. Some stakeholders in response to the GASB's Preliminary Views document questioned whether governments would be permitted to set policy thresholds for capitalization of their leases, similar to those commonly used for capital assets. The GASB viewed capitalization policies as methods to operationalize materiality; that is, those policies allow governments to specify amounts that they consider to be insignificant, individually and in the aggregate. The GASB believes that a policy similar to those that establish capitalization thresholds could be used for leases. However, establishing such a policy is within the purview of management. In practice, if management choses a threshold for recognizing a lease that is inconsistent with other capital assets, a question from an auditor could occur as to why management took such an action.

OBSERVATION: Capitalization policies are perhaps the most important part of capital asset operations as U.S. GAAP is principles-based rather than rules-based for capital assets. Consistent and rational capitalization polices are also very important for federal cost recovery. Title 2, Code of Federal Regulations, Part 200 (*The Uniform Administrative Requirements, Cost Principles, and Audit Requirements*) contains a relaxation of technology capitalization, allowing expenses of up to $5,000 per unit. But the requirements also emphasize consistency in policy so that the federal government is not unfairly charged. Capitalization policies should at the very least stipulate construction-in-process policies, cost-accumulation methods, adjustments, transfers, impairments, betterments, and disposals.

Valuation of Capital Assets

The governmental entity should report its capital assets in the various statements of net position, based on their original historical cost (including capitalized interest costs, if applicable) plus ancillary charges such as transportation, installation, and site preparation costs, and then depreciated if they are exhaustible. Capital assets that have been donated to a governmental entity must be capitalized at their acquisition value (plus any ancillary costs) at the date of receipt. Acquisition value is partially defined in GASB-72, pars. 79 and 86, as the price that would be paid to acquire an asset with an equivalent service potential in an orderly market transaction at the acquisition date (GASB-34, par. 18, as amended by GASB-72, pars. 78–79, 86, GASB-37, par. 6) [GASB Cod. Sec. 1400.102]. Impairment of capital assets is discussed later in this chapter.

Depreciation of Capital Assets

Capital assets depreciation methods and reporting of depreciation expense is discussed in detail in Chapter 18, "Expenses/Expenditures: Nonexchange and Exchange Transactions." Eligible infrastructure assets may also use a modified approach as long as certain provisions are met. This approach is discussed later in this chapter.

Reporting Capital Assets Where Ownership Is Unclear

All of a governmental entity's capital assets are reported in the government-wide financial statements. Footnote 67 to GASB-34 (*Basic Financial Statements—and Management's Discussion and Analysis—for State and Local Governments*) [GASB Cod. Sec. 1400.fn. 31] notes that a government that has the *primary responsibility for maintaining* a particular infrastructure asset should report the asset in its financial statements. GASB's *Implementation Guide 2015-1,* questions 7.12.2 to 7.12.4 [GASB Cod. Secs. 1400.735-2–4], makes it clear that the footnote applies only to situations in which it is unclear who owns a particular asset. For example, ambiguity of ownership may arise for infrastructure assets such as highways.

Some localities require homeowners to repair and maintain sidewalks adjacent to their properties, and localities establish regulations to determine when and how those sidewalks are to be maintained. Because the property owners, under this arrangement, are responsible for the maintenance of the sidewalks, the sidewalks should not be reported as assets by the government. The establishment of minimum maintenance standards by the governmental entity is not the same as accepting responsibility for the maintenance of the asset itself.

There may be an arrangement where one governmental entity maintains an asset but another governmental entity is responsible for the replacement of the asset. Under this arrangement, and when ownership is unclear, the government that is responsible for maintaining the capital asset should report the asset in its financial statements.

The *GASB Implementation Guide 2015-1*, question 7.9.6 [GASB Cod. Sec. 1400.735-1], addresses whether title and ownership are one and the same. Public assets are unique in that while title is held by the governmental entity, citizens and numerous other parties and entities have the right to use the property. Nonetheless, the governmental entity that holds title to an asset generally should report the asset in its financial statements. One exception to this generalization occurs when a lessee reports a capitalized lease based on the standards contained in GASB-62 (*Codification of Accounting and Financial Reporting Guidance Contained in Pre-November 30, 1989 FASB and AICPA Pronouncements*), which will be replaced by the concept of "right-to-use" that is contained in GASB-87 (*Leases*).

In many instances capital assets purchased by state or local government are financed or partially financed by federal awards, and the federal government can retain a reversionary interest in the asset. These assets (even though the federal government retains a reversionary interest in the asset's salvage value) should be reported by the state or local government because "the state or local government is the party that uses the assets in its activities and makes the decisions regarding when and how the assets will be used and managed." Except in the case of certain infrastructure assets (where the modified approach is used), depreciation expense should be recorded for these assets.

PRACTICE POINT: Title 2, Code of Federal Regulations, Part 200, Section 313(e), contains disposal requirements for equipment and other capital assets financed (or partially financed) by federal awards. Governments that need to dispose of capital assets in this situation must request disposition instructions from the federal awarding agency if the terms and conditions of the federal award require it. Items with a fair market value of less than $5,000 each may be retained, sold or otherwise disposed of with no further obligation to the federal agency. If the federal agency does not respond to the request for disposition instructions within 120 days, items above $5,000 per unit may be retained or sold. The federal agency is entitled to an amount from the proceeds of the sale in accordance with the agency's percentage of participation in the original cost. For example, if a piece of equipment was financed with 20% federal funds and 80% non-federal funds, then upon sale at auction for $10,000, $2,000 may be required to be paid to the federal agency, less $500 or 10% of the proceeds whichever is less for selling and handling expenses. Governments may transfer the property to the federal agency or to eligible third parties as well, as long as compensation is paid to the disposing government for its attributable percentage of the current fair market value of the property. Therefore, in the previous example, compensation should be $10,000.

Gifted or Donated Capital Assets

Often a governmental entity, as part of the agreement to allow the construction of residential or commercial property, requires that a real estate developer construct an asset (such as a street or park) that will be given to a local government. GASB-72 (*Fair Value Measurement and Application*) changed the provision in GASB-34, paragraph 18, which originally required fair value. Donated capital assets, works of art, historical treasures, and similar assets and capital assets that a government receives in a service concession arrangement are now required to be valued at **acquisition value** as of the date of transaction as previously discussed.

> **OBSERVATION:** The difference between acquisition value and fair value may be subtle. Acquisition value is an entrance price (meaning the government would have intended to buy a similar asset when received), whereas fair value is an exit price (meaning the government would have intended to sell the asset received). So one can assume that a piece of land that is 100 acres is donated to a government. A similar plot of land with similar characteristics is available for sale in the government's jurisdiction for $1 million. The government could then assume an acquisition value of $1 million. Fair value might be very different as it is based upon the concept of "highest and best use." (See Chapter 9, "Deposits, Investments, and Derivative Instruments," for a discussion on "highest and best use" and fair value). The same piece of land could be subdivided by a developer and realize a much higher fair value due to a different use.

Works of Art, Historical Treasures, and Similar Assets

Works of art, historical treasures, and similar assets (that are not donated—see above) generally have to be capitalized at their historical cost, "whether they are held as individual items or in a collection." However, such assets do not have to be capitalized if they are part of a collection and all of the following conditions are satisfied (GASB-34, par. 27, as amended by GASB-72, par. 9) [GASB Cod. Sec. 1400.109]:

- They are held for public exhibition, education, or research in furtherance of public service rather than financial gain.

- They are protected, kept unencumbered, cared for, and preserved.

- They are subject to an organizational policy that requires the proceeds from sales of collection items to be used to acquire other items for collections.

The GASB's *Implementation Guide 2015-1*, question 7.21.8 [GASB Cod. Sec. 1400.704-7], discusses the situation when a governmental entity has multiple collections, works of art, and historical treasures, the recognition provisions of paragraph 27 of GASB-34 may be applied for the entire entity or on a collection-by-collection basis. GASB-34 does not require that the organizational policy referred to in paragraph 27 of GASB-34 be formal; however, there should be some evidence to verify its existence.

If a governmental entity had capitalized collections as of June 30, 1999, those collections must remain capitalized and subsequent additions to the collections must be capitalized even if they satisfy the three conditions listed above.

Institutions of higher education and public schools may capitalize books due to their materiality and rare books due to their historical significance. Policies and procedures are necessary to delineate the depreciation method and useful lives of books and historical collections. A reevaluation of these policies may be necessary as more and more works are digitized.

The GASB's *Implementation Guide 2015-1*, question 7.21.1 [GASB Cod. Sec. 1400.704-1], describes collections of works of art and historical treasures as "generally . . . held by museums, botanical gardens, libraries, aquariums, arboretums, historic sites, planetariums, zoos, art galleries, nature, science and technology centers, and similar educational, research and public service organizations that have those divisions; however, the definition is not limited to those entities nor does it apply to all items held by those entities." For example, animals in a zoo are capital assets, and they could be considered a collection; however, question 7.21.3 [GASB Cod. Sec. 1400.704-3] adds "only successful breeding colonies of zoo animals would likely meet the requirements in paragraph 27 that collections be preserved."

In some instances, items in a collection are permanently attached to a structure and removing them might damage them or significantly reduce their value. Such items do not have to be subject to a written policy in order for them not to be capitalized, because the nature of how the items are displayed "demonstrates a commitment and probability that they will be maintained."

If a governmental entity capitalizes a collection that previously had not been reported at the date that GASB-34 was implemented, the capitalization should be reported as a change in an accounting principle (prior-period adjustment) and not as a correction of an error.

Works of art, historical treasures, and similar assets that were given to a governmental entity before the implementation of GASB-34 should be reported at the fair value of the asset at the date of gift and not at the date of implementation.

GASB's *Implementation Guide 2015-1*, question 7.21.9 [GASB Cod. Sec. 1400.704-8], reminds practitioners that GASB-34 does not provide a definition of inexhaustible collections or individual works of art or historical treasures; however, the *Guide* provides the following description of the items: "Those items with extraordinarily long useful lives that because of their cultural, aesthetic, or historical value, the holder of the asset (or assets) applies effort to protect and preserve the asset in a manner greater than that for similar assets without such cultural, aesthetic, or historical value."

Works of art, historical treasures, and similar assets that are received as donations must be recorded as revenue based on the standards established by GASB-33 (*Accounting and Financial Reporting for Nonexchange Transactions*). If these donated items are added to a noncapitalized collection, the governmental entity must simultaneously record a program expense equal to the amount of the donation recorded as revenue (GASB-34, par. 28) [GASB Cod. Sec. 1400.110].

As previously discussed, works of art, historical treasures, and similar assets that are "inexhaustible" do not have to be depreciated. All other capitalized items must be depreciated (GASB-34, par. 29) [GASB Cod. Sec. 1400.111].

Intangible Assets

As noted in GASB-34, certain intangible assets are included as a component or classification of capital assets. GASB-51 (*Accounting and Financial Reporting for Intangible Assets*), provides needed guidance regarding how to identify, account for, and report intangible assets. GASB-51 defines intangible assets and provides guidance on the proper reporting for different types of intangible assets, including whether they should be amortized. Prior to the issuance of GASB-51, questions were frequently raised regarding intangible assets and their inclusion as capital assets for accounting and financial reporting purposes.

GASB-51 defines an intangible asset as possessing the following characteristics:

- A lack of physical substance (i.e., the asset cannot be touched);

- A nonfinancial nature (i.e., the asset has value, but not in a monetary form such as cash, investments securities, a claim or right to monetary assets such as receivables, or prepayments of goods and services); and

- A multiple period useful life (i.e., the asset has an initial useful life extending beyond a single reporting period) (GASB-51, par. 2) [GASB Cod. Sec. 1400.138].

Examples of governmental intangible assets include easements, land and mineral use rights, computer software, patents, and trademarks.

Excluded from the scope of GASB-51 are the following:

- Intangible assets that are acquired or created primarily for the purpose of directly obtaining income or profit, which GASB-51 states should be treated and reported as investments. These may be patents or processes that the government has licensed potentially to third parties. A royalty stream may be an indicator of management's intent to obtain income or profit unless documented otherwise.

- Assets resulting from capital lease transactions, which GASB-51 states should be accounted for in accordance with the provisions contained in GASB-62 and in the process of being updated through the issuance of GASB-87 (see **PRACTICE ALERT**, above, and Chapter 14, "Leases and

Service Concession Arrangements") (GASB-51, par. 3, as amended by GASB-69, par. 39, and GASB-72, par. 64) [GASB Cod. Sec. 1400.139].

PRACTICE POINT: One of the exclusions from the scope of GASB-51 is "goodwill" created through the combination of a government and another entity. GASB-69 (*Government Combinations and Disposals of Government Operations*) discusses acquisitions. In an acquisition a government acquires another entity, or its operations, in exchange for significant consideration. The consideration provided is measured in relation to the assets and liabilities acquired. The acquired entity or operation becomes part of the acquiring government's legally separate entity. The acquiring government then recognizes the assets, deferred outflows of resources, liabilities, or deferred inflows of resources acquired or assumed at the acquisition date, in conformity with authoritative guidance for state and local governments. The acquiring government's application of recognition principles may result in recognizing assets, deferred outflows of resources, liabilities, or deferred inflows of resources that the acquired organization was not required to recognize. The acquired entity may have recognized deferred outflows of resources (or goodwill, by a nongovernmental entity) from previous acquisition transactions in which the consideration provided exceeded the net position acquired. The acquiring government should not recognize such deferred outflows of resources (or goodwill). If the consideration provided is greater than the net position acquired, the acquiring government reports the difference as a deferred outflow of resources. The deferred outflow is then amortized over future periods systematically and rationally with a length of amortization determined by considering remaining capital asset service lives, the expected length of contracts acquired or similar measures. There is also no such thing as "negative goodwill" for governmental acquisitions. If consideration is less than the net position acquired, the acquiring government eliminates the excess net position by reducing the acquisition values of non-current assets (other than financial assets) that are acquired. If the allocation reduces the acquisition value of the acquired non-current assets to zero, the remainder is recognized as a special item. If the intent of the "selling" government is to accept a lower price to provide aid without receiving equal value, a contribution exists.

GASB Statement No. 85 (*Omnibus 2017*), par. 5, clarifies GASB-69 for goodwill in existence prior to the issuance of GASB-69. For acquisitions that occurred prior to the effective date of GASB-69, the above guidance should be applied and negative goodwill should not be reported. GASB-85 became effective for periods beginning after June 15, 2017. Reclassification of any goodwill in existence may result in reclassifications to deferred outflows of resources or part of the restatement of net position required by GASB-85 (GASB-69, par. 39, as amended by GASB-85, par. 5) [GASB Cod. Sec. Co10.136].

GASB-51 generally requires that intangible assets (included within the scope of the statement) be reported as capital assets at historical cost. For intangible assets to be reported at historical cost in the financial statements, the asset must be "identifiable," which means the asset is separable, or the government can sell, rent, or transfer it to another party. Consequently, if the asset is not separable, it has to arise from contractual or other legal rights, such as water rights acquired from another government through a contract that cannot be transferred to another party (GASB-51, pars. 5–6, as amended by GASB-63, par. 8) [GASB Cod. Secs. 1400.140–.141].

Many intangible assets are purchased or received from other parties. However, certain intangible assets may be generated internally by a government itself, such as software systems. Outlays related to developing such assets may be incurred over time rather than at a single point in time when a purchase occurs. The accounting and reporting of these types of assets has been given special attention by the GASB. GASB-51 addresses three circumstances that must be met in order for outlays, which are related to internally generated intangible assets, to begin to be reported as a capital asset:

1. The government's specific objective for the project and the service capacity in which the asset is expected to be used upon completion of the project has to be determined.

2. The feasibility of completing the project so that it can be used in that capacity has to be demonstrated.

3. The government's intention to complete or to continue the development of the asset has to be demonstrated (GASB-51, par. 7) [GASB Cod. Sec. 1400.142].

GASB-51 provides specific guidance for capitalizing outlays related to internally generated computer software as intangible assets. This guidance involves classifying activities in developing and installing internally generated computer software into three stages: (1) preliminary project stage, (2) application development stage, and (3) post-implementation/operation stage. Different rules apply to outlays in each of the stages. The principles are as follows:

	Preliminary Stage	Development Stage	Post-Implementation/ Operation Stage
Definition	Determination of whether a project is technologically and financially feasible	Management authorizes and commits to funding	Software is accepted and operating
Characteristics of Stage	Demonstration that there is intent to complete the project	Software is coded, tested, implemented. INITIAL training occurs.	Ongoing maintenance that does NOT increase useful life
	Initial investigations or designs	Procurement and contracting	Ongoing training
GAAP Principles	Expense	Capitalize	Expense
Additional information			Betterments are capitalized if they increase useful life or service utility of the software

The above table can also be applied to many internally generated intangible assets other than software, including patents, trademarks, and other invented items.

> **OBSERVATION:** A government's accounting software or system needs to be flexible enough to properly account for these multiple phases and capitalize *all* related costs, including direct salaries, indirect costs, payroll, costs of consultants, and other design and build costs.

With regard to amortization, intangible assets that have no legal, contractual, regulatory, technological, or other factors limiting their useful life are considered to have an indefinite useful life and should not be amortized. Otherwise, similar to other depreciable capital assets, intangible assets are to be amortized. For example, water rights procured under a contract with no termination to the rights of the purchasing government would be considered an intangible asset with an indefinite useful life and would therefore be reported at historical cost and not be amortized. However, if an intangible asset originally considered to have had an indefinite useful life experiences an event that results in a subsequent determination that the useful life is no longer indefinite (e.g., a change in the terms of the water rights contract that provides a termination date for such rights), it must be amortized over its remaining useful life (GASB-51, par. 16) [GASB Cod. Sec. 1400.151].

Outlays in governmental funds associated with intangible assets should be reported as expenditures when incurred consistent with the current financial resources measurement focus. At the government-wide level of financial reporting, these intangible asset outlays of governmental funds would be capitalized and amortized in accordance with the provisions of GASB-51 and be a reconciling item between the fund financial statements and the government-wide financial statements (GASB-51, par. 19) [GASB Cod. Sec. 1400.153].

> **PRACTICE ALERT:** Many systems of government are so-called "cloud computing" arrangements, inclusive of a contract or software license. The user/government does not take possession of the software. Instead, the software application "resides" on the vendor or third party's hardware and access is provided to the software on an as-needed basis over the internet or a dedicated line.
>
> The GASB has not taken a position on "cloud computing" arrangements as of the date of publication, but is conducting pre-agenda research on such arrangements, inclusive of a literature review, surveys and interviews. It is unclear if a project will be pursued. FASB Accounting Standards Update 2015-05, updating FASB Accounting Standards Codification (ASC)™ Subtopic 350-40 (*Intangibles—Goodwill and Other—Internal Use Software*) contains *nonauthoritative* guidance for fees paid in a "cloud computing" arrangement. If such an arrangement includes a software license (which is common), the accounting is similar to other software licenses. For governments, the provisions are in GASB-51 as an intangible asset. If a license is not present, then the FASB Update requires the customer to account for the arrangement similarly to other service contracts.

Intangible Assets and Service Concession Arrangements

A government could be a party to a service concession arrangement (SCA) in accordance with GASB-60 [GASB Cod. Sec. S30]. A governmental operator reports an intangible asset for the right to access the facility and collect third-party fees from its operation at cost (e.g., the amount of an up-front payment or the cost of construction of or improvements to the facility). The cost of improvements to the facility made by the governmental operator during the term of the SCA should increase the governmental operator's intangible asset if the improvements increase the capacity or efficiency of the facility. The intangible asset should be amortized over the term of the arrangement in a systematic and rational manner. Service concession arrangements are further discussed in Chapter 14, "Leases and Service Concession Arrangements."

PRACTICE ALERT: GASB staff are in the midst of pre-agenda research on public-private partnerships, GASB-60. It is possible revisions are needed for arrangements where it is unclear if such arrangements are subject to GASB-60 or GASB-87 (*Leases*).

Items That Will Become Assets That Are Constructed by a Government but Not Ultimately Owned by That Government

There are many circumstances where an item that will become an asset is constructed by one government but not ultimately owned by that government. The first government may finance the construction of the ultimate asset by bonds or grants, but when it is completed, deed the finished item over to another government who will own or operate the capital asset. This frequently occurs in infrastructure construction where the infrastructure spans multiple jurisdictions or the recipient government(s) do not have the credit or other funds or expertise to construct it. Councils of governments that are established to receive tax monies for infrastructure construction are a prime example of these arrangements. In these arrangements, a capital asset is not established at the constructing government, even though construction in process may be used. Guidance provided by GASB-54, paragraph 33, implies that a capital projects fund may not be used in these arrangements, because a capital projects fund excludes "those types of capital-related outflows financed by proprietary funds or for assets that will be held in trust for individuals, private organizations, *or other governments*" (emphasis added). However, guidance is not succinctly provided as to accounting and financial reporting of these transactions. It is this author's opinion that an agency fund or a special revenue fund may be used for the outlays during construction of the capital asset, largely dependent on the financing source or practices of the government. A special revenue fund may be preferable if federal awards or bonds are the financing source as agency funds are not presented on the face of the basic financial statements.

To account for these types of transactions, instead of capital outlays, which imply a capital asset in process, it is better to recognize expenditures as construction occurs within a special revenue fund. These expenditures would not need to be reclassified to construction in process as construction progresses, because construction in process is an asset. Since the constructed item is not an item with present service capacity that the government presently controls, reclassification to construction in process is not proper. Certainly, a construction journal may be maintained and is needed for the project to establish total cost. Upon completion, as expenditures have occurred in the funds, no adjustment to fund balance or net position is needed via a transfer. The total cost is then shifted to the recipient government who would then recognize the asset at cost similarly to donated assets, as discussed previously. An increase would occur to contributed assets (a revenue account) and the type of capital asset (an asset account) to record the transfer. Contributed assets would then close to the net investment in capital assets account at the end of a fiscal year.

General Infrastructure Assets

"Infrastructure assets" are defined by GASB-34 as "long-lived capital assets that normally are stationary in nature and normally can be preserved for a significantly greater number of years than most capital assets" and include the following (GASB-34, par. 19) [GASB Cod. Sec. 1400.103]:

- Bridges;
- Dams;
- Drainage systems;
- Lighting systems;
- Roads;
- Tunnels; and
- Water and sewer systems.

Buildings are generally not considered infrastructure assets unless they "are an ancillary part of a network of infrastructure assets."

Capitalization Guidance for General Infrastructure Assets

The *GASB Implementation Guide 2015-1*, question 7.104.11 [GASB Cod. Sec. 1400.732-5], raises the issue of whether a governmental entity can selectively report portions of infrastructure networks that were acquired prior to the July 1, 1980. Infrastructure networks should be reported on a network-by-network basis and not as a portion of a network. It should be remembered that the selective reporting of network costs is available only when it is not practical to determine or reasonably estimate the cost of infrastructure assets acquired prior to the implementation of the standards established by GASB-34. As a practical matter, as of the date of this publication, it is likely that the infrastructure networks that were acquired prior to July 1, 1980 have either been recognized previously or if not recognized, assuming a 40-year useful life and not using the modified approach, have an immaterial carrying value for most governments.

Like other capital assets, infrastructure assets should be presented in the statement of net position at historical cost (or estimated cost) less accumulated depreciation. A single amount (net of accumulated depreciation) may be presented on the face of the financial statement, in which case accumulated depreciation and the major categories of capital assets (land, buildings, equipment, infrastructure etc.) must be reported in a note.

A governmental entity may have to estimate the cost of major general infrastructure assets. Although the GASB describes some methods that can be used to estimate historical cost under these circumstances, "governments may use any approach that complies with the intent of this Statement" (GASB-34, pars. 154–155) [GASB Cod. Secs. 1400.168–.169].

OBSERVATION: The governmental entity that has the primary responsibility for maintaining a particular infrastructure asset should report the asset in its financial statements. Infrastructure assets that are maintained through a contract with a third party must nonetheless be reported by a governmental entity (GASB-34, fn. 67) [GASB Cod. Sec. 1400.fn.31].

GASB *Implementation Guide 2015-1,* question 7.12.14 [GASB Cod. Sec. 1400.735-5], discusses when a county constructs a road that is financed by county bonds, but ultimately transitions the road to the state to manage future maintenance. If there is evidence as to which government owns the road, that government should report it. In many cases regarding infrastructure, there is no deed or title. When ownership is unclear, the government with the primary responsibility for managing an infrastructure asset reports the asset. In this case, the state would report the road. But the county would also have bonds outstanding without a related capital asset.

Methods of Calculating Infrastructure Depreciation

In order to compute depreciation expense on infrastructure assets, a governmental entity may use "any established depreciation method." There is no list of acceptable depreciation methods. In order for a depreciation method to be acceptable, it must meet the general conditions of being both *systematic* and *rational*. The systematic criterion requires that an established set of computational procedures be defined (essentially a formula) so that the application of the depreciation method results in the same pattern of depreciation expense under a specific set of circumstances (cost, salvage value, estimated life, etc.). The rationality criterion is poorly defined but it is generally interpreted to mean that the pattern of depreciation expense is based on a reasonable objective(s). For example, the objective might be to reflect more depreciation expense in the early life of the asset based on the assumption that the infrastructure asset will deteriorate more in its earlier life (GASB-34, pars. 161–162) [GASB Cod. Secs. 1400.161–.162].

OBSERVATION: Depreciation methods that might be used by governmental entities to account for infrastructure assets include the straight-line method, sum-of-the-years' digits method, and a variety of declining balance methods, such as the 150% declining method. The most common method used by governmental entities is the straight-line method.

Composite methods. For some infrastructure assets a group life depreciation method may be appropriate for tracking asset costs and to computing depreciation expense. Under a composite method, similar (all interstate highways in a state) or dissimilar infrastructure assets (such as roads, bridges, or tunnels) are combined in order to form a single historical cost basis for computing depreciation and accounting for the disposition of infrastructure assets. The composite method requires that an annual depreciation rate be determined for the collection of assets based on the relationship of depreciation expense to the total capitalized cost of the infrastructure assets that make up the group (GASB-34, par. 163) [GASB Cod. Sec. 1400.177].

There is no single set of procedures for employing composite depreciation methods. The GASB makes the following observations as to how the methods could be implemented (GASB-34, par. 164) [GASB Cod. Sec. 1400.178]:

- The composite life could be based on a simple average or weighted average life of the group assets utilizing the following formula:

    [1 ÷ {(sum of all the useful lives of the individual assets in the group) ÷

    the count of the assets}]

    = annual depreciation rate as a percentage

    For 6 highways with 10, 20, 30, 40, 50, and 60 years lives the formula would be:

    1 ÷ {(10+20+30+40+50+60 = 210) ÷ 6} = 2.85714% annual depreciation rate.

- The composite depreciation rate could be based on an assessment of the useful lives of the grouping of assets.

Once a composite depreciation rate is determined, it should be used throughout the life of the group assets. However, it may be necessary to change the rate if the composition of the group assets changes (assets are replaced) or the estimated composite life of the remaining assets changes significantly. The change in the composite depreciation rate under these circumstances would be accounted for as a change in an accounting estimate as defined in GASB-62, par. 69 [GASB Cod. Secs. 2250.101, .132], on accounting changes (GASB-34, pars. 165–166) [GASB Cod. Secs. 1400.179–.180].

Modified Approach for Infrastructure Assets

The GASB does not require that infrastructure assets that are part of a network or subsystem of a network (referred to as eligible infrastructure assets) be depreciated if the following conditions are satisfied (GASB-34, par. 23) [GASB Cod. Sec. 1400.105]:

- An asset management system is employed that:
  - Has an up-to-date inventory of eligible infrastructure assets,
  - Performs condition assessments of the assets and summarizes the results using a "measurable scale,"
  - Estimates, on an annual basis, the annual amount needed to "maintain and preserve the eligible infrastructure assets at the condition level established and disclosed by the government," and

- The government is preserving and maintaining the eligible infrastructure assets "approximately at (or above) a condition level established and disclosed by the government."

The documentation of condition assessments must be carefully done so that their results can be replicated. GASB-34 describes results as being subject to replication as "those that are based on sufficiently understandable and complete measurement methods such that different measurers using the same methods would reach substantially similar results." (GASB-34, fn.18) [GASB Cod. Sec. 1400.fn7].

As an example, the GASB's *Implementation Guide 2015-1*, question 7.12.7 [GASB Cod. Sec. 702-13], identifies the following as buildings that may be an ancillary part of a network or subsystem:

- Turnpike rest areas,
- Road maintenance buildings related to a highway system, and
- Water pumping buildings related to a water system.

The *Guide* also states that a subsystem makes up a part of a network (a collection of related assets). For example, a sewer system (the network) could comprise storm drains and retention ponds.

The condition level must be established and documented by governmental policy or legislative action, and the assessment itself may be made either by the governmental entity directly or by external parties. Professional judgment and good faith are the basis for determining what constitutes acceptable and accurate documentation of the condition of eligible infrastructure assets. However, GASB-34 states that governmental entities should document the following (GASB-34, par. 24) [GASB Cod. Sec. 1400.106]:

- Complete condition assessments of eligible infrastructure assets are performed in a consistent manner at least every three years; and
- The results of the three most recent complete condition assessments provide reasonable assurance that the eligible infrastructure assets are being preserved approximately at (or above) the condition level established and disclosed by the government.

GASB-34 points out that the condition level could be applied to a group of assets by using a condition index or "as the percentage of a network of infrastructure assets in good or poor condition."

If a governmental entity identifies a subsystem of infrastructure assets as "eligible" (and therefore the computation of depreciation is optional), the documentary requirements apply only to the subsystem and not to the entire network of infrastructure assets.

The GASB's *Implementation Guide 2015-1*, question 7.16.2 [GASB Cod. Sec. 1400.703-3], reminds practitioners that GASB-34 requires that the modified approach be applied to all assets in the network or subsystem; however, a governmental entity could decide to use the modified approach for one network but not for another network. On the other hand, if the eligible infrastructure assets are reported by two or more different departments, either all or none of the assets in the network or subsystem must be subjected to the modified approach.

The GASB's *Implementation Guide 2015-1,* question 7.19.4 [GASB Cod. Sec. 703-21], recognizes that numerous asset management systems are available to governmental entities. The GASB does not sanction management systems. It is the responsibility of the management of a governmental entity to assess a management system and determine whether that system can satisfy the standards established by paragraphs 23 and 24 of GASB-34.

A governmental entity may perform the condition assessment annually or may use a cycle basis. If a cyclical basis is used for networks or subsystems, all assets of these groups must be assessed during the cycle. However, rather than apply the condition assessment to all assets, a statistical sample approach may be employed in the annual approach or in the cycle approach.

Because eligible infrastructure assets do not have to be depreciated, all expenditures related to their maintenance should be recognized as a current expense when incurred. Expenditures that are capital in nature (additions and improvements) should be capitalized as part of the eligible infrastructure assets because they, by definition, increase the capacity or efficiency of the related infrastructure asset (GASB-34, par. 25) [GASB Cod. Sec. 1400.107].

The adequate maintenance of the condition of eligible infrastructure assets is a continuous process and if the conditions established by GASB-34 are initially satisfied but subsequently are not, the infrastructure assets are not considered "eligible" and depreciation expense must be computed for them and reported in the statement of activities. The change in accounting for depreciation expense should be reported as a change in an accounting estimate (GASB-34, par. 26) [GASB Cod. Sec. 1400.108].

OBSERVATION: The non-recognition of depreciation expense for eligible infrastructure assets is optional. A governmental entity can decide to depreciate all infrastructure assets that are exhaustible rather than carve out and identify "eligible infrastructure assets."

The GASB's *Implementation Guide 2015-1,* question 7.16.3 [GASB Cod. Sec. 1400.702-22], points out that parks are considered land and therefore are not infrastructure assets; however, a subsystem within a park (such as roads and trails) could be considered an infrastructure asset and therefore eligible for the modified approach.

When an infrastructure asset is subject to the modified approach, the transfer of the asset from one governmental entity to another is recorded by the transferring government as a functional expense, depending on the nature of the asset transferred.

Electing the Modified Approach

A governmental entity can begin to use the modified approach to account for eligible infrastructure assets if both of the following conditions are satisfied (GASB-34, par. 152) [GASB Cod. Sec. 1400.166]:

- One complete condition assessment is available.

- The governmental entity documents that the eligible infrastructure assets are being preserved approximately at (or above) the condition level identified.

GASB-34 points out that initially the three most recent complete condition assessments and the estimated and actual amounts to maintain and preserve the assets for the previous five reporting periods (as required by GASB-34, par. 132) [GASB Cod. Sec. 1400.118] may not be available. Under this circumstance, the governmental entity should present the information that is available (GASB-34, par. 153) [GASB Cod. Sec. 1400.167].

Reporting under the Modified Approach

Governmental entities that use the modified (depreciation) approach for certain eligible infrastructure assets must present the following schedules as required supplementary information (RSI) (GASB-34, pars. 132–133) [GASB Cod. Secs. 1400.118–.119]:

- The assessed condition of infrastructure assets (for at least the three most recent complete condition assessments) along with the date of the assessments.

- A comparison of (1) the estimated annual required amount at the beginning of the year needed to maintain and preserve the condition level established and disclosed in the financial statements and (2) the amount actually expensed for each of the past five reporting periods.

The schedules described above must be accompanied by the following related disclosures:

- The basis for the condition measurement and the measurement scale used to assess and report the condition.

- The condition level at which the government intends to preserve the eligible infrastructure assets.

- Factors that have a significant effect on trends related to the information presented in the schedules described above, including changes in the measurement scale, the basis for the condition measurement, or the condition assessment methods used.

- If there is a change in the condition level established by the governmental entity, the estimate of the effect of the change on the estimated annual amount needed to maintain and preserve the assets for the current period.

OBSERVATION: The GASB encourages governments that gather information that must be disclosed when they use the modified approach to disclose such information even if they do not use the modified approach.

The GASB's *Implementation Guide 2015-1*, question 7.20.11 [GASB Cod. Sec. 1400.710-2], provides the following guidance for performing the condition assessment related to the modified approach for reporting infrastructure assets:

- In performing the condition assessment, a governmental entity should use the same method, basis, and scale for the complete assessment period. If a three-year cycle is used, the consistency standard applies to the three-year period. The method, basis, or scale may be changed before an assessment period begins, but all changes must be disclosed in the notes to the RSI.

- The methods used to perform a condition assessment will change over time and new methods may be adopted before the beginning of the condition assessment period.

PRACTICE ALERT: As part of pre-agenda research for the GASB's *Financial Reporting Model—Reexamination* project, GASB staff did focus group research about the efficacy of the modified approach for infrastructure assets. At the time of publication, it is unclear if the GASB will reexamine the approach as part of the overall project.

ACCOUNTING AND FINANCIAL REPORTING FOR IMPAIRMENT OF CAPITAL ASSETS AND FOR INSURANCE RECOVERIES

Unlike the asset impairment accounting standards applicable to commercial accounting, until the issuance of GASB Statement No. 42 (*Accounting and Financial Reporting for Impairment of Capital Assets and for Insurance Recoveries*), there had been no guidance on how to measure or report the impairment of these assets for a governmental entity. Although GASB-42 applies to proprietary fund and government-wide financial statements, those standards do not apply to governmental funds. GASB-42 defines capital assets consistent with paragraph 19 of GASB-34 [GASB Cod. Sec. 1400.103].

For the purposes of GASB-42, land is considered a capital asset that is separate from buildings and depreciable improvements and therefore should be evaluated separately for impairment.

Definition of Capital Asset Impairment

GASB-42 describes the impairment of a capital asset as "a significant, unexpected decline in the service utility of a capital asset." The significant and unexpected decline is based on events or changes in circumstances that were not anticipated when the capital asset was placed into service. "Service utility" is the "usable capacity that at acquisition was expected to be used to provide service, as distinguished from the level of utilization, which is the portion of the usable capacity currently being used." (GASB-42, pars. 5–6) [GASB Cod. Secs. 1400.181–.182]

GASB-42 identifies the following five indicators of an impairment of a governmental capital asset (GASB-42, par. 9, GASB-51, par. 18) [GASB Cod. Sec. 1400.185]:

1. Evidence of physical damage, such as, for a building, damage by fire or flood, to the degree that restoration efforts are needed to restore service utility;

2. Change in legal or environmental factors, such as a water treatment plant that cannot meet (and cannot be modified to meet) new water quality standards;

3. Technological developments or evidence of obsolescence, such as that related to diagnostic equipment that is rarely used because new equipment is better;

4. A change in the manner or expected duration of usage of a capital asset, such as closure of a school prior to the end of its useful life; and

5. Construction stoppage, such as stoppage of construction of a building due to lack of funding.

The five examples listed above are identified as common indicators of impairment. The GASB recognizes that the list is not all-inclusive. Professional judgment must be used to identify other events and changes that give rise to capital asset impairments.

Impairment Test: Two-Step Process

The five common capital asset impairment indicators (and other events and changes as described above) do not have to be applied every time they arise. Such an approach would be prohibitively expensive to apply and the resulting financial reporting benefits would be marginal. For this reason, GASB-42 provides for the testing of capital asset impairment by determining whether both of the following factors are present (GASB-42, par. 11) [GASB Cod. Sec. 1400.187]:

1. The magnitude of the decline in service utility is significant; and

2. The decline in service utility is unexpected.

GASB-42 considers a significant decline to be evidenced by the continuing operating expenses related to the use of the impaired capital asset or the costs to restore the asset are significant in relationship to the current service utility.

All capital assets subject to depreciation generally reflect a decline in utility with age or usage; however, asset impairment arises when that decline is unexpected. For example, restoration costs are generally not part of a capital asset's normal life cycle and if they were later contemplated because of an event or change, that development would suggest an unexpected decline in the service utility of the capital asset. On the other hand, the incurrence of normal maintenance costs or preservation costs does not suggest the impairment of a capital asset.

Temporary Impairments

The impairment of a capital asset should generally be considered permanent. If an impairment of a capital asset is considered temporary, the historical cost of the capital asset should not be written down. However, impairments can be considered temporary only when there is evidence to support such a conclusion. The following illustrates an example of a temporary impairment:

> A middle school that is not being used due to declining enrollment should not be written down if future middle school enrollment projections substantiated by current elementary school enrollment demonstrate that the middle school

will be needed in a few years (GASB-42, par. 18, GASB-51, par. 18) [GASB Cod. Sec. 1400.194].

OBSERVATION: The carrying amount of impaired capital assets that are idle at year-end should be disclosed, regardless of whether the impairment is considered permanent or temporary (GASB-42, par. 20, GASB-72, pars. 80–81) [GASB Cod. Sec. 1400.196].

Measuring the Impairment of Capital Assets

When a capital asset is considered to be impaired based on the criteria in GASB-42, the amount of the impairment loss (based on historical cost) should be determined by using one of the following measurement approaches:

- Restoration cost approach (generally used to measure impairment losses from physical damage from fire, wind, and the like);

- Service units approach (generally used to measure impairment losses from environmental factors, technological changes, obsolescence, or change in the manner or duration of use); and

- Deflated depreciated replacement cost approach (generally used to measure impairment losses from change in the manner or duration of use).

OBSERVATION: GASB-42 suggests that impairment losses from construction stoppages be determined based on the lower of the carrying value or fair value of the impaired asset.

The specific method to be used should be the approach "that best reflects the decline in service utility of the capital asset." Once an approach has been used, that approach should also be used to measure subsequent impairment write-downs with similar characteristics (GASB-42, pars. 12–15) [GASB Cod. Secs. 1400.188–.191].

Restoration Cost Approach

Under the restoration cost approach, the write-down is based on the proportion of the capital asset impaired as expressed in current restoration cost. The current restoration cost is then converted to a historical cost basis under either a cost index or a ratio approach. The following steps are used for the ratio approach:

- *Step 1* Determine the restoration cost in current dollars.

- *Step 2* Determine the replacement cost in current dollars for the capital asset.

- *Step 3* Determine the carrying value of the impaired capital asset before adjustment (historical cost less accumulated depreciation).

- *Step 4* Determine the relationship between the restoration cost in current dollars and the replacement cost in current dollars for the capital asset.

- *Step 5* Determine the impairment lost by multiplying the carrying value of the asset by the percentage computed in Step 4.

OBSERVATION: The restoration cost approach can also be implemented by using an appropriate cost index.

The estimate of the restoration cost should be based on the amount of the impairment caused by the change or event and should exclude costs related to demolition, cleanup, additions, and improvements.

To illustrate the restoration cost approach, assume that a building originally cost $10,000,000, had an estimated useful life of 40 years (with a nominal residual value), and was 30% depreciated, when it was discovered that ceilings had been partially insulated with asbestos. The cost of restoring the ceilings is $3,000,000. The estimated current replacement cost for the building is $13,000,000. The computation of the impairment write-down is as follows:

Step	Amount
Step 1 – Restoration Cost in Current Dollars	$3,000,000
Step 2 – Replacement Cost in Current Dollars	13,000,000
Step 3 – ($10,000,000-$3,000,000) (Historical cost less depreciation before adjustment)	7,000,000
Step 4 ($3,000,000 ÷ $13,000,000) (Step 1 ÷ Step 2)	× 23%
= Impairment write-down	$1,610,000

If it is assumed that the event that caused the impairment was considered unusual in nature but not infrequent in occurrence and was not within the control of management, it would be considered a "special item" as defined in GASB-34 and would be recorded in proprietary fund or government-wide financial statements as follows:

	Debit	Credit
PROPRIETARY FUND		
Special Item—Impairment Loss	1,610,000	
Accumulated Depreciation—Building		1,610,000
To record impairment loss on building		

An impairment loss would not be recognized in a governmental fund, because the capital assets are not reported in such funds and because the event does not reduce current financial resources of the entity.

Service Units Approach

Under the service units approach, the write-down is based on the proportion of the capital asset, as expressed in service units, which has been lost due to the event or change that created the impairment. The total service units can be based on the maximum service units or total service units throughout the life of the capital asset and can be expressed in a variety of measurement units, including years of service, number of citizens benefited, and various outputs.

To illustrate the service units approach, assume that waste treatment equipment costs $1,000,000, and originally had an estimated useful life of 40 years (with a nominal residual value). After 10 years of use, new environmental regulations are established and the equipment can be used for only five more years before new equipment must be acquired. The amount of the service units lost, expressed in years, is 25 years, and the amount of the impairment loss is $625,000 [=$1,000,000 × (25 ÷ 40)].

Deflated Depreciated Replacement Cost Approach

The computation of the impairment loss using the deflated depreciated replacement cost approach is based on determining the current cost of an asset needed for the current level of service. Based on the assumed carrying value (cost minus accumulated depreciation) of the theoretical asset, that carrying value is deflated to the historical cost basis for when the original asset was acquired. For example, assume that a building had an original cost of $5,000,000 and was 40% depreciated. The building was to be used originally as a clinic but because of the construction of a new clinic, the building will be used instead as a warehouse. The cost of a suitable (based on the new usage) warehouse is approximately $1,500,000 and the replacement cost of the clinic is $7,000,000. The amount of the impairment loss is computed as follows:

Step	Amount
Deflator ($7,000,000 ÷ $5,000,000)	1.4
Assumed carrying amount of a new warehouse ($1,500,000 × 60%)	$900,000
Carrying amount of old building ($5,000,000 × 60%)	$3,000,000
Deflated assumed carrying amount of a new warehouse ($900,000 ÷ 1.4)	(642,857)
= Impairment loss	$2,357,143

Insurance Recoveries

GASB-42 provides the following presentation guidance for insurance recoveries related to impairments of capital assets:

- Restoration or replacement costs should be reported separately (as an expenditure) from any insurance recovery (as another financing source or extraordinary item) in the financial statements of a governmental fund.

- Restoration or replacement costs should be reported separately from the impairment loss and associated insurance recovery in the government-wide and proprietary fund financial statements.

- The impairment loss should be reported net of any insurance recovery when the recovery is realized or realizable in the same year as the impairment loss.

- Insurance recovery proceeds that are realized or realizable in a period subsequent to the recognition of the impairment loss should be reported as program revenue, non-operating revenue, or an extraordinary item (GASB-42, par. 21) [GASB Cod. Sec. 1400.197].

OBSERVATION: Insurance recoveries also are for noncapital assets. For example, assume a government loses $1 million due to a fraud scheme. The loss needs to be included as part of a program or general government expense as an extraordinary item, special item, or operating expense during the year the loss is discovered. The government, however, has antifraud insurance and recovers the funds in a subsequent year. The insurance recovery would use the same methodology as part of program revenue, non-operating revenue, or an extraordinary item.

Reporting Impairment Write-Down

When a capital asset impairment is determined to be permanent, the amount of the write-down must be evaluated and classified in the financial statements in one of the following categories as established by GASB-34:

- Program expense based on the guidance established by paragraphs 41–46 of GASB-34 [GASB Cod. Secs. 2200.129–.134, C50.121, 2300.107].

- Extraordinary item based on the guidance established by paragraph 55 of GASB-34 or GASB-62, pars. 45–49 [GASB Cod. Secs. 1800.145, .147–.151, 2200.143, .145–.149, C50.121].

- Special item based on the guidance established by paragraph 56 of GASB-34 or GASB-62, pars. 45–49 [GASB Cod. Secs. 1800.146–.151, 2200.144–.149, 2300.107, C50.121].

- Operating expense based on guidance established by paragraphs 101–102 of GASB-34 [GASB Cod. Secs. 1100, 1800, 2200.191–.192, P80.114–.115].

If the impairment write-down is related to a proprietary fund capital asset, the write-down is classified either as (1) an operating expense, (2) an extraordinary item, or (3) a special item. If the impairment is related to a governmental fund capital asset, no write-down is reported, because the write-down does not consume current financial resources of the governmental fund.

Impairments of Intangible Capital (and Non-Capital) Assets

GASB-51 amends the capital assets section of GASB-34. Therefore, intangible assets are also subject to impairment testing. Should an intangible asset be impaired, the same guidance is followed as if the asset were tangible.

PRACTICE ALERT: GASB-87 incorporates by reference the impairment standards contained in GASB-42 if leased assets become impaired.

Impairments as a Result of Combinations

GASB-69 (*Government Combinations and Disposals of Government Operations*) includes provisions for accounting and financial reporting for the capital assets involved in combinations. In a merger, impairment may occur in a number of ways, including a disposal of buildings and other capital assets due to redundancy. If two cities are merging, there is no need for a second city hall. Therefore, impairment is present. In this case, GASB-69 directs preparers and auditors to adjust carrying values in accordance with GASB-42 (GASB-69, par. 19) [GASB Cod. Sec. Co10.116]. Similarly, in a merger where one government continues but the other does not, an impairment may also occur (GASB-69, par. 26) [GASB Cod. Sec. Co10.123]. Even in a disposal or a transfer of operations, impairment may be present. For example, if a city police force is transferred to a county sheriff, chances are there are buildings, police cars, and other assets the former city no longer needs. The transferee (receiving) government will decide if impairment is present. There may also be decisions in any type of combination to change the manner of use or duration of use, which will also potentially cause impairment (GASB-69, par. 49) [GASB Cod. Sec. Co10.146].

Asset Retirement Obligations

PRACTICE POINT: This section discusses GASB-83 (*Certain Asset Retirement Obligations*). GASB-83 is effective for periods beginning after June 15, 2018. Changes adopted to conform to the provisions of GASB-83 require a retroactive restatement of financial statements for all prior periods presented if practicable.

GASB-83 establishes standards of accounting and financial reporting for *certain* asset retirement obligations (AROs) (not all asset retirement obligations). ARO is defined in GASB-83 as a legally enforceable liability associated with the retirement of a tangible capital asset. The tangible capital asset must be *permanently* removed from service. Retirement is similar to other disposals, including sale, abandonment, recycling or some other manner. The provisions of GASB-42 would apply for a temporary idling.

ARO's are a normal occurrence from operations, whether acquired or constructed. There must be a legally enforceable obligation with the retirement of the tangible capital asset or GASB-83 does not apply. GASB-83 also does not apply to:

- Obligations that arise solely from a plan to sell or otherwise dispose of a tangible capital asset;
- Obligations associated with the preparation of a tangible capital asset for an alternative use;
- Obligations for pollution remediation, such as asbestos removal, that result from the other-than-normal operation of a tangible capital asset;
- Obligations associated with maintenance, rather than retirement, of a tangible capital asset;

- The cost of a replacement part that is a component of a tangible capital asset;

- Landfill closure and postclosure care obligations, including those not covered by GASB-18 (*Accounting for Municipal Solid Waste Landfill Closure and Postclosure Care Costs*); and

- Conditional obligations to perform asset retirement activities (GASB-83, pars. 4–6) [GASB Cod. Secs. A10.102–.104].

Recognition of an ARO

Similarly to environmental remediation obligations recognized in accordance with GASB-49 (*Accounting and Financial Reporting for Pollution Remediation Obligations*) (see Chapter 16, "Other Liabilities"), GASB-83 requires governments to recognize an ARO liability upon incurrance and when reasonably estimable. External and internal obligating events may trigger an ARO. Such events include:

External Obligating Events including:

- Approval of federal, state, or local laws or regulations
- Creation of a legally binding contract
- Issuance of a court judgment.

Internal Obligating Events including:

- For contamination-related AROs, the occurrence of contamination that is the result of the normal operation of a tangible capital asset and is not in the scope of GASB-49. (For example, a nuclear vessel contamination as part of the normal operation of the plant.)

- For non-contamination-related AROs:
  - If the pattern of occurrence of the liability is due to normal use, placing the asset into service and consuming capacity would trigger an ARO.
  - If the pattern of incurrence of the liability is not based on the use, just placing the asset into service would trigger an ARO.
  - If the pattern of incurrence of the liability is not based on the use, just placing the asset into service would trigger an ARO.

ARO will generate a liability. The offset is a deferred outflow of resources unless the asset is abandoned prior to operation. If abandonment occurs, an expense is recognized (GASB-83, pars. 8–13) [GASB Cod. Secs. A10.105–.110].

Initial Measurement of an ARO

The ARO is determined based on legal requirements relevant to the asset's retirement. It is based on the best estimate of the *current value* of the outlays expected to be incurred. Similarly to the provisions of GASB-49, current value is the amount that would be paid if all equipment, facilities, and services included in the estimate were acquired at the end of the current period.

All available evidence should be used to determine the estimate. Similarly to the provisions of GASB-49, a probability weighting is used of potential outcomes when sufficient evidence is available or can be obtained at reasonable cost. If the cost to obtain the amount is unreasonable, the most likely amount is used.

EXAMPLE: A public utility is required to establish a liability to retire an electric plant. Assume the ARO related to the plant plant's retirement as of the reporting date has a variety of probabilities. There is a 10% chance the ARO will be $10,000,000, a 50% chance it will be $50,000,000 and a 40% chance it will be $100,000,000. The ARO at the reporting date would be as follows:

Probability (A)	Amount (B)	Total (A × B)
10%	$10,000,000	$1,000,000
50%	$50,000,000	25,000,000
40%	$100,000,000	40,000,000
100%	N/A	$66,000,000

Exception for Minority Interest Owners

It is a common occurrence for a state or local government to be a minority owner in a large-scale plant that would require an ARO. Minority shares are defined in GASB-83 as being less than 50% of an ownership interest in an undivided interest arrangement in which (*a*) the government and one or more other entities jointly own a tangible capital asset to the extent of each entity's ownership interest, and (*b*) each joint owner is liable for its share of the ARO. In many cases, the majority owner is not a governmental entity and uses FASB standards. Even in the case where no entity has a majority ownership stake, FASB standards may apply where a nongovernmental owner has operational responsibility for the asset.

In these situations, the previous discussion on the initial measurement of the ARO using GASB-83 would not apply. Instead, most likely, FASB standards would apply. The measurement of the initial ARO should occur no more than one year and one day prior to the government's reporting date (GASB-83, par. 17) [GASB Cod. Sec. A10.114].

EXAMPLE: A city is a 10% owner in a large scale nuclear plant. The City's fiscal year-end is June 30, 2020. The City may use the ARO information from the plant owner/operator as long as it is measured no earlier than June 29, 2019.

Subsequent Measurement of ARO and the Deferred Outflow of Resources

After the initial ARO calculation, recognition of a liability and the related deferred outflow of resources, the ARO should be adjusted at least annually based on the effects of general inflation or deflation. All relevant factors to determine the outlays associated with the ARO should also be remeasured. The factors may have changed since the last measurement due to new technology, changes in laws or regulation or changes in equipment needed to retire the asset.

Prior to retirement of the asset, any changes in the ARO also increase or decrease the deferred outflow of resources. After retirement of the capital asset, any change in the ARO is either an expense (or revenue).

Similar adjustments would occur for minority interest owners.

The deferred outflow of resources would be amortized systematically and rationally upon initial measurement in one of two ways:

1. Amortize the deferred outflow of resources over the estimated useful life of the asset.

2. Amortize over the *remaining* estimated useful life of an asset for assets placed into operation previously, but either implementation of GASB-83 or a change in law requires ARO recognition (GASB-83, pars. 19–23) [GASB Cod. Secs. A10.116–.120].

Recognition in Governmental Funds

ARO may occur in a governmental fund. Goods and services may have been provided related to the recognition of the ARO. The amounts that are normally expected to be liquidated with expendable available financial resources would be declared a liability. Facilities or equipment acquired related to ARO would be an outlay/expenditure (GASB-83, par. 24) [GASB Cod. Sec. A10.121].

Funding and Assurance Provisions

Laws, regulations, judgments and similar commonly require assets to be restricted for payment of AROs, especially in public utilities. Customers of the utility are billed on a monthly basis a rate or charge for the ARO. Amounts received should be placed in a restricted asset account for the purpose of ARO and additional disclosure is required of the balances. The asset accounts should not offset the ARO in external financial reports (GASB-83, pars. 25–26) [GASB Cod. Secs. A10-122–.123].

Note Disclosure of ARO

GASB-83 requires notes to the basic financial statements related to ARO including:

- A general description of the AROs and associated tangible capital assets, as well as the source of the obligations (whether they are a result of federal, state, or local laws or regulations, contracts, or court judgments);

- The methods and assumptions used to measure the liabilities;

- The estimated remaining useful life of the associated tangible capital assets;

- How any legally required funding and assurance provisions associated with AROs are being met; for example, surety bonds, insurance policies, letters of credit, guarantees by other entities, or trusts used for funding and assurance; and

- The amount of assets restricted for payment of the liabilities, if not separately displayed in the financial statements.

If amounts cannot be reasonably estimated and therefore, no ARO is recognized, the facts and circumstances should be disclosed with regard to what is known on the ARO.

For minority interest owners, disclosure is limited to:

- A general description of the ARO and associated tangible capital asset, including:

  — The total amount of the ARO shared by the nongovernmental majority owner or the nongovernmental minority owner that has operational responsibility, other minority owners, if any, and the reporting government,

    — The reporting government's minority share of the total amount of the ARO, stated as a percentage, and

    — The dollar amount of the reporting government's minority share of the ARO;

- The date of the measurement of the ARO produced by the nongovernmental majority owner or the nongovernmental minority owner that has operational responsibility, if that date differs from the government's reporting date;

- How any legally required funding and assurance provisions associated with the government's minority share of an ARO are being met; for example, surety bonds, insurance policies, letters of credit, guarantees by other entities, or trusts used for funding and assurance; and

- The amount of assets restricted for payment of the government's minority share of the ARO, if not separately displayed in the financial statements (GASB-83, pars. 27–28) [GASB Cod. Secs. A10.124–.125].

PRACTICE POINT: The auditing of ARO will likely focus on the process of estimating the liability, recognition of whether a law, regulation, contract or judgment exists on triggering ARO and disclosure. The estimation process may require governments to contract a specialist to calculate the ARO. Auditors will likely review the assumptions made by the specialist to determine if the ARO is fairly stated.

QUESTIONS

1. Which of the following is *not* a capital asset?
   a. Land and land improvements.
   b. Buildings and building improvements.
   c. Supplies.
   d. Works of art, historical treasures, and other similar assets.

2. Due to the measurement focus and basis of accounting in governmental funds, which accounting element would be used to record a purchase of a $30,000 police car that would ultimately become a capital asset?
   a. Payroll expenditure.
   b. Capital outlays.
   c. Capitalized lease expense.
   d. Due to other funds.

3. When ownership is unclear on an infrastructure asset between a state and a county government, which government should record the infrastructure asset?
   a. The federal government because it assisted in funding the infrastructure.
   b. The state government because the infrastructure is a state highway.
   c. The county government because the infrastructure traverses a county.
   d. Whichever government that has primary responsibility for maintaining the infrastructure.

4. Which of the following *is not* a characteristic of an intangible asset?
   a. The asset is acquired or created primarily for the purpose of directly obtaining income or profit.
   b. The asset has a lack of physical substance.
   c. The asset is of a nonfinancial nature.
   d. The asset has a multiple period useful life.

5. A state is undertaking a multiple year project to beginning in 20X1 acquire and implement a new accounting system. In the first year, the state performed an in-depth analysis to determine that the software would be feasible and did a fit analysis. The state legislature appropriated funds at the end of the year and a contract was awarded to a software company. During years two through four, the software was developed, customized, tested, and run parallel through various stress tests. Staff and management were trained. On July 1, 20X6, the software was accepted. Various maintenance procedures were performed throughout 20X6, but otherwise the software worked as expected. Ongoing training did occur for new employees and updates. When would capitalization occur for the software?

    a. Years two through four.

    b. Year one.

    c. Year five (20X6).

    d. Years one through five.

6. A city wants to use the modified approach for its infrastructure assets. Which of the following conditions would not allow the city to use the modified approach during 20X6?

    a. The city performs condition assessments of the assets and summarizes the results using a measurable scale annually.

    b. The city estimates annually the amount needed to preserve and maintain the assets at the condition level established and disclosed by the government.

    c. The city reports an annual certified engineering study completed on October 1, 20X6 confirming the level of condition assessment of the city's infrastructure as of June 30, 20X6.

    d. The city reports an inventory of infrastructure from the period of July 1, 19X4 to June 30, 19X5.

7. Which of the following is *not* an indicator of asset impairment?

    a. Evidence of physical damage.

    b. Change in fair value.

    c. Technological obsolescence.

    d. Change in the manner or expected duration of usage of an asset.

8. A high school shuts down a wing of classrooms due to lower than expected enrollment to save on costs. However, the city clerk reports an increase in births and migration into the city due to a new factory opening. The clerk works with the school board to estimate that the high school wing may reopen in two years. This activity is indicative of

    a. Restoration cost approach.

    b. Service units approach.

    c. Temporary impairment.

    d. Deflated depreciation replacement cost approach.

9. Which of the following accounting elements *would not* be used to write down an asset that is impaired?

    a. Transfer expense.

    b. Program expense.

    c. Extraordinary item.

    d. Special item.

10. GASB-69 discusses government combinations and disposals of government operations. What could be an outcome of a government combination with regard to asset impairment?

    a. If two cities combine, the new city makes a judgment that only one city hall is needed and shuts the other city hall, declaring an impairment.

    b. Assets may be repurposed for a new function.

    c. Both a and b.

    d. Neither a nor b.

Case (*Adapted from GASB-42*)
Assumptions

In 20X5, a federal agency adopts a regulation requiring all underground gas tanks to be rustproof double-walled tanks with spill-protection devices. The period for compliance with the regulation is 10 years. Castle Rock County installed new underground tanks in its public works fuel facility in 20X4, one year before the regulation was adopted. The new tanks do not meet the requirements that will go into effect in 20Y5 (ten years from now). The tanks installed in 20X5 cost $700,000 and had been expected to provide service for forty years. Management of the County does not consider this event unusual in nature but does consider it infrequent in occurrence, as defined by GASB-62. Management does not consider this event to be within its control.

Evaluation of impairment

The indicator of impairment is the adoption of a regulation that affects capital assets. The evaluation of magnitude would consider the cost of operating the capital asset, which includes capital costs as well as operating costs, in relation to its service potential. The cost of the capital asset has not changed as a result of the new regulation, but its service potential has. If service potential is measured by the estimated useful life of the underground tanks, their service potential has been reduced from forty years to eleven years. This magnitude would be evaluated as significant. The other test of not being part of the normal life cycle of the asset has also been met. If county management had known adoption of the regulation was imminent, they most likely would have installed tanks in 20X4 that would have met the requirements of the new regulation even if they cost more than the tanks they did install. Thus, in 20X5, impairment of the underground tanks should be reported. Impairment loss using the service units approach would be determined as follows:

Element	Amount
Historical cost	$700,000
Total service units—years	40
Cost per service unit	17,500
Number of service units made unusable by regulation (40 years -11 years) 29 Impairment loss	29
Impairment loss	**$507,500**

In your best judgment, how should the impairment loss be reported by the public works department in the statement of activities and in the notes to the basic financial statements?

ANSWERS

1. Which of the following is *not* a capital asset?

   Answer – C: Supplies. All others are capital assets.

2. Due to the measurement focus and basis of accounting in governmental funds, which accounting element would be used to record a purchase of a $30,000 police car that would ultimately become a capital asset?

   Answer – B: Capital outlays.

3. When ownership is unclear on an infrastructure asset between a state and a county government, which government should record the infrastructure asset?

   Answer – D: Whichever government that has primary responsibility for maintaining the records for the infrastructure in accordance with GASB-34.

4. Which of the following *is not* a characteristic of an intangible asset?

   Answer – A: If an asset is acquired or created primarily for the purpose of directly obtaining income or profit, then it is an investment.

5. A state is undertaking a multiple-year project, beginning in 20X1, to acquire and implement a new accounting system. In the first year, the state performed an in-depth analysis to determine that the software would be feasible and did a fit analysis. The state legislature appropriated funds at the end of the year and a contract was awarded to a software company. During years two through four, the software was developed, customized, tested, and run parallel through various stress tests. Staff and management were trained. On July 1, 20X6, the software was accepted. Various maintenance procedures were performed throughout 20X6, but otherwise the software worked as expected. Ongoing training did occur for new employees and updates. When would capitalization occur for the software?

   Answer – A: Years two through four. All other answers would either have expense elements in them or would be expensed.

6. A City wants to use the modified approach for its infrastructure assets. Which of the following conditions would not allow the City to use the modified approach during 20X6?

   Answer – D: To use the modified approach, an inventory must be kept current of the infrastructure. It appears that the inventory in item D is 100 years old.

7. Which of the following are *not* an indicator of asset impairment?

   Answer – B: Change in fair value is not an indicator of asset impairment. All other choices are.

8. A high school shuts down a wing of classrooms due to lower than expected enrollment to save on costs. However, the City clerk reports an increase in births and migration into the City due to a new factory opening. The clerk works with the school board to estimate that the high school wing may reopen in two years. This activity is indicative of

   Answer – C: Temporary impairment.

9. Which of the following accounting elements *would not* be used to write down an asset that is impaired?

   Answer – A: Transfer expense – all other items are acceptable, depending upon facts and circumstances.

10. GASB-69 discusses government combinations and disposals of government operations. What could be an outcome of a government combination with regard to asset impairment?

    Answer – C: Both a and b are possible outcomes of a combination.

Case (*Adapted from GASB-42*)
Assumptions

In 20X5, a federal agency adopts a regulation requiring all underground gas tanks to be rustproof, double-walled tanks with spill-protection devices. The period for compliance with the regulation is 10 years. Castle Rock County installed new underground tanks in its public works fuel facility in 20X4, one year before the regulation was adopted. The new tanks do not meet the requirements that will go into effect in 20Y5 (ten years from now). The tanks installed in 20X5 cost $700,000 and had been expected to provide service for forty years. Management of the County does not consider this event unusual in nature but does consider it infrequent in occurrence, as defined by GASB-62. Management does not consider this event to be within its control.

Evaluation of impairment

The indicator of impairment is the adoption of a regulation that affects capital assets. The evaluation of magnitude would consider the cost of operating the capital asset, which includes capital costs as well as operating costs, in relation to its service potential. The cost of the capital asset has not changed as a result of the new regulation, but its service potential has. If service potential is measured by the estimated useful life of the underground tanks, their service potential has been reduced from forty years to eleven years. This magnitude would be evaluated as significant. The other test of not being part of the normal life cycle of the asset has also been met. If County management had known adoption of the regulation was imminent, they most likely would have installed tanks in 20X4 that would have met the requirements of the new regulation even if they cost more than the tanks they did install. Thus, in 20X5, impairment of the underground tanks should be reported. Impairment loss using the service units approach was be determined as follows:

Element	Amount
Historical cost	$700,000
Total service units—years	40
Cost per service unit	17,500
Number of service units made unusable by regulation (40 years -11 years) 29 Impairment loss	29
Impairment loss	**$507,500**

In your best judgment, how should the impairment loss be reported by the public works department in the statement of activities and in the notes to the basic financial statements?

Answer – The impairment loss of $507,500 would be reported in the statement of activities as public works program expenses. The following disclosure would be presented in the notes to the financial statements:

> Public works expenses include an impairment loss of $507,500 on underground tanks due to federal environmental regulations.

CHAPTER 11
OTHER ASSETS AND DEFERRED OUTFLOWS OF RESOURCES

CONTENTS

INTRODUCTION

The accounting standards that are used to determine which assets should be presented in a governmental entity's financial statements and how they should be presented vary depending on whether an asset is presented in (1) governmental funds, (2) proprietary funds and fiduciary funds, or (3) the government-wide financial statements.

> **NOTE:** For a discussion of how cash and investments and capital assets should be presented, see Chapter 9, "Deposits, Investments, and Derivative Instruments," and Chapter 10, "Capital Assets," respectively.

GOVERNMENTAL FUNDS

The modified accrual basis of accounting and the current financial resources measurement focus should be used in accounting for assets within governmental funds.

Governmental fund assets (assets of the General Fund, Special Revenue Funds, Capital Project Funds, Debt Service Funds, and Permanent Funds) that are not considered current financial resources (e.g., capital assets) are presented only in the governmental entity's government-wide financial statements and not in the fund financial statements.

Materials and Supplies

Materials and supplies in inventory are current assets of a governmental fund, but they are not considered current financial resources. As discussed in Chapter 3, "Basis of Accounting and Measurement Focus," governmental funds, for the most part, measure the flow of current financial resources. However, one of the exceptions to this generalization is the accounting for inventories. Inventories may be accounted for by using either the consumption method (flow of economic resources) or the purchase method (flow of current financial resources). National Council on Governmental Accounting Statement No. 1 (NCGA-1) (*General Accounting and Financial Reporting Principles*) states that when the inventory amount is significant, that amount must be reported in the governmental fund's balance sheet regardless of the method used (NCGA-1, par. 73) [GASB Cod. Sec. 1600.127]. Principles of inventory accounting for proprietary funds are included in GASB-62 (*Codification of Accounting and Financial Reporting Guidance Contained in Pre-November 30, 1989 FASB and AICPA Pronouncements*), pars. 188–201 [GASB Cod. Secs. I40.101-.114].

> **PRACTICE ALERT:** As part of the GASB's *Financial Reporting Model—Reexamination* project, the Board has tentatively proposed the definition of *financial resources* to include "cash, resources that are expected to be converted to cash, and resources that are consumable in lieu of cash." The proposal is contained in the Preliminary Views due process document. Inventory and prepaid items may be retained as assets in governmental funds.

Consumption Method

The consumption method of accounting for inventories is not consistent with the fundamental governmental fund concept that only expendable financial resources should be presented in a fund's balance sheet. Under the consumption method, a governmental expenditure is recognized only when the inventory items are *used* rather than purchased. For example, if a governmental unit purchased $100,000 of supplies, the following entry would be made (NCGA-1, par. 73) [GASB Cod. Sec. 1600.127]:

	Debit	Credit
GENERAL FUND		
Supplies Inventory	100,000	
Vouchers Payable		100,000

At the end of the period, an inventory of supplies would be made, and the amount of inventory consumed would be recognized as a current expenditure. To continue with the example, assume that supplies worth $25,000 remain at the end of the accounting period. The current period's expenditure for supplies would be recorded in the following manner:

	Debit	Credit
GENERAL FUND		
Expenditures—Supplies	75,000	
Supplies Inventory		75,000

Because inventories are reported as an asset (even though *currently* they do not represent expendable financial resources), it is necessary to set aside fund balance by an amount equal to the carrying value of the inventory. Thus, in the above example, the following entry would be made at the end of the accounting period in accordance with GASB-54:

	Debit	Credit
GENERAL FUND		
Fund Balance—Unassigned	25,000	
Fund Balance—Nonspendable—Supplies Inventory		25,000

In the Basis for Conclusions of GASB-54, the Board concluded that balances of inventory are deemed to be nonspendable because they are not expected to be converted into cash. There could be some instances where a government has inventory that would be converted into cash through a sale. For example, if prisoners make furniture for sale, the raw materials for that furniture would be inventory. However, these sort of programs are accounted for in enterprise funds.

Purchase Method

The purchase method of accounting for inventories is consistent with the governmental fund concept of reporting only expendable financial resources. Under the purchase method, purchases of inventories are recognized as expenditures when the goods are received and the transaction is vouchered. To illustrate, assume the same facts as those used in the consumption method example presented earlier.

When the supplies are acquired, the transaction would be recorded as follows (NCGA-1, par. 73) [GASB Cod. Sec. 1600.127]:

	Debit	Credit
GENERAL FUND		
Expenditures—Supplies	100,000	
Vouchers Payable		100,000

At the end of the period, no adjustment is made to the expenditures account even though only $75,000 of goods was consumed. However, NCGA-1 requires that an inventory item must be presented on the balance sheet if the amount of inventory is considered significant. If it were concluded that the ending inventory of supplies was significant, the following entry would be made at the end of the accounting period under GASB-54:

	Debit	Credit
GENERAL FUND		
Supplies Inventory	25,000	
Fund Balance—Nonspendable—Supplies Inventory		25,000

Under both the consumption method and the purchase method, the nonspendable fund balance would be presented under the broad caption of fund balance in a manner similar to the following illustration:

	Amount
GENERAL FUND	
Fund Balance	
Fund Balance—Nonspendable for Supplies Inventory	$25,000
Fund Balance—Unassigned	400,000
Total Fund Balance	$425,000

Materials and Supplies Reported at the Lower of Cost or Market

GASB-62, paragraphs 188–201 [GASB Cod. Secs. I40.101–.114], contains guidance on when materials and supplies should be reported at the lower of cost or market. U.S. GAAP requires that inventories or supplies be subjected to the lower of cost or market test for possible write-down. That is, if the replacement cost of inventories or supplies is less than the cost of the items (using FIFO, LIFO, or the average cost method) a write-down is required.

The AICPA's Audit and Accounting Guide *State and Local Governments* points out that if a governmental entity does not choose to follow GASB-62 with respect to the lower of cost or market method, it should nonetheless write down inventories or supplies if they are affected by physical deterioration or obsolescence. This requirement applies to the use of either the consumption method or the purchase method. The purchase method could be affected by the need for a write-down because NCGA-1, par. 73 [GASB Cod. Sec. 1600.127], requires that a governmental fund record inventories or supplies when a significant amount of inventories or supplies exist at the end of the year. Under this circumstance, a write-down would require a reduction both in the asset balance and the non-spendable fund balance for inventory or supplies.

Prepayments and Deferred Outflows of Resources

Prepaid items may include items such as prepaid expenses, deposits, and deferred outflows of resources. Like inventory items, prepayments and deferrals do not represent expendable financial resources. However, NCGA-1 states that these items may be accounted for by using either the allocation method or the non-allocation method (NCGA-1, par. 73) [GASB Cod. Sec. 1600.127].

Allocation Method of Prepaid Amounts

NCGA-1 does not specifically refer to an allocation method and a non-allocation method but rather describes the process of allocation with regard to prepaid amounts.

When the allocation method is used to account for prepayments, an asset is established at the date of payment and subsequently amortized over the accounting periods that are expected to benefit from the initial payment. For example, if a state or local government purchased a three-year insurance policy for $45,000, the transaction would be recorded as follows under the allocation method (NCGA-1, par. 73) [GASB Cod. Sec. 1600.127]:

	Debit	Credit
GENERAL FUND		
Prepaid Insurance	45,000	
Vouchers Payable		45,000

At the end of each year, the partial expiration of the insurance coverage would be recorded as follows:

	Debit	Credit
GENERAL FUND		
Expenditures—Insurance	15,000	
Prepaid Insurance		15,000

Prepayments are reported as assets of the specific governmental fund that will derive future benefits from the expenditure. In the above example, the governmental unit's fund would report prepaid insurance as an asset of $30,000 at the end of the first year of the insurance coverage.

Because prepayments are not current financial resources, the fund's fund balance should be reserved by the amount presented in the asset balance. Thus, at the end of the first year in the current example, the following entry would be made in accordance with GASB-54:

	Debit	Credit
GENERAL FUND		
Fund Balance—Unassigned	30,000	
Fund Balance—Nonspendable—Prepaid Insurance		30,000

Similarly to inventory, prepaid insurance cannot be readily converted into cash and is therefore nonspendable. The balance in the nonspendable fund balance would fluctuate each year as a result of changes in the carrying value of the prepayment accounts.

The allocation method is not consistent with the basic governmental fund concept that only current financial resources should be presented in the fund's balance sheet.

Non-Allocation Method

The non-allocation method of accounting for prepayments and deferrals is consistent with the basic governmental fund concept that only expendable financial resources are reported by a specific fund. Payments for the prepaid items are fully recognized as an expenditure in the year of payment. Under the non-allocation method, no asset for the prepayment is created, and no expenditure allocation to future accounting periods is required. To continue with the previous example, the only entry that will be made if the nonallocation method is used is to recognize the expenditure in the year of payment as shown in the following illustration (NCGA-1, par. 73) [GASB Cod. Sec. 1600.127]:

	Debit	Credit
GENERAL FUND		
Expenditures—Insurance	45,000	
Vouchers Payable		45,000

Although NCGA-1 requires that significant amounts of inventories be recorded in the balance sheet no matter which accounting method is used, no similar requirement is extended to significant amounts of prepayments. It can be assumed that significant amounts of prepayments should also be reported in a fund's balance sheet.

If the expenditure account is closed to the fund balance account and no asset is recognized, there is no need to establish a nonspendable fund balance for prepaid insurance when the non-allocation method is used. However, if the nonallocation method is used and the decision is made to report significant amounts of prepayments at period end, a nonspendable fund balance should be recognized.

Escheat Property

Under certain conditions, state laws allow governmental entities to receive title to property without compensation to other parties. The assets received by the governmental entity are referred to as escheat property. One common example of the receipt of escheat property is when a deposit with a financial institution is inactive for a stated period of time. After certain procedures followed by the financial institution are performed, the balance in the account reverts to a governmental entity. Another circumstance under which a governmental entity receives escheat property is when an individual dies without a will and with no known heirs.

When property escheats to a governmental entity, state laws generally establish procedures under which claimants can assert their ownership of the property. In some states, potential claimants must assert their rights to property within a stated period of time. In other states, time restrictions are not imposed by the state.

The circumstances under which escheat property is received and held by a governmental entity create a number of accounting issues, which were addressed by the issuance of GASB-21 (*Accounting for Escheat Property*). GASB-21 defines the "escheat process" as "the reversion of property to a governmental entity in the absence of legal claimants or heirs." Governmental entities that receive escheat property may manage the receipts in a number of ways, including using the funds to finance current operations or investing the funds and using only the investment income to finance governmental activities (GASB-21, par. 3, GASB-34, par. 6, and GASB-37, par. 3) [GASB Cod. Sec. E70.101].

Appropriate Fund Type

When escheat property is received, it generally should be reported in the governmental fund or proprietary fund to which the property escheats; however, escheat property held for other parties (individuals, private organizations, or another governmental entity) should be reported in a fiduciary fund (Private-Purpose Trust Fund) or the governmental or proprietary fund that is normally used to account for escheat property, offset by a liability to the other party.

Accounting for escheat property in proprietary funds, government-wide financial statements, and fiduciary funds is discussed later in this chapter (GASB-34, par. 72, GASB-37, par. 3) [GASB Cod. Secs. 1300.113, E70.102].

Accounting and Reporting Standards

When escheat property is received during the year, the total amount received is apportioned between an escheat liability account and an escheat revenue account. The amount of the liability recorded is the estimated amount expected to be paid to claimants, and the balance is recorded as revenue. Similarly to any accounting estimate, the governmental entity should use relevant information and current circumstances to make its best estimate of total future payments to claimants. Generally, the estimated liability is based on the governmental entity's historical relationship between escheat property received and amounts paid to claimants, taking into consideration current conditions and recent trends. The estimated liability is based on projected payments to claimants and not on the amount that by law must be retained by the governmental entity for possible payment to claimants. Payments made to claimants reduce the escheat liability (GASB-21, par. 5, as amended by GASB-34, par. 6, and GASB-37, par. 3) [GASB Cod. Sec. E70.103].

To illustrate the accounting for escheat property in a General Fund, assume that a governmental entity receives $50,000 of escheat property during the year, pays out claims of $10,000, and estimates additional payments to claimants of $5,000 after the year. To record the activity for the year, the following entries are made in the governmental entity's General Fund:

	Debit	Credit
GENERAL FUND		
Cash	50,000	
Revenues—Escheat		50,000
To record the receipt of escheat property.		
Revenues—Escheat	10,000	
Cash		10,000
To record payments to escheat claimants.		
Revenues—Escheat	5,000	
Claimant Liability		5,000
To record estimated future payments to escheat claimants.		

Payments and estimated payments to claimants are recorded as reductions to revenue rather than as expenditures. This approach is similar to recording property tax revenue at a net amount (expected amount to be received), rather than using a bad debts expense account.

Deferred Outflows of Resources

GASB-65 (*Items Previously Reported as Assets and Liabilities*) discusses a number of areas where deferred outflows of resources can occur in both the funds and the government-wide financial statements:

Activity	Accounting and Financial Reporting Aspects
Current refundings and advance refundings resulting in the defeasance of debt	The difference between the reacquisition price and the net carrying amount of the old debt should be reported as a deferred outflow of resources (or a deferred inflow of resources depending on the math) and recognized as a component of interest expense in a systematic and rational manner over the remaining life of the old debt or the life of the new debt, whichever is shorter. Similarly, if a change in the provisions of a lease results from a refunding by the lessor of tax-exempt debt, including an advance refunding, in which *(a)* the perceived economic advantages of the refunding are passed through to the lessee and *(b)* the revised agreement is classified as a capital lease by the lessee, then the lessee should adjust the lease obligation to the present value of the future minimum lease payments under the revised lease. The adjustment of the lease obligation to present value should be made using the effective interest rate applicable to the revised agreement. The resulting difference should be reported as a deferred outflow of resources (or a deferred inflow of resources depending on the math). The deferred outflow of resources or the deferred inflow of resources should be recognized as a component of interest expense in a systematic and rational manner over the remaining life of the old debt or the life of the new debt, whichever is shorter.(GASB-23, par. 4, as amended by GASB-34, pars. 15 and 91, and GASB-65, par. 6) [GASB Cod. Sec. D20.111] **PRACTICE ALERT:** The Tax Cuts and Jobs Act of 2017 changes the status of advance refunding bonds to taxable transactions after December 31, 2017. It is unclear what effect, if any, the passage of the Act has on existing bonds and any changes in disclosure forthcoming from the GASB.
Government-mandated nonexchange transactions and voluntary nonexchange transactions	If resources are received by the grantee/recipient before time requirements are met, but after all other eligibility requirements have been met, the resources are reported as a deferred outflow of resources by the *provider* (and a deferred inflow of resources by the *grantee/recipient*) (GASB-33, par. 21, as amended by GASB-65, par. 10) [GASB Cod. Sec. N50.118].
Direct loan origination costs in lending transactions	Reported as deferred outflows of resources until the underlying loan is sold, at which time the deferred outflows are expensed. Fees paid to permanent investors at origination are deferred outflows of resources until the sale, at which time the deferred outflows are expensed (GASB-62, pars. 467 and 469, as amended by GASB-65, pars. 26-27) [GASB Cod. Sec. L30.131, .133].
Change in Lease Term	If a change in the provisions of a lease is as a result of a refunding by the lessor of tax-exempt debt, the previous provisions of refunding bonds currently apply (see above) (GASB-62, par. 221, as amended by GASB-65, pars. 7 and 15) [GASB Cod. Sec. L20.116].
Sale/Leaseback transaction	If there is a loss on a sale, a deferred outflow of resources occurs with recognition of expense/expenditures, in proportion to the related gross rental charged over the life of the lease term (GASB-62, par. 242, as amended by GASB-65, par. 18) [GASB Cod. Sec. L20.156].

PRACTICE POINT: GASB Statement No. 86 (*Certain Debt Extinguishment Issues*) makes improvements to existing guidance primarily found in GASB Statement No. 7 (*Advance Refundings Resulting in Defeasance of Debt*) and No. 23 (*Accounting and Financial Reporting for Refundings of Debt Reported by Proprietary Activities*), and relevant sections of GASB-62 for specific circumstances when resources are used to defease debt not related to bond refunding transactions. GASB-86 became effective for reporting periods beginning after June 15, 2017. Additional information on GASB-86 is contained in Chapter 12, "Long-Term Debt."

In the non-governmental fund statements, defined benefit pension activity in accordance with GASB-68 (as amended by GASB-71) and defined benefit OPEB activity in accordance with GASB Statement No. 75 (*Accounting and Financial Reporting for Postemployment Benefits Other than Pensions*) may include recognition of deferred outflows of resources when:

- Proportions change from one year to the next for a cost-sharing employer or between any type of employer and a nonemployer contributing entity in a special funding situation.
- Contributions occur after the measurement date.
- Differences occur between actual and expected experience due to the publication of an experience study.
- Differences occur between projected and actual investment earnings on plan investments (where projected earnings are higher than actual earnings).

Chapter 13, "Pension, Postemployment, and Other Employee Benefit Liabilities," contains a thorough discussion on pensions and other postemployment benefits other than pensions.

As of the date of publication, other deferred outflows of resources may also occur when:

- Consideration provided exceeds net position acquired in a government combination, the acquiring government should report the difference as a deferred outflow of resources in accordance with GASB Statement No. 69 (*Government Combinations*) (clarified by GASB-85 (*Omnibus 2017*)—see **PRACTICE POINT** in Chapter 10, "Capital Assets").
- An asset retirement obligation is required to be recognized while a tangible capital asset is in use in accordance with GASB Statement No. 83 (*Certain Asset Retirement Obligations*) (see **PRACTICE POINT** in Chapter 10, "Capital Assets").

PROPRIETARY AND FIDUCIARY FUNDS AND THE GOVERNMENT-WIDE FINANCIAL STATEMENTS

The accrual basis of accounting and economic resources measurement focus should be used to determine which assets should be presented on the balance sheet or statement of net position of a proprietary or fiduciary fund and in the statement of net position within the government-wide financial statements.

Materials and Supplies

Materials and supplies in inventory are current assets of proprietary and fiduciary funds and the government-wide financial statements under the accrual basis of accounting and economic resources measurement focus. Only the consumption method of accounting for inventories is consistent with the fundamental concept of the economic resources measurement focus. Under the consumption method, an expense is recognized only when the inventory items are used.

Prepayments

Prepaid items may include items such as prepaid expenses and inventory. As is the case for inventory items, prepayments and deferrals represent economic resources in proprietary and fiduciary funds and in the government-wide financial statements. Only the allocation method is used to account for prepayments and deferrals, with an asset established at the date of payment and subsequently amortized over the accounting periods that are expected to benefit from the initial payment.

Escheat Property

In order to prepare proprietary or fiduciary fund and government-wide financial statements, escheat property should be accounted for using the accrual basis of accounting and the economic resources measurement focus.

When a Private-Purpose Trust fund is used to account for escheat property, there may be transfers from that fund to a governmental fund or proprietary fund. Such transfers are recorded as transfers out by the Private-Purpose Trust Fund and transfers in by the governmental fund. During a period that has transfers, the remaining assets held by the Private-Purpose Trust Fund at the end of the year may be greater or less than the escheat liability account. If the amount of assets is greater than the liability, the Private-Purpose Trust Fund reports the difference as fund balance. If the amount of assets is less than the liability, the fund reports the difference as an asset (Advance to Governmental Fund), and the governmental fund reports the same amount as a liability (Advance from the Private-Purpose Trust Fund). Thus, a Private-Purpose Trust Fund used to account for escheat property can never show a deficit fund balance amount.

ALL FUNDS AND FINANCIAL STATEMENTS

Interfund Receivables/Payables

Governmental entities are generally involved in a variety of interfund transactions that may give rise to an interfund receivable or payable. For a discussion of the standards that apply to the reporting of interfund receivables and payables, see Chapter 5, "Terminology and Classification."

Fund Overdrafts in Internal Investment Pools

When a fund overdraws its position in an internal investment pool, the AICPA's Audit and Accounting Guide *State and Local Governments* requires that the fund that overdrew its position report an interfund payable and the fund that is assumed (based on management's discretion) to have funded the overdraft report an interfund receivable.

For example, assume that a Capital Projects Fund participates in an internal investment pool and withdraws $900,000 from the pool to pay for capital assets even though its equity position at the time of withdrawal is $850,000. If it is assumed that management deems the excess withdrawal to have been provided by the General Fund, the following entries would be made by the two funds:

	Debit	Credit
CAPITAL PROJECTS FUND		
Capital Expenditures	900,000	
Interest in Investment Pool		850,000
Due to General Fund		50,000
To record interfund payable due to overdrawn balance at fiscal year-end.		
GENERAL FUND		
Due from Capital Projects Fund	50,000	
Interest in Investment Pool		50,000
To record interfund receivable due to overdrawn balance at fiscal year-end.		

The accounting for the overdraft and assumed coverage of the overdraft is the same no matter which fund types are involved. For example, an overdraft between two funds of the governmental fund category (as shown above) would be treated in the same way as an overdraft between funds that do not belong to the same fund category (e.g., the General Fund may fund an overdraft by an Enterprise Fund).

The interfund loan would not be eliminated when the fund financial statements are prepared; however, the treatment of the interfund loan at the government-wide financial statement level would depend on the fund categories involved. For example, if the interfund loan was between two governmental funds, the interfund loan would be eliminated; however, if the interfund loan was between a governmental fund and an Enterprise Fund, the amounts would be reported as part of the internal balance presented on the statement of net position.

Disaggregation of Receivables and Payables

Much of the information contained in governmental as well as corporate financial statements is highly aggregated in that a single balance often represents a host of individual account balances. In many instances the aggregation does not obscure the nature of the reported balance, but in some cases a reader of the financial statement may be misinformed because of the aggregation.

In a limited way, current governmental reporting standards address the aggregation issue. For example, GASB-3 (*Deposits with Financial Institutions, Investments [Including Repurchase Agreements], and Reverse Repurchase Agreements*) requires reporting by investment type, and GASB-34 requires reporting capital asset and long-term liabilities by class and type.

GASB-38 requires that a governmental entity present in the notes to its financial statements the details of receivables and payables reported on the statements of net position and balance sheets "when significant components have been obscured by aggregation." In addition, significant receivable balances that are not expected to be collected within one year of the date of the financial statements should be disclosed.

The disclosure format depends on the complexity of the financial operations of a particular governmental entity and the amount of detail that it displays on the face of its financial statements. In some instances, there may be enough detail presented directly in the financial statements and the disclosure may simply be limited to identifying receivables that are not expected to be collected within one year, if any. In other situations, it may be necessary to present a fairly involved disclosure such as the following illustration (adapted from GASB-38, par. 73, GASB-63, par. 37) [GASB Cod. Sec. 2300.903].

EXHIBIT 11-1
ILLUSTRATION OF DISCLOSURE OF DISAGGREGATION OF RECEIVABLES AND PAYABLES

NOTE—Receivables and Payables

The major components of receivables as of June 30, 20X8, were as follows:

	Accounts	Taxes	Special Assessments	Due from Other Governments	Other	Total Receivables
Governmental Activities:						
General Fund	$10,935,000	$4,457,000	$—	$5,004,000	$235,000	$20,631,000
Utilities services tax	2,676,000	—	1,990,000	—	—	4,666,000
Gas Tax	347,000	—	22,000	1,841,000	—	2,210,000
Other governmental	141,000	—	—	653,000	182,000	976,000
Internal Service	215,000	—	—	—	—	215,000
Total-governmental activities	**$14,314,000**	**$4,457,000**	**$2,012,000**	**$7,498,000**	**$417,000**	**$28,698,000**
Amounts not scheduled for collection during the subsequent year	$—	$—	$1,650,000	$—	$—	$1,650,000
Business-Type Activities:						
Wastewater	$3,789,000	$—	$—	$1,825,000	$323,000	$5,937,000
Solid waste	1,199,000	—	—	—	—	1,199,000
Other proprietary	435,000	—	—	—	89,000	524,000
Total-business type activities	**$5,423,000**	**$—**	**$—**	**$1,825,000**	**$412,000**	**$7,660,000**

The major components of payables as of June 30, 20X8, were as follows:

	Vendors	Salaries and Benefits	Accrued Interest	Other	Total Payables
Governmental activities:					
General	$3,892,000	$3,651,000	$—	$415,000	$7,958,000
Gas tax	536,000	—	—	—	536,000
Community redevelopment	4,328,000	11,000	—	—	4,339,000
Other governmental	561,000	51,000	—	75,000	687,000
Internal Service	1,197,000	204,000	2,169,000	—	3,570,000
Reconciliation of balances in fund financial statements to government-wide financial statements	—	—	1,681,000	—	1,681,000
Total governmental activities	**$10,514,000**	**$3,917,000**	**$3,850,000**	**$490,000**	**$18,771,000**
Business-Type Activities:					
Wastewater	$6,523,000	$289,000	$3,525,000	$65,000	$10,402,000
Solid waste	870,000	132,000	—	—	1,002,000
Other proprietary	1,490,000	196,000	523,000	—	2,209,000
Total—business-type activities	**$8,883,000**	**$617,000**	**$4,048,000**	**$65,000**	**$13,613,000**

QUESTIONS

1. In accordance with the consumption method of valuing inventory in a governmental fund, which entry would be made to increase an asset when inventory is purchased?

   a. Debit vouchers payable

   b. Debit supplies inventory

   c. Credit supplies inventory

   d. Credit net position

2. At the end of a period in a governmental fund where inventory is accounted for using the consumption method, which of the following entries would be made to increase the amount consumed of inventory in the current period?

   a. Debit supplies inventory

   b. Debit expenditures—supplies

   c. Credit expenditures—supplies

   d. Credit cash

3. Under the purchase method of inventory accounting, in a governmental fund which entry would occur on the acquisition of inventory to increase account by the amount purchased?

   a. Debit expenditures—supplies

   b. Debit vouchers payable

   c. Credit expenditures—supplies

   d. Credit net position

4. In accordance with GASB-65 and GASB-68, which of the following would likely not be a deferred outflow of resources?

   a. The difference between the acquisition price and the carrying amount in a bond refunding transaction resulting in an economic gain.

   b. On the provider's books, where resources are received by a recipient from the provider before time requirements are met but after all other eligibility requirements have been met.

   c. Bond issuance costs.

   d. Differences between actual and expected experience with regard to defined benefit pensions.

5. When title to a property reverts to a state without compensation to an owner in an absence of legal claimants or heirs is the process of:

   a. Escheat

   b. Eminent domain

   c. Reversion

   d. Inversion

ANSWERS

1. In accordance with the consumption method of valuing inventory in a governmental fund, which entry would be made to increase an asset when inventory is purchased?

   Answer – B: Debit supplies inventory.

2. At the end of a period in a governmental fund where inventory is accounted for using the consumption method, which of the following entries would be made to increase the amount consumed of inventory in the current period?

   Answer – B: Debit expenditures—supplies.

3. Under the purchase method of inventory accounting, in a governmental fund which entry would occur on the acquisition of inventory to increase the amount purchased?

   Answer – A: Debit expenditures—supplies.

4. In accordance with GASB-65 and GASB-68, which of the following would likely not be a deferred outflow of resources?

   Answer – C: Bond issuance costs. (They are now expensed under GASB-65.)

5. When title to a property reverts to a state without compensation to an owner in an absence of legal claimants or heirs is the process of:

   Answer – A: Escheat. Eminent domain has compensation to the owner, potentially involving litigation.

CHAPTER 12
LONG-TERM DEBT

CONTENTS

INTRODUCTION

The accounting standards that are used to determine which long-term liabilities should be presented in a governmental entity's financial statements and how they should be presented vary depending on whether a liability is presented in (1) governmental funds, (2) proprietary or fiduciary funds, or (3) the government-wide financial statements.

This chapter discusses the accounting and reporting treatment for certain long-term obligations of state and local governments, including:

- Bonds and notes;
- Bond, tax, and revenue anticipation notes;
- Demand bonds;
- Conduit debt obligations;
- Arbitrage liability; and
- Extinguishment of debt and debt refunding/defeasance.

Certain long-term obligations are discussed in other chapters as follows:

- Accrued compensated absences, employer pension, and other postemployment benefit obligations (see Chapter 13, "Pension, Postemployment, and Other Employee Benefit Liabilities");
- Capital lease obligations (see Chapter 14, "Leases and Service Concession Arrangements");
- Claims and judgments (see Chapter 15, "Risk Management, Claims, and Judgments");
- Landfill closure and post-closure obligations (see Chapter 16, "Other Liabilities");
- Asset retirement obligations (see Chapter 10, "Capital Assets," and referred to in Chapter 16, "Other Liabilities"); and
- Pollution remediation obligation (see Chapter 16, "Other Liabilities").

PRACTICE ALERT: GASB Statement No. 88 (*Certain Disclosures Related to Debt, including Direct Borrowings and Direct Placements*) updates the definition of the word "debt" for purposes of disclosure in the notes to financial statements. Upon implementation, debt will be defined as:

A liability that arises from a contractual obligation to pay cash (or other assets that may be used in lieu of payment of cash) in one or more payments to settle an amount that is fixed at the date the contractual obligation is established. For disclosure purposes, debt does not include certain leases or accounts payable.

For purposes of this determination, interest to be accrued and subsequently paid (such as interest on variable-rate debt) or interest to be added to the principal amount of the obligation (such as interest on capital appreciation bonds) does not preclude the amount to be settled from being considered fixed at the date the contractual obligation is established.

GASB-88 excludes leases that may meet the updated definition of "debt" except in the case where ownership ultimately transfers in the lease (a financed purchase). In such a case, a debt *is present* (GASB-88, par. 4) [GASB Cod. Secs. 1500.129, 2300.120, .124].

In addition to other requirements to disclose information related to debt in the notes to the financial statements in other GASB statements, governments should disclose *summarized* information about the following items, if applicable:

- Amount of unused lines of credit,
- Collateral pledged as security for debt,
- Terms specified in debt agreements related to *significant*:

—Events of default with finance-related consequences,

—Termination events with finance-related consequences, and

—Subjective acceleration clauses (GASB-88, par. 5) [GASB Cod. Secs. 1500.130, 2300.124].

In the notes to the financial statements, disclosures will be separated regarding direct borrowings and direct placements from all other forms of debt (GASB-88, par. 6) [GASB Cod. Sec. 1500.129].

GASB-88 was required to be implemented for reporting periods beginning after June 15, 2018. It applies to the notes to the financial statements for all periods presented. If application for prior periods presented is not practicable, the reason for not applying the statement to prior periods presented should be disclosed.

TYPES OF LONG-TERM DEBT

General Obligation and Revenue Bonds and Notes

State and local governments generally issue long-term obligations in two forms:

1. General obligation bonds; and
2. Revenue bonds and notes.

General obligation bonds represent bonded indebtedness of the government entity to which repayment is supported by the full faith and credit of the government in the form of its taxing ability. General obligation bonds normally require voter approval and are typically repaid with property or other taxes levied for such purpose.

Revenue bonds and notes are obligations evidenced in the form of bonds or notes to which repayment is supported by specific revenue sources other than property taxes, such as utility revenues, hospital revenues, and other business-type activity revenue.

OBSERVATION: Some governments term revenue obligation bonds "special obligation bonds" due to a specific revenue stream. Others term specific portions of taxes that pay for bonds "tax allocation bonds." These are just some of the many variations of general and revenue obligation bonds. Governments that pool types of programs or uses that are bonded may issue "Certificates of

Participation." Within the pool, allocations are made to show the amount of debt that is attributable to the various programs or uses.

Demand Bonds

Demand bonds allow bondholders to require a governmental entity to redeem bonds on the basis of terms specified in the bond agreement. For example, the bond agreement may allow the bonds, based on action taken by bondholders, to be retired five years after their issuance.

When demand bonds are issued, the following key question arises because bondholders can redeem demand bonds on demand: should the governmental unit treat the debt as current or long-term? That is, (1) should a governmental fund account for the demand bonds in a specific fund, or classify the debt as a general long-term liability (i.e., is reported only in the entity's government-wide financial statements), or (2) should a proprietary fund classify the debt as a current liability or long-term liability? GASBI-1 (*Demand Bonds Issued by State and Local Governmental Entities*) addresses the issue.

PRACTICE POINT: Due to the provisions of GASB Statement No. 76 (*The Hierarchy of Generally Accepted Accounting Principles for State and Local Governments*) and as explained within the GASB's basis for conclusions, the GASB will no longer issue interpretations. The GASB believes that the purpose that GASB Interpretations serve can be met in the future through other accounting literature. As such, footnote 1 to GASB-76 explains: "All GASB Interpretations heretofore issued and currently in effect also are considered as being included within Category A and are continued in force until altered, amended, supplemented, revoked, or superseded by subsequent GASB pronouncements."

When demand bonds are redeemed, the funds needed to retire the debt may come from the governmental entity's available cash, proceeds from the resale of the redeemed bonds by remarketing agents, short-term credit arrangements, or long-term credit arrangements. A short-term credit agreement may be based on standby liquidity agreements or other arrangements entered into by the governmental unit. In instances where the redeemed bonds are not readily resold, there may be a take-out agreement whereby a financial institution agrees to convert the bond to long-term debt, such as installment notes. A key factor in determining the appropriate accounting for demand bonds is the existence of a "take-out agreement." In a take-out agreement, the government issuer makes arrangements with a financial institution to convert bonds presented to an installment agreement that is payable sometimes for five or ten years or more. Frequently a take-out agreement is made at the same time the bonds are sold (GASBI-1, par. 5) [GASB Cod. Sec. D30.104].

GASBI-1 concludes that the issues surrounding the accounting for demand bonds are similar to the issues associated with bond anticipation notes originally as discussed in NCGAI-9. NCGAI-9 stated that bond anticipation notes should be classified as general long-term liabilities "if all legal steps have been taken to refinance the bond anticipation notes and the intent is supported by an ability to consummate refinancing the short-term note on a long-term basis in accordance with the criteria" set forth in (FASB standards) (NCGAI-9, par. 12, as amended by GASB-34, pars. 15–16, 31, and 82, GASB 63, par. 8) [GASB Cod. Sec. D30.110].

GASBI-1 is applicable to demand bonds that have an exercisable provision for redemption at or within one year of the governmental unit's Statement of Net Position date. Such bonds should be reported as a long-term liability in the government-wide financial statements (or excluded from current liabilities of proprietary funds) when all of the following criteria are met (GASBI-1, par. 10, and GASB-34, pars. 12, 82, 91, and 97, as amended by GASB-62, pars. 29—43, and GASB-63, par. 8) [GASB Cod. Sec. D30.108]:

- Before the financial statements are issued, the issuer has entered into an arm's-length financing (take-out) agreement to convert bonds "put" but not resold into some other form of long-term obligation.

- The take-out agreement does not expire within one year from the date of the issuer's statement of net position.

- The take-out agreement is not cancelable by the lender or the prospective lender during that year, and obligations incurred under the take-out agreement are not callable by the lender during that year.

- The lender or the prospective lender or investor is expected to be financially capable of honoring the take-out agreement.

Even when a take-out agreement is cancelable or the obligation created by the take-out agreement is callable during the year, the demand bonds may be considered long-term debt if (1) violations of the agreement (if any) can be objectively determined and (2) no violations have occurred prior to the issuance of the financial statements. However, if violations have occurred and a waiver from the take-out agreement lender has been obtained, the debt should be considered long-term for financial reporting purposes.

When the conditions of GASBI-1 *have not been met*, demand bonds must be presented as a liability of the fund that received the proceeds from the issuance of the bonds. If demand bonds are issued and no take-out agreement has been executed at their issuance date or at the net position date, the bonds cannot be considered a long-term liability (GASBI-1, pars. 10 and 13, GASB-34, par. 82, as amended by GASB-63, par. 8) [GASB Cod. Sec. D30.109].

Conduit Debt Obligations

Governments sometimes issue conduit debt, which can be defined as certain limited-obligation bonds and other similar debt instruments that provide capital financing for third parties that are not a part of the issuing government's financial reporting entity. A significant distinguishing characteristic of conduit debt is that while conduit debt instruments generally bear the name of the governmental issuer, the issuer has no obligation for the debt beyond the repayment resources provided by the benefiting third party. The proceeds from the sale of conduit debt are used to accomplish or advance some public purpose (e.g., school expansion, or the expansion of a private business to increase employment or the government's tax base). Normally, such debt is repayable only from lease or loan agreements between the issuing government and the benefiting third party. Conduit debt explicitly states that the issuing government has no obligation other than possibly to help creditors exercise their rights in the event of default.

PRACTICE ALERT: As this book was going to press, the GASB released an exposure draft potentially updating the conduit debt provisions discussed in this section.

The GASB has tentatively concluded that conduit debt involves at least three participants: the government-issuer, the third-party obligor (borrower), and the bondholder(s) which are usually participating through a trustee. The third party obligor should not be in the same reporting entity. Conduit debt obligations not only involve capital financing but they may also involve operating issuances or leases. The final definition of conduit debt will not include the terms "revenue bonds, limited obligation" and similar terms. The GASB has tentatively concluded that a conduit debt obligations should not be reported as a liability of the issue. Instead, the issuer would only report a liability when a payment by the issuer is more likely than not (similarly to a nonexchange financial guarantee). Therefore, in many circumstances, the third-party obligor may be reporting their portion of the debt. Disclosure is also proposed to be revised.

Comments will be accepted until October 2018 with a final standard expected by April 2019.

As stated in GASBI-2 (*Disclosure of Conduit Debt Obligations*), "conduit debt obligations" are currently described as follows (GASBI-2, par. 2) [GASB Cod. Sec. C65.101]:

> Certain limited-obligation revenue bonds, certificates of participation, or similar debt instruments issued by a state or local governmental entity for the express purpose of providing capital financing for a specific third party that is not a part of the issuer's financial reporting entity.

As briefly discussed above, certificates of participation are widely used by local government to finance bundles of projects with each project having a dedicated revenue stream to pay for the project's participating portion. Other conduit debt forms are used for more specific purposes. For example, a governmental entity may issue revenue bonds for the purpose of financing the construction of an industrial plant by a private enterprise. In a conduit debt arrangement, the governmental entity issues the debt, debt proceeds are used to construct the facility, and the private enterprise signs a mortgage note or lease with the governmental entity. In the transaction, the governmental entity serves as a debtor (for the original issuance of the debt), and a lender or lessor (for the receipt of the mortgage note or lease from the nongovernmental entity). In the arrangement, even though the obligation bears the name of the governmental entity, the governmental entity is not responsible for the payment of the original debt but rather that debt is secured only by the cash payments agreed to be paid by the nongovernmental entity under the terms of the mortgage note or lease agreement.

Generally, the conduit debt transaction is arranged so that payments required by the nongovernmental entity (mortgage or lease payments) are equal to the mortgage payment schedule related to the original debt (entered into by the governmental entity). The nongovernmental entity benefits from the conduit debt transaction because interest rates are lower on the original loan entered into by the governmental entity, and the lower financing cost is the basis for arranging the mortgage or lease schedule payments to be made by the nongovernmental entity.

Generally the governmental entity should disclose the amount of the conduit debt outstanding as of its balance sheet date; however, if that amount is not determinable, the amount of the original balance of the debt may be disclosed for conduit debt issued prior to the effective date of the Interpretation. When the outstanding balance of conduit debt is composed of current balances and original issuance balances, the two amounts must be segregated for disclosure purposes. Specifically, GASBI-2 states that conduit debt obligations should be disclosed in the notes to the financial statements of the issuing entity and should include the following:

- A general description of the conduit debt transactions.

- The aggregate amount of all conduit debt obligations outstanding at the balance sheet date.

- A clear indication that the issuer has no obligation for the debt beyond the resources provided by related leases or loans (GASBI-2, par. 3) [GASB Cod. Sec. C65.102].

For conduit debt issued after the effective date of GASBI-2, the governmental entity must make arrangements (generally, by having access to the nongovernmental entity's debt amortization schedule and confirmation of subsequent payments) to track payments passed through by the nongovernmental entity to the original creditor.

GASBI-2 does not establish accounting standards for conduit debt. GASBI-2 and the AICPA Audit and Accounting Guide *State and Local Governments* both state that some issuers of conduit debt obligations currently report them as liabilities along with related assets (normally a lease financing receivable or note or loan receivable), whereas other governments do not. GASBI-2 does state that it does not alter that reporting or the reporting of future substantially similar conduit debt obligations for conduit debt issuers that have reported the obligations as liabilities. Therefore, in current practice the reporting of conduit debt obligations as liabilities along with their related assets is considered optional. However, for all issuers of conduit debt, GASBI-2 requires the specific note disclosures described above.

When conduit debt is presented on the governmental entity's balance sheet or statement of net position, debt disclosure requirements (such as debt service requirements until the debt matures) must be observed. However, no such payments to maturity disclosure requirements apply to conduit debt that is only disclosed in the financial statements (GASBI-2, par. 4, as amended by GASB-34, par. 6) [GASB Cod. Sec. C65.103].

Although not disclosed as conduit debt, utility commitments frequently have the characteristics of conduit debt even though the commitment may be technically a long term contractual liability. For example, if a city utility participates in what is called a "take or pay" contract, the city is obligated to pay the amortized cost of indebtedness regardless of the ability of the contracting agency to provide electricity and/or transmission, as applicable. The original indebtedness of the project is amortized by adding the financing costs to purchase energy over the life of the contract. More specifically, a nuclear plant is constructed and a number of city utilities participate in the finance of the plant by entering into "take or pay" contracts with the plant authority; $90 million in bonds are sold by the plant authority and $10 million in interest will accumulate over the life of the bonds, yielding a total debt service of $100 million. The city utility's take or pay contract stipulates that it is entitled to 4% of the output of the plant and in return will pay a stream of amounts to purchase that electricity at market over a certain period of time. Therefore, at a minimum, the 4% of the output has to pay for $4 million of the total debt service of the plant, with any amounts over $4 million deemed to pay for current costs and surpluses.

Arbitrage Liability

Arbitrage involves the simultaneous purchase and sale of the same or essentially the same securities with the object of making a profit on the spread between two markets. In the context of government finance, arbitrage describes the strategy of issuing tax-exempt debt and investing the proceeds in debt securities that have a higher rate of return; however, state and local governments are subject to rules and regulations established by Internal Revenue Code Section 148 and the U.S. Treasury that under certain conditions create an arbitrage rebate to be paid to the federal government.

Care must be taken in the structuring of tax-exempt bonds to avoid arbitrage unless a government can successfully navigate the various exceptions to paying an arbitrage rebate. The rebate tax is based on the differential of the interest yields and can be an up to 50% tax on the earnings payable every five years. Penalties for failing to calculate this spread include the loss of tax-exempt status.

In general, state and local governments should use the guidance contained in GASB-62 (*Codification of Accounting and Financial Reporting Guidance Contained in Pre-November 30, 1989 FASB and AICPA Pronouncements*), pars. 96–113 [GASB Cod. Secs. C50.151–.168, 2300.106], to determine whether an arbitrage liability must be recognized. The AICPA's Audit and Accounting Guide *State and Local Governments* (par. 5.10) requires that the arbitrage analysis be made annually "to determine whether it is material and thus should be reported in the financial statements."

OBSERVATION: The federal government has authorized various forms of subsidized bonds at the state and local levels (Build America, Recovery Zone Economic Development Bonds, Qualified Zone Economic Development Bonds, etc.). Although they are not guaranteed by the federal government, the bonds are subsidized by a revenue stream that reduces overall interest costs. The bonds are also not tax exempt and per GASB-62, footnote 6, they do not count in the calculation of capitalized interest. The GASB's *Implementation Guide 2015-1*, question Z.33.25 [GASB Cod. Sec. N50.710-3], notes that these subsidies should not reduce interest expense. Rather, the federal reimbursement is a separate nonexchange transaction and should be recognized as nonexchange revenue when all eligibility requirements are met. Thus, the payment of interest on the qualifying bonds is reported gross, not netted with the federal reimbursement.

PRACTICE ALERT: The 2017 Tax Cuts and Jobs Act eliminated the ability to sell qualified tax credit bonds after December 31, 2017. As of the date of publication, it is unclear if the GASB will need to change the guidance contained in question Z.33.25.

GOVERNMENTAL FUNDS

The measurement focus for governmental funds is generally the flow of current financial resources. Liabilities that will consume current financial resources of the fund responsible for payment during the fiscal period are presented in that fund's balance sheet. No explicit current liability classification exists on a fund's balance sheet (the financial statement is unclassified). However, the mere presentation of the liability in the balance sheet of the government's fund implies that the debt is current and will require the use of expendable financial resources (NCGA par. 18).

The definition of "current liabilities" differs significantly between a governmental entity and a commercial enterprise. For-profit GAAP describes "current liabilities" as those items that will be liquidated through the use of current assets. "Current assets" are defined as resources expected to be realized or consumed within the entity's operating cycle. Thus, the term to maturity of a current liability of a commercial enterprise could be a year or longer, depending on the entity's operating cycle. A liability of a governmental fund is considered current when it is expected to be liquidated with current financial resources. The term to maturity for a government's current liability is much shorter than that for a commercial enterprise.

GASB-62 incorporates the definitions of "current assets" and "current liabilities" extant in paragraphs 30–35 [GASB Cod. Secs. 1800.109–.114, 2200.175–.181, 1500.106–.107].

OBSERVATION: There is no requirement to implement a classified statement of net position. In fact, preparing a classified statement of net position may cause an audit to extend as the apportionment between current and long-term for elements beyond those that are readily determinable, such as long-term debt, may cause additional audit work. Care must be taken to decide whether or not a classified statement of net position is necessary due to bond covenants, laws, regulations, or ordinances.

See Chapter 16, "Other Liabilities," for a discussion of the definition of and accounting treatment for liabilities of governmental funds.

Tax, Revenue and Bond Anticipation Notes

NCGAI-9 (*Certain Fund Classifications and Balance Sheet Accounts*), as amended, addresses the issue of accounting for tax, revenue and bond anticipation notes. Anticipation notes are issued with the expectation that the government will receive specific resources in the near future and that these resources will be used to retire the liability. Tax anticipation notes are often issued as part of a cash management strategy that recognizes that certain taxes (such as property taxes) will not be collected evenly over the fiscal year. Bond anticipation notes may be issued with the understanding that as soon as the proceeds from the issuance of specific long-term bonds are received, the bond anticipation notes will be extinguished (NCGAI-9, par. 12, as amended by GASB-34, pars. 15–16, 31, and 82) [GASB Cod. Secs. 1100, 1500, 2200, B50.102–.103, C50.120, C60.109, D20.109–.110, D30.108–.110, J50.107, L10.109, L20, P21.112–.113, S40.116–.118].

PRACTICE POINT: Some governments have legislation that does not allow the issuance of anticipation notes that straddle a fiscal year. All such notes must be repaid at the end of a fiscal year. However, many governments may indeed have such legislation and retire the notes on the last day of a fiscal year only to reissue them the next day. The substance of this transaction in reality is that a long-term debt may exist instead of a short-term debt.

For governmental funds, notes issued in anticipation of the receipt of taxes or revenues should be presented as a liability of the fund that will actually receive the proceeds from the issuance of the notes. The tax or revenue anticipation note represents a governmental fund liability that will be extinguished through the use of expendable available resources of the fund.

Notes issued in anticipation of proceeds from the subsequent sale of bonds may be classified as general long-term obligations (and therefore presented only in the government-wide financial statements) when the conditions surrounding the notes satisfy the requirements contained in U.S. GAAP. Specifically, GASB-62, pars. 38–39 [GASB Cod. Secs. 1500.110–.111, 1800.117–.118, 2200.184–.185], state that what is typically considered a current liability may be treated as a long-term liability when (1) the intention is to refinance the debt on a long-term basis and (2) the intention can be substantiated through a post-balance-sheet issuance of the long-term debt or by an acceptable financing agreement.

The actual issuance of the bonds must occur after the balance sheet date but before the balance sheet is issued to satisfy the post-balance-sheet condition for a governmental unit. The amount of the bond anticipation notes that is included as general long-term debt and presented in the government-wide financial statements cannot be greater than the proceeds of the actual bond sale. In addition, the maturity date of the newly issued bonds (or serial bonds) must be sufficiently later than the balance sheet date so as not to require the use of a fund's available expendable resources to retire the maturing bonds (GASB-62, par. 40) [GASB Cod. Secs. 1500.112, 1800.119, 2200.186].

When the intent to refinance the bond anticipation notes is substantiated by a financing agreement, the maximum amount of the notes that can be presented as a general long-term obligation in the entity's government-wide financial statements is the amount of the estimated bond proceeds expected to be realized under the agreement. If a portion of the actual bond proceeds is restricted for purposes other than the extinguishment of the bond anticipation notes, the restricted portion must be classified as a governmental fund liability. For example, if the bond anticipation notes total $10,000,000 and the actual bonds when sold under the financing agreement are expected to yield $12,000,000, but $4,000,000 of the proceeds are restricted for other purposes, only $8,000,000 of the $10,000,000 bond anticipation notes can be classified as a general long-term liability. If the amount available under the financing agreement fluctuates depending on some measurable factor, the amount of the notes to be classified as long-term is based on a reasonable estimate of the minimum amount that will be available under the agreement. When a reasonable estimate cannot be made, none of the bond anticipation notes can be classified as long-term debt.

When a liability for bond anticipation notes meets the criteria for classification as a general long-term liability, a note to the financial statements must contain (1) a general description of the financing agreement and (2) the terms of any new debt incurred or expected to be incurred as a result of the agreement. If the criteria established by GASB-62 have not been satisfied, bond anticipation notes must be presented as a liability in the financial statements of the governmental fund that recorded the proceeds from the issuance of the notes.

To illustrate the accounting for bond anticipation notes, assume that $10,000,000 of bond anticipation notes is issued and the proceeds are recorded in the Capital Projects Fund. If the criteria are met, the following entries are made:

	Debit	Credit
Entry 1:		
CAPITAL PROJECTS FUND		
Cash	10,000,000	
Proceeds From Issuance Of Bond Anticipation Notes		10,000,000

If the GASB-62 criteria are not satisfied, the following entry is made:

	Debit	Credit
Entry 2:		
CAPITAL PROJECTS FUND		
Cash	10,000,000	
Bond Anticipation Notes Payable		10,000,000

PRACTICE ALERT: The status of the presentation of anticipation notes in governmental funds is one of the issues being deliberated in the GASB's *Financial Reporting Model Improvements—Reexamination* project. In substance, many of these transactions are similar to long-term debt. Anticipation notes that remain outstanding at year-end are shown as liabilities in governmental funds under the current model. Based on any final conclusion made by the GASB on the period of availability to declare a liability in a governmental fund, tax and revenue anticipation notes may continue to be presented as liabilities of funds, or may not be recognized due to their normally short-term nature.

Demand Bonds in Governmental Funds

To illustrate the accounting for demand bonds in governmental funds, assume that $4,000,000 of demand bonds is issued and the proceeds are to be used by a Capital Projects Fund. When the criteria established by GASBI-1 are met (a general long-term liability exists), the following entries are made:

	Debit	Credit
Entry 3:		
CAPITAL PROJECTS FUND		
Cash	4,000,000	
Proceeds from Issuance of Demand Bonds		4,000,000

When the demand bonds are issued and the criteria established in GASBI-1 are not met, the following entry is made:

	Debit	Credit
Entry 4:		
CAPITAL PROJECTS FUND		
Cash	4,000,000	
Bonds Payable on Demand		4,000,000

For the above entries, the following will occur:

Entry Number	Will/Will Not be shown as a long-term liability on the government-wide financial statements
Tax, Revenue and Bond Anticipation Notes	
1	Will
2	Will Not
Demand Bonds	
3	Will
4	Will Not

If the demand bonds are presented for redemption, the redemption should be recorded as an expenditure of the fund from which debt service is normally paid. To illustrate, assume that the $4,000,000 demand bonds are redeemed and paid out of the Debt Service Fund from funds transferred from the General Fund. The following entries would be made if the demand bonds were originally classified as general long-term debt, and the debt is converted to long-term installment notes as determined under the terms of a take-out agreement:

	Debit	Credit
GENERAL FUND		
Cash	4,000,000	
Proceeds From Issuance of Long-Term Installment Notes to Finance Redemption of Demand Bonds		4,000,000
Transfers out (to Debt Service Fund)	4,000,000	
Cash		4,000,000
DEBT SERVICE FUND		
Cash	4,000,000	
Transfers in (from General Fund)		4,000,000
Expenditures (for Redemption of Demand Bonds)	4,000,000	
Cash		4,000,000

Note: The debt would be removed from the government-wide financial statements since it has been liquidated.

If the demand bonds redeemed were originally recorded as a liability of the Capital Projects Fund (no take-out agreement), the following entries are made to redeem the demand bonds:

	Debit	Credit
GENERAL FUND		
Transfers out (to Debt Service Fund)	4,000,000	
Cash		4,000,000
DEBT SERVICE FUND		
Cash	4,000,000	
Transfers in (from General Fund)		4,000,000
CAPITAL PROJECTS FUND		
Bonds Payable on Demand	4,000,000	
Other Financing Sources—(Retirement of Fund Liabilities by Payments Made by Other Funds)		4,000,000

The liability of the Capital Projects Fund is reduced by simultaneously crediting "Other Financing Sources." That account would appear on the Capital Projects Fund's statement of revenues, expenditures and changes in fund balances.

Demand bonds that were originally classified as a long-term liability because a take-out agreement existed at the issuance date of the bonds would have to be reclassified if the original take-out agreement expires. Under this circumstance, it would be necessary to establish a liability in the fund that originally recorded the demand bond proceeds. For example, if the $4,000,000 demand bonds illustrated earlier were originally recorded as a long-term liability (in the government-wide financial statements), the following entries would be made if the take-out agreement expires (GASBI-1, par. 10, as amended by GASB-63, par.

8, GASB-34, pars. 12, 82, 91, 97, as amended by GASB-62, pars. 29–43) [GASB Cod. Sec. D30.108]:

	Debit	Credit
CAPITAL PROJECTS FUND		
Other Financing Uses (Reclassification of Long-Term Debt as a Fund Liability)	4,000,000	
Bonds Payable (on Demand)		4,000,000

Note: The debt is reported as a governmental fund liability and as an obligation in the government-wide financial statements.

Any actual bond redemption occurring after the debt is reclassified as the liability of a specific governmental fund should be recorded as an expenditure of the fund that accounts for the servicing of the debt (GASBI-1, par. 13, GASB-34, par. 82, as amended by GASB-63, par. 8) [GASB Cod. Sec. D30.109].

PRACTICE POINT: The date of reclassification is not the date the take-out agreement expires. If the take-out agreement expires within one year of the date of the balance sheet, the debt must be reclassified as the liability of a specific governmental fund.

PROPRIETARY FUNDS

The accrual basis of accounting and economic resources measurement focus is used to determine which liabilities should be presented on the statement of net position of a proprietary or fiduciary fund. In general, a proprietary or fiduciary fund should report liabilities in a similar manner that a commercial enterprise does assuming that the presentation is not inconsistent with standards established by the GASB. Fiduciary funds do not have long-term debt as the funds are being held for others.

Bond, Tax, and Revenue Anticipation Notes

GASB-62, par. 40 [GASB Cod. Secs. 1500.112, 1800.119, 2200.186], stipulates that a proprietary or fiduciary fund must determine whether bond, tax and revenue anticipation notes should be presented on the proprietary fund's balance sheet as a current or long-term liability.

Demand Bonds

GASBI-1 is applicable to demand bonds accounted for in a proprietary fund that have an exercisable provision for redemption at or within one year of the fund's balance sheet date. Such bonds may be reported as a long-term liability in the proprietary fund when all of the criteria of GASBI-1 are met.When the conditions of GASBI-1 have not been met, demand bonds must be presented as a current liability if the proceeds were received by a proprietary fund. If demand bonds are issued and no take-out agreement has been executed at their issuance date or at the balance sheet date, the bonds cannot be considered a long-term liability.

GOVERNMENT-WIDE FINANCIAL STATEMENTS

The accrual basis of accounting and the economic resources measurement focus are used to determine which liabilities should be presented in a governmental entity's statement of net position. Liabilities should be presented in the statement of net position based on their relative liquidity. The liquidity of liabilities is based on maturity dates or expected payment dates. Because of the significant degree of aggregation used in the preparation of government-wide financial statements, the GASB notes that the liquidity of an asset or liability account presented in the statement of net position should be determined by assessing the average liquidity of the class of assets or liabilities to which it belongs, "even though individual balances may be significantly more or less liquid than others in the same class and some items may have both current and long-term elements" (GASB-34, par. 31) [GASB Cod. Secs. 2200.116, B50.103, C50.120, C60.109, D30.110].

Both governmental activities and business-type activities should be presented in the statement of net position.

Bond, Tax, and Revenue Anticipation Notes

Bond, tax, and revenue anticipation notes should be presented in the government-wide financial statements. To determine the liquidity of these debts the criteria established by NCGAI-9 must be used to determine whether bond anticipation notes are current or noncurrent (due in more than one year). Tax and revenue anticipation notes are considered current liabilities (liabilities due within one year).

Demand Bonds

Demand bonds should also be presented in the government-wide financial statement. To determine the liquidity of this type of debt, the criteria established by GASBI-1 must be used to determine whether the demand bonds are current or noncurrent (due in more than one year).

EXTINGUISHMENT OF DEBT AND DEBT REFUNDING/ DEFEASANCE

A governmental unit may extinguish debt in a manner whereby the unit (1) has no further legal responsibilities under the original debt agreement or (2) continues to be legally responsible for the debt but the extinguishment is considered an in-substance defeasance (retirement).

PRACTICE POINT: GASB Statement No. 86 (*Certain Debt Extinguishment Issues*) effective for reporting periods that began after June 15, 2017, extends most of the provisions for extinguishment of debt to situations where resources *other than the proceeds of refunding debt* are placed in trust for the sole purpose of debt extinguishment.

An example of such a transaction would occur when a government building is sold. Non-callable bonds that financed the building are outstanding. The proceeds from the sale are placed in a defeasance trust to the extent needed to pay off the bonds (interest and principal) upon maturity.

The trust is restricted to owning only monetary assets that are essentially risk-free as to the amount, timing, and collection of interest. If the debt is payable in U.S. dollars, the trust should be funded with assets also in U.S. dollars. GASB-86 limits essentially risk free assets to: (1) direct obligations of the U.S. government; (2) obligations guaranteed by the U.S. government; and (3) securities backed by U.S. government obligations as collateral and for which interest and principal balances on the collateral generally flow immediately through to the security holder (commonly known as "SLGS"). Such assets are required to provide cash flows that approximately coincide with timing and amount of the defeased debt. If some of the securities are callable, they are not essentially risk-free and do not qualify for defeasance purposes.

Certain provisions regarding prepaid insurance related to the extinguished debt and note disclosure of the transaction are included as part of GASB-86. Once an escrow is properly funded and defeasance occurs, the debt is no longer shown as a liability. Any difference between the reacquisition price and the net carrying amount of the debt is shown as a gain or loss in the period of defeasance. Payments to the escrow agent are shown as debt service expenditures in governmental funds.

Once the defeasance occurs and as long as the debt remains outstanding, the information on the transaction is included with other defeasance transactions as discussed in this section.

Debt is considered to be extinguished under the following circumstances detailed in GASB-62, paragraphs 124–127 [GASB Cod. Secs. D20.101–.103, .501–.504], as well as GASB-7 [GASB Cod. Secs. D20.104–.117]:

- The debtor pays the creditor and is relieved of all its obligations with respect to the debt. This concludes the debtor's reacquisition of its outstanding debt securities in the public securities market, regardless of whether the securities are canceled or held as treasury bonds.

- The debtor is legally released from being the primary obligor under the debt either judicially or by the creditor and it is probable (as defined in GASB-62, par. 100a) that the debtor will not be required to make future payments with respect to the debt under any guarantees.

- The debtor irrevocably places cash or other assets in a trust to be used solely for satisfying scheduled payments of both interest and principal of a specific obligation and the possibility that the debtor will be required to make future payments with respect to that debt is remote. In this circumstance, debt is extinguished even though the debtor is not legally released from being the primary obligor under the debt obligation (in-substance defeasance).

When debt is extinguished as an in-substance defeasance transaction, only monetary assets can be contributed to the irrevocable trust. The monetary assets must be (1) denominated in the same currency in which the debt is payable, and (2) essentially risk free with respect to the timing, amount, and collection of principal and interest. GASB-7 (*Advanced Refundings Resulting in Defeasance of*

Debt) lists the following as examples of essentially risk free assets denominated in U.S. dollars (GASB-7, par. 4):

- Direct obligations of the U.S. government;

- Obligations guaranteed by the U.S. government; and

- Securities backed by U.S. government obligations as collateral under an arrangement by which the interest and principal payments on the collateral generally flow immediately through to the holder of security, commonly known as "SLGS" or "slugs."

The monetary assets must generate cash flows that approximate the debt service requirements of the original debt. That is, cash must be available from the trust to pay interest and make principal repayments as they become due. The cash flows must be sufficient to meet trustee fees and similar administrative expenditures if these expenditures are expected to be made from the assets of the trust. If the administrative expenditures are to be paid directly by the governmental unit, a liability for the total expected administrative expenditures should be recognized in the period in which the debt is considered extinguished (GASB-7, par. 4) [GASB Cod. Sec. D20.106].

The liability recognized based on the expected administrative expenditures financed by the governmental unit may be classified as general long-term debt and therefore presented only in the government-wide financial statements if the expenditures do not require current appropriation and expenditure of governmental fund financial resources.

The concept of in-substance defeasance was established in for-profit GAAP, where debt could be removed from an entity's financial statements (even though it is not legally retired) by creating an irrevocable trust and transferring certain types of assets to the fund that will be used to meet debt service requirements of the obligation over its remaining life. GASB-7 incorporated the standards established by for-profit GAAP with respect to in-substance defeasance and thus enabled governmental entities to remove debt from their financial statements even when the debt instrument is not legally surrendered by an investor.

The amount of the debt considered to be retired based on an in-substance defeasance transaction must be disclosed as long as the debt remains legally outstanding. In addition, disclosures should include a general description of the in-substance defeasance transaction (GASB-7, par. 11) [GASB Cod. Sec. D20.114].

When market interest rates decrease, governmental and commercial entities must decide if it is feasible to change their debt structure, thus reducing future debt service payments. When an entity uses the proceeds from the issuance of new debt to retire old debt before its maturity date, the process is referred to as a "refunding."

OBSERVATION: A third type of refunding occurs on rare occasions. A "crossover refunding" issuance is secured similarly to other refunding bonds, but even though the original bonds are refunded, the original revenue stream continues to pay for them until a call date. Effectively, the government is taking advantage of lower interest rates on new debt at the point of sale of these bonds.

But not all of the criteria for a defeasance are met. What usually occurs is that the new refunding bonds escrow is not sufficient to meet the debt service of the old debt until a future date. At that time, the pledged revenues "cross over" or swap to pay debt service on the refunding bonds and escrowed securities are used to pay the refunded bonds. During the period when both the refunded and the refunding bonds are outstanding, debt service on the refunding bonds is paid from interest earnings on the invested proceeds of the refunding bonds. However, for accounting purposes, because an accounting defeasance has not occurred, both issues are shown as outstanding debt and the related escrow is shown as part of restricted investments. With regard to the statement of net position, GASB has noted in the GASB *Implementation Guide 2015-1*, question 7.23.15 [GASB Cod. Sec. 2200.709-14] that in a crossover refunding bond issuance, the refunding debt is not capital related until it refunds (defeases) the old debt at the crossover date. Prior to that time, the refunding bond liability and the cash and investments balances should be approximately equal—therefore net position is not affected. After the defeasance occurs (after the crossover date), the refunding debt assumes the characteristics of the old debt and would be included in the calculation of net investment in capital assets.

Current and Advance Refundings

PRACTICE ALERT: The 2017 Tax Cuts and Jobs Act changes the status of advance refunding bonds to taxable transactions after December 31, 2017. Current refunding bonds are still allowed. As of the date of publication, it is unclear if the GASB will need to change the guidance contained in GASB-7 or GASB-23.

The refunding of old debt (defeasance) can be accomplished as either a current refunding or an advance refunding. Debt is defeased when either legal requirements (current refunding) or accounting requirements (advance refunding) are satisfied. Legal requirements are met and debt is defeased when debt holders are paid at the maturity date or at a call date stipulated in the debt agreement. When debt is paid before its maturity date (at a call date or retired by repurchasing the debt in the secondary market) and the retirement is financed by issuing new debt, the process is referred to as a current refunding of debt. Accounting requirements are met when debt is in-substance defeased. U.S. GAAP states that an in-substance defeasance occurs when cash and other assets are placed in an irrevocable trust that is to be used exclusively to service the future debt requirements of the (old) debt. When an in-substance defeasance is financed by issuing new bonds, the process is referred to as an "advance refunding of debt."

GASB-7 establishes both accounting standards and disclosure standards for advance refundings of debt. The accounting standards apply to funds whose measurement focus is the flow of current financial resources. Funds included in this category are the General Fund, Special Revenue Funds, Debt Service Funds, Capital Projects Funds, and Permanent Funds. An advance refunding of debt would be recorded in one of these funds and the related debt (both the new debt and the old debt) would be presented only in the governmental entity's government-wide financial statements (GASB-7, par. 7, as amended by GASB-34, pars.16 and 82, GASB-23, par. 3, GASB-34, par. 5, GASB-62, pars. 124 and 128, GASB-70, par. 12) [GASB Cod. Sec. D20.101].

The disclosure standards established by GASB-7 apply to all governmental entities and include state and local governments as well as public benefit corporations, public authorities, public employee retirement systems, governmental utilities, governmental hospitals, and public colleges and universities.

Advance Refundings in Governmental Funds

When general long-term debt that is reported in the government-wide financial statements but not a government fund is defeased through an advance refunding, the proceeds from the issuance of the new debt should be recorded as "Other Financing Source—Proceeds of Refunding Debt" in the governmental fund that receives the proceeds from the issuance of the new debt. The newly issued debt should also be recorded as a liability in the governmental unit's government-wide financial statements. When payments to the escrow agent to defease the old debt are made from the proceeds of the newly issued debt, the payments should be recorded as "Other Financing Use—Payment to Refunded Debt Escrow Agent." The defeased debt should be removed from the governmental unit's government-wide financial statements (GASB-7, pars. 8–9; GASB-34, pars. 16, 82, and 88, as amended by GASB-37, par. 16) [GASB Cod. Sec. D20.109].

NOTE: GASB-7 uses the term "bond" instead of the more general term *debt* in its account titles when referring to advance refundings resulting in defeasance of debt. The defeasance of the old debt could be accomplished through refinancing other than issuing bonds. (See also previous **PRACTICE ALERTS** on GASB-88.) Therefore, the general term "debt" is used for the term "bond" throughout this analysis and explanation.

For example, if a governmental unit defeased $500,000 of long-term notes by issuing $500,000 of long-term bonds and placed the proceeds in an irrevocable escrow, the following entries would be made assuming that the proceeds from the issuance of the new debt were recorded in the Debt Service Fund:

	Debit	Credit
DEBT SERVICE FUND		
Cash	500,000	
Other Financing Source—Proceeds of Refunding Debt		500,000
To record the issuance of long-term bonds.		
Other Financing Use—Payment to Refunded Debt Escrow Agent	500,000	
Cash		500,000
To record the payment to the escrow agent for debt defeasance.		

In the government-wide financial statements, long-term notes payable would be removed and bonds payable would be presented. If the cash is never deposited to the governmental entity's accounts, the first two entries may be combined to show only the source and use of the proceeds.

When payments made to the escrow agent to defease the debt are made from the governmental unit's resources and not from proceeds generated from the issuance of new debt, the payments should be recorded as a debt service expenditure and not as an other financing use. For example, if it is assumed in the previous illustration that the $500,000 debt was defeased by issuing $400,000 of bonds and using $100,000 from the General Fund, the following entries would be made (GASB-7, par. 8, GASB-34, pars. 82, 88, GASB-37, par. 16) [GASB Cod. Sec. D20.109]:

	Debit	Credit
DEBT SERVICE FUND		
Cash	400,000	
Other Financing Source—Proceeds of Refunding Debt		400,000
To record the issuance of long-term bonds.		
Other Financing Use—Payment to Refunded Debt Escrow Agent	400,000	
Cash		400,000
To record the issuance of long-term bonds.		
GENERAL FUND		
Expenditures—Principal	100,000	
Cash		100,000

In the government-wide financial statements, long-term notes of $500,000 would be removed and bonds payable of $400,000 would be presented. Payments made to the escrow agent from current governmental resources that represent accrued interest on the defeased debt should be recorded as a debt service expenditure (interest) and not as an other financing use.

Advance Refundings in Proprietary Funds

PRACTICE ALERT: The 2017 Tax Cuts and Jobs Act changes the status of advance refunding bonds to taxable transactions after December 31, 2017. Current refunding bonds are still allowed. As of the date of publication, it is unclear if the GASB will need to change the guidance contained in GASB-7 or GASB-23.

In December 1993, the GASB revised the accounting standards related to the refunding of debt by proprietary funds with the issuance of GASB-23 (*Accounting and Financial Reporting for Refundings of Debt Reported by Proprietary Activities*).

The standards established by GASB-23 apply to all funds maintained by state and local governmental entities that use proprietary fund accounting. This includes not only all states and municipalities, but also public benefit corporations and authorities, public utilities, and public hospitals and other public health-care providers.

GASB-23 applies to both current refundings and advance refundings of debt. Paragraph 4 of GASB-23, as amended by GASB-65, par. 6 [GASB Cod. Sec. D20.111], requires that the difference between the reacquisition price and the net carrying amount of the old debt be recognized as a deferred inflow of resources or deferred outflow of resources and amortized as a component of interest expense in a systematic and rational manner over the remaining life of the old debt or the life of the new debt, whichever is shorter.

When a governmental entity that uses proprietary fund accounting refunds debt (either a current refunding or an advance refunding), the difference between (1) the book value of the refunded (old) debt and (2) the amount required to retire the debt should be accounted for as a deferral and should not be reported as a gain or loss on the fund's operating statement.

The book value of the retired debt includes its maturity value and any related unamortized discount or premium. The amount required to retire the old debt (reacquisition price) depends on whether the transaction is a current re-funding or an advance refunding. For current refundings, the reacquisition price is the amount paid to debt holders (face value of the debt plus the premium amount, if any). For advance refundings, the reacquisition price is the amount of assets that must be placed in escrow to satisfy the in-substance defeasance criteria originally established by for-profit GAAP.

Transaction costs related to the issuance of the new debt that is the basis for the refunding are not considered when determining the difference between the book value of the old debt and the reacquisition price.

For an advance refunding, for-profit GAAP, states that if "it is expected that trust assets will be used to pay related costs, such as trustee fees, as well as to satisfy scheduled interest and principal payments of a specific debt, those costs shall be considered in determining the amount of funds required by the trust. On the other hand, if the debt incurs an obligation to pay any related costs, the debt shall accrue a liability for those probable future payments in the period that the debt is recognized as extinguished" (GASB-23, par. 5, as amended by GASB-65, par. 6) [GASB Cod. Sec. D20.112]. In the latter circumstance (accrual of future payments), the amount accrued should be used to determine the amount of the deferred inflow or outflow of resources, but not reported as a current expense. The deferred inflow or outflow of resources is presented separately from the balance of the refunding debt in the statement of net position.

OBSERVATION: GASB-65 (*Items Previously Reported as Assets and Lia-bilities*) characterizes the differential between the reacquisition price of the previously issued debt and the net carrying amount of the old debt to deferred inflows or deferred outflows of resources, depending on if the differential is positive or negative. This may also occur in the case of a lease that is refunded by using tax-exempt debt prior to the expiration of the lease term.

Subsequently, the deferred outflow (or inflow) of resources is amortized over the original remaining life of the old debt or the life of the new debt, whichever is less. The amount is amortized in a "systematic and rational manner" as a component of interest expense. If the amount is a deferred outflow of resources, interest expense is increased because of the periodic amortization. If the amount is a deferred inflow of resources resulting in an eventual gain, interest expense is decreased.

OBSERVATION: Amortization methods that satisfy the systematic and rational guideline include (1) the effective interest method, (2) the straight-line method for term bonds, and (3) the proportionate to stated-interest requirements method. In financial accounting, it is generally accepted that periodic interest expense should be determined on the basis of the effective interest method or the straight-line method if the results from applying the latter method are not materially different from the use of the effective interest method. GASB-23 does not use the effective interest method as the benchmark for determining the acceptability of periodic amortization. Because of the structure of the refunding and of the bonds that are refunded, other methods may reflect more of a fiscal reality than either the effective interest or the straight-line method.

OBSERVATION: Other methods can include amortizing when groups of principal amounts mature. This is preferable when the maturities are uneven. What constitutes "systematic and rational" is a matter of judgment. GASB does not attempt to provide a general definition of "systematic and rational" in any literature.

The standards established by GASB-23 for accounting for gains or losses that arise from refundings are significantly different from the standards applicable to similar transactions in the private sector. For government entities, any loss will be deferred, while in the private sector, a loss must be reported immediately on an entity's statement of operations.

Refunding Debt Previously Refunded

Debt that is used to refund previously issued debt may also be subsequently refunded. Any gain or loss from the subsequent refunding should be deferred and combined with any unamortized deferred gain or loss related to the original refunding. The combined deferral should be amortized over the shorter of (1) the remaining amortization period that was used in the original refunding or (2) the life of the newly issued debt. The standard applies to current refundings as well as to advance refundings. However, refunding debt that has been previously refunded may result in a taxable debt issuance.

To illustrate, assume that Debt A was issued on January 1, 20X2, with a maturity date in 7 years. On January 1, 20X4, Debt A is refunded by issuing Debt B with a maturity date in 10 years. If a deferred outflow of resources of $300,000 is created by the refunding, the deferral is amortized over 5 years (the lesser of the 5 years remaining in the original life of Debt A and the 10-year life of Debt B). Further, assume that on January 1, 20X5, Debt B is refunded by issuing Debt C with a maturity date in 2 years. If a deferred outflow of resources of $600,000 is created by the second refunding, that amount is combined with the previously unamortized deferred outflow of resources related to the original refunding ($300,000 - $120,000), and the combined amount of $780,000 ($600,000 + $180,000) is amortized over 2 years (the lesser of the 3 years remaining in the amortization period for the first refunding and the 2-year life of Debt C).

EXHIBIT 12-1
COMPREHENSIVE ILLUSTRATION: CURRENT REFUNDING

In a current refunding, proceeds from the newly issued debt are used to immediately retire the old debt. For proprietary funds, the computation of the deferred outflow of resources arising from a current refunding is shown in Illustration 1 of Appendix B of GASB-23, as amended by GASB-53 (discussed in more detail later in this chapter). The illustration is based on the following facts:

> Castle Rock County retires $20,000,000 in variable rate debt, paying $400,000 of a call premium. The county had an interest rate swap as an effective hedging derivative instrument that is also terminated as part of the transaction. As of the interest rate swap's termination date, the fair value of the swap represents a liability of $1,500,000, and the deferred outflow of resources amount is $1,500,000 (an effective hedge). The termination requires a $1,500,000 payment to the counterparty by the government. Costs of the transaction are immaterial to this discussion. New fixed-rate debt was issued for $20,000,000 to fund the transaction.

To record the transactions the following must occur:

1. The termination payment is a cash outflow of $1,500,000.

2. The net carrying amount of the refunded debt determined to calculate the deferred outflow of resources or deferred inflow of resources on the refunding should include the deferred outflow of resources or deferred inflow of resources amount related to the terminated hedging derivative instrument—a $1,500,000 deferred outflows of resources, computed as of the date of refunding. In many cases, the deferred outflow of resources or deferred inflow of resources approximates the hedging derivative instrument's termination payment.

3. The deferred outflow of resources on refunding in the circumstances described in the fact pattern is calculated as follows:

REACQUISITION PRICE:		
Old bonds outstanding	$ 20,000,000	
Call premium on old bonds	400,000	
Funds required to retire old bonds		$ 20,400,000
NET CARRYING AMOUNT OF OLD BONDS:		
Old bonds outstanding	$(20,000,000)	
Deferred outflow of resources—interest rate swap	1,500,000	
Net Carrying Amount		(18,500,000)
Deferred Outflow of Resources on Refunding		**$1,900,000**

To record the current refunding, the following entries would be made in the proprietary fund, irrespective of interest accruals on the new debt:

	Debit	Credit
Interest Rate Swap	1,500,000	
Cash		1,500,000
To record termination payment to counterparty.		
Variable Rate Bonds	20,000,000	
Deferred Outflow of Resources on Refunding	1,900,000	
Deferred Outflow of Resources— Interest Rate Swap		1,500,000
Cash (call premium on old bonds)		400,000
Fixed Rate Bonds		20,000,000
To retire variable rate debt, associated hedge, record call premium and issue fixed rate bonds.		

PRACTICE POINT: In a current refunding, a difference between the reacquisition price and the carrying amount of the old debt usually results from one or more factors, all related to the old debt: call premium and unamortized premium or discount because the new bonds effectively incorporate those factors into their pricing structure.

GASB-53 amended the calculation of the deferred outflow of resources (deferred) loss on early retirement of debt. In a refunding transaction, if there is a deferred amount related to a derivative transaction that hedged the prior bonds, the balance of the deferral account should be included in the net carrying amount of the old debt for purposes of calculating the difference between that amount and the reacquisition price of the old debt. GASB-53 requires that this method be used whether or not a termination of the related hedging derivative instrument occurs. The balance of the deferral account also is part of the economic gain or loss calculation (discussed below).

Based on the above analysis, the deferred outflow of resources arising from the early retirement of debt is $1,500,000. GASB-65 requires that the amount be capitalized as a deferred outflow of resources and be amortized in a systematic and rational manner over the lesser of the original remaining life of the old bonds or the life of the new bonds, whichever is shorter.

If the deferred outflow of resources amount is amortized using the straight-line method, the annual amortization is $300,000 ($1,500,000 ÷ 5 years). The amortization would be part of the interest expense the proprietary fund recognizes each year.

GASB-64: Derivative Instruments: Application of Hedge Accounting Termination Provisions—An Amendment of GASB Statement No. 53

GASB-64 (*Derivative Instruments: Application of Hedge Accounting Termination Provisions*) stipulates that instead of recognizing investment revenue immediately because of the release of the accumulated deferred charges when a derivative terminates, the derivative may not terminate when certain circumstances occur. Those circumstances include when a swap counterparty is replaced through an assignment or an in-substance assignment, as defined by the GASB-64, and the swap represents a liability of the government. If those criteria are met, the loss would continue to be deferred outflow of resources. The swap agreements would terminate and be replaced immediately with identical terms and conditions. Many of these instances occurred when the credit markets failed during the fall of 2008 and 2009. In the above example, should an in-substance assignment have occurred, the $1,500,000 would not have been released.

DISCLOSURES

Long-Term Debt Disclosures

GASB-38 (*Certain Financial Statement Note Disclosures*) requires debt service disclosure with separate presentations for each of the five years following the Statement of Net Position and in five-year increments thereafter through the year of maturity. The disclosure must identify the principal and interest components of debt service.

The disclosure requirement also applies to the minimum lease payments for capital leases and non-cancelable operating leases, as described in Chapter 14, "Leases and Service Concession Arrangements."

An illustration of the disclosure requirement for debt for the year ended June 30, 20X8, is as follows in accordance with GASB-88:

Note—Debt Service Requirements to Maturity—Primary Government (in thousands)

| Fiscal Year | Governmental Activities | | | | | | Business-Type Activities | | |
| | Certificates of Participation | | | General Obligation Bonds | | | Notes from Direct Borrowing—Airport | | |
	Principal	Interest	Total	Principal	Interest	Total	Principal	Interest	Total
20X9	$5,500	$3,551	$9,051	$11,210	$1,660	$12,870	$232	$14	$246
20Y0	5,645	3,352	8,997	11,610	1,268	12,878	239	7	246
20Y1	5,800	3,129	8,929	12,030	852	12,882	-	-	-
20Y2	5,970	2,896	8,866	4,050	400	4,450	-	-	-
20Y3	6,150	2,650	8,800	4,200	268	4,468	-	-	-
20Y4-Y8	28,755	9,042	37,797	6,255	308	6,563	-	-	-
20Y9-Z3	15,095	1,912	17,007	-	-	-	-	-	-
Total	$103,914	$183,292	$287,206	$49,355	$4,756	$54,111	$471	$21	$492

(Other debt disclosure requirements are discussed in Chapter 20, "Comprehensive Annual Financial Report.")

If a governmental entity has debt that carries a variable interest rate, the debt service disclosures should be based on the interest rate in effect as of the date of the current Net Position statement/balance sheet. In addition, the conditions that affect the determination of the variable interest rate should be disclosed.

The notes to the financial statements should focus on the primary government (which includes its blended component units) and support the information included in the government-wide financial statements and the fund financial statements. Note disclosures related to discretely presented component units should be presented based on the requirements established by GASB-14, paragraph 63, as amended by GASB-61, paragraph 11(b) [GASB Cod. Secs. 2300.105, 2600.123, C20.105, C50.146, I50.139, I55.108, P50.129].

OBSERVATION: Controversy has ensued as to how much debt disclosure to incorporate for discretely presented component units within a primary government's notes to the basic financial statements. GASB-14, paragraph 63, as amended, stipulates that for discretely presented component units, notes *essential* to fair presentation in the reporting entity's basic financial statements encompass only major discretely presented component units considering the nature and significance of each component unit's relationship to the primary government. Determining which discretely presented component unit disclosures are essential to fair presentation is a matter of professional judgment and should be done on a component unit-by-component unit basis. A specific type of disclosure might be essential for one component unit but not for another depending on the individual component unit's relationship with the primary government. For example, if a primary government is obligated in some manner for the debt of a particular component unit, it is likely that debt-related disclosures should be made for that component unit. On the other hand, for non-major component units, debt-related disclosures do not always need to be included in the primary government's notes to the basic financial statements if the primary government is not obligated in some manner for that debt. It is up to professional judgment and the policies and practices of the primary government. (See previous PRACTICE ALERT on GASB-88.)

Variable Interest Rate Debt Disclosure

Many governments have the opportunity to sell variable rate debt either with a corresponding derivative hedge or without a hedge (commonly known as "naked" variable rate debt). The purpose of issuing the debt is to lower interest costs and satisfy bondholders' needs. Typically, the bondholders for this type of debt are tax-exempt money market mutual funds.

Due to the variability in interest rates, disclosure is slightly different than fixed rate debt disclosure. GASB-38, par. 10 [GASB Cod. Secs. 1500.129, 2300.106], stipulates that the schedule of debt service requirements to maturity for variable rate debt should use interest determined using the rate in effect at the financial statement date and the terms by which interest rates change for variable rate debt.

The following is an example of variable interest rate debt disclosure:

As of June 30, 20X7, aggregate debt service requirements of the Castle Rock County's variable rate debt and net receipts/payments on associated hedging derivative instruments are as follows. These amounts assume that current interest rates on variable-rate bonds and the current reference rates of hedging derivative instruments will remain the same for their term. As these rates vary, interest payments on variable-rate bonds and net receipts/payments on the hedging derivative instruments will vary. Refer to Note X for information on derivative instruments (amounts in thousands).

Year Ended			Hedging Derivatives, Net	
June 30	Principal	Interest	Interest	Total
20X8	$6,000	$7,786	$(1,253)	$12,533
20X9	10,000	7,525	(1,211)	16,314
20Y0	27,000	7,090	(1,141)	32,949
20Y1	33,000	5,916	(952)	37,964
20Y2	15,000	4,480	(721)	18,759
20Y3-Y7	29,000	19,140	(3,080)	45,060
20Y8-Z2	15,000	12,385	1,475	28.860
20Z3-Z7	14,000	9,570	(528)	23,042
Total	$169,000	$73,892	$(7,411)	$215,481

Short-Term Debt Disclosures

GASB-34 requires that the activity in long-term debt presented in the statement of net position be summarized in a note to the financial statements, but there was no similar requirement for short-term debt. GASB-38 extends the analysis to the statement of net position and balance sheet for short-term debt outstanding during the year "even if no short-term debt is outstanding at year-end." GASB-38 does define short-term debt but notes that short-term debt "results from borrowings characterized by anticipation notes, use of lines of credit, and similar loans."

The schedule of changes in short-term debt is presented in a note to the financial statements and includes the following components:

- Beginning balance;
- Increases for the year;
- Decreases for the year; and
- Ending balance.

In addition, the disclosure should include the reason the short-term debt was issued during the year. An example of the disclosure is presented below:

Note—Short-Term Debt

During the year, the County issued bond anticipation notes in order to begin the reconstruction of a major bridge that had been heavily damaged by floodwaters. The proceeds from the short-term debt were needed immediately to begin the project, and these notes were paid off approximately three months later, when long-term bonds were issued to finance the capital project. Short-term debt activity for the year ended June 30, 20X7, is summarized as follows:

	Beginning Balance	Proceeds	Repayment	Ending Balance
Bond anticipation notes	$—	$12,000,000	$(12,000,000)	$—

Demand Bond Disclosures

When a governmental entity has demand bonds outstanding, irrespective of the exercisable date of the demand provision, GASBI-1 requires that the following information be disclosed (GASBI-1, par. 11) [GASB Cod. Sec. D30.111]:

- General description of the demand bond program;
- Terms of any letters of credit or other standby liquidity agreements outstanding;
- Commitment fees to obtain the letters of credit;
- Any amounts drawn on the letters of credit as of the balance sheet date;
- A description of the take-out agreement (expiration date, commitment fees to obtain the agreement, and terms of any new obligation under the take-out agreement); and
- Debt service requirements if the take-out agreement is exercised.

If installment notes arise from the exercise of the take-out agreement, the amount of the installment loan should be part of the schedule of debt service requirements.

The disclosures are in addition to the general long-term debt disclosures as required by other GASB Statements. These general disclosure requirements are discussed later in this chapter.

Conduit Debt Disclosures

The following information should be disclosed in the financial statements of the issuing entity related to conduit debt obligations (GASBI-2, par. 3) [GASB Cod. Sec. C65.102]:

- Description of the conduit debt transaction;
- Total amount of outstanding conduit debt as of the date of the balance sheet; and
- Statement that the governmental entity has no responsibility for the payment of the debt except for the payments received on the underlying lease or loan agreement.

Refunding Disclosures

GASB-7 established disclosure standards for advance refundings by all governmental entities but did not address disclosure requirements for current refundings. GASB-23 requires that the disclosure requirements established in GASB-7 be extended to current refundings.

GASB-7 disclosure standards are applicable to all advance refundings resulting in the defeasance of debt irrespective of whether the defeased debt is presented only as general long-term debt or as a liability of a specific fund.

A note to the financial statements should provide a general description of an advance refunding that results in debt defeasance. At a minimum, the note should contain the following disclosures (GASB-7, pars. 11–14, GASB-14, pars. 11, 62, and 63, as amended by GASB-34, pars. 82 and 113, and GASB-53, par. 24) [GASB Cod. Secs. D20.114–.117]:

- The difference between (*a*) the cash flow requirements necessary to service the old debt over its life and (*b*) the cash flow requirements necessary to service the new debt and other payments necessary to complete the advance refunding; and
- The economic gain or loss that arises because of the advance refunding.

The life of the old debt is based on its stated maturity date and not on its call date, if any.

OBSERVATION: The two disclosures described above are the only disclosure requirements for advance refunding mandated by GASB-7; however, Appendix A of GASB-7 notes that the GASB believes that, generally, disclosures should include (1) amounts of the old and new debt, (2) additional amounts paid to the escrow agent, and (3) management's explanation for an advance refunding that results in an economic loss. The GASB also states that ultimately the specific disclosures by a particular governmental entity are dependent on "such things as the number and relative size of the entity's advance refunding transactions, the fund structure of the reporting entity, and the number and type of refundings of its component units."

Difference in Cash Flow Requirements

The cash flow requirements of the old debt are simply the sum of all future interest and principal payments that would have to be paid by the governmental entity if the debt remained outstanding until its maturity date. The cash flow requirements of the new debt are the sum of all future interest and principal payments that will have to be paid to service the new debt in the future, and other payments that are made from the governmental entity's current resources rather than from proceeds from the issuance of the new debt. Any proceeds from the issuance of the new debt that represent accrued interest (when the bonds are sold between interest payment dates) should not be included as cash flow requirements related to the new debt, but should include the effects of a hedging derivative instrument, as applicable (GASB-7, pars. 11–14, GASB-14, pars. 11, 62, and 63, as amended by GASB-34, pars. 82 and 113, and GASB-53, par. 24) [GASB Cod. Secs. D20.114–.117].

When new debt is issued in an amount that exceeds the amount needed to defease the old debt, only the portion of the new debt needed to defease the old debt should be included as cash flow requirements related to the new debt, again, including the effects of a hedging derivative instrument, as applicable.

Economic Gain or Loss

The economic gain or loss is computed by determining the difference between the present value of cash flow requirements of the old debt and the present value of cash flow requirements of the new debt. The interest or discount rate used to determine the present value of the cash flows is a rate that generally must be computed through trial and error, either manually or by using a computer software package. The objective is to identify an interest rate that, when applied to the cash flow requirements for the new debt, produces an amount equal to the sum of the (1) proceeds of the new debt (net of premium or discount) and (2) accrued interest, less the underwriting spread.

Issuance costs related to the advance refunding may include such transaction costs as insurance, legal, administrative, and trustee costs. These costs may be recoverable through the yield in the escrow fund or may likely be expensed in accordance with GASB-65. Treasury Department regulations establish the maximum allowable yield of the escrow fund, and certain issuance costs (allowable costs) may be used to reduce the amount defined as proceeds from the issuance of the new debt. The effect of the Treasury Department regulations is to increase the allowable amount that can be legally earned in the escrow fund. Although issuance costs may be allowable under the Treasury Department regulations, they may not be recoverable through the escrow fund because (1) the interest rate on U.S. securities purchased by the escrow fund may be less than the legal maximum rate allowed by the Treasury Department or (2) the escrow fund may be used to liquidate the old debt on a call date and the investment period may be too short to allow for the full recovery of the allowable costs through escrow earnings. When issuance costs are considered allowable costs by the Treasury

Department and they are recovered through the escrow fund, the result is that such costs are not an actual cost to the governmental entity. These are referred to as recoverable costs and are not used to compute the interest or discount rate used to determine the present value of the cash flow requirements related to the old debt and new debt (GASB-7, par. 12) [GASB Cod. Sec. D20.115].

Computing the Required Refunding Disclosures

To clarify the computation of the differences in cash flow requirements and the economic gain or loss arising from an advance refunding, GASB-7 presented three examples in an appendix. The following sections present the steps that may be followed to compute the required disclosures. After a general description of the steps, Example II from GASB-7 is used to demonstrate how the following suggested four steps can be applied to a specific set of circumstances.

Step 1. Compute the amount of resources that will be required to (1) make a payment to the escrow agent in order to defease the debt and (2) pay issuance costs (to be expensed). The resources may be generated entirely from the issuance of new debt, or the refunding may be partially financed by using other resources of the governmental unit.

OBSERVATION: If the old debt is defeased entirely by using other resources of the governmental unit (no new debt is issued), the transaction is not subject to the accounting and disclosure standards established by GASB-7 because it does not satisfy the definition of an advance refunding. Although this method of financing the defeasance is not discussed in GASB-7, it would appear that the accounting standards established by GASB-7 would be appropriate— that is, funding of the irrevocable trust would be treated as a debt service expenditure. The disclosure standards established by GASB-7 would not be appropriate because there would be no new debt service requirements. On the other hand, if a governmental entity accumulates sufficient funds internally to pay off all or part of a debt, the debt would not be considered defeased because an irrevocable trust, as described in GASB-7, would not be established.

The payment to the escrow agent must be large enough to make all interest payments and the principal payment based on either the call date or maturity date of the old debt. Either the call date or the maturity date is used, depending on which is specified as the retirement date in the escrow fund agreement. The amount of the required payment to the escrow agent is also dependent on the rate of return that can be earned in the escrow fund. The escrow rate of return is determined by the market investment conditions and the allowable yield on the escrow investment as determined by Treasury Department regulations.

The amount of the issuance costs must be added to the amount paid to the escrow agent to determine the total amount of resources required to defease the debt.

Step 2. Compute the effective interest rate target amount. The effective interest rate target amount is computed by subtracting the amount of non-recoverable issuance costs from the amount of the resources required to defease the old debt and to pay issuance costs (computed in Step 1). By reducing the amount required to defease the old debt (and to pay issuance costs) by the non-recoverable issuance costs, the effective interest rate (to be computed in Step 3) will be decreased. If all issuance costs are recoverable and the new debt is sold at par, the coupon rate on the new debt will be the same as the effective interest rate.

Step 3. Compute the effective interest rate. The effective interest rate is the interest rate used to discount the debt service requirements on the new debt so that it is exactly equal to the effective interest rate target amount (computed in Step 2). The computation of the effective interest rate is relatively easy if you have access to a computer and a software program. If you do not have access to a computer, the computation of the effective interest rate is tedious because it must be determined through trial and error and by using interpolation.

Step 4. Compute (1) the difference between the cash flow required for service the old debt and the cash flow required to service the new debt and (2) the economic gain or loss resulting from the advance refunding. The difference between the cash flow requirements can be computed as follows:

Elements	*Amounts*
Total interest payments on old debt (using the maturity date of the old debt)	$X
Principal payment to retire old debt	X
Total cash flow requirements to service old debt	$X
Total interest payments on new debt	$X
Principal payments to retire new debt	X
Other resources used to defease old debt	X
Less: Accrued interest on new debt at date of issuance	–X
Total cash flow requirements to service new debt	–X
Difference in cash flow requirements	$X

The economic gain or loss on the advance refunding can be computed as follows:

Elements	*Amounts*
Present value of cash flow requirements to service old debt	$X
Present value of cash flow requirements to service new debt	$X
Other resources used to defease old debt	X
Less: Accrued interest on new debt at date of issuance	–X
Economic gain (loss) on advance refunding	$X

Many underwriters and financial advisers will compute these amounts and provide them for a government. As an alternative, GASB-7 contains a comprehensive illustration of these calculations; also, many spreadsheet programs will calculate the amounts to be presented.

Generally, the advance refunding disclosures required by paragraph 11 of GASB-7 should focus on the primary government, including its blended component units. Thus, disclosures related to governmental activities, business-type activities, major funds, and aggregated nonmajor funds (GASB-7, par. 13, as amended by GASB-14, pars. 11 and 63, and GASB-34, par. 113) [GASB Cod. Sec. D20.116].

For periods after an in-substance debt defeasance has occurred, the amount of the defeased debt outstanding should be disclosed with a distinction between amounts that apply to the primary government (including blended component units) and discretely presented component units (GASB-7, par. 14, as amended by GASB-14, par. 62, and GASB-34, par. 113) [GASB Cod. Sec. D20.117].

PRACTICE POINT: The required disclosures for defeased debt outstanding are applicable only to in-substance defeased debt and not to legally defeased debt.

PRACTICE ALERT: As introduced previously, GASB-86 adds similar disclosures for debt that has been defeased without using refunding bonds.

The following are examples of notes to a financial statement that provide disclosures for (1) an advance refunding resulting in defeased debt and (2) prior-year defeasance of debt outstanding.

Note X—Defeased Debt. On December 31, 20X8, Castle Rock County issued general obligation bonds of $111.44 (par value) with an interest rate of 10% to advance refund term bonds with an interest rate of 20% and a par value of $100. The term bonds mature on December 31, 20Y7, and are callable on December 31, 20Y0. The general obligation bonds were issued at par and, after paying issuance costs of $5.00, the net proceeds were $106.44. The net proceeds from the issuance of the general obligation bonds were used to purchase U.S. government securities and those securities were deposited in an irrevocable trust with an escrow agent to provide debt service payments until the term bonds are called on December 31, 20Y0. The advance refunding met the requirements of an in-substance debt defeasance and the term bonds were removed from the County's government-wide financial statements.

As a result of the advance refunding, the County reduced its total debt service requirements by $6.28, which resulted in an economic gain (difference between the present value of the debt service payments on the old and new debt) of $5.89.

PRACTICE ALERT: If the transaction in Note X occurred as a result of a defeasance using existing resources in accordance with GASB-86, the note would be as follows:

Note X—Defeased Debt Related to Sale of Convention Center. On December 31, 20X8, Castle Rock County sold the Castle Rock County Convention Center. As of that date, the Convention Center had $100 of outstanding noncallable bonds that mature on December 31, 20Y0. No outstanding insurance was connected to the bonds. To fund the payment of the outstanding noncallable bonds and related interest, the County placed $99.50 into an irrevocable debt defeasance trust held by the County's third-party trustee. The amount placed into escrow plus accrued interest will be sufficient to pay the entirety of principal and interest on the noncallable bonds at maturity. The assets held in escrow contain obligations guaranteed by the U.S. government denominated in U.S. dollars that are essentially risk free as the escrow's cash flows approximately coincide as to timing and amount with the scheduled interest and principal payments of the defeased debt. Due to the defeasance, the outstanding debt was removed from the liabilities of the County's government-wide financial statements.

Note Y—Prior Years' Debt Defeasance. In prior years, the County has defeased various bond issues by creating separate irrevocable trust funds. New debt has been issued and the proceeds have been used to purchase U.S. government securities that were placed in the trust funds. The investments and fixed earnings from the investments are sufficient to fully service the defeased debt until the debt is called or matures. For financial reporting purposes, the debt has been considered defeased and therefore removed as a liability from the County's government-wide financial statements. As of December 31, 20X7, the amount of defeased debt outstanding amounted to $795.

QUESTIONS

1. Debts that allow bondholders to require a governmental entity to redeem bonds on the basis of terms specified in the bond agreement at will are more commonly known as:

    a. General obligation bonds

    b. Revenue obligation bonds

    c. Special revenue bonds

    d. Demand bonds

2. Which of the following is not required to be met for a demand bond to be recorded as a long-term liability of the government?

    a. Before the financial statements are issued, the issuer has entered into an arm's-length financing (take-out) agreement to convert bonds "put" but not resold into some other form of long-term obligation.

    b. The take-out agreement does not expire within one year from the date of the issuer's statement of net position.

    c. Cash is deposited into an irrevocable trust to pay the entirety of principal and interest on the bonds.

    d. The take-out agreement is not cancelable by the lender or the prospective lender during that year, and obligations incurred under the take-out agreement are not callable by the lender during that year.

3. Certain limited-obligation revenue bonds, certificates of participation, or similar debt instruments issued by a state or local governmental entity for the express purpose of providing capital financing for a specific third party that is not a part of the issuer's financial reporting entity are known as:

    a. Conduit debt obligations

    b. General obligation bonds

    c. Revenue obligation bonds

    d. Special obligation bonds

4. Build America Bonds, Recovery Zone Economic Development Bonds, and similar instruments have subsidies paid on them from the federal government [if sold prior to December 31, 2017]. Although they are not guaranteed, GASB staff note that the accounting for the subsidies should be:

    a. A reduction of current-period interest expense.

    b. A separate nonexchange transaction and recognized as revenue when all eligibility requirements are met, therefore not netting against any other transaction.

    c. A deferred inflow of resources and systematically and rationally adjusted to interest expense over the life of the bonds.

    d. An offset to the bond liability.

5. Debt is considered to be extinguished under the following circumstances except when:

   a. The debtor pays the creditor and is relieved of all its obligations with respect to the debt. This concludes the debtor's reacquisition of its outstanding debt securities in the public securities market regardless of whether the securities are canceled or held as treasury bonds.

   b. The debtor is legally released from being the primary obligor under the debt either judicially or by the creditor and it is probable that the debtor will not be required to make future payments with respect to the debt under any guarantees.

   c. The old bonds are replaced with new refunding bonds.

   d. The debtor irrevocably places cash or other assets in a trust to be used solely for satisfying scheduled payments of both interest and principal of a specific obligation and the possibility that the debtor will be required to make future payments with respect to that debt is remote. In this circumstance, debt is extinguished even though the debtor is not legally released from being the primary obligor under the debt obligation.

6. Common types of short-term financing for cash-flow needs when taxes, grants, streams of revenue, bonds, or other types of financing will occur in the future are known as:

   a. Mezzanine financing

   b. Anticipation notes

   c. Participation notes

   d. Obligation notes

7. GASB-38 requires debt service to maturity for all types of debt (including capital leases) in which of the following patterns?

   a. Principal and interest requirements to maturity, presented separately, for each of the five subsequent fiscal years and in five-year increments thereafter.

   b. Total debt service to maturity only, presented separately, for each of the five subsequent fiscal years and in five-year increments thereafter.

   c. Principal and interest requirements to maturity, presented separately for all years until maturity.

   d. Total debt service to maturity only, presented separately for all years until maturity.

8. GASB-38 requires short-term debts to be disclosed using which of the following methods?

   a. In required supplementary information, a schedule of changes in short-term debt, disclosing beginning- and end-of-year balances, increases, and decreases along with the purpose for which the short-term debt was issued. Any outstanding balances at year-end would be presented in the Statement of Net Position.

   b. In the notes to the basic financial statements, a schedule of changes in short-term debt, disclosing beginning- and end-of-year balances, increases, and decreases along with the purpose for which the short-term debt was issued. Any outstanding balances at year-end would be presented in the Statement of Net Position.

   c. In other supplementary information, a schedule of changes in short-term debt, disclosing beginning- and end-of-year balances, increases, and decreases along with the purpose for which the short-term debt was issued. Any outstanding balances at year-end would be presented in the Statement of Net Position.

   d. In the introductory letter, a schedule of changes in short-term debt, disclosing beginning- and end-of-year balances, increases, and decreases along with the purpose for which the short-term debt was issued. Any outstanding balances at year-end would be presented in the Statement of Net Position.

9. A major difference in the accounting and financial reporting of long-term debt between governmental funds and proprietary funds (as well as the government-wide financial statements) is:

   a. The governmental funds present only the proceeds of debt issuances as other financing sources and the payment of debts as other financing uses. The proprietary funds and government-wide financial statements include debts as liabilities.

   b. None. There are no major differences.

   c. The proprietary funds present only the proceeds of debt issuances as other financing sources and the payment of debts as other financing uses. The governmental funds and government-wide financial statements include debts as liabilities.

   d. No debts are presented in the funds or the government-wide financial statements.

10. Castle Rock County sells debt. Underwriting and other issue costs are incurred as well as premiums and discounts. For the underwriting and other issuance costs, GASB-65 requires them to be recorded as:

    a. Deferred inflows of resources.

    b. Deferred outflows of resources.

    c. Expenses or expenditures.

    d. Restricted net position.

ANSWERS

1. Debts that allow bondholders to require a governmental entity to re-deem bonds on the basis of terms specified in the bond agreement at will are more commonly known as:

   Answer - D: Demand bonds.

2. Which of the following is not required to be met for a demand bond to be recorded as a long-term liability of the government?

   Answer - C: Answers A, B, and D are required to be met for a demand bond to be recorded as a long-term liability.

3. Certain limited-obligation revenue bonds, certificates of participation, or similar debt instruments issued by a state or local governmental entity for the express purpose of providing capital financing for a specific third party that is not a part of the issuer's financial reporting entity are known as:

   Answer – A: Conduit debt.

4. Build America Bonds, Recovery Zone Economic Development Bonds, and similar instruments have subsidies paid on them from the federal government [if sold prior to December 31, 2017]. Although they are not guaranteed, GASB staff note that the accounting for the subsidies should be:

   Answer – B: As a separate nonexchange transaction and recognized as revenue when all eligibility requirements are met, therefore not netting against any other transaction.

5. Debt is considered to be extinguished under the following circumstances except for:

   Answer – C: All other items are characteristics of debt extinguishment.

6. Common types of short-term financing for cash-flow needs when taxes, grants, streams of revenue, bonds, or other types of financing will occur in the future are known as:

   Answer – B: Taxes, grants, streams of revenue, or bonds may occur in the future, but if financing is needed today, anticipation notes are sold.

7. GASB-38 requires debt service to maturity for all types of debt (includ-ing capital leases) in which of the following patterns?

   Answer – A: GASB-38 requires presentation of principal and interest to maturity, presented separately for each of the five subsequent fiscal years and in five-year increments thereafter.

8. GASB-38 requires short-term debts to be disclosed using which of the following methods?

   Answer – B: In the notes to the basic financial statements, a schedule of changes in short-term debt, disclosing beginning- and end-of-year bal-ances, increases, and decreases along with the purpose for which the short-term debt was issued. Any outstanding balances at year-end would be presented in the Statement of Net Position.

9. A major difference in the accounting and financial reporting of long-term debt between governmental funds and proprietary funds (as well as the government-wide financial statements) is:

Answer – A: The governmental funds present only the proceeds of debt issuances as other financing sources and the payment of debts as other financing uses. The proprietary funds and government-wide financial statements include debts as liabilities.

10. Castle Rock County sells debt. Underwriting and other issue costs are incurred as well as premiums and discounts. For the underwriting and other issuance costs, GASB-65 requires them to be recorded as:

Answer – C: Expenses or expenditures.

CHAPTER 13
PENSION, POSTEMPLOYMENT, AND OTHER EMPLOYEE BENEFIT LIABILITIES

CONTENTS

INTRODUCTION

A state or local government often provides a number of pension, postemployment, and other employee benefits to its employees including the following:

- Termination benefits;
- Compensated absences benefits;
- Pension and retirement benefits; and
- Postemployment health-care and other benefits.

A common theme among the accounting requirements of these types of benefits is the measurement and recognition of the costs of the benefits at the time the employee works and earns them rather than when they are paid. This chapter addresses the accounting and financial reporting issues related to these types of benefits.

A reminder that care must be taken with regard to termination benefits funded by federal grants. Federal agencies scrutinize termination benefits because many governments will want to charge termination benefits to federal awards so that these benefits have a separate funding source. However, unless an employee worked predominantly for a federally funded program, these costs are not chargeable to a federal award, causing a questioned cost and potentially a refund of the costs to the federal program.

TERMINATION BENEFITS

GASB-47 (*Accounting for Termination Benefits*) [GASB Cod. Sec. T25] provides for the accounting and reporting of all forms of employment termination benefits for state and local governments, such as early-retirement incentives, severance pay, and other voluntary or involuntary benefits.

> **OBSERVATION:** In accordance with GASB-68, par. 8 (*Accounting and Financial Reporting for Pensions—an amendment of GASB Statement No. 27*) [GABS Cod. Secs. P20.106, P21.106], termination benefits are specifically excluded from the definition of "pensions." However, termination benefits effectively increase a pension liability immediately because no service life remains on the employee if the employee is eligible to receive a defined benefit pension. Postemployment benefits other than pensions (OPEB) *may or may not* include the effect of termination benefits. GASB-75, par. 8 (*Accounting and Financial Reporting for Postemployment Benefits Other than Pensions*) [GASB Cod. Sec. P51.104] requires employers to determine the effect of a termination benefit on liabilities for defined benefit OPEB and unused sick leave credits that are converted to provide or enhance defined benefit OPEB—a more common practice than converting to defined benefit pensions. GASB-74, par. 10 (*Financial Reporting for Postemployment Benefits Other Than Pension Plans*) [GASB Cod. Secs. P53.105, Po50.105, Po51.103] specifically excludes termination benefits or termination payments for sick leave, as they are *employer* charges, not plan charges. The effect of termination or sick leave benefits that are allowed to be converted to contributions for OPEB may necessitate an adjustment of information presented by a plan to employers, adjusting an employer's liability. Similar provisions are contained in GASB-73, par. 11 (*Accounting and Financial Reporting for Pensions and Related Assets That Are Not within the Scope of GASB Statement 68, and Amendments to Certain Provisions of GASB Statements 67 and 68*) [GASB Cod. Secs. P22.105, P23.103, P24.105].

Prior to GASB-47, guidance on governmental employer accounting and reporting for termination benefits was limited to only one form of termination benefits: voluntary short-term benefits. As a result, there has been significant variation among state and local governments in the accounting for termination benefits. In order to enhance both consistency of reporting of termination benefits and the comparability of financial statements, GASB-47 expands the guidance to address all forms of termination benefits, whether voluntary or involuntary, and requires that similar forms of termination benefits be accounted for in the same manner.

Termination benefits could be provided in a number of ways to departing employees. For example, employees could be offered extended health-care-related termination benefits for a specified period of time or enhanced defined pension benefits in exchange for early retirement.

GASB-47 makes a distinction between "voluntary" and "involuntary" termination benefits. However, the scope of GASB-47 does not include unemployment compensation, for which accounting requirements were established in NCGA-4 (*Accounting and Financial Reporting Principles for Claims and Judgments and Compensated Absences*) and have been amended since by GASB-10, GASB-34, GASB-59, GASB-62, and GASB-70. Financial reporting requirements for unemployment compensation programs are contained within GASB-34 (par. 67(b), footnote 34) [GASB Cod. Secs. 1300.109, Ca5.103, Ho5.103, In3.103, Sp20.103, Ut5.103, 1300.fn7, U50.101], which requires the programs to be presented in enterprise funds. Excluded from the scope of GASB-47 are postemployment benefits (pensions and OPEB), which are part of the compensation that employers offer in exchange for services received, except as explained above. As an employee is terminated, no further services are received. Therefore, termination benefits are different in nature from other forms of compensation for employee services, including postemployment benefits (GASB-47, par. 4, as amended) [GASB Cod. Sec. T25.102].

Voluntary Termination Benefits

Voluntary termination benefits are defined as benefits provided by employers to employees as an inducement to hasten the termination of services or as a result of a voluntary early termination. Examples of voluntary termination benefits include the following:

- Cash payments (one-time or installments); and
- Health-care coverage when none would otherwise be provided.

Involuntary Termination Benefits

Involuntary termination benefits are defined as benefits arising as a consequence of the involuntary early termination of services, such as layoffs. Examples of involuntary termination benefits include the following:

- Career counseling;
- Continued access to health insurance through the employer's group plan;
- Outplacement services; and
- Severance pay.

Other benefits, such as health-care continuation under the Consolidated Omnibus Budget Reconciliation Act (COBRA), are provided as a result of voluntary and involuntary terminations, in certain circumstances (GASB-47, par. 3) [GASB Cod. Sec. T25.101].

Measurement and Recognition of Termination Benefits

In general terms, the employer should account for termination benefits in accordance with the measurement and recognition requirements laid out in GASB-47, paragraphs 9 through 16, as amended by GASB-69, pars. 53 and 54 [GASB Cod. Secs. T25.105–.112], which are summarized below.

Measurement: Health-Care-Related Termination Benefits

Generally, the measurement criteria requires the employer to measure the cost of termination benefits by calculating the discounted present value of expected future benefit payments in accordance with the following requirements, as applicable: (1) projection of benefits, (2) health-care trend rate, and (3) discount rate. In certain circumstances the benefit cost may be based on unadjusted premiums.

The *GASB Implementation Guide 2015-1,* question Z.47.1 [GASB Cod. Sec. T25.704-1], addresses the effect of the Consolidated Omnibus Reconciliation Act (COBRA) when the former employee may continue to participate in an employer's active employee healthcare plan, as long as the former employee pays

100% of the blended premium rate. For financial reporting purposes. COBRA benefits are considered a form of health-care-related termination benefits, which would be calculated using the provisions of GASB-47. If the termination is not part of a large-scale, age related termination event, GASB-47 also allows the government to use blended premium rates as the basis for projection of benefits. The employer would have no expected future benefit payments as the former employee is expected to pay 100% of the blended premium rate. Therefore, no liability would be calculated. But if there were a large-scale layoff and the age-adjusted premium approximating claims costs is different than the former employee's contributions, a liability may be present.

OBSERVATION: As introduced previously related to sick-leave or other termination conversions, the effect of a termination benefit on an employer's defined benefit pension or other postemployment benefit (OPEB) liabilities should be carefully investigated to ascertain if the benefit is part of an ongoing benefit or a one-time benefit. A one-time benefit will use the standards contained in GASB-47. If a defined benefit or a defined contribution plan is in place for either pensions or other postemployment benefits, the provisions of GASB-68, GASB 73 (if a trust or equivalent arrangement is not present) or GASB-75 may apply. For example, an enhanced benefit formula for pensions or OPEB may be offered if the employee terminates. If that is the case, GASB-68, GASB-73, and/ or GASB-75 is applicable.

For healthcare-related termination benefits in a large-scale, age-related program (which are often discriminatory and potentially illegal), benefits are segregated between the terminated employees from the active employee group for the purposes of measurement. The employer's projected expected future benefit payments are based on the total claims costs, or age-adjusted premiums approximating claims costs for the terminated employees in a similar manner to OPEB projections (and discussed later in this chapter). The expected benefit payment for each period is the difference between the projected claims costs, or age-adjusted premiums approximating claims costs for the terminated employees and the payment(s) (if any) to be made by the terminated employees.

PRACTICE POINT: The payments made by the terminated employees are often zero.

If the termination is not a large-scale, age-related program (meaning nondiscriminatory), the employer segregates the benefits provided to the terminated employees (and their beneficiaries) similarly to a large-scale program. But in this case, the use projected claims costs, or age-adjusted premiums approximating claims costs is not required. Only unadjusted premiums are used as the basis for projecting expected benefit payments. Similarly to a large-scale program, the unadjusted premiums are netted against any payments made by the terminated employees.

The expected future benefit payments utilize a healthcare cost trend rate and a discount rate, both similarly to a defined benefit OPEB plan, but for only the timeframe for the termination payments. In many cases, this period is very short (GASB-47, par. 9) [GASB Cod. Sec. T25.105].

Measurement: Non-Health-Care-Related Termination Benefits

If the benefit terms establish an obligation to pay specific amounts on fixed or determinable dates, the cost of the benefits are required to be measured at the discounted present value of expected future payments. However, if the terms do not establish such an obligation to pay on fixed or determinable dates, the benefit cost may, alternatively, be measured at the undiscounted total of estimated future payments at current cost levels (GASB-47, pars. 10–11) [GASB Cod. Secs. T25.106–.107].

Recognition in Accrual-Basis Financial Statements

An employer is required to recognize a liability and expense for *voluntary* termination benefits, on the accrual basis of accounting, when the employees accept an offer and the amount can be estimated.

An employer is required to recognize a liability and expense for *involuntary* termination benefits, on the accrual basis of accounting, when a plan of termination has been approved by those in authority to commit the employer to the plan, the plan has been communicated to the employees, and the amount can be estimated. Termination expense associated with a disposal of governmental operations that is included in the period in which the operation is sold or transferred is included in the determination in the gain or loss reported for the disposal (GASB-47, pars. 12–15, as amended by GASB-69, par. 53) [GASB Cod. Secs. T25.108–.111].

Recognition in Modified Accrual Basis Financial Statements

In governmental fund financial statements prepared on the modified accrual basis of accounting, termination benefit liabilities and expenditures are recognized to the extent that the liabilities are normally expected to be liquidated with expendable available financial resources similar to other governmental fund liabilities. If a governmental operation is terminated, the benefit expenditures associated with the termination would be included as part of a special item related to the disposal of operations (GASB-47, par. 16, as amended by GASB-69, par. 54) [GASB Cod. Sec. T25.112].

Disclosures

GASB-47 requires the footnotes to include a description of the termination benefits arrangements, the costs of termination benefits in the period in which the employer becomes obligated if that information is not otherwise identifiable from information displayed on the face of the financial statements, and significant methods and assumptions used in determining the termination benefit liabilities and expenses. If an employer provides termination benefits that affect defined benefit pension or OPEB liabilities, the employer should disclose the change in those liabilities attributable to the termination benefit. If a termination benefit is not recognized as the expected benefits are not estimable, the event is disclosed with that fact, likely as a contingency (GASB-47, pars. 18–21, as amended by GASB-68, pars. 20, 59, 83, 92, and 120, and GASB-73, pars. 4, 7, 25, 68, and 78) [GASB Cod. Secs. T25.114–.117].

COMPENSATED ABSENCES

Many governmental and business entities provide a variety of compensated absences, such as paid vacations, paid holidays, sick pay, and sabbatical leaves, for their employees. Because of the nature of these commitments, compensated absences plans generally create an economic liability for a governmental entity.

The standards established by GASB-16 apply to all governmental entities without exception. Thus, the standards must be observed by governmental funds, proprietary funds, and fiduciary funds.

The accounting standards that are used to account for compensated absences depend on whether the liability is presented in a (1) governmental fund, (2) proprietary or fiduciary fund, or (3) the government-wide financial statements (GASB-16, pars. 1, 4, and 5, as amended by GASB-34, par. 3, and GASB-35, par. 5) [GASB Cod. Secs. C60.101–.102].

Recognition and Measurement Criteria

GASB-16 establishes the basic concept that a liability for compensated absences should be recorded when future payments for such absences have been earned by employees. Thus, GASB-16 establishes the basic principle that there should be no accrual for compensated absences that are dependent on the performance of future services by employees, or when payments are dependent on future events that are outside the control of the employer and employees.

GASB-16 takes the position that most sick-leave plans are based on the occurrence of a specific future event that is not controlled by the employer or the employee. The future event is sickness. Even though an employee has earned sick leave benefits, the benefits will not be paid (paid time off) unless the employee is sick. Due to the need for the occurrence of a future event, sick-leave benefits would generally not be accrued, but rather would be recorded as an expenditure/expense when sick leave is taken.

GASB-16 applies the accrual concept in the context of the following compensated absences (GASB-16, par. 6) [GASB Cod. Sec. C60.103]:

- Vacation leave and other compensated absences with similar characteristics;
- Sick leave and other compensated absences with similar characteristics; and
- Sabbatical leave.

Vacation Leave and Other Compensated Absences with Similar Characteristics

Compensated absences for vacation leave and benefits with similar characteristics should be recorded as a liability when earned by employees if the following conditions are satisfied:

- Compensated absence is earned on the basis of services already performed by employees.

- It is probable that the compensated absence will be paid (payment may be in the form of paid time off, cash payments at termination or retirement, or some other means) in a future period.

Fringe-benefit arrangements may allow employees to earn compensated absences, but employees may not be entitled to benefits until certain minimum conditions (such as minimum time of employment) are met. Under this arrangement, a governmental entity should accrue for compensated absences that are probable (i.e., likely to take place). Thus, a governmental entity must determine whether it is likely that benefits earned, but not payable until certain conditions are met, will be paid. On the other hand, benefits related to compensated absences that have been earned, but are expected to lapse, should not be accrued. For example, some benefits may lapse because there is a cap on the number of vacation days that can be carried forward from period to period.

Although the standards established in GASB-16 are discussed in the context of vacation leave, those standards are equally applicable to compensated absences that have characteristics similar to vacation leave. Thus, any compensated-absence benefit that is not dependent on an event outside of the control of the employer or the employee should be accounted for in a manner similar to vacation leave benefits. Generally, these types of benefits are granted to employees solely on the basis of the length of their employment. For example, a governmental entity that provides its employees with one personal day for each six months worked is providing a compensated absence benefit that should be accrued, because it is based on length of employment. On the other hand, an entity that provides its employees with military-leave benefits should not accrue this compensated absence, because the benefit will be paid only if an employee serves in the military at a future date (GASB-16, par. 7) [GASB Cod. Sec. C60.104]. See Exhibit 13-1.

EXHIBIT 13-1
ILLUSTRATION: VACATION LEAVE

To illustrate the use of compensated absences for vacation leave, assume the following:

- Each employee earns one day of vacation for each month worked starting with the hire date.

- An employee is entitled to use vacation leave after one year of employment.

- If an employee is terminated, all earned (but unused) vacation leave is paid at the employee's current pay rate. (Employees with less than one year of service receive no payment.)

The estimated liability for vacation leave is based on the following information: Number of current employees by length of service:

Employee Category	Members of the Category	Number of Members in Category
1	Employees who have worked for more than one year	70
2	Employees who have worked for less than one year	30

Characteristics of employee categories:

	Category 1	Category 2
Current average daily pay rate	$135	$75
Average number of vacation days accumulated	25	7

Based on prior experience, it is estimated that approximately 30% of employees with less than one year of experience will work at least one year and therefore be entitled to termination pay for accumulated vacation days.

The estimated liability for compensated absences liability for vacation leave is computed below:

Category	Number of Employees		Average Pay Rate		Average Vacation Days Accumulated		Probability Factor		Extended Amounts
1	70	×	$135	×	25	×	100%	=	$236,250
2	30	×	75	×	7	×	30%	=	4,725
Estimated liability for vacation leave									$240,975*

* The estimate should also include a provision for additional salary-related payments (see the section entitled "Liability Calculation").

The accrual of compensated absences for vacation leave is usually straight-forward. Most governmental entities impose few, if any, restrictions on an employee's right to take vacation days earned or to receive accumulated vacation pay when termination occurs. Thus, in most instances the number of vacation days earned to date should be the basis for the accrual for compensated absences for vacation leave. However, in some cases, the right to receive vacation leave may depend on some unfulfilled condition. For example, a new employee may have to work a minimum of six months before vacation days are earned. In this case, the governmental entity must determine whether it is probable that newly hired employees eventually will meet the minimum work criterion. If so, the entity must include these employees' past work experience in the calculation of the compensated-absence accrual. Including this type of work experience could be seen as a violation of GASB-16's basic premise that accrual is appropriate only when payments do not depend on events outside the control of the employer and employee. GASB-16 states that future employment is a condition controlled by the employer and employee—the employer could fire the employee or the employee could quit.

Sick Leave and Other Compensated Absences with Similar Characteristics

Sick-leave benefits often differ from other compensated absences in that sick-pay benefits are dependent on employee illness (a future event). However, sick-leave programs often allow employees to accumulate sick days, and if they are not used, employees may be paid for all or perhaps a maximum number of the accumulated sick days on termination or retirement, referred to as termination payments.

Due to the unique characteristics of sick-leave programs, the GASB addressed the issue separately. Thus, compensated absences for sick leave and other compensated absences with similar characteristics should be accrued only when it is probable that the employer will have to make termination payments. Sick-pay benefits that have been earned, but probably will be used only for sick leave, should not be accrued, but rather recorded as an expenditure/expense when employees are paid for days not worked due to illness.

Other compensated absences are considered similar to sick leave when the benefit is based on a specific future event that is not subject to control by the employer and employees. Examples of other compensated absences with this characteristic include leaves for military service, jury duty, and close-family funerals.

GASB-16 established two methods, the termination payment method and the vesting method, that can be used to calculate the liability related to compensated absences for sick leave. Neither method allows for the accrual of non-vesting (rights that cannot or will not vest) sick leave.

Termination Payment Method

Under the termination payment method, a governmental entity generally estimates its sick pay liability based on past history, adjusted for changes in pay rates, administrative policies, and other relevant factors. Thus, the accrual applies historical information or trends to a governmental entity's current workforce (GASB-16, par. 8) [GASB Cod. Sec. C60.105]. See Exhibit 13-2.

EXHIBIT 13-2
ILLUSTRATION: SICK LEAVE (TERMINATION PAYMENT METHOD)

To illustrate the termination payment method, assume the following:

- Sick leave can be used only for personal sickness or close-family sickness.
- Sick leave accumulates with no limit, and sick leave not taken before termination or retirement will be paid to an employee at the rate of 80% of the employee's current pay rate if the employee has 10 years or more of service.

- Each employee earns one day of sick leave for each month worked, and when sick leave is taken, the employee is paid at his or her current rate of pay.
- The estimated liability for sick leave is based on the following governmental entity's experience over the past five years:

Factor	Amount
Number of employees terminated or retired during past five years	10 employees
Number of sick days paid on termination or retirement for employees during past five years	90 sick days
Total number of years worked by all employees terminated or retired during past five years (all employees × hours worked past 5 years ÷ 365 (rounded))	180 years
Current average daily pay rate	$100

Currently the governmental entity's active labor force includes 100 employees who have accumulated 1,200 person-years of work.

The estimated liability for sick leave compensated absences is computed below:

Operation	Amount
Number of sick days paid on termination or retirement for employees during past five years	90
Multiply by average current pay rate	× $100
Subtotal	$9,000
Multiply by final payment percentage of current pay	× 80%
Subtotal	$7,200
Divide by number of years worked by retired and terminated employees	÷ 180 years
Equals	=$40
Multiply by number of years worked by current labor force	× 1,200
Estimated liability for sick leave	$48,000*

* The estimate should also include a provision for additional salary-related payments.

Although termination payments for sick leave are usually paid in cash to employees, some governmental entities allow an employee to forego direct payments for additional service credit in determining the amount of pension benefits or as a contribution to the cost of postemployment health care due to the employee. Such arrangements are not termination payments; however, they should be considered in determining the actuarial valuation of the governmental entity's pension obligations.

The estimation methodology is based on an example presented in Appendix C to GASB-16 [GASB Cod. Sec. C60.901]. However, there is no prescribed method that must be used to compute the estimate. A governmental entity must determine the most appropriate method to compute the estimate. For example, GASB-16 notes that a governmental entity could estimate the liability by "developing a ratio based on historical data of sick leave paid at termination compared with sick leave accumulated and by applying that ratio to the sick leave accumulated by current employees as of the (statement of net position) date."

Vesting Method

The termination payment method may be difficult for some governmental entities to apply. For example, in some instances relevant historical information may not be available or the workforce may be too small to successfully apply historical ratios or trends. The vesting method focuses on vesting sick leave. Vesting sick-leave rights include vested rights and those rights that will eventually vest, generally after a minimum number of years have been worked. The vesting method differs in the termination payment method in the following ways (GASB-16, par. 8) [GASB Cod. Sec. C60.105](see Exhibit 13-3).

EXHIBIT 13-3
ILLUSTRATION: SICK LEAVE (VESTING METHOD)

To illustrate the vesting method, assume the following:

- Sick leave can be used only for personal sickness or close-family sickness.
- Sick leave accumulates with no limit, and any sick leave accrued but not previously taken by the time of termination or retirement will be paid to an employee at the rate of 80% of the employee's current pay rate if the employee has 10 years or more of service.
- Each employee earns one day of sick leave for each month worked, and when sick leave is taken, the employee is paid at his or her current rate of pay.
- The estimated liability for sick leave is based on the following estimates:

Number of current employees by classification:

Employee Category	Members of the Category	Number of Members in Category
1	Administrative/professional	10
2	Uniformed	20
3	Clerical/secretarial	70
	Total	**100**

Characteristics of employee-categories:

Factor	Amounts		
	Category 1	Category 2	Category 3
Current average daily pay rate	$150	$130	$60
Average number of sick days accumulated	13	16	8
Probability employee will work at least 10 years	90%	95%	25%

The estimated liability for compensated absences liability for sick leave is computed below:

Category	Number of Employees		Average Pay Rate		Average Sick Days Accumulated		Probability Factor		Extended Amounts
1	10	×	$150	×	13	×	90%	=	$17,550
2	20	×	$130	×	16	×	95%	=	39,520
3	70	×	$60	×	8	×	25%	=	8,400
							Subtotal		$65,470
Multiply by percentage of final payment									80%
Estimated liability for sick leave									$52,376*

* Estimate should also include a provision for additional salary-related payments (see the section entitled "Liability Calculation"). The vesting method includes all vesting sick leave amounts for which payment is probable, not just the vesting amounts that will result in terminal payment. The vesting method is based on accumulated benefits as of a statement of net position date, not on amounts accruing over expected periods of services.

Although the termination payment method is more consistent with the termination payment concept used to account for sick leave, the GASB believes that "the vesting method also provides a reasonable estimate of anticipated termination payments."

The vesting method is somewhat deficient in that the liability may include a provision for sick leave that will be satisfied by employee absences because of sickness rather than amounts paid at termination or retirement. GASB-16 recognizes the deficiency but states that the approach is acceptable "because of concerns about the cost-benefit of trying to estimate the extent to which such use might occur."

Sabbatical Leave

Governmental fringe benefits may include earning sabbatical leaves, especially in public institutions of higher education and healthcare facilities. In determining whether compensated absences for sabbatical leaves should be accrued, the criteria discussed earlier must be satisfied (see discussion in section titled "Vacation Leave and Other Compensated Absences with Similar Characteristics"). In applying those criteria, the purpose of the leave must be evaluated. If sabbatical leave provides employees with unrestricted time off, a liability for compensated absences should be accrued. The amount of the accrual should be based on the periods during which the rights to sabbatical leaves are earned and the probable amounts that will be paid (through paid time off or by other means) to employees under the sabbatical program.

Some sabbatical-leave benefits provide restricted leaves. The nature of the duties performed by governmental personnel change, but the governmental entity dictates the services or activities to be performed by employees on sabbatical. For example, employees may be required to perform research or participate in continuing professional education programs. Compensated-absences liability for sabbatical-leave programs based on restricted leaves should not be accrued. Instead, it should be reported as a current expenditure/expense during periods that employees perform their directed duties as required under sabbatical programs.

Liability Calculation. The accrual of compensated absences should be based on pay rates that are in effect as of the statement of net position date, unless a specific rate is established by contract, regulation, or policy. For example, some governmental contract agreements may entitle employees to sick-pay termination settlements at one-half of employees' current pay rates (GASB-16, par. 9) [GASB Cod. Sec. C60.106].

In addition to the basic pay rate, the accrual of compensated absences should include estimated employer payments related to the payroll. GASB-16 describes these payments as items for which a government is "liable to make a payment directly and incrementally associated with payments made for compensated absences on termination" (incremental salary-related payments). To meet the standard of being directly and incrementally associated with payment of termination payments for compensated absences, the related payroll payments must be (1) a function of the employee's salary amount and (2) payable as part of salary for compensated-absences balances at the date an employee takes time off, retires, or is terminated.

Salary-related payments include the employer's share of Social Security and Medicare payroll taxes because those taxes are a function of an employee's level of salary and are also paid to the federal government when employees receive payments for compensated absences. However, all of an employee's salary may not be subject to payroll taxes, a fact the employer should take into consideration when estimating the compensated absences accrual.

Another salary-related payment is the employer's share of contributions to pension plans. When the pension plan is a defined contribution plan or a cost-sharing, multiple-employer defined benefit pension plan, the employer's share of the contribution should be part of the accrual for compensated absences if the employer is liable for contributions to the plan based on termination payments made to employees for compensated absences. The salary-related pension contribution must be part of the accrual, because it is included in the base used to determine the employer's share of contributions to the pension plan. On the other hand, the accrual should not include contributions to single-employer plans and agent multiple-employer defined benefit plans, in which case the actuarial computation for employer contributions takes into consideration termination payments for compensated absences (GASB-16, par. 11) [GASB Cod. Sec. C60.108].

PRACTICE POINT: GASB-16 (par. 11, footnote 7) [GASB Cod. Secs. C60.108, fn.6] is slightly amended by GASB-68. An additional accrual should not be made relating to single-employer or agent multiple-employer defined benefit pensions, or for the required contribution to a cost sharing multiple-employer defined benefit plan.

In addition, the *GASB Implementation Guide 2015-1*, questions 5.255.1 and Z.16.1, as amended by GASB Implementation Guide 2016-1, question 5.37 [GASB Cod. Secs. C60.707-1–2], clarify the situation when a government includes cash payments to retiring employees for unused compensated absences (vacation leave and sick leave to the extent settled by means of a termination payment) as part of the employees' compensation for the final year of service for the purposes of determining employees' defined pension benefits and the employer's contractually required contributions to the cost-sharing pension plan. GASB-16, paragraph 11, as amended *does not apply*. Instead, the projected effects of the termination payment for compensated absences in an employee's compensation in the final year of service on benefit payments is required to be included in the projection of benefit payments for determining the employer's pension liability under GASB-68.

Recognition of compensated absences liabilities and expenditures in modified accrual-basis financial statements is discussed in GASB Interpretation No. 6, par. 14 (*Recognition and Measurement of Certain Liabilities and Expenditures in Governmental Fund Financial Statements—an Interpretation of NCGA Statements 1, 4, and 5; NCGA Interpretation 8; and GASB Statements No. 10, 16, and 18*), as amended. GASBI-6 generally excludes pension liabilities and expenditures, as such, from its scope but nevertheless does apply to the portion of contractually required pension contributions of a cost-sharing employer that is within the definition of a defined benefit plan because GASB-16, as amended, includes that portion of the contributions as part of the measurement of compensated absences liabilities and expenses.

Other fringe benefits should be evaluated to determine whether they are directly and incrementally related to the payment of salaries at termination. For example, health-care insurance fringe benefits are generally based on the governmental entity's claims experience and characteristics of its labor force rather than on the salary level of an employee. Therefore, the compensated absences accrual should not include an estimate for health-care insurance costs. Additionally, life insurance benefits should not be part of the accrual unless (1) the insurance benefit is a function of the salary earned by an employee and (2) the life insurance premium for the last month of employment (termination date) is based on the total amount paid rather than on a normal salary amount.

The amount accrued for salary-related payments should be based on rates in effect as of the statement of net position date and should be applied to the total accrual for compensated absences. For example, salary related payments applicable to the accrual of vacation leave should apply to the total accrual for vacation leave even though most of the earned leave will usually be satisfied as paid time off rather than as termination pay (GASB-16, par. 10) [GASB Cod. Sec. C60.107].

OBSERVATION: GASB-16 does not attempt to address all compensated absences that might be part of a governmental entity's fringe-benefit package. If a governmental entity has such fringe benefits, those benefits should be accounted for using the broad concepts established in the GASB-16. Also, each compensated absence benefit should be accounted for on the basis of the substance of the benefit plan, not on its name. For example, a fringe benefit may be labeled as sick leave when in fact employees can be absent from work for reasons other than illness. In this case, standards related to vacation-leave absences should be observed rather than the standards related to sick leave.

Accounting and Reporting

Presentation in Governmental-Wide Financial Statements

The accrual basis of accounting and the economic resources measurement focus should also be used to determine the amount of the liability related to compensated absences that should be presented in a governmental entity's statement of net position. Liabilities should be presented in the statement of net position based on their relative liquidity. In determining the amount of the liability the guidance discussed earlier in the context of governmental funds should be followed, except the total amount of the estimated debt should be presented as a liability (not just the portion of the debt that will use expendable financial resources) (GASB-34, pars. 16 and 92, as amended by GASB-63, par. 8, GASB-34, par. 31) [GASB Cod. Sec. C60.109].

Presentation in Proprietary and Fiduciary Fund Financial Statements

The accrual basis of accounting should be used to determine the amount of the liability related to compensated absences that should be presented on the statement of net position of a proprietary or fiduciary fund. In determining the amount of the liability the guidance discussed earlier in the context of governmental funds should be followed, except the total amount of the estimated debt should be presented as a liability (not just the portion of the debt that will use expendable financial resources) (NCGA-1, par. 42, as amended by GASB-16, pars. 6–11, GASB-34, pars. 92 and 107) [GASB Cod. Sec. C60.110].

Presentation in Government Fund Financial Statements

While GASB-16 establishes standards for the measurement of the compensated absences liability, the amount that should be reported as an expenditure in a governmental fund is based on the modified accrual basis of accounting and current financial resources measurement focus. Thus, only the portion of the estimated future payments for compensated absences *that will use current expendable resources should be reported as a liability of a governmental fund;* however, the entire amount would be presented in the governmental entity's statement of net position (GASB-16, par. 13, as amended by GASB-34, pars. 6, 69, 79, and 82, GASB-I6, pars. 14 and 16) [GASB Cod. Sec. C60.111].

EMPLOYER PENSION AND OTHER POSTEMPLOYMENT BENEFIT OBLIGATIONS

Governmental employers may provide postemployment benefits through either a defined benefit pension plan or a defined contribution plan. For the most part, the standards address issues related to defined benefit pension or defined benefit other postemployment benefit (OPEB) plans, which are common types of plans adopted by state or local governmental employers.

The following GASB standards are applicable for various pensions and OPEB obligations (excluding amendments issued subsequent to these standards to clarify provisions):

	GASB-67 (Financial Reporting for Pension Plans)	GASB-68 (Accounting and Financial Reporting for Pensions)	GASB-73 (Accounting and Financial Reporting for Pensions That Are Not within the Scope of GASB Statement No. 68)	GASB–74 (Financial Reporting for Postemployment Benefit Plans Other than Pensions)	GASB-75 (Accounting and Financial Reporting for Postemployment Benefits Other than Pensions)
GASB Codification Section	Pe5	P20	P22	Po50	P51
Defined Benefit Plan with an irrevocable Trust	Yes			Yes	
Defined Contribution Plan with an irrevocable trust	Yes			Yes	
Defined Benefit Plan without an irrevocable Trust			Yes	Yes	
Defined Contribution Plan without an irrevocable trust			Yes	Yes	
Employer that is a member / sponsor of a defined benefit plan		Yes	Yes		Yes
Employer that is a member / sponsor of a defined contribution plan		Yes	Yes		Yes
Special Funding Situations		Yes	Yes		Yes

Since these original statements were issued by the GASB, the GASB has amended them as follows:

- GASB-71 (*Pension Transition for Contributions Made Subsequent to the Measurement Date—an amendment of GASB-68*),

- GASB-73 (*Accounting and Financial Reporting for Pensions and Related Assets That Are Not within the Scope of GASB Statement 68, and Amendments to Certain Provisions of GASB Statements 67 and 68*) (had both new and amended guidance),

- GASB-78 (*Pensions Provided through Certain Multiple-Employer Defined Benefit Pension Plans*),

- GASB-82 (*Pension Issues—an amendment of GASB Statements No. 67, No. 68, and No. 73*), and

- GASB-85 (*Omnibus 2017*) (amends certain provisions of GASB-74 and GASB-75).

As indicated above, all the statements in some capacity also provide guidance for defined contribution plans. In a defined contribution plan, future payments to a particular employee are based on the amounts contributed to the plan, earnings on those investments, and forfeitures allocated to an employee's account. A defined contribution plan does not create the difficult accounting and reporting issues raised by a defined benefit plan.

PRACTICE POINT: In a special funding situation, a participating non-employer has a possibility of more than one liability. Typically, this occurs in teachers' retirement systems where a state pays some (or all) of the pension benefits.

GASB-67 and GASB-68 and the Basic Provisions of Pensions

GASB-67 and GASB-68 contain sweeping changes for governmental defined benefit pension plans and government employers that are members of single employer, agent-multiple-employer or cost-sharing-multiple employer plans. Chapter 22, "Pension and Other Postemployment Benefit Plans," contains further information on GASB-67 (and GASB-74).

GASB-68 (*Accounting and Financial Reporting for Pensions—an amendment of GASB-27*) retains the similar scope of the former GASB-27. Only entities that administer defined benefit pension plans through trusts are included within the scope of GASB-68. GASB-68 includes standards for measurement and recognition of liabilities, deferred outflows of resources, deferred inflows of resources and the calculation of annual expense or expenditures. Methods and assumptions are included in the standard to project benefit payments, discount the payments to their actuarial present value and to attribute the present value to periods of pensionable service. Note disclosure and required supplementary information changes are included in GASB-68. Note disclosure and required supplementary information differ based on the type of plan the employer is included in.

"Defined benefit" pensions are pensions whose income or other benefits that the employee will receive at or after separation from employment are defined by the benefit terms. The pensions may be stated as a specified dollar amount or as an amount that is calculated based on one or more factors such as age, years of service, and compensation.

"Defined contribution" pensions have terms that include:

- An individual account for each employee;

- The contributions that an employer is required to make (or the credits that it is required to provide) to an active employee's account are for periods in which that employee renders service; and

- There are provisions that the pensions an employee will receive will depend only on the contributions (or credits) to the employee's account, actual earnings on investments of those contributions (or credits), and the effects of forfeitures of contributions (or credits) made for other employees, as well as pension plan administrative costs, that are allocated to the employee's account.

Defined benefit pension plans include three types of employers:

1. *Single employers* are those whose employees are provided with defined benefit pensions through single-employer pension plans—pension plans in which pensions are provided to the employees of *only one employer*. An example of this is where a city public safety force has its own pension plan.

2. *Agent employers* are those whose employees are provided with defined benefit pensions through agent multiple-employer pension plans. Agent-multiple-employer pension plans are entities where plan assets are pooled for investment purposes but separate accounts are maintained for each individual employer so that each employer's share of the pooled assets is legally available to pay the benefits of *only the employer's employees and no other employer in the plan*. Many local governments are members of larger statewide plans that are agent-multiple-employer plans.

3. *Cost-sharing employers* are those whose employees are provided with defined benefit pensions through cost-sharing multiple-employer pension plans. These pension plans are where the pension obligations to the employees of more than one employer are pooled and plan assets can be used to pay the benefits of the employees *of any employer* that provides pensions through the pension plan. Some local governments are members of countywide cost-sharing plans (GASB-68, pars. 11–13).

The types of defined contribution plans vary by law and contract, but the most prevalent ones used in state and local governments include the following:

- *Internal Revenue Code Section 403(b) plans.* These tax deferred annuity plans are funded by salary reductions. They are usually found in public institutions of higher education and hospitals. However, some governments use them to receive lump-sum payments at retirement from defined benefit plans. The risk of having enough funds at retirement then shifts to the retiree. Elementary and secondary public and private school systems also often offer 403(b) plans to their employees.

- *Internal Revenue Code Section 457 plans* are common in government. A plan administrator invests plan assets at the direction of plan participants. Due to the provisions of the plan, the participant has the risk of loss of value.

Upon occasion, so-called "hybrid plans" may be found in state and local governments. These plans include the following:

- *Cash balance plans.* In these plans, hypothetical accounts are maintained for participants. The government then credits the accounts with funds annually and promises earnings at a particular rate. The rate may be different than actual earnings and the formula may be changed annually.

- *Money purchase plans.* In these plans, contributions are determined for and allocated for specific individuals as a percentage of compensation. The employer's contributions are based on a formula.

- *Target benefit plans.* In these plans, the employees contribute on an actuarial basis knowing a certain date of retirement. There is no guarantee of a balance or return. Many mutual funds sell these types of plans.

- *Deferred Retirement Option Program (DROP)* allows an employee to elect a calculation of benefit payments based on service credits and salary as of a certain date (the DROP date). The employee continues to provide service to the employer and is paid for that service by the employer after the DROP entry date; however, the pensions that would have been paid to the employee (if the employee had retired and not entered the DROP) are credited to an individual employee account within the defined benefit pension plan until the end of the DROP period.

PRACTICE POINT: In some cases, governments may offer Internal Revenue Code Section 401(k) plans and may even file a Form 5500 *Annual Return/ Report of Employee Benefit Plan* with the United States Department of Labor. The governments that offer such plans are mainly Tribal Nations, educational institutions and similar. The AICPA Audit and Accounting Guide *State and Local Governments*, Chapter 13, notes: "Although many of the audit objectives for governmental plans are similar to those for private-sector pension plans, the Employee Retirement Income Security Act of 1974 (ERISA) does not apply to most governmental entities." In such cases where a non-Tribal Nation, educational institutions, and similar that offer a 401(k) plan to employees, the offering is likely a vestige of a practice that existed prior to 1974 and has continued to the current time, even though the filing of a Form 5500 is not necessary.

Requirements for Trust or Equivalent Arrangement

To receive the advantages of using a trust or equivalent arrangement, GASB-67 and GASB-68 (and for OPEB, GASB-74 and GASB-75) require the following:

- Contributions from employers and nonemployer contributing entities to the pension plan and earnings on those contributions are irrevocable.

- Pension (or OPEB) plan assets are dedicated to providing pensions (or OPEB) to plan members in accordance with the benefit terms.

- Pension (or OPEB) plan assets are legally protected from the creditors of employers, nonemployer contributing entities, and the pension (or OPEB) plan administrator. If the plan is a defined benefit pension (or OPEB) plan, plan assets also are legally protected from creditors of the plan members. (GASB-67, par. 3, GASB-68, par. 4, as amended by GASB-78, par. 2, GASB-74, par. 3, GASB-75, par. 4) [GASB Cod. Secs. Pe5.101, P20.101, Po50.101, P51.101].

The advantages to using a trust or equivalent arrangement are primarily monetary and security. If assets are accumulated in the trust, investment earnings are generated that may in the long-term, offset a portion, if not all, of a related pension (or OPEB) liability. As the assets are protected from creditors, shielding occurs in bankruptcy.

GASB-68 introduces the aspect of operations where employers make contributions to satisfy *employee* contribution requirements. In GASB-68, footnote 2 [GASB Cod. Secs. P20.fn2, P21.fn2], if the contribution amounts are recognized by the employer as salary expense, those contributions should be classified as employee contributions for purposes of GASB-68. Otherwise, those contributions should be classified as employer contributions. (See discussion on Employer Paid Member Contributions or "pick-ups" in relation to GASB Statement 82 (*Pension Issues*) later in this chapter along with a discussion of the AICPA nonauthoritative paper *Emerging Pension Issues*.) If contributions are returned to employers or a nonemployer contributing entity (e.g., a State on behalf of a school district) due to an employee leaving service, the forfeited amounts that are returned do not violate the aspects of a trust. Finally, it is a common practice to have plan assets pay for the administrative costs of the trust, typically out of investment earnings. The use of plan assets to pay for administrative costs of the trust or to refund employee contributions in accordance with benefit terms also do not violate the aspects of a trust.

Should the pension or OPEB plan not have a trust or an equivalent arrangement, the provisions of GASB-73 would then apply for pensions, GASB-74 for OPEB plans and GASB-75 for OPEB employers. These statements are discussed in later sections of this chapter.

Required Actuarial Valuations and Common Aspects of Valuations

GASB-68 requires actuarial valuations at least every two years. Once set, the valuation must occur on the same day in the same pattern. For example, if a government has the valuations every two years as of December 31st, December 31st must be used for the valuations in the future or else a change in accounting principle will occur, requiring a beginning balance restatement for all periods presented. More frequent valuations are encouraged within GASB-68. Actuarial valuations can value assets and liabilities at a date different from the measurement date (defined as the date of the measurement of the net pension liability). If a valuation is not performed as of the measurement date, the total pension liability is based on update procedures to roll forward amounts from an earlier actuarial valuation (as long as it is performed as of a date no more than 30 months and 1 day prior to the employer's most recent year-end). Many government valuations *are not* performed as of the measurement date.

PRACTICE POINT: The reason why one day was added to the actuarial valuation limit is due to many plans allowing for additional creditable service if serving one day into the next period. For example, some plans may allow for an additional month or even an additional year by serving just one day into the next period. Therefore, the actuarial valuation would potentially be materially misstated if a large number of employees retire as of the first day of a period without this adjustment.

PRACTICE POINT: GASB-67 and GASB-68 stipulate that only the entry-age actuarial cost methods may be used *for financial reporting purposes.* Any other method may be used for operating purposes; however, translation between the two methods may be needed for decision makers to understand their differences. The entry-age actuarial cost method is applied as follows:

- Attribution should be made on an employee-by-employee basis rather than on an entire group.
- Service costs should be level as a percentage of an employee's projected payroll.
- The beginning of the attribution period should be the period in which the employee was hired.
- A single exit age, based on retirement, should be used for all benefits.
- The service costs attributed to all periods should be based on a single measure of the present value of the employee's projected benefit payments.
- Differences between actual and expected experience should reduce or increase the total pension liability of the employer(s).

Benefit projections are required to be based on the plan provisions existing at the measurement date. The provisions may be in contract or law. Similar to the standards in the former GASB-27, the effects of projected salary changes, projected service credits, and projected automatic benefit changes (including cost of living adjustments (COLAs)) are included in the calculations. If COLAs are not automatically provided, if there is a pattern of granting that is "substantially automatic," then these "ad hoc" COLAs are also included to the extent of their granting (GASB-68, par. 22) [GASB Cod. Sec. P20.121].

Benefit payments are discounted to their actuarial present value using a formula comprising a single rate that is derived from:

- A long-term expected rate of return on pension plan investments to the extent that the pension plan's fiduciary net position is projected to be sufficient to pay benefits and pension plan assets are expected to be invested using a strategy to achieve that return; and

- A tax-exempt, high-quality municipal bond rate to the extent that the conditions for use of the long-term expected rate of return are not met.

These two rates are compared using cash flows to the point where funds available to pay benefits in the future are insufficient to pay benefits. At that point, the high-quality (typically AA or better) municipal bond rate is used. The two rates are then solved together to provide one stream of cash flows at the updated discount rate until all benefits are paid as of the measurement date (GASB-68, pars. 26–31) [GASB Cod. Secs. P20.125 –.130]. Determining the discount rate is an iterative process performed by actuaries that will build a table consisting of:

- *Payroll*—current employees with projected salary increases and future employees expected to be hired with *their* salary increases into the future.

- *Employee Contribution percentages*—employee contribution percentages are based on current statute or plan provisions (which may be different for current versus future employees that have different rates dependent upon date of hire). If employees are noncontributory, zero would be used. The percentages contributed would be multiplied by the payroll amounts.

- *Employer Contribution percentages*—similarly to employee contributions, the percentages are based upon current statute or plan provisions.

- *Benefit payments*—these would be projected by the actuary in accordance with the entry age actuarial cost method, as described previously.

- *Service costs*—this is the annual expense that an employee earns based upon service and the current statute or plan provisions.

- *Beginning plan fiduciary net position*—this would be the beginning balance held in trust for the payment of benefits.

- *Administrative expense*—this would be the current administrative expense and projected forward with increases into the future.

- *The Long-Term Expected Rate of Return on Plan Assets*—this would be used to provide an estimate of investment rate of return on plan assets.

- *The Tax-Exempt High Quality General Obligation Rate*—this needs to be known if indeed the plan will run out of funds to pay remaining benefits to be paid as of the valuation date.

A very high level view of the calculation is as follows:

- Beginning fiduciary net position *plus.*

- Projected total contributions from employers, including nonemployer contributing entities, along with current as well as future employees (if applicable) based upon the rates *less.*

- Projected benefit payments *less.*

- Projected administrative expense *plus.*

- Projected investment earnings *equals.*
- Ending fiduciary net position.

For each year into the future, the projected beginning fiduciary net position and the projected benefit payments are then compared. If the projected benefit payment for the year is *less than* the beginning fiduciary net position, then it is "funded" with plan assets. This calculation continues the same way until the fiduciary net position is insufficient to fund projected benefits however many years into the future. The point when fiduciary net position is *insufficient* to fund benefit payments that are remaining is known as the "cross-over" point. The remainder of the benefit payments must then be funded by investments at the tax-exempt high quality general obligation rate. Both streams of projected benefit payments are then discounted at the present value of each rate until all projected benefits are paid for current and future employees, which may be many decades into the future. The GASB *Implementation Guide 2015-1*, Appendix B5-2, Illustration 1 [GASB Cod. Sec. P20.901, Illustration 1] contains a thorough example of how to calculate the discount rate.

PRACTICE POINT: An example of the calculation is not shown in the *Governmental GAAP Guide* due to its complexity. GASB's OPEB standards use a similar calculation for the discount rate (however for OPEB, the discount rate in many cases is not a large driver of healthcare costs). In practice, actuaries usually perform the calculation, but management is ultimately responsible for its reasonableness.

PRACTICE POINT: If a plan has a significant amount of fiduciary net position in relation to its total pension liability, the "cross-over" point is well into the future. In some cases where law stipulates "full funding," the cross-over point may never occur, allowing the use of the long-term expected rate of return on plan assets. If a plan does not have a significant amount of fiduciary net position, the "cross-over" point will be more current, therefore lowering the discount rate and raising the pension liability. If there is no trust present, there is likely no fiduciary net position (assets), necessitating a lower discount rate and higher total pension (or OPEB) liability.

The present value of the projected benefit payments is then required to be attributed to periods of employee service using the entry age actuarial cost method with each period's service cost determined as a level percentage of pay. The actuarial present value is required to be attributed for each employee individually, from the period when the employee first accrues pensions through the period when the employee retires (GASB-68, par. 32) [GASB Cod. Sec. P20.131].

Single and Agent-Multiple-Employers: Financial Reporting, Notes, and Required Supplementary Information

For single and agent-multiple-employers, the employers recognize and record a liability on their statements of net position equal to the net pension liability. The liability is calculated as the present value of the projected benefit payments, less the value of assets available to pay those benefits. For most governments, the net amount will result in a liability. If the assets are larger than the present value of the projected benefit payments, the net amount will result in an asset (GASB-68, pars. 20–21) [GASB Cod. Secs. P20.119–.120].

PRACTICE POINT: The impact of reporting a net pension liability cannot be minimized. For some governments, the amount may be the largest number on the entire statement of net position. Financial reporting, analysis and stakeholder perception may be changed by the recording of this liability. The *GASB Implementation Guide 2015-1*, question 7.23.10 [GASB Cod. Sec. 2200.708-12], reminds practitioners, in part, to discuss the issue of recording a net pension liability and the effect on unrestricted net position. If the effect on unrestricted net position is significant, the government may disclose additional details of unrestricted net position in the notes to the financial statements to isolate the effect of the net pension liability. The government may also address these circumstances in the management's discussion and analysis (MD&A). Alternatively, if a net pension asset is present, it is also a best practice to address how the elements are estimated and how a net pension asset should not be securitized through a debt issuance, nor is it available for operating purposes and finally, how it is contingent upon plan provisions and statutes being adhered to into the future.

Annual pension expense is calculated by the summation of work multiplied by the items contained within the benefit plan structure and resulting in changes to the components of the net pension liability. Deferred outflows of resources and deferred inflows of resources change by amortization of changes between estimated amounts and actual amounts of various aspects of the liability, including investments, demographics, and plan structure.

Succinctly, the following are elements of pension expense:

Element of Pension Expense	Element Increases/Decreases Pension Expense
Service cost, excluding employee contributions	Increases
Employee contributions	Decreases
Interest on beginning total pension liability	Increases
Changes in benefit terms	May increase or decrease
Plan administrative costs	Increase
Projected earnings on plan investments	Decreases
Amortization of deferred outflows of resources (or deferred inflows of resources) for differences between expected and actual experience, changes in assumptions, net differences between projected and actual earnings, changes in proportion (in cost-sharing multiple-employer plans), or differences between actual contributions and proportionate share (also in cost-sharing multiple employer plans)	Increases (or decreases in the case of amortizations of deferred inflows of resources)
Other adjustments	May increase or decrease

Most changes to the net pension liability will occur in the period of change, especially in a change of a plan that only affects retirees or beneficiaries with no remaining service to the employer. Current-period service cost, interest on the total pension liability also are expensed immediately. However, projected earnings on the pension plan's investments are also included in the determination of the annual pension expense.

Demographic and economic assumption changes and differences between expected and actual experience are recorded as deferred inflows of resources or deferred outflows of resources and amortized to pension expense annually in a systematic and rational manner over a closed period equal to the average of the expected remaining service lives of all employees that are provided with benefits through the pension plan (active employees and inactive employees), beginning with the current period. The effect on the net pension liability of differences between the projected earnings on pension plan investments and actual experience with regard to those earnings is required to be included in pension expense in a systematic and rational manner over a closed period of five years, beginning with the current period. Changes in the net pension liability not included in pension expense are required to be reported as deferred outflows of resources or deferred inflows of resources related to pensions. Finally, if employer contributions are made subsequent to the measurement date of the net pension liability, they are required to be reported as deferred outflows of resources not only in the government-wide financial statements, but potentially in the fund financial statements that paid the contributions (GASB-68, pars. 33–34) [GASB Cod. Secs. P20.132–.133].

OBSERVATION: One of the major changes in mind-set with the implementation of GASB-68 was the annual required contribution (ARC), which still may be prepared for management (internal) purposes and in terminology used by management (or in law). In its basis for conclusions to GASB-68, the GASB explains that by (a) requiring employers to report measures such as the ARC introduced in GASB-27 and the extent to which they contributed the ARC and (b) establishing parameters (including a maximum amortization period for unfunded actuarial liabilities) for the calculation of those measures, the GASB was viewed as having established de-facto contribution policy standards. Many governments accepted this and even had the calculation of an ARC written into law or similar ordinance, even though it was not meant to be required and with the ability to do biennial actuarial valuations written into GASB-27, the ARC was certainly not meant to be an annual requirement.

GASB-68 makes clear the separation between its objectives related to establishing standards for the financial reporting of pensions by employers, on the one hand, and public policy matters such as pension contribution policy, on the other. Consistent with this distinction, GASB did not establish an ARC or similar measure in GASB-68. As a result, the GASB did not believe that it would be appropriate to require disclosures in GASB-68 about a standardized measure of the amount an employer would need to contribute to a pension plan each year as part of a systematic contribution pension plan in order to reach projected objectives (GASB-68, par. 323).

PRACTICE POINT: For agent-multiple employers, receiving the information from an agent-multiple employer plan to record in the basic financial statements, notes to the basic financial statements, and required supplementary information appears to be a challenge. The plans need to present each employer with a financial statement, the note disclosure, and required supplementary information. If the plan has hundreds of employers and performs allocations of investment revenues and administrative expenses to the various employers, the timely presentation of this information is a challenge. The AICPA's Audit & Accounting Guide, *State and Local Governments,* chapter 13, Part II and especially Appendix A to chapter 13, paragraphs A-16 through A-22, contain guidance requiring the information to be transmitted from the plans to the employers to be audited separately from the audit of the plan's financial statements. As an alternative, an internal controls engagement may be performed in accordance with AT Section 801 (*Reporting on Controls at a Service Organization*).Controls may be required to be tested based on management's assertion that internal controls are suitably designed and have been operating effectively for an entire year under audit. (Also known as a Type 2 report.) For single employer plans, increased testing on census data and the information transfer will also be required. Therefore, in both cases time should be increased to prepare this data, unless it can be prepared off-cycle to the date of the basic financial statements.

Within governmental fund statements, a net pension liability may be recorded, but only to the extent that it would be liquidated with current financial resources (potentially the accrued amount for the next fiscal period). Pension expenditures include the amounts that have been paid by the employer to the pension plan and the change in the beginning and ending net pension liability as recorded in the funds, not on the government-wide financial statements (GASB-68, par. 36) [GASB Cod. Sec. P20.135].

PRACTICE POINT: GASB Statement No. 85 (*Omnibus 2017*) amended these provisions slightly. In governmental fund financial statements, liabilities to employees for defined benefit pensions should be measured as of the end of the reporting period. All expenditures for defined benefit pensions (including amounts for payables to a pension plan and amounts for costs incurred by the employer related to the administration of defined benefit pensions) should be measured for a reporting period. This appears to clarify if there is a liability in a governmental fund.

For single and agent-multiple employers, the notes to the basic financial statements include descriptive information similar to what was provided under GASB-27. Tables are included for the current-year changes in the net pension liability and significant assumptions and items included in the calculation of the total pension liability (COLAs, inflation, salaries, discount rates, experience study results, etc.). Finally, the notes contain information about the date of the actuarial valuation and any changes to the assumptions and benefit terms and how contributions are determined (GASB-68, pars. 37–45) [GASB Cod. Secs. P20.136–.144].

Required supplementary information includes presentations of 10 years of data as of the *measurement date* of the sources of changes in the net pension liability, the components of the net pension liability, ratios of the pension plan's fiduciary net position as a percentage of the total pension liability (similar to the former "funded ratio"), and the net pension liability as a percentage of covered-employee payroll (See **PRACTICE POINT** on GASB-82 (*Pension Issues—an amendment of GASB Statements No. 67, No. 68, and No. 73*) later in this chapter). If the contributions of a single or agent-employer are actuarially determined, the employer should also present in required supplementary information 10-year schedules that include information about the actuarially determined contribution, contributions to the pension plan, and related ratios. If the contributions are established in a statute or by contract, a 10-year schedule is presented instead with information about the statutorily or contractually required contribution rates, contributions to the pension plan, and related ratios. In all cases, a footnote to the required supplementary information includes significant methods and assumptions used in calculating the actuarially determined contribution. In addition, employers are required to explain factors that significantly affect trends in the amounts reported in the schedules, such as changes of benefit terms, changes in the size or composition of the population covered by the benefit terms, or the use of different assumptions (GASB-68, pars. 46–47) [GASB Cod. Secs. P20.145–.146].

OBSERVATION: As part of GASB-73 (*Accounting and Financial Reporting for Pensions and Related Assets That Are Not within the Scope of GASB Statement 68, and Amendments to Certain Provisions of GASB Statements 67 and 68*) provisions of required supplementary information have been amended. The GASB is now limiting the information about factors that significantly affect trends in the investment-related amounts reported for those factors the participating governments have influence over (e.g., changes in investment policies). Information about external economic factors (e.g., changes in market prices) is not required to be disclosed. Furthermore, the schedules that would include disclosure of a receivable/payable for contractually deferred contributions with a separate payment schedule would not be classified as a separately financed specific liability of an individual employer or nonemployer contributing entity to the pension plan. The full amount of the pension plan receivable/employer or nonemployer contributing entity payable to a plan for contractually deferred contributions with a separate payment schedule is a contribution in the reporting period in which the receivable/payable arises.

The various contribution amounts disclosed exclude amounts, if any, associated with payables to the pension plan that arose in a prior fiscal year and *separately financed specific liabilities* of the individual employer or nonemployer contributing entity. A single employer that has a special funding situation would recognize additional revenue for the portion of expense recognized by the governmental nonemployer contributing entity. A cost-sharing employer that has a special funding situation recognizes additional revenue and pension expense for the portion of expense recognized by the governmental nonemployer contributing entity for the change in the total pension liability associated with a separately financed specific liability of the individual governmental nonemployer contributing entity that is associated with the employer. Expense recognized by a cost-sharing employer or nonemployer contributing entity in a special funding situation should be reduced by the employer or nonemployer contributing entity's proportionate share of contributions to the pension plan to separately finance specific liabilities of others—effectively recording a subsidy. Finally, employers recognize revenue for the support of a nonemployer contributing entity that is not in a special funding situation in the reporting period in which the contribution of the nonemployer contributing entity is reported as a change in the net pension liability or collective net pension liability, as applicable.

Cost Sharing Employers: Financial Reporting, Notes and Required Supplementary Information

Cost-sharing employers are required to present their *proportionate share* of the net pension liability of the plan, *as determined by the plan*. If a special funding situation exists (where a non-employer funds a portion—if not all—of the employer's portion), the proportion that is allocated to the cost-sharing employer may be reduced as long as the funding situation meets certain irrevocable tests. The employer's portion is determined on a basis that is consistent with the manner in which contributions to the pension plan are determined, and consideration should be given to separate rates, if any, related to separate portions of the collective net pension liability. The use of the employer's projected long-term contribution effort as compared to the total projected long-term contribution effort of all employers as the basis for determining an employer's proportion is encouraged.

OBSERVATION: The long-term contribution effort is somewhat ambiguous and can be misleading. If a proportion changes, all amounts would change, including the net pension liability and other elements. As with other GASB Statements, the term "long-term" is undefined and left to professional judgment. Some relatively stable plans (without governments joining or leaving very often), may use a historical view of at least the prior year's contributions as a basis for the allocation. Others may use an actuarial analysis, especially if employers join or leave the plan at some point. In any event, the allocation method will need to be disclosed by the plan.

OBSERVATION: The AICPA is concerned with the ability to audit the transfer of information from a cost-sharing multiple-employer plan to the employers in the plan. The AICPA Audit and Accounting Guide *State and Local Governments*, Chapter 13, Appendix B, particularly paragraphs B-11-B-19, discuss how to communicate information from a cost sharing plan to employers. The schedules are separately audited. A "Schedule of Employer Allocations" details by employer the allocation percentages based on contributions, including when a nonemployer funds a portion of the liability in a special funding situation.

The Schedule of Employer Allocations is presented as follows:

	Contributions	Allocation
Employer 1	$2,143,842	36.3748%
Employer 2	268,425	4.5544%
Employer 3	322,142	5.4658%
Employer 4	483,255	8.1994%
Employer 5	633,125	10.7423%
Employer 6	144,288	2.4481%
Employer 7	95,365	1.6181%
Employer 8	94,238	1.5989%
Employer 9	795,365	13.4950%
Employer 10	267,468	4.5382%
Employer 11	403,527	6.8467%
Employer 12	165,886	2.8146%
Employer 13	68,454	1.1615%
Employer 14	6,240	0.1059%
Employer 15	2,144	0.0364%
Total	**$5,893,764**	**100.00%**

As discussed in Chapter 7, "Proprietary Funds," each employer should create a similar schedule within the government and for component units that contribute through the government to the plan to properly allocate the pension elements to those funds/employers that are expected to contribute to funding the government's pension elements in accordance with NCGA-1, paragraph 42 (see "*Allocations of Pension Elements within Reporting Entities*" later in this chapter).

A "Schedule of Pension Amounts by Employer" has two alternative presentations. Alternative 1 lists all employers in the plan and the allocation for every accounting element that needs to be transferred to the employers, based on the allocations in the previous schedule. For very large cost-sharing multiple employer plans with more than a handful of employers, Alternative 1 yields a very onerous schedule for plans with many employers. A second alternative contains only the aggregated amounts for each accounting element, including:

- Net pension liability;
- Deferred Outflows of Resources, including, but not limited to:
  - Differences between Expected and Actual Experience;
  - Net Difference between Projected and Actual Investment Earnings on Pension Plan Investments;
  - Changes of Assumptions;
  - Changes in Proportion and Differences between Employer Contributions and Proportionate Share of Contributions; and
  - Total Deferred Outflows of Resources;

- Deferred Inflows of Resources, including, but not limited to:
  - Differences between Expected and Actual Experience;
  - Changes of Assumptions;
  - Changes in Proportion and Differences between Employer Contributions and Proportionate Share of Contributions; and
  - Total Deferred Inflows of Resources;
- Proportionate Share of Plan Pension Expense;
- Net Amortization of Deferred Amounts from Changes in Proportion and Differences between Employer Contributions and Proportionate Share of Contributions; and
- Total Employer Pension Expense.

It is up to the employer to use the information in the allocation schedule and multiply the allocation against the aggregated amounts for each element. Upon receipt of each of the schedules, the employers can then rely on this information to be placed in their basic financial statements, notes to the basic financial statements and required supplementary information because it will contain an audit opinion. Similarly to agent multiple-employer plan information, time should be increased to prepare this data, unless it can be prepared off-cycle to the date of the basic financial statements.

Further discussion of these schedules is found in Chapter 22, "Pension and Other Postemployment Benefit Plans."

PRACTICE POINT: The AICPA State and Local Government Expert Panel has issued a follow-up white paper article on *Emerging Pension Issues*. The article is **non-authoritative** as it has not been approved, disapproved, or otherwise acted on by any senior technical committee of the AICPA and does not represent the official position of the AICPA. However, various aspects of the article may give rise to additional information in the Schedules from cost-sharing multiple employer plans into the future. The AICPA is reminding practitioners that a change in proportionate shares will likely occur annually which will necessitate a deferred inflow or outflow of resources and an annual amortization, if material. It is also suggesting that additional information should be included involving pension expense related to specific liabilities of individual employers (see further discussion later in this chapter). Finally, the Schedule should exclude pension expense attributable to Employer Paid Member Contributions ("pick-ups"). (See discussion on GASB-82 (*Pension Issues—an amendment of GASB Statements No. 67, No. 68, and No. 73*) later in this chapter.) Therefore, the total pension expense noted above will be split into four columns:

1. Proportionate share of allocable plan pension expense;
2. Pension expense related to specific liabilities of individual employers;
3. Net amortization of deferred amounts from changes in proportion and differences between employer contributions and proportionate share of contributions; and
4. Total pension expense, excluding that attributable to employer-paid member contributions (equating to the sum of the previous three elements).

As summarized above, changes in the employer's proportion of the collective net pension liability as well as differences between the individual employer's contributions and the employer's proportionate share of total contribution from all employers must be determined. The effect of this is declared as a deferred inflow of resources or a deferred outflow of resources and amortized to pension expense over the remaining service lives of all employees (active and inactive) (GASB-68, pars. 48–58) [GASB Cod. Secs. P20.147–.158]..

EXHIBIT 13-4
ILLUSTRATION: CALCULATION OF CHANGES IN PROPORTION OF A COST-SHARING EMPLOYER AND RELATED JOURNAL ENTRIES

To illustrate the calculation of changes in proportion for a cost-sharing employer, the following information must be used (adapted from the GASB *Implementation Guide 2015-1, Appendix B5-2,* Illustration 8b) [GASB Cod. Sec. P20.901, Illustration 3b]:

Step 1: Collective balances at December 31, 20X7 and 20X8, are as follows:

Measurement Date	12/31/20X7	12/31/20X8
Collective deferred outflows of resources for the Plan	$1,373,691	$2,185,960
Collective deferred inflows of resources for the Plan	$1,538,565	$1,233,001
Collective net pension liability	$6,178,023	$7,455,024
District's proportion	0.19%	0.20%

The collective pension expense for the measurement period ended December 31, 20X8, is $1,163,898. The average of the expected remaining service lives of all employees that are provided pensions through the pension plan (active and inactive employees) determined as of the beginning of the measurement period (January 1, 20X8) is 9.3 years.

Step 2: Additional information for the fiscal year ended *June 30, 20X9* is as follows:

- Contributions from the school district to the plan from January 1, 20X8 to June 30, 20X8 were $1,030, reported as a deferred outflow of resources in the prior year, due to the provisions of GASB-68, par. 57, as amended by GASB-71 and GASB-73, par. 122) [GASB Cod. Sec. P20.157]. From July 1, 20X8 to December 31, 20X8, contributions were also $1,030. From January 1, 20X9 to June 30, 20X9, contributions subsequent to the measurement date but prior to the district's year-end were $1,065.

- The beginning deferred outflows related to changes in proportion and contributions in prior periods was $170. The amount to be recognized as an increase to pension expense in the next measurement period (ended December 31, 20X9) is $30.

- The beginning deferred inflows of resources related to changes in proportion and contributions in prior periods was $192. The amount to be recognized as a *decrease* to pension expense for the next measurement period (ended December 31, 20X9) is $36.

Step 3: The following amounts would be recognized as debits and credits related to the change in proportionate share:

	Proportionate Share at 12/31/20X7 (0.19%)	Proportionate Share at 12/31/20X8 (0.20%)	Debits	Credits
Deferred Outflows of Resources	$2,610 = ($1,373,691× 0.19%)	$4,372 = ($2,185,960× 0.20%)	$1,762	
Deferred Inflows of Resources	$2,923 = ($1,538,565× 0.19%)	$2,466 = ($1,233,001× 0.20%)		($457)
Net Pension Liability	$11,738 = ($6,178,023× 0.19%)	$14,910 = ($7,455,024× 0.20%)		$3,172

NOTE: The ($457) is the result of a lowering of a "natural credit"—the deferred inflows of resources. In reality, this would be a debit. As the deferred outflows of resources increases a "natural debit," a further debit is needed. Finally, the net pension liability increases a "natural credit" resulting in a further credit. The above debits and credits are not meant to balance as further information is needed in Step 4.

Step 4: The pension expense for the measurement period ended December 31, 20X8 is $2,327, which would be $1,163,898 × 0.20%. The beginning balances as of 12/31/20X7 for the period reflected $137 in debit balances for deferred outflows of resources, $154 in deferred inflows of resources and $618 in net pension liability related to the change in proportion. As the $154 + $618 equals total credits of $772, $635 must be the amount recognized as the net effect of the change in proportion on beginning balances ($772 - $137 = $635). Therefore, this difference of $635 would have to be deferred and amortized over the remaining service lives of active and inactive members, beginning with this year. ($635 ÷ 9.3 years = $68 in pension expense, the remaining $567 would be a deferred outflow of resources.)

Finally, contributions from employers to the Plan during the period ending December 31, 20X8 were $1,004,730. The district's proportionate share (0.20%) should have been $2,009. However, the district contributed $2,060 ($1,030 from January 1, 20X8 to June 30, 20X8 and another $1,030 from July 1, 20X8 to December 31, 20X8). Therefore, a difference exists of $51 that would need to be deferred and amortized over the remaining service lives of active and inactive members. ($51 ÷ 9.3 years = $5 in pension expense, the remaining $46 would be a deferred outflow of resources.)

Therefore, the Journal Entries for the District for the Fiscal Year Ended June 30, 20X9 (December 31, 20X8 measurement date) would be:

	Debits	Credits
Deferred Outflows of Resources – proportionate share of collective deferred outflows of resources (from Step 3)	$1,762	
Pension Expense ($2,327+68+5 all from Step 4)	2,400	
Deferred Inflows of Resources – proportionate share of collective deferred inflows of resources (from Step 3) (proportion lowered)	457	
Deferred Outflows of Resources –($567 + 46 from Step 4)	613	
Proportionate share of net pension liability (from Step 3)		$3,172
Deferred outflows of resources – District contributions from 1/1/X8 – 6/30/X8		1,030
Cash (likely already recorded) – District contributions from 7/1/X8 – 12/31/X8		1,030

> **NOTE:** The only pension element that is not presented in the Statement of Net Position on the government-wide financial statements is Pension Expense. Therefore, the results of Steps 1 through 3 all "close" to pension expense. This closing may change pension expense as reported in the Schedule of Pension Amounts by Employer.

A second set of journal entries would recognize the amortization of deferred outflows of resources and deferred inflows of resources for the year calculated in Step 2:

	Debits	Credits
Deferred Inflows of Resources (from Step 2)	$36	
Deferred Outflows of Resources (from Step 2)		$30
Pension expense		6

Finally, per GASB-68, par. 57, as amended by GASB-71 and GASB-73, par. 122 [GASB Cod. Sec. P20.157], the district's contributions from 1/1/X9 to 6/30/X9 would be recognized as deferred outflows of resources to be adjusted to net pension liability in the next measurement period:

	Debits	Credits
Deferred Outflows of Resources – district contributions from 1/1/X9 to 6/30/X9 (from Step 2)	$1,065	
Cash		$1,065

Similar to single and agent-multiple employer plans, governmental fund statements include the cost-sharing employer's proportionate share of the net pension liability that will be liquidated with current financial resources. Pension expenditures are calculated similarly (GASB-68, par. 73) [GASB Cod. Sec. P20.173].

The notes to the basic financial statements of cost-sharing employers include similar descriptive information and annual information. GASB-68 requires cost-sharing employers to present in required supplementary information 10-year schedules containing the net pension liability and certain related ratios and, if applicable, information about statutorily or contractually required contributions, contributions to the pension plan, and related ratios (GASB-68, pars. 74–82, as amended by GASB-73, pars. 117 and 119, and GASB-82, par. 6) [GASB Cod. Secs. P20.174–.182].

Special Funding Situations

If the employer is involved in a "special funding situation," the amount that a nonemployer entity is legally and irrevocably required to fund (e.g., a state on behalf of a school district) becomes a liability of the nonemployer entity rather than that of the employer. If a state funds 50% of a school district's pension liability on an ongoing basis, then 50% of the liability is recorded on the state's statement of net position, while the remainder is recorded on the school district's statement of net position (GASB-68, pars. 83–91) [GASB Cod. Secs. P20.183–.191]. Special funding situations may occur in all types of plans and funding may be received from non-governmental employers.

For employers that receive support of nonemployer contributing entities in a special funding situation, revenue is recognized in an amount equal to the nonemployer contributing entities' total proportionate share of the collective pension expense that is associated with that employer (GASB-68, par. 95) [GASB Cod. Sec. P20.196]. Special funding situations are common in pensions that are for school districts and are managed by statewide plans.

The nonemployer contributing entity recognizes its proportionate share of all accounting elements, including net pension liability, deferred outflows of resources, deferred inflows of resources, and pension expense. Changes in proportionate share may occur at each measurement date. The pension expense should then be reported to each employer in the plan in *their proportion*, which would result in additional expense and subsidy revenue to that employer.

OBSERVATION: Special funding situations are different than separately financed specific liabilities. A section on separately financed specific liabilities occurs later in the chapter.

EXHIBIT 13-5
ILLUSTRATION: SPECIAL FUNDING SITUATION AND RELATED JOURNAL ENTRIES

To illustrate a special funding situation, based upon contributions in the prior year, School District #19080 has a 0.063% employer proportionate share of total statewide teachers cost-sharing multiple employer plan calculated employer contributions. However, the state has a special funding situation and contributes 37.65% of total statewide teachers cost-sharing multiple employer plan calculated employer contributions.

The plan reports a pension expense that would be recognized by all employers of $1,389,000,000 (rounded). Therefore, School District #19080 would recognize a pension expense of $875,070 as follows:

Element	Amount
Annual pension expense reported by the plan	$1,389,000,000
School District #19080's proportion	× 0.063%
School District #19080's proportion of annual pension expense	**$875,070**

However, the District would not recognize the same amount in revenue. 0.063% is 0.101043% of the total statewide teachers' contributions, *without* the state's portion. Therefore, they must recognize revenue as follows:

Element	Amount
Annual pension expense reported by the plan	$1,389,000,000
State's portion of annual pension expense	× 37.65%
Aggregated state's proportion of annual pension expense (to be reported by all School Districts as the State participates in a special funding situation) (the State would report this as pension expense)	$522,958,500
School District #19080's proportion	0.063%
The total of the proportions of all employers for which support is provided by the State (aggregated employer contributions) (1– 37.65%)	62.350%
Proportion of the State's total proportionate share of collective pension expense associated with School District #19080 (0.063% ÷ 62.350%)	× 0.101043%
In conformity with paragraphs 94 and 95 of GASB-68 [GASB Cod. Secs. P20.196–.197], the District recognizes revenue and pension expense that is associated with School District #19080 ($522,958,500 × 0.101043%) (Debit pension expense, credit revenue – state aid)	**$528,410**

The School District also needs to record its share of deferred outflows of resources, deferred inflows of resources, and net pension liability. Using the 0.063%, the following is its share of other accounting elements as reported by the plan:

Element	Plan Amounts	District #19080 (0.063%) Amounts
Net Pension Liability	$58,437,000,000	$36,815,310
Deferred Outflows of Resources	-	-
Deferred Inflows of Resources – representing unamortized differences between projected and actual earnings on plan investments	$14,390,000,000	$9,065,700

Due to GASB-71, any contributions made subsequent to the measurement date by the District to the Plan would be recognized as a deferred outflow of resources, reducing pension expense. At the next measurement date, the contributions previously reclassed to deferred outflows of resources would be recognized as part of the net pension liability. Therefore, pension expense would be recognized as part of a reversing entry of the reclassed deferred outflows of resources.

Then, to record the expense and subsidy as of the end of the year:

	Debit	Credit
Pension Expense ($875,070 + $528,410)	$1,403,480	
Revenue – State Aid		$528,410
Cash (or payables that already adjusted net position)		875,070

PRACTICE POINT: GASB-85 (*Omnibus 2017*) clarifies the presentation of revenue and expenditures for on-behalf payments in governmental funds. If the above transactions were in a governmental fund, expenditures would be recognized for on-behalf payments for pensions equalling the total of (*a*) amounts paid during the reporting period by the nonemployer contributing entities to the pension plan or for benefits as they come due, and (*b*) the change between the nonemployer contributing entities' beginning and ending receivable balances of amounts normally expected to be liquidated with expendable available financial resources. Items (*a*) and (*b*) could include payables to a pension plan. Unless payments are not legally required for defined contribution pensions, revenue is recognized equal to the expenditures calculated in this step. GASB-85 was effective for periods beginning after June 15, 2017.

Allocations of Pension Elements within Reporting Entities

Since 1979, U.S. GAAP has required long-term liabilities directly related to and expected to be paid from proprietary and fiduciary funds to be presented in said funds (NCGA-1, par. 42, as amended) [GASB Cod. Secs. 1100.108, 1500.102, C60.110]. Recording the accounting elements required by GASB-68 in funds that are in the full accrual basis of accounting presents a challenge for preparers and auditors. GASB-68 contains no specific guidance for allocation of the net pension liability or other pension related measures to individual funds.

Amounts are required to be allocated to component units. GASB *Implementation Guide 2015-1*, questions 5.125.1 through 5.125.3 [GASB Cod. Secs. P20.707-1–3], discuss the issue of allocating to component units as follows:

Fact Pattern	Guidance
A single-employer defined benefit pension plan is used to provide pensions to the employees of a state government and several governments that are component units of the state. In their stand-alone financial reports, should each of the component units report as a single employer?	No. Component units would apply the cost-sharing employer requirements for GASB-68 for their own stand-alone reports. Therefore, each government would report their own proportionate share of the collective net pension liability (or asset), taking into account if a special funding situation is present. The reporting entity (the state and component units) would include just note disclosures and RSI for a single employer.
If the component units do not issue stand-alone financial reports, is a portion of the accounting elements required to be allocated to the component units as if they were cost-sharing employers for the purposes of the reporting entity's financial report?	Yes. Regardless of whether the financial data (in this case, the net pension liability and related measures) is issued in stand-alone financial reports of the component units, the reporting entity's financial report should include that data as if it had been. GASB-68, par. 18 requires that in stand-alone financial statements, the component units account for and report their participation in the pension plan as if they were cost-sharing employers. Therefore, the financial report of the reporting entity should include the primary government's and the component units' proportionate shares of the collective net pension liability and related measures as if the entities were cost-sharing employers.
In a single employer or agent multiple-employer plan, does it matter if the component unit is discretely presented or blended?	No. Each should account for and report its participation in the plan as if it was a cost-sharing employer, regardless of status.

As there is minimal guidance as to the allocations, employers need to consider if a basis of allocation is systematic and rational. For example, if a cost-sharing multiple employer plan uses employer contributions as a basis for allocations, the employers should use the same and using the same measurement period information in allocating to enterprise, internal service or fiduciary funds. As a reminder, if proportions change from year to year, if material, a deferred inflow of resources or deferred outflow of resources may result, requiring a "due to" or "due from" entry between funds. This also presents a problem for separately audited departments or funds. U.S. GASB standards rightfully do not discuss separately audited departments that present GAAP-based departmental financial statements. The AICPA Audit & Accounting Guide, *State and Local Governments* recommends consideration of long-established practices in these presentation applying all relevant GAAP.

PRACTICE POINT: Allocating to fiduciary funds raises a further problem. There are no provisions in fiduciary fund reporting to declare deferred inflows of resources nor deferred outflows of resources, even in the newly released GASB-84. Furthermore, for plans that are fiduciary component units, allocating pension elements back to the plan may result in a circular accounting entry or an inability to post pension-related information. Plans routinely expense administrative expense including employee benefits. These expenses are funded from investment return or in some cases budgetary funding. Therefore, there is inconsistent U.S. GAAP for this issue. For most plans and fiduciary funds, an allocation of pension elements would likely be immaterial to the rest of the reporting entity. In most cases, the reporting government may be better served to report the information in the governmental activities and note disclose the allocation stating as part of the summary of significant accounting policies with regard to pensions: "amounts that would normally be allocated to fiduciary funds have been reported as part of governmental activities" or something similar.

Separately Financed Specific Liabilities

GASB-68, footnote 15 [GASB Cod. Sec. P20.546] describes separately financed specific liabilities with regard to a cost-sharing pension plan. A *separately financed specific liability* to a defined benefit pension plan is a *one-time* assessment to an *individual employer or nonemployer contributing entity* of an amount resulting from an increase in the total pension liability due to:

- An individual employer joining a pension plan;

- A change in benefit terms to an individual employer; or

- A contractual commitment for a nonemployer contributing entity to make a one-time contribution to finance a reduction in the net pension liability.

Examples of separately financed liabilities to the pension plan include cash payments or long-term payables for amounts assessed to an individual employer upon joining the pension plan or for increases in the total pension liability for changes of benefit terms specific to the employer.

If a long-term installment contract is used to finance an employer joining a plan, the *GASB Implementation Guide 2015-1*, question 5.165.2, requires for the portion of past service cost associated with employees that exceeds assets to the plan, the amount of the installment contract is a payable to the new plan. Both the amount of the installment contract and the amount of assets to the new plan should be accounted for as contributions from the employer for a separately financed specific liability of the individual employer.

GASB-68 requires separately financed specific liabilities to be excluded from required supplementary information related to actuarially determined contributions and contributions made from single and agent employers (GASB-68, par. 46(c)) [GASB Cod. Sec. P20.145(c)]. The *GASB Implementation Guide 2015-1*, question 5.157.10 [GASB Cod Cod. Sec. P20.727-11), magnifies this issue by restating the measure of the actuarially determined contribution that is required by paragraph 46c(1) of GASB-68 [GASB Cod. Sec. P20.145(c)] or the statutorily or contractually required contribution that is required by GASB-68, paragraph 46d(1) [GASB Cod. Sec. P20.145(d)(1)] excludes amounts, if any, to separately finance specific liabilities of the individual employer to the pension plan. Similarly, the amount of contributions presented in relation to the actuarially determined or statutorily or contractually required contribution, as applicable, should exclude amounts recognized as additions to the pension plan for separately financed specific liabilities of the individual employer to the pension plan.

Separately financed specific liabilities are also required to be excluded from determining a cost-sharing employer's proportion (GASB-68, par. 48) [GASB Cod. Sec. P20.147]. For the cost-sharing employer, pension expense must also be adjusted. For contributions to the pension plan to separately finance specific liabilities of the individual employer to the pension plan, the difference during the measurement period between both of the elements below calculates the employer's pension expense as follows:

- The amount of such contributions from the employer (and amounts associated with the employer from nonemployer contributing entities that are not in a special funding situation); and

- The amount of the employer's proportionate share of the total of the contributions determined using the employer's proportion of the collective net pension liability.

This is a similar calculation for determining the contributions to recognize to the pension plan for a cost-sharing employer with separately financed specific liabilities. It is also similar for governmental nonemployer contributing entities in the calculation of their proportionate share of the collective net pension liability.

PRACTICE POINT: GASB-73, pars. 118–121 [GASB Cod. Secs. P20.220, .546, Pe5.536, P20.145, .181, .216, Pe5.128, P20.fn21, P20.156, .195, .207], amended GASB-68 with regard to separately financed specific liabilities, including from contributions made by others. Contributions made by others to a pension plan during the measurement period to separately finance specific liabilities to the pension plan should be recognized as follows:

- For a cost-sharing employer, the amount of the employer's proportionate share of the total of such contributions (excluding amounts associated with the employer from nonemployer contributing entities not in a special funding situation) determined using the employer's proportion of the collective net pension liability should be recognized as a reduction of the employer's pension expense.

- For a governmental nonemployer contributing entity in a special funding situation, the amount of the governmental nonemployer contributing entity's proportionate share of the total of such contributions determined using the governmental nonemployer contributing entity's proportion of the collective pension liability should be recognized as a reduction of the governmental nonemployer contributing entity's expense.

- For an employer that has a special funding situation, the amounts required to be recognized in conformity with GASB-68, as applicable, should be reduced by the employer's proportionate share of the total of the amounts recognized by nonemployer contributing entities in conformity with item (b) above that are associated with the employer.

Accordingly, the governmental nonemployer in a special funding situation contributing to an entity for separately financed specific liabilities also generates revenue at the employer receiving the benefits. Therefore, the proportionate shares would be affected.

Separately financed specific liabilities are different than normal payables arising in defined benefit pension plans. GASB-68 requires payables to the pension plan for unpaid (legal, contractual, or statutory) financing obligations associated with a pooled total pension liability to be separated from separately financed specific liabilities even if separate payment terms have to be established. Payables are recognized as contributions in the reporting period as any payable to the pension plan arises. However, for the purposes of required supplementary information presented in contribution-related schedules, these amounts are excluded.

GASB Statement No. 73

As discussed previously, GASB-67 and GASB-68 excluded all pension plans that did not use trusts or equivalent arrangements. As a reminder, a trust or equivalent arrangement is present when:

- Contributions from employers and nonemployer contributing entities to the pension plan and earnings on those contributions are irrevocable.

- Pension (or OPEB) plan assets are dedicated to providing pensions (or OPEB) to plan members in accordance with the benefit terms.

- Pension (or OPEB) plan assets are legally protected from the creditors of employers, nonemployer contributing entities, and the pension (or OPEB) plan administrator. If the plan is a defined benefit pension (or OPEB) plan, plan assets also are legally protected from creditors of the plan members.

GASB-73 (*Accounting and Financial Reporting for Pensions and Related Assets That Are Not within the Scope of GASB-68, and Amendments to Certain Provisions of GASB Statements 67 and 68*) expands the approach of GASB-67 and GASB-68 to all pensions, regardless of the presence of a trust. However, without a trust, there is only a minimal chance of assets available to pay for plan benefits (fiduciary net position). Without fiduciary net position, the discount rate is much lower as there are no assets to generate a long-term expected rate of return. Therefore, the related net pension liability maybe much higher than a plan with similar characteristics using a trust. Defined contribution plan provisions, special funding situations and other aspects of GASB-73 are similar to GASB-67 and GASB-68, with reductions in note disclosure due to the lack of fiduciary net position. However, in the note to the required supplementary information, there is a clear disclosure about the lack of assets to fund the benefits.

Assets Held

If a pension plan has assets that are not held in trust, the assets are not part of fiduciary net position. Therefore, they are still part of the employer's (or the nonemployer contributing entity's) assets. In this situation, a government that holds assets accumulated for pension purposes in a fiduciary capacity should report the assets in an agency fund. The amount of assets accumulated in excess of liabilities for benefits due to plan members and accrued investment and administrative expenses should be reported as a liability to participating employers or nonemployer contributing entities.

If the agency fund is included in the financial report of an employer whose employees are provided with benefits through the pension plan or a nonemployer contributing entity that pays benefits as the pensions come due, balances reported in the agency fund *should exclude* amounts that pertain to the employer or nonemployer contributing entity that reports the agency fund.

Insured Plans—GASB-73

Many of the plans and employers that may be subject to GASB-73 are insured plans. Insured plans are defined benefit pension plans in which pensions are financed through an arrangement whereby premiums are paid to an insurance company while employees are in active service, in return for which the insurance company unconditionally undertakes an obligation to pay the pensions as defined in the pension plan terms. The pensions provided through insured plans are classified as insured benefits (GASB-73, pars. 14–17) [GASB Cod. Secs. P22.108–.110].

In the accrual basis of accounting, insured plans recognize an expense equal to the amount of premiums or other payments required for the reporting period in accordance with the agreement with the insurance company and a change in the liability to the insurer equal to the difference between the amount of pension expense and the amount paid to the insurer. For governmental fund financial statements, the amounts would be similar as they would likely be only amounts expended with current available financial resources (GASB-73, pars. 99–100) [GASB Cod Cod. Secs. P22.190–.191].

PRACTICE POINT: The provisions of GASB-85 (*Omnibus 2017*) noted for governmental funds previously (the calculation of expenditures and on-behalf payments) also apply to GASB-73 and governmental funds.

For insured plans, the notes to the basic financial statements only describe the benefits and the benefit provisions, including the authority under which the provisions are established or may be amended. The notes describe the transfer of the payment of benefits from the employer to one or more insurance companies. They should also describe if there is a retained obligation if the insurance company becomes insolvent. Finally, they should also present the current year pension expense/expenditure for the insured benefits (GASB-73, par. 101) [GASB Cod. Sec. P22.192].

GASB Statement No. 78

During the implementation of GASB-68, employers raised concerns regarding the scope and applicability of GASB-68 as it relates to pensions provided through certain multiple-employer defined benefit pension plans (e.g., certain cost-sharing pension plans that are not state or local governmental plans, such as "Taft-Hartley" plans and plans that have similar characteristics) and to state and local governmental employers whose employees are provided with such pensions. Specifically, employers focused on the inability to obtain the measurements and other information needed to comply with the requirements of GASB-68 due to the nature of a government's involvement in and relationship with the pension plan that is nongovernmental. "Taft-Hartley" plans are usually administered by organized labor.

GASB-78 (*Pensions Provided through Certain Multiple-Employer Defined Benefit Pension Plans*) amended GASB-68 for these types of arrangements. GASB-78 applies when a cost-sharing multiple-employer defined benefit pension plan is in place for employees of state or local government employers that *is not* a state or local government pension plan. The plan is used to provide benefits to both employees of state or local government employers and to non-governmental employees and employers. Finally, the plan has no predominant state or local government employers.

Due to the nature of the employer and plan relationship, only pension expense is recognized equal to the employer's required contributions to the pension plan for the reporting period. A payable is reported for any unpaid contributions. Separate liabilities to the plan are handled similarly to the separately financed specific liabilities related to GASB-68 and GASB-73. Pension expenditures in governmental funds are handled similarly to pension expense.

Due to the minimal information required to be generated by the plan, note disclosure and required supplementary information focuses on the contribution aspects, beyond the basic descriptions of the plan arrangements, benefits, contributions and availability of separate reports (GASB-78, pars. 5–10) [GASB Cod. Secs. P22.224–.229].

GASB Statement No. 82

GASB-82 (*Pension Issues—an amendment of GASB Statements No. 67, No. 68, and No. 73*) amends GASB-67, GASB-68, GASB-73, and certain questions in the *GASB Implementation Guide 2015-1* in three different areas of practice: Payroll-related measures in required supplementary information, selection of assumptions in actuarial standards of practice, and employer-paid member contributions. GASB-82 became effective for periods beginning after June 15, 2016 and except for the provisions regarding actuarial standards of practice, required a retroactive restatement of financial statements for all prior periods presented.

Payroll-related Measures in Required Supplementary Information

Since the implementation of GASB-67 and GASB-68, there has been widespread confusion on the definition of "covered-employee payroll" as used in required supplementary information.

As used in GASB-67 and GASB-68, "covered-employee payroll" is defined as the payroll of employees that are provided pensions through the pension plan. The former definition in GASB-27 of "covered payroll" referred to all elements included in *compensation* paid to active employees on which contributions to a pension plan are based. For example, if pension contributions are calculated on base pay including overtime, covered payroll includes overtime compensation.

The change made in GASB-67 and GASB-68 was a challenge to many governments that were required to make adjustments in their calculation to adhere to the updated definition. For example, if a public institution of higher education included the value of a housing allowance for the chancellor of the institution as part of compensation and therefore, as part of a pension, this amount would have been excluded in the presentation for GASB-67 and GASB-68 purposes, if the allowance is *not* part of compensation. Another possibility is when a state contributes a percentage of tax revenues to a plan which has no relationship to compensation. GASB-82 reverts the presentation back to covered payroll specifically for the presentation in required supplementary information for many situations if contributions are based on a measure of payroll (GASB-82, pars. 5–6) [GASB Cod. Secs. P20.523, .114, .145, .181, Pe5.514].

PRACTICE POINT: The differences between "covered-employee payroll" and "covered payroll" cannot be emphasized enough. For single employer and cost-sharing pension plans that are administered through trusts, the measure of payroll required to be used by *the plan* is covered payroll. Covered payroll is the payroll on which contributions to a plan are based. So if contributions are based on something other than payroll, *to the plan*, there is not much of an effect. GASB-82, paragraph 5, does not mention agent-multiple employer plans because the ratio is not presented. Agent pension plans only present a 10-year schedule presenting for each fiscal year the annual money-weighted rate of return on plan investments.

For *the employer*, there could be a very material change. For employers that provide pensions through pension plans that are administered through trusts, the measure of payroll should also be covered payroll.

An even more significant change could occur in the implementation of GASB Statement No. 85, which incorporates some of this language for postemployment benefits other than pensions reporting. Many OPEB plans that have contributions do not base the contributions on any measure of pay. A discussion of those provisions occurs later in this chapter.

Selection of Assumptions

Management of a plan may direct an actuary to financially engineer contributions to meet a budgetary challenge. For some governments and plans, this is almost routine. This engineering may result in an actuarial deviation from guidance in Actuarial Standards of Practice. GASB-82 emphasizes that actuaries cannot deviate from the requirements of GASB-67, GASB-68, and GASB-73 for financial reporting purposes (GASB-82, par. 7) [GASB Cod. Sec. P20.122, .161, P22.119, Pe5.134].

Employer-Paid Member Contributions

Perhaps the most important aspect of GASB-82 has to do with employer-paid member contributions as they are widespread and misunderstood. A government may need to terminate an employee, but to do so, has agreed with the employee to make their portion of pension contributions for a period of time. This may be allowed in law or in the plan provisions. However, the agreement made has an impact to the net pension liability of the government and of course financial reporting. It also may have an income tax impact for the employee depending upon the circumstances of the contributions. This issue was also extensively discussed in the AICPA's article *Emerging Pension Issues*.

GASB-82 summarizes the changes as follows:

- For the *plan*, if payments are made by the *employer* to satisfy contribution requirements that are supposed to be from the plan member/employee, those amounts should be classified as *plan member contributions* in the statement of changes of fiduciary net position and for the purposes of calculating the net pension liability in accordance with GASB-67.

- For the *employer*, for the purposes of applying GASB-68, including for the purposes of determining a cost-sharing employer's proportion, the amounts should be classified as employee contributions. An employer's expense and expenditures for those amounts should be recognized in the period for which the contribution is assessed and classified in the same manner as the employer classifies similar compensation other than pensions – such as salaries and wages or as fringe benefits (GASB-82, par. 8) [GASB Cod. Sec. 20.fn2, P21. fn2, P22.fn2, P24.fn2, Pe5.fn2, Pe6.fn2].

Internal Revenue Code Section 414(h)(2) Election

If an employer makes payments to satisfy employee contribution, this is known as a "pick up." GASB-82 requires a discussion of any pick-up provisions to be included as note disclosure, likely in the text regarding contributions.

The AICPA's article discusses the impact of Internal Revenue Code Section 414(h)(2), which is specific to state and local governments where contributions of employers are designated employee contributions, but the employer picks up the contributions. If there are "pick ups" in place, where the employer pays the employee's contributions and designates them as employer contributions, the IRS requires tests to be met so that the contributions are not taxed. These provisions are contained in IRS Revenue Ruling 2006-43 (*Government Pick-Up Plans; Employer Contributions; Income Tax; Prospective Application*).

The provisions are:

- Employing units must take formal action (such as through the issuance of a resolution by a City Council or other governing body) to provide that the contributions on behalf of a specific class of employees, although designated as employee contributions, will be paid by the employing unit in lieu of employee contributions.

- Participating employees, from the date of the *pick-up* and later, are not permitted to have a cash right or deferred election right with respect to the designated employee contributions. Participating employees must not be permitted to opt out of the *pick-up*, or to receive the contributed amounts directly instead of having them paid by the employing unit to the plan.

By not having a cash right, the employee may not draw on the funds that were not taxed to them. The employee cannot change this election once this is made.

PRACTICE POINT: Many governments may have knowingly or unknowingly made this election, or made in agreement with an employee or group of employees without knowing the IRS consequences. There may be very real tax implications for employees depending upon whether or not contributions were made pre-tax or post-tax. If contributions were made pre-tax, an election may have been made.

Furthermore, the employer may not have been involved with the election and it may have been made at the plan level. Or the plan may not have been involved and an election may have been made at an employer level. If an election was made at an employer level in a cost-sharing multiple-employer plan, this raises an issue of whether proportional shares were calculated properly.

To gather information, the plan should survey all member governments. The survey can (1) determine if the employer has made the election (or if they are making employer-paid member contributions without making the election) and (2) gather supporting information behind the contributions made since the first actuarial valuation in accordance with the provisions of GASB-67 and GASB-68.

Based on these provisions and GASB-82, the following potential impacts may occur to plan and employer reporting:

Alternatives	Plan Reporting in Accordance with GASB-67 or GASB-73, as amended by GASB-82	Employer Reporting in Accordance with GASB-68 or GASB-73, as amended by GASB-82
Employer-paid member contribution is recognized by the employer as salary expense (no IRC § 414(h)(2) election has been made).	• Contributions are *member/employee contributions* in statement of changes in fiduciary net position and for the purposes of calculating the net pension liability in accordance with GASB-67.	• Contributions are salary expense and excluded from pension expense.
Employer – paid member contribution is recognized by the employer as *other than salary expense* (IRC § 414(h)(2) election *has been made*).	• Contributions are *employer contributions* in statement of changes in fiduciary net position and for the purposes of calculating the net pension liability in accordance with GASB-67.	• Contributions are employer pension expense. If contributions are made subsequent to measurement period but before year-end, contributions would be included as part of deferred outflows of resources adjustment in accordance with GASB-68, as amended by GASB-71.

As discussed previously, the AICPA's schedules of Employer Allocations and Pension Amounts by Employer would have to change if employer paid member contributions are present.

Effect on Required Supplementary Information

The change from covered-employee payroll to covered payroll and the effect of employer-paid member contributions may necessitate a restatement of previously issued required supplementary information. The schedule of changes in the net pension liability (or proportionate share of net pension liability) and related ratios and the schedule of contributions all contain information that would be changed by GASB-82.

PRACTICE POINT: Example disclosures may be found in CCH's 2018 *Governmental GAAP Disclosure Manual*, Chapter 19.

Defined Contribution Reporting in Accordance with GASB-68 (and GASB-73)

Defined contribution reporting is far simpler than defined benefit reporting due to the nature of the plan. In financial statements prepared using the economic resources measurement focus and accrual basis of accounting, pension expense includes the amount of contributions or credits to employees' accounts that are defined by the benefit terms as attributable to employees' services in the period. This amount is reported net of forfeited amounts that are removed from employees' accounts. Amounts that are reallocated to the accounts of other employees should not be considered forfeited amounts for this purpose. A change in the pension liability is then recognized equal to the difference between amounts recognized as pension expense as calculated above and amounts paid by the employer to the pension plan (GASB-68, par. 123) [GASB Cod. Sec. P21.110].

For governmental funds, pension expenditures are the total of amounts paid by the employer to the plan and the change in the beginning and ending balances of amounts normally expected to be liquidated with expendable available financial resources. A fund liability is then declared for any unpaid contributions expected to be liquidated with expendable available financial resources. These liabilities are due and payable in accordance with the plan and legal requirements (GASB-68, par. 124) [GASB Cod. Sec. P21.111].

Also, due to the type of plan, the notes to the financial statements for plans where the employer contributes include the following:

- Name of the plan and identification of the administrator of the plan and the plan as a defined contribution plan.

- Brief description of the benefit terms (including vesting, forfeitures, and the policy related to the use of forfeited amounts) and establishment and amendment of benefit terms authority.

- The contribution (or crediting) rates (dollars or percentages) for employees, the employer, and nonemployer contributing entities, if any, and the authority under which those rates are established or may be amended.

- The pension expense, forfeitures reflected in pension expense, and the amount of the employer's liability outstanding at the end of the period (if any) (GASB-68, par. 126) [GASB Cod. Sec. P21.113].

457 Plans (and Similar)

Until the implementation of GASB-84 (*Fiduciary Activities*) (see **PRACTICE ALERT**), GASB-32 (*Accounting and Financial Reporting for Internal Revenue Code Section 457 Deferred Compensation Plans—a rescission of GASB Statement No. 2 and* *an amendment of GASB Statement No. 31*) contains the guidance for reporting 457 plan arrangements. A 457 plan that meets the criteria for a pension (and other employee benefit) trust fund should be reported in that fund type in the statements of fiduciary net position and changes in fiduciary net position. 403(b) plans are similar. Most investments are reported at fair value. If it is impractical to obtain investment valuation information from the plan administrator as of the reporting government's financial report date, the most recent report of the administrator should be used—for example, reports ending within the reporting government's fiscal year or shortly thereafter, adjusted for interim contributions and withdrawals (GASB-32, pars. 4–6) [GASB Cod. Secs. D25.101, I50.108, D25.fn1].

PRACTICE ALERT: A fiduciary activity that is *not a component unit* is present if the government controls the assets of the arrangement (described herein) *and* is any of the following in accordance with GASB-84:

- A pension plan that is administered through a trust in accordance with the provisions of GASB Statement No. 67 (*Financial Reporting for Pension Plans*) (see Chapter 22, "Pension and Other Postemployment Benefit Plans"),

- An other postemployment benefits (OPEB) plan administered through a trust in accordance with the provisions of GASB Statement No. 74 (*Financial Reporting for Postemployment Benefit Plans Other than Pension Plans*) (also see Chapter 22, "Pension and Other Postemployment Benefit Plans"), or

- A circumstance in which assets from entities that are *not* part of the reporting entity are accumulated for pensions as described in GASB Statement No. 73 (*Accounting and Financial Reporting for Pensions and Related Assets That Are Not within the Scope of GASB Statement 68, and Amendments to GASB Statements 67 and 68*) or OPEB as described in GASB-74.

If the activity is not a pension or OPEB plan or where assets are accumulated for pensions or OPEB as described, the activity is a fiduciary activity if all of the following criteria are met:

1. The assets associated with the activity are controlled by the government.

2. The assets associated with the activity are *not* derived either:

   a. Solely from the government's *own—source revenues,* or

   b. From government-mandated nonexchange transactions or voluntary nonexchange transactions with the exception of pass-through grants for which the government does *not* have administrative or direct financial involvement (see Chapter 17, "Revenues, Nonexchange and Exchange Transactions").

3. The assets associated with the activity have *one or more* of the following characteristics:

    a. The assets are (like many trusts or benefit plans):

        (1) Administered through a trust agreement or equivalent arrangement in which the government *itself* is not a beneficiary,

        (2) Dedicated to providing benefits to recipients in accordance with the benefit terms, and

        (3) Legally protected from the creditors of the government.

    b. The assets are for the benefit of individuals and the government does *not* have administrative involvement with the assets or direct financial involvement over the assets. In addition, the assets are *not* derived from the government's provision of goods or services to those individuals (situations where governments may serve as a custodian of funds).

    c. The assets are for the benefit of organizations or other governments that *are not* part of the financial reporting entity. In addition, the assets are *not* derived from the government's provisions of goods or services to those organizations or other governments (e.g., Internal Revenue Code Section 529 plans).

A government *controls* the assets of an activity if the government (a) holds the assets or (b) has the ability to direct the use, exchange or employment of the assets in a manner that provides benefits to the specified or intended recipients. Restrictions from legal or other external constraints that stipulate the assets can be used only for a specific purpose do not negate control.

Own-source revenues are revenues generated by the government itself like water and sewer charges, investment earnings, sales and income taxes, property taxes and other inflows.

Implementation of GASB-84 will be for periods beginning after December 15, 2018. For June 30th governments, implementation will begin for the period beginning on July 1, 2019. Earlier application is encouraged. Changes adopted to conform to the provisions of GASB-84 should be applied retroactively by restating financial statements, if practicable, for all prior periods presented. If restatement for prior periods is not practicable, the cumulative effect, if any, of applying GASB-84 should be reported as a restatement of beginning net position (or fund balance or fund net position, as applicable) for the earliest period restated. In the first period that this Statement is applied, the notes to the financial statements should disclose the nature of the restatement and its effect. Also, the reason for not restating prior periods presented should be disclosed. Upon implementation, GASB-32 will be repealed.

For 457 plans and similar, the major questions about implementation will be:

1. Is there a trust or equivalent arrangement present? Usually the answer is yes.

2. Are the assets controlled by the government? In most 457 plans, by virtue of using a third-party administrator where the government signs the contract, control may be present, answering point 1 above.

3. The assets of a 457 plan are not derived from the government's own source revenues. They are derived from participants in the plan. Therefore, the answer is yes to item 2(a) above.

4. In most 457 plans, the assets are within a trust where the government is not the beneficiary, the assets are used to fund benefits in accordance with the plan provisions and there is legal protection. Therefore, point 3(a) above is met.

Therefore, in all likelihood, a fiduciary activity exists unless the government does not have control of the assets. To do so, the employees would have control, including of contract provisions. If a fiduciary activity *does* exist, reporting would likely be in a pension or other postemployment benefit fund. In the case of multiple funds, a combining schedule should be used.

PRACTICE POINT: The effect of GASB-84's implementation may be pervasive for many governments. Agency fund activity will now be converted to custodial funds. Business-type activities that hold resources with a corresponding liability that should be reported in a custodial fund will report such activity that will be held three months or less as a liability and not a separate custodial fund. The presentation of a statement of fiduciary net position and a statement of changes in fiduciary net position will be clarified. The recognition of fiduciary component units are expected to also be more standardized.

OTHER POSTEMPLOYMENT BENEFITS: EMPLOYER REPORTING

In addition to pension benefits, postemployment benefits may include payments to retirees or their beneficiaries for life insurance benefits, health insurance benefits, and other pension-related benefits. The obligation related to these postemployment benefits in many cases is significant and may exceed the amount related to an employer's pension obligation.

In governmental funds, when a governmental employer's obligation related to postemployment benefits is long term, the liability should not be presented in a government fund but should be presented as part of the general liabilities in the entity's government-wide financial statements. On the other hand, if the obligation or a portion of the obligation is to be extinguished by using current expendable resources, the obligation (or portion of the obligation) should be classified as a liability of the fund responsible for the payment, and a current expenditure should be reflected in the fund's operating statement (NCGA-1, pars. 33 and 42) [GASB Cod. Secs. 1100.108, 1500.101–.102, C60.110].

Overview of GASB-74 and GASB-75

GASB-74 and GASB-75 largely conform to the OPEB plan and employer standards previously contained in GASB-43 and GASB-45, as well as the alternative measurement method in GASB-57 with the recent changes contained in GASB-67, GASB-68, GASB-71, and GASB-73.

GASB-74 (*Financial Reporting for Postemployment Benefits Other Than Pension Plans*) supersedes the requirements of GASB-43 (*Financial Reporting for Postem-*

ployment Benefit Plans Other Than Pension Plans), as amended, and GASB-57 (*OPEB Measurements by Agent Employers and Agent Multiple-Employer Plans*), for defined benefit OPEB plans. GASB-74 also supersedes the requirements of GASB-25 (*Financial Reporting for Defined Benefit Pension Plans and Note Disclosures for Defined Contribution Plans*), as amended, GASB-43, and GASB-50 (*Pension Disclosures*), for defined contribution OPEB plans. The accounting, financial reporting, and note disclosure provisions largely mirror those contained in GASB-67 as they would apply to OPEB plans.

GASB-75 (*Accounting and Financial Reporting for Postemployment Benefits Other Than Pensions*) replaces the requirements of GASB-45 (*Accounting and Financial Reporting by Employers for Postemployment Benefits Other Than Pensions*), as amended, and GASB-57 (*OPEB Measurements by Agent Employers and Agent Multiple-Employer Plans*), for OPEB that is provided to the employees of state and local governmental employers. The standard largely mirrors the provisions of GASB-68 and GASB-71 because they would apply to employers participating in OPEB plans. GASB-75 became effective for fiscal years beginning after June 15, 2017. Earlier application is encouraged.

GASB-74

Nearly every provision of GASB-67, as amended by GASB-73 is replicated wherever possible in the provisions of GASB-74, except of course GASB-74 updates the principles for postemployment benefits other than pensions (OPEB), whereas GASB-67 as amended focuses on pensions.

GASB-74 contains provisions of defined benefit and defined contribution OPEB plans that are administered through trusts and equivalent arrangements similarly to GASB-67. To have a trust or equivalent arrangement, the following must be present:

- Contributions from employers and nonemployer contributing entities to the OPEB plan and earnings on those contributions must be irrevocable. Refunds to an employer or nonemployer contributing entity of the nonvested portion of contributions that are forfeited by plan members in a defined contribution OPEB plan do not violate this requirement.

- OPEB plan assets are dedicated to providing OPEB to plan members in accordance with benefit terms. It is common that OPEB plan assets pay OPEB administrative costs or to refund plan member contributions consistent with benefit terms. The payment of administrative costs and refunds do not violate this criterion.

- Plan assets are legally protected from the creditors of employers, nonemployer contributing entities and the OPEB plan administrator. In a defined benefit OPEB plan, plan assets are also legally protected from the creditors of the individual plan members.

In addition, if a trust not be present, GASB-74 contains the standards primarily established in GASB-73 with regard to plan assets accumulated for the purposes of OPEB (GASB-74, par. 4) [GASB Cod. Sec. P53.101].

PRACTICE POINT: The provisions of GASB-74 apply in situations where the plan is presented in a stand-alone OPEB plan financial report as well as when OPEB plan information is including in the financial report of another government, such as a sponsor, typically as a fiduciary fund (GASB-74, par. 5) [GASB Cod. Sec. Po50.102]. The provisions of GASB-74 *do not* apply to defined benefit OPEB plans in which benefits are financed through an arrangement where premiums are paid to insurance company *while the employees are in active service* and the insurance company *unconditionally* obligates itself to pay the OPEB of employees as defined in the plan terms (otherwise known as an insured plan) (GASB-74, par. 8) [GASB Cod. Sec. Po50.104]. In many situations, OPEB is provided as an insured plan.

Types of OPEB and OPEB Plans

The most common form of OPEB has to do with postemployment healthcare benefits. These include, but are not limited to medical, dental, vision, hearing and other health-related benefits whether provided separately from a pension plan or included as part of a pension plan. It may also include death benefits, life insurance, disability and long-term care. There are also plans where legal services and other forms of postemployment benefits are made available to members.

OPEB does not include termination or sick leave benefits as discussed earlier in this chapter. However, the effects of either may be included in measures of OPEB liabilities as frequently, they may be used as contributions on the employees' behalf.

Defined benefit OPEB plans and defined contribution OPEB plans have similar definitions to pensions and similar structures. The most common OPEB plan is for a single employer. Multiple-employer OPEB plans may use an agent-multiple employer or a cost-sharing employer model. Again, trusts may or may not be used (GASB-74, pars. 10–18) [GASB Cod. Secs. P53.103–.106, Po50.105–.112, Po51.103–.106].

Required OPEB Plan Financial Statements

Similarly to the provisions of GASB-67, a defined benefit OPEB plan administered through a trust is required to present:

- A *Statement of Fiduciary Net Position* including assets, deferred outflows of resources, liabilities, deferred inflows of resources, and fiduciary net position; and

- A *Statement of Changes in Fiduciary Net Position* inclusive of additions to, deductions from and the net increase or decrease to fiduciary net position for the reporting period, similarly to and inclusive of similar information required by GASB-67 (GASB-74, par. 20) [GASB Cod. Sec. Po50.114].

The statement of fiduciary net position should exclude the effects of allocated insurance contracts. Allocated insurance contracts irrevocably transfer the responsibility for providing plan benefits to the insurer. All required payments to acquire the contracts have been made and it is unlikely that the employer, nonemployer contributing entities, or the OPEB plan will be required to make additional payments to satisfy benefits that were supposed to be included in the contract (GASB-74, par. 25) [GASB Cod. Sec. Po50.119].

Note Disclosure

Irrespective of the type of OPEB plan, note disclosures include the following:

- Description of the plan inclusive of the type of plan, number of employers, information on the GASB, number of plan members by type, the authority under which benefit terms are established or may be changed, whether the plan is closed to new entrants and contribution requirements.

- OPEB plan investments, describing investment policies, concentrations, the money-weighted rate of return, and similar items, in addition to the disclosures required by other GASB statements including GASB-3, GASB-40, and GASB-72.

- Details of receivables from investments, plan members, employers, or nonemployer contributing entities.

- Details of allocated insurance contracts that are excluded from plan assets.

- Details of reserves (GASB-74, par. 34).

Single employer and cost-sharing multiple-employer plan note disclosures include additional information on:

- The components of the liability to the employer(s) and noncontributing entities to plan members for benefits (the net OPEB liability or NOL).

- Significant assumptions and other inputs to measure the total OPEB liability (TOL) including applicable actuarial assumptions, especially the healthcare cost trend rates.

- A sensitivity analysis increasing and decreasing the healthcare cost trend rates by 1%.

- Information on the discount rate, calculated similarly to pensions.

PRACTICE POINT: Many OPEB plans do not contain a large amount of assets held in trust in comparison to their total OPEB liabilities. As such, the discount rate for OPEB plans will likely be much different than a similar pension plan.

- The date of the actuarial valuation and if roll forward procedures are used (GASB-74, par. 35) [GASB Cod. Secs. Po50.129, 2300.107].

Required Supplementary Information—Single and Cost-Sharing Multiple Employer OPEB Plans

Similar to pensions, 10-year schedules are required showing:

- Changes in the NOL, presenting the beginning and ending TOL balances, the OPEB plan's fiduciary net position and the NOL and the effects of additions and deductions during the year. For those plans using the alternative measurement method, amounts that arise from differences and changes in assumptions may be aggregated.

- A schedule of the TOL, the OPEB plan's fiduciary net position, the NOL and the percentage of the TOL that is fiduciary net position. This includes the *covered-employee payroll* and the NOL as a percentage of *covered-employee payroll*.

- If actuarially determined, statutorily or contractually required contributions are used, a 10-year schedule showing such contributions and contributions made by the employers or nonemployer contributing entities. As discussed earlier in this chapter, separately financed specific liabilities (in this case to the OPEB plan) are excluded. The differences between the contributions determined or required and the contributions made is compared to *covered-employee payroll* along with a percentage (GASB-74,par. 36) [GASB Cod. Sec. Po50.130].

Agent OPEB plans only have to present a 10-year schedule of the annual money-weighted rate of return by fiscal year (GASB-74, par. 37) [GASB Cod. Sec. Po50.131].

Notes to the required supplementary information are also required similarly to those in pension plans. The significant methods and assumptions to actuarially determined contributions (if any) are included. Also factors that significantly affected trends such as changes in benefits and assumptions should be included. Information about investment-related factors should be excluded under the amendments to GASB-67 and GASB-68 provided by GASB-73 (GASB-74, par. 38) [GASB Cod. Sec. Po50.132].

Measuring the OPEB Liability

The measurement of the TOL uses the same process as pensions with significant exceptions, including the use of the healthcare cost trend rate. The entry-age normal actuarial method must be used to attribute the actuarial present value of benefit payments to each plan member. The valuation must be made no more than 24 months earlier than the OPEB *plan's* most recent fiscal year end. (GASB-75, par. 28 allows an additional six months plus one day for the *employer's most recent fiscal year-end* in a similar manner to GASB-68.) Actuarial standards of practice must be used with deviations excluded (similarly to the provisions of GASB-82). The discount rate setting process is the same as for pensions (GASB-74, pars. 39–44) [GASB Cod. Secs. Po50.133–.138].

In addition to the healthcare cost trend rate, OPEB has a few important differences from pensions. Projected benefit payments should be based on claims costs or *age adjusted premiums approximating claims costs* in conjunction with actuarial standards of practice.

OBSERVATION: The provision of using age adjusted premiums approximating claims costs replaced the former *implicit rate subsidy* calculation contained in GASB-43 and GASB-45.

It is common to have legal or contractual caps on OPEB benefits. Caps may limit the plan or its members from a larger liability. These must be taken into consideration when calculating the TOL.

Furthermore, projected benefit payments should also include taxes or other assessment expected to be imposed on benefit payments using the rates in effect at the OPEB plan's year end, or if different rates have been approved by the assessing government to be applied in future periods, the rates approved by the assessing government associated with the periods when the assessments will be imposed (GASB-74, pars. 45–47) [GASB Cod. Secs. Po50.139–.141].

PRACTICE ALERT: The Patient Protection and Affordable Care Act (PL 111-148) (commonly known as "Obamacare") contained provisions that may affect the calculation of OPEB defined benefit liabilities for state and local governments. So-called "Cadillac Plans" are taxed using a 40% excise of premium amounts in excess of $27,500 for families and $10,200 for individuals beginning on January 1, 2020 for ages less than 55 or greater than 64. For ages between 55 and 65, the amounts are $11,850 for individuals and $30,950 for all other coverage types. It is unclear as of the date of publication the ultimate resolution of the uncertainties surrounding the future of the entire Act. Many governmental plans exceed these amounts and would be subject to taxation under the current provisions of the Act. Many actuaries are including the potential taxation in the calculation of the total OPEB liability. Depending upon plan provisions and medical claims cost inflation, the effect of such taxation on a net OPEB liability may be significant.

PRACTICE POINT: The provisions of GASB Technical Bulletin 2006-1, *Accounting and Financial Reporting by OPEB Plans for Payments from the Federal Government Pursuant to the Retiree Drug Subsidy Provisions of Medicare Part D*, as established by the Medicare Prescription Drug, Improvement, and Modernization Act of 2003, have largely been absorbed into GASB-74. The retiree drug subsidy (RDS) payments from the federal government to an employer as part of an OPEB plan administered as a trust are a voluntary nonexchange transaction between the federal government and the employer. The accounting for contributions by the employer does not change as a result of the RDS. Therefore, the net OPEB liability calculation made by the plan does not take into account the RDS payment to the employer. If the plan receives the RDS payment instead of the employer, in the statement of changes in plan fiduciary net position, the RDS payment is shown separately from the contributions from the employer(s). The total OPEB liability calculation also excludes the effect of the RDS payments. Such payments are shown separately in the RSI schedules. (GASBTB 2006-1, pars. 1, 4, 5, 9, and 10, as amended by GASB-74, pars. 3, 5, 20, 28, and 36) [GASB Cod. Sec. P050.601].

Measurement of the OPEB liability raises a number of concerns that are different than the measurement of the net pension liability in the following areas:

Actuarial Assumption	Pensions	OPEB
Long-term rate of return	A main driver of the discount rate in the calculation of the net pension liability.	Many OPEB plans are not funded (also known as pay-as-you-go) or only provide subsidies as pass-through transactions. Therefore, the long-term rate of return is not a large concern.
Mortality	This vital assumption determines the payment period of benefits.	This is not as vital as the liability is largely driven by claims. Furthermore, if the retiree is required to transfer to a Medicare plan at an eligible age, mortality is likely not an issue.
Salary inflation	Salary is a large driver of benefits and therefore, inflation is a factor.	Salary is not a driver of benefits and therefore, not a factor.
Retirement age or retirement rate	Similarly to salary level, payments may be based on age at retirement.	The rate of retirement is a major factor in terms of eligibility to receive benefits and the calculation of cash flow to determine the liability.
Cost of living adjustments (COLAs) and healthcare cost trends	COLAs are only applicable if offered by the plan.	The healthcare cost trend rate is the main driver of OPEB, even more so than other assumptions.
Plan options	Options chosen by participants are dependent upon law, regulations and plan provisions.	Many plans have multiple options of healthcare providers, limits, plans, deductibles and similar. Many plans only provide subsidies.
Utilization rate (rate that plan resources are used to pay benefits)	Applicable, but pension plans tend to have more assets to pay benefits, even if benefits adjust, than OPEB plans.	A very large factor as the older a beneficiary becomes, the more healthcare is needed.
Participation rate (the likelihood that a participant will retire based on plan provisions and for OPEB, select healthcare coverage)	Based on vesting requirements.	Retirees are often required to pay into the plan. Higher premiums may result in lower participation as the beneficiary has the option of paying for their own healthcare, including Medicare (if eligible).
Taxation	Not applicable.	In certain plans, a federal excise tax may be due in accordance with provisions of the Patient Protection and Affordable Care Act (see previous PRACTICE POINT).

Alternative Measurement Method

The former provisions of GASB-43 as well as GASB-57 (*OPEB Measurements by Agent Employers and Agent Multiple-Employer Plans*) are included in GASB-74 to address issues for small employers within agent plans that use the alternative measurement method to determine their liabilities as well as the frequency and timing of measurements by employers that are part of agent multiple-employer OPEB plans. GASB-74 continues the provisions, including when an agent multiple-employer plan that has just one member employer plan with fewer than 100 plan members to use the alternative measurement method, irrespective of the number of total plan members in the plan. All members of an agent multiple-employer OPEB plan should use a common valuation date and at a minimum frequency to satisfy the plan's financial reporting requirements.

PRACTICE POINT: It is the author's view that the alternative measurement method may be more difficult to use and to audit than to have an actuary prepare the information, except for the very smallest employers. Though it is U.S. GAAP, the information that is calculated may be very suspect. Luckily, for the very smallest employers, it is likely that the amounts calculated by the alternative measurement method may be immaterial.

Defined Contribution OPEB Plans

Similarly to pensions, defined contribution OPEB plans that are administered as trusts have limited note disclosure. The plan should be identified as a defined contribution plan, along with the authority under which the OPEB plan is established or amended. Classes of plan members and the number of plan members are also disclosed (GASB-74, par. 60) [GASB Cod. Sec. Po51.106].

PRACTICE POINT: The AICPA has released requirements related to a plan's reporting to employers. Similar auditing and reporting standards between the OPEB plan and employer(s) are required, including schedules of employer allocations and schedules of employer OPEB amounts for cost-sharing multiple employer plans and more stringent auditing provisions regarding census data and similar information. The CCH publication *Knowledge Based Audits™—State and Local Governments* contains information on the auditing provisions.

PRACTICE POINT: Many cost-sharing multiple-employer OPEB plans have a tremendous burden of providing a systematic and rational way to allocation of the OPEB employers' accounting elements to employers. In contrast to defined benefit pension plans, cost-sharing multiple-employer OPEB plans do not have as well-defined plan provisions and may not have contributions currently to afford an allocation based upon contributions. Therefore, an actuarial model based upon claims data may be the only solution for such cost-sharing multiple-employer OPEB plans, causing difficulty in auditing the allocations. Fortunately, it appears the preponderance of OPEB plans are single-employer plans.

GASB-75

GASB-75 (*Accounting and Financial Reporting for Postemployment Benefits Other Than Pensions*) has similar provisions to the pension standards contained in GASB-68, GASB-71, and GASB-73 (for non-trust provisions). As previously stated, most OPEB plans (and employers) are likely single-employer plans. As such, this section of the chapter focuses primarily on single employer provisions, noting any changes for agent-employer and cost-sharing employer situations. Since so many of the provisions are duplicative to GASB-68, GASB-71, and GASB-73, as well as the background information contained in GASB-75 that is largely from GASB-74, only the elements particular to employers are contained in this section.

Special Funding Situations

Similarly to pensions, special funding situations are circumstances when a nonemployer entity is *legally responsible* for providing financial support of OPEB of the employees of another entity by making contributions *directly to an OPEB plan*. Having a trust is not as important as making the contributions or making the payments when due. The amount of contributions or benefit payments must not be dependent upon events or circumstances unrelated to OPEB. Examples of dependency and nondependency are as follows (GASB-75, par. 18) [GASB Cod. Secs. P51.106, P52.108]:

Not Dependent— Special Funding Situation Likely	Dependent– Special Funding Situation Unlikely
• Nonemployer entity is required by statute to contribute a defined percentage of an employer's payroll directly to an OPEB plan that is administered through a trust.	• Nonemployer entity is required to make contributions to an OPEB plan that is administered through a trust based on a specified percentage of a given revenue source or equal to the amount by which the nonemployer entity's ending fund balance exceeds a defined threshold amount.
• Nonemployer entity is required to pay retiree health insurance premiums as the premiums come due.	• The amount of benefit payments required to be made by the nonemployer entity as OPEB comes due is limited by a given revenue source or by the amount by which the nonemployer entity's fund balance exceeds a defined threshold.
• Nonemployer entity is required by the terms of an OPEB plan to contribute directly to the OPEB plan a statutorily defined proportion of the employer's required contributions to the OPEB plan.	• Resources provided to the employer, regardless of the purpose for which those resources are provided.

Defined benefit and defined contribution OPEB may have special funding situations.

NOTE: The vast majority of GASB-75, as amended, has not been fully codified as of the date of publication. Wherever possible, codification references are inserted.

OPEB Expense, Deferred Outflows of Resources and Deferred Inflows of Resources Related to OPEB, and Support of Nonemployer Contributing Entities

For employers, changes in the Net OPEB Liability (NOL) should be recognized as OPEB expense in the current reporting period. Changes in the NOL include service costs determined using the entry age actuarial cost method, interest on the beginning TOL, the differences outlined below, net investment income and administrative expense.

Each of the following should be recognized in OPEB expense, beginning in the current reporting period, using a systematic and rational method over a closed period equal to *the average of the expected remaining service lives* of all employees that are provided with OPEB through the OPEB plan (active employees and inactive employees) determined as of the beginning of the measurement period (portions of which may be recognized as deferred outflows of resources or deferred inflows of resources):

- Differences between expected and actual experience with regard to economic and demographic factors in the measurement of TOL.
- Changes in assumptions about future economic or demographic factors.
- The difference between projected and actual earnings on OPEB plan investments should be recognized in OPEB expense using a systematic and rational method over a closed *five-year period*, beginning in the current reporting period. The amount not recognized in OPEB expense should be reported as deferred outflows of resources or deferred inflows of resources related to OPEB. Deferred outflows of resources and deferred inflows of resources arising from differences between projected and actual OPEB plan investment earnings in different measurement periods should be aggregated and reported as a net deferred outflow of resources related to OPEB or a net deferred inflow of resources related to OPEB.

Contributions to the OPEB plan from the employer should not be recognized in OPEB expense. Contributions to the OPEB plan from nonemployer contributing entities that are not in a special funding situation are recognized as revenue. Employer contributions after the measurement date, but before the employer's fiscal year-end are recognized as deferred outflows of resources (GASB-75, par. 43-44).

For governmental funds, the measurement of OPEB expenditures is similar to the measurement in pensions. OPEB expenditures are equal to the total of the amounts paid by the employer to the OPEB plan and the change between beginning and ending balances of amounts normally expected to be liquidated with expendable available financial resources (GASB-75, par. 46).

Note Disclosures—Single and Agent Employers

Note disclosures for OPEB information is similar to the information required by single and agent employers related to pensions. U.S. GAAP allows information to be aggregated wherever possible to avoid unnecessary duplication. However, OPEB information should not be included in the same footnote element as pension information. The total (aggregate for all OPEB, regardless of the type of OPEB plans through which the OPEB is provided and whether the OPEB plans are administered through a trust) of the employer's OPEB liabilities, net OPEB assets, deferred outflows of resources and deferred inflows of resources related to OPEB, and OPEB expense/expenditures for the period associated with defined benefit OPEB liabilities to employees, as applicable, should be disclosed if the total amounts are not otherwise identifiable from information presented in the financial statements, similarly to the provisions that have been in place since GASB-38. If note disclosures include the primary government and component units, the note disclosures should separately identify the primary government inclusive of blended component units from discretely presented component units (GASB-75, pars. 47–49).

For single and agent employers, note disclosures include:

- OPEB plan description, name and type of plan, the benefit terms, classes of employees covered, types of benefits, contribution information, key elements of OPEB formulas, changes in terms, COLAs, the number of employees covered by benefit terms and their classes, contribution requirements and the availability of a stand-alone report from the plan.

- Information about the NOL including assumptions and other inputs, healthcare cost trend rate, discount rate, mortality, experience studies and a sensitivity analysis of the healthcare cost trend rate as discussed previously.

- Information about the OPEB Plan's fiduciary net position (largely from the plan's financial statements).

- Changes in the NOL for the year (likely formatted as a table or schedule in the notes). If the employer has a special funding situation, the nonemployer's proportionate share information should be included in this section.

- Information on the measurement of the NOL including the actuarial valuation information, expense and similar information presented for pensions. As with pensions, separately financed specific liabilities to the OPEB plan are excluded from employer's contributions.

- Schedules showing the balances and amortization of deferred inflows and outflows of resources similarly to pensions (GASB-75, pars. 50–56).

Required Supplementary Information and Related Note Disclosure—Single and Agent Employers

Required supplementary information for single and agent employers for OPEB is similar to that of pensions. The schedules include 10 fiscal years of information on:

- Changes in the NOL. The schedule includes information in the notes as well as related ratios to *covered-employee payroll*. (See previous discussion on *covered-employee payroll* and discussion in GASB-82 and additional **PRACTICE ALERT** and section below on GASB-85.)

- If actuarially determined, statutorily or contractually required contributions are calculated, a schedule of such contributions and contributions made, excluding those associated with separately financed specific liabilities of the individual employer to the OPEB plan. Related ratios inclusive of *covered-employee payroll* are calculated (GASB-75, par. 57).

Note disclosure is similar to that of pensions. The disclosure is inclusive of significant methods and assumptions used in calculating the actuarially determined contributions, if any. Information should be presented about factors that significantly affect trends in the amounts reported (e.g., changes of benefit terms, changes in the size or composition of the population covered by the benefit terms, or the use of different assumptions). Information about investment-related factors that significantly affect trends in the amounts reported should be limited to those factors over which the OPEB plan or the participating governments have influence (e.g., changes in investment policies), which is similar to the changes made by GASB-73. Information about external, economic factors (e.g., changes in market prices) should not be presented. (The amounts presented for prior years should not be restated for the effects of changes—for example, changes of benefit terms or changes of assumptions—that occurred subsequent to the measurement date of that information.)

Cost-Sharing Employers

As discussed previously with regard to pensions, cost-sharing employers report a proportionate share of the OPEB accounting elements. This proportion will likely change from year to year, requiring a deferred outflow of resources or deferred inflow of resources to be declared and amortized over the remaining service life of employees. Other than the use of proportions, the measurement and valuation parameters are the same as single and agent-employers.

Note Disclosure—Cost-Sharing Employers

For cost-sharing employers, note disclosures include (focusing on the employer's proportionate share of the plan):

- OPEB plan description, name and type of plan, the benefit terms, contribution information, classes of employees covered, types of benefits, key elements of OPEB formulas, changes in terms, COLAs, the number of employees covered by benefit terms and their classes, contribution requirements and the availability of a stand-alone report from the plan.

- Information about the collective NOL including assumptions and other inputs, healthcare cost trend rate, discount rate, mortality, experience studies and a sensitivity analysis of the healthcare cost trend rate as discussed previously.

- Information about the OPEB Plan's fiduciary net position (largely from the plan's financial statements).

- Changes in the NOL for the year (likely formatted as a table or schedule in the notes). If the employer has a special funding situation, the nonemployer's proportionate share information should be included in this section.

- Information on the measurement of the NOL including the actuarial valuation information, expense and similar information presented for pensions. As with pensions, separately financed specific liabilities to the OPEB plan are excluded from employer's contributions.

- Schedules showing the balances and amortization of deferred inflows and outflows of resources similarly to pensions (GASB-75, pars. 89–96).

Required Supplementary Information and Related Note Disclosure—Cost-Sharing Employers

Required supplementary information for cost-sharing employers for OPEB is similar to that of pensions, again focusing on the proportionate share. The schedules include 10 fiscal years of information on:

- Changes in the NOL. The schedule includes information in the notes as well as related ratios to *covered-employee payroll*. (See previous discussion on *covered-employee payroll* and discussion in GASB-82 and additional information below in the **PRACTICE ALERT** on GASB-85.)

- If actuarially determined, statutorily or contractually required contributions are calculated, a schedule of such contributions and contributions made, excluding those associated with separately financed specific liabilities of the individual employer to the OPEB plan. Related ratios inclusive of *covered-employee payroll* are calculated (GASB-75, par. 98).

Note disclosure is similar to that of pensions and single and agent employers.

Employers that have a special funding situation or that are governmental nonemployer contributing entities in a special funding situation have similar calculations, note disclosure and required supplementary information.

OPEB Provided through OPEB Plans Not Administered through Trusts

Many employers provide OPEB outside of a trust for many reasons. The GASB has applied the provisions of GASB-73 as previously detailed to OPEB. The TOL, timing and frequency of actuarial valuations, assumptions and projection of benefit payments, OPEB expense calculation and other items are all the same as previously discussed with regard to OPEB and pensions.

A major difference is in the discount rate setting process. As no fiduciary net position is available without a trust, in this situation, the discount rate is a yield or index rate for 20-year tax-exempt general obligation municipal bonds with an average rating of AA/Aa or higher (or equivalent quality on another rating scale) (GASB-75, par. 155) [GASB Cod. Sec. P52.122].

Note Disclosure for OPEB Provided through OPEB Plans Not Administered through Trusts

Note disclosure is also very similar to the previously mentioned OPEB, dependent upon the type of plan. However, it must be noted that there are no assets accumulated in a trust. Each criterion for a trust previously described should be noted that the particular OPEB plan does not meet (GASB-75, pars. 162–169) [GASB Cod. Secs. P52.129–.136].

Required Supplementary Information and Notes for OPEB Provided through OPEB Plans Not Administered through Trusts

As there are no assets/fiduciary net position, the 10 year schedules for required supplementary information are limited. They include the 10 year schedule of changes in the TOL and related notes to the required schedule. No contribution schedule is necessary (GASB-75, pars. 170–171) [GASB Cod. Secs. P52.137–.138].

Insured Benefits

As with pensions, defined benefit OPEB plans in which benefits are financed through an arrangement whereby premiums are paid to an insurance company while employees are in active service, in return for which the insurance company unconditionally undertakes an obligation to pay the OPEB of those employees as defined in the OPEB plan terms, are insured plans, and the OPEB provided through those plans is classified as insured benefits (GASB-75, par. 11) [GASB Cod. Sec. P52.106].

The accounting and financial reporting for insured benefits is very simple. In the government-wide or business-type activity financial statements, an employer that provides OPEB through an insured plan should recognize OPEB expense equal to the amount of premiums or other payments required for the reporting period in accordance with the agreement with the insurance company for such OPEB and a change in the liability to the insurer equal to the difference between amounts recognized as OPEB expense and amounts paid by the employer to the insurer. For governmental funds, OPEB expenditures related to insured benefits should be recognized equal to the total of the amount of premiums paid or other payments made by the employer to the insurer and the change between the beginning and ending balances of amounts normally expected to be liquidated with expendable available financial resources. A liability for insured benefits is normally expected to be liquidated with expendable available financial resources to the extent that the payments are due and payable pursuant to legal requirements, including contractual arrangements (GASB-75, pars. 227–228).

Notes to the financial statements for insured benefits only require a brief description of the benefits, the fact that the obligations are insured by one or more insurance companies, details of retained obligations and the current-year OPEB expense/expenditure for the insured benefits.

Defined Contribution OPEB

Defined contribution OPEB is also very similar to defined contribution pension reporting. OPEB expense is equal to the amount of contributions or credits to employees' accounts that are defined by the benefit terms as attributable to employees' services in the period, net of forfeited amounts that are removed from the employees' accounts. Amounts that are reallocated to the accounts of other employees should not be considered forfeited amounts for this purpose.

Added to the expense is a change in the OPEB liability. If a trust is used, the difference between the amounts recognized as OPEB expense and the amounts paid is added to the expense. If no trust is used, the difference between amounts recognized as OPEB expense and amounts paid by the employer as the benefits come due during the fiscal year is added to expense.

Governmental fund reporting is similar to governmental fund reporting for pensions. OPEB expenditures equal the total of amounts paid by the employer for OPEB as the benefits come due and the change between the beginning and ending balances of amounts normally expected to be liquidated with expendable available financial resources. A liability for defined contribution OPEB is recognized to the extent the liability is normally expected to be liquidated with expendable available financial resources. A liability for defined contribution OPEB is normally expected to be liquidated with expendable available financial resources to the extent that contributions are due and payable pursuant to legal requirements, including contractual arrangements.

For multiple defined contribution OPEB plans, aggregated OPEB liabilities should be displayed separately from aggregated OPEB assets. The notes to financial statements about each defined contribution OPEB plan to which an employer is required to contribute include:

- The name of the OPEB plan, identification of the entity that administers the OPEB plan, and identification of the OPEB plan as a defined contribution OPEB plan.

- A brief description of the benefit terms (including terms, if any, related to vesting and forfeitures and the policy related to the use of forfeited amounts) and the authority under which benefit terms are established or may be amended.

- If the OPEB is provided through a defined contribution OPEB plan that is administered through a trust the contribution (or crediting) rates (in dollars or as a percentage of salary) for employees, the employer, and nonemployer contributing entities, if any, and the authority under which those rates are established or may be amended.

- If the OPEB is provided through a defined contribution OPEB plan that is not administered through a trust, disclosure includes the fact that there are no assets accumulated in a trust that meets the criteria. If OPEB is provided through an OPEB plan *that is* administered through a trust and that trust does not meet the criteria for a trust, each criterion in paragraph 4 that the trust does not meet should be disclosed.

- Identification of the authority under which requirements for the employer and nonemployer contributing entities, if any, to pay OPEB as the benefits come due are established or may be amended. Also, the amount paid by the employer for OPEB as the benefits came due during the reporting period, if not otherwise disclosed.

- The amount of OPEB expense recognized by the employer in the reporting period.

- The amount of forfeitures reflected in OPEB expense recognized by the employer in the reporting period.
- The amount of the employer's liability outstanding at the end of the period, if any (GASB-75, pars. 230–234) [GASB Cod. Secs. P51.109–.112].

Effect of GASB-85 on GASB-74 and GASB-75

PRACTICE ALERT: GASB-85 clarifies the provisions of GASB-74 and GASB-75 in six key elements:

1. The timing of the measurement of pension and OPEB liabilities and related expenditures recognized in governmental fund financial statements;

2. The recognition of on-behalf payments for pensions or OPEB on employer financial statements;

3. Presentation of payroll-related measures in required supplementary information for purposes of reporting by OPEB plans and employers that provide OPEB;

4. Classification of employer paid member contributions for OPEB;

5. Simplifications related to the alternative measurement method for OPEB; and

6. Accounting and financial reporting for OPEB provided through *certain* multiple-employer defined benefit OPEB plans.

Nearly all of these provisions originated in GASB-78 and GASB-82 and have been modified for the purposes of OPEB. GASB-85 became effective for fiscal years beginning after June 15, 2017. For the most part, changes required to implement GASB-85 are applied retroactively by restating beginning balances, if practicable for all prior periods presented.

For governments that are in the process of implementing GASB-75, it is important that the applicable provisions of GASB-85 are implemented at the same time.

GASB 85 was issued to resolve certain practice issues, six of which have impact on GASB-74 and GASB-75, with certain other impacts on GASB-68 and GASB-73 previously discussed in **PRACTICE POINTS**. For governmental funds, liabilities to employees for defined benefit pensions should be measured as of the end of the reporting period. All expenditures for defined benefit pensions (including amounts for payables to a pension plan, and amounts for costs incurred by the employer related to the administration of defined benefit pensions) should be measured for a reporting period. This appears to provide clarification as to whether there is a liability in a governmental fund (GASB-75, par. 46, as amended by GASB-85, par. 8) [GASB Cod. Sec. P50.142].

On-behalf payments are also addressed, which are common in OPEB arrangements. If they occur in a governmental fund, expenditures would be recognized for on-behalf payments for pensions equalling the total of (*a*) amounts paid during the reporting period by the nonemployer contributing entities to the pension plan or for benefits as they come due, and (*b*) the change between the nonemployer contributing entities' beginning and ending receivable balances of amounts normally expected to be liquidated with expendable available financial resources. Items (a) and (b) could include payables to a pension plan. Unless payments are not legally required for defined contribution pensions, revenue is recognized equal to the expenditures calculated in this step (GASB-24, pars. 3, 9, and 12, GASB-75, par. 25, as amended by GASB-85, pars. 9–12) [GASB Cod. Secs. N50.134–.138, P50.120–.121].

Payroll Measures in Required Supplementary Information—Plan Reporting

Similarly to the provisions of GASB-82, GASB-85 amends the measures of payroll. For single-employer and cost-sharing multiple employer defined benefit OPEB plans, the measure of payroll that is required to be used *for the plan* is covered payroll. Covered payroll is the payroll on which contributions to the OPEB plan are based (GASB-74, par. 36, as amended by GASB-85, par. 13) [GASB Cod. Sec. Po50.130].

PRACTICE POINT: Many OPEB arrangements that have contributions to a plan are *not* based on a measure of pay. Therefore, no measure of payroll should be presented as part of required supplementary information of the plan. The notes to the required supplementary information should explain this, if not already explained in the notes to the basic financial statements with regard to the OPEB arrangement.

Payroll Measures in Required Supplementary Information—Employer Reporting

Also similar to GASB-82, for employers that provide OPEB through OPEB plans that are administered through trusts, the measure of payroll to be presented in required supplementary information (and used in the ratios presented) have two possible alternatives:

- *Covered payroll* if the contributions to the OPEB plan are based on a measure of pay, or

- *Covered-employee payroll* if the contributions to the OPEB plan are *not* based on a measure of pay. Covered-employee payroll is the payroll of employees that are provided OPEB through the OPEB plan. In practice, *covered-employee payroll* may be the more prevalent measure (GASB-85, par. 14) [GASB Cod. Sec. P50.154].

Employer-Paid Member Contributions for OPEB

Employer-paid member contributions are common in OPEB arrangements. For the OPEB plan, such contributions are plan member contributions. However, for the employer, they are employee contributions. An employer's expense and expenditures for those such amounts are recognized in the period of contribution assessment and classified either as salaries or wages or fringe benefits (GASB-74, fn.2, as amended by GASB-85, par. 15) [GASB Cod. Sec. Po50.150].

PRACTICE POINT: See previous discussion on Internal Revenue Service Revenue Ruling 2006-43 and Internal Revenue Code Section 414(h)(2) for potential consequences of employer-paid member contributions.

Alternative Measurement Method Adjustment in GASB-85

GASB-85 contains various adjustments to the alternative measurement method. For plans, the adjustments entail the expected point in time at which plan members (employees) will exit from active service and with regard to turnover. For employers, a change in proportion may occur and a differential between contributions during the measurement period and the proportionate share of contributions required. Either may be required to be recognized as additional OPEB elements, as applicable (GASB-74, as amended by GASB-85, pars. 16–17) [GASB Cod. Sec. Po50.151].

OPEB Provided through Certain Multiple-Employer Defined Benefit OPEB Plans

Similarly to the provisions of GASB-78, described earlier in this chapter, OPEB may be provided by a plan that is not a governmental plan. The plans are typically managed by organized labor and may be organized as voluntary employee benefit associations (VEBAs) where employees of nongovernmental entities may join. These provisions apply when a cost-sharing multiple-employer defined benefit pension plan is in place for employees of state or local government employers that *is not* a state or local government OPEB plan. The plan is used to provide benefits to both employees of state or local government employers and to non-governmental employees and employers. Finally, the plan has no predominant state or local government employers.

Due to the nature of the employer and plan relationship, only OPEB expense is recognized equal to the employer's required contributions to the pension plan for the reporting period. A payable is reported for any unpaid contributions. Separate liabilities to the plan are handled similarly to the separately financed specific liabilities related to GASB-75 as described previously. OPEB expenditures in governmental funds are handled similarly to OPEB expense.

Due to the minimal information required to be generated by the plan, note disclosure and required supplementary information focuses on the contribution aspects, beyond the basic descriptions of the plan arrangements, benefits, contributions and availability of separate reports (GASB-75, pars. 4, 6, 9, as amended by GASB-85, pars. 18–25) [GASB Cod. Secs. P50.101, .103, .105, .111, .112].

QUESTIONS

1. According to GASB-47, examples of involuntary termination benefits usually do not include which of the following?

   a. Career counseling

   b. Continued access to health insurance through the employer's group plan

   c. Return to work at 60% of former hours

   d. Severance pay

2. GASB-16 applies the accrual concept in the context of financial reporting and disclosure except for of which of the following compensated absences:

   a. Vacation leave

   b. Sick leave

   c. Sabbatical leave

   d. Unpaid leave

3. Which type of pensions are where income or other benefits that the employee will receive at or after separation from employment are known by the benefit terms and they may be stated as a specified dollar amount or as an amount that is calculated based on one or more factors such as age, years of service, and compensation?

   a. Defined contribution plan

   b. Defined benefit plan

   c. Hybrid plan

   d. Cash balance plan

4. Which type of pensions have terms including, an individual account for each employee, the contributions that an employer is required to make (or the credits that it is required to provide) to an active employee's account are for periods in which that employee renders service; and there are provisions that the pensions an employee will receive will depend only on the contributions (or credits) to the employee's account, actual earnings on investments of those contributions (or credits), and the effects of forfeitures of contributions (or credits) made for other employees, as well as pension plan administrative costs, that are allocated to the employee's account?

   a. Defined contribution plan

   b. Defined benefit plan

   c. Hybrid plan

   d. Cash balance plan

5. An employer is in which type of defined benefit plan where plan assets are pooled for investment purposes but separate accounts are maintained for each individual employer so that each employer's share of the pooled assets is legally available to pay the benefits of only the employer's employees and no other employer in the plan?

   a. Hybrid plan.

   b. Single employer defined benefit plan.

   c. Agent multiple employer defined benefit plan.

   d. Cost sharing multiple employer defined benefit plan.

6. An employer is in which type of defined benefit plan where the pension obligations to the employees of more than one employer are pooled and plan assets can be used to pay the benefits of the employees *of any employer* that provides pensions through the pension plan?

   a. Hybrid plan.

   b. Single employer defined benefit plan.

   c. Agent multiple employer defined benefit plan.

   d. Cost sharing multiple employer defined benefit plan.

7. For a cost sharing employer, what is one of the major differences in the implementation of GASB-68 from what was the guidance in GASB-27?

   a. GASB-68 requires an ARC, but GASB-27 does not.

   b. GASB-68 requires the net pension liability, pension expense, deferred inflows of resources and deferred outflows of resources positions as well as expanded note disclosure and required supplementary information.

   c. GASB-68 requires statistical information from all employers.

   d. GASB-68 requires restatement back to the implementation date of GASB-27.

8. GASB-68's discount rate is based upon which of the following?

   a. The long term rate of return to the point at which there are assets no longer available to pay plan benefits. At that time, a AA bond index rate (or better) is used. The two cash flows are combined into a single discount rate that satisfies all cash flows to pay plan benefits.

   b. The risk free rate of return is used.

   c. The long term rate of return is used as established by the plan.

   d. LIBOR is used.

9. Circumstances in which a nonemployer entity (including potentially a for-profit or not-for-profit entity) is legally responsible for making contributions directly to a pension plan used to provide pensions to the employees of another entity or entities is an example of:

   a. A cost sharing multiple employer plan.

   b. A special funding situation.

   c. A hybrid plan.

   d. A defined contribution plan.

Case – Adapted from GASB-68

Facts: The State of Centennial reports a substantial liability, deferred outflows of resources and deferred inflows of resources, and expense as a result of its contributions to the Teachers' Pension Plan (TPP).

The following is information about TPP.

General Information about the Pension Plan

Plan description. TPP is a cost-sharing multiple-employer defined benefit pension plan administered by the Teachers Retirement System (TRS) that provides benefits for teaching-certified employees of participating school districts. Article 33 of the State of Centennial Statutes grants the authority to establish and amend the benefit terms to the TRS Board of Trustees (TRS Board). TRS issues a publicly available financial report that can be obtained at [Internet address].

Benefits provided. TPP provides retirement, disability, and death benefits. Retirement benefits are determined as 2.5% of the employee's final three-year average compensation times the employee's years of service. Employees with 10 years of continuous service are eligible to retire at age 60. Employees are eligible for service-related disability benefits regardless of length of service. Five years of service is required for non-service-related disability eligibility. Disability benefits are determined in the same manner as retirement benefits but are payable immediately without an actuarial reduction. Death benefits equal the employee's final full-year salary.

1. What type of activity would cause the State of Centennial to report the accounting elements indicated in the facts?

2. If during the year, instead of retirement benefit determined at as 2.5% of the employee's final three-year average compensation times the employee's years of service, they are now determined at 3% of the employee's final five-year average compensation times the employee's years of service, what type of adjustment and disclosure would occur?

3. What type of actuarial cost method must be used in accordance with GASB-68?

4. How are differences between the projected earnings on pension plan investments and actual experience with regard to those earnings amortized and reported?

5. What is contained in the Required Supplementary Information of the State about this activity?

ANSWERS

1. According to GASB-47, examples of involuntary termination benefits usually do not include which of the following?

   Answer – C: All others are examples of involuntary termination benefits.

2. GASB-16 applies the accrual concept in the context except for of which of the following compensated absences:

   Answer – D: If leave is unpaid, it is not accrued.

3. Which type of pensions are where income or other benefits that the employee will receive at or after separation from employment are known by the benefit terms and they may be stated as a specified dollar amount or as an amount that is calculated based on one or more factors such as age, years of service, and compensation?

   Answer – B: All others are not defined benefit arrangements.

4. Which type of pensions have terms including, an individual account for each employee, the contributions that an employer is required to make (or the credits that it is required to provide) to an active employee's account are for periods in which that employee renders service; and there are provisions that the pensions an employee will receive will depend only on the contributions (or credits) to the employee's account, actual earnings on investments of those contributions (or credits), and the effects of forfeitures of contributions (or credits) made for other employees, as well as pension plan administrative costs, that are allocated to the employee's account?

   Answer – A: This is the definition of a defined contribution plan. All others do not fit this definition.

5. An employer is in which type of defined benefit plan where plan assets are pooled for investment purposes but separate accounts are maintained for each individual employer so that each employer's share of the pooled assets is legally available to pay the benefits of only the employer's employees and no other employer in the plan?

   Answer – C: This is the definition of an agent multiple-employer plan. All others do not fit this definition.

6. An employer is in which type of defined benefit plan where the pension obligations to the employees of more than one employer are pooled and plan assets can be used to pay the benefits of the employees *of any employer* that provides pensions through the pension plan?

   Answer – D: This is the definition of a cost-sharing multiple employer plan. All others do not fit this definition.

7. For a cost sharing employer, what is one of the major differences in the implementation of GASB-68 from what was the guidance in GASB-27?

   Answer – B: All other answers are not contained in GASB-68, as amended.

8. GASB-68's discount rate is based upon which of the following?

   Answer – A: The answer is based upon the provisions of GASB-68. None of the other answers are U.S. GAAP.

9. Circumstances in which a nonemployer entity (including potentially a for-profit or not-for-profit entity) is legally responsible for making contributions directly to a pension plan used to provide pensions to the employees of another entity or entities is an example of:

   Answer – B: This meets the definition contained within GASB-68. All others are not U.S. GAAP.

Case – Adapted from GASB-68

Facts: The State of Centennial reports a substantial liability, deferred outflows of resources and deferred inflows of resources, and expense as a result of its contributions to the Teachers' Pension Plan (TPP).

The following is information about TPP.

General Information about the Pension Plan

Plan description. TPP is a cost-sharing multiple-employer defined benefit pension plan administered by the Teachers Retirement System (TRS) that provides benefits for teaching-certified employees of participating school districts. Article 33 of the State of Centennial Statutes grants the authority to establish and amend the benefit terms to the TRS Board of Trustees (TRS Board). TRS issues a publicly available financial report that can be obtained at [Internet address].

Benefits provided. TPP provides retirement, disability, and death benefits. Retirement benefits are determined as 2.5% of the employee's final three-year average compensation times the employee's years of service. Employees with 10 years of continuous service are eligible to retire at age 60. Employees are eligible for service-related disability benefits regardless of length of service. Five years of service is required for non-service-related disability eligibility. Disability benefits are determined in the same manner as retirement benefits but are payable immediately without an actuarial reduction. Death benefits equal the employee's final full-year salary.

1. What type of activity would cause the State of Centennial to report the accounting elements indicated in the facts?

   Answer – Special Funding Situation.

2. If during the year, instead of retirement benefits determined at as 2.5% of the employee's final three-year average compensation times the employee's years of service, they are now determined at 3% of the employee's final five-year average compensation times the employee's years of service, what type of adjustment and disclosure would occur?

   Answer – This is a change in benefit terms. For active employees, the amount of the change in the liability would be deferred and amortized over the estimated remaining service life of their employment. For inactive employees and retirees, the amount would be expensed immediately.

3. What type of actuarial cost method must be used in accordance with GASB-68?

   Answer – Entry Age Normal Actuarial Cost method.

4. How are differences between the projected earnings on pension plan investments and actual experience with regard to those earnings amortized and reported?

   Answer – Differences between the projected earnings on pension plan investments and actual experience with regard to those earnings are deferred and amortized over a closed five-year period. So for example, if earnings are projected to be 8% and they are 13%, then the 5% difference is divided by 5 and amortized to pension expense over five years. The next year the calculation is reperformed.

5. What is contained in the Required Supplementary Information of the State about this activity?

   Answer – The required supplementary information should be presented separately for each defined benefit pension plan for which the State recognizes a substantial proportion of the collective net pension liability. The information should be determined as of the measurement date of the collective net pension liability. Contributions should be determined as of the governmental nonemployer contributing entity's most recent fiscal year-end.

   Schedule A. A 10-year schedule presenting the following for each year:

   (1) The State's proportion (percentage) of the collective net pension liability.

   (2) The State's proportionate share (amount) of the collective net pension liability.

   (3) The pension plan's fiduciary net position as a percentage of the total pension liability.

   Schedule B. If the contribution requirements of the State are statutorily or contractually established, a 10-year schedule presenting the following for each year:

   (1) The State's statutorily or contractually required contribution. For purposes of this schedule, statutorily or contractually required contributions should exclude amounts, if any, to separately finance specific liabilities of the pension plan.

   (2) The amount of contributions recognized by the pension plan in relation to the State's statutorily or contractually required contribution. For purposes of this schedule, contributions should include only amounts recognized as additions to the pension plan's fiduciary net position during the State's fiscal year resulting from actual contributions and from contributions recognized by the pension plan as current receivables.

   (3) The difference between the State's statutorily or contractually required contribution and the amount of contributions recognized by the pension plan in relation to its statutorily or contractually required contribution.

Notes to required schedules would include information about factors that significantly affect trends in the amounts reported in the schedules (e.g., changes of benefit terms, changes in the size or composition of the population covered by the benefit terms, or the use of different assumptions) should be presented as notes to the schedules. (The amounts presented for prior years should not be restated for the effects of changes—for example, changes of benefit terms or changes of assumptions—that occurred subsequent to the measurement date of that information.)

CHAPTER 14
LEASES AND SERVICE CONCESSION ARRANGEMENTS

CONTENTS

INTRODUCTION

A governmental entity, like business enterprises, may enter into lease agreements in which it acquires property rights (lessee) through a lease agreement or is obligated to provide property rights (lessor) to another party. The accounting standards that are used to account for lease transactions vary to some degree depending on whether the liability is presented in a (1) governmental fund, (2) proprietary fund or fiduciary fund, or (3) the government-wide financial statements. Governmental accounting and reporting standards for lease agreements are based on the following pronouncements:

- National Council on Governmental Accounting (NCGA) Statement No. 5 (NCGA-5) (*Accounting and Financial Reporting Principles for Lease Agreements of State and Local Governments*), as amended by GASB-14, GASB-34, and GASB-38.

- GASB-13 (*Accounting for Operating Leases with Scheduled Rent Increases*), as amended by GASB-34 and GASB-65.

- GASB-62 (*Codification of Accounting and Financial Reporting Guidance Contained in Pre-November 30, 1989 FASB and AICPA Pronouncements*), pars. 211–271, as amended by GASB-63, GASB-65, and GASB-66 [GASB Cod. Sec. L20].

GASB-87 *Leases*—Introduction

PRACTICE ALERT: The GASB recently approved Statement No. 87, *Leases.* This wide-ranging change in practice will likely have a material effect on lease operations. Implementation is for periods beginning after December 15, 2019. For June 30th governments, implementation will occur on July 1, 2020. Due to the lengthy implementation period, information on GASB-87 is contained in Appendix A to this chapter so as not to confuse users. The 2020 edition of the *Governmental GAAP Guide* will move this information into the body of this chapter.

LESSEE ACCOUNTING

PRACTICE POINT: The remainder of this chapter is based on the current U.S. GAAP as of the date of publication. The elements herein do not reflect changes contained in GASB-87. Please see the **Appendix** to this chapter for those changes.

A lease agreement conveys property rights to the lessee for a specific period of time. Although actual title to the property is not transferred to the lessee, a lease agreement must be evaluated to determine whether the transaction should be treated as an in-substance purchase. From the lessee's perspective, the lease may be classified as a capital lease or as an operating lease.

Capital Leases

A lease agreement is classified as a capital lease (in-substance purchase) when substantially all of the risks and benefits of ownership are assumed by the lessee. A capital lease is, for the most part, viewed as an installment purchase of property rather than the rental of property (NCGA-5, par. 12).

GASB-62, par. 213, requires that a lease be capitalized if any one of the following four criteria is a characteristic of the lease transaction [GASB Cod. Sec. L20.105]:

Criterion #	Definition #
1.	The lease transfers ownership of the property to the lessee by the end of the lease term.
2.	The lease contains a bargain purchase option.
3.	The lease term is equal to 75% or more of the estimated economic life of the leased property.
4.	The present value of the minimum lease payments at the inception of the lease, excluding executory costs, equals at least 90% of the fair value of the leased property.

A bargain purchase option exists when the lessee can exercise a provision in the lease and buy the property sometime during the term of the lease at an amount substantially less than the estimated fair value of the property. Judgment must be used in determining whether the purchase option price will be a bargain price at the option date. If there is reasonable assurance at the inception of the lease that the purchase option will be exercised, the option is considered a bargain purchase option.

Lease payments include the minimum rental payments based on the term of the lease, exclusive of executory costs, such as payments for insurance and property taxes. Contingent rental payments are not included as part of the lease payments unless they are based on an existing index or rate, such as the prime interest rate. The lease payments include any residual value guaranteed by the lessee (or related party) at the end of the term of the lease. Also, any penalty payment that must be made because of a failure to renew or extend the lease is considered a lease payment.

When the lease contains a bargain purchase option, the minimum lease payments include only (1) the minimum rental payments over the term of the lease and (2) the bargain purchase option.

GASB-62, par. 270 [GASB Cod. Sec. L20.184], defines "lease term" as the fixed non-cancelable term of the lease plus the following periods, if applicable:

- Periods for which failure to renew the lease imposes a penalty on the lessee in an amount such that at the inception of the lease renewal appears to be reasonably assured;

- Periods covered by a bargain renewal option;

- Periods covered by ordinary renewal options during which a guarantee by the lessee of the lessor's debt related to the leased property is expected to be in effect;

- Periods covered by ordinary renewal options preceding the date as of which a bargain purchase is exercisable; and

- Periods that represent renewals or extensions of the lease at the lessor's option (however, the lease term cannot extend beyond the date of a bargain purchase option).

When determining the present value of the lease payments, the lessee should use its incremental borrowing rate. However, the lessee should use the lessor's implicit interest rate to determine the present value of the lease payments if:

1. The lessee can determine the lessor's implicit interest rate; and

2. The lessor's implicit interest rate is less than the lessee's incremental borrowing rate.

The lessee's incremental borrowing rate is the estimated interest rate the lessee would have had to pay if the leased property had been purchased by the lessee and financed over the period covered by the lease.

Operating Leases—Lessee

When a lease does not satisfy any one of the four capitalization criteria, the agreement is classified as an operating lease in accordance with GASB-62, par. 213 [GASB Cod. Sec. L20.105]. An operating lease does not require the capitalization of minimum lease payments. Therefore, neither an asset nor a liability is recorded at the inception of the lease in the government's financial statements for the lessee. For all operating leases, rental expense/expenditure is presented for each period for which a statement of revenues, expenditures, and changes in fund balance or a statement of revenues, expenses, and changes in net position or a statement of activities is presented. Disclosures should include separate amounts for minimum rentals, contingent rentals, and sublease rentals, if material (GASB-62, par. 223) [GASB Cod. Sec. L20.127].

Fiscal Funding Clauses

Non-cancelation is a precondition to the capitalization of a lease. In general, a lease subject to cancelation cannot be capitalized; however, if the lease is subject to cancelation based on the occurrence of a *remote* event, the lease may be capitalized if one of the four capitalization criteria is met (NCGA-5, pars. 18 and 20) [GASB Cod. Secs. L20.108–.109].

A lease with a governmental unit may contain a clause stating that the lease is cancelable if the governmental unit does not appropriate the funds necessary to make the required lease payments during the budgeting period. U.S. GAAP draws the following conclusion with respect to the existence of fiscal funding clauses in lease agreements:

> The existence of a fiscal funding clause in a lease agreement would necessitate an assessment of the likelihood of lease cancelation through exercise of the fiscal funding clause. If the likelihood of exercise of the fiscal funding clause is assessed as being remote, a lease agreement containing such a clause would be considered a non-cancelable lease; otherwise, the lease would be considered cancelable and thus classified as an operating lease.

LESSOR ACCOUNTING

When a governmental unit is the lessor in a lease agreement, the agreement must be reviewed to determine whether the transaction should be treated as an in-substance sale of the property. From the lessor's perspective, the lease may be classified as a sales-type lease, direct financing lease, leveraged lease, or an operating lease.

Sales-type leases are contracts that give rise to a potential gain (or loss) at the inception of the lease. A gain or loss is generated if the fair value of the leased property at the inception of the lease is greater or less than its carrying amount. Leases involving real estate have to meet certain criteria to be a sales-type lease. If the lessor is primarily engaged in financing operations (such as mortgage-financing authorities) sales-type leases are rare. Rather, direct financing leases are used. If a sales-type lease is renewed or extended, it is effectively converted to a direct financing lease, unless the renewal or extension is near the end of the original lease term.

Direct financing leases do not give rise to a potential gain or loss, because the cost and the fair value of the property are the same at the inception of the lease. If there is a renewal or extension, the carrying amount of the property at the end of the original lease term is likely different from its fair value. Similarly to above, this should not preclude the renewal or extension being classified as a direct financing lease (GASB-62, par. 212(b)) [GASB Cod. Sec. L20.104].

Leveraged leases involve three parties: a lessee, a long-term creditor, and a lessor (which may be known as an equity participant). The financing provided by the long-term creditor is nonrecourse to the credit position of the lessor, although the creditor may have recourse to the property being leased. The amount of the financing is sufficient to provide the lessor with leverage. The lessor's net investment (rentals receivable, net of applicable principal and interest and estimated residual value) may fluctuate throughout the lease (GASB-62, par. 265) [GASB Cod. Sec. L20.179].

Sales-Type Leases

In a sales-type lease, the amount to be recorded as the gross investment in the lease by the lessor equals the:

- The minimum lease payments (net of executory costs including insurance, maintenance, and other items paid by the lessor) plus
- The *unguaranteed* value to the benefit of the lessor.

The difference between the gross investment in the lease in and the sum of the present values of the two components of the gross investment should be recorded as a liability. The discount rate to be used in determining the present values should be the interest rate implicit in the lease. The net investment in the lease should consist of the gross investment less the related liability. The liability should be recognized as revenue over the lease term so as to produce a constant periodic rate of return on the net investment in the lease. The net investment in the lease should be subject to the same considerations as other assets in classification as current or noncurrent assets in a classified statement of net position. Contingent rentals should be included in the flows statement when accruable.

The present value of the minimum lease payments, net of executory costs, computed at the interest rate implicit in the lease, should be recorded as the sales price. The cost or carrying amount, if different, of the leased property, plus any initial direct costs, less the present value of the unguaranteed residual value accruing to the benefit of the lessor, computed at the interest rate implicit in the lease, should be recognized in the same period.

The estimated residual value should be reviewed at least annually. If the review results in a lower estimate than had been previously established, a determination should be made as to whether the decline in estimated residual value is other than temporary. If the decline in estimated residual value is judged to be other than temporary, the accounting for the transaction should be revised using the changed estimate. The resulting reduction in the net investment should be recognized as a loss in the period in which the estimate is changed. An upward adjustment of the estimated residual value should not be made.

In leases containing a residual guarantee or a penalty for failure to renew the lease at the end of the lease term, following the method of amortization described above will result in a balance of minimum lease payments receivable at the end of the lease term that will equal the amount of the guarantee or penalty at that date. In the event that a renewal or other extension of the lease term renders the guarantee or penalty inoperative, the existing balances of the minimum lease payments receivable and the estimated residual value should be adjusted for the changes resulting from the revised agreement (subject to the limitation on the residual value), and the net adjustment should be charged or credited to a liability (GASB-62, pars. 224a–e) [GASB Cod. Sec. L20.128].

Direct Financing Leases

A direct financing lease transfers substantially all of the risks and benefits of ownership from the lessor to the lessee. In a direct financing lease, the lessor finances the in-substance purchase of the property by the lessee (NCGA-5, par. 15) [GASB Cod. Sec. L20.131].

GASB-62 requires that a lease be classified as a direct financing lease (1) when any one of the four capitalization criteria used to define a capital lease for the lessee is met and (2) when both of the following criteria are satisfied (GASB-62, par. 214) [GASB Cod. Sec. L20.106]:

- Collectability of the minimum lease payments is reasonably predictable.
- No important uncertainties surround the amount of the unreimbursable costs yet to be incurred by the lessor under the lease.

Minimum lease payments are considered collectible even though it may be necessary to estimate them based on past experience with uncollectible amounts from specific groupings of similar receivables.

An important uncertainty with respect to unreimbursed future costs is an indication that the risks of ownership have not been transferred to the lessee. For example, if the lessor guarantees to replace obsolete property, the lease should not be treated as a direct financing lease. On the other hand, if the lessor is responsible for executory costs that may vary in future periods, this uncertainty alone does not preclude classifying the lease as a direct financing lease.

The lessor's minimum lease payments are the same as the lessee's minimum lease payments plus any (1) residual values or (2) rental payments guaranteed by a third-party not related to the lessor or lessee. In determining the present value of the minimum lease payments, the lessor should use its implicit interest rate. GASB-62, par. 271 [GASB Cod. Sec. L20.510], defines "interest rate implicit in the lease" as follows:

> The discount rate that, when applied to (1) the minimum lease payments, excluding that portion of the payments representing executory costs to be paid by the lessor, together with any gain thereon, and (2) the unguaranteed residual value accruing to the benefit of the lessor, causes the aggregate present value at the beginning of the lease term to be equal to the fair value of the leased property to the lessor at the inception of the lease, minus any investment tax credit retained by and expected to be realized by the lessor. (This definition does not necessarily include all factors that a lessor might recognize in determining the lessor's rate of return.)

For the lessor, direct financing leases should be accounted for as follows:

- The sum of the minimum lease payments, executory costs (if any) to be paid by the lessor, and any gain plus the unguaranteed residual value accruing to the benefit of the *lessor* would be the gross investment in the lease at inception.
- The difference between the gross investment in the lease and the cost or carrying amount of the leased property is recorded as a liability by the lessor (GASB-62, par. 226) [GASB Cod. Sec. L20.130].

Operating Leases—Lessor

When a lease agreement does not satisfy at least one of the four criteria (common to both lessee and lessor accounting) and both of the criteria for a lessor (collectability and no uncertain reimbursable costs), the lease is classified as an operating lease. In an operating lease there is no simulated sale and the lessor simply records rent revenues as they become measurable and available. In addition, the leased property is not removed from the capital assets of the government. Any initial direct costs in an operating lease are recorded as an expense/expenditure by the lessor (GASB-62, par. 227, as amended by GASB-63, par. 8, GASB-65, par. 17, and GASB-66, par. 4) [GASB Cod. Sec. L20.132].

LEASES INVOLVING REAL ESTATE

Governments lease real estate as lessees or lessors. Some of these are complex transactions. Four categories of leases involving real estate are common: leases involving land only, leases involving buildings and land, leases involving equipment and real estate, and leases involving a part or parts of a building (GASB-62, par. 232) [GASB Cod. Sec. L20.140].

Land Leases

To be a capital lease involving *only land*, only one of the following criteria is needed:

1. The lease transfers ownership of the property to the lessee by the end of the lease term; or

2. The lease contains a bargain purchase option.

If neither of these is met, the lease of the land is an operating lease. If there is a transfer of ownership only and a gain (or loss) is present, then the lessor would classify the lease as a sales-type lease as previously discussed, as the economic substance of the transaction is a sale. If there is no gain or loss, then direct financing or leveraged lease accounting is used.

If there is a bargain purchase option and both collectability of the minimum lease payments is predictable and no important uncertainties surround the amount of unreimbursed costs yet to be incurred by the lessor, the lessor records the lease as a direct financing lease, leveraged lease or operating lease. Otherwise it is an operating lease. Finally, if ownership of the land is expected to the lessee if either the lease transfers ownership, or a bargain purchase is involved, then the asset recorded on the capital lease is not amortized (GASB-62, par. 233) [GASB Cod. Sec. L20.141].

Leases Involving Buildings and Land

Leases involving buildings and land may result in two separate transactions. For the lessee, if either a transfer of ownership or a bargain purchase is involved, the land and building should be separately capitalized. The following is an example of determining the values of a land and building:

A lease is signed involving a piece of land and a building on July 1, 20X9. The present value of the minimum lease payments on the 20 year lease is $1,234,000. Executory costs were $10,000. No gain on the lease was reported. An independent appraisal was done at signing. The fair value of the building on July 1, 20X9 was $2,000,000. The fair value of the land was $500,000.

Elements	Amounts and Allocations
Present Value of the Lease Payments	$1,234,000
Less: Executory Costs	$(10,000)
Less: Gain on sale	-
Net Adjustments	(10,000)
Net Present Value	$1,224,000

Elements	Amounts and Allocations		
Fair Value of Building at Date of Lease	2,000,000	80%	979,200
Fair Value of Land at Date of Lease	500,000	20%	244,800
Total Fair Value	$2,500,000	100%	$1,224,000

The building will be amortized similarly to other owned assets. The capitalized land would not be amortized as it will ultimately become the property of the lessee.

For the lessor, if the land gives rise to a gain or loss, it is a sales type lease. If there is no gain or loss and similarly to land, if collectability of the minimum lease payments is predictable and no important uncertainties surround the amount of unreimbursed costs yet to be incurred by the lessor, the lessor records the lease as a direct financing lease, leveraged lease, or operating lease. Otherwise it is an operating lease.

However, special provisions apply if there is neither a transfer of ownership nor a bargain purchase. If the fair value of the land is less than 25% of the total fair value of the property at the date of the lease, both the lessee and lessor consider the transaction as a single unit for the purposes of consideration whether the lease term is 75% or more of the estimated economic life of the leased property and consideration of whether the present value of the lease payments equals or exceeds 90% of the fair value of the leased property. For the lessee, if either of the percentages is met, the lessee would capitalize the land and building as a single unit and amortize over the life of the lease; otherwise, it is an operating lease as neither of the percentages are met. For the lessor, if either is met, it is a direct financing lease, leveraged lease or an operating lease. Otherwise, it is an operating lease.

If the fair value of the land is greater than 25% of the total fair value of the leased property, the land and the building is considered separately in considering the economic life or the present value of the lease payments.

Leases Involving Equipment and Real Estate

Leases often include equipment with real estate. If this occurs, the portion of the minimum lease payments applicable to the equipment should be estimated. Consideration of each of the criteria for capital leasing would then be made on the equipment separately from the real estate.

Leases Involving Only Part or Parts of a Building

Leases often occur of parts of a building, including single floors or parts of a floor. Usually the fair value of the leased portion may not be determinable. If it is determinable, then the allocation method discussed in the previous section on leases of land and buildings would be used. To determine the value, an appraisal may be done. This should be done if a capital lease maybe present. However, the smaller the portion of a building, the less meaningful an appraisal may be.

If the value is determinable, the lessee will calculate the value using the allocation method discussed in the previous section. If it is not determinable, then if the fair value of the asset is more than 25% of the total fair value of the property at the date of the lease, it is capitalized. For the lessor, it is an operating lease. This is a common scenario in airports with a further factor of the gate operations being highly regulated by the federal aviation administration (GASB-62, pars. 236–238) [GASB Cod. Secs. L20.144–.146].

OPERATING LEASES WITH SCHEDULED RENT INCREASES

Governmental entities may enter into operating lease agreements that include scheduled rent increases. Although the FASB has addressed the accounting for operating leases with scheduled rent increases, the GASB concluded that the FASB guidance was inappropriate for governmental entities and therefore issued GASB-13.

The reporting standards established by GASB-13 apply to all governmental units, including state and local governments, public benefit corporations and authorities, public employee retirement systems, and governmental utilities, hospitals, colleges, and universities (GASB-13, par. 4) [GASB Cod. Sec. L20.121].

Measurement and Recognition Criteria

An operating lease contract may include scheduled rent increases. For example, the prescribed rental payments may be $50,000 per year for the first three years and $70,000 per year for the final two years of the contract. If the rental increases are considered to be systematic and rational, rental expenditure/expense (for the lessee) or rental revenue (for the lessor) should be recognized in accordance with the operating lease contract. Thus, in the previous example, the amounts recognized would be $50,000 in each of the first three years and $70,000 in the last two years of the lease contract.

What constitutes "systematic and rational" is a matter of judgment. Similarly to other GASB pronouncements, although the GASB does not attempt to provide a general definition of systematic and rational, the following examples are offered as illustrations (GASB-13, par. 5) [GASB Cod. Sec. L20.122]:

- Scheduled rent increases are established to reflect the anticipated increase in the value of the property rented or the expected cost increases caused by inflation.

- Lease payments are structured to reflect the time pattern of the availability of the property to the lessee (such as the anticipated increase in the use of the property in later periods or the increase in the amount of property available to the lessee in later periods).

Although GASB-13 establishes the basic standard that an operating lease with scheduled rent increases should be measured consistent with the terms of the lease contract, there is an exception. This exception arises when lease payments for a year(s) are considered artificially low in relationship to other lease payments that must be made during the course of the lease agreement. Although "artificially low" is not defined in GASB-13, the term implies that the lessee is making payments during a particular time period that are substantially less than the rental value of the property being leased. GASB-13 provides the following examples as illustrations of artificially low lease payments:

- The lessor reduces or eliminates lease payments for a period of time based on the strategy that subsequent lease payments are not equal to the rental value of the property and the transaction is in effect a financial arrangement between the two parties (e.g., the lessor may require no lease payments for the first year but the remaining lease payments are increased accordingly to allow for the repayment of the loan to the lessee and an interest factor related to the loan).

- The lessor reduces or eliminates lease payments during the first part of the lease agreement to entice the lessee to enter into the lease agreement.

When an operating lease with scheduled rent increases is evaluated as having artificially low payments in a particular year(s), the rental expenditure/expense (for the lessee) and rental income (for the lessor) should be measured using either one of the following methods (GASB-13, par. 6) [GASB Cod. Secs. L20.123, .133]:

- The straight-line method; or
- The estimated fair rental method.

Under the straight-line method of accounting for operating leases with scheduled rent increases, the periodic rental expenditure/expense and rental revenue are equal to the total lease payments divided by the number of periods covered by the agreement. During the periods when lease payments are not equal to the amount of rental expenditure/expense or rental revenue, an accrual account (either a payable or a receivable) should be used to record the transaction. For example, if the amount of the rental payment is $110,000 and the amount of the rental revenue is $120,000, the following entry should be made (GASB-13, par. 5) [GASB Cod. Sec. L20.122]:

	Debit	Credit
Cash	110,000	
Lease Payments Receivable	10,000	
Rental Revenue		120,000

OBSERVATION: A governmental fund would accrue the lease payment of $10,000 only if it is both measurable and available. If the revenue recognition criteria are not satisfied, the "revenue" should be reported as a deferred inflow of resources in accordance with GASB-65. Rental income would be recorded in proprietary funds, government-wide financial statements, and fiduciary funds without regard to the availability criterion.

Under the estimated fair rental method, the periodic rental expenditure/expense and rental revenue are recorded based on the estimated fair rental value of the property. The difference between the fair rental value of the property and the lease payments should be accounted for using the interest method, where interest (interest expense/expenditure or interest revenue) is recorded at a constant rate based on the amount of the outstanding accrued lease receivable or payable (GASB-13, par. 7) [GASB Cod. Secs. L20.124, .134].

If a reasonable estimate of the fair rental value of the leased property cannot be made, the straight-line method should be used to account for an operating lease with scheduled rent increases (GASB-13, par. 6) [GASB Cod. Secs. L20.123, .133].

GOVERNMENTAL FUNDS

Liabilities and assets of a long-term nature that are not specifically related to proprietary funds or fiduciary funds are not recorded in a governmental fund, but rather are reported in the governmental activities column of the government-wide financial statements.

Recording a Capital Lease by the Lessee

A state or local government lessee should record a capital lease at an amount equal to the present value of the minimum lease payments excluding that portion of the payments representing executory costs such as insurance and maintenance to be paid by the lessor, together with any gain on the lease; however, the amount recorded cannot exceed the fair value of the leased property. If the lease exceeds the fair value, then the amount recorded as both the asset and obligation is the fair value (GASB-62, par. 216) [GASB Cod. Secs. L20.108, .111].

As general capital assets do not represent current financial resources available for appropriation and expenditure, the property rights capitalized should not be reported in a governmental fund but instead should be reported in the entity's government-wide financial statements. Likewise, the long-term obligation created by the capitalized lease does not require the use of current financial resources, and therefore should be reported only in the government-wide financial statements. In addition, NCGA-5 states that when the capitalized lease represents the purchase or construction of general capital assets, the transaction should be shown as an expenditure and other financing sources in a governmental fund. It is not necessary to account for the capital lease in a separately created Debt Service Fund or Capital Projects Fund unless these funds are legally mandated to record capital lease transactions. A Debt Service Fund would be used when resources are being accumulated for payment of the lease payments in future periods (NCGA-5, pars. 13–14) [GASB Cod. Secs. L20.119, .120, 1800.128].

To illustrate the accounting for a capital lease, assume that Castle Rock County leases computer equipment from a large corporation for a five-year period, which is the economic life of the equipment. The lease is signed on December 19, 20X8. As a promotion, the corporation gives a discount of $152,009.50 on the equipment along with forgiveness of $42,550.77 of interest, for a total of $194,560.27. This $194,560.27 equates to the amount of interest that will be received over the life of the lease. Therefore, effectively, the lease is a zero interest lease to the lessor (rounded).

Starting on April 19, 20X9, five annual payments of $322,590.99 will be made. The governmental unit's incremental borrowing rate is 5.796%, and the fair value of the property is $1,612,956 at the inception of the lease before the discount. The present value of the minimum lease payments is also $1,612,956, as shown in the following illustration:

Elements	Rounded Amounts
Annual lease payments	$322,591
Present value of an annuity, interest rate is 5.796% and the number of periods is five	×4.52879
Subtotal	$1,460,946
Discount borne by the corporation at inception	152,010
Present value of minimum lease payments	$1,612,956

The capitalized lease would be recorded as follows in the General Fund at inception, assuming no separate Debt Service Fund or Capital Projects Fund is used to account for the transaction:

GENERAL FUND	Debit	Credit
Expenditures – Capital Outlay-Computer Equipment	$1,612,956	
Other Financing Sources – Capitalized Leases		$1,460,946
Other Financing Sources – Discount on Equipment		152,010
To record capital lease on computer equipment.		

Note: The capital assets ($1,612,596) would be reported in the governmental activities column of the government-wide financial statements. As a practical matter, the discount would likely be combined with the capitalized lease's other financing source. The interest expense of $42,550.77 would also likely be combined with the discount to reduce the principal.

Note: A net liability of $1,460,946 ($1,612,956 - $152,010) would be reported in the government activities column of the government-wide financial statements. As the interest forgiveness is also received, the additional $42,551 forgiven would reduce the $1,460,946 to $1,418,395.

In subsequent periods, the lease payments are recorded as expenditures of the governmental fund that makes the lease payment (assumed in this example to be the General Fund). If the expenditure is recorded by object class (as described in NCGA-1, par. 116) [GASB Cod. Sec. 1800.137], an amortization schedule must be prepared to distinguish the principal and interest portions of the lease payment. An amortization schedule based on the example discussed above is presented in the following illustration:

		Amortization Schedule		
Date	Lease Payment	Interest expenditure @5.796%	Principal	Balance of Lease at Beginning of Period
12/19/x8	-0-	-0-	-0-	$1,418,395.73
4/19/x9	$322,590.99	27,252.53	$295,338.46	1,123,057.27
4/19/y0	322,590.99	65,090.68	257,500.31	865,556.96
4/19/y1	322,590.99	50,166.36	272,424.63	593,132.33
4/19/y2	322,590.99	34,377.04	288,213.95	304,918.38
4/19/y3	322,590.99	17,672.61	304,918.38	-0-

The second lease payment (4/19/x9) would be recorded in the following manner:

	Debit	Credit
GENERAL FUND		
Expenditures—Capital Lease Principal	295,338.46	
Expenditures—Capital Lease Interest	27,252.53	
Cash		322,590.99
To record lease payment on 4/19/x9 for computer equipment.		

Note: The amount of the lease liability presented in the government-wide financial statements would be reduced by $295,338.46 and interest expense of $27,252.53 would also be reported. An additional accrual for interest would be made for the time period from 4/19/x9 to the fiscal year-end. In the General Fund, no amount would be due, because they are not paid from current financial resources unless they meet the definition of those resources set in policy or law.

If the lease payments are to be paid from a Debt Service Fund, any transfers from the General Fund to the Debt Service Fund are treated as transfers and not as expenditures of the General Fund (NCGA-5, pars. 13–14) [GASB Cod. Secs. L20.119–.120, 1800.128].

In general, contingent rental amounts are not used to determine minimum lease payments that are to be capitalized. For example, the following amounts are not part of minimum lease payments:

- Escalation of minimum lease payments because of increases in construction or acquisition cost of leased property;
- Escalation of minimum lease payments because of increases in some measure of cost or value during the construction or preconstruction period; and
- Lease payments that are based on future use of the property (such as number of machine hours).

When the lease payments are based on an existing index or rate (such as the consumer price index), the estimated future lease payments should be included in the minimum lease payments using the position of the index or rate at the inception of the lease. Subsequent changes in the rental payments are contingent rentals and should be accrued as the index or rate changes (GASB-62, par. 271) [GASB Cod. Sec. L20.504].

Increases or decreases in lease payments caused by the passage of time are not contingent rental payments and must be included as part of the minimum lease payments.

To illustrate the accounting for contingent rentals, assume a governmental unit signs a 10-year lease agreement for which annual payments are to be $300,000 plus or minus $5,000 for each percentage point that the average prime interest rate exceeds or is less than 6%. If the prime interest rate is 7% at the inception of the lease, the minimum lease payments to be capitalized are $305,000 ($300,000 + $5,000). If the actual prime interest rate is 10% during the second year of the lease, the additional $15,000 is treated as an expenditure of the second period, assuming the payment will be made from current available financial resources.

Recording a Direct Financing Lease by the Lessor

A governmental unit should normally record as a lease receivable (or gross investment) the total minimum lease payments plus the unguaranteed residual value of the leased property. NCGA-5 states that "only the portion of the lease receivable that represents revenue/other financing sources that are measurable and available" is to be reflected in the current statement of revenues and expenditures as revenue/other financing sources. "Measurable" refers to the ability to estimate the amount of the lease payment that will actually be collected from the lessee. "Available" means that the cash flow must be collected during the current accounting period or shortly after the end of the period but in time to pay liabilities of the current period (NCGA-5, par. 15) [GASB Cod. Sec. L20.131].

The carrying value of the leased property should be removed from the government-wide financial statements and the total lease payments receivable should be reported in both the governmental fund and the government-wide financial statements. In a direct financing lease, the difference between the total lease receivable and the carrying value of the leased property represents interest income to be received in the future, therefore not earned as of inception. The future interest income is amortized over the lease term using the effective interest method through the passage of time. The interest income is recognized only when the measurable and available criteria are satisfied (NCGA-5, par. 14) [GASB Cod. Secs. L20.120, 1800.128].

Accounting for a direct financing lease can be illustrated by referring to the earlier example used to demonstrate the accounting for a lessee's capital lease, but switching from a for-profit corporation to where the equipment is leased from another government. The total amount of the lease receivable recorded by the other government is as follows, assuming the payments under the lease will be available to the General Fund:

	Debit	Credit
GENERAL FUND		
Lease Payments Receivable ($322,591 × 5 years) (rounded)	1,612,956	
Deferred Inflows of Resources—Lease Principal Payments		1,612,956
To record direct financing lease to lessee for computer equipment.		

Due to the discount of the lease at inception, effectively the lease would be a zero interest lease as well from the governmental lessor to the lessee.

In the governmental fund, the amount of the last four lease payments ($322,591) (rounded) is part of the deferred inflow of resources because the payments are not available financial resources. As payments are collected, the receivable account is reduced and the appropriate revenue and other financing sources amounts are recognized. As each payment is received, the deferred inflow of resources is debited and revenue is credited.

If a state or local government executes several leases that are accounted for as direct financing leases, it may be necessary to provide an estimate for uncollectible payments. Because the governmental accounting model is based on the modified accrual basis, the use of a bad debts expense account is inappropriate; however, an allowance account can be established by reducing the amount of deferred revenue initially recognized when the direct financing lease was recorded. If a portion of the lease receivable has been recognized as earned at the end of the period based on the measurable and available criteria, revenue would be debited instead of deferred inflows of resources.

Costs directly related to the negotiation and consummation of the lease are referred to as initial direct costs and include expenditures such as legal fees, costs of credit investigations, and commissions. A provision for bad debts related to lease payments is not considered an initial direct cost. Initial direct costs should be recognized as expenditures when incurred, and an equal amount of unearned revenue should be recognized in the same period. For example, in the previous illustration, if the initial direct costs were $6,500, the following entries would be made (GASB-62, par. 226, as amended by GASB-63, par. 8) [GASB Cod. Sec. L20.130]:

	Debit	Credit
GENERAL FUND		
Expenditures—Initial Direct Cost of Leases	6,500	
Accounts Payable		6,500
To record payable for initial direct cost (recording fee) *of the direct financing lease of computer equipment.*		

The implicit interest rate used by the lessor should be computed after deducting the amount of initial direct costs. Thus, in the current example, the implicit interest rate would be less than 5.796%.

Contingent rentals are generally not included in the lessee's minimum lease payments. Contingent rentals are recognized by the lessor as revenue when they become measurable and available. Contingent rentals are disclosed separately from minimum rentals and sublease rentals for operating leases (if applicable) for each period for which a flows statement is presented. Within the notes, a general description of the leasing arrangement would include the basis on which contingent rentals are determined (NCGA-5, par. 27, GASB-62, par. 223c–d) [GASB Cod. Sec. L20.127].

Recording an Operating Lease by the Lessor

The lessor should include the leased property with or near capital assets in the statement of net position. The property should be depreciated following the lessor's normal depreciation policy, and in the statement of net position, the accumulated depreciation should be deducted from the investment in the leased property.

Rent should be reported as revenue over the lease term as it becomes receivable according to the provisions of the lease. However, if the rentals vary from a straight-line basis, the revenue should be recognized on a straight-line basis unless another systematic and rational basis is more representative of the time pattern in which use benefit from the leased property is diminished, in which case that basis should be used.

Initial direct costs should be deferred and allocated over the lease term in proportion to the recognition of rental revenue. If, at the inception of the lease, the fair value of the property in an operating lease involving real estate that would have been classified as a sales-type lease except that it did not meet the criterion that transfers ultimate ownership at the end of the lease and the lease is recorded at less than its cost or carrying amount, then a loss equal to that difference should be recognized at the inception of the lease (GASB-62, par. 227, as amended by GASB-63, par. 8, GASB-65, par. 17, and GASB-66, par. 4) [GASB Cod. Sec. L20.132].

To illustrate the accounting for an operating lease by a lessor in a governmental fund, assume that the lease agreement requires monthly rental payments of $5,000 and is classified as an operating lease. At the time the payment is due, the lease would be recorded as follows:

	Debit	Credit
GENERAL FUND		
Cash	5,000	
Revenue—Rent		5,000
To record rent received on operating lease.		

U.S. GAAP states that rent revenue receipts that vary in amount over the life of the lease should be recognized on a straight-line basis, unless "another systematic and rational basis is more representative of the time pattern in which use benefit from the leased property is diminished." If the rent payments are greater in the earlier life of the lease, part of the payment must be deferred. To illustrate, assume that a three-year lease agreement provides for rent payments of

$15,000, $13,000, and $8,000 over the three-year period. The operating lease would be accounted for in the following manner (GASB-13, par. 6) [GASB Cod. Sec. L20.133]:

	Debit	Credit
GENERAL FUND		
Year 1:		
Cash	15,000	
Revenue—Rent		12,000
Deferred Inflows of Resources—Rent		3,000
To record rent received on operating lease with scheduled rent increases, deferring a portion until future years.		
Year 2:		
Cash	13,000	
Revenue—Rent		12,000
Deferred Inflows of Resources—Rent		1,000
To record rent received on operating lease with scheduled rent increases, deferring a portion until future years.		
Year 3:		
Cash	8,000	
Deferred Inflows of Resources—Rent	4,000	
Revenue—Rent		12,000
To record rent received on operating lease in final year.		

In most instances, uneven lease payments are characterized by higher payments in the early part of the lease. However, if the payments in the early part of the lease are not smaller, the straight-line revenue recognition method cannot be used, because the accrued rent does not meet the availability criterion.

GASB-66 amended GASB-62's provisions on operating leases and purchases of loans or a group of loans. The change allowed the fair-value method of recognition.

Recording an Operating Lease by the Lessee

To illustrate the accounting for an operating lease by the lessee, assume that the lease agreement requires monthly rental payments of $5,000 and is classified as an operating lease. At the time the payment is due, the lease would be recorded as follows:

	Debit	*Credit*
GENERAL FUND		
Expenditures—Rent	5,000	
Accounts Payable		5,000
To record rent payable on operating lease (monthly prior to disbursement).		

PROPRIETARY FUNDS, FIDUCIARY FUNDS, AND THE GOVERNMENT-WIDE FINANCIAL STATEMENTS

The accrual basis of accounting and the economic resources measurement focus should be used to determine how lease transactions should be reported in government-wide financial statements. That is, lease transactions are reported in proprietary and fiduciary funds and the government-wide financial statements in a manner similar to how commercial enterprises report lease transactions, which is based on the guidance in NCGA-5 and in GASB-62.

Capital assets and the related obligations arising from capital lease transactions should be reported in proprietary and fiduciary funds, and the governmental entity's government-wide financial statements in the statement of net position (NCGA-5, pars. 16–17, GASB-13, pars. 4–7, GASB-34, pars. 69, 92, 106–107, GASB 62, pars. 216–221) [GASB Cod. Secs. L20.117–.118].

RELATED-PARTY LEASE TRANSACTIONS

Leases between related parties of government are common. Leases between related parties may be classified as a capital lease or an operating lease in accordance with the criteria discussed previously referencing GASB-62, pars. 213–214 [GASB Cod. Secs. L20.105–.106]. For the financial statements of the related parties, the accounting and classification in *both* parties should be symmetrical, except in certain circumstances.

Such a circumstance may be where it is clear that the terms and conditions of the lease have been significantly affected by the fact that the parties are related. For example, the discount rate is significantly different than market. In such cases, the economic substance of transaction will be very different from the legal form. As U.S. GAAP always sides with the economic substance of such transactions, the parties will need to record the lease differently. Disclosure will also be required of the nature and extent of the leasing transactions between the parties. (GASB-62, par. 239) [GASB Cod. Sec. L20.153].

In the circumstance where a related party lease is an investment in accordance with the definition of an investment in GASB-72 [GASB Cod. Sec. I50], and the investee related party is accounted for using the equity method, a gain or loss on the transaction is accounted for using the equity method (GASB-62, par. 240) [GASB Cod. Secs. I50.109–.116, .145, L20.154].

A governmental related party transaction may arise between a state or local government and a public authority. A public authority is created to raise funds through the issuance of debt, the proceeds of which will be used to purchase or construct fixed assets. These assets may be leased by the public authority to the state or local government with title passing to the governmental entity at the end of the lease term (NCGA-5, par. 22, as amended by GASB-34, par. 80, GASB-62, pars. 211–271) [GASB Cod. Sec. L20.147].

The accounting treatment of a lease between a state or local government and a public authority is dependent on whether the public authority is part of the overall governmental reporting entity. GASB-14 (*The Financial Reporting Entity*) defines the "reporting entity" as the primary government and all related component units (GASB-14). For a more thorough discussion of the financial reporting entity, see Chapter 4, "Governmental Financial Reporting Entity."

OBSERVATION: Related-party leases are a sign of a potential blended component unit in accordance with GASB-61, especially if the lease mirrors the amount of debt service due.

If the public authority is considered part of the primary government of the reporting entity, the lease classification criteria are not applied. The capital assets and long-term obligations arising from a capital lease transaction would not be reported by the primary government. Instead, the public authority's debt and assets should be reported as a part of the primary government's debt and assets. For example, the leased capital assets would be reported as capital assets in the government-wide statement of net position and related debt would be reported as a long-term liability in the government-wide statement of net position. The debt service activity of the public authority would be reported as a debt service activity of the primary government (NCGA-5, par. 24, GASB-14, par. 58, GASB-34, pars. 80 and 82, GASB-62, pars. 211–271, GASB-63, par. 8) [GASB Cod. Secs. L20.149–.150].

In the unlikely occurrence that a lease exists between a discretely presented component unit and a primary government where the lease does not mirror in any way debt service, then the lease is considered similarly to any other lease of the government. Otherwise, they are long-term contracts. Any receivables and payables between the entities should not be netted with other receivables and payables. Depending upon the substance of the transaction, a lease between the primary government and the public authority may be a related-party transaction that should also be disclosed in the notes to the basic financial statements.

On the other hand, when the public authority is *not* considered part of the overall reporting entity, GASB-13 and now the provisions of GASB-62 must be used to classify the lease. Specifically, the criteria are applied to determine if the state or local government should capitalize the lease and if the public authority should treat the lease as a direct financing lease (NCGA-5, par. 25) [GASB Cod. Sec. L20.151].

Finally, the nature and extent of the leasing agreement between a state or local government and a public authority should be disclosed in the financial statements of the parties involved in the lease (NCGA-5, par. 26, as amended by GASB-56, pars. 4–7, and GASB-62, par. 239) [GASB Cod. Sec. L20.152].

Sale—Leaseback Transactions

Sale-Leaseback transactions are when a property is sold by a government and then the government leases the property (or part of the property) back from the new owner. The new owner receives potential tax benefits from the transaction which are not available to the government. The government is potentially relieved of the burden of owning and maintaining the property.

If the lease meets the criteria for a capital lease, the selling government (the new lessee) will account for the lease portion as a capital lease. Otherwise, the selling government (the new lessee) will account for the lease portion as an operating lease.

The gain or loss on the sale of the property from the selling government is recorded as a deferred inflow of resources or deferred outflow of resources, respectively and amortized systematically and rationally in proportion to the recognition of the leased asset (likely using the effective interest method). If land is involved, the amortization is on a straight-line basis.

If the lease is an operating lease, the proportion is the related gross rental charged to expenses/expenditures over the lease term, unless:

1. The seller (new lessee) relinquishes the right to *substantially all* of the remaining use of the property. (*Substantially all* is used in GASB-62 to mean 90% or more of the present value of the rental). If this is the case, the leaseback is a separate transaction based on the respective terms and therefore not "netted." If the amount of rentals contained in the lease is unreasonable under market condition at inception (off-market lease), an amount is adjusted to deferred inflow of resources or deferred outflow of resources adjusting the gain or loss for the off-market terms. Or,

2. The seller retains more than a minor amount of the property, but less than substantially all, and realizes a gain on the sale in excess of the present value of the minimum lease payments over the lease term, if the lease is classified as an operating lease, *or* the recorded amount of the leased asset in a capital lease. In such a case, the gain on the sale is recognized as of the date of the sale. Or,

3. The fair value of the property at the time of the transaction is less than its undepreciated cost (at a bargain). In such a case, the loss is recognized immediately based on the difference between the undepreciated cost and fair value.

The buyer (new lessor) records the transaction as a purchase and a direct financing lease, or as an operating lease, dependent upon which of the criteria are met. (GASB-62, pars. 241–242, as amended by GASB-65, par. 18) [GASB Cod. Secs. L20.155–.157].

Real Estate Sale-Leaseback Transactions

Sale–leaseback transactions may involve real estate, real estate with equipment, plant, buildings, furniture and fixtures. In most cases, such transactions are packaged, no matter what the value of each of the individual components may be. Improvements may be involved in the transactions and in many cases, the seller-lessee may retain the underlying land. Finally, in some cases, the transaction may occur within the same reporting entity or with related parties, consummated at or near simultaneously, suggesting a package may exist (GASB-62, par. 244) [GASB Cod. Sec. L20.158].

Sale–leaseback accounting only is used by a seller government-lessee if it includes *all of the following*:

- A *normal* leaseback (described in the following paragraph),
- Payment terms and provisions that demonstrate the buyer–lessor's initial and continuing investment in the property (will operate, pay for and not neglect the property), and
- Terms and conditions that transfer all of the risks and rewards to the buyer–lessor.

A *normal* leaseback is a lessee–lessor relationship that exists when there is active use of the property by the seller government-lessee in exchange for rent. If a sublease exists, it is deemed to be a minor factor, as long as the present value is 10% or less than the fair value of the land sold. (GASB-62, pars. 245–246) [GASB Cod. Secs. L20.159–.160].

Terms of the Lease

The terms of the lease should be considered and compared to market rates that would be received from an independent party. If the terms are off-market, the seller government-lessee may have continuing involvement with the property. If continuing involvement is present, sale-leaseback accounting may be disqualified (GASB-62, par. 247) [GASB Cod. Sec. L20.161].

Continuing Involvement

If continuing involvement exists, the transaction may not qualify for a sale-leaseback, unless a normal leaseback is available. A disqualified sale-leaseback should be accounted for similarly to a financing. Continuing involvement may be evidenced by:

- The seller-lessee has an obligation or an option to repurchase the property or the buyer-lessor can compel the seller-lessee to repurchase the property, or
- The seller-lessee guarantees the buyer-lessor's investment or a return on that investment for a limited or extended period of time.

In cases where there may be guarantees and therefore no full transfer of the risks of ownership, continuing involvement may be evidenced by:

- The seller-lessee is required to pay the buyer-lessor at the end of the lease term for a decline in the fair value of the property below the estimated residual value on some basis other than excess wear and tear of the property levied on inspection of the property at the termination of the lease. Or,
- The seller-lessee provides nonrecourse financing to the buyer-lessor for any portion of the sales proceeds or provides recourse financing in which the only recourse is to the leased asset. Or,
- The seller-lessee is not relieved of the obligation under any existing debt related to the property. Or,

The seller-lessee provides collateral on behalf of the buyer-lessor other than the property directly involved in the sale-leaseback transaction, the seller-lessee or a related party to the seller-lessee guarantees the buyer-lessor's debt, or a related party to the seller-lessee guarantees a return of or on the buyer-lessor's investment. Or,

- The seller-lessee's rental payment is contingent on some predetermined or determinable level of future operations of the buyer-lessor.

There may be other evidences of continuing involvement by the seller-lessee, including sharing of any of the property's future appreciation in value or gains on a future sale. (GASB-62, pars. 248–251) [GASB Cod. Secs. L20.162–.165].

Sales-Leasebacks in Regulated Entities

Regulated entities such as airports, utilities, and similar should apply the provisions of regulated accounting as outlined in statutes. The regulations may adjust the timing of recognition of gains and losses, interest rates, and allowable costs. (GASB-62, pars. 252–254) [GASB Cod. Secs. L20.166–.168].

Subleases

Subleases are characterised by transactions when:

1. The leased property is then subsequently leased to a third party, with the original lease agreement intact.

2. A new lessee is substituted under the original lease agreement (stepping into the shoes). The new lessee is now primarily obligated to the lessor and the original lessee may or may not be still liable.

3. A new lessee is substituted under the original lease agreement and the original lease agreement is cancelled.

The original lessor does not change the accounting on the original lease, unless the lease is terminated (see previous discussion on terminations). If the original lease was a capital lease, the lessee removes the asset and the remaining obligation for the lease with a gain or loss recognized for the difference. If the original lessee remains liable, a loss contingency may be in place. Any consideration payments made or received should be included as part of the determination of gain or loss. If the original lease was an operating lease and the original lessee remains liable to the lessor, a loss contingency also may exist.

If the original lessee is *not* relieved of the primary obligation, the transaction is accounted for by the original lessee as follows:

- The classification provisions of a capital lease or operating lease should be reconsidered. If the new lease meets the criteria for a sales-type or direct financing lease, the unamortized balance of the asset is the cost of the leased property. Otherwise, the property is an operating lease. However, the original lessee still has a lease obligation to the lessor.

- An exception to capital lease accounting may be in place if circumstances surrounding the sublease suggest the sublease was part of the original transaction and the original lessee is merely an intermediary. In that case, the fair value of the leased property carries to the sublease.

- If the original lease was an operating lease, it continues to be so in the sublease.

Losses may be recognized by the original lessee who disposes of leased property or mitigates the cost of an existing lease commitment by subleasing the property, similarly to a debt defeasance. The new sub-lessee should classify the lease as an operating lease or a capital lease accordingly. (GASB-62, pars. 257–263) [GASB Cod. Secs. L20.171–.177].

Leveraged Leases

A leveraged lease meets all of the following characteristics:

- Except for when no gain or loss exists for a lessor in a direct financing lease or sales-type leases, most direct financing leases or sales-type leases are leveraged.

- It involves at least a lessee, a long-term creditor, and a lessor (the equity participant).

- The financing provided by the creditor is nonrecourse and sufficient to provide the lessor with substantial "leverage" in the transaction. And,

- The net investment declines during the early years once the investment has been completed and rises during the later years of the lease before its final elimination.

A lease not meeting this definition is a sales-type lease.

Lessors with leveraged leases record an investment in a leveraged lease, net of the recourse debt. The balances result in the initial and continuing investment in the leases with entries to rental receivable (net of the portion of the rental applicable to principal and interest on the debt) and the estimated residual value of the leased asset. Lessors compute the rate of return on the lease based on the cashflows and disbursements. If the rate is positive, revenue exists and the revenue is apportioned to the years of the lease using an implicit rate. The difference between the cash flow and the amount of revenue recognized increases or reduces the net investment balance.

If the rate is negative, a deficiency exists and a loss is recognized at inception. If the rates change during the lease and loss occurs, it is also recognized immediately. Assumptions should be reviewed at least annually to determine if a loss exists. (GASB-62, pars. 264–270, NCGA-5, par. 27) [GASB Cod. Secs. L20.178–.184].

SERVICE CONCESSION ARRANGEMENTS

Service Concession Arrangements (SCAs) are common, especially in situations where governments are willing to sacrifice temporary control of capital assets to monetize their value currently or over a long term. Infrastructure (toll roads or bridges), buildings and operations of government (recreation, utilities and information technology) are common areas for service concession arrangements. GASB-60 (*Accounting and Financial Reporting for Service Concession Arrangements*) established the financial reporting and accounting principles when capital assets are leased from one government to either an operator or another government in exchange for certain revenue streams or other contractual value. They are a type of public-private or public-public partnership. In an SCA, (1) the transferor government conveys to an operator the right and related obligation to provide services through the use of infrastructure or another public asset in exchange for significant consideration and (2) the operator collects and is compensated by fees from third parties. The transferor government reports the capital asset facility subject to an SCA as its capital asset, not the operator's, generally following existing measurement, recognition, and disclosure guidance for capital assets. Any new facilities constructed or acquired by the operator or improvements to existing facilities made by the operator are reported at fair value by the transferor. A liability is recognized, for the present value of significant contractual obligations to sacrifice financial resources imposed on the transferor government, along with a corresponding deferred inflow of resources. Revenue is recognized by the transferor government in a systematic and rational manner over the term of the arrangement. Therefore, up-front, lump-sum payments must be reported at present value, even though cash is received.

In the case of a third-party governmental operator, an intangible asset exists at cost for its right to access the facility and collect third-party fees in accordance with GASB-51. The governmental operator amortizes the intangible asset over the term of the arrangement in a systematic and rational manner. For existing facilities, a governmental operator's cost may be the amount of an up-front payment or the present value of installment payments. For new or improved facilities, a governmental operator's cost may be its cost of improving an existing facility or constructing or acquiring a new facility.

For a service concession arrangement to exist, four criteria must be met. These are similar in nature to the capital lease criteria:

1. The transferor government conveys to the operator the right and related obligation to provide public services through the use and operation of a capital asset in exchange for significant consideration, such as an up-front payment, installment payments, a new facility, or improvements to an existing facility.

2. The operator collects and is compensated by fees from third parties (usually the general public).

3. The transferor government determines or has the ability to modify or approve what services the operator is required to provide, to whom the operator is required to provide the services, and the prices or rates that can be charged for the services.

4. The transferor government is entitled to significant residual interest in the service utility of the facility at the end of the arrangement (GASB-60, par. 4) [GASB Cod. Sec. S30.101].

Any deviation from these four criteria results in a service management agreement, which is a contract rather than an SCA. SCAs are common in toll roads, water and sewer facilities, recreational facilities such as golf courses, stadiums, parking facilities, buildings, data centers, and they are being discussed for various other capital assets including parklands. SCAs are entered into because they can provide a medium to long-term budgetary solution to a current fiscal problem. Also, certain risks may be transferred to the operator depending on the terms and conditions of the contract. For example, in the case of a toll road SCA, the operator may be required to operate and maintain the road at a certain condition for the period of the SCA.

OBSERVATION: GASB Statement No. 72 (*Fair Value Measurement and Application*) modified paragraph 9 of GASB-60. For a newly purchased or constructed facility associated with an SCA, previously the facility was reported by the transferor government as a capital asset at fair value when placed in operation, along with any contractual obligations as liabilities and a deferred inflow of resources for the difference. Paragraph 79(c) of GASB-72 modifies the requirement to report at fair value to *acquisition value*. GASB-72 defines acquisition value as the price that would be paid to acquire an asset with equivalent service potential in an orderly market transaction at the acquisition date, *or* the amount at which a liability could be liquidated with the counterparty at the same date. In practice, the difference between the fair value and acquisition value of a capital asset involved in an SCA may not seem significant. However, U.S. GAAP requires the change.

If an SCA is transacted with an existing capital asset, the capital asset rules, including valuation, disclosure, impairment and depreciation, apply. Even if the operator improves on an asset involved in an SCA, the transferor government reports the improvement at fair value when it is placed in operation. However, if any embedded liabilities are contained within the SCA, the transferor should report the liability as well. Any differential would be a deferred inflow of resources that would reduce as the *book value* of the capital asset lowers, net of any services provided related to the liability. Liabilities related to an SCA may be first responder services, insurance, maintenance, or other ongoing items that are defined in the contract (GASB-60, pars. 8-12) [GASB Cod. Secs. S30.104-.108].

Care must be taken to understand the terms of the contract. For example, if the asset involved with the SCA is to be returned to the government in the same condition or better than at the date of transfer, then the capital asset for the transferor becomes a non-depreciable capital asset and therefore may be best reported on a separate line in the statement of net position and in the notes to the basic financial statements (GASB-60, par. 11) [GASB Cod. Sec. S30.107].

When an up-front payment, or installment payments are received related to an SCA, either must be reported at present value. Contractual liabilities are netted against the payments and any difference is recorded as deferred inflows of resources. Revenue is then recognized as the deferred inflow of resources is reduced (GASB-60, par. 12) [GASB Cod. Sec. S30.108].

LEASE AND SERVICE CONCESSION ARRANGEMENTS DISCLOSURE REQUIREMENTS

Disclosures: Capital Leases by Lessees

GASB-62, par. 223(a) [GASB Cod. Sec. L20.127(a)], requires the following information for capital leases to be disclosed in a state or local government's financial statements:

- The gross amount of assets recorded under capital leases as of the date of each set of financial statements presented by major classes according to nature or function. This information may be combined with the comparable information for owned assets.

- The total of minimum sublease rentals to be received in the future under non-cancelable subleases as of the date of the latest financial statements presented.

- Total contingent rentals actually incurred for each period for which a flows statement is presented.

- Assets recorded under capital leases and the accumulated amortization of those assets under capital leases. Unless the expense resulting from amortization of assets recorded under capital leases is included with depreciation expense and the fact that it is so included is disclosed, the amortization expense should be disclosed in the notes to the financial statements.

In addition to these disclosures, the financial statements should include a general description of the lease agreement, including items such as the existence of renewal or purchase options, and restrictions imposed by the lease agreement.

GASB-38 (*Certain Financial Statement Note Disclosures*) requires separate presentations for each of the five years following the date of the balance sheet and in five-year increments thereafter through the last year of the lease agreement (GASB-38, par. 11) [GASB Cod. Sec. L20.126]. The disclosure must identify the principal and interest components of the lease payments:

Fiscal Year Ending June 30,	Amount
20X3	$3,261,946
20X4	3,040,720
20X5	2,457,417
20X6	1,764,332
20X7	1,392,132
20X8–20Y2	937,833
Total minimum lease payments	12,854,380
Less: interest	(1,453,498)
Present value minimum lease payments	$11,400.882

Disclosures: Direct Financing Leases

When leasing is a significant part of the *lessor's* activities, the following information with respect to leases should be disclosed in the notes to financial statements. For *both* sales-type and direct financing leases, the lessor should disclose, the components of the net investment in sales-type and direct financing leases as of the date of each set of financial statements presented. This includes:

- Future minimum lease payments to be received, with separate deductions for (1) amounts representing executory costs, including any gain, included in the minimum lease payments and (2) the accumulated allowance for uncollectible minimum lease payments receivable; and
- The unguaranteed residual values accruing to the benefit of the lessor.

In direct financing leases, initial direct costs are also disclosed. Furthermore, disclosure would include any related liability as well as the future minimum lease payments to be received for each of the five succeeding fiscal years as of the date of the latest financial statements presented. The total contingent rentals that are to be included in the flows statement for each period are also to be presented (GASB-62, par. 231).

In addition, there should be a general description of the direct financing lease agreements.

Exhibit 14-1 is an example of a note to the financial statements describing a governmental unit's direct financing lease operations.

EXHIBIT 14-1
EXAMPLE NOTE DESCRIBING DIRECT FINANCING LEASE

The County's leasing operations consist exclusively of leasing various computer units and support equipment that were purchased in previous years but are no longer used. These leases are classified as direct financing leases and expire at various intervals over the next seven years.

The following lists the components of the net investment in direct financing leases as of June 30:

	20X8	20X7
Total minimum lease payments to be received	$450,000	$520,000
Less: Amounts representing estimated executory costs	(5,000)	(7,000)
Minimum lease payments receivable	445,000	513,000
Less: Allowance for uncollectible amounts	(40,000)	(43,000)
Net minimum lease payments receivable	405,000	470,000
Estimated residual values of leased property	15,000	20,000
Subtotal	420,000	490,000
Less: Income attributable to future periods	(105,000)	(125,000)
Net investment in direct financing leases	$315,000	$365,000

Minimum lease payments do not include contingent rentals which may be received as stipulated in the lease contracts. These contingent rental payments occur only if the use of the equipment exceeds a certain level of activity each year. Contingent rentals amounted to $12,000 in 20X8 and $18,000 in 20X7. At June 30, 20X8, minimum lease payments for each of the five succeeding fiscal years are as follows:

Year	Amount
20X9	$80,000
20Y0	80,000
20Y1	75,000
20Y2	70,000
20Y3	65,000
Total	$370,000

OBSERVATION: In most in-substance sale lease agreements, a governmental unit would account for the transaction as a direct financing lease because the governmental unit is seldom involved in a lease agreement that gives rise to a manufacturer's or dealer's profit. However, a sales-type lease may occur even when the lessor is not a manufacturer or dealer. U.S. GAAP notes that a sales-type lease arises when the lessor realizes a profit or loss on the lease transaction. This would occur when the fair value of the lease property at the inception of the lease is greater or less than the carrying value of the property. For a governmental unit, the accounting for a sales-type lease is essentially the same as the accounting for a direct financing lease because no operating profit or loss is recognized when the lease is recorded.

Disclosures: Operating Leases

When a governmental unit has operating leases as a lessor, there must be a disclosure in the financial statements describing the general characteristics of the lease agreements. In addition, the following disclosures must be made in accordance with NCGA-5, par. 27, as amended by GASB-62, par. 231 [GASB Cod. Sec. L20.139]:

- The cost and carrying amount, if different, of property on lease or held for leasing organized by major classes of property according to nature or function and the amount of accumulated depreciation in total as of the date of the latest balance sheet presented;

- Minimum future rentals on non-cancelable leases as of the date of the latest balance sheet presented, in the aggregate and for each of the five succeeding fiscal years; and

- Total contingent rentals included in income for each period for which an activity statement is presented.

PRACTICE POINT: Additional disclosure examples are included in CCH's *2018 Governmental GAAP Disclosure Manual*, Chapter 23.

QUESTIONS

1. To qualify as a capital lease under current U.S. GAAP, any one of the following conditions must be met except for:

   a. The lease transfers ownership of the property to the lessee by the end of the lease term.

   b. The lease is 12 months or less.

   c. The lease term is equal to 75% or more of the estimated economic life of the leased property.

   d. The present value of the minimum lease payments at the inception of the lease, excluding executory costs, equals at least 90% of the fair value of the leased property.

2. GASB-62 defines "lease term" as the fixed non-cancelable term of the lease plus the following periods, if applicable, except for:

   a. Periods for which failure to renew the lease imposes a penalty on the lessee in an amount such that at the inception of the lease renewal appears to be reasonably assured.

   b. Periods covered by ordinary renewal options during which a guarantee by the lessee of the lessor's debt related to the leased property is expected to be in effect.

   c. Periods from the beginning of the lease to the end of the first year of the lease.

   d. Periods that represent renewals or extensions of the lease at the lessor's option (however, the lease term cannot extend beyond the date of a bargain purchase option).

3. Which type of lease does not give rise to a potential gain or loss because the cost and the fair value of the property are the same at the inception of the lease?

   a. Direct financing lease.

   b. Sales type lease.

   c. Leveraged lease.

   d. Operating lease.

4. In accordance with GASB-65, in an operating lease, initial direct costs of the lease are:

   a. Recorded as part of a capital asset and amortized.

   b. Recorded as a deferred outflow of resources.

   c. Recorded as a deferred inflow of resources.

   d. Recorded as an expenditure/expense.

5. To meet the criteria for a service concession arrangement (SCA) in accordance with GASB-60, four criteria must be met, not including which of the following:

   a. The concessioneer must be a related party or part of the reporting entity of the transferor government.

   b. The transferor government conveys to the operator the right and related obligation to provide public services through the use and operation of a capital asset in exchange for significant consideration, such as an up-front payment, installment payments, a new facility, or improvements to an existing facility.

   c. The operator collects and is compensated by fees from third parties (usually the general public).

   d. The transferor government is entitled to significant residual interest in the service utility of the facility at the end of the arrangement

CASE

Castle Rock County agrees to enter into a lease for a computer system. The term of the non-cancelable lease is 10 years. The lease gives the County options to purchase the system at years 3, 5, 7, and 10 at a bargain purchase price. Annual payments are $2,191,201 (rounded) beginning one year after the lease signing, reflecting a $16 million loan (at fair value of the asset) and an interest rate of 6%.

1. What are the journal entries to reflect the lease agreement on the County's general fund statements and government-wide statements?

2. What are the entries to record the first year's lease payment and depreciation (assume that the asset depreciates with the same life of the lease [10 years])?

(Adapted from Michael H. Granof. 2007. *Government and Not-for-Profit Accounting, Concepts and Practices.* 4th ed. New York: Wiley, pp. 317–318, 328–329.)

ANSWERS

1. To qualify as a capital lease under current U.S. GAAP, any one of the following conditions must be met except for:

   Answer – B: All others are criteria of capital leases.

2. GASB-62 defines "lease term" as the fixed non-cancelable term of the lease plus the following periods, if applicable, except for:

   Answer – C: All others may be added to the fixed non-cancelable term of the lease.

3. Which type of lease does not give rise to a potential gain or loss because the cost and the fair value of the property are the same at the inception of the lease?

   Answer – A.

4. In accordance with GASB-65, in an operating lease, initial direct costs of the lease are:

   Answer – D.

5. To meet the criteria for a service concession arrangement (SCA) in accordance with GASB-60, four criteria must be met, not including which of the following:

   Answer – A: All others are part of the criteria for an SCA.

CASE

Castle Rock County agrees to enter into a lease for a computer system. The term of the non-cancelable lease is 10 years. The lease gives the County options to purchase the system at years 3, 5, 7, and 10 at a bargain purchase price. Annual payments are $2,191,201 (rounded) beginning one year after the lease signing reflecting a $16 million loan (at fair value of the asset) and an interest rate of 6%.

Answers:

1. General Fund:

	Debit	Credit
GENERAL FUND		
Expenditures—Capital assets expenditures (or capital outlay)	16,000,000	
Other financing sources—capital lease		16,000,000

Government - Wide:

	Debit	Credit
GOVERNMENT—WIDE		
Equipment under capital lease	16,000,000	
Capital lease obligations		16,000,000

3. During the first year, $960,000 represents interest ($16,000,000 $\times$ 6%). The remainder, $1,231,201 ($2,191,201 - $960,000), represents principal on the lease. Therefore, the journal entry is as follows in the General Fund:

	Debit	Credit
GENERAL FUND		
Expenditures—Capital Leases—Interest	960,000	
Expenditures—Capital Leases—Principal	1,231,201	
Cash		2,191,201

In the Government-Wide financial statements, the following occurs related to the payment on the lease:

	Debit	Credit
GOVERNMENT-WIDE		
Interest expense—capital leases	960,000	
Capital lease obligations	1,231,201	
Cash		2,191,201

To record depreciation on the leased asset:

	Debit	Credit
GOVERNMENT-WIDE		
Depreciation expense—equipment ($16,000,000 $\div$ 10)	1,600,000	
Accumulated depreciation—equipment		1,600,000

(Adapted from Michael H. Granof. 2007. *Government and Not-for-Profit Accounting, Concepts and Practices*. 4th ed. New York: Wiley, pp 317–318, 328–329.)

APPENDIX–GASB STATEMENT NO. 87 *(LEASES)*

PRACTICE ALERT: As the *Governmental GAAP Guide* went to press, the GASB approved Statement No. 87 (*Leases*). Upon implementation, a lease will be defined as a contract that conveys the right to use a nonfinancial asset (the underlying asset) for a period of time in an exchange or exchange-like transaction. "Exchange" and "exchange-like" transactions have the same definitions as presented in GASB Statement No. 33 (*Accounting and Financial Reporting for Nonexchange Transactions*). Examples of nonfinancial assets include buildings, land, vehicles, and equipment, as defined in GASB-72. Any contract that meets this definition would be accounted for under the updated guidance, unless specifically excluded. The broad approach to including any contract may update the accounting and financial reporting for contracts not specifically labeled leases, but in substance are leases.

Many paragraphs of existing GASB standards will be either modified or superseded upon implementation, including but not limited to: NCGA-1, NCGA-5, NCGAI-1, GASBI-6, portions of GASB-14, GASB-34, GASB-37, GASB-38, GASB-42, GASB-44, GASB-51, GASB-58, GASB-62, GASB-65 and various questions in *Implementation Guide 2015-1*.

Exclusions from GASB-87

GASB-87 specifically excludes the following types of assets:

- Lease contracts for intangible assets (including lease contracts concerning the rights to explore for or to exploit natural resources such as oil, gas, etc.), licensing contracts (most notably computer software), and other than sublease contracts for intangible right-to-use lease assets;

- Leases of biological assets;

- Leases where the underlying asset in a lease meets the definition of an investment in accordance with GASB-72;

- Contracts that meet the definition of a service concession arrangement; and

- Leases in which the underlying asset is financed with outstanding conduit debt, unless both the underlying asset and the conduit debt are reported by the lessor.

Certain regulated leases have limited treatment, most notably aviation leases between airports and airlines that are regulated by the U.S. Department of Transportation. The concessions at airports that do not include the airlines are subject to the provisions of GASB-87.

Lease Term

GASB-87 defines the lease term to be defined as the period of time during which a lessee has a noncancellable right to use an underlying asset, plus the following periods of time, if applicable, covered by a lessee's option to:

- Extend the lease if it is reasonably certain, based on all relevant factors, that the lessee will exercise that option; or

- Terminate the lease if it is reasonably certain, based on all relevant factors, that the lessee will not exercise that option.

All relevant factors need to be considered to determine the likelihood that the lessee will exercise an option to extend the lease. These are embedded in the contract or may be dependent upon the asset, the market for similar property, or government-specific reasons. The factors required to be considered include, but are not limited to:

- A significant economic incentive, such as contractual terms and conditions for the optional periods that are favorable compared with current market rates;

- A significant economic disincentive, such as costs to terminate the lease and sign a new lease (e.g., negotiation costs, relocation costs, abandonment of significant leasehold improvements, costs of identifying another suitable underlying asset, costs associated with returning the underlying asset in a contractually specified condition or to a contractually specified location, or a substantial cancellation penalty);

- The lessee's history of exercising renewal or termination options; and
- The extent to which the lease is essential to the provision of government services.

Fiscal Funding, Lease Cancellation, and Remeasurement

A fiscal funding or cancellation clause would be considered in determining the lease term only when it is reasonably certain that the clause will be exercised. Lessees and lessors would reassess the lease term only if the lessee does *either* of the following:

- Elects to exercise an option even though the lessor or lessee had previously determined that it was not reasonably certain that the lessee would do so; or
- Does not elect to exercise an option even though the lessor or lessee had previously determined that it was reasonably certain that the lessee would do so.

Current U.S. GAAP contains different language with regard to fiscal funding clauses that in many cases, results in an operating lease. The "reasonably certain" clause may result in capitalizing many of these arrangements.

Leases That Transfer Ownership

If a lease transfers ownership from lessor to lessee and does not contain termination options, GASB-87 continues the current model of direct financing. A note receivable would be recognized along with a transfer of the asset. A gain or loss may occur.

Accounting Model—Lessees

A lessee will account for a lease by recognizing a lease liability and a right-to-use intangible lease asset at the beginning of a lease, unless it is a short-term lease or transfers ownership of the underlying asset. The lease liability will be measured at the present value of payments to be made for the lease term. The lease asset would be measured at the amount of the initial measurement of the lease liability plus any payments made to the lessor at or before the beginning of the lease and certain indirect costs. The lease liability is reduced as payments are made and an outflow of resources for interest on the liability is recognized. The lessee would amortize the lease asset in a systematic and rational method over the term of the agreement. Notes to the financial statements will include a description of leasing arrangements, the amount of lease assets recognized, and a schedule of future lease payments to be made.

The following elements are used to determine the initial value of the lessee's liability:

- Fixed payments, less any lease incentives (such as a cash payment or reimbursement of moving costs) receivable from the lessor;
- Variable lease payments that depend on an index or a rate (such as the Consumer Price Index or a market interest rate), initially measured using the index or rate as of the beginning of the lease;
- Variable lease payments that are fixed in substance;

- Amounts that are reasonably certain of being required to be paid by the lessee under residual value guarantees;
- The exercise price of a purchase option if it is reasonably certain that the lessee will exercise that option;
- Payments for penalties for terminating the lease, if the lease term reflects the lessee; exercising an option to terminate the lease or a fiscal funding or cancellation clause; and
- Any other payments that are reasonably certain of being required based on an assessment of all relevant factors.

Variable payments based on future performance or usage are not included. Instead, they are an expense for the period.

Example: A coffee stand at an airport leases space in the terminal lobby. The lease is based on 3% of sales, paid monthly 15 days after each monthly period and subject to audit by airport internal audit staff. The lessee will record the monthly payment as an expense. However, if the coffee stand pays the lesser of a minimum monthly payment, or 3% of sales, then the payment is in substance fixed at the minimum monthly payment.

Example of Accounting Model for Lessees: Assume that a government is leasing a piece of equipment. The initial term is five years with two options to renew at two years each. Payments are $1,000 a month for the initial term and do not rise upon renewal. The estimated useful life of the equipment is seven years. It is reasonably certain that the government will lease the equipment for the seven years, using one renewal period. This is based on all relevant factors, including the useful life of the equipment and past history of the government's pattern of leasing equipment. Similar pieces of equipment from the same source have a 6% borrowing rate, determined using the provisions for imputation of interest contained in GASB-62, paragraphs 173–187 (see further discussion below on implicit interest). The entry for the lessee at inception would be:

	Debit	Credit
Leased Asset–Equipment (Intangible)	$68,453	
Lease Liability		$68,453

To record the value of the right to use the equipment at inception and the present value of the liability (Present value of $1,000 per month for {5 + 2 years} at 6%).

In the first month, the entry would be:

	Debit	Credit
Amortization expense	$815	
Lease Liability	658	
Interest expense	342	
Accumulated amortization		$815
Cash		1,000

To record the straight-line amortization of the right to use the equipment ($68,453 / 84). The interest expense is [$68,453 x (6% / 12 months)]. The payment on the lease liability is $1,000 less the interest expense and both the interest and the principal will adjust monthly using the effective interest method.

If the lease were to occur in a governmental fund, the following would be the initial entry, even though there is no capital asset that results, but there is an intangible asset:

	Debit	Credit
GENERAL FUND		
Capital outlay—(expenditure) (leased equipment)	$68,453	
Other financing source—leased equipment		$68,453

The first month's entry in a governmental fund would be:

	Debit	Credit
GENERAL FUND		
Other Financing Use—lease payments	$658	
Interest expense	342	
Cash		$1,000

The Effect of a Lease Incentive

Lease incentives are common to entice lessees to contract. Lease incentives are a payment to, or on behalf of, the lessee, for which the lessee has a right of offset with its obligation to the lessor. These are equivalent to rebates or discounts. They may include reimbursement of the lessee's costs, assumption of a pre-existing lease obligation to a third party, or similar. Some incentives may be immediate, while others are delayed.

Example: A government is deciding on a five year lease with five equal payments of $23,740 paid at the end of each year. The implicit rate in the lease is 6%. The present value of the lease payments is $100,000. The lessor agrees to pay $5,000 to the government at the end of the first year, reducing the net payment for the first year to $18,740. The lowering of the payment reduces the net present value of the liability to $95,283. The government agrees to the lease. The following is an amortization schedule of the lease:

Fiscal Year	Liability at Beginning of Year	Interest Expense for Year	Net Payment	Liability at End of Year	Reduction of Principal
X1	$95,283	$5,717	$18,740	$82,260	$13,023
X2	82,260	4,960	23,740	63,456	18,804
X3	63,456	3,807	23,740	43,524	19,932
X4	43,524	2,611	23,740	22,396	21,128
X5	22,396	1,344	23,740	-	22,396
					$95,283

Note: Interest expense for the year = Liability at Beginning of Year x 6%. The net payment less the interest = the reduction of principal annually. $5,000 at the end of the year equates to $4,717 at present value, with an interest rate of 6% as of the date of lease signing. $100,000 - $4,717 = $95,283.

The accounting model for this lease incentive payment would be as follows for the first year:

	Debit	Credit
1/1/X1		
Right to use asset	$95,283	
Lease Liability		$95,283
12/31/X1		
Interest expense	$5,717	
Lease Liability	$13,023	
Cash		$18,740
Amortization expense	19,057	
Right to use asset		19,057
($95,283 ÷ 5 year assumed life)		

Liability Remeasurement Requirements

Remeasurement of the lease liability will occur at subsequent financial reporting dates if any of the following have occurred and are expected to significantly affect the lease liability:

- There is a change in the lease term;
- An assessment of all relevant factors indicates that the likelihood of a residual value guarantee being paid has changed from reasonably certain to not reasonably certain, or vice versa;
- An assessment of all relevant factors indicates that the likelihood of a purchase option being exercised has changed from reasonably certain to not reasonably certain, or vice versa;
- There is a change in the estimated amounts for payments already included in the liability; and
- There is a change in the rate the lessor charges the lessee, if used as the initial discount rate.

The change in a rate would be implemented from the date of the rate change forward and does not require a restatement of prior periods.

The leased asset at the beginning of the lease is determined as follows:

Elements		Amounts
Amount of lease liability at inception		$XX,XXX
Less: Payments made to the lessor at or before the beginning of the lease	($x,xxx)	
Plus: Any lease incentives received from the lessor	Xxx	
Plus: Any initial direct costs that are ancillary charges to place the leased asset into service.	Xxx	
Total adjustments		X,XXX
Leased asset value at inception		$XX,XXX

Amortization of the leased asset is systematic and rational over the *shorter* of the lease term or the useful life of the asset. If the lease contains a purchase option that the lessee has determined will be reasonably certain of being exercised, the leased asset would be amortized over the useful life of the underlying asset. Land would not be amortized. In practice, the amortization expense will likely be combined with other forms of depreciation.

Note Disclosure—Lessees

Similarly to current lease disclosure, other than short-term leases (as described later), lessee should include: a general description of leasing arrangements, the total amount of lease assets and related amortization (disclosed separately from other capital assets), the amount of lease assets by major class of asset, the outflows for the period, principal and interest requirements for the next five years and five year increments thereafter, commitments under leases, and the components of any impairment losses. A lessee is not required to disclose collateral pledged under a lease if that collateral is solely the lease asset underlying the lease.

Accounting Model—Governmental Lessors

Governmental lessors will recognize a lease receivable and a deferred inflow of resources at the beginning of a lease, with certain exceptions (such as a short-term lease or a lease that transfers ownership of the underlying asset). A lessor will not derecognize the asset underlying the lease. The lease receivable will be measured at the present value of lease payments to be received for the lease term. The deferred inflow of resources will be measured at the value of the lease receivable plus any payments received at or prior to the beginning of the lease that relate to future periods.

A governmental lessor will recognize interest revenue on the lease receivable and an inflow of resources from the deferred inflow of resources on a systematic and rational basis over the term of the lease. Notes to the financial statements would include a description of lease arrangements, the total amount of revenue recognized from leases, and a schedule of future lease payments to be received.

Example of Accounting Model—Governmental Lessor: For a governmental lessor, the proposed accounting model for the same piece of equipment discussed previously, leased by a government to another government not in the same reporting entity would be as follows, assuming no uncollectable amounts, no transfer of ownership and no down payment:

	Debit	Credit
Lease Receivable—Equipment	$68,453	
Deferred Inflow of Resources—Leased Equipment		$68,453

To record the value of leased equipment at inception and the present value of the liability (Present value of $1,000 per month for [{5 + 2 years} × 12 months = 84 months] at 6%).

In the first month, the entry would be:

	Debit	Credit
Cash	$1,000	
Depreciation Expense—Equipment	815	
Deferred Inflow of Resources—Leased Equipment	658	
Lease Receivable—Equipment		$ 658
Miscellaneous Revenue—Leases		658
Interest revenue		342
Accumulated Depreciation—Equipment		815

Depreciation on the equipment would continue as it is still owned by the government ($68,453 / 84). The interest expense is [$68,453 x (6% / 12 months)].

If the governmental lessor accounts for the lease in a governmental fund, the entry would be similar to above, except for the depreciation expense and accumulated depreciation entries.

Contracts with Multiple Components

Generally, a government would account for the lease and nonlease components of a lease as separate contracts. If a lease involves multiple underlying assets, lessees and lessors generally would account for each underlying asset as a separate lease contract. To allocate consideration required under the contact to different components, lessees and lessors would use contract prices for individual components based on observable stand-alone prices, if reasonable. These situations are commonly known as "triple-net" leases.

If a contract does not include prices for individual components, or if those prices are not reasonable, lessors and lessees should use professional judgment to determine their best estimate for allocating the contract price to each component, maximizing the use of observable information; for example, using readily available observable stand-alone prices. If it is not practicable to determine a best estimate for price allocation, a government may account for the entire contract as a single lease unit.

Under certain circumstances, multiple components in a lease contract would be accounted for as a single lease unit. Contracts that are entered into at or near the same time with the same counterparty and meet certain criteria would be considered part of the same lease contract and would be evaluated in accordance with the guidance on contracts with multiple components.

A set of decisions needs to be made if indeed multiple components exist:

1. Does the contract have individual prices? If yes, go to step 2. If no, then:

    a. Is it practicable to obtain the best estimate to allocate the considera-tion between components, maximizing observable information (e.g., using readily available observable stand-alone prices for compo-nents)? If yes, use the best estimate to allocate the consideration between components. If no, then account for entire contract as a single lease unit.

2. Are the prices reasonable based on other standalone prices? If no, go to step 1a. If yes, use the contract prices.

Observable information may include pricing for utilities, security, mainte-nance, and similar other items that are normally paid separately from leases. To obtain this information, a similar process is used when needed to determine values of investments that are not readily available (Level 3) in accordance with GASB-72. The information should be *reasonably* available, in other words, quickly and easily without extraordinary efforts.

Short-term Leases

A short-term lease will be defined as a lease that, at the beginning of the lease, has a maximum possible term under the contract of 12 months or less, including any options to extend. Lessees and lessors would recognize short-term lease payments based on the payment provisions of the contract.

Modifications

An amendment to a lease contract will be considered a lease modification, unless the lessee's right to use the underlying asset decreases, in which case it would be a partial termination. A lease termination will be accounted for by reducing the carrying values of the lease liability and lease asset by a lessee, or the lease receivable and deferred inflow of resources by the lessor, with any difference being recognized as a gain or loss. A lease modification generally would be accounted for by remeasuring the balances of the related lease liability and lease asset by a lessee, or the related lease receivable and deferred inflow of resources by a lessor.

Subleases, Sale-Leaseback, and Lease-Leaseback Transactions

Subleases will be treated as transactions separate from the original lease. The original lessee that becomes the lessor in a sublease will account for the original lease and the sublease as separate transactions as a lessee and lessor, respectively.

A sale-leaseback transaction will be accounted for under sale-leaseback accounting if the transaction includes a qualifying sale. The sale and leaseback portions of a transaction will be accounted for as separate sale and lease transactions, except that any gain or loss on the sale will be reported as a deferred inflow of resources or deferred outflow of resources and recognized over the term of the leaseback. A lease-leaseback transaction would be recognized as a net transaction. The gross amounts of each portion of the transaction would be disclosed.

Intra-Entity Leases and Leases with Related Parties

Leases with or between blended component units largely retains the accounting model previous to GASB-87. If eliminations are required, these eliminations should be made prior to aggregation with the primary government. The remaining entries would result in inflows and outflows of resources.

For leases with related parties, the substance of the transaction will be recognized instead of the transaction's legal form, including the length of the lease. All of the proposed elements would then apply.

Note Disclosure—Governmental Lessors

Similarly to lessee, other than short-term leases, the following will be disclosed, which may be grouped for purposes of disclosure:

- A general description of its leasing arrangements, including the basis, terms, and conditions on which any variable lease payments not included in the lease receivable are determined;

- The carrying amount of assets on lease or held for leasing, by major classes of assets, and the amount of accumulated depreciation;

- The total amount of inflows of resources (for example, lease revenue, interest revenue, and any other lease-related inflows) recognized in the reporting period from leases, if the total is not displayed on the face of the financial statements;

- The amount of inflows of resources recognized in the reporting period for variable lease payments and other payments not previously included in the lease receivable, including inflows of resources related to residual value guarantees and termination penalties; and

- The existence, terms, and conditions of options by the lessee to terminate the lease or abate lease payments if the lessor government has issued debt for which the principal and interest payments are secured by the lease payments.

If the primary operations of a lessor is to lease assets to other entities, like financing authorities, housing authorities and similar, a schedule of future lease payments that are included in the lease receivable, along with the initial five years of principal and interest and five year increments thereafter are disclosed.

For regulated leases, other than short-term leases, the disclosure is limited to:

- A general description of its agreements;
- The carrying amount of assets subject to exclusive use by one counterparty under agreements, by major class of assets, and the amount of accumulated depreciation;
- The total amount of inflows of resources (for example, lease revenue, interest revenue, and any other lease-related inflows) recognized in the reporting period from agreements, if the total is not displayed on the face of the financial statements;
- A schedule of expected future minimum payments under the agreement for each of the subsequent five years and in five-year increments thereafter;
- The amount of inflows of resources recognized in the reporting period for variable payments not included in expected future minimum payments; and
- The existence, terms, and conditions of options by the lessee to terminate the lease or abate lease payments if the lessor government has issued debt for which the principal and interest payments are secured by the lease payments.

Effective Date and Transition

GASB-87 has an effective date of a final standard for reporting periods beginning after December 15, 2019. For June 30th governments, the effective date would be for periods beginning after July 1, 2020. Leases will be recognized and measured using the facts and circumstances that exist at the beginning of the period of implementation (or, if applied to earlier periods, the beginning of the earliest period restated). However, lessors would not restate the assets underlying their existing sales-type or direct financing leases. Any residual assets for those leases would become the carrying values of the underlying assets.

Changes required to conform to GASB-87 will result in a retroactive restatement of all prior periods presented. If restatement is not practicable, the cumulative effect, if any, of applying GASB-87 will be reported as a restatement of beginning net position (or fund balance or fund net position, as applicable) for the earliest period presented.

CHAPTER 15
RISK MANAGEMENT, CLAIMS, AND JUDGMENTS

CONTENTS

INTRODUCTION

State and local governments encounter essentially the same accounting and reporting issues as commercial enterprises that purchase insurance coverage (insured). GASB-10 (*Accounting and Financial Reporting for Risk Financing and Related Insurance Issues*) was issued to provide guidance for governmental entities that assume the role of the insurer and the role of the insured.

> **NOTE:** For a discussion of the accounting standards established by GASB-10 and amended by GASB-30 that apply to governmental entities that assume the role of an insurer and pool resources of other governments, see Chapter 23, "Public Entity Risk Pools."

Most governmental entities are exposed to a variety of risks that may result in losses. These risks include possible loss from acts of God, injury to employees, or breach of contract. GASB-10 addresses risk of loss that arises from events where the government (not a pool) bears the risk, such as the following:

- Torts (wrongful acts, injuries, or damages—not involving breach of contract—for which a civil action can be brought);
- Theft of, damage to, or destruction of assets;
- Business interruptions;
- Errors and omissions (such as the publication of incorrect data or the failure to disclose required information);
- Job-related illnesses or injuries to employees (not a pool for workers' compensation);
- Acts of God (events beyond human origin or control—natural disasters such as lightning, windstorms, and earthquakes); and
- Losses resulting from providing accident, health, dental, and other medical benefits to employees and retirees and their dependents and beneficiaries (but excluding all postemployment benefits).

In addition, liabilities for environmental remediation and landfill post-closure costs follow the provisions of GASB-49 and GASB-18, respectively. Specifically, GASB-49 introduced an expected cash flow and weighted average probability of loss model to calculate liabilities. GASB-49 also has separate guidance on insurance recoveries, including those expected in future periods.

> **PRACTICE POINT:** The GASB has released Statement No. 83 (*Certain Asset Retirement Obligations*). A complete discussion of GASB-83 is presented in Chapter 10, "Capital Assets."

Some large governments only self-insure, and only up to a certain dollar threshold set in law (e.g., $100,000). This affords some relief from frivolous lawsuits and exorbitant billing by legal teams. Self-insurance means that settlements and judgments are paid out of current appropriated funds rather than out of a trust or pool of funds. In certain circumstances, the settlement or judgment is structured to pay out over a period of years and the court orders that such amounts be appropriated annually.

On certain large construction projects, one way to mitigate risk is to have all construction contractors pool their resources and have the government control the pool (known as an owner-controlled insurance program, or OCIP). OCIPs may be very effective in reducing workers' compensation losses. Depending on how the law is written creating the OCIP, any unspent assets may inure to the government, with the government assuming risk after a certain time, or the assets may inure to a private insurance carrier or the contractors. If the sponsoring government assumes the risk, then the provisions of GASB-10 and GASB-30 may apply.

The common theme to managing risk is that a governmental entity must decide how to finance losses that may arise from these and other events. From an accounting perspective, potential losses related to these events require that a governmental entity consider whether an accrual for possible losses should be recognized at the end of an accounting period. Again, the consideration for a possible accrual for losses by a governmental entity is no different from the evaluation that a commercial enterprise must make. For this reason, GASB-10 includes many of the standards also codified in GASB-62, pars. 96–113 [GASB Cod. Secs. C50.151–.168], on contingencies, to provide guidance to state and local governments for the accrual of losses related to risk activities.

The accounting standards that are used to determine the amount of the liability that should be presented in a governmental entity's financial statements vary depending on whether a liability is presented in a (1) governmental fund, (2) proprietary and fiduciary funds, or (3) the government-wide financial statements.

ACCOUNTING FOR RISK MANAGEMENT LIABILITIES

General Principles of Liability Recognition

Except when an internal service fund is used, if a risk of loss from the events listed above has not been transferred to a third party, an accrual for a claim should be recognized if both of the following conditions exist:

1. On the basis of information available before the financial statements are issued, it is probable (likely to occur) that an asset has been impaired or a liability has been incurred as of the date of the financial statements; and

2. The loss can be reasonably estimated.

GASB-10 identifies the date of the financial statements as "the end of the most recent accounting period for which financial statements are being presented" (GASB-10, par. 53) [GASB Cod. Sec. C50.110].

To determine whether a loss is probable, all relevant information available prior to the issuance of the financial statements should be evaluated. An accrual for a loss is made only if the loss was based on an event or a condition that existed on or before the date of the balance sheet (GASB-10, par. 54) [GASB Cod. Sec. C50.111].

The accrual of a loss in a current period implies that an event will occur in a subsequent period that will substantiate the recognition of the accrual. The accrual of a loss due to an event that suggests that the governmental entity will be held liable for the loss will eventually be confirmed when the entity agrees (or is forced) to pay the injured party. Of course, an accrual of a loss is based on a prediction that the future event will in fact occur. GASB-10 uses the following definitions to describe the various probabilities of whether a loss will eventually be confirmed by a future event (GASB-10, par. 55) [GASB Cod. Sec. C50.112]:

> *Probable*—The future event or events confirming the fact that a loss has occurred are likely to occur.
>
> *Reasonably possible*—The chance of the future event or events occurring is more than remote but less than likely.
>
> *Remote*—The change of the future event or event occurring is slight.

GASB-70 (*Accounting and Financial Reporting for Nonexchange Financial Guarantee Transactions*), paragraphs 7 through 9, includes a "more likely than not" (MLTN) measurement technique. If there are qualitative, historical, or quantitative factors that exist that indicate that a guarantee may have to be exercised, then a liability would be declared for the amount of the guarantee. GASB-70 also uses GASB-49's technique that if no measure of probability is better than another in a range of possible liabilities, then the minimum probability is used to measure the liability.

There are innumerable examples of loss contingencies for governmental entities. The AICPA's Audit and Accounting Guide *State and Local Governments* lists the following as examples of loss contingencies that should be evaluated for possible accrual:

- Contractual actions (such as claims for delays or inadequate specifications on contracts);
- Guarantees of other entities' debt;
- Unemployment compensation claims;
- Property tax appeals;
- Tax refund claims; and
- Refunds of nonexchange revenues when the recipient government does not satisfy a provider's requirements.

The last three items listed above (property tax appeals, tax refund claims, and other refunds) should be evaluated in the context of GASB-33 (*Accounting and Financial Reporting for Non-Exchange Transactions*).

GASB-10 does not address the method(s) that may be used to allocate a loss among funds once the amount of the loss is determined. A governmental entity is free to allocate (or not allocate) the loss in any manner it deems appropriate (GASB-10, pars. 53–57, as amended by GASB-30, par. 9, GASB-34, par. 6) [GASB Cod. Secs. C50.110–.114].

The criterion that the loss must be subject to reasonable estimation before an accrual is appropriate does not imply that there must be only a single amount that is likely to be incurred. A reasonable amount can be expressed in terms of a range of possible losses. If one specific amount within the range is the most likely to occur, that amount should be accrued as a loss and the excess (the maximum amount in the range minus the amount accrued), as discussed later, should be disclosed in the financial statements.

When no single amount within the range of possible losses is most likely to occur, the minimum amount in the range should be accrued as a loss and the excess should be disclosed in the financial statements.

Incurred But Not Reported Claims

A governmental entity must evaluate its exposure to incurred but not reported (IBNR) conditions. IBNR claims are claims that have not yet been asserted, as of the financial statements issuance date, even though they may have occurred before the date of the statement of net position. These types of claims are common in Medicaid, earthquake, or hurricane insurance and similar programs. The valuation of the claims are discussed in the next section.

If the governmental entity concludes that it is not probable that IBNR claims will be asserted, the loss should not be accrued or disclosed in the financial statements. On the other hand, if the entity concludes that it is probable that an IBNR claim will be asserted by another party, the loss should be accrued if a reasonable estimate of the loss can be made (GASB-10, par. 56) [GASB Cod. Sec. C50.113].

IBNR claims include three components:

1. Known loss events that are expected to be presented as claims.
2. Unknown loss events that are expected to become claims.
3. Expected future development on claims already reported.

Governmental entities must evaluate their exposure to liabilities related to unpaid claims costs, which includes both (1) claims that have been reported and (2) claims incurred but not reported. GASB-30 requires that the liability for unpaid claims costs should be based on the following factors (GASB-30, pars. 8–9) [GASB Cod. Secs. C50.101, .114]:

- Total ultimate costs of settling a claim, including provisions for inflation and other societal and economic factors;
- Past experience of settling claims; and
- Factors needed to make past experience trends consistent with current conditions.

Valuation of Claims Cost Liabilities

The estimated liability for claims costs should include all costs related to the ultimate settlement of claims. In addition to an estimate for actual payments to claimants, the estimated liability for claims costs should include specific, incremental claims adjustment expenditures/expenses. Specific claims adjustment expenditures/expenses represent costs that are incurred by a governmental entity only because it is attempting to dispose of a specific claim. For example, a claim may require the governmental entity to hire an individual with a certain type of expertise to evaluate the government's legal responsibility as it relates to the claim. On the other hand, claims costs that would otherwise be incurred—for example, salaries of administrative personnel in the department that processes claims and other similar overhead costs—would generally not be considered incremental. Other allocated or unallocated claim adjustment expenditures/ expenses may be included in the estimated liability for claims costs, but GASB-30 does not require their inclusion.

The estimated liability for claims costs for a public entity risk pool must include a provision for other allocated or unallocated claim adjustment expenditures/expenses. The GASB implied that such expenditures/expenses are conceptually part of the estimated liability for claims costs for entities other than pools. GASB-30 includes a provision for allocated or unallocated claim adjustment expenditures/expenses in the accrual for claims costs to be optional. The composition of the accrual must be disclosed in the financial statements.

The estimated liability for claims costs should be reduced by estimated recoveries that may arise from unsettled claims. GASB-30 refers to two broad categories of recoveries, "salvage" and "subrogation," and GASB-10 provides the following definitions of these terms (the definitions have been slightly modified to reflect the discussion of governmental entities other than public entity risk pools):

> *Salvage*—The amount received by a governmental entity *other than a pool* from the sale of property (usually damaged) on which the entity has paid a total claim to the claimant and has obtained title to the property.

> *Subrogation*—The right of a governmental entity *other than a pool* to pursue any course of recovery of damages, in its name, against a third party who is liable for costs of an event that have been paid by the governmental entity.

In addition to claims that have not been settled, the governmental entity may also anticipate recoveries from claims that have already been settled. Anticipated recoveries on settled claims should be netted (reduced) against the estimated liability for claims costs.

The accrual for claims costs may be based on a case-by-case review, an overall approach of applying historical experience to all claims outstanding, or a combination of both approaches. GASB-30 notes that the accrual for IBNR losses must be based on historical experience. When historical experience is used to estimate the accrual, claims should be appropriately categorized by amount and type of claim to ensure that relevant historical experience is applied to similar claims.

Discounting

The GASB does not specify whether the accrual of claims liabilities should be discounted. Thus, it is acceptable to report the accrual at either a gross amount or a discounted amount, with one exception: structured settlements should be discounted if the amount to be paid to the claimant is fixed by contract and the payment dates are fixed or determinable (GASB-10, par. 59) [GASB Cod. Sec. C50.116].

When claims liabilities are presented in the financial statements at discounted amounts, the rate selected to compute the discounted amounts should take into consideration factors such as the following (GASB-10, par. 60) [GASB Cod. Sec. C50.117]:

- Settlement rate (the rate at which a monetary liability with uncertain terms can be settled or a monetary asset [receivable] with uncertain terms can be sold); and

- Investment yield rate (the expected rate of return on investments held by the governmental entity during the period in which the expected payments to the claimant will occur).

OBSERVATION: The discount rate used may be different from other yields, including bond yields and discount rates used for defined benefit pensions and OPEB, respectively. Auditors of the government will want to test the rate used for claims liabilities for reasonableness.

Public Entity Risk Pools in Comparison with Risk Management

The GASB *Implementation Guide 2015-1*, question 3.4.1 [GASB Cod. Sec. Po20.704-1], discusses the factors to determine whether an entity is a public entity risk pool. In making the determination, all of the following factors should be considered together defining a risk pool:

- A cooperative group of governmental entities joining together to finance an exposure, liability, or risk. Risk may include property and liability, workers' compensation, or employee health care. A pool may be a stand-alone entity or included as part of another governmental entity that acts as the pool's sponsor.

- A governmental entity that is a pool's sponsor may also participate in the pool for its own risk management function.

- Stand-alone pools are established under authorizing statute by agreement of any number of state and local governmental entities. Stand-alone pools are sometimes organized or sponsored by municipal leagues, school associations, or other types of associations of governmental entities. Stand-alone pools are frequently operated by a board that has as its membership one member from each participating government. They typically have no publicly elected officials or authority to tax.

If a government provides insurance or risk management coverage separate from its own risk management activities to individuals or organizations outside the governmental reporting entity and there is material transfer or pooling of risk among the participants, that activity should be accounted for as a public-entity risk pool. If a government provides risk transfer or pooling coverage combined with its own risk management activities to individuals or organizations outside its reporting entity, those activities should continue to be reported in a governmental fund or an internal service fund only as long as the entity is the predominant participant in the fund. If the entity is not the predominant participant in the fund, then the combined activities should be reported as a public entity risk pool, using an enterprise fund and the accounting and reporting requirements of an enterprise fund. In summary:

- *Pools should comprise primarily governmental entities.* It was intended that the provisions of GASB-10, as amended, apply to risk financing groups of primarily state and local governments, while recognizing that there may be some cases where a group has a minority of participants—in terms of both representation and risk coverage—that are nongovernmental.

- *Pools should be a cooperative effort.* It was intended that participants would work together to finance risk. Evidence of a cooperative effort may be voluntary participation in the activity—even if participation is a participant's last recourse. If a cooperative effort does not exist, then a governmental program may actually exist, and contributions from participants may actually be fees, assessments, or taxes—not premiums (required contributions). A governmental program could be accounted for in the general fund, a special revenue fund, or an enterprise fund depending on its nature.

Entities Participating in Public Entity Risk Pools with Transfer or Pooling of Risk

Premiums (or required contributions) paid by a governmental entity to a public entity risk pool that result in the transfer or sharing of risk should be reported as an expenditure/expense by the governmental entity.

If the governmental entity is subject to supplemental premium assessment by the public entity risk pool, consideration should be given to whether an additional expenditure or expense should be accrued or disclosed in the financial statements. An accrual for the supplemental premium assessment should be made if the following conditions exist:

- A supplemental premium assessment will probably be made.

- A reasonable estimate of the supplemental premium assessment can be made.

When a possible supplemental premium assessment, including a supplemental assessment in excess of an accrued supplemental assessment, does not satisfy the criteria for accrual (probable and subject to reasonable estimation), the potential supplemental premium assessment should be evaluated to determine whether it should be disclosed in the governmental entity's financial statements. Any potential supplemental premium assessment that can be classified in one of the following categories should be disclosed:

- The occurrence of assessment is probable but no reasonable estimate (or estimate range) of the assessment can be made.

- The likelihood of assessment is reasonably possible.

When a possible supplemental premium assessment is disclosed in the financial statements, the following should be part of the disclosure (GASB-10, par. 69) [GASB Cod. Sec. C50.132]:

- A description of the possible supplemental premium assessment; and
- An estimate (or estimate range) of the assessment (or, if no estimate can be made, disclosure of this fact is required).

When a public entity risk pool does not have the authority to assess additional premiums and the pool has incurred a deficit, the economic viability of the pool should be evaluated. The governmental entity must be concerned with the possibility that the public entity risk pool will not be able to pay claims as they are settled. If the following conditions exist, the governmental entity should record a liability for estimated claims costs:

- The public entity risk pool appears not to be able to pay the claims related to the governmental entity as they become due.
- It is probable that the governmental entity will be required to pay its own claims.
- A reasonable estimate of the amount of claims that will be paid by the governmental entity can be made.

When the likelihood of payment of claims that cannot be paid by a public entity risk pool, including any payment in excess of an accrued amount, does not satisfy the criteria for accrual (probable and subject to reasonable estimation), the potential payment should be evaluated to determine whether disclosure is appropriate. Any potential payments that can be classified in one of the following categories should be disclosed:

- Potential payment is probable but no reasonable estimate (or estimate range) of the payment can be made.
- Potential payment is reasonably possible.

When a potential payment is disclosed in the financial statements, the following should be disclosed (GASB-10, par. 70) [GASB Cod. Sec. C50.133]:

- Nature of the potential payment; and
- Estimate (or estimate range) of the potential payment (or, if no estimate can be made, disclosure of this fact is required).

Capitalization Contributions Made to Public Entity Risk Pools with Transfer or Pooling of Risk

When a governmental entity makes a capital contribution to a public entity risk pool where risk has been transferred or pooled, a determination must be made regarding whether to record the contribution as an asset or as an expenditure/ expense. The contribution may be accounted for as an asset if "it is probable that the contribution will be returned to the entity upon either the dissolution of or the approved withdrawal from the pool." The judgment as to whether an asset exists should be based on the written contract that governs the relationship between the governmental entity and the public entity risk pool. In addition, an asset exists only if the public entity risk pool has the financial capacity to return the capital contribution to the governmental entity (GASBI-4, pars. 4–8) [GASB Cod. Secs. C50.134–.138]. Footnote 1 to GASBI-4 [GASB Cod. Sec. C50.fn9] explains when state and local governmental entities join to form a public entity risk pool or when those entities join an established pool and if capitalization contributions are required, they are usually in the form of cash.

The assessment of whether to recognize an asset when a governmental entity makes a capital contribution to a public entity risk pool should not occur only at the date of contribution. If the public entity risk pool's financial condition changes in a period subsequent to the contribution, it may be necessary to remove the asset from the governmental entity's financial statements and recognize an expenditure/expense.

When the capital contribution made to a public entity risk pool is accounted for as an asset in a governmental fund, the entity's fund balance must be classified as nonspendable to disclose that the asset is not available for expenditure in the following budgetary period.

If management concludes that it is probable that the contribution to the public entity risk pool will not be returned and the contribution is made by a governmental fund, the contribution may be accounted for using either the allocation method or the non-allocation method. When the allocation method is used, a prepayment is established at the date of the contribution and is subsequently amortized over the period for which it is expected the contribution will be used to determine the amount of premiums the contributor must pay. Again, if the period is not readily determinable, the amortization period should not exceed 10 years. Because the prepayment is not a current financial resource, the fund's fund balance account should be classified as nonspendable by the amount presented for prepaid insurance.

When the non-allocation method of accounting is used in a government fund, the capital contribution is reported immediately as an expenditure. Under this approach no asset is created, and thus there is no need to establish a fund balance reserve at the end of the accounting period.

Entities Participating in Public Entity Risk Pools without Transfer or Pooling of Risk

A governmental entity may participate in a public entity risk pool when the relationship is not characterized by a transfer or pooling of risk. For example, there is no transfer or pooling of risk in a banking pool or a claims-servicing (account) pool.

When there is no transfer or pooling of risk in the relationship with the public entity risk pool, the governmental entity must evaluate and recognize losses from incurred claims as if there were no participation in the public entity risk pool. Specifically, standards discussed earlier, in the section titled "General Principles of Liability Recognition," must be observed.

Payments made to a public entity risk pool (including capitalization contributions) to which there has been no transfer or pooling of risk should be accounted for as either a deposit or a reduction of the claims liabilities account. A deposit should be recorded when the payment is not expected to be used to pay claims. A reduction of the claims liabilities account should be made when payments to the pool are to be used to pay claims as they are incurred (GASB-10, par. 71, and GASBI-4, par. 9) [GASB Cod. Sec. C50.139].

Insurance Related Transactions

Claims-Made Policies

A governmental entity may purchase a claims-made policy. GASB-10 defines a "claims-made policy" as follows:

> *Claims-made policy or contract*—A type of policy that covers losses from claims asserted (reported or filed) against the policyholder during the policy period, regardless of whether the liability-imposing events occurred during the current or any previous period in which the policyholder was insured under the claims-made contract or other specified period before the policy period (the policy retroactive date).

In a claims-made policy, the risk of loss to which the governmental entity is exposed is not entirely transferred. Specifically, the governmental entity is liable for claims that have occurred but were not reported nor filed during the period covered by the claims-made policy. The exposure to loss resulting from a claims-made policy should be evaluated using the standards discussed in the previous section titled "General Principles of Liability Recognition" to determine whether such exposure requires an accrual or disclosure in the financial statements.

The risk exposure related to a claims-made policy can be avoided by acquiring a tail-coverage insurance policy. GASB-10 defines "tail coverage" as follows:

> *Tail coverage*—A type of insurance policy designed to cover claims incurred before, but reported after, cancellation or expiration of a claims-made policy. (The term "extended discovery coverage" is used in the commercial insurance industry.)

When tail coverage is acquired, a governmental entity does not have to evaluate the possible accrual or disclosure of losses arising from claims-made policies (GASB-10, par. 72) [GASB Cod. Sec. C50.140].

Retrospective-Rated Policies and Contracts

A governmental entity may purchase a retrospective-rated policy (or contract). GASB-10 defines a "retrospective (experience) rating" as follows:

> *Retrospective (experience) rating*—A method of determining the final amount of an insurance premium by which the initial premium is adjusted based on actual experience during the period of coverage (sometimes subject to maximum and minimum limits). It is designed to encourage safety by the insured and to compensate the insurer if larger-than-expected losses are incurred.

When a retrospective-rated policy is acquired, the minimum premium should be recognized as an expenditure or expense over the period covered by the contract. In addition, the standards discussed in the section titled "General Principles of Liability Recognition" should be used to accrue for reported and unreported claims in excess of the minimum premium. If there is a maximum premium identified in the contract, the accrual should not exceed the amount of the maximum premium (GASB-10, par. 73) [GASB Cod. Sec. C50.141].

In some circumstances, the conditions for recognizing a loss contingency may not exist. If this is the case, no accrual for additional premium payments should be made. However, the governmental entity should refer to the standards discussed in the section titled "Disclosure of Loss Contingencies" to determine whether the possibility of additional premiums being charged under the retrospective-rated policy should be disclosed in the notes to the financial statements.

Some governmental entities purchase retrospective-rated policies that are based on the experience of a group of policyholders. When a retrospective-rated policy is based on group experience, the initial premium should be amortized as an expenditure or expense over the period of time covered by the contract. The governmental entity should accrue supplemental premiums or refunds that arise from the experience of the group to date. The accrual should be based on the ultimate cost of reported and unreported claims as of the date of the financial statements. In addition, the following disclosures should be made:

- Insurance coverage is based on retrospective-rated policies.

- Premiums are accrued on the basis of the experience to date of the ultimate claims cost of the group of which the governmental entity is a participant.

The governmental entity will have to rely on the insurer entity to provide the information necessary to accrue additional premiums or refunds as of the date of the statement of net position.

When an entity cannot accrue estimated losses from reported or unreported claims related to a retrospective-rated policy using group experience because the accrual criteria are not satisfied, the disclosure criteria should be used to determine whether disclosure is appropriate (GASB-10, par. 74) [GASB Cod. Sec. C50.142].

Policyholder or Pool Dividends

A governmental entity may be entitled to a policyholder dividend (or return of contribution) based on the terms of its insurance contract or its participation in a public entity risk pool. GASB-10 provides the following definition of "policyholder dividends" (GASB-10, par. 75) [GASB Cod. Sec. C50.143]:

> *Policyholder dividends*—Payments made or credits extended to the insured by the insurer, usually at the end of a policy year that result in reducing the net insurance cost to the policyholder. These dividends may be paid in cash to the insured or applied by the insured to reduce premiums due for the next policy year.

A policyholder dividend should be recorded by the governmental entity as a reduction of expenditures or expenses as of the date the dividend is declared by the insurer.

Entities Providing Claims Servicing or Insurance Coverage to Others

Governmental entities may provide insurance or risk-management coverage to individuals or entities that are not part of the governmental reporting entity (primary government and all related component units). For example, a governmental entity may provide insurance coverage under a workers' compensation plan. If there is a material transfer or pooling of risk and the activities are separate from its own risk-management activities, the governmental entity should account for these activities in a public entity risk pool by following the standards discussed in Chapter 23, "Public Entity Risk Pools."

On the other hand, a governmental entity may provide insurance or risk-management coverage to individuals or entities that are not part of the governmental reporting entity, but these services may be part of its own risk-management activities. Under this circumstance and assuming the governmental entity is the predominant participant in the fund, all of the activities should be accounted for in either the General Fund or an Internal Service Fund, and the standards discussed in this chapter should be followed. If the governmental entity is not the predominant participant, the activities should be accounted for in an Enterprise Fund, and the standards discussed in Chapter 23, "Public Entity Risk Pools," should be followed.

OBSERVATION: Although the General Fund can be used to account for the risk-management activities when the governmental entity is the predominant participant, the author believes it may be preferable to account for such activities in an Internal Service Fund to limit the activities reported in the General Fund to revenues and expenses related to routine governmental transactions in accordance with GASB-10, par. 63. GASB-66 (*Technical Corrections—2012—an amendment of GASB Statements No. 10 and No. 62*) removed the limitation to the General Fund or an Internal Service Fund. Instead, governments should base their fund type classification decisions on the nature of the activity to be reported, as required in GASB-54 and GASB-34.

Finally, some governmental entities may service claims and provide no insurance coverage to individuals or entities that are not part of the governmental reporting entities. Under this arrangement, amounts collected or due from, and amounts paid or due to the individuals or other entities should be netted and reported as a net asset or liability determined on the accrual basis. Operating revenue and administrative costs arising from the claims-servicing activities should be accounted for consistently with the standards discussed in Chapter 23, "Public Entity Risk Pools" (see the section titled "Pools Not Involving Transfer or Pooling of Risks") (GASB-10, par. 76, as amended by GASB-66, par. 3) [GASB Cod. Sec. C50.144].

Annuity Contracts

A governmental entity may satisfy its obligation to a claimant by purchasing an annuity in the claimant's name. If the possibility of making additional payments to the claimant is remote, the claim should be removed as a liability. Under this circumstance, the claim would not be presented as a liability and the purchase of the annuity contract would not be presented as an asset.

When claims have been removed from the claims liability account because of the purchase of an annuity contract, the amount removed should be disclosed as a contingent liability. The disclosure should continue as long as there is a legal possibility that the claimant could demand payment from the governmental entity. Disclosure is not required for annuity contracts purchased if both of the following conditions exist (GASB-10, par. 61, as amended by GASB-34, par. 6) [GASB Cod. Sec. C50.118]:

- The claimant has signed an agreement releasing the governmental entity from further obligation.

- The likelihood of future payments to the claimant is remote.

If a claim had been removed from the claims liability account because an annuity contract was purchased in a previous period, but in the current period it was determined that the governmental entity is now primarily liable for the claim, the claim should be reestablished as a claims liability.

GOVERNMENTAL FUNDS

The modified accrual basis of accounting and current financial resources measurement focus should be applied to accounting for claims and judgments in governmental funds.

For example, assume that an entity identifies a probable loss and that a reasonable estimate of the loss ranges from $100,000 to $400,000. Assume that the most likely amount of the loss is $150,000. The amount of the claims liability that should be accrued in a governmental fund is based on the application of the modified accrual basis of accounting. If none of the $150,000 estimate is expected to use expendable available financial resources, no claims expenditure (liability) would be accrued, but the full amount ($150,000) would be presented in the government-wide financial statements (GASB-34, pars. 6, 79, 92, and 107) [GASB Cod. Sec. C50.124].

Use of a Single Fund

Prior to GASB-66, when a governmental entity used a single fund to account for its risk financing activities, either the General Fund or an Internal Service Fund was required to be used. GASB-66 ended this requirement.

However, it still appears that the more logical fund to account for an entity's risk financing activities is an Internal Service Fund, because an Internal Service Fund and the Enterprise Fund required by the GASB to account for a public entity risk pool have the same measurement focus and basis of accounting. The GASB allowed the use of the General Fund to account for risk financing activities to be consistent with the general concept that a governmental entity should use the minimum number of funds appropriate for its operations. The following discussion assumes the risk financing activities are accounted for in the entity's General Fund.

Risk Retention

When the General Fund is used to account for a governmental entity's risk financing activities, claims liabilities and the related expenditure or expense should be recognized on the basis of standards discussed in the earlier section entitled "General Principles of Liability Recognition." These standards require that the standards contained in GASB-62 related to the accrual of loss contingencies be applied to claims arising from risk financing activities. Any accrual of claims liabilities should be reduced by amounts expected to be paid through excess insurance.

OBSERVATION: This section refers to the recognition of expenditures when the General Fund is used. In the General Fund, only expenditures can be recorded; however, as discussed later, the total amount of the liability can be determined in the General Fund and then allocated to other funds, including those that record expenses rather than expenditures.

If it is concluded that a loss related to risk financing activities should not be accrued because the occurrence of the loss is not probable or the amount of the loss is not subject to reasonable estimation, the loss should be evaluated to determine whether disclosure in the financial statements is necessary. The standards discussed in the earlier section titled "Disclosure of Loss Contingencies" should be applied when deciding whether to disclose the loss.

When the General Fund is used to account for a governmental entity's risk financing activities, the amount of the loss may be allocated to other funds in any appropriate manner. For example, assume a loss of $500,000 is computed and the loss is allocated to an Enterprise Fund, Capital Projects Fund, and General Fund, in the amounts of $50,000, $70,000, and $380,000, respectively. To record the recognition and allocation of the loss, the following entries would be made in the affected funds:

	Debit	Credit
GENERAL FUND		
Expenditures—Claims Costs	$380,000	
Due from Enterprise Fund	50,000	
Due from Capital Projects Fund	70,000	
Estimated Claims Costs Payable		$500,000
To record risk financing and allocate loss on risk financing.		
ENTERPRISE FUND		
Expenses—Claims Costs	50,000	
Due to General Fund		50,000
To record risk financing and allocated loss on risk financing.		
CAPITAL PROJECTS FUND		
Expenditures—Claims Costs	70,000	
Due to General Fund		70,000
To record risk financing and allocated loss on risk financing.		

When the General Fund allocates the loss expenditure or expense to other funds and the total allocation, including the amount allocated to the General Fund, exceeds the accrual computed using the guidelines discussed in the section titled "General Principles of Liability Recognition," the excess amount should be treated as a transfer. To illustrate this requirement, assume the same facts as the previous example except assume that the Enterprise Fund and Capital Projects Fund are allocated an additional cost of $10,000 each. To record the allocation, the following entries are made:

	Debit	Credit
GENERAL FUND		
Expenditures—Claims Costs	$380,000	
Due from Enterprise Fund	60,000	
Due from Capital Projects Fund	80,000	
Estimated Claims Costs Payable		$500,000
Transfers in—Enterprise Fund		10,000
Transfers in—Capital Projects Fund		10,000
To record risk financing and allocate loss on risk financing along with transfers for funding.		
ENTERPRISE FUND		
Expenses—Claims Costs	50,000	
Transfers Out—General Fund	10,000	
Due to General Fund		60,000
To record risk financing and allocated loss on risk financing and transfers.		
CAPITAL PROJECTS FUND		
Expenditures—Claims Costs	70,000	
Transfers Out—General Fund	10,000	
Due to General Fund		80,000
To record risk financing and allocated loss on risk financing and transfers.		

If one fund reimburses another fund for expenditures or expenses paid, the reimbursement should be recorded as a reduction of expenditures or expenses by the reimbursed fund and as an expenditure or expense by the reimbursing fund. This classification problem most often occurs when (1) the General Fund does not allocate loss expenditures or expenses to other funds (or the amount allocated is too small) and another fund reimburses the General Fund for the payment of a claim related to the activities of the other fund or (2) the General Fund pays insurance premiums for another fund and, at a later date, the other fund reimburses the General Fund for a portion of the premiums paid (GASB-10, par. 64, as amended by GASB-66, par. 3, GASB-34, pars. 79, 112) [GASB Cod. Sec. C50.126].

PROPRIETARY AND FIDUCIARY FUNDS

The accrual basis of accounting and the economic resources measurement focus should be used to determine which claims should be presented in a proprietary or fiduciary fund. That is, the guidance contained in GASB-62 (as discussed earlier in the section titled "General Principles of Liability Recognition") should be followed to determine the amount of the claim. If a claims liability is considered to be incurred, the liability should be presented both in the proprietary or fiduciary fund and in its business activities columns of the statement of net position.

OBSERVATION: A governmental entity that reports its operating activities in a proprietary or trust fund may participate in a risk-financing Internal Service Fund if the proprietary or trust fund is a component unit of the governmental entity that has established the Internal Service Fund. On the other hand, a proprietary or trust fund should not account for its risk financing activities in an Internal Service Fund if the proprietary or trust fund is not a component unit of the governmental entity (GASB-10, fn. 12, GASB-14, par. 66, GASB-34, pars. 6, 138, 139) [GASB Cod. Sec. C50.127, fn8].

Internal Service Fund

When an Internal Service Fund is used to account for a governmental entity's risk financing activities, claims liabilities and the related expenses should be recognized either on the basis of the standards discussed in the section titled "General Principles of Liability Recognition," or by such liabilities and expenses being actuarially determined. Any accrual of claims liabilities should be reduced by amounts expected to be paid through excess insurance.

If it is concluded that a loss related to risk financing activities should not be accrued because the occurrence of the loss is not probable or the amount of the loss is not subject to reasonable estimation, the loss should be evaluated to determine whether disclosure in the financial statement is necessary. The standards discussed in the section titled "Disclosure of Loss Contingencies" should be applied to make the decision of whether to disclose (GASB-10, par. 65) [GASB Cod. Sec. C50.127].

NCGA-1 states that the purpose of an Internal Service Fund is "to account for the financing of goods or services provided by one department or agency to other departments or agencies of the governmental unit, or to other governmental units, on a cost-reimbursement basis." Thus, the risk financing services provided by an Internal Service Fund should be billed to those funds for those services provided. GASB-10 states that an Internal Service Fund may use any method it considers appropriate to determine the amounts charged to the various other funds as long as the following guidelines are satisfied:

- The total amount for service charges to other funds is equal to the amount of liability computed in complying with the standards discussed in the previous section titled "General Principles of Liability Recognition," or

- The total amount for service charges to other funds is computed using an actuarial method or historical cost information, and that amount is adjusted over time so that the expenses and revenues of the Internal Service Fund are approximately the same.

- If the second approach is used (actuarial method or historical cost information method), an additional charge may be made to other funds that represents a reasonable provision for expected future catastrophic losses.

OBSERVATION: Internal Service Funds are also used to allocate centralized overhead costs that are reimbursed by the federal government (either directly or indirectly). The overhead costs are accumulated in the fund, reimbursed by the federal government, and then allocated back to funds based on approved formulas in accordance with *the Uniform Administrative Requirements, Cost Principles, and Audit Requirements for Federal Awards* (Title 2 Code of Federal Regulations, Part 200). Preparers of indirect cost proposals should also review Appendix VII to 2CFR200 *States and Local Government and Indian Tribe Indirect Cost Proposals* for detailed guidance.

GASB-10 defines "actuarial method" as follows:

> *Actuarial method*—Any of several techniques that actuaries use to determine the amounts and timing of contributions needed to finance claims liabilities so that the total contributions plus compounded earnings on them will equal the amounts needed to satisfy claims liabilities. It may or may not include a provision for anticipated catastrophe losses.

The first method (based on standards discussed in the section titled "General Principles of Liability Recognition") requires that the amount billed to other funds by the Internal Service Fund be equal to the amount of liability recognized under the accrual concepts. Thus, under the first method, the amount of billings must be based on the incurrence of liabilities based on specific events.

The second method (actuarial method or historical cost information method) is not based on the evaluation of events that have actually occurred. Under the second method, the amount billed can be based on projected claims that *may* occur.

OBSERVATION: U.S. GAAP does not allow for "smoothing" of expenses or expenditures as allowed by the second method. A loss contingency is accrued based on the incurrence of a liability as of the date of the statement of net position. It is arguable that the concept of interperiod equity cannot be achieved because U.S. GAAP does not allow for the "averaging of losses" so that any one period would not have a significantly larger amount of recognized expenditures than any other period. The GASB provided a solution to the interperiod equity problem by allowing governmental entities to use an actuarial method that results

in level charges and to charge an optional amount for expected future catastrophic losses.

The amount billed by the Internal Service Fund to the other funds should be
recognized as revenue, and each fund should recognize either expenditures or an
expense based on the amount of the billing. For example, if an Internal Service
Fund charged the General Fund and an Enterprise Fund $400,000 and $50,000,
respectively, the following entries would be made (GASB-10, par. 66) [GASB
Cod. Sec. C50.128]:

	Debit	Credit
INTERNAL SERVICE FUND		
Due from General Fund	$400,000	
Due from Enterprise Fund	50,000	
Revenue—Charges for Services		$450,000
To record internal billing for claims and judgments.		
GENERAL FUND		
Expenditures—Payments in Lieu of Insurance Premiums	400,000	
Due to Internal Service Fund		400,000
To record risk financing premiums.		
ENTERPRISE FUND		
Expenses—Payments in Lieu of Insurance	50,000	
Due to Internal Service Fund		50,000
To record risk financing premiums.		

GASB-10 recognizes that when an actuarial method or historical cost information method is used (with or without an additional charge for expected future
catastrophic losses), in any one period, the amount of the claims costs expense
recognized and the amount of billings to the other funds may not be the same.
The difference between the cumulative claims costs recognized and the cumulative billings does not have to be charged back to the other funds if adjustments
are made over a reasonable period of time to reduce the difference. When a fund
balance deficit arises, the deficit should be disclosed in the notes to the governmental entity's financial statements. Any amount in the Internal Service Fund's
net position that arose from an optional additional charge for catastrophic losses
should be reported as restricted net position equity for future catastrophic losses
in notes to the financial statements (GASB-10, par. 67, as amended by GASB-63,
par. 8, GASB-34, par. 98) [GASB Cod. Sec. C50.129].

If the Internal Service Fund bills other funds for a total amount that is
greater than the total amount as discussed earlier in this section, the excess
should be accounted for as interfund transfers by the Internal Service Fund and
the other funds. The Internal Service Fund would report a transfer in and the
other funds would report a transfer out.

The amounts billed over time and the amounts of expenses recognized by
the Internal Service Fund should be approximately the same over a reasonable

period. If the Internal Service Fund incurs a deficit that is not eliminated over a reasonable period of time, the deficit should be billed to the participating funds to cover the full costs of claims recognized as expenses. When a chargeback occurs, the Internal Service Fund should recognize revenue and the other funds should record either an expenditure or an expense (GASB-10, par. 68, as amended by GASB-34, par. 112, GASB-63, par. 8) [GASB Cod. Sec. C50.130].

GOVERNMENT-WIDE FINANCIAL STATEMENTS

The accrual basis of accounting and the economic resources measurement focus should be used to determine which claims and assessments should be presented in a governmental entity's statement of net position. If a claims liability is considered to be incurred, the liability should be presented as a debt obligation of the governmental entity in its governmental and business activities columns of the statement of net position. As required by GASB-34, liabilities that have an average maturity greater than one year must be reported in two components, namely, the amount due within one year and the amount due in more than one year.

When a claims expense is recorded, the expense must be evaluated to determine how the expense should be presented in the statement of activities. That is, a determination should be made as to whether the claims expense is a direct expense (expenses that are specifically associated with a service, program, or department). In some instances a claims expense may be an extraordinary item (unusual and infrequent) and therefore should be presented in the lower section of the statement of activities. When a claims expense is either unusual or infrequent, but not both, the item should be disclosed in a note to the financial statements (GASB-34, pars. 16, 31) [GASB Cod. Sec. C50.120].

Reporting Risk Financing Internal Service Fund Balances and Activity

If an Internal Service Fund is used to account for risk management activities, such activities should be eliminated to avoid "doubling-up" expenses and revenues in the government activities column of the statement of activities. The effect of this approach is to adjust activities in an Internal Service Fund to a break-even balance. That is, if the Internal Service Fund had a "net profit" for the year, there should be a pro rata reduction in the charges made to the funds that used the Internal Service Fund's services for the year. Likewise, a net loss would require a pro rata adjustment that would increase the charges made to the various participating funds. After making these eliminations any residual balances related to the Internal Service Fund's assets and liabilities should be reported in the government activities column in the statement of net position (GASB-34, pars. 59 and 62, as amended by GASB-63, pars. 7–8) [GASB Cod. Secs. C50.122–.123].

DISCLOSURES

Disclosure of Loss Contingencies

When a possible future loss, including any loss in excess of an accrued amount, does not satisfy the criteria for accrual (probable and subject to reasonable estimation), the loss should be evaluated to determine whether it should be disclosed in the governmental entity's financial statements. Any loss that can be classified in one of the following categories should be disclosed:

- Loss is probable but no reasonable estimate (or estimate range) of the loss can be made.
- Loss is reasonably possible.

When a loss is disclosed in the financial statements, the following should be disclosed:

- Nature of the loss; and
- Estimate (or estimate range) of the loss (or, if no estimate can be made, the disclosure should state so).

Possible losses arising from unreported claims or unreported assessments do not have to be disclosed unless the following conditions exist:

- It is probable that a claim will be asserted or an assessment will be made.
- It is reasonably possible that a loss will arise from the asserted claim or assessment.

When a loss is based on a future event whose likelihood of occurring is remote, the loss should not be accrued or disclosed in the financial statements (GASB-10, par. 58) [GASB Cod. Sec. C50.115].

Risk Management Disclosures

The following disclosures should be made in the financial statements of entities that are not public entity risk pools (GASB-10, par. 77; GASB-30, par. 10) [GASB Cod. Sec. C50.145]:

- Describe the types of risk to which the governmental entity is exposed.
- Identify the methods used for risk financing (such as self-insurance, transfer of risk by purchasing insurance from a commercial enterprise, or transfer to or pooling of risk in a public entity risk pool). If the governmental entity has acquired commercial insurance that is insignificant in relation to the risk exposure, the governmental entity has in substance retained the risk of loss.
- Describe significant reductions in insurance coverage from the previous year, arranged by major category of risk, and indicate whether settlements exceeded insurance coverage for each of the past three years.
- Disclose whether the entity participates in a public entity risk pool and the nature of participation, if any, including rights and obligations of the governmental entity and the pool.

- Disclose whether the governmental entity has retained the risk of loss (risk is not transferred when activities are accounted for in an Internal Service Fund), and describe the following:

  — Basis of estimating liabilities for unpaid claims including the effects of specific, incremental claim adjustment expenditures/expenses, and recoveries related to salvage and subrogation, as well as the effects of other components of the estimated amount, and whether the accrual includes a provision for other allocated or unallocated claim adjustment expenditures/expenses;

  — Carrying amount of unpaid claims liabilities that have been computed on a present-value basis and the range of discount rates used to make the computation; and

  — Total amount of outstanding liabilities that have been removed from the balance sheet because of the purchase of annuity contracts from third parties in the name of claimants (amount should not include amounts related to settlements for which claimants have signed an agreement releasing the entity from further obligation and the chance of further payment is remote).

- Present a total claims liabilities reconciliation, including changes in aggregate liabilities for claims in the current year and prior year using the following tabular format:

  — Beginning balance of claims liabilities;

  — Provision for incurred claims expenses for the year and increases or decreases in the provision for events that were incurred in prior years;

  — Payments made for claims arising during the current year and prior fiscal years;

  — Explanation of other material reconciling items; and

  — Ending balance of claims liabilities.

Level of Disclosure

Professional judgment must be exercised to determine the most appropriate level of disclosure. The notes to the financial statements should focus on the primary government (which includes its blended component units) and support the information included in the government-wide financial statements and the fund financial statements.

OBSERVATION: Note disclosures related to discretely presented component units should be presented based on the requirements established by GASB-14, paragraph 63, as amended by GASB-61. However, for the most part, unless they are material, the notes to the basic financial statements of a primary government do not carry disclosures on risk from discretely presented component units unless the primary government assumes a contingent portion of the risk (see Component Unit Disclosures, below).

In some situations, it may be appropriate for the governmental entity to make disclosures for the entity as a whole. Separate or additional disclosures by individual major funds may be appropriate in other situations.

When the financial statements of a public entity risk pool are presented separately and also included in a primary government's financial report, disclosures in the primary government's financial statements should emphasize the nature of the primary government's participation in the pool. The primary government's financial report should note that the public entity risk pool presents separate financial statements (GASB-10, par. 78, as amended by GASB-34, par. 6, GASB-14, pars. 11 and 63, as amended by GASB-61, par. 11, GASB-68, par. 18, GASB-73, par. 24, GASB-34, par. 113) [GABS Cod. Sec. C50.146].

Subsequent Events

To ensure that the financial statements are not misleading, the governmental entity should consider the need to disclose subsequent events, which are events or transactions related to risk management that occur after the date of the balance sheet. Disclosure should be made for material items that have one of the following characteristics:

- The subsequent event resulted in the impairment of an asset or the incurrence of a liability (actual loss, such as damage from an earthquake).
- A reasonable possibility exists that a subsequent event resulted in the impairment of an asset or the incurrence of a liability (contingent loss, such as the personal injury claims to parties in which it has been alleged that the governmental entity's negligence contributed to the injuries).

If a governmental entity concludes that a subsequent event should be disclosed, the following information should be presented in the disclosure:

- The nature of the actual loss or loss contingency; and
- An estimate (or range of estimates) of the actual loss or contingent loss (or, if no estimate can be made, disclose appropriately).

In unusual circumstances, a subsequent event may result in the presentation of pro forma financial statements to supplement the historical financial statements. This should be limited to the occurrence of an actual loss that is subject to reasonable estimation. Pro forma statements are prepared by modifying the historical financial statements as if the loss had occurred on the last day of the fiscal year. Usually, only a pro forma balance sheet is presented and may be most informative if the pro forma and historical financial statements are presented on a comparative (columnar) basis (GASB-10, par. 80, as amended by GASB-34, par. 12, and GASB-63, par. 8) [GASB Cod. Sec. C50.149].

Component Unit Disclosures

The following disclosures should be made by a component unit that issues separate financial statements and participates in its primary government's risk-management Internal Service Fund (GASB-10, par. 79, as amended by GASB-14, par. 65) [GASB Cod. Sec. C50.148]:

- Describe the risks of loss to which the entity is exposed and the way(s) in which those risks of loss are handled (e.g., purchase of commercial insurance, participation in a public entity risk pool, risk retention).

- Describe significant reductions in insurance coverage from coverage in the prior year by major categories of risk. Also indicate whether the amount of settlements exceeded insurance coverage for each of the past three fiscal years.

- Disclose that the component unit participates in the Internal Service Fund.

- Describe the nature of the participation.

- Describe the rights and responsibilities of both the component unit and the primary government.

PRACTICE POINT: Examples of disclosures may be found in the CCH 2018 *Governmental GAAP Disclosure Manual*, Chapters 17 and 31.

QUESTIONS

1. In making the determination whether or not a government is either a participant in or operating a risk pool rather than managing risk, the following factors need to be considered except for:

   a. A cooperative group of governmental entities joining together to finance an exposure, liability, or risk. Risk may include property and liability, workers' compensation, or employee health care. A pool may be a stand-alone entity or included as part of another governmental entity that acts as the pool's sponsor.

   b. A governmental entity that is a pool's sponsor may also participate in the pool for its own risk management function.

   c. A governmental entity is managing risk through regular contributions to a fund based on an actuarial study.

   d. Stand-alone pools are established under authorizing statute by agreement of any number of state and local governmental entities. Stand-alone pools are sometimes organized or sponsored by municipal leagues, school associations, or other types of associations of governmental entities. Stand-alone pools are frequently operated by a board that has as its membership one member from each participating government. They typically have no publicly elected officials of their own or power to tax.

2. Unless a state or local governmental entity has not transferred the risk of loss to an unrelated third party or used an internal service fund, when should an accrual for a claim be recognized?

   a. On the basis of information available before the financial statements are issued, it is probable (likely to occur) that an asset has been impaired or a liability has been incurred as of the date of the financial statements and the loss can be reasonably estimated.

   b. Cash is paid to settle the claim.

   c. The claim is being adjudicated in a court of law; however, the government's legal counsel indicates that the risk of loss is remote.

   d. The claim is being adjudicated in a court of law; however, the government's legal counsel indicates that the risk of loss is probable but not estimable.

3. According to GASB-10, when should claims liabilities be discounted?

   a. In all settlement circumstances.

   b. When structured settlements are in place because the amount to be paid to the claimant is fixed by contract and the payment dates are fixed or determinable.

   c. When structured settlements are not in place because the amount to be paid to the claimant is variable by contract but the payment dates are fixed or determinable.

   d. When structured settlements are required to be paid to an irrevocable trust.

4. Payments made or credits extended to the insured by the insurer, usually at the end of a policy year, that result in reducing the net insurance cost to the policyholder either paid in cash to the insured or applied by the insured to reduce premiums due for the next policy year are examples of:

   a. Net settlements.

   b. Structured settlements.

   c. Unearned revenue.

   d. Policyholder dividends.

5. Incurred but not reported claims include the following components except for:

   a. Recoveries from subrogation.

   b. Known loss events that are expected to be presented as claims.

   c. Unknown loss events that are expected to become claims.

   d. Expected future development on claims already reported.

Case – Adapted from the *GASB Comprehensive Implementation Guide*

For each set of facts, indicate whether the organization is a public entity risk pool.

1. The State of Centennial has a fund through which it offers health care coverage for active employees of local governments that elect to participate. Employees are eligible to receive benefits only for covered illnesses and events that occur during active employment. Required annual contributions to the fund are actuarially determined. Participants (the governments) pay a pro-rata share of the required annual contributions based on total payroll costs for the prior year. Claims are paid from the fund up to an aggregate limit. Excess insurance is purchased for the remainder of claims. The state is not a participant in the fund. It uses a separate fund to account for the health care costs of its active employees.

2. The State of Centennial pension system has a fund through which it accumulates assets contributed by the state and participating local governments for future retiree health care benefits.

3. Castle Rock County has a fund through which it offers workers' compensation coverage to local schools, both public and private (nongovernmental not-for-profit), that elect to participate. Required annual contributions to the fund are actuarially determined. Participants pay a pro-rata share of the required annual contributions based on total payroll costs for the prior year. Eighty percent of covered payroll costs are attributable to public schools; the remainder is attributable to private schools. The county does not participate in this fund for its own workers' compensation costs.

4. Castle Rock County has a fund through which it offers workers' compensation coverage to all local governments and not-for-profit organizations within the county's geographic boundaries that elect to participate. Required annual contributions to the fund are actuarially determined. Participants pay a pro-rata share of the required annual contributions based on total payroll costs for the prior year. The county participates in this fund for its own workers' compensation costs. It has 30% of the covered payroll; the local governments have 65% of the covered payroll, and not-for-profit organizations have 5% of the covered payroll.

5. The State of Centennial League of Municipalities administers a program that provides workers' compensation coverage to all member local governments that elect to participate. Required annual contributions to the program are actuarially determined. Participants pay a pro-rata share of the required annual contributions based on total payroll costs for the prior year.

ANSWERS

1. In making the determination whether or not a government is either a participant or operating a risk pool rather than managing risk, the following factors need to be considered except for:

   Answer – C: All others are factors in making the determination.

2. Unless a state or local governmental entity has not transferred the risk of loss to an unrelated third party or used an internal service fund, when should an accrual for a claim be recognized?

   Answer – B: An accrual is made irrespective of the timing of cash payments to settle the claim.

3. According to GASB-10, when should claims liabilities be discounted?

   Answer – B: Structured settlements and similar may not be discounted in accordance with GASB-10, as amended.

4. Payments made or credits extended to the insured by the insurer, usually at the end of a policy year, that result in reducing the net insurance cost to the policyholder either paid in cash to the insured or applied by the insured to reduce premiums due for the next policy year are examples of:

   Answer – D: Settlements and unearned revenue do not reduce net insurance costs.

5. Incurred but not reported claims include the following components except for:

   Answer – A: The remaining answers are part of incurred but not reported claims.

Case – Adapted from the *GASB Comprehensive Implementation Guide*

For each set of facts, indicate whether the organization is a public entity risk pool.

1. The State of Centennial has a fund through which it offers health care coverage for active employees of local governments that elect to participate. Employees are eligible to receive benefits only for covered illnesses and events that occur during active employment. Required annual contributions to the fund are actuarially determined. Participants (the governments) pay a pro-rata share of the required annual contributions based on total payroll costs for the prior year. Claims are paid from the fund up to an aggregate limit. Excess insurance is purchased for the remainder of claims. The state is not a participant in the fund. It uses a separate fund to account for the health care costs of its active employees.

   Answer – Pool.

2. The State of Centennial pension system has a fund through which it accumulates assets contributed by the state and participating local governments for future retiree health care benefits.

   Answer – Not a pool.

3. Castle Rock County has a fund through which it offers workers' compensation coverage to local schools, both public and private (nongovernmental not-for-profit), that elect to participate. Required annual contributions to the fund are actuarially determined. Participants pay a pro-rata share of the required annual contributions based on total payroll costs for the prior year. Eighty percent of covered payroll costs are attributable to public schools; the remainder is attributable to private schools. The county does not participate in this fund for its own workers' compensation costs.

   Answer – Pool.

4. Castle Rock County has a fund through which it offers workers' compensation coverage to all local governments and not-for-profit organizations within the county's geographic boundaries that elect to participate. Required annual contributions to the fund are actuarially determined. Participants pay a pro-rata share of the required annual contributions based on total payroll costs for the prior year. The county participates in this fund for its own workers' compensation costs. It has 30% of the covered payroll; the local governments have 65% of the covered payroll, and not-for-profit organizations have 5% of the covered payroll.

   Answer – Pool: Because the county is not the predominant participant.

5. The State of Centennial League of Municipalities administers a program that provides workers' compensation coverage to all member local governments that elect to participate. Required annual contributions to the program are actuarially determined. Participants pay a pro-rata share of the required annual contributions based on total payroll costs for the prior year.

   Answer – Pool.

CHAPTER 16
OTHER LIABILITIES

CONTENTS

INTRODUCTION

The accounting standards that are used to determine which liabilities should be presented in a governmental entity's financial statements vary depending on whether a liability is presented in (1) governmental funds, (2) proprietary funds or fiduciary funds, or (3) the government-wide financial statements.

Note: Certain liabilities incurred by state and local governments are specifically addressed in other chapters as follows:

- Liabilities arising from certain asset retirement obligations (GASB-83) (see Chapter 10, "Capital Assets") (but introduced in this chapter as well);

- Liabilities arising from long-term debt transactions (see Chapter 12, "Long-Term Debt");

- Liabilities arising from pension and employee benefit transactions (see Chapter 13, "Pension, Postemployment, and Other Employee Benefit Liabilities");

- Liabilities arising from lease and service concession transactions (see Chapter 14, "Leases and Service Concession Arrangements"); and

- Liabilities arising from risk management activities (see Chapter 15, "Risk Management, Claims, and Judgments").

This chapter discusses other liabilities of governmental funds, such as payables and accruals unique to the modified accrual basis of accounting and current financial resources measurement focus. In addition, the chapter discusses the accounting and reporting of liabilities arising from operation or responsibility for a municipal solid waste landfill, state lottery obligations, and pollution remediation obligations.

GASB Concepts Statement No. 6 (GASB:CS-6) (*Measurement of Elements of Financial Statements*) addresses both measurement approaches and measurement attributes. A measurement approach determines whether an asset or liability presented in a financial statement should be either (*a*) reported at an amount that reflects a value at the date that the asset was acquired or the liability was incurred or (*b*) remeasured and reported at an amount that reflects a value at the date of the financial statements. A measurement attribute is the feature or characteristic of the asset or liability that is measured.

GASB:CS-6 established the two measurement approaches that are to be used in financial statements, as follows:

1. *Initial-Transaction-Date-Based Measurement (Initial Amount)*—This is commonly known as "historical cost." GASB:CS-6 defines the "initial amount" as the transaction price or amount assigned when an asset was acquired or a liability was incurred, including subsequent modifications to that price or amount, such as through depreciation or impairment.

2. *Current-Financial-Statement-Date-Based Measurement* (Remeasured Amount)—This is commonly known as "current value" but may be at fair value, replacement value, or settlement price. The commonality among the values is that they are defined as the amount assigned when an asset or liability is remeasured as of the financial statement date.

GASB:CS-6 established the four measurement attributes that are to be used in financial statements, as follows:

1. *Historical cost* is the price paid to acquire an asset or the amount received pursuant to the incurrence of a liability in an actual exchange transaction.

2. *Fair value* is the price that would be received to sell an asset or paid to transfer a liability in an orderly transaction between market participants at the measurement date.

3. *Replacement cost* is the price that would be paid to acquire an asset with equivalent service potential in an orderly market transaction at the measurement date.

4. *Settlement amount* is the amount at which an asset could be realized or a liability could be liquidated with the counterparty other than in an active market.

GOVERNMENTAL FUND LIABILITIES

The measurement focus for governmental funds is the flow of current financial resources. Liabilities that will consume current financial resources of the fund responsible for payment during the fiscal period are presented in that fund's balance sheet. No explicit current liability classification exists on a fund's balance sheet (the financial statement is unclassified). However, the mere presentation of the liability in the balance sheet of the government's fund implies that the debt is current and will require the use of expendable financial resources. Therefore, the governmental fund's measurement focus is based upon determination of financial position and changes in financial position encompassing sources, uses, and balances of financial resources (NCGA-1 par. 18) [GASB Cod. Sec. 1300.102].

The definition of "current liabilities" differs significantly between a governmental fund and a commercial enterprise. GASB-62, par. 34 [GASB Cod. Secs. 1500.106, 1800.113, 2200.180], describes "current liabilities" as those items that will be liquidated through the use of current assets. "Current assets" are defined as resources expected to be realized or consumed within the entity's operating cycle. Thus, the term to maturity of a current liability of a commercial enterprise could be a year or longer, depending on the entity's operating cycle. A liability of a governmental fund is considered current when it is expected to be liquidated with current financial resources. The term to maturity for a government's current liability is much shorter than that for a commercial enterprise.

Long-term liabilities not accounted for in proprietary or fiduciary funds of a governmental reporting entity are presented in the entity's government-wide financial statements (NCGA-1, par. 33, as amended by GASB-34, pars. 6, 82, as amended by GASB-63, par. 8) [GASB Cod. Sec. 1500.101].

Recording Fund Liabilities and Expenditures

As described earlier, governmental funds generally record a liability when it is expected that the liability will be paid from revenues recognized during the current period. Liabilities that are normally expected to be paid with current financial resources should be presented as a fund liability, and liabilities that have been incurred but that are not normally expected to be paid with current financial resources should be considered long-term liabilities. Long-term liabilities are presented in the government-wide financial statements (statement of net position) and not in a fund balance sheet.

For many years accountants have criticized the definitions of governmental revenues/assets and expenditures/liabilities because they are based on circular reasoning. That is, revenue can only be accrued at the end of a period if the revenue will be collected in time to pay accrued liabilities; however, liabilities can be accrued at year-end only when they are paid from revenues recognized during the current period. GASB Interpretation No. 6 (GASBI-6) (*Recognition and Measurement of Certain Liabilities and Expenditures in Governmental Fund Financial Statements*) was issued to provide guidance for determining when liabilities should be accrued in governmental funds (not proprietary funds, fiduciary funds, or the government-wide financial statements).

GASB-76 (*The Hierarchy of Generally Accepted Accounting Principles for State and Local Governments*) reduced the U.S. GAAP hierarchy to two categories of authoritative U.S. GAAP, moving GASB interpretations into Category A. GASB *Interpretations* have been infrequently issued and are largely incorporated into Statements. GASB-76 includes a footnote to Category A on the status of interpretations:

> All GASB Interpretations heretofore issued and currently in effect also are considered as being included within Category A and are continued in force until altered, amended, supplemented, revoked, or superseded by subsequent GASB pronouncements. Category A standards, including GASB Interpretations heretofore issued and currently in effect, are the subject of the Accounting Principles Rule of the American Institute of Certified Public Accountants' (AICPA) *Code of Professional Conduct*, and this Statement does not affect the application of that rule.

To address the accrual of liabilities, GASBI-6 categorizes governmental fund liabilities as follows:

- Liabilities that are generally recognized when due;
- Liabilities that are recognized when they are "*normally expected to be liquidated with expendable available financial resources*"; and
- Liabilities that have no specific accrual modification (GASBI-6, par. 11, as amended by GASB-47, par. 3, and GASB-49, par. 24) [GASB Cod. Sec. 1500.119].

The Interpretation does not apply to operating leases that include scheduled rent increases (the standards established by GASB-13 (*Accounting for Operating Leases with Scheduled Rent Increases*) should be followed) (see **Appendix** in Chapter 14, "Leases and Service Concession Arrangements" discussing the sweeping changes coming in the future in GASB Statement No. 87 (*Leases*)).

The basic guidance for determining when a governmental fund should accrue an expenditure/liability is found in NCGA-1 (*Governmental Accounting and Financial Reporting Principles*), paragraph 70, which states that "most expenditures and transfers out are measurable and should be recorded when the related liability is incurred." GASBI-6 expands on this general guidance by noting the following (GASBI-6, par. 12) [GASB Cod. Sec. 1500.103]:

> Governmental fund liabilities and expenditures that should be accrued include liabilities that, once incurred, normally are paid in a timely manner and in full from current financial resources—for example, salaries, professional services, supplies, utilities, and travel.

These transactions give rise to fund liabilities that are considered mature liabilities because they are "normally due and payable in full when incurred."

However, GASBI-6 points out that there are several significant exceptions to this general guidance established in NCGA-1. Specifically, NCGA-1 states that "unmatured long-term indebtedness" should not be reported as a fund liability (except for debts that are related to proprietary and trust funds). "Unmatured long-term indebtedness" is defined as "the portion of general long-term indebtedness that is not yet due for payment," and includes debts such as the following (GASBI-6, pars. 9–11) [GASB Cod. Secs. 1500.117–.119]:

- Formal debt agreements such as bonds and notes;
- Liabilities "normally expected to be liquidated with expendable available financial resources"; and
- Other commitments that are not current liabilities properly recorded in governmental funds.

Although the term "liability" appears easy to understand, it is often misunderstood, as it contains the concepts of obligations, and to some extent, time. An obligation is a social, legal, or moral requirement, such as a duty, contract, or promise that compels one to follow or avoid a particular course of action. Obligations can be legally enforceable as exemplified when a court compels the government to fulfill its obligation. Obligations could arise from legislation or contractual obligations; they may differ, however, based on whether exchange transactions (value for value) or nonexchange transactions take place. Constructive liabilities may occur in exchange transactions when resources are transferred to a government. In this case, the government must fulfill its obligations. The concept of "little or no discretion to avoid" arises when no power exists to decline sacrificing of resources or penalty/consequences of not doing the action is more than minor. One of the consistent themes in all of these nuances is that the parties to an obligation that may be a liability are usually external to the government.

The language contained in GASB Interpretation 6 (GASBI-6) (*Recognition and Measurement of Certain Liabilities and Expenditures in Governmental Fund Financial Statements*) was one of the reasons why the clarification of the concepts of the terms "liability" and "obligation" needed to be released. GASBI-6, par. 10 [GASB Cod. Sec. 1500.118], describes "matured liabilities" in governmental funds only (not associated with proprietary funds) as those that are normally due and payable in full when incurred or the matured portion of general long-term indebtedness (the portion that has come due for payment). GASBI-6, par. 11,as amended by GASB-47, par. 3, and GASB-49, par. 24) [GASB Cod. Sec. 1500.119], also interpreted "matured liabilities" to include debt service on formal debt issued when due (matured) and compensated absences, claims and judgments, special termination benefits, and landfill closure and postclosure care costs. All of these should be recognized as governmental fund liabilities and expenditures to the extent the liabilities are "normally expected to be liquidated with expendable available financial resources." In its basis for conclusions, the GASB considered but rejected an alternative interpretation that "other commitments" are the long-term portion of any other liabilities, provided that the government has entered into a multilateral agreement to defer payment to a future period. The GASB concluded that there is no accrual modification that would permit deferring to a future period the recognition of fund liabilities (such as salaries and utilities) that normally are paid in a timely manner and in full from current financial resources when incurred. Rather, the GASB proposed that such transactions should be reported as governmental fund liabilities and expenditures when incurred.

OBSERVATION: The controversy stems somewhat from the changing landscape of government operations. For example, post-retirement health care benefits in many jurisdictions may be changed in law without collective bargaining, leading to the notion that these benefits may not be liabilities. The GASB's conclusions mentioned above are also leading to the interpretation (perhaps rightfully so) that no liability would exist in a governmental fund that normally pays salary escalations that cannot be paid out of current financial resources due to economic conditions. The escalations are then renegotiated to be paid in a future period even though in a statement of net position a liability may be declared for the same circumstance.

Exceptions

GASBI-6 points out that the three specified categories listed above are exceptions to the general rule that a liability is recorded as a fund liability and "in the absence of an explicit requirement to do otherwise, a government should accrue a governmental fund liability and expenditure in the period in which the government incurs the liability."

Most expenditures are measurable and should be recorded when the related fund liability is incurred. An exception to this generalization is the treatment of interest and principal payments for general long-term indebtedness. Interest and principal on long-term debt are not recorded as expenditures as they accrue, but when they become due and payable. For example, if a governmental entity issues a 30-year bond, the liabilities would not be reported as a *fund liability* until the debt is actually due and payable, which would be thirty years after issuance.

Current accounting standards provide for an exception to the basic concept that general long-term indebtedness is not reported as expenditures until the amounts become due and payable. When funds have been transferred to the Debt Service Fund during the fiscal year in anticipation of making debt service payments "shortly" after the end of the period, it is acceptable to accrue interest and debt in the Debt Service Fund as an expenditure in the year the transfer is made. Prior to the issuance of GASBI-6, there was a considerable amount of confusion as to what is meant by shortly. The Interpretation states that "shortly" means "early in the following year"; however, the period of time after the end of the year cannot be greater than one month.

The exception does not apply to the following situations:

- The financial resources that will be used to pay the indebtedness early in the following year are held in a fund other than a Debt Service Fund.
- The financial resources represent "non-dedicated financial resources" that have been transferred to a Debt Service Fund based on management discretion.

The accumulation of resources under the two strategies described above should not be reported as an expenditure but as part of the governmental fund's fund balance.

It should be emphasized that this exception applies only when a Debt Service Fund is used to account for servicing the debt.

Although NCGA-1 implies that a fund liability should be recorded when the obligation is incurred, one of the most important concepts that forms the basis for preparing the financial statements of a governmental fund is that liabilities are recorded only when they are normally expected to be liquidated with expendable available financial resources. As described in GASBI-6, this exception to the broad accrual assumption is based on the same guidance established for formal debt agreements as described in the previous section. That is, "governments, in general, are normally expected to liquidate liabilities with expendable available financial resources to the extent that the liabilities mature (come due for payment) each period." In order to apply this broad generalization to current practice, GASBI-6 notes that "a series of specific accrual modifications have been established pertaining to the reporting of certain forms of long-term indebtedness." These exceptions include formal debt agreements as described in the previous section as well as the following debt arrangements:

- Debts that arise from compensated absences, pensions, other postemployment benefits, and termination benefits (see Chapter 13, "Pension, Postemployment, and Other Employee Benefit Liabilities");

- Capital lease agreements (see Chapter 14, "Leases and Service Concession Arrangements");

- Claims and judgments (see Chapter 15, "Risk Management, Claims, and Judgments"); and

- Landfill closure and post-closure obligations, discussed later in this chapter.

OBSERVATION: GASBI-6 uses the phrase "normally expected to be liquidated with expendable available financial resources," which is interpreted to be equivalent to other, similar variations, including "normally would be liquidated with expendable available financial resources" and "payable with expendable available financial resources."

PRACTICE ALERT: Reducing or eliminating these exceptions to the conceptual framework for reporting governmental fund liabilities is one of the many goals of the GASB's *Financial Reporting Model—Reexamination* project.

The third broad exception to the basic concept that government fund liabilities are recognized on an accrual basis relates to possible new forms of debt. In a dynamic economy, new forms of debt may be created that have not been addressed by a specific governmental accounting standard. GASBI-6 points out that these "other commitments" should be reported as a fund liability when due and payable. The total amount of the debt, regardless of when due, would be reported in the government-wide financial statements.

Accumulation of Resources

GASBI-6 clarifies the funding strategy with respect to unmatured liabilities that are not reported as fund obligations. Some governmental entities have established the practice of budgeting these obligations on an accrual basis or otherwise funding the eventual payment of these liabilities on something other than a budgetary basis.

For example, compensated absences may be reported as a fund expenditure of $100,000 based on the concept of "normally expected to be liquidated with expendable available financial resources" but the governmental entity may budget for and accumulate fund resources in the amount of $300,000, which is the amount of the accrual based on the standards established by GASB-16.

GASBI-6 states that the accumulation of resources that will be used eventually to pay for unmatured general long-term indebtedness cannot be reported in a governmental fund as an expenditure or obligation of the fund because that funding strategy does not result in the outflow of current financial resources. Thus, in the previous example the governmental fund would record an expenditure of $100,000 for compensated absences and the additional $200,000 ($300,000 – $100,000) should be reported as part of the assigned fund balance of the governmental (debt service) fund. If appropriate action has been taken by the management of the governmental entity, the assigned fund balance may be identified for the funding of compensated absences, but that transaction does not result in expenditure recognition. Nor is it reported due to the constraints of GASB-54. However, if the government is legally required to fund these obligations, a committed or a restricted fund balance would be appropriate. A restricted fund balance would be proper if the legal requirement was made by an entity other than the government itself (e.g., a state law or a bond indenture).

GASBI-6 points out that the GASB does not establish strategies for funding obligations. That is the responsibility of the governmental entity's management; however, the GASB is not unsympathetic with those governmental entities that believe that it is advantageous and appropriate to fund certain liabilities on an accrual basis rather than on a strict budgetary basis. For example, the GASB notes that "if a government wishes to report employee benefits such as compensated absences or special termination benefits on the accrual basis in fund financial statements, as well as in government-wide financial statements, it would not be precluded from reporting them through an employee benefit trust fund, if a proper trust is established."

LANDFILL CLOSURE AND POST-CLOSURE CARE COSTS

Many governmental entities are involved with the onerous task of collecting and disposing of an ever increasing volume of refuse. One method of disposing of this material is through landfill operations. Like other entities, landfills have cash inflows and outflows during their operating lives. However, landfills are unique because when they close, their cash inflows cease but their cash outflows generally must continue to ensure that the surrounding environment is not damaged by tainted water and other residues.

Governmental accounting and reporting standards for landfill operations are provided in GASB-18 (*Accounting for Municipal Solid Waste Landfill Closure and Post-Closure Care Costs*).

In the past, operators and owners were not mandated to provide funds to protect the environment after closing a landfill, but the environmental protection movement fostered legislation that requires such funding. Specifically, in 1991, the U.S. Environmental Protection Agency (EPA) issued a rule (Solid Waste Disposal Facility Criteria) that applies to municipal solid waste landfills (MSWLFs). The EPA ruling establishes closure requirements for MSWLFs that accept solid waste after October 9, 1991, and "location restrictions, operating criteria, design criteria, groundwater monitoring and corrective action requirements, post-closure care requirements, and financial assurance requirements" for MSWLFs that receive solid waste after October 9, 1993.

The unique character of landfills and the EPA rule raise the accounting issues of how and when costs expected to be incurred after the close of a landfill should be recorded. Based on research conducted by GASB, it is apparent that a variety of accounting practices were being used to account for closure and post-closure care costs. GASB-18 was specifically issued to reduce the diversity of acceptable accounting practices in this area. With the issuance of GASB-18, the GASB took the position that the EPA rule provided very specific requirements and that the time is appropriate to establish accounting standards related to solid waste landfill closure and post-closure care costs.

Although the EPA rule concerning municipal solid waste landfill closure and post-closure care costs applies to private and public owners and operators of landfills, GASB-18 does not apply to private entities.

GASB-18 applies to all governmental MSWLFs irrespective of what type of accounting model they use to account for the activities of a landfill. The costs incurred by the governmental entity may arise from regulations established by a federal, state, or local governmental agency. The guidance established by GASB-18 applies to both closure and post-closure care costs (GASB-18, par. 3, as amended by GASB-34, par. 3, and GASB-35, par. 5) [GASB Cod. Sec. L10.101].

In footnote 2 of GASB-18, as amended by GASB-34 [GASB Cod. Sec. L10.fn2], the GASB defines costs to encompass "both an economic and a financial resources perspective." Under current governmental accounting standards, a proprietary fund recognizes as expenses both economic (e.g., the depreciation of a capital asset) and financial resources (e.g., cash expenditures) used in operations, while a governmental fund's measurement of expenditures is limited to the consumption of financial resources. Thus, because the costing standards established by GASB-18 are somewhat different from those associated with governmental funds, the GASB used footnote 2 to clarify the cost-recognition approach established in GASB-18.

Definition of Closure and Post-Closure Care Costs

The basic objective of GASB-18 is to recognize all landfill costs by the time a landfill is closed (no longer accepts solid waste). Of course, once it is closed, there will be expenditures associated with the landfill (post-closure care), but those costs should have been estimated by the closure date and recognized as such in the governmental entity's financial statements. The degree to which the accounting standards established by GASB-18 are satisfied is directly related to a governmental entity's ability to accurately estimate all future costs. (These costs could extend over a long period of time).

The starting point in satisfying the standards established by GASB-18 is to identify "the estimated total current cost of MSWLF closure and post-closure care." Current cost refers to the cost of buying, in the current year, capital assets and services related to closure and post-closure care, even though those costs will actually be incurred in future periods. Specifically, the estimated total current cost of MSWLF closure and post-closure care should include the current cost of (1) capital assets, (2) final cover, and (3) monitoring and maintenance activities.

Based on the current design plans of the MSWLF, capital asset costs should include expenditures related to the acquisition and installation of equipment and the construction of facilities. Such costs should be limited to capital assets that will be acquired, installed, or built (1) at or near the date the landfill ceases to accept waste and (2) after the landfill ceases to accept waste. In addition, capital asset costs should include only those assets that will be used exclusively for the MSWLF activity. However, when a capital asset is used by more than one MSWLF, the costs should be allocated between or among the MSWLFs on the basis of usage.

Once the landfill is full, it will generally be necessary to cap the facility. The current cost of the capping should be included as part of the estimated total current cost of the MSWLF (GASB-18, par. 4) [GASB Cod. Sec. L10.103].

Even after the landfill no longer accepts solid waste, the governmental entity will continue to incur costs related to the monitoring and maintenance of facilities and the landfill itself. Federal, state, or local regulations mandate how long the monitoring and maintenance period must last. These ongoing (future) costs are part of the estimated total current cost of the MSWLF. GASB-18 requires that the estimate be based on the "expected usable landfill area," which is the area expected to receive the solid waste during the life of the MSWLF. However, estimation of the landfill capacity should take into consideration a number of factors such as MSWLF permit periods (including the probability of renewals) and geological factors. For example, the capacity of the landfill may decrease if, in a subsequent year, it is determined that a portion of the area has geological characteristics that make it unsuitable to accept solid waste.

Federal, state, or local laws and regulations will mandate what measures must be used to ensure that the landfill is properly closed and monitored when solid waste is no longer accepted. These laws and regulations should be the basis for estimating the total current cost of MSWLF closure and post-closure care. Furthermore, the closure and post-closure costs should be based on the laws and regulations that have been approved as of the statement of net position date (GASB-18, par. 5, as amended by GASB-34, pars. 13 and 91, as amended by GASB-63, par. 8) [GASB Cod. Sec. L10.104].

OBSERVATION: Under specified circumstances, the EPA rule can be modified by allowing state or local landfill requirements to apply to a landfill owner or operator. In this case, state or local requirements would dictate which equipment, facilities, and services must be acquired with respect to closure and post-closure care, and the accounting by the governmental entity should be consistent with the modified requirements.

PRACTICE ALERT: As of the date of publication, it is unclear if the EPA rule will change or be repealed given the sweeping changes occurring in the federal government. Practitioners and auditors should monitor the status of the Solid Waste Disposal Facility Criteria closely if they have a MSWLF. If the rule is repealed, it would be up to the GASB to decide if changes are necessary in GASB-18.

Reporting MSWLFs

Proprietary Funds

When MSWLF activities are accounted for in a proprietary fund, a portion of the estimated total current cost of closure and post-closure care should be recognized each year as an expense. The cost basis for determining the amount of expense to be recognized is based on the definition of "estimated total current cost."

The amortization or allocation period starts the day the landfill accepts solid waste and continues until it no longer accepts waste. The amount of annual expense recognition is based on usage (similar to the units-of-production depreciation method). If 20% of the landfill is filled during the current year, 20% of the estimated total current cost of closure and post-closure care should be reported as a current expense. If no solid waste is accepted during a period, there should be no expense recognition for that period.

It is likely that cost estimates will change from year to year, and for this reason, the computation of the annual expense must take into consideration the capacity used and the amount of expense recognized in previous years. Thus, the analysis that should be used each year to determine the amount of expense to be recognized is based on the following formula:

$$\frac{[\text{Estimated Total Current Cost} \times \text{Cumulative Capacity Used}]}{\text{Total Estimated Capacity}} - \text{Amount of Expense Previously Recognized}$$

For example, if the estimated total current cost is \$1,000,000, the cumulative capacity used is 100,000 cubic yards, the total estimated capacity is 500,000 cubic yards, and the amount of expense recognized in all previous years is \$125,000, the expense to be recorded in the current year is computed as follows:

[$1,000,000 × 100,000 cubic yards]

$$\div \qquad - \ \$125,000 \quad = \ \$75,000$$

500,000 cubic yards $\qquad\qquad\qquad$ (current expenses)

Since the computation is based on expected or future cost, there is no capital asset on the records of the proprietary fund that can be amortized. For this reason, the current expense related to the estimated total current cost of MSWLF closure and post-closure care is recorded by debiting an expense account and crediting a liability. For example, the expense computed in the previous paragraph would be recognized by making the following journal entry (GASB-18, par. 7, as amended by GASB-34, par. 6) [GASB Cod. Sec. L10.106]:

	Debit	Credit
LANDFILL ENTERPRISE FUND		
Expenses—Landfill Closure and Post-Closure Care Costs	75,000	
Estimated Liability for Landfill Closure and Post-Closure Care Costs		75,000
To record landfill closure current costs and liability.		

Acquisitions of equipment and facilities that will occur near or after the date the landfill no longer accepts waste are part of the estimated total current cost of the MSWLF. When these items are purchased (at or near the end of the life of the landfill), they should not be reported as capital assets but rather should be accounted for as a reduction to the estimated liability for landfill closure and post-closure care costs (GASB-18, par. 8) [GASB Cod. Sec. L10.107].

A landfill operator may acquire capital assets used exclusively for a MSWLF that do not meet the definition of "disbursements near or after the date that the MSWLF stops accepting solid waste and during the post-closure period." These capital expenditures, based on the guidance established by GASB-18, are not a component of the estimated total current cost of MSWLF closure and post-closure care and, therefore, must be capitalized and depreciated over the estimated remaining life of the landfill. The total estimated life of the landfill is the period from the date on which waste is first accepted until the date on which waste is no longer accepted. Thus, once the facility is filled, expenditures that have been capitalized must be fully depreciated (GASB-18, par. 9) [GASB Cod. Sec. L10.108]. See Exhibit 16-1 for a complete illustration of the costs and related liabilities.

Governmental Funds

When MSWLF activities are accounted for in a governmental fund, the basic measurement approach used by a proprietary fund should also be used by the governmental fund. A portion of the estimated total current cost of closure and post-closure care should be recognized each year using the estimated life of the landfill and the usage of the landfill for a particular period. However, due to the difference in the measurement focus and basis of accounting of a governmental fund as compared to a proprietary fund, the annual cost recognition related to estimated closure and post-closure care costs generally will not affect a governmental fund's activity statement.

The basic facts used to illustrate the accounting for MSWLF activities in a proprietary fund can be used to illustrate the activity in a governmental fund. As computed earlier, the amount of closure and post-closure care costs recognized was $75,000. This amount must be analyzed to determine whether it is to be paid with current expendable resources of the governmental entity. In almost all instances, it is unlikely that any of the estimated closure and post-closure care costs will use current expendable resources because those costs are based on "disbursements near or after the date that the MSWLF stops accepting solid waste." Assuming that none of the $75,000 is due and payable from current expendable resources, the governmental entity will report the total amount of the current cost as a general long-term liability in the governmental activities of the government-wide financial statements.

Capital acquisitions that are included in estimated total current cost should be reported as closure and post-closure care expenditures (GASB-18, pars. 10–11, as amended by GASB-34, pars. 18, 82, 119, as amended by GASB-63, par. 8, also GASBI-6, pars. 14–16) [GASB Cod. Sec. L10.109].

Government-Wide Financial Statements

Account balances and transactions related to MSWLFs should be reported in government-wide financial statements, similar to proprietary funds, based on the standards established in paragraphs 7, 10, and 11 of GASB-18, as amended by GASB-34 (as discussed above) [GASB Cod. Sec. L10.110].

Changes in Estimates

At the end of each year, a governmental entity should evaluate its estimate of the total current cost related to closure and post-closure care of a MSWLF. Changes in expected cost may arise from a number of factors, including inflation or deflation, technological advancements, and modifications to legal requirements at the local, state, or national level (GASB-18, par. 6) [GASB Cod. Sec. L10.105].

Closure and post-closure care costs generally extend over a lengthy period. For this reason, it is likely that there will be a number of changes in the components used to compute the annual costs of MSWLF closure and post-closure care. For example, the estimated cost of a landfill cap, control facilities, and maintenance services will undoubtedly change from year to year. The accounting for such changes is dependent on the period in which the change takes place. If the change in estimated costs occurs before the landfill is filled, the change is a "change in accounting estimate" and should be reported on a prospective basis. The effect of the change is allocated over the remaining estimated life of the landfill. For example, in the previous illustration, if it is assumed that in the following year the estimated total current cost is $1,000,000 (no change), the cumulative capacity used is 200,000 cubic yards, the total estimated capacity is 400,000 cubic yards (a change in estimate), and the amount of expense recognized in all previous years is $200,000 ($125,000 + $75,000), the amount of costs to be recognized for the year is computed as follows:

[$1,000,000 × 200,000 cubic yards]

$$\div \ \frac{}{400{,}000 \text{ cubic yards}} \quad - \ \$200{,}000 \quad = \quad \$300{,}000$$
(current expenses)

The use of the formula established by GASB-18 takes into consideration changes in accounting estimates (GASB-18, par. 13) [GASB Cod. Sec. L10.111].

When changes in estimates occur after the landfill no longer accepts solid waste, the effects of the changes should be recorded as a current year cost and not allocated over the remaining life of the closed landfill (the number of years mandated by law or regulation that the governmental entity must monitor and maintain the closed landfill). These costs should be recognized when they are probable and subject to reasonable estimation (i.e., they must satisfy the criteria within GASB-62, pars. 96–113, on contingencies). Whether those costs are to be reported by a governmental fund as an expenditure on its activity statement depends on whether the cost is due and payable from current expendable resources (GASB-18, par. 14) [GASB Cod. Sec. L10.112].

Some costs may relate to the horizontal expansion of the landfill. Because these costs arise from the expansion of the landfill capacity, they should not affect the factors used to compute the current cost of MSWLF closure and post-closure care for the original landfill. It would be necessary under this circumstance to make two separate computations for estimated total current cost for closure and post-closure care: one for the costs related to the original landfill dimensions, and one for costs related to the (new) expanded landfill area.

Accounting for Assets Placed in Trust

Under requirements of the EPA rule, some owners or operators of landfills will have to provide financial assurances concerning the future landfill closure and post-closure care costs. The purpose of the EPA requirement is to make sure that landfill owners or operators will have the capability to provide resources to assure that the financial burden of a filled landfill will not become the responsibility of taxpayers. The EPA rule can be achieved by putting assets in various forms of trusts.

When a governmental entity makes payments to the trust, those payments should not be treated as expenditures/expenses, but rather should be reported on the statement of net position as assets with an appropriate title such as "Amounts Held by Trustee." The assets should be reported in the fund that accounts for the landfill activities. Earnings on amounts held by the trustee (or otherwise set aside) should be reported as investment income and not as a reduction to the estimated total current cost of closure and post-closure care (GASB-18, par. 15) [GASB Cod. Sec. L10.113].

OBSERVATION: GASB-18 establishes accounting and reporting standards for MSWLFs, but the funding strategies must be established by the governmental entity's management team, and those strategies must be in compliance with applicable laws and regulations.

Responsibility Assumed by Another Entity

Under some circumstances the financial obligation related to closure and post-closure care of a landfill may be transferred from the governmental entity to another party, such as a private enterprise. If the responsibility has been legally transferred and the private enterprise is financially capable of meeting the financial obligation imposed by the closure and post-closure care responsibilities, the governmental entity is not required to recognize the annual portion of estimated total current cost of MSWLF closure and post-closure care.

When it is concluded that the financial responsibility for the landfill has been transferred to a private enterprise, the governmental entity should continue to assess the ability of the enterprise to fulfill its obligation. If federal, state, or local laws or regulations require that the governmental entity retain contingent liability for closure and post-closure care costs, and a question regarding the ability of the assuming entity to meet its obligation arises, the governmental entity should determine whether provisions should be made for the closure and post-closure care costs. When it is determined that it is *probable* that the governmental entity will have to assume the financial responsibility because of the poor financial condition of the assuming entity, the related obligation should be recognized on the governmental entity's financial statements. The liability should be computed using the guidelines discussed earlier, depending on whether the landfill activities are accounted for in a proprietary fund or in a governmental fund (GASB-18, par. 16, as amended by GASB-34, par. 82, and GASB-35, par. 5) [GASB Cod. Sec. L10.114].

Disclosures

GASB-18 requires that the following note(s) to a governmental entity's financial statements be presented (GASB-18, par. 17) [GASB Cod. Sec. L10.115]:

- Describe the laws, regulations, etc., that establish requirements for landfill closure and post-closure care.
- State that the liability for landfill closure and post-closure care costs is based on the amount of landfill used to date.
- Disclose the amount of the estimated liability for landfill closure and post-closure care costs (if not presented on the face of a financial statement) and the balance to be recognized in subsequent periods.
- Disclose the percentage of landfill used to date and the estimated remaining life (years) of the landfill.
- Describe how closure and post-closure care costs are being funded (if at all).
- Disclose the amount of assets that have been restricted for the payment of closure and post-closure costs (if not presented on the face of a financial statement).
- Describe the nature of the estimates used and the potential for changes in estimates that may result from inflation, technological changes, or regulatory changes.

PRACTICE POINT: An example of disclosure is contained in Wolter's Kluwer's *2018 GAAP Governmental GAAP Disclosures Manual*, Chapter 52.

Landfills Reported as Component Units

When landfills are considered to be component units of the primary government, the guidelines established by GASB Statement No. 14 (*The Financial Reporting Entity*) must be followed to determine how the financial statements and related notes of the landfill should be reported. GASB-14 adopts the basic philosophy that the financial information pertaining to the primary government (which could include landfill component units that are blended) and similar information pertaining to discretely presented landfill component units should be distinguishable. This philosophy is extended to disclosures in notes and the presentation of required supplementary information in the financial statements of the financial reporting entity. Determining what should be disclosed in notes to the financial statements is a question of professional judgment. A determination must be made as to which disclosures are essential to the fair presentation of the basic financial statements (GASB-18, par. 18) [GASB Cod. Sec. L10.116].

EXHIBIT 16-1
ILLUSTRATION: LANDFILL CLOSURE AND POST-CLOSURE-CARE COSTS CALCULATIONS

This example is based on Appendix C of GASB-18, and is intended to illustrate the application of the standards established. Assume the following information:

According to its operating plan filed with the state, ABC Landfill will open in 20X4 and will operate on a cell basis, opening one cell at a time and installing liners and leachate collection systems before the cell receives any waste. Construction on new cells will begin before older cells reach capacity. When a cell reaches capacity, gas collection wells will be installed, and final cover, including vegetative cover, will be put in place. Water monitoring wells, erosion control systems, and a leachate treatment plant will be constructed during the first and second years of landfill operations.

Other Assumptions

- Landfill construction begins in 20X6; opens January 1, 20X7.
- Projected landfill life in years: 33.
- The landfill will be operated on a cell basis.
- Total landfill area: 150 acres.
- Initial expected usable landfill area: 100 acres/33 cells.
- Initial estimated capacity based on expected usable landfill area: 4.5 million cubic yards (capacity per cell = 136,364 cubic yards).
- Landfill usage:

Year	Cubic Yards
20X7	90,000
20X8	120,000
20X9	135,000

- The postclosure monitoring period required by current state law is 30 years after the entire landfill receives final cover.

- In 20X8, the entity opened an area of the landfill that was subsequently determined to be unusable because of its location on unstable sediment. For this reason, estimated capacity and expected usable landfill area were reduced by approximately 5% to 4,275,000 cubic yards and 31 cells, as of December 31, 20X8. (This reduction also affects expected leachate output from the landfill.)

- Estimates are based on current costs in 20X8, adjusted using the state-provided inflation rate of 1.5% in 20X8 and 1.85% in 20X9.

Estimated Total Current Cost of Closure and Post-Closure Care—20X7

	Element	Amount
1.	Equipment and Facilities Cost	
	Near date landfill stops accepting waste during closure/postclosure	$ -
	Maintenance and upgrading of on-site leachate treatment facility (costs projected to be paid principally at the end of 30 years)	375,000
	Expected renewals and replacements of storm water and erosion control facilities ($50,000 per year)	1,500,000
	Monitoring well replacements (30 at $25,000 each)	750,000
2.	Final Cover Cost	
	(Final cover, including vegetative cover, installed as cells are filled)	-
3.	Post-Closure Care Cost	
	Inspection and maintenance of final cover ($75,000 per year)	2,250,000
	Groundwater monitoring ($100,000 per year)	3,000,000
	Gas monitoring ($5,000 per year)	150,000
	On-site leachate pretreatment cost and off site treatment (30,000,000 gallons total × $.05 per gallon)	1,500,000
	Projected remediation cost based on statistical average at similarly sited landfills	250,000
	Total estimated current cost of closure and post-closure care	$9,775,000

Estimated Total Current Cost of Closure and Post-Closure Care—20X8

	Element	Amount
1.	Equipment and Facilities Cost	
	Near date landfill stops accepting waste during closure/postclosure	$ -

Element	Amount
Maintenance and upgrading of on-site leachate treatment facility (costs projected to be paid principally at the end of 30 years)	380,625
Expected renewals and replacements of storm water and erosion control facilities ($50,750 per year)	1,522,500
Monitoring well replacements (30 at $25,375 each)	761,250
2. Final Cover Cost	
(Final cover, including vegetative cover, installed as cells are filled)	-
3. Post-Closure Care Cost	
Inspection and maintenance of final cover ($76,125 per year)	2,283,750
Groundwater monitoring ($101,500 per year)	3,045,000
Gas monitoring ($5,075 per year)	152,250
On-site leachate pretreatment cost and off-site treatment (28,500,000 gallons total × $.05075 per gallon)	1,446,375
Projected remediation cost based on statistical average at similarly sited landfills	253,750
Total estimated current cost of closure and post-closure care	$9,845,500

Estimated Total Current Cost of Closure and Post-Closure Care—20X9

Element	Amount
1. Equipment and Facilities Cost	
Near date landfill stops accepting waste	$ -
During closure/postclosure	
Maintenance and upgrading of on-site leachate treatment facility (costs projected to be paid principally at the end of 30 years)	387,667
Expected renewals and replacements of storm water and erosion control facilities ($51,689 per year)	1,550,670
Monitoring well replacements (30 at $25,844 each)	775,320
2. Final Cover Cost	
(Final cover, including vegetative cover, installed as cells are filled)	-
3. Post-Closure Care Cost	
Inspection and maintenance of final cover ($77,533 per year)	2,325,990
Groundwater monitoring ($103,378 per year)	3,101,340
Gas monitoring ($5,169 per year)	155,070
On-site leachate pretreatment cost and off-site treatment (28,500,000 gallons total × $.05169 per gallon)	1,473,165
Projected remediation cost based on statistical average at similarly sited landfills	258,444
Total estimated current cost of closure and post-closure care	$10,027,666

Proprietary Fund Assumption

If it is assumed that the MSWLF activities are accounted for in a proprietary fund, the following entries would be made:

Entry for 20X7

The following entry would be made in 20X7, the first year of operating activity for the landfill.

	Debit	Credit
LANDFILL ENTERPRICE FUND		
Expenses—Landfill Closure and Post-Closure Care Costs	195,500	
Estimated Liability for Landfill Closure and Post-Closure Care Costs		195,500
To record landfill closure current costs and liability changes for 20X7. [$ 9,775,000 × 90,000 cubic yards]÷ 4,500,000 cubic yards – $0 = $195,500		

Entry for 20X8

The following entry would be made in 20X8. It should be noted that the computation takes into consideration two changes in estimates. One change occurs due to the increase in the estimated total current cost of MSWLF closure and post-closure care ($9,845,500), and the other change relates to a reduction in the estimated capacity of the landfill (4,275,000 cubic yards).

	Debit	Credit
LANDFILL ENTERPRICE FUND		
Expenses—Landfill Closure and Post-Closure Care Costs	288,114	
Estimated Liability for Landfill Closure and Post-Closure Care Costs		288,114
To record landfill closure current costs and liability changes for 20X8. [$ 9,775,000 × 90,000 + 120,000 cubic yards]÷ 4,275,000 cubic yards – $195,500 = $288,114		

Entry for 20X9

The following entry would be made in 20X9. At the end of 20X9, the estimated total current cost of MSWLF closure and post-closure care has been increased to $10,027,666. The $483,614 below is the sum of $195,500 and $288,114.

	Debit	Credit
LANDFILL ENTERPRICE FUND		
Expenses—Landfill Closure and Post-Closure Care Costs	325,636	
Estimated Liability for Landfill Closure and Post-Closure Care Costs		325,636
To record landfill closure current costs and liability changes for 20X9. [$ 9,775,000 × 90,000 + 120,000 + 135,000 cubic yards]÷ 4,275,000 cubic yards – $483,614		

The estimated liability for landfill closure and post-closure care costs as of December 31, 20X9, would be reported as a long-term liability in the proprietary fund's statement of net position at $809,250.

OBSERVATION: So-called "Financial Assurance Letters" are frequently required by regulatory entities of MSWLFs, including the United States Environmental Protection Agency (EPA). These letters are required to demonstrate that the operator of the MSWLF will be able to pay for the required closure and post-closure care activities, and any corrective action that might become necessary due to releases of contaminants into the surrounding environment. EPA believes that requiring these financial assurance demonstrations ensures proper long-term financial planning by owner/operators so that sites will be closed properly and maintained and monitored in a manner that protects human health and the environment. State and federal government entities are exempt from these requirements. However, municipal entities are not. Many auditors are engaged to help prepare these letters. They are not an audit function. Rather, they are an agreed-upon procedures engagement. The letters are based upon a site-specific cost estimate. They are prepared at the commencement of operations and adjusted annually during the life of the MSWLF to account for inflation and other factors. Corrective action cost estimates are prepared when a release is detected, and also must be adjusted annually during the period of corrective action.

PRACTICE POINT: Many of the aspects of GASB-18 and GASB-49 (discussed in the next section) are replicated in GASB Statement No. 83 (*Certain Asset Retirement Obligations*). GASB-83 is effective for periods beginning after June 15, 2018. Changes adopted to conform to the provisions of GASB-83 require a retroactive restatement of financial statements for all prior periods presented if practicable. A complete discussion of GASB-83 is contained in Chapter 10, "Capital Assets."

POLLUTION REMEDIATION OBLIGATIONS

A number of governments face the responsibility for cleaning up or remediating pollution such as asbestos, brownfields, and the like. GASB-49 (*Accounting and Financial Reporting for Pollution Remediation Obligations*) provides specific guidance on accounting and financial reporting for these obligations.

Obligation Event Triggers

Under GASB-49, state and local governments are required to determine whether they should report a liability in their financial statements for pollution remediation obligations if any of the following five events (triggers) has occurred:

1. Pollution poses an imminent danger to the public or environment *and* a government has little or no discretion to avoid fixing the problem.

2. A government has violated a pollution-prevention permit or license.

3. A regulator has identified (or evidence indicates that a regulator will identify) a government as responsible or potentially responsible for cleaning up pollution or has stated that the government must pay all or some of the cleanup costs.

4. A government is named or evidence exists that it will be named in a lawsuit to compel it to address the pollution.

5. A government legally obligates itself to or begins to clean up pollution or perform post-cleanup activities (GASB-49, par. 11) [GASB Cod. Sec. P40.109].

If none of the foregoing events has occurred, a government is not required to calculate or report a pollution-remediation liability. However, if one or more of the events has occurred and a range of potential outlays can be reasonably estimated, then a government is required to calculate and report a liability within the financial statements that are reported using the full accrual basis of accounting. The government is only required to estimate and report liabilities for activities that are reasonably estimable. For example, if in the early stages of pollution remediation, only legal fees and site testing costs were reasonably estimable, then only those costs would be accrued. Once any further remediation costs were reasonably estimable, then they would be accrued at that time. Similar to current landfill closure and post-closure obligation standards, the pollution-remediation liabilities would be reevaluated periodically and estimated liabilities adjusted.

Measurement of the Obligation

GASB-49 uses an "expected cash flow" measurement technique to measure pollution-remediation liabilities using an estimate of ranges of potential outlays required to remediate the pollution (GASB-49, par. 16) [GASB Cod. Sec. P40.114].

> **Example:** Assume a school district has been notified by a regulator that it is responsible for the entire cost of cleaning up asbestos in its school buildings. Also assume the district estimates that there is a 10% chance that cleanup will cost $1,000,000, a 50% chance the cleanup will cost $5,000,000 and a 40% chance the costs will be $10,000,000. The expected cash flow technique would calculate the estimated liability as follows:

Estimated Cost	Probability	Weighted Amount
$1,000,000	10%	$100,000
5,000,000	50%	2,500,000
10,000,000	40%	4,000,000
		$6,600,000

Using this expected cash flow technique, $6,600,000 would be reported by the government as a liability in its financial statements.

The expected cash flow technique is a new way to estimate liabilities. Because a probability measure is used of possible outlays, even a 1% chance of an outlay needs to be accrued. This has been controversial in implementation because the legal community that defends governments against lawsuits was initially wary of a government recording even a 1% possibility of loss and thereby admitting some amount of liability. Care must be taken in these estimations of loss, and potentially a professional resource may be needed to give a reliable estimate, if any.

In situations where the government cannot reasonably estimate the liability for all portions of the remediation effort, it would only be required to report liabilities for the amounts that can be reasonably estimated.

Disclosures

GASB-49 requires certain note disclosures, including the following:

- The nature and source of the pollution-remediation obligation;
- The amount of estimated liabilities for remediation if it is not separately disclosed on the face of the financial statements;
- The methods and assumption used to estimate the liability;
- The potential for estimate changes due to external factors; and
- An estimate of the amount of any expected cost recovery from insurance or other parties.

If a liability was not reasonably estimable, then the government would be required to disclose only the nature of the pollution-remediation activities (GASB-49, pars. 25–26) [GASB Cod. Secs. P40.123–.124].

> **Example:** Assume that Castle Rock County contracted with a state-licensed contractor to remove specified, nonhazardous solid and liquid industrial waste from its public works and shops for disposal off-site at a state-licensed disposal facility. The contractor complied with all applicable laws and regulations. In 20X6, the County was contacted by EPA, who believed that hazardous materials were on the site. The EPA then listed the site on its National Priorities List. Those materials were generated by the County from various agencies. The county was named as a potentially responsible party (PRP) and directed by EPA to respond to questions and to research its records to further the investigation. The County researched its records and in late 20X6 determined that it had indeed contaminated the site. However, the County could not determine the significance of the waste. Although the County could not reasonably estimate a range of all legal outlays, it estimated that the current value of outlays for legal services to prepare for preliminary negotiations ranged from $50,000 to $80,000. No amounts within this range were considered to be better estimates than any other amounts.
>
> Because the county admitted that it was a party to the waste, the legal services need to be accrued, and because no amounts were considered to be better estimates than other amounts, the following entry is needed:

	Debit	Credit
GOVRNMENT-WIDE FINANCIAL STATEMENTS		
Expenses—Environmental Remediation [(50,000 + 80,000)/2]	65,000	
Estimated Liability for Environmental Remediation		65,000
To record estimated liability for environmental waste disposal from DPW.		

The expense could also be charged to the service or agency that is responsible for the pollution.

During 20X7, the EPA identified other possible transporters and polluters on the site, but little else went on. Therefore no further entry is needed.

During 20X8, the EPA asserted that there were major issues with the site and issued an order to the county and other potentially responsible parties to remediate the site. The County initially estimated the outlay that would be incurred to perform the cleanup to be between $1 million and $2 million in current dollars. The County initially estimated that its ultimate share of this outlay would prove to be in the range of 20% to 50%. Stated another way, the county initially estimated that other PRPs would ultimately reimburse 50% to 80% of this outlay. The county also estimated that it would incur outlays for legal services related to the remediation effort ranging from $200,000 to $2 million in current dollars, in addition to any legal service outlays that might be incurred by any PRP group that might be formed. No amounts within any of these ranges were considered to be better estimates than any other amounts. Because of a lack of information about the type and extent of the remediation effort that could be required, no range of outlays for the overall remediation effort could be developed at the time.

Because of this activity, the following needs to be accrued:

Element	Amount
Expected Cleanup Costs ($1,000,000 + $2,000,000) / 2	$1,500,000
Less, estimated recoveries from third parties [({50% + 80%} / 2)×$1,500,000]	(975,000)
Net expected outlays to remediate site	525,000
Expected legal costs [$200,000 + $2,000,000) / 2]	1,100,000
Total remediation expense	$1,625,000

As each piece of the remediation is completed, the liability is remeasured and adjusted as needed.

PRACTICE POINT: An example of disclosure is contained in Wolter's Kluwer's *2018 GAAP Governmental GAAP Disclosures Manual,* Chapter 53.

STATE LOTTERY OBLIGATIONS AND GAMING

Generally, a state lottery satisfies one or more of the three conditions listed earlier for determining whether an activity should be reported as an Enterprise Fund. In many lottery games, a fixed percentage of ticket sales must be paid out as winnings. The AICPA's Audit and Accounting Guide *State and Local Governments* points out that lottery prize costs under this or similar payout arrangements are subject to accrual based on their relationship to total ticket sales and that accrual-based accounting may be appropriate under conditions such as the following:

- Prizes have been won and claimed but have not been paid.
- Prizes have been won but not claimed.
- Games are in process at the end of the year.

Some lotteries allow a winner to either take an immediate lump sum payment or receive payments over a specified period of time. If the lottery winner chooses to receive the winnings over a period of time and the state purchases an annuity from an insurance company in the name of the winner, the AICPA's *State and Local Governments* guide points out that no related liability or asset should be reported on the state's financial statements.

When the state does not purchase an annuity in the name of the winner, the liability should be presented at its present value. When determining the liability to be discounted, the amount should include amounts won as well as amounts won but not yet claimed and amounts that will be won and claimed for games in progress at the end of the year.

Furthermore, the state might decide to finance the periodic payments to the winner by "purchasing U.S. Treasury securities matched in timing and amount to the future payments." Under this arrangement, the investment in securities should be reported as an asset on the state's financial statements. The lottery liability and the investment cannot be offset against one another. When the state has financed the periodic payments to the lottery winner through the purchase of an annuity from an insurance company, the state should consider whether a contingent liability should be disclosed in its financial statements. A contingent liability may arise if there is some default in payment from the escrow of securities [GASB Cod. Secs. Sp20.801–.804].

Gaming

Gaming has proliferated in many state and local governments in recent years. There are revenue recognition issues and compliance issues involved with gaming. (The compliance issues are beyond the scope of this *Guide*.)

Gaming involves activities in which a gaming entity participates in games of chance with customers (players), with both the gaming entity and the customer having the chance to win or lose money or other items of economic value based on the outcome of the game (commonly referred to as *banked games*). Such activities are referred to as *gaming activities* [GASB Cod. Sec. Sp20.805].

Additional examples of banked games and gaming activities are as follows:

Banked Games	Gaming Activities	Gaming Related Activities
Poker and similar games	Slot tournaments in which players play with real money and retain any payouts from machines during the tournament.	Card games
Blackjack		Tournaments
Keno		Lotteries
Sports betting		Pari-mutuel race betting
Non-pari-mutuel race betting		

Games in which the player has the chance to win or lose money or other items of economic value, with the gaming entity receiving a fee (typically either a fixed fee or a percentage of play) for administering the game, rather than the gaming entity being at risk to win or lose based on the outcome of the game, *are neither banked games nor gaming activities.* Such activities are referred to as gaming related activities.

Certain games may be either gaming activities or gaming related activities, depending on the facts and circumstances. For example, gaming activities games include play as part of tournaments in which customers play with real money or equivalents, and the entity is at risk to win or lose based on the outcome of the game.

However, a slot tournament in which customers play with credits or other designated machine input other than cash and cash equivalents and accumulate points that determine their standing in the tournament, *but retain no cash or other items of economic value* as payouts from the machine, *is not a banked game* and, therefore, *not a gaming activity* [GASB Cod. Sec. Sp20.806].

For some gaming related activities, *the entity may have the chance to win or lose money* or other items of economic value based on factors other than the outcome of the game, such as business risk [GASB Cod. Sec. Sp20.807]. For other activities, *the entity has neither business risk nor gaming risk and has no opportunity to make a profit directly from tournament play.* A casino may hold a tournament with no banked games, no entry fee, and prizes that are not directly funded by tournament members. For example, the winner of a tournament with no entry fee and no banked games may receive a cash prize or an automobile. Such activities are neither gaming activities nor gaming related activities [GASB Cod. Sec. Sp20.808].

Revenue Recognition in Gaming

Revenue recognized and reported by a casino is generally defined as the win from gaming activities, that is, the difference between gaming wins and losses, not the total amount wagered (a net amount). State lotteries that use *video gaming* use similar provisions. However, lotto and instant game ticket sales have revenue separated from prize payouts and expenses, which are reported as expenses or deductions from revenue [GASB Cod. Secs. Sp20.809–.810].

Gross gaming revenue, or win, is the difference between:

- Gaming wins from banked games, less

- Gaming losses from banked games, less

- Incentives and adjustments for changes in progressive jackpot liability accruals.

Gross gaming revenue is generally not reported by gaming entities in their external financial statements; rather, net gaming revenue is generally reported

[GASB Cod. Sec. Sp20.811]. However, gross gaming revenue is typically a compliance element for regulatory purposes.

Net gaming revenue equals:

- Gross gaming revenue (as defined previously) minus

- Incentives that are charged to gaming revenue, plus or minus

- The change in accrued jackpot liabilities, plus

- Revenue from gaming related activities [GASB Cod. Sec. Sp20.812].

Gaming entities generally report all payouts and prizes related to banked games as a component of net gaming revenue. Accordingly, prizes or payouts resulting from banked games, even if not built into a payout table, should not be reported as marketing or promotional expense. For example, customers hitting a particular slot machine combination within a specified time period may win an automobile in addition to the stated jackpot for the particular combination. The cost of that automobile should be reported as a component of net gaming revenue [GASB Cod. Sec. Sp20.813].

Special circumstances from certain gaming related activities result in different revenue recognition provisions. Examples are as follows [GASB Cod. Secs. Sp20.814–.816]:

Fact Pattern	Example	Recognition
Gaming entity is at no risk to win or lose, gaming entity pays out prizes directly funded by tournament members.	• Tournament members may each pay $1,000 as an entry fee, with $950 included in the tournament prize pool and $50 as a fee to a casino.	• The *prize pool* should be reported as a component of net gaming revenue and the fee to the casino included in net gaming revenue.
Gaming entity has no gaming risk *but has business risk*.	• A slot tournament may include no banked games and have a grand prize of $100,000, *regardless of the fees collected from the number of entrants*.	• The entity may have the chance to win or lose money, and the gaming entity's *net profit or loss* from such activities should be reported as a component of net gaming revenue.

The gaming entity has no opportunity or intention of making a profit directly from tournament play.

- A casino may sponsor a tournament with no banked games, no entry fee, and prizes that are not directly funded by tournament members. The winner of a tournament with no entry fee and no banked games may receive a $100,000 cash prize (or an automobile).

- Activities are neither gaming activities nor gaming related activities. Prizes from these types of activities are typically reported as marketing or promotional expense, rather than as a component of net gaming revenue.

OBSERVATION: According to the AICPA's Audit and Accounting Guide *State and Local Governments*, Chapter 12, lottery activities *generally* meet the criteria in GASB-34, par. 67 [GASB Cod. Secs. 1300.109, Ca5.103, Ho5.103, In3.103, Sp20.103, and Ut5.103], requiring the use of enterprise funds. However, some states report them as a governmental fund as they provide a cash flow mechanism for programs and services of the general government, such as education. Legally separate state lotteries may be reported as discretely presented component units, as they do not meet the criteria for blending in paragraph 53 of GASB-14, as amended [GASB Cod. Sec. 2600.113]. This is due to the ability of anyone to participate in the lottery by choice and potentially benefit from winnings. Lotteries may also issue fund or departmental financial statements separately from the state as a whole. Finally, additional guidance is available in the AICPA's Audit and Accounting Guide *Gaming*, also in Chapter 12. The *Gaming* guide discusses the basic financial statements and required supplementary information that may be presented for lotteries, how resources flow between lotteries and sponsoring governments, assets and liabilities, impairment of capital assets, and segment reporting. Tribal government casinos should also review the *Gaming* guide for additional guidance.

ACCOUNTING AND FINANCIAL REPORTING FOR NONEXCHANGE FINANCIAL GUARANTEE TRANSACTIONS

GASB-70 requires governments that extend nonexchange financial guarantees to recognize a liability when qualitative factors or historical data indicate that is more likely than not that the government will make a payment on the guarantee.

Many governments participate either as a guarantor or a recipient of a guarantee. Guarantees extend to non-governmental entities including not for profit and for-profit enterprises. Frequently, these guarantees are exercised by non-financial or qualitative events (e.g., violation of an agreement). A common action occurs in nearly every governmental nonexchange guarantee: a government commits to indemnify the holder of the obligation if the entity that issued the obligation does not fulfill its payments.

Qualitative and historical factors must be used to decide whether or not a payment on the guarantee is *more likely than not* to be made. These factors include, but are not limited to, the following:

- Initiation of the process of entering into bankruptcy or a financial reorganization;

- Breach of a debt contract in relation to the guaranteed obligation, such as a failure to meet rate covenants, failure to meet coverage ratios, or default or delinquency in interest or principal payments; and

- Indicators of significant financial difficulty, such as the failure to transfer deposits from debt service funds to paying agents or trustees; the draw on a debt service reserve fund; the initiation of the process by a creditor to intercept receipts to make a debt service payment; debt holder concessions; significant investment losses; loss of a major revenue source; significant increase in noncapital disbursements in relation to operating or current revenues; or commencement of financial supervision by another government (GASB-70, par. 7) [GASB Cod. Sec. N30.103].

If a group of guarantees exist, the government that makes the guarantees as part of a group must review historical data to determine whether a guarantee will be exercised. This may occur in home mortgage guarantees (GASB-70, par. 8) [GASB Cod. Sec. N30.104].

When it is more likely than not (as defined as greater than 50%) that the guaranteeing government will have to make a payment on the guarantee, a liability and an expense in the government-wide financial statements is recognized. The amount recognized should be the best estimate of the discounted present value of the future outflows expected to be incurred as a result of the guarantee. If a range of estimates is evident and no particular value in the range is better than another amount, then the minimum amount in the range is used (GASB-70, par. 9) [GASB Cod Cod. Sec. N30.105].

A fund liability may exist to the extent that the guarantee is expected to be paid with current financial resources. Liabilities for nonexchange financial guarantees extended are normally expected to be liquidated with expendable available financial resources when payments are due and payable on the guaranteed obligation (GASB-70, par. 10) [GASB Cod. Sec. N30.106].

For the government receiving the guarantee, when a government is required to repay a guarantor for payments made on the government's obligations, the government should reclassify that portion of its liability for the guaranteed obligation as a liability to the guarantor, instead of to a debt holder. The government that issued the guaranteed obligation should continue to report the obligation as a liability until all or a portion of the liability is legally released, such as when a Plan of Adjustment is confirmed by the court in the case of bankruptcy. The release of the obligation triggers revenue for the government receiving the release (GASB-70, pars. 11–12) [GASB Cod. Secs. N30.107–.108].

There could be a situation where debt is recorded twice within the same reporting entity. A component unit may have debt outstanding that is guaranteed by a primary government. The guarantee is exercised, yet the component unit still is obligated to pay the debt. However, GASB-70 also has a liability with the primary government for the guarantee. To relieve this problem, GASB-70 allows a *blended component unit* (not a discretely presented component unit) to record a receivable when the guarantor records a liability.

Example of a Guarantee between Governments: The Castle Rock County Convention Center is a government that is separately reported from Castle Rock County. State of Centennial statute allows counties to extend nonexchange financial guarantees on bonds issued by special districts to provide for facilities improvements. Both the County and the Center have June 30th fiscal year-ends. On November 1, 20X5, the Board of the Center authorized and approved $10 million in general obligation bonds to be issued 30 days later for Center improvements. The bonds mature annually through December 1, 20Y1, with semiannual interest payments. Also on November 1, 20X5, the County approved to extend a nonexchange financial guarantee on the issuance with no requirements for the Center to repay the County if there is a default and the guarantee is exercised.

During the last half of fiscal year 20X8, the Center's revenue from operations began to decrease due to a new center opened in the neighboring city of Lafayette, in Stone County. A violation of revenue coverage covenants occurred with the Center's bonds. On June 1, 20X8, the semiannual interest payment was made by the Center. However, the Center had to liquidate the bond reserve account to do so—another violation of a bond covenant.

Castle Rock County determined that as of June 30, 20X8, the Center is more likely than not unable to make any of the remaining required debt service payments on the bonds. The County determined that the present value of the future debt service payments is $4.020 million using a discount rate of 5%—equal to the bond's true interest rate. On December 1, 20X8, the County made the entire debt service payment on the bonds.

Castle Rock County's Financial Statements:

	Debit	Credit
GOVERNMENT–WIDE FINANCIAL STATEMENTS		
Expenses—Guarantee on Castle Rock County Convention Center Bonds	4,020,000	
Guarantee Payable—Castle Rock County Convention Center Bonds		4,020,000
To record estimated liability for Convention Center Bonds Guaranteed by the County.		

GASB-70 requires disclosure in the notes to the basic financial statements by the guaranteeing government (the County) to include the facts and terms of the guarantee, along with the beginning balance, increases, decreases and the ending balance of the debts that are guaranteed. Amounts paid and amounts expected to be recovered are also disclosed. The Center would have similar, symmetrical disclosure, including amounts owed to the County to repay the guarantee (if any) (GASB-70, par. 14) [GASB Cod. Sec. N30.110].

PRACTICE POINT: An example of disclosure is contained in Wolter's Kluwer's *2018 GAAP Governmental GAAP Disclosures Manual*, Chapter 89.

QUESTIONS

1. GASB Interpretation 6 categorizes governmental fund liabilities with the following elements except for:

    a. Liabilities that are normally deferred.

    b. Liabilities that are generally recognized when due.

    c. Liabilities that are recognized when they are "normally expected to be liquidated with expendable available financial resources."

    d. Liabilities that have no specific accrual modification.

2. The estimated total current cost of a municipal solid waste landfill closure and post-closure care should include the following, except for:

    a. Capital assets.

    b. Final cover.

    c. Monitoring and maintenance activities.

    d. Tipping fees.

3. At the end of each year, a governmental entity should evaluate its estimate of the total current cost related to closure and post-closure care of a municipal solid waste landfill. If an adjustment is needed from prior years, the change would be recorded as a

    a. Prior period adjustment.

    b. Change in estimate.

    c. Change in accounting principle.

    d. Change in contingency.

4. Under GASB-49, state and local governments are required to determine whether they should report a liability in their financial statements for pollution remediation if any of the following events have occurred except for:

    a. Pollution poses an imminent danger to the public or environment and a government has little or no discretion to avoid fixing the problem.

    b. A government is named or evidence exists that it will be named in a lawsuit to compel it to address the pollution.

    c. A government is located on a river that contains PCBs.

    d. A government legally obligates itself to or begins to clean up pollution or perform post-cleanup activities.

5. Under GASB-49, if the government cannot reasonably estimate the liability for all portions of the remediation effort, what is the government required to disclose?

    a. Nothing.

    b. Liabilities for amounts that can reasonably estimated.

    c. The maximum amount of liability possible.

    d. The minimum amount of liability possible.

Case – Adapted from GASB Standards

In an effort to revitalize its downtown area, Silver City in Castle Rock County purchases vacant buildings and properties, performs pollution remediation, and resells the buildings and property. State of Centennial statute holds that the owner of polluted property is responsible for pollution remediation. In 20X4, the city completed a site assessment for a parcel of land with a building and concluded that the property could be cleaned for between $100,000 and $130,000. No amounts within the range were considered to be better estimates than any other amounts. In late 20X4, the city entered into an agreement with the owner of the building and a prospective buyer wherein the city would purchase the property for $80,000, perform pollution remediation, and sell the property to the buyer for $175,000. The city purchased the property that year and placed the remediation work out for bid. Bids were received in early 20X5. The lowest acceptable bid was $125,000. The city accepted the bid and remediation work commenced and was completed in 20X5. State regulations required the city to notify the state environmental protection department of the results of the site assessment and of the transfer of ownership of the property to the city. Based on the results of the site assessment, the city was aware that the level of pollution was such that the State of Centennial environmental protection department would require remediation of the pollution.

What would be the reporting in 20X4 and 20X5 for Silver City?

ANSWERS

1. GASBI-6 categorizes governmental fund liabilities with the following elements except for:

   Answer – A: All others are categories of governmental fund liabilities.

2. The estimated total current cost of a municipal solid waste landfill closure and post-closure care should include the following except for:

   Answer – D: Tipping fees are charges to garbage haulers, so they are revenue to the landfill.

3. At the end of each year, a governmental entity should evaluate its estimate of the total current cost related to closure and post-closure care of a municipal solid waste landfill. If there is an adjustment needed from prior years, the change would be recorded as a

   Answer – B: GASB-18 requires the change to be a change in estimate.

4. Under GASB-49, state and local governments are required to determine whether they should report a liability in their financial statements for pollution remediation if any of the following events have occurred except for:

   Answer – C: There's no evidence presented that the government will be named or potentially is a responsible party.

5. Under GASB-49, if the government cannot reasonably estimate the liability for all portions of the remediation effort, what is the government required to disclose?

   Answer – B: Only the amounts that can be reasonably estimated are used.

Case – Adapted from GASB Standards

In an effort to revitalize its downtown area, Silver City in Castle Rock County purchases vacant buildings and properties, performs pollution remediation, and resells the buildings and property. State of Centennial statute holds that the owner of polluted property is responsible for pollution remediation. In 20X4, the city completed a site assessment for a parcel of land with a building and concluded that the property could be cleaned for between $100,000 and $130,000. No amounts within the range were considered to be better estimates than any other amounts. In late 20X4, the city entered into an agreement with the owner of the building and a prospective buyer wherein the city would purchase the property for $80,000, perform pollution remediation, and sell the property to the buyer for $175,000. The city purchased the property that year and placed the remediation work out for bid. Bids were received in early 20X5. The lowest acceptable bid was $125,000. The city accepted the bid and remediation work commenced and was completed in 20X5. State regulations required the city to notify the state environmental protection department of the results of the site assessment and of the transfer of ownership of the property to the city. Based on the results of the site assessment, the city was aware that the level of pollution was such that the State of Centennial environmental protection department would require remediation of the pollution.

What would be the reporting in 20X4 and 20X5 for Silver City?

Answer:

20X4

This example illustrates two obligating events: Silver City voluntarily obligated itself to commence remediation by purchasing the property in 20X4. Additionally, at the time the city purchased the property it became aware that it will be named as a responsible party for pollution remediation. The pollution remediation obligation is measured at its expected outlay of $115,000, which is the weighted average of the estimate of the range of cleanup outlays (($100,000 + $130,000)/2). The purchase price and expected remediation outlays for the property ($80,000 + $115,000) exceed the fair value ($175,000) by $20,000. Because amounts in excess of fair value do not qualify for capitalization, the city should record a pollution remediation liability and expense of $20,000 in 20X4. No accounting entry should be made for the amount of expected pollution remediation outlays that would be capitalized, because those outlays do not meet the criteria for recognition until incurred.

The City would provide a general description of its brownfield remediation program and would disclose, for example, the fact that, "based on the level of pollution present, state law requires the city to perform pollution remediation because the property was acquired." The city also may need to disclose, for example, that "the city measured the liability by estimating a reasonable range of potential outlays and multiplying those outlays by their probability of occurring." The city would separately disclose the amount of the estimated liability or liabilities (if not apparent from the financial statements).

20X5

The City's expected outlays rise to $125,000 (the bid for the remediation work). This $10,000 increase is in excess of the fair value of the property and, therefore, is recorded as an increase in the remediation liability and expense. Depending on the City's policy, the first progress billings from the contractor reduce the remediation liability, create a capital asset, or are ratably applied to both.

The City would update its disclosure for current information. For example, the City could disclose that "the liability is measured at the cost of the construction contract" and that "the amount assumes no unexpected change orders."

CHAPTER 17

REVENUES: NONEXCHANGE AND EXCHANGE TRANSACTIONS

CONTENTS

INTRODUCTION

Most governmental entities are involved in a number of nonexchange and exchange (and exchange-like) transactions. This chapter discusses the basic rules that governmental entities should follow to report these sources of revenues in governmental funds, proprietary funds, fiduciary funds, and government-wide financial statements.

To provide the framework for establishing accounting principles related to the elements of financial statements and their measurement and recognition within the financial statements, the GASB has issued GASB:CS-4 (*Elements of Financial Statements*).

GASB:CS-6 (*Measurement of Elements of Financial Statements*) discusses both measurement approaches and measurement attributes. A measurement approach determines whether an asset or liability presented in a financial statement should be (1) reported at an amount that reflects a value at the date that the asset was acquired or the liability was incurred or (2) remeasured and reported at an amount that reflects a value at the date of the financial statements. A measurement attribute is the feature or characteristic of the asset or liability that is measured. Changes in remeasured or initial amounts, as defined here, would potentially be an indicator of an increase of inflows, outflows, deferred inflows of resources, deferred outflows of resources, assets, or liabilities.

There are two measurement approaches in U.S. GAAP:

1. *Initial-transaction-date-based measurement (initial amount).* This is the transaction price or amount assigned when an asset was acquired or a liability was incurred, including subsequent modifications to that price or amount, such as through depreciation or impairment. This approach is more commonly known as "historical cost" or "entry price," but those terms are not quite accurate.

2. *Current-financial-statement-date-based measurement (remeasured amount).* This is the amount assigned when an asset or liability is remeasured as of the financial statement date. This is sometimes known as "fair value," "current value," or "carrying value." However, that is also not quite accurate, because those values are attributes.

Therefore, there are four measurement attributes that are used in U.S. GAAP:

1. Historical cost is the price paid to acquire an asset or the amount received pursuant to the incurrence of a liability in an actual exchange transaction. The understanding of this attribute is well-known and documented.

2. Fair value is the price that would be received to sell an asset or paid to transfer a liability in an orderly transaction between market participants at the measurement date.

3. Replacement cost is the price that would be paid to acquire an asset with equivalent service potential in an orderly market transaction at the measurement date. This concept was largely introduced in GASB-42 (*Accounting and Financial Reporting for Impairment of Capital Assets and for Insurance Recoveries*).

4. Settlement amount is the amount at which an asset could be realized or a liability could be liquidated with the counterparty, other than in an active market. This attribute was largely introduced in GASB-53 (*Accounting and Financial Reporting for Derivative Instruments*).

GASB-72 (*Fair Value Measurement and Application*) clarifies when fair value should be used and measured, following the concepts contained in GASB:CS-6. Chapter 9, "Deposits, Investments, and Derivative Instruments," contains a full discussion of GASB-72, and Chapter 22, "Pension and Other Postemployment Benefit Plans," contains required additional disclosure for governments that have complex investments.

GASB-72 also introduced "acquisition value" which is an entry price. Acquisition value is the price that *would be* paid to acquire an asset with equivalent service potential in an orderly market transaction at the acquisition date, or the amount at which a liability could be liquidated with the counterparty at the acquisition date. Acquisition value is limited to donated capital assets, donated works of art, historical treasures and similar assets, or capital assets that a government receives in a service concession arrangement. Previous to GASB-72, donated items were to be measured at fair value.

In GASB:CS-4, the GASB identified and defined seven elements, stating that the elements' definitions are to be applied to a governmental unit. The seven elements are the fundamental components of financial statements and can be organized by the specific financial statement they relate to.

GASB:CS-4 provides that the revenue element of the "resource flows (change) statements" be defined as an "inflow of resources" resulting in an acquisition of net position by the entity that is applicable to the reporting period.

The acquisition of net position (inflow) is defined as net position coming under the control of the entity or net positions becoming newly available to the entity even if the resources are consumed directly when acquired. An acquisition of net position results in (1) an increase in assets in excess of any related increase in liabilities or (2) a decrease in liabilities in excess of any related decrease in assets. Examples of acquisition of net position include (1) imposing a tax (because the resources have newly come under the control of the entity) and (2) performing under the conditions of a grant received in advance (because liabilities of the entity have been satisfied, thereby increasing the entity's net position).

REVENUES: NONEXCHANGE TRANSACTIONS

PRACTICE ALERT: In January 2018, the GASB staff released an Invitation to Comment, *Revenue and Expense Recognition*, requesting feedback on a modified version of the current revenue recognition model that focuses on whether the transaction is an exchange or a nonexchange transaction as well as introducing a new model based on the existence of a performance obligation. Assuming the project progresses, final provisions may not be released by the GASB until 2023.

"Exchange transactions" are defined as the simultaneous transfer of approximately equal goods or services between parties. On the other hand, governmental entities are involved in a number of "nonexchange transactions," which are characterized by the transfer of goods or services that are *not equal* between parties. For governmental entities, nonexchange transactions range from taxes raised by governmental entities (recipient of the resources) to grants made by one governmental entity (providers of the resources) to another governmental or nongovernmental entity.

OBSERVATION: A transaction comprising $1 of compensation for a piece of land is not an exchange transaction. Exchange transactions should be those in which each party essentially receives equal values.

In December 1998, the GASB issued GASB-33 (*Accounting and Financial Reporting for Nonexchange Transactions*) to provide guidance for nonexchange transactions involving financial or capital resources. The standards established by GASB-33 do not apply to food stamps or to on-behalf services for fringe benefits and salaries, which are addressed in GASB-24 (*Accounting and Financial Reporting for Certain Grants and Other Financial Assistance*), but the standards do apply to pass-through grants, which are defined in GASB-24. GASB-24 did not address the issue of when pass-through grants should be recognized; therefore, the standards established by GASB-33 should be observed to determine the timing of these grants.

The standards established by GASB-33 do not apply to the acquisition of goods and services in an exchange transaction that were funded through a nonexchange transaction (GASB-33, footnote 3). For example, the standards established by GASB-33 would not apply to the acquisition of computers from a commercial enterprise (an exchange transaction) even though the governmental entity receives the resources to pay for the computers from a state grant (a nonexchange transaction). GASB-33 does not apply to nonexchange transactions involving contributed services (GASB-33, par. 5) [GASB Cod. Secs. 1600.111, .126, N50.103].

OBSERVATION: Revenue recognition in a government is sometimes very difficult to understand because of the various types of exchanges between citizens and other stakeholders, other governments, and the government itself. Furthermore, many governments have statutory provisions regarding when revenue is recognized for statutory or budgetary purposes, which may be quite different from U.S. GAAP. This is highly unlike for-profit enterprises that have exchange transactions between customers, resellers, clients, and the entity. Care must be taken to understand the revenue stream to see if the inflows process has been completed before revenue is recognized.

The Nature of Nonexchange Transactions

The two parties in a nonexchange transaction are the provider of the resources and the receiver of the resources. The provider of the resources could be the federal government, a state or local government, or a nongovernmental entity (such as an individual or a business entity). The receiver of the resources could be a state or local government or a nongovernmental entity. As noted earlier, what distinguishes a nonexchange transaction from an exchange transaction is that in a "nonexchange transaction" a government "either gives value (benefit) to another party without directly receiving equal value in exchange or receives value (benefit) from another party without directly giving equal value in exchange" (GASB-33, par. 7) [GASB Cod. Secs. 1600.111, .126, N50.104]. Ostensibly, these are "one-way" transactions rather than a fee for a good or service.

GASB-33 provides accounting and reporting standards for the following four categories of nonexchange transactions:

- Derived tax revenues;
- Imposed nonexchange revenues (fees, assessments, etc.);
- Government-mandated nonexchange transactions (grants with performance or eligibility requirements); and
- Voluntary nonexchange transactions (grants and donations).

GASB-70 (*Accounting and Financial Reporting for Nonexchange Guarantee Financial Transactions*) introduced a fifth category of nonexchange transaction. The extension of a financial guarantee for the obligations of another government, a not-for-profit entity, or a for-profit entity without directly receiving consideration of equal value in exchange is a form of a nonexchange transaction. As a part of this nonexchange financial guarantee, a government commits to indemnify the holder of the obligation if the entity that issued the obligation does not fulfill its payment requirement. Governments also receive financial guarantees for obligations it has issued in which equal value is not provided by the government in return.

PRACTICE POINT: See Chapter 16, "Other Liabilities," in this *Guide* for a discussion of GASB-70.

The standards of GASB-33, for the most part, apply to the four categories of nonexchange transactions and not to specific types of nonexchange transactions. For example, the GASB does not specifically prescribe how sales tax revenue should be measured but rather established general standards for derived tax revenues that apply to all revenues considered to be part of the category, including sales tax revenue. For this reason, GASB-33 requires a governmental entity to evaluate each of its nonexchange transactions and decide which of the four categories should be used to classify a particular transaction (GASB-33, par. 8) [GASB Cod. Secs. 1600.111, N50.105, P70.101].

The GASB established general rather than specific standards in order to provide a flexible approach that addresses current implementation problems as well as future developments in governmental activities. The GASB could not realistically establish recognition standards for every possible type of nonexchange transaction that is currently experienced by a governmental entity. By providing general standards, the GASB enables a specific governmental entity to apply them to all of its nonexchange transactions and not just for a few specific situations. Another advantage of general standards is that they apply to "new kinds of transactions that governments may encounter or establish in the future."

In determining which category is appropriate for each nonexchange transaction, a governmental entity must look at the substance of the transaction rather than at its "label." The entity should not group a nonexchange transaction in one of the four Statement categories based on whether the transaction is described as a tax, a grant, or by some other name. For example, the GASB notes that a grant provided by a governmental entity could be designated as a voluntary contribution (i.e., a voluntary nonexchange transaction); however, another governmental entity's grant could be designated as a government-mandated nonexchange transaction.

In a similar fashion, a governmental entity's overreliance on the "label" to name a transaction may result in misclassifying a nonexchange transaction as an exchange transaction, or vice versa. For example, a source of revenue for a governmental entity may be described as a fee (implying an exchange transaction) but the transaction may have the characteristics of a tax (a nonexchange transaction).

From a practical point of view, classifying a transaction as a nonexchange transaction or an exchange transaction can be difficult and requires close analysis. For example, the GASB defines an "exchange-like transaction" as "an identifiable exchange between the reporting government and another party, but the values exchanged may not be quite equal or the direct benefits of the exchange may not be exclusively for the parties to the exchange." Examples of exchange-like transactions include the following (GASB-33, par. 9) [GASB Cod. Secs. N50.106, P70.101]:

- Fees for professional licenses and permits;
- Passenger facility charges;
- Certain tap fees;
- Certain developer contributions; and
- Certain grants and donations.

If after careful evaluation the governmental entity determines that the items listed are exchange-like transactions, the standards established by GASB-33 do not apply. Exchange-like transactions should be accounted for in the same manner as exchange transactions.

To illustrate the difficulty of distinguishing between a nonexchange transaction and an exchange transaction, the GASB uses the example of a "grant" made by a commercial enterprise to a public university. If the university has exclusive rights to any benefits that may derive from the research effort, the transaction is a nonexchange transaction. However, if the commercial enterprise retains the right of first refusal on the results of the research, it is likely that the transaction is an exchange or exchange-like transaction. In other instances, the GASB notes that the relationship between the university and the commercial enterprise may suggest that the transaction should be divided into two separate parts: an exchange transaction portion and a nonexchange transaction portion. The standards established by GASB-33 would then apply only to the nonexchange portion of the transaction (GASB-33, par. 10) [GASB Cod. Sec. N50.107].

OBSERVATION: The GASB's *Implementation Guide 2015-1*, question 4.22.8 [GASB Cod. Sec. 2100.715-13], notes that a nonexchange transaction between a potential component unit and a primary government is an indicator of financial burden, which may indicate a component unit.

Therefore, a governmental entity must determine whether a transaction is a nonexchange transaction or an exchange transaction, and if it is a nonexchange transaction, the entity must evaluate the transaction's characteristics in order to properly classify it into one of the four categories based on the guidance established by the GASB, which is discussed later (GASB-33, pars. 9–10) [GASB Cod. Secs. N50.106–.107, P70.101].

Revenue Recognition and Expenditure Criteria

The GASB takes the position that all nonexchange transactions are fundamentally controlled by either legislation or contractual requirements or both, and these factors are essential in determining when revenues from nonexchange transactions should be recognized. For example, a governmental entity should recognize derived tax revenues when the related exchange transaction has occurred as defined by the enabling legislation. On the other hand, the entity should recognize imposed nonexchange revenues when it has an enforceable legal claim to receive the revenues. That enforceable legal claim is generally based on the governmental entity's legislative authority to impose and collect the tax. In addition, enabling legislation often identifies the period in which the resources can be used by the entity and the purposes for which the resources can be expended (GASB-33, pars. 16–18) [GASB Cod. Secs. N50.113–.115, P70.105, 1400.155]. GASB-33 defines "enabling legislation" as legislation that "authorizes the government to assess, levy, change, or otherwise mandate payment of resources (from external resource providers)" (GASB-33, footnote 4) [GASB Cod. Sec. N50.fn3].

This was further clarified in GASB-46, which stipulates that a legally enforceable enabling legislation restriction is one that a party external to a government—such as citizens, public interest groups, or the judiciary—can compel a government to honor. GASB-46 states that the legal enforceability of an enabling legislation restriction should be reevaluated if any of the resources raised by the enabling legislation are used for a purpose not specified by the enabling legislation or if a government has other cause for reconsideration. Although the determination that a particular restriction is not legally enforceable may cause a government to review the enforceability of other restrictions, it should not necessarily lead a government to the same conclusion for all enabling legislation restrictions (GASB-46, par. 3) [GASB Cod. Sec. 1800.158].

On the other hand, the governmental entity should recognize government-mandated nonexchange transactions and voluntary nonexchange transactions when the entity, or entities involved in the transaction, satisfies all eligibility requirements. The relevant eligibility requirements in a government-mandated nonexchange transaction are generally based on enabling legislation and related regulations. Those laws and regulations often identify purpose restrictions that apply to the resources provided under the program. The relevant eligibility requirements in a voluntary nonexchange transaction may arise from enabling legislation or from contractual agreements with a nongovernmental entity. For example, a nongovernmental entity, such as a corporation or an individual, may provide resources to a governmental entity but the provisions of those resources may depend on a number of eligibility factors contained in the donor agreement (GASB-33, par. 21) [GASB Cod. Sec. N50.118].

GASB-65 (*Items Previously Reported as Assets and Liabilities*) did not make large changes in revenue recognition in governmental funds. However, certain liabilities that were formerly deferred and recognized as deferred revenue are now recognized as deferred inflows of resources.

Simultaneous Expenditure Recognition

The standards established by GASB-33 generally apply to both revenue and expenditure recognition at the same time. That is, when both parties to the nonexchange transactions are governmental entities, the same standards that the recipient government used to determine whether revenue should be recognized should be used by the provider governmental entity to determine when an expense should be recognized.

This so-called symmetrical approach does not always mean that the two participating governmental parties will record the revenue and the expense/expenditure in the same period. For example, if one governmental entity uses the accrual basis of accounting and the other entity uses the modified accrual basis of accounting, the timing of the revenue and the expense/expenditure may not be the same. On the other hand, even if both parties use the same basis of accounting, the concept of conservatism may change the timing of the transaction for the recipient government. That is, conservatism may require that the provider government recognize an expense but that the recipient government not recognize revenue because there is too much uncertainty as to whether the revenue will be realized. However, in general, when both governmental entities use the same basis of accounting, they should recognize the revenue (recipient government) and the expenditure (provider government) in the same accounting period.

> **OBSERVATION:** The symmetry concept does not apply to revenue and expenditure recognition under the modified accrual basis of accounting in that the availability criterion must be satisfied for revenue recognition but that criterion is not applicable to expenditure recognition. For example, a state government may provide expenditure-driven grants to local governments and therefore the criteria for expenditure-driven grants (see a later discussion in this chapter for the criteria) must be satisfied before expenditures can be recognized by the state government. Likewise revenue can be recognized by the local governments only if the same criteria that are used for expenditure recognition by the state government are satisfied. However, the local governments must also apply the availability criterion to the nonexchange transaction before revenue can be recorded, but the availability criterion is not relevant to determining when expenditures are to be recorded by the state government under the modified accrual basis of accounting.

The concept of symmetrical recognition applies only to transactions between state and local governmental entities. The recognition standards can be different when one of the parties to the transaction is the federal government or a non-governmental entity due to eligibility, time, and purpose requirements.

Time Requirements and Purpose Restrictions

To determine when nonexchange transactions should be recorded and how those transactions should be presented in the financial statements, the governmental entity needs to consider time requirements and purpose restrictions. Time requirements and purpose restrictions do not have the same effect on the timing of revenue recognition or expense recognition that arises from nonexchange transactions.

Time Requirements

Resources may be provided by one governmental entity or another party to a governmental entity with the requirement that the resources be used in (or begin to be used in) a specified period(s). GASB-33 notes that "time requirements specify the period or periods when resources are required to be used or when use may begin." Time requirements may be imposed by enabling legislation or by a nongovernmental party that provides the resources to governmental entities. For example, legislation may identify the period in which a recipient governmental entity can use a grant or it may require that resources be used over a specified number of years. In other instances, time requirements imposed by either the provider government or the provider nongovernmental entity may require that the resources provided may never be used (e.g., permanent endowment) or that the resources cannot be used until a specified event has occurred (GASB-33, par. 12) [GASB Cod. Sec. N50.109].

When a nonexchange transaction is subject to a timing requirement, that requirement generally affects the period in which revenue is recognized by the governmental entity. Also, the effect that a timing requirement has on a nonexchange transaction is dependent on whether the transaction is (1) a government-mandated nonexchange transaction or a voluntary nonexchange transaction or (2) an imposed nonexchange revenue transaction. Generally, derived tax revenues are not subject to time requirements (GASB-33, par. 13) [GASB Cod. Sec. N50.110].

Purpose Restrictions

Purpose restrictions relate to the use of resources that arise from a nonexchange transaction. For example, gasoline taxes may be earmarked specifically and exclusively for road maintenance. Because of the nature of purpose restrictions, a governmental entity should recognize assets, liabilities, revenues, and expenses related to nonexchange transactions in its financial statements without taking into consideration purpose restrictions. That is, a purpose restriction does not affect the timing of the recognition of a nonexchange transaction. In fact, the GASB notes that a purpose restriction cannot be met unless a nonexchange transaction has taken place (GASB-33, par. 12) [GASB Cod. Sec. N50.109]. In summary, a purpose restriction means that a particular stream of revenue can only be used for a particular purpose.

OBSERVATION: In accordance with GASB-54, a purpose, time, or eligibility restriction can be an indicator of a restricted fund balance for any unspent amounts at year-end.

During the period between when a governmental entity records a nonexchange transaction that has purpose restrictions and when the entity uses those resources, the entity should indicate in the equity section of its statement of position the amount of resources that is restricted. Governmental funds should report the restriction as restricted fund balance, and funds that use proprietary fund accounting should refer to the purpose restriction as a "restriction" of their net position balance (GASB-33, par. 14) [GASB Cod. Sec. N50.114].

Purpose restrictions can arise from derived tax revenues, imposed nonexchange revenues, government-mandated nonexchange transactions, and voluntary nonexchange transactions.

Derived Tax Revenue

"Derived tax revenues" are revenues from taxes that are imposed on exchange transactions. Although the tax is imposed on an exchange transaction, the source of revenue is considered revenue from a nonexchange transaction because the exchange transaction is between two parties that do not include a governmental entity. Derived tax revenue has the following principal characteristics (GASB-33, par. 7a) [GASB Cod. Secs. 1600.111, .126, N50.104]:

- A governmental entity imposes the tax on the provider (the individual or enterprise that acquires the income, goods, or services); and
- The imposition of the tax is based on an exchange transaction.

For example, revenue obtained from a retail sales tax is derived tax revenue because the tax is imposed by the governmental entity on an exchange (the sale) between a retailer (collector of the tax resource) and a customer. Other examples of derived tax revenues include personal income taxes and corporate income taxes. Under a personal income tax the governmental entity imposes a tax on an exchange transaction (wages earned from an employer). Likewise, when a corporate income tax is imposed by a governmental entity, the business entity is the provider of the tax resource based on the numerous exchanges that occur with customers and vendors.

A governmental entity should recognize derived tax revenue when (1) the exchange that the tax is based on has occurred, (2) the amount is measurable, and (3) the tax is expected to be collected (realizable). For example, when a retail sale occurs, a governmental entity should record the sales tax derived from that sale as revenue, irrespective of when the cash is expected to be received from the retailer. However, in order to recognize revenue under this concept, a governmental entity will often use estimates in order to make an appropriate revenue accrual at the end of the year. For example, certain retail merchants are required to remit sales tax collections during the month after they actually collect the tax from customers. Under this circumstance, the governmental entity will have to estimate at the end of its fiscal year the tax collections that it will receive subsequent to year-end and that were based on sales that occurred on or before the entity's year-end date. In other instances, a governmental entity will have to estimate refunds that it must make after its fiscal year-end. For example, a governmental entity that imposes a personal income tax will generally have to make some refunds (due to overpayments) to individuals who file their tax returns after the end of the governmental entity's fiscal year (GASB-33, par. 16) [GASB Cod. Sec. N50.113].

A governmental entity usually cannot collect all taxes that are legally due and, therefore, it should report as revenue only the estimated tax that it expects to realize. Under this circumstance, the governmental entity will again need to use various estimation methods in order to report net revenues from derived tax sources. For example, a governmental entity that imposes a personal income tax may use historical trend information (adjusted for current economic and enforcement conditions) in order to provide an appropriate allowance for uncollectible derived tax receivables.

OBSERVATION: GASB-33, pars. 16 and 18 [GASB Cod. Secs. N50.113, .115, 1400.155], requires that derived taxes and imposed nonexchange revenues be reported in the statement of activities, net of estimated refunds and estimated uncollectible amounts, respectively. A bad debts expense account should not be used. However, the notes to the basic financial statements would show any amounts receivable net of those uncollectible amounts.

A governmental entity must record an asset arising from a derived tax revenue transaction when the related exchange transaction occurs or when the entity receives resources, whichever comes first. That asset will be recorded as cash when tax receipts are collected during the accounting period, but it will take the form of a receivable when revenue is accrued at the end of the year. However, if the entity collects taxes before the conditions of revenue recognition (as described above) are satisfied, it should record the receipt of cash as tax revenue received in advance (a liability account) in accordance with GASB-65.

In its basis for conclusions for GASB-65, in paragraph 53, the GASB concluded that resources received in advance in relation to a derived tax revenue nonexchange transaction (such as taxes) are still liabilities. Curiously, the GASB did not classify or name the liability. Therefore, a description of what is occurring, as in the aforementioned "tax revenue received in advance," should be adequate. However, GASB-65, paragraph 31 [GASB Cod. Secs. 1800.109, 1800.110, 2200.175, 2200.176, 2250.132, 2250.137, 2450.129, F60.101, L30.114, N50.112, N50.113, S20.110, S20.113], limits the use of the word "deferred" only to those items that are deferred outflows of resources or deferred inflows of resources.

Only one governmental entity is involved in a derived tax revenue transaction. For this reason, this type of nonexchange transaction will give rise only to governmental revenue and not governmental expenditure. The GASB notes that generally derived tax revenues are not subject to time restrictions (GASB-33, footnote 8) [GASB Cod. Secs. N50.113, fn7]. If derived tax revenue is subject to time restrictions, a governmental entity should use the guidance that applies to imposed nonexchange revenue transactions.

As noted earlier, purpose restrictions do not affect the timing of revenues related to nonexchange transactions; however, because resources are restricted the governmental entity must disclose that fact in its financial statements. This disclosure requirement may be accomplished by establishing a fund balance restriction (for governmental fund types) or a restriction of net positions (for proprietary or fiduciary fund types). For example, assume that a governmental entity recognizes $100,000 of derived tax revenues (net of uncollectible amounts) during the period (based on exchange transactions covered by the tax legislation) and that the amount is restricted because of a court judgment against the government for the purchase of computers for the entity's library. Such transactions would be recorded in a governmental fund in the following manner:

	Debit	Credit
GENERAL FUND		
Cash (or taxes receivable)	100,000	
Revenues—Derived Taxes		100,000
To record the recognition of derived tax revenues, net of uncollectible amounts.		
Fund Balance—Unassigned (or Assigned)	100,000	
Fund Balance Restricted for the Purchase of Computers		100,000
To record the restriction of fund balance due to court judgment.		

OBSERVATION: The purpose restriction does not delay the recognition of the revenue.

Imposed Nonexchange Revenues

"Imposed nonexchange revenues" are based on assessments imposed by a government on a non-governmental entity (other than assessments that are based on exchange transactions). The principal characteristic of these sources of revenue is that they are "imposed by that government on an act committed or omitted by the provider (such as property ownership or the contravention of a law or regulation) that is not an exchange transaction". GASB-33 identifies the following as imposed nonexchange revenues:

- Property (ad valorem) taxes assessed by a governmental entity;
- Fines and penalties imposed by a governmental entity;
- Property seized by a governmental entity; and
- Property that escheats to a governmental entity.

A governmental entity should recognize imposed nonexchange revenues (1) in the period when use of the resources is required or is first permitted by time requirements, (2) when the amount is measurable, and (3) when the tax is expected to be collected (realizable). However, the application of these revenue recognition criteria depends to some extent on the type of revenue source.

Property Taxes (and Other Ad-Valorem Taxes)

Generally, the most important example of an imposed nonexchange revenue stream is property taxes. GASB-33 notes that the date that a governmental entity has an enforceable legal claim against a property owner is usually included in the enabling legislation. The legislation may refer to the enforceable legal claim date using a variety of terms, including the lien date, assessment date, or some other descriptive term. The term used in the legislation is not the controlling factor in determining when property tax revenue should be recognized. The basic principle adopted by GASB-33 is that a "receivable should be recognized as soon as the government has a legal claim to a provider's resources that is enforceable through the eventual seizure of the property." The entity should record the revenue/receivable at that date even if the property owner has the right to appeal the assessment or has other due process rights.

The amount of the property taxes receivable is based on the assessed value of the property and the current property tax rate used by the governmental entity. Even though a governmental entity has an enforceable legal claim against property owners, all property taxes assessed will not be collected, and the entity will need to make a reasonable estimate of the amount of uncollectible property taxes and to provide an appropriate allowance.

OBSERVATION: For revenue recognition, GASB-33 emphasizes that the lien date is not the important date. The critical date is the date of an enforceable legal claim. Another important factor is that the enforceable legal claim date does not require that a governmental entity formally place a lien on the property as of that date.

There is one exception to the enforceable legal claim date. In some instances a governmental entity levies property taxes for one particular period but the enforceable legal claim date or the payment due date(s) occurs in another period. Under this circumstance, GASB-33 requires the entity to record the property taxes as revenue in the period in which it levied the taxes (GASB-33, pars. 17–18) [GASB Cod. Secs. N50.114–.115, P70.105, 1400.155].

Property taxes are assessed for a fiscal year and are expected to finance expenditures of the year of assessment. Usually on the assessment date or levy date, the property taxes become a lien against the assessed property (demand date criterion), but the actual amounts paid to the governmental unit may be made on a quarterly or monthly basis during the year covered by the assessment. Property taxes should be recorded as revenue on a modified accrual basis and, therefore, recorded when they are both measurable and available (NCGA-1, par. 62, as amended by GASB-38, par. 7) [GASB Cod. Secs. 1600.106, 2300.106, P70.104].

The amount of the property taxes receivable is based on the assessed value of the property and the current property tax rate used by the governmental unit. All property taxes assessed will not be collected, and the measurability criterion can be satisfied only if the governmental unit can make a reasonable estimate of the amount of uncollectible property taxes (GASB-33, par. 18, as amended by GASB-65, par. 9) [GASB Cod. Sec. N50.115].

When reasonable estimates can be made, the property tax levy may be recorded as follows:

	Debit	Credit
GENERAL FUND		
Property Taxes Receivable	400,000	
Property Tax Revenue		370,000
Allowance for Uncollectible Property Taxes		30,000

To record the recognition of property tax receivable, along with allowance for uncollectible amounts.

The property tax levy revenues are recorded net of the estimated amount of uncollectible property taxes. No bad debts expense account is used because only expenditures, not expenses, are recorded by governmental funds. In the above example, a deferred inflow of resources is recorded as the government may not utilize the funds until after the fiscal year.

The revenue is reported as a net amount because only the net amount is expected to be available during the fiscal period. Since revenues are reported net, it is not appropriate to record a bad debt expense because the expense does not represent an actual expenditure of current financial resources during the period. Reporting revenues on a net basis does not mean that a governmental unit cannot budget for bad debt expense and monitor the expense through its financial accounting system. When this is done, however, the bad debt expense account used for budgeting or internal purposes must be netted against the related gross revenue account and reported as net revenue for financial reporting purposes. In the following illustration, bad debt expense is not recorded, but the example journal entries could easily be modified to accommodate the use of a bad debts expense account for internal reporting purposes.

During the fiscal year, the routine transactions (such as write-offs of accounts and collections on account) affecting the receivables and allowance accounts may be recorded as follows, assuming $350,000 is collected. Interest receivable and revenues for delinquent accounts would be recorded similarly:

	Debit	Credit
GENERAL FUND		
Cash	350,000	
Property Taxes Receivable—Current		350,000
To record the recognition of property taxes.		

GASB-33, par. 18, as amended by GASB-65, par. 9 [GASB Cod. Sec. N50.115], states that deferred inflows of resources should be reported when resources associated with imposed nonexchange revenue transactions are received or reported as a receivable before (*a*) the period for which property taxes are levied or (*b*) the period when resources are required to be used or when use is first permitted for all other imposed nonexchange revenues in which the enabling legislation includes *time requirements* (not purpose requirements). Recognition of an allowance was not affected by GASB-65.

It may be determined during the fiscal year that the allowance for uncollectible accounts was either over-provided for or underprovided for. When this conclusion is reached, the allowance account and the revenue account are appropriately adjusted to reflect the change in the accounting estimate. For example, in the current illustration, if it were decided that the allowance provision for the year should have been $27,000 and not $30,000, the following entry would be made:

	Debit	Credit
GENERAL FUND		
Allowance for Uncollectible Property Taxes—Current	3,000	
Property Taxes Receivables—Current		3,000
To record the recognition of property tax reductions due to amounts that will never be collected.		

At the end of the year, it may be decided to transfer the balance in the current receivables account to a delinquent account for internal control and analysis. The transfer does not substitute for the write-off of an account when a specific account has been identified as uncollectible. In fact, for reporting purposes, the current and delinquent balances are usually combined since they both represent specific accounts that are expected to ultimately be collected. To continue with the illustration, assume that all of the remaining net receivables are considered collectible, but they are technically delinquent at the end of the fiscal year. In this case, the following entry would be made, assuming a lien is recorded:

	Debit	Credit
GENERAL FUND		
Property Taxes Receivable—Delinquent Tax Liens	47,000	
Property Taxes Receivable—Current		47,000
Property Tax Revenue	47,000	
Unavailable Tax Revenue—Tax Liens		47,000
To record the recognition of property taxes that are deemed delinquent and related reductions in revenue to close the fiscal year.		

The results from the above transactions would show Property Taxes Receivable—Delinquent Tax Liens for $47,000 along with an offsetting Unavailable Tax Revenue—Tax Liens, also for $47,000. The Allowance for Uncollectible Property Taxes—Current account would carry forward to the next year amounting to $20,000. Assuming $30,000 in Tax Liens were collected in the next year, irrespective of interest and penalties, the entry would be as follows:

	Debit	Credit
GENERAL FUND		
Cash	30,000	
Property Taxes Receivable—Delinquent Tax Liens		30,000
Unavailable Tax Revenue—Tax Liens	30,000	
Revenue—Tax Liens		30,000
To record the payment on delinquent property taxes, prior to interest and penalties.		

After this entry, a best practice is to reassess the allowance account.

In general, NCGA-1 (*Governmental Accounting and Financial Reporting Principles*) requires that the modified accrual basis of accounting be used to recognize revenues in government funds and provides the following guidance:

> Revenues and other governmental fund financial resources increments (e.g., bond issue proceeds) are recognized in the accounting period in which they become susceptible to accrual—that is, when they become both *measurable* and *available* to finance expenditures of the fiscal period. "Available" means collectible within the current period or soon enough thereafter to be used to pay liabilities of the current period. Application of the "susceptibility to accrual" criterion requires judgment, consideration of the materiality of the item in question, and due regard for the practicality of accrual, as well as consistency in application (NCGA-1, par. 62, GASB-38, par. 7) [GASB Cod. Sec. 1600.106].

GASB-65 modified the accounting slightly by adding the following sentence from paragraph 30:

> When an asset is recorded in governmental fund financial statements but the revenue is not available, the government should report a deferred inflow of resources until such time as the revenue becomes available (NCGA-1, par. 119, as amended by GASB-33, par. 17, GASB-54, par. 5, GASB-65, par. 30) [GASB Cod. Sec. 1600.114].

In order to establish common criteria for the recognition of revenue under the modified accrual basis of accounting, in November 1997, the GASB issued GASBI-5 (*Property Tax Revenue Recognition in Governmental Funds*), which inserted the following sentence defining "available" with regard to property tax revenue:

> *Available* means collected within the current period or expected to be collected soon enough thereafter to be used to pay liabilities of the current period.

OBSERVATION: The revised wording established by the Interpretation uses the terminology "collected or expected to be collected," whereas NCGA-1, par. 62, refers to "collectible." The GASB recognizes the different phraseology but states that "modifying the terminology in paragraph 62 of NCGA Statement 1 is beyond the scope of this Interpretation." As of the end of a fiscal year, a governmental entity must estimate the amount of property taxes that are expected to be collected within no more than 60 days of the end of the period. In most instances a reasonable estimate can be made (the measurability criterion). In other circumstances, the financial statements will not have to be finalized until after the 60-day period, so that actual collections during the "stub" period can be the basis for the year-end accrual. In any event, governments should have a consistent, clear policy as to what is meant by "collected or expected to be collected." Many large governments with robust revenue-estimation systems can pinpoint collection periods by tax type.

The effect of the Interpretation is to eliminate the due date criterion originally established by NCGAI-3 and superseded. Thus, in order for property taxes to be reported as revenue (1) the levy must apply to the current year and (2) they must be "collected within the current period or expected to be collected soon enough thereafter to be used to pay liabilities of the current period."

PRACTICE ALERT: The concepts of "measurable" and "available" with regard to revenue recognition is one of the focus areas of the GASB's *Financial*

Reporting Model—Reexamination project. For a further discussion, see Chapter 3, "Basis of Accounting and Measurement Focus."

When it is concluded that assessed property tax revenue will not be available, the revenue cannot be recognized in the current assessment period. Continuing with the current illustration, if it is concluded that $4,000 of the property taxes receivable at the end of the fiscal year will not be collected until more than 60 days after the close of the period, the following entry would be made (GASB-33, par. 18, as modified by GASB-65, par. 9):

	Debit	Credit
GENERAL FUND		
Property Tax Revenue	4,000	
Deferred Inflows of Resources—Property Taxes		4,000
To reclassify property tax revenues to be collected more than 60 days after the close of the fiscal year.		

OBSERVATION: As previously stated, the term "deferred" in financial statements has changed due to the implementation of GASB-65. For example, in prior practice "deferred revenue" resulting from grant funds received in advance of an entity's meeting the eligibility requirements, other than those related to the passage of time, is actually a liability, not a deferred inflow of resources as defined in GASB:CS-4. This amount does not meet the definition of a deferred inflow of resources, because an acquisition of net positions has not occurred. An asset (cash) increased at the same time that the liability to perform under the terms of the grant increased. Thus, net positions are unchanged. The GASB believes that items such as these should be described in financial statements without using the term "deferred" in the caption. For instance, in the foregoing example, the caption "grant advances" or "unearned revenue" could be used, rather than "deferred revenue." GASB did not define captions for deferred items that do not meet the definition of deferred inflows of resources. The GASB believes that financial statements would be more understandable to users if the term "deferred" was restricted for items meeting the definition of deferred inflows or outflows of resources.

When property taxes are received in advance of the actual levy or assessment date, the receipt should be recorded as deferred inflows of resources upon implementation of GASB-65. Subsequently, the revenue is recognized in the period that the tax is levied, assuming the measurable and available criteria are met (NCGA-1, par. 66; GASB-65, par. 9) [GASB Cod. Sec. N50.115].

When property taxes are delinquent but are expected to be collected, they should be reported as deferred inflows of resources—property taxes if it is estimated that the taxes will not be available to pay current obligations of the governmental fund. Generally, this would mean that the delinquent property taxes are not expected to be collected within 60 days of the close of the fiscal year.

The governmental unit must disclose the important dates associated with assessed property taxes. These dates may include the lien dates, due dates, and collection dates. In addition, some units may be prohibited from recognizing property tax revenues based on the measurable and available criteria. When this circumstance exists, the nature of the prohibition should be disclosed in a note to the financial statements. Moreover, the fund balance should be committed or assigned (depending on law) by the amount of the property tax revenue recognized under generally accepted accounting principles, but this is not consistent with the legal requirement that must be observed by the governmental unit.

Other Imposed Nonexchange Revenues

All other imposed nonexchange revenues should be recorded in the governmental entity's financial statements as of the date an enforceable legal claim arises unless the enabling legislation establishes a time requirement. When a time requirement is imposed, the entity should recognize revenue when the resources are permitted to be used (GASB-33, pars. 17–18) [GASB Cod. Secs. N50.114–.115, P70.105, 1400.155] and in accordance with GASB-65, paragraph 9, defer the inflows of resources until that time.

OBSERVATION: GASB-33 notes that the enforceable legal claim date for other imposed nonexchange revenues can generally be determined by the enabling legislation or related regulations.

A governmental entity must record an asset from imposed nonexchange transactions when the entity has an enforceable legal claim to the asset (as explained above) or when the entity receives resources, whichever comes first. That asset will be in the form of cash from tax receipts, fines, and so on, which are collected during the accounting period, but the asset will take the form of a receivable when revenue is accrued at the end of the year. However, if the entity collects imposed nonexchange revenue before the revenue recognition criteria are satisfied, the entity should record the receipt of cash as deferred inflows of resources. In the case of property taxes and other ad-valorem taxes, it is possible for the entity to recognize a receivable before revenue is recognized. That is, it can record property taxes as a receivable/deferred inflow of resources when the entity has an enforceable legal claim (as described earlier) even if it levies the taxes after the date of the enforceable legal claim. Because the entity receives cash before the period for which the taxes were levied, the government reduces the receivable but its deferred inflow of resources remains the same.

Only one governmental entity is involved in an imposed nonexchange revenue transaction. For this reason, this type of nonexchange transaction will give rise only to governmental revenue and not governmental expenditures.

A time restriction arises when a resource provider requires that a recipient governmental entity use the resources in a specific time period or requires that they not be used until a specified date or event has occurred. When a governmental entity receives resources that are subject to a time restriction, it should record the asset (cash) but recognize a liability (an advance) rather than revenue.

Once the time restriction has occurred or been met, the entity can recognize the imposed nonexchange revenue.

A purpose restriction does *not* affect the recognition of imposed nonexchange revenues. A governmental entity can record those revenues when the criteria described above are satisfied; however, the entity must indicate in its financial statements that the restricted resources received from an imposed nonexchange revenue source are to be used for a specified purpose. This is accomplished by establishing a fund balance restriction (for governmental fund types) or a restriction of net position (for proprietary or fiduciary fund types). For example, an entity recognizes $1,000,000 of property taxes during the accounting period (based on the enforceable legal claim concept) and the amount is restricted for the construction of a public school library. At the end of the accounting period, the entity would have to restrict $1,000,000 of fund balance.

Government-Mandated Nonexchange Transactions

Revenues from government-mandated nonexchange transactions arise when a governmental entity provides resources to a governmental entity that is at a lower level than the governmental entity that is providing the resources and the provider entity "requires [the recipient] government to use them for a specific purpose or purposes established in the provider's enabling legislation." An example of this is when the federal government (provider government) makes resources available to a state (recipient government), or a state government (provider government) makes resources available to a municipality or other local governmental entity (recipient government). GASB-33 notes that government-mandated nonexchange revenues have the following principal characteristics (GASB-33, par. 7c) [GASB Cod. Secs. 1600.111, .126, N50.104]:

- The provider government requires that the recipient government institute a specific program (or facilitate the performance of a specific program) conducted by the recipient government or nongovernmental entity (secondary recipient entity or *subrecipient(s)*).

- Certain performance requirements must be fulfilled (other than the provision of cash or other assets in advance).

A secondary recipient in a government-mandated nonexchange transaction can be a governmental entity or a nongovernmental entity. For example, the federal government mandates that states have a drug rehabilitation program and provides some funds to be used directly by the states (recipient government), and some of the funding is passed through the state to counties and certain not-for-profit organizations. In this example, the counties and not-for-profit organizations are secondary recipients.

Because the resources received by the recipient government must be used for a particular purpose, such resources always create a purpose restriction. In many instances, the resources are also subject to eligibility requirements, including time restrictions. An example of a government-mandated nonexchange transaction is the federal government requiring a state government to use federal funds to provide educational counseling to certain disadvantaged groups.

OBSERVATION: Simply mandating that a lower-level governmental entity establish a specific program does *not* create a government-mandated nonexchange transaction itself. The higher-level government must fund the program. The standards established by GASB-33 do not apply to unfunded mandates established by the federal government or state governments, because these types of programs do not involve the exchange of resources (GASB-33, footnote 5) [GASB Cod. Sec. N50.fn6].

In a government-mandated nonexchange transaction, if the two governmental entities that are involved in the transaction are state and local governments, they are both subject to GASB accounting and reporting standards. For this reason, the standards established by GASB-33 will apply to the recognition of revenue (by the recipient government) and the recognition of expenditures (by the provider government). However, if the provider government is the federal government or if a secondary recipient of the resources is a nongovernmental entity, then these entities are not subject to the standards established by GASB-33.

In a government-mandated nonexchange transaction, the recipient government should recognize revenue when all eligibility requirements (which include time requirements) are satisfied. The eligibility requirements are categorized as follows (GASB-33, par. 20) [GASB Cod. Sec. N50.117]:

- Required characteristics of recipients;
- Time requirements; and
- Reimbursements.

All eligibility requirements must be satisfied before the recipient government in a government-mandated nonexchange transaction can recognize an operating transaction. If cash or another asset is provided before the eligibility requirements are satisfied, the recipient government records the transaction as an advance rather than as an operating transaction (a transaction that affects the operating statement) (GASB-33, par. 19) [GASB Cod. Sec. N50.116].

A government-mandated nonexchange transaction may have an eligibility requirement that stipulates that the recipient (or secondary recipient) must have specific characteristics that have been adopted by the provider government. For example, a state government passed legislation that provides resources to local school districts to make certain expenditures that were mandated in the legislation. Under this eligibility requirement, a government-mandated nonexchange transaction can occur only if the recipient government is a school district. The GASB notes that most government-mandated nonexchange transactions have an eligibility requirement that relates to the required characteristics of recipients or secondary recipients.

Provider governments, either through enabling legislation, related regulations, or as part of the appropriations, may identify the period during which recipient governments may expend resources provided by provider governments or they may identify the period when recipient governments can begin expending the resources (and be expended in one or more periods). A recipient government should not recognize resources that it received or expects to receive as operating transactions (i.e., presented on the statement of activity) until the recipient government satisfies the time requirements (and all other eligibility requirements), except as explained in the following paragraph:

When a recipient government receives government-mandated nonexchange transactions to finance operations or to acquire capital assets in or beginning in a specific period, the provider government should recognize an expense/liability and the recipient government should recognize revenues/receivable when the specified period begins, assuming all other eligibility requirements are satisfied.

In accordance with GASB-65, par. 10, resources transmitted before the eligibility requirements are met (excluding time requirements) should be reported as assets by the provider and as liabilities by the recipient. Resources received before time requirements are met but after all other eligibility requirements have been met, should be reported as a deferred inflow of resources by the recipient. Resources transmitted before the eligibility requirements are met (excluding time requirements) should be reported as liabilities (advances) by the recipient. Footnote 4 to GASB-65 reminds preparers that recognition of assets and revenues should not be delayed pending completion of purely routine requirements, such as the filing of claims for allowable costs under a reimbursement program or the filing of progress reports with the provider (GASB-33, par. 20) [GASB Cod. Sec. N50.117].

A prevalent example of when assets would be reported by a provider and liabilities would be reported by a recipient would be in relation to federal grant funds passed from one level of government to another where there would be a potential for disallowed costs (e.g., in primary education funds). Given that there is a high incidence of disallowed costs due to student eligibility in primary education, funds received during a fiscal year but before a school year prior to eligibility requirements being met, would be recorded as an asset (advances to school districts) by the providing government and a liability (advances from the state department of education) until eligibility requirements are met by the receiving government.

In some instances, the time requirement may be permanent (e.g., permanent endowment) or the restriction may state that resources may not be spent until the expiration of a specified number of years or until a specified event has occurred. Examples of this include a governmental unit of a local government receiving a permanent addition to its endowment or other trusts, or a local public museum receiving contributions of "works of art, historical treasures, and similar assets to capitalized collections." Often during the interim period, the governmental entity may derive benefits from the resources (investment income or display the artwork or historical relics). The recipient government should recognize government-mandated nonexchange transactions of this type as revenue when they are received, assuming the recipient government has satisfied all other eligibility requirements. The time requirement is considered to be satisfied when "the recipient begins to honor the provider's stipulation not to sell, disburse, or consume the resources and continues to be met for as long as the recipient honors that stipulation." However, during the time restriction period (which means indefinitely for a permanent endowment), the recipient government should note in its statement of position the fund balance restriction for a governmental fund type or net position restriction or similar description for a proprietary or fiduciary fund type (GASB-33, par. 22 and footnote 12) [GASB Cod. Sec. N50.119, fn.11].

OBSERVATION: If a governmental entity receives contributions of works of art, historical treasures, or other, similar assets to be added to capitalized collections, the entity should not capitalize those receipts if the collection the assets are being added to has not previously been capitalized. Rather, these amounts are recognized as program expense equal to the amount of revenues recognized. (See previous discussion on acquisition value and donated items in accordance with GASB-72.) If the collections are capitalized, then donations are increases in capital assets.

For administrative or practical purposes, a governmental entity may receive resources early from another governmental entity. The receipt of these resources under this circumstance is not considered the receipt of an endowment or other similar receipts as described in the previous paragraph. Therefore, a recipient government should *not* record this type of receipt as revenue until all eligibility requirements that apply to government-mandated nonexchange transactions are satisfied (GASB-33, par. 23) [GASB Cod. Sec. N50.120].

When the provider government does not establish time requirements, the recipient of the resources and the provider of the resources should recognize the government-mandated nonexchange transaction when all other eligibility requirements are satisfied. Assuming no other eligibility requirements exist, both the recipient government and the provider government should recognize revenue/expenditure based on the first day of the fiscal year of the provider government. For example, the relevant fiscal year of the provider government is generally the first day the appropriation becomes effective. Thus, under that circumstance, both the provider government and the recipient government should record the entire amount related to the government-mandated transaction based on the first day of the provider government's fiscal year (applicable period), unless the provider government has a biennial budgetary process. When the provider government has a biennial budgetary process, each year of the biennial period should be considered a separate year (applicable period), and "the provider and the recipients should allocate one-half of the resources appropriated for the biennium to each applicable period, unless the provider specifies a different allocation" (GASB-33, par. 24) [GASB Cod. Sec. N50.121].

When a secondary recipient government is involved in a government-mandated transaction, the primary recipient government's fiscal year should be used rather than the original provider government's fiscal year. For example, the federal government provides a state government with resources and a local government also receives some of the resources. The local government would use the state government's fiscal year to determine when to recognize revenue; however, the state government would use the federal government's fiscal year to determine when it should recognize revenue under the government-mandated program (GASB-33, footnote 14) [GASB Cod. Sec. N50.fn.12].

GASB-33 notes that some grant programs may be established by a state whereby "the required period of disbursement often is specified through the appropriation of resources under the enabling legislation, rather than as part of the legislation or related regulations." In this circumstance an explicit appropriation must be made by state legislature (the existence of the program under the enabling legislation is not enough) and the period to which the appropriation applies must have begun before a local government can recognize revenue (assuming all eligibility criteria are satisfied). The *GASB Implementation Guide 2015-1*, question Z.33.16 [GASB Cod. Sec. N50.710-1], applies this general guidance by noting that a city that receives a grant award (but not the resources) from a state cannot recognize grant revenue unless the state has appropriated resources for the grant. However, the *GASB Implementation Guide 2015-1*, in the same question, notes that, for example, if "state law requires the state treasurer to pay the grant whether or not the legislature appropriates resources," the city should recognize the grant when it is awarded.

Some government-mandated nonexchange transactions are based on a reimbursement arrangement. These transactions are referred to as "reimbursement-type transactions" or "expenditure-driven grant programs." The fundamental characteristic of these types of programs is that the provider government "stipulates that a recipient cannot qualify for resources without first incurring allowable costs under the provider's program." When government-mandated nonexchange transactions are subject to a reimbursement eligibility requirement, the recipient government should not recognize revenue until the recipient has incurred eligible costs that are reimbursable under the program (GASB-33, pars. 15 and 20, both as amended by GASB-65) [GASB Cod. Secs. N50.112, .117]. It is important to remember that a reimbursement eligibility requirement is not a purpose restriction and, therefore, is not subject to financial statement presentation requirements that apply to purpose restrictions.

The recognition of revenue by the recipient government and expenditures by the provider government should not be delayed because routine administrative procedures have not been completed. GASB-33 notes that these procedures could include filing claims for reimbursements under an expenditure-driven program or completing progress reports required by the provider government (GASB-33, footnote 10) [GASB Cod. Sec. N50.fn9]. However, in practice, most categorical grants require claims to be filed for reimbursement. Furthermore, large governments need to be careful not to receive reimbursement too far in advance of expenditure or else they may be in violation of an agreement with the United States Treasury under the federal Cash Management Improvement Act of 1990 (as amended). If a government draws funds too early, the United States Treasury may be entitled to interest on a daily basis between when the funds were received and when the funds were expended.

Voluntary Nonexchange Transactions

Voluntary nonexchange transactions arise from "legislative or contractual agreements, other than exchanges, entered into willingly by two or more parties." A voluntary nonexchange transaction can be based on either a written or an oral agreement, assuming the latter is verifiable. The principal characteristics of voluntary nonexchange transactions are listed below (GASB-33, par. 7d and footnote 6) [GASB Cod. Secs. 1600.111, .126, N50.104, N50.fn.5]:

- They are not imposed on the provider or the recipient; and
- Satisfaction of eligibility requirements (other than the provision of cash or other assets in advance) is necessary for a transaction to occur.

In a voluntary nonexchange transaction, a governmental entity may be the recipient or the provider of the resources, and the second party of the transaction may be another governmental entity or a nongovernmental entity, such as an individual or a not-for-profit organization. Examples of voluntary nonexchange transactions include certain grants, some entitlements, and donations. Voluntary nonexchange transactions may involve purpose restrictions and/or time requirements, and they often require that resources be returned to the provider if purpose restrictions or eligibility requirements are contravened after the voluntary nonexchange transaction has been recognized by a governmental entity.

NOTE: For convenience, in the following discussion of voluntary nonexchange transactions it is assumed that both parties to the nonexchange transaction are governmental entities. When one of the parties to the nonexchange transaction is not a governmental entity, that nongovernmental entity is not required to follow the standards established by GASB-33. The GASB established the same (with one exception) accounting standards for government-mandated nonexchange transactions and voluntary nonexchange transactions. These standards are explained in the previous section. (The accounting standard exception for voluntary nonexchange transactions is that there are four possible eligibility requirements instead of three. The additional requirement—contingency eligibility—is discussed later in this section.)

In a voluntary nonexchange transaction, the provider and the recipient should recognize the nonexchange transaction when all eligibility requirements (which include time requirements) are satisfied. The eligibility requirements are categorized as follows (GASB-33, par. 20) [GASB Cod. Sec. N50.117]:

- Required characteristics of recipients (discussed earlier);
- Time requirements (discussed earlier);
- Reimbursements (discussed earlier); and
- Contingencies (discussed below).

All eligibility requirements must be satisfied before the parties to a voluntary nonexchange transaction can record an operating transaction. Resources transmitted before the eligibility requirements are met (excluding time requirements) should be reported as assets (advances to another government) by the provider and as liabilities by the recipient (advances from another government).

Resources received before time requirements are met but after all other eligibility requirements have been met, should be reported as a deferred outflow of resources by the provider and a deferred inflow of resources by the recipient, with cash inflows or cash outflows being the credits or debits, respectively.

OBSERVATION: In some instances where the provider of the resources is a nongovernmental entity, resources may be made on an installment basis. If there is no time restriction(s) (or other eligibility requirements) that applies to the donation, the GASB requires that the recipient government recognize the full amount of the donation as revenue. If the installments are spread over more than one year, the entity should recognize the amount of revenue as the present value of the future cash flows.

The final possible eligibility requirement for a voluntary nonexchange transaction is based on a contingency imposed by the provider. That is, the right to receive resources by the recipient can occur only if the recipient has performed the specified requirement. For example, a state university has been promised resources by a private donor if the university can persuade its alumni to match dollar-for-dollar the promised gift of the original donor. Under this circumstance, the university can recognize an operating transaction only if the university obtains the appropriate resources from its alumni.

An asset (receivable) must be recorded by the recipient when it has satisfied the revenue criteria for voluntary nonexchange transactions described above. If the recipient collects resources from a voluntary nonexchange transaction before the recipient satisfies the revenue recognition criteria, the recipient should record the receipt of cash as either a deferred inflow of resources or a liability, as explained previously.

Voluntary nonexchange transactions often involve pledges (promises to pay) from nongovernmental entities (e.g., individuals, business enterprises, or not-for-profit organizations). Such promises may involve cash, works of art, and various other assets, and they may or may not involve purpose restrictions or time requirements. The recipient government should record pledges as revenue by the recipient government when "all eligibility requirements are met, provided that the promise is verifiable and the resources are measurable and probable of collection." The governmental entity may have to establish an allowance account before the entity can recognize pledges as revenue so that the total pledges are reported at their expected realizable value (GASB-33, par. 25) [GASB Cod. Sec. N50.122].

The standards established by GASB-33, paragraph 22 [GASB Cod. Sec. N50.119], apply to pledges. The recipient government should recognize pledges of resources that *cannot* be sold, disbursed, or consumed until after a passage of a specified period of time or the occurrence of a specified event as revenue when they are received, assuming the government has satisfied all other eligibility requirements. For example, if a government receives a pledge that involves additions to the governmental entity's permanent endowment, term endowments, or contributions of works of art, historical treasures, and similar assets to be included in the entity's collection, the governmental entity should not recognize the pledge as revenue until it receives the pledged property (GASB-33, footnote 15) [GASB Cod. Sec. N50.fn13].

When the provider of resources in a voluntary nonexchange transaction is a government, that government should recognize expenditures based on the same criteria that are used by the recipient government to recognize revenues (as discussed above). If the expenditure recognition criteria are not satisfied and the provider government has made a cash payment to the recipient government, the provider government should record the payment as an advance (asset) or potentially a deferred outflow of resources.

OBSERVATION: Similarly to government-mandated nonexchange transactions, for voluntary nonexchange transactions in accordance with GASB-65, paragraph 10, resources that are received before time requirements are met but after all other eligibility requirements have been met should be reported as a deferred inflow of resources by the recipient. Resources transmitted before the eligibility requirements are met (excluding time requirements) should be reported as liabilities (advances) by the recipient. Frequently, these may occur with deposit transactions.

Subsequent Contravention of Eligibility Requirements or Purpose Restrictions

A recipient government may record a nonexchange transaction as an operating transaction, but subsequent events indicate that resources will not be transferred in a manner originally anticipated by both parties or that resources transferred will have to be returned to the provider. This situation may arise because (1) eligibility requirements related to a government-mandated transaction or a voluntary nonexchange transaction are no longer being satisfied or (2) the recipient will not satisfy a purpose restriction within the time period specified (GASB-33, par. 26).

When it is *probable* (likely to occur) that the recipient will not receive the resources or will be required to return all or part of the resources already received, the following procedures should be observed:

- The provider government should recognize as revenue (1) the amount of resources that will not be provided to the recipient (but that have already been recognized as expenditures by the provider) and/or (2) the amount of resources already provided to the recipient but expected to be returned; and

- The recipient government should recognize as expenditures (1) the amount of resources that have been promised by the provider (and already recognized as revenue by the recipient) and/or (2) the amount or resources already received by the recipient but expected to be returned to the provider.

The AICPA's *State and Local Governments* Guide states that a similar situation arises when grant revenues are subject to a grant audit and the possibility of an adjustment has arisen. Under this development, the recipient governmental entity should consider whether a loss contingency arises based on the standards codified in GASB-62, paragraphs 96–113, to determine whether a liability should be reported (or netted against a related receivable) or a note disclosure should be made.

Nonexchange Revenues Administered or Collected by Another Government

A governmental entity may collect derived tax revenues or imposed nonexchange revenues on behalf of a recipient government that imposes the tax. For example, a state government administers a local sales tax (imposed by the locality) in conjunction with the state sales tax it imposes. In this circumstance, GASB-33 requires that the recipient government apply the relevant revenue recognition standards that apply to derived tax revenues and imposed nonexchange revenues. The state government would not record revenue for the portion of the tax due to the recipient governmental entity but, rather, would recognize a liability. In some instances, the recipient government may need to estimate the amount of revenue to be accrued in a particular accounting period. The GASB assumes that the recipient government, because it imposes the tax, will have sufficient information to make an appropriate accrual at the end of the year (GASB-33, par. 27).

Derived tax revenues and imposed nonexchange revenues of one governmental entity that are shared with another governmental entity (but not imposed by the recipient government) are based on two transactions, namely, (1) events or actions that give rise to the derived tax revenue or the imposed nonexchange revenue and (2) the sharing of the revenue by one governmental entity (provider government) with another governmental entity (recipient government).

In the first transaction, a governmental entity would record revenue based on the criteria established by GASB-33, depending on whether the revenue is from derived taxes or imposed nonexchange transactions. The second transaction results in both the recording of an expenditure/expense (by the provider government) and revenue (by the recipient government) and represents either a government-mandated or a voluntary nonexchange transaction. GASB-36 requires that both the provider government and the recipient government record the expenditure/expense and revenue, respectively based on the government-mandated nonexchange or voluntary nonexchange criteria. Thus, the two governments would record the sharing of the tax revenue (as an expenditure/expense and revenue in the same period (GASB-36, par. 2).

In some instances, shared nonexchange revenues may be based on a continuing appropriation. A continuing appropriation is an "appropriation that, once established, is automatically renewed without further legislative action, period after period, until altered or revoked." When shared revenues are based on continuing appropriations, the eligibility requirement (which is the basis for recording the government-mandated or voluntary nonexchange transaction) is satisfied when either (1) the underlying transaction occurs (for derived tax revenue) or (2) the period when resources were required to be used or the first period that use was permitted has occurred (for imposed nonexchange transactions). For example, GASB-36 points out that "when a state shares its sales taxes under the requirements of a continuing appropriation, the recipient should record revenues and receivables when the underlying sales occur, regardless of whether the guidance for derived tax revenues or for government-mandated and voluntary nonexchange transactions applies."

When revenue sharing occurs based on a continuing appropriation, the recipient government should make any accrual of revenue based on information supplied by the provider government. For example, in the case of shared sales taxes, the provider government should make available to the recipient governments information about sales tax revenues that have been earned in the current period but that will not be collected from merchants until the following period. GASB-36 points out "if notification by the provider government is not available in a timely manner, recipient governments should use a reasonable estimate of the amount to be accrued."

> **OBSERVATION:** When shared revenue includes allocations of taxes between one level of government and another as a voluntary nonexchange transaction and if at the lower level the allocation is restricted to a program, the *GASB Implementation Guide 2015-1*, question 7.34.5, discusses how the tax at the lower level should be recognized as general revenue as long as it is not restricted for any purpose. If the tax revenue contains a purpose restriction for education, for example, then it should be program revenue.

> **OBSERVATION:** Revenue sharing could occur in a service concession arrangement. If the operator is another government, then the transferor government reports all revenue earned and expenses incurred—including the amount of revenues shared with the transferor—that are associated with the operation of the facility. The transferor government should recognize only its portion of the shared revenue when it is earned in accordance with the terms of the arrangement. If revenue-sharing arrangements contain amounts to be paid to the transferor government regardless of revenues earned (e.g., $100,000 annually), then the present value of those amounts should be reported by the transferor and governmental operator as if they were installment payments at the inception of the arrangement.

Revenue Recognition Using the Modified Accrual Basis of Accounting

The standards established by GASB-33 retain the current fundamental criterion for revenue recognition that applies to the modified accrual basis of accounting, namely that revenue be recorded when it is both available and measurable. In addition, GASB-33 specifically states that revenue should be recognized only when it is probable (likely to occur) that it will be collected. As discussed below, the same standards for the recognition of revenue under the accrual basis of accounting should be used to record revenue under the modified accrual basis of accounting, except the revenue must be available (GASB-33, pars. 29–30) [GASB Cod. Secs. N50.126–.127].

As described above, the availability criterion requires that resources only be recorded as revenue if those resources are expected to be collected or otherwise realized in time to pay liabilities reported in the governmental fund at the end of the accounting period. In practice, the period of collectibility has generally ranged from thirty days to as much as a year. GASB-38 (*Certain Financial Statement Note Disclosures*) did not attempt to define the availability criterion in a more restricted manner, but it does require a governmental entity to specifically disclose what period of time is used to implement the standard. For example, the disclosure requirement could be met by simply stating "the city considers receivables collected within sixty days after year-end to be available and recognizes them as revenues of the current year" (GASB-38, par. 7) [GASB Cod. Secs. 1600.106, 2300.106, P70.104].

Derived Tax Revenues

GASB-33 requires that derived tax revenues be recorded in the same period in which the exchange transaction that generates the tax revenue occurs. Thus, once the taxable transaction has occurred, the governmental entity has an enforceable legal claim to the tax resources. If the resources related to the enforceable legal claim are available to the governmental entity, then, under the modified accrual basis of accounting, the governmental entity should record revenue.

Imposed Nonexchange Revenues

As defined earlier, imposed nonexchange revenue is characterized by an assessment implemented by a governmental entity "on an act committed or omitted by the provider (such as property ownership or the contravention of a law or regulation) that is not an exchange transaction."

For property taxes, the standards established by GASB-33 require that governmental entities continue to use the criteria established by NCGAI-3, as amended, in order to record revenues related to property taxes. For imposed nonexchange revenues that are derived from sources *other than property taxes*, the governmental entity should record deferred inflows of resources when resources associated with imposed nonexchange revenue transactions are received or reported as a receivable before (*a*) the period for which property taxes are levied or (*b*) the period when resources are required to be used or when use is first permitted for all other imposed nonexchange revenues in which the enabling legislation includes time requirements in accordance with GASB-65, par. 9.

Government-Mandated Nonexchange Transactions

Under the modified accrual basis of accounting, a recipient governmental entity should record resources received from another governmental entity that are considered government-mandated nonexchange transactions as revenue when the recipient entity has satisfied all eligibility requirements and the related resources are available to the entity. Resources received before time requirements are met but after all other eligibility requirements have been met, should be reported as a deferred outflow of resources by the provider and a deferred inflow of resources by the recipient. Resources transmitted before the eligibility requirements are met (excluding time requirements) should be reported as liabilities by the recipient, all in accordance with GASB-65, par. 10 [GASB Cod. Secs. N50.116, .118].

Voluntary Nonexchange Transactions

The characteristics of a voluntary nonexchange transaction are that (1) it is not imposed on the provider or the recipient and (2) eligibility requirements (including time requirements) must be satisfied before the transaction can occur. GASB-33 requires that the governmental entity record revenues related to a voluntary nonexchange transaction when all eligibility requirements have been satisfied and the related resources are available to the entity. Similar to mandated nonexchange transactions, resources received before time requirements are met but after all other eligibility requirements have been met, should be reported as a deferred outflow of resources by the provider and a deferred inflow of resources by the recipient.

Exhibit 17-1 summarizes the revenue recognition criteria established by GASB-33 and modified for the provisions of GASB-65 where necessary.

EXHIBIT 17-1
REVENUE AND EXPENDITURE RECOGNITION CRITERIA IN ACCORDANCE WITH GASB-65

	Derived Tax Revenue	Imposed Nonexchange Revenues	Government-Mandated Nonexchange Transactions	Voluntary Nonexchange Transactions
Revenue Recognition Criteria[A]	The exchange that the tax is based on has occurred.[B]	Deferred inflows of resources are reported when resources are received or reported as a receivable before (a) the period for which property taxes are levied or (b) the period when resources are required to be used or when use is first permitted for all other imposed nonexchange revenues in which the enabling legislation includes time requirements.[C]	Resources *received* before time requirements are met but after all other eligibility requirements have been met should be reported as a deferred inflow of resources by the recipient. Resources *transmitted* before the eligibility requirements are met (excluding time requirements) should be reported as liabilities by the recipient and assets by the provider.	Resources *received* before time requirements are met but after all other eligibility requirements have been met should be reported as a deferred inflow of resources by the recipient. Resources *transmitted* before the eligibility requirements are met (excluding time requirements) should be reported as liabilities by the recipient and assets by the provider.
Expenditure Recognition Criteria	Due to the parties involved in the transaction, no expenditure can arise for a governmental entity.	Due to the parties involved in the transaction, no expenditure can arise for a governmental entity.	Resources transmitted before the eligibility requirements are met (excluding time requirements) should be reported as assets by the provider and liabilities by the recipient. Resources received before time requirements are met but after all other eligibility requirements have been met should be reported as a deferred outflow of resources by the provider.	Resources transmitted before the eligibility requirements are met (excluding time requirements) should be reported as assets by the provider and liabilities by the recipient. Resources received before time requirements are met but after all other eligibility requirements have been met should be reported as a deferred outflow of resources by the provider.
Effect of a Time Restriction	Generally not subject to time restrictions	Revenue should not be recognized until the time restriction is satisfied.	Revenue should not be recognized until the time restriction is satisfied.[D]	Revenue should not be recognized until the time restriction is satisfied.[D]
Effect of a Purpose Restriction	The restriction should be disclosed in the financial statements.	The restriction should be disclosed in the financial statements.	The restriction should be disclosed in the financial statements.	The restriction should be disclosed in the financial statements.

(A) When revenue is recognized under the modified accrual basis of accounting, the available criterion must be satisfied.

(B) In addition, revenue can be recognized only if the amount is *measurable* (subject to reasonable estimation) and *realizable* (expected to be collected). Nonexchange transactions that are not recognizable because they are not measurable must be disclosed in the governmental entity's financial statements.

(C) When property taxes are levied for one particular period but the enforceable legal claim date or the payment due date(s) occurs in another period, GASB-33 requires that property tax revenue be recorded in the period for which the property tax is levied, subject to the provisions of GASB-65, paragraph 9 [GASB Cod. Sec. N50.115].

(D) When the provider of the resources prohibits the sale, disbursement, or consumption of resources for a specified period of time (or indefinitely, as in permanent endowment), or until a specified event has occurred, revenue should be recorded when the asset is received but the restriction should be disclosed in the entity's financial statements.

Certain Grants and Other Financial Assistance

GASB-24 (*Accounting and Financial Reporting for Certain Grants and Other Financial Assistance*) establishes standards for grants and other financial assistance that are classified as (1) pass-through grants, (2) food stamps, and (3) on-behalf payments for fringe benefits and salaries.

Pass-Through Grants

Pass-through grants are "grants and other financial assistance received by a governmental entity to transfer to or spend on behalf of a secondary recipient." A secondary recipient is "the individual or organization, government or otherwise, that is the ultimate recipient of a pass-through grant, or another recipient organization that passes the grant through to the ultimate recipient." The governmental entity that receives the grant that is distributed to a secondary recipient is the recipient government.

For example, the federal government (the grantor government) may make a grant to a state government (recipient governmental entity) that is to be distributed by the state government to certain municipal governments (secondary recipients) within the state. The secondary recipient does not have to be a governmental entity, but rather could be individuals or nongovernmental organizations.

GASB-24 requires that cash pass-through grants generally be recorded simultaneously as revenue and expenditures or expenses in a governmental fund, or proprietary fund. Only in those instances when the recipient government functions as a cash conduit should a pass-through grant be accounted for in an Agency Fund. The GASB describes cash conduit activity as transmitting grantor-supplied moneys "without having administrative or direct financial involvement in the program." Applying the standard requires that a governmental entity evaluate its administrative and financial roles in a grant program.

The GASB takes the position that administrative involvement is based on whether the recipient government's role in the grant program constitutes an operational responsibility for the grant program. While there is no attempt to formally define administrative involvement, the GASB notes that the following activities constitute such involvement:

- Monitoring secondary recipients for compliance with specific requirements established by the program;

- Determining which secondary recipients are eligible for grant payments (even if eligibility criteria are established by the provider government); and

- Exercising some discretion in determining how resources are to be allocated.

Administrative involvement may occur before the receipt of the grant by the recipient government or after the grant is received. Both pre-grant activities and post-grant activities should be evaluated to determine whether the recipient government is exercising administrative involvement in the grant program.

A recipient governmental entity's role in a grant program is considered more than custodial when the entity has a direct financial involvement in the program. While the GASB does not provide a definition of direct financial involvement, the following activities would suggest that the entity's role is beyond that of custodial responsibility:

- The recipient government is required to provide matching funds; and

- The recipient government is responsible for disallowed costs.

The GASB does not require a recipient government to consider payments for administrative costs (an indirect financial involvement) when determining whether its role is more than custodial. However, if the indirect financial payments are more than incidental, the recipient government's participation satisfies the administrative involvement criteria described in the standard and, therefore, it would be inappropriate to account for the pass-through grant in an Agency Fund.

Finally, the standards established by GASB-24 emphasize that all cash pass-through grants must be reported in the financial statements of the recipient government. Those grant programs considered strictly custodial in nature would be accounted for in an Agency Fund. Those grant programs that are characterized by either administrative involvement or direct financial involvement would be accounted for in a governmental fund, or a proprietary fund. It is not appropriate to record grant activity by establishing an asset and a related liability account, except in an Agency Fund. Even in an Agency Fund there must be a separate statement of changes in assets and liabilities that summarizes activity for the period (GASB-24, par. 5) [GASB Cod. Sec. N50.128].

The *GASB Implementation Guide 2015-1*, question 7.34.6 [GASB Cod. Sec. 2200.717-7], states that when a state receives a grant from the federal government and subsequently passes the resources to local governments for capital purposes, the state should report the receipt as an operational grant (program revenue) and not as a capital grant. A capital grant arises only "if it is restricted to the acquisition, construction, or improvement of the state's capital assets." The distributions to the localities are reported as an expenditure.

The AICPA's *State and Local Governments* Guide states that when a governmental entity receives a fee related to the administration of pass-through grants, the fee should be recorded as revenue.

Electronic Benefit Transfers (SNAP)

The supplemental nutrition assistance program (SNAP) (formerly known as food stamps) is defined in GASB-24 as "a federal program [Catalog of Federal Domestic Assistance (CFDA) program number 10.551] that is intended to improve the diets of members of low-income households by increasing their ability to purchase food." Currently, transfers of payments are provided by the federal government and are distributed directly to recipients by agents (including local governments) of the state governments. Recipients spend the assistance at retail establishments, and the retailers in turn deposit the spent assistance with their banks (GASB-24, par. 6) [GASB Cod. Sec. F60.101].

GASB-24 requires that receipts and disbursements under the program be accounted for by the states in the General Fund or a Special Revenue Fund. Expenditures are recognized when benefits are distributed by the state government or its agent to a low-income recipient. Recipients receive these benefits electronically through an electronic benefits transfer (EBT) system to a card that is usable in supermarkets and similar establishments.

The GASB takes the position that the SNAP program is expenditure-driven. Therefore, when expenditures are recognized there is an equal and simultaneous recognition of revenue.

On-Behalf Payments for Fringe Benefits and Salaries

GASB defines on-behalf payments for fringe benefits and salaries as "direct payments made by one entity (the paying entity or paying government) to a third-party recipient for the employees of another, legally separate entity (the employer entity or employer government)." They include payments made by governmental entities on behalf of nongovernmental entities and payments made by nongovernmental entities on behalf of governmental entities and may be made for volunteers as well as for paid employees of the employer entity.

Perhaps the best example of an on-behalf payment is a pension contribution made by a state government (paying government) to the state's teachers' pension fund (third-party recipient) for employees of a school district (employer government) within the state. On-behalf payments also include payments by a governmental entity to volunteers of another governmental entity. For example, a state government may make pension payments or other fringe benefit payments for individuals who serve as volunteer firefighters for rural fire districts (GASB-24, par. 7) [GASB Cod. Sec. N50.129].

PRACTICE ALERT: The provisions of GASB-24, pars. 7–13, with regard to on-behalf payment of defined benefit pensions were unchanged by GASB-68 (*Accounting and Financial Reporting for Pensions—an amendment of GASB Statement No. 27*). These situations are termed "special funding situations." GASB-68, par. 90, states that revenue should be recognized in an amount equal to the nonemployer contributing entities' total proportionate share of collective pension expense. GASB-68, par. 92, discusses how the proportionate share is determined. GASB-75 (*Accounting and Financial Reporting for Postemployment Benefits Other Than Pensions*) pars. 43(d), 69, 106, 113, and various other paragraphs and references. also deal with on-behalf payments in a similar manner to what is contained in GASB-68. These have been updated slightly due to the provisions of GASB-85 discussed at the conclusion of this practice alert.

If the effective pension plan terms define a specific relationship of the contribution requirements of a nonemployer contributing entity to those of the employer and other contributing entities, the employer's proportion should be established in a manner consistent with those terms, notwithstanding differences between the measurement basis used to determine contributions and that used to determine the collective net pension liability. Chapter 13, "Pension, Postemployment, and Other Employee Benefit Liabilities," discusses this issue further.

Further, if (*a*) the governmental nonemployer contributing entity's required contribution, consistently contributed, is defined in the pension plan terms to be the amount necessary to finance 100% of past service cost on the actuarial funding basis used by the employers and nonemployer contributing entities and (*b*) the employers' required contribution rate is defined in the pension plan terms to be an amount to satisfy the portion of the actuarially determined service cost of each period that is not offset by employee contributions, the employer's proportion of the collective net pension liability should be considered to be zero percent. In a zero percent situation, where another employer is contributing 100% of the pension liability in an irrevocable manner, then only revenues and expenses are declared, similarly to current practice in accordance with GASB-24. As a caution, however, with regard to pensions in accordance with GASB-68, the inflows and outflows will likely not match, because they are not based upon cash flows. An accrual for an expense will be made, which may not equal the subsidy receivable.

Finally, GASB Statement No. 85 (*Omnibus 2017*), paragraphs 9-12, amend the various paragraphs in GASB-75 as follows relating to on-behalf payments for pensions or OPEB in employer financial statements:

1. In financial statements prepared using the current financial resources measurement focus, an employer should recognize expenditures for on-behalf payments for pensions or OPEB equal to the total of

   a. Amounts paid during the reporting period by nonemployer contributing entities to the pension or OPEB plan (or for benefits as they come due) and

   b. The change between the nonemployer contributing entities' beginning and ending balances of amounts normally expected to be liquidated with expendable available financial resources. Both (a) and (b) include amounts for payables to a pension or OPEB plan.

2. Except for the circumstances identified in the next bullet, in financial statements prepared using the current financial resources measurement focus, an employer should recognize revenue equal to the amount of expenditures determined in accordance with the previous item.

3. For on-behalf payments that are *not legally required* for *defined contribution* pensions or OPEB, an employer *should apply the revenue*

recognition requirements GASB-24, paragraph 8 [GASB Cod. Sec. N50.130] (discussed below).

4. For on-behalf payments for pensions or OPEB, paragraphs 9–12 of GASB-24, as amended, *should not be applied* (see following discussion).

The employer entity and the paying entity may be either a governmental or a nongovernmental entity. The third-party recipient may be either an individual or an organization. Therefore, on-behalf payments addressed by GASB-24 include payments by nongovernmental entities made on behalf of governmental employees and payments made by governmental entities on behalf of nongovernmental employees. An example of the latter circumstance is the payment of faculty salaries at a public college or university by a private (not-for-profit) research foundation affiliated with the educational institution.

The standards established for on-behalf payments for fringe benefits and salaries must be observed by the employer government and the paying government (see previous **PRACTICE ALERT** on GASB-85).

GASB-24 requires that an on-behalf payment made by the paying governmental entity be recognized both as an expenditure or expense and as revenue by the employer governmental entity. The specific amount to be recorded depends on whether the employer government is legally responsible for payment of the fringe benefit or salary. "Legally responsible entity" is defined as follows:

> For on-behalf payments for fringe benefits and salaries, the entity is required by legal or contractual provisions to make the payment. Legal provisions include those arising from constitutions, charters, ordinances, resolutions, governing body orders, and intergovernmental grant or contract regulations.

When the employer government is not legally responsible for the payment, the amount to be recorded is determined by the amount actually paid by the paying governmental entity. Thus, if a state government makes a $100,000 contribution to the state pension fund on behalf of a locality, the locality would simultaneously record an expenditure or expense of $100,000 and an equal amount of revenue.

A measurement problem arises when the employer government is legally responsible for payment of expenditures or expenses that are being funded by the paying government. The question arises about whether the amount of the expenditure or expense should be based on the actual payment made by the paying government or whether it should be recorded using governmental U.S. GAAP that would otherwise apply to the particular transaction.

GASB-24 requires that on-behalf payments for fringe benefits and salaries be recorded as expenditures or expenses on the basis of applicable accounting standards when the employer government is legally responsible for the item. Using this approach, the employer government refers to existing accounting standards to determine the amount of the expenditure or expense and compares that amount with the on-behalf payments made by the paying governmental entity. Any difference between the two amounts is reflected in the employer government's financial statements as an asset or a liability. The amount of revenue recognized is equal to the on-behalf payments made by the paying government and any amounts receivable from the paying government at the end of the year (GASB-24, par. 8) [GASB Cod. Sec. N50.130].

When the employer government is legally responsible for the payment from a governmental fund and there is a difference between the expenditure computed under governmental U.S. GAAP and the payment made by the paying government, modified accrual accounting standards are used to determine the presentation of any resulting asset or liability. If a liability arises from the comparison, the employer government determines whether the liability will be liquidated with expendable available financial resources. An asset that arises from the comparison is reported in the entity's financial statements if the asset represents expendable financial resources that are available for appropriation and expenditure during the next accounting period.

The accounting for on-behalf fringe benefits and salaries as prescribed by GASB-24 encourages paying governmental entities to provide employer governments with information that enables the employer governments to properly record expenditures or expenses and related revenue. In some instances, paying governments will be unable to supply employer governments with the amounts of payments made specifically on their behalf. If the paying governmental entity or the third-party recipient cannot or will not provide such information, GASB-24 requires that the employer government estimate the amount of expenditure or expense and revenue that should be recorded.

A cost allocation problem arises when a paying government that provides funds to cost-sharing, multiple-employer pension plans makes a single payment that relates to many employer governments. In these circumstances, GASB-24 requires that the allocation method used to apportion the total funding among the employer governments be systematic and rational and be applied on a consistent basis. More specifically, the allocation should be based on "the ratio of an individual employer's covered payroll to the entire covered payroll related to the on-behalf payments" (GASB-24, par. 9) [GASB Cod. Sec. N50.131].

The *GASB Implementation Guide 2015-1*, question 7.34.4 [GASB Cod. Sec. 2200.717-5], states that items recognized as revenues based on the standards established by GASB-24 should be reported as program revenues.

Because an employer government's recognition of expenditures or expenses and revenue is based on the policies and actions of the paying government, a financial reporting problem arises when the two entities do not have the same fiscal year-end. In these circumstances, the employer government should attempt to obtain information from the paying government (or the third-party entity, if relevant) that would coincide with the employer government's year-end. If the employer government is unable to obtain such information, the employer government should base its expenditure or expense recognition on the paying government's year-end data. To make the computation, the employer government can use either (1) the paying government's year-end date that occurs during the employer government's same fiscal year or (2) the paying government's year-end date that occurs during the employer government's first quarter subsequent to its (the employer government's) current fiscal year-end date. Once the paying government's appropriate year-end date is selected, the approach should be applied consistently from year to year (GASB-24, par. 10) [GASB Cod. Sec. N50.132].

On-behalf payments create a potential allocation problem among an employer government's funds. A question arises about how an on-behalf payment made by a state government for a city should be allocated to the various individual funds that might benefit from the subsidy. For example, a state government may make a single payment for employees whose activities are associated with a Special Revenue Fund and an Enterprise Fund. GASB-24 states that no allocation is necessary. However, allocation is not prohibited.

Generally, when on-behalf payments are reported in only one fund, the fund used should be the General Fund (GASB-24, par. 11) [GASB Cod. Sec. N50.133].

OBSERVATION: Although GASB-24 recommends that the General Fund be used when a single fund is used to account for on-behalf payments, each situation should be examined to determine whether that guidance is reasonable. For example, GASB-24 notes that when all on-behalf payments for fringe benefits and salaries are related to an Enterprise Fund, the on-behalf payments should be accounted for in the Enterprise Fund and not in the reporting entity's General Fund.

An employer government should make the following disclosures regarding on-behalf payments in the notes to its financial statements (GASB-24, par. 12) [GASB Cod. Sec. N50.134]:

- Amounts of expenditure or expense and revenue recognized due to on-behalf payments for fringe benefits and salaries; and

- If on-behalf payments for pension plans have been made and the employer government is not legally responsible for the payments, the name of the plan and the name of the paying government.

GASB-24 requires the governmental entity that makes on-behalf payments for fringe benefits and salaries to classify the payments in the same way as other similar cash grants made to other entities. For example, if a state government makes on-behalf pension payments for public schoolteachers, the classification of those payments depends on how the state government classifies similar educational cash grants made to public school districts. If, for example, the latter are classified as education expenditures, the on-behalf payments should also be reported as education expenditures, not as pension expenditures (GASB-24, par. 13) [GASB Cod. Sec. N50.135].

The GASB states that the legal responsibility for the funding of on-behalf payments for fringe benefits and salaries has no effect on determining how the payments should be categorized on the paying government's financial statements.

A reporting problem arises when the two parties to pass-through grants or on-behalf payments for fringe benefits and salaries are part of the same reporting entity. The standards established in GASB-24 apply to pass-through grants and on-behalf payments for entities that are combined as part of a single reporting entity. Under these circumstances, expenditures or expenses and revenues recognized must be reclassified as transfers in a manner consistent with the standards established by GASB-14 (*The Financial Reporting Entity*) and further clarified by GASB-34, par. 61, as amended [GASB Cod. Secs. 1800.106, 2200.155, 2600.117]. However, receivables and payables between the primary government and its discretely presented component units or between those components should be reported on a separate line in the basic financial statements.

Recording Nonexchange Transactions

Governmental Funds

Although the standards established in GASB-33 are written in the context of the accrual basis of accounting, they provide a significant amount of general guidance for nonexchange transactions irrespective of the basis of accounting that is used by a governmental entity. For this reason, the GASB has decided that the general guidance provided in the GASB-33 applies to governmental activities (activities accounted for in such funds as the General Fund and Special Revenue Funds) except that they must be modified to observe the modified accrual basis of accounting. However, in applying the standards the availability criterion must be satisfied when revenue is recognized under the modified accrual basis of accounting. In addition, under both the accrual basis of accounting and the modified accrual basis of accounting, nonexchange transactions are recorded only when transactions are measurable (subject to reasonable estimation) and collection is probable (realizable). GASB-33 defines "probable" as likely to occur. Nonexchange transactions that are not recorded because the measurable criterion cannot be satisfied must be disclosed in a governmental entity's financial statements (GASB-33, par. 11) [GASB Cod. Sec. N50.108].

Proprietary and Fiduciary Funds

Revenues from nonexchange transactions should be recognized in proprietary and fiduciary funds based on accrual accounting concepts and be consistent with the standards established by GASB-33.

Government-Wide Financial Statements

Revenues presented in a governmental entity's statement of activities should be based on accrual accounting concepts and be consistent with the standards established by GASB-33.

REVENUES: EXCHANGE TRANSACTIONS

In an exchange transaction the governmental entity and the other party to the transaction exchange cash, goods, or services that are essentially of the same value. For example, revenue earned from providing water services to customers is an exchange transaction. Unlike nonexchange transactions, the GASB has not provided comprehensive guidance for the recognition of exchange transactions. The GASB has provided guidance for the recognition of investment income for certain investments; see Chapter 9, "Deposits, Investments, and Derivative Instruments."

PRACTICE ALERT: In January 2018, the GASB staff released an Invitation to Comment, *Revenue and Expense Recognition*, requesting feedback on a modified version of the current revenue recognition model that focuses on whether the transaction is an exchange or a nonexchange transaction as well as introducing a new model based on the existence of a performance obligation. Assuming the project progresses, final provisions may not be released by the GASB until 2023.

Recording Exchange Transactions

Governmental Funds

Like nonexchange transactions, exchange transactions should be recorded in a governmental fund when they are measurable, available, and collection is probable. For example, a governmental entity may sell a parcel of land to another party and receive a down payment and a three-year annual note for the balance of the purchase price. The down payment, because it is available to pay current expenditures, would be recorded as revenue of an "other source of financial resources" or a "special item" if it is unusual in nature and/or infrequent in occurrence and under the control of management in accordance with GASB-62, par. 46 [GASB Cod. Secs. 1800.148, 2200.146]; however, the subsequent installments would not be recorded as revenue until the cash is received.

Proprietary and Fiduciary Funds

A proprietary or fiduciary fund should recognize revenue on an accrual basis, meaning that revenue is considered realized when (1) the earning process is complete or virtually complete and (2) an exchange has taken place.

Government-Wide Financial Statements

Revenues related to exchange transactions in a governmental entity's statement of activities should be based on accrual accounting concepts. Governmental activities as presented in the government-wide financial statements should be accounted for and reported based on all applicable GASB pronouncements and remaining non-superseded NCGA pronouncements.

SALES, PLEDGES, AND INTRA-ENTITY TRANSFERS OF ASSETS AND FUTURE REVENUES

GASB-48 (*Sales and Pledges of Receivables and Future Revenues and Intra-Entity Transfers of Assets and Future Revenues*) provides financial statement users with consistent measurement, recognition, and disclosure across governments and within individual governments relating to the accounting for sales and pledges of receivables and future revenues and intra-entity transfers of assets and future revenues.

GASB-48 does not apply to a government's pledge of its "full faith and credit" as security whether it relates to its own debt or to the debt of a component. The GASB stated, "by backing the government's own debt with its full faith and credit, the government makes an *unconditional commitment* to pay principal and interest on that debt without specifying the resources that will be used for repayment." Because specific revenues are not specified in this situation, these full faith and credit situations were not included in the scope of GASB-48. See Chapter 16, "Other Liabilities," for a further discussion of guarantees that involve the exercising of a full faith and credit in accordance with GASB-70 (*Accounting and Financial Reporting for Nonexchange Financial Guarantees*) (GASB-48, par. 3) [GASB Cod. Sec. S20.101].

GASB-48 focuses specifically on financial reporting issues associated with pledges and sales of receivables and future revenues. It makes a distinction in determining whether a transaction is a sale or a collateralized borrowing. All transactions within the scope of GASB-48 should be reported as collateralized borrowings unless certain criteria are met.

Assessing a Government's Continuing Involvement in Receivables and Future Revenues

The right to future cash flows from receivables should be reported as a sale if the government's continuing involvement with those receivables is terminated. A government no longer has continuing involvement in receivables if all of the following criteria are met:

- The receivables are not limited by constraints imposed by the transferor government, such as the transferee's ability to subsequently sell or pledge the receivables.

- The transferor has no options or abilities to unilaterally substitute for or require specific accounts from the receivables transferred. There is no violation of the criterion if there are transfers made of defective accounts.

- The sale agreement is not cancelable by either party.

- The transferor government has been isolated from the receivables and the cash resulting from their collection. GASB-48 discusses the criteria used to determine whether receivables have been isolated from the transferor government (e.g., a separate legal standing between the transferee and the transferor).

A transaction relating to cash flows from specific future revenues that are exchanged for lump-sum proceeds should be reported as a sale if the government's continuing involvement with those revenues meets all of the following criteria:

- The future generation of revenues will not be maintained by active involvement of the transferor government. Active involvement generally requires a substantive action or performance, whereas, passive involvement in the generation of future revenues generally requires no substantive actions or performance by the government.

- The transferor government has released and has no restrictions on the transferee government's ability to subsequently sell or pledge the future cash flows.
- The transferor government has been isolated from cash resulting from the collection of the future revenues.
- There is no prohibition on the transfer or assignment of the original resources contained in the contract, agreement, or arrangement between the original resource provider and the transferor government.
- The sale agreement is not cancelable by either party (GASB-48, par. 6) [GASB Cod. Sec. S20.103].

Accounting Transactions That Do Not Qualify as Sales

In general terms, when the GASB-48 criteria required for sales reporting are not met, the transaction should be reported as a collateralized borrowing by the transferor. Rather than a sale, these sales and future revenues should be considered for financial statement purposes as pledged rather than sold.

If sale criteria are not met, then collateralized borrowing occurs and the following steps are taken by both the transferor and the transferee:

- Transferor government:
  — Does not derecognize receivables;
  — Continues recognition of revenues pledged;
  — Recognizes liability for the proceeds received; and
  — Payments reduce liability; and
- Transferee government should recognize a receivable for the amounts paid to the pledging government (GASB-48, pars. 11–12, as amended by GASB-63, par. 8) [GASB Cod. Secs. S20.108–.109].

Accounting for Transactions That Meet the Criteria to Be Reported as Sales

If the GASB-48 criteria required for sales reporting are met, the transaction should be reported as a sale:

- *Receivables*—In the sale of receivables, the selling government should remove the individual accounts at their carrying values and no longer recognize as assets the receivables sold.
- *Future revenues*—In the sale of future revenues, the proceeds should be reported by the selling government as either revenue, advances, or deferred inflows of resources in both the fund statements and the government-wide financial statements.

The transactions are handled differently for a transfer of assets within the same financial reporting entity as opposed to when the transferee is a government outside of the selling government's financial reporting entity.

If the conditions for sale treatment are met, then the following steps are taken by both the transferor and the transferee government:

- Transferor government (also known as the selling government):
  - Derecognizes receivables;
  - No asset to derecognize for future revenues; and
  - Difference between proceeds and carrying value is as follows: (1) on sale of receivables there is revenue recognition or a gain/loss and (2) on sale of future revenues there is generally deferred inflows of resources.
- Transferee government (also known as purchasing government):
  - Intra-entity sale treatment has purchased receivables reported at carrying value and payments to the selling government for rights to future revenues are reported as a deferred outflow of resources.
  - Outside of the reporting entity the asset (rights) are recorded at cost (GASB-48, pars. 13–14, as amended by GASB-65, pars. 12, 31) [GASB Cod. Secs. S20.110–.111].

GASB-65, par. 13, states that a transferee government should not report an asset and related revenue until recognition criteria appropriate to that type of revenue are met. Instead, the transferee government should report the amount paid as a deferred outflow of resources to be recognized over the duration of the sale agreement. The transferor government should report the amount received from the intra-entity sale as a deferred inflow of resources in its government-wide and fund financial statements and recognize the amount as revenue over the duration of the sale agreement.

Disclosure of Future Revenues Sold

GASB-48 states that in the year of the sale, governments that sell future revenue streams should disclose in the notes to financial statements information about the specific revenues sold, including:

- Identification of the specific revenue sold, including the approximate amount, and the significant assumptions used in determining the approximate amount;
- The period the sale applies to;
- The relationship of the sold amount to the total for the specific revenue, if estimable—that is, the proportion of the specific revenue stream that has been sold; and
- A comparison of the proceeds of the sale and the present value of the future revenues sold, including the significant assumptions used in determining the present value.

Disclosure of Future Revenues Pledged

Some governments may not receive resources in exchange for a pledge of future cash flows of specific revenues (i.e. not a sale of future revenues). However, the government may pledge future revenues for a specific purpose. There may be restrictions that prohibit the government entity from issuing debt or due to a charter, statute, or constitutional requirement it may be limited in the extent that it may issue debt. When primary governments are in this situation and are empowered to create separate component units or use existing component units to issue debt on their behalf, the primary government may pledge future revenue streams as security for the debt. Pledging governments should disclose revenues pledged that have been formally committed to directly collateralize or secure debt of the pledging government or directly or indirectly collateralize or secure debt of a component unit. These required disclosures do not apply to revenues that are shared by another government.

For purposes of the disclosures required by GASB-48 for future revenues pledged as collateral for debt repayment, pledged revenues are the specific revenues that have been formally committed to directly collateralize or secure debt of the pledging government, or directly or indirectly collateralize or secure debt of a component unit.

As defined in GASB-48, an indirect collateralization involves a pledged revenue agreement that is not directly between the pledging government and the bondholders. In other words, the pledging government's revenues do not secure the debt; rather, the debt is secured by the pledging government's payments (which are financed by that revenue) to the other legally separate entity (such as a component unit). In essence, the pledging government makes an annual debt service "grant" to the component unit, which in turn pledges that revenue as security for its debt.

For each period in which the secured debt remains outstanding, GASB-48 requires the pledging governments to disclose in the notes to financial statements information about specific revenues pledged, including:

- Identification of the specific revenue pledged and the approximate amount of the pledge. Generally, the approximate amount of the pledge would equal the remaining principal and interest requirements of the secured debt;
- Identification of, and general purpose for, the debt secured by the pledged revenue;
- The term of the commitment—that is, the period during which the revenue will not be available for other purposes;
- The relationship of the pledged amount to the total for the specific revenue, if estimable—that is, the proportion of the specific revenue stream that has been pledged; and
- A comparison between the pledged revenues recognized during the period and the principal and interest requirements for the debt that is directly or indirectly collateralized by those revenues. For this disclosure, pledged revenues recognized during the period may be presented net of specified operating expenses, based on the provisions of the pledge agreement; however, the amounts should not be netted in the financial statements.

The disclosure requirements for pledged future revenues are not required for legally separate entities (such as component units) that report as stand-alone business-type activities whose operations are financed primarily by a single major revenue source. For example, the disclosure requirements would not apply to the stand-alone financial statements of a water utility district whose single major source of revenue (water charges to customers) is pledged for repayment of collateralized debt of the district (GASB-48, pars. 21–22) [GASB Cod. Secs. S20.118–.119].

EXHIBIT 17-2
EXAMPLE: SALE OF DELINQUENT RECEIVABLES

Facts and assumptions: A County (the seller) enters into an agreement to sell delinquent taxes due to another governmental entity (the purchaser). The seller County received $2,500,000 in exchange for tax receivables/liens totaling $4,000,000. The County's allowance for uncollectible accounts pertaining to those tax receivables is $1,000,000, resulting in a net carrying value of $3,000,000. The sale agreement stipulates that the liens are sold without recourse except that the County has an obligation with respect to liens found to be defective. For defective liens, the County is required to (1) perfect the liens, (2) reacquire the liens from the purchaser, or (3) deliver to the purchaser substantially equivalent liens in substitution.

Conclusion: This transaction meets the criteria to be recognized as a sale.

Accounting in the year of the sale: The seller County reduces property taxes receivable by $4,000,000, reduces the allowance for uncollectible accounts by $1,000,000, and recognizes a loss on the sale of $500,000 (the carrying value of $3,000,000 less the proceeds of $2,500,000) in the government-wide statement of activities. In its governmental funds prior to the sale, the seller County was reporting a zero net carrying value for the delinquent taxes receivable because they were either deemed to be uncollectible ($1,000,000) or deferred under the availability criterion ($3,000,000). Therefore, the entire amount of the proceeds ($2,500,000) is recognized as revenue and the remaining net receivable and related deferred inflows of resource amounts are eliminated. The seller County has determined that if any liens are found to be defective, it would first attempt to perfect the liens and, if unable to do so, provide acceptable substitutions. The County believes it is not probable that it would repurchase defective liens and therefore does not recognize a liability.

Accounting in future years: If any of the tax liens are subsequently found to be defective and it is probable that the seller county would reacquire those liens, a liability and an expenditure/expense would be recognized, provided that the amount of the repurchase obligation is measurable. At the same time, the county would add back the reacquired tax liens receivable and reduce the expense by the estimated collectible value of those liens. In the governmental funds, either the expenditure would be reduced if the receivable were considered available or related deferred inflow of resources would be established.

PRACTICE POINT: An disclosure example of a sale of receivables is found in Wolters Kluwer's *2018 GAAP Governmental GAAP Disclosures Manual*, Chapter 65.

Irrevocable Split-Interest Agreements—GASB-81

PRACTICE POINT: The GASB has issued GASB Statement No. 81 (*Irrevocable Split-Interest Agreements*), which requires a government that receives resources pursuant to an irrevocable split-interest agreement to recognize assets, liabilities, and deferred inflows of resources. A government would also recognize as assets beneficial interests in irrevocable split-interest agreements that are administered by a third party, if those beneficial interests are under the control of the government and embody present service capacity.

An Irrevocable Split-Interest Agreement (ISIA) is a *split-interest agreement* in which the donor has not reserved, or conferred to another person, the right to terminate the agreement at will and have the assets returned to the donor or a third party. A split-interest agreement is where a donor enters into a trust or other legally enforceable agreement (with similar characteristics) under which the donor transfers resources to an intermediary to administer for the unconditional benefit of at least two beneficiaries, one of which could be a government.

Previous to GASB-81, the accounting and financial reporting for ISIAs was contained in the *GASB Implementation Guide 2015-1*, question 7.72.11, which expanded upon various provisions in GASB-31, GASB-33, and GASB-34. Such agreements could be very common not just in public institutions of higher education or health entities, but in general purpose governments, especially with regard to conservation lands, historical areas, and similar. Individual ISIAs may vary as to the parties who are beneficiaries, the order of beneficiaries or intermediaries.

Typical ISIAs

ISIAs usually have a lead interest and a remainder interest. A lead interest has the right to all or a portion of the benefits of resources while the ISIA is in effect. The remainder interest has just that—whatever is left in the ISIA at termination. Governments may be a lead interest, receiving an annuity or other stream of payments for a certain period, or a remainder interest, receiving what is left at the end of the period (GASB-81, par. 8) [GASB Cod. Sec. I70.105].

Some ISIAs have a specific number of years of life (a period-certain term) while others are life-contingent and are dependent upon an event, commonly the death of the donor or the lead-interest. Each of these aspects defines the accounting, financial reporting and disclosure (GASB-81, par. 9) [GASB Cod. Sec. I70.106].

If a Government Is the Intermediary

GASB-81 requires governments that are both intermediaries and beneficiaries of an ISIA to record an asset for resources received, a liability for the beneficiary's (-ies') interest(s) and a deferred inflow of resources for the difference, representing the unconditional beneficial interest to the government. Assets that are investments will be reported at fair value in accordance with GASB-72 (*Fair Value Measurement and Application*). Interest, dividends and changes in fair value would increase or decrease the deferred inflow of resources or the liability.

If a Government Is the Remainder Entity

If the government is both the intermediary and the remainder, assets again would be recognized for resources received. A liability would be recognized for the amounts assigned to other beneficiaries and a deferred inflow of resources for the government's unconditional interest (GASB-81, par. 10) [GASB Cod. Sec. I70.107].

How to Value the Liability

The amount recognized as the liability to the lead interest(s) should be measured at a settlement amount based on the stream of payments that is expected to be provided to other beneficiaries. Establishing the amount depends upon the payment provisions in the ISIA, the estimated rate of return, the mortality rate (if the term is life-contingent) and the discount rate if a present value technique is used.

Discounting

If no discounting is used, the liability would reduce for each disbursement. If discounting is used, as assets reduce, so would the deferred inflow of resources in the amount of the amortization of the discount. The liability would reduce by the difference, similarly to a mortgage.

Changes in assumptions may occur, which may require adjusting the settlement amount. However, upon termination, all balances would be recognized. The deferred inflows of resources balance would be recognized as revenue. The elimination of any remaining liability would be a gain or revenue (GASB-81, pars. 11–15) [GASB Cod. Secs. I70.108–.112].

Government as a Lead Beneficiary

The government may be in a lead position. Similar accounting would occur. However, the deferred inflow of resources would represent the government's unconditional interest, measured at a settlement amount and may or may not be discounted. At termination, when the assets are disbursed, any remaining liability and deferred inflow of resources would be eliminated (GASB-81, pars. 16–21) [GASB Cod. Secs. I70.113–.118].

Life Interests in Real Estate

Life interests are common. A residence may be near a public institution of higher education. The owner may enter into an ISIA with the college or university with the provision of the donor retaining the right to use the house until death. Upon death, the college or university receives the house. Depending upon the terms and conditions of the ISIA as well as management's intent, the house may be a capital asset or an investment. If a capital asset, the donation would be measured at acquisition value in accordance with GASB-72. Liabilities would be recognized for obligations to maintain the house during the ISIA, including for insurance, maintenance, repairs or similar. A deferred inflows of resources would represent the difference between the asset and liability. This is a similar model to a service concession arrangement (see Chapter 14, "Leases and Service Concession Arrangements").

If the house is intended to be investment property, any change in fair value would have to be recognized at each reporting period, along with an adjustment to the deferred inflow of resources. If a capital asset, depreciation would occur during the ISIA. Upon termination, the deferred inflow of resources balance would be recognized as an inflow (GASB-81, pars. 22–28) [GASB Cod. Secs. I70.122–.128].

Third Party Intermediaries

If the government is not the intermediary, but is a beneficiary, an asset and a deferred inflow of resources would be recognized. This assumes the ISIA has no variance power, the donor does not control the intermediary, and there is an unconditional interest held by the government. The asset would be measured at fair value. If the government is the lead interest, the asset is reduced by distributions and revenue recognized by reducing the deferred inflow of resources. If the government is the remainder, recognition of revenue would only occur upon termination (GASB-81, pars. 29–34) [GASB Cod. Secs. I70.129–.131].

PRACTICE POINT: Should a government believe it is involved in an ISIA, management focus should be on recognizing where the government is positioned in the ISIA. Is it the lead, remainder, intermediary, or a third party intermediary? Documenting the agreements carefully and recognizing the proper amounts may be key. A government should consider a survey of all agencies/ departments for such agreements and perhaps involving legal counsel to decipher the various aspects. A specialist may be required to value the assets and any liability.

The auditing of ISIAs will focus on completeness, recognition, valuation and disclosure. If discounting is used to value a liability, the assumptions will be tested. The government's decision-making on whether a life interest is an investment or a capital asset will also be tested. Of course, if the ISIA is immaterial, GASB-81 would not apply.

Example: A resident of Castle Rock County transfers title to her ranch land and buildings on the ranch to the County, retaining a right to use the land and buildings until their death. The resident will continue to pay the various costs of the property until their death, including maintenance costs, property taxes, insurance, utilities, and similar costs. The resident stipulates that the land and building be used by the County and the County's residents as open-space/ recreational/conservation land and not for investment property or royalty property. The County analyzes that the land will not be used ultimately for income or profit in accordance with the provisions of GASB-72 (*Fair Value Measurement and Application*) and, therefore, will be recorded as a donated capital asset. An assessment is performed at the date of transfer and the land is worth $20,000,000, while the buildings on the land are worth $1,000,000, yielding an acquisition value of $21,000,000 in accordance with the provisions of GASB-72 and GASB-81. The County makes the following entries:

	Debit	Credit
GOVERNMENT-WIDE		
Land—Irrevocable Split Interest Agreement	20,000,000	
Buildings—Irrevocable Split Interest Agreements	1,000,000	
Deferred Inflows of Resources—Irrevocable Split Interest Agreement		21,000,000
To record irrevocable split interest agreement for ranch and buildings donated.		

In this example, no liability exists as the resident continues to pay such costs. If a liability was recognized, it would be increased as costs are incurred and reduced as such costs are satisfied. It would also reduce the deferred inflow of resources at inception of the ISIA.

In this case, the Buildings are a capital asset. Throughout the life of the agreement, the buildings initial acquisition value will depreciate in accordance with the County's method of depreciation. Assuming an estimated five-year life remaining on the agreement (per the County's actuary), $200,000 annually would be recorded as depreciation (1,000,000 ÷ 5).

Had the Land and the Buildings been recorded as investment property, the property would have been reported at fair value in accordance with the provisions of GASB-72 as of the date of the ISIA. Changes in the fair value of the investment would increase or decrease the deferred inflow of resources.

Upon the donor's death, the ISIA terminates and the deferred inflow of resources would be recognized as revenue.

ACCOUNTING AND REPORTING ISSUES

Tax Abatement Disclosures—GASB-77

GASB Statement No. 77 (*Tax Abatement Disclosures*) was released in 2015. GASB-77 focuses on tax abatement *disclosures*, rather than the financial reporting of the effect of tax abatements. By focusing on the disclosure of tax abatements, the goal of GASB-77 is to:

- Assist users of financial statements to assess the sufficiency of current year revenues to pay for current year services (i.e., interperiod equity);

- Gauge compliance with finance-related legal and contractual obligations;

- Provide further exposure of financial inflows and outflows of resources; and

- Understand a government's financial position and economic condition.

Tax abatements for financial reporting are defined in GASB-77 as an agreement in which the government promises to forego tax revenues and the individual or entity promises to subsequently take a specific action that contributes to economic development or otherwise benefits the government or its citizens. A common example is a business receiving a tax abatement for a period of years for locating a factory in an area and hiring a specific minimum number of permanent full-time positions.

Many governments already produce reports about tax abatement information related to economic development. However, the reports may only provide a small amount of information about how the abatements may affect the government's financial position and results of operations or constrain the ability to raise taxes in the future. Another common practice is when a tax abatement is forced on a government by a larger government on the local government's behalf without its consent. Due to law or regulation, a state or a county may force a tax abatement on a city or special district, lowering its tax base temporarily (or permanently), with the hope of raising other forms of local taxation and fees through increased economic activity.

Tax abatements may also be disguised in many forms. They may be contained in a budget, regulation, ordinance, or law as a tax expenditure, tax credit, tax expense, or a similar action by the government. GASB-77 requires governments to consider a transaction's substance, not its form or title, in determining whether the activity meets the definition of a tax abatement for the purposes of the provisions of GASB-77.

Tax abatements may also be subject to nondisclosure provisions as part of a negotiation process between a business and a government until the agreement becomes final. This is so the government does not lose the business to another competing government.

PRACTICE POINT: One of the more important aspects of GASB-77 is it only requires *disclosure* and **not** an accounting event. Respondents to the Exposure Draft of what became GASB-77 asked for clarification related to the appropriate basis of accounting to be used in disclosing the amount of tax revenue foregone. The GASB could have required governments to report gross taxes levied, less abatements, to arrive at net tax revenues. However, the GASB concluded that once taxes are abated, a government has no expectation of a resource inflow related to the abatement account ever occurring. Therefore, the presentation of tax abatements is in accordance with the accrual basis of accounting, which would generate no additional revenue or expense related to these agreements currently or in the future for the duration of the agreement.

GASB-77 requires five broad categories of disclosure related to tax abatements in the notes to the financial statements:

1. Distinguish disclosures resulting from those entered into by the reporting government and those entered into by other governments that reduce the reporting government's tax revenues;

2. Present tax abatements either individually or aggregated;

3. rganize tax abatement agreements by each major tax abatement program (e.g., economic development, television, and film production);

4. Organize tax abatement agreements by the government that entered into the tax abatement and the specific tax being abated; and

5. Disclose the period in which a tax abatement is entered into and continue until the tax abatement agreement expires, unless there is a commitment made by the government other than to reduce taxes as part of a tax abatement agreement (e.g., a government may commit to improve a highway for better access to a stadium, rather than abating taxes) (GASB-77, par. 5) [GASB Cod. Sec. T10.103].

Governments may choose to disclose information about individual tax abatement agreements or present them in the aggregate. If a government chooses to present individual tax abatement agreements, it should be only those agreements that meet or exceed a quantitative threshold selected by the government. For example, a government may choose to present individual tax abatement agreements that exceed $100,000. This threshold should be disclosed as part of the notes (GASB-77, par. 6) [GASB Cod. Sec. T10.104].

Additional note disclosures will include the following information about tax abatements that governments enter into:

- A brief description, including the names and purposes of tax abatement programs, the specific taxes being abated, the authority under which the agreements are entered into, the criteria of eligibility, the mechanism of reducing taxes (e.g., by reducing assessed value, a specific dollar amount, or percentage of taxes), provisions for recapturing abated taxes, including the conditions when abated taxes become eligible for recapture, and finally the types of commitments made by the recipients of tax abatements;

- The gross dollar amount on an accrual basis that reduced tax revenues during the reporting period as a result of tax abatements;

- If amounts are received or are receivable from other governments in association with the abatement, the name(s) of the government(s), the authority under which the amounts were or will be paid, and the dollar amount received or receivable from other governments;

- If there are commitments made by the government other than to reduce taxes, a description of the types of commitments made and the most significant individual commitments made (this particular disclosure will be made until the government has fulfilled its commitment);

- As discussed above, the quantitative threshold set by the government used to determine which agreements to disclose individually; and

- If information is legally prohibited from being disclosed, the government would disclose the general nature of the tax abatement information omitted and the specific source of the legal prohibition (GASB-77, par. 7) [GASB Cod. Sec. T10.105].

Similar information will be disclosed for governments that are forced to abate taxes by other governments. Discretely presented component units may also disclose this information. However, the primary government would disclose a discretely presented component unit's tax abatements only when it is essential for fair presentation. Such component units may also force an abatement on a primary government. In these cases, the primary government would disclose the abatements similar to the description above (GASB-77, pars. 8–10) [GASB Cod. Secs. T10.105–.108].

PRACTICE POINT: GASB-77 may require a reporting government to analyze records in which such agreements exist, including legal documents, contracts, and similar agreements. These records may not be readily available to preparers due to confidentiality agreements and agreements made by other governments. Coordination within a government and between governments and larger governments may be needed when such coordination has not previously existed. The information required by GASB-77 may be difficult to obtain from other governments. Empirically, some of this information may already be disclosed in the media or on a website maintained by the government or a larger government. The disclosure of this information may point preparers to the source of where records are maintained for such abatements.

PRACTICE POINT: An example of disclosure is contained in Wolter's Kluwer's 2018 GAAP Governmental GAAP Disclosures ManualChapter 92

QUESTIONS

1. The major difference between nonexchange transactions and exchange transactions focuses on which of the following:

   a. The measurement approaches and measurement attributes in U.S. GAAP differ for nonexchange and exchange transactions.

   b. The conceptual framework for financial reporting differs for exchange and nonexchange transactions.

   c. In a nonexchange transaction, a government either gives value or a benefit to another party without directly receiving value in exchange while in an exchange transaction, the values are ostensibly equal.

   d. In a nonexchange transaction, the timing of recognition of the transaction may differ greatly from when an exchange transaction occurs.

2. What are the fundamental control mechanisms in revenue recognition for nonexchange transactions?

   a. Legislation, contractual requirements, or both, with a further caveat that imposed nonexchange revenues (taxes) are recognized when the government has an enforceable claim to receive the revenues.

   b. Management uses professional judgment to determine when revenue recognition should occur for nonexchange transactions.

   c. Revenue recognition in accordance with GASB-33 occurs when goods or services are transferred to a party outside of the reporting entity of the government.

   d. Revenue recognition is mostly dependent on fund types.

3. Which of the following is not a category of a nonexchange transaction?

   a. Derived tax revenues.

   b. Allowances for debts.

   c. Imposed nonexchange revenues.

   d. Voluntary nonexchange transactions.

4. In accordance with U.S. GAAP, which of the following is not an example of an exchange-like transaction?

   a. Fees for professional licenses and permits.

   b. Passenger facility charges.

   c. Certain developer contributions.

   d. Nonexchange guarantee financial transactions.

5. In a government-mandated nonexchange transaction, in accordance with GASB-65, what accounting element is recognized by a government when resources are received before time requirements are met but after all other eligibility requirements are met?

   a. Deferred inflow of resources.

   b. Deferred revenue.

   c. Revenue.

   d. Unearned revenue.

Cases – Adapted from U.S. GAAP

1. The State of Centennial (recipient) imposes a tax on sales of goods by retail merchants. The tax is 5% of the sale amount and is collected by merchants from customers (providers) at the time of sale. Most merchants are required to submit sales tax receipts to the state on a weekly basis; however, small retail sales merchants are required to submit receipts only on a quarterly basis.

   a. What type of nonexchange transaction is occurring here?

   b. When should the state recognize revenue?

2. Castle Rock County (recipient) through its Board of Supervisors adopts a property tax levy ordinance that explicitly links the taxes to the appropriation ordinances for the fiscal year May 1, 20X6 through April 30, 20X7. In accordance with State of Centennial statutes, the County has an enforceable legal claim to the taxes as of the assessment date, which is defined in the statutes as the first day of the fiscal year to which the appropriation ordinance applies (May 1, 20X6 in this example). However, none of the taxes are collected until July 1, 20X7 or later.

   a. What type of nonexchange transaction is occurring here?

   b. When should the county recognize revenue?

3. The State of Centennial (provider) provides seed funds and reimburses school districts (recipients) for specific costs related to special education, up to a maximum amount for each school district in each school year. To obtain reimbursement for allowable costs, the school districts submit quarterly reports to the state.

   a. What type of nonexchange transaction is occurring here?

   b. When should a school district recognize revenue?

4. The State of Centennial (provider) distributes money to counties and cities (recipients) for use in county road repairs and city street repairs, respectively. Part of the money is allocated to the counties and cities based on population. The remainder is awarded on a competitive basis to certain small cities. Potential recipients of the competitive awards apply for funding for specific safety improvement projects, and the state, in consultation with certain representative organizations, determines which projects to finance. For the competitive awards only, the state indicates that the resources may be used at any time after the awards are made. The state's fiscal year ends on June 30. County and city fiscal years end on December 31.

   a. What type of nonexchange transaction is occurring here?

   b. When should recipients recognize revenue?

ANSWERS

1. The major difference between nonexchange transactions and exchange transactions focuses on which of the following:

   Answer – C: In a nonexchange transaction, a government either gives value or a benefit to another party without directly receiving value in exchange, whereas in an exchange transaction, the values are ostensibly equal.

2. What are the fundamental control mechanisms in revenue recognition for nonexchange transactions?

   Answer – A: Legislation, contractual requirements, or both, with a further caveat that imposed nonexchange revenues (taxes) are recognized when the government has an enforceable claim to receive the revenues.

3. Which of the following is not a category of a nonexchange transaction?

   Answer – B: The rest are nonexchange transactions in accordance with U.S. GAAP.

4. In accordance with U.S. GAAP, which of the following is not an example of an exchange-like transaction?

   Answer – D: The rest are exchange-like transactions in accordance with U.S. GAAP.

5. In a government-mandated nonexchange transaction, in accordance with GASB-65 what accounting element is recognized by a government when resources are received before time requirements are met but after all other eligibility requirements are met?

   Answer – A: The rest do not fit the definition as outlined in GASB-65.

Cases – Adapted from U.S. GAAP

1. The State of Centennial (recipient) imposes a tax on sales of goods by retail merchants. The tax is 5% of the sale amount and is collected by merchants from customers (providers) at the time of sale. Most merchants are required to submit sales tax receipts to the state on a weekly basis; however, small retail sales merchants are required to submit receipts only on a quarterly basis.

   a. What type of nonexchange transaction is occurring here?

   b. When should the state recognize revenue?

   Answer – This illustrates the characteristics of derived tax revenues. (The sales are exchange transactions.) The state should recognize assets and revenues, net of estimated refunds, as each sales transaction occurs. (From a practical standpoint, the state will likely base the amount to be recognized on total merchants' sales as reported or estimated for the weeks or quarters that make up the state's fiscal year.) Derived tax revenues are largely unaffected by GASB-65.

2. Castle Rock County (recipient) through its Board of Supervisors adopts a property tax levy ordinance that explicitly links the taxes to the appropriation ordinances for the fiscal year May 1, 20X6 through April 30, 20X7. In accordance with State of Centennial statutes, the county has an enforceable legal claim to the taxes as of the assessment date, which is defined in the statutes as the first day of the fiscal year to which the appropriation ordinance applies (May 1, 20X6 in this example). However, none of the taxes are collected until July 1, 20X7 or later.

   a. What type of nonexchange transaction is occurring here?

   b. When should the County recognize revenue?

   Answer – These are imposed nonexchange revenues. (The tax is imposed on property ownership, which is not an exchange transaction.) The county should recognize property taxes receivable on May 1, 20X6 (the date that the enforceable legal claim arises), and it should recognize revenues over the period May 1, 20X6 through April 30, 20X7 (the period for which the tax is levied). Had revenues been received *before* the period for which the property taxes are levied *or* the period when resources are required to be used or when use is first permitted, GASB-65, par. 9, requires a receivable and a deferred inflow of resources declared.

3. The State of Centennial (provider) provides seed funds and reimburses school districts (recipients) for specific costs related to special education, up to a maximum amount for each school district in each school year. To obtain reimbursement for allowable costs, the school districts submit quarterly reports to the state.

   a. What type of nonexchange transaction is occurring here?

   b. When should a school district recognize revenue?

   Answer – These are voluntary nonexchange transactions. (The program is not a mandate on the state or the school districts.) However, fulfillment of two eligibility requirements is necessary for a transaction to occur (in addition to the requirement that the recipients be school districts): The applicable period (school year) should have begun and the school districts should have incurred allowable costs. The second requirement indicates that the transaction has the characteristics of grants commonly referred to as reimbursement-type or expenditure-driven grants.

   After the school year has begun, the school districts should recognize receivables and revenues as they incur allowable costs, up to the maximum specified for the year. Had resources been received before time requirements are met but after all other eligibility requirements were met, a deferred inflow of resources would be declared in accordance with GASB-65.

4. The State of Centennial (provider) distributes money to counties and cities (recipients) for use in county road repairs and city street repairs, respectively. Part of the money is allocated to the counties and cities based on population. The remainder is awarded on a competitive basis

to certain small cities. Potential recipients of the competitive awards apply for funding for specific safety improvement projects, and the state, in consultation with certain representative organizations, determines which projects to finance. For the competitive awards only, the state indicates that the resources may be used at any time after the awards are made. The state's fiscal year ends on June 30. County and city fiscal years end on December 31.

a. What type of nonexchange transaction is occurring here?

b. When should recipients recognize revenue?

Answer – These are voluntary nonexchange transactions. (The program is not a mandate on the state or the counties and cities.) However, fulfillment of certain eligibility requirements is necessary for a transaction to occur: For the awards based on population, the recipients are required to be counties or cities and the applicable period should have begun. (Unless the state specifies otherwise, the applicable period begins on the first day of the state's fiscal year.) For the competitive awards, the eligibility requirements are that (*a*) the recipients are required to be small cities, (*b*) the state should have selected the recipients, based on the selection criteria, and (*c*) the applicable period should have begun. (In this case, the applicable period begins when the award is made and may continue into subsequent periods; there is no time limit on the use of the resources.) The requirement to use the resources for road and street repairs and improvements is a purpose restriction.

All counties and cities in the program should recognize receivables and revenues for the full amount of their awards when their respective eligibility requirements have been met. Because of the purpose restriction, they also should report resulting net position (or equity or fund balance) as restricted until used. As above, if resources were received before time requirements were met but after all other eligibility requirements were met, a deferred inflow of resources would be declared in accordance with GASB-65.

CHAPTER 18
EXPENSES/EXPENDITURES: NONEXCHANGE AND EXCHANGE TRANSACTIONS

CONTENTS

INTRODUCTION

With the issuance of GASB-34 (*Basic Financial Statements—and Management's Discussion and Analysis—for State and Local Governments*), governmental entities must measure and report in their financial reports the transactions that give rise to both expenses and expenditures. Like revenues, expenses and expenditures may arise from nonexchange transactions as well as exchange transactions.

To provide the framework for establishing accounting principles related to the elements of financial statements and their measurement and recognition within the financial statements, the GASB has issued GASB:CS-4 (*Elements of Financial Statements*).

GASB:CS-6 (*Measurement of Elements of Financial Statements*) discusses both measurement approaches and measurement attributes. A measurement approach determines whether an asset or liability presented in a financial statement should be (1) reported at an amount that reflects a value at the date that the asset was acquired or the liability was incurred or (2) remeasured and reported at an amount that reflects a value at the date of the financial statements. A measurement attribute is the feature or characteristic of the asset or liability that is measured. Changes in remeasured or initial amounts, as defined here, would potentially be an indicator of an increase of inflows, outflows, deferred inflows of resources, deferred outflows of resources, assets, or liabilities.

There are two measurement approaches in U.S. GAAP:

1. *Initial-transaction-date-based measurement (initial amount)*. This is the transaction price or amount assigned when an asset was acquired or a liability was incurred, including subsequent modifications to that price or amount, such as through depreciation or impairment. This approach is more commonly known as "historical cost" or "entry price," but those terms are not quite accurate.

2. *Current-financial-statement-date-based measurement (remeasured amount)*. This is the amount assigned when an asset or liability is remeasured as of the financial statement date. This is sometimes known as "fair value," "current value," or "carrying value." However, that is also not quite accurate, because those values are attributes.

Therefore, there are four measurement attributes that are used in U.S. GAAP:

1. *Historical cost* is the price paid to acquire an asset or the amount received pursuant to the incurrence of a liability in an actual exchange transaction. The understanding of this attribute is well-known and documented.

2. *Fair value* is the price that would be received to sell an asset or paid to transfer a liability in an orderly transaction between market participants at the measurement date.

OBSERVATION: GASB-72 (*Fair Value Measurement and Application*) has been issued. Contained within the standard is an additional measurement attribute—*acquisition value*. Acquisition value is only applicable to donated capital assets, donated works of art, historical treasures, and similar assets, as well as capital assets that a government receives in a service concession arrangement. Chapter 9, "Deposits, Investments, and Derivative Instruments," contains a thorough discussion of the new standard.

---

3. *Replacement cost* is the price that would be paid to acquire an asset with equivalent service potential in an orderly market transaction at the measurement date. This concept was largely introduced in GASB-42 (*Accounting and Financial Reporting for Impairment of Capital Assets and for Insurance Recoveries*).

4. *Settlement amount* is the amount at which an asset could be realized or a liability could be liquidated with the counterparty other than in an active market. This attribute was largely introduced in GASB-53 (*Accounting and Financial Reporting for Derivative Instruments*).

In GASB:CS-4, the GASB has identified and defined seven elements, stating that the elements' definitions are to be applied to a governmental unit (i.e., a separate legal entity that is an organization created, for example, as a body corporate or a body corporate and politic). The seven elements are the fundamental components of financial statements and can be organized by the specific financial statement they relate to.

GASB:CS-4 provides that the expenditure/expense element of the "resource flows (change) statements" be defined as an "outflow of resources" that results in a consumption of net position by the entity that is applicable to the reporting period.

The consumption of net position (outflow) is defined as the using up of net position that result in (1) a decrease in assets in excess of any related decrease in liabilities or (2) an increase in liabilities in excess of any related increase in assets. Examples of consumption of resources include (1) using cash resources to make direct aid payments to eligible recipients (because existing cash resources of the entity have been consumed) and (2) using the labor of employees to provide government services for which payment will be made in the next reporting period (because the entity has consumed employee labor resources that were directly acquired from the employees).

Governmental entities that provide resources that are based on nonexchange transactions must record both expenses (for proprietary and fiduciary funds, and government-wide financial statement purposes) and expenditures (for governmental fund financial statement purposes). GASB-33 (*Accounting and Financial Reporting for Nonexchange Transactions*) takes the position that the same-timing recognition criteria for determining an expense under the accrual basis of accounting are applicable to determining when expenditures should be recognized under the modified accrual basis of accounting. This chapter discusses the basic rules that governmental entities should follow to report these transactions in governmental funds, proprietary and fiduciary funds, and the government-wide financial statements.

PRACTICE ALERT: In January 2018, the GASB staff released an Invitation to Comment, *Revenue and Expense Recognition*, requesting feedback on a modified version of the current revenue recognition model that focuses on whether the transaction is an exchange or a nonexchange transaction as well as introducing a new model based on the existence of a performance obligation. Assuming the project progresses, final provisions may not be released by the GASB until 2023.

EXPENSES/EXPENDITURES: NONEXCHANGE TRANSACTIONS

The two parties in a nonexchange transaction are the provider of the resources and the receiver of the resources. The provider of the resources could be the federal governmental, a state or local government, or a non-governmental entity (such as an individual or business entity). The receiver of the resources could be a state or local government, or a nongovernmental entity. What distinguishes a nonexchange transaction from an exchange transaction is that in a *non* exchange transaction a government "either gives value (benefit) to another party without directly receiving equal value in exchange or receives value (benefit) from another party without directly giving equal value in exchange" (GASB-33, par. 7) [GASB Cod. Secs. 1600.111, .126, N50.104].

GASB-33 provides accounting and reporting standards for the following four categories of nonexchange transactions:

1. Derived tax revenues;

2. Imposed nonexchange revenues;

3. Government-mandated nonexchange transactions; and

4. Voluntary nonexchange transactions.

The first two categories (derived tax revenue and imposed nonexchange revenues) do not give rise to governmental expense or expenditure because the governmental entity is always the recipient of resources and never the provider of resources under these types of nonexchange transactions.

The GASB takes the position that all nonexchange transactions are fundamentally controlled by legislation, contractual requirements, or both, and this factor is essential in determining when expense and expenditures from nonexchange transactions should be recognized. Thus, expenses and expenditures related to government-mandated nonexchange transactions and voluntary nonexchange transactions should be recognized when all eligibility requirements established by the relevant authority have been satisfied.

The relevant eligibility requirements in a government-mandated nonexchange transaction are generally based on enabling legislation and related regulations. Those laws and regulations often identify purpose restrictions that apply to how the resources provided under the program are to be used. The relevant eligibility requirements in a voluntary nonexchange transaction may arise from enabling legislation or from contractual agreements with a nongovernmental entity. For example, a nongovernmental entity, such as a corporation or an individual, may provide resources to a governmental entity, but the provisions of those resources may depend on a number of eligibility factors contained in the donor agreement (GASB-33, par. 21) [GASB Cod. Sec. N50.118].

The standards established by GASB-33 generally apply to both revenue and expense recognition at the same time. That is, when both parties to the nonexchange transactions are governmental entities, the same standards that are used to determine whether revenue should be recognized by the recipient government are used to determine when an expense should be recognized by the provider governmental entity.

Time Requirements and Purpose Restrictions

To determine when expenses or expenditures related to nonexchange transactions should be recorded and presented in a governmental entity's financial statements, time requirements and purpose restrictions should be taken into consideration. Time requirements and purpose restrictions do not have the same effect on the recognition of expense or expenditure in a governmental entity's financial statements.

Time Requirements

Resources may be provided by one governmental entity to another governmental entity with the requirement that the resources be used in (or begin to be used in) a specified period(s). GASB-33 notes that "time requirements specify the period or periods when resources are required to be used or when use may begin." Time requirements may be imposed by enabling legislation. For example, legislation may identify the period in which a recipient government can use a grant or it may require that resources be used over a specified number of years. In other instances, time requirements imposed by the provider government may require that the resources provided never be used (permanent endowment) or that they cannot be used until a specified event has occurred.

When a nonexchange transaction is subject to a timing requirement, that requirement generally affects the period in which expenses and expenditures are recognized by the provider government. As discussed later, the effect that a timing requirement has on a nonexchange transaction is dependent on whether the transaction is (1) a government-mandated nonexchange transaction or a voluntary nonexchange transaction or (2) an imposed nonexchange revenue transaction.

Purpose Restrictions

Purpose restrictions relate to the use of resources that arise from a nonexchange transaction. For example, a party may receive a grant that may be used only to purchase an emergency communication system. Because of the nature of purpose restrictions, expenses and expenditures (as well as the related liability) related to nonexchange transactions should be recognized in a governmental entity's financial statements without taking into consideration purpose restrictions. That is, a purpose restriction does not affect the timing of the recognition of a nonexchange transaction. In fact, the GASB notes that a purpose restriction cannot be met unless a nonexchange transaction has taken place (GASB-33, par. 12) [GASB Cod. Sec. N50.109].

Although purpose restrictions do not affect the timing of an expense or expenditures by the provider government, a recipient government must disclose the restriction in its financial statements. For a discussion of how this is accomplished, see the discussion in Chapter 17, "Revenues: Nonexchange and Exchange Transactions."

Purpose restrictions can be related to both government-mandated nonexchange transactions and voluntary nonexchange transactions.

Government-Mandated Nonexchange Transactions

Expenditures/expenses from government-mandated nonexchange transactions arise when a governmental entity at one level provides resources to another governmental entity at a lower level, and the higher level governmental entity "requires [the other] government to use them for a specific purpose or purposes established in the provider's enabling legislation." For example, a state government (provider government) may make resources available to a county government (recipient government). GASB-33 notes that government-mandated nonexchange expense or expenditure transactions have the following principal characteristics (GASB-33, par. 7c) [GASB Cod. Secs. 1600.111, .126, N50.104]:

- The provider government requires that the recipient government institute a specific program (or facilitate the performance of a specific program) conducted by the recipient government or nongovernmental entity (secondary recipient entity); and
- Certain performance requirements must be fulfilled (other than the provision of cash or other assets in advance).

Because the resources provided by the providing government must be used for a particular purpose, resources received under a government-mandated nonexchange transaction always create a purpose restriction. In many instances, the resources are also subject to eligibility requirements, including time restrictions. An example of a government-mandated nonexchange transaction includes the requirement by a state government that a local government provide educational counseling to certain disadvantaged groups.

Simply mandating that a lower-level government entity establish a specific program does not create a government-mandated nonexchange transaction itself. The higher-level government must fund the program. The standards established by GASB-33 do not apply to unfunded mandates established by a government because these types of programs do not involve the exchange of resources (GASB-33, footnote 5) [GASB Cod. Sec. N50.fn4].

In a government-mandated nonexchange transaction, when the two governmental entities that are involved in the transaction are the state and a local government, they are both subject to GASB accounting and reporting standards. For this reason, the standards established by GASB-33 will apply to the recognition of revenue (by the recipient government) and the recognition of an expenditure/expense (by the provider government).

In a government-mandated nonexchange transaction, the provider government should recognize an expense or expenditure when all eligibility requirements (which include time requirements) are satisfied. The eligibility requirements are categorized as follows (GASB-33, par. 20) [GASB Cod. Sec. N50.117]:

- Required characteristics of recipients;
- Time requirements; and
- Reimbursements.

These requirements are discussed in detail in Chapter 17, "Revenues: Nonexchange and Exchange Transactions."

As a reminder, GASB-65 (*Items Previously Reported as Assets and Liabilities*), par. 10 [GASB Cod. Secs. N50.116, .118], requires resources transmitted *before the eligibility requirements are met* (excluding time requirements) to be reported as assets by the provider, instead of expenses/expenditures. GASB does not name the account for this transaction, but something similar to "advances provided to other governments" may be usable. Outflows of resources before time requirements are met but after all other eligibility requirements have been met should be reported as a deferred outflow of resources by the provider government.

Voluntary Nonexchange Transactions

Voluntary nonexchange transactions arise from "legislative or contractual agreements, other than exchanges, entered into willingly by two or more parties." A voluntary nonexchange transaction can be based on either a written or oral agreement, assuming the oral agreement is verifiable. The principal characteristics of voluntary nonexchange transactions are listed below (GASB-33, par. 7d, and footnote 6) [GASB Cod. Secs. 1600.111, .126, N50.104, N50.fn5]:

- They are not imposed on the provider or the recipient.

- Satisfaction of eligibility requirements (other than the provision of cash or other assets in advance) is necessary for a transaction to occur.

In a voluntary nonexchange transaction, a governmental entity may be the recipient or the provider of the resources, and the parties to the transaction may be another governmental entity or a nongovernmental entity, such as an individual or a not-for-profit organization. Examples of voluntary nonexchange transactions include certain grants, some entitlements, and donations. These types of nonexchange transactions may involve purpose restrictions and/or time requirements and often the arrangement requires that resources must be returned to the provider if purpose restrictions or eligibility requirements are contravened after the voluntary nonexchange transaction has been recognized by a governmental entity.

In a voluntary nonexchange transaction, the provider and the recipient should recognize the nonexchange transaction when all eligibility requirements (which include time requirements) are satisfied. The eligibility requirements are categorized as follows (GASB-33, par. 20) [GASB Cod. Sec. N50.117]:

- Required characteristics of recipients;

- Time requirements;

- Reimbursements; and

- Contingencies.

These requirements are discussed in detail in Chapter 17, "Revenues: Nonexchange and Exchange Transactions." Paragraph 10 of GASB-65 [GASB Cod. Secs. N50.116, .118] has a similar treatment of voluntary nonexchange transactions as government-mandated nonexchange transactions. Outflows of resources before time requirements are met but after all other eligibility requirements have been met should be reported as a deferred outflow of resources by the provider.

Sharing Government-Mandated and Voluntary Nonexchange Revenues—GASB Statement No. 36

GASB Statement No. 36, par. 2 (*Recipient Reporting for Certain Shared Nonexchange Revenues*) [GASB Cod. Secs. N50.125, fn14], superseded paragraph 28 of GASB-33 with regard to government-mandated and voluntary nonexchange transactions. Previous to GASB-36, an exception allowed governments to recognize revenues for certain transactions equal to cash received for those transactions during the period. GASB-36 replaces this paragraph.

Governments may collect derived tax revenues or imposed nonexchange revenues and share those revenues with other governments. If shared revenues occur, both the provider and recipient governments need to comply with the requirements of GASB-36 for voluntary or government-mandated nonexchange transactions, as appropriate. The revenues may be subject to a continuing appropriation, which may require notification by the provider government to the recipient government for accrual-based information. If the notification does not occur, an accrual estimate is allowed under GASB-36.

Recording Nonexchange Transactions

Governmental Funds

Although the standards established in GASB-33 are written in the context of the accrual basis of accounting, they provide a significant amount of general guidance for nonexchange transactions irrespective of the basis of accounting that is used by a governmental entity. For this reason, the GASB states that the general guidance provided in GASB-33 applies to governmental funds (activities accounted for in funds such as the General Fund and Special Revenue Funds). Expenditures of governmental funds are accounted for under the current financial resources measurement focus and modified accrual basis of accounting. Expenditures are decreases or outflows of *financial resources* and are recognized in the accounting period in which the fund liability is incurred, if measurable, except for unmatured interest on long-term debt, which is recognized when due.

Proprietary and Fiduciary Funds

Expenses from nonexchange transactions should be recognized in proprietary and fiduciary funds based on accrual accounting concepts and be consistent with the standards established by GASB-33.

Government-Wide Financial Statements

Expenses related to nonexchange transaction that are presented in a governmental entity's statement of activities should be based on accrual accounting concepts and be consistent with the standards established by GASB-33.

EXPENSES/EXPENDITURES: EXCHANGE TRANSACTIONS

In an exchange transaction the governmental entity and the other party to the transaction exchange cash, goods, or services that are essentially of the same value. For example, the purchase of a vehicle by a governmental entity from a car dealer is an exchange transaction. Unlike nonexchange transactions, the GASB has not provided comprehensive guidance for the recognition of exchange transactions.

PRACTICE ALERT: As introduced previously, a major component of the GASB's reexamination of the financial reporting model, and in particular revenues and expenses, is whether additional guidance needs to be developed for exchange transactions. The *Revenue and Expense Recognition* Invitation to Comment discusses a modified recognition utilizing the existing exchange/nonexchange model as well as a model based on the presence of a performance obligation. A performance obligation exists when the government has to do something in advance of revenue recognition. (In such a case, an example of an exchange transaction with a performance obligation may be the delivery of a patient to a hospital utilizing the government's ambulance service.)

Recording Exchange Transactions

Governmental Funds

GASB-34 requires that governmental entities produce government-wide financial statements that are based on the accrual accounting basis and the flow of all economic resources; however, GASB-34 also requires that governmental fund financial statements continue to be presented based on the modified accrual accounting basis and the flow of current financial resources.

The GASB believes that retaining the modified accrual basis of accounting for governmental funds was an important aspect of satisfying financial accountability, which is one of the foundations of governmental financial reporting. In general, a proprietary or fiduciary fund should record an expense when incurred; however, the recognition must be consistent with any relevant standards established by the GASB.

Government-Wide Financial Statements

Expenses related to exchange transactions in a governmental entity's statement of activities should be based on accrual accounting concepts. Governmental activities as presented in the government-wide financial statements should be accounted for and reported based on all applicable GASB pronouncements and all non-superseded NCGA pronouncements.

DEPRECIATION AND AMORTIZATION EXPENSE

An exchange transaction occurs when a governmental entity acquires capital assets. The expense related to that exchange transaction arises when depreciation expenses are recorded in the government-wide financial statements. In proprietary and fiduciary funds and the government-wide financial statements, the cost (net of estimated salvage value) of capital assets (except for certain infrastructure assets, which are discussed later) should be depreciated over their estimated useful lives. Inexhaustible capital assets (such as land, land improvements, and certain infrastructure assets) should not be depreciated (GASB-34, par. 21) [GASB Cod. Secs. 1100.107, 1400.104].

OBSERVATION: Because governmental funds report transactions on the modified accrual basis of accounting and current financial resources measurement focus, capital assets are not reported as fund assets of governmental funds. Therefore, capital assets are reported as fund expenditures when acquired and depreciation expense is not applicable to governmental funds.

The *GASB Implementation Guide 2015-1*, question 7.14.1 [GASB Cod. Sec. 1400.702-21], discusses, in part, that the estimated useful life of an asset is the period of time that the governmental entity believes the asset will be used in its activities based upon the government's own experience and plans for the assets. The question further discusses that factors that are relevant to making this determination include the following:

- The asset's present state of condition;
- How the asset will be used;
- Construction type;
- Maintenance policy; and
- Relevant service and technology demands.

The answer to the question does caution governments not to compare with other governments. The GASB notes the experience of other governmental entities is relevant only if the expected experience is anticipated to be the same.

The GASB's *Implementation Guide 2015-1*, question 7.14.2 [GASB Cod. Sec. 1400.705-11], further discusses that there is not a generally accepted schedule of useful lives that can be used to determine depreciation expense for governmental entities. Although informal schedules or guidance are provided by professional organizations, it is the responsibility of management to determine the estimated useful life of a capital asset. Furthermore, the Internal Revenue Service's schedule of lives for property classes related to the Modified Accelerated Cost Recovery System is not based on the actual estimated economic lives of assets.

The GASB suggests that the following may be used to estimate the useful lives of depreciable assets in *Implementation Guide 2015-1*, question 7.14.3 [GASB Cod. Sec. 1400.705-12]:

- General guidelines obtained from professional and industry organizations;
- Information for comparable assets of other governments; and
- Internal information.

These sources are starting points and should be modified based on the specific characteristics and expected use of a newly acquired capital asset.

GASB further discusses, in general, the lives of capital assets should be reviewed each year. In practice, most governments only review those lives that may have changed during the year as a result of some of the following events that may have occurred:

- Property replacement policies have changed;
- Preventive maintenance policies have changed; and
- Unexpected technological changes have occurred.

If it is concluded that the life of a capital asset should be changed, GASB-62, pars. 63–89 [GASB Cod. Secs. 2250.101–.152, 2300.107], requires that the asset's undepreciated cost (less the revised residual value) be allocated over the remaining life of the asset. This is a change in an accounting estimate.

As with commercial accounting, there is no specific list of acceptable depreciable methods; however, the method selected must be systematic and rational. GASB-34 notes that depreciation may be applied in the following manner (GASB-34, par. 22) [GASB Cod. Secs. 1100.107, 1400.113]:

- To a class of assets;
- To a network of assets;
- To a subsystem of a network assets; and
- To individual assets.

OBSERVATION: The composite depreciation method, which was illustrated in GASB-34 in the context of infrastructure assets, can also be used to compute depreciation expense for other capital assets; however, the method should not be applied across classes of assets. In grouping assets for the purpose of computing depreciation expense, the GASB's *Implementation Guide 2015-1*, questions 7.15.1, .3–.4 [GASB Cod. Secs. 1400.705-14–16], discuss how assets should not be grouped in a manner that would not enable a governmental entity to report depreciation expense as a direct expense for particular functions as required by paragraph 44 of GASB-34 [GASB Cod. Sec. 2200.132] or note disclosures required by paragraph 117d [GASB Cod. Secs. 2300.106, .118]. The composite method is discussed later in this chapter.

In the rare event when infrastructure assets are sold or the more common event of when infrastructure assets are disposed of (outside of the scope of GASB-69 (*Government Combinations and Disposals of Government Operations*)), the *GASB Implementation Guide 2015-1,* question 7.12.12 [GASB Cod. Sec. 1400.702-16], requires the gain or loss to be reported on the statement of activities as the difference between the net book value of the capital asset (original cost or estimated cost minus accumulated depreciation) and the proceeds from the disposition. If the infrastructure is not being depreciated (as allowed under the modified method under certain conditions), the gain or loss is the difference between the original cost (or estimated cost) and the proceeds.

OBSERVATION: If a service concession arrangement includes a provision that the capital asset be returned to the transferor government in "as good or better" condition than at the date of the arrangement, then theoretically deprecia-tion stops. It is suggested that the capital asset involved should be reported with nondepreciable capital assets as "Assets Involved in Service Concession Arrangements."

Amortization Periods for Intangible Assets

Intangible assets are described in GASB-51, par. 2 (Accounting and Financial Reporting for Intangible Assets) [GASB Cod. Sec. 1400.118] as those that lack physical substance, are of a nonfinancial nature and have an *initial* useful life extending beyond a single reporting period. They may be internally or externally generated.

GASB-51, pars. 16–17 [GASB Cod. Secs. 1400.151–.152], describe the amorti-zation of intangible assets. Similar to tangible assets, the guidance is based upon service capacity. The useful life of an intangible asset that arises from contractual or other legal rights should not exceed the period to which the service capacity of the asset is limited by contractual or legal provisions. Renewal periods related to contractual or legal rights may be considered in determining the useful life of the intangible asset if there is evidence that the government will be able to renew the contract and that any anticipated outlays incurred as part of achieving the renewal are nominal in relation to the level of service capacity expected to be obtained through the renewal.

Similar to a tangible asset, an intangible asset could have an indefinite useful life if there are no legal, contractual, regulatory, technological, or other factors that limit it. GASB-51, par. 17 [GASB Cod. Sec. 1400.152], prohibits intangible assets with indefinite useful lives to be amortized. If changes in factors and conditions result in the useful life of an intangible asset no longer being indefi-nite, the asset should be tested for impairment because a change in the expected duration of use of the asset has occurred in accordance with GASB-42 (*Accounting and Financial Reporting for Impairment of Capital Assets and for Insurance Recoveries*). The carrying value of the intangible asset, if any, following the recognition of any impairment loss would then be amortized in subsequent reporting periods over the remaining estimated useful life of the asset.

PRACTICE ALERT: An appendix to Chapter 14, "Leases and Service Concession Arrangements," describes the provisions of GASB Statement No. 87 (*Leases*), which will be implemented for periods beginning after December 15, 2019. The updated lease accounting and financial reporting model uses a "right-to-use" asset (an intangible asset) for the vast majority of leases. The amortiza-tion of the leased asset by a lessee will be in a systematic and rational manner over the *shorter* of the lease term or the useful life of the asset. If the lease contains a purchase option that the lessee has determined will be reasonably certain of being exercised, the leased asset would be amortized over the useful life of the underlying asset. Land would not be amortized. In practice, the amortization expense will likely be combined with other forms of depreciation.

Infrastructure Depreciation: Modified Approach

PRACTICE ALERT: A component of the GASB's reexamination of the financial reporting model includes measuring the effectiveness of the Modified Approach. If the modified approach is found not to meet the needs of the stakeholders of a state or local government's financial reports, the GASB may choose to discontinue its use, based on feedback received from due process. Initial surveys have been performed by GASB staff, but no tentative conclusions drawn as of the date of publication of this *Guide*.

The GASB does not require that infrastructure assets that are part of a network or subsystem of a network (referred to as eligible infrastructure assets) be depreciated if the following conditions are satisfied (GASB-34, par. 23) [GASB Cod. Sec. 1400.105]:

- An asset management system is employed that:
  - — Has an up-to-date inventory of eligible infrastructure assets;
  - — Performs condition assessments of the assets and summarizes the results using a "measurable scale";
  - — Estimates, on an annual basis, the annual amount needed to "maintain and preserve the eligible infrastructure assets at the condition level established and disclosed by the government"; and
- The government documents that the eligible infrastructure assets are being "preserved approximately at (or above) a condition level established and disclosed by the government."

A governmental entity that adopts the modified approach may continue to use it as long as the two conditions listed above are met. The GASB's *Implementation Guide 2015-1*, question 7.18.1 [GASB Cod. Sec. 1400.703-15], discusses how the second criterion listed refers to the conditions of the asset, not the amount of resources expended to maintain the asset at a particular condition. For example, if a governmental entity originally estimated that a specific amount was needed to maintain the asset but did not actually expended those funds, that does not mean that the entity can no longer use the modified approach—as long as the condition of the asset does not fall below the established condition level.

OBSERVATION: The documentation of condition assessments must be carefully done so that their results can be replicated. GASB-34 describes results being subject to replication as "those that are based on sufficiently understandable and complete measurement methods such that different measurers using the same methods would reach substantially similar results."

The condition level must be established and documented by governmental policy or legislative action and the assessment itself may be made either by the governmental entity directly or by external parties. Professional judgment and good faith are the basis for determining what constitutes acceptable and accurate documentation of the condition of eligible infrastructure assets. However, GASB-34 states that governmental entities should document the following (GASB-34, par. 24) [GASB Cod. Sec. 1400.106]:

- Complete condition assessments of eligible infrastructure assets are performed in a consistent manner at least every three years; and

- The results of the three most recent complete condition assessments provide reasonable assurance that the eligible infrastructure assets are being preserved approximately at (or above) the condition level established and disclosed by the government.

GASB-34 points out that the condition level could be applied to a group of assets by using a condition index or "as the percentage of a network of infrastructure assets in good or poor condition."

If a governmental entity identifies a subsystem of infrastructure assets as "eligible" (and therefore the computation of depreciation is optional), the documentary requirements apply only to the subsystem and not to the entire network of infrastructure assets.

A governmental entity may perform the condition assessment annually or may use a cycle basis. If the entity uses a cyclical basis for networks or subsystems, it must assess all assets of these groups during the cycle. However, rather than apply the condition assessment to all assets, the entity may employ a statistical sample approach in the annual approach or in the cycle approach.

Because eligible infrastructure assets do not have to be depreciated, all expenditures related to their maintenance should be recognized as a current expense when incurred. Expenditures that are capital in nature (additions and improvements) should be capitalized as part of the eligible infrastructure assets because they, by definition, increase the capacity or efficiency of the related infrastructure asset (GASB-34, par. 25) [GASB Cod. Sec. 1400.107].

The adequate maintenance of the condition of eligible infrastructure assets is a continuous process and if the conditions established by GASB-34 are initially satisfied but subsequently are not, the infrastructure assets are not considered "eligible" and depreciation expense for them must be computed and reported in the statement of activities. The change in accounting for depreciation expense should be reported a change in an accounting estimate in accordance with GASB-62, pars. 69–70 [GASB Cod. Secs. 2250.101, .132–.133]. A change in estimate is accounted for on a prospective basis. That is, the balances in the infrastructure assets (net of residual values, if any) are to be depreciated over the remaining lives of the assets when the governmental entity no longer qualifies to use the modified approach (GASB-34, par. 26) [GASB Cod. Sec. 1400.108].

While GASB-34 provides guidance for a change from not depreciating certain infrastructure assets to the recognition of annual depreciation expense on those assets, it does not address how the reverse situation should be reported in a governmental entity's financial statements. A change from depreciating infrastructure assets to not depreciating them could arise for reasons such as the following:

- Business-type activities might decide on a non-depreciating strategy when they implement the standards established by GASB-34.

- Infrastructure networks or subsystems may be transferred from an Enterprise Fund to general capital assets.

- At a date after the implementation of the standards established by GASB-34 a governmental entity may decide to change from depreciating infrastructure assets to the modified approach because it now satisfies the requirements established by paragraph 23 of GASB-34.

GASB-37, par. 8, as modifying GASB-34, par. 25, footnote b [GASB Cod. Sec. 1400.fn10], requires that a change from the depreciating approach to the non-depreciating approach (modified approach) for certain infrastructure assets be accounted for on a prospective basis (change in an accounting estimate). Thus, when this type of change is made, the carrying amount of the asset remains the same and that amount provides the basis for computing subsequent depreciation expense.

The GASB considered whether to account for this type of change as a change in an accounting principle, but rejected this approach which would have required that "the carrying amount of the asset . . . be restated to remove previously recorded accumulated depreciation and previously capitalized preservation costs, if any."

The GASB's *Implementation Guide 2015-1*, question 7.17.1 [GASB Cod. Sec. 1400.703-9], discusses the treatment of maintenance costs (i.e., routine repairs) for the modified approach and the traditional depreciation approach. That is, under both approaches, maintenance costs are expensed.

The treatment of preservation costs is different under the two approaches. Preservation costs are not defined in GASB-34 but are described in question 7.17.2 of the GASB *Implementation Guide 2015-1* [GASB Cod. Sec. 1400.703-10] as cost that "generally are considered to be those outlays that extend the useful life of an asset beyond its original estimated useful life, but do not increase the capacity or efficiency of the asset." Some accountants refer to preservation costs as "major repairs." Under the modified approach preservation costs are expensed; under the traditional depreciation approach preservation costs are capitalized. Under both approaches additions and improvements are capitalized. Of course, differentiating among these costs (preservation, additions, and improvements) is often difficult. The governmental entity should use "any reasonable approach" to make the cost allocation.

Therefore, the differences between the modified approach and depreciation for maintenance, preservation and general additions and improvements are as follows:

	Modified Approach	Depreciation
Maintenance costs	Expense	Expense
Preservation costs	Expense	Capitalize
Additions and improvements	Capitalize	Capitalize

Question 7.17.3 of the *GASB Implementation Guide 2015-1* [GASB Cod. Sec. 1400.703-11] demonstrates how the above guidance should be applied by raising the question of whether the cost of removing and replacing or resurfacing an existing roadway should be capitalized if the modified approach is used. The results arising from the removing and replacing or resurfacing must be evaluated

to determine whether the activity is considered (1) maintenance or preservation or (2) an increase in the capacity or efficiency of the roadway. If the costs are related to maintenance or preservation, they should be expensed under the modified approach. If the costs increase the capacity or efficiency of the roadway, they must be capitalized. Capacity is increased when a capital asset can provide more services or goods. Efficiency is increased when a capital asset can accomplish the same level of service at a lower cost.

OBSERVATION: Deferred maintenance of infrastructure has become an important issue for state and local governments. However, there is currently no U.S. GAAP standard with regard to measuring and recognizing deferred maintenance in the basic financial statements. Within the basis for conclusions to GASB-42 (*Accounting and Financial Reporting for Impairment of Capital Assets and for Insurance Recoveries*), the GASB remarks as follows in paragraph 34 of that Statement's Basis for Conclusions: "The Board recognizes that users of financial statements are concerned about these issues; however, these issues could not be included in the scope of this Statement. The GASB believes that additional time to study the results of Statement 34 implementation efforts and to allow condition assessment approaches to further develop is necessary before additional guidance on these issues can be considered." The financial reporting model is currently in the process of reexamination. It is likely that deferred maintenance of infrastructure may be further considered.

QUESTIONS

1. Eligibility requirements in government-mandated nonexchange transactions include all the following except for:

   a. Required characteristics of recipients.

   b. Time requirements.

   c. Reimbursements.

   d. Whether participation is voluntary or not.

2. In a voluntary nonexchange transaction, the provider and the recipient should recognize the nonexchange transaction when all eligibility requirements are met. The eligibility requirements include all of the following except for:

   a. Required characteristics of recipients.

   b. Time requirements.

   c. Whether participation is voluntary or not.

   d. Contingencies.

3. In accordance with GASB-65, what accounting element is likely recognized when resources are transmitted from the government where financial statements are being prepared to another before time requirements are met but after all other eligibility requirements are met?

   a. Deferred inflows of resources.

   b. Deferred outflows of resources.

   c. Inflows.

   d. Outflows.

4. In the determination of useful life to record depreciation expense, the *GASB Implementation Guide 2015-1* states that the period of time that the governmental entity believes the asset will be used in its activities is key. Which of the following factors is not relevant to making this determination?

   a. Historical cost.

   b. How the asset will be used.

   c. Maintenance policy.

   d. The asset's present state of condition.

5. To use the modified approach, U.S. GAAP does not require depreciation if all of the following conditions are met for an asset management system except for:

   a. An up-to-date inventory of eligible assets is kept.

   b. The inventory system must be computerized.

   c. Condition assessments of the assets are performed using a measurable scale.

   d. Estimates are made annually for the amount needed to maintain and preserve the eligible infrastructure assets at the condition level established and disclosed by the government.

ANSWERS

1. Eligibility requirements in government-mandated nonexchange transactions include all the following except for:

   Answer – D: The transaction is mandated. All the rest are eligibility requirements.

2. In a voluntary nonexchange transaction, the provider and the recipient should recognize the nonexchange transaction when all eligibility requirements are met. The eligibility requirements include all of the following except for:

   Answer – C: The voluntary nature of the transaction does not have any bearing on eligibility. All the rest are characteristics of voluntary nonexchange transactions.

3. In accordance with GASB-65, what accounting element is likely recognized when resources are transmitted from the government where financial statements are being prepared to another before time requirements are met but after all other eligibility requirements are met?

   Answer – B: Deferred outflows of resources. The rest of the answers are not in accordance with U.S. GAAP.

4. In the determination of useful life to record depreciation expense, the *GASB Implementation Guide 2015-1* states that the period of time that the governmental entity believes the asset will be used in its activities is key. Which of the following factors is not relevant to making this determination?

   Answer – A: The remaining answers are not key determinants.

5. To use the modified approach, U.S. GAAP does not require depreciation if all of the following conditions are met for an asset management system, except for:

   Answer – B: Systems are not required to be computerized. All the rest are requirements of the modified approach.

CHAPTER 19
SPECIAL ASSESSMENTS

CONTENTS

INTRODUCTION

A governmental entity may raise resources assessing only the properties of taxpayers who would directly benefit either from the construction or improvement of a capital asset or from the provision for special services. For example, a city may assess property owners in order to improve water or sewer lines in a specific location within the city or a local government may assess businesses in a downtown area in order to provide special sanitation maintenance on an ongoing basis, commonly known as "tax incremental financing" (TIFs). These special assessment activities provided by a governmental entity are generally characterized by their narrow scope and the method by which they are financed.

Governmental accounting and reporting standards for special assessments are based on the guidance established by GASB-6 (*Accounting and Financial Reporting for Special Assessments*).

GASB-6 significantly reduced the likelihood of fund balance deficits resulting from special assessments by treating special assessment debt like all other debt issued by a governmental unit. The proceeds of the special assessment debt should be recorded as another source of financing, and the debt should be reported as part of the governmental unit's general long-term debt if the unit is directly liable or in some manner liable for the special assessment debt.

Another significant accounting standard established by GASB-6 is the prohibition of the use of Special Assessment Funds for governmental financial reporting. The rationale for the prohibition is that special assessment transactions and balances are no more unique than capital expenditures, debt service expenditures, and special levies that are accounted for in the other governmental funds or in Enterprise Funds. Special assessment transactions and balances generally will be accounted for in a number of different funds.

TYPES OF SPECIAL ASSESSMENTS

Services Financed by Special Assessments

Special assessments used to finance special types of service or special levels of service should be accounted for generally in the General Fund, a Special Revenue Fund, or an Enterprise Fund. The GASB states that the number of separate funds established should be kept to the minimum level that will satisfy legal and administrative requirements. Therefore, in some cases, services financed by special assessments may be accounted for in the General Fund. Assessment revenues and related expenditures/expenses should use the accounting basis that is appropriate for the fund used. The activities related to the special assessment should be reported in the government-wide financial statements, using the accrual basis of accounting, in either the governmental or business-type activities depending on the nature of the service provided (GASB-6, par. 14, as amended by GASB-33, GASB-34, pars. 6, 15–16) [GASB Cod. Sec. S40.114]).

The GASB's *Implementation Guide 2015-1*, question 7.36.1 [GASB Cod. Sec. 2200.717-8], notes that special assessment activities provided by a governmental entity are generally characterized by their narrow scope and the method by which they are financed. For financial reporting purposes operating special assessments revenues are not considered general revenues like property taxes. Operating special assessments are program revenues (charges for services) because they are assessed against those specific parties who are entitled to the specific service. In many cases, revenues are recorded as user fees to indicate that users are directly benefiting from the services financed by special assessments.

Capital Improvements Financed by Special Assessments

Generally, capital improvements financed by special assessments have two distinct phases: the construction phase and the debt service phase. When a governmental unit is directly liable or obligated in some manner (as defined in the section titled "Governmental Liability for Debt") for the special assessment debt, the capital construction and related debt service transactions should be accounted for in a manner similar to other governmental capital outlays and debt service payments. For this reason, special assessment transactions related to capital improvements may be accounted for in a Capital Projects Fund or Debt Service Fund. If there are no legal or administrative requirements that necessitate the use of a separate Capital Projects Fund or Debt Service Fund, the General Fund can be used.

If special assessment revenue is generated, a fund balance remaining at the end of a fiscal year could be restricted if accounted for in a governmental fund. The provisions of the assessment would have to align with the guidance provided in GASB-54 (*Fund Balance Reporting and Governmental Fund Type Definitions*), paragraph 8(a), because the restriction would occur through a debt covenant or paragraphs 8(b) and 9 [GASB Cod. Secs. 1800.168–.169], which discuss and define enabling legislation. In some instances, depending on local laws, regulations, and ordinances, if the assessment were generated by an action of the government's highest level of decision-making authority, any fund balance would show as a committed fund balance.

When a governmental entity is obligated in some manner to make debt repayments in the case of default by property owners, the expenditures (expenses) "should be reported in the same manner and on the same basis of accounting, as any other capital improvement and financing transaction." Revenues from special assessment capital improvement transactions should be accounted for based on the standards established by GASB-33 (*Accounting and Financial Reporting for Nonexchange Transactions*) (GASB-6, par. 15, as amended by GASB-33, pars. 12–13, 17–18, GASB-34, pars. 80–82, GASB-63, par. 8, GASB-65, par. 30) [GASB Cod. Sec. S40.118].

The GASB's *Implementation Guide 2015-1*, question 7.36.2 [GASB Cod. Sec. 2200.717-9], discusses how capital special assessments are program revenues (program-specific capital grants and contributions) because the property owners derive a direct benefit from the contributions they make to the program.

ACCOUNTING AND REPORTING FOR SPECIAL ASSESSMENTS

Governmental Liability for Debt

Because property owners are generally obligated to finance all or part of the repayment of special assessment debt, a question arises whether the special assessment debt should be reported as debt of the governmental entity. When the governmental unit is primarily liable for the special assessment debt, the debt should be reported as debt by the governmental entity. In addition, special assessment debt should be reported as such when the governmental unit is "obligated in some manner" to repay the debt in cases where property owners default. GASB-6 states that a governmental unit is obligated in some manner to pay the special assessment debt if one of the following two circumstances exists:

- The governmental unit is legally obligated to assume all or part of the special assessment debt if property owners default.

- The governmental unit, although not required to do so, may assume secondary responsibility for all or part of the special assessment debt, and the governmental unit has either taken such action in the past or indicated that it will take such action.

The following eight specific conditions indicate that a governmental unit is obligated in some manner to repay the special assessment debt:

1. When lien foreclosure proceeds are inadequate and the governmental unit is required to fund the deficiencies;

2. When reserves, guarantees, or sinking funds must be established by a governmental unit;

3. When delinquencies occur and the governmental unit is required to fund such delinquencies until proceeds are received from foreclosures;

4. When properties put up for sale because of delinquencies are not sold at public auction and must be acquired by the governmental unit;

5. When the governmental unit is authorized to and in fact establishes reserves, guarantees, or sinking funds (even if an authorized fund has not yet been established, the governmental unit may still be obligated in some manner with respect to the special assessment debt based on the conditions described in 7 and 8, below);

6. When the governmental unit is authorized to and in fact establishes a separate fund to be used to purchase or redeem special assessment debt (even if an authorized fund has not yet been established, the governmental unit may still be obligated in some manner with respect to the special assessment debt based on the conditions described in 7 and 8, below);

7. When it is explicitly indicated by contract that the governmental unit may finance delinquencies, although there is no legal duty to do so; and

8. When it is probable that the governmental unit will accept responsibility for defaults based on either legal decisions within the state or action previously taken by the governmental unit with respect to special assessment defaults.

As the above conditions suggest, the GASB takes a very broad approach in identifying special assessment debt that should be reported by a governmental unit as debt. This broad approach to debt classification is further endorsed in GASB-6 when the phrase "obligated in some manner" is described as including all situations except for the following:

- The governmental unit is prohibited from assuming responsibility for the special assessment debt in case of default.

- The governmental unit is not legally liable to assume the special assessment debt in case of default and has in no way indicated that it will or may assume the debt (GASB-6, par. 16) [GASB Cod. Sec. S40.115].

NOTE: GASB-70 (*Accounting and Financial Reporting for Nonexchange Guarantees*) specifically does not apply to special assessment debt.

Classification of Special Assessment Debt

When property owners are responsible for paying all or a portion of special assessment debt issued to finance capital improvements, the accounting for the special assessment is dependent on whether (1) the debt is general obligation debt, (2) the governmental unit is obligated in some manner to repay the debt, or (3) the governmental unit is in no way obligated to repay the debt.

General Obligation Debt

General obligation debt is backed by the full faith and credit of a governmental unit. When special assessment debt is backed by a governmental unit, the debt should be reported like any other general obligation debt in the statement of net position.

Obligated in Some Manner

A governmental unit is obligated in some manner to pay special assessment debt when (1) the governmental unit is legally obligated to assume all or part of the special assessment debt if property owners default or (2) the governmental unit may assume secondary responsibility for all or part of the debt and the unit has either taken such action in the past or indicated that it will take such action. Special assessment debt that a governmental unit is obligated for in some manner should be reported similarly to any other general obligation debt in the statement of net position, but the debt should be referred to as "Special Assessment Debt with Governmental Commitment" (GASB *Implementation Guide 2015-1*, question 7.22.13) [GASB Cod. Sec. S40.709-1].

The portion of special assessment debt (for which a governmental unit is somewhat obligated) that is a direct obligation of an Enterprise Fund or is to be repaid from operating revenues of an Enterprise Fund should be recorded as a liability of the Enterprise Fund and reported as debt in the business-type activities column in the statement of net position (GASB-6, pars. 17, 23 GASB-34, pars. 15–16, 18, 30, and 82, as amended by GASB-63, par. 8) [GASB Cod. Sec. S40.116]).

No Obligation to Pay Debt

In some cases, special assessment debt may be issued with the governmental unit having no obligation to repay the debt. Under this circumstance, the special assessment debt would not be reported as an obligation by the governmental entity. However, if a portion of the special assessment is to be paid by the governmental unit based on the public benefit portion of the capital improvement or because the governmental unit owns property that is subject to the special assessment, this portion of the special assessment debt would be recorded as a general long-term debt in the statement of net position.

When a governmental unit is in no way obligated for the special assessment debt, the debt is not reported in the unit's financial statements. However, transactions related to the financing and construction of the capital asset must be reported by the governmental entity. The receipt of the funds is reported in an Agency Fund (statement of fiduciary net position). (See previous **PRACTICE ALERTS** on GASB-84 on Agency Funds in Chapter 8, "Fiduciary Funds.") Construction expenditures should be accounted for in a Capital Projects Fund and the receipt of resources should be reported as "contribution from property owners" rather than described as "bond proceeds." The capital asset should be reported in the governmental activities column in the statement of net position (GASB-6, par. 19; GASB-34, pars. 16 and 50) [GASB Cod. Sec. S40.125].

Special Assessment Reserve, Guarantee, or Sinking Fund

A governmental unit may be required or authorized to establish a reserve, guarantee, or sinking fund to accumulate resources in case property owners default on their special assessments. A debt service fund should be used when resources are accumulated for principal and interest payments due in future years. As a reminder, reserves are not presented on the face of the basic financial statements, because they are components of net position and fund balance.

Financing Special Assessments with Current Resources

A capital improvement may be initially financed with currently available resources of the governmental unit rather than with proceeds from the issuance of special assessment debt. Payments that are made directly from a governmental fund (usually the General Fund) for capital improvements should be recorded as capital expenditures in the fund making the payments. Resources transferred from a governmental fund to a Capital Projects Fund should be recorded as interfund transfers, and capital outlays eventually made by the Capital Projects Fund should be recorded as capital expenditures.

The levy of the special assessment against property owners should be recorded in the governmental fund that initially provided the resources used to finance the capital improvement. The portion of the special assessment that should be recorded as revenue is the amount that is both measurable and available (GASB-6, par. 22, as amended by GASB-65, par. 30) [GASB Cod. Sec. S40.120].

In accordance with GASB-65, amending GASB-33 and discussed in the *GASB Implementation Guide 2015-1*, question Z.33.12 [GASB Cod. Sec. N50.708-3], if an entity levies amounts in its current property tax levy for future debt service payments, the future amounts are not reported as deferred inflows of resources until those future periods start. Unless a legal requirement specifies otherwise, the period for which these amounts are levied is the same as the period for which the rest of the taxes are levied. If a special assessment is a component of property taxation, then this guidance may be followed for this situation.

Reporting Special Assessments Financed with Current Resources in Governmental Funds

Capital assets constructed for an Enterprise Fund and financed by special assessments should be accounted for in a manner similar to other capital improvements financed by special assessments. However, the capital asset should be recorded both by the Enterprise Fund and in the business-type activities column of the statement of net position.

The cost of the capital asset should be capitalized, net of special assessment revenues. The special assessment debt related to the construction of the capital asset should be recorded as a liability of the Enterprise Fund only if one of the following conditions exists:

- The Enterprise Fund is directly liable for the special assessment debt.
- The Enterprise Fund is not directly liable for the special assessment debt, but the debt is expected to be repaid from revenues of the Enterprise Fund.

Debt expected to be repaid by an Enterprise Fund should be reported as debt of the Enterprise Fund even though the debt may be backed by the full faith and credit of the governmental unit. The debt must also be reported in the government-wide statement of net position.

Although GASB-6 states that most capital assets constructed for an Enterprise Fund and financed by special assessments will be accounted for as described in the previous paragraph, it is acceptable to record all special assessment transactions solely in the Enterprise Fund. Under this approach, the special assessment levy would be recorded as a receivable and contributed capital revenue. Special assessment debt for which the Enterprise Fund is directly liable or expected to repay from its revenues would be accounted for in the Enterprise Fund. The accrual basis of accounting should be used to account for special assessments receivable and the related interest income, and special assessment debt and the related interest expense (GASB-6, par. 23) [GASB Cod. Sec. S40.116].

Even though the GASB accepted two methods of accounting for special assessment capital projects that benefit Enterprise Funds, it did not suggest that one method was preferable to the other. The GASB did state that, generally, the guidance provided by GASB-6, par. 15, should be followed (see previous section titled "Capital Improvements Financed by Special Assessments"). The GASB stated in an appendix that "reporting all transactions and balances in an Enterprise Fund is not appropriate in many instances" (par. 42 of the original standard). The basic concern by the GASB is that project cash and receivables, and the special assessment debt, often do not meet the definitions of assets and liabilities of the enterprise fund itself. Thus, even though it is not suggested in the accounting standards paragraphs of GASB-6, the preparer of governmental financial statements must carefully review the facts related to the special assessment to determine whether there is any justification for reporting all special assessment transactions and balances in an Enterprise Fund.

Reporting Capital Assets Financed by Special Assessment Debt in Government-Wide Financial Statements

As noted earlier, capital assets or improvements financed by special assessment debt for which the entity is obligated in some manner must be reported as capital assets in either the governmental or business-type activities column in the statement of net position. The related special assessment revenue and receivables must be accounted for on the accrual basis of accounting.

When the governmental entity is not obligated for the special assessment debt, the capital asset must be reported on the statement of net position and an equal amount of program revenue (capital contributions) should be reported on the statement of activities (GASB-6, par. 19; GASB-34, pars. 16,50) [GASB Cod. Sec. S40.125].

Special Assessment Districts of Component Units

A component unit applies the criteria established by GASB-6 to determine how special assessment transactions and accounts should be reported. When the component unit's financial statements are blended with the primary government's financial statements to form the reporting entity, the component unit's special assessment debt should be reported as a liability in the reporting entity's financial statements based on GASB-6 criteria even though the primary government may not be responsible in any way for the component unit's special assessment debt (GASB-6, par. 24, as amended by GASB-14, par. 13) [GASB Cod. Sec. S40.128].

PRACTICE POINT: Special assessment debt issued by component units is frequently found in redevelopment agencies or business improvement districts. Depending on the organization of such agencies/districts, if the entities are component units, they are commonly blended, especially if the primary government is the sole corporate entity of the agency/district organized as a not-for-profit organization or the primary government is obligated in some manner for the debt. Additional information is included in Chapter 4, "Governmental Financial Reporting Entity."

DISCLOSURES

The disclosures in the governmental unit's financial statements with respect to special assessment debt depend on whether the unit is responsible for the debt.

Governmental Unit Obligated for Debt

When the governmental unit is primarily obligated or obligated in some manner for the repayment of special assessment debt, the following disclosures that are applicable to all general obligation debt should be made in the unit's financial statements:

- Nature of governmental unit's obligation for special assessment debt;
- Description of individual special assessment debt issues;
- Description of requirements or authorizations for the establishment of guarantees, reserves, or sinking funds if defaults occur;
- Changes in general long-term debt (special assessment debt for which the unit is primarily responsible) and special assessment debt with governmental commitment (special assessment debt for which the unit is obligated in some manner);
- Summary of debt service requirements to maturity; and
- Special assessment debt authorized but unissued.

In addition, the amount of the special assessments receivable that is delinquent should be disclosed on the face of the Balance Sheet (or the statement of net position as discussed previously) or in a note to the financial statements (GASB-6, par. 20) [GASB Cod. Sec. S40.126].

Governmental Unit Not Obligated for Debt

When the governmental unit is not obligated in any manner for repayment of the special assessment debt, the following disclosures should be made in the unit's financial statements (GASB-6, par. 21) [GASB Cod. Sec. S40.127]:

- Present amount of special assessment debt outstanding;
- Statement that the governmental unit is in no manner obligated to repay the special assessment debt; and
- Statement that the governmental unit functions as an agent for the property owners by collecting assessments, forwarding collections to special assessment debt-holders, and, if appropriate, beginning foreclosure.

The *GASB Implementation Guide 2015-1*, question 7.5.12 [GASB Cod. Sec. 2200.704-10], clarifies that U.S. GAAP does not require governments to include in the management's discussion and analysis (MD&A) a section on special assessment debt for which the government is not obligated. However, the debt may be discussed in connection with capital asset activity if the proceeds are to be used to build or acquire significant infrastructure assets for the government.

QUESTIONS

1. Special assessments are usually levied for improvements except for which of the following:
   a. Sidewalks
   b. Operational purposes
   c. Water and sewer lines
   d. Roads

2. Capital improvements funded by special assessments are likely accounted for in which type of fund?
   a. Capital projects fund
   b. Special revenue fund
   c. Special assessment fund
   d. Debt service fund

3. Conditions where a government is obligated to pay for special assessment debt include the following except for:
   a. When reserves, guarantees, or sinking funds must be established by a governmental unit.
   b. When delinquencies occur and the governmental unit is required to fund such delinquencies until proceeds are received from foreclosures.
   c. When it is more likely than not that a government will have to pay on nonexchange financially guaranteed debts of another government.
   d. When properties put up for sale because of delinquencies are not sold at public auction and must be acquired by the governmental unit.

4. If the government is not obligated for the debt but simply collects the assessments from property owners and forwards them to the bondholders, reporting is as follows except for:
   a. Present amount of special assessment debt outstanding.
   b. Statement that the government intends to fund the debt through a debt service fund.
   c. Statement that the governmental unit is in no manner obligated to repay the special assessment debt.
   d. Statement that the governmental unit functions as an agent for the property owners by collecting assessments, forwarding collections to special assessment debt holders, and, if appropriate, beginning foreclosure.

ANSWERS

1. Special assessments are usually levied for improvements except for which of the following:

   Answer – B.

2. Capital improvements funded by special assessments are likely accounted for in which type of fund?

   Answer – A.

3. Conditions where a government is obligated to pay for special assessment debt include the following except for:

   Answer – C: Those provisions are in GASB-70, which is not applicable to special assessment debt.

4. If the government is not obligated for the debt but simply collects the assessments from property owners and forwards them to the bondholders, reporting is as follows except for:

   Answer – B.

IV. FINANCIAL REPORTING BY GENERAL-PURPOSE GOVERNMENTS

CHAPTER 20
COMPREHENSIVE ANNUAL FINANCIAL REPORT

CONTENTS

INTRODUCTION: COMPREHENSIVE ANNUAL FINANCIAL REPORT

The GASB takes the position that every governmental entity should prepare and publish a comprehensive annual financial report (CAFR) "as a matter of public record." The CAFR is a governmental entity's official annual report and should include the following sections:

- Introductory section.
- Financial section
  - Auditor's report;
  - Management's discussion and analysis (MD&A);
  - Basic financial statements; and
  - Notes to the basic financial statements.
- Required supplementary information (other than MD&A) (RSI).
- Supplementary Information.
  - Combining statements and individual fund statements and schedules.
- Statistical section.

Other information may be presented in a CAFR, including an organizational chart, a table of acknowledgements, and various title, explanatory, and divider pages.

OBSERVATION: Chapters 21 through 24 of the *Governmental GAAP Guide* discuss stand-alone financial reporting by special-purpose governments including public colleges and universities, pension and other postemployment benefit plans and public entity risk pools. Many of these entities prepare CAFRs. As some of the sections named above are not applicable, the following would be presented as sections in a special-purpose government CAFR:

Element	Public Colleges and Universities (using enterprise fund accounting)	Pension and Other Post-Employment Benefit Plans	Public Entity Risk Pools	Other Special Districts (using enterprise fund accounting) (for example— public utilities and hospitals)
Introductory Section:	Yes	Yes	Yes	Yes
Financial Section:				
Auditor's Report	Yes	Yes	Yes	Yes
MD&A	Yes	Yes	Yes	Yes
Basic Financial Statements	Yes	Yes	Yes	Yes
RSI (other than MD&A)	Yes	Yes	Yes	Yes
Supplementary Information:				
Combining Statements	If Applicable	If Applicable	If Applicable	If Applicable
Investment Section	Not Applicable	Yes	Not Applicable	Cash and Investment Pools Only
Actuarial Section	Not Applicable	Yes	Not Applicable	Not *Usually* Applicable
Compliance Information—Debt Disclosure Related to Bond Covenants	If Applicable	If Applicable	If Applicable	If Applicable
Statistical Section	Yes	Yes	Yes	Yes

In the Statistical section, for special purpose governments, different schedules and analyses are used due to the non-general nature of the government.

Although the GASB *encourages* (but *does not* require) the preparation of a CAFR, it identifies certain components as the minimum required presentation for proper financial reporting in accordance with generally accepted accounting principles. These minimum required components include:

- MD&A;

- Basic Financial Statements;

- Notes to the Basic Financial Statements; and

- RSI (other than MD&A).

PRACTICE ALERT: The GASB is in the midst of a wide-ranging multiple-year project reexamining the financial reporting model, a related project reexamining revenue and expense recognition principles and note disclosure. In late 2016, the GASB issued an Invitation to Comment, *Financial Reporting Model Improvements—Governmental Funds.* The release represented the first due process document and asked respondents for comment on a large portion of the current financial reporting model. An Invitation to Comment is a GASB staff document, asking for comments at a relatively early stage of a project prior to the GASB Board reaching a consensus view. The topics considered in this initial phase included:

- Recognition approaches (measurement focus and basis of accounting) for governmental funds,
- The format of the governmental funds statement of resource flows (also known as the statement of revenues, expenditures, and changes in fund balances),
- Specific terminology,
- Reconciliation of the governmental fund statements to the government-wide statements, and
- For certain recognition approaches, a statement of cash flows.

In September 2018, the GASB released a second due process document consisting of the Board's Preliminary Views on the *Financial Reporting Model—Reexamination* project. Most notably, the GASB is focusing on a proposed one-year (operating cycle) period of availability for governmental funds with a goal of resolving inconsistencies in the recognition of prepaid items, inventory, tax and revenue anticipation notes, and grant receivables. Topics considered included:

- Refinement of the management's discussion and analysis
- The format of the government-wide statement of activities, including whether additional information should be presented in a "natural classification" (salaries, employee benefits, etc.) schedule in the notes
- Debt service fund presentations, potentially elevating them to major fund status, similarly to the general fund
- The status and reporting of permanent funds
- Proprietary fund and business-type activity financial statements, especially the presentation of operating and non-operating revenues and expenses
- The presentation of fiduciary fund financial statements and whether the statements should be presented in the basic financial statements
- Consistency of presentation of budgetary comparisons within required supplementary information.

The project may not be fully completed until at least 2021. Other related project, *Revenue and Expense Recognition*, was just began due process in 2018 with an Invitation to Comment and note disclosure.

PRACTICE POINT: To reiterate, U.S. GAAP *does not require* a CAFR. For some governments, the costs of preparation and auditing a CAFR outweigh its benefits. Furthermore, the preparation and the auditing of a CAFR may take significantly more time than only a set of basic financial statements. Still other governments are required to prepare CAFRs due to a law or policy. If a government has the option to prepare a CAFR and chooses not to, to some, the lack of a CAFR diminishes availability of information necessary to place a government's financial position in a proper perspective. It is expected that the discussion over the usability of governmental financial reporting, including the usability of the current financial reporting model, will continue well into the future.

PRACTICE POINT: The AICPA Accounting and Review Services Committee (ARSC) has issued clarified standards on the preparation of financial statements. ARC Section 70, *Preparation of Financial Statements*, applies when an accountant in public practice (*not in public service*) is engaged to prepare financial statements. ARC Section 70 does not apply when the accountant prepares financial statements *and is engaged* to audit, review, or compile the statements (a separate engagement). The engagement is a non-attest service and *does not require* a determination about whether the accountant is independent of the entity. In addition, there is no requirement for the accountant to verify the accuracy or completeness of the information provided by management or otherwise gather evidence to express an opinion or a conclusion on the financial statements or otherwise report on the financial statements. As a practicality measure, accountants in government who are members of the AICPA should apply ET Section 2.320.001 (Accounting Principles Rule), wherever possible, even though they may not be expressing an opinion. ET Section 2.320.001.01 states: "A *member* shall not (1) express an opinion or state affirmatively that the *financial statements* or other financial data of any entity are presented in conformity with generally accepted accounting principles or (2) state that he or she is not aware of any material modifications that should be made to such statements or data in order for them to be in conformity with generally accepted accounting principles, if such statements or data contain any departure from an accounting principle promulgated by bodies designated by *Council* to establish such principles that has a material effect on the statements or data taken as a whole. If, however, the statements or data contain such a departure and the *member* can demonstrate that due to unusual circumstances the *financial statements* or data would otherwise have been misleading, the *member* can comply with the rule by describing the departure, its approximate effects, if practicable, and the reasons why compliance with the principle would result in a misleading statement." For protection and to comply with ARC Section 70, accountants should include an indication on each page of the financial statements that they prepare where it is known that the financial statements will be given to an independent auditor, at a minimum, "no assurance is provided" on the financial statements. If the accountant is not able to include such a statement, the accountant should issue a disclaimer that makes clear that no assurance is provided or perform a compilation engagement.

INTRODUCTORY SECTION

Generally, the introductory section of the CAFR contains items such as a title page, a table of contents, a letter of transmittal, and other material deemed appropriate by management. A letter of transmittal is a cover letter that summarizes the basis for the financial report, highlights financial activity for the period, and may refer to other significant events that have occurred during the period. The letter may contain a translation document that records the differences between any budgetary presentation that citizens, executives, and legislative members may more readily understand and U.S. GAAP showing the fluctuation between a legal basis of accounting and U.S. GAAP. The letter is usually addressed to the chief executive of the governmental unit, the legislative body, or the citizens of the government, and it is usually signed by the chief financial officer of the state or local government that prepared the CAFR.

OBSERVATION: The GASB's *Implementation Guide 2015-1*, question 7.5.2, as amended by GASB *Implementation Guide Update 2016-1*, paragraph 5.10 [GASB Cod. Sec. 2200.704-1], discusses how the GASB encourages governmental entities not to report information in the letter of transmittal of the CAFR that is included in the MD&A section of the basic financial statements. Duplication can be minimized by making a brief reference to an item in the letter of transmittal with an appropriate reference to the further discussion of the item in the MD&A. A governmental entity has significant flexibility in determining what should be included in the letter of transmittal because there are no U.S. GAAP rules that apply to it.

Although most governments intend for their CAFR's transmittal letter to be devoid of political or marketing statements, some governments use the transmittal letter to tout various achievements, services, and things that make a particular government stand out. As discussed in question 7.5.2 [GASB Cod. Sec. 2200.704-1], the transmittal letter provides a forum for government officials to discuss plans and other information that may not meet the criteria of GASB-34, paragraph 11(h) [GASB Cod. Sec. 2200.109(h)], which requires discussion of "currently known facts, decisions or conditions." Hence, there is no U.S. GAAP and no auditing of transmittal letters beyond articulating whether data contained within the letter reiterates other financial information contained elsewhere within the CAFR or the government's other financial data. For example, the transmittal letter is a good place to include a summary of service efforts and accomplishments information (NCGA-1, par. 139, as amended by GASB-6, par. 25, GASB-34, fn.7) [GASB Cod. Sec. 2200.105, fn.7].

FINANCIAL SECTION

The financial section of the CAFR includes the auditor's report, MD&A, the basic financial statements, RSI (other than the MD&A), and supplementary information (NCGA-1, par. 139, as amended by GASB-6, par. 25, GASB-34) [GASB Cod. Sec. 2200.105].

Auditor's Report

Generally accepted auditing standards (GAAS) and in certain cases *Government Auditing Standards*, issued by the comptroller general of the United States of

America (GAGAS), are applicable to audits of governmental entities performed by an independent auditor. The independent auditors report on the fair presentation of the reporting entity's various opinion units as defined in the AICPA's Audit and Accounting Guide for *State and Local Governments*. Various types of audit reports may be found in CCH's *Knowledge-Based Audits™ of State and Local Governments with Single Audits*, Chapters 12 (Auditor's Reports—GAAS) and 24 (Auditor's Reports Required by the Single Audit—GAGAS).

Management's Discussion and Analysis (MD&A)

The basic financial statements should be *preceded* by management's discussion and analysis (MD&A), which the GASB classified as required supplementary information (RSI). MD&A information should "provide an objective and easily readable analysis of the government's financial activities based on currently known facts, decisions, or conditions." The MD&A discusses information on all activities of the government, addressing both governmental activities and business-type activities, the major funds activities and results of operations in comparison to prior periods, capital asset and debt transactions, budgetary activity and other elements.

For the purposes of the MD&A, *currently known facts* generally includes information that the government is *aware of* as of the date of the auditor's report. As explained in the GASB *Implementation Guide 2015-1*, question 7.5.13 [GASB Cod. Sec. 2200.704-11], the key word is *known* and therefore it should not be speculative. Typically, these events or decisions should have already occurred or have been enacted, adopted, agreed upon, or contracted. Governments should not discuss in MD&A the possible effect of events that might happen as that would be speculative. If a government wants to discuss speculative matters, they could be addressed in the letter of transmittal. The question discusses things that might be included in an MD&A that might have a significant effect on financial position or results of operations, if known such as:

- The award and acceptance of a major grant,
- The adjudication of a significant lawsuit,
- A significant change in the property tax base,
- The completion of an agreement to locate a major manufacturing plant in a city,
- An adopted increase in a state's sales tax rate,
- An approved increase in a university's tuition,
- A flood that caused significant damage to a government's infrastructure, and
- A renegotiated labor contract with government.

On the other hand, predicting how much sales tax revenues would increase if a planned shopping mall is built or that a data-processing system under consideration "will pay for itself" over a certain period of time would be examples of statements that are not based on currently known facts, decisions, or conditions and therefore, best discussed in the transmittal letter.

In some instances, issues discussed in MD&A as "currently known facts" will also be disclosed in the notes to the financial statements as subsequent events or contingencies. The discussion in MD&A should highlight but not repeat the information required to be disclosed in the notes.

Information in the MD&A should provide a broad overview of both the short-term and long-term analyses of the government's activities based on information presented in the financial report and fiscal policies that have been adopted by the governmental entity. Although the analysis provided by management should be directed to current-year results in comparison with the previous year's results, the emphasis should be on the current year. The MD&A presentation should not be viewed as a public relations opportunity for the governmental entity but rather should be based on factual information and incorporate both positive and negative developments. In an attempt to make the information meaningful and understandable to constituents of the governmental entity, it may be appropriate to use graphs, multiple-color presentations, or other presentation strategies that might provide insight into the analysis (GASB-34, pars. 8–9) [GASB Cod. Secs. 2200.106–.107, fns. 6–7].

The MD&A information should focus on the primary government's activities (both governmental and business-type activities) and distinguish between its activities and the government's discretely presented component units. Professional judgment must be exercised to determine whether MD&A should include comments related to a specific discretely presented component unit. Factors that may be relevant in making that determination include the relationship between the component unit and the primary government and the significance of the component unit in comparison to all discretely presented component units. In some instances, it may be appropriate to refer readers to the separately presented financial statements of the component unit (GASB-34, par. 10) [GASB Cod. Sec. 2200.108]. Finally, the MD&A should answer the common question through each element: "why?" For example, "The overall balance of capital assets increased due to the initiation of construction on the new wing of the Castle Rock County offices, offset by normal end-of-life disposals and accumulated depreciation."

The GASB emphasizes that management of the governmental entity should see the MD&A section of the financial report as an opportunity to communicate with interested parties, and it warns against preparing boilerplate material that adds little insight into the financial position and activity of the government. However, this emphasis on flexibility by the GASB is tempered in that, at a minimum, the following issues should be discussed (GASB-34, par. 11) [GASB Cod. Sec. 2200.109]:

    a. Brief discussion of the basic financial statements;

    b. Presentation of condensed financial information;

    c. Analysis of the overall financial position and results of operations;

    d. Analysis of balances and transactions of individual funds;

    e. Analysis of significant budget variations;

    f. Discussion of significant capital assets and long-term debt activity;

g. Discussion of modified depreciation approach (if employed by the governmental entity); and

h. Description of currently known facts, decisions, or conditions.

PRACTICE POINT: The (a)–(h) listing *contains the minimum*, not the maximum elements to be included in the MD&A. Governments can provide additional details on the above topics in (a)–(h). Information that does not relate to those topics is likely provided elsewhere, including the transmittal letter or other supplementary information and should not be in the MD&A (GASB-37, par. 4) [GASB Cod. Sec. 2200.fn8].

PRACTICE ALERT: The effectiveness of the MD&A is one of the focus areas of the GASB's *Financial Reporting Model—Reexamination project*. The GASB may explore options to enhance the MD&A, including consideration of elimination of requirements that result in boilerplate language. Some elements may be deemed no longer necessary for understanding the financial reporting model. The GASB may also clarify guidance for presenting currently known facts, decisions, or conditions that are expected to have a significant effect on financial position or results of operations (GASB-34, par. 11(h)).

The GASB's *Implementation Guide 2015.1,* questions 7.5.4 and 7.5.6 [GASB Cod. Secs. 2200.704-3, 704-4], discuss when a government with both governmental and business-type activities may present *comparative* data (inclusive of total reporting entity columns for the current and a previous year) in its basic financial statements.

MD&A is not required for the previous year's presentation because that presentation does not constitute a complete set of financial statements (basic financial statements, notes, and RSI). On the other hand, most governmental entities do not present comparative financial statements (basic financial statements, notes, and RSI for two years) because of the complexity of such presentations; however, if comparative financial statements are presented, MD&A must be presented for each year. That does not mean that there must be two completely separate MD&A presentations. Question 7.5.4 requires, when comparative financial statements are presented, *three years* of comparative information should be presented in the MD&A—the current year, the prior year, and the year preceding the prior year. The analysis only needs to cover two years—from the year preceding the prior year to the prior year and from the prior year to the current year.

Condensed financial information in MD&A for both years could be presented on a comparative basis with the analysis of the overall financial position and results of operations for each year included in the same paragraph or section. Governmental entities that might have the space to present comparative financial statements include governments that have a single program or a business-type activities only entity.

The MD&A presentations, because they are RSI, should be limited to the eight elements listed above. For example, service efforts and accomplishments (SEA) or performance data *should not* be presented as a separate category (because it is not listed as such in the "a through h" listing). However, SEA or performance data could be introduced in a "listed" category if that information helps to explain the required MD&A. That is, performance data could be discussed in item c if it clarifies why certain operating results change from one year to the next. If it is concluded that it is inappropriate to include an item in MD&A, that information could be included in supplementary information or the letter of transmittal. The degree of detail related to the eight elements will vary from governmental entity to governmental entity. At a minimum, however, the specific requirements addressed in these elements, and described below, must be presented in MD&A.

Some readers of GASB-34 interpreted this requirement to mean that MD&A had to include at least these eight components (a through h) but that a financial statement preparer was free to add other components. GASB-37 discusses how the language in paragraph 11 should have been interpreted to mean that "the information presented should be confined to the topics discussed in a through h."

OBSERVATION: GASB-34, as amended by GASB-37, par. 4, encourages governments to avoid "boilerplate" discussions within the MD&A and only report the most relevant financial information. A frequent complaint of users of financial statements is that boilerplate information is used too often in the MD&A Preparers of the MD&A should take the MD&A seriously and focus on it as the primary communication tool to users of financial statements and decision-makers.

Discussion of the Basic Financial Statements

The MD&A information should include a description of the basic financial statements and how the government-wide financial statements relate to the fund financial statements. This discussion should explain how fund financial statements either "reinforce information in government-wide statements or provide additional information." Topics that may be included in this section of MD&A may include the following:

- The broad scope and overall perspective of government-wide financial statements (statement of net position and the statement of activities);

- The nature of major fund financial statements for governmental funds (balance sheet and statement of revenues, expenditures, and changes in fund balances) and proprietary fund activities (statement of net position, statement of revenues, expenses, and changes in fund net position, and statement of cash flows); and

- The fiduciary role of the governmental entity and the nature of the related financial statements (statement of fiduciary net position and statement of changes in fiduciary net position).

The GASB's *Implementation Guide 2015-1*, questions 7.5.9 and 7.57.3 [GASB Cod. Secs. 2200.704-7 and .730-4], discuss aspects of how the totals in the government-wide financial statements will generally not equal the totals in the fund financial statements, because different measurement focuses and bases of accounting are used to prepare the financial statements. For this reason, GASB-34 (par. 77) [GASB Cod. Sec. 2200.160], requires that at the bottom of the fund financial statements or in a separate schedule there be a summary reconciliation between the fund financial statements and the government-wide financial statements. Specifically, the amount shown as the "total fund balances" in the "total governmental funds" column on the fund balance sheets must be reconciled to the "net position" for governmental activities presented on the statement of net position. Also, the amount shown as "net changes in fund balance" in the "total governmental funds" column on the statements of revenues, expenditures, and changes in fund balances must be reconciled to the "changes in net position" for governmental activities presented on the statement of activities. Requirement 11(a) focuses on the same concept as paragraph 77, but MD&A should provide only an overview of the differences, and that overview should be in a narrative form. If the totals on the government-wide financial statements and fund financial statements are essentially the same, MD&A should note that they are similar.

Presentation of Condensed Financial Information

The MD&A information should include *condensed* government-wide financial statements and comments on the significant changes from the previous year to the current year, not an entire copy of the basic financial statements in the MD&A. The condensed presentation should include information, at a minimum, that supports the analysis of the overall financial position and results of operations (which is the next topic discussed below). GASB-34, par. 11(b) [GASB Cod. Sec. 2200.109(b)] contains a list of the condensed information elements in the MD&A, which includes the following:

- Total assets, distinguishing between capital and other assets;
- Total liabilities, distinguishing between long-term debt outstanding and other liabilities;
- Total net position, distinguishing between amounts presented as the net investment in capital assets, restricted amounts, and unrestricted amounts;
- Total program revenues (by major sources);
- General revenues (by major sources);
- Total revenues;
- Program expenses (by functional category, at a minimum);
- Total expenses;
- Excess (deficiency) before contributions to term and permanent endowments or permanent fund principal, special and extraordinary items, and transfers;
- Contributions;
- Extraordinary and special items;

- Transfers;
- Change in net position; and
- Beginning and ending net position.

OBSERVATION: The use of the term "major sources" by GASB-34 is important. "Major sources" is undefined in U.S. GAAP, but is generally construed by preparers to mean greater than 10% of each particular accounting element.

OBSERVATION: Presentation of a segment does not mean that separate management's discussions and analyses (MD&A) are presented. The MD&A should present aggregated information. GASB-34, does not specifically mention aggregation in the MD&A, but presentation of more than one MD&A would lead to confusion.

The GASB's *Implementation Guide 2015-1*, question 7.5.10 [GASB Cod. Sec. 2200.704-8], discusses how paragraph 9 of GASB-34 encourages the use of charts and graphs in the MD&A, comparison of condensed financial information should not be presented as charts and graphs; however, charts and graphs may be used to elaborate on the presentation of the condensed information.

Analysis of the Overall Financial Position and Results of Operations

There should be an analysis of the overall improvement or deterioration of financial position and results of operations of the governmental entity based on government-wide financial statements. The analysis should focus on both governmental activities and business-type activities. The emphasis on the comments about the condensed government-wide financial statements should be analytical and not just computational. For example, percentage changes from the previous year to the current year should be supplemented with a discussion of important economic factors, such as interest rate changes and changes in regional economic activity, which affected the governmental entity's operating results for the year.

Analysis of Balances and Transactions of Individual Funds

Part of MD&A should concentrate on significant changes in balances and transactions that are related to individual funds. Information concerning the availability of resources for future use should be discussed, taking into consideration restrictions, commitments, and other factors.

Analysis of Significant Budget Variations

The analysis of budgetary information should focus on significant differences between (1) the original budget and the final budget and (2) actual budgetary results and the final budget. The commentary should include analysis of currently known reasons that are expected to have a significant effect on future services or liquidity.

OBSERVATION: The GASB's *Implementation Guide 2015-1*, question 7.5.11 [GASB Cod. Sec. 2200.704-9], discusses in part how the MD&A should not merely point out the obvious. For example, stating that there was an increase from the original budget in order to "cover higher-than-expected expenditures" is not helpful. The analysis should explain what factors led to the increase in expenditures. For example, a record snowfall total for the year increased the need for snow-and ice-clearing appropriations for the department of public works.

OBSERVATION: The analyses portions of the MD&A should not be taken lightly as the analyses should answer the question "why." All too often, practitioners perform the analysis by stating that a balance increased or decreased from the prior year, without answering the question "why." In many instances, the practitioner may state a balance increased, when in fact, it decreased or vice versa. In some instances, analysis is copied from a peer government, with editing not performed to remove that government's name, or the text has no bearing on the element being analysed. Governments should take the time to properly perform the analyses sections of the MD&A as it usually is a focus area of the users of the financial statements.

Discussion of Significant Capital Assets and Long-Term Debt Activity

MD&A information should describe activity that affected capital assets and long-term debt during the period. The discussion should include commitments for capital expenditures, changes in credit ratings, and whether debt limitations may affect future planned activities. In this analysis there is no need to repeat the information that is contained in the notes to the financial statements that relate to capital assets and long-term liabilities; however, the information may be presented in a summary form.

The GASB's *Implementation Guide 2015-1,* question 7.5.12 [GASB Cod. Sec. 2200.704-10], exempts special assessment debt from discussion in the MD&A when the governmental entity is not obligated in any manner (as described in GASB-6 (*Accounting and Financial Reporting for Special Assessments*)). However, the *Guide* notes that special assessment debt may be included in the MD&A discussion "if, for example, the proceeds were used to build or acquire significant infrastructure assets for the government." (See Chapter 19, "Special Assessments," for an additional discussion on such debt.)

PRACTICE POINT: As stated previously, governments often copy information available elsewhere into the MD&A (e.g., tables in the notes to the basic financial statements related to capital assets and long-term debt activity. Again, this is not proper. The term "significant" is heavily used in U.S. GAAP, but is largely undefined. For auditing purposes, "significant" usually means less than qualitatively material (which is defined as the point where a misstatement is possible relative to size and nature) and more than insignificant (an item of a clearly inconsequential nature).

Discussion of Modified Depreciation Approach (If Employed by the Governmental Entity)

As discussed earlier, a governmental entity may choose not to depreciate certain "eligible" infrastructure assets but rather may use the modified approach. For governments that use the modified approach, the MD&A information should discuss the following:

- Any significant changes in the assessed level of condition of eligible infrastructure assets from previous condition assessments;

- A comparison of the current level of asset condition with the condition level that the government has established; and

- Any significant difference between the actual amounts spent to maintain the current level and condition and the estimated annual amount needed to maintain or preserve eligible infrastructure assets at an appropriate level of condition.

OBSERVATION: The nation's aging infrastructure has brought into focus the issue of deferred maintenance disclosure. The modified approach has some aspects of an assessment of deferred maintenance; however, it is not widely used. It is also one of the areas that may be reexamined as part of the GASB's *Financial Reporting Model—Reexamination* project. Many users of financial statements have commented to the GASB that this issue should be explored. For example, common interest realty associations (CIRAs) (commonly known as condominium associations) operate similarly to governments and even use funds. CIRAs often present disclosure of the level of deferred maintenance in the complex and are required to present supplementary information on funding renewals and replacements. For governments, the level of deferred maintenance may be a large unrecorded future obligation. Therefore, it may be beneficial to the users of the government's financial statements to disclose estimates of deferred maintenance by type of infrastructure (roads, dams, bridges, etc.) that are disclosed elsewhere in engineering reports to decision-makers. This may be accomplished by a table in the MD&A.

For example, the City of San Jose, California disclosed the following in a recent report from the City's Transportation and Environment Committee to the City Council, which could be used in an MD&A as long as the disclosure is auditable:

Infrastructure Backlog (amounts in thousands):

Program	Current Backlog of Deferred Needs	Annual Ongoing Unfunded Needs
Airport	$14,814	$12,750
Buildings	121,000	17,830
City Facilities Operated by Others	8,800	TBD
Convention Center and Cultural Facilities	17,500	TBD
Fleet	8,000	1,900
Parks, Pools and Open Space	122,841	30,590

Sanitary Sewer	TBD	5,700
Service Yards	17,000	2,900
Storm Sewer	30,000	TBD
Information Technology	5,171	2,972
Transportation Infrastructure	646,900	100,500
Total	**$992,026**	**$175,142**

Description of Currently Known Facts, Decisions, or Conditions

MD&A should describe currently known facts, decisions, or conditions that are expected to have a significant effect on the entity's financial position (net position) and operations results (revenues, expenses, and other changes in net position). GASB-34 emphasizes that currently known facts do not constitute prospective information, such as forecasted financial statements.

> **OBSERVATION:** As discussed previously, the GASB's *Implementation Guide 2015-1*, question 7.5.13 [GASB Cod. Sec. 2200.704-11], clarifies how currently known facts must be based on events that have taken place. This aspect is also the most commonly overlooked requirement in an MD&A. Many preparers insert that the government has passed a budget for the next fiscal period. Nearly every government has some currently known facts and conditions at the date of the financial statements that are qualitative as well as quantitative. For example, gain or loss of a major employer, restructuring of operations, pension or OPEB plan, major change in taxation or other revenues, status of a large construction project or the anticipated level of deferred maintenance are all potential currently known facts and conditions that could be inserted into an MD&A.

Basic Financial Statements

GASB-34 lists the following as the components of a governmental entity's basic financial statements (NCGA-1, par. 139, as amended by GASB-6, par. 25, GASB-34) [GASB Cod. Sec. 2200.105):

- Government-wide financial statements;
- Fund financial statements; and
- Notes to the basic financial statements.

GASB-34 provides that the required budgetary comparison schedules may be presented as a component of the basic financial statements rather than as RSI. However in practice, most practitioners include budgetary information as part of RSI. When the budgetary comparison schedules are presented as a basic financial statement, the schedules should be reported within the governmental fund financial statements and they are subjected to a different level of auditing than as RSI.

Government-Wide Financial Statements

The focus of government-wide financial statements is on the overall financial position and activities of the government as a whole. These financial statements are constructed around the concept of a primary government as defined by

GASB-14 (*The Financial Reporting Entity*), as amended by GASB-39 and GASB-61, and therefore encompass the primary government and its component units, except for fiduciary funds of the primary government and component units that are fiduciary in nature. Financial statements of fiduciary funds are not presented in the government-wide financial statements but are included in the fund financial statements (GASB-34, par. 13).

PRACTICE ALERT: The financial statements of Fiduciary Funds are excluded from government-wide financial statements because resources of these funds cannot be used to finance a governmental entity's activities. The financial statements of a Fiduciary Fund are included in the entity's fund financial statements because the governmental entity is financially accountable for those resources even though they belong to other parties. The GASB has issued Statement No. 84 (*Fiduciary Activities*). For a complete discussion on GASB-84 and the effects of implementation for periods beginning after December 15, 2018, see Chapter 8, "Fiduciary Funds."

The GASB believes that government-wide financial statements provide user groups with the following (GASB-34, par. 12, as amended by GASB-63, pars. 7 and 8) [GASB Cod. Sec. 2200.110]:

- Present financial information about the overall government without presenting information about individual funds or fund types;

- Exclude financial information about fiduciary activities;

- Differentiate between financial information that applies to the primary government and that of discretely presented component units;

- Differentiate between the primary government's governmental activities and business-type activities; and

- Measure and present all financial balances and activities based on the economic resources measurement focus and the accrual basis of accounting.

PRACTICE POINT: A governmental entity cannot simply issue only government-wide financial statements or only fund financial statements and deem them a complete set of financial statements. However, the reporting requirements for certain special-purpose governments are somewhat different, as described in GASB-34. In addition, generally governments cannot combine the government-wide and fund financial statements; however, single-program governments may combine the government-wide and fund financial statements. This exception is discussed in GASB-34 (GASB-34, pars. 129, 138, 139, as amended by GASB-63, par. 8) [GASB Cod. Secs. Sp20.107–.108].

In order to achieve some of the objectives listed above, GASB-34 requires that government-wide financial statements be formatted following these guidelines (GASB-34, pars. 14–15) [GASB Cod. Secs. 2200.112–.113]:

- Separate rows and columns should be used to distinguish between the primary government's governmental activities and business-type activities.

- A total column should be used for the primary government.

- Separate rows and columns should distinguish between the total primary government (governmental activities plus business-type activities) and its discretely presented component units.

- A total column may be used for the reporting entity (primary government and discretely presented component units), but this is optional.

- A total column may be used for prior-year information, but this is optional.

GASB-34, paragraph 15, describes how governmental activities are "generally financed through taxes, intergovernmental revenues, and other nonexchange revenues," and business-type activities are financed to some degree by charging external parties for the goods or services they acquire. Governmental activities are generally accounted for in governmental funds and Internal Service Funds. Business-type activities are usually reported in Enterprise Funds.

A total column should be used to combine the governmental activities and the business-type activities of a governmental entity. A separate column that combines the government and its component units (discretely presented) may or may not be used. However, if a separate column is used, it should not be titled "memorandum only." The "memorandum only" columnar heading is appropriate only when columns with different measurement focuses and bases of accounting are added together. The government-wide financial statements are based on a single measurement focus and basis of accounting.

The government-wide financial statements have separate columns for governmental activities and business-type activities. In general, governmental funds are combined to form the governmental activities column and Enterprise Funds are combined to form the business-type activities column; however, an activity and a fund are not the same. An "activity" refers to a program or service but a "fund" is an accounting and reporting vehicle. For this reason, an activity (governmental or business-type) could be performed in one or more funds, and a fund could perform one or more activities. For example, an Enterprise Fund could perform an activity that is governmental, rather than business, in nature and that activity should be presented in the governmental activities column in the government-wide financial statements. If this occurs, the activity would represent a reconciling item between the fund financial statements and the government-wide financial statements as required by GASB-34, paragraph 77 [GASB Cod. Sec. 2200.160].

As a reminder, the GASB's *Implementation Guide 2015-1* points out that GASB-34 *does not require* that comparative prior-year data be presented but that it *may* be presented. For this reason, GASB-34 provides no guidelines for the presentation of prior-year data. Presenting comparative data in governmental financial statements, as opposed to corporate financial statements, is very problematic because of the complicated structure of governmental statements. For example, reporting a comparative statement of net position for many governmental entities requires eight columns or more. Trying to format a statement of activities for many governmental entities would probably be too unwieldy. If a governmental entity is not a complex reporting entity (e.g., if it has only governmental activities and no component units), presenting prior-year data might not be cumbersome. The GASB'S *Guide* points out that for more complicated reporting entities the best way to present prior-year data may be by reproducing the prior-year financial statements in the current-year's financial statements.

PRACTICE POINT: Some of these presentation provisions are not applicable to entities that are subjected to regulatory accounting, such as public utilities and insurance entities. The provisions of GASB-62, pars. 476–500 [GASB Cod. Sec. Re10], include provisions for entities subject to regulatory accounting provisions. The provisions primarily stem from the former FAS-71 as it existed prior to November 31, 1989. (Now codified as FASB Accounting Standards Codification® (ASC) Topic 980, *Regulated Operations*, but significantly amended since then.) Regulatory accounting is discussed in Chapter 24, "Other Special-Purpose Governments."

The flow of economic resources measurement focus and accrual accounting (which are the concepts upon which commercial enterprises prepare their financial statements) are the basis upon which government-wide financial statements are prepared. Under the flow of economic resources measurement focus and accrual basis of accounting, revenues are recognized when earned and expenses are recorded when incurred when these activities are related to exchange and exchange-like activities. In addition, long-lived assets (such as buildings and equipment) are capitalized and depreciated over their estimated economic lives (GASB-34, pars. 6 and 16) [GASB Cod. Secs. 2200.102, .114].

Unlike commercial enterprises, much of the revenue received by governments is not based on an exchange or an exchange-like transaction (i.e., the selling of a product or service and receiving something of approximate equal value) but rather arises from the entity's taxing powers or as grants from other governmental entities or individuals (nonexchange transactions). For these nonexchange transactions, the standards established by GASB-33 (*Accounting and Financial Reporting for Nonexchange Transactions*) are used.

The government-wide financial statements include the following:

- Statement of net position; and
- Statement of activities.

NOTE: A government-wide statement of cash flows is not required.

Statement of Net Position

GASB-63 *Financial Reporting of Deferred Outflows of Resources, Deferred Inflows of Resources, and Net Position* introduced a Statement of Net Position for all accrual basis financial statements. The formula for deriving a statement of net position is as follows:

$$Assets$$
$$+ Deferred\ Outflows\ of\ Resources$$
$$- Liabilities$$
$$- Deferred\ Inflows\ of\ Resources$$
$$= Net\ Position$$

Net position is comprised of net investment in capital assets, restricted net position and unrestricted net position.

Although the GASB recommends that the net position format be adopted for the statement of net position, the GASB does not prohibit formatting the statement so that a net position section (equity) is presented whereby total assets plus deferred outflows of resources equals total liabilities plus deferred inflows of resources plus the residual balance. Irrespective of how the statement of net position is formatted, the difference between total assets and total liabilities must be referred to as "net position" rather than "fund balances" or "equity" (GASB-34, par. 30, as amended by GASB-63, pars. 7 and 8, GASB-62, par. 501 and fn. 232) [GASB Cod. Sec. 2200.115].

Presentation of Assets, Deferred Outflows of Resources, Liabilities and Deferred Inflows of Resources

Assets, deferred outflows of resources, liabilities, and deferred inflows of resources should be presented in the statement of net position based on their relative liquidity. The liquidity of assets is determined by their ability to be converted to cash and the absence of any restriction that might limit their conversion to cash. The liquidity of liabilities is based on maturity dates or expected payment dates. Because of the significant degree of aggregation used in the preparation of government-wide financial statements, the GASB notes that the liquidity of an asset or liability account presented in the statement of net position should be determined by assessing the average liquidity of the class of assets or liabilities to which it belongs, "even though individual balances may be significantly more or less liquid than others in the same class and some items may have both current and long-term element" (GASB-34, par. 31) [GASB Cod. Sec. 2200.116].

Most governmental entities prepare an unclassified statement of net position that lists assets based on their liquidity. Alternatively, GASB-34 notes that assets, deferred outflows of resources, liabilities, and deferred inflows of resources may be presented in the statement of net position using a classified financial statement format whereby accounts are grouped in current and noncurrent categories similar to the presentation used by business enterprises (GASB-34, fn. 23, as amended by GASB-63, par. 8) [GASB Cod. Sec. 2200.fn13].

Neither GASB-63, GASB-65, nor Concepts Statement 4 (GASB:CS-4) (which introduced the elements of deferred outflows of resources and deferred inflows of resources) discussed whether there is a possibility of a current portion of a deferred outflow of resources or a deferred inflow of resources. Because these are now presented in separate sections in the statement of net position, it is not proper to commingle these with other assets or liabilities even if a classified statement of net position is used.

When a governmental entity presents a classified statement of net position, the question arises as to whether the amount that represents restricted net position (in the equity section) requires that specific assets be identified as "restricted assets" (in the asset section). In preparing financial statements, there is no general requirement that specific equity accounts be traceable to specific assets. Therefore, when a classified statement of net position is presented, there is no need to establish a subcategory of assets identified as restricted; however, a financial statement preparer should carefully evaluate the ramifications of restrictions to determine whether they are determinant in categorizing an asset as current or noncurrent.

GASB-62 notes that current assets should not include "cash and claims to cash that are restricted as to withdrawal or use for other than current operations, are designated for expenditure in the acquisition or construction of noncurrent assets, or are segregated for the liquidation of long-term debt." The GASB's *Implementation Guide 2015-1*, question 7.22.2 [GASB Cod. Sec. 2200.708-2], states that "resources accounted for in the General Fund, Special Revenue Funds, and Debt Service Funds are generally expected to be used in current operations or to liquidate current obligations and thus generally would be considered current assets." On the other hand, cash presented in a Capital Projects Fund or a Permanent Fund, due to the nature of each fund type, should be evaluated to determine whether the amount or a portion of the amount should be reported as a current or noncurrent asset.

The AICPA's Audit and Accounting Guide *State and Local Governments* addresses the issue of how "assets restricted for debt retirement [that] include amounts due from other funds" should be reported in the statement of net position. For example, the assets of a Debt Service Fund may include an amount due from the General Fund. When all governmental funds are consolidated to create the government activities column in the statement of net position, the interfund receivable and payable are eliminated, but care must be taken that the implied restriction on cash for debt retirement is considered when a classified statement of net position is prepared (differentiating between current and noncurrent assets) and when an unclassified statement of net position is prepared (listing assets based on their liquidity).

Once individual liabilities are grouped into titles for financial statement presentation, account groupings that have an average maturity of greater than one year must be reported in two components—the portion due within one year and the portion due beyond one year. For example, if several individual general ledger accounts have been grouped for financial statement purposes in the account titled "notes payable" and on average this grouping has an average maturity greater than one year, the presentation on the statement of net position could appear as follows:

Partial Statement of Net Position	
Liabilities	
Notes Payable:	
Due within one year	$1,000,000
Due beyond one year	6,000,000

If several liability groupings have an average maturity life beyond one year, the detail information by account title (e.g., notes payable, bonds payable) does not have to be made on the face of the statement of net position but rather may be presented in a note to the financial statements with appropriate reference.

The GASB's *Implementation Guide 2015-1*, question 7.22.4 [GASB Cod. Sec. 2200.708-4], discusses how a governmental entity must make an estimate of compensated absences that may be paid within one year based on factors such as (1) historical experience, (2) budgeted amounts, and (3) personnel policies concerning the length of accumulation.

The governmental entity should report all of its capital assets in the statement of net position, based on their original historical cost plus ancillary charges such as transportation, installation, and site preparation costs. Capital assets that have been donated to a governmental entity must be capitalized at their estimated fair value (plus any ancillary costs) at the date of receipt. Capital assets are discussed in Chapter 10, "Capital Assets."

The liquidity of assets is determined by their ability to be converted to cash and the absence of any restriction that might limit their conversion to cash. If an asset is restricted, the nature of the restriction must be evaluated to determine the appropriate location within the asset classification. The following are common examples of how restrictions would affect asset presentation:

- *Cash restricted for the servicing of debt.*   If the cash is expected to be used to pay "current maturities," the cash could be reported with unrestricted cash.

- *Permanently restricted assets.*   If assets are permanently restricted, they are not available to pay a governmental entity's expenses and are therefore as illiquid as capital assets.

- *Term restrictions.*   The term of the restriction determines where assets subject to term restrictions are presented. If the restriction ends within a short period after the date of the financial statements, the assets would be relatively liquid. On the other hand, if the time restriction is longer than one year, the assets are as illiquid as long-term receivables that have a similar "maturity" date.

Presentation of Long-Term Liabilities

In the government-wide financial statements, both short-term and long-term liabilities of a governmental entity are presented as described earlier. Long-term liabilities may include debts such as notes, mortgages, bonds, and obligations related to capitalized lease agreements. In addition, operating liabilities related to activities such as compensated absences and claims and assessments must be reported in the statement of net position.

Presentation of Components of Net Position

Net position represents the difference between a governmental entity's total assets plus its deferred outflows and its total liabilities plus its deferred inflows. The statement of net position must identify the components of net position, namely (1) net investment in capital assets, (2) restricted net position, and (3) unrestricted net position.

PRACTICE POINT: The GASB's *Implementation Guide 2015-1*, question 7.22.7 [GASB Cod. Sec. 7.22.7], specifically notes that other terms, such as "equity," "net worth," and "fund balance" should not be used in the statement of net position.

Net Investment in Capital Assets

The portion of net position consisting of net investment in capital assets includes capital assets of the government, net of accumulated depreciation. Accumulated depreciation also includes the amortization of intangible assets. The amount is further reduced by the outstanding balances of all forms of debt attributable to the improvement of those assets. Forms of debt issued for construction of assets for other governments or other operating borrowings are excluded.

Deferred outflows of resources and deferred inflows of resources that are attributable to the acquisition, construction, or improvement of those assets or related debt also should be included in this component of net position. If there are significant unspent related debt proceeds or deferred inflows of resources at the end of the reporting period, the portion of the debt or deferred inflows of resources attributable to the unspent amount should not be included in the calculation of net investment in capital assets. Instead, that portion of the debt or deferred inflow of resources should be included in the same net position component (restricted or unrestricted) as the unspent amount (GASB-63, par. 9, GASB-51, par. 5) [GASB Cod. Sec. 2200.118, fn. 14].

The GASB's *Implementation Guide 2015-1*, in questions 7.23.1–16 [GASB Cod. Secs. 2200.708-9–12, 709-10–15], makes the following observations about net investment in capital assets:

- All capital assets, regardless of any restrictions (e.g., federal surplus property), must be considered in the computation of net investment in capital assets. The purpose of identifying net position as restricted and unrestricted is to provide insight into the availability of *financial*, not capital, resources.

- As discussed, the net investment in capital assets component of net position consists of (1) capital assets, net of accumulated depreciation then (2) reduced by the outstanding balances of bonds, mortgages, notes, or other borrowings that are attributable to the acquisition, construction, or improvement of those assets. Deferred outflows of resources and deferred inflows of resources that are attributable to the acquisition, construction, or improvement of those assets or related debt should also be included in this component of net position. If there are significant unspent related debt proceeds or deferred inflows of resources at the end of the reporting period, the portion of the debt or deferred inflows of resources attributable to the unspent amount should not be included in the calculation of net investment in capital assets. Instead, that portion of the debt or deferred inflows of resources should be included in the same net position component (restricted or unrestricted) as the unspent amount—for example, *restricted for capital projects*.

- Many governmental entities create (1) a Capital Projects Fund to account for capital debt proceeds to be used to acquire, construct, or improve infrastructure assets and buildings (including land) and (2) specific accounts in the General Fund or other funds for capital debt proceeds to be used to acquire capital assets other than infrastructure assets. When these approaches are used, it is relatively simple to identify the unspent portion of capital debt proceeds. For those governmental entities that do not use these two approaches and commingle funds, they must "use their best estimates—in a manner that can be documented—to determine the unspent portion."

- When debt is issued to refund existing capital-related debt, the newly issued debt is considered capital-related and is used to compute the net investment in capital assets component.

OBSERVATION: *Implementation Guide Update 2016-1*, paragraph 5.14, which amended GASB *Implementation Guide*, question 7.23.6 [GASB Cod. Sec. 2200.709-6], discusses the effect of refunding existing capital-related debt on net investment in capital assets. Even though the direct connection between the capital assets and the debt issued to finance the construction or acquisition has been eliminated, the replace debt assumes the capital characteristics of the original issue. However, if the new issue is refunding capital appreciation debt, only the portion of the new debt that refunds the original principal of the old debt should be considered capital related.

- When a governmental entity has capital assets but no related debt, the net position component should be simply identified as "investment in capital assets."

- When a general purpose government issues bonds to construct school buildings for its independent school districts and the repayment of the bonds is the responsibility of the general purpose government, because the debt was not used to acquire, construct, or improve capital assets for the governmental entity, the outstanding debt is not capital-related and is not used to compute the amount of net investment in capital assets of the general purpose government. The effect is to reduce unrestricted net position. If doing so has a significant effect on the unrestricted net position component, the circumstances may be further explained in a note to the financial statements.

With the inclusion of deferred inflows of resources or deferred outflows of resources in the calculation of net investment in capital assets, borrowings become more important. For example, in a debt refunding transaction, the borrowing portion presumably is now included as part of related debt. Unamortized positions of up-front payments in hybrid derivative instruments related to debt issued to fund capital assets are also included in the calculation of net investment in capital assets. Some view securities lending transactions as borrowings; however, they would not be germane in the calculation of net investment in capital assets. The borrowings related to sales of future revenues would also not be germane, because they also do not involve capital assets—they involve receivables.

Restricted net position arises if either of the following conditions exists (GASB-34, par. 34, GASB-46, par. 6, as amended by GASB-63, pars. 8 and 10) [GASB Cod. Sec. 2200.119]:

- Externally imposed by creditor (such as through debt covenants), grantors, contributors, or laws or regulations of other governments; or

- Imposed by law through constitutional provisions or enabling legislation.

GASB-34 points out that enabling legislation "authorizes the government to assess, levy, charge, or otherwise mandate payment of resources (from external resource providers)" and includes a legally enforceable requirement that those resources be used only for the specific purposes stipulated in the legislation. Enabling legislation also commonly places restrictions on asset use in governmental utility operations, if the utility reports in accordance with a regulatory framework (GASB-34, fn. 25, as amended by GASB-62, pars. 476–500) [GASB Cod. Sec. 2200.fn16]. (Also see Chapter 24, "Other Special-Purpose Governments.")

GASB-46 defines "legal enforceability" as meaning that a government can be compelled by an external party—citizens, public interest groups, or the judiciary—to use resources created by enabling legislation only for the purposes specified by the legislation. However, enforceability cannot ultimately be proven unless tested through the judicial process; therefore, professional judgment must be exercised (GASB-46, par. 3) [GASB Cod. Sec. 2200.120].

When a state legislature passes a law to earmark a percentage of specific tax proceeds (e.g., a percent of its sales taxes) for a specific purpose, this is not the same as enabling legislation. The enabling-legislation criterion is satisfied only when the same law creates both the tax and the restriction on how the resulting resources may be used.

The specific purpose of the enabling legislation may be changed from time to time by the government. *From the point of change forward*, the resources accumulated under the new enabling legislation should be reported as restricted to the purpose specified by the new enabling legislation. Professional judgment should be used to determine if remaining balances accumulated under the original enabling legislation should continue to be reported as restricted for the original purpose, restricted to the purpose specified in the new legislation, or unrestricted (GASB-46, par. 4) [GASB Cod. Sec. 2200.121].

If there is a violation of the restriction established in the enabling legislation, or if the government reconsiders, the restriction needs to be reevaluated as it may no longer be enforceable. If it is determined that the restriction is no longer enforceable, then the balances are reclassed to unrestricted net position *from the beginning of the period* (GASB-46, par. 5) [GASB Cod. Sec. 2200.122].

Restricted net position should be identified based on major categories that make up the restricted balance. These categories could include items such as net position restricted for capital projects and net position restricted for debt service. Supporting details of restricted net position should be presented in the body of the financial statements and not in the notes to the financial statements.

The liabilities related to restricted assets must be considered in determining restricted net position as presented on the statement of net position. For example, the statement of net position would generally identify net assets restricted for capital projects. In order to determine that amount, the starting point would be to identify total net position (total assets and deferred outflows of resources less total liabilities and deferred inflows of resources) in all Capital Projects Funds. Additionally, because a Capital Projects Fund is on the modified accrual basis and the statement of net position is on the accrual basis, it would be necessary to take into consideration any "conversion" adjustments that would increase or decrease the liabilities in the Capital Projects Funds. However, a negative (deficit) balance in restricted net position cannot be displayed on the statement of net position. Any negative amount would be used to reduce the unrestricted net position balance.

In some instances, net position may be restricted on a permanent basis (in perpetuity). Under this circumstance, the restricted net position must be subdivided into expendable and nonexpendable restricted net position. This is common with permanent endowments such as land trusts, permanent fund principal amounts, minority interests in component units, and similar. (GASB-34, par. 35, as amended by GASB-61, par. 12, and GASB-63, par. 8) [GASB Cod. Sec. 2200.123].

GASB-34 points out that, generally, the amount of net position identified as restricted on the statement of net position will not be the same as the amount of restricted fund balance or restricted net position presented on the fund balance sheets/statement of net position because (1) the financial statements are based on different measurement focuses and bases of accounting and (2) there are different definitions for restricted net position and restricted fund balance. (Fund financial statements are discussed later.)

The GASB *Implementation Guide 2015-1*, questions 7.24.1-30 [GASB Cod. Secs. 2200.710-2–16, 711-1, 712-1–8], have the following common themes about restricted net position:

- Paragraph 34 of GASB-34 is the starting point for determining whether net position is restricted. In addition, in order to be considered restricted net position, the restriction must be narrower than the "reporting unit in which it is reported." For example, if the resources are restricted to "public safety," then the resources are considered to be restricted. On the other hand, if the resources are to be used "for the benefit of the citizens," that restriction is as broad as the governmental entity and there is effectively no restriction on net position.

- The requirements of paragraph 35 apply only to permanent endowments or permanent fund principal because restrictions imposed on term endowments will at some point be expendable.

- The liabilities related to restricted assets must be considered in determining restricted net position.

- Earmarking an existing revenue source is not the same as enabling legislation. The enabling legislation criterion is satisfied only when the same law creates a tax or other source of revenue and the restriction on how the resulting resources may be used.

Unrestricted Net Position

Assets that are not classified as net investment in capital assets or restricted are included in the category unrestricted net position. Portions of the entity's net position may be identified by management to reflect tentative plans or commitments of governmental resources. The tentative plans or commitments may be related to items such as plans to retire debt at some future date or to replace infrastructure or specified capital assets. Designated amounts are not the same as restricted amounts because designations represent planned actions, not actual commitments. For this reason, designated amounts should not be classified with restricted net position but rather should be reported as part of the unrestricted net position component. In addition, designations cannot be disclosed as such on the face of the statement of net position (GASB-34, pars. 36–37, as amended by GASB-54, pars. 10–16, GASB-63, pars. 8, 11) [GASB Cod. Secs. 2200.124–.125].

OBSERVATION: A common problem that occurred in implementing GASB-68 was the explanation of an unrestricted net deficit (negative unrestricted net position) to non-accountants. The problem will increase should a government have a OPEB liability with the implementation of GASB-75. The amount of a net pension and/or net OPEB liability may be very significant in comparison to the balance of unrestricted net position excluding pension and or OPEB amounts. Preparers should be very careful in the language that is used to explain the unrestricted net deficit. The *GASB Implementation Guide 2015-1*, question 7.23.10 [GASB Cod. Sec. 2200.708-12], discusses in part, how a preparer should notify users of the financial statements information related to such amounts that may mask other information due to the magnitude of the amounts. If the effect of the implementation of a GASB standard is *significant*, the GASB encourages additional details of unrestricted net position in the notes to the financial statements to isolate its effect. The government may also address these circumstances in the MD&A as part of either the net position or, in this case, the liabilities discussions. The author of this volume encourages governments to include this disclosure in both the notes to the financial statements *and* the MD&A if the effect is significant.

The statement of net position illustrated in this chapter (Exhibit 20-1) is unclassified and presented in accordance with GASB-34, as amended by GASB-63. Alternatively, GASB-34 notes that assets and liabilities *may be* presented in the statement of net position using a classified financial statement format whereby accounts are grouped in current and noncurrent categories similar to the presentation used by business enterprises. When a governmental entity presents a classified statement of net position, the question arises as to whether the amount that represents restricted net position (in the equity section) requires that specific assets be identified as "restricted assets" (in the asset section). In preparing financial statements there is no general requirement that specific equity accounts be traceable to specific assets. Therefore, when a classified statement of net position is presented there is no need to establish a subcategory of assets identified as restricted; however, a financial statement preparer should carefully evaluate the ramifications of restrictions to determine whether they are determinant in categorizing an asset as current or noncurrent. GASB-62 notes that current assets should not include "cash and claims to cash that are restricted as to withdrawal or use for other than current operations, are designated for expenditure in the acquisition or construction of noncurrent assets, or are segregated for the liquidation of long-term debt."

The GASB's *Implementation Guide 2015-1*, question 7.22.2 [GASB Cod. Sec. 2200.708-2], discusses how "resources accounted for in the General Fund, Special Revenue Funds, and Debt Service Funds are generally expected to be used in current operations or to liquidate current obligations and thus generally would be considered current assets." On the other hand, cash presented in a Capital Projects Fund or a Permanent Fund, due to the nature of each fund, should be evaluated to determine whether the amount or a portion of the amount should be reported as a current or noncurrent asset.

A fund with restrictions, such as a Special Revenue Fund, may include an asset balance that exceeds the requirements of the related restriction. Under this circumstance, the excess amount should be used to compute the amount of unrestricted net position. Furthermore, in this example involving a Special Revenue Fund, the fund itself would likely have a restricted fund balance, as well as either a committed or assigned fund balance for the excess portion in accordance with the provisions of GASB-54.

In some instances, a state statute may exist that requires that "revenues derived from a fee or charge shall not be used for any purpose other than that for which the fee or charge was imposed." Therefore, if a local government has imposed such a fee or charge (e.g. for the replacement of infrastructure assets), the unspent resources accumulated from the fee or charge represents a restricted net position (the equity account component).

A state legislature may change an existing law that previously restricted the use of tax revenue to a particular type of expenditure. Question 7.24.12 of the GASB *Implementation Guide 2015-1* [GASB Cod. Sec. 2200.712-2] clarifies that although "the new restriction is not established by the original enabling legislation, the net position arising from the changed legislation is nonetheless restricted for purposes of financial statement disclosure even though the new tax revenues are to be used for a purpose different from that identified in the original legislation."

A Special Revenue Fund may include resources that are unrestricted (e.g., a transfer from the General Fund) and resources that are restricted (e.g., revenues from a state shared motor fuel tax that must be used for street repair and maintenance). Because the resources (cash) are fungible, a revenue flow assumption must be made by the governmental identify to identify whether unrestricted or restricted resources are used first. U.S. GAAP allows either approach; however, the financial statements must disclose the accounting policy adopted.

Under some circumstances a governmental entity may report capital debt but not report the capital asset that was purchased with the debt proceeds. For example, the originally classified so-called Phase 3 governments were encouraged but not required to report major general infrastructure assets retroactively when they implemented GASB-34; however, the related debt had to be reported. Under this circumstance, the question arises as to whether the capital debt should be considered in determining the amount to be reported as net investment in capital assets. U.S. GAAP requires capital debt must be used to compute the amount of net investment in capital assets even though the related capital asset is not reported in the statement of net position. Furthermore, if the total capital debt is greater than the reported capital assets, the net investment in capital assets will have a negative (debit) balance; however, that negative amount must nonetheless be reported in the governmental entity statement of net position.

In some instances, a governmental entity may specifically restrict assets that are to be used to pay the current portion of bonds that were issued to finance the acquisition of capital assets. Even though the restricted assets are used to determine the amount of restricted net position, the related current portion of the maturing debt must be used to determine the amount of net investment in capital assets rather than restricted net position.

Costs related to the issuance of debt must be expensed and gains and losses related to the refunding of debt must be amortized. For reporting purposes, the unamortized portion of these accounts is used to determine the amount of the related net position based on the purpose of issuing the debt. For example, if debt was issued to finance the construction of a capital asset, any unamortized balances are used to compute the reported amount of net investment in capital assets. On the other hand, if debt was issued for a specific purpose and the proceeds have not been expended, the unamortized balances are used to determine the amount of restricted net position. If the debt was issued and the proceeds were not restricted, the unamortized balances are used to compute unrestricted net position.

Question 7.25.1 of the *GASB Implementation Guide 2015-1* [GASB Cod. Sec. 708-13] clarifies the effect of an equity interest in a joint venture in unrestricted net position. The investment does not reflect capital assets (1) held directly by the governmental entity or (2) restricted as defined in paragraph 34 of GASB-34 [GASB Cod. Sec. 2200.119]. Therefore, the unrestricted net position category is the default category. If an item does not qualify for classification as net investment in capital assets or restricted net position, then it must be classified as unrestricted net position.

EXHIBIT 20-1
CASTLE ROCK COUNTY
STATEMENT OF NET POSITION AS OF
DECEMBER 31, 20XX

	Primary Government			Component Units	
	Governmental Activities	Business-type Activities	Total Primary Government	Public Library	Public Health
Assets					
Cash, pooled cash and investments	$190,696,456	$5,840,364	$196,536,820	$13,708,926	$967,870
Taxes receivable	179,801,359	13,765	179,815,124	33,034,868	-
Other receivables	9,364,060	126,760	9,490,820	6,811	109,048
Internal balances	1,832,008	(1,832,008)	-	-	-
Due from other governments	7,687,432	434,692	8,122,124	-	1,541,129
Inventories	855,008	-	855,008	82,529	-
Other current assets	1,607,487	1,123	1,608,610	357,499	179,948
Assets held for resale	-	210,999	210,999	-	-
Depreciable capital assets and infrastructure, net	337,802,069	49,099,752	386,901,821	19,410,933	30,032
Land and non-depreciable infrastructure	687,407,377	13,828,215	701,235,592	1,248,056	-
Construction in Progress	56,969,903	33,364	57,003,267	-	315,482
Total assets	**1,474,023,159**	**67,757,026**	**1,541,780,185**	**67,849,622**	**3,143,509**
Deferred Outflows of Resources					
Refunding of debt, net	3,147,855	-	3,147,855		
Net difference between projected and actual investment earnings on pension plan Investments	838,320	-	838,320		
Employer contributions subsequent to measurement date of net pension liability	1,228,657	-	1,228,657		
Total deferred outflows of resources	**5,214,832**	**-**	**5,214,832**	**-**	**-**
Liabilities					
Accounts and retainage payable	9,714,676	188,581	9,903,257	192,209	191,741
Accrued salaries	10,383,670	82,170	10,465,840	716,469	537,750
Other accrued liabilities	2,649,577	91,288	2,740,865	-	100
Matured Bonds Interest payable	681,885	-	681,885		
Due to other governments	30	-	30		
Funds held in custody for others	374,038	-	374,038		
Advances from other governments	823,895	565,691	1,389,586	-	330,853
Net pension liability	8,179,594	-	8,179,594		
Noncurrent liabilities:					
Due within one year	19,675,791	259,028	19,934,819	101,888	102,623
Due in more than one year	148,544,346	516,722	149,061,068	854,569	532,261
Total liabilities	**201,027,502**	**1,703,480**	**202,730,982**	**1,865,135**	**1,695,328**
Deferred Inflow of Resources					
Unavailable property tax revenue	170,192,606	-	170,192,606	33,173,453	
Total deferred inflow of resources	**170,192,606**	**-**	**170,192,606**	**33,173,453**	
Net Position					
Net investment in capital assets	943,170,744	62,264,972	1,005,435,716	20,658,989	345,514
Restricted for:					
Road and bridge	11,332,785	-	11,332,785		
Social services	5,095,579	-	5,095,579		

	Primary Government			Component Units	
	Governmental Activities	Business-type Activities	Total Primary Government	Public Library	Public Health
Open space	28,622,095	-	28,622,095	-	-
Traffic impact	10,285,647	-	10,285,647	-	-
Public safety	2,667,227	-	2,667,227	-	-
Welfare	423,428	-	423,428	-	-
Debt service	13,377,217	-	13,377,217	-	-
Capital projects	12,897,518	1,175,000	14,072,518	-	-
Emergencies	7,998,083	-	7,998,083	-	-
Other	11,466,091	-	11,466,091	-	-
Unrestricted	60,681,469	2,613,574	63,295,043	2,152,045	1,097,667
Total net position	**$1,108,017,883**	**$66,053,546**	**$1,174,071,429**	**$32,811,034**	**$1,443,181**

NOTE: The above table is based upon a real government (a county). Certain adjustments were made to magnify the elements related to GASB-68 or GASB-75, as amended as the county does not have a defined benefit plan. In addition, no adjustments have been made for any business-type activities or component units that may rightfully should include a portion of any pension elements in accordance with NCGA-1, paragraph 42, as amended, which requires long-term liabilities that are "directly related to and expected to be paid from" those funds to be reported in the statement of net position or statement of fiduciary net position, respectively. Theoretically, a sub-allocation could have been made based upon employer contributions, pensionable compensation, or similar items. However, since the government underlying the schedules in this chapter does not have a defined benefit plan, any further allocation potentially may be misleading to the reader. Further details are contained in CCH's *Governmental GAAP Practice Manual* and in Chapter 13, "Pensions, Postemployment, and Other Employee Benefit Liabilities."

Statement of Activities

The format for the government-wide statement of activities is significantly different from any operating statement previously used in governmental financial reporting. The focus of the statement of activities is on the net cost of various activities provided by the governmental entity. The statement begins with a column that identifies the cost of each governmental activity. Another column identifies the revenues that are specifically related to the classified governmental activities. The difference between the expenses and revenues related to specific activities computes the net cost or benefits of the activities, which "identifies the extent to which each function of the government draws from the general revenues of the government or is self-financing through fees and intergovernmental aid" (GASB-34, pars. 38, as amended by GASB-37, par. 11, GASB-63, par. 8) [GASB Cod. Sec. 2200.126].

The GASB established the unique presentation format for the statement of activities in part because it believes that format provides an opportunity to provide feedback on a typical budgetary question that is asked when a program is adopted; namely, "What will the program cost and how will it be financed?" Due to this presentation format, expenses and revenues should be reported "gross" or "broad" on the statement of activities.

> **PRACTICE ALERT:** One of the aspects of the GASB's Financial Reporting Model—Reexamination project is to explore alternatives for the format of the statement of activities. An alternative may be in the Preliminary Views document to be released in 2018, potentially as supplementary information portraying expenses in a so-called natural classification format, utilizing expense categories relating to object classes (payroll, employee benefits, contractor payments, etc.). This format is commonly used by public institutions of higher education and not-for-profit organizations.

The governmental entity must determine the level at which governmental activities are to be presented; however, the level of detail must be at least as detailed as that required in the governmental fund financial statements (which are discussed later). Generally, activities would be aggregated and presented at the functional category level; however, entities are encouraged to present activities at a more detailed level, such as by programs. Due to the size and complexities of some governmental entities it may be impractical to expand the level of detail beyond that of functional categories. (The discussion that follows assumes that the level of detail presented in the statement of activities is at the functional category level.)

The minimum level of detail for expenses presented on the statement of activities is, for governmental activities, by function (e.g., "public safety," "public health"), and for business-type activities by different identifiable activities (e.g., "water," "sewer," "refuse collection"). The level of detail for presentation on the statement of activities is the required minimum level and not the actual level of detail used to prepare the fund financial statements. That is, fund financial statements could be prepared at a more detailed level than the minimum required and the statement of activities could reflect a lesser level (e.g., the minimum level required) (GASB-34, par. 40) [GASB Cod. Sec. 2200.128].

GASB-34 requires that business-type activities be separately reported at least by segment on the statement of activities (government-wide financial statement). Rather than define a segment in the context of the statement of activities, GASB-34 used the definition of a segment, which is reproduced as follows, established for the presentation of segment information in a note to the financial statements for Enterprise Funds:

> [A] segment is considered to exist when "an identifiable activity reported as or within an Enterprise Fund or another stand-alone entity for which one or more revenue bonds or other revenue-backed debt instruments (such as certificates of participation) are outstanding." A segment has a specific identifiable revenue stream pledged in support of revenue bonds or other revenue-backed debt and has related expenses, gains and losses, assets, and liabilities that can be identified.

The GASB's objective for reporting disaggregated information in the business-type activities section of the statement of activities was not to identify segment information but rather to have a separate presentation for activities that are different. In order to better achieve this objective, GASB-37 amends GASB-34 by requiring that the statement of activities present "activities accounted for in

Enterprise Funds by different identifiable activities," which is described as follows (GASB-37, par. 10) [GASB Cod. Sec. 2200.127]:

> An activity within an Enterprise Fund is identifiable if it has a specific revenue stream and related expenses and gains and losses that are accounted for separately. Determining whether an activity is different may require the use of professional judgment, but is generally based on the goods, services, or programs provided by an activity.

In the statement of activities presented for an Enterprise Fund, the *GASB Implementation Guide 2015-1*, question 7.26.3 [GASB Cod. Sec. 2200.714-2], discusses potential criteria for reporting separate activities. "Generally the difference between activities in the goods, services or programs provided" is obvious, but in some circumstances professional judgment must be used to determine which activities should be reported separately. For example, the *Guide* discusses how unemployment compensation (for a state) is different from a housing loan program of the state and therefore, they should be separate activities. But for public institutions of higher education, an athletic program may be separate or integrated, depending upon the school's operations. Ultimately, the question gives guidance to preparers to present the level of detail that provides the most meaningful information to meet user needs.

The GASB's objective is "to present a level of detail that will provide useful information to meet the needs of users of the financial statements." For example, GASB-37 points out that an Enterprise Fund may be used to account for natural gas services and electric services. Although both of these services are considered "utility services," they are different activities and should be presented as such on the statement of activities if separate assets and liabilities can be identified for each activity. On the other hand, a public college accounted for as an Enterprise Fund would likely have revenues from residence halls, food services, and a bookstore. GASB-37 suggests that these revenue-producing functions would generally not be considered separate activities because they are all related to the single activity of providing the higher education service.

Expenses—Direct and Indirect. Once the level of detail is determined, the primary government's expenses for each governmental activity should be presented. It should be noted that these are expenses and not expenditures and are based on the concept of the flow of economic resources, which includes depreciation expense. As noted earlier, the minimum level of detail allowed by GASB-34 is functional program categories, such as general government, public safety, parks and recreation, and public works. At a minimum, each functional program should include "direct expenses," which are defined as "those that are specifically associated with a service, program, or department and, thus, are clearly identifiable to a particular function" (GASB-34, par. 41) [GASB Cod. Sec. 2200.129].

Some functional categories, namely general government and administrative support, are by their very nature indirect expenses and GASB-34 does not require that these indirect expenses be allocated to other functional categories. However, if these indirect expenses are in fact allocated (either partially allocated or fully allocated) to the other functional expense categories, the statement of activities must be expanded to include separate columns for direct and indirect expenses so that the presentation format provides a basis for comparison with other governmental entities that choose not to allocate their indirect expenses (GASB-34, par. 42) [GASB Cod. Sec. 2200.130].

When a governmental entity allocates part or all of its indirect costs (and therefore presents columns for direct and indirect costs), a column that presents the total of these two columns may be presented on the statement of activities, but a total column is not required.

In some instances, a governmental entity will charge (through the General Fund or an Internal Service Fund) other funds or programs an overhead rate that is based on general administrative expenses. GASB states that under this circumstance it is not necessary to identify and eliminate these charges from the various direct program expenses presented in the statement of activities; however, the summary of significant accounting policies should state that the direct program expenses include such charges (GASB-34, par. 43) [GASB Cod. Sec. 2200.131]. A common example of an item in an overhead rate charged to programs would be pension expense.

Question 7.28.4 of the *GASB Implementation Guide 2015-1* [GASB Cod. Sec. 2200.715-5] discusses how indirect expenses *could be* allocated to business-type activities as well as governmental activities assuming there is a reasonable basis for doing so. However, if those expenses are allocated to business-type activities, the allocation creates an additional item that has to be disclosed as a reconciling item between the fund financial statements and the government-wide financial statements. For example, there may be no basis to allocate interest on long-term debt to business-type activities if the business-type activity is not expected to pay the principal on the long-term debt.

At the other extreme, the indirect expenses of the "general government" functional category presented in the statement of activities may be allocable to both governmental and business-type activities. But in the allocation, there may be an inappropriate change to the net positions in both types of activities. As a result, a transfer from governmental activities to business-type activities would be required to balance the effect on net position, even though there is no expectation of internal reimbursements for indirect-expense allocations, nor may the transfer be lawful in some jurisdictions.

When a governmental entity performs a common support activity (e.g., vehicle maintenance) for a variety of programs (public safety, streets, etc.), to the extent possible the common activity costs should be allocated as a direct expense of the specific programs. Question 7.28.1 of the *GASB Implementation Guide 2015-1* [GASB Cod. Sec. 2200.715-2] notes that any costs that cannot be allocated to a specific function should be reported as "general government or a similar indirect cost center" on the statement of activities.

GASB-34 requires that each functional program include direct expenses, which are defined as "those that are specifically associated with a service, program, or department and, thus, are clearly identifiable to a particular function." U.S. GAAP requires that non-enterprise fund employee benefit costs (such as pension costs, vacation pay, etc.) should be allocated to functional programs (such as public safety, streets, etc.) if the employee's wage is also considered a direct expense.

A governmental entity may negotiate indirect costs rates under various federal governmental grants and contracts whereby those rates are used to transfer the costs (reimbursement) from the General Fund to specific governmental funds that administer the federal awards. As the rates are based on indirect costs, they cannot be reported as direct expenses of a particular function but, rather, must be reported as "general government" expenses (or an equivalent caption) on the statement of activities.

Generally, the cost (net of estimated salvage value) of capital assets should be depreciated over their estimated useful lives. (For a discussion of depreciation expense, see Chapter 18, "Expenses/Expenditures: Nonexchange and Exchange Transactions.") Depreciation expense should be reported as a direct expense of the specific functional category if the related capital asset can be identified with the functional category. For example, depreciation expense related to a police vehicle should be reported, along with other direct expenses, at the appropriate functional expense category (e.g., public safety). Depreciation on capital assets that are shared by two or more functions should be reported as a direct expense based on a pro rata allocation to the appropriate functional expense categories. For example, if a building houses the administrative office of the police department and the public assistance department, the depreciation expense for the office building would be allocated on an appropriate basis to the two functional expense categories (e.g., public safety and health and welfare) (GASB-34, par. 44) [GASB Cod. Sec. 2200.132].

Depreciation expense for infrastructure should not be allocated to the various functions of government and should be reported as a direct expense. For example, streets, highways, and related infrastructure assets may be reported as part of public works or transportation. Water and sewer mains or electrical lines may be reported as part of a utility department. The reporting is generally associated with the function where the capital outlay occurs or the maintenance of the infrastructure is recorded (GASB-34, par. 45) [GASB Cod. Sec. 2200.133].

Depreciation expense related to capital assets that are not identified with a particular functional category (such as the depreciation of city hall) does not have to be reported as a direct expense to specific functions but rather may be presented as a separate line item in the statement of activities or included in the general government functional category. However, when unallocated depreciation expense is reported as a separate line in the statement of activities, it should be indicated on the face of the statement that the amount reported as depreciation expense represents only unallocated depreciation expense and not total depreciation expense.

Question 7.29.4 of the *GASB Implementation Guide 2015-1* [GASB Cod. Sec. 2200.715-9] requires unallocated depreciation expense to be on the face of the statement of activities. That can be achieved by using an appropriate description of the line item, such as "Unallocated Depreciation Expense," or by labeling the line item "Depreciation Expense" with a reference (such as an asterisk) to the bottom of the statement that states that "the amount represents only unallocated depreciation expense and not total depreciation expense."

Generally, interest expense on general long-term debt is considered an indirect expense and should not be allocated as a direct expense to specific functional categories but rather should be presented as a single line item, appropriately labeled. However, GASB-34 notes that "when borrowing is essential to the creation or continuing existence of a program and it would be misleading to exclude the interest from direct expenses of that program," the related interest expense should be reported as a direct expense with the appropriate functional classification (GASB-34, par. 46) [GASB Cod. Sec. 2200.134].

Question 7.30.2 of the *GASB Implementation Guide 2015-1* [GASB Cod. Sec. 2200.715-11] provides the following example of a financing arrangement whereby interest expense is considered a direct expense and allocated to a particular function or program:

> A state government has a program to make reduced-rate loans to school districts in the state. The initial funding for the program was provided by a large bond issue. Since the bond issue is fundamental to the school district loan program and is an integral part of the cost of providing the program to local districts, the interest expense should be allocated to this activity.

If part of interest expense is reported as a direct expense of a functional line item, it should be indicated on the face of the statement if the amount reported as interest expense represents only unallocated interest expense and not total interest expense. The amount of total interest expense must be determinable on the face of the statement of activities or it must be disclosed in a note to the financial statements.

OBSERVATION: The GASB takes the position that treating interest expense as a direct expense is inconsistent with the nature of financing projects. For example, a capital asset related to one project may be purchased with existing funds, and a similar asset for another project may be financed. Under a direct allocation approach, one project would have more expenses than the other even though the determination of the interest expense is based on management discretion rather than the nature of each project.

With regard to reporting interest expense on the statement of activities, U.S. GAAP requires:

- Interest expense related to a capital lease is not a direct expense of the function that uses the capital assets subject to the lease. The use of a capital lease is just another financing option and should be evaluated like any other borrowing arrangement.

- Under most circumstances no interest on general long-term liabilities is reported as a direct expense; therefore, using the caption "interest on long-term debt" is sufficient to indicate that all interest expense is indirect. The amount of total interest expense must be determinable on the face of the statement of activities or it must be disclosed in a note to the financial statements.

Similarly, interest expense for Enterprise Funds and component units does not have to be reported as a separate line item in the business-type activities section of the statement of activities because the expense is considered to be a direct expense for each of these operating units.

A state's constitution might not allow for the issuance of debt except by a constitutional amendment approved by voters. Under this circumstance the debt is issued only for a specific activity. However, GASB-34, paragraph 46 [GASB Cod. Sec. 2200.134], discusses, in part, how the interest on the debt is still considered indirect and should not be allocated to the specific function or activity. If the state government is concerned that a functional activity should in fact include interest expense, the alternative format for the statement of activities (see paragraph 42 of GASB-34) [GASB Cod. Sec. 2200.130]may be used whereby indirect expenses are allocated (either partially allocated or fully allocated) to the other functional expense categories. Under this format the statement of activities must be expanded to include separate columns for direct and indirect expenses so that the presentation format provides a basis for comparison with other governmental entities that choose not to allocate their indirect expenses.

Revenues and other resource inflows. A fundamental concept in the formatting of the statement of activities, as described above, is the identification of resource inflows to the governmental entities that are related to specific programs and those that are general in nature. GASB-34, par. 47 [GASB Cod. Sec. 2200.135]notes that governmental programs are generally financed from the following sources of resource inflows:

- Parties who purchase, use, or directly benefit from goods and services provided through the program (e.g., fees for garbage collections, transportation fares, fees for using recreational facilities, building permits and hunting permits);

- Outside parties (other governments and nongovernmental entities or individuals) who provide goods and services to the governmental entity (e.g., a grant to a local government from a state government);

- The reporting government's constituencies (e.g., property taxes); and

- The governmental entity (e.g., investment income).

The first source of resources listed above is always program revenue. The second source is program revenue if it is restricted to a specific program, otherwise the item is considered general revenue. The third source is always general revenue, even when restricted. The fourth source of resources is usually general revenue.

GASB-34 provides definitions for program revenues (charges for services, operating grants and contributions, and capital grants and contributions) in pars. 48–51 (as amended by GASB-37, pars. 12–13), and general revenues in paragraph 52 [GASB Cod. Secs. 2200.136–.140]. The definitions for the various types of revenues are mutually exclusive and therefore a particular source of revenue can only meet the definition of one type of revenue.

The definitions contained in GASB-34 are as follows, as amended:

Type of Revenue	Definition in GASB-34, as Amended
Program Revenues	• Those that are derived directly from the program itself or from parties outside the reporting government's taxpayers or citizenry, as a whole; they reduce the net of the function to be financed from the general government's general revenues.
Charges for services	• Revenues based on exchange or exchange-like transactions. These revenues arise from charges to customers or applicants who purchase, use, or directly benefit from the goods, services, or privileges provided. Revenues in this category include fees charged for specific services, such as: — Water use; — Garbage collection; — Licenses and permits (dog licenses, liquor licenses, and building permits); and — Operating special assessments, such as for street cleaning or special street lighting; and any other amounts charged to service recipients. Payments from other governments that are exchange transactions—for example, when County A reimburses County B for boarding County A's prisoners—also should be reported as charges for services.

Type of Revenue	Definition in GASB-34, as Amended
Program-specific grants and contributions (operating and capital)	• Revenues arising from mandatory and voluntary nonexchange transactions with other governments, organizations, or individuals that are restricted for use in a particular program. Some grants and contributions consist of capital assets or resources that are restricted for capital purposes—to purchase, construct, or renovate capital assets associated with a specific program. These should be reported separately from grants and contributions that may be used either for operating expenses or for capital expenditures of the program at the discretion of the reporting government. These categories of program revenue are specifically attributable to a program and reduce the net expense of that program to the reporting government. For example, a state may provide an operating grant to a county sheriff's department for a drug-awareness-and-enforcement program or a capital grant to finance construction of a new jail.
	Multipurpose grants (those that provide financing for more than one program) should be reported as program revenue if the amounts restricted to each program are specifically identified in either the grant award or the grant application. Multipurpose grants that do not provide for specific identification of the programs and amounts should be reported as general revenues. Preparers of the financial statements should review the terms and conditions of the grant award contained in the grant application or award letter to determine the ultimate purpose of a grant.

Using this classification scheme, the governmental entity should format its statement of activities based on the following broad categories of resource inflows (GASB-34, par. 47) [GASB Cod. Sec. 2200.135]:

- Program revenues
  - Charges for services;
  - Operating grants and contributions; and
  - Capital grants and contributions;
- General revenues
- Contributions to permanent funds
- Extraordinary items
- Special items
- Transfers

Program revenues arise because the specific program with which they are identified exists, otherwise the revenues would not flow to the governmental entity. Program revenues are presented on the statement of activities as a subtraction from the related program expense in order to identify the net cost (or benefit) of a particular program. This formatting scheme enables a reader of a governmental entity to identify those programs that are providing resources that may be used for other governmental functions or those that are being financed from general revenues and other sources of resources.

Lotteries and Revenue Classification

Lotteries generate various types of revenues for states. As discussed in the AICPA's Audit & Accounting Guide *State and Local Governments*, the activities may be part of the primary government or a component unit. Generally, they use enterprise funds. However, they may not meet the criteria to use an enterprise fund and therefore are a governmental activity. If the lottery is a component unit, it may not meet the criteria for blending as described in GASB-14, paragraph 53, as amended [GASB Cod. Sec. 2600.113]. The GASB's *Implementation Guide 2015-1*, question 4.32.5 [GASB Cod. Sec. 2600.706-17], discusses when state lotteries are created to primarily generate revenue for a state, the services provided by a lottery result in the opportunity for financial gain to anyone who chooses to participate. When prizes occur, the lottery operation does not exclusively, or almost exclusively benefit the primary government. Therefore, if a lottery is a component unit, it is likely discretely presented.

Questions routinely occur about how revenues raised by one function / activity but used by another function / activity should be classified in the statement of activities. For example, if revenue generated by a state lottery (one function / activity) must be used to finance education (an other function / activity) should the proceeds from the lottery be reported as revenue for the lottery or for education?

GASB-37 states that the following factors are to be used to determine which revenue should be related to a program (GASB-37, pars. 11–13) [GASB Cod. Secs. 2200.136–.137] as well as *Implementation Guide 2015-1*, question 7.39.3 [GASB Cod. Secs. 2200.717–.12]:

- For charges for services, the determining factor is which function generates the revenue.
- For grants and contributions, the determining factor is the function to which the revenue is restricted.

Thus, in the lottery example, the proceeds from the lottery would be reported as charges for services of the lottery activity because the educational activity used the resources but did not charge for the services.

Other Program Revenue Classification Issues

In some instances, it is impractical to classify the program that should report a particular item of program revenue, in which case the governmental entity may establish a policy for classifying the program revenue if the policy is consistently applied.

The language used in GASB-34 strongly implied that only three categories could be used to identify program revenues, namely (1) charges for services, (2) operating grants and contributions, and (3) capital grants and contributions.

GASB-37 states that the formatting of the statement of activities is more flexible than originally conveyed in GASB-34. For example, more than one column could be included under one of the three program revenue columns. Furthermore, the columnar heading may be modified to be more descriptive. For example, a program revenue column could be labeled "operating grants, contributions, and restricted interest."

PRACTICE POINT: Identifying revenues with a particular function does not mean that revenues must be allocated to a function. Revenues are related to a function only when they are directly related to the function. If no direct relationship is obvious, the revenue is general revenue, not program revenue.

A governmental entity that classifies its expenses by *function* may receive a state grant (which meets the definition of program revenue) that is to be used for specified programs. The fact that the grant is based on one classification scheme and a governmental entity's statement of activities is based on another does not change the original character of the revenue. That is, the grant is still classified as program revenue (not general revenue) even though it must be allocated to a variety of functions in the statement of activities.

The GASB's *Implementation Guide 2015-1*, in various questions contained in 7.39 [GASB Cod. Secs. 2200.717-12–16, 720-2–3], provides the following to illustrate how potential program revenues should be evaluated based on the guidance established in GASB-34:

Fact Pattern	Suggested Guidance
State law requires that 20% of the state's lottery sales revenue be used for elementary and secondary education programs in the state. Should the 20% be allocated to the education function as program revenue?	No. The proceeds from the sales of lottery tickets are related to the "lottery" program and not to the education program. Presenting the net revenues of a program on a statement of activities does not imply that those net proceeds are used for that particular program. In this instance, the net revenue from the lottery program is a "profit" that reduces the governmental entity's need to finance other programs (including educational programs) through general revenues.
State gas taxes are shared with eligible local governments. The local governments have discretion over when and how the money is spent, as long as it is for road and highway projects. Even though a high percentage of the revenue will likely be spent for capital purposes, maintenance and repair expenses are also allowable. How should the revenue (grants and contributions) be reported by the local governments—capital, operating, or some combination?	GASB-34 (par. 50) [GASB Cod. Sec. 2200.138] notes that if a grant or contribution can be used either for operating or capital purposes, at the discretion of the governmental entity, it should be reported as an operating contribution.

Fact Pattern	Suggested Guidance
A government charges indirect expenses to its human services program through an indirect cost plan and is reimbursed by the federal and state grant agencies for the costs of the program. However, in the statement of activities, the government does not allocate the indirect expenses to the human services program, but rather, reports them in the general government function. Should the portion of the grant that reimburses the indirect expense be reported as program revenues of the human services or general government function?	In this instance there should be a "matching" of program revenues and program expenses. If the indirect expenses are allocated to the human services program, the portion of the grant that reimburses the indirect expenses should be reported as program revenues. If the indirect expenses are not allocated to the human services program, the portion of the grant that reimburses the indirect expenses should be reported as program revenues for the general government function.

Investment revenue that qualifies as program revenues (legally restricted for a particular purpose) should be reported as program revenue. Depending on the nature of the restriction, the restricted investment revenue should be reported either as operating, or capital grants and contributions in the statement of activities.

Charges for services revenues that are characterized as charges for services are based on exchange or exchange-like transactions and arise from charges for providing goods, services, and privileges to customers or applicants who acquire goods, services, or privileges directly from a governmental entity. Generally, these and similar charges are intended to cover, at least to some extent, the cost of goods and services provided to various parties. GASB-34, as amended by GASB-37 lists the following as examples of charges for services revenue:

- Service charges (such as water usage fees and garbage collection fees);
- Licenses and permit fees (such as dog licenses, liquor licenses, and building permits);
- Operating special assessments (such as street-cleaning assessments or special street-lighting assessments); and
- Intergovernmental charges that are based on exchange transactions (such as one county being charged by another that houses its prisoners).

With the issuance of GASB-34, some financial statement preparers were unsure about how revenues related to fines and forfeitures should be classified in the statement of activities. Charges for services (program revenues) include revenues based on exchange or exchange-like transactions, which implies that the fines and forfeitures might not be classified as program revenue. However, fines and forfeitures should be reported as charges for services because fines and forfeitures are generated by the program, they are more like charges for services than grants and contributions.

GASB-37 modified GASB-34 by specifically stating that fines and forfeitures are to be classified as charges for services because "they result from direct charges to those who are otherwise directly affected by a program or service, even though they receive no benefit." However, GASB-37 recognizes that there is an element of confusion and arbitrariness in classifying fines and forfeitures as charges for services by noting that the statement of activities could be formatted (1) in order to present a separate column labeled "Fines and Forfeitures" under the "Charges for Services" column or (2) by retitling the column "Charges for Services, Fees, Fines, and Forfeitures" (GASB-37, par. 13) [GASB Cod. Sec. 2200.137].

In some instances, a state law might prohibit the use of fines for particular purposes (e.g., public safety expenses and other expenses that are related to the generation of the fine revenue). Even though the uses of the fine revenues (or in general, all charges for services) are somewhat limited, they are nonetheless program revenues and not general revenues.

The size or importance of a program's revenue does not change the character of the revenue for classification purposes on the statement of activities. For example, a community that has a substantial amount of fines that are used to fund a variety of programs does not make the fine revenue general revenue. The net cost of a function or program is the difference between (1) expenses and (2) the charges, fees, and fines that derive directly from it and the grants and contributions that are restricted to it. A particular function may generate a "profit" that can be used in a variety of ways. That fact does not make the revenue general.

Some public schools charge tuition fees for programs such as out-of-district students, vocational education, and adult educational programs where the fee is intended to cover the direct instructional cost of the program plus indirect administrative and support services. Therefore, the tuition revenue should be classified with the appropriate program revenue classification on the statement of activities. None of the revenue should be allocated to the indirect functional classification.

Governmental entities may receive mandatory and voluntary grants or contributions (nonexchange transactions) from other governments or individuals that must be used for a particular governmental activity. For example, a state government may provide grants to localities that are to be used to reimburse costs related to adult literacy programs. These and other similar sources of assets should be reported as program-specific grants and contributions in the statement of activities but they must be separated into those that are for operating purposes and those that are for capital purposes. If a grant or contribution can be used either for operating or capital purposes, at the discretion of the governmental entity, it should be reported as an operating contribution (GASB-34, par. 50) [GASB Cod. Sec. 2200.138].

Grants and contributions that are provided to finance more than one program (multipurpose grants) should be reported as program-specific grants "if the amounts restricted to each program are specifically identified in either the grant award or the grant application." (The grant application should be used in this manner only if the grant was based on the application.) If the amount of the multipurpose grants cannot be identified with particular programs, the revenue should be reported as general revenue rather than program-specific grants and contributions.

Earnings related to endowments or permanent fund investments are considered program revenues if they are restricted to a specific program use; however, the restriction must be based on either an explicit clause in the endowment agreement or contract. Likewise, earnings on investments that do not represent endowments or permanent fund arrangements are considered program revenues if they are legally restricted to a specific program. Investment earnings on endowments or permanent fund investments that are not restricted and, therefore, are available for general operating expenses are not program revenues but rather should be reported as general revenues in the "lower" section of the statement of activities.

A Permanent Fund may be managed and controlled by one function (such as the transportation function) but a portion of the investment income may be restricted for use in another function (such as the public safety function). The portion of the investment income restricted to the other function should be reported as program revenue for the other function and not the function that is managing the Permanent Fund. That is, restricted resources are program revenues of the function to which they are restricted in accordance with the *GASB Implementation Guide*, question 7.37.2 [GASB Cod. Sec. 2200.717-11]. Also, earnings on invested accumulated resources of a specific program that are legally restricted to the specific program should be reported as program revenues (GASB-34, par. 51) [GASB Cod. Sec. 2200.139].

Question 7.34 [GASB Cod. Secs. 2200.716-4–716-10] of the *GASB Implementation Guide 2015-1* provides the following to illustrate how potential grants and contributions should be evaluated based on the guidance established in GASB-34:

Fact Pattern	Suggested Guidance
A school district is awarded an operating grant from the state department of education. The grant agreement states that the department will reimburse the school district for all eligible expenses of three specific programs. The grant award, however, does not specifically identify the amounts restricted to each program, as required by paragraph 50, because they will not be known until the school district submits its after-the-fact request for funding. Can the school district report the grant as program revenues for the three programs, or should it be reported as general revenue?	The grant should be reported by the school district as program revenue and allocated to specific functions based on the amounts of reimbursable expenses incurred for each program. Since the reimbursements are known (even though they were not known at the time of the state grant) before the financial statements are prepared, the state grants do relate to a specific program.
A local government is awarded a categorical grant that finances a large number of its programs. The grant award lists the programs covered but does not restrict any specific amounts to specific programs. Should the government allocate the grant amount to covered programs and report it as program revenue?	Grants and contributions that are provided to finance more than one program (multipurpose grants) should be reported as program-specific grants "if the amounts restricted to each program are specifically identified in either the grant award or the grant application." The grant application should be used in this manner only if the grant was based on the application. If the amount of the multipurpose grants cannot be identified with particular programs, the revenue should be reported as general revenues rather than program-specific grants and contributions. In this case the grants must be reported as general revenues.
State law allocates a percentage of the state's sales tax revenues to local governments. A portion of the local share is restricted to education. At the local level, is the sales tax allocation to education program or general revenue?	The local government should classify the shared sales tax revenue as a voluntary contribution and not as a tax, as required by GASB-36. The portion of the shared revenue for a local school district would be reported as a general revenue because the resources are available for "education" and not for a particular program within the educational activities.

Fact Pattern	Suggested Guidance
A local government receives a large bequest from the estate of a wealthy benefactor. The corpus of the donation cannot be spent, but instead is required to be invested to provide earnings that are restricted to a special use. Because the principal amount can never be spent, how should it be reported?	The receipt of the gift should be accounted for in a Permanent Fund and reported as revenue in the fund's statement of revenues, expenditures, and changes in fund balances. The principal amount would be reported as restricted on the fund's balance sheet. When a governmental entity receives contributions to its term and permanent endowments or to permanent fund principal, those contributions should be reported as separate items in the lower portion of the statement of activities. These receipts are not considered to be program revenues (such as program specific grants), because in the case of permanent contributions, the principal can never be expended. On the statement of net position, the principal would be reported as restricted.

OBSERVATION: *GASB Implementation Guide 2015-1*, question 7.34.4, as amended by *Implementation Guide Update 2016-1*, paragraph 5.15 [GASB Cod. Sec. 2200.716-7], discusses revenue recognition from pass-through grants, on-behalf payments and food stamp revenues, along with revenue recognized as a result of a special funding situation in accordance with GASB-68 or GASB-73 (or when implemented, GASB-75). Revenues should be recognized as program revenues because they are specifically attributable to a program and reduce the net cost of that program to the reporting government.

Losses related to changes in the fair value of investments subject to the standards established by GASB-31 (*Accounting and Financial Reporting for Certain Investments and for External Investment Pools*), as amended by GASB-72 (*Fair Value Measurement and Application*), paragraph 75 [GASB Cod. Secs. 1600.109, D40.116, I50.101, 124, In3.136, Po20.141, Po20.144].

All investment income, including changes in the fair value of investments (gains or losses), should be recognized as revenue in the operating statement (or other statement of activities). When identified separately as an element of investment income, the change in the fair value of investments should be captioned "net increase (decrease) in the fair value of investments." Realized gains and losses should not be displayed separately from the net increase (decrease) in the fair value of investments in the financial statements, except that realized gains and losses may be separately displayed in the separate reports of governmental external investment pools. GASB-53 (*Accounting and Financial Reporting for Derivative Instruments*), paragraph 20 [GASB Cod. Secs. D40.116, I50.101, I50.108, In5.102, Po20.141], as amended, also requires similar treatment when derivative instruments become ineffective.

Changes in fair value, including losses be reported as an offset to program revenues when the earnings from the investments are restricted for a specific purpose. If no restriction exists, the losses would be reported as a loss or an offset to investment income in the general revenue section of the statement of activities.

OBSERVATION: GASB-72, paragraph 79 [GASB Cod. Secs. 1100.fn1, 1400.fn1, S30.fn6], requires donated capital assets, works of art, historical treasures and similar assets to be recorded at acquisition value at the acquisition date, rather than fair value. Acquisition value is defined as the price that would be paid to acquire an asset with equivalent service potential in an orderly market transaction at the acquisition date, or the amount at which a liability could be liquidated with the counterparty. Capital assets that a government receives in a service concession arrangement would also be at acquisition value.

General revenues should be reported in the "lower" portion of the statement of activities. Such revenues include resource flows related to income taxes, sales taxes, franchise taxes, and property taxes, and they should be separately identified in the statement. Nontax sources of resources that are not reported as program revenues must be reported as general revenues. This latter group includes unrestricted grants, unrestricted contributions, and unrestricted investment income (GASB-34, par. 52) [GASB Cod. Sec. 2200.140].

General revenues are used to offset the net (expense) revenue amounts computed in the "upper" portion of the presentation, and the resulting amount is labeled as excess (deficiency) of revenues over expenses before extraordinary items and special items.

OBSERVATION: All taxes, including dedicated taxes (e.g., motor fuel taxes), are considered general revenues rather than program revenues. The GASB takes the position that only charges to program customers or program-specific grants and contributions should be characterized as reducing the net cost of a particular governmental activity.

Careful analysis is sometimes needed to properly classify a revenue source as either program revenue or general revenue. For example, the GASB's *Implementation Guide 2015-1*, question 7.35.5, [GASB Cod. Sec. 2200.718-5] provides an illustration where a developer is required to make a one-time contribution to a municipality based on the assessed value of a recently completed project and those resources are to be used to help maintain the infrastructure related to the project. The revenue source is not a program revenue but, rather, a general revenue because it "arises from an imposed nonexchange transaction that is, in substance, a tax." Therefore, the contribution would be presented in the lower portion of the statement of activities and could be labeled as "restricted for infrastructure maintenance."

In some instances, a governmental entity may establish a prerequisite fee or license that must be paid before a business or other party is subject to another charge or tax. The character of each revenue source must be evaluated independently to determine whether it is program revenue or a tax (general revenue). For example, a local governmental entity may require a business to obtain a business license and in order to maintain the license, the business must also pay a "business license tax" that is based on the entity's gross receipts. The license and any license renewal fee are program revenues (charges for services), whereas the business license tax is general revenue (gross receipts tax) even though it is related to maintaining the business license.

Not all program revenues create restricted net position. By their nature, grants and contributions (both operational and capital) give rise to restricted net position, but charges for services may be unrestricted, restricted to the program that gave rise to the charge, or restricted to a program that is unrelated to the revenue generated service. On the other hand, a tax revenue could be restricted for a particular use (e.g., taxes levied specifically to pay debt service) but nonetheless reported as general revenue, perhaps under a heading that identifies it as restricted for a particular purpose.

Taxes imposed by another government are not a tax receipt (by the recipient government) but, rather, a nonexchange transaction as defined by GASB-33. The characteristics of the shared tax revenue must be examined to determine whether it is a program revenue (as defined by paragraph 50) or general revenue (as defined by paragraph 52).

All taxes are considered general revenues rather than program revenues with the following illustrations (in each case the tax receipt is reported as general revenue):

- A county government imposes a separate sales tax, the proceeds of which are required to be used for public safety or health and welfare programs. Because of the restrictions on use, these taxes are not "discretionary" revenues.

- A city levies a special tax that is restricted for use within a specific program or function (a separate property tax levied to pay debt service costs, for example).

- A county government has enacted a transient occupancy (hotel, motel) tax, a percentage of which is required to be used for "tourism" programs in the county. The county has significant tourism activity and reports it as a separate function in its statement of activities. The county maintains that the revenue comes from "those who directly benefit from the goods or services of the program," and consequently should be reported as charges for services.

GASB-33 requires that derived taxes and imposed nonexchange revenues (both general revenues) be reported net of estimated refunds and estimated uncollectible amounts, respectively. Uncollectible exchange transactions revenues related to governmental activities on the statement of activities should also be recorded net of any uncollectible amounts. That is, a bad-debts expense account should not be used for presentation purposes.

When a governmental entity receives contributions to its term and permanent endowments or to permanent fund principal, those contributions should be reported as separate items in the lower portion of the statement of activities. These receipts are not considered to be program revenues (such as program-specific grants) because, in the case of term endowments, there is an uncertainty of the timing of the release of the resources from the term restriction and, in the case of permanent contributions, the principal can never be expended (GASB-34, par. 53, as amended by GASB-63, par. 8) [GASB Cod. Sec. 2200.141].

GASB-34 also discusses when the earnings of a Permanent Fund are required to be used for a specific purpose but are not distributed in the current year, those earnings (even though they are not distributed or spent) should be reported as program revenues.

The next section of the statement of activities includes a category where extraordinary items (gains or losses) are to be presented. GASB-34 incorporates the definition of "extraordinary items" (unusual in nature and infrequent in occurrence) as originally provided in APB-30. GASB-62, paragraphs 45 through 49 [GASB Cod. Secs. 1800.147–.151, 2200.143–.149], confirms and expands these definitions.

PRACTICE POINT: One of the aspects of the GASB's Financial Reporting Model—Reexamination project is to explore whether the definition for extraordinary items should be clarified. The FASB recently clarified its definition of extraordinary items in FASB Accounting Standards Update 2015-1, *Income Statement—Extraordinary and Unusual Items* (Subtopic 225-20): Simplifying Income Statement Presentation by Eliminating the Concept of Extraordinary Items. The FASB is eliminating the concept of extraordinary items to simplify income statement presentation. Instead, items that are unusual or infrequently occurring will be presented. It is unclear if the GASB will adopt a similar approach.

An event is unusual in nature if it possesses a high degree of abnormality and therefore is not related to the entity's normal operations. An event is infrequent in occurrence if it is not expected to occur again in the foreseeable future. These concepts must be applied in the context of the characteristics of a particular entity, and their application is highly judgmental. Thus, what is considered unusual or frequent for one governmental entity, may not be unusual or frequent for another governmental entity.

There is no comprehensive list of extraordinary items, because that determination must be made on a case-by-case basis using professional judgment. The following *may* qualify as extraordinary items:

- Costs related to an environmental disaster caused by a large chemical spill in a train derailment in a small city.

- Significant damage to the community or destruction of government facilities by natural disaster (tornado, hurricane, flood, earthquake, and so forth) or terrorist act. Geographic location of the government may determine if a weather-related natural disaster is infrequent.

- Restoration of an impaired capital asset financed by insurance proceeds, which may be reported in the governmental fund financial statements as another financing source or an extraordinary item.

- A large bequest to a small government by a private citizen.
- Re-measurement of assets and liabilities resulting in gains or losses from municipal bankruptcy under the provisions of Chapter 9 of the United States Bankruptcy Code, as are adjustment of new payment terms that result in adjustment of fund liabilities (or assets) (see GASB-58) [GASB Cod. Sec. Bn5].

GASB-62, paragraph 49 [GASB Cod. Secs. 1800.151, 2200.149], discusses transactions that should not be extraordinary items, including:

- Write-down or write-off of receivables, inventories, equipment leased to others, or intangible assets;
- Gains or losses from exchange or translation of foreign currencies, including those relating to major devaluations and revaluations;
- Other gains or losses from sale or abandonment of capital assets used in operations;
- Effects of a strike, including those against major suppliers; and
- Adjustment of accruals on long-term contracts.

GASB-34 introduced a new classification of transactions—"special items." Subsequent statements further provided examples of them including those related to certain occurrences of asset impairment (GASB-42) and environmental remediation (GASB-49), as well as certain prior-period adjustment information (GASB-62). Special items are described as "significant transactions or other events within the control of management that are either unusual in nature or infrequent in occurrence." Special items should be reported separately and before extraordinary items. If a significant transaction or other event occurs but is not within the control of management and that item is either unusual or infrequent, the item is not reported as a special item but the nature of the item must be described in a note to the financial statements (GASB-34, par. 56) [GASB Cod. Sec. 2200.144].

The following *may* qualify as special items:

- Sales of certain general governmental capital assets.
- Special termination benefits resulting from workforce reductions due to sale of utility operations.
- Early-retirement program offered to all employees.
- Significant forgiveness of debt, other than within an order of municipal bankruptcy.
- Sale of a large governmental asset that resulted in a minimal gain or loss.

An item can only satisfy the criteria of either an extraordinary item or a special item, but not both. For example, if an item is both unusual and infrequent it must be reported as an extraordinary item regardless of whether it was subject to management control.

An extraordinary or special item to one government may not be an extraordinary or special item to another government. For example, consider the following:

Question: Example County is located on the Florida coastline and has sustained significant damage to the entire county, including county government facilities, from a recent hurricane. The County has incurred approximately $110,000,000 in expenses in the current year related to recovery from the hurricane damage. Do these expenses qualify to be reported as extraordinary or special items on the County's statement of activities?

Response: These expenses do not qualify as either special items or extraordinary items. Expenses incurred resulting from natural disasters, such as hurricanes, are never considered "special items" because they are not *within the control of management*. Therefore, these hurricane recovery expenses do not qualify for special item reporting treatment. Management should consider whether these hurricane recovery expenses may be reported as "extraordinary items." Part of the answer to question 7.43.2 of the *GASB Implementation Guide 2015-1* [GASB Cod. Sec. 2200.721-1] discusses that geographic location of the government may determine whether a weather-related natural disaster is infrequent. Because Example County is located on the Florida coastline and hurricanes are not infrequent at this location, these expenses would not qualify for reporting treatment as extraordinary items.

Transfers should be reported in the lower portion of the statement of activities (GASB-34, par. 53, as amended by GASB-63, par. 8) [GASB Cod. Sec. 2200.141]. The standards that determine how transfers should be reported in the statement of activities are discussed later in the context of fund statements.

Gains and losses arising from the disposition of capital assets that are related to specific programs should be reported as either general revenues (gains) or general government-type expenses (losses) because they are peripheral activities and not derived directly from a program. If the gains or losses are insignificant, they could be offset against depreciation expense for the period. Governmental entities that use group or composite depreciation methods would generally close disposition gains and losses to accumulated depreciation.

Eliminations and Reclassifications

As suggested earlier, the preparation of government-wide financial statements is based on a consolidating process (similar to corporate consolidations) rather than a combining process. Eliminations and reclassifications related to the consolidation process are based on (1) internal balances—statement of net position, (2) internal activities—statement of activities, (3) intra-entity activity, and (4) Internal Service Fund balances (GASB-34, par. 57) [GASB Cod. Sec. 2200.151].

Internal balances. The government-wide financial statements present the governmental entity and its blended component units as a single reporting entity. Based on this philosophy, most balances between funds that are initially recorded as interfund receivables and payables at the individual fund level should be eliminated in the preparation of the statement of net position within each of the two major groups of the primary government (the government activities and business-type activities). The purpose of the elimination is to avoid the grossing-up effect on assets and liabilities presented on the statement of net position.

For example, if there is an interfund receivable / payable between the General Fund and a Special Revenue Fund, those amounts would be eliminated in order to determine the balances that would appear in the governmental-activities column. Likewise, if there is an interfund receivable/payable between two proprietary funds of the primary government, those amounts would also be eliminated in the business-type activities column. However, the net residual interfund receivable/payable between governmental and business-type activities should not be eliminated but, rather, should be presented in each column (government activities and business-type activities) and labeled as "internal balances" or a similar description. These amounts will be the same and will therefore cancel out when they are combined (horizontally) in the statement of net position in order to form the column for total primary government activities (GASB-34, par. 58, as amended by GASB-63, par. 8, and GASB-65, par. 13) [GASB Cod. Sec. 2200.152].

> **OBSERVATION:** Generally, a governmental entity will maintain its accounting transactions using the conventional fund approach and convert this information to a government-wide basis using the flow of economic resources and accrual basis of accounting. Thus, at the fund level the internal balance between a government fund (modified accrual basis) may not equal the related balance with a proprietary fund (accrual basis); however, once the government fund is adjusted (through a worksheet) to the government-wide (accrual) basis, those adjusted amounts will equal the amounts presented in the proprietary funds.

There also may be interfund receivables / payables that arise because of transactions between the primary government and its fiduciary funds. These amounts should not be eliminated but rather should be reported on the statement of net position as receivables from and payables to external parties. As a reminder, the financial statements of fiduciary funds are not consolidated as part of the government-wide financial statements.

Internal activities. In order to avoid the doubling-up effect of internal activities among funds, interfund transactions should be eliminated so that expenses and revenues are recorded only once. For example, a fund (generally the General Fund or an Internal Service Fund) may charge other funds for services provided (such as insurance coverage and allocation of overhead expenses) on an internal basis. When these funds are consolidated in order to present the functional expenses of governmental activities in the statement of activities, the double counting of the expense (with an offset to revenue recorded by the provider fund) should be eliminated in a manner so that "the allocated expenses are reported only by the function to which they were allocated" (GASB-34, par. 59) [GASB Cod. Sec. 2200.153].

Internal activities should not be eliminated when they are classified as "interfund services provided and used." For example, when a municipal water company charges a fee for services provided to the general government, the expense and revenues related to those activities should not be eliminated (GASB-34, par. 60) [GASB Cod. Sec. 2200.154]. This type of internal activity is more fully discussed later in the section titled "Fund Financial Statements."

Intra-entity activity. Transactions (and related balances) between the primary government and its blended component units should be reclassified based on the guidance discussed later in the section titled "Fund Financial Statements." Transactions (and related balances) between the primary government and its discretely presented component units should not be eliminated in the government-wide perspective financial statements. That is, the two parties to the transactions should report revenue and expense accounts as originally recorded in those respective funds. Amounts payable and receivable between the primary government and its discretely presented component units should be reported as a separate line item on the statement of net position. Likewise, payables and receivables among discretely presented component units must also be reported separately (GASB-34, par. 61, as amended by GASB-63, par. 8, and GASB-65, par. 13) [GASB Cod. Sec. 2200.155].

Internal Service Fund balances. As described above (see "internal activities" [statement of activities]) internal service fund and similar activities should be eliminated to avoid doubling-up expenses and revenues in preparation of the government-activities column of the statement of activities. The effect of this approach is to adjust activities in an Internal Service Fund to a break-even balance. That is, if the Internal Service Fund had a "net profit" for the year there should be a pro rata reduction in the charges made to the funds that used the Internal Service Fund's services for the year. Likewise, a net loss would require a pro rata adjustment that would increase the charges made to the various participating funds. After making these eliminations, any residual balances related to the Internal Service Fund's assets and liabilities should be reported in the government-activities column in the statement of net position (GASB-34, par. 62, as amended by GASB-63, pars. 7 and 8) [GASB Cod. Sec. 2200.156].

In some instances, an internal service might not be accounted for in an Internal Service Fund but, rather, is accounted for in another governmental fund (probably the General Fund or a Special Revenue Fund). Furthermore, the internal-service transaction might not cut across functional expense categories. That is, there is a "billing" between different departments but the expenses of those departments are all included in the same functional expenses. Conceptually, the same break-even approach as described earlier should be applied so as not to gross-up expenses and program revenues of a particular functional expense; however, the GASB does not require that an elimination be made (unless the amounts are material), because the result of this non-elimination is that direct expenses and program revenues are overstated by equal amounts but net (expense) revenue related to the function is not overstated.

OBSERVATION: The GASB takes the position that activities conducted with an Internal Service Fund are generally government activities rather than business-type activities even though an Internal Service Fund uses the flow of economic resources and the accrual basis of accounting. However, when Enterprise Funds account for all or the predominant activities of an Internal Service Fund, the Internal Service Fund's residual assets and liabilities should be reported in the business-type activities column of the statement of net position.

Exhibit 20-2 illustrates a statement of activities consistent with the standards established by GASB-34. An alternative format creates a separate column for indirect activities. For example, if a government has a cost allocation plan for indirect costs, they may prefer to present these in a separate column from direct costs. This alternative format is not shown in this chapter, because the presentation is self-evident. (See also previous **PRACTICE ALERT** on the GASB's *Financial Reporting Model—Reexamination* project which may reformat the statement of activities entirely.)

Alternative presentation for statement of activities. As shown in Exhibit 20-2, the format of the statement of activities is unwieldy. When an entity has only governmental activities and a few functions, it may be possible to simplify the presentation of the statement by starting with a total column and then adding columns to the right of the total column that identify expenses and program revenues. The formatted statement could look something like the following:

	Total	Function #1	Function #2	Function #3
Expenses:				
Details	$XXX	$XXX	$XXX	$XXX
Total expenses	**XXX**	**XXX**	**XXX**	**XXX**
Program revenues:				
Charges for services	XXX	XXX	XXX	XXX
Operating grants and contributions	XXX	XXX	XXX	XXX
Capital grants and contributions	XXX	XXX	XXX	XXX
Net Program expense	**XXX**	**$XXX**	**$XXX**	**$XXX**
General revenues:				
Taxes:	XXX			
Real estate	XXX			
Others	XXX			
Unrestricted grants and contributions	XXX			
Unrestricted investment earnings	XXX			
Total general revenues	**XXX**			
Change in net position	XXX			
Net position—beginning	XXX			
Net position—ending	**$XXX**			

EXHIBIT 20-2
STATEMENT OF ACTIVITIES

Castle Rock County
Statement of Activities for the year
ended December 31, 20XX

Functions / Programs	Expenses	Program Revenues — Charges for Services	Program Revenues — Operating Grants and Contributions	Program Revenues — Capital Grants and Contributions	Net (Expense) Revenue — Primary Government — Governmental Activities	Net (Expense) Revenue — Primary Government — Business-Type Activities	Net (Expense) Revenue — Primary Government — Total	Net (Expense) Revenue — Component Units — Public Library	Net (Expense) Revenue — Component Units — Public Health
Governmental Activities:									
General government	$49,564,426	$24,837,014	$3,638,039	$-	$ (21,089,373)	$-	$(21,089,373)	$-	$-
Public safety	130,531,604	10,754,353	8,609,075	1,610	(111,166,566)	-	(111,166,566)	-	-
Highways and streets	45,044,210	5,931,700	1,403,495	1,047,375	(36,661,640)	-	(36,661,640)	-	-
Culture and recreation	27,707,260	776,531	1,415,656	-	(25,515,073)	-	(25,515,073)	-	-
Economic development and assistance	7,484,526	368,474	7,093,096	-	(22,956)	-	(22,956)	-	-
Welfare	61,171,256	116,099	40,714,491	-	(20,340,666)	-	(20,340,666)	-	-
Sanitation	648,401	493,824	-	-	(154,577)	-	(154,577)	-	-
Interest on long-term debt	6,667,395	-	-	-	(6,667,395)	-	(6,667,395)	-	-
Total governmental activities	328,819,078	43,277,994	62,873,852	1,048,985	(221,618,247)	-	(221,618,246)		
Business-type activities:									
Airport	6,381,280	3,344,070	-	1,230,677		(1,806,533)	(1,806,533)		
Total Primary Government	$335,200,358	$46,622,064	$62,873,852	$2,279,662	(221,618,247)	(1,806,533)	(223,424,780)		
Component Units:									
Public Library	$27,479,992	$816,704	$363,204	$679,016				(25,621,068)	
Public Health	13,170,414	2,086,606	11,474,444	-				-	390,636
Total Component Units	$40,650,406	$2,903,310	$11,834,648	$679,016				(25,621,068)	390,636

| | Program Revenues | | | | Net (Expense) Revenue and Change in Net Position | | | | |
| | | | | | Primary Government | | | Component Units | |
Functions / Programs	Expenses	Charges for Services	Operating Grants and Contributions	Capital Grants and Contributions	Governmental Activities	Business-Type Activities	Total	Public Library	Public Health
General Revenues:									
Taxes:									
Property					178,916,658		178,916,658	23,623,522	
Sales					61,305,362	239,672	61,545,034		
Investment income					2,161,945	99,529	2,261,474	172,372	4,763
Miscellaneous					2,079,294	1,667,633	3,746,927		
Total General Revenues					**244,463,259**	**2,006,834**	**246,470,093**	**23,795,894**	**4,763**
Change in Net Position					22,845,012	200,301	23,045,313	(1,825,174)	395,399
Net Position - January 1 20XX					1,085,172,871	65,853,245	1,151,026,116	34,636,208	1,047,782
Net Position - December 31 20XX					**$1,108,017,883**	**$66,053,546**	**$1,174,071,429**	**$32,811,034**	**$1,443,181**

Fund Financial Statements

Reporting Major Funds in Governmental and Proprietary Fund Financial Statements

A governmental entity should report (1) financial statements for its governmental funds and (2) proprietary funds, but the basis for reporting these funds is not by fund type but rather by major funds (GASB-34, par. 74) [GASB Cod. Sec. 2200.157].

GASB-34 requires that a governmental fund or Enterprise Fund be presented in a separate column in the fund financial statements if the fund is considered a major fund. A major fund is one that satisfies *both* of the following criteria (GASB-34, pars. 75–76, as amended by GASB-37, par. 15, and GASB-65, par. 33) [GASB Cod. Secs. 2200.158–.159]:

1. 10% Threshold—Total assets and deferred outflows, liabilities and deferred inflows, revenues, or expenditures/expenses (excluding extraordinary items) of the individual governmental or enterprise fund are equal to or greater than 10% of the corresponding element total (assets, liability, and so forth) for all funds that are considered governmental funds or enterprise funds.

2. 5% Threshold—The same element that met the 10% criterion in (*a*) is at least 5% of the corresponding element total for all governmental and enterprise funds combined.

In establishing major fund criteria, the GASB intended that a major fund arises when a particular element (assets, for example) of a fund meets both the 10% and the 5% threshold. Some preparers read the requirement as originally stated in GASB-34 to mean that a major fund arises when one element (assets, for example) satisfies the 10% threshold and another element (revenues, for example) satisfies the 5% threshold. GASB-37 clarifies the GASB's original intent. That is, a single element must satisfy both criteria. Revenue, net of discounts and allowance (rather than gross revenues) should be used in applying the major fund criteria to governmental fund and Enterprise Fund activities. Also, in determining total revenues and expenditures/expenses, extraordinary items would be excluded. Finally, GASB-34, par. 76 [GASB Cod. Sec. 2200.159], does allow some latitude if the government's officials believe that presentation of a fund is particularly important to financial statement users even if mathematically it wouldn't be considered a major fund.

PRACTICE POINT: In some instances, a governmental entity may account for all of its activities in only governmental funds or, alternatively, may use only Enterprise Funds. Under either of these two circumstances, only the 10% test is relevant because if the 10% test is satisfied, obviously the 5% test will also be satisfied.

PRACTICE POINT: Part of the *Financial Reporting Model—Reexamination* project includes whether the major fund criteria and tests should be changed in some manner to include more debt service fund reporting, which users find to be inconsistently reported as a major fund.

The General Fund is always considered a major fund and therefore must be presented in a separate column. Major fund reporting requirements do not apply to Internal Service Funds.

Based on research conducted by the GASB, it appears that major funds represent a significant percentage of a governmental entity's account balances and transactions. However, the major fund concept is a minimum threshold. If a governmental entity believes that a fund that is not considered a major fund is, important to readers of the financial statements, the entity should present that fund in a separate column.

A governmental entity must apply the major fund criteria each year to determine which funds are major funds. Thus, for example, a particular Capital Projects Fund might be reported as a major fund one year and the next year considered a nonmajor fund; however, if a fund does not satisfy the conditions for a major fund, it can still be presented as a major fund if the governmental entity believes that for consistency it is important to do so.

Internal Service Funds cannot be presented as major funds. They should be aggregated and presented in a separate column on the face of the proprietary fund financial statements, just to the right of the total column for Enterprise Funds. If a governmental entity wants to present additional detail about Internal Service Funds, that information can be presented in combining statements, but those statements are optional and they are not considered to be part of the basic external financial statements. They are part of the CAFR.

All other funds that are not considered major funds must be aggregated in a separate column and labeled as nonmajor funds. Therefore, more than one column cannot be used to present nonmajor funds, for example, by fund type.

GASB-34 does not require interfund balances and activities to be eliminated when nonmajor funds are aggregated; however, a governmental entity may choose to do so.

The *GASB Implementation Guide 2015-1,* questions 7.56.1-14 [GASB Cod. Secs. 2200.729-11–24], provide the following illustrations for identifying major funds:

Fact Pattern	Suggested Guidance
A city has a component unit that meets the criteria for blending and is included with its special revenue funds. Do the major fund reporting requirements apply to blended component units?	If a governmental entity chooses to report a component unit's balances and transactions as a separate fund, then the major fund reporting requirements apply to the fund.
Paragraph 76a states that governments should apply the 10% criterion for one element (total assets, liabilities, revenues, or expenses/expenditures), major fund criterion to all funds of that category or type. When should "category" be used and when should "type" be used?	The major fund criteria apply to the totals that represent (1) the governmental activities (a category) (General Fund, Special Revenue Funds, Capital Projects Funds, Debt Service Funds, and Permanent Funds) and (2) Enterprise Funds (a fund type). Internal Service Funds are not included in with Enterprise Funds when applying the criteria.
If an individual governmental or Enterprise Fund meets the initial 10% criterion for one element (total assets, liabilities, revenues, or expenses/expenditures), and meets the 5% benchmark for a different element, is that fund required to be presented as a major fund?	No. A fund is considered a major fund when the element satisfies both the 10% and the 5% criteria, not just one of the criteria.
In applying the major fund criteria to Enterprise Funds, should the government consider both operating and non-operating revenues and expenses?	Yes. The application of the tests requires that both operating and non-operating revenues and expenses be considered for an Enterprise Fund.
For determining major governmental funds, are other financing sources and uses included in the calculations?	No. In performing the criteria tests for governmental funds, other financing sources and uses would be excluded.
Can a non-GAAP budgetary basis of accounting be used to determine major funds?	No. The modified accrual basis for governmental funds and the accrual basis for Enterprise Funds must be used to apply the major funds test.
For major fund determination, should total assets, liabilities, revenues, or expenditures/ expenses include the effects of the items in the reconciliation of the fund statements to the government-wide statements?	No. The importance of a particular fund is based on the basis of accounting used to report the fund in the fund financial statements, not the government-wide financial statements.

Fact Pattern	Suggested Guidance
Are interfund balances and transactions required to be eliminated from the totals in the major fund test?	Interfund balances should not be eliminated to perform the major fund test. However, if there are interfund receivables and payables, a governmental entity could adopt a policy (if applied consistently) of netting receivables and payables (for the purpose of the test only). Thus the balance sheet totals for a fund and for the total fund category or fund type would be the basis for performing the test. (The question is not relevant to performing the major fund test for operating statements because transfers in and transfers out are not used to determine revenues and expenditures/expenses. It should be noted that interfund services provided and used are considered other revenues and expenditures/expenses.)

The totals in the government-wide financial statements for governmental activities will not equal the totals in the governmental fund financial statements because different measurement focuses and bases of accounting are used to prepare the financial statements. For this reason, the GASB requires that at the bottom of the fund financial statements or in a separate schedule a summary reconciliation between the fund financial statements and the government-wide financial statements be provided. That is, the amount shown as the "total fund balances" in the column "total governmental funds" on the fund balance sheets must be reconciled to the "net position" column for governmental activities presented on the statement of net position. Also, the amount shown as "net changes in fund balance" in the column, "total governmental funds" on the statements of revenues, expenditures, and changes in fund balances must be reconciled to the "changes in net position" column, for governmental activities presented on the statement of activities (GASB-34, par. 77) [GASB Cod. Sec. 2200.160].

In many instances, the GASB believes that summary reconciliation can achieve the objective of tying the financial statements together with simple explanations that appear on the face of the fund financial statements or in an accompanying schedule. However, the GASB points out that "if the aggregated information in the summary reconciliation obscures the nature of the individual elements of a particular reconciling item, governments should provide a more detailed explanation in the notes to the financial statements." The *GASB Implementation Guide 2015-1*, question 7.57.3 [GASB Cod. Sec. 2200.730-4], discusses how this could occur when a reconciling item is "a combination of several similar balances or transactions, or is a net adjustment." For example, the reconciling item could be described as arising because liabilities are reported on the fund financial statements only when they are due and payable in the current period but appear on the government-wide financial statements when they are incurred. If this reconciling item includes a variety of liabilities (such as compensated absences, bonds, litigation, and accrued interest), a governmental entity may decide to further explain the nature of the reconciling item and its components in a note.

The financial statement preparer must be careful not to present lengthy explanations on the face of the financial statements or in the accompanying schedules that detract from the financial statements themselves. For this reason, it is best to present the detailed explanations in a note to the financial statements.

OBSERVATION: Summary reconciliation provides a "crosswalk" between government-wide financial statements and fund financial statements in order to facilitate an understanding by financial statement readers who may be concerned that two different measurement approaches are reflected in a governmental entity's financial report.

Question 7.57.1 in the *GASB Implementation Guide 2015-1* [GASB Cod. Sec. 2200.730-2] discusses the issue of whether the accounting records for governmental funds should include the adjustment necessary to report governmental activities on an accrual basis because it is usually assumed that financial statements should be derived from account balances in the accounting records. The formal accounting records should not include adjustments of this nature. Governmental funds are typically accounted for on a cash, modified accrual, or budgetary basis of accounting, and if necessary, worksheet adjustments are made to convert these balances to a GAAP-basis (modified accrual) for financial reporting purposes. The modified accrual based financial statements are the basis for preparing the fund financial statements required by GASB-34. Once the governmental funds have been converted to the modified accrual basis, they are combined for internal purposes, and various worksheet conversion adjustments are made to convert them to an accrual basis for reporting governmental activities in the government-wide financial statements.

A governmental entity may apply the major fund criteria to its activities (governmental or enterprise funds) and determine that all of its funds are major funds except one. For example, it may have a single Special Revenue Fund that is a major fund, a single Capital Projects Fund that is a major fund, a General Fund (which is always a major fund) and a remaining Permanent Fund that is not a major fund. Based on the reporting requirements established by GASB-34 there will be a separate column that reports the Permanent Fund even though it is not a major fund; however, as explained in the *GASB Implementation Guide 2015-1*, question 7.56.8 [GASB Cod. Sec. 2200.729-18], U.S. GAAP requires the financial statements to "clearly distinguish between major and nonmajor funds." This could be accomplished by providing (1) a super-heading labeled "Major Funds" and placing beneath it the separate columns for the General Fund, the Special Revenue Fund, and the Capital Projects Fund and (2) a super-heading labeled "Other Fund" and placing beneath it a single separate column for the Permanent Fund.

Required Financial Statements: Governmental Funds

The measurement focus and the basis of accounting used to prepare financial statements for governmental funds is the current financial resources measurement focus and the modified accrual basis of accounting.

Based on the fundamental concepts discussed above, the following financial statements must be prepared for governmental funds (GASB-34, par. 78) [GASB Cod. Sec. 2200.161]:

- Balance sheet; and
- Statement of revenues, expenditures, and changes in fund balances.

Balance sheet. A governmental fund's balance sheet should be prepared using the "balance sheet format," where assets equal liabilities plus fund balances. The balance sheet should report the governmental entity's current financial resources and the claims to those resources for each major governmental fund and for the nonmajor funds. A total column should be used to combine all of the major funds and nonmajor funds (GASB-34, par. 83, as amended by GASB-63, pars. 7 and 12) [GASB Cod. Sec. 2200.162].

The provisions of GASB-63 (*Financial Reporting of Deferred Outflows of Resources, Deferred Inflows of Resources, and Net Position*) may apply to governmental funds. Paragraph 12 of GASB-63 discusses how deferred outflows of resources and deferred inflows of resources that are required to be reported in a governmental fund balance sheet should be presented in a format that displays assets plus deferred outflows of resources, equals liabilities plus deferred inflows of resources, plus fund balance.

PRACTICE POINT: Deferred outflows of resources are rare in governmental funds as of the date of this publication due to the measurement focus and basis of accounting for such funds. Deferred inflows of resources are common based on the provisions of GASB-65 and other standards.

The equity of a governmental fund (fund balance) should be identified as nonspendable, restricted, committed, assigned, or unassigned amounts. The restricted fund balances of the combined nonmajor funds must be presented in appropriate detail to inform the reader of the nature of the restrictions and to identify the amount of the other current financial resources that are available for future appropriation. For example, the fund balance for nonmajor Debt Service Funds may be described as restricted for debt service. In addition, the remaining fund balances for nonmajor funds must be at least identified by fund type on the face of the balance sheet, or if aggregated, disaggregated in the notes to the basic financial statements (GASB-54, pars. 22 and 25) [GASB Cod. Sec. 2200.163].

As noted earlier, there must be a summary reconciliation between the total fund balances on the balance sheet and the total net position as presented on the statement of net position for governmental activities (government-wide financial statement). Some of the typical items that may be needed to reconcile the two amounts are as follows (GASB-34, par. 85, as amended by GASB-63, par. 8, and GASB-65, par. 31) [GASB Cod. Sec. 2200.164]:

- The difference between reporting capital assets (net of accumulated depreciation) on the statement of net position and the non-recognition of those assets on the fund balance sheets.
- The difference between reporting long-term liabilities on the statement of net position and the non-recognition of those liabilities on the fund balance sheets.
- The difference between the recognition of other liabilities on the statement of net position when they are incurred and the recognition on the fund balance sheets of only those liabilities that are payable with current financial resources.
- The difference between reporting the net position balances of Internal Service Funds on the statement of net position and the non-recognition of those net position on the fund balance sheets.

Exhibit 20-3 provides an illustration of fund balance sheets for governmental funds consistent with the standards established by GASB-34.

EXHIBIT 20-3
FUND BALANCE SHEETS FOR GOVERNMENTAL FUNDS

CASTLE ROCK COUNTY
BALANCE SHEET - GOVERNMENTAL FUNDS
DECEMBER 31, 20XX

	General	Road and Bridge	Social Services	Capital Expenditures	Other Governmental	Total
Assets						
Cash, pooled cash and investments	$78,910,392	$11,126,937	$86,166	$8,426,930	$57,797,450	$156,347,875
Taxes receivable	125,013,046	11,038,075	10,469,191	7,551,285	25,729,762	179,801,359
Other receivables	1,647,430	822	37,045	24,190	1,585,710	3,295,197
Due from other funds	2,089,154	-	500,000	-	-	2,589,154
Due from other governments	1,269,969	234,743	4,641,057	-	1,541,663	7,687,432
Inventories	330,469	-	-	-	-	330,469
Other current assets	752,980	-	-	-	12,839	765,819
Restricted cash	-	-	280,211	-	-	280,211
Restricted investments	-	-	3,552,588	6,302,656	2,153,995	12,009,239
Advances	1,608,882	-	-	-	-	1,608,882
Total Assets	**$211,622,322**	**$22,400,577**	**$19,556,258**	**$22,305,061**	**$88,821,419**	**$364,715,637**
Liabilities and Deferred Inflows of Resources						
Accounts and retainage payable	$3,556,649	$408,714	$492,173	$291,639	$4,237,401	$8,986,576
Accrued salaries	5,749,242	654,828	1,793,874	-	2,059,132	10,257,076
Other accrued liabilities	64,061	-	-	-	8	64,069
Due to other funds	-	-	1,500,000	-	866,028	2,366,028
Due to other governments	14	-	-	-	16	30
Funds held in custody for others	107,223	-	215,441	-	51,374	374,038
Unearned amounts	559,422	-	-	-	264,473	823,895
Total Liabilities	**$10,036,611**	**$1,063,542**	**$4,001,488**	**$291,639**	**$7,478,432**	**$22,871,712**

	General	Road and Bridge	Social Services	Capital Expenditures	Other Governmental	Total
Deferred Inflows of Resources						
Unavailable property tax revenue	125,013,046	10,004,250	10,469,191	7,551,285	17,154,834	170,192,606
Other unavailable revenue	-	-	-	-	1,300,000	1,300,000
Total Deferred Inflows of Resources	125,013,046	10,004,250	10,469,191	7,551,285	18,454,834	171,492,606
Fund Balances						
Nonspendable	2,692,331	-	-	-	-	2,692,331
Restricted	6,990,700	11,332,885	5,095,579	14,462,137	62,888,153	100,769,354
Assigned	25,940,524	-	-	-	-	25,940,524
Unassigned	40,949,110	-	-	-	-	40,949,110
Total Fund Balances	76,572,665	11,332,785	5,095,579	14,462,137	62,888,153	170,351,319
Total Liabilities, Deferred Inflows of Resources and Fund Balances	$211,622,322	$22,400,577	$19,556,258	$22,305,061	$88,821,419	$364,715,637

Note that in the above fund balance section, management has been delegated the highest level of decision-making for financial reporting purposes by the County Board of Supervisors. Therefore, no committed fund balance is shown.

A reconciliation between the total fund balances balance sheet and the governmental activities net position as portrayed in the statement of net position is as follows:

CASTLE ROCK COUNTY
RECONCILIATION OF TOTAL GOVERNMENTAL FUND BALANCES TO THE
STATEMENT OF NET POSITION AS OF
DECEMBER 31, 20XX

Total Governmental Fund Balances		**$170,351,319**
Amounts reported for governmental activities in the statement of net position are different because:		
Capital assets used in governmental activities excluding internal service funds that are not financial resources and therefore are not reported in the funds.		1,066,141,114
Certain receivables and revenues are deferred in the governmental funds as they are not current financial resources. These revenues are accrued under the economic resources basis of accounting.		
Long-term receivables	6,000,000	
Deferred inflows of resources—unavailable revenues	1,300,000	7,300,000
Long-term liabilities are not due and payable in the current period and therefore are not reported in the funds.		
Certificates of participation	(78,285,000)	
Notes and bonds payable	(68,500,000)	
Accrued interest payable	(661,885)	
Estimated liability for landfill postclosure costs	(1,278,636)	
Compensated absences	(18,168,263)	(166,893,784)

Deferred outflows of resources:		
Losses to be recognized in a future period for the funding of debt that occurred in a prior period	3,147,855	
Net difference between projected and actual investment earnings on pension plan investments	838,320	
Employer contributions to pension plan subsequent to the measurement date of the collective net pension liability, but prior to the fiscal year end	1,228,657	5,214,832
Net pension liability		(8,179,594)
Amortization of bond premiums, recognized in full in the governmental funds when the debt is first issued, is recorded in the statement of net position.	(1,674,116)	
Internal service funds are used by management to charge the costs of insurance and other services to individual funds. The assets and liabilities of the internal service funds are included in governmental activities in the statement of net position.	35,758,112	
Net Position of Governmental Activities		**$1,108,017,883**

Statement of Revenues, Expenditures, and Changes in Fund Balances

This operating statement for governmental funds measures the flow of current financial resources and therefore would essentially follow the current standards used to prepare governmental financial statements. The operating statement would have columns for each major fund, one for all (combined) non-major funds and a total column. NCGA-1 illustrates three distinct formats that can be used to prepare the statement of revenues, expenditures, and changes in fund balances for governmental funds; however, GASB-34 mandates that the following format be observed (GASB-34, par. 86) [GASB Cod. Sec. 2200.165].

	Major Fund #1	Major Fund #2	Nonmajor Funds	Total
Revenues (detailed)	$XXX	$XXX	$XXX	$XXX
Expenditures (detailed)	XXX	XXX	XXX	XXX
Excess (deficiency) of revenues over (under) expenditures	XXX	XXX	XXX	XXX
Other financing sources and uses, including transfers (detailed)	XXX	XXX	XXX	XXX
Special and extraordinary items (detailed)	XXX	XXX	XXX	XXX
Net change in fund balance	XXX	XXX	XXX	XXX
Fund balances—Beginning of period	XXX	XXX	XXX	XXX
Fund balances—End of period	$XXX	$XXX	$XXX	$XXX

The above format is selected because the GASB believes that most readers of the financial statements focus on (1) the excess (deficiency) of revenues over expenditures and (2) the overall change in the fund balance. Also, the GASB noted that the format is one of the formats most commonly used by governmental entities. The fund balance portion of the statement should be in the format prescribed by GASB-54, par. 22 (GASB-34, fn. 38, as amended by GASB-54, par. 22) [GASB Cod. Sec. 2200.fn30].

Revenues and expenditures presented in the statement of revenues, expenditures, and changes in fund balances are classified consistent with the standards discussed in NCGA-1, paragraphs 110–116 [GASB Cod. Secs. 1800.131–.137]. GASB-34 requires debt issuance costs paid out of the proceeds of debt issuance should be reported as expenditures rather than netted against the proceeds (and presented as an other financing source). Debt issuance costs paid from resources other than debt proceeds should be recorded as expenditures at the same time the related debt proceeds are recorded (GASB-34, par. 87) [GASB Cod. Sec. 2200.166].

The category "other financing sources and uses" would include items such as (1) sale of long-term debt (including the effects of premiums and discounts), (2) certain payments to escrow agents related to bond refundings, (3) proceeds from the sale of capital assets (unless these items are special items), and (4) transfers (GASB-34, par. 88, as amended by GASB-37, par. 16) [GASB Cod. Sec. 2200.167].

GASB-34 originally required that the "proceeds" from the sale of long-term debt be reported as another financing source and that any related discount or premium or debt issuance costs be separately reported. Taken literally, that cannot be accomplished, because the term "proceeds" generally means that any discount or premium and the related cost is netted against the face amount of the debt. GASB-37 amended GASB-34 by substituting the term "proceeds" with "face amount." Thus, under the clarified language, if debt with a face amount of $1,000,000 was issued for $1,100,000, the transaction would be presented as follows in a governmental fund's operating statement:

Portion of Statement of Revenues, Expenditures and Changes in Fund Balances	
Other financing sources and uses:	
Long-term debt issued	$1,000,000
Premium on long-term debt issued	100,000

Special and extraordinary items (defined earlier) are presented after the category titled "other financing sources and uses." If a governmental entity has both special items and extraordinary items, they should be reported under the single heading labeled "special and extraordinary items." That is, there should not be separate broad headings for each item type (GASB-34, par. 89) [GASB Cod. Sec. 2200.168].

When a significant transaction or other event occurs that is either unusual or infrequent, but not both, and is not under the control of management, that item should be reported in one of the following ways:

- Presented and identified as a separate line item in either the "revenue" category or "expenditures" category.
- Presented but not identified as a separate line item in either the "revenue" category or "expenditures" category and described in a note to the financial statements.

OBSERVATION: An extraordinary gain or loss related to the early extinguishment of debt cannot occur on a statement of revenues, expenditures, and changes in fund balances because this statement presents only the changes in *current financial resources* (as part of other financing sources and uses) and not gains and losses from events and transactions.

There must be a summary reconciliation between the total net change in fund balances (total governmental funds) as shown on the statement of revenues, expenditures, and changes in fund balances and the change in net position as presented in the governmental activities column of the statement of activities. Some of the typical items that will be needed to reconcile the two amounts are (GASB-34, par. 90, as amended by GASB-63, par. 8) [GASB Cod. Sec. 2200.169]:

- The difference between reporting revenues and expenses on the accrual basis on the statement of activities and the reporting of revenues and expenditures on the modified accrual basis on the statement of revenues, expenditures, and changes in fund balances.
- The difference between reporting depreciation expense on the statement of activities and reporting the acquisition of capital assets as an expenditure on the statement of revenues, expenditures, and changes in fund balances.
- The difference between reporting proceeds from the issuance of long-term liabilities as another source of financing on the statement of revenues, expenditures, and changes in fund balances and the non-recognition of those proceeds on the statement of activities.
- The difference between reporting the repayment of the principal of long-term liabilities as an expenditure on the statement of revenues, expenditures, and changes in fund balances and the non-recognition of those payments on the statement of activities.
- The difference between reporting the net revenue (expenses) of Internal Service Funds on the statement of activities and the non-recognition of those activities on the statement of revenues, expenditures, and changes in fund balances.

Exhibit 20-4 illustrates a statement of revenues, expenditures, and changes in fund balances for governmental funds consistent with the standards established by GASB-34.

EXHIBIT 20-4

CASTLE ROCK COUNTY
STATEMENT OF REVENUES, EXPENDITURES, AND CHANGES IN FUND BALANCES FOR GOVERNMENTAL FUNDS
STATEMENT OF REVENUES, EXPENDITURES AND CHANGES IN FUND BALANCES - GOVERNMENTAL FUNDS
FOR THE YEAR ENDED DECEMBER 31, 20XX

	General	Road and Bridge	Social Services	Capital Expenditures	Other Governmental	Total
Revenues						
Taxes and special assessments	$122,737,158	$36,444,702	$10,104,682		$63,644,969	$240,222,021
Licenses and permits	3,814,924	762,518			1,522,989	6,100,431
Intergovernmental	9,148,548	547,252	37,155,730	2,351,260	12,660,846	61,863,636
Charges for services	41,098,225	1,635,512	88,089	1,611,599	2,135,166	46,568,591
Fines and forfeitures	213,483				587,490	800,973
Investment income	1,110,361	110,980	13,483	91,308	610,634	1,936,766
Donations and contributions	97,854	303,090	575		608,695	1,010,214
Other	1,009,450	3,985	17,466	24,084	300,558	1,445,543
Total Revenues	179,320,003	39,808,039	47,380,025	11,368,761	82,071,347	359,948,175
Expenditures:						
General government	43,960,529			1,880,871	2,383	45,843,783
Public safety	98,900,079				27,693,537	126,593,616
Highways and streets	4,371,701	23,692,490			477,993	28,542,184
Sanitation					484,192	484,192
Welfare			47,636,647		4,698,813	52,335,460
Culture and Recreation	1,698,536				11,313,007	13,011,543
Economic development and assistance					4,870,493	4,870,493
Health	4,769,983					4,769,983
Capital Outlay:						
General government	1,688,836				2,074,355	3,763,191
Public safety	1,937,441				101,731	2,039,172
Highways and streets	630,529	11,388,218			4,043,261	16,062,008
Welfare			233,157			233,157
Culture and Recreation	17,927				12,147,371	12,165,298

	General	Road and Bridge	Social Services	Capital Expenditures	Other Governmental	Total
Debt Service:						
Principal	-	-	-	5,240,000	11,580,000	16,820,000
Interest	-	-	-	3,908,470	2,606,924	6,515,394
Fiscal and other charges	-	-	-	4,607	500	5,107
Intergovernmental	1,968,697	3,436,196	1,403,375	-	23,131,219	29,939,487
Total Expenditures	**159,944,258**	**38,516,904**	**49,273,179**	**13,108,303**	**103,151,424**	**363,994,068**
Excess (Deficiency) of Revenues Over Expenditures	**19,375,745**	**1,291,135**	**(1,893,154)**	**(1,739,542)**	**(21,080,077)**	**(4,045,893)**
Other Financing Sources (Uses)						
Proceeds from the sale of capital assets	601,127	-	60,590	-	661,717	661,717
Transfers—in	572,345	-	1,936,501	1,696,097	21,058,947	24,263,890
Transfers—out	(20,497,644)	(36,496)	(103,935)	-	(3,625,815)	(24,263,890)
Transfers from Internal Service Funds	31,837					31,837
Total Other Financing Sources (Uses)	**(19,292,335)**	**(36,496)**	**1,893,156**	**1,696,097**	**16,433,132**	**693,554**
Net Change in Fund Balance	83,410	1,254,639	2	(43,445)	(4,646,945)	(3,352,339)
Fund Balance - January 1	76,489,255	10,078,146	5,095,577	14,505,582	67,535,098	173,703,658
Fund Balance - December 31	**$76,572,665**	**$11,332,785**	**$5,095,579**	**$14,462,137**	**$62,888,153**	**$170,351,319**

The required reconciliation between the net change in fund balance and the net change in governmental activities contained in the statement of activities would be as follows:

CASTLE ROCK COUNTY
RECONCILIATION OF THE STATEMENT OF REVENUES, EXPENDITURES AND CHANGES IN FUND BALANCES OF GOVERNMENTAL FUNDS TO THE STATEMENT OF ACTIVITIES
FOR THE YEAR ENDED DECEMBER 31, 20XX

Net Change in Fund Balances - Total Governmental Funds		**$(3,352,339)**
Amounts reported for governmental activities in the statement of activities are different because:		
Governmental funds report capital outlays as expenditures. However, in the statement of activities the cost of those assets is allocated over their estimated useful lives and reported as depreciation expense. This is the amount by which capital outlays exceeded depreciation in the current period.		
Capital asset additions	34,262,827	
Depreciation expense	(24,943,049)	
Construction in progress capitalized in previous years, expensed in current year	(305,612)	9,014,166
Revenues in the governmental funds that provide current financial resources were previously accrued in the statement of activities when they were earned.		(50,000)
Some revenues/expenses reported in the statement of activities do not provide/require the use of current financial resources and therefore are not reported as revenues/expenditures in governmental funds.		
Donation of capital assets	(679,016)	
Capital contributions from other entities	1,048,985	
Accrued bond interest	86,126	
Amortization of bond premium and refunding loss	(106,565)	
Change in estimated liability for landfill postclosure costs	(18,636)	
Accrued compensated absences	654,904	985,798
Net book value of disposed assets is reported as revenues in the governmental funds and not reported as revenues in the statement of activities.		(641,278)
Debt service principal payments		16,820,000
Internal service funds are used by management to charge the costs of certain activities, such as insurance and fleet services, to individual funds. The net revenue (expense) of internal service funds is reported with governmental activities.		68,665
Change in Net Position of Governmental Activities		**$22,845,012**

Required Financial Statements: Proprietary Funds

Financial statements for proprietary funds should be based on the flow of economic resources (measurement focus) and the accrual basis of accounting. The proprietary fund category includes Enterprise Funds and Internal Service Funds. Proprietary fund activities should be accounted for and reported based on all applicable GASB pronouncements.

Based on the fundamental concepts discussed above, the following financial statements must be prepared for proprietary funds (GASB-34, par. 91, as amended by GASB-63, par. 8) [GASB Cod. Sec. 2200.170]:

- Statement of net position;

- Statement revenues, expenses, and changes in net position; and

- Statement of cash flows.

The major fund reporting requirement does not apply to internal service funds even though they are proprietary funds. However, all internal service funds should be combined into a single column and presented on the face of the proprietary funds' financial statements. This column must be presented to the right of the total column for all enterprise funds. The internal service funds column and the enterprise funds total column should not be added together (GASB-34, par. 96) [GASB Cod. Sec. 2200.171].

Statement of Net Position

Assets and liabilities presented on the statement of net position of a proprietary fund should be classified as current and long-term, based on the guidance codified in GASB-62, paragraphs 29 to 43. The statement of net position may be presented in either one of the following formats (GASB-34, pars. 97–98, as amended by GASB-62, par. 501 and fn. 232, GASB-63, pars. 7–8) [GASB Cod. Secs. 2200.172–.173]:

- Net position format (where assets plus deferred outflows of resources, less liabilities less deferred inflows of resources equal net position); or

- Balance sheet format (where assets and deferred outflows equal liabilities and deferred inflows plus net position).

Net position should be identified as (1) net investment in capital assets; (2) restricted; and (3) unrestricted. The guidance discussed earlier (in the context of government-wide financial statements) should be used to determine what amounts should be related to these three categories of net position. GASB-34 notes that capital contributions should not be presented as a separate component of net position. Also, designations of net position cannot be identified on the face of the statement of net position.

In the basis for conclusions to GASB-34, paragraph 430 in explaining paragraph 98 of the statement, contributed capital should not be separately identified, even as a "subcomponent" under a broader classification. As further explained in question 7.70.1 of the *GASB Implementation Guide 2015-1* [GASB Cod. Sec. 2200.742-1], the focus of reporting in government should not be on a historical record of equity transactions, but on reporting net position available to finance future services. Governments that wish to continue to provide information about the extent to which a particular enterprise fund has received capital subsidies may do so in the notes to the financial statements.

Current Assets

The term *current assets* is used to apportion cash and other assets and resources commonly identified as those that are *reasonably* expected to be realized in cash or sold or consumed within one year. They may be inclusive of:

1. Cash available for current operations and items that are the equivalent of cash;

2. Inventories of merchandise, raw materials, goods in process, finished goods, operating supplies, and ordinary maintenance material and parts;

3. Trade accounts, notes, and acceptances receivable;

4. Receivables from taxpayers, other governments, vendors, customers, beneficiaries, and employees, if collectible within a year;

5. Installment or accounts and notes receivable if they conform generally to normal trade practices and terms within the business-type activity;

6. Marketable securities representing the investment of cash available for current operations; and

7. Prepayments such as insurance, interest, rents, unused royalties, current paid advertising service not yet received, and operating supplies.

Prepayments are current assets due to the requirement to use the current assets within a year, but not ostensibly the conversion into cash within a year. (GASB-62, par. 30, as amended by GASB-65, par. 31) [GASB Cod. Sec. 2200.175].

As discussed in GASB-62, paragraph 31, and amended by GASB-65, par. 31 [GASB Cod. Sec. 2200.176], current assets do not include cash and claims to cash when they are restricted under the following conditions:

• Amounts cannot be used for current operations.

• Amounts are to be used to acquire noncurrent assets.

• Amounts are to be used to pay long-term debts.

Footnote 11 to GASB-62 [GASB Cod. Sec. 2200.fn32] further comments that even though they are not actually set aside in special accounts, resources that are clearly to be used in the near future for the liquidation of long-term debts, payments to sinking funds, or for similar purposes should also, under this concept, be excluded from current assets. However, where such resources are considered to offset maturing debt that has properly been set up as a current liability, they may be included within the current asset classification.

Unearned discounts, finance charges, and interest on receivables are shown as reductions of the related receivables. Asset valuation allowances for losses, similarly to those on receivables are deducted from the assets or groups they relate, with disclosure (GASB-62, pars. 32–33) [GASB Cod. Secs. 2200.177–.178].

In a proprietary fund it is assumed that assets (especially current assets) are unrestricted in that there are no conditions that would prevent the governmental entity from using the resources for unrestricted purposes. Generally, assets are reported as restricted assets when the nature and amount of those assets satisfy applicable legal or contractual provisions or when restrictions on asset use change the nature or normal understanding of the availability of the asset. For example, cash and cash equivalents are normally considered unrestricted current assets available to pay current liabilities. However, an amount of cash may be restricted pursuant to a debt covenant to be a debt service reserve that must be maintained throughout the life of the outstanding bonds at a specific contractual amount; therefore, it would be misleading to report this restricted cash with all other cash (classified as current asset). Under this circumstance, the cash should be reported as restricted cash in the financial statement category labeled "noncurrent assets." If the name of the asset account does not adequately explain the normally perceived availability of that asset, the item should be identified as a restricted asset on the statement of net position. On the other hand, although equipment is not available to pay liabilities, the title of the account adequately describes the availability (or lack of liquidity) of the asset and therefore there is no need to identify the asset as restricted (GASB-34, par. 99, as amended by GASB-63, par. 8) [GASB Cod. Sec. 2200.179].

Many governmental entities have assets that are restricted to specific purposes, but if those purposes are related to current operations, they should be reported as current assets.

OBSERVATION: With regard to net position (equity) classifications, restricted net positions arise only when assets are (1) externally imposed by a creditor (such as through debt covenants), grantors, contributors, or laws or regulations of other governments or (2) imposed by law through constitutional provisions or enabling legislation.

Current Liabilities

Current liabilities are principally obligations whose liquidation is expected to require the use of existing resources that are classified as current assets, or the creation of other current liabilities. Typically, current liabilities include, but are not limited to:

- Payables incurred in the acquisition of materials and supplies to be used in providing services;
- Collections received in advance of the performance of services; and
- Debts that arise from operations directly related to the operating cycle, such as accruals for wages, salaries, commissions, rentals, and royalties.

If the liability's regular and ordinary liquidation is expected to occur within one year, current liabilities may also include:

- Short-term debts arising from the acquisition of capital assets,
- Serial maturities of long-term obligations,

- Amounts required to be expended within one year under sinking fund provisions, and
- Certain agency obligations arising from the collection or acceptance of cash or other assets for the account of third parties.

There may be many other elements of current liabilities, including long-term obligations that are (or will be) callable by a creditor due to covenant violations as of the date of the financial statements and not cured within a grace period. They may also include advance ticket sales for entertainment facilities (stadiums), security deposits (unless for long-term deliveries of service), and many other potential transactions. (GASB-62, pars. 34–35, fns. 12–19, as amended by GASB-63, par. 8) [GASB Cod. Secs. 2200.180–.181].

There is no requirement that there be a specific one-to-one relationship between assets and liabilities presented and the amounts presented in the three categories of net position. In other words, a reader will not generally be able to look at the statement of net position and identify the specific assets and liability accounts that are reported as, for example, unrestricted net assets.

Exhibit 20-5 illustrates a statement of net position for proprietary funds consistent with the standards established by GASB-34 as amended.

EXHIBIT 20-5
CASTLE ROCK COUNTY
STATEMENT OF NET POSITION
PROPRIETARY FUND AS OF
DECEMBER 31, 20XX

	Business-Type Activities	Governmental Activities
	Enterprise Fund Airport	Internal Service Funds
ASSETS		
Current assets:		
Cash, pooled cash, and investments	$5,840,364	$22,059,131
Taxes receivable	13,765	—
Other receivables	126,760	68,863
Due from other governments	434,692	—
Inventories	—	524,539
Other current assets	1,123	841,668
Assets held for resale	210,999	—
Total current assets	6,627,703	23,494,201
Noncurrent assets:		
Depreciable capital assets and infrastructure, net	49,099,752	16,038,235
Land and non-depreciable infrastructure	13,828,215	—
Construction in progress	33,364	—
Total noncurrent assets	62,961,331	16,038,235
TOTAL ASSETS	$69,589,034	$39,532,436
LIABILITIES		
Current liabilities:		
Accounts and retainage payable	188,581	728,100
Accrued salaries	82,170	126,594
Other accrued liabilities	91,288	2,585,508
Advances	565,691	—
Due to other funds	223,126	—
Loans payable	225,293	—
Compensated absences	33,735	28,230
Total current liabilities	1,409,884	3,468,432
Noncurrent liabilities:		
Due to other funds — long term	1,608,882	—
Loans payable	471,066	—
Compensated absences	451,656	285,892
Total noncurrent liabilities	2,125,604	285,892

	Business-Type Activities	Governmental Activities
	Enterprise Fund Airport	Internal Service Funds
TOTAL LIABILITIES	3,535,488	3,754,324
NET POSITION		
Net investment in capital assets	62,264,972	16,038,235
Restricted for:		
Capital projects	1,175,000	—
Fleet replacement	—	11,466,091
Unrestricted	2,613,574	8,273,786
TOTAL NET POSITION	**$66,053,546**	**$35,778,112**

OBSERVATION: The element assets held for resale is not classified as an investment in accordance with GASB-72, paragraph 68 [GASB Cod. Secs. 1400.102, I50.101, I50.107]. In this example, it is a capital asset reclassified at carrying value as the sale has not been completed as of the date of the financial statements.

Statement of Revenues, Expenses, and Changes in Fund Net Position

The operating statement of a proprietary fund is the statement of revenues, expenses, and changes in fund net position. In preparing this statement, the following standards should be observed (GASB-34, par. 100, as amended by GASB-48, par. 21, and GASB-63, par. 8) [GASB Cod. Sec. 2200.190]:

- Revenues should be reported by major source.
- Revenues that are restricted for the payment of revenue bonds should be identified.
- Operating and non-operating revenues should be reported separately.
- Operating and non-operating expenses should be reported separately.
- Separate subtotals should be presented for operating revenues, operating expenses, and operating income.
- Non-operating revenues and expenses should be reported after operating income.
- Capital contributions and additions to term and permanent endowments should be reported separately.
- Special and extraordinary items should be reported separately.
- Transfers should be reported separately.

OBSERVATION: Revenues should be reported net of related discounts or allowances. The amount of the discounts or allowances must be presented on the operating statement (either parenthetically or as a subtraction from gross revenues) or in a note to the financial statements. Furthermore, if there is a right of return, U.S. GAAP require that revenue should be recognized only if prices are fixed, if the sale is not contingent on another sale, if there is no recourse if there is a theft of the item, if the sale was at more than an "arm's length," there are no future obligations between the parties, and the amount of returns can be reasonably estimated (GASB-34, fn. 41, GASB-62, pars. 26–28) [GASB Cod. Secs. 1600.134–.136, 2200.fn.44].

GASB-34 requires that the statement of revenues, expenses, and changes in fund net position should be presented in the following sequence (GASB-34, par. 101, as amended by GASB-63, par. 8) [GASB Cod. Sec. 2200.191]:

	Major Fund #1	Major Fund #2	Nonmajor Funds	Total
Operating revenues (detailed)	$XXX	$XXX	$XXX	$XXX
Total operating revenues	XXX	XXX	XXX	XXX
Operating expenses (detailed)	XXX	XXX	XXX	XXX
Total operating expenses	XXX	XXX	XXX	XXX
Operating income (loss)	**XXX**	**XXX**	**XXX**	**XXX**
Non-operating revenues and expenses (detailed)	XXX	XXX	XXX	XXX
Income before other revenues, expenses, gains, losses, and transfers	XXX	XXX	XXX	XXX
Capital contributions, additions to permanent and term endowments, special and extraordinary items (detailed), and transfers	XXX	XXX	XXX	XXX
Change in net position	**XXX**	**XXX**	**XXX**	**XXX**
Net position—Beginning of period	XXX	XXX	XXX	XXX
Net position—End of period	**$XXX**	**$XXX**	**$XXX**	**$XXX**

Operating versus Nonoperating Revenues and Expenses

An important element of the statement of revenues, expenses, and changes in fund net position is that there must be a differentiation between operating revenues and non-operating revenues, and operating expenses and non-operating expenses based on policies established by the governmental entity. Those policies should be disclosed in the entity's summary of significant accounting policies and must be applied consistently from period to period. GASB-34 states that, in general, differentiations between operating and non-operating transactions should follow the broad guidance established by GASB-9 (*Reporting Cash Flows of Proprietary and Nonexpendable Trust Funds and Governmental Entities That Use Proprietary Fund Accounting*). For example, transactions related to (1) capital and related financing activities, (2) noncapital financing activities, (3) investing activities, and (4) nonexchange revenues, such as tax revenues, generally would be considered non-operating transactions for purposes of preparing the statement of revenues, expenses, and changes in net position (GASB-34, par. 102) [GASB Cod. Sec. 2200.192].

In addition, GASB-34 provides the following guidance:

Revenue and expense transactions normally classified as other operating cash flows from operations in most proprietary funds should be classified as operating revenues and expenses if those transactions constitute the reporting proprietary fund's principal ongoing operations. For example, interest revenue and expense transactions should be reported as operating revenue and expenses by a proprietary fund established to provide loans to first-time homeowners (GASB-34, fn.42) [GASB Cod. Sec. 2200.fn45].

PRACTICE POINT: The GASB's *Implementation Guide 2015-1*, in question 2.22.2 [GASB Cod. Sec. 2450.708-4], emphasizes that a governmental entity must decide how to define its operating and non-operating activities for proprietary funds. The reference in GASB-34 to the guidance provided in GASB-9 pars. 17–19, as amended by GASB-34, par. 112 [GASB Cod. Secs. 2450.114–.116] simply provides general concepts but they should not be viewed as requirements. This definition should be disclosed in the summary of significant accounting policies section of the notes to the basic financial statements.

In the question, property taxes are levied by a hospital district for care of indigent patients. The property taxes would *not* be an operating activity, unless they are levied for capital purposes. The operating activity of a hospital involves patient care. However, the GASB concludes that even if the amount levied is calculated to finance estimated care of the indigent, it is not a charge for services. Instead, property taxpayers are financing the care of the indigent, which is a subsidy as defined in GASB-9, paragraph 21(d) [GASB Cod. Sec. 2450.118(d)], and presentation as a noncapital financing inflow. For the statement of revenues, expenses and changes in net position purposes, the tax revenue may indeed be defined as operating per the hospital's policies and procedures. However, it would be reclassified in the statement of cash flows to noncapital financing.

PRACTICE ALERT: The GASB's *Financial Reporting Model—Reexamination* project includes research if the GASB should establish a definition of operating and non-operating activities. Some stakeholders would like the definition to be established by industry or peers. For example, colleges and universities may have a different definition of operations than airports, housing entities, finance entities, hospitals, stadiums, transit systems, and lotteries. Other stakeholders desire some form of consistency across all types of operations. This aspect of the project is among the more controversial topics. The GASB's Preliminary Views contains the Board's tentative view on the subject.

The GASB tentatively decided to propose that the definition of nonoperating revenues and expenses include subsidies received and provided, revenues and expenses of financing, resources from the disposal of capital assets and inventory, and investment income and expenses. Sale of inventory held for resale in the ordinary course of operations is not considered a disposal of inventory for purposes of this definition. This definition could change throughout the remainder of the project, but it should be followed closely by the stakeholders it may effect.

Based on the standards established by GASB-34, the statement of revenues, expenses, and changes in fund net position must reflect the "all-inclusive" concept. That is, except for prior period adjustments and the effects of certain changes in accounting principles, all resources inflows (except for liabilities) must be reported on a proprietary fund's operating statement. Thus, additions to permanent and term endowments can no longer be shown as direct additions to a fund capital. The guidance for determining when these items should be recognized is based on GASB-33 [GASB Cod. Sec. N50] (GASB-34, par. 103, as amended by GASB-63, pars. 8–9) [GASB Cod. Sec. 2200.193].

The fact that capital contributions are reported on a proprietary fund's operating statement does not mean that the contribution results in an increase in unrestricted net position. The transactions must be evaluated to determine whether the amount is appropriately presented as part of net investment in capital assets.

As described earlier, there must be reconciliations between the government-wide financial statements and the governmental fund financial statements. Generally, there is no need for a similar reconciliation between the government-wide financial statements and proprietary fund financial statements because both sets of financial statements are based on the same measurement focus and basis of accounting (GASB-34, par. 104, as amended by GASB-63, par. 8) [GASB Cod. Sec. 2200.194].

Typically, there are no reconciling items between business-type activities as they appear on the government-wide financial statements and the fund financial statements because both statements are prepared on the accrual basis of accounting and economic resources measurement focus. In general, the following are common reconciling items between business-type activities and government-wide financial statements:

- When enterprise funds are the only or predominant participants in an internal service fund, the balances related to the internal service fund must be included in the business-type activities column (not the governmental activities column, which is the typical presentation). Because internal service funds are not included in the totals of the enterprise funds (but rather, are presented in a column to the right of those funds) in the fund financial statements, a reconciling item arises.

- When enterprise funds participate in an internal service fund and the internal service fund is not at a "break even" position, a look-back adjustment must modify the expenses in the business-type activities column. This creates a difference between the expenses as presented in the fund financial statements and the expenses presented in the government-wide financial statements.

- When a governmental activity is performed in an enterprise fund (or vice versa), the results of the activity are presented in an enterprise fund financial statement, but those same results are also presented in the governmental activity column of the government-wide financial statements. This creates a difference between the two financial statements.

Exhibit 20-6 illustrates a statement of revenues, expenses, and changes in net position for proprietary funds consistent with the standards established by GASB-34.

EXHIBIT 20-6
CASTLE ROCK COUNTY
STATEMENT OF REVENUES, EXPENSES, AND CHANGES IN NET POSITION: PROPRIETARY FUNDS
FOR THE YEAR ENDED DECEMBER 31, 20XX

	Business-Type Activities	Governmental Activities
	Enterprise Fund Airport	Internal Service Funds
Revenues		
Operating Revenues:		
Insurance charges	$—	$33,054,376
Fleet rental charges	—	7,984,085
Rental income	2,948,066	—
Other	396,004	262,991
Total operating revenues	**3,344,070**	**41,301,452**
Operating Expenses:		
Salaries and related costs	1,375,686	2,513,459
Supplies	551,403	2,496,539
Other services and charges	636,636	33,219,321
Depreciation	3,421,290	2,925,263
Intergovernmental	2,430	—
Interdepartmental charges	305,870	700,064
Total operating expenses	**6,293,315**	**41,854,646**
Operating income (loss)	**($2,949,245)**	**$(553,194)**
Non-operating revenues (expenses)		
Fuel taxes	239,672	—
Investment income	99,529	225,183
Interest expense	(87,965)	-
Gain on disposal of capital assets	1,667,633	428,513
Total Non-operating revenues (expenses)	**1,918,869**	**653,696**
Contributions:		
Capital grants	1,230,677	—
Transfers out	—	(31,837)
Change in Net Position	**200,301**	**68,665**
Net Position — January 1	65,853,245	35,709,447
Net Position — December 31	**$66,053,546**	**$35,778,112**

Statement of cash flows. Proprietary funds should prepare a statement of cash flows based on the guidance established by GASB-9, except the statement of cash flows should be formatted based on the direct method in computing cash flows from operating activities. The statement of cash flows would be supplemented with a reconciliation of operating cash flows and operating income (GASB-34, par. 105) [GASB Cod. Sec. 2200.195].

Exhibit 20-7 illustrates a statement of cash flows for proprietary funds consistent with the standards established by GASB-34.

EXHIBIT 20-7
CASTLE ROCK COUNTY
STATEMENT OF CASH FLOWS:
PROPRIETARY FUNDS
FOR THE YEAR ENDED DECEMBER 31, 20XX

	Business-Type Activities	Governmental Activities
	Enterprise Fund Airport	Internal Service Funds
Cash flows from operating activities		
Cash received from:		
Insurance charges	$—	$33,047,139
Rental income	2,948,227	7,997,106
Other	395,664	278,855
Cash payments to or on behalf of:		
Employees	(1,382,340)	(2,542,637)
Suppliers	(1,564,371)	(35,310,509)
Others	(420,291)	(1,736,530)
Net cash provided by (used by) operating activities	**(23,111)**	**1,733,424**
Cash flows from noncapital financing activities		
Fuel taxes	243,556	-
Transfers Out	-	(31,837)
Net cash provided by (used by) noncapital financing activities	**243,556**	**(31,837)**
Cash flows from capital and related financing activities		
Cash proceeds from the sale of capital assets	1,667,633	428,513
Cash paid for acquisition of capital assets	(1,694,957)	(3,566,935)
Payment to the general fund for capital loan	(216,247)	-
Capital grants	3,404,185	-
Interest payments	(87,965)	-
Loan payments	(218,731)	-

	Business-Type Activities	Governmental Activities
	Enterprise Fund Airport	Internal Service Funds
Net Cash Flows provided by (used by) Capital and Related Financing Activities	2,853,918	(3,138,422)
Cash Flows from Investing Activities		
Investment income	99,529	225,183
Net Cash Flows from Investing Activities	99,529	225,183
Net Increase (Decrease) in Cash and Cash Equivalents	3,173,892	(1,211,652)
Cash and Cash Equivalents—Beginning of Year	2,666,472	23,270,783
Cash and Cash Equivalents—End of Year	$5,840,364	$22,059,131
Reconciliation of Operating Loss to Net Cash provided by (used by) Operating Activities		
Operating income (loss)	$ (2,949,245)	$(553,194)
Adjustments to reconcile operating loss to net cash provided by operating activities:		
Depreciation expense	3,421,290	2,925,263
(Increase) decrease of assets:		
Receivables	161	5,784
Inventories	-	(13,490)
Other current assets	(340)	5,248
Increase (decrease) of liabilities:		
Accounts payable	(1,012,968)	418,841
Accrued salaries and benefits	(6,654)	(29,178)
Other accrued liabilities	524,645	(1,025,850)
Net cash provided by (used by) operating activities	$(23,111)	$1,733,424

Noncash transactions consisted of an acquisition of capital assets in the accounts payable balance of the airport in the amount of $117,119 and capital grants due from other governments, also in the airport in the amount of $434,692.

Required Financial Statements: Fiduciary Funds and Similar Component Units

Assets held by a governmental entity for other parties (either as a trustee or as an agent) and that cannot be used to finance the governmental entity's own operating programs should be reported in the entity's fiduciary fund financial statement category. The financial statements for fiduciary funds should be based on the flow of economic resources measurement focus and the accrual basis of accounting (with the exception of certain liabilities of defined benefit pension plans until the implementation of GASB-68 and certain postemployment health-care plans). Fiduciary fund financial statements are not reported by major fund (which is required for governmental funds and proprietary funds) but must be reported based on the following fund types (GASB-34, par. 106, as amended by GASB-63, par 8, GASB-73, pars. 115–116, GASB-74, par. 20) [GASB Cod. Sec. 2200.196]:

- Pension (and other employee benefit) Trust Funds;
- Private-Purpose Trust Funds;
- Investment Trust Funds; and
- Agency Funds.

The financial statements of a fiduciary component unit should be included in one of the four fund types listed above. GASB's *Implementation Guide 2015-1*, question 7.55.5 [GASB Cod. Sec. 2200.729-8], emphasizes that a fiduciary fund that a governmental entity believes is particularly important cannot be presented in a separate column in the fund financial statements. If a governmental entity wants to present additional detail about its fiduciary funds, that information can be presented in combining statements. However, those statements are optional and are not considered to be part of the basic external financial statements. They are part of the CAFR.

PRACTICE ALERT: As discussed previously, see Chapter 8, "Fiduciary Funds," for an extensive discussion of GASB-84 (*Fiduciary Activities*).

Current GAAP (prior to GASB-84) require fiduciary fund reporting for assets held in a trustee or agency capacity for others and therefore cannot be used to support the government's own programs. If a government is a member/sponsor of a statewide pension plan for example, it may not be in a trustee or agency capacity for the plan. The plan's trustees would likely serve that purpose. Even in accordance with the various GASB pronouncements related to pensions and other post-employment benefits (OPEB), minimal (if any) reporting may be needed in pension trust funds for member/sponsoring governments in statewide cost-sharing multiple employer plans as the government has no managerial, trustee, or agency responsibility.

The following financial statements should be included for fiduciary funds:

- Statement of fiduciary net position; and
- Statement of changes in fiduciary net position.

PRACTICE POINT: Only a statement of fiduciary net position is prepared for an Agency Fund in accordance with current U.S. GAAP.

Statement of fiduciary net position. The assets, liabilities, and net position of fiduciary funds should be presented in the statement of fiduciary net position. There is no need to divide net position into the three categories (net investment in capital assets, restricted net position, and unrestricted net position) that must be used in the government-wide financial statements (GASB-34, par. 108, as amended by GASB-63, pars. 7–8, GASB-67, pars. 15–21, GASB-73, pars. 115–116, GASB-74, pars. 21–27) [GASB Cod. Sec. 2200.197], because all net position is ultimately in trust for beneficiaries.

Statement of changes in fiduciary net position. The statement of changes in fiduciary net position should summarize the additions to, deductions from, and net increase or decrease in net position for the year. GASB-34 also requires the statement to provide information "about significant year-to-year changes in net position" (GASB-34, par. 109, as amended by GASB-63, par. 8, GASB-67, pars. 22–29, GASB-73, pars. 115–116, and GASB-74, pars. 20–33) [GASB Cod. Sec. 2200.198].

Exhibit 20-8 is a statement of fiduciary net position and Exhibit 20-9 is a statement of changes in fiduciary net position.

Because an Agency Fund is established to account for assets of another party, only a statement of fiduciary net position should be reported for these funds. Furthermore, since the governmental entity has no equity in an Agency Fund, a statement of fiduciary net position should report only assets and liabilities (no amount for net position).

Under current U.S. GAAP (until GASB-84 is implemented) an Agency Fund is used when an irrevocable trust is not in place, plan assets are not dedicated to providing benefits to their retirees and their beneficiaries in accordance with the terms of the plan, and plan assets are not legally protected from creditors of the employer(s) or the plan administrator, yet assets are being accumulated that could ultimately be for retirees and beneficiaries (GASB-34, par. 110, as amended by GASB-63, par. 8, GASB-73, pars. 8 and 116, GASB-74, pars. 7 and 59) [GASB Cod. Secs. 2200.199, P53, Pe5.101, Po50].

Note: The underlying government that was used as the basis for these illustrations has no pension trust funds or private purpose trusts, only agency funds. The pension trust funds column below is for illustrative purposes only.

EXHIBIT 20-8
STATEMENT OF FIDUCIARY NET POSITION
AS OF DECEMBER 31, 20XX

	Pension Trust Funds	Agency Funds
ASSETS		
Cash, pooled cash and investments	$191,184,274	$25,658,261
Taxes receivable (net)	-	45,918
Interest receivable	200,421	—
Other assets		

	Pension Trust Funds	Agency Funds
Investments at Fair Value:		
U.S. Government and agencies	22,206,282	—
Corporate Obligations	16,518,383	—
Real estate investment trust (REIT)	9,660,250	—
Corporate stocks	53,693,510	—
Total investments	102,078,425	—
Total assets	**$293,463,120**	**$25,704,179**

LIABILITIES AND NET POSITION

	Pension Trust Funds	Agency Funds
Current liabilities:		
Accounts payable and accrued liabilities	65,514	3,853,710
Other accrued liabilities	-	145,178
Due to other governments	-	10,040,554
Due to bondholders	-	11,664,737
Total liabilities	**65,514**	**$25,704,179**

NET POSITION

Net Position restricted for pensions	**$293,397,606**

EXHIBIT 20-9
STATEMENT OF CHANGES IN FIDUCIARY NET POSITION
FOR THE YEAR ENDED DECEMBER 31, 20XX

	Pension Trust Funds
Additions:	
Contributions:	
Employer	$8,036,000
Plan members	14,016,063
Total Contributions	22,052,063
Net investment income:	
Investment earnings	42,688,837
Dividends	898,571
Gross investment income	43,587,408
Investment expenses	(365,264)
Net investment income	43,222,144
Total additions	**65,274,207**

	Pension Trust Funds
Deductions:	
Benefits paid to participants	26,675,878
Administrative expenses	241,635
Total deductions	26,917,513
Net increase (decrease)	38,356,694
Net Position Restricted for Pensions:	
Beginning of year	255,040,912
End of year	$293,397,606

Under current U.S. GAAP, an Agency Fund may be used as a clearing account when one governmental entity collects or receives financial resources that are to be distributed to other funds and other governmental entities. For example, a county government may collect property taxes that are to be allocated to the county government and to school districts, fire districts, or other governmental entities that are not part of the county government. Under this circumstance, the portion of the assets that belong to the county government (the reporting entity) should not be reported in an Agency Fund but rather should be reported as assets of the appropriate county governmental fund (GASB-34, par. 111) [GASB Cod. Sec. 2200.200].

Reporting Interfund Activity

In order to determine how intergovernmental transfers within and among governmental funds, proprietary funds, and fiduciary funds should be presented in the government-wide and fund financial statements, transfers must be categorized as follows (GASB-34, par. 112) [GASB Cod. Secs. 1100.112, 1300.120, 1800.101–.102, 2450.114–.115, .118, .120, .128, C50.126]:

- Reciprocal interfund activity
  —Interfund loans; and
  —Interfund services provided and used;
- Nonreciprocal interfund activity
  —Interfund transfers; and
  —Interfund reimbursements.

Reciprocal interfund activities are internal fund activities that have many of the same characteristics of exchange and exchange-like transactions that occur with external parties. Nonreciprocal interfund activities are internal fund activities that have many of the same characteristics of nonexchange transactions that occur with external parties.

Interfund loans. The concept of a loan as envisioned by GASB-34 is based on the expectation that the loan will be repaid at some point. Loans should be reported as interfund receivables by the lender fund and interfund payables by the borrower fund. That is, the interfund loan should not be eliminated in the preparation of financial statements at the fund level. Thus, the proceeds from interfund loans should not be reported as "other financing sources or uses" in the operating statements in the fund financial statements. If a loan or a portion of a loan is not expected to be repaid "within a reasonable time," the interfund receivable / payable should be reduced by the amount not expected to be repaid, and that amount should be reported as an interfund transfer by both funds that are a party to the transfer.

The GASB's *Implementation Guide 2015-1*, question 7.59.2 [GASB Cod. Sec. 1800.702-5], points out that professional judgment must be used to determine what constitutes "expected within a reasonable time." For example, the past history of repayment or lack of history can be relevant in making the determination. In other circumstances, the ability of a fund to make repayment could help make the determination.

Interfund services provided or used. Interfund receivables/payables may arise from an operating activity (i.e., the sale of goods and services) between funds rather than in the form of a loan arrangement. If the interfund operating activity is recorded at an amount that approximates the fair value of the goods or services exchanged, the provider/seller fund should record the activity as revenue and the user/purchaser fund should record an expenditure/expense. Any unpaid balance at the end of the period should be reported as an interfund receivable/payable in the fund statements. GASB-34 points out that GASB-10 (*Accounting and Financial Reporting for Risk Financing and Related Insurance Issues*), paragraph 64, requires when the General Fund is used to account for risk-financing activities, interfund charges to other funds must be accounted for as reimbursements.

Interfund transfers. This type of nonreciprocal transaction represents interfund activities where the two parties to the events do not receive equivalent cash, goods, or services. Governmental funds should report transfers of this nature in their activity statements as other financing uses and other financing sources of funds. Proprietary funds should report this type of transfer in their activity statements after non-operating revenues and non-operating expenses. Based on the standards established by GASB-34, there is no differentiation between operating transfers and residual equity transfers. Thus, no transfers can be reported as adjustments to a fund's beginning equity balance. GASB-34 points out that most payments "in lieu of taxes" should be reported as interfund transfers, unless the payments and services received are equivalent in value based on the exchange of specific services or goods. If the two are equivalent in value, the disbursing fund may treat the payment as expenditures (expense) and the receiving fund may record revenue. It is unlikely that current *in lieu of tax* arrangements involve the payments for identifiable services that are based on the value of services rendered.

The GASB's *Implementation Guide 2015-1*, question 7.72.7 [GASB Cod. Sec. 1800.702-7], discusses how a governmental entity should report a "payment in lieu of taxes" from an Enterprise Utility Fund to its General Fund. The nature of the payment must be examined to determine whether it approximates a fair value exchange. If the interfund operating activity is recorded at an amount that approximates the fair value of the goods or services exchanged, the General Fund (provider/seller fund) should record the activity as revenue and the

Enterprise Utility Fund (user/purchaser fund) should record an expenditure/expense. It is unlikely that this type of transaction would involve an exchange of services of equivalent value because of the indirect nature of the services provided through the General Fund. For this reason, it is probable that the payment would be treated as a transfer-out by the Enterprise Utility Fund and transfer-in by the General Fund.

Interfund reimbursements. A fund may incur an expenditure or expense that will subsequently be reimbursed by another fund. Reimbursements should not be reported in the governmental entity's financial statements in order to avoid "double counting" revenues and expense/expenditure items.

Notes to the Basic Financial Statements

The notes to the financial statements should focus on the primary government (which includes its blended component units) and support the information included in the government-wide financial statements and the fund financial statements (GASB-34, par. 113) [GASB Cod. Secs. 2300.102, .106, 2600.123, C50.146, D20.116].

OBSERVATION: Note disclosures of discretely presented or blended component units *should only be those that are essential to fair presentation in the reporting government's basic financial statements.* Deciding what is "*essential*" is based on the government's professional judgment and should be done on a component unit-by-component unit basis. A specific type of disclosure might be essential for one component unit but not for another depending on the individual component unit's relationship with the primary government. For example, if a primary government is obligated in some manner for the debt of a particular component unit, it is likely that debt-related disclosures should be made for that component unit.

PRACTICE POINT: Wolters Kluwer's *2018 Governmental GAAP Disclosures Manual* contains the entirety of required disclosures contained in GASB statements as of the date of publication and numerous examples. Included with the manual is a financial statement disclosures checklist from the perspective of the preparer and a suggested disclosure sequence.

PRACTICE ALERT: A somewhat parallel project to the *Financial Reporting Model—Reexamination* project being performed by the GASB is to reexamine note disclosures, focusing on requirements in existence prior to the issuance of GASB Statement No. 72 (*Fair Value Measurement and Application*). As of the date of publication, the project is finalizing initial research to present to the GASB for approval as a full-scale project. If approved, initial due process documents may not be released until 2019, at the earliest.

GASB-34, as amended by GASB-38 and many other standards, contains required note disclosures. NCGAI-6, as amended, contains the following non-authoritative sequence of note disclosures [GASB Cod. Sec. 2300.901]:

I. Summary of significant accounting policies (including departures from GAAP, if any).

PRACTICE POINT: If budgetary comparison information is reported in a budgetary comparison statement as part of the basic financial statements, rather than as RSI, the following should be inserted after subparagraph I.E:

F. Budgetary data.

    1. Budget basis of accounting.

    2. Excess of the expenditures over appropriations.

A. Description of the government-wide financial statements and exclusion of fiduciary activities and similar component units.

B. A brief description of the component units of the financial reporting entity and their relationships to the primary government. This should include a discussion of the criteria for including component units in the financial reporting entity and how the component units are reported. Also include information about how the separate financial statements for the individual component units may be obtained. In component unit separate reports, identification of the primary government in whose financial report the component unit is included and a description of its relationship to the primary government.

C. Basis of presentation—Government-wide financial statements.

    1. Governmental and business-type activities, major component units.

    2. Policy for eliminating internal activity.

    3. Effect of component units with differing fiscal year-ends.

D. Basis of presentation—fund financial statements.

    1. Major and nonmajor governmental and enterprise funds, internal service funds, and fiduciary funds by fund type.

    2. Descriptions of activities accounted for in the major funds, internal service fund type, and fiduciary fund types.

    3. Interfund eliminations in fund financial statements not apparent from headings.

E. Basis of accounting.

    1. Accrual—government-wide financial statements.

    2. Modified accrual—governmental fund financial statements, including the length of time used to define *available* for purposes of revenue recognition.

      3. Accrual—proprietary and fiduciary fund statements.

  F. Assets, liabilities, and net position and fund balances described in the order of appearance in the statements of net assets/balance sheet.

      1. Definition of cash and cash equivalents used in the proprietary fund statement of cash flows.

      2. Disclosure of valuation bases.

      3. Capitalization policy, estimated useful lives of capital assets.

      4. Description of the modified approach for reporting infrastructure assets (if used).

      5. Significant or unusual accounting treatment for material account balances or transactions.

      6. Policy regarding whether to first apply restricted or unrestricted resources when an expense is incurred for purposes for which both restricted and unrestricted net assets are available.

  G. Revenues, expenditures/expense.

      1. Types of transactions included in program revenues in the government-wide statement of activities.

      2. Policy for allocating indirect expense to functions in the government-wide statement of activities.

      3. Unusual or significant accounting policy for material revenue, expenditures, and expenses.

      4. Property tax revenue recognition.

      5. Vacation, sick leave, and other compensated absences.

      6. Policy for defining operating revenues and operating expenses in proprietary fund statements of revenues, expenses, and changes in fund net position.

II. Stewardship, compliance, and accountability.

  A. Significant violations of finance-related legal and contractual provisions and actions taken to address such violations.

  B. Deficit fund balance or fund net assets of individual funds.

III. Detail notes on all activities and funds.

PRACTICE POINT: If aggregated information in the summary reconciliations to government-wide statements obscures the nature of individual elements of a particular reconciling item, a more detailed explanation should be inserted after the Summary of Significant Accounting Policies.

  A. Assets.

      1. Cash deposits and pooling of cash and investments.

      2. Investments.

3. Reverse repurchase agreements.

4. Securities lending transactions.

5. Receivable balances.

6. Property taxes.

7. Due from other governments—grants receivable.

8. Required disclosures about capital assets.

B. Liabilities.

1. Payable balances.

2. Pension plan obligations and postemployment benefits other than pension benefits.

3. Other employee benefits.

4. Construction and other significant commitments.

5. Claims and judgments.

6. Lease obligations (capital and operating).

7. Short-term debt and liquidity.

8. Long-term debt.

   a. Description of individual bond issues and leases outstanding.

   b. Required disclosures about long-term liabilities.

   c. Summary of debt service requirements to maturity.

   d. Terms of interest rate changes for variable-rate debt.

   e. Disclosure of legal debt margin.

   f. Bonds authorized but unissued.

   g. Synopsis of revenue bond covenants.

   h. Special assessment debt and related activities.

   i. Debt refundings and extinguishments.

   j. Demand bonds.

   k. Bond, tax, and revenue anticipation notes.

9. Landfill closure and postclosure care.

C. Interfund receivables and payables and interfund eliminations.

D. Revenues and expenditures / expenses.

1. On-behalf payments for fringe benefits and salaries.

2. Significant transactions that are either unusual or infrequent, but not within the control of management.

E. Donor-restricted endowment disclosures.

F. Interfund transfers.

G. Encumbrances outstanding.

IV. Segment information—enterprise funds.

V. Individual major component unit disclosures (if not reported on the face of the government-wide statements or in combining statements).

VI. The nature of the primary government's accountability for related organizations.

VII. Joint ventures and jointly governed organizations.

VIII. Related party transactions.

IX. Summary disclosure of significant contingencies.

    A. Litigation.

    B. Federally assisted programs—compliance audits.

X. Significant effects of subsequent events.

The foregoing illustrative note disclosures are not a comprehensive illustration of all disclosure requirements. In other circumstances, governments may be required to provide additional disclosures related to, for example, the following:

- Accounting policies
- Asset Retirement Obligations
- Bond, revenue, and tax anticipation notes
- Chapter 9 bankruptcies
- Claims and judgments
- Commitments and contingencies
- Component units
- Conduit debt
- Defeased Debt with Existing Resources
- Deferred outflows of resources or deferred inflows of resources
- Deficit fund balances
- Demand bonds
- Deposits and investments
- Derivatives
- Disposal of government operations
- Encumbrances
- External investment pools
- Governmental fund balances
- Government combinations
- Impairment of capital assets and insurance recoveries
- Interfund eliminations
- Joint ventures and jointly governed organizations
- Nonexchange financial guarantees
- Nonexchange transactions that are not measurable
- Operating leases
- On-behalf payments

- Pension and other postemployment benefit plans
- Pollution remediation
- Related organizations
- Related-party transactions
- Reporting entity considerations
- Repurchase and reverse repurchase agreements
- Sales and pledges of revenue
- Securities lending
- Segment information
- Service concession arrangements
- Special assessments
- Tax Abatement Disclosures
- Termination benefits
- Violations of legal provisions

PRACTICE ALERT: Upon implementation of GASB Statement No. 84 (*Fiduciary Activities*), the above description is amended to note that fiduciary activities are *not* included. For a further discussion of GASB-84, see Chapter 8, "Fiduciary Funds."

PRACTICE POINT: The item on pensions references the alignment of the bases of accounting between the government and the plan(s). The bases of accounting may not be in alignment when the government (or the plans) use(s) a special purpose framework. If a government uses a special purpose framework, a reconciliation between the framework and the plan's information would be inserted in the subsection. An example disclosure in the Summary of Significant Accounting Policies is as follows:

For purposes of measuring the net pension liability, deferred outflows of resources and deferred inflows of resources related to pensions, and pension expense, information about the fiduciary net position of the State Employees' Pension Plan (SEPP) and additions to/deductions from SEPP's fiduciary net position have been determined on the same basis as they are reported by SEPP. For this purpose, benefit payments (including refunds of employee contributions) are recognized when due and payable in accordance with the benefit terms. Investments are reported at fair value.

The GASB's *Implementation Guide 2015-1*, question 7.84.3 [GASB Cod. Sec. 2300.703-4], discusses GASB-34, paragraph 115(h), as amended, with regard to the use of restricted resources disclosure. Governments are required to state their policy for *when* they use restricted resources. That is, are restricted resources used only after unrestricted resources have been spent for a particular purpose or are restricted resources assumed to be spent first? This sort of disclosure should be in a policy and if significant, discussed in the summary of significant accounting policies.

Required Note Disclosures about Fund Types and Activities of Funds

As introduced previously, GASB-38 requires that the summary of significant accounting policies include a description of the activities accounted for in the following columns of fund financial statements presented in the basic financial statements, assuming the columnar titles used in the fund financial statements are not sufficiently descriptive of the activities accounted for in a specific fund or fund type (GASB-38, par. 6) [GASB Cod. Secs. 1300.125, 2300.106]:

- Major funds (governmental and proprietary funds). Descriptions should also include references to special revenue fund restrictions (potentially including legal references as options).
- Internal Service Funds.
- Fiduciary Fund Types (Pension [and other employee benefit] Trust Funds, Investment Trust Funds, Private-Purpose Trust Funds, and Agency Funds).

The description should not focus on the definition of the fund type used to account for the activity but, rather, should describe the nature of the activities specifically accounted for in the fund. For example, if a restricted grant is accounted for in a Special Revenue Fund, the description should not simply present the definition of a Special Revenue Fund as provided by GASB-54 but, rather, should describe the source, purpose, and the restrictive nature of the grant. Because the Internal Service Fund column and the columns for each of the four fiduciary fund types could be made up of two or more separate funds, the description should include the major activities combined in each of these financial statement columns.

The followings are examples of fund titles and related descriptions that more fully describe the activities of a fund:

Major Fund Title	Disclosure (description of fund activity)
Governmental Funds	
Road and Bridge Fund	This fund records costs related to County road and bridge construction and maintenance except for engineering and public works administration, which are recorded in the general fund. By State of Centennial law, counties are required to maintain a road and bridge fund, and a portion of road and bridge taxes is allocated to cities and towns for their use in road and street activities. Most of this fund's revenues come from property, auto ownership, and highway users' taxes.

Major Fund Title	Disclosure (description of fund activity)
Social Services Fund	This fund administers human services programs under federal and state regulations. Programs include, but are not limited to, Medicaid, Food Stamps, Child Welfare Program, Aging and Adult Services Programs, Job Training Services, Temporary Assistance to Needy Families (TANF), and similar programs. Counties are required by state law to maintain a Social Services Fund. Besides receiving federal and state grant funds, this fund receives property taxes to fund any county matching requirements.
Capital Expenditure Fund	This fund is used to accumulate and provide monies for major capital expenditures in the County. The fund is also used to pay debt service for bonds issued in 20W9 in accordance with that series' bond indenture. The proceeds from the 20W9 bonds were used to fund an animal shelter and court and detention facilities.
Proprietary Fund	
Airport Fund	This fund (the only proprietary fund) accounts for the operations and results of the Castle Rock County Metropolitan Airport.

OBSERVATION: Based on the standards established by GASB-34, the General Fund is always considered a major fund. Because of the nature of a General Fund, its description could be limited to a general statement such as "this fund is the municipality's primary operating fund and it is used to account for all financial resources of the general government except those required to be accounted for in another fund." However, in some instances a governmental entity may decide the title (General Fund) is sufficiently descriptive and provide no description of the fund in the summary of significant accounting policies.

Required Note Disclosures about Capital Assets and Long-Term Liabilities

In order to support information included in a governmental entity's statement of net position prepared on a government-wide basis, disclosures related to capital assets and long-term liabilities should be included in the governmental entity's notes. The disclosures should observe the following guidance (GASB-34, par. 116) [GASB Cod. Secs. 2300.106, .117]:

- The presentations should be based on major classes of capital assets and long-term liabilities.

- Capital assets and long-term liabilities should be segregated into governmental activities and business-type activities.

- Non-depreciable capital assets, such as land, must be presented separately from depreciable capital assets.

Capital Asset Disclosures Note disclosures that relate to capital assets should include the following information (GASB-34, par. 117) [GASB Cod. Secs. 2300.106, .118]:

- Beginning and year-end balances (regardless of whether prior-year data are presented on the face of the government-wide financial statements), with accumulated depreciation separately identified;
- Capital acquisitions for the period;
- Sales or other dispositions for the period; and
- Current-period depreciation expense, supported by identifying amounts allocated to each functional expense presented in the statement of activities.

If a governmental entity chooses not to capitalize collection items (as discussed earlier), the following disclosures should be made (GASB-34, par. 118) [GASB Cod. Secs. 2300.106, .119]:

- A description of the capital assets not capitalized; and
- The reason the assets are not capitalized.

OBSERVATIONS: If collections are capitalized, the disclosures that apply to all other capital assets must be observed. If a service concession arrangement exists, the capital assets involved in the service concession arrangement may be disclosed on a separate line in the capital assets note to the basic financial statements, if material. The arrangement itself is best disclosed with the leases of the government (see lease disclosure herein).

Exhibit 20-10 illustrates a note that incorporates the disclosure requirements for capital assets established by GASB-34.

EXHIBIT 20-10
CAPITAL ASSET DISCLOSURES

	Beginning Balance	Increases	Transfers	Decreases	Ending Balance
Governmental Activities:					
Capital Assets Not Being Depreciated:					
Land and Land Improvements	$682,806,981	$5,125,396	$ -	$(525,000)	$687,407,377
Construction in Progress	51,254,390	15,539,832	(8,839,690)	(984,629)	56,969,903
Total Capital Assets Not Being Depreciated	734,067,371	20,665,228	(8,839,690)	(1,509,629)	744,377,280
Capital Assets Being Depreciated:					
Buildings and Improvements	253,983,248	577,384	207,283	-	254,767,915
Machinery and Equipment	104,850,621	6,827,529	430,391	(4,946,474)	107,152,067
Infrastructure	334,841,951	10,978,676	8,212,016	(5,836,103)	348,196,540
Total Capital Assets Being Depreciated	693,675,820	18,383,589	8,839,690	(10,782,577)	710,116,522
Less: Accumulated Depreciation:					
Buildings and Improvements	(102,168,814)	(6,064,495)	-	-	(108,233,309)
Machinery and Equipment	(66,511,485)	(8,244,003)	-	4,660,124	(70,095,364)
Infrastructure	(186,262,070)	(13,559,813)	-	5,836,103	(193,985,780)
Total Accumulated Depreciation	(354,942,369)	(27,868,311)	-	10,496,227	(372,314,453)
Total Capital Assets Being Depreciated, Net	338,733,451	(9,484,722)	8,839,690	(286,350)	337,802,069
Total Governmental Activities	$1,072,794,822	$11,180,506	$ -	$(1,795,979)	$1,082,179,349

Depreciation expense was charged to functions / programs of the primary government as follows:

Governmental Activities	Depreciation
General Government	$9,660,383
Public Safety	3,239,607
Highways and Streets	12,925,404
Culture and Recreation	1,629,835
Welfare	404,148
Sanitation	8,934
Total Depreciation Expense—Governmental Activities	**$27,868,311**

Capital Asset activity of the business-type activities for the year ended December 31, 20X6 was as follows:

	Beginning Balance	Increases	Transfers	Decreases	Ending Balance
Business-Type Activities:					
Capital Assets Not Being Depreciated:					
Land and Land Improvements	$13,828,215	$-	$-	$-	$13,828,215
Construction in Progress	23,144,875	33,364	(23,144,875)	-	33,364
Total Capital Assets Not Being Depreciated	36,973,090	33,364	(23,144,875)	-	13,861,579
Capital Assets Being Depreciated:					
Buildings and Improvements	8,333,927	-	-	-	8,333,927
Machinery and Equipment	5,114,624	42,725	-	-	5,157,349
Infrastructure	61,798,040	914,502	23,144,875	(9,112)	85,848,305
Total Capital Assets Being Depreciated	75,246,591	957,227	23,144,875	(9,112)	99,339,581
Less Accumulated Depreciation:					
Buildings and Improvements	(5,126,525)	(235,403)	-	-	(5,361,928)
Machinery and Equipment	(2,976,836)	(260,707)	-	-	(3,237,543)
Infrastructure	(38,720,228)	(2,925,180)	-	5,050	(41,640,358)
Total Accumulated Depreciation	(46,823,589)	(3,421,290)	-	5,050	(50,239,829)
Total Capital Assets Being Depreciated, net	28,423,002	(2,464,063)	23,144,875	(4,062)	40,099,752
Total Business-Type Activities	$65,396,092	$(2,434,699)	$-	$(4,062)	$62,961,331

Note that there is no standard format for the placement of parenthesis or dollar signs in any schedule in the basic financial statements, the notes to the basic financial statements, or any other schedule in the annual financial report. Some governments use parentheses for debits or for credits. Finally, in accordance with GASB-61, it is up to the primary government to decide whether or not to include capital asset information from component units in with this disclosure.

Long-Term Liabilities Disclosures

The disclosures related to long-term debt should encompass both long-term debt instruments (such as bonds, loans, and capitalized leases) and other long-term liabilities (such as estimated liabilities related to compensated absences and claims and judgments). These disclosures should include the following information (GASB-34, par. 119) [GASB Cod. Secs. 2300.106, .120, L20.125, .135]:

- Beginning and year-end balances (regardless of whether prior-year data are presented on the face of the government-wide perspective financial statements);

- Increases and decreases (separately presented) for the period;

- The part of each liability that is due within one year; and

- The governmental fund that has been generally used to pay other long-term liabilities (i.e., items such as compensated absences and claims and judgments).

GASB-34, paragraph 119(d), requires a governmental entity that has changed its policy concerning which governmental fund has been used in the past to liquidate certain long-term liabilities to discuss the change in the notes to the basic financial statements. The discussion is required as it provides readers with additional information about future claims against financial resources to assist them in assessing balances of funds.

Information related to net pension liabilities is reported in a separate note in accordance with GASB-68 and GASB-75, rather than with the overall long-term liabilities disclosures.

PRACTICE ALERT: GASB Statement No. 88 (*Certain Disclosures Related to Debt, including Direct Borrowings and Direct Placements*) is effective for reporting periods beginning after June 15, 2018. Additional information on GASB-88 is contained in Chapter 12, "Long-Term Debt."

Exhibit 20-11 illustrates a note that incorporates the disclosure requirements for long-term liabilities as well as other forms of debt.

EXHIBIT 20-11
LONG-TERM DEBT DISCLOSURES

	Beginning Balance	Increases	Decreases	Ending Balance	Due Within One Year
Governmental Activities					
Certificates of Participation:					
Series 20W9	$58,170,000	$—	$(3,325,000)	$54,845,000	$3,420,000
Series 20X3	22,115,000	—	(2,045,000)	18,070,000	2,080,000
Bonds Payable:					
Open Space 20W9	30,655,000	—	(7,220,000)	23,435,000	7,505,000
Open Space 20X0	12,245,000	—	(1,895,000)	10,350,000	1,940,000
Open Space 20X3	17,285,000	—	(1,715,000)	15,570,000	1,765,000
Northwest County District Imp. 20X2	8,315,000	—	(1,205,000)	7,110,000	1,240,000
Unamortized Premiums	1,674,116	—	(434,211)	1,239,905	434,211

	Beginning Balance	Increases	Decreases	Ending Balance	Due Within One Year
Landfill liability	1,278,636	392,254	(78,700)	1,592,190	97,970
Compensated absences	18,482,385	1,642,217	(1,853,270)	18,271,332	1,853,270
Total Governmental Activities	**$168,220,137**	**$2,034,471**	**$(19,771,181)**	**$150,483,427**	**$20,335,451**
Business-Type Activities					
Loans payable	$696,359	$ —	$(225,293)	$471,066	$232,052
Compensated absences	79,391	1,094	(12,092)	68,393	12,092
Total Business-Type Activities	**$775,750**	**$1,094**	**($237,285)**	**$539,459**	**$244,144**

As discussed previously, professional judgment must be used to determine the degree to which, if any, disclosures related to capital assets and long-term liabilities of discretely presented component units should be made.

Disclosures about Interfund Balances and Transfers

Various interfund transfers occur within most governmental reporting entities. For example, an interfund balance may arise from the sale of goods or services, the reimbursement of expenditures or expenses, or the provision of operating capital. These transfers can be an important resource for governmental services performed, and for this reason an analysis of interfund balances and transfers can provide insight into the viability of a particular governmental activity. GASB-38 requires that the following information for interfund balances included in fund financial statements be disclosed in a note to the financial statements:

- Identification of the amounts due from other funds by (1) individual major funds, (2) aggregated nonmajor governmental funds, (3) aggregated nonmajor Enterprise Funds, (4) aggregated Internal Service Funds, and (5) fiduciary fund types.
- The purpose for interfund balances.
- Interfund balances that are not expected to be repaid within one year of the date of the balance sheet (or Statement of Net Position).

The presentation should include interfund balances that are considered material. Those that are immaterial should be aggregated and presented as a single amount. However, the total of all balances should agree with the total interfund balances presented in the balance sheet for governmental funds and statement of net position of proprietary funds.

The focus of the aforementioned analysis is on the debtor fund rather than the creditor fund because the GASB believes that it is important for readers to be able to assess the likelihood that a particular interfund loan can be repaid. On the other hand, the explanations for interfund balances that are not expected to be paid within a year can alert readers of the financial statements to loan arrangements that are more or less long-term in nature, recurring, or unusual.

GASB-38 also requires that interfund activity for the year be summarized in a note to the financial statements that includes the following:

- Disclosure of amounts transferred from other funds by:
  - Individual major funds,
  - Aggregated nonmajor governmental funds,

- — Aggregated nonmajor Enterprise Funds,
- — Aggregated Internal Service Funds, and
- — Fiduciary fund types.
- • General description of the principal reasons for the government's interfund transfers.
- • The purpose and amount of significant transfers that satisfy either or both of the following criteria:
  - — Do not occur on a routine basis; or
  - — Are inconsistent with the activities of the fund making the transfer.

The focus of the disclosure of interfund transfers for the period is on the fund that provides the resources to another fund. The GASB believes that this focus is justified because it will help readers to determine whether the provider fund has the ability to continue to make subsidies to the recipient fund. However, the scope of the disclosure is limited in that there is no requirement to disclose the nature of *all* interfund transfers except in general terms. For example, the principal reasons for interfund transfers could include subsidy strategies, debt service requirements, and the need to match grants received from other governmental entities. However, if during the year there has been an interfund transfer that is not routine, financial statements readers should be informed of the size and nature of the transfer. In a similar fashion, when an interfund transfer is not consistent with the nature of the provider fund, readers should also be informed of that matter. For example, if a Debt Service Fund makes a transfer to an Enterprise Fund, that interfund transfer generally must be explained.

The presentation should include transfers that are considered material. Those that are immaterial should be aggregated and presented as a single amount. However, the total of all transfers should agree with the total transfers presented in the financial statements of governmental funds and proprietary funds.

PRACTICE POINT: Examples of these footnotes are contained in Wolters Kluwer's 2018 *Governmental GAAP Disclosure Manual*, Chapter 28.

Reporting Component Units

The reporting of component units in a primary government's basic external financial statements is discussed in Chapter 4, "Governmental Financial Reporting Entity."

Required Supplementary Information Other Than MD&A

Required supplementary information (RSI) is not part of the basic financial statements, but the GASB considers RSI to be an important part of a governmental entity's financial report. All RSI (with the exception of MD&A information) must be presented immediately after the notes to the basic financial statements (GASB-34, pars. 6, 129, GASB-67, pars. 32–34, GASB-68, pars. 46–47, 81–82, 114–

115, and 117, GASB-73, pars. 45–46, 66–67, 93–94, 96, and 115–116, GASB-74, pars. 36–38 and 59, GASB-75) [GASB Cod. Sec. 2200.205].

Currently, the GASB has established the following RSI standards in various GASB statements:

- MD&A (see earlier discussion in this chapter);
- Budgetary comparison schedules (see the following discussion);
- Reporting infrastructure assets under the modified approach (see Chapter 10, "Capital Assets");
- Public entity risk pools revenue and claims development information (see Chapter 23, "Public Entity Risk Pools"); and
- Employee benefit related information as detailed in Chapter 13, "Pension, Postemployment, and Other Employee Benefit Liabilities," especially with regard to disclosures required by GASB-68 (*Accounting and Financial Reporting for Pensions—an amendment of GASB Statement No. 27*), GASB-73 (*Accounting and Financial Reporting for Pensions and Related Assets That Are Not within the Scope of GASB Statement 68, and Amendments to Certain Provisions of GASB Statements 67 and 68*), GASB-74 (*Financial Reporting for Postemployment Benefit Plans Other than Pensions*), and GASB-75 (*Accounting and Financial Reporting for Postemployment Benefits Other than Pensions*).

OBSERVATION: There is a minor inconsistency in U.S. GAAP with regard to the statistical section and whether or not it is required supplementary information. In the preparation of a CAFR, not a set of basic financial statements, a statistical section is an integral part of information provided for a CAFR. However, the GASB has not definitely said that a statistical section is RSI when preparing a CAFR, even though in the implementation guide the GASB deems statistical data to be an essential part of reporting. But, if a public entity risk pool is part of the reporting entity, U.S. GAAP requires that if the pool does not issue a separate report, the information required by that paragraph should be reported in the statistical section of the financial reporting entity's comprehensive annual financial report. Therefore, at the very least, the statistical section is supplementary information.

Budgetary Comparison Schedules

GASB-34 requires that the budgetary comparison schedules for the General Fund and each major Special Revenue Fund that has a legally adopted annual budget be presented as RSI or as a basic financial statement. The schedule should include columns for the following (GASB-34, par. 130, as amended by GASB-41, par. 3) [GASB Cod. Sec. 2200.206]:

- The original budget;
- The final appropriated budget; and
- Actual results (presented on the government's budgetary basis).

PRACTICE ALERT: An integral part of the GASB's *Financial Reporting Model—Reexamination* project is to deliberate whether budgetary comparison schedules should be standardized as either RSI or as a basic financial statement. The GASB has tentatively concluded to standardize reporting as part of RSI and has included the provision in the GASB's preliminary views released in September 2018.

Question 7.91.10 [GASB Cod. Sec. 2200.763-12]in the GASB *Implementation Guide 2015-1* applies the requirements of GASB-34, paragraph 130, to governments that budget on a biennial basis. There is no exemption. The phrase *legally adopted* in paragraph 130 applies to the general fund as well as major special revenue funds. As explained in question 7.91.13 [GASB Cod. Sec. 2200.763-15], if a special-purpose government maintains a general fund (or its equivalent), but it is not legally required to adopt or does not legally adopt a budget, the budgetary comparison schedule would not be presented in the basic financial statements or required supplementary information. Nonmajor special revenue funds, capital projects and debt service funds are *not required* to be presented.

The following budgetary descriptions are established by GASB-34, par. 130, as amended by GASB-41, par. 3 [GASB Cod. Sec. 2200.206]:

Original budget—The first complete appropriated budget. The original budget may be adjusted by reserves, transfers, allocations, supplemental appropriations, and other legally authorized legislative and executive changes before the beginning of the fiscal year. The original budget should also include actual appropriation amounts automatically carried over from prior years by law.

Final budget—The original budget adjusted by all reserves, transfers, allocations, supplemental appropriations, and other legally authorized legislative and executive changes applicable to the fiscal year, whenever signed into law or otherwise legally authorized.

Appropriated budget—The expenditure authority created by the appropriation bills or ordinances which are signed into law and related estimated revenues.

The GASB encourages (but does not require) governmental entities to present an additional column that reflects the differences between the final budget and the actual amounts. An additional column may present the differences between the original budget and the final budget.

The comparative budgetary information described above can be presented as a basic financial statement rather than as RSI (schedule presentation). When the information is presented as a basic financial statement, the information should be reported with fund financial statements after the statement of changes in revenues, expenditures, and changes in fund balances. All of the budgetary information must be presented in one place. That is, a governmental entity may not present budgetary comparison information for its General Fund as a basic financial statement and present similar information related to its major Special Revenue Funds as required supplementary information. In some instances, a governmental entity might not be required to legally adopt an annual budget for its General Fund or a Special Revenue Fund that is a major fund and therefore there is no requirement to present the budgetary comparison information. If that is the case, GASB-34 requires that the fact that budgetary comparison information is not presented for a particular fund be included in the notes to RSI. However, the AICPA's *State and Local Governments* Guide points out that "if the government chooses to present its required budgetary comparison information in the basic financial statements, which disclosure should be made in the notes to the financial statements."

The comparative budgetary information may be presented "using the same format, terminology, and classifications as the budget document, or using the format, terminology, and classifications in a statement of revenues, expenditures, and changes in fund balances." In either case, there must be a reconciliation (presented in a separate schedule or in notes to RSI) between the budgetary information to U.S. GAAP information. Any excess of expenditures over appropriations in an individual fund must be disclosed in a note to the RSI. If the governmental entity presents the comparative budgetary information as a basic financial statement, the note related to the excess of expenditures over appropriations must be reported as a note to the financial statements rather than as a note to RSI (GASB-34, par. 131, GASB-37, par. 19) [GASB Cod. Sec. 2200.207].

Some other factors need to be weighed in the disclosure of original and final budgets:

- Some governmental entities initially use an interim budget (e.g., three months) that provides temporary spending authority. The original budget (as described above) must cover the entire fiscal period.

- GASB-34, paragraph 130a, specifically states that "the original budget includes actual appropriation amounts automatically carried over from prior years by law." If prior-year encumbrances are rolled forward by law, the current (original) budget includes those items. The amount of the encumbrances will be known or a reasonable estimate of them can be made in time to prepare the financial information.

- GASB-34, paragraph 130b, specifically states that amendments (such as transfers of appropriations between line items) must be included in the final budget, regardless of when they are "signed into law or otherwise legally authorized."

In some instances, a governmental entity is, for budgetary purposes, required to account for an activity in a particular fund type but based on the definitions established by GASB-34 must report that activity in another fund type. The reporting and disclosure requirements established by GASB-34 apply to the fund type that is actually used to report the activity and not to the fund type required for internal budgetary purposes.

Disclosure of Budgetary Policies

The appendix to NCGAI-6 recommended that the financial statements include a description of general budgetary policies. To comply with this recommendation, some governmental entities disclose their budgetary calendar and the legal level of budgetary control.

OBSERVATION: The GASB believes that sufficient presentation of budgetary information is achieved by the requirements established previously by NCGA pronouncements and GASB-34. These presentation requirements include (1) budgetary comparison schedules, (2) reconciliation of budgetary information to

U.S. GAAP information, (3) disclosure of the budgetary basis of accounting, and (4) disclosure of violations of legal provisions.

Budgetary Comparison Schedules for Other Funds

Some governmental entities may include in the financial section of their CAFR budgetary comparisons for debt service, capital projects, nonmajor special revenue funds, and other funds that have legally adopted budgets. However, GASB-34 establishes standards for the basic financial statements, MD&A, and certain RSI, but that its scope does not cover other components of the CAFR. If a governmental entity decides to present budgetary comparison schedules for debt service, capital projects, nonmajor special revenues funds, and other funds, the guidance established by GASB-34 (pars. 130–131, as amended) [GASB Cod. Secs. 2200.206–.207] may but does not have to be followed.

Excess of Expenditures over Appropriations

GASB-34 requires that budgetary comparison schedules be presented only for the General Fund and each major Special Revenue Fund that has a legally adopted annual budget. Additionally, paragraph 131 of GASB-34 [GASB Cod. Sec. 2200.207] establishes disclosure requirements for budgetary comparison schedules. One of the requirements states that any excess of expenditures over appropriations in an individual fund must be disclosed. The question has arisen regarding whether the required disclosure applies to only those funds that are presented in the budgetary comparison schedule. GASB-37 clarifies the standards established by GASB-34 by limiting the disclosures related to budgetary comparison schedules to the funds that are part of the required supplementary information. Paragraph 4(g) of NCGAI-6 established a requirement for governments to disclose material violations of finance-related legal and contractual provisions. GASB-38 expanded this requirement to include actions taken by the governmental entity to remedy the violations.

OBSERVATION: Any excess of expenditures over appropriations must be disclosed in the notes to the RSI; however, if the amount is considered a "material violation of finance-related legal provisions," the violations must also be disclosed in a note to the basic financial statements.

Reconciling Budget and U.S. GAAP Information

Budgetary comparison schedules should be accompanied by information that reconciles U.S. GAAP information and budgetary information. These differences may arise because of (1) entity differences, (2) perspective differences, (3) basis differences, (4) timing differences, or (5) other differences (NCGAI-10, par. 15; NCGAI-6, par. 5; and GASB-34, par. 131) [GASB Cod. Sec. 2200.207].

Entity differences. The reporting entity may include component units whose activities are not part of the appropriated budget. For example, a component unit may be subject to a legal non-appropriated budget and, thus, be excluded from the appropriated budget. But based on the criteria established in GASB-14 (*The*

Financial Reporting Entity), the component may be part of the overall reporting entity.

Perspective differences. The structure of the budget itself determines its perspective. The financial information contained in the budget may be constructed to reflect various points of view including the governmental unit's organizational structure, fund structure, or program structure. For example, budgetary information may be prepared on a program basis whereby all expenditures associated with a particular objective may be grouped irrespective of which organizational unit or fund makes the expenditure.

OBSERVATION: When there is a difference between the perspective for budgeting purposes and for financial reporting purposes, it is often difficult to reconcile the two sets of financial information. For example, if the budgetary system uses a program basis and the financial reporting system uses the fund basis, it is unlikely that a meaningful reconciliation can be prepared. In this case, the reconciliation between the GAAP-basis financial statements and the budgeted financial statements would be limited to entity, basis, and timing differences.

In most instances perspective differences are minor and can easily be isolated in order to prepare the necessary reconciliation between the budgetary and U.S. GAAP information. However, GASB-41 points out that some governmental entities have "budgetary structures that prevent them from associating the estimated revenues and appropriations from their legally adopted budget to the major revenue sources and functional expenditures that they report in their General Fund and major Special Revenue Funds" and therefore are not able to prepare budgetary comparison schedules (or statements) required by GASB-34. For example, assume that a governmental entity's budgetary focus (not related to the data elsewhere in this chapter) is referred to as the "Comprehensive Statutory Budget" and its budget is as follows:

	Budgeted per Statutory (in thousands of dollars) Ordinance
REVENUES:	
Taxes	$ 121,434
Licenses and permits	2,695
Intergovernmental revenues	8,343
Charges for services	22,387
Fines and forfeits	127
Investment earnings	640
Rental income	795
Miscellaneous	19,303
Total Revenues	**175,724**

	Budgeted per Statutory (in thousands of dollars) Ordinance
EXPENDITURES:	
General government	54,955
Public safety	89,791
Highways and Streets	4,145
Culture and leisure	1,166
Interdepartmental	27,088
Non-departmental health	5,868
Intergovernmental	2,606
Total Expenditures	**185,619**
Estimated Surplus (Deficit)	**$ (9,895)**

In this case, the government only passes a budget for the General Fund, similar to many other governments. A legally adopted budget schedule should be presented for any fund where a budget is passed. Within each category may be many other categories. For example, taxes may have separate entries for property, automobile excise, interest and penalties, gasoline and other categories. Charges for services may have budgeted revenues from every type of charge that the government assesses. Every category of expenditures may be disaggregated in a manner in which the government operates. For example, general government may have each department within general government and then further delineated by personnel services, supplies, other services and charges and even more detail, depending up on how the government manages its operations. There is no specific requirement in paragraphs 130 and 131 of GASB-34 for specific categories of revenues and expenditures in the schedule, other than compliance with the definitions of *original budget, final budget,* and actual amounts as discussed previously. However, paragraph 131 allows a government to present the budgetary comparison schedule using the same format, terminology, and classifications as the budget document in a similar manner to the statement of revenues, expenditures and changes in fund balances for the General Fund and each major Special Revenue Fund. In practice, governments include a schedule that is in sufficient detail necessary for the users of the schedule.

If a budgetary comparison schedule is prepared that compares the Comprehensive Statutory Budget to a statement of revenues, expenditures, and change in fund balance, a number of reconciling items are needed to explain the differences between budgetary inflows and outflows on an actual basis and those amounts reported in the General Fund on a U.S. GAAP basis.

The standards established by GASB-41 require (as was required previously) a comparative schedule for the General Fund and for each major Special Revenue Fund that has a legally adopted annual budget but allows one exception: A governmental entity that has perspective differences of the nature described above may prepare a budgetary comparison schedule as RSI based on the fund organization, or program structure that the entity uses as a basis for the legally adopted budget. The foundation for this exception is that the focus of the comparison schedule will be based on activities that are reported in the entity's General Fund or in a Special Revenue Fund. That is, when an activity (or collection of activities) is not presented as part of the General Fund or a Special Revenue Fund, the budgetary unit that includes various activities cannot be the focus for presenting budgetary comparison schedules.

PRACTICE POINT: The exception perspective that is allowed for comparative budgetary information can only be in the form of budgetary comparison schedules presented as RSI and not as financial statements.

Under the alternative comparison schedule focus approach, most of the items on the reconciliation would be similar to other reconciliations, but the following two items (based on the example presented above) would be used to remove the budgetary amounts for the various other funds (it is assumed in this example that the Special Revenue Fund is not a major fund and therefore does not require a separate budgetary comparison schedule) from the actual amounts reported on the budgetary comparison schedule.

Basis differences. The budgeting basis may differ from the accounting basis. For example, the governmental unit may be required by law to use the cash basis for budgeting purposes, but may be required by financial reporting purposes to use the modified accrual basis U.S. (GAAP basis).

Timing differences. There may be differences between the budgetary amounts and the U.S. GAAP basis amounts due to the different treatment of items such as continuing appropriations and biennial budgeting. For example, a governmental unit may treat encumbrances that are outstanding at the end of the year as expenditures of the current period for budgetary purposes, but, for reporting purposes, they cannot be classified as expenditures of the current period.

Other differences. NCGAI-10 notes that differences not classified in the previous four categories also should be included in the reconciliation between the entity's budgetary practices and U.S. GAAP practices.

Additional reporting. The prior discussion has been concerned exclusively with budgetary reporting on a comparative basis with actual results for funds that adopt an annual appropriated budget. NCGA-1 recognizes that governmental units may be subject to control through the implementation of other types of budgets. For example, NCGAI-10 defines a "non-appropriated budget" as follows (NCGAI-10, par. 11) [GASB Cod. Secs. 1700.114, 2400.108]:

> A financial plan for an organization, program, activity, or function approved in a manner authorized by constitution, charter, statute, or ordinance but not subject to appropriation and therefore outside the boundaries of the definition of "appropriated budget."

The NCGA takes the position that "more comprehensive budget presentations are generally to be preferred over the minimum standards." Thus, the existence of the minimum presentation requirements should not inhibit a reporting entity from presenting additional budgetary information. Even if additional budgetary disclosures are not made, there should be a disclosure in notes to the financial statements describing budgetary controls, including appropriated budgets and other budget or financial control plans used by the reporting entity (NCGAI-10, par. 13) [GASB Cod. Sec. 2400.120].

Some governmental entities establish various levels of budgetary control through multiple appropriation bills and ordinances. When budgetary comparison schedules required by GASB-34 are presented, the budgetary control classification scheme can be aggregated based on functional or program costs and "sources" of revenue (such as taxes, licenses and permits, intergovernmental revenues, charges for services, fines and forfeits, and miscellaneous items). However, when reporting individual funds on a budgetary basis at the CAFR level, the presentation generally requires a level of account detail that is consistent with actual budgetary control within the entity. NCGAI-10 states that in an "extreme" circumstance, the reporting entity may need to prepare a separate report in order to present revenues and expenditures in enough detail that is consistent with the budgetary control. When the entity must present a separate report, the notes to the RSI should refer to the separate report (NCGAI-10, par. 14, and GASB-34, pars. 6 and 131) [GASB Cod. Secs. 2200.207, 2400.121].

OBSERVATION: The level of detail included in the separate report cannot be greater than that used to present the budgetary information included in the RSI.

Exhibit 20-12 illustrates a budget-to-actual comparison schedule in a format allowed by GASB-34. (Note: the amounts in the schedule do not relate to the previous schedules and are for illustrative purposes only.)

EXHIBIT 20-12
BUDGET-TO-ACTUAL COMPARISON SCHEDULE

General Fund Example Government for the Year Ended December 31, 20XX

	Budgeted Amounts		Actual Amounts (Budgetary Basis See Note X)	Variance with Final Budget Positive (Negative)
	Original	Final		
Budgetary Fund Balance, January 1, 20XX	**$53,177,187**	**53,177,187**	**53,177,187**	—
Resources (Inflows):				
Taxes	116,845,801	116,845,801	113,809,641	(3,036,160)
Licenses and permits	2,660,160	2,660,160	2,471,544	(188,616)
Intergovernmental revenues	13,075,703	14,146,734	14,570,521	423,787
Charges for services	33,169,497	33,194,497	32,092,354	(1,102,143)
Fines and forfeits	6,311,000	6,311,000	6,362,062	51,032
Investment earnings	21,010,000	21,010,000	22,927,674	1,917,674
Rental income	1,126,773	1,126,773	1,073,420	(53,353)
Miscellaneous	2,105,342	2,105,342	2,307,555	202,213
Total Revenues	**196,304,276**	**197,400,307**	**195,614,741**	**(1,785,566)**
Amounts Available for Appropriation	**$249,481,463**	**250,577,494**	**248,791,928**	**(1,785,566)**
Charges to Appropriations (Outflows):				
General government	26,562,059	34,998,059	39,277,386	(4,279,327)
Public safety	99,252,660	99,696,764	97,209,499	2,487,265
Transportation	23,612,253	24,353,258	23,026,269	1,326,989
Culture and leisure	13,729,395	13,768,865	13,783,967	(15,102)
Community development	8,533,597	8,210,177	8,104,996	105,181
Total expenditures	**171,689,915**	**181,027,074**	**181,402,037**	**(374,963)**
Excess of Amounts Available for Appropriation over expenditures	**77,791,548**	**69,450,520**	**67,389,891**	**(2,160,629)**
Transfers in	18,258,197	26,294,197	26,931,281	637,084
Transfers out	(49,201,438)	(51,666,438)	(47,756,165)	3,910,273
Budgetary Fund Balance, December 31, 20X8	**$46,848,307**	**$44,278,179**	**$46,565,007**	**$2,386,728**

Exhibit 20-13 illustrates a budget-to-GAAP reconciliation required by GASB-34.

EXHIBIT 20-13
BUDGET TO GAAP RECONCILIATION

General Fund

Example Government

for the Year Ended December 31, 20XX

NOTE X: Explanation of differences between budget and U.S. GAAP.

In the above example, the government has no perspective differences as they budget on a U.S. GAAP basis. Common differences include, but are not limited to:

- The fund balance at the beginning of the year is a budgetary resource but is not a current-year revenue for financial reporting purposes.

- Transfers from other funds are inflows of budgetary resources but are not revenues for financial reporting purposes.

- The proceeds from the sale of real estate are budgetary resources but are considered a special item, rather than revenue, for financial reporting purposes.

- Transfers to other funds are outflows of budgetary resources but are not expenditures for financial reporting purposes.

Combining Financial Statements

Although it is not required in the minimum presentation in order to be in accordance with U.S. GAAP, a CAFR should include combining statements for the following situations:

- Combining financial statements by fund type for the primary government when there is more than one nonmajor fund; and

- Combining financial statements for discretely presented component units when the reporting entity has more than one nonmajor component unit (fund financial statements for individual component units are required if the financial information is not available to readers in separately issued reports).

Each of the individual financial statements in the combining is in the same format and contains the same content as its respective fund type as previously discussed in this chapter.

More Than One Nonmajor Fund

The focus of the fund statements included in the basic financial statements is on the major funds. As noted earlier, each major fund is presented in the fund statements in a separate column. Nonmajor funds are aggregated and presented in a single column. There is no requirement to present combining statements for nonmajor funds in the basic external financial statements but the information may be presented as supplementary information to the financial statements. If the nonmajor funds are not presented as supplementary information they must be presented as part of the CAFR in combining financial statements by fund type for the primary government.

The combining statements could have a section for all Special Revenue Funds, Capital Projects Funds, and so on. For instance, a governmental unit may have five nonmajor Special Revenue Funds and three nonmajor Capital Projects Funds. The combining financial statements would include a separate column for each of the eight nonmajor funds and a total column that can be traced into the fund financial statements that present major funds and aggregated nonmajor funds. In addition, the overall format and terminology used in the fund financial statements and the combining financial statements should be similar to provide a basis for easy cross-reference between the two sets of information.

The concept of a major fund does not apply to an Internal Service Fund. For this reason, all Internal Service Funds are presented in combining financial statements as part of the CAFR rather than as part of the basic external financial statements in a manner similar to the presentation described in the previous paragraph.

OBSERVATION: If a governmental entity has only a single Internal Service Fund, it is presented in the fund financial statements as a separate column and there would be no need to present its financial information in a combining financial statement.

More Than One Nonmajor Discretely Presented Component Unit

GASB-34 was written in a manner that satisfies the financial reporting entity standards originally established by GASB-14 (*The Financial Reporting Entity*) with respect to component units. Relevant guidance established by GASB-14 is as follows:

> The financial statements of the reporting entity should allow users to distinguish between the primary government and its component units by communicating information about the component units and their relationships with the primary government rather than creating the perception that the primary government and all of its component units are one legal entity (GASB-14, par. 42) [GASB Cod. Secs. 2100.142, 2600.105].

In addition, paragraph 51 of GASB-14 [GASB Cod. Sec. 2600.108]requires that information related to each major component unit be presented in the reporting entity's basic financial statements. To satisfy this standard, any one of the following approaches can be used:

- Present each major component unit in a separate column in the government-wide financial statements;

- Present combining statements (with a separate column for each major unit and a single column for the aggregated nonmajor units); or

- Present condensed financial statements in a note to the financial statements (with a separate column for each major unit and a single column for the aggregated nonmajor units).

OBSERVATION: The requirement for major component unit information does not apply to component units that are fiduciary in nature.

Each of these three presentation methods creates information that is part of the basic external financial statements; however, if there is more than one nonmajor component unit, the information concerning these nonmajor units must be presented in combining financial statements.

Individual Fund Financial Statements

The CAFR should include individual fund statements for the following situations:

- When the primary government has a single nonmajor fund of a given fund type; and
- When it is necessary to present comparative budgetary information about the previous year and the current year, if it is not presented in RSI.

Content of Combining Statements and Individual Fund Statements

As discussed, GASB-34 requires that a primary government present its major governmental and major enterprise and combined internal service funds on the face of the fund financial statements. In addition, the following combining and individual fund statements must be included in the financial section of a CAFR. In accordance with GASB-54, combining balance sheets for governmental funds also have to be in GASB-54 format, segregating nonspendable, restricted, committed, assigned, and unassigned balances. Required statements are as follows unless the entity presents only the basic financial statements (NCGA-1, pars. 143, 147, as amended by GASB-34, pars. 12, 75, 78, 80, 82, 86, 91, 96, 106–107, 112, and 130, and GASB-63, par. 9, GASB-9, par. 6) [GASB Cod. Sec. 2200.208]:

- *Nonmajor governmental funds:*
  - Combining balance sheets.
  - Combining statements of revenues, expenditures, and changes in fund balances.
  - Individual fund balance sheets and statements of revenues, expenditures, and changes in fund balances and schedules necessary to demonstrate compliance with finance-related legal and contractual provision of governmental funds.
- *Internal Service Funds and Nonmajor Enterprise Funds:*
  - Combining statements of fund net position.
  - Combining statements of revenues, expenses, and changes in fund net position.
  - Combining statements of cash flows.

— Individual statements of revenues, expenses, and changes in fund net position and individual statements of cash flows and schedules necessary to demonstrate compliance with finance-related legal and contractual provisions.

- *Fiduciary Funds:*

  — A combining statement of fiduciary net position.

  — A combining statement of changes in fiduciary net position.

Other Supplementary Schedules

The CAFR should include other schedules for the following situations:

- When it is necessary to demonstrate compliance with finance related legal and contractual provisions;

- When it is useful to bring together information that is spread throughout the financial statements and present the information in more detail; and

- When it is useful to present more detail for a line item that is presented in a financial statement.

Under certain circumstances, these schedules may be used to present data that is on a legally or contractually prescribed basis that is different from U.S. GAAP and/or may include data that management wants to present that is not required by U.S. GAAP. A common schedule may be used to comply with bond covenants. (NCGA-1, par. 131) [GASB Cod. Sec. 2200.210].

Narrative descriptions that facilitate the understanding of information in combining financial statements, individual fund and component unit financial statements, and schedules may be included directly on divider pages, the financial statements or schedules, or in an accompanying section appropriately labelled (NCGA-1, par. 159, as amended by GASB-34, pars. 6, 80, 82, 126 and fn.50) [GASB Cod. Sec. 2200.211].

PRACTICE POINT: The Government Finance Officers Association (GFOA) Certificate of Achievement in Financial Reporting program includes additional supplementary schedules as part of the program for different types of entities. For postemployment benefit plans as well as cash and investment pools, schedules of administrative expenses, investment expenses and payments to consultants for fees paid to other professionals other than investment providers are included. Postemployment benefit plans also include an investment section and an actuarial section. In addition, some governments that are required to have a single audit performed may include a section attached to their financial reports with a schedule of expenditures of federal awards, required reporting and other schedules. Finally, state and local governments may have additional schedules presented that are required by law, regulation or bond indenture. Unless a GASB statement requires these schedules, they are not RSI, they are supplementary information only.

STATISTICAL SECTION

Information included in the statistical tables section is not part of the governmental unit's basic financial statements even though the material is part of the CAFR. Statistical tables may include non-accounting information and often cover ten years or more information. In general, the purpose of presenting statistical tables is to give the user a historical perspective that will enhance the analysis of the governmental unit's financial condition (NCGA-1, pars. 132, 160, and 161) [GASB Cod. Sec. 2200.212].

GASB-44 (*Economic Condition Reporting—The Statistical Section*) [GASB Cod. Sec. 2800] establishes the reporting requirements for the statistical section of governments' annual reports when a CAFR is presented. Governments that prepare a statistical section for the first time in response to GASB-44, or that previously prepared a statistical section but did not present certain information, are encouraged but not required to report all required years of information retroactively. Governments are also encouraged but not required to implement the government-wide information required by GASB-44 retroactively to the year they implemented GASB-34.

GASB-44 defines the objectives of reporting statistical section information as follows:

> To provide financial statement users with additional historical perspective, context, and detail to assist in using the information in the financial statements, notes to financial statements, and required supplementary information to understand and assess a government's economic condition (GASB-44, par. 5) [GASB Cod. Sec. 2800.104].

GASB-44 separates the statistical information into five categories (GASB-44, par. 6) [GASB Cod. Sec. 2800.105]:

1. *Financial trends information* is intended to assist users in understanding and assessing how a government's financial position has changed over time. Examples for general purpose governments are:

   a. Net position by component and changes in net position by component for the last 10 fiscal years; and

   b. Fund balances for governmental funds and changes in fund balances for governmental funds for the last 10 fiscal years.

PRACTICE POINT: Many of these schedules may change with the implementation of any U.S. GAAP standard that requires a beginning balance restatement or a change in accounting practice. As examples, GASB-54 restated fund balance and fund types and GASB-68 restated how pension accounting and financial reporting is performed. In both cases, beginning balance changes, new accounting elements, or reformatting occurred.

---

2. *Revenue capacity information* is intended to assist users in understanding and assessing the factors that affect a government's ability to generate its own revenues. Examples for general purpose governments include, but are not limited to, the following:

    a. Assessed and actual values of taxable property for the last 10 fiscal years;

    b. Direct and overlapping property tax rates for the last 10 fiscal years;

    c. Principal property taxpayers for the current year and nine years ago; and

    d. Property tax levies and collections for the last 10 fiscal years.

3. *Debt capacity information* is intended to assist users in understanding and assessing a government's debt burden and its ability to issue additional debt. Examples for general purpose governments are:

    a. Ratios of outstanding debt by type for the last 10 fiscal years;

    b. Ratios of general bonded debt outstanding for the last 10 fiscal years;

    c. Direct and overlapping governmental activities debt as of current year-end;

    d. Legal debt margin for the last 10 fiscal years; and

    e. Pledged revenue coverage for the last 10 fiscal years.

4. *Demographic and economic information* is intended to assist users in understanding the socioeconomic environment that a government operates within, and it provides information that facilitates comparisons between governments over time. Examples for general purpose governments are:

    a. Demographic and economic statistics for the last 10 calendar years; and

    b. Principal employers for the current year and nine years ago.

5. *Operating information* is intended to provide contextual information about a government's operations and resources in order for users to understand and assess its economic condition. Examples for general purpose governments are:

    a. Full-time equivalent employees by function/program for the last 10 fiscal years;

    b. Operating indicators by function/program for the last 10 fiscal years; and

    c. Capital asset statistics by function/program for the last 10 fiscal years.

Appendix C to GASB-44 provides comprehensive illustrated examples of statistical schedules for both general purpose governments and special purpose governments. Many of the schedules are *optional.* These are further expanded in the *GASB Implementation Guide 2015-1*, Appendix B9-2 [GASB Cod. Sec. 2800.901], including dozens of schedules for:

- General purpose local governments;
- General purpose county governments;
- General purpose state governments;
- School districts;

- Governments engaged only in business-type activities including universities, airports, water and sewer systems; and

- A library district.

PRACTICE POINT: An exhibit set for retirement systems and similar fiduciary activities is *not* included in the *GASB Implementation Guide 2015-1*, Appendix B9-2, due to the changes in GASB-67, GASB-73, and GASB-75, but is included in *Implementation Guide Update 2016-1*, Appendix C. This update should be reviewed for guidance on such entities.

Professional judgment should be used to determine whether statistical tables other than the ones listed should be presented in the CAFR.

The statistical tables should include information for blended component units by combining the primary governmental statistics and the component units' statistics. Professional judgment should be used to determine whether statistical data related to discretely presented component units should be presented.

BASIC FINANCIAL STATEMENTS REQUIRED FOR SPECIAL-PURPOSE GOVERNMENTS

The standards established by GASB-34 are written in the context of general purpose governmental entities, such as state and local governments. However, these standards also apply, with some modification, to special-purpose governments that are "legally separate entities and may be component units or other stand-alone governments." GASB-34 provides the following definitions of these entities (GASB-34, par. 134) [GASB Cod. Secs. Ca5.101, Co5.101, Ho5.101, In3.101, Sp20.101, Ut5.101]:

> Component units are legally separate organizations for which elected officials of the primary government are financially accountable. In addition, a component unit can be another organization for which the nature and significance of its relationship with a primary government are such that exclusion would cause the reporting entity's financial statements to be misleading or incomplete.

> An "other stand-alone government" is a legally separate governmental organization that (a) does not have a separately elected governing body and (b) does not meet the definition of a component unit. Other stand-alone governments include some special-purpose governments, joint ventures, jointly governed organizations, and pools.

GASB-34 does not provide a definition of special-purpose governments; however, the GASB's *Implementation Guide 2015-1*, question 7.95.1 [GASB Cod. Sec. Sp20.701-1], notes that such governments "generally provide a limited (or sometimes a single) set of services or programs, for example, fire protection, library services, mosquito abatement, and drainage." It is important to distinguish between a general government and a special-purpose government because under certain circumstances identified in GASB-34 not all of the reporting standards established by GASB-34 must be observed by special-purpose governments.

See Chapter 21, "Public Colleges and Universities"; Chapter 22, "Pension and Other Postemployment Benefit Plans"; and Chapter 23, "Public Entity Risk Pools," for further discussion and examples of financial statements for certain special-purpose governments.

APPENDIX 20A
CONVERTING FROM FUND FINANCIAL STATEMENTS TO GOVERNMENT-WIDE STATEMENTS UNDER GASB-34

Perhaps the most complex task facing those who prepare governmental financial statements based on the standards established by GASB-34 is the development of system procedures that facilitate the presentation of the two levels of financial statements. Most governmental entities solve this problem by maintaining accounting systems necessary to prepare the fund financial statements, and then use a worksheet approach to convert the fund financial statements' basis of accounting and measurement focus as needed in order to prepare the government-wide financial statements.

The purpose of this appendix is to demonstrate how fund financial statement information can be converted to government-wide financial statement information through the use of worksheet conversion entries. The following conversion issues are addressed:

- Issuance of debt;

- Debt service transactions;

- Capital expenditures;

- Lease agreements;

- Accrual of certain operating expenses;

- Nonexchange transactions; and

- Previous years' transactions.

NOTE: The emphasis of this appendix is governmental funds (General Fund, Special Revenue Funds, Capital Projects Funds, Debt Service Funds, and Permanent Funds) rather than proprietary funds because the presentation basis for the proprietary fund category is already accrual accounting and economic resources focus. Fiduciary funds are not discussed, because they are presented in the fund financial statements but are not incorporated into the government-wide financial statements. The individual entries contained in the appendix do not result in the elements contained in the previous schedules. A more complete, referenced presentation is contained in CCH's *Governmental GAAP Practice Manual.*

ISSUANCE OF DEBT

Generally, liabilities that do not consume the current financial resources of a governmental fund are not reported at the fund financial statement level. However, the proceeds from the issuance of debt are recorded as another financing source in a governmental fund. On the other hand, in the government-wide financial statements, both short-term and long-term liabilities of a governmental entity are presented. Long-term liabilities may include such debts as notes, mortgages, bonds, and obligations related to capitalized lease agreements (discussed later).

In order to illustrate the worksheet entries necessary to convert the issuance of debt from the fund-financial statements to the government-wide financial statements, assume that on October 1, 20X0, a governmental entity issued bonds with a maturity value of $10,000,000 for $9,328,956. The bonds carry a stated interest rate of 7% and were sold at an effective interest rate of 8%. Interest is paid annually. That transaction was recorded at issuance as follows in a governmental fund:

	Debit	Credit
Cash	9,328,956	
Discount on Long-Term Debt Issued (Other Financing Uses)	671,044	
Long-Term Debt Issued (Other Financing Sources)		10,000,000

In the governmental fund financial statements, the issuance of the debt is presented on the statement of revenues, expenditures, and changes in fund balances as an "other financing source," but the amount is not presented in the balance sheet at the fund statement level. In order to convert the transaction from a fund perspective to a government-wide perspective, the following worksheet entry is made:

	Debit	Credit
Long-Term Debt Issued (Other Financing Sources)	10,000,000	
Discount on Long-Term Debt Issued (Other Financing Uses)		671,044
Long-term Liabilities		9,328,956

PRACTICE POINT: The above entry records the net proceeds as a long-term liability. It would also be acceptable to create a separate discount account (contra liability account) and record the maturity value of the debt in a separate account.

The effect of the worksheet entry is to report the transaction as a long-term general obligation in the government-wide financial statements (governmental activities column).

DEBT SERVICE TRANSACTIONS

NCGA-1 points out that most expenditures are measurable and should be recorded when the related governmental fund liability is incurred. An exception to this generalization is the treatment of interest and principal payments for general long-term indebtedness. Interest and principal on governmental fund long-term debt are not recorded as expenditures as they accrue but, rather, when they become due and payable. However, for the government-wide financial statements, interest expense is subject to accrual.

For example, the following bond discount amortization schedule would be prepared for the $10,000,000 bonds that were issued at a discount in the previous section:

Date	Cash	Interest	Amortization	Book Value
10/1/X1				$9,328,956
10/1/X2	$700,000	$746,316	$(46,316)	9,375,272
10/1/X3	700,000	750,022	(50,022)	9,425,294
10/1/X4	700,000	754,024	(54,024)	9,479,318
10/1/X5	700,000	758,345	(58,345)	9,537,663
10/1/X6	700,000	763,013	(63,013)	9,600,676
10/1/X7	700,000	768,054	(68,054)	9,668,730
10/1/X8	700,000	773,498	(73,498)	9,742,229
10/1/X9	700,000	779,378	(79,378)	9,821,607
10/1/Y0	700,000	785,729	(85,729)	9,907,336
10/1/Y1	700,000	792,664R	(92,664)	10,000,000

R = rounded

Based on the above amortization schedule, no interest is recorded during the fiscal year ended June 30, 20X2. However, in order to convert the transaction to an accrual basis the following worksheet entry is made:

	Debit	Credit
Interest Expense ($746,316 × 9/12)	559,737	
Interest Payable ($700,000 × 9/12)		525,000
Long-term Liabilities		34,737

The credit to the account "Long-Term Liabilities" represents the amortization of the discount for the partial year.

PRACTICE POINT: If a separate discount is created, the credit is to the discount account.

If long-term debt has been repaid during the year, the principal repayment is recorded as expenditures in the fund financial statements, but a worksheet entry is necessary to convert the principal payment from an expenditure to a reduction to the governmental entity's general debt.

CAPITAL EXPENDITURES

When capital assets are acquired by governmental funds, payments related to acquisitions are recorded as expenditures at the fund statement level. In order to convert the fund financial statements from a fund perspective to a government-wide perspective, the expenditure must be capitalized and any related depreciation expense recorded.

To illustrate the conversion of capital expenditures to the government-wide perspective, assume that on November 1, 20X6, a purchase order for $900,000 for various vehicles for the following governmental programs was signed to be paid from the General Fund (the vehicles have estimated useful lives of three years and no residual values):

Program	Outlay Amount
General government	$100,000
Public safety activities	300,000
Transportation department	400,000
Parks department	100,000
Total payments	$900,000

Further assume that the vehicles ordered on November 1 were received on December 1, and that the vendor was paid on December 15. These transactions are recorded in the appropriate governmental fund in the following manner (note that in accordance with GASB-54, encumbrance reserves are not presented in financial statements; however, they may be used by the government during the year as control mechanisms):

	Debit	Credit
11/1/X6		
Encumbrances	900,000	
Reserve for Encumbrances		900,000
12/1/X6		
Reserve for Encumbrances	900,000	
Encumbrances		900,000
Expenditures—General Government	100,000	
Expenditures—Public Safety	300,000	
Expenditures—Streets	400,000	
Expenditures—Recreation and Parks	100,000	
Accounts Payable		900,000
12/15/X6		
Accounts Payable	900,000	
Cash		900,000

In order to report the capital assets (vehicles) illustrated in this example as required by GASB-34, in the government-wide financial statements, the following worksheet entry is made to the amounts reported in the fund financial statements:

	Debit	Credit
12/31/X6 Vehicles—Capital Assets	900,000	
Expenditures—General Government		100,000
Expenditures—Public Safety		300,000
Expenditures—Streets		400,000
Expenditures—Recreation and Parks		100,000

Depreciation expense should be reported as a direct expense of the specific functional categories if the related capital asset can be identified with the functional category. For example, depreciation expense related to police vehicles should be reported (along with other direct expenses) as part of the appropriate functional expense category (e.g., public safety). Depreciation on capital assets that are shared by two or more functions should be reported as a direct expense based on a pro rata allocation to the appropriate functional expense categories. Depreciation expense related to capital assets that are not identified with a particular functional category does not have to be reported as a direct expense to specific functions but, rather, may be presented as a separate line item in the statement of activities or included in the general governmental functional category.

In the current example, the depreciation expense on the various vehicles to be reported in the government-wide financial statements is directly related to specific governmental programs. In order to reflect the relevant costs of these programs, the following worksheet entry is made:

	Debit	Credit
12/31/X6		
Expenses—General Government (1/9)	19,445	
Expenses—Public Safety (3/9)	58,333	
Expenses—Transportation (4/9)	77,778	
Expenses—Recreation and Parks (1/9)	19,448	
Accumulated Depreciation—Vehicles ($900,000 × 1/3 × 7/12)		175,000

LEASE AGREEMENTS

Rather than purchase a capital asset directly from a vendor, a governmental entity might lease the item. If the agreement is considered a capitalized lease as defined in NCGA-5 (*Accounting and Financial Reporting Principles for Lease Agreements of State and Local Governments*) and amended in GASB-62, pars. 211–271 [GASB Cod. Sec. L20], the transaction is accounted for in a governmental fund as both a resource from the issuance of debt and a capital expenditure (both of which are discussed earlier in this Appendix). Thus, in order to convert the fund financial statements to the government-wide statements, the expenditure must be capitalized, any related depreciation expense must be recorded, and the debt must be recognized along with the accrual of any related interest expense.

PRACTICE ALERT: As previously discussed in various chapters of CCH's *Governmental GAAP Guide*, GASB-87 (*Leases*) will change this reporting model somewhat. Further discussion of GASB-87 is contained in Chapter 14, "Leases and Service Concession Arrangements."

To illustrate the capitalization of a lease, assume a governmental entity, a city, leases office equipment that has an economic life of five years and no residual value. Lease payments of $100,000 to be paid from a government fund are to be made in five annual installments beginning on August 1, 20X6. The city's incremental borrowing rate is 8%. The capitalized value of the lease is computed as follows:

Information		Amount
$100,000 \times (n = 4; i = 8\%)$ 3.31213	=	$331,213
First payment on first day of contract	=	100,000
Total present value		$431,213

The following amortization schedule applies to the lease:

Date	Cash	Interest	Amortization	Book Value
8/1/X6				$431,213
8/1/X6	$100,000	-	-	331,213
8/1/X7	100,000	$26,497	$73,503	257,710
8/1/X8	100,000	20,617	79,383	178,327
8/1/X9	100,000	14,266	85,734	92,593
8/1/Y0	100,000	7,407	92,593	-

The equipment is part of the general government overhead costs.

The execution of the lease is recorded on August 1, 20X6, in the governmental fund as follows:

	Debit	Credit
8/1/X6		
Capital Expenditures—General Government	431,213	
Other Financing Sources—Capital Leases		431,213

In the governmental fund financial statements, the issuance of the debt component of the lease is presented on the statement of revenues, expenditures, and changes in fund balances as another financing source, but the amount is not presented in the balance sheet as a liability at the fund statement level. Likewise, the capital expenditure component of the lease is presented as an expenditure. In order to convert the transaction from a fund financial statement perspective to the government-wide perspective, the following worksheet entries are prepared:

	Debit	Credit
8/1/X6		
Other Financing Sources—Capital Leases	431,213	
Capital Expenditures—General Government		431,213
Leased Equipment—Capital Assets	431,213	
Lease Obligation Payable—due within one year		73,503
Lease Obligation Payable—due beyond one year		357,710
Depreciation:		
Expenses—General Government (60%)	47,434	
Expenses—Public Safety (20%)	15,812	
Expenses—Transportation (10%)	7,906	
Expenses—Recreation and Parks (5%)	3,953	
Expenses—Health and Welfare (5%)	3,953	
Accumulated Amortization—Leased Equipment ($431,213 \times 1/5 \times 11/12$)		79,058
Accrual for Interest		
Interest Expense	24,260	
Interest Payable ($\$26,497 \times 11/12$)		24,290

The entries above reflect the allocation (which is assumed) for depreciation expenses to various governmental programs (general, public safety, streets, etc.). Upon the lease payment, the payables for interest and the lease obligation due within one year would be debited, and cash would be credited.

ACCRUAL OF CERTAIN OPERATING EXPENSES

The basic guidance for determining when a governmental fund should accrue an expenditure/liability is found in NCGA-1, paragraph 70, which states that "most expenditures and transfers out are measurable and should be recorded when the related liability is incurred." GASBI-6 Recognition and Measurement of Certain Liabilities and Expenditures in Governmental Fund Financial Statements expands on this general guidance by noting the following:

> Governmental fund liabilities and expenditures that should be accrued include liabilities that, once incurred, normally are paid in a timely manner and in full from current financial resources—for example, salaries, professional services, supplies, utilities, and travel. These transactions give rise to fund liabilities that are considered mature liabilities because they are "normally due and payable in full when incurred."

To illustrate this approach, assume that a governmental entity's legal department evaluates a $5,000,000 claim that has been raised by an individual based on alleged property damages caused by an emergency vehicle. It is probable that the claim will have to be paid, and the estimate of the loss is about $300,000. It is also believed that the claim will probably be settled in approximately 24 months. This event represents a loss contingency of $300,000, but because the loss will not use current expendable financial resources it is not accrued in the governmental fund. However, the long-term liability amount ($300,000) is reported in the governmental activities column of the government-wide financial statements.

NONEXCHANGE TRANSACTIONS

GASB-33 (*Accounting and Financial Reporting for Nonexchange Transactions*) provides accounting and reporting standards for the following four categories of nonexchange transactions:

- Derived tax revenues;
- Imposed nonexchange revenues;
- Government-mandated nonexchange transactions; and
- Voluntary nonexchange transactions.

The standards established by GASB-33 retained the current fundamental criteria for revenue recognition that applies to the modified accrual basis of accounting, namely, that revenue is to be recorded when it is both available and measurable. NCGA-1 defines available as "collectible within the current period or soon enough thereafter to be used to pay liabilities of the current period." Revenue is measurable when it is subject to reasonable estimation. The recognition of revenue that was deferred changed upon implementation of GASB-65 (*Items Previously Reported as Assets and Liabilities*).

Many of the transactions previously reported as deferred revenues became deferred inflows of resources depending on whether the delay in recognition is caused by timing or eligibility issues. Other chapters in this CCH's *Governmental GAAP Guide*, primarily Chapter 17, review GASB-65 in more detail.

In preparing government-wide financial statements, the same standards established by GASB-33 (*Accounting and Financial Reporting for Nonexchange Transactions*) should be used to determine when revenue related to nonexchange transactions should be recognized except that the available criterion does not have to be satisfied. Thus nonexchange transactions need to be analyzed at the end of the accounting period to identify those that would require a worksheet adjustment to convert from the modified accrual to the accrual basis of accounting. For example, assume that a state government approved unrestricted operating grants for various localities for the calendar year ended December, 31 20X6, and that a particular municipality's share of the grant is $24,000,000, to be paid in four equal installments with no further eligibility requirements. If the last installment ($6,000,000) does not meet the definition of "available" but the terms of the grant satisfy the accrual standards as established by GASB-33, only $18,000,000 of the grant would be reported in the governmental fund financial statements. However, at the end of the period a worksheet entry is made for the $6,000,000 (fourth installment) as shown below, in order to convert the information to an accrual basis:

	Debit	Credit
Intergovernmental Grants Receivable	6,000,000	
General Revenues—Unrestricted Grants		6,000,000

PREVIOUS YEARS' BALANCES

In addition to current year transactions, previous years' balances are analyzed to determine how permanent balances (balance sheet/net position accounts) that appeared on last year's government-wide financial statements affect the current year's government-wide financial statements. Worksheet entries arising from this analysis are made through the beginning balance of net position.

PRACTICE POINT: These entries are for worksheet purposes only to roll-forward the prior year balances and to establish opening balances in the New Year. Entries to net position should not be made on the face of the financial statements when published, unless allowable by U.S. GAAP, usually through a restatement of prior year balances.

For example, assume that a governmental entity had the following general long-term debt items outstanding as of the beginning of the current year:

Liability	Amount
Bonds Payable	$10,000,000
Notes Payable	1,000,000
Compensated absences	750,000
Claims and judgments	220,000
Total	$11,970,000

Based on the above obligations the following worksheet entry is made to establish the beginning balances related to the governmental activities column in the statement of net position:

	Debit	Credit
Net Position	11,970,000	
Bonds Payable		10,000,000
Notes Payable		1,000,000
Compensated Absences liability		750,000
Claims and Judgments liability		220,000

In addition, a governmental entity will generally have to analyze its capital assets at the beginning of the year in a similar manner. For example, assume that a governmental entity had the following capital assets at the beginning of the year:

	Cost	Accumulated Depreciation
Land	$100,000,000	-
Buildings (60% depreciated)	400,000,000	$240,000,000
Equipment (70% depreciated)	200,000,000	140,000,000
Total	$700,000,000	$380,000,000

Based on the above analysis the following worksheet entry is made to establish the beginning balances related to the governmental activities column in the statement of net position:

	Debit	Credit
Land	100,000,000	
Buildings	400,000,000	
Equipment	200,000,000	
Accumulated Depreciation—Buildings		240,000,000
Accumulated Depreciation—Equipment		140,000,000
Net Position—Beginning		320,000,000

V. STAND-ALONE FINANCIAL REPORTING BY SPECIAL-PURPOSE GOVERNMENTS

CHAPTER 21
PUBLIC COLLEGES AND UNIVERSITIES

CONTENTS

INTRODUCTION

As originally issued, the standards established by GASB-34 (*Basic Financial Statements—and Management's Discussion and Analysis—for State and Local Governments*) did not apply to public colleges and universities (PCUs). GASB-35 (*Basic Financial Statements—and Management's Discussion and Analysis—for Public Colleges and Universities*), amended GASB-34, by requiring PCUs to report as special-purpose governments when they are legally separate entities as defined by GASB-14 (*The Financial Reporting Entity*). Special-purpose entities may be a component unit of a primary government or may be a stand-alone government. GASB-35 amended many GASB statements issued before it, and it is usually amended with each GASB statement that amends GASB-34.

BASIC REPORTING MODELS

GASB-35 requires that, in general, PCUs use the same accounting and financial reporting standards that are used by all other governmental entities. Specifically, PCUs that issue separate financial reports should observe the guidance established in GASB-34 for special-purpose governmental entities (paragraphs 134-138), depending on which of the following reporting environments is appropriate:

- Reporting only business-type activities (Enterprise Fund Model);
- Reporting both business-type and governmental activities; and
- Reporting only governmental activities.

PRACTICE ALERT: GASB Statement No. 84 (*Fiduciary Activities*) may change some reporting of endowments of PCUs. Implementation of GASB-84 will be for periods beginning after December 15, 2018. For June 30th governments, implementation will begin for the period beginning on July 1, 2019. Earlier application is encouraged. Changes adopted to conform to the provisions of GASB-84 should be applied retroactively by restating financial statements, if practicable, for all prior periods presented. If restatement for prior periods is not practicable, the cumulative effect, if any, of applying GASB-84 should be reported as a restatement of beginning net position (or fund balance or fund net position, as applicable) for the earliest period restated. In the first period that this Statement is applied, the notes to the financial statements should disclose the nature of the restatement and its effect. Also, the reason for not restating prior periods presented should be disclosed. Chapter 8, "Fiduciary Funds," contains a complete discussion of GASB-84.

PCUs engaged in *more* than one governmental program or that have *both* governmental and business-type activities provide *both* fund financial statements and government-wide financial statements. Some of these PCUs may even levy taxes. In such cases, *all* requirements for basic financial statements and required supplementary information (RSI) may apply (GASB-34, par. 135) [GASB Cod. Sec. Co5.103].

In some of these cases, PCUs may only have a single governmental program (such as a federal grant program reported in a special revenue fund). There is relief from some of the presentation required for fund financial statements for governmental funds as discussed in previous chapters. Such single governmental program PCUs may use a columnar format that reconciles individual line items of fund data to government-wide data, rather than at the bottom of the statements or in an accompanying reconciling schedule (as portrayed in Chapter 20, "Comprehensive Annual Financial Report"). The PCU may also present a statement of activities using a single column that reports expenses first followed by major revenue sources. The difference between the amounts is net revenue (expense) which is then adjusted by contributions to permanent and term endowments, special and extraordinary items, transfers and beginning and ending net position (GASB-34, par. 136, as amended by GASB-63, par. 8) [GASB Cod. Sec. Co5.104].

REPORTING ONLY BUSINESS-TYPE ACTIVITIES (ENTERPRISE FUND MODEL)

GASB-34 states that an Enterprise Fund must be used to account for an activity if *any one of the following criteria* is satisfied:

- The activity is financed with debt that is secured solely by a pledge of the net revenues from fees and charges of the activity.

- Laws or regulations require that the activity's costs of providing services, including capital costs (such as depreciation or capital debt service), be recovered with fees and charges rather than with taxes or similar revenues.

- The pricing policies of the activity establish fees and charges designed to recover its costs, including capital costs (such as depreciation, debt service or amortization of intangible assets) (GASB-34, pars. 67, fns. 33–34, GASB-37, par. 14, GASB-51, par. 5) [GASB Cod. Sec. 1300.109].

The first condition refers to debt secured solely by fees and charges. If that debt is secured by a pledge of fees and charges from the activity and the full faith and credit of the PCU or the component unit, this arrangement does not satisfy the "sole source of debt security" criterion and the activity does not have to be accounted for (assuming the other two criteria are not satisfied) in an Enterprise Fund. This conclusion is not changed even if it is anticipated that the PCU or the component unit is not expected to make debt payments under the arrangement. On the other hand, debt that is secured partially by a portion of its own proceeds does satisfy the "sole source of debt security" criterion.

Although the criteria established above identify those conditions under which an activity must be accounted for in an Enterprise Fund, GASB-34 also states that an Enterprise Fund may be used to "report any activity for which a fee is charged to external users for goods or services." The GASB believes that many PCUs can report as an Enterprise Fund because they generally charge tuition fees and various other fees for their educational services.

A PCU that reports only business-type activities must follow GASB-62 (*Codification of Accounting and Financial Reporting Guidance Contained in Pre-November 30, 1989 FASB and AICPA Pronouncements*). All applicable provisions of FASB Statements and Interpretations, APB Opinions, and Accounting Research

Bulletins that were not in conflict with GASB Statements are included in GASB-62, as amended.

OBSERVATION: Footnote 4 to GASB Statement No. 14 (*The Financial Reporting Entity*) (as amended by GASB-61, par. 4) [GASB Cod. Sec. 2100.fn3] discusses how component units and other related entities to a government may be organized as not-for-profit or for-profit entities. Not-for-profit entities (e.g., foundations) are typically related to public healthcare and higher education institutions. For-profit component units may be limited liability corporations related to the public healthcare, higher education, or postemployment benefit fund entities. Paragraph 43 of GASB-14 [GASB Cod. Sec. 2100.143] requires governments to apply "the definition and display provisions of this section." To accomplish this, translation may have to occur between the basis of accounting of the component units and the primary government. Questions 4.33.1–4.33.4 of the *GASB Implementation Guide 2015-1* [GASB Cod. Secs. 2600.701-3, 704-12–14] discuss translation between the bases of accounting and presentation. However, there is no requirement to change the recognition, measurement, or disclosure standards applied in a nongovernmental component unit's separately issued financial statements. A portion of this issue with not-for-profit component units was solved through the issuance of GASB Statement No. 80 (*Blending Requirements for Certain Component Units—an amendment of GASB Statement No. 14*). An additional blending criteria is added for component units that are organized as not-for-profit corporations in which (in this case the PCU) is the sole corporate member. Blending is required for such entities due to the changes made by GASB-80.

Preparers should also be aware that the not-for-profit reporting model is changing. The FASB has issued Accounting Standards Update 2016-14 (*Not-for-Profit Entities (Topic 958): Presentation of Financial Statements of Not-for-Profit Entities*), which, among many other things, incorporates a direct method statement of cash flows and elimination of the separate reporting of temporary net asset restrictions. The update is effective for periods that began after December 15, 2017, and for interim periods within years for periods that began after December 15, 2018. Further discussion on these issues may be found in Chapter 4, "Governmental Financial Reporting Entity."

PRACTICE POINT: As discussed in GASB-68 and GASB-75, if a stand-alone business-type activity contributes to the pension (or OPEB) contribution either directly or indirectly through a primary government to a plan, or contributes directly to a plan, the provisions of GASB-68 and GASB-75 apply. A net pension (or OPEB) liability, pension expense, and deferred inflows and deferred outflows of resources will be presented on the face of the basic financial statements, along with significant changes in note disclosure and required supplementary information. The financial information may be either directly presented (if the stand-alone business-type activity) contributes directly to a plan or it may be an allocation of activities from a primary government. Therefore, communication and coordination is essential between the stand-alone business-type activity and the plan or the primary government to receive this information on a timely basis.

For a further discussion, see Chapter 13, "Pension, Postemployment, and Other Employee Benefit Liabilities."

One of the advantages of a PCU reporting only business-type activities is that the resulting financial statements are to some degree similar to those required by not-for-profit colleges and universities that must observe the standards contained in the FASB's Accounting Standards Codification® (ASC) Topic 958 (*Not-for-Profit Entities*). However, there are some differences, including the structure of the net asset section of the statement of net position. As noted earlier, a PCU's net position must be categorized as (1) net investment in capital assets, (2) restricted, or (3) unrestricted, and a not-for-profit college or university must label its net asset section as (1) temporarily restricted, (2) permanently restricted, or (3) unrestricted. Also, there are significant differences in the structure of the activity statements under the two reporting models.

When a PCU is engaged in only business-type activities, it must observe only some of the standards established by GASB-34. Specifically, a PCU under this circumstance must observe the standards established by the following paragraphs of GASB-34 :

GASB-34 *Paragraphs* (as amended)	*Codification References*	*Topic*
91–105	GASB Cod. Secs. 2200.170–.195 (and many other related sections)	Enterprise Fund financial statements
113–123	GASB Cod. Sec. 2300.106	Notes to the financial statements
8–11 (as appropriate)	GASB Cod. Secs. 2200.106–.109	MD&A information
132–133 (if applicable)	GASB Cod. Secs. 1400.118–.119	RSI (other than MD&A)

Enterprise Fund Model Financial Statements

The financial statements of a PCU that is engaged only in business-type activities should include the following statements in addition to MD&A and RSI:

- Statement of net position;
- Statement of revenues, expenses, and changes in net position; and
- Statement of cash flows (GASB-34, pars. 129, 138, as amended by GASB-63, par. 8) [GASB Cod. Sec. Co5.106].

Statement of Net Position

Assets and liabilities presented in the statement of net position of a PCU reported as an Enterprise Fund should be classified as current and long-term, based on the guidance codified in GASB-62.

GASB-63 (*Financial Reporting of Deferred Outflows of Resources, Deferred Inflows of Resources, and Net Position*) introduced a Statement of Net Position format that incorporates the Deferred Outflows and Inflows of Resources. Net position includes three elements: (1) net investment in capital assets, (2) restricted net position, and (3) unrestricted net position. Net Position is the sum of assets and deferred outflows of resources reduced by liabilities and deferred inflows of resources (deferred positions presented separately from assets and liabilities).

Exhibit 21-1 is an illustration of a statement of net position for a PCU consistent with the standards required by GASB-35, as amended by GASB-63.

EXHIBIT 21-1
STATEMENT OF NET POSITION

Castle Rock College Statement of Net Position as of June 30, 20XX

	Castle Rock College	Castle Rock College Foundation
Assets		
Current Assets		
Cash and cash equivalents	$19,251,737	$244,559
Restricted cash and cash equivalents—current	3,073,652	—
Investments in marketable securities	7,771,848	7,369,720
Accounts receivable, net	1,584,213	—
Contributions receivable, net	—	72,377
Loans receivable—current portion	4,591	—
Other Current Assets	268,387	19,976
Total Current Assets	31,954,428	7,708,632
Noncurrent Assets		
Restricted cash and cash equivalents	11,009,502	—
Endowment investments	—	1,332,859
Investments in marketable securities	20,211,799	—
Contributions receivable, net	—	155,215
Loans receivable—net of current portion	2.303.011	—
Capital assets, net	88,197,783	—
Total Noncurrent Assets	121,722,095	1,488,074
Total Assets	$153,676,523	$9,196,706
Liabilities		
Current Liabilities		
Accounts payable and accrued liabilities	$2,499,980	$104,441
Accounts payable—construction	991,141	—
Accrued workers' compensation—current portion	114,499	—
Compensated absences—current portion	2,932,979	—
Faculty payroll accrual	2,502,575	—
Advances	2,760,910	—
Deposits	365,885	—
Other current liabilities	366,117	—
Long-term debt—current	1,589,046	—
Total Current Liabilities	14,123,132	104,441

	Castle Rock College	Castle Rock College Foundation
Noncurrent Liabilities		
Long-term debt (Note XX)	40,380,931	—
Accrued workers' compensation—net of current portion	441,461	—
Compensated absences, net of current portion	1,636,695	—
Loans payable—federal financial assistance program	1,877,907	—
Total Noncurrent Liabilities	**44,336,994**	—
TOTAL LIABILITIES	**58,460,126**	—
Deferred Inflows of Resources		
Service Concession Arrangement	468,589	—
Total Deferred Inflows of Resources	**468,589**	—
Net Position		
Net Investment in Capital Assets	$52,034,054	—
Restricted for:		
Non- 1,970,057 expendable— scholarships and academic purposes	1,332,859	
Expendable		
Scholarships	1,434,327	359,465
Academic purposes	—	2,448,404
Research	209,259	—
Loans	452,043	—
Debt service	82,880	—
Other	1,727,090	—
Unrestricted	36,838,098	4,951,537
TOTAL NET POSITION	**$94,747,808**	**$9,092,265**

Statement of Revenues, Expenses, and Changes in Fund Net Position

The operating or change statement of an Enterprise Fund is the statement of revenues, expenses, and changes in fund net position.

When a PCU has only business-type activities, the formatting of its statement of revenues, expenses, and changes in fund net position must differentiate between operating and non-operating transactions and events.

PRACTICE ALERT: As discussed in Chapter 20, the GASB's *Financial Reporting Model—Reexamination* project includes research if the GASB should establish a definition of operating and non-operating activities. Some stakeholders would like the definition to be established by industry or peers. For example, colleges and universities may have a different definition of operations than airports, housing entities, finance entities, hospitals, stadiums, transit systems, and lotteries. Other stakeholders desire some form of consistency across all types of operations. This aspect of the project is among the more controversial topics. The GASB's Preliminary Views contains the Board's tentative view on the subject.

The GASB tentatively decided to propose that the definition of nonoperating revenues and expenses include subsidies received and provided, revenues and expenses of financing, resources from the disposal of capital assets and inventory, and investment income and expenses. Sale of inventory held for resale in the ordinary course of operations is not considered a disposal of inventory for purposes of this definition. This definition could change throughout the remainder of the project, but it should be followed closely by the stakeholders it may affect.

Exhibit 21-2 is an illustration of a statement of revenues, expenses, and changes in fund net position for a PCU consistent with the standards established by GASB-35.

EXHIBIT 21-2
STATEMENT OF REVENUES, EXPENSES, AND CHANGES IN NET POSITION

Castle Rock College Statement of Revenues, Expenses, and Change in Net Position For the Year Ended June 30, 20XX

	Castle Rock College	Castle Rock College Foundation
Operating Revenues		
Student tuition and fees	$41,218,000	—
Less: Scholarship allowances	(7,576,655)	—
Net Student Tuition and Fees	**33,641,345**	—
Federal grants and contracts	6,278,275	—
State and local grants and contracts	1,005,846	—
Private grants	196,023	—
Sales and services of educational department	692,883	—
Gifts and contributions	—	191,209
Auxiliary enterprises: Residential life	13,739,521	—
Other operating revenues	1,394,650	33,231
TOTAL OPERATING REVENUES	**56,948,543**	**224,440**

	Castle Rock College	Castle Rock College Foundation
Operating Expenses		
Educational and general:		
Instruction	24,274,404	—
Academic support	9,241,661	—
Student services	9,656,265	—
Institutional support	11,635,665	402,109
Operations and maintenance of plant	12,063,644	—
Depreciation	3,986,967	—
Scholarships	155,356	404,875
Auxiliary enterprises: Residential life	11,907,599	—
Total Operating Expenses	**82,921,541**	**806,984**
Operating Income (Loss)	**(25,972,998)**	**(582,544)**
Nonoperating Revenues (Expenses)		
State appropriations	30,676,068	—
Gifts	809,513	—
Investment income, net of investment expense	3,637,537	1,309,149
Interest expense on debt	(628,616)	—
Debt issuance costs	(16,533)	—
Net nonoperating revenues before capital and endowment additions (reductions)	**34,477,969**	**1,309,149**
Income before capital and endowment additions (reductions)	**8,504,971**	**726,605**
State capital appropriations	—	—
Capital grants	8,400,165	—
Transfers (to)/from state agencies	(1,315,343)	—
Private gifts to endowment	—	146,846
Total capital and endowment additions (reductions)	**7,084,822**	**146,846**
Increase/(Decrease) in Net Position	**15,589,793**	**873,451**
Net Position–Beginning of Year	79,158,015	8,218,814
Net Position–End of Year	**$94,747,808**	**$9,092,265**

The GASB's *Implementation Guide 2015-1,* question 7.72.5 [GASB Cod. Sec. Co5.703-3], discusses when a PCU that is a special-purpose government engaged only in business-type activities may report its expenses using either natural or functional classifications, noting that neither GASB-34 nor GASB-35 specifies which classification scheme should be used. It should be noted that GASB-34 requires that the basic financial statements be preceded by MD&A (which is discussed later in this chapter). Paragraph 11 of GASB-34 [GASB Cod. Sec.

2200.109] lists the specific components that should comprise MD&A, and one of the components relates to condensed institution-wide financial statements and comments on the significant changes from the prior year to the current year. Furthermore, the condensed presentation should include information that, at a minimum, supports the analysis of the overall financial position and results of operations. One of the specific items that must be presented as condensed financial information is "program expenses, at a minimum by function." Thus, it may appear that there is a conflict between the requirements of GASB-34 (reporting program expenses) and the statement that a PCU could report its expenses using a natural rather than a functional classification. GASB-34 requires special-purpose governments engaged only in business-type activities to follow the requirements for MD&A (paragraphs 8–11) [GASB Cod. Secs. 2200.106–.109] only as appropriate. Thus, a PCU could report its expenses on a natural basis, but if it does so, the MD&A related to condensed expenses should also be based on a natural classification discussion rather than on a program basis.

Statement of Cash Flows

A PCU should prepare a statement of cash flows based on the guidance established by GASB-9, except the statement of cash flows should be formatted based on the direct method in computing cash flows from operating activities. The statement of cash flows should be supplemented with a reconciliation of operating cash flows and operating income (the indirect method).

Exhibit 21-3 provides an illustration of a statement of cash flows consistent with the standards established by GASB-35. Note that the College Foundation is a fiduciary activity and, therefore, is not required to present a Statement of Cash Flows.

EXHIBIT 21-3
STATEMENT OF CASH FLOWS

Castle Rock College
Statement of Cash Flows
For the Year Ended June 30, 20XX

	Castle Rock College
Cash Flows From Operating Activities	
Tuition and fees	$32,699,610
Research grants and contracts	8,048,517
Private grants	279,306
Payments to suppliers	(25,492,422)
Payments to utilities	(3,076,039)
Payments to employees	(41,238,727)
Payments for benefits	(2,250,968)
Payments for scholarships	(443,336)
Loans issued to students	(462,593)
Collections of loans to students	350,778

	Castle Rock College
Auxiliary enterprise receipts—Residential life	13,739,521
Receipts from sales and services of educational departments	677,175
Room and parking fees	34,535
Other receipts	1,345,072
Net Cash Provided (Used) by Operating Activities	**(15,789,571)**
Cash Flows From Noncapital Financing Activities	
State appropriations	25,785,452
Tuition remission to the State	(1,511,564)
Gifts from grants for other than capital purposes	371,034
Net Cash Flows Provided (Used) by Noncapital Financing Activities	**24,644,922**
Cash Flows from Capital and Related Financing Activities	
Perkins loan program net funds received	6,918
Purchases of capital assets	(15,041,600)
Proceeds from debt issuances	3,560,863
Principal repayments	(1,540,340)
Interest payments	(1,566,476)
Transfer of funds to State Agencies	(1,315,343)
Debt issuance costs	(16,533)
Net Cash Provided (Used) by Capital and Related Financing Activities	**(15,912,511)**
Cash Flows from Investing Activities	
Proceeds from sales of investments	2,482,275
Interest and other income	897,957
Purchases of securities investments	(7,228,231)
Net Cash Provided (Used) by Investing Activities	**(3,847,999)**
Net Increase (Decrease) in cash and cash equivalents	**(10,905,159)**
Cash and cash equivalents—Beginning of Year	44,240,050
Cash and cash equivalents—End of Year	**$33,334,891**
Cash and cash equivalents include:	
Cash and cash equivalents—current	$19,251,737
Restricted cash and cash equivalents—current	3,073,652
Restricted cash and cash equivalents	11,009,502
Cash and cash equivalents—End of Year	**$33,334,891**

During the year the College had significant noncash investing and financing activities, including $23,990,403 in the acquisition of capital assets and payments made by a state agency on behalf of the College for $8,400,165. An additional $2,739,580 resulted from fair value changes in securities. $6,402,180 was paid for fringe benefits on the College's behalf by the State. The College's service concession arrangement deferred inflow of resources position was amortized by $468,595 during the year.

Castle Rock College

Reconciliation of Net Operating Income (loss) to Net Cash Provided (Used) by Operating Activities:	
Net operating income (loss)	$(25,971,998)
Adjustments to reconcile net operating income (loss) to net cash provided (used) by operating activities:	
Depreciation expense	3,986,967
Bad debt expense realized on student loans	21,775
On-behalf fringe benefit payments made by the State	6,402,180
Changes in assets, liabilities and deferred inflows of resources:	
Receivables, net	(371,031)
Other current assets	(384)
Accounts payable and accrued liabilities	93,152
Compensated absences	100,188
Accrued faculty payroll	(28,591)
Advances	(456,987)
Student deposits	34,535
Other current liabilities	(42,320)
Student loans	(111,815)
Net Cash Provided (Used) by Operating Activities	**$(15,789,571)**

> **PRACTICE POINT:** GASB Statement No. 9, paragraph 8, discusses how the total amounts of cash and cash equivalents at the beginning and end of the period shown in the Statement of Cash Flows should be easily traceable to similarly titled line items or subtotals shown in the statement of net position as of those dates. As the College has multiple amounts for cash and cash equivalents, a reconciliation is included in the schedule. Otherwise, if only one line item for cash and cash equivalents is in the Statement of Net Position, the reconciliation included above is not necessary as long as the amounts agree.

Notes to the Financial Statements

GASB-35 does not change the general note disclosures required of PCUs from those of other governmental entities. See Chapter 20, "Comprehensive Annual Financial Report," for details on required notes to the financial statements.

Required Supplementary Information

A PCU should present the following RSI:

- Management's discussion and analysis information;
- Infrastructure assets (if the modified approach is used); and

- Pension plan or other post-employment benefits (OPEB) plan, schedules (if applicable) (see Chapter 13, "Pension, Postemployment, and Other Employee Benefit Liabilities".

OBSERVATION: GASB-34 requires that certain funds disclose budgetary comparison schedules as RSI; however, it would generally be inappropriate for a PCU that reports as an Enterprise Fund to do so.

See Chapter 20, "Comprehensive Annual Financial Report," for a detailed discussion of RSI.

COMPONENT UNITS OF PCUs AND PCUs THAT ARE COMPONENT UNITS

Reporting Component Units

GASB-34 was written in a manner that satisfies the financial reporting entity standards originally established by GASB-14 with respect to component units. Relevant guidance established by GASB-14 is as follows:

> The financial statements of the reporting entity should allow users to distinguish between the primary government and its component units by communicating information about the component units and their relationships with the primary government rather than creating the perception that the primary government and all of its component units are one legal entity. To accomplish this goal, *the reporting entity's financial statements should present the fund types ... of the primary government (including its blended component units, which are, in substance, part of the primary government) and provide an overview of the discretely presented component units* (GASB-14, par. 11) [GASB Cod. Sec. 2100.110]. *Financial statements of the reporting entity should provide an overview of the entity based on financial accountability, yet allow users to distinguish between the primary government and its component units* (GASB-14, par. 42) [GASB Cod. Sec. 2100.142] [emphasis added].

This general guidance established by GASB-14 is incorporated in GASB-35 and therefore applies to PCUs. The financial reporting concepts expressed in GASB-14 are accomplished by the display of discretely presented component units in the institutional-wide financial statements. Blended component units are folded into the financial statements of the primary institution as required by GASB-14, paragraphs 52–54, as amended by GASB-61, paragraph 9 [GASB Cod Cod. Secs. 2600.112–.114].

In addition, GASB-14 (par. 51, as amended by GASB-61, par. 7) [GASB Cod Cod. Sec. 2600.108] requires that information related to each major component unit be presented in the reporting entity's basic financial statements. To satisfy this standard, any one of the following approaches may be used:

- Present each major component unit in a separate column in the basic financial statements;
- Present combining statements of the major component units (separate columns) and a single column for all nonmajor component units; or
- Present condensed financial statements in a note to the financial statements.

PRACTICE POINT: As discussed previously, GASB Statement No. 80 (*Blending Requirements for Certain Component Units—an amendment of GASB Statement No. 14*) introduces an additional blending criteria is added for component units that are organized as not-for-profit corporations in which (in this case the PCU) is the sole corporate member.

PRACTICE POINT: The requirement for major component unit information does not apply to component units that are fiduciary in nature.

PRACTICE POINT: If the combining statement method is used, the totals in the combining statements should be consistent with the information presented in the component unit column in the institution-wide financial statements. Also, if this approach is used, a combining statement for nonmajor component units may be presented as supplementary information (but this is not a requirement).

If the note disclosure method is used, the following disclosures must be made:

- *Condensed statement of net position*
  - Total assets, distinguishing between capital assets and other assets (Amounts receivable from the primary institution or from other component units of the same reporting entity should be reported separately.)
  - Total liabilities, distinguishing between long-term debt outstanding and other liabilities (Amounts payable to the primary institution or to other component units of the same reporting entity should be reported separately.)
  - Total net position, distinguishing between restricted, unrestricted, and the amount of net investment in capital assets;
- *Condensed* statement of revenues, expenses, and changes in fund net position
  - Expenses, with separate identification of depreciation expense and amortization of long-lived assets
  - Other nontax general revenues
  - Contributions to endowments and permanent fund principal
  - Extraordinary and special items
  - Change in net position
  - Beginning and ending net position.

The notes to the financial statements should also describe the nature and amount of significant transactions between major component units and the primary government and other component units.

Exhibits 21-1 through 21-2 illustrate a fiduciary component unit (College Foundation) using a discrete presentation format. The GASB's *Implementation Guide 2015-1*, question 4.28.4 [GASB Cod. Sec. 2600.704-4], raises the issue of whether component units' financial information that is presented in combining financial statements (the second reporting approach) or notes to the financial statements (the third reporting approach) must be presented on a PCU's basic financial statements. If the second or third reporting approach is used, the PCU must nonetheless report all of its PCUs in a single column in the basic financial statements (GASB-14, pars. 13, 54, 65–66, GASB-34, pars. 6, 75, 80, 82, GASB-61, pars. 4 and 9, as amended by GASB-63, pars. 7–8) [GASB Cod. Secs. Co5.107–.110].

PRACTICE POINT: The requirement for major component unit information does not apply to component units that are fiduciary in nature.

Nongovernmental Component Units

The GASB's *Implementation Guide 2015-1* further raises the issue of how a PCU should report a component unit's financial statements for a component unit that uses a nongovernmental U.S. GAAP reporting model in questions 4.33.1-4 [GASB Cod Cod. Secs. 2600.701-3, 704-12–14]. Based on the guidance established by GASB-39 (*Determining Whether Certain Organizations Are Component Units*), many organizations classified as component units under GASB-39 are expected to be organizations that prepare their financial statements based on the not-for-profit reporting model described in the FASB ASC™ 958 (*Not-for-Profit Entities*). This not-for-profit reporting model is currently not the same as the reporting model used by primary governments to prepare their government-wide financial statements (see the discussion about such entities at the beginning of this chapter). Although both models are based on accrual accounting concepts (component units are presented only in the government-wide financial statements), there are differences. GASB-39 states that these reporting model incompatibilities can be addressed in the following ways:

- Present the not-for-profit organization's financial statements separately from the primary government's statement of net position and statement of activities; and

- Directly integrate the not-for-profit organization's financial statements into the primary government's statement of net position and statement of activities.

If the primary government decides that the accounting and reporting model for a not-for-profit organization is too dissimilar from the governmental accounting and reporting model, the not-for-profit organization's financial statements should be presented separately from the primary government's government-wide financial statements. This alternative is supported by the Chapter 4 of the

GASB's *Implementation Guide 2015-1* in its discussion of the financial reporting entity, which states the following:

> If the reporting entity's financial statements do not include a statement of activities, the nongovernmental component unit's financial statement data should be reconfigured into a display that is compatible with the reporting entity's change statement format and be presented in a discrete column to the right of the financial statement data of the primary government. However, if it is impractical to reformat the nongovernmental component unit's change statement data, they need not be reported on the same page as that of the primary government, but may be reported on a separate following page in accordance with the GASB *Implementation Guide*'s (CIG), question 4.33.1 [GASB Cod. Sec. 2600.704-12].

Under this approach, the (not-for-profit) component unit's financial statements would not be presented in the primary government's statement of net position or statement of activities, but rather would be presented immediately after those financial statements using the accounting standards and reporting format for a not-for-profit organization.

If a PCU has a nongovernmental fund-raising organization that meets the criteria in GASB-39 for discrete presentation in the PCU's financial reporting entity, the GASB CIG also contains guidance as to how to present the foundation. Question 4.33.4 [GASB Cod. Sec. 2600.704-14] discusses the subject as follows:

> If the foundation's statement of net [position]is not presented in a classified format, its assets and liabilities should be reclassified into their current and noncurrent components, based generally on the guidance in Statement No. 62 (*Codification of Accounting and Financial Reporting Guidance Contained in Pre-November 30, 1989 FASB and AICPA Pronouncements*), paragraphs 29–44. Also, the foundation's net assets should be redistributed among the three Statement 34 required components—net investment in capital assets, restricted (distinguishing between expendable and nonexpendable and between major categories of restrictions), and unrestricted. The data in the foundation's statement of activities may need to be realigned to distinguish between operating and nonoperating revenues and expenses and generally relocated to their appropriate positions in the GASB's required format. Also, because the university can present its operating expenses by either natural classification or functional categories, the foundation's expenses may need to be reconfigured to conform to the approach used by the university. In addition, the foundation's revenues may need to be reduced by related discounts and allowances, if reported separately as expenses, to be consistent with the university's presentation.

GASB-39 discusses that the primary government might decide that the financial statements of the (not-for-profit) component unit are not "completely incompatible" with the governmental financial reporting model. Under this circumstance, the component unit's financial statements could be "reconfigured to allow for a side-by-side columnar presentation" with the primary government.

OBSERVATION: GASB-61 also discusses equity interests in component units, amending paragraph 55 of GASB-14. PCUs may have equity interests in for-profit entities that the PCU establishes with a student (or a professor, private corporation, etc.) with the goal of investment return. Paragraph 55 is amended to stipulate that if a government (the PCU) owns a majority of the equity interest in a legally separate organization (e.g., through acquisition of its voting stock), the

PCU's intent for owning the equity interest should determine whether the organization should be presented as a component unit or an investment of the PCU. If the PCU's intent for owning a majority equity interest is to directly enhance its ability to provide services, the organization should be reported as a component unit. For example, a PCU that purchases 100% of the stock of an energy plant to provide a controlled source of energy for its capital assets should report the energy company as a component unit. When such a component unit is discretely presented, the equity interest should be reported as an asset of the fund that has the equity interest. If the interest is reported in a governmental fund, it may be reported as a joint venture. Changes in the equity interest should be reported pursuant to the requirements of either governmental funds or proprietary funds, depending on how the interest is reported. When such a component unit is blended, in the period of acquisition the purchase typically should be reported as an outflow of the fund that provided the resources for the acquisition and, in that and subsequent reporting periods, the component unit should be reported pursuant to the blending requirements of GASB-14, as amended by GASB-61.

If, however, the PCU owns the equity interest for the purpose of obtaining income or profit rather than to directly enhance its ability to provide services, it should report its equity interest as an investment, regardless of the extent of its ownership. For many research institutions, there is likely an equity interest as an investment, rather than to provide services. An example of this would be if a Public Hospital was affiliated with Castle Rock College, discussed in Exhibits 21-1 through 21-3, which is a common occurrence with PCUs. Medical Centers often create a separate corporation to assist in funding breakthroughs in medical technology, therefore allowing the research physicians to potentially capitalize on the research while potentially sheltering the PCU from liability. Care must be taken in the accounting and financial reporting of the research center. For example, if the center produces or obtains patents, if the patents were to be used in the center's operations, the patents may be recorded as intangible assets. However, if the patents were produced or obtained for income or profit, they would be recorded as investments and would need to be valued annually at fair value.

PRACTICE ALERT: The GASB recently released GASB Statement No. 89 *(Accounting and Financial Reporting for Majority Equity Interests—an amendment of GASB Statement No. 14)*. This statement seeks to improve the consistency of reporting a government's majority equity interest in a legally separate organization. If the definition of an investment is met, the majority equity interest would be reported using the equity method, unless the interest is engaged only in fiduciary activities, or a permanent fund (a governmental fund). In such cases, the interest would be reported at fair value. Any other holding would be reported as a component unit. The asset related to the majority equity interest would be reported by the fund that holds the interest. If a 100% equity interest is acquired, acquisition value is used to measure the various accounting elements of the acquired entity, similarly to the provisions contained in GASB Statement No. 69 *(Government Combinations and Disposals of Government Operations)* [GASB Cod. Sec. Co10]. The effective date of GASB-89 is for periods beginning after December 15, 2018. For June 30th governments, the period begins on July 1, 2019. The requirements are proposed to be applied retroactively, except for the provisions related to (1) reporting a majority equity interest in a component unit and (2) reporting a component unit in which the primary government acquired a 100% equity interest. Those provisions would be applied on a prospective basis.

OTHER MEASUREMENT AND REPORTING ISSUES

Eliminations and Reclassifications in Institutional-Wide Financial Statements

A PCU may use a variety of funds to account for transactions during an accounting period. The preparation of institution-wide financial statements is based on a consolidating process (similar to corporate consolidations) rather than a combining process, whereby the PCU is reported as a single operating entity. These eliminations and reclassifications related to the consolidation process are based on (1) internal balances (statement of net position), (2) internal activities (operating statement), and (3) intra-entity activity.

Internal Balances

The institution-wide financial statements present the primary institution and its blended component units, if any, as a single reporting entity. Based on this philosophy, most balances between funds that are initially recorded as interfund receivables and payables at the individual fund level should be eliminated when preparing the statement of net position. The balances are eliminated to avoid the "grossing-up" effect on assets and liabilities presented on the statement of net position. For example, if there is an interfund receivable/payable between two proprietary funds of the primary institution, those amounts would be eliminated.

There also may be interfund receivables/payables that arise because of transactions between the primary institution and its fiduciary funds. These amounts should not be eliminated but rather should be reported on the statement of net position as receivables from and payables to external parties.

Internal Activities

In order to avoid the "doubling-up" effect of internal activities among funds, interfund transactions should be eliminated so that expenses and revenues are recorded only once. For example, a fund may charge other funds for services provided (such as insurance coverage and allocation of overhead expenses) on an internal basis. When these funds are consolidated in order to present the operating expenses of institutional activities, the double counting of the expense (with an offset to revenue recorded by the provider fund) should be eliminated in a manner so that "the allocated expenses are reported only by the function to which they were allocated."

Interfund Activities between a PCU and Its Auxiliary Enterprises

The reporting of interfund activities between a PCU and its auxiliary enterprises is dependent upon which reporting model is used by the PCU. A PCU that is engaged in both business-type and governmental activities essentially must follow all of the standards established by GASB-34. The GASB's *Implementation Guide 2015-1* in question 7.47.23 [GASB Cod. Sec. 2200.725-17]notes that, under this reporting model, interfund activities between the PCU and its auxiliary enterprises should be accounted for based on the guidance established by paragraphs 59, 60, and 112 [GASB Cod. Secs. 1800.102, .104–.105]. Paragraph 59 [GASB Cod. Sec. 1800.104]requires that the doubling-up effect of Internal Service Fund activities and similar internal events be eliminated in the institution-wide financial statements. However, paragraph 60 [GASB Cod. Sec. 1800.105]requires that transactions based on "interfund services provided and used" between functions not be eliminated. Paragraph 112 [GASB Cod. Sec. 1800.102] provides guidance for reporting (1) interfund loans, (2) inter-fund services provided and used, (3) interfund transfers, and (4) interfund reimbursements in the proprietary funds.

The GASB's *Implementation Guide 2015-1* continuing in question 7.47.23 notes that a PCU that is engaged in only business-type activities and reports as single-column business-type activity should eliminate internal transactions between the PCU and its auxiliary enterprises.

Intra-Entity Activity

Transactions (and related balances) between the primary institution and its discretely presented component units should not be eliminated in the institutional-wide perspective financial statements. That is, the two parties to the transactions should report revenue and expense accounts as originally recorded in those respective funds. Amounts payable and receivable between the primary government and its discretely presented component units should be reported as separate line items on the statement of net position. Likewise payables and receivables between discretely presented component units must also be reported separately.

Pell Grants

GASB-24 (*Accounting and Financial Reporting for Certain Grants and Other Financial Assistance*) establishes standards for pass-through grants, which includes Pell Grants. GASB-35 superseded GASB-19, which had required Pell Grants to be accounted for as restricted revenues. On the other hand, the GASB's *Implementation Guide 2015-1*, question 7.72.10 [GASB Cod. Sec. Co5.702-1], discusses whether Pell Grants can be reported in an Agency Fund (until the implementation of GASB-84) (See PRACTICE ALERT below.).

GASB-24 describes pass-through grants, including Pell Grants, as "grants and other financial assistance received by a governmental entity to transfer to or spend on behalf of a secondary recipient." GASB-24 requires that cash pass-through grants generally be recorded simultaneously as revenue and expenditures or expenses in a governmental fund or proprietary fund. Only in those instances when the recipient government functions as a cash conduit should a pass-through grant be accounted for in an Agency Fund. The GASB describes cash conduit activity as transmitting grantor-supplied moneys "without having administrative or direct financial involvement in the program."

Administrative involvement is based on whether the recipient government's role in the grant program constitutes an operational responsibility for the grant program, such as the following:

- Monitoring secondary recipients for compliance with specific requirements established by the program;

- Determining which secondary recipients are eligible for grant payments (even if eligibility criteria are established by the provider government); and

- Exercising some discretion in determining how resources are to be allocated.

PRACTICE ALERT: In GASB-84 (*Fiduciary Activities*), paragraph 8, one of the key determinants of a non-pension or OPEB potential fiduciary component unit is whether or not the assets within the organization are for the benefit of individuals and the government does *not* have administrative involvement or direct financial involvement with the assets. The provisions from GASB-24 are referred to in footnote 1 to GASB-84. Similarly, one of the criteria in paragraph 11 of GASB-84 discusses when a non-component unit activity could be fiduciary in nature if the assets associated with the activity are *not* derived from government-mandated nonexchange transactions or voluntary nonexchange transactions with the exception of pass-through grants for which the government *does not* have administrative involvement or direct financial involvement. Other required criteria in paragraph 11 also refer to GASB-24. Further discussion of administrative involvement and GASB-84 is contained in Chapter 8, "Fiduciary Funds."

As part of the answer to question 7.72.10 [GASB Cod. Sec. Co5.702-1], which was slightly amended by GASB-84, paragraph 5, the GASB states that because of the administrative involvement under the current Pell Grant program, "public institutions should record Pell Grant receipts as revenue in their financial statements, and any amounts applied to student receivable accounts should be recorded as scholarship discounts or allowances."

With the implementation of GASB-35 there was some discussion by public college and university business officers as to the treatment of Pell Grants and student loans in statements of cash flows and statements of revenues, expenses, and changes in net position. Due to the administrative involvement with Pell Grant requirements and because Pell Grants are nonexchange transactions, public institutions should record Pell Grant receipts as nonoperating revenues in their financial statements, and any amounts applied to student receivable accounts should be recorded as scholarship discounts or allowances. However, most other student loans are operational in nature and therefore are shown in the operating activities section of a statement of cash flows. Furthermore, in GASB-9 (*Reporting Cash Flows of Proprietary and Nonexpendable Trust Funds and Governmental Entities That Use Proprietary Fund Accounting*), paragraph 19 [GASB Cod. Sec. 2450.116], the GASB concluded that certain "loan programs" are the operating activities of a governmental enterprise. The loans are not typical investments, because they are not necessarily intended to earn a profit. There are only two examples of qualifying loan programs in paragraph 19, including student loan programs. In the examples provided, loans are made to individuals who might not otherwise qualify for loans. The program is intended to directly benefit the individuals receiving the loans. Usually, the interest rate on a loan provided by this type of program is below the market rate. A student loan program provides direct benefits to individuals: students in need of financing their education.

The GASB expected few types of loan programs or finance authorities to meet the spirit of the exception provided in paragraph 19, even if making and collecting loans are the primary operations of the enterprise. A finance authority that facilitates financing by serving as an intermediary or conduit would not usually qualify even if the project to be financed indirectly benefits the institution or its students. For example, an authority created to finance institution building projects (such as classroom buildings or dormitories) would not qualify, because the direct beneficiary is the institution rather than individual students. Debt is issued by the authority and the proceeds are loaned to universities for their building or dormitory construction projects. Although the students who eventually live in the dorms will benefit from the activity, the direct beneficiary of the dormitory authority is the university itself, which is part of the governmental financial reporting entity. Such an arrangement merely facilitates the government's financing process. The substance of the arrangement is that the institution issued bonds to serve its own needs.

Other Forms of Lending and GASB-62, pars. 431–451 (as amended by GASB-65)

Student loans are integral to most PCU operations. GASB-62, paragraphs 431–451 [GASB Cod. Sec. L30], as amended by GASB-65, describes the accounting and financial reporting for nonrefundable fees and costs associated with lending activities and loan purchases. Lending, committing to lend, refinancing or restructuring loans, which many PCUs arrange are "lending activities" for purposes of applying paragraphs 431–451. If the PCU is only an indirect recipient of the loan, rather than making the loan to the student, then GASB-62 likely doesn't apply. If the PCU does make direct loans, then the PCU should use the applicable provisions, which are largely from for-profit standards. In summary, the following is the accounting and financial reporting standards for activities that are likely to occur at PCUs:

Item	Accounting and Financial Reporting Principles	GASB-62 and GASB-65 references	GASB Codification Sections
Loan Origination Fees and Costs	Loan origination fees except for the portion related to points should be recognized as revenue in the period received. Likewise, direct loan origination costs should be expensed in accordance with GASB-65.	Pars. 434–436 (as amended by GASB-65, par. 22).	GASB Cod. Secs. L30.105–.107
Loan Commitment Fees	Fees received for a commitment to originate a loan or group of loans should be recorded as a liability and, if the commitment is exercised, recognized as revenue in the period of exercise. If the commitment expires unexercised, the commitment fees should be recognized as revenue upon expiration of the commitment. Exceptions to this are:	Pars. 437 and 451 (as amended by GASB-65, par. 23)	GASB Cod. Secs. L30.108 and .501, .502, .506, and .509.

Item	Accounting and Financial Reporting Principles	GASB-62 and GASB-65 references	GASB Codification Sections
	a. If the PCU's experience with similar arrangements indicates that the likelihood that the commitment will be exercised is remote, the commitment fee should be recognized as revenue in the period received.		
	b. If the amount of the commitment fee is determined retrospectively as a percentage of the line of credit available but unused in a previous period, if that percentage is nominal in relation to the stated interest rate on any related borrowing, and if that borrowing will bear a market interest rate at the date the loan is made, the commitment fee should be recognized as revenue as of the determination date.		

In the unlikely occurrence that a PCU is engaged in mortgage banking activities, GASB-62 (pars. 452–475, as amended by GASB-65) [GASB Cod. Secs. L30.101–.138] discusses the accounting and financial reporting for those activities.

Split-Interest Agreements—GASB-81

A PCU may receive a gift from a donor structured as a split-interest agreement, where the PCU acts as the trustee. Generally, a split-interest agreement takes one of two forms: (1) an annuity trust or (2) a unitrust. Under an annuity trust, the donor receives an annual fixed payment during the period covered by the trust agreement. Under a unitrust, the donor receives an annual payment based on a specified percentage of the fair value of the market value of the trust's assets.

As discussed in Chapter 17, "Revenues: Nonexchange and Exchange Transactions," the GASB has issued Statement No. 81 (*Irrevocable Split-Interest Agreements*), superseding the provisions of question 7.72.11. GASB-81 requires that a government that receives resources pursuant to an irrevocable split-interest agreement recognize assets, liabilities, and deferred inflows of resources. GASB-81 also requires that a government recognize assets representing its beneficial interests in irrevocable split-interest agreements that are administered by a third party, if those beneficial interests are under the control of the government and embody present service capacity.

If a government is *both* the intermediary *and* intermediary *and* a beneficiary of an irrevocable split-interest agreement (ISIA), the government should recognize an asset for resources received, a liability for the beneficial interest that is assigned to other beneficiaries and a deferred inflow of resources for the beneficial interest that will unconditionally benefit the government. Assets that meet the definition of an investment would be measured in accordance with the provisions of GASB-72 (*Fair Value Measurement and Application*) as appropriate. Investment income, as defined in GASB-72 may increase or decrease the deferred inflow of resources if the remainder interest benefit is assigned to the government. If it is assigned to other beneficiaries, the changes in assets would recognize an increase or decrease to the related liability.

If a government is *just the remainder interest beneficiary*, the government would recognize an asset for the resources received, a liability for the lead interest that is assigned to other beneficiaries and a deferred inflow of resources for the government's unconditional remainder interest. The liability is calculated based on a settlement amount, using a valuation technique contained in the agreement. Several assumptions may be used to value the interest including the payment provisions in the agreement, the estimated rate of return on assets, and the mortality rate if the term is life-contingent, or a discount rate if a present value technique is used. If the valuation is discounted, then payments to the beneficiaries would reduce the liability for the period. The amount reported as the liability should be remeasured at each reporting date, based on changes in the assumptions that determined the settlement amount. Upon termination of the agreement, the deferred inflows of resources balance would be debited and revenue recognized.

If a government is *the lead interest beneficiary and beneficiary and the intermediary*, the government would recognize assets, a deferred inflow of resources for the unconditional lead interest and a liability for the remainder interest that is assigned to the other beneficiaries. Similar measurement and remeasurement techniques would apply as previously discussed.

Governments, especially PCU's, may also receive a life interest in real estate that are life-contingent. An asset would be recognized as a capital asset or investment, depending upon management intent at the time of the donation. Therefore, it may be measured at *either* acquisition value if a capital asset or fair value if an investment in accordance with GASB-72. If the government is responsible for activities such as insurance, maintenance or repairs on the asset during the life of the agreement, a liability is recorded and reduced based on the satisfaction of the obligations. A related deferred inflow of resources would be recorded as the difference between the asset and a recognized liability.

The following is an example of accounting for in irrevocable split-interest agreement involving a life interest in real estate that may be common in a PCU:

Example: In the beginning of 20X8, Mrs. Mary Smith, a widowed graduate of Castle Rock College in 19S7 decided to contact the Chief Endowment Officer of the College seeking to donate her house to the College. Her house is adjacent to the Castle Rock College campus. Mrs. Smith seeks to retain the right to use the house until she passes away. The Chief Endowment Officer presented this offer to the College Board of Trustees which quickly accepted the gift. The Board intends to use the house as the new President of the College's house. The house will be used for official functions and meetings. Therefore, Castle Rock College's Chief Financial Officer documented that the house should be classified as a capital asset in accordance with the provisions of GASB-81. An appraisal was done and an acquisition value of $2,500,000 was determined in accordance with the provisions of GASB-72. As Mrs. Smith is elderly, the College agreed to pay to insure the house and for regular maintenance and necessary repairs. The Chief Financial Officer calculates the liability for such expenses for the next five years (her estimated remaining life) to be $500,000. The following is then entered into the books and records of the College at the day of closing of the irrevocable split-interest agreement:

	Debit	Credit
Capital Asset—Smith House (ISIA)	$2,500,000	
Estimated Liability—Insurance, Maintenance, Repairs—Smith House (ISIA)		$500,000
Deferred Inflow of Resources—Smith House (ISIA)		$2,000,000

At the end of 20X8, $100,000 had been paid for the insurance, maintenance and repairs on the Smith House. Depreciation occurred as well, using a 40 year estimated useful life, per Castle Rock College's policy. The following is then entered:

	Debit	Credit
Depreciation Expense—Smith House (ISIA)	$62,500	
Estimated Liability—Insurance, Maintenance, Repairs—Smith House (ISIA)	100,000	
Deferred Inflow of Resources—Smith House (ISIA) ($2,000,000 ÷ 40)	50,000	
Cash (assumed)		$100,000
Accumulated depreciation—Smith House (ISIA)		62,500
Revenue—Smith House		50,000

Five years after the signing of the ISIA, Mrs. Smith dies. All liabilities had been paid previous to her death. $250,000 had been amortized to revenue from the deferred inflow of resources, leaving $1,750,000 to recognize as follows:

	Debit	Credit
Deferred Inflow of Resources—Smith House (ISIA) Termination	$1,750,000	
Revenue—Smith House (ISIA)—Termination		$1,750,000

GASB-81 contains additional provisions if a third party is an intermediary. The type of agreement characterizes the accounting and financial reporting in such circumstances.

Investment Income Restricted to Permanent or Term Endowments

One of the classifications established by GASB-34 (and therefore incorporated into GASB-35) was "additions to permanent and term endowments." When a PCU receives contributions to its term and permanent endowments or to permanent fund principal, those contributions should be reported as separate items in the lower portion of the statement of activities or statement of revenues, expenses, and changes in fund net position (depending upon which reporting model is used by the PCU). These receipts are not considered to be program revenues (such as program-specific grants) because, in the case of term endowments, there is an uncertainty of the timing of the release of the resources from the term restriction and, in the case of permanent contributions the principal can never be expended.

A question arises as to whether investment income that is restricted to permanent or term endowments could be reported as additions to permanent and term endowments. The GASB's *Implementation Guide 2015-1*, question 7.74.3 [GASB Cod. Sec. 2200.753-3], discusses how investment income of this nature should not be reported as additions to permanent and term endowments. If the PCU reports as a special-purpose governmental entity and reports only business-type activities (Enterprise Fund Model), investment income restricted to permanent or term endowments should be reported as nonoperating revenue. If the PCU reports governmental activities and therefore prepares a statement of activities, the income should be reported as general revenues in the lower portion of the financial statement.

Investments in Land and Other Real Estate Held by Endowments

A PCU may acquire or receive from a donor income-producing real estate (or a partial interest in such real estate) as a permanent or term endowment.

GASB-52 (*Land and Other Real Estate Held as Investments by Endowments*) requires that land and other real estate held as investments by endowments be reported at fair value at the reporting date. Any changes recorded in fair value during the period should be reported as investment income. GASB-52 applies to all state and local governments (GASB-52, par. 4) [GASB Cod. Secs. I50.108, .124].

GASB-52 amends paragraph 2 of GASB-31 (*Accounting and Financial Reporting for Certain Investments and for External Investment Pools*), requiring that investments in land and other real estate held by endowments be added to the disclosure provisions in paragraph 15 of GASB-31. Accordingly, disclosures should include the methods and significant assumptions used to determine the fair value of such investments and provide other information that is currently presented for other investments reported at fair value (GASB-52, par. 5) [GASB Cod. Sec. I50.101].

Accrual of Tuition and Fees Revenue

PCUs often receive revenues for tuition and fees in one year for services that must be delivered across more than one fiscal year. The GASB's *Implementation Guide 2015-1*, question 7.72.13 [GASB Cod. Sec. 2200.751-6], states that tuition and fees should be reported as revenue in the period they are earned.

QUESTIONS

1. Public colleges and universities (PCUs) that issue separate financial reports, in accordance with the guidance established in GASB-34 for special-purpose governmental entities should follow any of the following reporting environments, except for:

   a. Reporting only business-type activities (Enterprise Fund Model).

   b. Reporting both business-type and governmental activities.

   c. Reporting only governmental activities.

   d. Not-for-profit basis of accounting.

2. The financial statement of a PCU that is engaged only in business-type activities should include the following statements except for:

   a. Statement of net position.

   b. Reconciliation between statement of revenues, expenses, and changes in net position to the statement of activities.

   c. Statement of revenues, expenses, and changes in fund net position.

   d. Statement of cash flows.

3. U.S. GAAP requires that information related to each major component unit be presented in the reporting entity's basic financial statements. To satisfy this standard, any one of the following approaches can be used except for:

   a. Present each major component unit consolidated into the general fund.

   b. Present each major component unit in a separate column in the basic financial statements.

   c. Present combining statements of the major component units (separate columns) and a single column for all nonmajor component units.

   d. Present condensed financial statements in a note to the financial statements.

4. GASB-65 requires that loan origination fees be:

   a. Recognized as deferred inflows or outflows of resources and amortized over the remaining life of the loan.

   b. Recognized as assets or liabilities and amortized over the remaining life of the loan.

   c. Except for the portion related to points, recognized as revenue in the period received. Direct loan origination costs should be expensed.

   d. Including the portion related to points, recognized as revenue in the period received. Direct loan origination costs should be expensed.

5. U.S. GAAP requires that land and other real estate held as investments by endowments be reported at:

   a. Carrying value

   b. Historical cost

   c. Settlement value

   d. Fair value

ANSWERS

1. Public colleges and universities (PCUs) that issue separate financial reports, in accordance with the guidance established in GASB-34 for special-purpose governmental entities should follow any of the following reporting environments except for:

   Answer – D.

2. The financial statement of a PCU that is engaged only in business-type activities should include the following statements except for:

   Answer – B.

3. U.S. GAAP requires that information related to each major component unit be presented in the reporting entity's basic financial statements. To satisfy this standard, any one of the following approaches can be used except for:

   Answer – A.

4. GASB-65 requires that loan origination fees be:

   Answer – C.

5. U.S. GAAP requires that land and other real estate held as investments by endowments be reported at:

   Answer – D.

CHAPTER 22
PENSION AND OTHER POSTEMPLOYMENT BENEFIT PLANS

CONTENTS

INTRODUCTION

State and local governments often administer and/or account for pension and other employee benefit plans and report such plans in stand-alone special-purpose reports or as fiduciary funds within the financial statements of the sponsoring government. The employee benefit plans addressed in this chapter are follows:

- Pension plans and public employee retirement systems;
- IRC 457 deferred compensation plans; and
- Postemployment benefit plans other than pensions.

GASB-67

The primary function of a plan is to administer benefits and invest contributions into the plan to fund benefits currently and in the future. The administration of the benefits entails an actuarial valuation; investing in accordance with approved allocation methodology; and compliance with the plan provisions, laws, and regulations in a particular jurisdiction.

PENSION PLANS AND PUBLIC EMPLOYEE RETIREMENT SYSTEMS

The Scope of GASB-67

GASB Statement No. 67 (*Financial Reporting for Pension Plans*) is applicable for defined benefit pension plans that are administered through trusts or equivalent arrangements. To have a trust or equivalent arrangement, the following must be present:

- Contributions from employers and nonemployer contributing entities to the pension plan and earnings on those contributions must be irrevocable. In some situations, payments are made by the employer to satisfy contribution requirements, identified in the plan provisions as *plan member contributions*. (See section on employer-paid member contributions later in this chapter, at Communication Issues from the Plan to Employers/Sponsors.) Such amounts are classified by the plan as plan member contributions.

- Plan assets are dedicated to providing pensions to plan members in accordance with benefit terms.

- Pension plan assets are legally protected from the creditors of the employers, the nonemployer contributing entities, plan members, and the pension plan administrator (GASB-67, pars. 3, fn2, as amended by GASB-82, par. 8) [GASB Cod. Sec. Pe5.101].

Similar provisions are in place for defined contribution plans (GASB-67, par. 3) [GASB Cod. Sec. Pe6.101].

PRACTICE POINT: GASB Statement No. 73 (*Accounting and Financial Reporting for Pensions and Financial Reporting for Pension Plans That Are Not Administered through Trusts That Meet Specified Criteria and Amendments to Certain Provisions of GASB Statements 67 and 68*) contains provisions related to pension plans that do not benefit from irrevocable trusts being in place. Many of the disclosures and schedules required in either GASB-67 or GASB-68 are applicable in the disclosure of such arrangement. GASB-73 also amends certain provisions of GASB-67 and GASB-68 with regard to the following issues:

1. Information that is required to be presented as notes to the 10-year schedules of required supplementary information about investment-related factors that significantly affect trends in the amounts reported are now limited to those over which the employer has control.

2. Accounting and financial reporting for separately financed specific liabilities of individual employers and nonemployer contributing entities for defined benefit pensions is clarified.

3. The timing of employer recognition of revenue for the support of nonemployer contributing entities *not in a special funding situation* is also clarified.

Included in GASB-73 is a limitation about information about factors that significantly affect trends in the investment-related amounts reported to those factors over which the participating governments have influence (e.g., changes in investment policies). Information about external, economic factors (e.g., changes in market prices) is not required to be disclosed. Furthermore, the schedules that would include disclosure of a receivable/payable for contractually deferred contributions with a separate payment schedule would not be classified as a separately financed specific liability of an individual employer or nonemployer contributing entity to the pension plan. The full amount of the pension plan receivable/employer or nonemployer contributing entity payable to a plan for contractually deferred contributions with a separate payment schedule is a contribution in the reporting period in which the receivable/payable arises.

The various contribution amounts disclosed would exclude amounts, if any, associated with payables to the pension plan that arose in a prior fiscal year and separately financed specific liabilities of the individual employer or nonemployer contributing entity. A single employer that has a special funding situation would recognize additional revenue for the portion of expense recognized by the governmental nonemployer contributing entity. A cost-sharing employer that has a special funding situation should recognize additional revenue and pension expense for the portion of expense recognized by the governmental non-employer contributing entity for the change in the total pension liability associated with a separately financed specific liability of the individual governmental nonemployer contributing entity that is associated with the employer. Expense recognized by a cost-sharing employer or nonemployer contributing entity in a special funding situation should be reduced by the employer or nonemployer contributing entity's proportionate share of contributions to the pension plan to separately finance specific liabilities of others—effectively recording a subsidy. Finally, employers would recognize revenue for the support of a nonemployer contributing entity that is not in a special funding situation in the reporting period in which the contribution of the nonemployer contributing entity is reported as a change in the net pension liability or collective net pension liability, as applicable.

If pension plans provided through a defined benefit plan contain *both* assets held in trust and assets that are not held in trust, the pension plan is reported in accordance with the provisions of GASB-67, as amended. This may occur if employer reserves for future rate increases (as an example) are held by a plan, but not held in trust and are instead currently reported as an Agency Fund at the plan (until the implementation of GASB-84) (GASB-73, par. 18) [GASB Cod. Sec. Pe5.102].

The provisions of GASB-67, as amended, are applicable if the plan issues a stand-alone financial report (usually from a public employee retirement system) or the plan is included as part of a pension trust fund of an employer (typical for single employer plans). GASB-67 does not discuss other post-employment benefit plans (mainly retiree health care or OPEB), nor does it discuss termination benefits. When used in the context of GASB-67, the term "pensions" includes retirement income and death, insurance, and disability benefits that are administered through a pension plan (GASB-67, pars. 4–6, as amended by GASB-73, par. 9) [GASB Cod. Secs. Pe5.103–.105].

An important distinction to understand is the difference between a defined benefit and a defined contribution. In a defined benefit, an employee contributes and is matched by an employer based on a formula approved in advance. In many cases, the employer pays the majority or even 100% of the employee contribution. The pensions due to the employee upon retirement may be stated as a specified dollar amount or as an amount that is calculated based on one or more factors such as age, years of service, and compensation. In a defined contribution plan, an account is established for the employee. The employer may or may not contribute to the account based on service or some other formula. Earnings then are held in the employee's account, net of fees (GASB-67, par. 7) [GASB Cod. Sec. Pe5.106].

Obligations to employees may be pooled and sent to an employers' single plan, a larger plan that is a separate entity that invests and administers the pensions on behalf of the employers and employees while maintaining separate accounts for each employer, or to a plan that pools not only the investments but also the liabilities. These types of plans are single employer plans, agent-multiple employer plans, or cost-sharing multiple employer plans, respectively. Distinctions are made regarding particular requirements depending on the type of plan administered as follows:

Type of Plan	Definition and Example
Single employer pension plans	• Pensions provided to employees of one employer: Castle Rock County Fire and Police Retirement Plan.
Agent-multiple employer pension plans	• Plans where plan assets are pooled for investment purposes, but separate accounts are maintained for each individual employer so that each employer contributions must be only for each employer's employee benefits: State of Centennial Public Employees Retirement System.
Cost-sharing multiple employer pension plans	• Plans where assets are pooled for investment purposes and can also be used to pay for benefits of any employer within the plan: Castle Rock County Employees Retirement Association (includes the County, Cities, and Special Districts within the County).

There are many variations of these and certain large statewide entities may have an agent-multiple employer plan or multiple agent-multiple employer plans along with cost-sharing multiple employer plan or plans. These are all dependent on enabling statutes and other provisions of contracts and other laws (GASB-67, pars. 8–11) [GASB Cod. Secs. Pe5.107–.110].

Variations Due to Numbers of Plans

If all assets accumulated in a defined benefit pension plan for the payment of benefits may legally be used to pay benefits (including refunds of plan member contributions) to *any* of the plan members, the total assets should be reported as assets of one defined benefit pension plan even if:

- Administrative policy requires that separate reserves, funds, or accounts for specific groups of plan members, employers, or types of benefits be maintained (e.g., a reserve for plan member contributions, a reserve for disability benefits, or

- Separate accounts for the contributions of state government versus local government employers) or

- Separate actuarial valuations are performed for different classes of plan members (e.g., general employees and public safety employees) or

- Different groups of plan members because different contribution rates may apply for each class or group depending on the applicable benefit structures, benefit formulas, or other factors.

These variations are especially prevalent in governments at all levels, which may have different structures, classes, benefits, etc. If any of the plan members may receive assets to pay benefits irrespective of class etc., *then one plan is present with different classes*. If members can't receive assets to pay benefits outside of their class, structure, etc., then multiple plans may exist (GASB-67, par. 13) [GASB Cod. Sec. Pe5.111].

Defined Benefit Plan Financial Reporting

GASB-67 requires the following accrual basis of accounting financial statements in exactly the same manner as fiduciary funds (GASB-67, par. 14) [GASB Cod. Sec. Pe5.112]:

Statement	Elements
Statement of fiduciary net position	• Assets, deferred outflows of resources, liabilities, deferred inflows of resources, and fiduciary net position, as applicable, as of the end of the pension plan's reporting period.
Statement of changes in fiduciary net position	• Additions to, deductions from, and net increase (or decrease) in fiduciary net position for the pension plan's reporting period.

Within each of these, the various accounting elements include the following (GASB-67, pars. 15–21) [GASB Cod. Secs. Pe5.113–.119], starting with the *statement of fiduciary net position*:

Elements	Transactions and Amounts Included
Assets	• The major categories of assets, including, but not limited to, (*a*) cash and cash equivalents, receivables, investments, and assets used in pension plan operations and (*b*) the principal components of the receivables and investments categories.
Receivables	• Receivables are only short-term amounts due from employers, non-employer contributing entities, and plan members, and investments. Amounts recognized as receivables for contributions should include only those due pursuant to legal requirements and investments. Amounts due in more than one year should be recognized as the receivable arises. Discounting and the effective interest method may be used if the receivable is due in more than one year.
Investments	• Investments are reported on a trade date basis at fair value in accordance with the provisions of GASB-31 (*Accounting and Financial Reporting for Certain Investments and for External Investment Pools*) as amended by GASB-59 (*Financial Instruments Omnibus*) and GASB-72 (*Fair Value Measurement and Application*) as applicable (see Chapter 9, "Deposits, Investments, and Derivative Instruments). Unallocated insurance contracts should be reported as interest-earning investment contracts. Synthetic guaranteed investment contracts that are fully benefit responsive are reported at contract value.
Liabilities	• Liabilities are only benefits (including refunds of plan member contributions) due to plan members and accrued investment and administrative expenses.
Fiduciary Net Position	• Assets + Deferred outflows of resources − Liabilities − Deferred inflows of resources = Net position restricted for pensions at the end of a reporting period.

OBSERVATION: Note that the classes of assets do not include capital assets such as buildings. Many plans purchase the building where the administrative offices are and attempt to deem it an asset. However, if the building was purchased with contributions, then the asset really is an investment in a title as the benefits of ownership (and sale) will ultimately inure to the beneficiary, not to the plan. But, the provisions of GASB-72, par. 66 [GASB Cod. Secs. I50.101, .105], in defining an investment specifically exclude capital assets *held for sale*. If the plan holds the real estate as part of their portfolio, ultimately, the highest and best use of the building may be for income or profit and, therefore, would be an investment. Most plans do include real estate as part of their portfolios and the administrative building and its contents may be included as part of that invest-ment. In other cases, the building where the plan is located was purchased by a separate government or private entity and leased to the plan. Care must be taken to present these transactions properly.

PRACTICE ALERT: GASB Statement No. 84 (*Fiduciary Activities*) changes the recognition of a liability in a fiduciary fund. A liability to the beneficiaries of a fiduciary activity should be recognized in a fiduciary fund when an event has occurred that *compels the government* to disburse fiduciary resources. Events that compel a government to disburse fiduciary resources occur when a demand for the resources has been made or when no further action, approval, or condition is required to be taken or met by the beneficiary to release the assets. In essence, for a pension or OPEB trust, a liability would be declared when benefits are demanded. GASB-84 will be implemented for periods beginning after December 15, 2018. For further information on GASB-84, see Chapter 8, "Fiduciary Funds."

The example of a statement of fiduciary net position shown in GASB-67 is reproduced in Exhibit 22-1.

PRACTICE POINT: The statement of fiduciary net position shown below includes GASB-74 OPEB information.

EXHIBIT 22-1:
STATE OF TREASURE PUBLIC EMPLOYEES RETIREMENT SYSTEM
STATEMENT OF FIDUCIARY NET POSITION
AS OF DECEMBER 31, 20XX (in thousands)

	Base Plan	Firefighters Retirement	Judges Retirement	Defined Contribution 1	Defined Contribution 2	Retiree Health Benefits	20XX Total
Assets							
Cash and cash equivalents	$2,671	$66	$292	$38	$423	$54	$3,544
Investments, at fair value:							
Fixed income—domestic	3,713,96	91,345	20,122	-	-	127,507	3,952,937
Fixed income—international	10,450	257	59	-	-	-	10,766
Commercial mortgages	645,620	15,879	3,498	-	-	-	664,997
Short-term	220,071	5,413	1,192	-	1,405	-	228,081
Real estate	606,993	14,929	3,289	-	-	-	625,211
Domestic stocks	6,019,999	148,063	32,619	-	-	271,898	6,472,579
Global stocks	3,132,891	77,054	16,976	-	-	69,082	3,296,003
Private equities	905,712	22,276	4,907	-	-	-	932,897
Mutual funds	-	-	-	57,532	773,567	-	831,099
Total investments	15,255,699	375,216	82,662	57,532	774,972	468,487	17,014,570
Receivables	121,540	-	-	-	-	-	121,540
Other assets including prepaid benefits	80,429	-	-	-	-	3,473	83,902
Total assets	15,460,338	378,232	83,595	57,730	778,050	472,014	17,299,960
Liabilities							
Accrued liabilities	11,193	270	59	12	206	44	11,783
Benefits and refunds payable	376	9	-	-	-	-	385
In transit amounts	2,072	51	-	1	13	-	2,138
Investments purchased	110,752	2,724	600	-	-	-	114,076
Total liabilities	124,392	3,054	659	13	219	44	128,382
Net position restricted for pension benefits, postemployment benefits other than pensions and amounts held in trust	$15,335,946	$375,178	$82,936	$57,717	$777,831	$471,970	$17,101,578

Statement of Changes in Fiduciary Net Position

A pension plan should prepare an operating statement that reports the net increase or decrease in fiduciary net position from the beginning of the year until the end of the year. The statement of changes in fiduciary net position should be prepared on the same basis of accounting used to prepare the pension plan's statement of fiduciary net position. The two financial statements are interrelated (in a manner similar to an income statement and a balance sheet) in that (1) the net increase as reported on the statement of changes in fiduciary net position, when added to (2) the beginning balance of fiduciary net position on the statement of fiduciary net position, is equal to (3) the net plan assets as reported at the end of the year on the statement of fiduciary net position. The components of the inflows and outflows are as follows (GASB-67, pars. 22–29) [GASB Cod. Secs. Pe5.120–.125]:

Elements	Transactions and Amounts Included
Additions	• Contributions from employers, contributions from non-employer contributing entities (e.g., state government contributions to a local government pension plan), contributions from plan members, including those transmitted by the employers, Net investment income, including separate display of (1) investment income and (2) investment expense, including investment management and custodial fees and all other significant investment-related costs.
Investment Income	• Investment income includes changes in the fair value of investments, interest, dividends, and other income that is displayed separately or aggregated if immaterial. The net increase (decrease) in the fair value of investments should include realized gains and losses on investments that were both bought and sold during the period. Realized and unrealized gains and losses should not be separately displayed in the financial statements. Realized gains and losses, computed as the difference between the proceeds of sale and the original cost of the investments sold, *may be disclosed in notes to financial statements.* The disclosure also should state that the calculation of realized gains and losses is independent of the calculation of the net change in the fair value of pension plan investments and the realized gains and losses on investments that had been held in more than one reporting period and sold in the current period were included as a change in the fair value reported in the prior period(s) and the current period. Interest income is reported at the stated rate without including amortized premiums and discounts.
Investment Expense	• Reported to net out of investment income *if* investment expense is separable from (*a*) investment income and (*b*) the administrative expense of the pension plan.
Deductions	• At a minimum, (*a*) benefit payments to plan members (including refunds of plan member contributions) and (*b*) total administrative expense. Some plans may disaggregate benefit payments to retirees and survivors. If matching amounts are refunded along with accumulated interest, the refund caption may state this. Disability payments and claims may also be paid out of a defined benefit plan.
Net Increase (or Decrease) in Fiduciary Net Position	• Additions − Deductions = Net Increase (Decrease) in Fiduciary Net Position

PRACTICE POINT: GASB Statement No. 82 (*Pension Issues—an amendment of GASB Statement No. 67, No. 68, and No. 73*) was released just prior to publication. An issue addressed by GASB-82 is the classification of employer-paid member contributions (EPMCs). Commonly, payments are made by employers to satisfy contribution requirements that are *identified by the plan terms as plan member contribution requirements.* For GASB-67's purposes, those amounts should remain as plan member contributions. However, for the employer and employer reporting (see later in this chapter), the reporting may be different..

PRACTICE POINT: GASB Statement No. 85 (*Omnibus 2017*) carries forward similar provisions for OPEB arrangements.

PRACTICE POINT: Unrealized gains and losses must be recorded as part of investment income because fair value is the basis for measuring investments held by the pension plan. When debt securities are held by the pension plan, any related discount or premium should not be amortized as part of investment income, and interest income should be based on the stated interest rate. If the plan has a net investment loss for the year, the caption in the statement of changes in plan net position might be labeled "net investment (loss) income." Some plans segregate the unrealized portion of investment income (loss) from the realized portion for analysis and trend information.

The example of a statement of changes in plan net position shown as required by GASB-67 (and GASB-74) is reproduced in Exhibit 22-2.

EXHIBIT 22-2:
STATE OF TREASURE PUBLIC EMPLOYEES RETIREMENT SYSTEM
STATEMENTS OF CHANGES IN FIDUCIARY NET POSITION
AS OF DECEMBER 31, 20XX
(in thousands)

	Base Plan	Firefighters Retirement	Judges Retirement	Defined Contribution 1	Defined Contribution 2	Retiree Health Benefits	20XX Total
Additions							
Contributions from members	$237,033	$4	$630	$-	$48,333	$-	$286,000
Contributions from employers	356,367	7,453	3,947	-	5,475	21,900	395,142
Transfers and rollovers	-	-	-	-	14,837	-	14,837
Total contributions	593,400	7,457	4,577	-	68,645	21,900	695,980
Investment income:							
Net appreciation in fair value	1,411,349	34,527	7,613	6,193	69,443	54,697	1,583,820
Interest, dividends and other	330,011	8,074	1,781	47	15,434	-	355,347
Less: investment expenses	(45,467)	(1,112)	(240)	(149)	(1,648)	(190)	(48,807)
Total investment income-net	1,695,892	41,489	9,153	6,091	83,229	54,507	1,890,360
Other-net	29	-	-	5	-	2	37
Total Additions	2,289,321	48,946	13,735	6,091	151,874	76,409	2,586,377
Deductions							
Benefits and refunds	865,272	19,294	6,173	3,764	38,822	18,166	951,491
Administrative expenses	8,810	43	74	10	116	104	9,158

	Base Plan	Firefighters Retirement	Judges Retirement	Defined Contribution 1	Defined Contribution 2	Retiree Health Benefits	20XX Total
Total Deductions	874,082	19,337	6,247	3,774	38,937	18,270	960,649
Increase/(Decrease) in Net Position	1,415,239	29,609	7,487	2,317	112,937	58,139	1,625,728
Beginning of Year	13,920,707	345,569	75,449	55,400	664,894	413,831	15,475,850
Net position restricted for pension benefits, postemployment benefits other than pensions and amounts held in trust, End of Year	$15,335,946	$375,178	$82,936	$57,717	$777,831	$471,970	$17,101,578

Totals may not add due to rounding.

Notes to the Financial Statements

GASB-67 requires that the following be disclosed by all defined benefit pension plans as applicable (GASB-67, par. 30) [GASB Cod. Sec. Pe5.126]:

Plan Description

- Type of pension plan (single-employer, agent multiple-employer, or cost-sharing multiple-employer);

- Number of governmental employers participating in the plan and other entities contributing to the plan;

- Information regarding the board's composition, including the number of trustees by source of selection and the types of constituencies or credentials applicable to the selection;

- Type of governmental employees covered by the plan and their plan status (such as active members, retirees and beneficiaries receiving benefits, and terminated employees not yet receiving benefits, who some plans term "inactives") (When the plan is closed to new entrants, that fact should be disclosed.);

- Description of plan provisions such as types of benefits provided and policies concerning cost-of-living adjustments (automatic or discretionary);

- Authority under which benefits are provided or may be amended; and

- Descriptions of contribution requirements, including the authority under which contribution requirements of employers, non-employer contributing entities, if any, and plan members are established or may be amended and the contribution rates (in dollars or as a percentage of covered payroll) of those entities for the reporting period. If the pension plan or the entity that administers the pension plan has the authority to establish or amend contribution requirements, disclose the basis for determining contributions (e.g., statute, contract, an actuarial basis, or some other manner).

Summary of Significant Accounting Policies—Pension Plan Investments

- The investment policies of the plan, including the following:

  — Procedures and authority for establishing and amending investment policy decisions;

  — The policies pertaining to asset allocation;

— A description of any significant investment policy changes during the reporting period;

— A brief description of how the fair value of investments is determined, including the methods and significant assumptions used to estimate the fair value of investments if that fair value is based on other than quoted market prices;

— Identification of investments (other than those issued or explicitly guaranteed by the U.S. government) in any one organization that represent 5% or more of the pension plan's fiduciary net position (concentrations); and

— The annual money-weighted rate of return on pension plan investments.

OBSERVATION: The annual money-weighted rate of return on plan investments is relatively new to governmental accounting. The GASB has inserted a calculation as follows: The money-weighted return on investments is the internal rate of return on pension plan investments, net of pension plan investment expense, adjusted for the changing amounts actually invested. Pension plan investment expense should be measured on the accrual basis of accounting. Inputs to the internal rate of return calculation should be determined at least monthly. The use of more frequently determined inputs is encouraged.

PRACTICE POINT: GASB-72 adds the following for disclosures for investments that will most likely be present in plans and similar endowments. Disclosures are for recurring fair value measurements (measured each period), nonrecurring fair value measurements (measured in only particular circumstances such as an asset impairment), and for those investments that are measured by a net asset value per share (such as private equity). For recurring and nonrecurring fair value measurements, the following is disclosed:

• The fair value measurement at the end of the reporting period;

• The level of the fair value hierarchy within which the fair value measurements are categorized in their entirety (Level 1, 2, or 3);

• A description of the valuation techniques used in the fair value measurement; and

• If there has been a change in valuation technique that has a significant impact on the result (e.g., changing from an expected cash flow technique to a relief from royalty technique or the use of an additional valuation technique), that change and the reason(s) for making it.

Finally, for nonrecurring fair value measurements: the reason(s) for the measurement, such as asset impairment. For investments in entities that (*a*) calculate a NAV per share (or its equivalent) (regardless of whether the method of determining fair value has been applied), (*b*) do not have a readily determinable fair value, and (*c*) are measured at fair value on a recurring or nonrecurring basis during the period, a government should disclose information that addresses the nature and risks of the investments and whether the investments are probable of being sold at amounts different from the NAV per share. To meet that objective, a government should disclose the following information for each type of investment:

- The fair value measurement of the investment type at the reporting measurement date and a description of the significant investment strategies of the investee(s) in that type.

- For each type of investment that includes investments that can never be redeemed with the investees, but the government receives distributions through the liquidation of the underlying assets of the investees: the government's estimate of the period of time over which the underlying assets are expected to be liquidated by the investees.

- The amount of the government's unfunded commitments related to that investment type.

- A general description of the terms and conditions upon which the government may redeem investments in the type (e.g., quarterly redemption with 60 days' notice).

- The circumstances in which an otherwise redeemable investment in the type (or a portion thereof) might not be redeemable (e.g., investments subject to a redemption restriction, such as a lockup or gate).

- For those otherwise redeemable investments that are restricted from redemption as of the government's measurement date, the estimate of when the restriction from redemption might lapse should be disclosed and, if an estimate cannot be made, that fact and how long the restriction has been in effect should be disclosed.

- Any other significant restriction on the ability to sell investments in the type at the measurement date.

If a government determines that it is probable that it will sell an investment(s) for an amount different from NAV per share, the total fair value of all investments that meet the criteria and any remaining actions required to complete the sale.

If a group of investments would otherwise meet the criteria for NAV but the individual investments to be sold have not been identified (e.g., if a government decides to sell 20% of its investments in private equity funds but the individual investments to be sold have not been identified), such that the investments continue to qualify for the method of estimating fair value, the government's plans to sell and any remaining actions required to complete the sale(s).

Receivables

Policies and information on receivables to be disclosed will consist of any long-term contracts for contributions to the pension plan between (1) an employer or non-employer contributing entity and (2) the pension plan, and the balances outstanding on any such long-term contracts at the end of the pension plan's reporting period.

Allocated Insurance Contracts That Are Omitted from Plan Net Position

The notes to the basic financial statements should include the amount reported in benefit payments in the current period that is attributable to the purchase of allocated insurance contracts, a brief description of the pensions for which allocated insurance contracts were purchased in the current period, and the fact that the obligation for the payment of benefits covered by allocated insurance contracts has been transferred to one or more insurance companies. This information is only inserted if allocated insurance contracts are in use during the year or at year end.

Reserves

- A description of the policy related to the reserve(s);

- Authority under which pension plan funding sources are established and may be amended;

- The policy and conditions under which the reserves may be used; and

- Balances reported as legally required reserves at the reporting dates, their purposes, and whether they are fully funded. (Balances reported as "designations," as defined in NCGA-1, also may be reported but should not be reported as reserves.)

OBSERVATION: Reserve accounts have many different aspects. They are not required by U.S. GAAP, but they are used by management to segment operations. The largest reserves tend to be the summation of amounts contributed by member employees and those funded by amounts contributed by member employers. There may be contribution credit reserves, where any excess contributions are reserved for periods when member employers cannot fully fund or decide not to fully fund required contributions. There may be other reserves to fund various benefits, including cost of living adjustments. Other reserves may be for contingencies, differentials between market value and historical cost of investments and other items. These reserves should be approved by the plan's governing board or in statute and, ultimately, they should reconcile to the plan's net position. In practice, there may be some assets that are not part of an actuarial valuation, meaning that they are not part of the actuarially calculated value of assets to be used to pay benefits due to some governing board's decision. However, those "non-valuation" assets will ultimately become part of those assets to pay benefits. Therefore, depending on statute or trust agreement and market value smoothing patterns, there could be some instances where the market value of the entirety of assets does not equate to those in reserves to pay plan benefits.

Deferred Retirement Option Programs (DROPS)

These programs are prevalent. DROPs are programs that permit a plan member to elect a calculation of benefit payments based on service credits and salary, as applicable, as of the DROP entry date. The plan member continues to provide service to the employer and is paid for that service by the employer after the DROP entry date; however, the pensions that would have been paid to the plan member (if the plan member had retired and not entered the DROP) are credited to an individual member account within the defined benefit pension plan until the end of the DROP period. If a DROP is used as part of the plan, then the notes to the basic financial statements should include a description of the DROP terms and conditions and the balance of the amounts held by the pension plan pursuant to the DROP.

Disclosures Specific to Single-Employer and Cost Sharing Multiple Employer Plans (Not Agent Multiple-Employer Plans)

In addition to the above, the following items are added to the notes to the basic financial statements for single-employer pension plans and cost sharing multiple employer pension plans, but not agent multiple-employer plans (GASB-67, par. 31) [GASB Cod. Sec. Pe5.127]:

- The components of the liability of the employers and non-employer contributing entities to plan members for benefits provided through the pension plan, including the total pension liability, the pension plan's fiduciary net position and the pension plan's fiduciary net position as a percentage of the total pension liability (formerly known as the "funded ratio").

- Significant assumptions and other inputs used to measure the total pension liability, including assumptions about inflation, salary changes, and ad-hoc postemployment benefit changes (including ad-hoc COLAs).

- With regard to mortality assumptions, the source of the assumptions (e.g., the published tables on which the assumption is based or that the assumptions are based on a study of the experience of the covered group) should be disclosed.

- The dates of experience studies on which significant assumptions are based also should be disclosed. If different rates are assumed for different periods, information should be disclosed about what rates are applied to the different periods of the measurement.

- Discount rate information, including:

  — The discount rate applied in the measurement of the total pension liability and the change in the discount rate since the pension plan's prior fiscal year-end, if any;

  — Assumptions made about projected cash flows into and out of the pension plan, such as contributions from employers, non-employer contributing entities, and plan members;

  — The long-term expected rate of return on pension plan investments and a description of how it was determined, including significant methods and assumptions used for that purpose;

  — If the discount rate incorporates a municipal bond rate, the municipal bond rate used and the source of that rate;

  — The periods of projected benefit payments to which the long-term expected rate of return and, if used, the municipal bond rate applied to determine the discount rate;

  — The assumed asset allocation of the pension plan's portfolio, the long-term expected real rate of return for each major asset class, and whether the expected rates of return are presented as arithmetic or geometric means, if not otherwise disclosed;

  — Sensitivity measures of the net pension liability calculated using a discount rate that is 1-percentage-point higher than that required and a discount rate that is 1-percentage-point lower than that required by GASB-67; and

— The date of the actuarial valuation on which the total pension liability is based and, if applicable, the fact that update procedures were used to roll forward the total pension liability to the pension plan's fiscal year-end.

Communication Issues from the Plan to Employers/Sponsors

For agent-multiple employers, receiving the information from an agent-multiple employer plan to record in the basic financial statements, notes to the basic financial statements, and required supplementary information might be a challenge. The plans need to present each employer with a financial statement, the note disclosure, and required supplementary information discussed therein. If the plan has hundreds of employers and performs allocations of investment revenues and administrative expenses to the various employers, the timely presentation of this information is a challenge. The AICPA has proposed a "best practice" requiring the information to be transmitted from the plans to the employers to be audited separately from the audit of the plan's financial statements. A separate internal controls engagement may also ensue in accordance with AT Section 801 (*Reporting on Controls at a Service Organization*). Controls may be required to be tested based on management's assertion that internal controls are suitably designed and have been operating effectively for an entire year under audit (also known as a Type 2 report). For single employer plans, increased testing on census data and the information transfer will also be required. Therefore, in both cases, time should be increased to prepare this data, unless it can be prepared "off-cycle" to the date of the basic financial statements.

The AICPA is also concerned with the ability to audit the transfer of information from a cost-sharing multiple-employer plan to the employers in the plan. The state and local government expert panel has released a set of white papers detailing schedules that the plan should produce as "best practices." Additionally, a set of auditing interpretations have been released including these schedules and additional guidance for evidence gathering. The schedules would be separately audited. A "Schedule of Employer Allocations" detailed by employer the allocation percentages based on contributions, including when a nonemployer funds a portion of the liability in a special funding situation.

The schedule contained in the AICPA interpretation is as follows:

	20X7 Contributions	Allocation
Employer 1	$2,143,842	36.3748%
Employer 2	268,425	4.5544%
Employer 3	322,142	5.4658%
Employer 4	483,255	8.1994%
Employer 5	633,125	10.7423%
Employer 6	144,288	2.4481%
Employer 7	95,365	1.6181%
Employer 8	94,238	1.5989%

	20X7 Contributions	*Allocation*
Employer 9	795,365	13.4950%
Employer 10	267,468	4.5382%
Employer 11	403,527	6.8467%
Employer 12	165,886	2.8146%
Employer 13	68,454	1.1615%
Employer 14	6,240	0.1059%
Employer 15	2,144	0.0364%
Total	$5,893,764	100.00%

PRACTICE POINT: An issue addressed by GASB-82 is the classification of employer-paid member contributions (EPMCs). Commonly, payments are made by employers to satisfy contribution requirements that are *identified by the plan terms as plan member contribution requirements.* For GASB-67's purposes, those amounts should remain as plan member contributions. However, for the employer, the reporting may be different. Therefore, the allocation percentages above need to address employer paid member contributions, *depending upon the treatment of such contributions at the employer.* The possibilities are as follows:

- For payments made by the employer to satisfy contribution requirements that are identified by the pension plan as plan member contributions, *for the employer,* such amounts should be classified as *employee* contributions for the purposes of determining a cost-sharing employer's proportion. An employer's expense and expenditures for those amounts should be included in the salaries and wages of the period *for which the contribution is assessed* (meaning included in the employee's Internal Revenue Service Form W-2).

- If the employer makes payments to satisfy employee contribution requirements (commonly known as "picks ups") in connection with an election made in accordance with Internal Revenue Code Section 414(h)(2) as described in Revenue Ruling 2006-43 (*Government Pick-Up Plans; Employer Contributions; Income Tax; Prospective Application*), the employer should disclose information about that arrangement.

The AICPA has discussed this issue in a *non-authoritative article, Emerging Pension Issues.* In accordance with Revenue Ruling 2006-43, the following must be in place for the employer *not* to report additional income to the employee on their Form W-2:

- Employing units must take formal action (such as through the issuance of a resolution by the governing body) to provide that the contributions on behalf of a specific class of employees, although designated as employee contributions, will be paid by the employing unit in lieu of employee contributions.

- Participating employees, from the date of the *pick-up* and later, *are not permitted* to have a cash right or deferred election right with respect to the designated employee contributions. Participating employees *must not be permitted to opt out* of the *pick-up*, or to receive the contributed amounts directly instead of having them paid by the employing unit to the plan.

If the employer has made the election to pick-up, the contributions relative to that employer are employer contributions.

The effect of the presence of a pick up or not will also affect the calculation of other pension elements as follows:

Scenario	Effect on Pension Expense	Effect on Deferred Outflow of Resources for Contributions Made After the Measurement Date
Employer paid member contribution is treated by *the employer* as salary expense (no election made)	Contributions reported as salary expense and excluded from employer's pension expense.	No effect
Employer contribution paid is treated *by the employer* as other than salary expense (e.g., pension benefits) (election has been made in accordance with IRC § 414(h)(2)).	Contributions reported as additional employer pension expense, if made during the measurement period.	If contributions made after the measurement period, but before the employer year-end, additional deferred outflows of resources declared.

See additional changes below on the Schedule of Pension Amounts by Employer.

As discussed in Chapter 7, "Proprietary Funds," and Chapter 13, "Pension, Postemployment, and Other Employee Benefit Liabilities," each employer would then have to produce a similar schedule within the government and for component units that contribute through the government to the plan.

A "Schedule of Pension Amounts by Employer" contains two alternative presentations. Alternative 1 lists all employers in the plan and the allocation for every accounting element that needs to be transferred to the employers, based on the allocations in the previous schedule. For very large cost-sharing multiple employer plans with more than a handful of employers, Alternative 1 may yield a very onerous schedule. A second alternative contains just the aggregated amounts for each accounting element, including:

- Net pension liability;
- Deferred Outflows of Resources, including, but not limited to:
  - Differences between Expected and Actual Experience;
  - Net Difference between Projected and Actual Investment Earnings on Pension Plan Investments;
  - Changes of Assumptions;
  - Changes in Proportion and Differences between Employer Contributions and Proportionate Share of Contributions; and
  - Total Deferred Outflows of Resources;

- Deferred Inflows of Resources, including, but not limited to:
  - Differences between Expected and Actual Experience;
  - Changes of Assumptions;
  - Changes in Proportion and Differences between Employer Contributions and Proportionate Share of Contributions; and
  - Total Deferred Inflows of Resources;
- Proportionate Share of Plan Pension Expense;
- Net Amortization of Deferred Amounts from Changes in Proportion and Differences between Employer Contributions and Proportionate Share of Contributions; and
- Total Employer Pension Expense.

It is then be up to the employer to use the information in the allocation schedule and multiply the allocation against the aggregated amounts for each element. Upon receipt of each of the schedules, the employers can then rely on this information to be placed in their basic financial statements, notes to the basic financial statements, and required supplementary information because it will contain an audit opinion. Similar to agent multiple-employer plan information, time should be increased to prepare this data, unless it can be prepared "off-cycle" to the date of the basic financial statements.

PRACTICE POINT: Should "pick ups" be present as described previously, the "Schedule of Pension Amounts by Employer" from a cost-sharing multiple employer plan to its employers may change. New information may be included, as applicable:

- A new column to reflect pension expense related to specific liabilities of individual employers due to their joining the plan or leaving the plan; and
- Revisions to the column headings to be clear as to whether the pension expense includes or excludes the effect of employer paid member contributions as follows:
  - "Proportionate Share of Pension Expense" is changed to "Proportionate Share of Allocable Pension Expense"; and
  - "Pension Expense" is changed to "Pension Expense Excluding That Attributable to Employer-Paid Member Contributions."

PRACTICE POINT: Wolters Kluwer's *2018 Governmental GAAP Disclosure Manual*, Chapter 43, contains complete disclosures for a pension plan in both separately issued financial statements and employer statements. Chapter 16 contains investment disclosures.

Required Supplementary Information (RSI) for Single-Employer and Cost-Sharing Multiple Employer Plans Only

---

OBSERVATION: Footnote 11 to GASB-67 emphasizes that RSI should include all information whether the basic financial statements are presented in a stand-alone report or solely in the financial report of another government as a pension trust fund. No duplication is necessary for a government that presents similar information in accordance with GASB-68 (see Chapter 13), "Pension, Postemployment, and Other Employee Benefit Liabilities".

The RSI for plans extends to 10 years of information. The first two schedules discussed below can be combined if practical. The schedules should be as of a fiscal year-end and for cost-sharing plans the information disclosed should be for the plan as a whole.

The RSI should include the following 10-year schedules (GASB-67, par. 32, as amended by GASB-73, par. 119, and GASB-82, par. 5) [GASB Cod. Sec. Pe5.128]:

- A 10-year schedule of changes in the net pension liability, with annual beginning and ending balances of the total pension liability, the pension plan's fiduciary net position and the net pension liability. These amounts are then shown with the effects on those items during the year for service costs, interest on the total pension liability, changes of benefit terms, differences between expected and actual experience with regard to economic or demographic factors in the measurement of the total pension liability, changes of assumptions about future economic or demographic factors or of other inputs, contributions from all sources, delineated by source (including from non-employer contributing entities, pension plan net investment income, benefit payments, including refunds of plan member contributions, pension plan administrative expense, and, finally, other changes, separately identified if individually significant).

- If possible, the above schedule can be combined with a similar 10-year schedule showing the total pension liability, the pension plan's fiduciary net position, the net pension liability, the pension plan's fiduciary net position as a percentage of the total pension liability, and, finally, the covered payroll and the net pension liability as a percentage of covered payroll.

PRACTICE POINT: GASB-82 changed the divisor for the percentage calculation in RSI for single employer and cost-sharing multiple employer pension plans that are administered through trusts. The measure of payroll to be presented should be now *covered payroll*. Covered payroll is defined to be the portion of compensation paid to active employees on which contributions to a pension plan are based. The measure should also be used by employers. Therefore, the schedules to employers that plans deliver may need to be restated, as well the RSI of the Plan for all years presented.

- A 10-year schedule presenting if an *actuarially determined contribution* is calculated for employers or non-employer contributing entities. The schedule should identify whether the information relates to the employers, non-employer contributing entities, or both. The schedule should include the actuarially determined contributions of employers or non-employer contributing entities. These may include long-term receivables recognized for contractually deferred contributions with separate payment schedules, and cash receipts or long-term receivables for amounts assessed to an individual employer upon joining a multiple-employer pension plan or for increases in the total pension liability for changes of benefit terms specific to an employer in a multiple-employer pension plan. For cost-sharing pension plans, the contractually required contribution of employers or non-employer contributing entities would be included. The amount of contributions recognized during the fiscal year by the pension plan in relation to the actuarially determined contribution should also be disclosed. For purposes of this schedule, contributions should include only amounts recognized as additions to the pension plan's fiduciary net position resulting from cash contributions and from contributions recognized by the pension plan as current receivables. The difference between the actuarially determined contribution in and the amount of contributions recognized by the pension plan in relation to the actuarially determined contribution is then calculated. Covered-employee payroll is then disclosed along with the amounts of contributions recognized by the pension plan in relation to the actuarially determined contribution as a percentage of covered payroll.

PRACTICE POINT: The 10-year schedule only presents information when an actuarially determined contribution is used. If a statutory rate is used (e.g., a percentage of taxation) for contributions to the pension plan, no comparison is made.

PRACTICE POINT: GASB-73, paragraph 119, amended GASB-67's RSI with regard to the contribution-related schedules. The schedules should exclude amounts, if any, associated with payables to the pension plan that arose in a prior fiscal year and those associated with separately financed specific liabilities of the individual employer or nonemployer contributing entity, as applicable, to the pension plan.

- Finally, a 10-year schedule presenting for each fiscal year the annual money-weighted rate of return on pension plan investments.

RSI for Agent-Multiple Employer Plans

The only RSI for Agent-Multiple Employer Plans is a 10-year schedule presenting for each fiscal year the annual money-weighted rate of return on pension plan investments (GASB-67, par. 33) [GASB Cod. Sec. Pe5.129].

Notes to the RSI

The notes to the RSI should include significant methods and assumptions used in calculating the actuarially determined contributions, if any. In addition, for each of the schedules, information should be presented about factors that significantly affect trends in the amounts reported (e.g., changes of benefit terms, changes in the size or composition of the population covered by the benefit terms, or the use of different assumptions). (The amounts presented for prior years should not be restated for the effects of changes—for example, changes of benefit terms or changes of assumptions—that occurred subsequent to the end of the fiscal year for which the information is reported.) (GASB-67, par. 34, as amended by GASB-73, par. 117) [GASB Cod. Sec. Pe5.130].

PRACTICE POINT: GASB-73, par. 117, amended the notes to RSI. Investment-related factors that significantly affect trends in the amounts reported should be limited to those factors over which the pension plan or participating governments have influence (e.g., changes in investment policies). Information about external, economic factors (e.g., changes in market prices) should not be presented.

The example of a schedule of funding progress shown in GASB-67 is reproduced in Exhibit 22-3. Exhibit 22-4 is a schedule of employer contributions. Exhibit 22-5 is a schedule of investment returns using a money-weighted rate of return. **Note—the amounts in the following exhibits are not meant to agree to those contained in Exhibits 22-1 and 22-2.**

EXHIBIT 22-3
SCHEDULE OF CHANGES IN THE EMPLOYERS' NET PENSION LIABILITY AND RELATED RATIOS

Last 10 fiscal years (Dollar Amounts in Thousands) (only 2 years shown)

	20X8	20X7
Total Pension Liability		
Service cost	$75,864	$74,276
Interest	216,515	205,038
Changes in benefit terms	-	-
Differences between actual and expected experience	(37,539)	(15,211)
Changes in assumptions	-	-
Benefit payments, including refunds of member contributions	(119,434)	(112,603)
Net Change in Pension Liability	135,406	151,500
Total Pension Liability—Beginning	48,868,199	48,716,699
Total Pension Liability—Ending - (a)	$49,003,605	$48,868,199
Plan Fiduciary Net Position		
Contributions—employer	$1,015,397	$1,024,426
Contributions—member	690,355	886,525
Net investment income	4,702,603	724,563
Benefit payments, refunds	(3,707,349)	(3,885,835)
Administrative expense	(28,669)	(48,527)
Other	(15,217)	6,691
Net change in plan fiduciary net position	2,657,120	(1,292,157)
Plan fiduciary net position—Beginning	37,222,014	38,514,171
Plan fiduciary net position—Ending (b)	$39,879,134	$37,222,014
Employers' Net Pension Liability (a-b)	$9,124,471	$11,646,185
Plan's fiduciary net position as a Percentage of the Total Pension Liability	81.38%	76.17%
Covered Payroll	$4,492,930	$4,364,240
Employers' Net Pension Liability as a Percentage of Covered Payroll	203.09%	266.85%

The notes to the schedule explain any differences and changes from previous years' estimates.

EXHIBIT 22-4
SCHEDULE OF EMPLOYER CONTRIBUTIONS

Last 10 fiscal years (Dollar Amounts in Thousands) (only 2 years shown)

	20X8	20X7
Actuarially Determined Contributions	$1,705,752	$1,910,951
Contributions in relation to the Actuarially Determined Contribution	1,705,752	1,910,951
Contribution Deficiency (Excess)	$ -	$ -
Covered Payroll	$4,492,930	$4,364,240
Contributions as a Percentage of covered payroll	37.97%	43.79%

EXHIBIT 22-5
SCHEDULE OF INVESTMENT RETURNS

Last 10 fiscal years (only 2 years shown)

	20X8	20X7
	20X8	**20X7**
Annual Money-Weighted Rate of Return, Net of Investment Expense	8.19%	11.23%

In addition, notes to required supplementary information are included for the year ended (in this case December 31, 20X8). The notes would include any changes between years that may affect comparability, including at a minimum descriptions of changes in benefit terms, assumptions, and methods and assumptions used in calculating actuarially determined contributions.

Additional Items in Postemployment Benefit Plan CAFRs

CAFRs are frequently released for separately issued defined benefit postemployment benefit plans, although they are not required by U.S. GAAP. Should a plan prepare a CAFR, the components of the document are similar to those of general purpose governments. They include the following:

- Introductory section (letter of transmittal and various other introductory items).
- Financial section (report of the independent auditor, management's discussion and analysis, basic financial statements, and notes to basic financial statements).
- Required supplementary information (other than management's discussion and analysis).

- Supplementary information (schedules of administrative, investment, and consultant's expenses).

- An investment section detailing the plan's investments at fair value, investment return, investment allocation and other items.

PRACTICE POINT: The investment section amounts need to reconcile to the investments on the statement of plan net position because both are presented at fair value as of fiscal year-end.

- An actuarial section presenting the actuarial valuation of the plan with amounts that apportioned to members, assumptions, and other items, including an actuary's certification letter.

- The statistical section.

CAFR preparation for defined benefit plans is very important because the information contained in them may help management make better decisions. A CAFR for a plan may inform users of the financial statements even more than a general purpose government's CAFR. However, care must be taken that the information contained within a defined benefit plan CAFR is timely and succinct because a large portion of the information may be needed to produce a timely CAFR in a member general purpose government's CAFR.

Other Aspects of GASB-67

Separately Financed Liabilities to the Plan

Many plans are subject to state laws and regulations that allow for new employers to join the plan and in some cases, leave the plan. In most cases, leaving a plan is not economically feasible as most plans are subject to laws and regulations that require employers who want to leave a plan, to "buy out" at the risk free rate of return, thereby inflating any liability.

If an employer joins a plan, a liability is established at the employer based on the plan provisions for the existing employees that are subject to those conditions. Assets are usually required to be contributed to fund the liability either immediately or through a payment plan. If a payment plan is established, they are excluded from the RSI schedule of actuarially determined contributions to the pension plan as they are separate payment schedules from normal contributions (GASB-67, par. 32(c)(1-2), footnote 12, as amended by GASB-73, par. 119, and GASB-82, par. 5) [GASB Cod. Sec. Pe5.128]

The resulting contributions to the plan to finance such separately financed specific liabilities during the measurement period are recognized as follows:

- For cost-sharing employer, the amount of the employer's proportionate share of the total of such contributions (excluding nonemployer contributions) reduces the employer's pension expense.

- For a governmental nonemployer contributing entity in a special funding situation (e.g., a state contributing to a teacher's retirement plan on behalf of school districts), the amount of the governmental nonemployer contributing entity's proportionate share would also have its pension expense reduced (GASB-73, par. 121) [GASB Cod. Secs. P20.156, .195, .207].

Valuation Aspects

For most plans that have annual actuarial valuations on the same day, implementing GASB-67 from an actuarial standpoint will not have very pervasive changes. However, there are some elements of calculating the total pension liability in accordance with GASB-67 that are changing.

The timing of the valuations was one of the reasons why GASB-67 is more than just an amended version of the former GASB-25. GASB-67 requires that the actuarial valuation be performed either as of the pension plan's most recent fiscal year-end or the use of an update to "roll forward" to the most recent fiscal year-end from an actuarial valuation no more than 24 months earlier than the pension plan's most recent fiscal year-end.

Example:

Pension Plan's most recent fiscal year-end	December 31, 2019
Actuarial Valuation Date can be as of	December 31, 2019 *or*
Can be between	January 1, 2017 and December 31, 2019 *with Roll-forward procedures in between.*

Note that the employers' fiscal year-end is not taken into account. Those provisions are within GASB-68. If update procedures are used and *significant* changes occur between the actuarial valuation date and the pension plan's fiscal year-end, professional judgment should be used to determine the extent of procedures needed to roll forward the measurement from the actuarial valuation to the pension plan's fiscal year-end, and consideration should be given to whether a new actuarial valuation is needed. Significant changes could include the effects of changes in the discount rate resulting from changes in the pension plan's fiduciary net position or from changes in the municipal bond rate (GASB-67, par. 37) [GASB Cod. Sec. Pe5.133].

PLANNING POINT: The significant changes aspect seems to take into account any sort of major change in index rates similar to what occurred in the fall of 2008 with the collapse of the credit markets. However, other qualitative aspects could be construed as significant, including closing of the plan to entrants or a major shift in investment strategy.

The GASB also left up to the plan in consultation with the actuary the various assumptions that are used in developing the total pension liability. GASB-67 switches course in stating that the selection of all assumptions used in determining the total pension liability should be made in conformity with Actuarial Standards of Practice issued by the Actuarial Standards Board. However, the plan and all member employer(s) in the plan, should use the same assumptions or else the valuation would not be relevant (GASB-67, par. 38, as amended by GASB-82, par. 7) [GASB Cod. Sec. Pe5.134]. This aspect seemingly leaves the administration of the development of the liability squarely with the plan and not with the member employer(s).

PRACTICE POINT: GASB-82 requires the selection of assumptions used in determining the total pension liability to be in conformity with the provisions in U.S. GAAP. A *deviation*, as the term is used in Actuarial Standards of Practice issued by the Actuarial Standards Board, from the guidance in Actuarial Standards of Practice should not be considered in conformity with U.S. GAAP.

Benefits are projected, including all benefits measured in accordance with the benefit terms of the plan and all legal or contractual agreements that are in place as of the pension plan's fiscal year-end (not the employers'). Projected benefit payments should include the effects of automatic postemployment benefit changes (service credits, for example), including automatic cost of living adjustments (COLAs).

If benefits have adjustments that are made more on an ad-hoc basis, including benefit changes or COLAs, they are also included to the extent that they are "substantially automatic." Footnote 14 to GASB-67 [GASB Cod. Sec. Pe5.fn10] explains that "substantially automatic" is somewhat up to professional judgment, but relevant considerations may include the historical pattern of granting the changes, the consistency in the amounts of the changes or in the amounts of the changes relative to a defined cost-of-living or inflation index, and whether there is evidence to conclude that changes might not continue to be granted in the future despite what might otherwise be a pattern that would indicate such changes are substantively automatic.

Benefit changes should be projected, including projected salary changes (in circumstances in which the pension formula incorporates future compensation levels); and projected service credits (both in determining a plan member's probable eligibility for benefits and in the projection of benefit payments in circumstances in which the pension formula incorporates years of service). Excluded from the calculation would be any benefits to be paid from allocated insurance contracts (GASB-67, par. 39) [GASB Cod. Sec. Pe5.135].

As previously stated, the discount rate to be used is derived through a cash flow model. It is a single rate that initially uses the long-term expected rate of return on pension plan investments that are expected to be used to finance the payment of benefits, to the extent that the pension plan's fiduciary net position is projected to be sufficient to make projected benefit payments and pension plan assets are expected to be invested using a strategy to achieve that return. This rate is then matched to a yield or an index rate for 20-year, tax-exempt general obligation municipal bonds with an average rating of AA/Aa or higher (or equivalent quality on another rating scale), to the extent that the conditions are such that the plan cannot finance its benefits through the pension plan's fiduciary net position. The point of "crossover," therefore, becomes important because after that point, an AA/Aa index is used (GASB-67, pars. 40 and 44) [GASB Cod. Secs. Pe5.136 and .140].

PRACTICE POINT: The discount rate aspect was a large point of discussion in the development of what became GASB-67. Many users of governmental financial statements desired a "risk-free" rate of return as a discount rate similar to that for for-profit defined benefit plans. However, use of a "risk-free" rate of return would have two effects: (1) The liability would have been far larger than what is being presented today because it would assume that all benefits would be due and payable immediately to the extent that no funds would be available to pay the liability and (2) the discount rate would not have assumed the long-term aspect of governmental operations and the long-term aspect of the employer-employee relationship to fund the liability.

The issue continues to be deliberated, especially with regard to the perceived insolvency of the Employees Retirement System of the Government of the Commonwealth of Puerto Rico and other systems in New Jersey, Illinois and elsewhere. A Senator continues to advocate to require pension systems to file annual reports with the United States Treasury using an assumed rate of return adjusted to a United States Treasury rate—a rate that is far different than most discount rates in use. Many state and local government groups have voiced opposition to this plan. A compromise may be to voluntarily disclose the differences in the management's discussion and analysis as the differences in the liability is a currently known fact in accordance with GASB Statement No. 34 (*Basic Financial Statements—and Management's Discussion and Analysis—for State and Local Governments*), par. 11(h).

OBSERVATION: Due to the provisions of certain laws, many plans may never hit a "crossover point," because there are strong laws that force employers to fund contributions or else the plan may seize tax revenues or similar elements. If that is the case, a higher discount rate might be able to be used. Professional judgment should be used, but an indicator of sufficiency may include the most recent five-year contribution history of the employers and non-employer contributing entities as a key indicator of future contributions from those sources and should reflect all other known events and conditions (GASB-67, par. 42) [GASB Cod. Sec. Pe5.138]. The GASB included this provision to smooth out any contribution "spikes" due to pension obligation bond proceeds funding current cash flows.

The discount rate should be calculated annually or with each valuation. The cash flows to be included in the calculation would not only include the employer and employee's contributions and benefit payments, but also any non-employer contributions intended to finance benefits of current active and inactive plan members (status at the pension plan's fiscal year-end). Future cash inflows from all sources are only used to the extent that they are projected to exceed service costs for those plan members. The application of the cash flows is then matched to service costs of plan members in the current period (as there is no ability to fund future costs if service costs exceed cash inflows). Then, past service costs are funded with any remaining balance unless the effective pension plan terms related to contributions indicate that a different relationship between contributions to the pension plan from non-employer contributing entities and service costs should be applied. Contributions from members should be considered to be applied to service costs before contributions from employers and non-employer contributing entities (GASB-67, par. 41) [GASB Cod. Sec. Pe5.137].

Finally, unlike OPEB (see below), which does allow multiple types of actuarial methods under current U.S. GAAP, the GASB concluded that the entry age actuarial cost method should be used to attribute the actuarial present value of projected benefit payments of each plan member to periods. The attribution is made on an individual plan-member-by-plan-member basis. Each plan member's service costs should be level as a percentage of that member's projected pay. For purposes of this calculation, if a member does not have projected pay, the projected inflation rate should be used in place of the projected rate of change in salary. The beginning of the attribution period should be the first period in which the member's service accrues pensions under the benefit terms, notwithstanding vesting or other similar terms. The service costs of all pensions should be attributed through all assumed exit ages, through retirement. In pension plans in which the benefit terms include a DROP, the date of entry into the DROP is considered to be the plan member's retirement date (see previous discussion on DROPs) (GASB-67, par. 46) [GASB Cod. Sec. Pe5.142].

OBSERVATION: Because the calculation is performed on a member-by-plan-member basis, theoretically, members may be able to determine individual net pension liabilities (total pension liability less assets), thereby making defined benefit plans "more portable" between systems. Theoretically, a member would know what the liability is and be able to transfer that liability to another system and have that system assume or bill the previous system for the liability. Though this actuarial theory has yet to be tested, if successful, it could make the administration of large pension systems somewhat easier if members move to different employers throughout their careers. Currently, many systems employ a "wherever you work last pays" strategy. The new calculation method would allow each employer to have a piece of the final pension benefit payment stream for an employee.

Defined Contribution Plans

Although GASB-67 primarily focuses on accounting and reporting issues related to defined benefit pension plans, it does mandate some disclosures for defined contribution plans. In accordance with footnote 15 to GASB-67, the notes to financial statements of a defined contribution pension plan should include all disclosures required by below, as applicable, when the financial statements are presented, in a stand-alone pension plan financial report or solely in the financial report of another government (as a pension trust fund). If a defined contribution pension plan is included in the financial report of a government that applies the requirements of GASB-68 for benefits provided through the pension plan and similar information is required by GASB-67 and GASB-68, the government should present the information in a manner that avoids unnecessary duplication. The following should be included (GASB-67, par. 47) [GASB Cod. Sec. Pe6.108]:

- Identification of the pension plan as a defined contribution pension plan;

- Classes of plan members covered (e.g., general employees or public safety employees), the number of plan members, participating employers (if the pension plan is a multiple-employer pension plan), and, if any, non-employer contributing entities; and

- The authority under which the pension plan is established or may be amended.

IRC SECTION 457 DEFERRED COMPENSATION PLANS

In order to treat assets and income related to IRC Section 457 plans similar to other employee deferred compensation plans, Congress passed legislation in 1996 that governs IRC Section 457 plans. Specifically, the legislation states that a plan "shall not be treated as an eligible deferred compensation plan unless all assets and income of the plan described in subsection (b)(6) are held in trust for the exclusive benefit of participants and their beneficiaries." The federal law applies to all newly formed deferred compensation plans created as of August 20, 1996. In addition, existing IRC Section 457 plans were required to be modified to comply with the legislative requirements by January 1, 1999. In October 1997, the GASB issued GASB-32 (*Accounting and Financial Reporting for Internal Revenue Code Section 457 Deferred Compensation Plans*) in order to address the financial reporting ramifications of the new federal legislation.

GASB-32 superseded standards established by GASB-2 and in so doing eliminated all financial accounting and reporting guidance related to IRC Section 457 plans. The GASB takes the position that IRC Section 457 plans are no different (from a financial reporting perspective) from other deferred compensation plans. (There are no specific GASB standards that apply to 403(b) and 401(k) deferred compensation plans.) In addition, GASB-32 also amended GASB-31 (*Accounting and Financial Reporting for Certain Investments and for External Investment Pools*). Thus, governmental entities that report IRC Section 457 plan must observe the valuation and disclosure standards established by the following GASB pronouncements:

- GASB-3 (*Deposits with Financial Institutions, Investment (Including Repurchase Agreements), and Reverse Repurchase Agreements*)
- GASB-14 (*The Financial Reporting Entity*)
- GASBI-3 (*Financial Reporting for Reverse Repurchase Agreements*)
- GASB-28 (*Accounting and Financial Reporting for Securities Lending Transactions*)
- GASB-31 (*Accounting and Financial Reporting for Certain Investments and for External Investment Pools*)
- GASB-72 (*Fair Value Application and Measurement*)

Fund Reporting

Depending on how a deferred compensation plan, under the new statute, is administered, its creation may place a governmental employer in a fiduciary role. GASB-32 points out that NCGA-1, paragraph 26(3)(8), provides the following definition of a "fiduciary fund" (Trust Funds and Agency Funds):

Fiduciary Funds are used to account for assets held by a governmental unit in a trustee capacity or as an agent for individuals, private organizations, other governmental units, and/or other funds.

The governmental entity must exercise judgment to determine whether a fiduciary relationship exists between the entity and the IRC Section 457 deferred compensation pension plan.

OBSERVATION: Factors that may be considered in determining whether a fiduciary relationship exists include the presence of a formal trust agreement between the governmental entity and the Section 457 plan (trustees), the provision of investment advice, and governmental involvement in the administration of the plan. The GASB notes that, based on its research, most governmental entities that have established Section 457 plans neither provide administrative services to the plan nor investment advice for the plans. Although the GASB does not provide specific guidance (see **PRACTICE ALERT** below) as to what constitutes a fiduciary relationship between the governmental entity and the Section 457 plan, it notes that determining a fiduciary relationship applies to all trust fund arrangements, not just to Section 457 plans.

If such a fiduciary relationship does exist, the standards established by GASB-32 require that the balances and transactions related to the plan be accounted for in an Other Employee Benefit Trust Fund. If no fiduciary relationship exists, the balances and activities of the Section 457 plan would not be reported in the governmental entity's financial statements.

Generally, a valuation report should be obtained from the plan administrator and ideally the administrator's valuation date should coincide with the governmental entity's reporting date. When it is impractical to obtain a report that measures plan assets as of the governmental entity's reporting date, the most recent report should be used and adjusted for contributions and withdrawals subsequent to the date of the valuation report.

PRACTICE ALERT: GASB-84 (*Fiduciary Activities*) supersedes GASB-32 upon implementation for periods beginning after December 15, 2018. When GASB-32 was implemented, the GASB recognized that the definition of fiduciary funds that had been in existence since NCGA-1 would not be sufficient to assist governments in determining whether an activity should be reported as a fiduciary activity. The GASB believes with the clarifications provided in GASB-84, practitioners should be able to decide whether a 457 plan should be reported in a primary government's fiduciary funds or not. (See Chapter 8, "Fiduciary Funds," for additional information on GASB-84.)

Financial Statements

When an IRC Section 457 plan is reported in an Other Employee Benefit Trust Fund or stand-alone report, the following financial statements should be presented:

- Statement of fiduciary net position; and
- Statement of changes in fiduciary net position.

Fiduciary financial statements are presented in the fund financial statement section of the governmental entity's financial report. Fiduciary fund financial statements are not presented in the government-wide financial statements (GASB-32, pars. 4–6) [GASB Cod. Secs. D25.101, fn.1, I50.108].

POSTEMPLOYMENT BENEFIT PLANS OTHER THAN PENSION PLANS

Postemployment health-care benefits include medical, dental, vision, and other health-related benefits provided to terminated or retried employees and their dependents and beneficiaries.

PRACTICE POINT: Many practitioners do not focus on the element of termination or retirement and believe that GASB-74 and the related GASB-75 and GASB-85 apply to active employees as well as retirees. Indeed, if a subsidy occurs from an active employee to a terminated or retired beneficiary, then there are some elements that are germane to active employees. However, the vast majority of these statements are the calculation of assets or liabilities on behalf of terminated or retired employees and their beneficiaries in accordance with plan provisions.

OPEB may be provided in a defined benefit OPEB plan or a defined contribution plan. A defined benefit OPEB plan has "terms that specify the amount of benefits to be provided at a future date or after a certain period of time. The amount specified usually is a function of one or more factors such as age, years of service, and compensation." A defined contribution plan is an OPEB plan that has "terms that specify how contributions to a plan member's account are to be determined, rather than the amount of benefit the member is to receive. The amounts received by a member will depend only on the amount contributed to the member's account, earnings on investments of those contributions, and forfeitures of contributions made for other members that may be allocated to the member's account."

Some OPEB plans have characteristics of both defined benefit OPEB plans and defined contributions plans. GASB-74, paragraph 12 [GASB Cod. Sec. Po50.107], defaults to a defined benefit OPEB plan unless all three of the following characteristics are met, which would be indicative of a defined contribution plan. A defined contribution plan has these characteristics:

— Provides an individual account for each plan member;

— Defines the contributions that an employer or nonemployer contributing entity is required to make (or credits that it is required to provide) to an active plan member's account for periods in which that member renders service; and

— Provides that the OPEB a plan member will receive will depend only on the contributions (or credits) to the plan member's account, actual earnings on investments of those contributions (or credits), and the effects of forfeitures of contributions (or credits) made for other plan members, as well as OPEB plan administrative costs, that are allocated to the plan member's account.

Similar to pensions, the defined benefit OPEB standards proposed apply to single-employer, agent multiple-employer, and cost-sharing multiple-employer plans, which are defined as follows:

- *Single-employer plan*—A plan that covers the current and former employees, including beneficiaries, of only one employer.

- *Agent multiple-employer plan*—An aggregation of single-employer plans, with pooled administrative and investment functions. Separate accounts are maintained for each employer so that the employer's contributions provide benefits only for its employees. A separate actuarial valuation is performed for each individual employer's plan to determine the employer's period contribution rate and other information for the individual plan, based on the benefit formula selected by the employer and the individual plan's proportionate share of the pooled assets. The results of the individual valuations are aggregated at the administrative level.

- *Cost-sharing multiple-employer plan*—A single plan with pooling (cost-sharing) arrangements for the participating employers. All risks, rewards, and costs, including benefit costs, are shared and are not attributed individually to the employers. A single actuarial valuation covers all plan members, and the same contribution rate(s) applies for each employer.

The former provisions of GASB-57 (*OPEB Measurements by Agent Employers and Agent Multiple-Employer Plans*) are now included in GASB-74. The provisions address issues for small employers within agent plans that use the alternative measurement method to determine their liabilities as well as the frequency and timing of measurements by employers that are part of agent multiple-employer OPEB plans. The provisions allow an agent multiple-employer plan that has just one member employer plan with fewer than 100 plan members to use the alternative measurement method, irrespective of the number of total plan members in the plan. It also clarifies that all members of an agent multiple-employer OPEB plan should use a common valuation date and at a minimum frequency to satisfy the plan's financial reporting requirements.

Administering Public Employee OPEB Systems

A Public Employee Retirement System (PERS) may administer numerous defined benefit pension plans, defined contribution plans, deferred compensation plans, as well as OPEB plans. The standards in GASB-74 apply to a particular OPEB plan and not to a particular PERS, similar to the application of pensions in GASB-67. However, when a PERS presents the separate financial statements of a defined OPEB plan in its financial report, the standards in GASB-74 must be observed for that particular plan.

Defined benefit OPEB plans (other than insured plans) are classified first according to the number of employers whose employees are provided with OPEB through the OPEB plan. Similar to pensions, a primary government and its component units are considered to be one employer. If a defined benefit OPEB plan is used to provide OPEB to the employees of only one employer, the OPEB plan should be classified for financial reporting purposes as a single-employer defined benefit OPEB plan (single-employer OPEB plan) as described above. If a defined benefit OPEB plan is used to provide OPEB to the employees of more than one employer, the OPEB plan should be classified for financial reporting purposes as a multiple-employer defined benefit OPEB plan.

If the financial statements of more than one defined OPEB are included in the PERS report, the standards must be applied separately to each plan. The financial statements for each plan should be presented separately in the combining financial statements of the PERS along with appropriate schedules and other required disclosures. Thus, the standards apply to the individual plans administered by the PERS but the PERS itself must follow the standards established by GASB-34 in order to prepare its financial statements. Specifically, the PERS would report as a special-purpose government engaged only in fiduciary activities as defined by GASB-34.

To determine whether a PERS is administering a single OPEB plan or two or more OPEB plans (thus requiring separate reporting), the custody of the assets held must be analyzed to determine whether they are (1) available to pay benefits for all of the members of the OPEB plans or (2) available to pay benefits only to certain plan members.

401(h) Accounts

Some PERS manage both pensions and OPEB plans. In many situations, a single contribution is paid from the employer(s) (and/or employees) to the plan. Assets should be allocated between the pension plan and the OPEB plan. This requires, in part, allocation of the employer's total contribution between the pension plan and the OPEB plan and separate reporting of each plan's fiduciary net position. GASB-74 does not specify the manner in which the allocations should be made because that depends on the specific circumstances, including the benefit structure and terms and the method(s) of financing the pension and postemployment healthcare benefits. Therefore, an accounting policy should be adopted and applied consistently from period to period (GASB *Implementation Guide* 2017-2, question 4.18) [GASB Cod. Sec. Po50.8.97-4].

Separate reporting is required for pension and postemployment healthcare plan that meets the criteria of a trust and is administered by a plan. (GASB *Implementation Guide* 2015-1, question 5.64.2, as amended by GASB *Implementation Guide* 2016-1, question 5.6 [GASB Cod. Sec. Po50.701-2].

Assets Available to All Plan Members

If assets held by the PERS are legally available to pay benefits for all of the plan members, the OPEB plan is a single plan, and only a single set of financial statements needs to be prepared. GASB-74 notes that an OPEB plan is a single employer plan even if the following circumstances exist:

- Legally or because of administrative policy, the OPEB plan must maintain separate accounts based on such factors as specified groups, specific employers, or benefits provided by the plan.
- Separate actuarial valuations are made for classes or groups of covered employees.

Assets Available Only to Certain Plan Members

If any portion of the assets held by the PERS can be paid legally only to certain classes of employees (e.g., public safety officers) or employees of certain employers (e.g., only to state government employees), more than one plan is being administered and separate financial statements must be prepared for each plan (GASB-74, par. 19 [GASB Cod. Sec. Po50.113].

The assets availability criterion must also be applied to a governmental employer's CAFR. Separate reporting is required in the governmental employer's (or sponsor's) CAFR when more than one OPEB plan is being presented in the CAFR.

Financial Reporting

GASB-74 requires that the following financial statements be presented by a defined benefit OPEB plan, similarly to GASB-67 (GASB-74, par. 20) [GASB Cod. Sec. Po50.114]:

- Statement of fiduciary net position;
- Statement of changes in fiduciary net position; and

Statement of Fiduciary Net Position

The statement of fiduciary net position is prepared on an accrual basis and reports the plan's assets, liabilities, and net position. The statement should identify the major assets of the OPEB plan (e.g., cash, receivables, investments, and operating assets), and the receivables and investments categories should be further divided into their significant components. Reported liabilities should be subtracted from total assets and the difference reported as "net position held in trust for OPEB."

Exhibits 22-1 and 22-2 include GASB-74 compliant information.

Investments reported in the statement should be recorded on a trade-date basis, applying all the other applicable U.S. GAAP provisions regarding investments. Allocated insurance contracts are excluded from plan assets, similarly to pension reporting, if (GASB-74, pars. 24–25) [GASB Cod. Secs. Po50.118–.119]:

- The contract irrevocably transfers to the insurer the responsibility for providing the benefits;
- All required payments to acquire the contracts have been made; and
- The likelihood is remote that the employer, nonemployer contributing entities, or OPEB plan will be required to make additional payments to satisfy the benefit payments covered by the contract.

Statement of Changes in Fiduciary Net Position

An OPEB plan should prepare an operating statement that reports the net increase or decrease in net plan position from the beginning of the year until the end of the year. The statement of changes in plan net position should be prepared on the same basis of accounting used to prepare the OPEB plan's statement of fiduciary net position. The two financial statements are interrelated in that (1) the net increase as reported on the statement of changes in plan net position when added to (2) the beginning balance of fiduciary net position on the statement of fiduciary net position is equal to (3) the fiduciary net position as reported at the end of the year on the statement of fiduciary net position.

The statement of changes in fiduciary net position should present separate categories for additions and deductions in fiduciary net position for the year.

The additions section of the statement of changes in fiduciary net position should include the following components:

- Contributions received from an employer(s);

- Contributions received from employees (including those received via the employer);

- Contributions received from those other than employer(s) and employees;

- Net investment income for the year (includes the net appreciation or depreciation of the fair value of the plan assets) and investment income and other increases not reported as net appreciation or depreciation (these two components of investment income may be separately reported or reported as a single amount); and

- Total investment expenses (including investment fees, custodial fees, and "all other significant investment-related costs") (GASB-74, pars. 28–30) [GASB Cod. Secs. Po50.122–.124].

As above, payments to an insurance company for an allocated insurance contract that is excluded from OPEB plan assets, including purchases of annuities with amounts allocated from existing investments with the insurance company, should be included in amounts recognized as benefit payments. Dividends from an allocated insurance contract should be recognized as a reduction of benefit payments recognized in the period. Benefit payments should not include benefits paid by an insurance company in accordance with such a contract.

Deductions on the statement of changes in plan net position should include OPEB payments to retirees and beneficiaries, and administrative expenses. These items should not be combined but rather separately presented on the statement. Administrative expenses, such as depreciation expense and operating expenses, should be measured using accrual accounting and reported as deductions from net position (GASB-74, pars. 31–33) [GASB Cod. Secs. Po50.125–.127].

Notes to the Financial Statements

The notes of a defined benefit OPEB plan that is administered through a trust should include all the following disclosures, as applicable, or if the financial statements are presented in a stand-alone OPEB plan financial report or solely in the financial report of another government. If a defined benefit OPEB plan is included in the financial report of a government that also applies the requirements of GASB-75 for benefits provided through the OPEB plan and similar information is required by GASB-74 *and* GASB-75, the government should not duplicate the disclosures (GASB-74, footnote 8). The following should be disclosed in the notes, as applicable:

Plan description:

- The name of the OPEB plan, identification of the entity that administers the OPEB plan, and identification of the OPEB plan as a single-employer, agent, or cost-sharing OPEB plan.
- The number of participating employers (if the OPEB plan is an agent or cost-sharing OPEB plan) and the number of nonemployer contributing entities, if any.
- Information regarding the OPEB plan's board and its composition (e.g., the number of trustees by source of selection or the types of constituency or credentials applicable to selection).
- The number of plan members, separately identifying numbers of the following:
  - Inactive plan members currently receiving benefit payments;
  - Inactive plan members entitled to but not yet receiving benefit payments;
  - Active plan members; and
  - If the OPEB plan is closed to new entrants, that fact should be disclosed.
- The authority under which benefit terms are established or may be amended, the types of benefits provided through the OPEB plan, and the classes of plan members covered. If the OPEB plan or the entity that administers the OPEB plan has the authority to establish or amend benefit terms, a brief description should be provided of the benefit terms, including the key elements of the OPEB formulas and the terms or policies, if any, with respect to automatic postemployment benefit changes, including automatic cost-of-living adjustments (automatic COLAs); ad hoc postemployment benefit changes, including ad hoc cost-of-living adjustments (ad hoc COLAs); and the sharing of benefit-related costs with inactive plan members.
- A brief description of contribution requirements, including (*a*) identification of the authority under which contribution requirements of employers, nonemployer contributing entities, if any, and plan members are established or may be amended; (*b*) the contribution rates (in dollars or as a percentage of covered payroll) of the employer, nonemployer contributing entities, if any, and plan members for the reporting period; and (*c*) legal or contractual maximum contribution rates, if applicable. If the OPEB plan or the entity that administers the OPEB plan has the authority to establish or amend contribution requirements, disclose the basis for determining contributions (e.g., statute, contract, an actuarial basis, or some other manner).

OPEB Plan Investments

- Investment policies, including:
  - Procedures and authority for establishing and amending investment policy decisions;
  - Policies pertaining to asset allocation; and
  - Description of significant investment policy changes during the reporting period.
- Identification of investments (other than those issued or explicitly guaranteed by the U.S. government) in any one organization that represent 5% or more of the OPEB plan's fiduciary net position (concentrations).
- The annual money-weighted rate of return on OPEB plan investments calculated as the internal rate of return on OPEB plan investments, net of OPEB plan investment expense, and an explanation that a money-weighted rate of return expresses investment performance, net of OPEB plan investment expense, adjusted for the changing amounts actually invested. OPEB plan investment expense should be measured on the accrual basis of accounting. Inputs to the internal rate of return calculation should be determined at least monthly. The use of more frequently determined inputs is encouraged.

Receivables

The plan should disclose the terms of any long-term contracts for contributions to the OPEB plan between (1) an employer or nonemployer contributing entity and (2) the OPEB plan, and the balances outstanding on any such long-term contracts at the end of the OPEB plan's reporting period.

Allocated Insurance Contracts Excluded from OPEB Plan Assets

- The amount reported in benefit payments in the current period that is attributable to the purchase of allocated insurance contracts.
- A brief description of the OPEB for which allocated insurance contracts were purchased in the current period.
- The fact that the obligation for the payment of benefits covered by allocated insurance contracts has been transferred to one or more insurance companies.

Reserves

In circumstances in which there is a policy of setting aside, for purposes such as benefit increases or reduced employer contributions, a portion of the OPEB plan's fiduciary net position that otherwise would be available for existing OPEB or for OPEB plan administration:

A description of the policy related to such reserves.

- The authority under which the policy was established and may be amended.
- The purposes for and conditions under which the reserves are required or permitted to be used.
- The balances of the reserves (GASB-74, par. 34) [GASB Cod. Sec. Po50.128].

Specifically for Single-Employer and Cost-Sharing OPEB Plans

Specifically for single-employer and cost-sharing OPEB plans, additional information is needed in the notes as follows:

- The components of the liability of the employers and nonemployer contributing entities to plan members for benefits provided through the OPEB plan (net OPEB liability) calculated in accordance with the provisions of GASB-74, including:
  — The total OPEB liability (TOL);
  — The OPEB plan's fiduciary net position;
  — The net OPEB liability (NOL); and
  — The OPEB plan's fiduciary net position as a percentage of the TOL.

The notes should also describe significant assumptions and other inputs used to measure the TOL, including assumptions about:

- Inflation;
- Healthcare cost trend rates;
- Salary changes;
- Ad hoc postemployment benefit changes (including ad hoc COLAs); and
- Sharing of benefit-related costs with inactive plan members.

With regard to the sharing of benefit-related costs, if projections are based on an established pattern of practice, that fact should be disclosed. With regard to mortality assumptions, the source of the assumptions (e.g., the published tables on which the assumptions are based or that the assumptions are based on a study of the experience of the covered group) should be disclosed. The dates of experience studies on which significant assumptions are based also should be disclosed. For all significant assumptions, if different rates are assumed for different periods, information should be disclosed about what rates are applied to the different periods of the measurement. In addition, if the alternative measurement method is used to measure the total OPEB liability, the source or basis for all significant assumptions should be disclosed.

A sensitivity analysis is also presented in two different tables, one for the healthcare cost trend rate and one for the discount rate. With regard to the healthcare cost trend rate, measures of the *NOL* calculated using (*a*) a healthcare cost trend rate that is 1-percentage-point higher than the assumed healthcare cost trend rate and (*b*) a healthcare cost trend rate that is 1-percentage-point lower than the assumed healthcare cost trend rate should be disclosed.

For the discount rate, similar to GASB-67 and defined benefit pensions, the discount rate applied in the measurement of the TOL and the change in the discount rate since the OPEB plan's prior fiscal year-end, if any should be disclosed. The note should include assumptions made about projected cash flows into and out of the OPEB plan, such as contributions from employers, nonemployer contributing entities, and plan members, the long-term expected rate of return on OPEB plan investments and a description of how it was determined, including significant methods and assumptions used for that purpose, if the discount rate incorporates a municipal bond rate, the municipal bond rate used and the source of that rate, the periods of projected benefit payments to which the long-term expected rate of return and, if used, the municipal bond rate are applied in determining the discount rate and finally, the assumed asset allocation of the OPEB plan's portfolio, the long-term expected real rate of return for each major asset class, and whether the expected rates of return are presented as arithmetic or geometric means.

After this note disclosure on the discount rate, the second sensitivity analysis table is included with measures of the NOL calculated using a discount rate that is 1-percentage- point higher and 1-percentage-point lower.

Finally, the note should conclude with the date of the actuarial valuation or alternative measurement method calculation on which the TOL is based and, if applicable, the fact that update procedures were used to roll forward the TOL to the OPEB plan's fiscal year-end. If the alternative measurement method permitted by GASB-74 is used to measure the TOL, the fact that this alternative method was used in place of an actuarial valuation also should be disclosed (GASB-74, par. 35) [GASB Cod. Sec. Po50.129].

PRACTICE POINT: A complete set of note disclosures for an OPEB plan is contained in Wolters Kluwers' 2018 *Governmental GAAP Disclosures Manual*, Chapter 44. Investment disclosures are contained in Chapter 16.

Required Supplementary Information: Defined Benefit Single Employer and Cost-Sharing OPEB Plans

Except as noted in the following paragraph, GASB-74 requires a schedule of changes in the net OPEB liability and a schedule of contributions (if applicable) along with notes to the required supplementary information (RSI).The RSI should be presented immediately after the notes to the financial statements.

PRACTICE POINT: Upon implementation of GASB-74, the RSI applicable to GASB-43 and GASB-57 should be removed. Plans may wish to continue the information as users may be accustomed to seeing the information, but it will not articulate to the information contained in the basic financial statements or the notes. If the prior schedules need to be continued, it may be better placed in supplementary information.

Information for each year should be measured as of the OPEB plan's most recent fiscal year-end. Information about cost-sharing OPEB plans should be presented for the OPEB plan as a whole (GASB-74, par. 36) [GASB Cod. Sec. Po50.130].

Schedule of Changes in the Net OPEB Liability

The schedule will be presented for 10 years, presenting each year, the beginning and ending balances of the TOL, the OPEB plan's fiduciary net position and the NOL, along with the effects of the following items, as applicable:

- Service cost;
- Interest on the TOL;
- Changes of benefit terms;

- Differences between actual and expected experience with regard to economic or demographic factors in the measurement of the TOL;

- Changes of assumptions about future economic or demographic factors or other inputs;

- Contributions from employers, including amounts for OPEB benefits come due that will not be reimbursed to the employers using OPEB plan assets;

- Contributions from nonemployer contributing entities, including amounts for OPEB as the benefits come due that will not be reimbursed to the nonemployer contributing entities using OPEB plan assets;

- The total of contributions from active plan members and inactive plan members not yet receiving benefit payments;

- The total of contributions from active plan members and inactive plan members not yet receiving benefit payments;

- OPEB plan net investment income; and

- Benefit payments (including refunds of plan member contributions and amounts from employers or nonemployer contributing entities for OPEB as the benefits come due).

OPEB plan administrative expense and other changes, separately identified if individually significant, finish the initial part of the schedule.

If the alternative measurement method is used, differences between expected and actual experience with regard to economic or demographic factors in the measurement of the TOL and changes of assumptions about the future economic or demographic factors or other inputs may be combined.

The schedule then is continued, again for 10 years, presenting the following each year, similar to pensions:

- The TOL;
- The OPEB plan's fiduciary net position;
- The NOL;
- The OPEB plans' fiduciary net position as a percentage of the TOL;
- The *covered-employee payroll;* and
- The NOL as a percentage of the *covered-employee payroll* (see **PRACTICE ALERT**).

PRACTICE ALERT: GASB-85 (*Omnibus 2017*) changes the reporting for these payroll measures. For single-employer defined benefit OPEB plans and cost-sharing multiple-employer defined benefit OPEB plans, the measure of payroll that will be required to be presented should be *covered payroll.* Covered payroll is the payroll on which contributions to the OPEB plan are based. If contributions to the OPEB plan *are not based on a measure of pay, no measure of payroll should be presented.* Many OPEB plans receive a percentage of taxation or similar for their contributions. As such, no measure of pay would be presented. GASB-85 was implemented for periods beginning after June 15, 2017 with a retroactive restatement required.

Schedule of Employer Contributions

A 10-year schedule of employer contributions will be presented for each year *if an actuarially determined contribution* is calculated for employers or nonemployer contributing entities. The schedule includes:

- The actuarially determined contributions of employers or nonemployer contributing entities. For purposes of this schedule, actuarially determined contributions should exclude amounts, if any, associated with payables to the OPEB plan that arose in a prior fiscal year and those associated with separately financed specific liabilities to the OPEB plan.

- *For cost-sharing OPEB plans:* the statutorily or contractually required contribution of employers or nonemployer contributing entities, if different. For purposes of this schedule, statutorily or contractually required contributions should include amounts from employers or nonemployer contributing entities for OPEB as the benefits come due that will not be reimbursed to the employers or nonemployer contributing entities using OPEB plan assets and should exclude amounts, if any, associated with payables to the OPEB plan that arose in a prior fiscal year and those associated with separately financed specific liabilities to the OPEB plan.

- The amount of contributions, including amounts from employers or nonemployer contributing entities for OPEB as the benefits come due that will not be reimbursed to the employers or nonemployer contributing entities using OPEB plan assets, recognized during the fiscal year by the OPEB plan in relation to the actuarially determined contribution. For purposes of this schedule, contributions should exclude amounts resulting from contributions recognized by the OPEB plan as noncurrent receivables.

- The difference between the actuarially determined contribution and the amount of contributions recognized by the OPEB plan in relation to the actuarially determined contribution.

- *The covered-employee payroll* (see previous **PRACTICE ALERT**).

- The amount of contributions recognized by the OPEB plan in relation to the actuarially determined contribution as a percentage of *covered-employee payroll* (see previous **PRACTICE ALERT**).

PRACTICE ALERT: GASB-85 includes similar language to GASB-82 with regard to employer-paid member contributions (EPMCs). EPMCs may be more prevalent for OPEB than for pensions. If payments are made by the employer to satisfy contribution requirements that are identified by the OPEB plan terms as plan member requirements, they remain as plan member contributions. Employer reporting will change including for the purposes of determining a cost-sharing employer's proportion. For the employer, those amounts will be employee contributions.

Finally, a 10-year schedule is included each year presenting the annual *money-weighted* return on OPEB plan investments. This is the only required schedule *for agent OPEB plans*(GASB-74, par. 37) [GASB Cod. Sec. Po50.131].

Notes to the Required Schedules

The notes to RSI are similar to those required for pension plans, as discussed in GASB-67 and amended by GASB-73. Significant methods and assumptions used in calculating the actuarially determined contributions, if any, should be presented as notes to the schedule. In addition, for each of the schedules, information should be presented about factors that significantly affect trends in the amounts reported (e.g., changes of benefit terms, changes in the size or composition of the population covered by the benefit terms, or the use of different assumptions). Information about investment-related factors that significantly affect trends in the amounts reported should be limited to those factors over which the OPEB plan or the participating governments have influence (e.g., changes in investment policies). Information about external, economic factors (e.g., changes in market prices) should not be presented. (The amounts presented for prior years should not be restated for the effects of changes—for example, changes of benefit terms or changes of assumptions—that occurred subsequent to the end of the fiscal year for which the information is reported.) (GASB-74, par. 38) [GASB Cod. Sec. Po50.132]

Differences between Pension Valuations and OPEB Valuations for Defined Benefit Plans

For OPEB, the actuarial valuation is very similar to that used for pensions, as amended by the provisions in GASB-82 with regard to deviations. The former methods allowable in accordance with GASB-43 and GASB-45 are no longer allowed. Only the entry-age normal actuarial method is allowed.

PRACTICE POINT: Unlike pensions, few OPEB plans have high amounts of assets. Therefore, the "crossover" point will occur much sooner than in pensions. Therefore, the same discount rate as a pension plan might not be able to be used.

Unlike pensions, projected benefit payments also should include taxes or other assessments expected to be imposed on benefit payments using the rates in effect at the OPEB plan's fiscal year-end. If different rates have been approved by the assessing government to be applied in future periods, the rates approved by the assessing government associated with the periods in which the assessments on the benefit payments will be imposed. This aspect will include any effect of the Patient Protection and Affordable Care Act excise (when and if implemented, the so-called "Cadillac tax") as well as any effect a Medicare program may have on the valuation. Projected benefit payments should be based on claims costs, or *age adjusted premiums* approximating claims costs, in accordance with actuarial standards of practice. (This is the former *implicit rate subsidy* used in accordance with the provisions of GASB-43 and GASB-45.) A legal or contractual cap on benefit payments for OPEB will also be considered in projecting benefit payments. A consideration must be made if the cap has been enforced in the past and other relevant factors and circumstances (GASB-74, pars. 45–47) [GASB Cod. Secs. Po50.139–.141].

Alternative Measurement Method: Small Plans

In general, the measurement standards required by GASB-74 apply 74 to all OPEB plans; however, the GASB did continue the attempt to simplify the implementation of OPEB standards for a single-employer plan that has fewer than 100 plan members. For such plans, the OPEB plan may (1) apply all of the measurement standards without modification or (2) apply the measurement standards with one or more of the following modifications:

- *Assumptions in general*—Assumptions should be based on actual past experience, but grouping techniques may be used where assumptions may be based on combined experience data for similar plans as explained below (see "use of grouping").

- *Expected point in time at which benefits will begin to be provided*—This assumption may be based on a single assumed retirement age or that all employees will retire at a particular age.

- *Health-care cost trend rate*—This assumption should be based on an objective source.

- *Marital and dependency status*—This assumption may be based on the current marital status of employees or historical demographic data for the covered group.

- *Mortality*—This assumption should reflect current published mortality tables.

- *Plans with coverage options*—Employers with postemployment benefit plans where the employee has coverage options should base the coverage option on past experience but also take into consideration the choices of pre- and post-Medicare-eligible members.

- *Qualification for benefits assumption*—This assumption, when past experience data are not available, may be based on the simplifying assumption that the longer an employee works, the greater the probability he or she will work long enough to qualify for benefits. For example, if an employee must work for 10 years to qualify for benefits, then the probability of qualification increases 10% for each year the employee works.

- *Use of grouping*—Rather than consider each participant, participants may be grouped into categories based on such factors as an age range or length of service range.

- *Use of health insurance premiums*—Employers that have postemployment health-care plans where the employer makes premium payments to an insurer may use the current premium structure in order to project future health-care benefit payments (GASB-74, pars. 56–57) [GASB Cod. Secs. Po50.150–.151].

PRACTICE ALERT: GASB-85 amends the factors for the expected point in time at which plan members (employees) will exit from active service and turnover. For the expected point in time at which plan members will exit active service, the assumption should reflect past experience and future expectations for the covered group. For active plan members (employees) covered under the terms of the OPEB plan, the assumption *may* incorporate (1) a single assumed age at which plan members (employees) will exit from active service *or* (2) an assumption that plan members (employees) will exit from active service upon attaining a certain number of years of service. The turnover factor may be applied to determine the assumed probability that an active plan member (employee) will remain employed until the assumed age at which the plan member (employee) will meet employment-related eligibility requirements to receive benefits.

Plans that are Not Administered as Trusts or Equivalent Arrangements

GASB-74 continues the provisions for OPEB introduced in GASB-73 for pensions. Any assets accumulated for OPEB purposes should continue to be reported as assets of the employer or nonemployer contributing entity. If an OPEB plan is not administered through a trust, a government that holds assets accumulated for OPEB purposes in a fiduciary capacity should report the assets in an agency fund. The amount of assets accumulated in excess of liabilities for benefits due to plan members and accrued investment and administrative expenses should be reported as a liability to participating employers or nonemployer contributing entities. If the agency fund is included in the financial report of an employer whose employees are provided with benefits through the OPEB plan or a nonemployer contributing entity that makes benefit payments as OPEB comes due, balances reported by the agency fund should exclude amounts that pertain to the employer or nonemployer contributing entity that reports the agency fund (GASB-74, pars. 58–59) [GASB Cod. Secs. P53.107-.108, 2200.199].

Defined Contribution OPEB Plans

When an OPEB is a defined contribution plan, it should prepare its financial statements based on the general guidance for fiduciary funds as required by GASB-34. If the plan is administered as a trust or equivalent arrangement, it should disclose:

- Identification of the OPEB plan as a defined contribution OPEB plan;

- The authority under which the OPEB plan is established or may be amended;

- The classes of members covered; and

- The number of plan members, participating employers (if a multiple-employer plan) and, if any, any nonemployer contributing entities (GASB-74, par. 60) [GASB Cod. Sec. Po51.106].

QUESTIONS

1. GASB-67 is applicable for which type of entity:
   a. Defined contribution employers.
   b. Defined benefit employers.
   c. Defined benefit and contribution plans administered through trusts.
   d. Defined benefit and contribution plans not administered through trusts.

2. What type(s) of plans must use GASB-67 as a basis for accounting and financial reporting?
   a. Single employer pension plans.
   b. Agent multiple-employer pension plans and cost-sharing multiple employer pension plans.
   c. None of the above.
   d. A and B.

3. Statements of fiduciary net position contain all of the following accounting elements except for:
   a. Reserves.
   b. Assets and deferred outflows of resources.
   c. Liabilities and deferred inflows of resources.
   d. Fiduciary net position.

4. Statements of changes in fiduciary net position contain all of the following accounting elements except for:
   a. Additions such as contributions from employers and net investment income.
   b. Additions to reserves.
   c. Deductions such as benefit payments and administrative expense.
   d. Net increase (decrease) in fiduciary net position.

5. For an agent-multiple employer defined benefit *pension* plan, which of the following schedules is included in required supplementary information?
   a. A 10-year schedule showing changes in net pension liability.
   b. A 10-year schedule showing actuarially determined contributions, contributions made, and other data (if applicable).
   c. A 10-year schedule showing the annual money-weighted rate of return only.
   d. A 10-year schedule of funding progress.

ANSWERS

1. GASB-67 is applicable for which type of entity:

   Answer – C.

2. What type(s) of plans must use GASB-67 as a basis for accounting and financial reporting?

   Answer – D.

3. Statements of fiduciary net position contain all of the following accounting elements except for:

   Answer – A: Reserves are not presented on the face of basic financial statements.

4. Statements of changes in fiduciary net position contain all of the following accounting elements except for:

   Answer – B: Reserves are not presented on the face of basic financial statements. Also, additions to reserves result in a debit and a credit contained within fiduciary net position.

5. For an agent-multiple employer defined benefit pension plan, which of the following schedules is included in required supplementary information?

   Answer – C.

CHAPTER 23
PUBLIC ENTITY RISK POOLS

CONTENTS

PUBLIC ENTITY RISK POOLS

State and local governments encounter essentially the same accounting and reporting issues as commercial enterprises that provide insurance coverage (insurer) and that purchase insurance coverage (insured). GASB-10 (*Accounting and Financial Reporting for Risk Financing and Related Insurance Issues*) was issued to provide guidance for governmental entities that assume the role of the insurer and the role of the insured.

When a governmental entity is organized as a public entity risk pool, it may take on many of the characteristics of an insurer.

GASB-10 describes a *public entity risk pool* as a cooperative group of governmental entities joining together to finance an exposure, liability, or risk. Risk may include property and liability, workers' compensation, and employee health care. A pool may be a standalone entity or be included as part of a larger governmental entity that acts as the pool's sponsor.

The activities of a public entity risk pool vary, but in general they can be classified as follows:

Type of Pool	Definition	Example
Risk-sharing pool	Governmental entities join together to share in the cost of losses.	Statewide municipal league intergovernmental risk pool.
Insurance-purchasing pool (risk-purchasing group)	Governmental entities join together to acquire commercial insurance coverage.	Counties excess insurance authority (that contracts with a commercial insurance entity through a competitive bid process).
Banking pool	Governmental entities are allowed to borrow funds from a pool to pay losses.	Statewide deposit insurance trust fund.
Claims-servicing or account pool	Governmental entities join together to administer the separate account of each entity in the payment of losses.	Municipal health trust administered by a state as a claims paying agent.

An individual public entity risk pool can perform one or more of the above activities, but the latter two activities (banking pool and claims-servicing or account pool) do not result in the transfer of risk from the participating governmental entity to the public entity risk pool.

A public entity risk pool must be evaluated to determine the rights and responsibilities of the pool and the governmental entities that participate in the pool. The agreement between a public entity risk pool and the governmental entity may transfer part or all of the risk of loss to the risk pool or may retain all of the risk.

In addition to the agreement between the pool and the participants, the laws of a particular jurisdiction and the economic resources of the ultimate insurer should be taken into consideration when determining to what extent, if any, there has been a transfer of risk to the public entity risk pool from a governmental entity. For example, if a public entity risk pool has insufficient resources to pay claims as incurred, the risk of loss is retained by the individual governmental entity, irrespective of the agreement between the two parties. On the other hand, if an agreement has a deductible amount clause per claim, only the risk related to the amount of the loss in excess of the deductible amount is transferred to the public entity risk pool (GASB-10, par. 17) [GASB Cod. Sec. Po20.113].

The accounting and reporting standards established for public entity risk pools are essentially the same as the standards as codified in the FASB's Accounting Standards Codification® (ASC) Subtopic 944, *Financial Services—Insurance Activities*, as amended. The GASB states that the accounting and reporting of risk activities are essentially the same regardless of whether the entity related to the activities is a public entity or a commercial enterprise.

Irrespective of whether a public entity risk pool is involved in risk-sharing activities or insurance-purchasing activities, those activities should be accounted for in an Enterprise Fund (GASB-10, par. 18) [GASB Cod. Sec. Po20.115].

> **OBSERVATION:** As the accounting and reporting standards applicable to public entity risk pools are similar to a commercial enterprise, an Enterprise Fund is the appropriate fund to account for such entities.

ACCOUNTING AND REPORTING

Premium Revenue

A public entity risk pool should recognize premium revenue (or required contributions) over the contract period based on the amount of risk protection provided to the insured entity. In those instances where the risk protection for each period is the same, premium revenue should be recognized on a straight-line basis. For example, if a public entity risk pool charges $110,000 to a participating governmental entity for $5,000,000 of coverage for losses over a two-year period, the amount of premium revenue recognized each year is $55,000. On the other hand, if coverage for losses is $5,000,000 in year 1 and $6,000,000 in year 2, premium revenue is computed as follows (GASB-10, par. 19):

	Premium Revenue	
	Year 1	Year 2
($110,000 × $5,000,000) ÷ $11,000,000	$50,000	—
($110,000 × $6,000,000) ÷ $11,000,000	—	$60,000

In most instances, the period of risk and the contract period are the same; however, when they are significantly different, the premium revenue should be recognized over the period of risk (GASB-10, par. 19) [GASB Cod. Sec. Po20.116]. (See additional discussion of capitalization contributions and GASB Interpretation 4 later in this chapter.)

It may not be possible to determine the exact amount of the premium until after the end of the contract period. For example, a premium may be based on the amount of actual claims incurred during a period. An example of an experience-based premium contract is a contract that uses "retrospective rating," which GASB-10 defines as follows (GASB-10, par. 20) [GASB Cod. Sec. Po20.117]:

> *Retrospective (experience) rating*—A method of determining the final amount of an insurance premium by which the initial premium is adjusted based on actual experience during the period of coverage (sometimes subject to maximum and minimum limits). It is designed to encourage safety by the insured and to compensate the insurer if larger-than-expected losses are incurred.

In other instances, the premium may be based on the value of property covered during a contract period. An example of a value-based contract is a "reporting-form contract," which is defined as follows (GASB-10, par. 20) [GASB Cod. Sec. Po20.117]:

Reporting-form contract—A contract or policy in which the policyholder is required to report the value of property insured to the insurer at certain intervals. The final premium on the contract is determined by applying the contract rate to the average of the values reported.

In most instances of experience-based or valuation-based premiums, the public entity risk pool should be able to determine a reasonable estimate of the total premium. In this case, the premium revenue should be recognized over the contract period, based on the amount of risk protection provided. Estimates of the total premium should be revised as the public entity risk pool accumulates experience statistics from participants or receives revised property valuation reports from participants.

In accordance with GASB-62 (*Codification of Accounting and Financial Reporting Guidance Contained in Pre-November 30, 1989 FASB and AICPA Pronouncements*), pars. 69–70 [GASB Cod. Secs. 2250.101, 132–.133], changes in accounting estimates should be treated in a prospective manner. Thus, any adjustment to estimated total premiums would be reflected in any current and future financial statements in which the premium revenue is recognized. For example, assume that a premium of $150,000 for fire insurance is charged for a three-year period, given that the amount of property covered by the contract is expected to be $20,000,000 in year 1, $25,000,000 in year 2, and $30,000,000 in the final year (year 3) of the contract. The amount of premium revenue to be recognized in each of the three years under a reporting-form contract that is retrospectively rated is computed as follows:

	Premium Revenue		
	Year 1	Year 2	Year 3
($150,000 × $20,000,000) ÷ $75,000,000	$40,000	—	—
($150,000 × $25,000,000) ÷ $75,000,000	—	$50,000	—
($150,000 × $30,000,000) ÷ $75,000,000	—	—	$60,000

During year 2, assume that the estimated amounts of property covered in years 2 and 3 increase to $28,000,000 and $33,000,000, respectively, and that the total premium is estimated to be $172,000. In this circumstance, the amount of premium revenue to be recognized in years 2 and 3 would be as follows:

	Premium Revenue	
	Year 1	Year 2
([$172,000 – $40,000] × $28,000,000) ÷ $61,000,000	$60,590	—
([$172,000 – $40,000] × $33,000,000) ÷ $61,000,000	—	$71,410

If the public entity risk pool cannot reasonably estimate the total premium, premium revenue should be recognized using either the cost-recovery method or the deposit method. GASB-10 describes these two methods as follows (GASB-10, par. 20) [GASB Cod. Sec. Po20.117]:

Cost recovery method—Under the cost recovery method, premiums are recognized as revenue in an amount equal to estimated claims costs as insured events occur until the ultimate premium is reasonably estimable, and recognition of income is postponed until that time.

Deposit method—Under the deposit method, premiums are not recognized as revenue and claims costs are not charged to expense until the ultimate premium is reasonably estimable; recognition of revenue is postponed until that time.

To illustrate the cost-recovery method and the deposit method, assume that a public entity risk pool decides to bill a governmental entity the following amounts, but the billings are tentative because the total premium is based on retrospective rating and is not subject to reasonable estimation at the end of year 1:

Year	Amount
Year 1	$100,000
Year 2	110,000
Year 3	130,000
	$340,000

If estimated claims costs are $90,000 at the end of year 1, the following entries would be made by the risk pool under each of the two revenue recognition methods:

	Debit	Credit
COST-RECOVERY METHOD (YEAR 1):		
Premiums Receivable	100,000	
Premium Revenue		90,000
Unearned Premium Revenue		10,000
Expenses—Claims Costs	90,000	
Estimated Claims Costs Payable		90,000

	Debit	Credit
DEPOSIT METHOD (YEAR 1):		
Premiums Receivable	100,000	
Unearned Premium Revenue		100,000
Expenses—Claims Costs	90,000	
Estimated Claims Costs Payable		90,000

OBSERVATION: Due to the provisions of GASB-65 (*Items Previously Reported as Assets and Liabilities*), par. 31, which amended many section in the Codification, the use of the term "deferred" is limited to those items reported as deferred outflows of resources and deferred inflows of resources. The use of the term "unearned" is largely limited to insurance activities. Finally, GASB-10, par. 28, is amended by GASB-65, par. 20 [GASB Cod. Secs. Po20.131–.132, .134,

.146, .527], changing what had previously been recognized as deferred claims costs to expenses.

Assume that during year 2, the following reasonable estimates of premium revenue are made:

Year	Amount
Year 1	$130,000
Year 2	150,000
Year 3	170,000
	$450,000

Based on the fact that the public entity risk pool can reasonably estimate premium revenues, the following entries would be made in year 2:

	Debit	Credit
COST-RECOVERY METHOD (YEAR 2):		
($130,000 + $150,000 −		
Premiums Receivable $100,000)	180,000	
Unearned Premium Revenue	10,000	
Premium Revenue		190,000
DEPOSIT METHOD (YEAR 2):		
Unearned Premium Revenue	100,000	
Premiums Receivable	180,000	
Premium Revenue ($130,000 + $150,000)		280,000
Expenses—Claims Costs	90,000	
Estimated Claims Costs Payable		90,000

A public entity risk pool may collect a premium (or required contribution) that is specifically identified for coverage of future catastrophic losses. GASB-10 defines "catastrophe" as follows (GASB-10, par. 21) [GASB Cod. Sec. Po20.118]:

Catastrophe—A conflagration, earthquake, windstorm, explosion, or similar event resulting in substantial losses *or* an unusually large number of unrelated and unexpected losses occurring in a single period.

The accounting problem with respect to premiums related to catastrophic loss protection is that it is difficult to match the recognition of premium revenues and the recognition of losses that arise from future catastrophic losses. Specifically, should the premium related to catastrophic losses be recorded as deferred revenue until the actual loss occurs? The GASB states that premiums specifically related to future catastrophic losses should be recognized as premium revenue over the period covered by the contract. However, premium revenue related to catastrophic losses should be separately reported in the statement of net position as a restriction of net position if either one of the following conditions exists:

- The premium is contractually restricted for catastrophic losses; or

- The premium is legally restricted for catastrophic losses by an outside organization or individual (for instance, by pool participants).

OBSERVATION: Although GASB-10 refers specifically to the conditions necessary for the identification of a reservation of public entity risk pool equity, in the absence of such conditions, a pool could designate a portion of its equity for future catastrophic losses.

Claims Costs

Claims costs to be paid by a public entity risk pool should be evaluated using the fundamental criteria contained in GASB-62, pars. 96–113 [GASB Cod. Secs. C50.151—.168]. Thus, claims costs should be accrued at the end of the accounting period if the following conditions exist:

- Information available prior to issuance of the financial statements indicates that it is probable (the likely occurrence of the future event(s) that confirms that a loss has occurred) that a liability has been incurred at the date of the financial statements.

- The amount of the loss can be reasonably estimated.

Estimated claims costs become liabilities for the public entity risk pool when the covered event occurs. The occurrence of a fire or the injury of an individual covered by an agreement with the pool represents the critical date for determining a liability. In addition, some coverage (and therefore the recognition of a liability) is based on claims-made policies. This type of policy is defined as follows:

> *Claims-made policy or contract*—A type of policy that covers losses from claims asserted (reported or filed) against the policyholder during the policy period, regardless of whether the liability-imposing events occurred during the current or any previous period in which the policyholder was insured under the claims-made contract or other specified period before the policy period (the policy retroactive date).

Using the criteria for loss contingencies contained in GASB-62, pars. 96–113 [GASB Cod. Secs. C50.151—.168], and the critical event (date of occurrence or claims-made policy criterion) for liability recognition, the public entity risk pool must estimate a liability for unpaid claims costs. GASB-10 defines "liability for unpaid claims costs" in the following manner:

> *Liability for unpaid claims costs*—The amount needed to provide for the estimated ultimate cost of settling claims for events that have occurred on or before a particular date (ordinarily, the statement of net position date). The estimated liability includes the amount of money that will be needed for future payments on both (a) claims that have been reported and (b) incurred but not reported (IBNR) claims.

The above definition includes estimates for costs related to filed claims as well as incurred but not reported (IBNR) claims. "IBNR claims" are defined as follows:

> *Incurred but not reported (IBNR) claims*—Claims for insured events that have occurred but have not yet been reported to the governmental entity, public entity risk pool, insurer, or reinsurer as of the date of the financial statements. IBNR claims include (a) known loss events that are expected to later be presented as claims, (b) unknown loss events that are expected to become claims, and (c) expected future development on claims already reported.

The estimated liability for unpaid claims costs must be evaluated periodically to determine whether current factors make it necessary to adjust the liability for unpaid claims costs. For example, recent settlements may suggest that claims that have not been settled are understated. Adjustments of this nature are considered to be a change in an accounting estimate and, therefore, the resulting adjustment should be accounted for as an increase (or decrease) to current expenses of the public entity risk pool.

The estimated liability for unpaid claims costs should be reduced by estimated recoveries that may arise from unsettled claims. GASB-10 provides the following examples of recoveries (GASB-10, par. 22) [GASB Cod. Sec. Po20.119]:

> *Salvage*—The amount received by a public entity risk pool from the sale of property (usually damaged) on which the pool has paid a total claim to the insured and has obtained title to the property.

> *Subrogation*—The right of an insurer to pursue any course of recovery of damages, in its name or in the name of the policyholder, against a third party who is liable for costs of an insured event that have been paid by the insurer.

When a liability for unpaid claims is recognized, a related accrual should also be made for claim adjustment expenses. Claim adjustment expenses should include an estimate for all future adjustment expenses that arise in connection with the settlement of unpaid claims. Both allocated and unallocated claim adjustment expenses should be part of the accrual.

Allocated claim adjustment expenses are directly related to the settlement or processing of specific claims, and include expenses such as fees paid to adjusters and legal fees. Unallocated claim adjustment expenses are related to the settlement and processing of claims but are not traceable to a specific claim. Overhead costs of the public entity risk pool's claims department, such as administrative personnel salaries, allocations of depreciation, and utilities costs, are examples of unallocated claim adjustment expenses (GASB-10, par. 23) [GASB Cod. Sec. Po20.120].

The requirement to include unallocated expenses in the accrual for claim adjustment expenses presents a difficult allocation problem for most public entity risk pools. For example, what portion of the forthcoming year's overhead costs for the claims department should be included in the accrual? In addition, should only the future unallocated expenses of a single year be considered if it is likely that it may take years to settle some claims? A practical solution to the allocation problem is to estimate the percentage of claims identified and settled in one year and consider the balance to be the basis for the portion of overhead costs to be included in the year-end accrual. To illustrate, assume that a public entity risk pool has budgeted $500,000 for its overhead costs during the forthcoming year and it is estimated that about 80% of the claims processed are identified and settled in the same year. In this illustration, the liability for claim adjustment expenses should include an accrual of $100,000 ($500,000 × 20%) for unallocated claim adjustment expenses. Other more sophisticated allocation schemes are possible, but it is unlikely that the difference in amounts accrued between another allocation scheme and the one described here would have a material effect on the entity's financial statements.

In part, the accrual for claims liabilities represents estimates of cash flows that may occur several months or years into the future. The existence of such deferred payments raises the question of whether future cash flows related to the settlement of claims should be reported at gross value or at a discounted amount. The GASB does not take a position of whether future cash flows should be discounted. Thus, the accrual for claims liabilities can be reported either at a gross amount or at a discounted value.

OBSERVATION: The public entity risk pool should disclose the method (gross method or discounting method) used to measure the accrual for claims liabilities.

The GASB provides one exception to its neutral position with respect to discounting. Structured settlements should be discounted if the payout amounts and payment dates are fixed by contract. The GASB provides the following definition for "structured settlement" (GASB-10, par. 24) [GASB Cod. Sec. Po20.121]:

> *Structured settlement*—A means of satisfying a claim liability, consisting of an initial cash payment to meet specific present financial needs combined with a stream of future payments designed to meet future financial needs, generally funded by annuity contracts.

To illustrate a structured settlement, assume that a public entity risk pool agrees in a written settlement to pay $100,000 immediately and to purchase three annuities of $200,000 (representing various payments to the claimant spread over a period of years) at the end of year 2, year 4, and year 5. If a 10% discount rate is assumed, the claims liability should be recorded for $526,000 as follows:

Year	Future Cash Flows As Required by Contract	10% Present Value Factor	Present Value
1	$100,000	1.000	$100,000
2	200,000	0.826	165,200
4	200,000	0.683	136,600
5	200,000	0.621	124,200
			$526,000

The following entry would be made to record the structured settlement:

	Debit	Credit
Expenses—Claims Costs	526,000	
Estimated Claims Costs Payable		526,000

At the end of each year, it is necessary to record the amount of increase in the estimated liability due to the effects of discounting. For example, at the end of year 1, the following entry should be made:

	Debit	Credit
Expenses—Claims Costs	42,600	
Estimated Claims Costs Payable		42,600
($526,000–$100,000) × 10%		

If the public entity risk pool uses the discounting technique to measure claims liabilities, the GASB recommends that factors such as the pool's settlement rate and its investment yield rate be considered in establishing a discount rate. The "settlement rate" is defined as follows (GASB-10, par. 25) [GASB Cod. Sec. Po20.122]:

> *Settlement rate*—The rate at which a monetary liability with uncertain terms can be settled or a monetary asset (receivable) with uncertain terms can be sold.

The investment yield rate is the rate that the public entity risk pool is earning or expects to earn on its portfolio of investments over the period covered by the structured settlement.

Some claims against the public entity risk pool may be settled by the purchase of an annuity contract. GASB-10 defines "annuity contract" as "a contract that provides fixed or variable periodic payments made from a stated or contingent date and continuing for a specified period, such as for a number of years or for life."

When a claim is settled by the purchase of an annuity contract, the claim should be removed from the accrued liability account if the possibility of additional payments to the claimant are remote (likelihood of future payment is slight). Thus, neither the claim nor the investment in the annuity contract is reported in the public entity risk pool's statement of net position. Under this arrangement, the claim is accounted for as an in-substance defeasance of the debt. Thus, the responsibility for payment of the claim has been met, although the claim is still legally an outstanding obligation.

To illustrate the in-substance payment of a claim through the purchase of an annuity contract, assume that a claim with a recorded value of $250,000 is settled with the purchase of an annuity contract at a cost of $260,000. To record the purchase of the annuity contract, the following entry would be made:

	Debit	Credit
Estimated Claims Costs Payable	250,000	
Expenses—Claims Costs	10,000	
Cash		260,000

OBSERVATION: It is unlikely that the cost of purchasing an annuity will equal the recorded value of the claim. For example, a difference will arise if the public entity risk pool does not use discounting to measure its claims. Even when discounting is used (e.g., in a structured settlement), the rate used to discount a claim is not likely to be the rate that will be charged by the commercial enterprise from which the annuity is acquired. Any difference should be accounted for as an increase (decrease) in the claims costs expense for the year.

When claims have been removed from the claims liability account due to settlement by the purchase of an annuity contract, there is still a contingent liability. If the commercial enterprise could not fulfill its contractual requirements, the responsibility for payment would revert to the public entity risk pool. For this reason, GASB-10 requires the disclosure of the amount of claims removed from the claims liability account due to settlement by the purchase of annuity contracts, and that this disclosure continue for as long as the pool's contingent liability exists. Disclosure is not required if both of the following conditions exist (GASB-10, par. 26) [GASB Cod. Sec. Po20.123]:

- The claimant has signed an agreement releasing the public entity risk pool from further obligation.
- The likelihood of future payments to the claimant is remote.

Loss Contingencies

The conditions for recording a claim are that it is probable (likely to occur) that a liability has been incurred and a reasonable estimate of the liability can be made. If either of these conditions does not exist and there is at least a reasonable possibility (more than remote but less than probable) that a loss or an additional loss may have been incurred, the claim must be disclosed. The disclosure should include the following:

- Nature of the claim; and
- Estimate of the possible loss or range of loss (or state that an estimate cannot be made).

Similar disclosures should be made for any excess over amounts of claims accrued, if there is a reasonable possibility that an amount in excess of the accrued amount may have to be paid by the public entity risk pool (GASB-10, par. 27) [GASB Cod. Sec. Po20.124].

Acquisition Costs

Acquisition costs represent costs that arise from the acquisition of new contracts or the renewal of new contracts, including commissions, inspection fees, and salaries of employees involved in the underwriting process (process of selecting, classifying, evaluating, rating, and assuming risks) (GASB-10, par. 28) [GASB Cod. Sec. Po20.125].

GASB-65 updated the originally issued methodology of accounting and financial reporting for acquisition costs. Acquisition costs are not capitalized. As previously discussed, paragraph 20 of GASB-65 requires the costs to be recognized as an expense in the period incurred. Because of the expensing of these costs, though not specifically amended by GASB-65, the grouping and tracking of contracts by type of contract originally required in GASB-10 is not necessary.

Other Costs

Other costs should be expensed as incurred. Costs subject to immediate expense include gains or losses related to the management of the pool's portfolios of investments, administrative costs, and policy maintenance. "Policy maintenance costs" are "costs associated with maintaining records relating to insurance contracts and with the processing of premium collections and commissions" (GASB-10, par. 31) [GASB Cod. Sec. Po20.126].

Policyholder Dividends and Experience Refunds

A public entity risk pool may return a portion of the original premium paid based on the experience of the pool or a class of policies issued by the pool. A policyholder dividend (or return of contributions), as distinguished from an experience refund, is not determined based on the actual experience of an individual policyholder or pool participant but is instead *based on the experience of the pool or of a class of policies*.

Policyholder dividends should be accrued as dividends expense using an estimate of the amount to be paid. Dividends used by policyholders to reduce premiums should also be reported as premium income. Policyholder dividends include amounts returned to pool participants from excess premiums for future catastrophe losses.

Alternatively, experience refunds are based on the experience of individual policyholders or pool participants. If experience refund arrangements exist under experience-rated contracts, a separate liability should be accrued for those amounts, based on experience and the provisions of the contract. Instead, revenue should be reduced by amounts that are expected to be paid in the form of experience refunds (ostensibly a credit) (GASB-10, pars. 32–33) [GASB Cod. Secs. Po.128–.129].

For example, assume that an experience refund of $5,000 for a particular policyholder is estimated. To record the estimate, the following entry would be made:

	Debit	Credit
Premium Revenue	5,000	
Estimated Liability for Experience Refunds		5,000

Premium Deficiency

GASB-10 requires that a net realizable value test be made to determine whether there is a loss on existing contracts. If future expenses, plus any unamortized acquisition costs, exceed future premiums, then a loss or expense should be recognized (GASB-10, par. 34) [GASB Cod. Sec. Po20.130].

Contracts should be grouped and evaluated to determine whether the public entity risk pool has incurred a premium deficiency. The contracts should be grouped on the basis of common characteristics, such as the manner of acquisition, policy servicing, and measuring the revenue and expense related to the contracts. A premium deficiency is recognized if the following formula results in an amount greater than zero:

Element	Operation
Total expected claims costs including IBNR	+
Expected claim adjustment expenses	+
Expected dividends to policyholders or pool participants	=
Subtotal	Sum
Less: Related unearned premiums	-
Net amount is greater than zero, then premium deficiency is recognized	>0

To illustrate a premium deficiency calculation, assume the following non-authoritative example from the GASB *Implementation Guide 2015-1*, appendix B3-3 [GASB Cod. Sec. Po20.901]:

- For the premium deficiency calculation, policies are grouped consistent with the manner of acquiring, servicing, and measuring revenue and expense elements of the policies in the pool.

- Policyholder dividends are based on the experience of the entire pool, not on groups of policies. Therefore, if the overall pool experience is favorable, it is possible that dividends *may* be paid to policyholders with policies in a group in which a premium deficiency exists.

- Anticipation investment income is included in the determination and all amounts are in thousands. All accrued amounts are reported in the financial statements prior to the effect of the premium deficiency. Expected or anticipated amounts are related to events that are expected to occur (e.g., claims filed against a claims-made policy or claims against an occurrence based policy) after the statement of net position date and through the expiration of policy terms.

Element	Accrued Amounts	Expected or Anticipated Amount
Unearned premium	$100	$-
Unpaid claims costs (including IBNR claims costs)	110	105
Claim adjustment expense	7	5
Policyholder dividends	0	5
Investment income	4	5

Therefore, the following would be the deficiency:

Element		Calculation
Unearned premium		$100
Less:		
Expected claims costs	$105	
Expected claim adjustment expense	5	
Expected policyholder dividends	5	
Investment income	(5)	
Total costs		(110)
Premium deficiency expense		$10

If the premium deficiency is reasonably estimable, the pool has a legal and enforceable right to assess policyholders for the deficiency, and the collectability is probable and reasonably estimable, revenues and receivables should be declared by the pool for the assessments.

GASB-10 does not provide guidance as to whether expected investment income related to the grouping of contracts should be used to determine a premium deficiency. If expected investment income is used as part of the determination of a premium deficiency, the calculation should be disclosed (GASB-30, par. 4) [GASB Cod. Sec. Po20.131].

If a premium deficiency exists, then the unamortized acquisition costs are expensed as shown above. Deficiencies in excess of the amount are recognized as a liability as of the reporting date and as an expense. The liability adjusts in future periods as expected costs are incurred so that no liability exists by the end of the insurance contract. If deficiencies exist as a result of risk-sharing pool participation contracts, the deficiency is reported as revenue and assessments receivable as long as (GASB-30, par. 5) [GASB Cod. Sec. Po20.132]:

- A reasonable estimate of the additional contributions due can be made.
- The public entity risk pool has a legally enforceable claim to additional contributions.
- The collectibility of the additional contributions is probable.

Reinsurance

A public entity risk pool may enter into reinsurance contracts. The GASB defines "reinsurance" as follows (GASB-10) [GASB Cod. Sec. Po20.532]:

> *Reinsurance (reinsurer)*—A transaction in which an assuming enterprise (reinsurer), for a consideration (premium), assumes all or part of a risk undertaken originally by another insurer (ceding enterprise). However, the legal rights of the insured are not affected by the reinsurance transaction, and the ceding enterprise issuing the original insurance contract remains liable to the insured for payment of policy benefits.

The purpose of reinsurance is to spread the risk of loss, especially unusual losses that may occur, to more than one insurer.

The public entity risk pool must evaluate the terms of the reinsurance contract to determine how certain accounts should be presented in its financial statements.

When the public entity risk pool (ceding enterprise) can recover amounts from reinsurers (or excess insurers) based on paid claims and claim adjustment expenses, a receivable should be recorded and claims costs expense should be reduced. If it is expected that the total amount due from reinsurers will not be collected, an allowance for estimated uncollectible amounts should be established.

When amounts due from reinsurers are related to unpaid claims and claim adjustment expenses, the estimated amount due should be netted against the estimated claims costs liability and the claims costs expense should be reduced.

To account for the premium given by the public entity risk pool to the reinsurer, the portion (or all) of the unearned ceded premiums should be offset against the unearned premiums received from policyholders or pool participants. For example, assume a public entity risk pool receives unearned premiums of $700,000 from policyholders and 40% of these premiums are due to the reinsurer. These two transactions are recorded as follows:

	Debit	Credit
Cash	700,000	
Unearned Premium Revenue		700,000
To record premiums received from policyholder.		
Unearned Premium Revenue Ceded	280,000	
Ceded Premiums Payable ($700,000 × 40%)		280,000
To record ceded premiums due to reinsurer.		

For financial reporting purposes, receivables due from and payables due to the same reinsurer should be netted. In addition, (1) reinsurance premiums paid and related earned premiums and (2) reinsurance recoveries on claims and incurred claims costs may be netted on the public entity risk pool's operating statements (GASB-10, par. 37) [GASB Cod. Sec. Po20.133].

Amounts received from reinsurance transactions that represent the recovery of acquisition costs incurred by the public entity risk pool should be netted against the unamortized acquisition costs. The net amount of acquisition costs (original acquisition costs less recoveries related to reinsurance transactions) should be expensed. The public entity risk pool may agree to service all of the ceded insurance contracts while being reasonably compensated by the reinsurer. Under this circumstance, an accrual should be made for the estimated future (excess) maintenance costs related to the ceded contracts (GASB-10, par. 38, as amended by GASB-65, par. 20) [GASB Cod. Sec. Po20.134].

Some agreements may be a reinsurance transaction in form but not in substance. The risk of economic loss may not be shifted from the public entity risk pool to the reinsurer. In this case, amounts paid to the reinsurer should be treated as a deposit. If the amount received from a reinsurer exceeds the amount of the deposit, a net liability should be presented on the public entity risk pool's statement of net position (GASB-10, par. 39) [GASB Cod. Sec. Po20.135].

Capitalization Contributions Made to Other Public Entity Risk Pools

A public entity risk pool may have a relationship with another public entity risk pool that is similar to the relationship between a governmental entity and a public entity risk pool (as described earlier). For example, a public entity risk pool (the participant pool) may share a portion of its risk with another public entity risk pool (the excess pool). When this arrangement exists, and the participant pool makes a capitalization contribution to the excess pool, the participant pool should observe the accounting standards established in paragraphs 3–6 of GASBI-4 [GASB Cod. Secs. C50.134–.136]. In addition, the participant pool must also observe the accounting standards that relate to reinsurance contracts.

The guidance related to reinsurance may require the participant pool to net some balances related to the excess pool, or to treat certain payments to the excess pool as a deposit.

Capitalization Contributions Received

If it is probable that a capitalization contribution made to a public entity risk pool will be returned to the participant in the pool, the public entity risk pool (with transfer or pooling of risk) should account for the receipt of the contribution as a liability. If it is as probable that the contribution will *not* be returned, the receipt of the contribution should be reported as unearned premiums (a liability). The unearned premiums should be amortized and reported as premium revenue over the period for which it is expected that the capital contribution will be used to determine the amount of premiums the contributor must pay. However, if the period for which it is expected that the capital contribution will be used to determine the amount of premiums is not readily determinable, the amortization period cannot exceed 10 years (GASBI-4, pars. 11–12) [GASB Cod. Secs. Po20.137–.138].

The standards established by GASBI-4 require that all capitalization contributions received by a public entity risk pool that had previously been recorded as a component of capital be reclassified as a liability. Any capitalization contribution that had previously been recorded as revenue should be accounted for as a prior-period adjustment, with the restatement of the beginning balance of retained earnings for each period reported on a comparative basis.

Investments

Public entity risk pools, like commercial insurance companies, acquire a variety of investments to partially finance their costs of operations. A discussion of the method of accounting for these investments and other related issues is provided in Chapter 9, "Deposits, Investments, and Derivative Instruments."

PRACTICE POINT: Investments in risk pools are now to be reported at fair value per GASB-72 (*Fair Value Measurement and Application*).

Pools Not Involving Transfer or Pooling of Risks

Because of the arrangement between the public entity risk pool and participants, there may be no risk transfer or risk pooling among the participants. Under this arrangement, the public entity risk pool does not assume the role of an insurer but rather takes on the role of an agent for participants by performing the administrative duties of a claims servicer. Furthermore, under this arrangement, each participant is responsible for its own incurred claims.

When there is no transfer or pooling of risks, standards established in the previous section do not apply. Although the transactions and events related to the public entity risk pool (claims-servicing pool) are accounted for in an Enterprise Fund, no liability for incurred claims costs is reported. The pool's statement of net position reflects amounts due from participants as receivables and amounts due to participants as payables. In addition, GASBI-4 states that the receipt of a capitalization contribution should be netted against any related amount and a single asset or liability should be reported. That is, the pool's statement of net position reflects amounts due from participants as receivables and amounts due to participants as payables, after the amount of the capitalization contribution is taken into consideration. On the income statement, revenue from performing claims-servicing activities and related administrative expenses are reported (GASB-10, par. 51) [GASB Cod. Sec. Po20.148].

FINANCIAL STATEMENTS

As public entity risk pools are accounted for as Enterprise Funds, the financial statement requirements applicable to Enterprise Funds are applicable to governmental public entity risk pools. See Chapter 7, "Proprietary Funds," for a discussion of these required financial statements.

DISCLOSURES

The following additional information should be disclosed in the public entity risk pool's financial statements (GASB-10, par. 49; GASB-30, par. 6; and GASB-65, par. 20) [GASB Cod. Sec. Po20.146]:

- A description of the nature of risk transfer or the pooling agreement, including the rights and responsibilities assumed by both the public entity risk pool and its participants;

- A description of the number and types of participants;

- An explanation of the basis used to estimate the liabilities for unpaid claims and claim adjustment expenses, and an explicit statement that the estimate of the liabilities is based on the ultimate cost of settling the claims and includes the effects of inflation and other societal and economic factors;

- A description of the nature of acquisition costs that are capitalized, the method used to amortize such costs, and the amount of acquisition costs amortized for the period;

- Disclosure of the face (gross) amounts and carrying amounts of liabilities for unpaid claims and claim adjustment expenses presented on a present-value basis and the range of annual interest rates used to determine their present value;

- A statement of whether the public entity risk pool takes into consideration estimated investment income when determining if premium deficiencies exist;

- A description of the importance of excess insurance or reinsurance transactions to the public entity risk pool, including the following:

  — Type of coverage;

  — Reinsurance premiums ceded; and

  — Estimated amounts recoverable from excess insurers and reinsurers as of the statement of net position date that reduce the unpaid claims and claim adjustments expenses;

- A presentation of a total claims liabilities reconciliation, including changes in aggregate liabilities for claims and claim adjustment expenses from the prior year to the current year using the following tabular format (see the example in Exhibit 23-2):

  — Beginning balance of liabilities for unpaid claims and claim adjustment expenses;

  — Incurred claims and claim adjustment expenses for the year (with separate disclosure for the provision for insured events related to the current year and increases or decreases in the provision for events that were incurred in prior years);

  — Payments made (with separate disclosure for payments of claims and claim adjustment expenses related to insured events of the current year and payments of claims and claim adjustment expenses related to incurred events of prior years);

  — Explanation for other material reconciling items; and

  — Ending balance of liabilities for unpaid claims and claim adjustment expenses; and

- Disclosure of the total amount of outstanding liabilities that have been settled by purchasing annuity contracts from third parties in the name of claimants and the amount of liabilities that have been omitted from the statement of net position. (The disclosure should not include amounts related to settlements in which claimants have signed agreements releasing the pool from further obligation and the chance of further payment is remote.)

REQUIRED SUPPLEMENTARY INFORMATION

GASB-30 (*Risk Financing Omnibus—an amendment of GASB Statement No. 10*) requires reporting premium or required contribution revenue and claims development information (GASB-30, par. 7) [GASB Cod. Sec. Po20.147].

When a public entity risk pool presents separate financial statements, the revenue and claims development information should be presented as required supplementary information immediately after the notes to the financial statements. Required supplementary information is not considered to be part of the basic financial statements, because such information is not deemed essential to achieving the objective of adequate disclosure as required by governmental generally accepting accounting principles. On the other hand, required supplementary information is considered to be useful to various interested parties that must make assessments about a reporting entity.

When a public entity risk pool presents separate financial statements, the revenue and claims development information should be presented as required supplementary information immediately after the notes to the financial statements. When a public entity risk pool does not present separate financial statements, but rather presents its statements as part of another general governmental reporting entity's financial report, the revenue and claims development information may be presented as statistical information in the combined entity's comprehensive annual financial report (CAFR).

The standards established by GASB-30 supersede paragraph 50 of GASB-10, which described the format for required supplementary information for revenue and claims development information. The purpose of the presentation is to provide a basis for interested parties to identify and track trends related to current claims and developments in prior years' claims. In addition, the presentation provides a basis for determining the success of a pool's underwriting function and its ability to estimate its loss reserve over time.

Claims Development Information

The required supplementary information should be presented in a 10-year schedule (including the latest fiscal year) and include seven components (seven separate lines). The seven components are discussed in the following section and are cross-referenced to Exhibit 23-1, which is part of the illustration in Appendix D of GASB-30f [GASB Cod. Sec. Po20.901].

Line 1 The first line of the schedule of required supplementary information for revenue and claims development information focuses on revenues. A public entity risk pool should present (1) the amount of gross premium (or required contributions) revenue and reported investment revenue, (2) the amount of premium (or required contributions) revenue ceded, and (3) the amount of net reported premium (or required contributions) revenues (net of excess insurance or reinsurance) and reported investment revenue.

Line 2 The second line in the required supplementary information schedule discloses the amount of reported unallocated claim adjustment expenses and other costs.

OBSERVATION: Allocated claim adjustment expenses are directly related to the settlement or processing of specific claims, and they include expenses such as fees paid to adjusters and legal fees. Unallocated claim adjustment expenses are related to the settlement and processing of claims, but are not traceable to a specific claim. Overhead costs of the public entity risk pool's claims department, such as administrative personnel salaries, allocations of depreciation, and utilities costs, are examples of unallocated claim adjustment expenses.

OBSERVATION: Other costs that are not capitalized as acquisition costs for new contracts or renewed contracts should be expensed as incurred. Costs subject to immediate expense include gains or losses related to the management of the pool's portfolios of investments, administrative costs, and policy maintenance costs. "Policy maintenance costs" are "costs associated with maintaining records relating to insurance contracts and with the processing of premium collections and commissions."

Line 3 The third line in the schedule should present (1) the gross amount of incurred claims and allocated claim adjustment expenses, (2) the loss assumed by excess insurers or reinsurers, and (3) the net amount of incurred claims and allocated claim adjustment expenses. These three disclosures should include both paid and accrued amounts.

Incurred claims and allocated claim adjustment expenses may be internally developed by a public entity risk pool using various reporting methods. GASB-30 allows a public entity risk pool to present its claims information on an accident-year basis for occurrence-based policies, and a report-year basis for claims-made policies. Alternatively, the information may be presented on a policy-year basis. These alternatives are given the following definitions in GASB-10:

Claims-made policy—A type of policy that covers losses from claims asserted (reported or filed) against the policyholder during the policy period, regardless of whether the liability-imposing events occurred during the current or any previous period in which the policyholder was insured under the claims-made contract or other specified period before the policy period (the policy retroactive date).

Policy-year basis—For disclosure purpose as used in this Statement, a method that assigns incurred losses and claim adjustment expenses to the year in which the event that triggered coverage under the pool insurance policy or participation contract occurred. For occurrence-based coverage for which all members have a common contract renewal date, the policy year basis is the same as the accident-year basis. For claims-made coverage, policy year basis is the same as the report-year basis.

Amounts included in incurred claims and allocated claim adjustment expenses for a particular year should result only from events that triggered coverage under the policy or participation contract.

Once a method of developing the incurred claims and allocated claim adjustment expenses is adopted by a public entity risk pool, the method should be used consistently throughout each period.

OBSERVATION: The acceptability of more than one reporting basis (accident-year basis, report-year basis, and policy-year basis) raises the question of whether required supplementary information presented by public entity risk pools will be comparable. The GASB states that since the information is presented on a 10-year basis, trends for one public entity risk pool can be identified and compared to trends for other public entity risk pools. Furthermore, the GASB noted that some public entity risk pools have already developed trend information on an accident-year basis for statutory reporting, and therefore it is not necessary to require these pools to develop the information on another basis.

Line 4 The fourth line in the 10-year trend schedule relates the amount of incurred claims and allocated expense amounts recognized for a year and actual subsequent payments related to those amounts. The amounts should be presented on a cumulative basis from year to year, and should extend out for up to 10 years. For example, in Exhibit 23-1 the net amount that was originally estimated in 20W9 ($287,000) resulted in actual cash payments in 20W9 of $118,000, and actual cash payments over the 10-year period of $473,000.

Line 5 The fifth line in the schedule discloses the re-estimated amount for losses assumed by excess insurers or reinsurers based on the information available as of the end of the most current year. For example, in Exhibit 23-1 the original estimated ceded claims and expenses made in 20W9 was $52,000, but the most recent estimate of that amount (as of 20X8) is $104,000.

Line 6 The sixth line in the schedule presents the re-estimated net incurred claims and expenses based on the information available as of the end of the most current year. For example, in Exhibit 23-1 the original estimate of net incurred claims and expenses made in 20W9 was $235,000; however, the estimates change in subsequent years as the public entity risk pool gains more experience (settlement of actual claims) with the policies. By the seventh year of experience, there estimated net incurred claims and expenses are equal to the net amount paid ($473,000), which suggests that the public entity risk pool follows that no additional liability exists related to policy claims initiated in 20W9.

Line 7 The seventh line in the 10-year schedule provides insight into the public entity risk pool's ability to estimate claims and expenses by relating the original estimate of claims and expenses to the most recent estimate. For example, in Exhibit 23-1 the original estimate of estimated claims and expenses was $235,000 (Line 3) for 20W9, but the most recent reestimated amount as of 20X8 was $473,000 (Line 6). The difference of $238,000 ($473,000 − $235,000) is presented in Line 7 and labeled as the "increase in estimated net incurred claims and expenses from end of policy year."

OBSERVATION: The information developed for Line 4, Line 5, Line 6, and Line 7 should be based on the same reporting method(s) used in Line 3 (accident year, report year, or policy year).

The dollar amounts presented in the 10-year required supplementary information by public entity risk pools may be supplemented by the presentation of the same information on a percentage basis, although the latter presentation is not required. Also, percentage presentations cannot be substituted for dollar amount presentations (dollar amounts are illustrated only in Exhibit 23-1). GASB-10 notes that the presentation of percentage information "should not obscure or distort required elements of the table."

See Exhibits 23-2 and 23-3.

EXHIBIT 23-1
TEN-YEAR CLAIMS DEVELOPMENT INFORMATION

Fiscal and Policy Year Ended (In Thousands of Dollars)

	20W9	20X0	20X1	20X2	20X3	20X4	20X5	20X6	20X7	20X8
1. Required contribution and investment revenue:										
Earned	$908	$957	$1,357	$1,493	$1,479	$1,595	$1,811	$1,993	$2,192	$2,411
Ceded	366	387	559	615	624	686	754	830	913	1,004
Net earned	542	570	798	878	855	909	1,057	1,163	1,279	1,407
2. Unallocated expenses	64	68	81	91	70	81	92	110	123	131
3. Estimated claims and expenses, end of policy year:										
Incurred	287	303	453	503	569	651	780	909	1,092	1,512
Ceded	52	54	96	111	129	148	168	186	210	251
Net incurred	235	249	357	392	440	503	612	723	882	1,261
4. Net paid (cumulative) as of:										
End of policy year	118	124	179	196	220	251	306	361	450	641
One year later	177	186	268	294	330	377	459	542	675	
Two years later	254	268	385	422	474	542	660	779		
Three years later	304	321	461	506	568	649	790			
Four years later	359	379	545	597	671	766				
Five years later	404	427	614	673	756					

Six years later	445	469	674	740						
Seven years later	473	499	717							
Eight years later	473	499								
Nine years later	473									
5. Re-estimated ceded claims and expenses	104	109	160	174	184	195	211	217	234	251
6. Re-estimated net incurred claims and expenses:										
End of policy year	235	249	357	392	440	503	612	723	882	1,261
One year later	294	311	447	490	550	628	765	898	1,102	
Two years later	338	357	513	563	632	722	874	1,028		
Three years later	380	401	577	632	710	811	982			
Four years later	422	446	641	703	789	902				
Five years later	449	474	682	748	840					
Six years later	468	494	710	779						
Seven years later	473	499	717							
Eight years later	473	499								
Nine years later	473									
7. Increase in estimated net incurred claims and expenses from end of policy year	238	250	360	387	400	399	370	305	220	0

EXHIBIT 23-2
NOTE DISCLOSURE FOR UNPAID CLAIMS LIABILITIES

Unpaid Claims Liabilities

As discussed in Note A, the Fund establishes a liability for both reported and unreported insured events, which includes estimates of both future payments of losses and related claim adjustment expenses, both allocated and unallocated. The following represents changes in those aggregate liabilities for the Fund during the past two years (in thousands):

	20X8	20X7
Unpaid claims and claim adjustment expenses at beginning of year	**$1,421**	**$1,189**
Incurred claims and claim adjustment expenses:		
Provision for insured events of current year	1,282	900
Increases in provision for insured events of prior years	649	540
Total incurred claims and claim adjustment expenses	**1,931**	**1,440**
Payments:		
Claims and claim adjustment expenses attributable to insured events of current year	641	450
Claims and claim adjustment expenses attributable to insured events of prior years	904	758
Total payments	**1,545**	**1,208**
Total unpaid claims and claim adjustment expenses at end of year	**$1,807**	**$1,421**

At year-end 20X8, $718,000 of unpaid claims and claim adjustment expenses are presented at their net present value of $576,000. These claims are discounted at annual rates ranging from $8^{1}/_{2}\%$ to 11%. Unpaid claims expenses of $249,000 are not reported in the 20X8 year-end balances because the Fund has purchased annuities in claimants' names to settle those claims.

EXHIBIT 23-3
REQUIRED SUPPLEMENTARY INFORMATION FOR RECONCILIATION
OF CLAIMS LIABILITIES BY TYPE OF CONTRACT

Reconciliation of Claims Liabilities by Type of Contract

The schedule below presents (in thousands) the changes in claims liabilities for the past two years for the Fund's two types of contracts: property and casualty and employee health and accident benefits.

	Property and Casualty		Employee Health and Accident		Totals	
	20X8	20X7	20X8	20X7	20X8	20X7
Unpaid claims and claim adjustment expenses at beginning of year	$762	$716	$659	$473	$1,421	$1,189
Incurred claims and claim adjustment expenses:						
Provision for insured events of current year	513	360	769	540	1,282	900
Increases in provision for insured events of prior fiscal years	389	324	260	216	649	540
Total incurred claims and claim adjustment expenses	902	684	1,029	756	1,931	1,440
Payments:						
Claims and claim adjustment expenses attributable to insured events of current fiscal year	256	180	385	270	641	450
Claims and claim adjustment expenses attributable to insured events of prior fiscal years	542	455	362	303	904	758
Total payments	798	635	747	573	1,545	1,208
Total unpaid claims and claim adjustment expenses at end of fiscal year	$866	$765	$941	$656	$1,807	$1,421

QUESTIONS

1. The activities of a public entity risk pool may vary, but in general, they may be classified as the following except for:

    a. Pooled investment fund.

    b. Insurance purchasing pool.

    c. Banking pool.

    d. Claim servicing or account pool.

2. The method of estimating insurance premiums where premiums are not recognized as revenue and claims costs are not charged to expense until the ultimate premium is reasonably estimable; recognition of revenue is postponed until that time is an example of what:

    a. Retrospective rating.

    b. Cost recovery method.

    c. Deposit method.

    d. Reporting form contract.

3. Premium revenue is recorded separately in the statement of net position as restricted net position if which of the following conditions exists related to a catastrophe?

    a. Management restricts the premium for catastrophic losses.

    b. The premium is legally restricted for catastrophic losses by pool participants.

    c. The premium is restricted due to the passage of time.

    d. The premium is restricted due to the potential magnitude of the catastrophic losses.

4. The right of an insurer to pursue any course of recovery of damages in the name of the policyholder against a third party who is liable for the costs of an insured event that have been paid by the insurance is the definition of

    a. Premium deficiency.

    b. Indemnification.

    c. Salvage.

    d. Subrogation.

5. In accordance with GASB-65, acquisition costs of insurance are reported as a (an):

    a. Asset.

    b. Deferred outflow of resources.

    c. Deferred inflow of resources.

    d. Expense.

ANSWERS

1. The activities of a public entity risk pool may vary, but in general they may be classified as the following except for:

   Answer – A.

2. The method of estimating insurance premiums where premiums are not recognized as revenue and claims costs are not charged to expense until the ultimate premium is reasonably estimable; recognition of revenue is postponed until that time is an example of what:

   Answer – C.

3. Premium revenue is recorded separately in the statement of net position as restricted net position if which of the following conditions exists related to a catastrophe?

   Answer – B.

4. The right of an insurer to pursue any course of recovery of damages in the name of the policyholder against a third party who is liable for the costs of an insured event that have been paid by the insurance is the definition of

   Answer – D.

5. In accordance with GASB-65, acquisition costs of insurance are reported as a (an):

   Answer – D.

CHAPTER 24
OTHER SPECIAL-PURPOSE GOVERNMENTS

CONTENTS

INTRODUCTION

The majority of the *Governmental GAAP Guide* focuses on general purpose governments, which were introduced in Chapter 1, "Foundation and Overview of Governmental Generally Accepted Accounting Principles," as those entities that provide a wide range of services (often including both governmental and business-type activities.) They include states, counties, cities, towns, villages, and similar governmental entities. Although recognized Indian tribes may not specifically meet the criteria to be defined as a governmental entity, most tribal governments prepare their financial statements in accordance with the principles applicable to general-purpose state and local governments. Also included in the description of general-purpose governments are U.S. territories and the District of Columbia.

Special-purpose governments also were introduced in Chapter 1 as legally separate governmental entities that perform only one or a few activities and include colleges and universities, school districts, water and other utility districts or authorities, fire protection districts, cemetery districts, public employee retirement systems, public entity risk pools, governmental hospital or health-care organizations, public housing authorities, airport authorities, and similar entities.

In the previous chapters to the *Guide*, the focus has been on Public Colleges and Universities (PCUs) (Chapter 21) Pension and Other Postemployment Benefit Plans (Chapter 22) and Public Entity Risk Pools (Chapter 23). In addition, specific transactions were discussed in Chapter 16, "Other Liabilities," with regard to state lotteries and gaming entities. These are all very common activities. However, other special-purpose governments have specific GAAP contained in GASB Statements, primarily GASB Statement No. 62 (*Codification of Accounting and Financial Reporting Guidance Contained in Pre-November 30, 1989 FASB and AICPA Pronouncements*).

Special-purpose governments with specific GAAP provisions discussed in this chapter include:

- Public broadcasters and cable systems,

- Public hospitals and other healthcare providers,

- Insurance entities, other than public entity risk pools, and

- Regulated entities.

Each have slightly different GAAP based upon the provisions of GASB-62 and other GASB Statements. For example, GASB Statement No. 83 (*Asset Retirement Obligations*) is likely applicable for public utilities more than other governments and may be subject to regulatory accounting. Specific provisions are also in GAAP for customer and developer deposits at utilities. GASB Statement No. 81 (*Irrevocable Split-Interest Agreements*) is likely more applicable to public hospitals and public colleges and universities with endowments more than general purpose governments.

PRACTICE POINT: Asset retirement obligations are discussed in Chapter 10, "Capital Assets," and irrevocable split-interest agreements are discussed in Chapter 17, "Revenues: Nonexchange and Exchange Transactions."

OTHER SPECIAL-PURPOSE GOVERNMENTS

Public Broadcasters and Cable Systems

PCUs and some general-purpose governments own broadcast facilities. In certain areas of the country, cable television systems may be owned by governments.

Beyond the capital assets of the broadcast facility generally including technology, transmitters, the intangible asset of a license to broadcast and other elements which would be accounted for and reported similarly to other governments, broadcast facilities may license program material. They may also barter time blocks for programming. They likely also pay various fees for network programming (such as from the Public Broadcasting System—PBS). The facility may also have a related foundation for fundraising.

GAAP require a broadcast licensee to report an asset and liability for a broadcast license agreement either (*a*) at the present value of the liability using an imputed interest cost or (*b*) at the gross amount of the liability. If the present value of the liability is used, the difference between the gross and the net liability is accounted for as interest (GASB-62, par. 386) [GASB Cod. Sec. Br10.102].

As an example, radio station KLMN is a discretely presented component unit of Castle Rock State University. KLMN signs an agreement to broadcast a two-hour daily program of news from the national news service for seven years, paying $1,000 per month. The agreement is noncancellable unless either party ceases broadcasting. The present value of the liability is $68,453, using an imputed interest rate of 6% in accordance with the provisions of GASB-62, pars. 173–186 [GASB Cod. Sec. I30]. The radio station's comptroller would make the following entry:

	Debit	Credit
Right to broadcast national news	$68,453	
Broadcast rights obligation		$68,453
To record asset for intangible right to broadcast nightly news and liability for rights fees due monthly for next seven years.		

The first monthly installment would be as follows, including amortization of the right:

	Debit	Credit
Broadcast rights obligation ($1,000 – interest expense)	$658	
Interest expense ($68,453 × 6% / 12)	342	
Cash		1,000
Amortization Expense—broadcast rights	815	
Accumulated amortization— broadcast rights		815
To record monthly payment for nightly news and amortize right to broadcast using the effective interest method.		

Bartering

It is common for broadcasting stations to barter time blocks or advertising segments. For example, a station may have a promotion for concert tickets received as a barter from a recording company. The station would then run a contest with winners going to the concert.

In other situations, unused blocks of time are bartered with companies. For example, a CPA firm wants to promote its financial advisory services. The CPA firm barters the time on the station, receiving calls from listeners for financial advice. The CPA firm promotes its business and the station utilizes time not normally used. In other situations, the station exchanges advertising time for network programming. The affiliated broadcast station does not sell the related advertising time, but since it licenses the time from the federal communications commission, it has a cost. Therefore, the network pays for the services in accordance with the agreement. This arrangement is common in sports programming.

GAAP require all barter transactions *except those involving the exchange of advertising time for network programming* to be reported at the estimated fair value of the product or service received, as a nonmonetary exchange.

PRACTICE POINT: Nonmonetary exchanges are discussed in detail in Chapter 1 of the *Governmental GAAP Practice Manual*.

Barter revenue is reported when commercials are broadcast and merchandise or services received should be reported when received or used. If the merchandise or services are received prior to the commercial, a liability is reported. If the opposite is true, a receivable is reported (GASB-62, par. 387) [GASB Cod. Sec. Br10.103].

Cable Television Services

Cable television services may be provided by a general government or a special purpose government. They may utilize governmental activities or business-type activities (or both). For a governmental activity, either taxation or intergovernmental revenues utilizing an internal service fund is used. For example, a special district also operates a cable television service in a small village. The board meetings are broadcast on the system. The cost of the broadcast is likely in an internal service fund.

More likely though, external fees are charged to ratepayers. The monthly fees are a business-type activity usually reported in an enterprise fund (GASB-34, pars. 15, 69, and 135) [GASB Cod. Sec Ca5.102].

GAAP accounting for the system operated as an enterprise fund would be the same for any other enterprise fund. The financial statements required for business-type activities would be required (GASB-34, pars. 67, 129, 138, as amended by GASB-63, par. 8) [GASB Cod. Secs. Ca5.103–.104]. If the system engaged in both governmental and business-type activities, a complete set of financial statements, including required reconciliations, would be required. If the system was a component unit, all component unit provisions would apply (GASB-34, pars. 135–137, GASB-14, pars. 13 and 65–66) [GASB Cod. Secs. Ca5.105–.109].

Specific transactions unique to cable television systems include recognition of revenue during the "prematurity period," recognition of subscriber-related costs, depreciation of capitalized costs, and proper recording of hookup revenue and related costs.

Management of the system must establish the beginning and the end of the prematurity period which usually lasts less than two years. This period may last longer in cities due to the complexity of wiring a system. During this period, the system is partially under construction and partially in service. Similarly to other capital assets being placed in service, the achievement of a predetermined subscriber level ends the prematurity period. At that time, no additional invest-ment is required other than for cable television plants. The government that operates the system must clearly distinguish the periods and in some cases areas of the system may be in the prematurity period while other areas may be fully operational. The areas may have:

- Geographic differences,
- Mechanical differences (utilizing different "head-ends" or plants),
- Timing differences, likely based on construction elements or marketing,
- Different break-even points or return on investment decisions that will start or stop construction, or
- Separate accounting and reporting records (GASB-62, par. 391) [GASB Cod. Sec. Ca5.112].

Similarly to other capital assets, during the prematurity period, the costs of the cable television plant, materials, direct labor, and overhead are capitalized. Subscriber-related costs and other general and administrative costs are period costs. Programming costs that benefit the prematurity period and fully opera-tional periods are allocated (GASB-62, par. 391) [GASB Cod. Sec. Ca5.113].

The allocation of costs during the prematurity period is based on a formula determining a fraction. The numerator is *the greater of*:

- The average number of subscribers expected that month as of the beginning of the prematurity period, *or*
- The average number of subscribers that would be attained using at least equal (i.e., straight-line) monthly progress in adding new subscribers toward the estimate of subscribers at the end of the prematurity period, *or*
- The average number of actual subscribers.

The denominator is the total number of subscribers expected at the end of the prematurity period. In practice, this is similar to the percentage of completion method for construction accounting. The fraction then derives depreciation and amortization expense during the prematurity period. Costs that have been capitalized should be depreciated over the same period used to depreciate the plant (GASB-62, pars. 393–394, 396) [GASB Cod. Secs. Ca5.114–.115, .117].

Initial hookup revenue is recognized as revenue to the extent of direct selling costs incurred. Any remainder is recognized as a deferred inflow of resources and amortized to revenue over the estimated average remaining period that subscribers are expected to remain connected to the system. The individual subscriber installation costs (labor, materials, overhead) are capitalized similarly. Any costs of disconnecting and reconnecting a subscriber are expensed (GASB-62, pars. 397–398) [GASB Cod. Secs. Ca5.118–.119].

Public Hospitals and Other Healthcare Providers

Hospitals and other healthcare providers are commonly governments. Such facilities may be engaged in either governmental or business-type activities or both. Governmental activities are generally financed through taxes, intergovernmental revenues, and other nonexchange revenues. They are usually reported in governmental funds and internal service funds. Business-type activities are financed in whole or in part by fees charged to external users for goods or services. They are usually reported in enterprise funds (GASB-34, pars. 15, 69, and 135) [GASB Cod. Sec. Ho5.102]. Hospitals may be component units, likely to shield the primary government from liability.

If organized as a governmental activity, a business-type activity and/or as a component unit, all related GAAP accounting and financial reporting applies.

PRACTICE POINT: The following sections on charity care, accounting for joint activities, purpose, audience, content, allocation methods, incidental activities, and disclosures of allocated joint costs are from the AICPA *Audit and Accounting Guide*—Healthcare Entities and the AICPA Statement of Position 98-2, which have been cleared by the GASB and included in the GASB *Codification*. Only the *Codification* references are included in these sections as the individual paragraphs in the AICPA literature change.

Charity Care

Charity care includes healthcare services provided to patients, but never expected to result in cash flows. No revenue is recognized. For financial reporting purposes, gross service revenue does not include charity care and net service revenue is reported net of contractual and other adjustments in the statement of revenues, expenses, and changes in net position [GASB Cod. Sec. Ho5.802].

Governmental healthcare entities are required to disclose management's policy for providing charity care and the level of charity care provided, based on some measure of the entity's costs, units of service, or some other measure [GASB Cod. Sec. Ho5.803].

Accounting for Joint Activities—Fundraising versus Program or Management and General

Joint activities are those that are allocable between fundraising and an appropriate program or management and general function. Joint activities have criteria of *purpose, audience,* and *content.* If any of the criteria are *not* met, all joint costs are fundraising, including those that are usually management and general functions. The exception is costs of goods or services provided in exchange transactions that are part of joint activities, such as costs of direct donor benefits of a special event (e.g., a meal), which should not be reported as fundraising [GASB Cod. Sec. Ho5.804].

The criteria are fairly complex and are only applicable if fundraising costs of the healthcare entity are also required to be allocated to programmatic functions [GASB Cod. Secs. Ho5.805–.812]. Any cost allocation should be systematic and rational, resulting in a reasonable joint cost that can be applied consistently given similar facts and circumstances [GASB Cod. Sec. Ho5.813].

Disclosures of Allocations of Joint Costs

Entities that allocate joint costs should disclose the following in the notes in addition to all other applicable GAAP disclosure:

- The types of activities for which joint costs have been incurred,
- A statement that such costs have been allocated,
- The total amount allocated during the period and the portion allocated to each functional expense category [GASB Cod. Sec. Ho5.815].

Insurance Entities—Other Than Public Entity Risk Pools

PRACTICE POINT: Public Entity Risk Pools are discussed in Chapter 23.

Similarly to the other entities discussed in this chapter, insurance entities may be engaged in either governmental or business-type activities or both. Governmental activities are financed primarily through taxes, intergovernmental revenues, and other nonexchange revenues. They are generally reported in governmental funds and internal service funds. Business-type activities are financed in whole or in part by fees charged to external users for goods or services. They are usually reported in enterprise funds (GASB-34, pars. 15, 69, and 135) [GASB Cod. Sec. In3.102]. All GAAP apply to insurance entities as applicable, including if the entity is a component unit and/or produces a stand-alone financial statement.

In general, such insurance entities initiate short-duration insurance contracts (GASB-62, par. 400) [GASB Cod. Sec. In3.110].

PRACTICE POINT: This section does not apply to contracts for the purpose of providing coverage for OPEB. Such contracts are discussed in Chapter 13, "Pension, Postemployment, and Other Employee Benefit Liabilities," or Chapter 22, "Pension and Other Postemployment Benefit Plans." See following section on insurance entities that are regulated operations.

General Principles

Insurance contracts are classified as *short-duration* if the contract provides insurance protection for a fixed period of short duration and enables the insurer to cancel the contract or to adjust the provisions of the contract at the end of any contract period, such as adjusting the amount of premiums charged or coverage provided.

Examples of short-duration contracts include most **property and liability insurance contracts** and **workers' compensation programs**, as well as certain government **credit enhancement and mortgage guaranty contracts**. Accident and health insurance contracts may be short-duration or long-duration depending on whether the contracts are expected to remain in force for an extended period.

For example, individual and group insurance contracts that are noncancelable or guaranteed renewable (renewable at the option of the insured), or collectively renewable (individual contracts within a group are not cancelable), ordinarily are *long-duration contracts* (GASB-62, pars. 401–402) [GASB Cod. Secs. In3.111–.112].

Premium Revenue

Similarly to public entity risk pools, premiums from short-duration insurance contracts are recognized as revenue over the period of the contract in proportion to the amount of insurance protection provided. A liability for unpaid claims (including estimates of costs for claims relating to insured events that have occurred but have not been reported to the insurer) and a liability for claim adjustment expenses should be accrued when insured events occur. Variable costs that are related to the acquisition of the contracts are capitalized and charged to expense in proportion to the premium revenue recognized. Other investment, administrative, and policy-related costs are expensed (GASB-62, pars. 403–404) [GASB Cod. Secs. In3.113–.114].

If premiums are subject to adjustment (e.g., retrospectively rated or other experience-rated insurance contracts for which the premium is determined after the period of the contract based on claim experience or reporting-form contracts for which the premium is adjusted after the period of the contract based on the value of insured property), premium revenue should be recognized as follows:

1. If, as is usually the case, the ultimate premium is reasonably estimable, the estimated ultimate premium should be recognized as revenue over the period of the contract. The estimated ultimate premium should be revised to reflect current experience.

2. If the ultimate premium *cannot be reasonably estimated*, the cost recovery method or the deposit method may be used until the ultimate premium becomes reasonably estimable (GASB-62, pars. 405–406) [GASB Cod. Secs. In3.115–.116].

Recognizing Claims Costs

Liabilities for unpaid claims costs related to insurance contracts, including estimates of incurred but not reported claims are accrued when insured events occur. The liability for unpaid claims is based on the estimated ultimate cost of settling the claims (including the effects of inflation and other societal and economic factors), using past experience adjusted for current trends, and any other factors that would modify past experience. Changes in estimates of claim costs resulting from the continuous review process and differences between estimates and payments for claims should be recognized in the period in which the estimates are changed or payments are made.

Estimated recoveries on unsettled claims, such as salvage, subrogation, or a potential ownership interest in real estate, are evaluated in terms of their estimated realizable value and deducted from the liability for unpaid claims. Estimated recoveries on settled claims other than mortgage guaranty claims are also deducted from the liability for unpaid claims (GASB-62, pars. 407–408) [GASB Cod. Secs. In3.117–.118].

A liability for all costs expected to be incurred in connection with the settlement of unpaid claims (*claim adjustment expenses*) is accrued when the related liability for unpaid claims is accrued. Claim adjustment expenses include costs associated directly with specific claims paid or in the process of settlement, such as legal and adjusters' fees. Claim adjustment expenses also include other costs that cannot be associated with specific claims but are related to claims paid or in the process of settlement, such as internal costs of the claims function. Other costs that do not vary and not primarily related to acquisition are expensed as incurred. Commissions and other costs (e.g., salaries of certain employees involved in the underwriting and policy issue functions, and medical and inspection fees) that are primarily related to insurance contracts issued or renewed during the period in which the costs are incurred should be considered acquisition costs and are expensed (GASB-62, pars. 409–413, as amended by GASB-65, par. 20) [GASB Cod. Secs. In3.119–.123].

Premium Deficiencies

A premium deficiency is recognized as a liability if the sum of expected claim costs, claim adjustment expenses, and expected dividends to policyholders exceeds related unearned premiums. Disclosure is required if the insurance entity considers investment revenue in the determination of a premium deficiency. The liability is adjusted in future periods as costs incur so that no liability remains at the end of the contract period (GASB-62, pars. 415–417, as amended by GASB-65, par. 20, fn. 201) [GASB Cod. Secs. In3.124–.126, fn. 12].

Reinsurance

Similarly to public entity risk pool operations, any amount that is recoverable from reinsurers relating to *paid* claims and claims adjustments expenses are recorded as assets, adjusted for estimated uncollectible amounts. If amounts recoverable relate to *unpaid* claims, they are netted against such liabilities. Ceded unearned premiums should also be netted against unearned premiums. Any amounts from the same reinsurer that result in net receivables and net payables are netted as well. Reinsurance premiums ceded and related recoveries on claims are also netted against the related premiums and incurred claims costs in either the statement of activities or the statement of revenues, expenses, and changes in fund net position. Further adjustments may be made for estimated excess future servicing costs under the reinsurance contract and the effects of indemnification (GASB-62, pars. 418–420, fn.202) [GASB Cod. Secs. In3.127–.129, fn.13]

Policyholder Dividends

Policyholder dividends are accrued using an estimate of the amounts to be paid. Dividends declared or paid to policyholders reduce the related liability. Any amounts paid in excess of the dividend liability are expensed (GASB-62, pars. 421–422) [GASB Cod. Secs. In3.130–.131].

Investments and Mortgage Loans, Real Estate Used in Operations

Insurers may hold mortgage loans as investments or not as investments. Such loans that are *not* investments are reported at outstanding balances of principal, if at par, or at amortized cost if acquired at a discount or premium, adjusting for uncollectible amounts. All other mortgage loans that are investments are reported at fair value. Changes in fair value, amortizations, related charges and credits are also reported at fair value. Real estate that is held as an investment is also reported at fair value. Loan origination and commitment fees may also occur and are recorded similarly to other lending activities. Finally, real estate used in operations are recorded as capital assets with related depreciation occurring (GASB-62, pars. 423–428, as amended by GASB-63, par. 8, GASB-72, pars. 64 and 75) [GASB Cod. Secs. In3.132–.137].

Disclosures

Required disclosures for insurance entities other than public entity risk pools include the following:

1. The basis for estimating the liabilities for unpaid claims and claim adjustment expenses,

2. The carrying amount of liabilities for unpaid claims and claim adjustment expenses relating to contracts that are presented at present value in the financial statements and the range of interest rates used to discount those liabilities,

3. Whether the insurance enterprise considers anticipated investment revenue in determining if a premium deficiency exists,

4. The nature and significance of reinsurance transactions to the insurance enterprise's operations, including reinsurance premiums assumed and ceded, and estimated amounts that are recoverable from reinsurers and that reduce the liabilities for unpaid claims and claim adjustment expenses,

5. The relative percentage of participating insurance, the method of accounting for policyholder dividends, the amount of dividends, and the amount of any additional revenue allocated to participating policyholders, and

6. The fair value disclosures similarly to other investments, as applicable (GASB-62, par. 429, as amended by GASB-65, par. 20, GASB-72, pars. 80–82) [GASB Cod. Sec. In3.138].

REGULATED OPERATIONS

Regulatory accounting and financial reporting is common for entities such as public utilities or insurance entities that are subject to a third-party regulator, typically a state or a federal entity. The basis of accounting is a special-purpose framework.

> **PRACTICE POINT:** Should an entity be required to report using regulatory provisions, a modified independent auditors report is produced as the underlying balances and results of operations are not presented in accordance with GAAP as promulgated by the GASB. If there are no other issues with the entity requiring a modified report, the report will be issued unmodified with regard to the regulatory provisions and an adverse opinion in accordance with GAAP.

> **PRACTICE POINT:** This section *does not apply* to governmental entities that are either required or allowed to elect a statutory framework. Such frameworks are approved in legislation by a state and are primarily budgetary, cash, modified cash, or some other statutory basis of accounting which is not GAAP. A similar auditors report to regulated operations is presented for such entities.

Applicability of Regulatory Accounting and Reporting

Regulated operations are usually business-type activities that meet *all* of the following criteria:

1. The regulated business-type activity's rates for regulated services provided to its customers are established by or are subject to approval by an independent, third-party regulator or by its own governing board empowered by statute or contract to establish rates that bind customers.

2. The regulated rates are designed to recover the specific regulated business-type activity's costs of providing the regulated services.

3. In view of the demand for the regulated services or products and the level of competition, direct and indirect, it is reasonable to assume that rates set at levels that will recover the regulated business-type activity's costs can be charged to and collected from customers. This criterion requires consideration of anticipated changes in levels of demand or competition during the recovery period for any capitalized costs

Entities may have partially regulated operations and partially unregulated operations. These are usually utility enterprise funds contained within a general purpose government. Should this occur, the regulatory provisions continue to apply to those regulated operations. All other provisions in GAAP apply to the unregulated operations. Price controls or inflationary accounting are not regulatory accounting. If an entity is required to report using contractual accounting (which is a special-purpose framework), regulatory accounting applies. Contractual accounting may be required by certain grants (GASB-62, pars. 3 and 476–479) [GASB Cod. Secs. Re10.101–.103].

General Standards for Regulatory Accounting

Assets and Capitalization of Costs

Regulatory provisions require recognition of an asset based on certain conditions and rate actions. A regulated business-type activity should capitalize all or part of an incurred cost that otherwise would be charged to expense if both of the following criteria are met:

1. It is probable that future revenue in an amount at least equal to the capitalized cost will result from inclusion of that cost in allowable costs for rate-making purposes. The term "probable" is utilized similarly to the measurement of other contingencies, and

2. Based on available evidence, the future revenue will be provided to permit recovery of the previously incurred cost rather than to provide for expected levels of similar future costs. If the revenue will be provided through an automatic rate-adjustment clause, this criterion requires that the regulator's intent clearly be to permit recovery of the previously incurred cost.

Regulators also have the ability to reduce or eliminate the value of an asset by disallowing rates and charges. If a regulator excludes all or part of a cost from allowable costs and it is *not probable* that the cost will be included as an allowable cost in a future period, the cost cannot be expected to result in future revenue through the rate-making process. Accordingly, the carrying amount of any related asset is reduced to the extent that the asset has been impaired. Whether the asset has been impaired should be judged the same as for governments in general (GASB-62, pars. 480–481) [GASB Cod. Secs. Re10.105–.106].

Liabilities and Deferred Inflows of Resources

Regulators can also impose liabilities or deferred inflows of resources. Liabilities are usually obligations to the regulated business-type activity's customers and deferred inflows of resources represent an acquisition of net position from the regulated business-type activity's customers that is applicable to a future reporting period. The usual ways in which a transaction results in a liability or a deferred inflow of resources and the resulting accounting are as follows:

1. A regulator may require refunds to customers. Refunds that meet the criteria for the accrual of loss contingencies should be recorded as liabilities and as reductions of revenue or as expenses of the regulated business-type activity.

2. A regulator can provide current rates intended to recover costs that are expected to be incurred in the future with the understanding that if those costs are not incurred, future rates will be reduced by corresponding amounts. If current rates are intended to recover such costs and the regulator requires the regulated business-type activity to remain accountable for any amounts charged pursuant to such rates and not yet expended for the intended purpose, the regulated business-type activity should not recognize as revenues amounts charged pursuant to such rates. Those amounts are reported as a deferred inflow of resources and recognized as revenue when the associated costs are incurred.

3. A regulator can require that a gain or other reduction of net allowable costs be given to customers over future periods. That would be accomplished, for rate-making purposes, by allocating in a systematic and rational manner, the gain or other reduction of net allowable costs over those future periods and adjusting rates to reduce revenues in approximately the amount of the allocation. If a gain or other reduction of net allowable costs is to be allocated over future periods for rate-making purposes, the regulated business-type activity should not recognize that gain or other reduction of net allowable costs in the current period. Instead, it should be reported as a deferred inflow of resources for future reductions of charges to customers that are expected to result.

The actions of a regulator can eliminate a liability only if the liability was imposed by actions of the regulator (GASB-62, pars. 482–483, as amended by GASB-65, par. 29) [GASB Cod. Secs. Re10.107–.108].

PRACTICE POINT: Certain regulators may not recognize deferred inflows of resources. Practitioners should understand the regulatory language prior to utilizing these provisions.

Derivatives and Hedging

Utilities may utilize hedging activities in its operations. The GASB *Implementation Guide 2015-1*, question 10.13.7 [GASB Cod. Sec. Re10.701-2], discusses regulatory accounting and hedging.

Non-regulated utilities should test potential hedging derivative instruments for effectiveness and if effective, apply hedging.

In order to apply the regulatory accounting provisions, a regulated utility is required to determine the amount that otherwise should be reported as revenue or expense. That determination occurs only after consideration of whether a derivative instrument is a hedging derivative instrument, that is, only after the derivative instrument is determined to be effective in significantly reducing an identified risk. For example, a regulated gas utility purchases futures contracts to hedge price risk associated with a future natural gas purchase. Whether the futures contracts are effective hedges of future natural gas purchases should first be evaluated, for example, by employing the synthetic instrument method. If the futures contracts are effective, any fair value increases and decreases on the futures contracts should be reported as deferred inflows of resources or deferred outflows of resources, having no impact on the statement of revenues, expenses and changes in fund net position.

Customer Deposits—Utilities

Many electric, water, gas, sewer, and other utility operations require customer deposits to assure timely payment for services. Customer deposits to secure service payments normally are required before service starts and are refunded when service is terminated. Utility operations also may require land developers or individual property owners to make deposits as advance payments of system development fees to extend utility service lines to their properties. Utility operations generally are reported in enterprise funds (and may be regulated). Unearned customer and developer deposits initially are recorded as liabilities in those funds and in the government-wide financial statements. Customer deposits remain as liabilities until they are applied against unpaid billings or refunded to customers. Developer deposits remain as liabilities until they are recognized as revenue from system development fees [GASB Cod. Sec. Ut5.801].

PRACTICE POINT: This provision is from AICPA literature cleared by the GASB.

Specific Regulated Operations Standards Based on General Standards

Costs of Construction

A regulator may require capitalization of the cost of financing construction as part of the cost of capital assets. The cost may be financed partially by borrowings and partially by fund equity. A computed interest cost and a designated cost of equity funds are capitalized, and the change in net position for the current period is increased by a corresponding amount. After the construction is completed, the resulting capitalized cost is the basis for depreciation and unrecovered investment for rate-making purposes. In such cases, the amounts capitalized for rate-making purposes as part of the cost of acquiring the assets should be capitalized for financial reporting purposes instead of the amount of interest that would be capitalized. Those amounts should be capitalized only if their subsequent inclusion in allowable costs for rate-making purposes is probable. The statement of revenues, expenses and changes in fund net position (or the statement of activities or the regulatory equivalent) should include an item of other revenue, a reduction of interest expense, or both, in a manner that indicates the basis for the amount capitalized (GASB-62, par. 485, as amended by GASB-63, par. 8) [GASB Cod. Sec. Re10.110].

PRACTICE ALERT: GASB Statement No. 89 (*Accounting for Interest Cost during the Period of Construction—an amendment of GASB Statements No. 37 and No. 62*) [Various elements of GASB Cod. Secs. 1100, 1400, 2200, I30, and Re10] modifies the interest capitalization provision, simplifying accounting for interest cost during periods of construction. GASB-89 requires that interest cost be recognized in the period in which the cost is incurred as an expense. GASB-89's effective date is for periods beginning after December 15, 2019. For June 30th governments, the period would begin on July 1, 2020. Changes adopted to conform to the provisions of any final statement would be applied *prospectively*. For construction-in-progress, interest cost incurred after the beginning of the reporting period of application would not be capitalized and instead, expensed. Care must be taken by practitioners however as in some cases, the regulator may require interest to continue to be capitalized and part of a regulatory asset for financial reporting purposes.

Intra-Entity Profit

Profit on intra-entity sales to other entities that are in the same reporting entity as the regulated business-type activity *should not* be eliminated in general-purpose external financial statements if *both* of the following criteria are met:

1. The sales price is reasonable.

2. It is probable that, through the rate-making process, future revenue *approximately equal* to the sales price will result from the regulated business-type activity's use of the services.

The sales price usually should be considered reasonable if the price is accepted or not challenged by the regulator that governs the regulated affiliate. Otherwise, reasonableness should be considered in light of the circumstances. For example, reasonableness might be judged by the return on investment earned by operations or by a comparison of the transfer prices with prices available from other sources (GASB-62, pars. 486–487) [GASB Cod. Secs. Re10.111–.112].

Asset Impairment

When an operating asset or an asset under construction of a regulated business-type entity becomes impaired, the impairment should be accounted for in accordance with the provisions of GASB Statement No. 42 (*Accounting and Financial Reporting for Impairment of Capital Assets and for Insurance Recoveries*) [GASB Cod. Sec. 1400] as discussed in Chapter 10, "Capital Assets," of this *Guide*. In addition, the regulated business-type activity should determine whether recovery of any allowed cost is likely to be provided with either of two scenarios:

1. Full return on investment *during the period* from the time the asset is impaired to the time when recovery is completed or

2. Partial or no return on investment *during that period*.

Determination of which scenario applies should focus on the facts and circumstances related to the specific impairment and also should consider the past practice and current policies of the applicable regulatory jurisdiction on impairment situations. Based on that determination, the regulated business-type activity should account for the impairment as follows (GASB-62, pars. 488–491) [GASB Cod. Secs. Re10.113–.116]:

Element	Full Return on Investment Likely to be Provided	Partial or No Return on Investment Likely to Be Provided
Cost of the impaired plant	Any disallowance of all or part of the cost of the impaired plant that is *both probable* and *reasonably estimable* (similarly to other loss contingencies) should be recognized as a loss, and the carrying basis of the recorded asset should be correspondingly reduced. The remainder of the cost of the impaired plant should be reported as a separate new asset.	Any disallowance of all or part of the cost of the impaired plant that is both probable and reasonably estimable (similarly to other loss contingencies) should be recognized as a loss. The present value of the future revenues expected to be provided to recover the allowable cost of that impaired plant and return on investment, if any, should be reported as a separate new asset. Any excess of the remainder of the cost of the impaired plant over that present value also should be recognized as a loss. The discount rate used to compute the present value should be the regulated business-type activity's incremental borrowing rate, that is, the rate that the regulated business-type activity would have to pay to borrow an equivalent amount for a period equal to the expected recovery period. In determining the present value of expected future revenues, the regulated business-type activity should consider such matters as: (1) The probable time period before such recovery is expected to begin, and (2) The probable time period over which recovery is expected to be provided. If the estimate of either period is a range, the loss contingency guidance should be applied to determine the loss to be recognized. Accordingly, the most likely period within that range should

Element	Full Return on Investment Likely to be Provided	Partial or No Return on Investment Likely to Be Provided
		be used to compute the present value. If no period within that range is a better estimate than any other, the present value should be based on the minimum time period within that range.
Adjustment of Asset Carrying Amount— Change in Rates	A rate equal to the allowed overall cost of capital in the jurisdiction in which recovery is expected to be provided should be used.	The rate that was used to compute the present value should be used.
New Asset Amortization during Recovery Period	The asset should be amortized in the same manner as that used for rate-making purposes.	The asset should be amortized in a manner that will produce a constant return on the unamortized investment in the new asset equal to the rate at which the expected revenues were discounted.

Disallowed Costs of Construction

Regulators will likely audit material construction projects subject to regulation. When it becomes *probable* that part of the cost of a recently completed plant will be disallowed for rate-making purposes and a reasonable estimate of the amount of the disallowance can be made, the estimated amount of the probable disallowance should be deducted from the reported cost of the plant and recognized as a loss. If part of the cost is explicitly, but indirectly, disallowed (e.g., by an explicit disallowance of return on investment on a portion of the plant), an equivalent amount of cost should be deducted from the reported cost of the plant and recognized as a loss (GASB-62, par. 491) [GASB Cod. Sec. Re10.117].

Sale-leaseback Transactions

Sale-leaseback transaction accounting may result in a difference between the timing of revenue and expense required by GASB-62, pars. 211–271, relating to such transactions [GASB Cod. Sec. L20]. The timing of revenue and expense recognition related to the sale-leaseback transaction should be modified as necessary to conform to this section. That modification is required for a transaction that is accounted for by the deposit method or as a financing.

If a sale-leaseback transaction is accounted for by the deposit method but the sale is recognized for rate-making purposes, the amortization of the asset should be modified to equal the total of the rental expense and the gain or loss allowable for rate-making purposes. Similarly, if the sale-leaseback transaction is accounted for as a financing and the sale is recognized for rate-making purposes, the total of interest imputed under the interest method for the financing and the amortization of the asset should be modified to equal the total rental expense and the gain or loss allowable for rate-making purposes.

The difference between the amount of revenue or expense recognized for a transaction that is accounted for by the deposit method or as a financing and the amount of revenue or expense included in allowable cost for rate-making purposes is capitalized or accrued as a separate regulatory-created asset or liability, as appropriate, if that difference meets the criteria of the regulatory provisions (GASB-62, pars. 252–254) [GASB Cod. Secs. Re10.118–.120].

PRACTICE POINT: For a further discussion of leases, see Chapter 14 "Leases and Service Concession Arrangements." Chapter 14 also discusses GASB Statement No. 87 (*Leases*).

Refunds

For refunds that are recognized in a period other than the period in which the related revenue was recognized, the regulated business-type activity should disclose the effect on the change in net position and indicate the years in which the related revenue was recognized. Such effect may be disclosed by including it as a line item in the statement of revenues, expenses and changes in fund net position or the statement of activities, as applicable (GASB-62, par. 493, as amended by GASB-63, par. 8) [GASB Cod. Sec. Re10.121].

Recovery without Return on Investment

In some cases, a regulator may permit a regulated business-type activity to include a cost that would be charged to expense by an unregulated business-type activity as an allowable cost over a period of time by amortizing that cost for rate-making purposes, but the regulator does not include the unrecovered amount in the rate base. That procedure does not provide a return on investment during the recovery period. If recovery of such major costs is provided without a return on investment during the recovery period, the regulated business-type activity discloses the remaining amounts of such assets and the remaining recovery period applicable to them (GASB-62, par. 494) [GASB Cod. Sec. Re10.122].

Discontinuation of Regulatory Accounting—(Deregulation)

Discontinuance of regulatory accounting may be caused by:

1. Deregulation,
2. A change in the regulator's approach to setting rates from cost-based rate making to another form of regulation,
3. Increasing competition that limits the regulated business-type activity's ability to sell utility services at rates that will recover costs, or
4. Regulatory actions resulting from resistance to rate increases that limit the regulated business-type activity's ability to sell utility services at rates that will recover costs if the regulated business-type activity is unable to obtain (or chooses not to seek) relief from prior regulatory actions through appeals to the regulator or the courts.

These instances are required to be reported in the basic financial statements as they may represent a material change in operations.

When a regulated business-type activity determines that its operations in a regulatory jurisdiction no longer meet the criteria for application of regulated operations, that regulated business-type activity should discontinue these accounting provisions to its operations in that jurisdiction immediately. Similar actions should occur if the portion that fails to meet the criteria is separable from other operations that demonstrably continue to meet the criteria.

When a regulated business-type activity discontinues regulatory accounting to all or part of its operations, that regulated business-type activity should eliminate from its statement of net position prepared for general-purpose external financial reporting the effects of any actions of regulators that had been recognized as assets and liabilities as discussed in this section, but would not have been recognized as assets and liabilities by business-type activities in general.

However, the carrying amounts of capital assets and inventory measured and reported in accordance with the regulatory provisions should not be adjusted unless those assets are impaired, in which case the carrying amounts of those assets should be reduced to reflect that impairment. Whether those assets have been impaired should be judged in the same manner as for business-type activities in general. The net effect of the adjustments should be recognized in the period in which the discontinuation occurs and should be classified as a special or extraordinary item if they meet the criteria for such elements.

The carrying amounts of capital assets and inventory for regulated business-type activities applying regulatory accounting differ from those for business-type activities in general only because of the allowance for resources used during construction, intra-entity profit, and disallowances of costs of recently completed plants. If any other amounts that would not be includable in the carrying amounts of capital assets or inventory by business-type activities in general are included in or netted against the carrying amounts of capital assets or inventory, those amounts should be accounted for as part of the deregulation action.

Finally, a regulated business-type activity that discontinues application of regulatory accounting should no longer recognize the effects of actions of a regulator as assets or liabilities unless the right to receive payment or the obligation to pay exists as a result of past events or transactions and regardless of future transactions (GASB-62, pars. 496–499, as amended by GASB-63, par. 8, fn.231) [GASB Cod. Secs. Re10.124–.127, fn.11].

Disclosure of Deregulation

In a discontinuance of regulatory accounting involving all or a portion of operations, disclosure is required of the reasons and identification of which portion (or all) of the operations the deregulation applies (GASB-62, par. 500) [GASB Cod. Sec. Re10.128].

Glossary

This glossary has been developed to assist users of the *Governmental GAAP Guide* to understand terms that are commonly used in state and local governments. It is not meant to be all-inclusive, nor is it meant to be authoritative. Certain terms were introduced by GASB Standards that have been rescinded, but the term is included as it still may be utilized in practice. The reference to the rescinded standard is not made. The GASB Standard referenced is the latest GASB Statement that includes the definition in a glossary or in the text of the Statement.

Item	GASB Standard[1]	Definition
2a7-like pool	GASB-59	An external investment pool that is not registered with the SEC as an investment company, but nevertheless has a policy that it will, and does, operate in a manner consistent with the SEC's Rule 2a-7 of the Investment Company Act of 1940 (17 *Code of Federal Regulations* § 270.2a-7). Rule 2a-7 allows SEC-registered mutual funds to use amortized cost rather than market value to report net assets to compute share prices if certain conditions are met. Those conditions include restrictions on the types of investments held, restrictions on the term-to-maturity of individual investments and the dollar-weighted average of the portfolio, requirements for portfolio diversification, and requirements for divestiture considerations in the event of security downgrades and defaults, and required actions if the market value of the portfolio deviates from amortized cost by a specified amount. (See "External Investment Pool" and "Qualified External Investment Pool.")
AAA general obligations index	GASB-53	An index published by Municipal Market Data composed of interest rates of the highest quality state and local debt issuers.
Accountability (accountable)	GASB-14	The relationship that results from the appointment of a voting majority of an organization's governing board.

Item	GASB Standard[1]	Definition
Accounting change	GASB-62	A change in (a) an accounting principle, (b) an accounting estimate, or (c) the reporting entity. The correction of an error in previously issued financial statements is not an accounting change.
Accounting principle	GASB-62	Accounting principles and practices but also the methods of applying them.
Acquisition costs (government combinations)	GASB-69	Acquisition costs are the costs the acquiring government incurs to effect a government acquisition. Acquisition costs include, but are not limited to, fees for legal, accounting, valuation, professional, or consulting services.
Acquisition costs (insurance entities other than public entity risk pools)	GASB-62	Costs incurred in the acquisition of new and renewal insurance contracts. Acquisition costs include those costs that vary with and are primarily related to the acquisition of insurance contracts (for example, agent and broker commissions, certain underwriting and policy issue costs, and medical and inspection fees).
Acquisition value	GASB-72	The price that would be paid to acquire an asset with equivalent service potential in an orderly market transaction at the acquisition date, or the amount at which a liability could be liquidated with the counterparty at the acquisition date.
Act of God	GASB-10	An event beyond human origin or control, natural disasters. Lighting, windstorms, and earthquakes are examples.
Active employees	GASB-75	Individuals employed at the end of the reporting or measurement period, as applicable.
Active market	GASB-72	A market in which transactions for an asset or liability take place with sufficient frequency and volume to provide pricing information on an ongoing basis.
Active plan members	GASB-74	Employees in active service that are covered under the terms of an OPEB plan.
Actual contributions	GASB-68	Cash contributions recognized as additions to a pension plan's fiduciary net position.

Item	GASB Standard[1]	Definition
Actual synthetic rate	GASB-53	If the hedged item is an existing financial instrument or an expected transaction that is intended to be a financial instrument, the rate achieved by a synthetic instrument considering its cash flows for a period of time.
Actuarial accrued liability (AAL)		That portion, as determined by a particular Actuarial Cost Method, of the Actuarial Present Value of pension plan benefits and expenses which is not provided for by future Normal Costs.
Actuarial assumptions		Assumptions as to the occurrence of future events affecting pension costs, such as: mortality, withdrawal, disablement and retirement; changes in compensation and government-provided pension benefits; rates of investment earnings and asset appreciation or depreciation; procedures used to determine the Actuarial Value of Assets; characteristics of future entrants for Open Group Actuarial Cost Methods; and other relevant items.
Actuarial cost method		A procedure for determining the Actuarial Present Value of pension plan benefits and expenses and for developing an actuarially equivalent allocation of such value to time periods, usually in the form of a Normal Cost and an Actuarial Accrued Liability.
Actuarial experience gain and loss		A measure of the difference between actual experience and that expected based upon a set of Actuarial Assumptions, during the period between two Actuarial Valuation dates, as determined in accordance with a particular Actuarial Cost Method.
Actuarial method	GASB-10	Any of several techniques that actuaries use to determine the amounts and timing of contributions needed to finance claims liabilities so that the total contributions plus compounded earnings on them will equal the amounts needed to satisfy claims liabilities. It may or may not include a provision for anticipated catastrophe losses.
Actuarial present value of projected benefit payments	GASB-75	Projected benefit payments discounted to reflect the expected effects of the time value (present value) of money and the probabilities of payment.

Item	GASB Standard[1]	Definition
Actuarial valuation	GASB-75	The determination, as of a point in time (the actuarial valuation date), of the service cost, total pension or OPEB liability, and related actuarial present value of projected benefit payments for pensions performed in conformity with Actuarial Standards of Practice unless otherwise specified by the GASB.
Actuarial valuation date	GASB-75	The date as of which an actuarial valuation is performed.
Actuarial value of assets		The value of cash, investments and other property belonging to a pension plan, as used by the actuary for the purpose of an Actuarial Valuation.
Actuarially determined contribution	GASB-75	A target or recommended contribution to a defined benefit pension or OPEB plan for the reporting period, determined in conformity with Actuarial Standards of Practice based on the most recent measurement available when the contribution for the reporting period was adopted.
Actuarially equivalent		Of equal Actuarial Present Value, determined as of a given date with each value based on the same set of Actuarial Assumptions.
Ad hoc cost-of-living adjustments (ad hoc COLAs)	GASB-75	Cost-of-living adjustments that require a decision to grant by the authority responsible for making such decisions.
Ad hoc postemployment benefit changes	GASB-75	Postemployment benefit changes that require a decision to grant by the authority responsible for making such decisions
Administrative involvement	GASB-84	With regard to fiduciary activities, a government has administrative involvement with the assets if, for example, it (a) monitors compliance with the requirements of the activity that are established by the government or by a resource provider that does not receive the direct benefits of the activity, (b) determines eligible expenditures that are established by the government or by a resource provider that does not receive the direct benefits of the activity, or (c) has the ability to exercise discretion in how assets are allocated.

Item	GASB Standard[1]	Definition
Advance refunding (of bonds)	GASB-7	In an *advance refunding* transaction, new debt is issued to provide monies to pay interest on old, outstanding debt as it becomes due, and to pay the principal on the old debt either as it matures or at an earlier call date. An advance refunding occurs before the maturity or call date of the old debt, and the proceeds of the new debt are invested until the maturity or call date of the old debt. Most advance refundings result in defeasance of debt. Defeasance of debt can be either legal or in substance. [See **PRACTICE ALERT** in Chapter 12 "Long-Term Debt" in the *Governmental GAAP Guide* –issuance prohibited after December 31, 2017 by federal Tax Cuts and Jobs Act].
Agency funds (until the implementation of GASB-84-see custodial funds herein)	GASB-34	Use to report resources held by the reporting government in a purely custodial capacity (assets equal liabilities).Agency funds typically involve only the receipt, temporary investment, and remittance of fiduciary resources to individuals, private organizations, or other governments.
Agent employer	GASB-75	An employer whose employees are provided with pensions or OPEB through an agent multiple-employer defined benefit pension or OPEB plan.
Agent fees	GASB-28	Amounts paid by a lender to its securities lending agent as compensation for managing its securities lending transactions.
Agent multiple-employer defined benefit pension or OPEB plan (agent pension or OPEB plan)	GASB-75	A multiple-employer defined benefit pension (or OPEB) plan in which pension plan assets are pooled for investment purposes but separate accounts are maintained for each individual employer so that each employer's share of the pooled assets is legally available to pay the benefits of only its employees.

Item	GASB Standard[1]	Definition
Aggregate actuarial cost method		A method under which the excess of the Actuarial Present Value of Projected Benefits of the group included in an Actuarial Valuation over the Actuarial Value of Assets is allocated on a level basis over the earnings or service of the group between the valuation date and assumed exit. This allocation is performed for the group as a whole, not as a sum of individual allocations. That portion of the Actuarial Present Value allocated to a valuation year is called the Normal Cost. The Actuarial Accrued Liability is equal to the Actuarial Value of Assets. This method is not widely used.
AICPA		American Institute of Certified Public Accountants
Allocated insurance contract	GASB-74	A contract with an insurance company under which related payments to the insurance company are currently used to purchase immediate or deferred annuities for individual employees. Also may be referred to as an annuity contract.
Allotment (or allot)	NCGAI-10	Where spending authority is apportioned for a particular period by an approving authority.
Amenities (real estate)	GASB-62	Examples of amenities include golf courses, utility plants, clubhouses, swimming pools, tennis courts, indoor recreational facilities, and parking facilities.
Amortization (of unfunded actuarial accrued liability)		Systematic and rational manner of allocating liability amounts to future periods, based upon an accepted methodology. Amortization payments include payments of interest on and to amortize a liability.

Item	GASB Standard[1]	Definition
Annexation	GASB-69	Changes in the territorial boundaries of governments. An annexation may also be known as reorganization. In a government annexation arrangement, one government extends the bounds of its geographic footprint to include new incorporated or unincorporated areas. Often, annexations result only in changes in boundaries, and the annexed governments generally do not give up assets or gain relief from liabilities. However, in annexations in which assets, deferred outflows of resources, liabilities, and deferred inflows of resources comprising an operation are transferred, those items are required to be recognized at the carrying amounts reported by the transferring government.
Annual OPEB cost		An accrual-basis measure of the periodic cost of an employer's participation in a defined benefit OPEB plan (no longer utilized for general-purpose external financial reporting).
Annual required contributions of the employer(s) (ARC)		The employer's periodic required contributions to a defined benefit OPEB plan, calculated in accordance with the parameters (no longer utilized for general-purpose external financial reporting).
Annuity contract	GASB-10	A contract that provides fixed or variable periodic payments made from a stated or contingent date and continuing for a specified period, such as for a number of years or for life.
Appoint	GASB-14	To select members of a governing body (as long as the ability to do so is not severely limited by a nomination process) or confirm appointments made by others (provided that the confirmation is more than a formality or part of a ministerial responsibility).
Appropriated budget	NCGAI-10	The expenditure authority created by a bill or ordinance that is in law. It may also include revenues, transfers, allocations, allotments and program changes. It may be for a single period or for multiple years and for capital or for operating purposes or both.

Item	GASB Standard[1]	Definition
Appropriation	NCGAI-10	A line item giving spending authority in a budget.
Asset impairment	GASB-42	A significant, unexpected decline in the service utility of a capital asset.
Asset-backed securities	GASB-31	Assets that are composed of, or collateralized by, loans or receivables. Collateralization can consist of liens on real property, leases, or credit card debt.
Asset retirement obligation (ARO)	GASB-83	A legally enforceable liability associated with the retirement of a tangible capital asset.
Assets	GASB-65 (also GASB:CS-4)	Resources with present service capacity that the government presently controls.
Assigned fund balance	GASB-54	Amounts that are constrained by the government's *intent* to be used for specific purposes, but are neither restricted nor committed. Intent should be expressed by (a) the governing body itself or (b) a body (a budget or finance committee, for example) or official to which the governing body has delegated the authority to assign amounts to be used for specific purposes.
Assignment	GASB-64	An assignment occurs when a swap agreement is amended to replace an original swap counterparty, or the swap counterparty's credit support provider, but all of the other terms of the swap agreement remain unchanged.
At the market	GASB-53	The prevailing market price or rate. For example, an at-the-market swap is entered into at no cost to the government.
Attained age actuarial cost method		A method under which the excess of the Actuarial Present Value of Projected Benefits over the Actuarial Accrued Liability in respect of each individual included in an Actuarial Valuation is allocated on a level basis over the earnings or service of the individual between the valuation date and assumed exit. The portion of this Actuarial Present Value which is allocated to a valuation year is called the Normal Cost. The Actuarial Accrued Liability is determined using the Unit Credit Actuarial Cost Method (no longer utilized for general-purpose external financial reporting).

Item	GASB Standard[1]	Definition
Authoritative GAAP	GASB-76	Category A GAAP and Category B GAAP. Authoritative GAAP is incorporated periodically into the *Codification of Governmental Accounting and Financial Reporting Standards* (Codification), and when presented in the Codification, it retains its authoritative status.
Automatic cost-of-living adjustments (automatic COLAs)	GASB-75	Cost-of-living adjustments that occur without a requirement for a decision to grant by a responsible authority, including those for which the amounts are determined by reference to a specified experience factor (such as the earnings experience of the pension or OPEB plan) or to another variable (such as an increase in the consumer price index).
Automatic postemployment benefit changes	GASB-75	Postemployment benefit changes that occur without a requirement for a decision to grant by a responsible authority, including those for which the amounts are determined by reference to a specified experience factor (such as the earnings experience of the pension or OPEB plan) or to another variable (such as an increase in the consumer price index).
Available (property taxes)	GASBI-5	Collected within the current period or expected to be collected soon enough thereafter to be used to pay liabilities of the current period.
Balance sheet	GASB-34	Report of information about the current financial resources (assets, liabilities, and fund balances) of each major governmental fund and for nonmajor governmental funds in the aggregate and totaled as of the reporting date.
Bank holding company	GASB:TB 97-1	A company that controls one or more banks and may contain subsidiaries with operations related to banking.
Bankers' acceptances	GASB-3	Bankers' acceptances generally are created based on a letter of credit issued in a foreign trade transaction. Bankers' acceptances are short-term, non-interest-bearing notes sold at a discount and redeemed by the accepting banks at maturity for face value.
Banking pool	GASB-10	Risk financing arrangement in which monies are loaned to pool members in the event of a loss.

Item	GASB Standard[1]	Definition
Bargain purchase option (leases)	GASB-62	A provision allowing the lessee the option to purchase the leased property for a price that is sufficiently lower than the expected fair value of the property at the date the option becomes exercisable such that exercise of the option appears, at the inception of the lease, to be reasonably assured.
Bargain renewal option (leases)	GASB-62	A provision allowing the lessee the option to renew the lease for a rental sufficiently lower than the fair rental of the property at the date the option becomes exercisable such that exercise of the option appears, at the inception of the lease, to be reasonably assured.
Barter (broadcasting)	GASB-62	The exchange of unsold advertising time for products or services. The broadcaster benefits (providing the exchange does not interfere with its cash sales) by exchanging otherwise unsold time for such things as programs, fixed assets, merchandise, other media advertising privileges, travel and hotel arrangements, entertainment, and other services or products.
Basic financial statements	GASB-34	The core required financial statements of a government including management's discussion and analysis, government-wide financial statements, fund financial statements, notes to the financial statements and required supplementary information other than the management's discussion and analysis.
Basis differences	NCGAI-10	Differences that may arise when the basis of budgeting is different than GAAP.
Basis risk	GASB-53	The risk that arises when variable rates or prices of a hedging derivative instrument and a hedged item are based on different reference rates.
Benchmark interest rate	GASB-53	A widely recognized and quoted rate in an active financial market that is broadly indicative of the overall level of interest rates attributable to high-credit-quality obligors in that market. It is a rate that is widely used in a given financial market as a basis for determining the interest rates of financial instruments and commonly referenced in interest-rate-related transactions.

Item	GASB Standard[1]	Definition
Beneficial interest	GASB-81	The right to a portion of benefits from donated resources pursuant to split-interest agreements in which the interest is placed into a trust or other legally enforceable agreement with characteristics that are equivalent to an irrevocable split interest agreement and transfers the resources to an intermediary.
Blending (blended)	GASB-14	The method of reporting the financial data of a component unit that presents the component unit's balances and transactions in a manner similar to the presentation of the balances and transactions of the primary government.
Book entry	GASB-3	A system that eliminates the need for physically transferring bearer-form paper or registering securities by using a central depository facility.
Borrower	GASB-28	A broker-dealer or other entity that transfers collateral to a governmental entity in a securities lending transaction.
Borrower rebate	GASB-28	Payments from the lender to the borrower as compensation for the use of cash collateral provided by the borrower.
Broadcaster	GASB-62	An entity or an affiliated group of entities that transmits radio or television program material.
Brokered market	GASB-72	A market in which brokers attempt to match buyers with sellers but do not stand ready to trade for their own account. In other words, brokers do not use their own capital to hold an inventory of the items for which they make a market. The broker knows the prices bid and asked by the respective parties, but each party is typically unaware of another party's price requirements. Prices of completed transactions are sometimes available. Brokered markets include electronic communication networks, in which buy and sell orders are matched, and commercial and residential real estate markets.

Item	GASB Standard[1]	Definition
Budgetary comparison schedules	GASB-34	Schedules presented as required supplementary information for the general fund and for each major special revenue fund that has a legally adopted annual budget. The budgetary comparison schedule should present both (a) the original and (b) the final appropriated budgets for the reporting period as well as (c) actual inflows, outflows, and balances, stated on the government's budgetary basis. A separate column to report the variance between the final budget and actual amounts is encouraged but not required. Governments may also report the variance between original and final budget amounts.
Business enterprise capital assets	GASB-42	Assets that are used to produce revenues by selling goods or services. They are established as, and are expected to be, a self-supporting enterprise. Revenues produced are subject to market influences. Examples include power generation and transmission and casino enterprises.
Business-type activities	GASB-34	Activities financed in whole or in part by fees charged to external parties for goods and services.
Cable television plant	GASB-62	The cable television plant required to render service to the subscriber includes the following equipment: a. *Head-end*—This includes the equipment used to receive signals of distant television or radio stations, whether directly from the transmitter or from a microwave relay system. It also includes the studio facilities required for operator-originated programming, if any. b. *Cable*—This consists of cable and amplifiers (which maintain the quality of the signal) covering the subscriber area, either on utility poles or underground.

Item	GASB Standard[1]	Definition
		c. *Drops*—These consist of the hardware that provides access to the main cable, the short length of cable that brings the signal from the main cable to the subscriber's television set, and other associated hardware, which may include a trap to block particular channels.
		d. *Converters and descramblers*—These devices are attached to the subscriber's television sets when special services are provided, such as "pay cable" or 2-way communication.
Call option	GASB-53	An option that gives its holder the right but not the obligation to purchase a financial instrument or commodity at a certain price for a period of time.
Capital and related financing activities	GASB-9	The (a) acquiring and disposing of capital assets used in providing services or producing goods, (b) borrowing money for acquiring, constructing, or improving capital assets and repaying the amounts borrowed, including interest, and (c) paying for capital assets obtained from vendors on credit.
Capital assets	GASB-34	Assets including land, improvements to land, easements, buildings, building improvements, vehicles, machinery, equipment, works of art and historical treasures, infrastructure, and all other tangible or intangible assets that are used in operations and that have initial useful lives extending beyond a single reporting period.
Capital improvement assessment	GASB-6	Increase on taxes for capital asset acquisition or construction for a specific amount of time, for specific debts for specific property owners.
Capital projects funds	GASB-54	Funds used to account for and report financial resources that are restricted, committed, or assigned to expenditure for capital outlays, including the acquisition or construction of capital facilities and other capital assets. Capital projects funds exclude those types of capital-related outflows financed by proprietary funds or for assets that will be held in trust for individuals, private organizations, or other governments.

Item	GASB Standard[1]	Definition
Capping	GASB-18	The cost of final cover expected to be applied near or after the date that the landfill stops accepting solid waste.
Carrying amount (book value)	GASB-3	The amount at which assets and liabilities are reported in the financial statements.
Cash	GASB-9	Currency.
Cash conduit	GASB-24	A grantee that transmits grantor-supplied monies to subrecipients without having administrative or direct financial involvement in the program.
Cash equivalents	GASB-9	Cash equivalents are defined as short-term, highly liquid investments that are both: a. Readily convertible to known amounts of cash. b. So near their maturity that they present insignificant risk of changes in value because of changes in interest rates.
Cash flow hedge	GASB-53	A hedge that protects against the risk of either changes in total variable cash flows or adverse changes in cash flows caused by variable prices, costs, rates, or terms that cause future prices to be uncertain.
Catastrophe	GASB-10	A conflagration, earthquake, windstorm, explosion, or similar event resulting in substantial losses *or* an unusually large number of unrelated and unexpected losses occurring in a single period.
Category A GAAP	GASB-76	Officially established accounting principles—Governmental Accounting Standards Board (GASB) Statements.
Category B GAAP	GASB-76	GASB Technical Bulletins; GASB Implementation Guides; and literature of the AICPA cleared by the GASB.
Cede	GASB-10	To transfer all or part of an insurance risk to another enterprise through reinsurance.
CFDA		Catalog of Federal Domestic Assistance

Item	GASB Standard[1]	Definition
Change in accounting estimate	GASB-62	Changes in estimates used in accounting are necessary consequences of periodic presentations of financial statements. Preparing financial statements requires estimating the effects of future events. Accounting estimates change as new events occur, as more experience is acquired or as additional information is obtained.
Change in accounting principle	GASB-62	Adoption of a generally accepted accounting principle different from the one used previously for reporting purposes.
Change in the fair value of investments	GASB-31	The difference between the fair value of investments at the beginning of the year and at the end of the year, taking into consideration investment purchases, sales, and redemptions.
Chapter 9 (U.S. Bankruptcy Code)	GASB-58	Section of the Uniform Commercial Code (UCC) intended to protect a financially distressed government from its creditors while it develops and negotiates a plan for adjusting its debts. Chapter 9 must be approved by a state prior to usage by a government. In states where Chapter 9 is not approved, other mechanisms may be used including fiscal oversight.

Item	GASB Standard[1]	Definition
Charges for services	GASB-37	*Charges for services* is the term used for a broad category of program revenues that arise from charges to customers, applicants, or others who purchase, use, or directly benefit from the goods, services, or privileges provided, or are otherwise directly affected by the services. Revenues in this category include fees charged for specific services, such as water use or garbage collection; licenses and permits, such as dog licenses, liquor licenses, and building permits; operating special assessments, such as for street cleaning or special street lighting; and any other amounts charged to service recipients. Fines and forfeitures are also included in this category because they result from direct charges to those who are otherwise directly affected by a program or service, even though they receive no *benefit*. Payments from other governments for goods or services—for example, when County A reimburses County B for boarding County A's prisoners—also should be reported in this category.
Charity Care	GASB-76 (GASB Cod Sec 1000.802)	Charity care represents health care services that are provided but never expected to result in cash flows; therefore, charity care does not qualify for recognition as revenue.
Claim (insurance entities other than public entity risk pools)	GASB-62	A demand for payment of a policy benefit because of the occurrence of an insured event, such as the death or disability of the insured; the incurrence of hospital or medical bills; the destruction or damage of property and related deaths or injuries; defects in or liens on real estate; or the occurrence of a surety loss.
Claim adjustment expenses	GASB-62	Expenses incurred in the course of investigating and settling claims. Claim adjustment expenses include any legal and adjusters' fees, and the costs of paying claims and all related expenses. Unallocated claim adjustment expenses include other costs that cannot be associated with specific claims but are related to claims paid or in the process of settlement, such as salaries and other internal costs of the pool's claims department.

Item	GASB Standard[1]	Definition
Closed amortization period (closed basis) (the opposite is an open amortization period)		A specific number of years that is counted from one date and, therefore, declines to zero with the passage of time. For example, if the amortization period initially is thirty years on a closed basis, twenty-nine years remain after the first year, twenty-eight years after the second year, and so forth. In contrast, an open amortization period (open basis) is one that begins again or is recalculated at each actuarial valuation date. Within a maximum number of years specified by law or policy (for example, thirty years), the period may increase, decrease, or remain stable.
Closed period	GASB-75	A specific number of years that is counted from one date and declines to zero with the passage of time. For example, if the recognition period initially is five years on a closed basis, four years remain after the first year, three years after the second year, and so forth.
Closed-end mutual fund	GASB-31	An SEC-registered investment company that issues a limited number of shares to investors which are then traded as an equity security on a stock exchange. See also Open-end mutual fund.
Collateral	GASB-28	The cash, securities, or letters of credit received by the lender from the borrower as protection against the borrower's failure to return the underlying securities.
Collateral investment pool	GASB-28	An agent-managed pool that for investment purposes commingles the cash collateral provided on the securities lending transactions of more than one lender.
Collective deferred outflows of resources and deferred inflows of resources related to pensions or OPEB	GASB-75	Deferred outflows of resources and deferred inflows of resources related to pensions arising from certain changes in the collective net pension or OPEB liability.

Item	GASB Standard[1]	Definition
Collective net pension liability (Collective net OPEB liability)	GASB-75	The net pension or OPEB liability for benefits provided through (1) a cost-sharing pension plan or (2) a single-employer or agent pension or OPEB plan in circumstances in which there is a special funding situation.
Collective pension or OPEB expense	GASB-75	Pension or OPEB expense arising from certain changes in the collective net pension or OPEB liability.
Collective total OPEB liability	GASB-75	The total OPEB liability for benefits provided through a defined benefit OPEB plan that is *not administered* through a trust and (a) is used to provide benefits to the employees of a primary government and its component units or (b) in which there is a special funding situation.
Collective total pension liability	GASB-73	The total pension liability for benefits provided through (a) a pension plan that is used to provide pensions to the employees of a primary government and its component units or (b) a pension plan in circumstances in which there is a special funding situation.
Commercial paper	GASB-3	An unsecured promissory note issued primarily by corporations for a specific amount and maturing on a specific day. The maximum maturity for commercial paper is 270 days, but most is sold with maturities of up to 30 days. Almost all commercial paper is rated as to credit risk by rating services.
Commitment fees (lending activities)	GASB-62	Fees charged for entering into an agreement that obligates the government to make or acquire a loan or to satisfy an obligation of the other party under a specified condition. May include fees for letters of credit and obligations to purchase a loan or group of loans.

Item	GASB Standard[1]	Definition
Committed fund balance	GASB-54	Amounts that can only be used for specific purposes pursuant to constraints imposed by formal action of the government's highest level of decision-making authority should be reported as committed fund balance. Those committed amounts cannot be used for any other purpose unless the government removes or changes the specified use by taking the same type of action (for example, legislation, resolution, ordinance) it employed to previously commit those amounts. The authorization specifying the purposes for which amounts can be used should have the consent of both the legislative and executive branches of the government, if applicable. Committed fund balance also should incorporate contractual obligations to the extent that existing resources in the fund have been specifically committed for use in satisfying those contractual requirements.
Commodity swap	GASB-53	A swap that has a variable payment based on the price or index of an underlying commodity.
Common costs (real estate)	GASB-62	Costs that relate to two or more units within a real estate project.
Companion instrument	GASB-53	The element of a hybrid instrument, such as a borrowing, that as a separate instrument would be measured on a basis other than fair value. A hybrid instrument consists of an embedded derivative instrument and a companion instrument.
Comparative financial statements	GASB-62	When a statement of net [position] and the flows statement are presented for one or more preceding periods, as well as the current period, along with notes to the financial statements for the preceding periods that are repeated to the extent that they continue to be of significance.
Compensated absences	GASB-16	Accrued vacation and sick leave (and similar absences) that will be paid in accordance with the terms and conditions of laws, regulations, and contracts based on services already rendered.

Item	GASB Standard[1]	Definition
Completed-contract method (construction contracts)	GASB-62	The completed-contract method recognizes revenue only when the contract is completed, or substantially so. Accordingly, costs of contracts in process and current billings should be accumulated, but no interim revenue or expenses should be recognized other than provisions for losses. A contract should be regarded as substantially completed if remaining costs are not significant in amount.
Component Units	GASB-14	Legally separate organizations for which the elected officials of the primary government are financially accountable. In addition, a component unit can be another organization for which the nature and significance of its relationship with a primary government is such that exclusion would cause the reporting entity's financial statements to be misleading or incomplete.
Comprehensive Annual Financial Report (CAFR)	GASB:CS-1	CAFRs are more detailed reports containing the basic financial statements and other information and are intended for users who need a broad range of information. CAFRs may include such nonfinancial information as statistical data, analytical data, demographic information, forecasts, economic and service delivery statistics, legally required data, narrative explanations, and graphic displays. It includes an introductory, financial, and statistical sections (actuarial section on postemployment benefit plans) and other combining information on funds.
Concentration of credit risk	GASB-40	The risk of loss attributed to the magnitude of a government's investment in a single issuer.

Item	GASB Standard[1]	Definition
Conduit debt	GASBI-2	Certain limited-obligation revenue bonds, certificates of participation, or similar debt instruments issued by a state or local governmental entity for the express purpose of providing capital financing for a specific third party that is not a part of the issuer's financial reporting entity. Although conduit debt obligations bear the name of the governmental issuer, the issuer has no obligation for such debt beyond the resources provided by a lease or loan with the third party on whose behalf they are issued.
Consistent critical terms method	GASB-53	A method of evaluating effectiveness by qualitative consideration of the uniformity of the significant terms of the hedgeable item with the terms of the potential hedging derivative instrument.
Contamination	GASB-83	An event or condition normally involving a substance that is deposited in, on, or around a tangible capital asset in a form or concentration that may harm people, equipment, or the environment due to the substance's radiological, chemical, biological, reactive, explosive, or mutagenic nature.
Contingency	GASB-62	An existing condition, situation, or set of circumstances involving uncertainty as to possible gain (referred to as a gain contingency) or loss (referred to as a loss contingency) to a government that will ultimately be resolved when one or more future events occur or fail to occur. Resolution of the uncertainty may confirm the acquisition of an asset or the reduction of a liability or the loss or impairment of an asset or the incurrence of a liability.

Item	GASB Standard[1]	Definition
Contingent rentals	GASB-62	The increases or decreases in lease payments that result from changes occurring subsequent to the inception of the lease in the factors (other than the passage of time) on which lease payments are based, except as provided in the following sentence. Any escalation of minimum lease payments relating to increases in construction or acquisition cost of the leased property or for increases in some measure of cost or value during the construction or pre-construction period should be excluded from contingent rentals. Lease payments that depend on a factor directly related to the future use of the leased property, such as machine hours of use or sales volume during the lease term, are contingent rentals and, accordingly, are excluded from minimum lease payments in their entirety. However, lease payments that depend on an existing index or rate, such as the consumer price index or the prime interest rate, should be included in minimum lease payments based on the index or rate existing at the inception of the lease; any increases or decreases in lease payments that result from subsequent changes in the index or rate are contingent rentals and thus affect the determination of revenue or expense/expenditure as accruable.
Contract value		The value of an unallocated contract that is determined by the insurance company in accordance with the terms of the contract.
Contribution deficiencies (excess contributions)		The difference between the annual required contributions of the employer(s) (ARC) and the employer's actual contributions in relation to the ARC (no longer utilized for general-purpose external financial reporting).
Contributions	GASB-75	Additions to a pension or OPEB plan's fiduciary net position for amounts from employers, nonemployer contributing entities (for example, state government contributions to a local government pension or OPEB plan), or employees.

Item	GASB Standard[1]	Definition
Control (of assets)	GASB-84	A government controls the assets of an activity if the government (a) holds the assets or (b) has the ability to direct the use, exchange, or employment of the assets in a manner that provides benefits to the specified or intended recipients. Restrictions from legal or other external restraints that stipulate the assets can be used only for a specific purpose do not negate a government's control of the assets.
Correction of an error	GASB-62	Changes to previously issued financial statements after discovering mathematical mistakes, mistakes in the application of accounting principles, or oversight or misuse of facts that existed at the time the financial statements were prepared.
COSO		Committee of Sponsoring Organizations
Cost approach	GASB-72	A valuation technique that reflects the amount that would be required currently to replace the service capacity of an asset (often referred to as current replacement cost).
Cost method (investments in common stock)	GASB-62	When an investor records an investment in the stock of an investee at cost and recognizes as revenue dividends received that are distributed from net accumulated earnings of the investee since the date of acquisition by the investor. The net accumulated earnings of an investee subsequent to the date of investment are recognized by the investor only to the extent distributed by the investee as dividends. Dividends received in excess of earnings subsequent to the date of investment are considered a return of investment and are recorded as reductions of cost of the investment. A series of operating losses of an investee or other factors may indicate that a decrease in value of the investment has occurred that is other than temporary and should accordingly be recognized.
Cost recovery method (insurance entities other than public entity risk pools)	GASB-62	Under the cost recovery method, premiums are recognized as revenue in an amount equal to estimated claim costs as insured events occur until the ultimate premium is reasonably estimable, and recognition of revenue is postponed until that time.

Item	GASB Standard[1]	Definition
Cost-of-living adjustments	GASB-75	Postemployment benefit changes intended to adjust benefit payments for the effects of inflation.
Costs incurred to rent real estate projects	GASB-62	Examples of such costs include costs of model units and their furnishings, rental facilities, semi-permanent signs, rental brochures, advertising, "grand openings," and rental overhead including rental salaries.
Costs INCURRED TO *SELL* REAL ESTATE Projects	GASB-62	Examples of such costs include costs of model units and their furnishings, sales facilities, sales brochures, legal fees for preparation of prospectuses, semi-permanent signs, advertising, "grand openings," and sales overhead including sales salaries.
Cost-sharing employer	GASB-75	An employer whose employees are provided with pensions or OPEB through a cost-sharing multiple-employer defined benefit pension or OPEB plan.
Cost-sharing multiple-employer defined benefit pension or OPEB plan (cost-sharing pension or OPEB plan)	GASB-75, GASB-78	A multiple-employer defined benefit pension or OPEB plan that is administered through an irrevocable trust and which the pensions or OPEB obligations to the employees of more than one employer are pooled and pensions or OPEB assets can be used to pay the benefits of the employees of any employer that provides pensions or OPEB through the pension or OPEB plan. (*Note*—As used solely in GASB-78, it is a multiple-employer defined benefit pension plan in which the pension obligations to the employees of more than one employer are pooled and pension plan assets can be used to pay the benefits of the employees of any employer that provides pensions through the pension plan.)
Counterparty	GASB-42	The party that pledges collateral or repurchase agreement securities to the government or that sells investments to or buys them for the government.

Item	GASB Standard[1]	Definition
Coverage ratio	GASB-44	A measure of the magnitude of resources available to pay the interest on and repay the principal of debt backed by pledged revenues. For each type of debt backed by pledged revenues, a coverage ratio is generally calculated by dividing gross pledged revenues or pledged revenues net of specific operating expenses by the sum of interest expenses and principal repayments.
Covered group		Plan members included in an actuarial valuation (no longer utilized for general-purpose external financial reporting).
Covered-employee payroll	GASB-75	The payroll of employees that are provided with pensions or OPEB through the pension or OPEB plan, respectively.
Covered payroll	GASB-82	The portion of compensation paid to active employees on which contributions to a pension plan are based.
CPA		Certified public accountant
Credit risk	GASB-72	The risk that a counterparty will not fulfill its obligations.
Critical term	GASB-53	A significant term of the hedgeable item and potential hedging derivative instrument that affects whether their changes in cash flows or fair values substantially offset. Examples are the notional or principal amounts, payment dates, and, in some cases, fair values at inception, indexes, rates, and options.
Current (normal) servicing fee rate (mortgage banking)	GASB-62	A servicing fee rate that is representative of servicing fee rates most commonly used in comparable servicing agreements covering similar types of mortgage loans.

Item	GASB Standard[1]	Definition
Current assets	GASB-62	For accounting and financial reporting purposes, the term *current assets* is used to designate cash and other assets or resources commonly identified as those that are reasonably expected to be realized in cash or sold or consumed within a year. Therefore, current assets generally include such resources as (a) cash available for current operations and items that are the equivalent of cash; (b) inventories of merchandise, raw materials, goods in process, finished goods, operating supplies, and ordinary maintenance material and parts; (c) trade accounts, notes, and acceptances receivable; (d) receivables from taxpayers, other governments, vendors, customers, beneficiaries, and employees, if collectible within a year; (e) installment or deferred accounts and notes receivable if they conform generally to normal trade practices and terms within the business-type activity; (f) marketable securities representing the investment of cash available for current operations; and (g) prepayments such as insurance, interest, rents, unused royalties, current paid advertising service not yet received, and operating supplies. Prepayments are not current assets in the sense that they will be converted into cash but in the sense that, if not paid in advance, they would require the use of current assets within a year. [Current assets excludes] such resources as (a) cash and claims to cash that are restricted as to withdrawal or use for other than current operations, that are designated for disbursement in the acquisition or construction of noncurrent assets, or that are segregated for the liquidation of long-term debts; (b) receivables arising from unusual transactions (such as the sale of capital assets) that are not expected to be collected within 12 months; (c) cash surrender value of life insurance policies; (d) land and other natural resources; (e) depreciable assets; and (f) long-term prepayments that are applicable to the operations of several years, or deferred charges such as bonus payments under a long-

Item	GASB Standard[1]	Definition

term lease.

Current liabilities GASB-62

Used principally to designate obligations whose liquidation is reasonably expected to require the use of existing resources properly classifiable as current assets, or the creation of other current liabilities. As a category in the statement of net [position], the classification is intended to include obligations for items that have entered into the operating cycle, such as payables incurred in the acquisition of materials and supplies to be used in providing services; collections received in advance of the performance of services; and debts that arise from operations directly related to the operating cycle, such as accruals for wages, salaries, commissions, rentals, and royalties. Other liabilities whose regular and ordinary liquidation is expected to occur within one year also are intended for inclusion, such as short-term debts arising from the acquisition of capital assets, serial maturities of long-term obligations, amounts required to be expended within one year under sinking fund provisions, and certain agency obligations arising from the collection or acceptance of cash or other assets for the account of third parties. The current liability classification also is intended to include obligations that, by their terms, are due on demand or will be due on demand within one year from the date of the financial statements, even though liquidation may not be expected within that period. It also is intended to include long-term obligations that are or will be callable by the creditor either because the debtor's violation of a provision of the debt agreement at the date of the financial statements makes the obligation callable or because the violation, if not cured within a specified grace period, will make the obligation callable. Accordingly, such callable obligations should be classified as current liabilities unless one of the following conditions is met:

Item	GASB Standard[1]	Definition
		a. The creditor has waived or subsequently lost the right to demand repayment for more than one year from the date of the financial statements.
		b. For long-term obligations containing a grace period within which the debtor may cure the violation, it is probable that the violation will be cured within that period, thus preventing the obligation from becoming callable.
Current refunding	GASB-23	Refunding transaction when the issuance of new debt immediately replaces previously outstanding issued debt.
Current value	GASB-83	The amount that would be paid if all equipment, facilities, and services included in the estimate were acquired during the current period.
Current-financial-statement-date-based measurement (remeasured amount)	GASB:CS-6	The amount assigned when an asset or liability is remeasured as of the financial statement date.
Custodial agreement	GASB-3	A written contract establishing the responsibilities of a custodian holding collateral for deposits with financial institutions, investment securities, or securities underlying repurchase agreements.
Custodial credit risk	GASB-40	The custodial credit risk for *deposits* is the risk that, in the event of the failure of a depository financial institution, a government will not be able to recover deposits or will not be able to recover collateral securities that are in the possession of an outside party. The custodial credit risk for *investments* is the risk that, in the event of the failure of the counterparty to a transaction, a government will not be able to recover the value of investment or collateral securities that are in the possession of an outside party.

Item	GASB Standard[1]	Definition
Custodial funds	GASB-84	Used to report fiduciary activities that are *not* required to be in pension (and other employee benefit) trust funds, investment trust funds, or private-purpose trust funds. The external portion of investment pools that are *not held in a trust* should be reported in a separate *external investment pool fund* column under the custodial funds classification.
Daily liquid assets	GASB-79	For purposes of GASB-79, only the following are daily liquid assets: a. Cash, including demand deposits and certificates of deposit that mature within one business day b. U.S. government securities that are direct obligations c. Securities that will mature within one business day, with maturity determined without taking into account the maturity shortening features d. Securities subject to a demand feature that is exercisable and payable within one business day e. Amounts receivable and due unconditionally within one business day on pending sales of portfolio securities.
Dealer market	GASB-72	A market in which dealers stand ready to trade (either buy or sell for their own account), providing liquidity by using their capital to hold an inventory of the items for which they make a market. Typically, bid and ask prices (representing the price at which the dealer is willing to buy and the price at which the dealer is willing to sell, respectively) are more readily available than closing prices. Over-the-counter markets (for which prices are publicly reported, for example, by the National Association of Securities Dealers Automated Quotations systems or by OTC Markets Group, Inc.) are dealer markets. The market for U.S. Treasury securities is another example of a dealer market. Dealer markets also exist for some other assets and liabilities, including other financial instruments, commodities, and physical assets (for example, used equipment).

Item	GASB Standard[1]	Definition
Debt	GASB-88	For the purposes of disclosure in notes to financial statements, debt is a liability that arises from a contractual obligation to pay cash (or other assets that may be used in lieu of payment of cash) in one or more payments to settle an amount that is fixed at the date the contractual obligation is established. For disclosure purposes, debt does not include leases (unless they are financed purchases) or accounts payable.
Debt security	GASB-31	Any security that represents a creditor relationship with an entity. It also includes (a) preferred stock that either is required to be redeemed by the issuing entity or is redeemable at the option of the investor and (b) a collateralized mortgage obligation (CMO) or other instrument that is issued in equity form but is accounted for as a nonequity instrument. However, it excludes option contracts, financial futures contracts, and forward contracts.

• Thus, the term *debt security* includes, among other items, U.S. Treasury securities, U.S. government agency securities, municipal securities, corporate bonds, convertible debt, commercial paper, negotiable certificates of deposit, securitized debt instruments (such as CMOs and real estate mortgage investment conduits—REMICs), and interest-only and principal-only strips.

• Trade accounts receivable arising from sales on credit and loans receivable arising from real estate lending activities of proprietary activities are examples of receivables that do not meet the definition of a security; thus, those receivables are not debt securities. (If, however, they have been securitized, they then meet the definition.)

Item	GASB Standard[1]	Definition
Debt service funds	GASB-54	Funds used to account for and report financial resources that are restricted, committed, or assigned to expenditure for principal and interest. Debt service funds should be used to report resources if legally mandated. Financial resources that are being accumulated for principal and interest maturing in future years also should be reported in debt service funds.
Deferred inflow(s) of resources	GASB-65 (also GASB:CS-4)	An acquisition of net assets by the government that is applicable to a future reporting period. A deferred inflow of resources has a negative effect on net position, similar to liabilities.
Deferred outflow(s) of resources	GASB-65 (also GASB:CS-4)	A consumption of net assets by the government that is applicable to a future reporting period. A deferred outflow of resources has a positive effect on net position, similar to assets.
Deferred retirement option program (DROP)	GASB-73	A program that permits an employee to elect a calculation of benefit payments based on service credits and salary, as applicable, as of the DROP entry date. The employee continues to provide service to the employer and is paid for that service by the employer after the DROP entry date; however, the pensions that would have been paid to the employee (if the employee had retired and not entered the DROP) are credited to an individual employee account within the defined benefit pension plan until the end of the DROP period.
Defined benefit pension plans (or OPEB)	GASB-75	Pension or OPEB plans that are used to provide defined benefit pensions or OPEB.

Item	*GASB Standard*[1]	*Definition*
Defined benefit pensions (or OPEB)	GASB-75, GASB-78	Pensions or OPEB for which the income or other benefits that the employee will receive at or after separation from employment are defined by the benefit terms. The pensions or OPEB may be stated as a specified dollar amount or as an amount that is calculated based on one or more factors such as age, years of service, and compensation. (*Note*— Solely as used in GASB-78, pensions for which the income or other benefits that the employee will receive at or after separation from employment are defined by the benefit terms. The pensions may be stated as a specified dollar amount or as an amount that is calculated based on one or more factors such as age, years of service, and compensation.)
Defined contribution pension plans (or OPEB)	GASB-75	Pension or OPEB plans that are used to provide defined contribution pensions or OPEB.
Defined contribution pensions (or OPEB)	GASB-75	Pensions or OPEB having terms that: (a) provide an individual account for each employee; (b) define the contributions that an employer is required to make (or the credits that it is required to provide) to an active employee's account for periods in which that employee renders service; and (c) provide that the pensions an employee will receive will depend only on the contributions (or credits) to the employee's account, actual earnings on investments of those contributions (or credits), and the effects of forfeitures of contributions (or credits) made for other employees, as well as pension plan administrative costs, that are allocated to the employee's account.

Item	GASB Standard[1]	Definition
Deflated depreciated replacement cost approach	GASB-42	With regard to accounting for impaired capital assets, this approach replicates the historical cost of the service produced. A current cost for a capital asset to replace the current level of service is estimated. This estimated current cost is depreciated to reflect the fact that the capital asset is not new, and then is deflated to convert it to historical cost dollars.
Demand bond	GASBI-1	Long-term debt issuances with demand ("put") provisions that require the issuer to repurchase the bonds upon notice from the bondholder at a price equal to the principal plus accrued interest. To assure its ability to redeem the bonds, issuers of demand bonds frequently enter into short-term standby liquidity agreements and long-term "take out" agreements.
Deposit	GASB-10	Money placed with a banking or other institution or with a person, sometimes for a specific purpose.
Deposit method (insurance entities other than public entity risk pools)	GASB-62	Under the deposit method, premiums are not recognized as revenue and claim costs are not charged to expense until the ultimate premium is reasonably estimable.
Depository institution	GASB-79	A bank, credit union, or savings institution.
Depository insurance	GASB-40	Depository insurance includes: a. Federal depository insurance funds, such as those maintained by the Federal Deposit Insurance Corporation (FDIC or FDICIA). b. State depository insurance funds. c. Multiple financial institution collateral pools that insure public deposits. In such a pool, a group of financial institutions holding public funds pledge collateral to a common pool.
Derivative instrument	GASB-53	A derivative instrument is a financial instrument or other contract that has all of the following characteristics:

Item	*GASB Standard*[1]	*Definition*
		a. *Settlement factors.* It has (1) one or more reference rates and (2) one or more notional amounts or payment provisions or both. Those terms determine the amount of the settlement or settlements and, in some cases, whether or not a settlement is required.
		b. *Leverage.* It requires no initial net investment or an initial net investment that is smaller than would be required for other types of contracts that would be expected to have a similar response to changes in market factors.
		c. *Net settlement.* Its terms require or permit net settlement, it can readily be settled net by a means outside the contract, or it provides for delivery of an asset that puts the recipient in a position not substantially different from net settlement.
Derived tax revenues	GASB-33	Assessments imposed on exchange transactions (for example, income taxes, sales taxes, and other assessments on earnings or consumption.
Deviation (Actuarial Standards of Practice)	GASB-82	As used in actuarial standards of practice, a selection of assumptions that deviate from the guidance in an actuarial standard of practice as released by the Actuarial Standards Board.
Difference	GASB-62	In an extinguishment of debt, the excess of the reacquisition price over the net carrying amount or the excess of the net carrying amount over the reacquisition price.
Direct administrative involvement	GASB-84	For fiduciary activities, a recipient government has administrative involvement if, for example, it (a) monitors secondary recipients for compliance with program-specific requirements, (b) determines eligible secondary recipients or projects, even if using grantor-established criteria, or (c) has the ability to exercise discretion in how funds are allocated. A recipient government has direct financial involvement if, for example, it finances some direct program costs because of a grantor-imposed matching requirement or is liable for disallowed costs.

Item	*GASB Standard*[1]	*Definition*
Direct borrowing	GASB-88	Borrowing directly from a lender instead of through a public placement.
Direct debt	GASB-44	The outstanding long-term debt instruments – including bonds, notes, certificates of participation, loans, and capital leases – of the government preparing the statistical section.
Direct financial involvement	GASB-84	For fiduciary activities, a government has direct financial involvement with the assets if, for example, it provides matching resources for the activities.
Direct placement	GASB-88	Issuing a debt security directly to an investor.
Direct rate	GASB-44	An amount or percentage applied to a unit of a specific revenue base by the government preparing the statistical section information— for example, a property tax rate of $1 per $1,000 of assessed property value, a sales tax rate of 5 percent of a retail sale, or a water charge of a certain amount per 100 gallons of water used.
Direct the use	GASB-84	**See USE**
Direct selling costs (cable television systems)	GASB-62	Direct selling costs include commissions, the portion of a salesperson's compensation other than commissions for obtaining new subscribers, local advertising targeted for acquisition of new subscribers, and costs of processing documents related to new subscribers acquired. Direct selling costs do not include supervisory and administrative expenses or indirect expenses, such as rent and costs of facilities.
Discount rate (investment return assumption)	GASB-75	The single rate of return that, when applied to all projected benefit payments, results in an actuarial present value of projected benefit payments equal to the total of the following:

1. The actuarial present value of benefit payments projected to be made in future periods in which:

   a. the amount of the pension plan's fiduciary net position is projected to be greater than the benefit payments that are projected to be made in that period and

Item	GASB Standard[1]	Definition
		b. pension plan assets up to that point are expected to be invested using a strategy to achieve the long-term expected rate of return, calculated using the long-term expected rate of return on pension plan investments.
		2. The actuarial present value of projected benefit payments not included in (1), calculated using the municipal bond rate.
Discount rate (as used in GASB-73)	GASB-73	A yield or index rate for 20-year tax-exempt general obligation municipal bonds with an average rating of AA/Aa or higher (or equivalent quality on another rating scale).
Discount rate (non-trust arrangements)	GASB-75	The municipal bond rate.
Discounting	GASB-10	A method used to determine the present value of a future cash payment or series of payments that takes into consideration the time value of money.
Discrete presentation (discretely presented)	GASB-14	The method of reporting financial data of component units in a column(s) separate from the financial data of the primary government. An integral part of this method of presentation is that individual component unit supporting information is required to be provided either in condensed financial statements within the notes to the reporting entity's basic financial statements or in combining statements in the basic financial statements.
Dividends to policyholders (insurance entities other than public entity risk pools)	GASB-62	Amounts distributable to policyholders of participating insurance contracts as determined by the insurer. Under various state insurance laws, dividends are apportioned to policyholders on an equitable basis. The dividend allotted to any contract often is based on the amount that the contract, as one of a class of similar contracts, has contributed to the changes in net assets available for distribution as dividends.

Item	GASB Standard[1]	Definition
Dollar purchase–reverse repurchase agreement	GASB-3	A repurchase–reverse repurchase agreement that involves the transfer of securities in which the parties agree that the securities returned usually will be of the same issuer but will not be the same certificates. Fixed coupon and yield maintenance agreements are the most common types of dollar agreements.
Dollar-offset method	GASB-53	A quantitative method of evaluating effectiveness that compares the changes in expected cash flows or fair values of the potential hedging derivative instrument with the changes in expected cash flows or fair values of the hedgeable item.
DTC	GASB:TB 87-1	Depository Trust Company
Duration	GASB-40	A measure of a debt investment's exposure to fair value changes arising from changing interest rates. It uses the present value of cash flows, weighted for those cash flows as a percentage of the investment's full price.
Embedded derivative instrument	GASB-53	A derivative instrument that is an element of a hybrid instrument. A hybrid instrument consists of a companion instrument and an embedded derivative instrument. When separated, an embedded derivative instrument, such as an interest rate swap, is measured at fair value. May be an embedded option.
Employer entity	GASB-24	The entity that employs the individuals for whom a paying entity makes on-behalf payments for fringe benefits and salaries. The employer entity may be governmental or nongovernmental.

Item	GASB Standard[1]	Definition
Employer's contributions		Contributions made in relation to the annual required contributions of the employer (ARC). An employer has made a contribution in relation to the ARC if the employer has (a) made payments of benefits directly to or on behalf of a retiree or beneficiary, (b) made premium payments to an insurer, or (c) irrevocably transferred assets to a trust, or an equivalent arrangement, in which plan assets are dedicated to providing benefits to retirees and their beneficiaries in accordance with the terms of the plan and are legally protected from creditors of the employer(s) or plan administrator (ARC is no longer utilized in general-purpose external financial reporting).
Employer-paid member contributions	GASB-82	Payments made by the employer to satisfy contribution requirements that are identified by the pension plan terms as plan member contributions. For the pension plan, these amounts are classified as plan member contributions. For the employer, these amounts are classified as employee contributions, including for determining a cost-sharing employer's proportion and deferred outflows of resources related to employer contributions subsequent to the measurement date. An employer's expense and expenditures for those amounts should be included in the salaries and wages of the period for which the contribution is assessed. If an employer makes payments to satisfy employee contribution requirements (for example, if an employer "picks up" employee contributions in connection with an election made in accordance with Internal Revenue Code Section 414(h)(2) and revenue ruling 2006-43), the employer does not include such amounts in salaries and wages of the employee. (See also "pick-ups.")
Enabling legislation	GASB-54	Authorization for a government to assess, levy, charge, or otherwise mandate payment of resources (from external resource providers) and includes a *legally enforceable* requirement that those resources be used only for the specific purposes stipulated in the legislation.

Item	GASB Standard[1]	Definition
Enterprise funds	GASB-34	Used to report any activity for which a fee is charged to external users for goods or services. Activities are *required* to be reported as enterprise funds if any one of the following criteria is met. Governments should apply each of these criteria in the context of the activity's *principal revenue sources*. a. The activity is financed with debt that is secured solely by a pledge of the net revenues from fees and charges of the activity. Debt that is secured by a pledge of net revenues from fees and charges *and* the full faith and credit of a related primary government or component unit—even if that government is not expected to make any payments—is not payable solely from fees and charges of the activity. (Some debt may be secured, in part, by a portion of its own proceeds but should be considered as payable "solely" from the revenues of the activity.) b. Laws or regulations require that the activity's costs of providing services, including capital costs (such as depreciation or debt service), be recovered with fees and charges, rather than with taxes or similar revenues. c. The pricing policies of the activity establish fees and charges designed to recover its costs, including capital costs (such as depreciation or debt service).
Entry age actuarial cost method	GASB-75	A method under which the actuarial present value of the projected benefits of each individual included in an actuarial valuation is allocated on a level basis over the earnings or service of the individual between entry age and assumed exit age(s). The portion of this actuarial present value allocated to a valuation year is called the *normal cost*. The portion of this actuarial present value not provided for at a valuation date by the actuarial present value of future normal costs is called the *actuarial accrued liability*.

Item	GASB Standard[1]	Definition
Equity interest	GASB-14	A financial interest in a joint venture evidenced by the ownership of shares of the joint venture's stock or by otherwise having an explicit, measurable right to the net resources of the joint venture that is usually based on an investment of financial or capital resources by a participating government. A majority equity interest is an investment in the majority of the ownership of the entity.
Equity method (investment in common stock)	GASB-62	When an investor initially records an investment in the stock of an investee at cost and adjusts the carrying amount of the investment to recognize the investor's share of the earnings or losses of the investee after the date of acquisition. The amount of the adjustment is included in the determination of the changes in net assets by the investor. Such amount reflects adjustments including adjustments to eliminate inter-entity gains and losses, and to amortize, if appropriate, any difference between investor cost and underlying equity in net assets of the investee at the date of investment. The investment of an investor is also adjusted to reflect the investor's share of changes in the investee's capital. Dividends received from an investee reduce the carrying amount of the investment. A series of operating losses of an investee or other factors may indicate that a decrease in value of the investment has occurred that is other than temporary and that should be recognized even though the decrease in value is in excess of what would otherwise be recognized by application of the equity method. The equity method of accounting for an investment in common stock should be followed by a government whose investment in voting stock gives it the ability to exercise significant influence over operating and financial policies of an investee even though the government holds 50 percent or less of the voting stock.

Item	GASB Standard[1]	Definition
Equity security	GASB-31	Any security that represents an ownership interest in an entity, including common, preferred, or other capital stock; unit investment trusts; and closed-end mutual funds. However, the term *equity security* does not include convertible debt or preferred stock that either is required to be redeemed by the issuing entity or is redeemable at the option of the investor.
Equivalent arrangement	GASB-84	For the purposes of implementing GASB-84 only, one that, although not a trust by name, has the same characteristics required of a trust: (a) assets are dedicated to providing benefits to recipients in accordance with the benefit terms and (b) assets are legally protected from the creditors of the government that is acting as a fiduciary.
Equivalent single amortization period		The weighted average of all amortization periods used when components of the total unfunded actuarial accrued liability are separately amortized and the average is calculated in accordance with the parameters (No longer utilized in general-purpose external financial reporting).
Escheat (abandoned) property	GASB-21	The reversion of property to a governmental entity in the absence of legal claimants or heirs. The laws of many governmental entities provide that a rightful owner or heir can reclaim escheat property into perpetuity, provided the claimant can establish his or her right to the property. This does not necessarily mean that governments hold all escheat property into perpetuity. Because large portions of escheat property are never reclaimed, most governments use some of the property to help finance either their general or specific operations.

Item	*GASB Standard*[1]	*Definition*
Estimated actual value of taxable property	GASB-44	The fair value of taxable real or personal property or a surrogate measure of fair value if actual fair value information is not available. In practice, fair value is often referred to as *market value*. The estimated actual value of taxable property may be determined in a variety of manners, such as through a system that tracks changes in market values by monitoring property sales or by dividing the assessed value of property by an assumed assessment percentage.
Estimated economic life of leased property	GASB-62	The estimated remaining period during which the property is expected to be economically usable by one or more users, with normal repairs and maintenance, for the purpose for which it was intended at the inception of the lease, without limitation by the lease term.
Estimated residual value of leased property	GASB-62	The estimated fair value of the leased property at the end of the lease term.
Excess insurance (insurer)	GASB-10	The transfer of risk of loss from one party (the insured) to another (the excess insurer) in which the excess insurer provides insurance (as defined in this glossary) in excess of a certain, typically large amount. For example, a public entity risk pool may purchase excess insurance to transfer risk of aggregate losses above $5 million by its pool participants.
Exchange-like transaction	GASB-33	Transactions between a government and another party(ies) where the values may not be equal or the direct benefits of the exchange may not be exclusive to the parties to the exchange. These tend to be licenses, permits. or similar documents.
Exchange (or exchange transaction)	GASB-62	A reciprocal transfer between a government and another entity that results in the government acquiring assets or services or satisfying liabilities by surrendering other assets or services or incurring other obligations.
Exchange market	GASB-72	A market in which closing prices are both readily available and generally representative of fair value. An example of such a market is the New York Stock Exchange.

Item	GASB Standard[1]	Definition
Exit price	GASB-72	The price that is received to sell an asset or paid to transfer a liability.
Expected cash flow technique	GASB-72	The probability-weighted average (that is, mean of the distribution) of possible future cash flows.
Expected transaction	GASB-53	A transaction that is probable of occurring that exposes a government to the risk of adverse changes in cash flows or fair values. An expected transaction also may be a firm commitment—a binding agreement for the exchange of a specified quantity of resources at a specified price on a specified future date or dates.
External investment pool	GASB-31	An arrangement that commingles (pools) the moneys of more than one legally separate entity and invests, on the participants' behalf, in an investment portfolio; one or more of the participants is not part of the sponsor's reporting entity. An external investment pool can be sponsored by an individual government, jointly by more than one government, or by a nongovernmental entity. An investment pool that is sponsored by an individual state or local government is an external investment pool if it includes participation by a legally separate entity that is not part of the same reporting entity as the sponsoring government. If a government-sponsored pool includes only the primary government and its component units, it is an internal investment pool and not an external investment pool. (See also "qualified external investment pool.")

Item	GASB Standard[1]	Definition
Extinguishment of debt	GASB-62	Using financial resources that did not arise from debt proceeds, the debtor pays the creditor and is relieved of all its obligations with respect to the debt. This includes the debtor's reacquisition of its outstanding debt securities in the public securities markets, regardless of whether the securities are cancelled or held as so-called treasury bonds. The debtor is legally released from being the primary obligor under the debt, either judicially or by the creditor, and it is probable that the debtor will not be required to make future payments with respect to that debt under any guarantees.
Extraordinary items	GASB-34	Transactions or other events that are both unusual in nature and infrequent in occurrence *not within the control of management.*
Fair value	GASB-72	The price that would be received to sell an asset or paid to transfer a liability in an orderly transaction between market participants at the measurement date.
Fair Value (*caution:* real estate only)	GASB-62	The amount in cash or cash equivalent value of other consideration that a real estate parcel would yield in a current sale between a willing buyer and a willing seller (selling price), that is, other than in a forced or liquidation sale. The fair value of a parcel is affected by its physical characteristics, its probable ultimate use, and the time required for the buyer to make such use of the property considering access, development plans, zoning restrictions, and market absorption factors.
Fair Value Hedge	GASB-53	A hedge that protects against the risk of either total changes in fair value or adverse changes in fair value caused by fixed terms, rates, or prices.
Fair value of the leased property	GASB-62	The price for which the property could be sold in an arm's-length transaction between willing parties, that is, other than in a forced or liquidation sale. The following are examples of the determination of fair value:

Item	GASB Standard[1]	Definition
		a. The fair value of the property at the inception of the lease, in some cases, will be its normal selling price, reflecting any volume or trade discounts that may be applicable. However, the determination of fair value should be made in light of market conditions prevailing at the time, which may indicate that the fair value of the property is less than the normal selling price and, in some instances, less than the cost of the property.
		b. The fair value of the property at the inception of the lease, in some cases, will be its cost, reflecting any volume or trade discounts that may be applicable. However, when there has been a significant lapse of time between the acquisition of the property by the lessor and the inception of the lease, the determination of fair value should be made in light of market conditions prevailing at the inception of the lease, which may indicate that the fair value of the property is greater or less than its cost or carrying amount, if different.
Federal Deposit Insurance Corporation (FDIC or FDICIA)	GASB-40	A corporation created by the federal government that insures deposits in banks and savings associations.
Federal Home Loan Mortgage Corporation (FHLMC) (Freddie Mac) (mortgage banking)	GASB-62	FHLMC is a private corporation authorized by Congress to assist in the development and maintenance of a secondary market in conventional residential mortgages. FHLMC purchases mortgage loans and sells mortgages principally through mortgage participation certificates (PCs) representing an undivided interest in a group of conventional mortgages. FHLMC guarantees the timely payment of interest and the collection of principal on the PCs.

Item	GASB Standard[1]	Definition
Federal National Mortgage Association (FNMA) (Fannie Mae) (mortgage banking)	GASB-62	FNMA is an investor-owned corporation established by Congress to support the secondary mortgage loan market by purchasing mortgage loans when other investor resources are limited and selling mortgage loans when other investor resources are available.
Fiduciary Activity	GASB-84	For activities other than fiduciary component units or pension or OPEB arrangements that are not component units, when *all of the following* criteria are met: the assets associated with the activity are controlled by the government; the assets associated with the activity are *not* derived *either* solely from the government's own source revenues *or* from government-mandated nonexchange transactions or voluntary nonexchange transactions with the exception of pass-through grants for which the government does *not* have administrative or direct financial involvement; the assets associated with the activity have *one or more* of the following characteristics: the assets are (a) administered through a trust agreement or equivalent arrangement in which the government itself is *not* a beneficiary, (b) dedicated to providing benefits to recipients in accordance with the benefit terms , and (c) legally protected from the creditors of the government, the assets are for the benefit of individuals and the government does *not* have administrative involvement with the assets or direct financial involvement over the assets. In addition, the assets are *not* derived from the government's provision of goods or services to those individuals, the assets are for the benefit of organizations or other governments that are *not* part of the financial reporting entity and the assets are *not* derived from the government's provisions of goods or services to those organizations or other governments.

Item	GASB Standard[1]	Definition
Fiduciary Component Unit	GASB-84	An organization that meets the component unit criteria and is either a pension or an OPEB plan administered through a trust or a circumstance in which assets that are *not* part of the reporting entity are accumulated for pensions or OPEB. In determining whether legally separate entities are component units, a primary government is considered to have a financial burden if it is legally obligated or has otherwise assumed the obligation to make contributions to the pension or OPEB plan. A component unit that is not a pension or OPEB arrangement is also a fiduciary activity if the assets have one or more of the following characteristics: The assets are administered through a trust or equivalent arrangement in which the government itself is not a beneficiary, dedicated to providing benefits to recipients in accordance with benefit terms and legally protected from the creditors of the government, *or* the assets are for the benefit of individuals and the government does not have administrative involvement with the assets or direct financial involvement with the assets, nor are the assets derived from the government's provision of goods or services to those individuals, or finally, the assets are for the benefit of organizations or other governments not part of the reporting entity, nor are the assets derived from the provisions of goods or services to those organizations or other governments.
Fiduciary Funds (and similar component units)	GASB-34	Funds consisting of pension (and other employee benefit trust funds, investment trust funds, private-purpose trust funds and agency funds. The funds are used to report assets held in a trustee or an agency capacity for others and therefore cannot be used to support the government's own programs.
Final budget	GASB-34	The original budget adjusted by all reserves, transfers, allocations, supplemental appropriations, and other legally authorized legislative and executive changes applicable to the fiscal year, whenever signed into law or otherwise legally authorized.

Item	GASB Standard[1]	Definition
Financial accountability (financially accountable)	GASB-14	The level of accountability that exists if a primary government appoints a voting majority of an organization's governing board *and* is either able to impose its will on that organization or there is a potential for the organization to provide specific financial benefits to, or impose specific financial burdens on, the primary government. A primary government may also be financially accountable for governmental organizations with a separately elected governing board, a governing board appointed by another government, or a jointly appointed board that is fiscally dependent on the primary government.
Financial asset	GASB-72	Cash, evidence of ownership interest in an entity, or a contract that conveys to one entity a right to do either of the following: a. Receive cash or another financial instrument from a second entity. b. Exchange other financial instruments on potentially favorable terms with the second entity (for example, an option).
Financial benefit	GASB-14	Legal entitlement to, or the ability to otherwise access, the resources of an organization.
Financial burden	GASB-14	An obligation, legal or otherwise, to finance the deficits of, or provide financial support to, an organization; an obligation in some manner for the debt of an organization.
Financial instrument	GASB-72	A financial instrument is cash, evidence of an ownership interest in an entity, or a contract that both: • Imposes on one entity a contractual obligation to deliver cash or another financial instrument to a second entity or exchange other financial instruments on potentially unfavorable terms with the second entity (for example, an option). • Conveys to that second entity a contractual right to receive cash or another financial instrument from the first entity or to exchange other financial instruments on potentially favorable terms with the first entity (for example, an option).

Item	*GASB Standard*[1]	*Definition*
Financial liability	GASB-72	A contract that imposes on one entity an obligation to do either of the following: a. Deliver cash or another financial instrument to a second entity b. Exchange other financial instruments on potentially unfavorable terms with the second entity (for example, an option).
Financial reporting entity	GASB-14	A primary government, organizations for which the primary government is financially accountable, and other organizations for which the nature and significance of their relationship with the primary government are such that exclusion would cause the reporting entity's financial statements to be misleading or incomplete. The nucleus of a financial reporting entity usually is a primary government. However, a governmental organization other than a primary government (such as a component unit, a joint venture, a jointly governed organization, or other stand-alone government) serves as the nucleus for its own reporting entity when it issues separate financial statements.
Fiscal accountability	GASB-34	Compliance with public decisions concerning the raising and spending of public funds within a reporting period.
Fiscal funding clause (lease)	NCGA-5	Provision in a lease that allows a cancellation if a governing body does not appropriate funds to pay for a lease in a given period.
Fiscally independent / fiscally dependent government	GASB-14	A government is fiscally *independent* if it can (a) determine its budget without another government having the substantive authority to approve and modify that budget, (b) levy taxes or set rates or charges without substantive approval by another government, and (c) issue bonded debt without substantive approval by another government. A government is fiscally *dependent* if it is unable to complete one or more of these procedures without the substantive approval of another government.

Item	GASB Standard[1]	Definition
Fixed coupon repurchase—reverse repurchase agreement	GASB-3	A dollar repurchase—reverse repurchase agreement in which the parties agree that the securities returned will have the same stated interest rate as, and maturities similar to, the securities transferred.
Foreign currency risk	GASB-53	The risk that changes in exchange rates will adversely affect the cash flows or fair value of a transaction.
Foreign currency transactions	GASB-62	Transactions whose terms are denominated in a currency other than the U.S. dollar. Foreign currency transactions arise when a government (a) buys or sells on credit goods or services whose prices are denominated in a foreign currency, (b) borrows or lends resources and the amounts payable or receivable are denominated in a foreign currency, or (c) for other reasons, acquires or disposes of assets, or incurs or settles liabilities denominated in a foreign currency.
Form over substance	GASB-56	Consideration of the underlying economic effect of a transaction, which may be different than the legal justification or organization of a transaction.
Forward contract	GASB-53	A contractual agreement to buy or sell a security, commodity, foreign currency, or other financial instrument, at a certain future date for a specific price. An agreement with a supplier to purchase a quantity of heating oil at a certain future time, for a certain price, and a certain quantity is an example of a forward contract. Forward contracts are not securities and are not exchange-traded. Some forward contracts, rather than taking or making delivery of the commodity or financial instrument, may be settled by a cash payment that is equal to the fair value of the contract.

Item	GASB Standard[1]	Definition
Frozen attained age actuarial cost method		A method under which the excess of the Actuarial Present Value of Projected Benefits of the group included in an Actuarial Valuation, over the sum of the Actuarial Value of Assets plus the Unfunded Frozen Actuarial Accrued Liability, is allocated on a level basis over the earnings or service of the group between the valuation date and assumed exit. This allocation is performed for the group as a whole, not as a sum of individual allocations. The Unfunded Frozen Actuarial Accrued Liability is determined using the Unit Credit Actuarial Cost Method. The portion of this Actuarial Present Value allocated to a valuation year is called the Normal Cost (No longer utilized in general-purpose external financial reporting).
Frozen entry age actuarial cost method		A method under which the excess of the Actuarial Present Value of Projected Benefits of the group included in an Actuarial Valuation, over the sum of the Actuarial Value of Assets plus the Unfunded Frozen Actuarial Accrued Liability, is allocated on a level basis over the earnings or service of the group between the valuation date and assumed exit. This allocation is performed for the group as a whole, not as a sum of individual allocations. The Frozen Actuarial Accrued Liability is determined using the Entry Age Actuarial Cost Method. The portion of this Actuarial Present Value allocated to a valuation year is called the Normal Cost (No longer utilized in general-purpose external financial reporting).
Fund balance	GASB-54	In a governmental fund, the residual of assets, less liabilities and deferred inflows of resources (if applicable). Fund balance has five components: nonspendable, restricted, committed, assigned, and unassigned.

Item	GASB Standard[1]	Definition
Fund financial statements	GASB-34	Display of information about major funds individually and nonmajor funds in the aggregate for governmental and enterprise funds. Fiduciary statements should include financial information for fiduciary funds and similar component units. Each of the three fund categories should be reported using the measurement focus and basis of accounting required for that category.
Funded ratio		The actuarial value of assets expressed as a percentage of the actuarial accrued liability (No longer utilized in general-purpose external financial reporting).
Funding excess		The excess of the actuarial value of assets over the actuarial accrued liability (No longer utilized in general-purpose external financial reporting).
Funding policy		The program for the amounts and timing of contributions to be made by plan members, employer(s), and other contributing entities (for example, state government contributions to a local government plan) to provide the benefits specified by an OPEB plan (No longer utilized in general-purpose external financial reporting).
Futures contract	GASB-53	An exchange-traded security to buy or sell a security, commodity, foreign currency, or other financial instrument at a certain future date for a specific price. A futures contract obligates a buyer to purchase the commodity or financial instrument and a seller to sell it, unless an offsetting contract is entered into to offset one's obligation. The resources or obligations acquired through these contracts are usually terminated by entering into offsetting contracts.
GAAP		Generally accepted accounting principles
GAAS		Generally accepted auditing standards
GAGAS		Generally accepted government auditing standards
GAN		Grant anticipation note
GAO		General accountability office
GASB		Governmental Accounting Standards Board

Item	GASB Standard[1]	Definition
GASB *Implementation Guides*	GASB-76	GASB Implementation Guides are used to provide guidance that is limited to clarifying, explaining, or elaborating on GASB Statements (or GASB Interpretations). GASB Implementation Guides provide the GASB with a mechanism to address a wide range of detailed issues in a single document.
GASB *Interpretations*	GASB-76	GASB Interpretations provide a means for the Board to clarify, explain, or elaborate on GASB Statements as an aid to understanding those Statements. (GASB concluded in GASB-76 that GASB Interpretations are no longer needed).
GASB *Statements*	GASB-76	The primary communication method for accounting and financial reporting standards for state and local governmental entities. GASB Statements meet a fundamental need in the application of GAAP.
GASB *Technical Bulletins*	GASB-76	GASB Technical Bulletins provide a means to (a) issue timely guidance to clarify, explain, or elaborate on GASB Statements and (b) address areas not directly covered by GASB Statements. GASB Technical Bulletins can be subjected to a shorter period of broad public exposure than proposed Statements and are issued when a majority of the Board does not object to their issuance.
Gaming (Governmental Gaming)	GASB-76 (Cod. Sec. 1000.811)	Gaming includes activities in which a gaming entity participates in games of chance with customers, with both the gaming entity and the customer having the chance to win or lose money or other items of economic value based on the outcome of the game (commonly referred to as banked games). Such activities are referred to as gaming activities. Examples of games that typically are played as banked games include, but are not limited to, table games, machines, keno, bingo, and sports and non-pari-mutuel race betting.
General Fund	GASB-54	The primary operating fund of a government. The General Fund accounts for and reports all financial resources not accounted for and reported in another fund.

Item	GASB Standard[1]	Definition
General obligation debt	GASB-6	Debt paid by and secured by general taxation, generally income or property taxation. The full faith and credit of the government secures the debt.
General purpose external financial reporting	GASB:CS-3	A means of communicating financial information to meet the common information needs of the primary users of a government's financial report.
General purpose government	GASB-34	States, cities, counties, towns and villages (and so on).
General revenues	GASB-34	All revenues are *general revenues* unless they are required to be reported as program revenues. All taxes, even those that are levied for a specific purpose, are general revenues and should be reported by type of tax—for example, sales tax, property tax, franchise tax, income tax. All other nontax revenues (including interest, grants, and contributions) that do not meet the criteria to be reported as program revenues should also be reported as general revenues. General revenues should be reported after total net expense of the government's functions.
GIC		Guaranteed investment contract.
Going concern	GASB-56	Significant information that is available raising doubts whether a legally separate entity can continue to meet its obligations as they become due without substantial disposal of assets outside the ordinary course of business, restructuring of operations and debts, oversight of a financial assistance, oversight or review board or similar intervention.
Government	GASB-76 (Cod. Sec. 1000.801)	Public corporations and bodies corporate and politic [are governmental entities]. Other entities are governmental entities if they have one or more of the following characteristics: • Popular election of officers or appointment (or approval) of a controlling majority of the members of the entity's governing body by officials of one or more state or local governments • The potential for unilateral dissolution by a government with the net assets reverting to a government

Item	GASB Standard[1]	Definition
		• The power to enact and enforce a tax levy. Furthermore, entities are presumed to be governmental if they have the ability to issue directly (rather than through a state or municipal authority) debt that pays interest exempt from federal taxation. However, entities possessing only that ability (to issue tax-exempt debt) and none of the other governmental characteristics may rebut the presumption that they are governmental if their determination is supported by compelling, relevant evidence.
Government acquisitions	GASB-69	A government combination in which a government acquires another entity, or the operations of another entity, in exchange for significant consideration. The consideration provided should be significant in relation to the assets and liabilities acquired. The acquired entity or operation becomes part of the acquiring government's legally separate entity.
Government Combinations	GASB-69	A variety of arrangements including mergers and acquisitions. Government combinations also include transfers of operations that do not constitute entire legally separate entities and in which no significant consideration is exchanged. Transfers of operations may be present in shared service arrangements, reorganizations, redistricting, annexations, and arrangements in which an operation is transferred to a new government created to provide those services.
Government mergers	GASB-69	A government merger is a government combination of legally separate entities in which no significant consideration is exchanged and either a. Two or more governments (or one or more governments and one or more nongovernmental entities) cease to exist as legally separate entities and are combined to form one or more new governments; or

Item	GASB Standard[1]	Definition
		b. One or more legally separate governments or nongovernmental entities cease to exist and their operations are absorbed into, and provided by, one or more continuing governments.
Government National Mortgage Association (GNMA) (Ginnie Mae) (mortgage banking)	GASB-62	GNMA is a U.S. governmental agency that guarantees certain types of securities (mortgage-backed securities) and provides resources for and administers certain types of low-income housing assistance programs.
Governmental capital assets	GASB-42	Assets that directly or indirectly are used in providing services that are not directly associated with fees or other revenues. Examples include roads, bridges, schools, and equipment used for fire protection.
Governmental funds	GASB-34	Funds (emphasizing major funds) consisting of the General Fund, Special Revenue Funds, Capital Projects Funds, Debt Service Funds and Permanent Funds, as applicable. The funds focus primarily on the sources, uses, and balances of current financial resources and often has a budgetary orientation.
Government-mandated nonexchange transactions	GASB-33	When a government at one level provides resources to a government at another level and requires the recipient to use the resources for a specific purpose (for example, federal programs that state or local governments are mandated to perform).
Government-wide financial statements	GASB-34	Display of information about the reporting government as a whole, except for its fiduciary activities. The statements should include separate columns for the governmental and business-type activities of the primary government as well as for its component units. Government-wide financial statements should be prepared using the economic resources measurement focus and the accrual basis of accounting. They consist of a statement of net [position] and a statement of activities.

Item	GASB Standard[1]	Definition
Grants and other financial assistance	GASB-24	Transactions in which one governmental entity transfers cash or other items of value to (or incurs a liability for) another governmental entity, an individual, or an organization as a means of sharing program costs, subsidizing other governments or entities, or otherwise reallocating resources to the recipients.
Group insurance (insurance entities other than public entity risk pools)	GASB-62	Insurance protecting a group of persons, usually employees of an entity and their dependents. A single insurance contract is issued to their employer or other representative of the group. Individual certificates often are given to each insured individual or family unit. The insurance usually has an annual renewable contract period, although the insurer may guarantee premium rates for two or three years. Adjustments to premiums relating to the actual experience of the group of insured persons are common.
Hazardous wastes or hazardous substances	GASB-49	Wastes and substances that are toxic, corrosive, ignitable, explosive, or chemically reactive, or appear on special U.S. Environmental Protection Agency lists. This includes wastes and substances listed in 33 U.S.C. § 2701(23), and 42 U.S.C. § 6903(5) and § 9601(14). The definition of hazardous *substance* under the Superfund law is broader than the definition of hazardous *wastes* under RCRA. As used in this Statement, the terms *hazardous waste* and *hazardous substance* also include materials designated by state environmental regulators.
Healthcare cost trend rates	GASB-74	The rates of change per capita health claims over time as a result of such factors such as medical inflation, utilization of health care services, plan design, and technological developments.
Hedge accounting	GASB-53	The financial reporting treatment for hedging derivative instruments that requires that the changes in fair value of hedging derivative instruments be reported as either deferred inflows or deferred outflows.

Item	GASB Standard[1]	Definition
Hedgeable item	GASB-53	An asset or liability, or expected transaction that may be associated with a potential hedging derivative instrument.
Hedging derivative instrument	GASB-53	A derivative instrument that is associated with a hedgeable item and significantly reduces an identified financial risk by substantially offsetting changes in cash flows or fair values of the hedgeable item.
Highest and best use	GASB-72	The use of a nonfinancial asset by market participants that maximizes the value of the asset or the group of assets and liabilities within which the asset is used.
Historical cost	GASB:CS-6	The price paid to acquire an asset or the amount received pursuant to the incurrence of a liability in an actual exchange transaction.
Hybrid instrument	GASB-53	An instrument that is composed of an embedded derivative instrument and a companion instrument.
Hypothetical derivative instrument	GASB-53	An assumed derivative instrument designed to have terms that exactly match the critical terms of the hedged item, other than its maturity date, which would be the same as that of the potential hedging derivative instrument.
Immediate family(ies) (related parties)	GASB-62	Family members whom an elected or appointed official or a member of management might influence or by whom they might be influenced because of the family relationship.
Imposed nonexchange revenues	GASB-33	Assessments imposed on nongovernmental entities, including individuals, other than assessments on exchange transactions (for example, property taxes and fines).
Imposition of will (impose its will)	GASB-14	The ability to significantly influence the programs, projects, activities, or level of services performed or provided by an organization.

Item	GASB Standard[1]	Definition
Inactive employees	GASB-75	Individuals no longer employed by an employer in the pension or OPEB plan or the beneficiaries of those individuals. Inactive employees include individuals who have accumulated benefits under the terms of a pension or OPEB plan but are not yet receiving benefits and individuals currently receiving benefits.
Inactive plan members	GASB-74	Employees no longer in active service (or their beneficiaries) who have accumulated benefits under the terms of an OPEB plan.
Inception of the lease	GASB-62	The date of the lease agreement or commitment, if earlier. For purposes of this definition, a commitment should be in writing, signed by the parties in interest to the transaction, and should specifically set forth the principal provisions of the transaction. If any of the principal provisions are yet to be negotiated, such a preliminary agreement or commitment does not qualify for purposes of this definition.
Incidental operations	GASB-62	Revenue-producing activities engaged in during the holding or development period to reduce the cost of developing the property for its intended use, as distinguished from activities designed to generate income or a return from the use of the property.
Income approach	GASB-72	A valuation technique that converts future amounts (for example, cash flows or income and expenses) to a single current (discounted) amount.
Income distributions	GASB-28	Interest, dividends, stock splits, and other distributions made by an issuer of securities. Income distributions on underlying securities are payable from the borrower to the lender, and income distributions on collateral securities are payable from the lender to the borrower.

Item	GASB Standard[1]	Definition
Incremental costs of incidental operations	GASB-62	Costs that would not be incurred except in relation to the conduct of incidental operations. Interest, insurance, security, and similar costs that would be incurred during the development of a real estate project regardless of whether incidental operations were conducted are not incremental costs.
Incremental direct costs (lending activities)	GASB-62	Costs to originate a loan that (a) result directly from and are essential to the lending transaction and (b) would not have been incurred by the lender had that lending transaction not occurred.
Incremental revenues from incidental operations	GASB-62	Revenues that would not be produced except in relation to the conduct of incidental operations.
Incurred but not reported claims (IBNR)	GASB-62	Claims relating to insured events that have occurred but have not yet been reported to the insurer or reinsurer as of the date of the financial statements. IBNR claims include (a) known loss events that are expected to later be presented as claims, (b) unknown loss events that are expected to become claims, and (c) expected future development on claims already reported.
Incurred claims	GASB-10	Claims (losses) paid or unpaid for which the entity has become liable.
Indemnification	GASB-28	A securities lending agent's (or other agent's) guarantee that it will protect the lender from certain losses.
Indirect expenses	GASB-34	Expenses that are not program-specific and are usually allocated based upon a systematic and rational formula.

Item	GASB Standard[1]	Definition
Indirect project costs	GASB-62	Costs incurred after the acquisition of the property, such as construction administration (for example, the costs associated with a field office at a project site and the administrative personnel that staff the office), legal fees, and various office costs, that clearly relate to projects under development or construction. Examples of office costs that may be considered indirect project costs are cost accounting, design, and other departments providing services that are clearly related to real estate projects.
Individual investment accounts	GASB-31	An investment service provided by a governmental entity for other, legally separate entities that are not part of the same reporting entity. With individual investment accounts, specific investments are acquired for individual entities and the income from and changes in the value of those investments affect only the entity for which they were acquired.
Inflows of resources	GASB-65 (also GASB:CS-4)	An acquisition of net position by the government that is applicable to the reporting period (revenues).
Infrastructure (or infrastructure assets)	GASB-34	Long-lived capital assets that normally are stationary in nature and normally can be preserved for a significantly greater number of years than most capital assets. Examples of infrastructure assets include roads, bridges, tunnels, drainage systems, water and sewer systems, dams, and lighting systems. Buildings, except those that are an ancillary part of a network of infrastructure assets, should not be considered infrastructure assets.

Item	GASB Standard[1]	Definition
Initial direct costs (lease)	GASB-62	Only those costs incurred by the lessor that are (1) costs to originate a lease incurred in transactions with independent third parties that (a) result directly from and are essential to acquire that lease and (b) would not have been incurred had that leasing transaction not occurred and (2) certain costs directly related to specified activities performed by the lessor for that lease. Those activities are evaluating the prospective lessee's financial condition; evaluating and recording guarantees, collateral, and other security arrangements; negotiating lease terms; preparing and processing lease documents; and closing the transaction. The costs directly related to those activities should include only that portion of the employees' total compensation and payroll-related fringe benefits directly related to time spent performing those activities for that lease and other costs related to those activities that would not have been incurred but for that lease. Initial direct costs should not include costs related to activities performed by the lessor for advertising, soliciting potential lessees, servicing existing leases, and other ancillary activities related to establishing and monitoring credit policies, supervision, and administration. Initial direct costs should not include administrative costs, rent, depreciation, any other occupancy and equipment costs and employees' compensation and fringe benefits related to activities described in the previous sentence, unsuccessful origination efforts, and idle time.
Initial-transaction date-based measurement (initial amount)	GASB:CS-6	The transaction price or amount assigned when an asset was acquired or a liability was incurred, including subsequent modifications to that price or amount that are derived from the amount at which the asset or liability was initially reported.
Inputs	GASB-72	The assumptions that market participants would use when pricing an asset or liability, including assumptions about risk, such as the following:

Item	GASB Standard[1]	Definition
		a. The risk inherent in a particular valuation technique used to measure fair value (such as a pricing model); and
		b. The risk inherent in the inputs to the valuation technique.
		Inputs may be observable or unobservable.
In-substance assignment	GASB-64	An in-substance assignment occurs when all of the following criteria are met: • The original swap counterparty, or the swap counterparty's credit support provider, is replaced. • The original swap agreement is ended, and the replacement swap agreement is entered into on the same date. • The terms that affect changes in fair values and cash flows in the original and replacement swap agreements are identical. These terms include, but are not limited to, notional amounts; terms to maturity; variable payment terms; reference rates; time intervals; fixed-rate payments; frequencies of rate resets; payment dates; and options, such as floors and caps. • Any difference between the original swap agreement's exit price and the replacement swap's entry price is attributable to the original swap agreement's exit price being based on a computation specifically permitted under the original swap agreement. Exit price represents the payment made or received as a result of terminating the original swap. Entry price represents the payment made or received as a result of entering into a replacement swap.
In-substance defeasance	GASB-7	When debt is considered defeased for accounting and financial reporting purposes, even though a legal defeasance has not occurred.

Item	GASB Standard[1]	Definition
Insurance	GASB-10	The transfer of risk of loss from one party (the insured) to another party (the insurer) in which the insurer promises (usually specified in a written contract) to pay the insured (or others on the insured's behalf) an amount of money (or services, or both) for economic losses sustained from an unexpected (accidental) event during a period of time for which the insured makes a premium payment to the insurer.
Insured Benefits	GASB-75	Defined benefit provisions provided through an insured plan.
Insured Plan	GASB-75	Defined benefit pension (or OPEB) plans in which benefits are financed through an arrangement where premiums are paid or other payments are made to an insurance company while employees are in active service, in return for which the insurance company unconditionally undertakes an obligation to pay the pensions (or OPEB) of those employees as defined in the pension (or OPEB) plan terms.
Intangible asset	GASB-51	An asset that possesses all of the following characteristics:
		a. Lack of physical substance. An asset may be contained in or on an item with physical substance, for example, a compact disc in the case of computer software. An asset also may be closely associated with another item that has physical substance, for example, the underlying land in the case of a right-of-way easement. These modes of containment and associated items should not be considered when determining whether or not an asset lacks physical substance.
		b. Nonfinancial nature. In the context of this Statement, an asset with a nonfinancial nature is one that is not in a monetary form similar to cash and investment securities, and it represents neither a claim or right to assets in a monetary form similar to receivables, nor a prepayment for goods or services.

Item	GASB Standard[1]	Definition
		c. Initial useful life extending beyond a single reporting period.
Interest rate implicit in a lease	GASB-62	The discount rate that, when applied to (1) the minimum lease payments, excluding that portion of the payments representing executory costs to be paid by the lessor, together with any gain thereon, and (2) the unguaranteed residual value accruing to the benefit of the lessor, causes the aggregate present value at the beginning of the lease term to be equal to the fair value of the leased property to the lessor at the inception of the lease, minus any investment tax credit retained by and expected to be realized by the lessor.
Interest rate risk	GASB-53	The risk that changes in interest rates will adversely affect the fair values of a government's financial instruments or a government's cash flows.
Interest rate swap	GASB-53	A swap that has a variable payment based on the price of an underlying interest rate or index.
Interest-earning investment contract	GASB-31	A direct contract, other than a mortgage or other loan, that a government enters into as a creditor of a financial institution, broker-dealer, investment company, insurance company, or other financial services company and for which it receives, directly or indirectly, interest payments. Interest-earning investment contracts include time deposits with financial institutions (such as certificates of deposit), repurchase agreements, and guaranteed and bank investment contracts (GICs and BICs).
Intermediary	GASB-81	The trustee, fiscal agent, government, or any other legal or natural person that is holding and administering donated resources pursuant to a split-interest agreement. For the purposes of GASB-80, an intermediary is not required to be at third party.
Internal activities (interfund transfers)	GASB-34	Transfers between funds or activities of a government during a period.

Item	GASB Standard[1]	Definition
Internal balances (interfund loans)	GASB-34	Receivables or payables between funds or activities of a government that exist at the reporting date.
Internal investment pool	GASB-31	An arrangement that commingles (pools) the moneys of more than one fund or component unit of a reporting entity. Investment pools that include participation by legally separate entities that are not part of the same reporting entity as the pool sponsor are not internal investment pools, but rather are external investment pools.
Internal reserve method (mortgage banking)	GASB-62	A method for making payments to investors for collections of principal and interest on mortgage loans by issuers of GNMA securities. An issuer electing the internal reserve method is required to deposit in a custodial account an amount equal to one month's interest on the mortgage loans that collateralize the GNMA security issued.
Internal service funds	GASB-34	Used to report any activity that provides goods or services to other funds, departments, or agencies of the primary government and its component units, or to other governments, on a cost-reimbursement basis. Internal service funds should be used only if the reporting government is the predominant participant in the activity. Otherwise, the activity should be reported as an enterprise fund.
Internally generated intangible asset	GASB-51	An intangible asset that is created or produced by the government or an entity contracted by the government, or if it is acquired from a third party but requires more than minimal incremental effort on the part of the government to begin to achieve its expected level of service capacity. Computer software is a common type of internally generated intangible asset.
In-the-money	GASB-53	In the case of a call option, an option that has a market price above its strike price. In the case of a put option, an option that has a market price below its strike price.
Intra-entity activity	GASB-34	Resource flows between a primary government and blended component units during a period.

Item	GASB Standard[1]	Definition
Intrinsic value	GASB-53	The value of an option if the option is exercised immediately. An option that has intrinsic value is in-the-money.
Inventory	GASB-62	The aggregate of those items of tangible personal property that (a) are held for sale in the ordinary course of operations, (b) are in process of production for such sale, or (c) are to be currently consumed in the production of goods or services to be available for sale. Operating materials and supplies (for example, property held for installation or use in the provision of services) of certain business-type activities usually are treated as inventory.
Investee	GASB-72	An entity that issued an equity instrument of which all or a portion is held by an investor.
Investing activities	GASB-9	Making and collecting loans and acquiring and disposing of debt or equity instruments.
Investment	GASB-72	A security or other asset that (a) a government holds primarily for the purpose of income or profit and (b) has present service capacity based solely on its ability to generate cash or to be sold to generate cash.
Investment derivative instrument	GASB-53	A derivative instrument that is entered primarily for the purpose of obtaining income or profit, or a derivative instrument that does not meet the criteria of a hedging derivative instrument.
Investment trust funds	GASB-84	Used to report the fiduciary activities from the external portion of investment pools and individual accounts that are held in a trust that are (a) administered through a trust agreement or equivalent arrangement in which the government itself is *not* a beneficiary, (b) dedicated to providing benefits to recipients in accordance with the benefit terms, and (c) legally protected from the creditors of the government.
Irrevocable Split-Interest Agreement	GASB-81	A split-interest agreement in which the donor has not reserved, or conferred to another person, the right to terminate the agreement at will and have the assets returned to the donor or a third party.

Item	GASB Standard[1]	Definition
Irrevocable trust	GASB-75	For defined benefit and defined contribution plans, where contributions from employers and nonemployer contributing entities to the (plan) and earnings on those contributions are irrevocable, where plan assets are dedicated to providing (benefits) to plan members in accordance with benefit terms and (plan) assets are legally protected from the creditors of employers, nonemployer contributing entities and the plan administrator. If the plan is a defined benefit plan, plan assets are also legally protected from creditors of the plan members.
Issuer	GASB-40	An issuer is the entity that has the authority to distribute a security or other investment. A *bond issuer* is the entity that is legally obligated to make principal and interest payments to bond holders. In the case of mutual funds, external investment pools, and other pooled investments, *issuer* refers to the entity invested in, not the investment company-manager or pool sponsor.
Joint venture	GASB-14	A legal entity or other organization that results from a contractual arrangement and that is owned, operated, or governed by two or more participants as a separate and specific activity subject to joint control, in which the participants retain (a) an ongoing financial interest or (b) an ongoing financial responsibility.
Jointly governed organizations	GASB-14	A regional government or other multi-governmental arrangement that is governed by representatives from each of the governments that create the organization, but that is not a joint venture because the participants do not retain an ongoing financial interest or responsibility.
Lead interest	GASB-81	The right (a type of beneficial interest) to all or a portion of the benefits of resources during the term of a split-interest agreement.

Item	GASB Standard[1]	Definition
Lease term	GASB-62	The fixed noncancelable term of the lease plus (1) all periods, if any, covered by bargain renewal options, (2) all periods, if any, for which failure to renew the lease imposes a penalty on the lessee in such amount that a renewal appears, at the inception of the lease, to be reasonably assured, (3) all periods, if any, covered by ordinary renewal options during which a guarantee by the lessee of the lessor's debt directly or indirectly related to the leased property is expected to be in effect or a loan from the lessee to the lessor directly or indirectly related to the leased property is expected to be outstanding, (4) all periods, if any, covered by ordinary renewal options preceding the date as of which a bargain purchase option is exercisable, and (5) all periods, if any, representing renewals or extensions of the lease at the lessor's option; however, in no case should the lease term be assumed to extend beyond the date a bargain purchase option becomes exercisable. A lease that is cancelable (a) only upon the occurrence of some remote contingency, (b) only with the permission of the lessor, (c) only if the lessee enters into a new lease with the same lessor, or (d) only if the lessee incurs a penalty in such amount that continuation of the lease appears, at inception, reasonably assured should be considered "noncancelable" for purposes of this definition.
Legal defeasance (of bonds)	GASB-7	When debt is legally satisfied based on certain provisions in the debt instrument even though the debt is not actually paid.
Legal enforceability	GASB-54	When a government can be compelled by an external party—such as citizens, public interest groups, or the judiciary—to use resources created by enabling legislation only for the purposes specified by the legislation.

Item	GASB Standard[1]	Definition
Legally responsible entity	GASB-24	For on-behalf payments for fringe benefits and salaries, the entity required by legal or contractual provisions to make the payment. Legal provisions include those arising from constitutions, charters, ordinances, resolutions, governing body orders, and intergovernmental grant or contract regulations.
Legally separate organization (separate legal standing)	GASB-14	An organization created as a body corporate or a body corporate and politic (also known as "separate body politic") or otherwise possessing similar corporate powers. An organization that has separate legal standing has an identity of its own as an "artificial person" with a personality and existence distinct from that of its creator and others.
Lender	GASB-28	A governmental entity that transfers its securities to a broker-dealer or other entity in a securities lending transaction.
Lessee's incremental borrowing rate	GASB-62	The rate that, at the inception of the lease, the lessee would have incurred to borrow over a similar term the resources necessary to purchase the leased asset.
Level 1 inputs	GASB-72	Quoted prices (unadjusted) in active markets for identical assets or liabilities that the government can access at the measurement date.
Level 2 inputs	GASB-72	Inputs other than quoted prices included within Level 1 that are observable for an asset or liability, either directly or indirectly.
Level 3 inputs	GASB-72	Unobservable inputs for an asset or liability.
Level dollar amortization method		The amount to be amortized is divided into equal dollar amounts to be paid over a given number of years; part of each payment is interest and part is principal (similar to a mortgage payment on a building). Because payroll can be expected to increase as a result of inflation, level dollar payments generally represent a decreasing percentage of payroll; in dollars adjusted for inflation, the payments can be expected to decrease over time (No longer utilized in general-purpose external financial reporting).

Item	GASB Standard[1]	Definition
Level of utilization	GASB-42	The portion of usable capacity of a capital asset being used.
Level percentage of projected payroll amortization method		Amortization payments are calculated so that they are a constant percentage of the projected payroll of active plan members over a given number of years. The dollar amount of the payments generally will increase over time as payroll increases due to inflation; in dollars adjusted for inflation, the payments can be expected to remain level.
Leverage	GASB-53	The means of enhancing changes in fair value while minimizing or eliminating an initial investment. A leveraged investment has changes in fair value that are disproportionate to the initial net investment. An unleveraged investment requires a far greater initial investment to replicate similar changes in fair values. Derivative instruments are leveraged instruments because their changes in fair value are disproportionate to the initial net investment. For example, an interest rate swap that has a notional value of $100 million is entered with no initial net investment. Thereafter, as interest rates change, the swap produces changes in fair value consistent with a $100 million fixed-rate financial instrument.
Liabilities	GASB-65 (also GASB:CS-4)	Present obligations to sacrifice resources that the government has little or no discretion to avoid.
Liability for claim adjustment expenses	GASB-62	The amount needed to provide for the estimated ultimate cost required to investigate and settle claims relating to insured events that have occurred on or before a particular date (ordinarily, the financial statement date), whether or not reported to the insurer at that date.

Item	GASB Standard[1]	Definition
Liability for unpaid claims	GASB-62	The amount needed to provide for the estimated ultimate cost of settling claims relating to insured events that have occurred on or before a particular date (ordinarily, the financial statement date). The estimated liability includes the amount of money that will be required for future payments on both (a) claims that have been reported to the insurer and (b) claims relating to insured events that have occurred but have not been reported.
Lien	GASB-33	An enforceable legal claim by a government. The date of the lien may be known as a lien date or an assessment date.
Life-contingent term	GASB-81	A term specifying that the termination of a split-interest agreement is contingent upon the occurrence of a specified event, commonly the death of either the donor or other lead interest beneficiary.
Loan commitment	GASB-53	Formal offer for a defined period of time by a lender to extend a loan to a borrower according to specified terms such as the amount of the borrowing and repayment terms, including interest rates.
Loan premium or fee	GASB-28	Payments from the borrower to the lender as compensation for the use of the underlying securities when the borrower provides securities or letters of credit as collateral.
London Interbank Offered Rate (LIBOR)	GASB-53	A daily reference rate published by the British Bankers' Association based on the interest rates at which banks offer to lend unsecured funds to other banks in the London wholesale money market (or interbank market). This is the taxable rate that the most creditworthy banks charge each other. It is a common reference rate used in derivative instruments.
Long-term obligations	GASB-62	Obligations scheduled to mature beyond one year from the date of a government's financial statements.
Maintenance costs (insurance entities other than public entity risk pools)	GASB-62	Costs associated with maintaining records relating to insurance contracts and with the processing of premium collections and commissions.

Item	*GASB Standard*[1]	*Definition*
Major fund	GASB-34	The general fund or its equivalent and any other fund where:
		a. Total assets, liabilities, revenues, or expenditures/expenses of that individual governmental or enterprise fund are at least 10 percent of the corresponding total (assets, liabilities, and so forth) for all funds of that category or type (that is, total governmental or total enterprise funds), *and*
		b. Total assets, liabilities, revenues, or expenditures/expenses of the individual governmental fund or enterprise fund are at least 5 percent of the corresponding total for all governmental and enterprise funds combined.
		In addition to funds that meet the major fund criteria, any other governmental or enterprise fund that the government's officials believe is particularly important to financial statement users (for example, because of public interest or consistency) may be reported as a major fund.
Management	GASB-62	Persons who are responsible for achieving the objectives of the government and who have the authority to establish policies and make decisions by which those objectives are to be pursued. Management normally includes the chief executive officer (for example, city manager), directors or secretaries in charge of principal government departments or functions (such as service provision administration or finance), and other persons who perform similar policymaking functions. Persons without formal titles also may be members of management.

Item	GASB Standard[1]	Definition
Management's discussion and analysis (MD&A)	GASB-34	A component of required supplementary information, an introduction to the basic financial statements providing an analytical overview of the government's financial activities. The MD&A should provide an objective and easily readable analysis of the government's financial activities based on currently known facts, decisions, or conditions. MD&A should discuss the current-year results in comparison with the prior year, with emphasis on the current year. This fact-based analysis should discuss the positive and negative aspects of the comparison with the prior year. The use of charts, graphs, and tables is encouraged to enhance the understandability of the information. MD&A should focus on the primary government. Comments in MD&A should distinguish between information pertaining to the primary government and that of its component units. Determining whether to discuss matters related to a component unit is a matter of professional judgment and should be based on the individual component unit's significance to the total of all discretely presented component units and that component unit's relationship with the primary government. When appropriate, the reporting entity's MD&A should refer readers to the component unit's separately issued financial statements.
Margin	GASB-3	The excess of the market value including accrued interest of the securities underlying a repurchase—reverse repurchase or a fixed coupon repurchase—reverse repurchase agreement over the agreement amount including accrued interest. It is common practice for a margin to be built into an agreement to protect against declines in the market value of the underlying securities
Market approach	GASB-72	A valuation technique that uses prices and other relevant information generated by market transactions involving identical or comparable (similar) assets, liabilities, or groups of assets and liabilities.

Item	GASB Standard[1]	Definition
Market maker	GASB-72	An entity or individual that provides both a bid and ask price and is willing and able to transact at those prices.
Market multiples	GASB-72	A valuation technique that relies on the use of ratios as an expression of market price relative to a key statistic, such as earnings, book value, or cash flows.
Market participants	GASB-72	Buyers and sellers that (1) are in the principal (or most advantageous) market for an asset or liability and (2) have all of the following characteristics: a. They are independent of each other. That is, they are not related parties, although the price in a related-party transaction may be used as an input to a fair value measurement if the government has evidence that the transaction was entered into at market terms. b. They are knowledgeable, having a reasonable understanding about the asset or liability and the transaction using all available information, including information that might be obtained through due diligence efforts that are usual and customary. c. They are able to enter into a transaction for the asset or liability. d. They are willing to enter into a transaction for the asset or liability. That is, they are motivated but not forced or otherwise compelled to do so.
Market risk	GASB-72	The risk that changes in market prices will reduce the fair value of an asset, increase the fair value of a liability, or adversely affect the cash flows of an expected transaction. Market risk comprises the following: a. Interest rate risk; b. Currency risk; and c. Other price risks.

Item	GASB Standard[1]	Definition
Market-access risk	GASB-53	The risk that a government will not be able to enter credit markets or that credit will become more costly. For example, to complete a derivative instrument's objective, an issuance of refunding bonds may be planned in the future. If at that time the government is unable to enter credit markets, expected cost savings may not be realized.
Market-corroborated inputs	GASB-72	Inputs that are derived principally from or corroborated by observable market data by correlation or other means.
Market-related value of plan assets	GASB-43	A term used with reference to the actuarial value of assets. A market-related value may be fair value, market value (or estimated market value), or a calculated value that recognizes changes in fair value or market value over a period of, for example, three to five years.
Master agreement	GASB-3	A written contract covering all future transactions between the parties to repurchase—reverse repurchase agreements that establishes each party's rights in the transactions. A master agreement will often specify, among other things, the right of the buyer-lender to liquidate the underlying securities in the event of default by the seller-borrower.

Item	GASB Standard[1]	Definition
Master Settlement Agreement (MSA)	GASB:TB 2004-1	In 1998, the U.S. tobacco industry reached an agreement (referred to as the Master Settlement Agreement, or MSA) with state governments releasing the tobacco companies from present and future smoking-related claims that had been, or potentially could be, filed by the states. In exchange, the tobacco companies agreed to make annual payments *in perpetuity* to the states, subject to certain conditions and adjustments. The states of California and New York entered into additional agreements with their county governments and selected major cities to allocate a specific portion of their ongoing annual settlement payments to those local governments. The states and the California and New York local governments are referred to in this Technical Bulletin as "settling governments." Some settling governments have created legally separate entities (referred to as Tobacco Settlement Authorities, or TSAs) to issue debt and to obtain the rights to all or a portion of the settling governments' future tobacco settlement resources (TSRs). TSRs are exchange transactions.
Matched position	GASB-3	A condition existing when reverse repurchase agreement proceeds are invested in securities that mature at or almost at the same time as the reverse repurchase agreement and the proceeds from those securities will be used to liquidate the agreement.
Matrix pricing	GASB-72	A valuation technique used to value securities based on their relationship to benchmark quoted prices.
Matured liabilities	GASBI-6	Liabilities that normally are due and payable in full when incurred or the matured portion of general long-term indebtedness (the portion that has come due for payment).
Measurement date	GASB-72	The date when the fair value of an asset or liability is determined.
Measurement period	GASB-75	The period between the prior and the current measurement dates.

Item	GASB Standard[1]	Definition
Minimum lease payments	GASB-62	a. From the standpoint of the lessee: The payments that the lessee is obligated to make or can be required to make in connection with the leased property. However, a guarantee by the lessee of the lessor's debt and the lessee's obligation to pay (apart from the rental payments) executory costs such as insurance and maintenance in connection with the leased property should be excluded. If the lease contains a bargain purchase option, only the minimum rental payments over the lease term and the payment called for by the bargain purchase option should be included in the minimum lease payments. Otherwise, minimum lease payments include the following:

(1) The minimum rental payments called for by the lease over the lease term.

(2) Any guarantee by the lessee of the residual value at the expiration of the lease term, whether or not payment of the guarantee constitutes a purchase of the leased property. When the lessor has the right to require the lessee to purchase the property at termination of the lease for a certain or determinable amount, that amount should be considered a lessee guarantee. When the lessee agrees to make up any deficiency below a stated amount in the lessor's realization of the residual value, the guarantee to be included in the minimum lease payments should be the stated amount, rather than an estimate of the deficiency to be made up.

Item	*GASB Standard*[1]	*Definition*
		(3) Any payment that the lessee is required to make or can be required to make upon failure to renew or extend the lease at the expiration of the lease term, whether or not the payment would constitute a purchase of the leased property. In this connection, it should be noted that the definition of lease term includes "all periods, if any, for which failure to renew the lease imposes a penalty on the lessee in an amount such that renewal appears, at the inception of the lease, to be reasonably assured." If the lease term has been extended because of that provision, the related penalty should not be included in minimum lease payments.
		b. From the standpoint of the lessor: The payments described in (a) above plus any guarantee of the residual value or of rental payments beyond the lease term by a third party unrelated to either the lessee or the lessor, provided the third party is financially capable of discharging the obligations that may arise from the guarantee.
Modified approach (to infrastructure financial reporting)	GASB-34	Alternative to depreciation of infrastructure assets as long as two requirements are met. First, the government manages the eligible infrastructure assets using an asset management system that has the characteristics set forth below; second, the government documents that the eligible infrastructure assets are being preserved approximately at (or above) a condition level established and disclosed by the government. To meet the first requirement, the asset management system should: a. Have an up-to-date inventory of eligible infrastructure assets; b. Perform condition assessments of the eligible infrastructure assets and summarize the results using a measurement scale; and

Item	GASB Standard[1]	Definition
		c. Estimate each year the annual amount to maintain and preserve the eligible infrastructure assets at the condition level established and disclosed by the government.
Monetary assets and liabilities	GASB-62	Assets and liabilities whose amounts are fixed in terms of units of currency by contract or otherwise. Examples are cash, short- or long-term accounts and notes receivable in cash, and short- or long-term accounts and notes payable in cash.
Money-weighted rate of return	GASB-74	A method of calculating period-by-period returns on pension or OPEB plan investments that adjusts for the changing amounts actually invested. Money-weighted rate of return is calculated as the internal rate of return on pension or OPEB plan investments, net of pension or OPEB plan investment expense.
Money market investment	GASB-31	A short-term, highly liquid debt instrument, including commercial paper, banker's acceptances, and U.S. Treasury and agency obligations. Asset-backed securities, derivatives, and structured notes are not included in this term.
Mortgage banking activity	GASB-62	An activity that is engaged primarily in originating, marketing, and servicing real estate mortgage loans for other than its own account. Mortgage banking activities, as local representatives of institutional lenders, act as correspondents between lenders and borrowers.
Most advantageous market	GASB-72	The market that maximizes the amount that would be received to sell an asset or minimizes the amount that would be paid to transfer a liability, after taking into account transaction costs and transportation costs.
MSWLF	GASB-18	Municipal solid waste landfill.

Item	*GASB Standard*[1]	*Definition*
Multi-period excess earnings technique	GASB-72	A valuation technique based on prospective financial information (for example, revenues, expenses, or cash flows) associated with a collection of assets. The initial amount is reduced for the contributions of supporting assets, with the residual amount being the excess earnings associated with the asset being valued.
Multiple-employer defined benefit pension or OPEB plan	GASB-78	A defined benefit pension or OPEB plan that is used to provide pensions or OPEB to the employees of more than one employer.
Net asset value per share	GASB-72	The amount of net assets attributable to each share of capital stock (other than senior equity securities; that is preferred stock) outstanding at the close of the period. It excludes the effects of assuming conversion of outstanding convertible securities, whether or not their conversion would have a diluting effect. Also used in external investment pool valuation.
Net carrying amount	GASB-62	In an extinguishment of debt, the amount due at maturity, adjusted for unamortized premium, discount and cost of issuance.
Net investment in capital assets	GASB-63	Capital assets, net of accumulated depreciation, reduced by the outstanding balances of bonds, mortgages, notes, or other borrowings that are attributable to the acquisition, construction, or improvement of those assets. Deferred outflows of resources and deferred inflows of resources that are attributable to the acquisition, construction, or improvement of those assets or related debt also should be included in this component of net position. If there are significant unspent related debt proceeds or deferred inflows of resources at the end of the reporting period, the portion of the debt or deferred inflows of resources attributable to the unspent amount should not be included in the calculation of net investment in capital assets. Instead, that portion of the debt or deferred inflows of resources should be included in the same net position component (restricted or unrestricted) as the unspent amount.

Item	GASB Standard[1]	Definition
Net OPEB liability	GASB-75	The liability of employers and nonemployer contributing entities to plan members for benefits provided through a defined benefit OPEB plan that is administered through an irrevocable trust.
Net pension liability	GASB-68	The liability of employers and nonemployer contributing entities to employees for benefits provided through a defined benefit pension plan.
Net position	GASB-63 (also GASB:CS-4)	The residual of assets, plus deferred outflows of resources, less liabilities, less deferred inflows of resources. Fiduciary activities net to *fiduciary net position*. Net position is displayed in three components—*net investment in capital assets; restricted* (distinguishing between major categories of restrictions); and *unrestricted*.
Net realizable value	GASB-62	The estimated selling price in the ordinary course of operations less estimated costs of completion (to the stage of completion assumed in determining the selling price), holding, and disposal.
Network affiliation agreement (broadcasting)	GASB-62	A broadcaster may be affiliated with a network under a network affiliation agreement. Under the agreement, the station receives compensation for the network programming that it carries based on a formula designed to compensate the station for advertising sold on a network basis and included in network programming. Program costs, a major expense of television stations, generally are lower for a network affiliate than for an independent station because an affiliate does not incur program costs for network programs.

Item	*GASB Standard*[1]	*Definition*
Nonauthoritative Accounting Literature	GASB-76	Sources of nonauthoritative accounting literature include GASB Concepts Statements; pronouncements and other literature of the Financial Accounting Standards Board, Federal Accounting Standards Advisory Board, International Public Sector Accounting Standards Board, and International Accounting Standards Board, and AICPA literature not cleared by the GASB; practices that are widely recognized and prevalent in state and local government; literature of other professional associations or regulatory agencies; and accounting textbooks, handbooks, and articles. (*Author's note— inclusive of the text of this book.*)
Noncapital financing activities	GASB-9	The borrowing of money for purposes other than to acquire, construct, or improve capital assets and repaying those amounts borrowed, including interest. This category includes proceeds from all borrowings (such as revenue anticipation notes) not clearly attributable to acquisition, construction, or improvement of capital assets, regardless of the form of the borrowing. Also included are certain other interfund and intergovernmental receipts and payments.
Nonemployer contributing entities	GASB-75	Entities that make contributions to a pension or OPEB plan that is used to provide pensions or OPEB to the employees of other entities, that is administered through a trust. Employees are not considered nonemployer contributing entities. For arrangements in which pensions are provided through a pension plan that is *not administered through a trust*, entities that make defined benefit payments directly as pensions come due for employees of other entities, including using the entity's assets held by others for the purpose of providing benefits. Employees are *not* considered nonemployer contributing entities.

Item	GASB Standard[1]	Definition
Non-exchange financial guarantee	GASB-70	A nonexchange financial guarantee is a guarantee of an obligation of a legally separate entity or individual, including a blended or discretely presented component unit, which requires the guarantor to indemnify a third-party obligation holder under specified conditions.
Nonexchange transaction	GASB-33	When a government gives (or receives) value without directly receiving (or giving) equal value in return. Four classes of nonexchange transactions are used: 1. Derived tax revenues; 2. Imposed nonexchange revenues; 3. Government-mandated nonexchange transactions; and 4. Voluntary nonexchange transactions.
Nonmonetary assets and liabilities	GASB-62	Assets and liabilities other than monetary ones. Examples are inventories, investments in common stocks, capital assets, and liabilities for rent collected in advance.
Nonperformance risk	GASB-72	The risk that an entity will not fulfill an obligation. Nonperformance risk includes, but may not be limited to, the government's own credit risk.

Item	GASB Standard[1]	Definition
Nonspendable fund balance	GASB-54	The nonspendable fund balance classification includes amounts that cannot be spent because they are either (a) not in spendable form or (b) legally or contractually required to be maintained intact. The "not in spendable form" criterion includes items that are not expected to be converted to cash, for example, inventories and prepaid amounts. It also includes the long-term amount of loans and notes receivable, as well as property acquired for resale. However, if the use of the proceeds from the collection of those receivables or from the sale of those properties is restricted, committed, or assigned, then they should be included in the appropriate fund balance classification (restricted, committed, or assigned), rather than nonspendable fund balance. The corpus (or principal) of a permanent fund is an example of an amount that is legally or contractually required to be maintained intact.
Normal cost (also known as service cost)		That portion of the Actuarial Present Value of pension plan benefits and expenses which is allocated to a valuation year by the Actuarial Cost Method. (Normal cost is no longer utilized in general-purpose external financial reporting, but service cost is).
Notes to the financial statements (notes to the basic financial statements)	GASB-34	Notes explaining the governments balances and results of operations, presented in accordance with GAAP.
Notional amount	GASB-53	The number of currency units, shares, bushels, pounds, or other units specified in the derivative instrument. It is a stated amount on which payments depend. The notional amount is similar to the principal amount of a bond.
Obligating event (pollution remediation)	GASB-49	An event that triggers the recognition of a liability for pollution remediation.

Item	GASB Standard[1]	Definition
Observable inputs	GASB-72	Inputs that are developed using market data, such as publicly available information about actual events or transactions, and which reflect the assumptions that market participants would use when pricing an asset or liability.
Off-market term	GASB-53	A provision in a derivative instrument, such as a rate, price, or term, that is not consistent with the current market for that type of contract.
OMB		White House Office of Management and Budget
On-behalf payments for fringe benefits and salaries	GASB-24	Direct payments made by one entity (the paying entity or paying government) to a third-party recipient for the employees of another, legally separate entity (the employer entity or employer government). They include payments made by governmental entities on behalf of nongovernmental entities and payments made by nongovernmental entities on behalf of governmental entities, and may be made for volunteers as well as for paid employees of the employer entity.
Ongoing financial interest	GASB-14	An equity interest or any other arrangement that allows a participating government to have access to a joint venture's resources.
Ongoing financial responsibility	GASB-14	a. A participating government is obligated in some manner for the debts of a joint venture. b. The joint venture's existence depends on continued funding by the participating government.
OPEB Plans	GASB-74	Arrangements through which OPEB is determined, assets dedicated for OPEB (if any) are accumulated and managed, and benefits are paid as they come due.
Open group / closed group		Terms used to distinguish between two classes of Actuarial Cost Methods. Under an Open Group Actuarial Cost Method, Actuarial Present Values associated with expected future entrants are considered; under a Closed Group Actuarial Cost Method, Actuarial Present Values associated with future entrants are not considered (No longer utilized in general-purpose external financial reporting).

Item	GASB Standard[1]	Definition
Open-end mutual fund	GASB-31	An SEC-registered investment company that issues shares of its stock to investors, invests in an investment portfolio on the shareholders' behalf, and stands ready to redeem its shares for an amount based on its current share price. An open-end mutual fund creates new shares to meet investor demand, and the value of an investment in the fund depends directly on the value of the underlying portfolio. Open-end mutual funds include governmental external investment pools that are registered as investment companies with the SEC and that operate as open-end funds.
Operating activities (cash flows)	GASB-9	Cash flows resulting from providing services and producing and delivering goods, and include all transactions and other events that are not defined as capital and related financing, noncapital financing, or investing activities. Cash flows from operating activities generally are the cash effects of transactions and other events that enter into the determination of operating income.
Operation	GASB-69	An operation is an integrated set of activities conducted and managed for the purpose of providing identifiable services with associated assets or liabilities. For example, an operation may include the assets and liabilities specifically associated with the activities conducted and managed by the fire department in a general purpose government. Conversely, fire engines donated to or acquired by a fire department would constitute only a portion of that activity and, therefore, would not constitute an operation.
Option	GASB-53	A contract that gives its holder the right but not the obligation to buy or sell a financial instrument or commodity at a certain price for a period of time.
Option pricing model	GASB-72	A valuation technique used to value an option contract that is based on the critical terms of the contract and implied volatility.

Item	GASB Standard[1]	Definition
Orderly transaction	GASB-72	A transaction that assumes exposure to the market for a period before the measurement date to allow for marketing activities that are usual and customary for transactions involving such assets or liabilities. It is not a forced transaction (for example, a forced liquidation or distress sale).
Original budget	GASB-34	The first complete adopted budget of a government. The original budget may be adjusted by reserves, transfers, allocations, supplemental appropriations, and other legally authorized legislative and executive changes *before* the beginning of the fiscal year. The original budget should also include actual appropriation amounts automatically carried over from prior years by law. For example, a legal provision may require the automatic rolling forward of appropriations to cover prior-year encumbrances.
Origination fees (lending activities)	GASB-62	Costs to originate a loan that (a) result directly from and are essential to the lending transaction and (b) would not have been incurred by the lender had that lending transaction not occurred.
Other postemployment benefits (OPEB)	GASB-75	Benefits other than retirement income (such as death benefits, life insurance, disability, and long-term care) that are paid in the period after employment and that are provided separately from a pension plan, as well as postemployment health care benefits paid in the period after employment (if any), regardless of the manner in which they are provided. Other postemployment benefits do not include termination benefits or termination payments for sick leave.
Other stand-alone government	GASB-14	A legally separate governmental organization that (a) does not have a separately elected governing body and (b) does not meet the definition of a component unit. Other stand-alone governments include some special-purpose governments, joint ventures, jointly governed organizations, and pools.

Item	GASB Standard[1]	Definition
Outflow of resources (or outlays)	GASB-65 (also GASB:CS-4)	A consumption of net position by the government that is applicable to the reporting period (expenses or expenditures).
Overlapping debt	GASB-44	The outstanding long-term debt instruments—including bonds, notes, certificates of participation, loans, and capital leases—of governments that overlap geographically, at least in part, with the government preparing the statistical section information.
Overlapping rate	GASB-44	An amount or percentage applied to a unit of a specific revenue base by governments that overlap geographically, at least in part, with the government preparing the statistical section information.
Own-source revenues	GASB-84	Revenues that are generated by a government itself, such as tax revenues and water and sewer charges. Investment income is also an own-source revenue. Intergovernmental aid and shared revenues are not own-source revenues.
Parameters		The set of requirements for calculating actuarially determined OPEB information included in financial reports (No longer utilized in general-purpose external financial reporting).
Participation	GASB-31	The ability of an investment to capture market (interest rate) changes through the investment's negotiability or transferability, or redemption terms that consider market rates.
Participation contract	GASB-10	A formal written contract between a public entity risk pool and a pool participant describing, among other things, the period, the amount of risk coverage the pool will provide for the participating governmental entity, and the required contribution the participant must pay for that coverage. (The term *policy* is used in the commercial insurance industry.)
Pass-through grants	GASB-24	Grants and other financial assistance received by a governmental entity to transfer to or spend on behalf of a secondary recipient.

Item	GASB Standard[1]	Definition
Pay-as-you-go (PAYGO)		A method of financing a pension plan under which the contributions to the plan are generally made at about the same time and in about the same amount as benefit payments and expenses becoming due.
Paying entity	GASB-24	The entity that makes on-behalf payments for fringe benefits and salaries for the employees of another, employer entity. The paying entity may be governmental or nongovernmental.
Payroll growth rate		An actuarial assumption with respect to future increases in total covered payroll attributable to inflation; used in applying the level percentage of projected payroll amortization method.
Penalty (leases)	GASB-62	Any requirement that is imposed or can be imposed on the lessee by the lease agreement or by factors outside the lease agreement to disburse cash, incur or assume a liability, perform services, surrender or transfer an asset or rights to an asset or otherwise forego an economic benefit, or suffer an economic detriment. Factors to consider when determining if an economic detriment may be incurred include, but are not limited to, the uniqueness of purpose or location of the property, the availability of a comparable replacement property, the relative importance or significance of the property to the continuation of the lessee's operations or service to its customers, the existence of leasehold improvements or other assets whose value would be impaired by the lessee vacating or discontinuing use of the leased property, adverse tax consequences, and the ability or willingness of the lessee to bear the cost associated with relocation or replacement of the leased property at market rental rates or to tolerate other parties using the leased property.

Item	GASB Standard[1]	Definition
Pension (and other employee benefit) trust funds	GASB-84	Used to report resources require to be held in trust for the members and beneficiaries of defined benefit pension plans, defined contribution plans, or other employee benefit plans, where the assets are (a) administered through a trust agreement or equivalent arrangement in which the government itself is not a beneficiary, (b) dedicated to providing benefits to recipients in accordance with the benefit terms, and (c) legally protected from the creditors of the government.
Pension plans	GASB-78	Arrangements through which pensions are determined, assets dedicated for pensions are accumulated and managed, and benefits are paid as they come due.
Pensions	GASB-78	Retirement income and, if provided through a pension plan, postemployment benefits other than retirement income (such as death benefits, life insurance, and disability benefits). Pensions do not include postemployment healthcare benefits and termination benefits.
Percentage-of-completion method (construction contracts)	GASB-62	The percentage-of-completion method recognizes revenue as work on a contract progresses. The recognized revenue should be that percentage of estimated total revenue that either: a. Incurred costs to date bear to estimated total costs after giving effect to estimates of costs to complete based upon most recent information; or b. May be indicated by such other measure of progress toward completion as may be appropriate, having due regard to work performed.

Item	GASB Standard[1]	Definition
Perfected security interest	GASB-3	An interest in property, including securities, that is superior to the interests of the general creditors. Possession of the security by the secured party or its agent is generally needed to create a perfected security interest. In addition, a perfected security interest can be created without taking possession of the security if the transferor of the security interest has signed a security agreement that contains a description of the collateral and the secured party pays for the investment. Such a security interest is perfected for a period of 21 days. However, the secured party risks loss or impairment of its security interest during the 21-day period, because the Uniform Commercial Code provides that a holder in due course of a negotiable instrument or a bona fide purchaser of the instrument will take priority over the secured party. After 21 days, the security interest becomes unperfected unless the secured party takes possession of the security.
Period-certain term	GASB-81	A term specifying that the termination of a split-interest agreement occurs after a specified number of years.
Permanent funds	GASB-54	Funds used to account for and report resources that are restricted to the extent that only earnings, and not principal, may be used for purposes that support the reporting government's programs—that is, for the benefit of the government or its citizenry. Permanent funds do not include private-purpose trust funds, which should be used to report situations in which the government is required to use the principal or earnings for the benefit of individuals, private organizations, or other governments.
Phase (real estate)	GASB-62	A parcel on which units are to be constructed concurrently.

Item	GASB Standard[1]	Definition
Pick-ups	GASB-82	If an employer makes payments to satisfy employee contribution requirements to a pension plan (for example, in connection with an election made in accordance with Internal Revenue Code Section 414(h)(2) and Revenue Ruling 2006-43), the employer does not include such amounts in salaries and wages of the employee. (See also employer-paid member contributions).
Plan assets		Resources, usually in the form of stocks, bonds, and other classes of investments, that have been segregated and restricted in a trust, or in an equivalent arrangement, in which (a) employer contributions to the plan are irrevocable, (b) assets are dedicated to providing benefits to retirees and their beneficiaries, and (c) assets are legally protected from creditors of the employer(s) or plan administrator, for the payment of benefits in accordance with the terms of the plan.
Plan liabilities		Obligations payable by the plan at the reporting date, including, primarily, benefits and refunds due and payable to plan members and beneficiaries, and accrued investment and administrative expenses. Plan liabilities do not include actuarial accrued liabilities for benefits that are not due and payable at the reporting date.
Plan members	GASB-75	Individuals that are covered under the terms of a pension or OPEB plan. Plan members generally include (a) employees in active service (active plan members) and (b) employees no longer in active service (or their beneficiaries) who have accumulated benefits under the terms of a pension plan (inactive plan members).
Plan net position (plan net position held in trust) (also fiduciary net position)		The difference between total plan assets and total plan liabilities at the reporting date.

Item	GASB Standard[1]	Definition
Plan of adjustment	GASB-58	Plan submitted to a bankruptcy judge that separates the government's claims and liabilities into classes that may or may not be adjusted as part of the bankruptcy.
Pledged receivables	GASB-48	Taxes or other types of receivables used to secure either a collateralized borrowing or sold to a third party in exchange for cash.
Pledged revenues	GASB-48	Revenues to be collected in the future securing either a collateralized borrowing or sold to a third party in exchange for cash.
Policy	GASB-10	A formal written contract of insurance between an insurer and an insured describing, among other things, the period and amount of risk coverage the insurer agrees to provide the insured.
Policyholder	GASB-10	The party to whom an insurance policy is issued and who pays a premium to an insurer for the insurer's promise to provide insurance protection.
Policyholder dividends	GASB-10	Payments made or credits extended to the insured by the insurer, usually at the end of a policy year that result in reducing the net insurance cost to the policyholder. These dividends may be paid in cash to the insured or applied by the insured to reduce premiums due for the next policy year.
Policy-year basis	GASB-10	For disclosure purposes, a method that assigns incurred losses and claim adjustment expenses to the year in which the event that triggered coverage under the pool insurance policy or participation contract occurred. For occurrence-based coverage where all members have a common contract renewal date, the policy-year basis is the same as the accident-year basis. For claims-made coverages, policy-year basis is the same as the report-year basis.

Item	GASB Standard[1]	Definition
Pollution	GASB-49	The U.S. Environmental Protection Agency provides the following discussion of the term *pollution* on its website: "Generally, the presence of a substance in the environment that because of its chemical composition or quantity prevents the functioning of natural processes and produces undesirable environmental and health effects. Under the Clean Water Act, for example, the term has been defined as the man-made or man-induced alteration of the physical, biological, chemical, and radiological integrity of water and other media."
Pollution remediation obligation	GASB-49	An obligation to address the current or potential detrimental effects of existing pollution by participating in pollution remediation activities. For example, obligations to clean up spills of hazardous wastes or hazardous substances and obligations to remove contamination such as asbestos are pollution remediation obligations.
Popular reports	GASB:CS-1	Less detailed reporting intended for users whose financial reporting needs are better satisfied through more condensed information.
Postemployment	GASB-75	The period after employment.
Postemployment benefit changes	GASB-75	Adjustments to the pension of an inactive employee (or plan member).
Postemployment healthcare benefits	GASB-75	Medical, dental, vision, and other health-related benefits paid subsequent to the termination of employment.
Potential hedging derivative instrument	GASB-53	A derivative instrument that is associated with a hedgeable item prior to the determination that the derivative instrument is effective in significantly reducing the identified financial risk.
Potentially responsible party (PRP)	GASB-49	An individual or entity—including owners, operators, transporters, or generators—that is held potentially responsible for pollution at a site. The term refers to a party that is held by law as potentially responsible for pollution at any site. It is not limited to parties associated with Superfund sites.

Item	GASB Standard[1]	Definition
Preacquisition costs (real estate)	GASB-62	Costs related to a property that are incurred for the express purpose of, but prior to, obtaining that property. Examples of preacquisition costs may be costs of surveying, zoning or traffic studies, or payments to obtain an option on the property.
Prematurity Period (cable television systems)	GASB-62	During the prematurity period, the cable television system is partially under construction and partially in service. The prematurity period begins with the first earned subscriber revenue. Its end will vary with circumstances of the system but will be determined based on plans for completion of the first major construction period or achievement of a specified predetermined subscriber level at which no additional investment will be required other than for cable television plants. The length of the prematurity period varies with the franchise development and construction plans.
Premium (insurance)	GASB-10	The consideration paid for an insurance contract.
Premium deficiency	GASB-10	The amount by which expected claims costs (including IBNR) and all expected claim adjustment expenses, expected dividends to policyholders or pool participants, unamortized acquisition costs, and incurred policy maintenance costs exceed related unearned premium revenue.
Preparer	GASB:CS-3	Those who are responsible for producing financial reports that recognize relevant events in the financial statements or that disclose or present messages about such events elsewhere in the financial report.
Present value	GASB-72	A valuation technique used to link future amounts (cash flows or values) to a present amount by employing a discount rate (an application of the income approach).

Item	GASB Standard[1]	Definition
Primary dealers	GASB-3	A group of government securities dealers included in the "List of Government Securities Dealers Reporting to the Market Reports Division of the Federal Reserve Bank of New York [NY Fed]" that submit daily reports of market activity and positions and monthly financial statements to the NY Fed and are subject to its informal oversight. Primary dealers include SEC-registered securities broker-dealers, banks, and a few unregulated firms.
Primary government	GASB-14	A state government or general purpose local government. Also, a special-purpose government that has a separately elected governing body, is legally separate, and is fiscally independent of other state or local governments.
Principal market	GASB-72	The market with the greatest volume and level of activity for an asset or liability.
Principal-to-principal market	GASB-72	A market in which transactions, both originations and resales, are negotiated independently with no intermediary. Little information about those transactions may be made available publicly.
Private purpose trust funds	GASB-84	Used to report escheat property or all other trust arrangements under which principal and income benefit individuals, private organizations or other governments, that are *not* pension arrangements, OPEB arrangements, or activities required to be reported in investment trust funds and are held in a trust that meets the following criteria: The assets are (a) administered through a trust agreement or equivalent arrangement (hereafter jointly referred to as a trust) in which the government itself is not a beneficiary, (b) dedicated to providing benefits to recipients in accordance with the benefit terms, and (c) legally protected from the creditors of the government.
Probable	GASB-62	Classification of a loss contingency where the future event or events are likely to occur.

Item	GASB Standard[1]	Definition
Productive assets	GASB-62	Assets held for or used in the production of goods or services by the government. Productive assets include an investment in another entity if the investment is accounted for by the equity method but exclude an investment not accounted for by that method.
Program revenues	GASB-34	Revenues derived directly from the program itself or from parties outside the reporting government's taxpayers or citizenry, as a whole; they reduce the net cost of the function to be financed from the government's general revenues. The statement of activities should separately report three categories of program revenues: (a) charges for services, (b) program-specific operating grants and contributions, and (c) program-specific capital grants and contributions.
Program-specific grants and contributions (operating and capital)	GASB-34	Revenues arising from mandatory and voluntary nonexchange transactions with other governments, organizations, or individuals that are restricted for use in a particular program.
Project Costs	GASB-62	Costs clearly associated with the acquisition, development, and construction of a real estate project.
Projected benefit payments	GASB-75	All benefits estimated to be payable through the pension or OPEB plan to current active and inactive employees as a result of their past service and their expected future service.
Projected salary increase assumption		An actuarial assumption with respect to future increases in the individual salaries and wages of active plan members; used in determining the actuarial present value of total projected benefits when the benefit amounts are related to salaries and wages. The expected increases commonly include amounts for inflation, enhanced productivity, and employee merit and seniority. (Sometimes known as payroll growth or inflation).

Item	*GASB Standard*[1]	*Definition*
Projected unit credit actuarial cost method (PUC)		A method under which the benefits (projected or unprojected) of each individual included in an Actuarial Valuation are allocated by a consistent formula to valuation years. The Actuarial Present Value of benefits allocated to a valuation year is called the Normal Cost. The Actuarial Present Value of benefits allocated to all periods prior to a valuation year is called the Actuarial Accrued Liability (No longer utilized in general-purpose external financial reporting).
Property and liability insurance	GASB-10	Insurance contracts that provide protection against (a) damage to, or loss of, property caused by various perils, such as fire and theft, or (b) legal liability resulting from injuries to other persons or damage to their property. Property and liability insurance companies also may issue accident and health insurance contracts. There is a broad insurance distinction between companies writing life and health insurance and those writing the property insurance or "nonlife" lines of fire, marine, casualty, and surety. Although no one definition has been fully established, some use the generic title "property and casualty" insurance, whereas others use "property and liability" insurance.
Proprietary funds	GASB-34	Funds consisting of enterprise funds (emphasizing major funds) and internal service funds. The funds focus on the determination of operating income, changes in net [position] (or cost recovery), financial position and cash flows.

Item	GASB Standard[1]	Definition
Public Corporation (See also Component Units)	GASB-76 (Cod Sec 1000.801 fn. 4)	*Black's Law Dictionary* defines a public corporation as: "An artificial person (for example, [a] municipality or a governmental corporation) created for the administration of public affairs. Unlike a private corporation it has no protection against legislative acts altering or even repealing its charter. Instrumentalities created by [the] state, formed and owned by it in [the] public interest, supported in whole or part by public funds, and governed by managers deriving their authority from [the] state." *Sharon Realty Co. v. Westlake, Ohio Com. Pl., 188 N.E. 2d 318, 323, 25, O.O.2d 322.* A public corporation is an instrumentality of the state, founded and owned in the public interest, supported by public funds and governed by those deriving their authority from the state. *York County Fair Ass'n v. South Carolina Tax Commission, 249 S.C. 337, 154 S.E. 2d 361, 362.*
Public employee retirement system	GASB-68	A special-purpose government that administers one or more pension plans; also may administer other types of employee benefit plans, including postemployment healthcare plans and deferred compensation plans.
Public entity risk pool	GASB-10	A cooperative group of governmental entities joining together to finance an exposure, liability, or risk. Risk may include property and liability, workers' compensation, or employee health care. A pool may be a stand-alone entity or included as part of a larger governmental entity that acts as the pool's sponsor.
Purpose restriction (eligibility)	GASB-33	The purpose for which resources are required to be used. All other purposes other than those required are unallowed (or disallowed).
Put option	GASB-53	An option that gives its holder the right but not the obligation to sell a financial instrument or commodity at a certain price for a period of time.

Item	*GASB Standard*[1]	*Definition*
Qualified External Investment Pool	GASB-79	An external investment pool that elects (and maintains) measurement for financial reporting purposes all investments at amortized cost, as long as it meets *all the following criteria*, as defined in GASB-79: • The pool transacts with participants at a stable net asset value per share (for example, all contributions and redemptions are transacted at $1 net asset value per share); • Portfolio maturity requirements are met; • Portfolio quality requirements are met; • Portfolio diversification requirements are met; • Portfolio liquidity requirements are met; and • Shadow pricing requirements are met. If an external investment pool is noncompliant with any of the criteria during the reporting period, it should measure investments at fair value in accordance with GASB-31, as amended, except for investments with remaining maturities that are 90 days or less, which may remain at amortized cost.
Quantitative method	GASB-53	A method of evaluating effectiveness using a mathematical relationship. Synthetic instrument, dollar-offset, and regression analysis are the quantitative methods specifically addressed in this Statement.
RAN		Revenue anticipation note
Reacquisition price	GASB-62	In extinguishments of debt, the amount paid on extinguishment, including a call premium and miscellaneous costs of reacquisition. If extinguishment is achieved by a direct exchange of new securities, the reacquisition price is the total present value of the new securities.
Readily determinable fair value	GASB-72	An equity security has a readily determinable fair value if it meets any of the following conditions:

Item	GASB Standard[1]	Definition
		a. The fair value of an equity security is readily determinable if sales prices or bid-and-asked quotations are currently available on a securities exchange registered with the U.S. Securities and Exchange Commission or in the over-the-counter market, provided that those prices or quotations for the over-the-counter market are publicly reported by the National Association of Securities Dealers Automated Quotations systems or by OTC Markets Group, Inc. Restricted stock meets that definition if the restriction terminates within one year.
		b. The fair value of an equity security traded only in a foreign market is readily determinable if that foreign market is of a breadth and scope comparable to one of the U.S. markets referred to in (a).
		c. The fair value of an investment in a mutual fund is readily determinable if the fair value per share (unit) is determined and published and is the basis for current transactions.
Real rate of return	GASB-75	The rate of return on an investment after adjustment to eliminate inflation.
Reasonably possible	GASB-62	Classification of a loss contingency where the change of the future event or events occurring is more than remote but less than likely.
Recipient government	GASB-24	In a pass-through grant, a governmental entity that receives grants and other financial assistance to transfer to or spend on behalf of a secondary recipient.
Redistricting	GASB-69	Redrawing of the territorial boundaries usually within a government and usually for political, census or other demographic purposes. For example, redistricting may be used in a school district's enrollment rebalancing efforts. Sometimes, however, redistricting may involve the transfer of operations from one district to another.

Item	GASB Standard[1]	Definition
Reference rate	GASB-53	The rate to which a derivative instrument's variable payment is linked. Common reference rates are LIBOR, the SIFMA swap index, the AAA general obligations index, and the pricing point of a commodity. For example, a commodity swap's variable payment may be linked to the price of No. 2 heating oil at the New York harbor pricing point. Other literature may refer to a reference rate as a reference index.
Refunding	GASB-23	Issuance of new debt when proceeds are used to repay previously outstanding debt. The proceeds may be used currently (current refunding) or placed in escrow until a later date (advance refunding).
Registered security	GASB-3	A security that has the name of the owner written on its face. A registered security cannot be negotiated except by the endorsement of the owner.
Regression analysis method	GASB-53	A statistical technique that measures the relationship between a dependent variable and one or more independent variables. The future value of the dependent variable is predicted by measuring the size and significance of each independent variable in relation to the dependent variable. Regression analysis included in the text of this Statement uses only one independent variable.
Reinsurance	GASB-62	A transaction in which a reinsurer (assuming enterprise), for a consideration (premium), assumes all or part of a risk undertaken originally by another insurer (government). However, the legal rights of the insured are not affected by the reinsurance transaction and the insurance enterprise issuing the insurance contract remains liable to the insured for payment of policy benefits.
Related organization	GASB-14	An organization for which a primary government is not financially accountable (because it does not impose will or have a financial benefit or burden relationship) even though the primary government appoints a voting majority of the organization's governing board.

Item	GASB Standard[1]	Definition
Related parties	GASB-62	A government's related organizations, joint ventures, and jointly governed organizations, as defined in Statement No. 14, *The Financial Reporting Entity*, as amended; elected and appointed officials of the government; its management; members of the immediate families of elected or appointed officials of the government and its management; and other parties with which the government may deal if one party can significantly influence the management or operating policies of the other to an extent that one of the transacting parties might be prevented from fully pursuing its own separate interests. Another party also is a related party if it can significantly influence the management or operating policies of the transacting parties (for example, through imposition of will as discussed in Statement 14, as amended) or if it has an ownership interest in one of the transacting parties and can significantly influence the other to an extent that one or more of the transacting parties might be prevented from fully pursuing its own separate interests.
Relative fair value before construction (real estate)	GASB-62	The fair value of each land parcel in a real estate project in relation to the fair value of the other parcels in the project, exclusive of value added by on-site development and construction activities.
Relative liquidity	GASB-34	Organization of the assets and liabilities in a statement of net position with the elements "closest to cash" placed at the top of each category, followed by elements by descending liquidity.

Item	*GASB Standard*[1]	*Definition*
Relief from royalty technique	GASB-72	A valuation technique used to value certain intangible assets (for example, trademarks and trade names) based on the premise that the only value that a purchaser of the assets receives is the exemption from paying a royalty for its use. Application of this method usually involves estimating the fair value of an intangible asset by quantifying the present value of the stream of market-derived royalty payments that the owner of the intangible asset is exempted from or "relieved" from paying.
Remainder interest	GASB-81	The right (a type of beneficial interest) to receive all or a portion of the resources remaining at the end of a split-interest agreement's term.
Remeasured amounts	GASB:CS-6	Remeasured amounts reflect the conditions in effect at the financial statement date and may be determined using a number of methods. Remeasurement changes the amount reported for an asset or liability from an initial amount or previous remeasured amount to an amount indicative of a value at the financial statement date. Remeasured amounts establish a new carrying value for the asset or liability that is determined without reference to previously reported amounts.
Remedial investigation and feasibility study (RI/FS)	GASB-49	Extensive technical studies to investigate the scope of site impacts (RI) and determine the remedial alternatives (FS) that, consistent with the National Contingency Plan provisions of the federal Superfund law or similar state laws, may be implemented at a polluted site. An RI/FS may include a variety of on- and off-site activities, such as monitoring, sampling, and analysis.
Remote	GASB-62	Classification of a loss contingency where the chance of the future event or events occurring is slight.
Replacement cost	GASB:CS-6	The price paid to acquire an asset with equivalent service potential in an orderly market transaction at the measurement date.
Reporting date		The date of the financial statements; the last day of the fiscal year.

Item	GASB Standard[1]	Definition
Reporting form contract	GASB-10	A contract or policy in which the policyholder is required to report the value of property insured to the insurer at certain intervals. The final premium on the contract is determined by applying the contract rate to the average of the values reported.
Repurchase agreement (repo)	GASB-3	An agreement in which a governmental entity (buyer-lender) transfers cash to a broker-dealer or financial institution (seller-borrower); the broker-dealer or financial institution transfers securities to the entity and promises to repay the cash plus interest in exchange for the *same* securities. A generic term for an agreement in which a governmental entity (buyer-lender) transfers cash to a broker-dealer or financial institution (seller-borrower); the broker-dealer or financial institution transfers securities to the entity and promises to repay the cash plus interest in exchange for the same securities (as in definition (a) above) or for different securities.
Required contribution	GASB-10	The consideration a pool participant pays a public entity risk pool for a participation contract. (The term *premium* is used in the commercial insurance industry.)
Required supplementary information (RSI)		Schedules, statistical data, and other information that are an essential part of financial reporting and should be presented with, but are not part of, the basic financial statements of a governmental entity. RSI is required by GAAP.
Reset date	GASB-40	The time, frequently quarterly or semiannually, that a bond's variable coupon is repriced to reflect changes in a benchmark index.
Resource Conservation and Recovery Act (RCRA)	GASB-49	A federal law that provides comprehensive regulation of hazardous wastes from point of generation to final disposal. All generators of hazardous waste, transporters of hazardous waste, and owners and operators of hazardous waste treatment, storage, or disposal facilities must comply with the applicable requirements of the statute.

Item	*GASB Standard*[1]	*Definition*
Restoration cost approach	GASB-42	With regard to an impaired capital asset, the amount of impairment is derived from the estimated costs to restore the utility of the capital asset. The estimated restoration cost can be converted to historical cost either by restating the estimated restoration cost using an appropriate cost index or by applying a ratio of estimated restoration cost over estimated replacement cost to the carrying value of the capital asset.
Restricted fund balance	GASB-54	Fund balance with constraints placed on the use of resources that are either: a. Externally imposed by creditors (such as through debt covenants), grantors, contributors, or laws or regulations of other governments; or b. Imposed by law through constitutional provisions or enabling legislation.
Restricted net position	GASB-63	Restricted assets reduced by liabilities and deferred inflows of resources related to those assets. Generally, a liability relates to restricted assets if the asset results from a resource flow that also results in the recognition of a liability or if the liability will be liquidated with the restricted assets reported.
Restricted stock	GASB-31	Equity securities whose sale is restricted at acquisition by legal or contractual provisions (other than in connection with being pledged as collateral) except if that restriction terminates within one year or if the holder has the power by contract or otherwise to cause the requirement to be met within one year. Any portion of the security that can reasonably be expected to qualify for sale within one year, such as may be the case under SEC Rule 144 (17 *Code of Federal Regulations* § 230.144) or similar rules of the SEC, is not considered restricted.
Retirement of a tangible capital asset	GASB-83	The permanent removal of a tangible capital asset from service.

Item	GASB Standard[1]	Definition
Retrospective (experience) rating	GASB-10	A method of determining the final amount of an insurance premium by which the initial premium is adjusted based on actual experience during the period of coverage (sometimes subject to maximum and minimum limits). It is designed to encourage safety by the insured and to compensate the insurer if larger-than-expected losses are incurred.
Return of contribution	GASB-10	Payments made or credits extended to the participant by a public entity risk pool, usually at the end of a participation contract year, that result in reducing the participant's net participation contribution. These returns may be paid in cash to the participant or applied by the pool to reduce participation contributions due for the next participation contract year. (The term *dividend* is used in the commercial insurance industry.) Returns of contributions are distinguished from experience refunds in that returns are not determined based on the actual experience of an individual pool participant but, instead, on the experience of the pool as a whole or of a class of participants.
Revenue obligation debt (also known as special obligation debt)	GASB-48	Debt issued secured by a stream of revenues. The debt may or may not be backed by the full faith and credit of the government.
Reverse repurchase agreement (reverse repo)	GASB-3	An agreement in which a broker-dealer or financial institution (buyer-lender) transfers cash to a governmental entity (seller-borrower); the entity transfers securities to the broker-dealer or financial institution and promises to repay the cash plus interest in exchange for the *same* securities. A generic term for an agreement in which a broker-dealer or financial institution (buyer-lender) transfers cash to a governmental entity (seller-borrower); the entity transfers securities to the broker-dealer or financial institution and promises to repay the cash plus interest in exchange for the same securities (as in definition (a) above) or for different securities.

Item	*GASB Standard*[1]	*Definition*
Risk	GASB-10	Defined variously as uncertainty of loss, chance of loss, or the variance of actual from expected results. Also, the subject matter of an insurance contract (for example, the insured property or liability exposure).
Risk adjustment	GASB-72	See "risk premium".
Risk management	GASB-10	The process of managing an organization's activities to minimize the adverse effects of certain types of losses. The main elements of risk management are risk control (to minimize the losses that strike an organization) and risk financing (to obtain finances to restore the economic damages of those losses).
Risk premium	GASB-72	Compensation sought by risk-averse market participants for bearing the uncertainty inherent in the cash flows of an asset or a liability. Also referred to as a risk adjustment.
Rollover risk	GASB-53	The risk that a hedging derivative instrument associated with a hedgeable item does not extend to the maturity of that hedgeable item. When the hedging derivative instrument terminates, the hedgeable item will no longer have the benefit of the hedging derivative instrument. An example is an interest rate swap that pays the government a variable-rate payment that is designed to match the term of the variable-rate interest payments on the government's bonds. If the hedging derivative instrument's term is 10 years and the hedged debt's term is 30 years, after 10 years the government will lose the benefit of the swap payments.
Salvage	GASB-62	The amount received by an insurer from the sale of property (usually damaged) on which the insurer has paid a total claim to the insured and has obtained title to the property.

Item	GASB Standard[1]	Definition
Secondary recipient (sub-recipient)	GASB-24	The individual or organization, governmental or otherwise, which is the ultimate recipient of a pass-through grant, or another recipient organization that passes the grant through to the ultimate recipient. All rights and responsibilities of the grant award are still with the recipient government which must monitor [and hold accountable] the secondary recipient (sub-recipient) for compliance with the terms and conditions of the grant award. (Sub-recipient monitoring.)
SEC-registered broker-dealer	GASB-3	A securities broker-dealer regulated by the Securities and Exchange Commission under the Securities Exchange Act of 1934. Broker-dealers may be "carrying" (holding depositors funds) or "non-carrying" (not holding depositors funds but regulated by the SEC).
Securities Industry and Financial Markets Association (SIFMA) swap index	GASB-53	An index sponsored by the Securities Industry and Financial Markets Association of seven-day high-grade tax-exempt variable-rate demand obligations, formerly known as The Bond Market Association swap index.
Securities lending agent	GASB-28	An entity that arranges the terms and conditions of loans, monitors the market values of securities lent and the collateral received, and often directs the investment of cash collateral.
Securities lending transactions	GASB-28	Transactions in which governmental entities transfer their securities to broker-dealers and other entities for collateral—which may be cash, securities, or letters of credit—and simultaneously agree to return the collateral for the same securities in the future.
Securitization	GASB-48	The pledging of all or a portion of a revenue stream to provide early access to future cash flows.
Security	GASB-31	A transferrable financial instrument that evidences ownership or creditor-ship, whether in physical or book entry form.

Item	GASB Standard[1]	Definition
Segment	GASB-37	An *identifiable activity* (or grouping of activities), reported as or within an enterprise fund or another stand-alone entity that has one or more bonds or other debt instruments (such as certificates of participation) outstanding, with a revenue stream pledged in support of that debt. In addition, the activity's revenues, expenses, gains and losses, assets, and liabilities are required to be accounted for separately.
Segmented time distributions	GASB-40	Segmented time distributions group investment cash flows into sequential time periods in tabular form.
Select and ultimate rates		Actuarial assumptions that contemplate different rates for successive years. Instead of a single assumed rate with respect to, for example, the investment return assumption, the actuary may apply different rates for the early years of a projection and a single rate for all subsequent years. For example, if an actuary applies an assumed investment return of 8 percent for year 20W0, 7.5 percent for 20W1, and 7 percent for 20W2 and thereafter, then 8 percent and 7.5 percent are select rates, and 7 percent is the ultimate rate.
Self-insurance	GASB-10	A term often used to describe an entity's retention of risk of loss arising out of the ownership of property or from some other cause, rather than transferring that risk to an independent third party through the purchase of an insurance policy. It is sometimes accompanied by the setting aside of assets to fund any related losses. Because no insurance is involved, the term *self-insurance* is a misnomer.

Item	GASB Standard[1]	Definition
Separately financed specific liabilities to the Pension (or OPEB) plan	GASB-75	Specific contractual liabilities to a defined benefit Pension or OPEB plan for one-time assessments to an individual employer or nonemployer contributing entity of amounts resulting from, for example, increases in the total Pension or OPEB liability due to an individual employer joining a Pension or OPEB plan or changes of benefit terms specific to an individual employer, or a contractual commitment for a nonemployer contributing entity to make a one-time contribution for purposes of reducing the net Pension or OPEB liability. The term *separately* financed is intended to differentiate these payables to the Pension or OPEB plan from payables to the Pension or OPEB plan that originate from the portion(s) of the total Pension or OPEB liability that is pooled by two or more employers (or by a single, agent, or cost-sharing employer and a nonemployer contributing entity in a special funding situation) for financing purposes. Payables to the pension or OPEB plan for unpaid (legal, contractual, or statutory) financing obligations associated with the pooled portion of the total pension OPEB liability are not considered to be separately financed specific liabilities, even if separate payment terms have been established for those payables.

Item	GASB Standard[1]	Definition
Service assessments	GASB-6	Service-type special assessment projects are for operating activities and do not result in the purchase or construction of fixed assets. Often the assessments are for services that are normally provided to the public as general governmental functions and that would otherwise be financed by the general fund or a special revenue fund. Those services include street lighting, street cleaning, and snow plowing. Financing for these routine services typically comes from general revenues. However, when routine services are extended to property owners outside the normal service area of the government or are provided at a higher level or at more frequent intervals than for the general public, special assessments are sometimes levied. Only the affected property owners are charged for the additional services.
Service concession arrangement	GASB-60	An arrangement between a transferor (a government) and an operator (governmental or nongovernmental entity) in which (1) the transferor conveys to an operator the right and related obligation to provide services through the use of infrastructure or another public asset (a "facility") in exchange for significant consideration and (2) the operator collects and is compensated by fees from third parties.
Service continuation	GASB-69	Where a new or continuing government intends to provide services similar to the formerly separate governments, organizations, or operations.
Service cost(s) (see also normal cost)	GASB-75	The portion(s) of the actuarial present value of projected benefit payments that are attributed to valuation years.
Service units approach	GASB-42	With regard to accounting for an impaired capital asset, the isolation of the historical cost of the service utility of the capital asset that cannot be used due to the impairment event or change in circumstances. The amount of impairment is determined by evaluating the service provided by the capital asset—either maximum estimated service units or total estimated service units throughout the life of the capital asset—before and after the event or change in circumstance.

Item	GASB Standard[1]	Definition
Servicing (mortgage banking)	GASB-62	Mortgage loan servicing includes collecting monthly mortgagor payments, forwarding payments and related accounting reports to investors, collecting escrow deposits for the payment of mortgagor property taxes and insurance, and paying insurance from escrow resources when due.
Settlement amount	GASB:CS-6	The amount at which an asset could be realized or a liability could be liquidated with the counterparty, other than in an active market.
Settlement rate	GASB-10	The rate at which a monetary liability with uncertain terms can be settled or a monetary asset (receivable) with uncertain terms can be sold.
Shadow price	GASB-79	The net asset value per share of a qualifying external investment pool, calculated using total investments measured at fair value at the calculation date.
Shared service arrangements	GASB-69	In a shared service arrangement, two or more governments agree to consolidate similar operations. For example, two governments may agree to consolidate the separate fire departments of each government into a single shared activity serving the constituents of both governments. The shared service arrangement could be in the form of a separate government, joint venture, jointly governed organization, joint operation, or cost-sharing arrangement.
Short-term obligations	GASB-62	Obligations that are scheduled to mature within one year after the date of a government's financial statements.
Similar productive assets	GASB-62	Productive assets that are of the same general type, that perform the same function, or that are employed in the same line of operations.
Simulation models	GASB-40	Simulation models estimate changes in an investment's or a portfolio's fair value, given hypothetical changes in interest rates. Various models or techniques may be used, such as "shock tests" or value-at-risk.
Single employer	GASB-75	An employer whose employees are provided with pensions or OPEB through a single-employer defined benefit pension or OPEB plan.

Item	GASB Standard[1]	Definition
Single-employer defined benefit pension or OPEB plan (single-employer pension or OPEB plan)	GASB-75	A defined benefit pension or OPEB plan that is used to provide pensions or OPEB to employees of only one employer.
Site Assessment	GASB-49	A site-specific baseline risk assessment that identifies hazards, assesses exposure to the hazards and their toxicity, and characterizes and quantifies the potential risks posed by the site. A site assessment may be noninvasive, involving inquiry into previous uses of a site, site reconnaissance, and interviews (a Phase I site assessment), or may involve invasive testing for pollution (a Phase II site assessment).
SLGS	GASB-7	State and local government securities issued by the U.S. Treasury to provide state and local governments with required cash flows at yields that do not exceed Internal Revenue Service (IRS) arbitrage limits.
Special assessments (special assessment debt)	GASB-6	Capital improvements or services provided by local governments are intended primarily to benefit a particular property owner or group of property owners rather than the general citizenry. The benefitting owners pay a regular assessment to the government through a lien on their property to pay the debt. The liens on assessed properties secure the debt which may or may not be also backed by the full faith and credit of the government as additional security.
Special funding situations	GASB-75	Circumstances in which a nonemployer entity is legally responsible for making contributions directly to a pension or OPEB plan that is used to provide pensions or OPEB to the employees of another entity or entities and either of the following criteria is met:
		a. The amount of contributions for which the nonemployer entity legally is responsible is *not* dependent upon one or more events or circumstances unrelated to the pensions.

Item	GASB Standard[1]	Definition
		b. The nonemployer entity is the only entity with a legal obligation to make contributions directly to a pension or OPEB plan.
Special item	GASB-62	Events and transactions that are distinguished either by their unusual nature or by the infrequency of their occurrence, or both, *within the control of management.*
Special purpose government	GASB-34	Governments engaged usually in a single (or small number of) governmental program(s).
Special revenue fund	GASB-54	Funds are used to account for and report the proceeds of specific revenue sources that are restricted or committed to expenditure for specified purposes other than debt service or capital projects. The term *proceeds of specific revenue sources* establish that one or more specific restricted or committed revenues should be the foundation for a special revenue fund. Those specific restricted or committed revenues may be initially received in another fund and subsequently distributed to a special revenue fund. Those amounts should not be recognized as revenue in the fund initially receiving them; however, those inflows should be recognized as revenue in the special revenue fund in which they will be expended in accordance with specified purposes. Special revenue funds should not be used to account for resources held in trust for individuals, private organizations, or other governments.
Special termination benefits		Benefits offered by an employer for a short period of time as an inducement to employees to hasten the termination of services. For example, to reduce payroll and related costs, an employer might offer enhanced pension benefits or OPEB to employees as an inducement to take early termination, for employees who accept the offer within a sixty-day window of opportunity.
Specific identification	GASB-40	In the context of interest rate risk disclosures, the specific identification method does not compute a disclosure measure but presents a list of each investment, its amount, its maturity date, and any call options.

Item	GASB Standard[1]	Definition
SPF		Special purpose framework (formerly known as OCBOA)
Split-interest agreement	GASB-81	Agreements in which the donor enters into a trust or other legally enforceable agreement (with characteristics that are equivalent to split-interest agreements) under which the donor transfers resources to an intermediary to administer for the unconditional benefit of at least two beneficiaries, one of which can be a government (in the case of GASB-81).
Sponsor		The entity that establishes a plan. The sponsor generally is the employer or one of the employers that participate in the plan to provide benefits for their employees. Sometimes, however, the sponsor establishes the plan for the employees of other entities but does not include its own employees and, therefore, is not a participating employer of that plan. An example is a state government that establishes a plan for the employees of local governments within the state, but the employees of the state government are covered by a different plan.
Sponsoring government	GASB-31	A governmental entity that provides investment services—whether an investment pool or individual investment accounts—to other entities and that therefore has a fiduciary responsibility for those investments.
Spot Price	GASB-53	Current delivery price of a commodity trading in the spot market at a specified location or pricing point. In the spot market, commodities sold or purchased for cash are immediately delivered.

Item	*GASB Standard*[1]	*Definition*
Stabilization arrangements (or stabilization funds or rainy day funds)	GASB-54	Amounts for use in emergency situations or when revenue shortages or budgetary imbalances arise. Those amounts are subject to controls that dictate the circumstances under which they can be spent. Many governments have formal arrangements to maintain amounts for budget or revenue stabilization, working capital needs, contingencies or emergencies, and other similarly titled purposes. The authority to set aside those amounts generally comes from statute, ordinance, resolution, charter, or constitution. Stabilization amounts may be expended only when certain specific circumstances exist. The formal action that imposes the parameters for spending should identify and describe the specific circumstances under which a need for stabilization arises. Those circumstances should be such that they would not be expected to occur routinely. For example, a stabilization amount that can be accessed "in an emergency" would not qualify to be classified within the committed category because the circumstances or conditions that constitute an emergency are not sufficiently detailed, and it is not unlikely that an "emergency" of some nature would routinely occur. Similarly, a stabilization amount that can be accessed to offset an "anticipated revenue shortfall" would not qualify unless the shortfall was quantified and was of a magnitude that would distinguish it from other revenue shortfalls that occur during the normal course of governmental operations.
Stand-alone pension or OPEB plan financial report (stand-alone plan financial report)	GASB-74	A report that contains the financial statements of a pension plan and is issued by the pension or OPEB plan or by the public employee retirement system that administers the plan. The term *stand-alone* is used to distinguish such a financial report from pension plan financial statements that are included as a pension or OPEB trust fund of another government.

Item	*GASB Standard*[1]	*Definition*
Statement of activities	GASB-34	Report of the results of operations of the reporting government presented in a format that reports the net (expense) revenue of its individual functions. An objective of using the net (expense) revenue format is to report the relative financial burden of each of the reporting government's functions on its taxpayers. This format identifies the extent to which each function of the government draws from the general revenues of the government or is self-financing through fees and intergovernmental aid. General revenues, contributions to term and permanent endowments, contributions to permanent fund principal, special and extraordinary items, and transfers should be reported separately after the total net expenses of the government's functions, ultimately arriving at the "change in net [position]" for the period.
Statement of cash flows	GASB-34	Required statement for proprietary funds directly showing the cash inflows and outflows of a period and reconciling operating cash flows to operating income.
Statement of Net [Position] (Statement of Fiduciary Net Position)	GASB-63	Report of all financial and capital resources. Governments are encouraged to present the statement in a format that displays assets plus deferred outflows of resources less liabilities plus deferred inflows of resources equal net [position], although the traditional balance sheet format (assets plus deferred outflows of resources equal liabilities plus deferred inflows of resources plus net position) may be used. Regardless of the format used, however, the statement of net [position] should report the difference between assets plus deferred outflows of resources and liabilities plus deferred inflows of resources as net position, not fund balances or equity.
Statement of revenues, expenditures, and changes in fund balances	GASB-34	A report of information about the inflows, outflows, and balances of current financial resources of each major governmental fund and for the nonmajor governmental funds in the aggregate. A total column should be presented as of the period ended by the reporting date.

Item	GASB Standard[1]	Definition
Statement of revenues, expenses, and changes in fund net position or fund equity (statement of revenues, expenses, and changes in fiduciary net position)	GASB-34	The operating statement for proprietary funds (or fiduciary funds).
Stock rights	GASB-31	Rights given to existing stockholders to purchase newly issued shares in proportion to their holdings at a specific date.
Stock warrants	GASB-31	Certificates entitling the holder to acquire shares of stock at a certain price within a stated period. Warrants often are made part of the issuance of bonds or preferred or common stock.
Strike price	GASB-53	In the case of a call option, the price at which the holder of a call option may purchase a financial instrument or commodity. In the case of a put option, it is the price at which the holder may sell a financial instrument or commodity. The strike price also is known as the exercise price.
Structured notes	GASB-31	Debt securities whose cash flow characteristics (coupon, redemption amount, or stated maturity) depend on one or more indexes, or that have embedded forwards or options.
Structured settlement	GASB-10	A means of satisfying a claim liability, consisting of an initial cash payment to meet specific present financial needs combined with a stream of future payments designed to meet future financial needs, generally funded by annuity contracts.
Subrogation	GASB-62	The right of an insurer to pursue any course of recovery of damages, in its name or in the name of the policyholder, against a third party who is liable for costs relating to an insured event that have been paid by the insurer.

Item	GASB Standard[1]	Definition
Subscriber related costs (cable television systems)	GASB-62	These are costs incurred to obtain and retain subscribers to the cable television system and include costs of billing and collection, bad debts, and mailings; repairs and maintenance of taps and connections; franchise fees related to revenues or number of subscribers; general and administrative system costs, such as salary of the system manager and office rent; programming costs for additional channels used in the marketing effort or costs related to revenues from, or number of subscribers to, per channel or per program service; and direct selling costs.
Subsequent event	GASB-56	Events or transactions that affect the financial statements after the reporting date. Recognized events require adjustment to the financial statements as they existed prior to the reporting date. Nonrecognized events may require disclosure.
Subsidized capital assets	GASB-42	Assets that are used to produce revenues through charges for services or fees, but that a government would subsidize, if needed, because the service provided by the capital assets is a public benefit. The revenues produced are set by the management of the government, perhaps based upon cost of services or political considerations, rather than set with consideration of market influences. Examples include water and sewer systems, stadiums, convention centers, metropolitan transportation systems, hospitals, and toll roads.
Substantive plan		The terms of an OPEB plan as understood by the employer(s) and plan members.

Item	GASB Standard[1]	Definition
Superfund	GASB-49	A federal law (the Comprehensive Environmental Response, Compensation, and Liability Act of 1980 [CERCLA], as amended by the Superfund Amendments and Reauthorization Act of 1986 [SARA], which together are referred to as Superfund) that provides the U.S. Environmental Protection Agency with broad authority to order liable parties to remediate polluted sites or use Superfund money to remediate them and then seek to recover its costs and additional damages.
Supporting (or supplementary) information (SI).	GASB:CS-3	Supporting information that is useful for placing basic financial statements and notes to basic financial statements in an appropriate operational, economic, or historical context. SI is presented with the basic financial statements, notes to basic financial statements, and RSI in a government's general purpose external financial report. Although the GASB does not require SI to be presented, preparers of governmental financial reports who elect to present SI (or are otherwise required by law or regulations to present SI) with their basic financial statements, notes to basic financial statements, and RSI should follow any applicable GASB-issued or GASB-cleared guidance regarding the format and content of that information.
Susceptible to accrual	NCGA-1	Revenues of governmental funds that are collected or collectible within the current period or soon enough thereafter to be used to pay liabilities of the current period.
Swap	GASB-53	A type of derivative instrument in which there is an agreement to exchange future cash flows. These cash flows may be either fixed or variable and may be either received or paid. Variable cash flows depend on a reference rate.

Item	GASB Standard[1]	Definition
Swaption	GASB-53	An option to enter into a swap. When a swaption is an interest rate option, it may be used to hedge long-term debt. When a government sells a swaption (also called writing a swaption), a cash payment may be received. Option pricing theory, including time and volatility measures, is used to value swaptions.
Synthetic instrument method	GASB-53	A method of evaluating effectiveness that combines a hedged item and a potential hedging derivative instrument into a hypothetical financial instrument to evaluate whether the hypothetical financial instrument pays a substantively fixed rate.
Synthetic price	GASB-53	The price of the existing or expected commodity transaction as adjusted by the effect of the potential hedging derivative instrument. That is, the net price considering both the actual price of the existing or expected commodity transaction and the effect of the potential hedging derivative instrument.
Taft-Hartley Plan	GASB-78	A type of multiple-employer defined benefit plan, where a state or local government *may* be an employer with employees provided pensions. As used in GASB-78, these types of plans utilize irrevocable trusts or equivalent arrangements, but are not managed by a state or local government, are used to provide defined benefit pensions *both* to employees of state or local governmental employers *and* to employees of employers that are *not* state or local government employers and there are no predominant state or local governmental employer, either individually or collectively with other state or local governmental employers that provide pensions through the pension plan. Typically, these plans are managed by labor unions, are subject to the provisions of ERISA and may have reporting to the Pension Benefit Guarantee Corporation (a U.S. government agency). Such plans have been in existence since the Taft-Hartley Act of 1947.

Item	GASB Standard[1]	Definition
Tail	GASB-10	The length of time between the occurrence of an event giving rise to a claim and the actual reporting and eventual settlement of that claim.
Tail coverage	GASB-10	A type of insurance policy designed to cover claims incurred before, but reported after, cancellation or expiration of a claims-made policy. (The term *extended discovery coverage* is used in the commercial insurance industry.)
Take out agreement	GASBI-1	Used to provide long-term financing in the event the remarking agent is unable to sell demand bonds within a specified period subsequent to the exercise of the demand by bondholders.
TAN		Tax anticipation note
Tax Abatement	GASB-77	A reduction in tax revenues that results from an agreement between one or more governments and an individual or entity in which (a) one or more governments promise to forgo tax revenues to which they are otherwise entitled and (b) the individual or entity promises to take a specific action after the agreement has been entered into that contributes to economic development or otherwise benefits the governments or the citizens of those governments.
Tax Deductions	GASB-77	Tax deductions are subtractions from the tax base (for example, gross income). Thus, deductions indirectly affect the amount of tax due by making the tax base smaller. In general, tax credits are directly applied to the amount of tax due. This is why tax credits are generally "more valuable" than deductions; they provide a dollar-for-dollar reduction in the amount of tax due.

Item	GASB Standard[1]	Definition
Tax Expenditure(s)	GASB-77	Governmental programs employed to lower the taxes of broad classes of taxpayers, or the taxes of individuals or entities based on the performance of specific actions. Tax expenditures include tax exemptions, tax deductions, and *tax abatements*, among other programs. Governments exempt certain individuals, entities, or activities from taxation. Common examples of *tax exemptions* include the exclusion of income earned on municipal bonds from income taxes and the full or partial exemption of senior citizens and military veterans from property taxes.
Terminal funding		A method of funding a pension plan under which the entire Actuarial Present Value of benefits for each individual is contributed to the plan's fund at the time of withdrawal, retirement or benefit commencement (No longer utilized in general-purpose external financial reporting).
Termination benefits	GASB-75	Inducements offered by employers to active employees to hasten the termination of services, or payments made in consequence of the early termination of services. Termination benefits include early-retirement incentives, severance benefits, and other termination-related benefits.
Termination risk	GASB-53	The risk that a hedging derivative instrument's unscheduled end will affect a government's asset and liability strategy or will present the government with potentially significant unscheduled termination payments to the counterparty. For example, a government may be relying on an interest rate swap to insulate it from the possibility of increasing interest rate payments. If the swap has an unscheduled termination, that benefit would not be available.
Third-party recipient	GASB-24	For purposes of on-behalf payments for fringe benefits and salaries, the individual or organization that receives the payment. For example, an employee who receives a salary supplement or a pension plan that receives pension contributions.

Item	GASB Standard[1]	Definition
Time requirements	GASB-33	Specification of (a) the period when resources are required to be used (sold, disbursed, or consumed) or when use may begin (for example, operating or capital grants for a specific period) or (b) that the resources are required to be maintained intact in perpetuity or until a specified date or event has occurred (for example, permanent endowments, term endowments, and similar agreements). Time requirements affect the timing of recognition of nonexchange transactions.
Time value of an option	GASB-53	The portion of an option's fair value that is attributable to the time remaining on the option before expiration. An option with time value but no intrinsic value is out-of- the-money or at-the-market. Time value is the difference between an option's fair value and its intrinsic value.
Tort	GASB-10	A wrongful act, injury, or damage (not involving a breach of contract) for which a civil action can be brought.
Total direct rate	GASB-44	The weighted average of all individual direct rates applied by the government preparing the statistical section information.
Total OPEB liability	GASB-75	The portion of the actuarial present value of projected benefit payments that is attributed to past periods of member service in conformity with the requirements of GAAP. The total OPEB liability is the liability of employers and nonemployer contributing entities to plan members for benefits provided through a defined benefit OPEB plan that *is not* administered through a trust.
Total pension liability	GASB-73	The portion of the actuarial present value of projected benefit payments that is attributed to past periods of employee service.
Transaction costs	GASB-72	The costs to sell an asset or transfer a liability in the principal (or most advantageous) market for the asset or liability that (1) are directly attributable to the disposal of the asset or the transfer of the liability and (2) meet both of the following criteria: a. They result directly from and are essential to that transaction.

Item	GASB Standard[1]	Definition
		b. They would not have been incurred by the entity had the decision to sell the asset or transfer the liability not been made.
Transaction date	GASB-62	The date at which a transaction (for example, a sale or purchase of merchandise or services) is recorded in accounting records in conformity with GAAP. A long-term commitment may have more than one transaction date (for example, the due date of each progress payment under a construction contract is an anticipated transaction date).
Transaction gain or loss (foreign currency transaction)	GASB-62	Transaction gains or losses result from a change in exchange rates between the U.S. dollar and the currency in which a foreign currency transaction is denominated. They represent an increase or decrease in (a) the actual U.S. dollar cash flows realized upon settlement of foreign currency transactions and (b) the expected U.S. dollar cash flows on unsettled foreign currency transactions.
Transfers of operations	GASB-69	A *transfer of operations* is a government combination involving the operations of a government or nongovernmental entity, rather than a combination of legally separate entities, in which no significant consideration is exchanged. Operations may be transferred to another existing entity or to a new entity.
Transition year		The fiscal year in which a new GAAP statement is first implemented.
Transportation costs	GASB-72	The costs that would be incurred to transport an asset from its current location to its principal (or most advantageous) market.
Troubled debt restructuring	GASB-62	When a creditor for economic or legal reasons related to the debtor's financial difficulties grants a concession to the debtor that it would not otherwise consider. That concession either stems from an agreement between the creditor and the debtor or is imposed by law or a court.

Item	GASB Standard[1]	Definition
Trust (or equivalent arrangement	GASB-84	Specifically for the purposes of implementation of GASB-84, where assets are (a) administered through an agreement or equivalent arrangement (hereafter jointly referred to as a trust) in which the government itself is not a beneficiary, (b) dedicated to providing benefits to recipients in accordance with the benefit terms, and (c) legally protected from the creditors of the government.
Type of contract	GASB-10	Classification of policies or participation contracts based on the nature of the coverages provided that distinguishes them as an identifiable class of contract. For example, types of contracts may include general liability, property, automobile liability, automobile physical damage, multi-peril, and workers' compensation.
Unallocated insurance contracts	GASB-67	Contracts with an insurance company under which payments to the insurance company are accumulated in an unallocated pool or pooled account (not allocated to specific plan members) to be used either directly or through the purchase of annuities to meet benefit payments when plan members retire. Monies held by the insurance company under an unallocated contract may be withdrawn and otherwise invested.
Unassigned fund balance	GASB-54	The residual classification for the general fund. This classification represents fund balance that has not been assigned to other funds and that has not been restricted, committed, or assigned to specific purposes within the general fund. The general fund should be the only fund that reports a positive unassigned fund balance amount. In other governmental funds, if expenditures incurred for specific purposes exceeded the amounts restricted, committed, or assigned to those purposes, it may be necessary to report a negative unassigned fund balance.
Uncollateralized deposit	GASB-40	An uncollateralized deposit does not have securities pledged to the depositor-government.

Item	GASB Standard[1]	Definition
Unconditional benefit	GASB-81	A right belonging to the government that cannot be taken away without the government's consent, such as an unconditional beneficial interest.
Underlying securities	GASB-28	The securities lent by the lender to the borrower.
Underlyings	GASB-53	A specified interest rate, security price, commodity price, foreign exchange rate, index of prices or rates, or other variable (including the occurrence or nonoccurrence of a specified event such as a scheduled payment under a contract). An underlying may be a price or rate of an asset or liability but is not the asset or liability itself.
Underwriting	GASB-10	The process of selecting, classifying, evaluating, rating, and assuming risks.
Undivided interest (joint operation)	GASB-14	An arrangement that resembles a joint venture but no entity or organization is created by the participants. An undivided interest is an ownership arrangement in which two or more parties own property in which title is held individually to the extent of each party's interest. Implied in that definition is that each participant is also liable for specific, identifiable obligations (if any) of the operation. Because an undivided interest is not a legal entity, borrowing to finance its operations often is done individually by each participant. An additional consequence of the absence of a formal organizational structure is that there is no entity with assets, liabilities, expenditures/expenses, and revenues—and thus, *equity*—to allocate to participants. A government participating in this type of arrangement should report its assets, liabilities, expenditures/expenses, and revenues that are associated with the joint operation.
Unfunded actuarial accrued liability (unfunded actuarial liability)	GASB-43	The excess of the Actuarial Accrued Liability over the Actuarial Value of Assets.

Item	GASB Standard[1]	Definition
Unguaranteed residual value (leases)	GASB-62	The estimated residual value of the leased property exclusive of any portion guaranteed by the lessee or by a third party unrelated to the lessor.
Unit of account	GASB-72	The level at which an asset or a liability is aggregated or disaggregated for recognition or disclosure purposes.
Unmatured long-term indebtedness	GASBI-6	The portion of general long-term indebtedness that is not yet due for payment reported as general long-term liabilities of the government, rather than as governmental fund liabilities. Applies not only to formal debt issues such as bonds, but also to other forms of general long-term indebtedness, including capital leases, compensated absences, claims and judgments, pensions, special termination benefits, landfill closure and postclosure obligations, and "other commitments that are not current liabilities properly recorded in governmental funds.
Unobservable inputs	GASB-72	Inputs for which market data are not available and that are developed using the best information available about the assumptions that market participants would use when pricing an asset or liability.
Unrestricted Net Position	GASB-63	The net amount of the assets, deferred outflows of resources, liabilities, and deferred inflows of resources that are not included in the determination of net investment in capital assets or the restricted component of net position.
Usable capacity	GASB-42	The service utility of a capital asset that at acquisition was expected to be used to provide service. Current usable capacity of a capital asset is the capacity in a current period. Original usable capacity was the capacity of a capital asset at inception. Maximum service capacity is a rate of use where the capital asset is utilized to its maximum potential. Surplus capacity is the difference between maximum service capacity and usable capacity.

Item	GASB Standard[1]	Definition
Use (direct the use of assets)	GASB-84	Expending or consuming an asset for the benefit of individuals, organizations, or other governments, outside of the government's provision of services to them.
Users (of financial reports)	GASB:CS-1	(a) Those to whom government is primarily accountable (the citizenry), (b) those who directly represent the citizens (legislative and oversight bodies), and (c) those who lend or who participate in the lending process (investors and creditors). The needs of intergovernmental grantors and other users are considered to be encompassed within the needs of the three primary user groups. Internal managers in the executive branch of government who have ready access to financial data through *internal* reporting are not considered *primary* users.
Valuation technique	GASB-72	A specific method or combination of methods used to determine the fair value of an asset or liability.
Variable rate investment	GASB-40	An investment with terms that provide for the adjustment of its interest rate on set dates (such as the last day of a month or calendar quarter) and that, upon each adjustment until the final maturity of the instrument or the period remaining until the principal amount can be recovered through demand, can reasonably be expected to have a fair value that will be unaffected by interest rate changes.
Variance power	GASB-81	The unilateral power to redirect the use of the transferred resources to another beneficiary, overriding the donor's instructions. This transfer would occur without the approval of the donor, specified beneficiaries, or any other interested party.

Item	GASB Standard[1]	Definition
Vesting method	GASB-16	An estimate of accrued sick leave liability based on the sick leave accumulated at the balance sheet date by those employees who currently are eligible to receive termination payments as well as other employees who are expected to become eligible in the future to receive such payments. To calculate the liability, these accumulations should be reduced to the maximum amount allowed as a termination payment. Accruals for those employees who are expected to become eligible in the future should be based on assumptions concerning the probability that individual employees or classes or groups of employees will become eligible to receive termination payments.
Voluntary nonexchange transaction	GASB-33	Legislative or contractual agreements, other than exchanges, entered into willingly by the parties to the agreement (for example, certain grants and private donations).
Voting majority	GASB-14	When the number of a government's appointees to a component unit's board is sufficient to exhibit control.
Weekly liquid assets	GASB-79	For purposes of GASB-79, only the following are weekly liquid assets:

For purposes of GASB-79, only the following are weekly liquid assets:

a. Cash, including demand deposits and certificates of deposit that mature within five business days and are expected to be held to maturity

b. U.S. government securities that are direct obligations

c. Securities that (1) are U.S. government securities that are not direct obligations, (2) are issued at a discount without provision for the payment of interest, and (3) have a remaining maturity of 60 days or less

d. Securities that will mature within five business days, with maturity determined without taking into account the maturity shortening features

e. Securities subject to a demand feature that is exercisable and payable within five business days

Item	GASB Standard[1]	Definition
		f. Amounts receivable and due unconditionally within five business days on pending sales of portfolio securities.
Weighted average maturity (WAM)	GASB-40	A weighted average maturity measure expresses investment time horizons—the time when investments become due and payable—in years or months, weighted to reflect the dollar size of individual investments within an investment type.
Wrap contract	GASB-53	A contract in which the issuer provides assurance that the adjustments to the interest crediting rate of a synthetic guaranteed investment contract will not result in a future interest crediting rate that is less than zero.
Written option	GASB-53	An option sold by a government. The purchaser of the option becomes the holder of it.
Yellow Book		GAGAS issued by GAO
Yield-maintenance repurchase–reverse repurchase agreement	GASB-3	A dollar repurchase—reverse repurchase agreement in which the parties agree that the securities returned will provide the seller-borrower with a yield as specified in the agreement.
Zero fair value	GASB-53	Value of a derivative instrument that is either entered into or exited with no consideration being exchanged. A zero fair value should be within a dealer's normal bid/offer spread.

[1] Latest GASB standard referencing the term.

Accounting Resources on the Web

Presented here are World Wide Web URLs of interest to practitioners. Because of the constantly changing nature of the Internet, addresses change and new resources become available every day. To find additional resources, use search engines such as Bing (http://www.bing.com/), Google (http://www.google.com/), and Yahoo! (http://search.yahoo.com).

PRACTICE POINT: The GASB has issued the full text of all of its pronouncements freely on the Internet, at www.gasb.org (click on "Pronouncements"). The full text can be accessed along with summaries and status. Interpretations and technical bulletins are also available. Text is offered as PDF files, but can be copied and pasted.

Accounting Research Manager® http://www.AccountingResearchManager.com

Accounting Today **magazine** http://www.accountingtoday.com

AICPA http://www.aicpa.org

AICPA Government Audit Quality Center http://www.aicpa.org/gaqc

American Accounting Association http://aaahq.org

American Legal Publishing Corp. http://www.amlegal.com/library

American Public Power Association (APPA) http://www.appanet.org

American Water Works Association http://www.awwa.org

Association for Budgeting and Financial Management (ABFM) http://www.abfm.org

Association of Certified Fraud Examiners (ACFE) http://www.acfe.com/

Association of College and University Auditors (ACUA) http://www.acua.org/ACUA/College_University_Auditors.asp

Association of Financial Guaranty Insurers (AFGI) http://www.afgi.org

Association of Government Accountants (AGA) http://www.agacgfm.org

Association of Latino Professionals in Finance and Accounting (ALPFA) http://www.alpfa.org

Association of Local Government Auditors http://www.GovernmentAuditors.org

Association of Public Pension Fund Auditors (APPFA) http://www.appfa.org

Association of School Business Officials International http://www.asbointl.org

Automated Clearing House https://www.fiscal.treasury.gov/fsservices/instit/pmt/ach/ach_home.htm

Bloomberg News on Municipal Bonds http://www.bloomberg.com/news/municipal-bonds

BoardSource http://www.boardsource.org

Bond Buyer (including municipal bond indexes) http://www.bondbuyer.com

Bureau of Labor Statistics http://www.bls.gov

Bureau of the Fiscal Service (Treasury Dept.) http://www.fiscal.treasury.gov

Catalog of Federal Domestic Assistance (CFDA) http://www.cfda.gov

CCH Incorporated http://CCHGroup.com

CCH Learning Center http://CCHGroup.com/LearningCenter

CCH Seminars http://CCHGroup.com/Seminars

Center for Retirement Research at Boston College http://crr.bc.edu/

Check Payment Systems Association http://www.cpsa-checks.org

Chief Financial Officers Council—2CFR200 *Uniform Administrative Requirements, Cost Principles, and Audit Requirements for Federal Awards* **(Uniform Guidance)** https://cfo.gov/grants/

Code of Federal Regulations http://www.gpo.gov/fdsys/browse/collectionCfr.action

Committee of Sponsoring Organizations of the Treadway Commission (COSO) http://www.coso.org

Congress.gov https://www.congress.gov/

Council of State Governments (CSG) http://www.csg.org

Council of the Inspectors General on Integrity & Efficiency (CIGIE) http://www.ignet.gov

Department of Education OIG's Non-Federal Audit Team https://www2.ed.gov/about/offices/list/oig/index.html

Electronic Municipal Market Access (EMMA) http://emma.msrb.org

Electronic Privacy Information Center http://epic.org

FASB http://www.fasb.org

Federal Accounting Standards Advisory Board (FASAB) http://www.fasab.gov

Federal Audit Clearinghouse http://harvester.census.gov/facweb

Federal Digital System (FDsys) http://www.govinfo.gov

Federal Register http://www.gpo.gov/fdsys/browse/collection.action?collectionCode=FR

FEDSTATS http://fedstats.sites.usa.gov

GASB http://www.gasb.org

General Services Administration http://www.gsa.gov

Governing **magazine** http://www.governing.com

Government Accountability Office http://www.gao.gov

Government Accounting Standards http://gao.gov/yellowbook/overview

Government Finance Officers Association (GFOA) http://www.gfoa.org

Government Publishing Office http://www.gpo.gov

Grants Portal http://www.grants.gov/

GuideStar http://www.guidestar.org

Harvard John F. Kennedy School of Government Executive Education https://exed.hks.harvard.edu/

Health and Human Services (HHS) Grants/Funding http://www.hhs.gov/grants

HUD Audit Guidance links https://www.hudoig.gov/reports-publications/audit-guides

HUD Office of Public and Indian Housing (PIH) https://www.hud.gov/program_offices/public_indian_housing

HUD Real Estate Assessment Center (REAC) https://www.hud.gov/program_offices/public_indian_housing/reac

Information for Tax-Exempt Organizations http://www.irs.gov/charities/index.html

Institute of Internal Auditors, The (IIA) http://www.theiia.org

Institute of Management Accountants (IMA) http://www.imanet.org

IntelliConnect® http://IntelliConnect.cch.com

Intergovernmental Audit Forums http://www.auditforum.org

Internal Revenue Service (IRS) http://www.irs.gov

International City/County Managers Association http://www.icma.org

International Institute of Municipal Clerks (IIMC) http://www.iimc.com

Investment Company Institute (ICI) http://www.ici.org

Legal Information Institute (Cornell Law School) http://www.law.cornell.edu/statutes.html

Minority Business Development Agency http://www.mbda.gov

Municipal Code Corporation (MCC) http://www.municode.com

Municipal Securities Rulemaking Board (MSRB) http://www.msrb.org

NACHA—The Electronic Payments Association http://www.nacha.org

National Association of Asian American Professionals (NAAAP) http://www.naaap.org

National Association of Black Accountants, Inc. http://www.nabainc.org

National Association of Bond Lawyers http://www.nabl.org

National Association of College and University Business Officers (NACUBO) http://www.nacubo.org

National Association of Counties (NACO) http://www.naco.org

National Association of Housing and Redevelopment Officials (NAHRO) http://www.nahro.org

National Association of Regional Councils http://www.narc.org

National Association of State Agencies for Surplus Property http://www.nasasp.org

National Association of State Auditors, Comptrollers, and Treasurers (NASACT) http://www.nasact.org

National Association of State Boards of Accountancy (NASBA) http://www.nasba.org

National Association of State Budget Officers http://www.nasbo.org

National Association of State Retirement Administrators http://www.nasra.org

National Conference of State Legislatures (NCSL) http://www.ncsl.org

National Federation of Municipal Analysts (NFMA) http://www.nfma.org

National Governors Association (NGA) http://www.nga.org

National Labor Relations Board http://www.nlrb.gov

National League of Cities (NLC) http://www.nlc.org

National Rural Development Partnership http://www.rd.usda.gov

Native American Finance Officers Association (NAFOA) http://www.nafoa.org

North American Industry Classification System (NAICS) http://www.census.gov/eos/www/naics

Occupational Employment Statistics http://stats.bls.gov/oes/home.htm

Office of Federal Contract Compliance Programs (OFCCP) http://www.dol.gov/ofccp

Office of Management and Budget http://www.whitehouse.gov/omb

Office of Women's Business Ownership (SBA) http://www.sba.gov/offices/headquarter/wbo

Privacy Foundation http://www.privacyfoundation.org

Prompt Payment Act Interest Rate http://www.fms.treas.gov/prompt/rates.html

Public Pension Financial Forum (P2F2) http://www.P2F2.org

Securities and Exchange Commission http://www.sec.gov

Securities Industry and Financial Markets Association (SIFMA) http://www.sifma.org

Software and Information Industry Association (SIIA) http://www.siia.net

Standards for Internal Control in the Federal Government (the Green Book) http://gao.gov/greenbook/overview

The Library of Congress http://www.loc.gov

USA CityLink http://www.usacitylink.com

USA.gov http://www.usa.gov

USA.gov for Nonprofits http://www.usa.gov/Business/Nonprofit.shtml

USA Spending.Gov http://www.usaspending.gov

U.S. Census Bureau: Federal, State, and Local Government Page http://www.census.gov/govs/

U.S. Code Search http://uscode.house.gov

U.S. Conference of Mayors http://www.usmayors.org

U.S. Department of Agriculture http://www.usda.gov

U.S. Department of Commerce http://www.commerce.gov

U.S. Department of Defense http://www.defense.gov

U.S. Department of Education http://www.ed.gov

U.S. Department of Energy http://www.energy.gov

U.S. Department of Health and Human Services http://www.hhs.gov

U.S. Department of Housing and Urban Development http://www.hud.gov

U.S. Department of Labor http://www.dol.gov

U.S. Department of State http://www.state.gov

U.S. Department of the Interior http://www.doi.gov

U.S. Department of the Treasury's Listing of Approved Sureties http://www.fiscal.treasury.gov/fsreports/ref/suretyBnd/c570.htm

U.S. Department of Transportation http://www.dot.gov

U.S. Department of Treasury Bureau of the Fiscal Service http://www.fiscal.treasury.gov

U.S. Department of Veterans Affairs http://www.va.gov

U.S. Environmental Protection Agency http://www.epa.gov

U.S. GAO Bid Protest Decisions http://www.gao.gov/decisions/bidpro/bidpro.htm

U.S. Government Forms http://www.gsa.gov/forms

U.S. House of Representatives http://www.house.gov

U.S. House of Representatives Current Floor Proceedings http://clerk.house.gov/floorsummary/floor.aspx

U.S. HUD Client Information and Policy System http://portal.hud.gov/hudportal/HUD?src=/program_offices/administration/hudclips

U.S. HUD Office of Inspector General http://www.hudoig.gov

U.S. Postal Service http://www.usps.com

U.S. Senate http://www.senate.gov

U.S. Small Business Administration http://www.sba.gov

U.S. Transportation and Safety Administration http://www.tsa.gov

U.S. Treasury http://www.treasury.gov

Wolters Kluwer http://www.wolterskluwer.com/Products/Tax-And-Accounting

CROSS-REFERENCE

ORIGINAL PRONOUNCEMENTS TO COMPREHENSIVE *GOVERNMENTAL GAAP GUIDE* CHAPTERS

This locator provides instant cross-reference between an original pronouncement and the chapter(s) in this publication where such pronouncement appears. Original pronouncements are listed chronologically on the left and the chapter(s) in which the pronouncement appears in CCH's *Governmental GAAP Guide* on the right. Primary Codification section references are in parentheses.

GOVERNMENTAL ACCOUNTING STANDARDS BOARD STATEMENTS

GASB Statements are issued by the Governmental Accounting Standards Board under the authority of ET Sections 1.320.001 and 2.320.001 (Accounting Principles Rule) of the AICPA's *Code of Professional Conduct—Revised*. (Part 1 is designated for members in public practice, part 2 is designated for members in business— defined in ET Section 0.400.32 as someone who is employed or engaged on a contractual or even volunteer basis in a(n) executive, staff, governance, advisory, or administrative capacity in such areas as industry, the public sector, education, the not-for-profit sector, and regulatory or professional bodies.) ET Sections 1.320.001 and 2.320.001 state the following:

> A member shall not (1) express an opinion or state affirmatively that the financial statements or other financial data of any entity are presented in conformity with generally accepted accounting principles or (2) state that he or she is not aware of any material modifications that should be made to such statements or data in order for them to be in conformity with generally accepted accounting principles, if such statements or data contain any departure from an accounting principle promulgated by bodies designated by Council to establish such principles that has a material effect on the statements or data taken as a whole. If, however, the statements or data contain such a departure and the member can demonstrate that due to unusual circumstances the financial statements or data would otherwise have been misleading, the member can comply with the rule by describing the departure, its approximate effects, if practicable, and the reasons why compliance with the principle would result in a misleading statement.

Unless otherwise specified, GASB Statements apply to financial reports of all state and local governmental entities, including public benefit corporations and authorities, public employee retirement systems, and governmental utilities, hospitals, colleges, and universities.

OBSERVATION: GASB *Implementation Guides* (including the *Comprehensive Implementation Guide*) are authoritative in accordance with GASB Statement No. 76, par. 4(b). Footnote 2 to that paragraph notes that authoritative material from the GASB's various implementation guides is incorporated periodically into the *Comprehensive Implementation Guide*. In the same paragraph, authoritative U.S. GAAP is incorporated periodically into the *Codification of Governmental Accounting and Financial Reporting Standards* and when presented in the *Codification*, it retains its authoritative status. Due to the breadth and depth of the *Implementation Guides*, codification references are not noted for the *Implementation Guides* in the following tables. Where necessary to clarify issues in U.S. GAAP questions, answers, and further analyses are included in the text of the *Governmental GAAP Guide*.

Original Pronouncement	*Governmental GAAP Guide Reference*
GASB Statement No. 1 (1984)	
Authoritative Status of NCGA Pronouncements and AICPA Industry Audit Guide (throughout)	Foundation and Overview of Governmental Generally Accepted Accounting Principles, Chapter **1**
GASB Statement No. 2 (1986)	
Financial Reporting of Deferred Compensation Plans Adopted under the Provisions of Internal Revenue Code Section 457 (D25)	Rescinded
GASB Statement No. 3 (1986)	
Deposits with Financial Institutions, Investments (Including Repurchase Agreements), and Reverse Repurchase Agreements (C20; I50; R10)	Deposits, Investments, and Derivative Instruments, Chapter **9**
GASB Statement No. 4 (1986)	
Applicability of FASB Statement No. 87, "Employers' Accounting for Pensions," to State and Local Governmental Employers	Rescinded
GASB Statement No. 5 (1986)	
Disclosure of Pension Information by Public Employee Retirement Systems and State and Local Governmental Employers	Rescinded
GASB Statement No. 6 (1987)	
Accounting and Financial Reporting for Special Assessments (S40)	Special Assessments, Chapter **19**
GASB Statement No. 7 (1987)	
Advance Refundings Resulting in Debt Defeased Debt (D20)	Long-Term Debt, Chapter **12**
GASB Statement No. 8 (1988)	
Applicability of FASB Statement No. 93, "Recognition of Depreciation by Not-for-Profit Organizations," to Certain State and Local Governmental Entities (Co5; Pu5)	Rescinded
GASB Statement No. 9 (1989)	
Reporting Cash Flows of Proprietary and Nonexpendable Trust Funds and Governmental Entities That Use Proprietary Fund Accounting (2450)	Proprietary Funds, Chapter **7**

Original Pronouncement	*Governmental GAAP Guide Reference*
GASB Statement No. 10 (1989)	
Accounting and Financial Reporting for Risk Financing and Related Insurance Issues (Po20; C50)	Public Entity Risk Pools, Chapter **23**
GASB Statement No. 11 (1990)	
Measurement Focus and Basis of Accounting—Governmental Fund Operating Statements	Rescinded
GASB Statement No. 12 (1990)	
Disclosure of Information on Postemployment Benefits Other Than Pension Benefits by State and Local Governmental Employers (P50)	Rescinded
GASB Statement No. 13 (1990)	
Accounting for Operating Leases with Scheduled Rent Increases (L20) (to be fully rescinded upon implementation of GASB-87)	Leases and Service Concession Arrangements, Chapter **14**
GASB Statement No. 14 (1991)	
The Financial Reporting Entity (2100, 2300; 2600, J50)	Governmental Financial Reporting Entity, Chapter **4**
GASB Statement No. 15 (1991)	
Governmental College and University Accounting and Financial Reporting Models (Co5)	Rescinded
GASB Statement No. 16 (1992)	
Accounting for Compensated Absences (C60)	Pension, Postemployment, and Other Employee Benefit Liabilities, Chapter **13**
GASB Statement No. 17 (1993)	
Measurement Focus and Basis of Accounting—Governmental Fund Operating Statements: Amendment of the Effective Dates of GASB Statement No. 11 and Related Statements	Rescinded
GASB Statement No. 18 (1993)	
Accounting for Municipal Solid Waste, Landfill Closure and Postclosure Care Costs (L10)	Other Liabilities, Chapter **16**
GASB Statement No. 19 (1993)	
Governmental College and University Omnibus Statement (Co5)	Rescinded
GASB Statement No. 20 (1993)	
Accounting and Financial Reporting for Proprietary Funds and Other Governmental Entities That Use Proprietary Fund Accounting (P80)	Rescinded
GASB Statement No. 21 (1993)	
Accounting for Escheat Property (E70)	Other Assets and Deferred Outflows of Resources, Chapter **11**

Original Pronouncement	*Governmental GAAP Guide Reference*
GASB Statement No. 22 (1993)	
Accounting for Taxpayer-Assessed Tax Revenues in Governmental Funds (1600)	Rescinded
GASB Statement No. 23 (1993)	
Accounting and Financial Reporting for Refundings of Debt Reported by Proprietary Activities (D20)	Long-Term Debt, Chapter **12**
GASB Statement No. 24 (1994)	
Accounting and Financial Reporting Certain Grants and Other Financial Assistance (F60, N50)	Revenues: Nonexchange and Exchange Transactions, Chapter **17**
GASB Statement No. 25 (1994)	
Financial Reporting for Defined Benefit Pension Plans and Note Disclosures for Defined Contribution Plans (Pe5)	Rescinded
GASB Statement No. 26 (1994)	
Financial Reporting for Postemployment Healthcare Plans Administered by Defined Benefit Pension Plans (Po50)	Rescinded
GASB Statement No. 27 (1994)	
Accounting for Pensions by State and Local Governmental Employers (P20)	Rescinded
GASB Statement No. 28 (1995)	
Accounting and Financial Reporting for Securities Lending Transactions (I60)	Deposits, Investments, and Derivative Instruments, Chapter **9**
GASB Statement No. 29 (1995)	
The Use of Not-for-Profit Accounting and Financial Reporting Principles by Governmental Entities (N80)	Rescinded
GASB Statement No. 30 (1996)	
Risk Financing Omnibus (C50 and Po20)	Risk Management, Claims, and Judgments, Chapter **15** Public Entity Risk Pools, Chapter **23**
GASB Statement No. 31 (1997)	
Accounting and Financial Reporting for Certain Investments and for External Investment Pools (I50)	Deposits, Investments, and Derivative Instruments, Chapter **9**
GASB Statement No. 32 (1997)	
Accounting and Financial Reporting for Internal Revenue Code Section 457 Deferred Compensation Plans (D25, I50)	Pension and Other Postemployment Benefit Plans, Chapter **22**
GASB Statement No. 33 (1998)	
Accounting and Financial Reporting for Nonexchange Transactions (N50)	Revenues: Nonexchange and Exchange Transactions, Chapter **17**

Original Pronouncement	*Governmental GAAP Guide Reference*
GASB Statement No. 34 (1999)	
Basic Financial Statements—and Management's Discussion and Analysis—for State and Local Governments (Entire Codification)	Comprehensive Annual Financial Report, Chapter **20** (most chapters reference aspects of GASB-34)
GASB Statement No. 35 (1999)	
Basic Financial Statements—and Management's Discussion and Analysis—for Public Colleges and Universities (Co5)	Public Colleges and Universities, Chapter **21**
GASB Statement No. 36 (2000)	
Recipient Reporting for Certain Shared Nonexchange Revenues (N50)	Revenues: Nonexchange and Exchange Transactions, Chapter **17** Expenses/Expenditures: Nonexchange and Exchange Transactions, Chapter **18**
GASB Statement No. 37 (2001)	
Basic Financial Statements—and Management's Discussion and Analysis—for State and Local Governments: Omnibus (Entire Codification)	Comprehensive Annual Financial Report, Chapter **20** (most chapters reference aspects of GASB-37 that amended GASB-34)
GASB Statement No. 38 (2001)	
Certain Financial Statement Note Disclosures	Budgetary Accounting, Chapter **2**
(Section 2300)	Revenues: Nonexchange and Exchange Transactions, Chapter **17**
	Other Assets and Deferred Outflows of Resources, Chapter **11**
	Other Liabilities, Chapter **16**
	Leases and Service Concession Arrangements, Chapter **14**
	Special Assessments, Chapter **19**
GASB Statement No. 39 (2002)	
Determining Whether Certain Organizations Are Component Units (Sections 2100, 2600)	Governmental Financial Reporting Entity, Chapter **4**
GASB Statement No. 40 (2003)	
Deposit and Investment Risk Disclosures (C20, I50)	Deposits, Investments, and Derivative Instruments, Chapter **9**
GASB Statement No. 41 (2003)	
Budgetary Comparison Schedules— Perspective Difference—an amendment of GASB Statement No. 34 (Section 2200, Section 2400)	Budgetary Accounting, Chapter **2**
GASB Statement No. 42 (2003)	
Accounting and Financial Reporting for Impairment of Capital Assets and for Insurance Recoveries (Section 1400)	Capital Assets, Chapter **10**, Other Special-Purpose Governments, Chapter **24** (for Regulated Operations)

Original Pronouncement	Governmental GAAP Guide Reference
GASB Statement No. 43 (2004)	
Financial Reporting for Postemployment Benefit Plans Other Than Pension Plans (Pe5, Pe6, Po50)	Rescinded
GASB Statement No. 44 (2004)	
Economic Condition Reporting: The Statistical Section—an amendment of NCGA Statement No. 1 (Section 2800)	Comprehensive Annual Financial Report, Chapter 20
GASB Statement No. 45 (2004)	
Accounting and Financial Reporting by Employers for Postemployment Benefits Other Than Pensions (P50)	Rescinded (implementation of GASB-75)
GASB Statement No. 46 (2004)	
Net Assets Restricted by Enabling Legislation—an amendment of GASB Statement No. 34 (Section 1800, Section 2200)	Terminology and Classification, Chapter 5
GASB Statement No. 47 (2005)	
Accounting for Termination Benefits (T25)	Pension, Postemployment, and Other Employee Benefit Liabilities, Chapter 13
GASB Statement No. 48 (2006)	
Sales and Pledges of Receivables and Future Revenues and Intra-Entity Transfers of Assets and Future Revenues (S20)	Revenues: Nonexchange and Exchange Transactions, Chapter 17
GASB Statement No. 49 (2006)	
Accounting and Reporting of Pollution Remediation Obligations (P40)	Other Liabilities, Chapter 16
GASB Statement No. 50 (2007)	
Pension Disclosures (P20, Pe5, Pe6)	Rescinded
GASB Statement No. 51 (2007)	
Accounting and Financial Reporting for Intangible Assets (Section 1400)	Capital Assets, Chapter 10
GASB Statement No. 52 (2007)	
Land and Other Real Estate Held as Investments by Endowments (I50)	Deposits, and Investments, and Derivative Instruments, Chapter 9
GASB Statement No. 53 (2008)	
Accounting and Financial Reporting for Derivative Instruments (D40)	Deposits, Investments, and Derivative Instruments, Chapter 9
GASB Statement No. 54 (2009)	
Fund Balance Reporting and Governmental Fund Type Definitions (Section 1300, Section 1800)	Foundation and Overview of Governmental Generally Accepted Accounting Principles, Chapter 1 Terminology and Classification, Chapter 5 Governmental Funds, Chapter 6

Original Pronouncement	Governmental GAAP Guide Reference
GASB Statement No. 55 (2009)	
The Hierarchy of Generally Accepted Accounting Principles for State and Local Governments (Section 1000)	Rescinded
GASB Statement No. 56 (2009)	
Codification of Accounting and Financial Reporting Guidance Contained in the AICPA Statements on Auditing Standards (Section 2250)	Foundation and Overview of Governmental Generally Accepted Accounting Principles, Chapter 1
GASB Statement No. 57 (2009)	
OPEB Measurements by Agent Employers and Agent Multiple-Employer Plans (PO5, Pe5)	Rescinded
GASB Statement No. 58 (2009)	
Accounting and Financial Reporting for Chapter 9 Bankruptcies (Bn5)	Foundation and Overview of Governmental Generally Accepted Accounting Principles, Chapter 1
GASB Statement No. 59 (2010)	
Financial Instruments Omnibus (D40, I50)	Deposits, Investments, and Derivative Instruments, Chapter 9
GASB Statement No. 60 (2010)	
Accounting and Financial Reporting for Service Concession Arrangements (S30)	Leases and Service Concession Arrangements, Chapter 14
GASB Statement No. 61 (2010)	
The Financial Reporting Entity: Omnibus—an amendment of GASB Statements No. 14 and No. 34 (Section 2100, Section 2600)	Governmental Financial Reporting Entity, Chapter 4
GASB Statement No. 62 (2011)	
Codification of Accounting and Financial Reporting Guidance Contained in Pre-November 30, 1989 FASB and AICPA Pronouncements (Entire Codification)	Most chapters in the guide including Other Special-Purpose Governments, Chapter 24
GASB Statement No. 63 (2011)	
Financial Reporting of Deferred Outflows of Resources, Deferred Inflows of Resources, and Net Position (Entire Codification)	Terminology and Classification, Chapter 5, Comprehensive Annual Financial Report, Chapter 20
GASB Statement No. 64 (2011)	
Derivative Instruments: Application of Hedge Accounting Termination Provisions—an amendment of GASB Statement No. 53 (D40)	Deposits, Investments, and Derivative Instruments, Chapter 9

Original Pronouncement	Governmental GAAP Guide Reference
GASB Statement No. 65 (2012)	
Items Previously Reported as Assets and Liabilities (Entire Codification)	Foundation and Overview of Governmental Generally Accepted Accounting Principles, Chapter 1 Leases and Service Concession Arrangements, Chapter 14 Revenues: Nonexchange and Exchange Transactions, Chapter 17 Expenses/Expenditures: Nonexchange and Exchange Transactions, Chapter 18
GASB Statement No. 66 (2012)	
Technical Corrections—2012—an amendment of GASB Statements No. 10 and No. 62 (C50, L20, L30)	Leases and Service Concession Arrangements, Chapter 14
GASB Statement No. 67 (2012)	
Financial Reporting for Pension Plans— an amendment of GASB Statement No. 25 (Pe5, Pe6)	Fiduciary Funds, Chapter 8 Pension, Postemployment, and Other Employee Benefit Liabilities, Chapter 13 Pension and Other Postemployment Benefit Plans, Chapter 22
GASB Statement No. 68 (2012)	
Accounting and Financial Reporting for Pensions—an amendment of GASB Statement No. 27 (P20)	Fiduciary Funds, Chapter 8 Pension, Postemployment, and Other Employee Benefit Liabilities, Chapter 13
GASB Statement No. 69 (2013)	
Government Combinations and Disposals of Government Operations (Co10)	Governmental Financial Reporting Entity, Chapter 4 Capital Assets, Chapter 10
GASB Statement No. 70 (2013)	
Accounting and Financial Reporting for Non-Exchange Financial Guarantee Transactions (N30)	Other Liabilities, Chapter 16 Special Assessments, Chapter 19
GASB Statement No. 71 (2013)	
Pension Transition for Contributions Made Subsequent to the Measurement Date—an amendment of GASB Statement No. 68 (P20)	Fiduciary Funds, Chapter 8 Pension, Postemployment, and Other Employee Benefit Liabilities, Chapter 13
GASB Statement No. 72 (2015)	
Fair Value Measurement and Application (Section 3100, I50, D40)	Deposits, Investments, and Derivative Instruments, Chapter 9 Pension and Other Postemployment Benefit Plans, Chapter 22
GASB Statement No. 73 (2015)	
Accounting and Financial Reporting for Pensions and Related Assets That Are Not within the Scope of GASB Statement 68 and Amendments to Certain Provisions of GASB Statements 67 and 68 (P20, P22, P23, P24, Pe5, 2200)	Fiduciary Funds, Chapter 8 Pension, Postemployment, and Other Employee Benefit Liabilities, Chapter 13

Original Pronouncement	*Governmental GAAP Guide Reference*

GASB Statement No. 74 (2015)

Financial Reporting for Postemployment Benefit Plans Other Than Pension Plans (Po50)

Fiduciary Funds, Chapter **8** Pension, Postemployment, and Other Employee Benefit Liabilities, Chapter **13** Pension and Other Postemployment Benefit Plans, Chapter **22**

GASB Statement No. 75 (2015)

Accounting and Financial Reporting for Postemployment Benefits Other Than Pensions (P51, P52, P54)

Fiduciary Funds, Chapter **8** Pension, Postemployment, and Other Employee Benefit Liabilities, Chapter **13**

GASB Statement No. 76 (2015)

The Hierarchy of Generally Accepted Accounting Principles for State and Local Governments (Section 1000)

Foundation and Overview of Governmental Generally Accepted Accounting Principles, Chapter **1**

GASB Statement No. 77 (2015)

Tax Abatement Disclosures (Section 2300, T10)

Revenues: Nonexchange and Exchange Transactions, Chapter **17**

GASB Statement No. 78 (2015)

Pensions Provided through Certain Multiple Employer Defined Benefit Pension Plans (P20)

Pension, Postemployment, and Other Employee Benefit Liabilities, Chapter **13**, Pension and Other Postemployment Benefit Plans, Chapter **22**

GASB Statement No. 79 (2015)

Certain External Investment Pools and Pool Participants (In5)

Deposits, Investments, and Derivative Instruments, Chapter **9**

GASB Statement No. 80 (2016)

Blending Requirements for Certain Component Units—an amendment of GASB Statement No. 14 (Section 2600)

Governmental Financial Reporting Entity, Chapter **4**, Public Colleges and Universities, Chapter **21**

GASB Statement No. 81 (2016)

Irrevocable Split-Interest Agreements (I70)

Revenues: Nonexchange and Exchange Transactions, Chapter **17**, Public Colleges and Universities, Chapter **21**

GASB Statement No. 82 (2016)

Pension Issues—an amendment of GASB Statements No. 67, No. 68 and No. 73 (P20, Pe5, Pe6)

Pension, Postemployment, and Other Employee Benefit Liabilities, Chapter **13**, Pension and Other Postemployment Benefit Plans, Chapter **22**

GASB Statement No. 83 (2016)

Certain Asset Retirement Obligations (1500, 1600, 2300, A10, C50, L10, P40)

Other Liabilities, Chapter **16**

GASB Statement No. 84 (2017)

Fiduciary Activities (Many Sections)

Fiduciary Funds, Chapter **8**

Original Pronouncement	Governmental GAAP Guide Reference
GASB Statement No. 85 (2017)	
Omnibus (I50, P20, P21, P22, P24 and other sections)	Deposits, Investments, and Derivative Instruments, Chapter 9 Pension, Postemployment, and Other Employee Benefit Liabilities, Chapter 13, Pension and Other Postemployment Benefit Plans, Chapter 22
GASB Statement No. 86 (2017)	
Certain Debt Extinguishment Issues (D20)	Long-Term Debt, Chapter 12
GASB Statement No. 87 (2017)	
Leases (L20)	Leases and Service Concession Arrangements, Chapter 14
GASB Statement No. 88 (2018)	
Certain Disclosures Related to Debt, Including Direct Borrowings and Direct Placements (1500, 2300, D30)*	Long-Term Debt, Chapter 12
GASB Statement No. 89 (2018)	
Accounting for Interest Cost during the Period of Construction (1400, 2200, Re10)*	Capital Assets, Chapter 10 Other Special-Purpose Governments, Chapter 24
GASB Statement No. 90 (2018)	
Accounting and Financial Reporting for Majority Equity Interests-an amendment of GASB Statement No. 14 (2100, 2600, I50)*	Governmental Financial Reporting Entity, Chapter 4 Deposits, Investments, and Derivative Instruments, Chapter 9

* Pending as of publication date

GOVERNMENTAL ACCOUNTING STANDARDS BOARD INTERPRETATIONS

GASB Interpretations are issued by the Governmental Accounting Standards Board. Footnote 1 to GASB Statement No. 76 includes interpretations as part of category "A" GAAP and are continued in force until altered, supplemented, revoked, or superseded by subsequent GASB pronouncements. Interpretations will likely no longer be issued as the *Implementation Guides* have largely replaced them.

Original Pronouncement	Governmental GAAP Guide Reference
GASB Interpretation No. 1 (1984)	
Demand Bonds Issued by State and Local Governmental Entities (D30)	Long-Term Debt, Chapter 12
GASB Interpretation No. 2 (1995)	
Disclosure of Conduit Debt Obligations (C65)	Other Liabilities, Chapter 16
GASB Interpretation No. 3 (1996)	
Financial Reporting for Reverse Repurchase Agreements (I55)	Deposits, Investments, and Derivative Instruments, Chapter 9

Original Pronouncement	*Governmental GAAP Guide Reference*
GASB Interpretation No. 4 (1996)	
Accounting and Financial Reporting for Capitalization Contributions to Public Entity Risk Pools (C50 and Po20)	Public Entity Risk Pools, Chapter **23**
GASB Interpretation No. 5 (1997)	
Property Tax Revenue Recognition in Governmental Funds (an Interpretation of NCGA Statement 1 and an Amendment of NCGA Interpretation 3) (P70)	Revenues: Nonexchange and Exchange Transactions, Chapter **17**
GASB Interpretation No. 6 (2000)	
Recognition and Measurement of Certain Liabilities and Expenditures in Governmental Fund Financial Statements (1500, 1600)	Other Liabilities, Chapter **16**

GOVERNMENTAL ACCOUNTING STANDARDS BOARD TECHNICAL BULLETINS

GASB Technical Bulletins are issued by the Governmental Accounting Standards Board. The GASB has authorized its staff to prepare Technical Bulletins to respond to governmental accounting issues on a timely basis. Technical Bulletins are not voted on formally by the GASB; however, a Technical Bulletin will not be issued if a majority of the members of the GASB object to its issuance. They are part of Category "B" GAAP.

Original Pronouncement	*Governmental GAAP Guide Reference*
GASB Technical Bulletin 84-1 (1984)	
Purpose and Scope of GASB Technical Bulletins and Procedures for Issuance	Foundation and Overview of Governmental Generally Accepted Accounting Principles, Chapter **1**
GASB Technical Bulletin 87-1 (1987)	
Applying Paragraph 68 of GASB Statement 3 (I50)	Superseded by GASB-40
GASB Technical Bulletin 92-1 (1992)	
Display of Governmental College and University Compensated Absences Liabilities (Co5)	Rescinded
GASB Technical Bulletin 94-1 (1994)	
Disclosures About Derivatives and Similar Debt and Investment Transactions (2300)	Rescinded
GASB Technical Bulletin 96-1 (1996)	
Application of Certain Pension Disclosure Requirements for Employers Pending Implementation GASB Statement 27 (P20)	Rescinded

Original Pronouncement	Governmental GAAP Guide Reference
GASB Technical Bulletin 97-1 (1997)	
Classification of Deposits and Investments into Custodial Credit Risk Categories for Certain Bank Holding Company Transactions	Superseded by GASB-40
GASB Technical Bulletin 98-1 (1998)	
Disclosures about Year 2000 Issues	Rescinded
GASB Technical Bulletin 99-1 (1999)	
Disclosures about Year 2000 Issues—An Amendment of Technical Bulletin 98-1	Rescinded
GASB Technical Bulletin 2000-1 (2000)	
Disclosures about Year 2000 Issues—A Rescission of GASB Technical Bulletins 98-1 and 99-1	No reference
GASB Technical Bulletin 2003-1 (2003)	
Disclosure Requirements for Derivatives Not Reported at Fair Value on the Statement of Net Assets	Superseded by GASB-53
GASB Technical Bulletin 2004-1 (2004)	
Tobacco Settlement Recognition and Financial Reporting Entity Issues	Partially superseded by GASB-48 and GASB-75. Revenues: Nonexchange and Exchange Transactions, Chapter 17
GASB Technical Bulletin 2006-1 (2006)	
Accounting and Financial Reporting by Employers and OPEB Plans for Payments from the Federal Government Pursuant to the Retiree Drug Subsidy Provisions of Medicare Part D	Pension, Postemployment, and Other Employee Benefit Liabilities, Chapter 13 Pension and Other Postemployment Benefit Plans, Chapter 22, partially superseded by GASB-75.
GASB Technical Bulletin 2008-1 (2008)	
Determining the Annual Required Contribution Adjustment for Postemployment Benefits	Rescinded

GOVERNMENTAL ACCOUNTING STANDARDS BOARD CONCEPTS STATEMENTS

GASB Concepts Statements are issued by the Governmental Accounting Standards Board; however, Concepts Statements do not establish generally accepted accounting principles for state and local governmental entities. Concepts Statements identify concepts that will be used by the GASB in establishing future governmental accounting and reporting standards.

Original Pronouncement	Governmental GAAP Guide Reference
GASB Concepts Statement No. 1 (1987)	
Objectives of Financial Reporting (100)	Foundation and Overview of Governmental Generally Accepted Accounting Principles, Chapter 1

Original Pronouncement	Governmental GAAP Guide Reference
GASB Concepts Statement No. 2 (1994)	
Service Efforts and Accomplishments Reporting (100)	Foundation and Overview of Governmental Generally Accepted Accounting Principles, Chapter 1
GASB Concepts Statement No. 3 (2005)	
Communication Methods in General Purpose External Financial Reports That Contain Basic Financial Statements	Foundation and Overview of Governmental Generally Accepted Accounting Principles, Chapter 1
GASB Concepts Statement No. 4 (2007)	
Elements of Financial Statements	Foundation and Overview of Governmental Generally Accepted Accounting Principles, Chapter 1
GASB Concepts Statement No. 5 (2008)	
Service Efforts and Accomplishments— an amendment of GASB Concepts Statement No. 2)	Foundation and Overview of Governmental Generally Accepted Accounting Principles, Chapter 1
GASB Concepts Statement No. 6 (2014)	
Measurement of Elements of Financial Statements	Foundation and Overview of Governmental Generally Accepted Accounting Principles, Chapter 1

NATIONAL COUNCIL ON GOVERNMENTAL ACCOUNTING STATEMENTS

NCGA Statements (NCGAs) were issued by the National Council on Governmental Accounting until 1984, when the GASB assumed the role of promulgating accounting principles for state and local governments. GASB Statement No. 1 states that NCGA Statements not otherwise superseded are considered authoritative support for determining generally accepted accounting principles for state and local governments.

Original Pronouncement	Governmental GAAP Guide Reference
NCGA Statement No. 1 (1979)	
Governmental Accounting and Financial Reporting Principles (throughout)	
• Accounting and Reporting Capabilities	Foundation and Overview of Governmental Generally Accepted Accounting Principles, Chapter 1
• Fund Accounting Systems	Foundation and Overview of Governmental Generally Accepted Accounting Principles, Chapter 1
• Fund Types	Comprehensive Annual Financial Report, Chapter 20

Original Pronouncement	Governmental GAAP Guide Reference
• Number of Funds	Foundation and Overview of Governmental Generally Accepted Accounting Principles, Chapter 1
• Reporting Capital Assets	Capital Assets, Chapter 10
• Valuation of Capital Assets	Capital Assets, Chapter 10
• Depreciation of Capital Assets	Capital Assets, Chapter 10
• Reporting Long-Term Liabilities	Other Liabilities, Chapter 16
• Measurement Focus and Basis of Accounting in the Basic Financial Statements	Basis of Accounting and Measurement Focus, Chapter 3
• Budgeting, Budgetary, Control, and Budgetary Reporting	Budgetary Accounting, Chapter 2
• Transfer, Revenue, Expenditure, and Expense Account Classification	Terminology and Classification, Chapter 5
• Common Terminology and Classification	Terminology and Classification, Chapter 5
• Annual Financial Reports	Foundation and Overview of Governmental Generally Accepted Accounting Principles, Chapter 1
NCGA Statement No. 2 (1980)	
Grant, Entitlement, and Shared Revenue Accounting by State and Local Governments (G60)	Rescinded
NCGA Statement No. 3 (1981)	
Defining the Governmental Reporting Entity (no reference)	Rescinded
NCGA Statement No. 4 (1982)	
Accounting and Financial Reporting Principles for Claims and Judgments and Compensated Absences (C50; C60)	Risk Management, Claims, and Judgments, Chapter 15 Governmental Funds, Chapter 6
NCGA Statement No. 5 (1983)	
Accounting and Financial Reporting Principles for Lease Agreements of State and Local Governments (L20)	Leases and Service Concession Arrangements, Chapter 14
NCGA Statement No. 6 (1983)	
Pension Accounting and Financial Reporting: Public Employee Retirement Systems and State and Local Government Employers (P20; Pe5)	Rescinded
NCGA Statement No. 7 (1984)	
Financial Reporting for Component Units within the Governmental Reporting Entity (no reference)	Rescinded

NATIONAL COUNCIL ON GOVERNMENTAL ACCOUNTING INTERPRETATIONS

NCGA Interpretations (NCGAIs) were issued by the National Council on Governmental Accounting until 1984, when the GASB assumed the role of promulgating accounting principles for state and local governments. GASB-1 states that NCGA Interpretations not otherwise superseded are considered authoritative support for determining generally accepted accounting principles for state and local governments.

Original Pronouncement	Governmental GAAP Guide Reference
NCGA Interpretation No. 1 (1976)	
GAAFR and the AICPA Audit Guide (no reference)	Rescinded
NCGA Interpretation No. 2 (1980)	
Segment Information for Enterprise Funds (2500)	Rescinded
NCGA Interpretation No. 3 (1981)	
Revenue Recognition—Property Taxes (P70)	Revenues: Nonexchange and Exchange Transaction, Chapter 17
NCGA Interpretation No. 4 (1981)	
Accounting and Financial Reporting for Public Employee Retirement Systems and Pension Trust Funds (no reference)	Rescinded
NCGA Interpretation No. 5 (1982)	
Authoritative Status of Governmental Accounting, Auditing, and Financial Reporting (1968) (1100)	Rescinded
NCGA Interpretation No. 6 (1982)	
Notes to the Financial Statements Disclosure (2300)	Comprehensive Annual Financial Report, Chapter 20
NCGA Interpretation No. 7 (1983)	
Clarification as to the Application of the Criteria in NCGA Statement 3, "Defining the Governmental Reporting Entity" (no reference)	Rescinded
NCGA Interpretation No. 8 (1983)	
Certain Pension Matters (P20; T25)	Risk Management, Claims, and Judgments, Chapter 15
NCGA Interpretation No. 9 (1984)	
Certain Fund Classifications and Balance Sheet Accounts (B50; U50)	Capital Assets, Chapter 10 Long-Term Debt, Chapter 12
NCGA Interpretation No. 10 (1984)	
State and Local Government Budgetary Reporting (2400)	Budgetary Accounting, Chapter 2
NCGA Interpretation No. 11 (1984)	
Claim and Judgment Transactions for Governmental Funds (C50)	Superseded by GASB-10

NATIONAL COUNCIL ON GOVERNMENTAL ACCOUNTING CONCEPTS STATEMENTS

NCGA Concepts Statements were issued by the National Council on Governmental Accounting until 1984, when the GASB assumed the role of promulgating accounting principles for state and local governments. NCGA Concepts Statement No. 1 was superseded by GASB Concepts Statement No. 1; however, the GASB concluded that NCGA Concepts Statement No. 1 is nonetheless a useful source for understanding the role of financial reporting by governmental entities.

Original Pronouncement	*Governmental GAAP Guide Reference*
NCGA Concepts Statement No. 1 (1982)	
Objectives of Accounting and Financial Reporting for Governmental Units (Appendix B)	Foundation and Overview of Governmental Generally Accepted Accounting Principles, Chapter 1

INDEX

FUN

M

THE